Psychological Science

Third Edition

Psychological Science

Third Edition

Michael S. Gazzaniga

University of California, Santa Barbara

Todd F. Heatherton

Dartmouth College

Diane F. Halpern

Claremont McKenna College

W. W. NORTON & COMPANY

NEW YORK ■ LONDON

W. W. Norton & Company has been independent since its founding in 1923, when William Warder Norton and Mary D. Herter Norton first published lectures delivered at the People's Institute, the adult education division of New York City's Cooper Union. The Nortons soon expanded their program beyond the Institute, publishing books by celebrated academics from America and abroad. By mid-century, the two major pillars of Norton's publishing program—trade books and college texts—were firmly established. In the 1950s, the Norton family transferred control of the company to its employees, and today—with a staff of four hundred and a comparable number of trade, college, and professional titles published each year—W. W. Norton & Company stands as the largest and oldest publishing house owned wholly by its employees.

Editor: Sheri L. Snavely
Managing Editor, College: Marian Johnson
Developmental Editor: Beth Ammerman
Manuscript Editors: Kurt Wildermuth, Chris Thillen, Alice Vigliani
Associate Editor, Art Development: Sarah England
Project Editor: Kurt Wildermuth
Editorial Assistant: Wamiq Jawaid
Production Manager: Chris Granville
Book Designer: Lissi Sigillo
Art Director: Rubina Yeh
Photo Researchers: Trish Marx and Elyse Rieder
Marketing Manager: Ken Barton
Emedia Editor: Dan Jost
Ancillary Editor: Rachel Comerford
Illustrators: Dragonfly Media Group
Compositor: Prepare, Emilcomp Inc.
Manufacturer: Courier Companies

Library of Congress Cataloging-in-Publication Data

Gazzaniga, Michael S.
  Psychological science / Michael S. Gazzaniga, Todd F. Heatherton, Diane F. Halpern. — 3rd ed.
    p. cm.
  Includes bibliographical references and indexes.

ISBN 978-0-393-93421-2

  1. Psychology—Textbooks. I. Heatherton, Todd F. II. Halpern, Diane F. III. Title.
  BF121.G393 2010
  150—dc22
                              2008039604

W. W. Norton & Company, Inc., 500 Fifth Avenue, New York, N.Y. 10110
                    www.wwnorton.com

W. W. Norton & Company Ltd., Castle House, 75/76 Wells Street, London W1T 3QT

2 3 4 5 6 7 8 9 0

We dedicate this book to
Lilly, Emmy, and Garth Tretheway
Sarah Heatherton and James Heatherton
Sheldon, Evan, Karen, Amanda, and Jason Halpern
and Jaye, Danny, and Belle Halpern-Duncan.

CONTENTS IN BRIEF

ABOUT THE AUTHORS

Michael S. Gazzaniga (PhD, California Institute of Technology) is Distinguished Professor and Director of the Sage Center for the Study of the Mind at the University of California, Santa Barbara. He founded and presides over the Cognitive Neuroscience Institute and is founding editor-in-chief of the *Journal of Cognitive Neuroscience*. He is past president of the American Psychological Society and a member of the American Academy of Arts and Sciences and the National Academies Institute of Medicine. His research focuses on split-brain patients. He has held positions at the University of California, Santa Barbara; New York University; the State University of New York, Stony Brook; Cornell University Medical College; and the University of California, Davis. He has written many notable books, including, most recently, *Human*.

Todd F. Heatherton (PhD, University of Toronto) is the Champion International Professor of Psychological and Brain Sciences at Dartmouth College. His recent research takes a social brain sciences approach, which combines theories and methods of evolutionary psychology, social cognition, and cognitive neuroscience to examine the neural underpinnings of social behavior. He has been on the executive committees of the Society of Personality and Social Psychology, the Association of Researchers in Personality, and the International Society of Self & Identity. He is Associate Editor of the *Journal of Cognitive Neuroscience* and serves on many editorial boards and grant review panels. He received the Petra Shattuck Award for Teaching Excellence from the Harvard Extension School in 1994, the McLane Fellowship from Dartmouth College in 1997, and the Friedman Family Fellowship from Dartmouth College in 2001. He is a Fellow of the American Psychological Association, the Association for Psychological Science, and the Society for Personality and Social Psychology.

Diane F. Halpern (PhD, University of Cincinnati) is Professor of Psychology at Claremont McKenna College. She has won many awards for her teaching and research, including the 2002 Outstanding Professor Award from the Western Psychological Association, the 1999 American Psychological Foundation Award for Distinguished Teaching, the 1996 Distinguished Career Award for Contributions to Education from the American Psychological Association, and the California State University's State-Wide Outstanding Professor Award. Halpern was president of the American Psychological Association in 2004 and is a past president of the Society for the Teaching of Psychology. She is author of *Thought and Knowledge: An Introduction to Critical Thinking* and *Sex Differences in Cognitive Abilities*. She is currently chairing an APS task force on redesigning undergraduate education in psychology. Her edited book, *Undergraduate Education in Psychology: A Blueprint for the Future of the Discipline* (APA Books), will be published in 2009.

PREFACE

When we, Mike and Todd, began the First Edition of this book, more than a decade ago, our primary motivation was to create a textbook that captured ongoing revolutionary changes in the field by focusing on cutting-edge psychological and brain sciences. Instead of an encyclopedic and homogenized textbook that dutifully covered worn themes and tired topics, we tried to create a readable book that captured the excitement of contemporary research and yet was respectful to the rich tradition of scientific research accumulated by the field. We sought and received excellent advice from countless colleagues about what was most important to them in introductory psychology courses and what they believed was of greatest value to students. It became clear that most instructors wanted a textbook that focused on material that students really needed to know at the introductory level rather than being bloated with unnecessary details. As we noted in the preface to the Second Edition, it was clear that there was an audience eager for a current and scientific treatment of psychology that was accessible for the majority of students.

We made a number of important revisions in the Second Edition, with students first and foremost in our minds. The Second Edition was more balanced in terms of level of detail, and it included many more vivid examples and case histories. Moreover, we expanded our coverage of critical thinking because it was clear that students needed more explicit instruction in how to think about and judge empirical research. However, we retained the features that appealed most to students and instructors, such as the declarative style that focused on answers to current scientific questions and the ask-and-answer approach that captured students' interest and kept the material engaging. We also continued to focus on research that crossed levels of analysis, from cultural and social context to genes and neurons. In the first half of the book, we included more social and cultural examples.

A New Coauthor for the Third Edition

Although we were enormously gratified by the response from instructors and students to our Second Edition, we also knew that there was room for improvement. One of the most important advantages we had was our editor extraordinaire, Jon Durbin, who was as personally invested in the project as we were and who worked tirelessly with us to improve the book. Given how favorably people responded to our enhanced discussion of critical thinking in the Second Edition, Jon sought out one of the world's leading experts on critical thinking to help us do even more with this important construct. Fortunately for us, the expert he sought was Diane Halpern, past president of the American Psychological Association; leader in the study of the science of learning; author of many critically acclaimed articles and books on cognition, culture, and gender; organizer of many important committees for examining learning objectives and training of students in psychology; and the acknowledged guru of critical thinking. Moreover, Diane had won many awards for her teaching, including the 2002 Outstanding Professor Award from the Western Psychological Association, the 1999 American Psychological Foundation Award for Distinguished Teaching, and the 1996 Distinguished Career Award for Contributions to Education given by the American Psychological Association. So when Diane spoke, we listened.

As it became clear that Diane could contribute to our book in many ways, Jon Durbin raised the idea of Diane joining us as a coauthor. Indeed, it was an intriguing idea, particularly with Mike recently being the President of the Association for Psychological Science and Diane recently being the President of the American Psychological Association. Although the two societies differ somewhat in their primary focuses, both are committed to educating students on the science of psychology, so Diane's joining our textbook would be symbolic of the core mission of APS and APA. Fortunately, Diane shared our interest and vision in creating a highly accessible, scientifically rigorous textbook and agreed to join us. What she also added, and we very much desired, was her expertise on the science of learning. Although we had both spent considerable time in the classroom and received awards for our teaching, Diane's empirical approach to the science of learning resonated for us. That, after all, is the point of our book: We learn how things work through careful scientific study.

The Third Edition Emphasizes the Science of Learning

Over the past few decades, by conducting empirical studies, researchers have discovered the best practices for learning. Researchers have studied the way people think, learn, and remember, yet this knowledge is not often applied to student learning. Diane's expertise in these areas brought many new science-based learning features to the Third Edition, such as an enhanced ask-and-answer approach and Critical Thinking modules that show students how to put critical thinking into action. Using scientific evidence about the cognitive, individual, and environmental factors that influence learning, the Third Edition brings this science into the classroom. Learning Objectives focus students on the central questions they should be able to answer after reading the chapter. The Learning Objectives are explicitly tied to the corresponding Summing Up/Measuring Up features at the end of each main section, which give students take-home messages as well as questions with which they can test their understanding. Practice Tests at the end of the chapters help students consolidate their knowledge. Thus we used knowledge from scientific research to design the pedagogical elements of the book.

The Visual Program

We followed a similar approach to improving the quality of the visual art program. The artwork in the First and Second Editions, like that in most introductory psychology textbooks, mainly consisted of static drawings, graphs of findings, pictures of researchers, and so forth—nothing really inspiring. We wanted to do better with this new edition. Because we value the scientific approach, we sought out one of the world's leading educational psychologists, Richard Mayer, whose research focuses on how people can learn more effectively using visual materials. Indeed, for his pioneering research in science education, Rich won the 2008 Distinguished Contribution of Applications of Psychology to Education and Training Award from the American Psychological Association. Fortunately, Rich was just down the hall from Mike's new office in Santa Barbara, so Diane and Todd flew to Santa Barbara to seek Rich's advice and counsel. This was an enormously productive meeting, as Rich helped us conceptualize new presentations of visual information in ways that will help students learn.

Active learning is not stimulated by text alone. The Third Edition supports visual learners with clear, attractive graphics that stimulate students' thinking skills and drive home their understanding of key concepts. Throughout this edition, new figures bring abstract concepts to life for students. "Try for Yourself" features encourage students to engage in demonstrations on their own, and "Scientific Method" illustrations carefully and consistently lead students through the steps of some of the most interesting experiments and studies. We are especially pleased with the new "How We" figures, in Chapter 5, which take students step by step through complex processes such as how we hear and how we see. We also carefully considered each piece of visual material in the book, making sure that captions were informative rather than descriptive, and we eliminated many figures that were simply uninspired, replacing them with art that is more meaningful for students.

The Third Edition Comes to Life

After considerable time, thought, and effort, we are pleased to present our new edition. We believe that our book gives students a thorough and interesting overview of contemporary psychological research using the best practices from the science-of-learning research. It develops psychological literacy by presenting the material in a way that is directly related to their lives. The Third Edition also invites students to consider the difficult new ethical dilemmas stemming from advances in psychological research. Mike's book *The Ethical Brain* raised many fundamental questions about how society needs to consider the implications of research in psychological and brain sciences. For each chapter of *Psychological Science*, Mike wrote a feature describing an ethical issue central to the theme of the chapter. Given the success of *The Ethical Brain*, we expect that students will find these features engaging and thought provoking.

The three of us feel that the revisions we have made to our textbook will have great appeal for students and instructors. We conducted focus sessions and conducted a large survey of users and potential users to canvas their thoughts, and we took these ideas into careful consideration as we crafted this new edition. There have been major changes to nearly every chapter; in particular, we have added more material related to gender, culture, and international issues. We also followed the advice of many faithful users by moving the social chapter up in the order, merging the motivation and emotions chapter, expanding the health coverage, adding a large section on positive psychology, increasing the coverage of consciousness, moving the brain anatomy material back to the "Biological Foundations" chapter, and combining attention and memory in one chapter. There are many good solutions for ordering and presenting material in introductory psychology, and we look forward to hearing from users about the solutions we arrived at in this edition.

At the same time, we stayed true to our primary goal—of creating an accessible book that focuses on contemporary research approaches within psychological science. This is an exciting time to work in psychological science, and we hope that our excitement is contagious to our students and readers. We are energized and inspired by the many undergraduate and graduate students we have the pleasure to interact with each day. This book is written for them, with our respect for their intelligence and our admiration for their inquisitiveness.

Acknowledgments

We begin by acknowledging the unwavering support we have received from our families. Writing a textbook is a time-consuming endeavor, and our family members have been generous in allowing us the time to focus on writing. We are also extremely grateful to the many colleagues who gave us constructive feedback and advice. Some individuals deserve special recognition. First and foremost is our good friend Margaret Lynch, who has shared marvelous advice across all three editions as well as helping out in numerous other ways. Margaret is an amazing advocate for students and reminds us never to take them for granted or underestimate them. (She has also remained steadfast in discouraging contractions.) We are also particularly indebted to Debra Mashek for creating the Practice Tests and Psychology and Society questions and contributing richly to the learning system, including advising us on Learning Objectives and other pedagogical features. Wendy Domjan took the time to provide detailed reviews across most of the book, and she really pushed us to make the material accessible.

We also benefited from the astute guidance of many reviewers and consultants over the past three editions, particularly Elizabeth Phelps, Howard Hughes, Peter Tse, Steven Heine, Richard Mayer, Jamie Pennebaker, Wendi Gardner, Tara Callaghan, Jim Enns, David Barlow, Lisa Best, Erin Hardin, Katherine Gibbs, Dana Dunn, Dawn Strongin, and numerous others who took the time to share with us their views about what works in teaching introductory psychology. We have been very pleased with the warm reception our book has received internationally and would like to recognize the thoughtful guidance and advice of our UK advisor, Jamie Ward, University of Sussex.

Producing a textbook requires a small army of people who are crucial at each step of the way. For instance, our ancillary team was instrumental in producing first-rate materials that will assist students and instructors in having a rich experience with the material. Gary Lewandowski joined our long-time friends and colleagues from Bloomsburg University Brett Beck and Eileen Astor-Stetson as the author of the Third Edition's Study Guide. Brett and Eileen also authored superb new content for the student StudySpace Web site. Pat Carroll once again assembled wonderful video offerings that contribute so much to classroom instruction. Likewise, Caton Roberts created brilliant PowerPoint lectures to accompany the text. Sue Franz, Robin Morgan, and Patrick Dyer wrote a truly spectacular Instructor's Manual, which also benefited from design ideas by Katherine Gibbs. We are so grateful to all these individuals, who lent their talent and time to create a strong support package for the Third Edition.

A special mention needs to be made of the Test Bank, which, as every instructor knows, is crucial to a successful course. Inadequate test banks with uneven or ambiguous items can frustrate students and instructors alike. For the Third Edition, we used a science-of-learning approach to assessment. First, we convened a focus group in July 2007 in La Jolla, California, composed of leading assessment researchers to discuss best practices for test item construction and assessment. Valerie Shute and Deigo Zapata-Rivera then wrote guidelines for assessment that were useful for all print and media support materials to ensure quality and consistency throughout. Subsequently, the highly accomplished team of Wendy Domjan, Bernard Beins, Valeri Farmer-Dugan, and Jessica Shryack did an amazing job of assembling the items. We cannot express the depth of our appreciation for their efforts.

Focus Group Participants

Throughout the planning process, we sought expert advice on many aspects of the textbook and the ancillary package. Two focus group sessions were particularly helpful. The first, as mentioned, was for test assessment. This group of academics and researchers included Dave Daniel (James Madison University), Peter Ewell (Vice President, National Center for Higher Education Management Systems), Kurt F. Geisinger (University of Nebraska, Lincoln; Center Director, Buros Center on Testing), Arthur Graesser (University of Memphis), Milt Hakel (Bowling Green State University), Mark McDaniel (Washington University, St. Louis), and Valerie Shute (Florida State University; Principal Research Scientist at Educational Testing Service, Research & Development Division).

We would also like to thank a group of first-rate introductory psychology instructors who met with us at APS in Washington, D.C., in May 2007: Thomas Capo (University of Maryland), Stephen Forssell (George Washington University), Cynthia S. Koenig (St. Mary's College of Maryland), Molly Lynch (Northern Virginia Community College), Beth Morling (University of Delaware), and Benjamin Walker (Georgetown University). This talented group of individuals gave us tough-minded, thoughtful critiques of our revision plan for the main text and teaching support materials. There is no doubt that they helped significantly tighten and improve our plans for this exciting new edition. We are ever grateful for their contributions.

The Norton Team

In the modern publishing world, where most books are produced by large multi-national corporations, W. W. Norton stands out as a beacon to academics and authors. Its employees own the company, and therefore every individual who worked on our book has a vested personal interest in its success; it shows in the great enthusiasm they bring to their work. Jon Durbin, a born motivational speaker, was our first editor. Jon absorbed so much psychological knowledge and came to know some many people in the field that at times it was easy to forget he wasn't a psychologist. Unfortunately for psychology, his first love is history, and Jon decided to shift his full-time attention to editing books in that field. However, he needs to be recognized as the person responsible for bringing Diane onto the team. We missed Jon's exuberant enthusiasm as we completed the Third Edition, and we wish him well as he toils away with all those dreary historians.

We are indebted to Roby Harrington for his unwavering support of our book, but we are especially grateful to him for hiring Sheri Snavely to head the psychology list and to serve as our new editor. Sheri is a highly experienced science editor, and she brought many excellent ideas to the book, particularly in terms of reconsidering the entire art program. We are grateful for her dedication to the project and for her unflagging commitment to its success. She has a way of bringing out our best work, and her care and passion show throughout this Third Edition. Sheri is one of a kind, and we are honored to have worked with her this past year.

Beth Ammerman served admirably in her role as developmental editor, pushing us to be crystal clear in how we describe concepts and ideas and making sure that the reader cannot distinguish the three authorial voices. Senior developmental editor Kurt Wildermuth, who served as lead manuscript editor and project editor, is a wordsmith of the highest order and one of the most organized people we have met. He possesses the rare talent to stay completely focused, even when dealing with the potential vagaries of jury duty. As senior production editor, Christopher Granville managed to keep us all on track in meeting critical timelines and did so without complaining about the authors' erratic and never-ending travel schedules. Sarah England did an amazing job creating the visual art program for the Third Edition. She worked with Rich Mayer to develop new interactive figures that encourage student involvement, and she created wonderful new illustrations throughout the book. Students will be forever grateful for her visual art that helps them understand some of the more complex and technical aspects of psychological science. We also thank Rachel Comerford for taking charge of the ancillaries to make sure we have the strongest possible support package and Dan Jost for working his usual magic with emedia. Peter Lesser played an especially important role on the assessment initiative, and we appreciate the efforts he made on our behalf.

If there were an award for the most disciplined, organized, efficient, and all-round master editorial assistant, Wamiq Jawaid would run away with the prize. Words cannot convey how grateful we are to Wamiq for working long hours to make sure we had all the materials we needed right when we needed them.

Special thanks go to our marketing manager, Ken Barton, who has racked up enough frequent flier points traveling for our book that he could probably fly to the moon and back. He is ever cheerful and ever thoughtful, which is truly a winning combination. Indeed, the entire sales management and marketing team at Norton, led by director of sales and marketing Stephen Dunn, have put together wonderful materials to demonstrate key features of the book. Sales managers Nicole Albas, Lib Triplett, Allen Clawson, Katie Incorvia, Annie Stewart, and Scott Berzon have inspired the Norton travelers. Of course, we are especially grateful to the travelers for taking the time to learn about our book in order to introduce it to our fellow instructors. We have enjoyed talking to so many of the travelers about the book, particularly Peter Ruscitti, John Darger, John Kelly, and Greg Leiman. Finally, we acknowledge Norton president Drake McFeely for inspiring a workforce that cares so deeply about publishing and for having continuing faith in us.

Third Edition Consultants and Reviewers

Mary J. Allen, *California State University–Bakersfield*

David H. Barlow, *Boston University*

Bernard C. Beins, *Ithaca College*

Lisa Best, *University of New Brunswick*

Elisabeth Leslie Cameron, *Carthage College*

Wendy Domjan, *University of Texas at Austin*

Michael Domjan, *University of Texas at Austin*

Dana S. Dunn, *Moravian College*

Howard Eichenbaum, *Boston University*

Naomi Eisenberger, *University of California–Los Angeles*

Howard Friedman, *University of California–Riverside*

David C. Funder, *University of California–Riverside*

Preston E. Garraghty, *Indiana University*

Katherine Gibbs, *University of California–Davis*

Jamie Goldenberg, *University of South Florida*

Raymond Green, *Texas A&M–Commerce*

Erin E. Hardin, *Texas Tech University*

Linda Hatt, *University of British Columbia–Okanagan*

Terence Hines, *Pace University*

Howard C. Hughes, *Dartmouth College*

Steve Joordens, *University of Toronto–Scarborough*

Gabriel Kreiman, *Harvard University*

Benjamin Le, *Haverford College*

Gary W. Lewandowski Jr., *Monmouth University*

Margaret F. Lynch, *San Francisco State University*

Debra Mashek, *Harvey Mudd College*

Tim Maxwell, *Hendrix College*

Douglas G. Mook, *University of Virginia, Emeritus*

Maria Minda Oriña, *University of Minnesota–Twin Cities Campus*

Dominic J. Parrott, *Georgia State University*

David Payne, *Wallace Community College*

Catherine Reed, *Claremont McKenna College*

Caton Roberts, *University of Wisconsin–Madison*

Juan Salinas, *University of Texas at Austin*

John J. Skowronski, *Northern Illinois University*

Andra Smith, *University of Ottawa*

Dawn L. Strongin, *California State University–Stanislaus*

Kristy L. vanMarle, *University of Missouri–Columbia*

Simine Vazire, *Washington University in St. Louis*

Athena Vouloumanos, *New York University*

Kenneth A. Weaver, *Emporia State University*

Jill A. Yamashita, *Saint Xavier University*

MEDIA & PRINT RESOURCES FOR INSTRUCTORS AND STUDENTS

For Instructors

Instructor's Resource Manual

by Sue Franz (Highline Community College), Robin Morgan (Indiana University Southeast), and Patrick Dyer (Kennesaw State University)

The Instructor's Resource Manual has been comprehensively integrated with the new edition of the text. The manual equips you with new Concept Maps for each chapter that are completely integrated with emedia features.

Test-Item File

by Wendy Domjan (University of Texas at Austin), Barney Beins (Ithaca College), Valeri Farmer-Dougan (Illinois State University), and Jessica Shryack (University of Minnesota)

This file has been completely revised, using an evidence-centered approach designed by Valerie Shute of Florida State University and Diego Zapata-Rivera of the Educational Testing Service. It includes over 3,000 questions structured around a Concept Map that is consistent with the Study Guide and Instructor's Resource Manual. Use it to evaluate student knowledge on factual, applied, and conceptual levels. The Test-Item File is available in print, ExamView® Assessment Suite, and Word formats.

The Norton Psychology DVD

This diverse collection of over 60 minutes of video clips, ranging from 3 to 7 minutes each, shows the science of psychology in action. The updated DVD includes a host of new clips that incorporate the Learning Objectives of the text with Critical Thinking questions—creating a truly effective teaching tool. Free to qualified adopters.

Instructor's Resource DVD

The Instructor's Resource DVD provides an array of resources for instructors to create easy and effective lecture presentations:

- Lecture PowerPoints with Clicker Questions
- Art PowerPoints
- Image Gallery of art from the text

Instructor's Resource Site

The Instructor's Resource Site is an online source of instructional content for use in lectures, modified classrooms, and distance education courses. The site includes:

- Lecture PowerPoints
- Clicker Questions in PowerPoint format
- Art PowerPoints
- Image Gallery of art from the text

- BlackBoard/WebCT Coursepack
- BlackBoard/WebCT Web Quizzes and Test Bank
- Computerized Test Bank and ExamView® Assessment Suite Software

For Students

StudySpace
wwnorton.com/studyspace

This free student Web site provides a rich array of multimedia resources and review materials within a proven, task-oriented study plan. Each chapter is arranged in an effective Organize, Learn, and Connect structure, with review materials such as chapter summaries, flashcards, and quizzes. The Norton Quiz+ Assessment Program gives students customized chapter-by-chapter study plans that target specific content areas for review. The StudySpace offers:

- **Chapter Audio Podcasts** that serve as chapter overviews and discussions of key concepts. The content is chapter-specific and is organized around the key Learning Objectives.

- **Scientific Method Tours with Review Questions** that help students understand the basic processes of psychological phenomena such as vision and hearing. Each process tour incorporates the new Scientific Method features in the text and is accompanied by review questions.

- **New Animations** that cover more topics and psychological processes in the text. They appear on StudySpace and can be accessed and launched from the ebook.

- **Drag-and-Drop Labeling Exercises** that use the line art from the text to help students understand key diagrams and complex structures.

- **Visual Quizzes** that integrate the revised art program from the text to help students review the details of important figures and diagrams.

Ebook
nortonebooks.com

Same great content, half the price!
The ebook links to StudySpace and offers many useful electronic tools, such as highlighting and sticky notes.

Study Guide
by Gary Lewandowski (Monmouth University)

The thoroughly revised Study Guide is based on new assessment principles. A Concept Map gives students a tour of each chapter; Learning Objectives and self-tests are also included. Exercises include quizzes in various question formats (with answer key), graphical concept models, key terms, and Critical Thinking questions based on the Critical Thinking Skills in the text.

ZAPS
wwnorton.com/zaps

The Norton Psychology Labs are online labs that allow students to participate in classic studies in psychology. ZAPS online gives students the theoretical background for each psychological experiment within an interactive, data-driven format.

STUDENT PREFACE

How Psychology Can Help You Learn

In this increasingly fast-paced world, we are constantly bombarded with information: News stories reach us in minutes from around the globe, new technologies replace old ones, and groundbreaking scientific studies alter long-held beliefs about the physical world. To succeed in college and in your career, you will need to develop powerful learning strategies that produce durable and flexible learning—learning that lasts well into the future and that you can transfer to new situations. The following study skills, based on psychological research, will help you work more productively, learn more efficiently, and apply what you have learned in a variety of settings. (You will find more about learning in several chapters in this book, especially in Chapter 7, "Attention and Memory," and Chapter 8, "Intelligence.")

1. The Right Goals Lead to Success

Throughout your life, you will set countless short-term and long-term goals for yourself: to get that enormous pile of laundry done, to run an eight-minute mile, to have a family, to succeed in your career. It's important to choose goals that are challenging yet attainable. If your goals are unrealistically high, you set yourself up for failure and discouragement, but if they are too low, you won't achieve your greatest potential. Divide each goal into specific, achievable steps, or subgoals, and reward yourself when you reach a milestone. Even a small achievement is worth celebrating!

2. A Little Stress Management Goes a Long Way

Let's face it: Stress is a fact of life. A moderate amount of stress can improve your performance by keeping you alert, challenged, and focused. However, too much stress has the opposite effect and can diminish your productivity, interfere with your sleep, and even take a toll on your health. When the pressure is on, seek healthy ways to manage your stress, such as exercising, writing in a journal, spending time with friends, practicing yoga, or meditating.

3. Cramming Is a Crummy Way to Learn

You have a busy life, and it is always tempting to postpone studying until the night or two before an exam. But in all of your classes there is too much to learn to cram your learning into a few days or late nights. You might be able to remember enough information to get a passing grade on an exam the following day, but plenty of research has shown that cramming does not produce learning that lasts. To make learning stick, you need to space out your study sessions over the semester and build in plenty of time for active reviews.

4. Learning Is Not a Spectator Sport

The more effort you put into your studying, the more benefit you will receive. Merely rereading a chapter or your class notes is not as effective as actively trying to remember what you have learned. Every time you learn something, you create "memory traces" in your brain. By retrieving the information that was learned, you strengthen the memory traces so that you will be more likely to recall the memory in the future. In this book, to encourage active studying, every major section heading is in the form of a question. When you go back to study each section, begin by writing out an answer to the question in the heading without looking at the book. Then check the accuracy and completeness of what you wrote.

5. Explaining Enhances Understanding and Memory

As you learn, focus on trying to explain and describe complicated topics in your own words, as opposed to just memorizing terms and definitions. For example, simply using flashcards to learn about visual perception may help you memorize individual parts of the eye and their functions, but doing so will not help you put the pieces together to understand the incredible process of how we see and recognize objects in the world. Memorizing isolated bits of information is also likely to result in shallow learning that is easily forgotten. A deeper level of learning based on explanation and description would give you a more holistic understanding and a greater ability to generalize the information.

6. There Is More Than One Way to Learn

As you will read in Chapter 7, people process information in two channels—visual and verbal. Another strategy for creating durable learning is to use both of these information formats. Try to supplement the notes you take with visual and spatial displays such as concept maps, graphs, flowcharts, and other types of diagrams. Doing so not only makes you more likely to remember the information but also helps you gain a better understanding of the big picture by emphasizing the connections among important ideas.

A knowledge of psychology can be useful to you in many ways, even if you do not pursue a career in the field. For this reason, we have tried to make all the material in *Psychological Science* accessible and interesting for you as well as directly applicable to your life. As you gain an integrated grounding in traditional and new approaches within psychological science, we hope that this book spurs your curiosity about psychological phenomena. We hope that, by thinking critically about issues and themes in psychological science and in aspects of your life, you will develop a greater understanding of yourself and others.

Mike, Todd, and Diane

CONTENTS

Chapter 2   Research Methodology 33

Chapter 3   Biological Foundations

Chapter 4   The Mind and Consciousness 133

Chapter 7   Attention and Memory 279

Chapter 15 Treating Disorders of the Mind and Body 665

Psychological Science

Third Edition

Introduction

AROUND MIDNIGHT ON FEBRUARY 4, 1999, four members of a plainclothes New York City police Street Crimes Unit drove down Wheeler Avenue in the Bronx, one of the city's five boroughs. They were looking for a rape suspect and saw 22-year-old Amadou Diallo (FIGURE 1.1A), a West African immigrant, standing in the doorway to his apartment building. On the sidewalk, the officers say, they told Diallo to freeze but then saw him reach into his pants pocket. Believing Diallo was reaching for a weapon, they opened fire. Within approximately five seconds, the four officers fired 41 shots at the unarmed Diallo, 19 of which struck him. Diallo died at the scene. His neighbors say Diallo probably did not understand the word *freeze*, since English was not his first language. Others believe Diallo was reaching for his wallet to prove his identity. No one will ever know. An innocent man died. The officers—Kenneth Boss, Sean Carroll, Edward McMellon, and Richard Murphy—were tried for murder and acquitted, but they are left to live with their feelings of guilt and remorse (FIGURE 1.1B).

What Are the Seven Themes of Psychological Science?

- Psychology Is an Empirical Science
- Nature and Nurture Are Inextricably Entwined
- The Brain and Mind Are Inseparable
- A New Biological Revolution Is Energizing Research
- The Mind Is Adaptive
- Psychological Science Crosses Levels of Analysis
- We Often Are Unaware of the Multiple Influences on How We Think, Feel, and Act

How Did the Scientific Foundations of Psychology Develop?

- Experimental Psychology Begins with Structuralism
- Functionalism Addresses the Purpose of Behavior
- Gestalt Psychology Emphasizes Patterns and Context in Learning
- Women Made Pioneering Contributions to Psychology
- Freud Emphasized the Power of the Unconscious
- Most Behavior Can Be Modified by Reward and Punishment

- Cognition Affects Behavior
- Social Situations Shape Behavior
- Psychological Therapy Is Based on Science

How Can We Apply Psychological Science?

- Psychological Knowledge Is Used in Many Professions
- People Are Intuitive Psychological Scientists
- Psychological Science Requires _____'s Thinking
- Psychologists Adh_____
- Psychology ___ Life

Psychologists seek to understand how people perceive, think, and act in a wide range of situations, including horrific ones such as the Diallo case. Among the psychological phenomena involved in this case are emotion, memory, visual perception, decision making, social interaction, cultural differences, prejudice, group behavior, and mental trauma. Psychologists would be interested in knowing, for example, how the officers' emotional states affected their decision making at the scene. They also would want to study the accuracy of the defendants' and eyewitnesses' accounts of the shooting. In addition, they would want to examine group behavior. Did the fact that the officers arrived at the scene together affect individual behavior? Did media coverage influence the trial (which was moved upstate, to Albany, because of the high-profile demonstrations outside the New York City courthouse)? Did prejudice affect the way the officers identified and approached Diallo? Did being the potential target of prejudice affect Diallo's reaction to the police? Did prejudice affect the jury's decision? The Bronx's population is approximately half African American. Many New York City residents charged that the Diallo shooting was motivated by racism. The defense lawyers asserted that race had little to do with the shooting. How can we know?

It is difficult to study the factors that underlie prejudice because most people deny holding such socially unacceptable beliefs. How, then, can we "peek inside" the mind to discover what people are thinking and feeling? Over recent decades—by employing strategies such as the self-reports of research participants, observational studies, and experiments—researchers have made numerous important discoveries about prejudice. For instance, prejudice not only influences the beliefs and behaviors of the prejudiced person but also has strong negative psychological effects on the targets of prejudice, whose behaviors are shaped in part by others' beliefs about them. Perhaps most important, psychologist scientists have discovered methods for reducing stereotyping and prejudice.

Several important developments in study methods are deepening psychological science's understanding of the human mind and human behavior. Methods now exist for observing the working brain in action. Various techniques known collectively as

(a)   (b)

FIGURE 1.1 **Asking Why** **(a)** Amadou Diallo was mistakenly shot and killed by police officers who were searching for a rapist. **(b)** Here **(left to right)**, officers Sean Carroll, Kenneth Boss, and Edward McMellon talk with reporters outside the courthouse. Richard Murphy is not pictured. A jury acquitted all four officers of murder, but did racism play a part in his death?

brain imaging show which parts of the brain are involved in particular behaviors or particular mental activities. For instance, the cognitive neuroscientist Elizabeth Phelps, the social psychologist Mahzarin Banaji, and their colleagues used brain imaging to study racial attitudes. In one study, they showed white college students pictures of unfamiliar black and white faces while, using *functional magnetic resonance imaging (fMRI),* they scanned the students' brains (Phelps et al., 2000). For some of the research participants, the unfamiliar black faces activated a structure in the brain called the *amygdala,* which is involved in detecting threat; this activation indicates a negative emotional response (FIGURE 1.2). These findings alone do not mean, however, that the (white) students who responded in this way necessarily are afraid of unfamiliar black people. This response occurred only in those participants whose scores on the *Implicit Association Test (IAT)* indicated negative attitudes toward blacks. The IAT, taken on a computer, measures reaction times (how quickly people respond) to assess indirectly whether people associate positive and negative words with certain groups of people. In a second study, the researchers showed a new group of white students pictures of famous black people, such as Denzel Washington and Michael Jordan; this time, the amygdala was not activated. This encouraging news suggests that increasing familiarity reduces the fear response, and this reduction in turn might reduce the likelihood of prejudice and discrimination.

The research on prejudice is one example of how psychologists explain human behaviors in real-life contexts. Most of us have a strong desire to figure out other people, to understand their motives, thoughts, desires, intentions, moods, actions, and so on. We want to know whether others are friends or foes, leaders or followers, likely to spurn us or fall in love with us. Our social interactions require us to use our impressions of others to categorize them and to make predictions about their intentions and actions. We want to know why they remember some details and conveniently forget others, or why they engage in self-destructive behaviors. Essentially, we constantly try to figure out what makes other people tick. People who do this for a living are *psychological scientists.*

Psychological science is the study of mind, brain, and behavior. But what exactly does each of these terms mean? *Mind* refers to mental activity. The perceptual experiences a person has while interacting with the world (sight, smell, taste, hearing, and touch) are examples of the mind in action—as are the person's memories, the person's thoughts, and the person's feelings. Mental activity results from biological processes—the actions of *nerve cells,* or *neurons,* and their associated chemical reactions—within the brain. Later, this chapter will discuss scholars' long-standing debate about the relationship between the brain and the mind. For now, note that the "mind is what the brain does" (Kosslyn & Koenig, 1995, p. 4). In other words, the physical brain enables the mind.

The term *behavior* is used to describe a wide variety of actions, from the subtle to the complex, that occur in all organisms. For many years, psychologists focused on behavior rather than on mental states, largely because they had few objective techniques for assessing the mind. The advent of technology to observe the working brain in action has allowed psychological scientists to study mental states such as consciousness and has led to a fuller understanding of human behavior.

psychological science The study of mind, brain, and behavior.

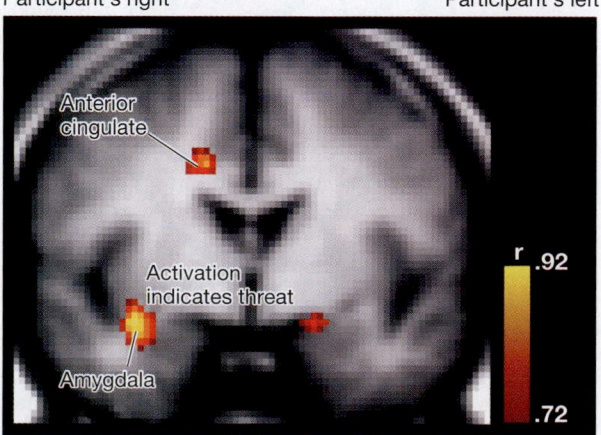

FIGURE 1.2 Brain Imaging and Racial Attitudes Phelps, Banaji, and their colleagues showed white college students pictures of unfamiliar black and white faces. When some of the participants viewed unfamiliar black faces, brain scans showed activation of the amygdala, a brain region associated with threat detection, and also of the anterior cingulate, which is associated with emotional response.

What Are the Seven Themes of Psychological Science?

This book highlights seven themes. Some of these themes traditionally have defined psychology, and all of them guide psychological scientists' study of the mind, brain, and behavior.

1. Psychology is an empirical science.
2. Nature and nurture are inextricably entwined.
3. The brain and mind are inseparable.
4. A new biological revolution is energizing research.
5. The mind is adaptive.
6. Psychological science crosses levels of analysis.
7. We often are unaware of the multiple influences on how we think, feel, and act.

Psychology Is an Empirical Science

Psychological scientists use the *scientific method* to understand how people think, feel, and act. As discussed in Chapter 2, the scientific method is the use of objective, systematic procedures that lead to an accurate understanding of what is being studied. It involves careful observations of the natural world to examine how things work. Although most people are not scientists, most people consume scientific research in some form, and to be savvy consumers of that research they must be able to distinguish between "good science," meaning well-conducted research, and "bad science," meaning flawed research. Understanding how science is conducted makes it possible to tell which studies are credible—that is, use sound scientific methods—and which ones are not. By understanding that psychology is an empirical science, in other words, you begin to learn how psychologists work and how you can become an intelligent consumer of research (**FIGURE 1.3**).

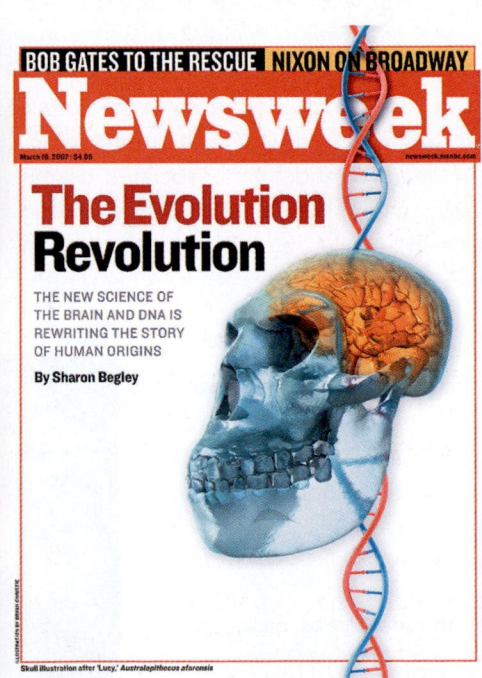
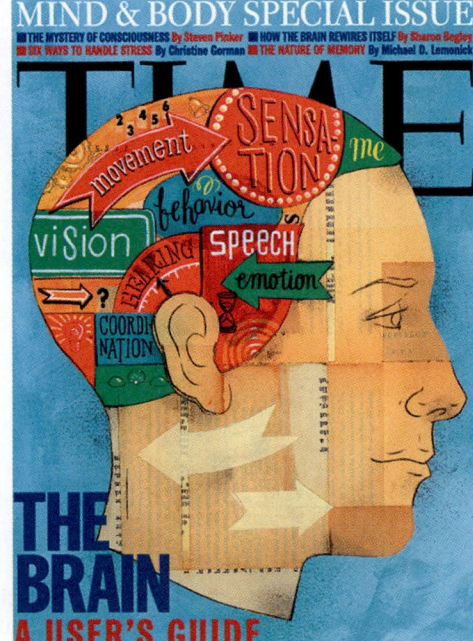

FIGURE 1.3 Psychology in the News Most people consume scientific research without even being aware of it, when it is presented in the latest intriguing news headline. Being a savvy consumer of scientific information means separating "good science" from "bad science."

Nature and Nurture Are Inextricably Entwined

From the time of the ancient Greeks, people have debated whether the individual's psychology is attributable more to *nature* or to *nurture*. That is, are psychological characteristics biologically innate or acquired through education, experience, and **culture** (the beliefs, values, rules, norms, and customs existing within a group of people who share a common language and environment). This **nature/nurture debate** has taken one form or another throughout psychology's history, and psychologists now widely recognize that both nature and nurture are important to humans' psychological development. Psychological scientists now study, for example, the ways that nature and nurture influence each other in shaping the brain, mind, and behavior. Many researchers explore how thoughts, feelings, and behaviors are influenced by genes and by culture. In examples throughout this book, nature and nurture are so enmeshed that they cannot be separated.

As an example of changing beliefs about the influences of nature and nurture, consider two mental disorders that are discussed further in Chapter 14: *Schizophrenia* causes a person to have unusual thoughts, such as believing he or she is God, or experience unusual sensations, such as hearing voices. *Bipolar disorder* causes a person to have dramatic mood swings, from feeling extremely sad (depressed) to feeling euphoric (manic). Before the 1950s, it was generally believed that these two mental disorders, among others, resulted from bad parenting or other environmental circumstances—that is, the causes were believed to be all nurture. But in the late 1950s and the 1960s, various drugs were discovered that could alleviate the symptoms of these disorders; more-recent research has shown that these conditions are heritable. Psychological scientists now believe that many mental disorders result as much from the brain's "wiring" (nature) as from how people are reared and treated within particular cultures (nurture). However, that schizophrenia and bipolar disorder are more likely in certain environments suggests they can be affected by context. People's experiences change their brain structures, which in turn influence people's experiences within their environments. Rapid advancements in understanding the biological and environmental bases of mental disorders are leading to effective treatments that allow people to live normal lives.

Take as another example *posttraumatic stress disorder (PTSD)*, a mental disorder generally believed to result from traumatic events that people experience, such as during military duty or in accidents. Sufferers of PTSD have intrusive and unwanted memories of their traumatic experiences. Although PTSD seems to arise from specific situations, recent research indicates that some people inherit a genetic predisposition to developing it—in this case, nurture activates nature (**FIGURE 1.4**). The social environment also plays an important role in whether treatment for these and other disorders is successful; for example, family members' negative comments tend to decrease a treatment's effectiveness. Psychological science depends on understanding human nature's genetic basis and how environment shapes any particular human's nature.

The Brain and Mind Are Inseparable

Close your eyes and think about your thoughts for a second. Where do your thoughts reside? If you are like most people, you have a subjective sense that your mind is floating somewhere in or near your head—perhaps inside your skull or a few inches above your forehead. Throughout history, the mind has been viewed as residing in many organs of the body, including the liver and the heart. What is the relationship between the mind's (mental) activity and the body's (physical)

culture The beliefs, values, rules, and customs that exist within a group of people who share a common language and environment and that are transmitted through learning from one generation to the next.

nature/nurture debate The arguments concerning whether psychological characteristics are biologically innate or acquired through education, experience, and culture.

FIGURE 1.4 Nurture and Nature Posttraumatic stress disorder (PTSD) seems to arise from traumatic events, but recent research indicates that some people inherit a genetic predisposition to developing it. Here, Jesus Bocanegra, 24, stands in front of a self-portrait he did during his military service in Iraq from 2003 to 2004. After returning from Iraq, Bocanegra was diagnosed with PTSD, and his nervousness in crowds forced him to leave college.

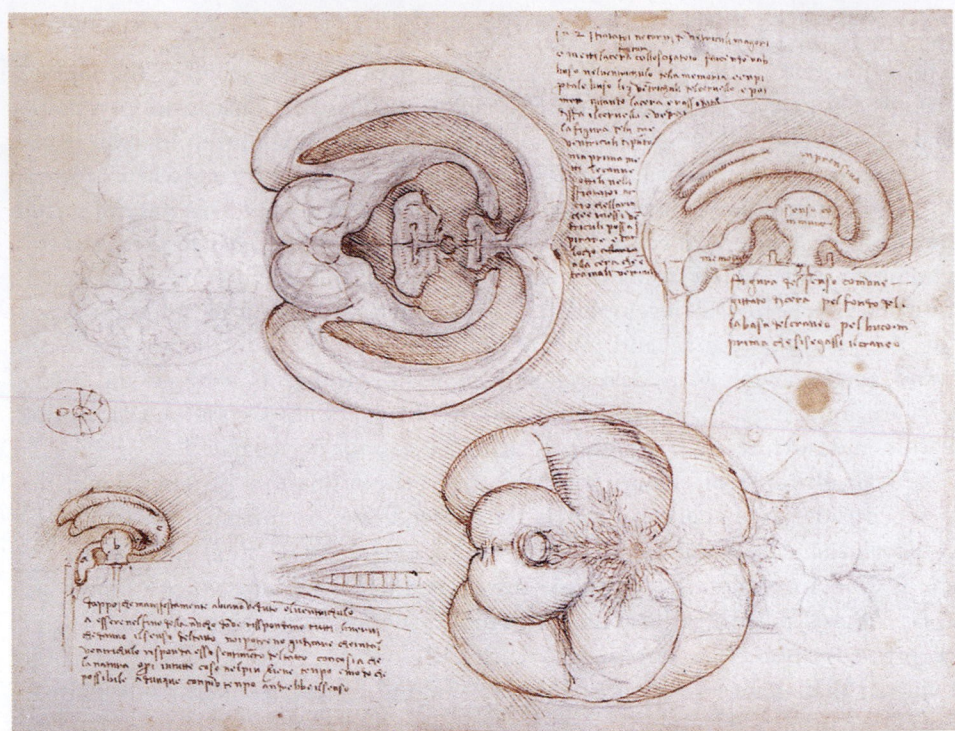

FIGURE 1.5 Da Vinci and the Brain This drawing by Leonardo da Vinci dates from around 1506. Using a wax cast to study the brain, da Vinci found that the various sensory images arrived in the middle region of the brain, which he called the *sensus communis*.

mind/body problem A fundamental psychological issue that considers whether mind and body are separate and distinct or whether the mind is simply the subjective experience of the physical brain.

FIGURE 1.6 René Descartes According to Descartes' theory of dualism, the mind and the body are separate yet intertwined. As discussed throughout this book, psychological scientists now reject that separation.

workings? The **mind/body problem** is perhaps the quintessential psychological issue: Are the mind and body separate and distinct, or is the mind simply the physical brain's subjective experience?

Through most of history, scholars believed the mind is separate from and in control of the body. They held this belief partly because of the strong theological belief that a divine and immortal soul separates humans from nonhuman animals. Around 1500, the artist Leonardo da Vinci challenged this doctrine when he dissected human bodies to make his anatomical drawings more accurate. (These experiments also offended the Church because they violated the human body's presumed sanctity.) Da Vinci's dissections led him to many conclusions about the brain's workings, such as that all sensory messages (vision, touch, smell, etc.) arrived at one location in the brain. He called that region the *sensus communis*, and he believed it to be the home of thought and judgment; its name may be the root of the modern term *common sense* (Blakemore, 1983). Da Vinci's specific conclusions about brain functions were not accurate, but his work represents an early and important attempt to link the brain's anatomy to psychological functions (**FIGURE 1.5**).

In the 1600s, the philosopher René Descartes promoted the first influential theory of *dualism,* the idea that mind and body are separate yet intertwined (**FIGURE 1.6**). The way Descartes connected mind and body was at the time quite radical. The body, he argued, was nothing more than an organic machine, governed by "reflex." For Descartes, many mental functions, such as memory and imagination, resulted from bodily functions. Linking some mental states with the body was a fundamental departure from earlier views of dualism, in which all mental states were separate from bodily functions. In keeping with prevailing religious beliefs, however, Descartes concluded that the rational mind, which controlled volitional action, was divine and separate from the body. Thus his view of dualism maintained the distinction between mind and body, but he assigned to the body many of the mental functions previously considered the mind's sovereign domain. As noted above, psychological scientists largely reject dualistic thinking, believing instead that the mind is what the brain does. (The link between brain activity and conscious experience is considered more fully in Chapter 4, "The Mind and Consciousness.")

A New Biological Revolution Is Energizing Research

A new and profoundly significant biological revolution is in progress, involving a deeper and somewhat different understanding of the human mind and human behavior as compared to views held only a few decades ago. Since the time of the ancient Greek philosopher Aristotle, scholars have asked questions about basic psychological phenomena. But they lacked the methods to examine scientifically many of these fundamental questions, such as *What is consciousness? Where does emotion come from? How does emotion affect cognitive processes? How are memories stored in the brain?* These early thinkers were left with philosophical speculation. This situation began to change around the beginning of the twentieth century, and the last 20 years or so have seen tremendous growth in the understanding of mental activities' biological bases. This interest in biology permeates all areas of psychological science: locating the *neural,* or brain, correlates of how we identify people, discovering the neurochemical problems that produce particular psychological disorders, and so on. As discussed below, three developments in particular have set the stage for the biological revolution and are contributing to the understanding of psychological phenomena.

BRAIN CHEMISTRY The first major development in the biological revolution is a growing understanding of brain chemistry. The brain works through the actions of *neurotransmitters,* chemicals that communicate messages between nerve cells (**FIGURE 1.7**). Over the last 30 years, psychological scientists have made tremendous progress in identifying these chemicals and their functions. Although it was long believed that only a handful of neurotransmitters were involved in brain functions, in fact hundreds of substances play critical roles in mental activity and behavior. For instance, people have better memories for events that happen when they are aroused than when they are calm, because chemicals involved in responding to the world influence the neural mechanisms involved in memory. Their understanding of the brain's chemical processes has provided researchers with many insights into both mental activity and behavior, and it has enabled them to develop treatments for various psychological disorders.

THE HUMAN GENOME The second major development in the biological revolution is the enormous progress in understanding genetic processes' influence on life. Scientists have mapped the *human genome*—the basic *genetic code,* or blueprint, for the human body—and they have developed various techniques for discovering the links between genes and behavior. For instance, to study particular genes' effects on memory, researchers bred mice that lacked a specific gene (and showed impaired memory—thus the gene is related to memory) and ones that included an additional specific gene (and showed improved memory—more evidence). By identifying the genes involved in memory, researchers soon may be able to develop therapies, based on genetic manipulation, that will assist people who have memory problems, including people with Alzheimer's disease.

   Of course, the idea that a single gene causes a specific behavior is overly simplistic. No one gene is solely responsible for memory, racist attitudes, and so on.

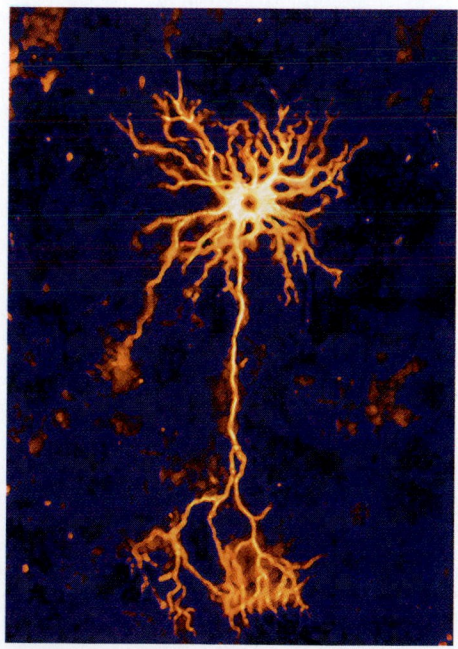

FIGURE 1.7 Human Nerve Cell Nerve cells, or neurons, like this one are the basic units of the human nervous system. The growing understanding of their chemistry has led to better explanations of mental activity and of behavior.

Great moments in evolution

evolutionary theory In psychological science, a theory that emphasizes the inherited, adaptive value of behavior and mental activity throughout the history of a species.

adaptations In evolutionary theory, the physical characteristics, skills, or abilities that increase the chances of reproduction or survival and are therefore likely to be passed along to future generations.

FIGURE 1.8 Charles Darwin Introduced in *On the Origin of Species*, Darwin's theory of evolution has had a huge impact on how psychologists think about the mind. This portrait reportedly was Darwin's favorite picture of himself.

Almost all psychological and biological activity is affected by multiple genes' actions. Nonetheless, as discussed in Chapter 3, many physical and mental characteristics are inherited to some degree. Scientists are beginning to understand how situational contexts, such as the presence or absence of particular people, influence how genes are expressed and therefore how they affect behavior. Mapping the human genome has given scientists the foundational knowledge for studying how specific genes affect thoughts, actions, feelings, and disorders. Although many possible corrections for genetic defects are decades away, the scientific study of genetic influences is providing fresh insights into mental activity.

WATCHING THE WORKING BRAIN The development of methods for assessing the brain in action has provided the third major force fueling the biological revolution in psychology. The way the brain influences behavior has been studied with increasing effectiveness for more than a century, but only since the late 1980s have researchers been able to study the working brain as it performs its vital psychological functions. Using the methods of *neuroscience,* psychological scientists can now address some of the most central questions of human experience, such as how different brain regions interact to produce perceptual experience, how various types of memory are similar or different, and how conscious experience involves changes in brain activity.

Knowing where in the brain something happens does not by itself reveal much, but the finding that consistent patterns of brain activation are associated with specific mental tasks suggests the two are connected. For over a century, scientists had disagreed about whether psychological processes are located in specific parts of the brain or distributed throughout the brain. We now know that there is some *localization* of function (some areas are important for specific feelings, thoughts, and actions) but that many brain regions participate to produce behavior and mental activity. Brain imaging has allowed researchers to make tremendous strides in understanding the mental states involved in many psychological abilities (Posner & DiGirolamo, 2000). The progress in understanding the neural basis of mental life has been rapid and dramatic. For good reason, the 1990s were labeled the decade of the brain.

The Mind Is Adaptive

The human mind has been shaped by evolution. That is, from the perspective of **evolutionary theory,** the brain has evolved over millions of years to solve problems related to survival and reproduction. The accumulating evidence indicates that the mind is adaptive in biological and cultural terms: In addition to helping us overcome challenges, it provides a strong framework for our shared social understandings of how the world works. During the course of human evolution, random genetic mutations endowed some of our ancestors with **adaptations**—physical characteristics, skills, and abilities—that increased their chances of survival and reproduction and ensured that their genes were passed along to future generations.

Among the major intellectual events that shaped the future of psychological science was the publication in 1859 of Charles Darwin's *On the Origin of Species* (**FIGURE 1.8**). Earlier philosophers and naturalists, including Darwin's grandfather, Erasmus Darwin, had discussed the possibility that species might evolve. But Charles Darwin first presented the mechanism of evolution, which he called

natural selection: the process by which organisms' random mutations that are adaptive are passed along and random mutations that hinder survival (and therefore reproduction) are not. Thus as species struggle to survive, those better adapted to their environments will leave more offspring, those offspring will produce more offspring, and so on. This idea has come to be known as the *survival of the fittest*.

Darwin's ideas have profoundly influenced many scientific fields, philosophy, and society. Modern evolutionary theory has driven the field of biology for years, but it has only recently begun to inform psychology. Rather than being a specific area of scientific inquiry, evolutionary theory is a way of thinking that can be used to understand many aspects of mind and behavior (Buss, 1999).

SOLVING ADAPTIVE PROBLEMS

Over the last five million years, adaptive behaviors and specialized mechanisms have been built into our bodies and brains through evolution. For instance, a mechanism that produces calluses has evolved to protect the skin from the abuses of the physical labor that humans sometimes need to engage in to survive. Likewise, specialized circuits, or structures, have evolved in the brain to solve adaptive problems (Cosmides & Tooby, 1997).

Evolutionary theory is especially useful for considering whether human mechanisms are adaptive—in other words, whether they affect survival and reproduction. For example, psychologists have known for decades that situational and cultural contexts influence the development of social behaviors and of attitudes. Now evidence is accumulating that many behaviors and attitudes can also be considered adaptive solutions to recurring human problems. For example, humans have a fundamental need to belong to a group, and therefore all societies discourage behaviors that may lead to social exclusion (Baumeister & Leary, 1995). People who lie, cheat, or steal may drain group resources and thereby decrease the chances of survival and reproduction for other group members. Some evolutionary psychologists believe humans have "cheater detectors" on the lookout for this sort of behavior in others (Cosmides & Tooby, 2000).

Another classic example of the way adaptive mechanisms develop involves the "visual cliff" (**FIGURE 1.9**). When infants old enough to crawl are placed on top of a clear piece of plastic that covers both a firm surface (such as a table) and a dropped surface (the clear plastic extends over the edge of the table), the infants may pat the surface that extends over the cliff and even accidentally back onto it, but they will not willingly crawl over the cliff, even if their mothers are standing on the other side of the cliff encouraging them to do so. Infants become wary of heights at about the same age they learn to crawl, even though they have little personal experience with heights or gravity. This fear of heights is surely an adaptive mechanism that will enhance their chances of survival.

MODERN MINDS IN STONE AGE SKULLS

According to evolutionary theory, we need to be aware of the challenges our early ancestors faced if we want to understand much of our current behavior, whether adaptive or maladaptive. Humans began evolving about five million years ago, but modern humans (*Homo sapiens*) can be traced back only about 100,000 years, to the Pleistocene era. If the human brain slowly adapted to accommodate the needs of Pleistocene hunter-gatherers, scientists should try to understand how the brain works within the context of the environmental pressures humans faced during the Pleistocene era. For instance, people like sweet foods, especially those high in fat. These foods are highly

natural selection Darwin's theory that those who inherit characteristics that help them adapt to their particular environments have a selective advantage over those who do not.

FIGURE 1.9 Adaptive Mechanism
Despite the plastic covering over the visual cliff, infants will not crawl over the cliff even if their mothers call to them from the other side.

caloric, and in prehistoric times eating them would have had great survival value. In other words, a preference for fatty and sweet foods was adaptive. Today, many societies have an abundance of foods, many of them high in fat and sugar. That we still enjoy them and eat them, sometimes to excess, may now be maladaptive in that it can produce obesity. Nonetheless, our evolutionary heritage encourages us to eat foods that had survival value when food was relatively scarce. Many of our current behaviors, of course, do not reflect our evolutionary heritage. Reading books, driving cars, using computers, instant messaging, and watching television are among the human behaviors that we have displayed only recently. (Further complexities in the evolutionary process are discussed in Chapter 3, "Biological Foundations.")

CULTURE PROVIDES ADAPTIVE SOLUTIONS For humans, many of the most demanding adaptive challenges involve dealing with other humans. These challenges include selecting mates, cooperating in hunting and in gathering, forming alliances, competing for scarce resources, and even warring with neighboring groups. This dependency on group living is not unique to humans, but the nature of relations among and between ingroup and outgroup members is especially complex in human societies. The complexity of living in groups gives rise to culture, and culture's various aspects are transmitted from one generation to the next through learning. For instance, our musical and food preferences, our ways of expressing emotion, our tolerance of body odors, and so on are strongly affected by the cultures we are raised in. Many of a culture's "rules" reflect adaptive solutions worked out by previous generations.

In contrast to human biological evolution, which has taken place over several million years, cultural evolution has occurred much faster, and the most dramatic cultural changes have come in the last few thousand years. Although humans have changed only modestly in physical terms in that time, they have changed profoundly in regard to how they live together. Even within the last century, there have been dramatic changes in how human societies interact. The flow of people, commodities, and financial instruments among all regions of the world, often referred to as *globalization,* has increased in velocity and scale over the past century in ways that were previously unimaginable. Even more recently, the Internet has created a worldwide network of humans, essentially a new form of culture with its own rules, values, and customs.

Over the past decade, recognition has grown that culture plays a foundational role in shaping how people view and reason about the world around them—and that people from different cultures possess strikingly different minds. Research by the social psychologist Richard Nisbett, for example, has demonstrated that people from most Asian countries have a worldview quite different from that of people from most European and North American countries. Metaphorically speaking, Nisbett's work has suggested that Westerners tend to miss the forest for the trees, focusing on single elements in the forefront, whereas those from Eastern cultures tend to overlook single trees, focusing on the entire forest in the background (**FIGURE 1.10**). Nisbett and his colleagues (2001) have documented many differences in these groups' thinking styles. The general pattern is that Westerners are much more analytic—they break complex ideas into simpler components, categorize information, and use logic and rules to explain behavior. Easterners tend to be more holistic in their thinking, seeing everything in front of them as an inherently complicated whole, with all elements affecting all other elements. In his book *The Geography of Thought* (2003), Nisbett argues that these essential cultural differences date back to ancient Greek and Chinese societies from roughly the eighth

FIGURE 1.10 Cultural Differences Westerners tend to be "independent" and autonomous, stressing their individuality. Easterners—such as this Cambodian family—tend to be more "interdependent," stressing their sense of being part of a collective.

through the third centuries BCE. He characterizes the Greeks of that time as focusing on personal freedom, logic, and debate; their Chinese contemporaries as focusing on harmonious relationships with family and with other villagers. Indeed, cross-cultural research has found that "family orientation" and "harmony" are two major dimensions of personality for the Chinese but not for people from Western cultures (Cheung, Cheung, & Leung, 2008). As psychological scientists come to better understand the relationship between culture and behavior, they make clear the importance of considering behavioral phenomena in their cultural contexts.

Psychological Science Crosses Levels of Analysis

Throughout the history of psychology, studying a phenomenon at one level of analysis has been the favored approach. Only recently have researchers started to explain behavior at several levels of analysis, providing an increasingly complete picture of behavioral and mental processes. Because mind and behavior can be studied on many levels of analysis, psychologists often collaborate with researchers from other scientific fields, such as biology, computer science, physics, anthropology, and sociology. *Interdisciplinary* efforts share the goal of understanding how biological, individual, social, and cultural factors influence our specific behaviors.

Four broadly defined levels of analysis reflect the most common research methods for studying mind and behavior (**FIGURE 1.11**). The *biological level of analysis* deals with how the physical body contributes to mind and behavior, as in the neuro-chemical and genetic processes occurring in the body and brain. The *individual level of analysis* focuses on individual differences in personality and in the mental processes that affect how people perceive and know the world. The *social level of analysis* involves how group contexts affect people's ways of interacting and influencing each other. The *cultural level of analysis* deals with how different cultures shape the thoughts, feelings, and actions of the people in them.

FIGURE 1.11 Levels of Analysis

	LEVEL	FOCUS	WHAT IS STUDIED?
	Biological	Brain systems	Neuroanatomy, animal research, brain imaging
		Neurochemistry	Neurotransmitters and hormones, animal studies, drug studies
		Genetics	Gene mechanisms, heritability, twin and adoption studies
	Individual	Individual differences	Personality, gender, developmental age groups, self-concept
		Perception and cognition	Thinking, decision making, language, memory, seeing, hearing
		Behavior	Observable actions, responses, physical movements
	Social	Interpersonal behavior	Groups, relationships, persuasion, influence, workplace
			Attitudes, stereotypes, perceptions
	Cultural	Thoughts, actions, behaviors—in different societies and cultural groups	Norms, beliefs, values, symbols, ethnicity

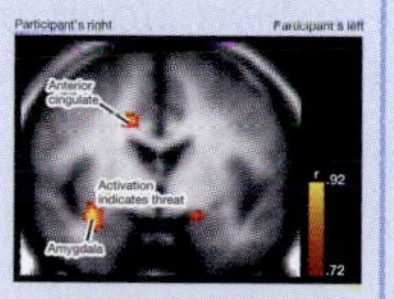

To understand how research is conducted at the different levels, consider the many ways psychological scientists have studied listening to music, a pastime important to most people (Renfrow & Gosling, 2003). Researchers have examined how musical preferences vary among individuals and across cultures, how music affects emotional states and thought processes, and even how the brain perceives sound as music rather than noise. For instance, studies of music's effects on mood at the biological level of analysis have shown that pleasant music may be associated with increased activation of one brain chemical, serotonin, that is known to be relevant to mood (Evers & Suhr, 2000). Other researchers have used *brain systems analysis* to study music's effects (Peretz & Zatorre, 2005). Does perceiving music use the same brain circuits as, say, perceiving the sounds of cars or of spoken language? Processing musical information turns out to be similar to general auditory processing, but it also may use different brain mechanisms. *Case studies* have indicated that some patients with certain types of brain injury become unable to hear tones and melody but not speech or environmental sounds. One 35-year-old woman who had brain damage lost the ability to recognize even familiar tunes—a condition known as *amusia*—even though other aspects of her memory system and language system were intact (Peretz, 1996).

In studies conducted at the individual level of analysis, researchers have used laboratory experiments to study music's effects on mood, memory, decision making, and various other mental states and processes (Krumhansl, 2002). They have discovered, for instance, that "Russia under the Mongolian Yoke" from Prokofiev's *Field of the Dead,* played at half speed, reliably puts people into negative moods. Mood may be affected not only by the tempo of the music but also by whether the music is in major or minor mode. At least in Western music, major mode is typically associated with positive moods and minor mode is associated with sad moods. This emotional response appears to be learned, at least in part, because very young children do not discriminate between modes. By age seven or eight, however, children can reliably distinguish the mood effects of major and minor modes (Gregory, Worrall, & Sarge, 1996).

A study of music at the social level of analysis might compare the types of music people prefer when they are in groups with the types they prefer when alone, or how group preferences for some types of music influence individuals' preferences when they are not in a group. For instance, when people are alone they might like quiet, contemplative music, whereas with others they might like more upbeat music that encourages dancing.

The cross-cultural study of music preferences has developed into a separate field, *ethnomusicology*. An ethnomusicologist has noted, for example, that African music has rhythmic structures different from those in Western music (Agawu, 1995), and these differences in turn may reflect the important role of dancing and drumming in African folktales. Ethnomusicologists also note that, as mentioned above, the influences of major and minor modes on mood hold only within certain cultures, because these associations are not innate and must be learned.

As these examples show, research across the levels of analysis is creating a greater understanding of the psychology of music. Adding to that understanding is innovative research combining two or more levels of analysis.

We Often Are Unaware of the Multiple Influences on How We Think, Feel, and Act

An important lesson from psychological research is that people are influenced by subtle factors in their environments, even when they largely are unaware of those influences. That is, some factors influence our thoughts, feelings, and behaviors at an unconscious level: They happen without our awareness and therefore leave us without knowledge (retrievable memories) of them. The idea that we are influenced by events and memories we are not consciously aware of has a long history in psychology; it is often associated with Sigmund Freud, whose work is discussed in more detail later in this chapter. More recently, John Bargh and his colleagues (Bargh, 2006; Bargh & Chartrand, 1999) have referred to these unconscious influences as the "automaticity of everyday life," because they occur automatically—without effort or intent. For example, after participants in a study read a list of words related to kindness, they rated a person they had just met as kinder than did the second group of participants, who had read words unrelated to kindness. Further, the first group had no conscious knowledge that their ratings were affected by the list of words (Srull & Wyer, 1979). After reading the words related to kindness, the first group's knowledge about the concept of *kindness,* in memory, was *primed,* or activated, and became more available for a short time (maybe 15 to 20 minutes), thus affecting their subsequent judgments. Likewise, in a recent study, participants who were shown negative facial expressions very quickly, so fast that they did not know they had seen them, reported being in worse moods than those reported by participants shown neutral facial expressions (Ruys & Stapel, 2008).

Priming can be done with a smell or a tactile (touch) sensation. In one study (Williams & Bargh, 2007), research participants held a cup of coffee for the researcher while he juggled an armful of textbooks, clipboards, and so on. Half the participants held a cup of hot coffee, and half held a cup of iced coffee. None of the participants believed that just holding the cup would affect their thoughts, feelings, or actions, but it did: The participants who held the hot coffee rated a third person as "warmer" and less selfish than did those who held the iced coffee. In short, as you will see throughout this book, we are aware of only a fraction of the environmental factors that influence us.

> ## SUMMING UP
>
> ### What Are the Seven Themes of Psychological Science?
>
> Psychological science is the study of mind, brain, and behavior. This book focuses on seven major themes that characterize psychological science: (1) Psychology is an empirical science that uses research methods as a way of knowing about how we think, feel, and behave. (2) Nature and nurture are inextricably entwined: We cannot consider either influence separately, because they work together. (3) The brain and mind are inseparable. (4) A biological revolution has been energizing psychological research into how the brain enables the mind. Among the revolutionary developments are increasing knowledge of the neurochemistry of mental disorders, the mapping of the human genome, and the invention of imaging technologies that allow researchers to observe the working brain in action. (5) The mind is adaptive. In recent years, psychological science has been influenced heavily by evolutionary psychology, which argues that the brain has evolved to solve adaptive problems. (6) Psychological scientists share the goal of understanding mind, brain, and behavior, but they do so by focusing on the same problems at different levels of analysis—biological, individual, social, and cultural. Most problems in psychology require studies at each level. (7) We often are unaware of the multiple influences on how we think, feel, and behave. Events can prime our minds so that we think, feel, and behave in ways suggested by the priming stimuli, even though we may not be aware of or remember those influences.

FIGURE 1.12 Confucius Ancient philosophers such as Confucius studied topics that remain important in contemporary psychology.

⊙ **MEASURING UP**

For each example below, indicate which of the seven themes of psychological science apply. For some examples, more than one theme may apply.

Themes:

1. Psychology is an empirical science.
2. Nature and nurture are inextricably entwined.
3. The mind and brain are inseparable.
4. A biological revolution is energizing psychological research.
5. The mind is adaptive.
6. Psychologists use different levels of analysis in their research.
7. We often are unaware of the influences on how we think, feel, and behave.

Examples:

a. In one study, some participants were asked to graph lines between endpoints near each other (e.g., −1, −3), and other participants were asked to graph lines between endpoints far from each other (e.g., −5, +12). All were then asked to judge the closeness of their relationship with a loved one. Participants who graphed short lines rated their relationship as closer than did those who graphed long lines (Williams & Bargh, 2008).

b. To understand the development of genius, psychologists study the heritability of genius and the experiences that help it develop.

c. Psychologists are skeptical of astrology as a way of knowing about a person's personality, because astrology violates a central principle in psychological science.

d. In a study of prejudice, psychologists used an attitudes test and brain imaging when participants looked at pictures of African Americans' faces and of Caucasians' faces.

e. When psychologists study a disorder of the mind, they frequently look at genetic factors that might be involved in causing the disorder.

f. Descartes' notion of dualism was replaced with this general theme.

How Did the Scientific Foundations of Psychology Develop?

People have always wanted to know why people do the things they do, so psychology as a field of inquiry has an extensive history, roots in every corner of the globe, and intellectual origins dating back to long before it was established as a formal discipline. Ancient Greek philosophers such as Aristotle and Plato pondered many of the same questions considered by contemporary psychological scientists. Ancient Greek physicians such as Hippocrates and ancient Roman physicians such as Galen recognized that the brain was important for mental activity. In China, the philosopher Confucius (551–479 BCE) emphasized human development, education, and interpersonal relations, all of which remain contemporary topics in psychology around the world (Higgins & Zheng, 2002; **FIGURE 1.12**). During the Han dynasty (206 BCE–220 CE), the Chinese developed multiple tests to select candidates for government jobs, and by the time of the Ming dynasty (1368–1644), multistage testing was used throughout the country. Only those with the highest test scores could serve in public office (Higgins & Zheng, 2002).

Similarly, there is a long history of psychological thought in Muslim countries; in fact, some scholars claim that Western notions of psychology can be found in the writings of early Muslim scholars (Haque, 2004). For example, Al Kindi

(801–866 CE) produced hundreds of writings about sorrow and grief. To combat depression, he used cognitive strategies—many of them similar to a type of psychotherapy, *cognitive therapy,* commonly used today. At-Tabari (838–870 CE) wrote about child psychology and emphasized the need for psychotherapy.

In the mid-1800s in Europe, psychology arose as a separate field of study using the experimental method. In *A System of Logic* (1843), John Stuart Mill declared that psychology should leave the realm of speculation and of philosophy and become a science of observation and of experiment. Indeed, he defined psychology as "the science of the elementary laws of the mind" and argued that only through the methods of science would the processes of the mind be understood. As a result, throughout the 1800s early psychologists increasingly studied mental activity through careful scientific observation. Like the shift from philosophy to experimentation, rapid increases in knowledge about basic physiology were central to the development of psychological science—though, as discussed above, the field is only now drawing on biology's full power to explain psychological phenomena.

As psychology developed from a young discipline to a vital field of science and a vibrant profession, different ways of thinking about the content of psychology emerged. These ways of thinking are called *schools of thought.* As is true in every science, one school of thought would dominate the field for a while; there would then be a backlash, and a new school of thought would take over the field. Today, as multiple levels of analysis are used to understand psychology, researchers rely on the scientific method to support their theories and to decide what is most likely true. The following section discusses some major figures and major schools of thought in the history of psychology.

Experimental Psychology Begins with Structuralism

In 1879, Wilhelm Wundt (**FIGURE 1.13**) established the first psychology laboratory and institute. At this facility, in Leipzig, Germany, for the first time students could earn advanced academic degrees in psychology. Wundt trained many of the great early psychologists, many of whom then established psychological laboratories throughout Europe, Canada, and the United States.

Wundt realized that psychological processes, the products of physiological actions in the brain, take time to occur. Therefore, he would present each research participant with a simple psychological task and a related but more complex one. By subtracting the time a participant took to complete the simple task from the time that participant took to complete the more complex task, Wundt could infer how much time a particular mental event—the common factor between the two tasks—took to occur. Researchers still widely use *reaction time* to study psychological processes, but their equipment is of course more sophisticated than Wundt's. Wundt was not satisfied with simply studying mental reaction times, however; he wanted to measure conscious experiences. To do so, he developed the method of **introspection,** a systematic examination of subjective mental experiences that requires people to inspect and report on the content of their thoughts. Wundt asked people to use introspection in comparing their subjective experiences as they contemplated a series of objects—for example, by stating which one they found more pleasant.

Edward Titchener, a student of Wundt's, used methods such as introspection to pioneer a school of thought that became known as **structuralism,** which is based on the idea that conscious experience can be studied when it is broken down into its underlying components. Titchener believed that an understanding of the basic elements of consciousness would provide the scientific basis for understanding the mind. He argued that one could take a stimulus such as a musical tone and by introspection analyze its "quality," "intensity," "duration," and "clarity." Wundt ultimately

FIGURE 1.13 Wilhelm Wundt Wundt founded modern experimental psychology.

introspection A systematic examination of subjective mental experiences that requires people to inspect and report on the content of their thoughts.

structuralism An approach to psychology based on the idea that conscious experience can be broken down into its basic underlying components or elements.

FIGURE 1.14 William James James was highly influenced by Darwin and (among many other accomplishments) is credited with "naturalizing" the mind.

stream of consciousness A phrase coined by William James to describe one's continuous series of ever-changing thoughts.

functionalism An approach to psychology concerned with the adaptive purpose, or function, of mind and behavior.

rejected such uses of introspection, but Titchener relied on the method throughout his career. The general problem with introspection is that experience is subjective; each person brings to introspection a unique perceptual system, and it is difficult for researchers to determine whether study participants are applying introspection to a study's criteria in similar ways. Accordingly, over time psychologists largely abandoned introspection, because it was not a reliable method for understanding psychological processes. Nonetheless, Wundt, Titchener, and other structuralists were important due to their goal of developing a pure science of psychology with its own vocabulary and set of rules.

Functionalism Addresses the Purpose of Behavior

One critic of structuralism was William James, a brilliant scholar whose wide-ranging work has had an enormous, enduring impact on psychology (**FIGURE 1.14**). In 1873, James abandoned a career in medicine to teach physiology at Harvard University. He was among the first professors at Harvard to openly welcome questions from students rather than having them listen silently to lectures. James's personal interests were more philosophical than physiological; he was captivated by the nature of conscious experience. In 1875, he gave his first lecture on psychology, and he later quipped that it was also the first lecture on psychology he had ever heard. To this day, psychologists find rich delight in reading James's penetrating analysis of the human mind, *Principles of Psychology* (1890), the most influential book in the early history of psychology. Many of the book's central ideas have held up over time.

In criticizing structuralism's failure to capture the most important aspects of mental experience, James argued that the mind was much more complex than its elements and therefore could not be broken down. For instance, he noted that the mind consisted of an ever-changing, continuous series of thoughts. This **stream of consciousness** could not be frozen in time, according to James, so the structuralists' techniques were sterile and artificial. He likened psychologists who used the structural approach to people trying to understand a house by studying each of its bricks individually. More important to James was that the bricks together formed a house and that a house has a particular function. The mind's elements mattered less than the mind's usefulness to people.

Heavily influenced by Charles Darwin's thinking, James argued that psychologists ought to examine the *functions* served by the mind—how the mind operates. According to his approach, which became known as **functionalism,** the mind came into existence over the course of human evolution, and it works as it does because it is useful for preserving life and passing along genes to future generations. In other words, it helps humans adapt to environmental demands.

Many functionalists applied psychological research to the real world. If a behavior serves a purpose, they argued, that purpose ought to be reflected in daily human life. Thus, for example, James applied the functional approach to the study of phenomena such as the nature of religious experience. The educator John Dewey tested functionalist theories in his classrooms, teaching according to how the mind processes information. This *progressive* approach to education emphasized divergent thinking and creativity rather than the repetitive drill learning of conventional knowledge (which might, after all, be incorrect; Hothersall, 1995). Yet the broad-ranging subjects to which functionalism was applied led to criticism that this school was not sufficiently rigorous, and therefore functionalism slowly lost momentum as a movement within psychology. Within the past few decades, however, the functional approach has returned to psychological science, as more and more researchers consider the adaptiveness of the behaviors and mental processes they study.

Gestalt Psychology Emphasizes Patterns and Context in Learning

Another school of thought that arose in opposition to structuralism was the *Gestalt* school, founded by Max Wertheimer in 1912 and expanded by Wolfgang Köhler, among others. According to **Gestalt theory,** the whole of personal experience is not simply the sum of its constituent elements; or in other words, *the whole is different from the sum of its parts.* So, for example, if a researcher shows people a triangle, they see a triangle—not three lines on a piece of paper, as would be the case for the trained observers in one of Titchener's structuralist experiments. (When you look at **FIGURE 1.15**, do you see the parts or the whole?) In experimentally investigating subjective experience, the Gestalt psychologists relied not on the reports of trained observers but on ordinary people's observations. This unstructured reporting of experience was called the *phenomenological* approach, referring to the totality of subjective conscious experience.

The Gestalt movement reflected an important idea that was at the heart of criticisms of structuralism: The perception of objects is subjective and dependent on context. Two people can look at an object and see different things. Indeed, one person

Gestalt theory A theory based on the idea that the whole of personal experience is different from simply the sum of its constituent elements.

*Many principles of psychological science are easy to experience. In each chapter of this book, **Try for Yourself** features will present you with the chance to be your own research participant.*

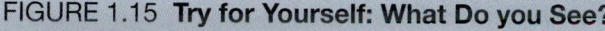

FIGURE 1.15 Try for Yourself: What Do you See?

The fragments make up a picture of a dog sniffing the ground.

Explanation: The mind organizes the picture's elements automatically to produce the perception of the dog. The picture is processed and experienced as a unified whole. Once you perceive the dog, you cannot choose to not see it.

FIGURE 1.16 **Try for Yourself: What Do you See?**

This drawing by the psychologist Roger Shepard can be viewed as either a face behind a candlestick or two separate profiles.

Explanation: The mind organizes the scene into one or another perceptual whole, so the picture looks a specific way each time it is viewed, but it is difficult to see both the single face and two profiles at the same time.

FIGURE 1.17 Mary Whiton Calkins
Calkins was an important pioneer of psychological science, despite having been denied the doctorate she earned in psychology.

can look at an object and see it in completely different ways. (When you look at **FIGURE 1.16**, how many possible views do you see?) The Gestalt perspective has influenced many areas of psychology, such as the study of vision and the understanding of human personality.

Women Made Pioneering Contributions to Psychology

Women's contributions to psychological science, like women's contributions to many other fields of science, were long underappreciated and for many years even ignored. Consider Mary Whiton Calkins (**FIGURE 1.17**). At Smith College, she studied philosophy and classics; at Wellesley College, she was employed initially on a temporary basis as a Greek instructor, then invited to become a professor of the new field of philosophical psychology, contingent on her completing advanced training in psychology. At the time, her options were quite limited because psychology was relatively new to North America. After canvassing the possibilities, she decided that studying with William James at Harvard University would provide her with the best training. James was enthusiastic about having her as a student. Unfortunately, Harvard's president, Charles Eliot, did not believe in coeducation, and only after great pressure from James, Calkins's father, and the president of Wellesley did Eliot relent and let Calkins enroll in the seminar as a guest. The male students withdrew from the seminar in protest, leaving Calkins with a private tutorial "at either side of a library fire," as she describes in her autobiography.

Calkins continued her psychological studies with several other mentors at Harvard, including the famous psychophysicist Hugo Munsterberg. With him, in 1895 she completed all the requirements for a PhD. Although she scored higher than her male classmates on the qualifying exam, Harvard denied her the degree, offering instead a PhD from Radcliffe, the women's school affiliated with Harvard. Calkins refused the degree, bristling at the unequal treatment she received and describing the differential education of men and women as artificial and illogical. Efforts to have Harvard overturn its earlier decision continue to this day, as does Harvard's refusal to grant her the degree she earned. (Harvard did not grant a PhD to a woman until 1963.)

Calkins had a productive career as a professor at Wellesley and wrote an introductory psychology textbook in 1901. She was the first woman to set up a psychology laboratory, published more than 100 articles, and in 1905 was elected the first woman president of the American Psychological Association. Calkins's major research interest was the self, which she believed could be studied using the methods of science. She made several other important contributions to the early science of psychology, although in her later years she became somewhat disenchanted by the rise of behaviorism and its dismissal of the concept of self.

Margaret Flay Washburn was the first woman to be officially granted a PhD in psychology. She was awarded her doctorate in 1921 at Cornell University, where she studied with Edward Titchener. In the same year, Washburn became the second woman president of the American Psychological Association. She spent most of her career at Vassar College, which she had attended as an undergraduate. Her passion for teaching was rewarded by her students, who raised $15,000 as a gift to celebrate her 25 years at Vassar. In keeping with her devotion to students, Washburn used the gift to set up a scholarship fund for women. Of course, many other women contributed to the history of psychology, and their contributions are now readily acknowledged. Today, women make up approximately 70 percent of psychology majors and nearly half of all new psychology doctorates in the workforce (Frincke & Pate, 2004).

Freud Emphasized the Power of the Unconscious

Twentieth-century psychology was profoundly influenced by one of its most famous thinkers, Sigmund Freud (**FIGURE 1.18**). Freud, who was trained in medicine, began his career working with people who had neurological disorders such as paralysis of various body parts. He found that many of his patients had few medical reasons for their paralysis, and he soon came to believe their conditions were caused by psychological factors.

Psychology was in its infancy at the end of the nineteenth century, when Freud deduced that much of human behavior is determined by mental processes operating below the level of conscious awareness, at the level of the **unconscious.** Freud believed these unconscious mental forces, often sexual and in conflict, produced psychological discomfort and in some cases even apparent psychological disorders. From his theories, Freud pioneered the clinical case study approach (discussed in Chapter 2, "Research Methodology") and developed the therapeutic method of **psychoanalysis,** which involves trying to bring the contents of a patient's unconscious into conscious awareness so their conflicts can be dealt with constructively. For example, he analyzed the apparent symbolic content in a patient's dreams in search of hidden conflicts. He also used *free association,* a technique in which a patient simply would talk about whatever he or she wanted to for as long as he or she wanted to. Freud believed that through free association, a person eventually would reveal the unconscious conflicts causing the psychological problems. He eventually extended his theories to account for general psychological functioning.

Freud's influence was considerable, affecting the psychologists who followed him as well as the public's view of psychology. The basic problem with many of Freud's original ideas, such as the meaning of dreams, is that they are extremely difficult to test using the methods of science. But although contemporary scientists no longer accept many of Freud's theories, Freud's idea that mental processes occur below the level of conscious awareness is now widely accepted in psychological science.

Most Behavior Can Be Modified by Reward and Punishment

In 1913, the psychologist John B. Watson challenged psychology's focus on conscious and unconscious mental processes as inherently unscientific (**FIGURE 1.19**). Watson believed that if psychology was to be a science, it had to stop trying to study mental events that could not be observed directly. Scorning methods such as introspection and free association, he developed **behaviorism**, an approach that emphasizes environmental effects on behavior.

The intellectual issue most central to Watson and his followers was the nature/nurture question. For Watson and other behaviorists, nurture was all. Heavily influenced by the work of the physiologist Ivan Pavlov (discussed further in Chapter 6, "Learning"), Watson believed that animals acquired, or learned, all behaviors through environmental factors: Understanding the environmental *stimuli,* or triggers, was all that was needed to predict a behavioral *response.* Psychologists greeted Watson's approach with great enthusiasm. Many had grown dissatisfied with the ambiguous methods used by those studying mental processes; instead, they believed, it was only by studying observable behaviors that psychologists would be taken seriously as scientists.

B. F. Skinner became famous for taking up the mantle of behaviorism. Like Watson, Skinner denied mental states' existence, writing in his provocative book

FIGURE 1.18 Sigmund Freud The father of psychoanalytic theory, Freud hugely influenced psychology in the twentieth century.

unconscious The mental processes that operate below the level of conscious awareness.

psychoanalysis A method developed by Sigmund Freud that attempts to bring the contents of the unconscious into conscious awareness so that conflicts can be revealed.

behaviorism A psychological approach that emphasizes the role of environmental forces in producing behavior.

FIGURE 1.19 John B. Watson Watson, who spent most of his adult life in advertising, was a proponent of behaviorism. His views were amplified by thousands of psychologists, including B. F. Skinner.

Beyond Freedom and Dignity (1971) that concepts referring to mental processes were of no scientific value in explaining behavior. Rather, Skinner believed that mental states were nothing more than an illusion. He wanted to understand how repeated behaviors were shaped or influenced by the events or consequences that followed them. For instance, an animal would learn to perform a behavior if doing so in the past had led to a positive outcome, such as receiving food.

Behaviorism dominated psychological research well into the early 1960s. In many ways, these were extremely productive times for psychologists. Many of the basic principles established by behaviorists continue to be viewed as critical to understanding the mind, brain, and behavior. At the same time, sufficient evidence has accumulated to show that thought processes influence outcomes, and few psychologists today describe themselves as strict behaviorists.

Cognition Affects Behavior

Much of psychology during the first half of the twentieth century was focused on studying observable behavior. But evidence slowly emerged showing that humans' perceptions of situations could influence behavior and that learning was not as simple as the behaviorists believed. In the late 1920s, the Gestalt theorist Wolfgang Köhler found that chimpanzees could solve the problem of how to get a banana that was out of reach. The chimpanzees had to figure out how to connect two sticks to form a longer stick, which would then allow them to reach the banana and draw it close. The animals tried various methods, until suddenly they seemed to have insight—as evidenced by their reaching the banana and using the strategy perfectly on subsequent tasks. At around the same time, learning theorists such as Edward Tolman were showing that animals could learn by observation. This finding made little sense (according to behaviorist theory) because the observing animals were not being rewarded—the connections were all being made in their heads. Other psychologists conducting research on memory, language, and child development showed that the simple laws of behaviorism could not explain such things as why cultural influences alter how people remember a story, why grammar develops systematically, and why children go through stages of development during which they interpret the world in different ways. All of these findings suggested that mental functions were important for understanding behavior.

In 1957, George A. Miller and colleagues launched the *cognitive revolution* in psychology (**FIGURE 1.20**). Ulric Neisser integrated a wide range of cognitive phenomena in his classic 1967 book *Cognitive Psychology*, which named and defined the field. **Cognitive psychology** (discussed further in Chapter 8, "Thinking and Intelligence") is concerned with higher-order mental functions such as intelligence, thinking, language, memory, and decision making. Cognitive research has shown that the way people think about things influences their behavior. Several events in the 1950s set the stage for the rise of cognitive science; perhaps the most important was the growing use of computers. Computers operate according to software programs, which dictate rules for how information is processed. Cognitive psychologists such as Alan Newell and the Nobel laureate Herbert Simon applied this process to their explanation of how the mind works. These *information processing* theories of cognition viewed the brain as the hardware that ran the mind, or mental processes, as the software; the brain takes in information as a code, processes it, stores relevant sections, and retrieves stored information as required. Some early cognitive psychologists recognized that the brain was important to cognition, but many cognitive psychologists preferred to focus exclusively on the software, with little interest in the specific brain mechanisms involved. In the early 1980s, cognitive psychologists joined forces with neuroscientists, computer scientists, and philosophers to develop an integrated view of mind and brain. The field of **cognitive neuroscience** emerged during the 1990s as one of the most exciting fields of science.

FIGURE 1.20 George A. Miller In 1957, Miller launched the cognitive revolution by establishing the Center for Cognitive Science at Harvard University.

cognitive psychology The study of how people think, learn, and remember.

cognitive neuroscience The study of the neural mechanisms that underlie thought, learning, and memory.

Social Situations Shape Behavior

At the turn of the twentieth century, many psychologists came to appreciate that people's behaviors were affected by the presence of others. During the 1920s, scholars such as Floyd Allport began to examine how people were affected by their social worlds. This approach received a boost as people sought to understand the atrocities committed in World War II. The behavior of Nazi soldiers led a number of psychologists to focus their research on topics such as authority, obedience, and group behavior. These topics are the province of **social psychology,** which focuses on the power of situation and on the way people are shaped through their interactions with others.

In 1962, Adolf Eichmann, one of Adolf Hitler's chief lieutenants, was hanged for "causing the killing of millions of Jews." Shortly before his death, Eichmann claimed, "I am not the monster I am made out to be. I am the victim of a fallacy." The atrocities committed in Nazi Germany compelled psychologists to consider whether evil is an integral part of human nature. Why had apparently normal Germans, Poles, Austrians, and many other people from the Axis nations during World War II willingly participated in the murders of innocents—men, women, and children? Why did some people in these countries resist and put their own lives at risk to save others? Researchers, many influenced by Freudian ideas, initially sought to understand what types of people would commit evil acts. They concluded that certain types, especially those raised by unusually strict parents, display a slightly greater willingness to follow orders. But as discussed in Chapter 12, almost everyone is strongly influenced by social situations. His behavior cannot be excused, but Eichmann was correct that people were overlooking the power of the situation in explaining his heinous actions.

In the 1930s and 1940s, Kurt Lewin, who was trained as a Gestalt psychologist, emphasized a scientific, experimental approach to social psychology (**FIGURE 1.21**). His *field theory* emphasized the interplay between people (biology, habits, beliefs) and their environments, such as social situations and group dynamics. This perspective allowed psychologists to begin examining some of the most complex forms of human mental activity, such as how people's attitudes shape behavior, why they are prejudiced against other groups, how they are influenced by other people, and why they are attracted to some people and repelled by others. Human beings navigate within a social world, and psychological science recognizes the importance of fully considering a situation to predict and understand the behavior within it.

Psychological Therapy Is Based on Science

In the 1950s, a humanistic approach to the treatment of psychological disorders, led by Carl Rogers and Abraham Maslow, emphasized how people can come to know and accept themselves in order to reach their unique potentials. Some of the techniques developed by Rogers, such as specific ways of questioning and listening during therapy, are staples of modern treatment. Only in the last four decades, however, has a scientific approach to the study of psychological disorders emerged.

Throughout psychology's history, the methods developed to treat psychological disorders mirrored advances in psychological science. For instance, behaviorism's rise led to a group of therapies designed to modify behavior rather than address underlying mental conflicts. Behavioral modification methods continue to be highly effective in a range of situations, from training those with intellectual impairments to treating patients who are especially anxious and fearful. The cognitive revolution in scientific thinking led therapists to recognize the important role of thought processes in mental disorders. Pioneers such as Aaron T. Beck developed therapies to correct faulty cognitions (faulty beliefs about the world); these cognitive therapies are especially effective for treating conditions such as anxiety disorders, depression, and eating disorders. For some mental disorders, such as schizophrenia, the most effective treatments are drugs

FIGURE 1.21 Kurt Lewin Lewin founded modern social psychology, pioneering the use of experimentation to test hypotheses and thus to form theories.

that alter brain chemistry. For people with these disorders, the biological revolution in psychological science has helped immensely. But for people with other disorders, drug therapy is less preferable than cognitive and behavioral therapies because drugs can produce side effects or lead to reliance on the drugs. In many situations, a combination of drugs and cognitive-behavioral therapy is the best treatment plan.

Today, most therapeutic approaches to dealing with psychological disorders consist of two key factors that reflect the field's origins: adopting a widely recognized treatment of choice that scientific research has demonstrated to be clinically effective and recognizing that each person is a unique individual with specific issues and needs. As discussed in Chapter 15, probably the greatest change in clinical psychology over the course of the twentieth century has come from the realization, through scientific research, that no universal treatment or approach fits all psychological disorders—contrary to the thinking of the early giants such as Freud, Skinner, and Rogers (Kazdin, 2008).

 ## SUMMING UP

How Did the Scientific Foundations of Psychology Develop?

Although people around the world have pondered psychological questions for thousands of years, the formal discipline of psychology began in Wilhelm Wundt's laboratory in Germany in 1879. Wundt believed it necessary to reduce mental processes into their constituent, "structural" parts, by using an approach known as structuralism. Other early psychologists argued that it was more important to understand how the mind functions than what it contains. During this period, most research was aimed at understanding the subjective mind. Freud, for example, emphasized the unconscious, and the Gestalt movement focused on perception. The behaviorists then claimed that the study of the mind was too subjective and therefore unscientific. Accordingly, for the first half of the twentieth century, most psychologists studied only observable behaviors. The cognitive revolution in the 1960s returned the mind to center stage, and research on mental processes such as memory, language, and decision making blossomed. Throughout the last century, some psychologists have emphasized the social contexts of behavior and of mental activity. Advances in psychological science have informed the treatment of psychological disorders.

MEASURING UP

Identify the school of thought that each of the following statements characterizes. The options here are behaviorism, functionalism, cognitive, social, Gestalt, structuralism, and psychoanalysis.

a. To be a respectable scientific discipline, psychology should be concerned with what people and other animals do—in other words, with observable actions.

b. Psychology should be concerned with the way behavior helps us adapt to environment.

c. Psychology should be concerned with the way thoughts affect behavior.

d. To understand behavior, psychologists need to understand the contexts in which people live and act.

e. Because the sum is greater than the parts, psychologists should study the entirety of how we make sense of the world.

f. Psychologists should study the "pieces" that make up the mind.

g. To understand behavior, psychologists should study people's unconscious mental processes.

How Can We Apply Psychological Science?

Psychology is one of the most popular majors at many colleges. The general usefulness of understanding mental activity may explain psychology's popularity as a major: This field can help you understand your motives, your personality, and even why you remember some things and forget others. Psychological science is more than fascinating and personally relevant, however; it also serves as excellent training for many professions. As you will discover, psychological science covers broad ground, touching on all aspects of human life.

Psychological Knowledge Is Used in Many Professions

Many types of researchers study the mind, brain, and behavior at different conceptual levels. For instance, physicians need to know much more than anatomy and chemistry; they need to know how to relate to their patients, how the patients' behaviors are linked to health, and what motivates or discourages patients from seeking medical care or following treatment protocols. Understanding the aging brain and how it affects visual perception, memory, and motor movement is vital for those who treat elderly patients. Indeed, psychological scientists make major contributions to research on human physical and mental health.

Psychological science is equally useful for anyone whose career involves understanding people. To persuade jurors, lawyers need to know how groups make decisions. Advertisers need to know how attitudes are formed or changed and to what extent people's attitudes predict their behavior. Politicians use psychological techniques of impression management to make themselves attractive to voters.

If you are thinking about a career in psychology or a related field, there is good news. According to the United States Department of Labor (Bureau of Labor Statistics, 2007), opportunities for people with graduate degrees in psychology are expected to grow approximately 15 percent between now and 2016. If you are wondering what you can do with an undergraduate degree in psychology, the answer is "almost everything." Prospective employers want their employees to have data analysis skills, communication skills, critical thinking skills, and the abilities to learn and to get along with others. These skills are all developed in psychology curricula. One survey of college graduates with bachelor's degrees in psychology found that they held a wide range of positions requiring psychological knowledge, including attorney's assistant, police officer, social worker, personnel director, hospital counselor, store manager, and research assistant (Morgan, n.d.).

People study psychology for many reasons, and some students become so fascinated by psychological science that they devote their lives to studying the mind and behavior (**FIGURE 1.22**). Psychological science is an exciting field—researchers are unraveling the very nature of what it means to be a human being. Although the scientific principles of brain, mind, and behavior have been established, the foundations of psychological science continue to grow, and there is still a tremendous amount to learn about issues such as how nature and nurture interact and how the brain enables the mind. Indeed, contemporary psychological science is providing new insights into problems and issues that the great scholars of the past struggled to solve.

People Are Intuitive Psychological Scientists

By nature, humans are intuitive psychological scientists, developing hypotheses about and trying to predict others' behavior. For example, people choose marriage partners they expect will best meet their

Real World PSYCHOLOGY

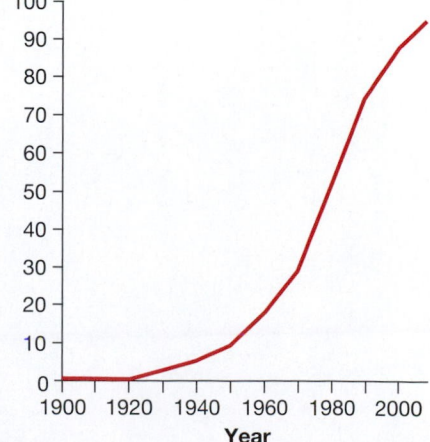

FIGURE 1.22 **Growth of the Field** This graph, adapted from data published by the American Psychological Association (APA), shows the great increase in this professional organization's membership from 1900 to 2004.

APA membership (thousands)

S. GROSS

"For God's sake, think! Why is he being so nice to you?"

emotional, sexual, and support needs. Defensive drivers rely on their intuitive senses of when other drivers likely will make mistakes. People seek to predict whether others are kind, are trustworthy, will make good caretakers, will make good teachers, and so on. But people cannot intuitively know if taking certain herbs will increase memory, for example, or whether playing music to newborns makes them more intelligent, or whether mental illness results from too much or too little of a certain brain chemical.

One of this textbook's most important goals is to provide a basic education about the methods of psychological science for students whose only exposure to psychology will be through an introductory course. Readers will become psychologically literate, with a good understanding of the major issues, theories, and controversies and the ability to apply that learning in a wide variety of settings. Psychologically literate people will also avoid common misunderstandings about psychological science. Although psychologists make important contributions to understanding and treating mental illness, most psychological science has little to do with such therapeutic clichés as couches and dreams. Instead, it is about understanding mental activity, social interactions, and how people acquire behaviors. To understand what makes you tick and what makes other people tick, you need a basic operating manual for the human mind and human behavior, a manual provided by psychological science.

Psychological Science Requires Critical Thinking

One of the hallmarks of a good scientist—or a savvy consumer of scientific research—is *amiable skepticism,* which involves a wariness of dramatic new scientific findings in the absence of convincing evidence, as well as an openness to new ideas when good evidence and sound reasoning support them. An amiable skeptic develops the habit of carefully weighing the evidence when deciding what to believe. The ability to think in this way is often referred to as **critical thinking**—a systematic way of evaluating information to reach reasonable conclusions. In other words, the term *critical thinking* "is used to describe thinking that is purposeful, reasoned, and goal directed—the kind of thing involved in solving problems, formulating inferences, calculating likelihoods, and making decisions, when the thinker is using skills that are thoughtful and effective for the particular context and type of thinking task" (Halpern, 2003, p. 6). Being a critical thinker involves considering alternative explanations, looking for holes in evidence, and using logic and reasoning to see whether the information makes sense. It also involves considering whether the information might be biased, such as by personal or political agendas. Critical thinking involves healthy questioning and keeping an open mind. Most people are quick to question information that does not fit with their worldviews, but as an educated person you also need to think critically about other information—perhaps especially the information that verifies your preconceptions. After all, you may be least motivated to think critically when evaluating such information.

Does eating too much sugar cause children to become hyperactive? Many people believe this connection has been established scientifically, but in fact a review of the scientific literature reveals that the relationship between sugar consumption and hyperactivity is essentially zero (Wolraich, Wilson, and White, 1995). Many people will argue that they have seen with their own eyes what happens when children eat large amounts of sweets. But consider the contexts of such firsthand observations. Might the children have eaten lots of sweets when they were at parties with many other children? Might the gatherings, rather than the sweets, have caused the children to be very excited and active? People often let their beliefs and their biases determine how they label observations: The highly active children's behavior, viewed in connection with the eating of sweets, becomes an example of sugar-induced

critical thinking A systematic way of evaluating information to reach reasonable conclusions.

hyperactivity. A critical thinker would consider such alternative explanations for behavior and seek quality research that takes such possibilities into account.

As you read this book, you will learn how to separate the believable from the incredible. You will learn to spot badly designed experiments, and you will develop the skills necessary to critically evaluate claims made in the popular media. The information in this book also provides a state-of-the-art background in psychological science, helping you form a better idea of whether a claim is consistent with current knowledge in psychology. The media love a good story, and findings from psychological research are often provocative. Unfortunately, media reports can be distorted or even flat-out wrong. Throughout your life, as a consumer of psychological science you will need to be skeptical of overblown media reports of word "brand-new" findings obtained by "groundbreaking" research.

Consider, for instance, a study conducted by a cognitive psychologist that found playing Mozart to research participants led them to score slightly higher on a test loosely related to intelligence. The media jumped onto the so-called Mozart effect with abandon; the result has been that many parents determinedly play Mozart to young infants—and even to fetuses (**FIGURE 1.23**). Indeed, governors of two U.S. states instituted programs that provided free Mozart CDs to every newborn. Web sites make bold claims about the power of Mozart, including fantastical assertions that listening to Mozart can cure neurological illness and other maladies. To understand the true power of Mozart for the developing mind, we need to step back and critically evaluate the research underlying the Mozart effect.

In 1993, researchers played the first 10 minutes of the Mozart Sonata for Two Pianos in D Major (K. 448) to a group of college students. Compared with students who listened to relaxation instructions or who sat in silence, those who heard Mozart performed slightly better on a task that involved folding and cutting paper, a task part of a larger overall measure of intelligence. This modest increase lasted for about 10 to 15 minutes (Rauscher, Shaw, & Ky, 1993). However, subsequent research largely failed to get the same results, even when using a similar research design. Having carefully reviewed the studies testing the Mozart effect, Christopher Chabris (1999) concluded that listening to Mozart is unlikely to increase intelligence among listeners. According to Chabris, listening to Mozart appears to enhance only certain types of motor skills, not measures more commonly associated with intelligence. Another important question from a critical thinking perspective is whether it was the music or some other aspect of the situation that led to better performance on the folding and cutting task. A team of researchers has shown that the effect may occur simply because listening to music is more uplifting than sitting in silence or relaxing, and therefore the increase in positive mood is largely responsible for better performance (Thompson, Schellenberg, & Husain, 2001). Recall from earlier in this chapter that music has been shown to affect mood and cognition.

Also note that all the studies to date have been conducted on college students, yet all the publicity focuses on whether listening to Mozart increases infants' intelligence. Most likely it does not. Of course, experiences during early life are important; but most of the claims about music go way beyond the data. Now that you are a bit more informed, what do you think?

A wide range of evidence shows that people can learn to improve how they think. For instance, before they have taken a psychology course, many students have false beliefs, or misconceptions, about psychological phenomena. One such false belief is that people use only 10 percent of their potential brain

FIGURE 1.23 The Mozart Effect A much publicized research study done in the early 1990s concluded that infants benefited from the "Mozart effect," and many products play on the assumption that babies benefit from hearing music. This Baby Einstein rocking chair can connect to CD players or iPods, enabling parents to develop music programs for their children.

power. (More misconceptions will be discussed in Chapter 2, "Research Methodology.") In an exemplary study, Kowalski and Taylor (2004) found that students who employ critical thinking skills will complete an introductory course with a more accurate understanding of psychology than that of students who complete the same course but do not employ the same skills. As you read this book, attend to the critical thinking skills and apply these skills in your other classes, your workplace, and your everyday life.

Psychologists Adhere to a Code of Ethics

As discussed in Chapter 2, ethics is central to psychological science, and all psychologists adhere to a code of ethical behavior. The American Psychological Association publishes a code of ethics that all its members must respect. The ethical code includes being respectful to all people, treating them with dignity, and protecting them from potential harm. The psychological associations in many countries around the world have similar codes of ethics.

Many scientific and societal changes are creating new ethical dilemmas for psychologists and for people in related fields such as medicine and anthropology. Some of the new ethical dilemmas arise from the biological revolution, which is causing psychologists to rethink the ethical use of drug therapies, the use of psychological data in the courtroom, and the need for new privacy laws for both data on DNA and the results of brain imaging. The line between right and wrong is often a fine one, because these dilemmas are created by rapid changes in what we know about psychology. In each chapter of this book, an "On Ethics" section discusses a specific ethical dilemma, providing the background information and outlining the problem. As a reader and critical thinker, you are encouraged to consider the possible solutions in each case.

Psychology Is Relevant to Every Person's Life

Sometimes people ask why they need to study psychology. After all, the material is just common sense, right? The answer is no. Sometimes, as noted earlier about misconceptions, the results are surprising and run counter to common beliefs. For example, many people at least initially reject the idea that some of what they think, feel, and do is determined by unconscious influences; but hundreds of studies show that such influences happen. We have no conscious knowledge of what is happening in our brains in the first fraction of a second when we see a baby's face, but we are attending to that baby's face differently than we attend to an adult's face (Kringelbach et al., 2008). Throughout this book you will read many such examples of psychology's surprising nature.

Perhaps the most important reason for studying psychology is that its insights are critical in almost every sphere of our lives and its content—in explicating how humans think, feel, and behave—is universal. It can help us be better parents, understand how our siblings affect our development, work more effectively in groups, and relieve chronic pain, just to name a few examples. As the world becomes smaller, as the Internet extends its reach, and as more people travel to farther places to visit, study, and live, we are moving toward a psychology of all people. Around the world, the popular press covers the topics you will learn about in this book: advances in the brain sciences, how DNA is being used to identify people with particular disorders and cure them of these disorders, how advances in the understanding of the sensory systems are helping people see and hear better, how the new knowledge of taste is being used to create new recipes, how group behavior can be understood, how the debilitating effects of depression can be alleviated, how memory can be maintained as we age. The list is virtually endless, but it encompasses important knowledge for helping people lead happier and healthier lives and for creating a healthier and better planet for all of us. Psychological science is about all of us—and therefore about you. We, the authors, invite you to enjoy this book!

How Can We Apply Psychological Science?

Psychological science's content is of interest and value to many professions. Perhaps for this reason, psychology is one of the most popular majors on many college campuses. Although most people function as intuitive psychological scientists, many of our intuitions and beliefs are wrong; so we need to understand the research methods psychologists use and to think critically about research findings. Psychologists in most places of the world adhere to strict codes of ethics that regulate how they act toward others and how they conduct research. New advances—in science, in society—have created new ethical dilemmas in psychology. The findings from psychological science are relevant to every person's life.

1. Critical thinking is _____.
   a. criticizing the way other people think
   b. using specific thinking skills to reach reasonable conclusions
   c. questioning everything you read or hear and refusing to believe anything you have not seen for yourself
   d. becoming an authority on everything so you never have to rely on other people's judgments

2. Psychology is relevant _____.
   a. in those parts of the world where it is a well-developed science
   b. in all aspects of life
   c. for people who are naturally inquisitive
   d. for the mentally ill but not for people who are mentally healthy

CONCLUSION

Psychological scientists use the methods of science to study the mind, brain, and behavior across different levels of analysis. Psychologists have replaced the age-old question about whether a trait or behavior is due to nature or nurture with the idea that nature and nurture cannot be separated. The rich history of psychology is marked by various schools of thought. The founders of psychology grappled with questions such as *How can we understand the mind? How does the brain function? How many of our traits are predetermined by our genes? How do our personalities affect our lives? What social forces influence personal decisions?*

The concept of natural selection, developed by Darwin over a century ago, is an integral part of psychological science because to understand a particular behavior, psychologists first must understand what advantage led humans to evolve that behavior. Did this behavior solve a problem for our evolutionary ancestors? Once psychologists gain a sense of what a behavior is for, they can better investigate how it works. These processes remain at the forefront of psychological research today as scientists seek to unravel the mysteries of brain, mind, and behavior. The basic questions apply to all levels of analysis: biological, individual, social, and cultural. Furthermore, research across the multiple levels of analysis is invigorating psychological science and providing new insights into age-old questions. In the following chapters, you will practice the skills of critical thinking and ponder ethical dilemmas. You will learn not only how psychological science operates but also many remarkable things about the brain, the mind, and behavior. It might just be one of the most fascinating explorations of your life.

■ CHAPTER SUMMARY

What Are the Seven Themes of Psychological Science?

- **Psychology Is an Empirical Science:** Psychological science relies on empirical evidence as a way of knowing about how we think, feel, and behave.

- **Nature and Nurture Are Inextricably Entwined:** Nature and nurture depend on each other, and their influences cannot be separated.

- **The Brain and Mind Are Inseparable:** Older dualist notions about the separation of the brain and mind have been replaced with the idea that the (physical) brain enables the mind; brain and mind cannot be separated.

- **A New Biological Revolution Is Energizing Research:** The scientific knowledge of brain activity has been enhanced by the discovery of more neurotransmitters. Mapping of the human genome has furthered genetics' role in analyzing both disease and behavior. Tremendous advances in brain imaging have revealed the working brain. These advances are changing how we think about psychology.

- **The Mind Is Adaptive:** The brain has evolved to solve survival problems and adapt to environments. Many modern behaviors are by-products of adaptation.

- **Psychological Science Crosses Levels of Analysis:** Psychological scientists examine behavior from various analytical levels: biological (brain systems, neurochemistry, and genetics), individual (personality as well as perception and cognition), social (interpersonal behavior), and cultural (within a single culture and across several cultures).

- **We Often Are Unaware of the Multiple Influences on How We Think, Feel, and Act:** Hundreds of studies show that subtle events in the environment can change how we think, feel, and act without our awareness of the way they influence us.

How Did the Scientific Foundations of Psychology Develop?

- **Experimental Psychology Begins with Structuralism:** Although psychology's intellectual history dates back thousands of years, psychology began as a formal discipline in 1879, in Wilhelm Wundt's laboratory in Germany. Using techniques of introspection, scientists attempted to understand conscious experience by reducing it to its structure.

- **Functionalism Addresses the Purpose of Behavior:** According to functionalists, the mind is best understood by examining its functions, not its structure.

- **Gestalt Psychology Emphasizes Patterns and Context in Learning:** The assertion that the whole experience (the Gestalt) is greater than the sum of its parts led to an approach emphasizing the subjective experience of perception.

- **Women Made Pioneering Contributions to Psychology:** Women's early contributions to psychological science, such as the achievements of Mary Calkins and of Margaret Washburn, have been underacknowledged.

- **Freud Emphasized the Power of the Unconscious:** The psychoanalytic assumption that unconscious processes are not readily available to our awareness but influence our behavior had an enormous impact on psychology.

- **Most Behavior Can Be Modified by Reward and Punishment:** Discoveries that behavior is changed by its consequences caused behaviorism to dominate psychology until the 1960s.

- **Cognition Affects Behavior:** The computer analogy of the brain and the cognitive revolution led to the information processing perspective.

- **Social Situations Shape Behavior:** Work in social psychology has highlighted how situations and other people are powerful forces in shaping behavior.

- **Psychological Therapy Is Based on Science:** Scientific research over the course of the twentieth century taught psychological scientists that there is no universal treatment for psychological disorders. Instead, different treatments are effective for different disorders.

How Can We Apply Psychological Science?

- **Psychological Knowledge Is Used in Many Professions:** Because psychology focuses on human behavior, it is of interest to many students and professionals and is used in virtually every profession.

- **People Are Intuitive Psychological Scientists:** Humans naturally explain and predict others' behavior, but biases and prejudices often lead to wrong conclusions, so we need to use scientific methods.

- **Psychological Science Requires Critical Thinking:** The use of critical thinking skills will improve how we think. Skepticism, an important element of science, requires a careful examination of how well evidence supports a conclusion. Using critical thinking skills and understanding the methods of psychological science are important for evaluating research reported in the popular media.

- **Psychologists Adhere to a Code of Ethics:** In most countries, psychologists are governed by a code of ethics. These codes require psychologists to treat people with respect and dignity and to show utmost concern for people's safety.

- **Psychology Is Relevant to Every Person's Life:** Psychology can help us be better students, parents, employees and employers, team members, peacemakers, and more. The field is broad with applications to all areas of life.

■ KEY TERMS

adaptations, p. 10

behaviorism, p. 21

cognitive neuroscience, p. 22

cognitive psychology, p. 22

critical thinking, p. 26

culture, p. 7

evolutionary theory, p. 10

functionalism, p. 18

Gestalt theory, p. 19

introspection, p. 17

mind/body problem, p. 8

natural selection, p. 11

nature/nurture debate, p. 7

psychoanalysis, p. 21

psychological science, p. 5

social psychology, p. 23

stream of consciousness, p. 18

structuralism, p. 17

unconscious, p. 21

■ PRACTICE TEST

1. When you mention to your family that you enrolled in a psychology course, your family members share their understanding of the field. Which comment best reflects the nature of psychological science?
   a. "You're going to learn how to get in touch with your feelings."
   b. "The concept of 'psychological science' is such an oxymoron. It is impossible to measure and study what goes on in peoples' heads."
   c. "I think you'll be surprised by the range of questions psychologists ask about the mind, the brain, and behavior, not to mention the methods they use to answer these questions."
   d. "By the end of the class, you'll be able to tell me why I am the way I am."

2. Match each definition with one of the following ideas from evolutionary theory: adaptations, natural selection, survival of the fittest.
   a. Gene mutations that endow physical characteristics, skills, and abilities can increase an organism's chances of survival and of reproduction.
   b. Individuals better adapted to their environment will leave more offspring.
   c. Organisms' adaptive random mutations are passed along, and mutations that hinder both survival and reproduction are not.

3. Titles of recent research articles appear below. Indicate which of the four levels of analysis—cultural, social, individual, or biological—each article likely addresses.
   a. Achievement motivation in adolescents: The role of peer climate and best friends (Nelson & DeBacker, 2008)
   b. Circadian affective, cardiopulmonary, and cortisol variability in depressed and nondepressed individuals at risk for cardiovascular disease (Conrad et al., 2008)
   c. Schooling in Western culture promotes context-free processing (Ventura et al., 2008)
   d. Severity of physical aggression reported by university students: A test of the interaction between trait aggression and alcohol consumption (Tremblay, Graham, & Wells, 2008)

4. True or false? Psychology as a field of inquiry developed almost exclusively from Western thinking.

5. Indicate which school or schools of thought each of the following scholars is associated with: John Dewey, William James, Wolfgang Kohler, Kurt Lewin, George Miller, B. F. Skinner, Edward Titchener, Edward Tolman, John B. Watson, Max Wertheimer, Wilhelm Wundt.
   a. structuralism
   b. functionalism
   c. Gestalt
   d. behaviorism
   e. cognitive
   f. social

6. Match each description with one of the following theoretical ideas: field theory, information processing theory, introspection, phenomenological approach, stream of consciousness.
   a. a systematic examination of subjective mental experience that requires people to inspect and report on the contents of their thoughts
   b. the interaction of biology, habits, and beliefs with environments to create behavior
   c. examining the totality of subjective conscious experience
   d. a continuous series of ever changing thoughts
   e. the view that the brain takes in information as a code, processes it, stores relevant bits, and retrieves stored information as required

7. Imagine you have decided to seek mental health counseling. You mention this to a few of your friends. Each friend shares an opinion with you. Based on your understanding of psychological science, which friend offers the strongest advice?
   a. "I wouldn't bother if I were you. All therapy is a bunch of psychobabble."
   b. "I know a therapist who uses this really cool method that can fix any problem. Seriously, she knows the secret!"
   c. "That's great! Psychologists do research to figure out which interventions are most helpful for people with different concerns."
   d. "Well, I guess if you like relaxing on couches and talking, you might get a lot out of therapy."

8. Which of the following practices are hallmarks of critical thinking? Check all that apply.
   a. asking questions
   b. considering alternative explanations
   c. considering the possibility that biases are coloring the evidence
   d. keeping an open mind
   e. looking for holes in evidence
   f. skepticism
   g. reasoning logically to see whether information makes sense

9. Your brother reads that research shows eating ice cream makes people more intelligent. He starts downing a pint of ice cream every day to increase his intelligence. To help your brother better understand this claim (and avoid obesity), which of the following questions would you ask? Check all that apply.
   a. "Does the article mention how much ice cream people had to eat to become more intelligent?"
   b. "Does the article say how the researchers measured intelligence?"
   c. "Does the article mention whether the person who conducted the research is a famous scholar?"
   d. "I wonder how the researchers designed the study. Were they doing good science?"
   e. "I'd want to know who sponsored the study. Would you believe these results if the study was paid for and conducted by researchers at the world's largest ice cream company?"

■ PSYCHOLOGY AND SOCIETY

1. Review the seven themes of psychological science. Write a brief essay about which two or three themes you are particularly excited to learn about during this course. Be sure to explain your interest in those themes.

2. Make a list of your roles (e.g., student, parent, activist) and interests (e.g., sports, computers, music). Describe at least one way psychology is relevant to each role and interest.

The answer key for all the Measuring Up exercises and the Practice Tests can be found at the back of the book.

Research Methodology

when the working day is done
girls—they want to have fun
oh girls just want to have fun . . .

　　　　—Cyndi Lauper, "Girls Just Want to Have Fun"
　　　　(released 1981; lyrics by Robert Hazard)

THESE LYRICS FROM CYNDI LAUPER'S SMASH HIT, which made it onto the Top 10 list in 15 countries and has been described as a "feminist anthem" for the 1980s, may seem like a strange opening for a chapter on research methodology. But the lyrics of "Girls Just Want to Have Fun," like those of most popular songs, tell a story about the way people think, feel, and behave in specific social contexts. In this case, the story is about the thoughts and feelings of women when they finish a day at work. (*Women*, rather than *girls*, because except

---

What Is Scientific Inquiry?
- The Scientific Method Depends on Theories, Hypotheses, and Research
- Unexpected Findings Can Be Valuable

What Are the Types of Studies in Psychological Research?
- Descriptive Studies Involve Observing and Classifying Behavior
- Correlational Designs Examine How Variables Are Related
- An Experiment Involves Manipulating Conditions
- Critical Thinking Skill: Identifying the Need for Control Groups

- Random Assignment Is Used to Establish Equivalent Groups
- Critical Thinking Skill: Recognizing That Large Samples Generate More Reliable Results Than Small Samples

What Are the Data Collection Methods of Psychological Science?
- Observing Is an Unobtrusive Strategy
- Case Studies Examine Individual Lives and Organizations
- Asking Takes a More Active Approach
- Response Performance Measures Information Processing

- Body/Brain Activity Can Be Measured Directly
- Research with Animals Provides Important Data
- There Are Ethical Issues to Consider

How Are Data Analyzed and Evaluated?
- Good Research Requires Valid, Reliable, and Accurate Data
- Descriptive Statistics Provide a Summary of the Data
- Correlations Describe the Relationships between Variables
- Inferential Statistics Permit Generalizations

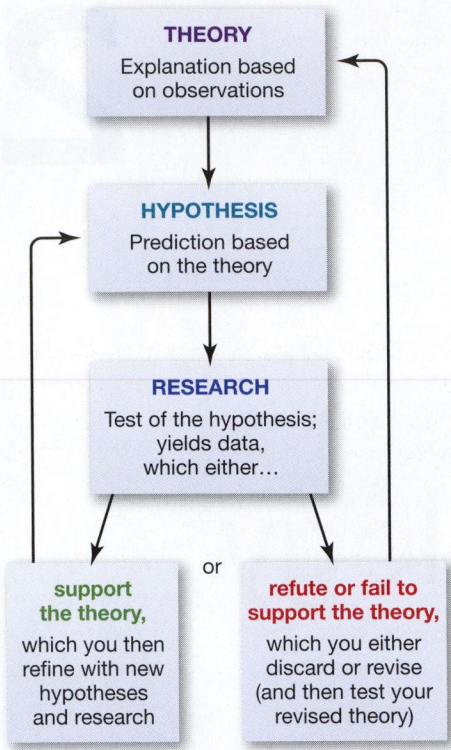

THEORY
Explanation based on observations

HYPOTHESIS
Prediction based on the theory

RESEARCH
Test of the hypothesis; yields data, which either...

support the theory, which you then refine with new hypotheses and research

or

refute or fail to support the theory, which you either discard or revise (and then test your revised theory)

FIGURE 2.1 The Scientific Method The scientific method reflects a cyclical relationship among a theory, a testable hypothesis (or testable hypotheses) derived from the theory, research conducted to test the hypothesis, and adjustments to the theory as findings prompt reevaluation. A good theory evolves over time, and the result is an increasingly accurate model of some phenomenon.

LEARNING OBJECTIVE
Explain the differences among theories, hypotheses, and research.

scientific method A systematic procedure of observing and measuring phenomena to answer questions about *what* happens, *when* it happens, *what* causes it, and *why*.

theory A model of interconnected ideas and concepts that explains what is observed and makes predictions about future events.

in unusual circumstances, any female who is at work all day must be an adult.) The idea of working women wanting to have fun probably came from repeated observations, by the lyricist or someone who inspired him, of real people saying and doing things after work.

Of course, psychological researchers usually do not look to the lyrics of popular songs for research ideas. Most researchers have more serious areas of interest, such as understanding how the brain changes when a child or adult experiences a traumatic event, discovering the ways that people learn new information, finding effective treatments for mental disorders, or identifying the age at which children become credible witnesses, to name just a few. But for the purposes of understanding the principles of research methodology, we will use the description of female behavior heard by countless people around the world in this *Billboard* hit.

Suppose you were asked to analyze this song as your research project. What study would you design to determine whether women just want to have fun after a day at work? Whom would you select as participants for your study? How would you measure "fun"? What theory would you be testing? This chapter addresses these sorts of questions.

During the last century, psychologists made many important discoveries about the mind, brain, and behavior. These discoveries emerged through careful scientific research. The scientific method is *systematic*, which means that it proceeds in orderly steps that are carefully planned. To answer research questions, scientists use objective procedures so that they can develop an accurate understanding of the phenomena they study. (*Phenomena* are things that can be observed—the singular is *phenomenon*.) An objective procedure is free from bias, so if another researcher uses the same procedure with the same sample of people, he or she would expect the same results.

As you read about research methods in the context of studying human behavior, here are some key questions to keep in mind.

- What are the goals of research?
- What are the steps for conducting a research study?
- What kinds of ethical issues are involved in conducting research?
- How well do the data support the conclusion?
- Are there alternative explanations?

What Is Scientific Inquiry?

Scientific inquiry is a way of finding answers to empirical questions—questions that can be answered by observing the world and measuring aspects of it. Scientific inquiry has four basic goals, which correspond to describing *what* happens, predicting *when* it happens, controlling *what causes* it to happen, and explaining *why* it happens. To be more confident in the conclusions drawn from their observations, researchers in the various fields of science use a general approach known as the **scientific method**, which is more objective than casual observations.

The Scientific Method Depends on Theories, Hypotheses, and Research

Formally speaking, the scientific method reflects a dynamic interaction among three essential elements: theories, hypotheses, and research (**FIGURE 2.1**). A **theory** is an explanation or a model of how something in the world works, consisting of interconnected ideas and concepts. It is used to explain prior observations and to make predictions about future events.

A good theory should generate a **hypothesis** (or multiple hypotheses), a specific, testable prediction about the outcome that would best support the theory. If the theory is reasonably accurate, the prediction framed in the hypothesis should be supported. To see how theories lead to testable hypotheses, imagine you are beginning a study of the "women and fun" question discussed above. You theorize that working women want to have fun because they need a break from the monotony at work. To test this theory, you might hypothesize that women who have more fun at work will less likely engage in fun activities after work than those who have boring jobs.

Once you have developed hypotheses to test your theory, you must do **research,** which involves the systematic and careful collection of **data,** or objective information that provides a test of whether the hypothesis—and ultimately, the corresponding theory—is likely to be supported. To test the hypothesis about women's desire for fun after work, for example, you might ask women to rate how much fun they have at work and how often they do something fun after work. Or you could use brain imaging techniques to see if women who have low levels of arousal when they perform work tasks (suggesting they are the most bored while working) are most likely to exhibit fun-seeking behaviors when they finish work for the day.

Once the research findings are in, you would return to the original theory to evaluate the implications of the data that were collected. The findings either support your theory or require that your theory be modified or discarded. Then the process starts all over again, as good research reflects a cyclical process whereby a theory is continually refined by new hypotheses and tested by new research methods (**FIGURE 2.2**). Often, more than one theory can explain human behavior, so no single study can provide a definitive answer. In general, we can have more confidence in scientific findings when research outcomes are replicated. **Replication** involves repeating a study and getting the same (or similar) results. When the results from two or more studies are the same, or at least support the same conclusion, confidence in the findings increases.

hypothesis A specific prediction of what should be observed in the world if a theory is correct.

research Scientific process that involves the systematic and careful collection of data.

data Objective observations or measurements.

replication Repetition of an experiment to confirm the results.

FIGURE 2.2 The Scientific Method in Action

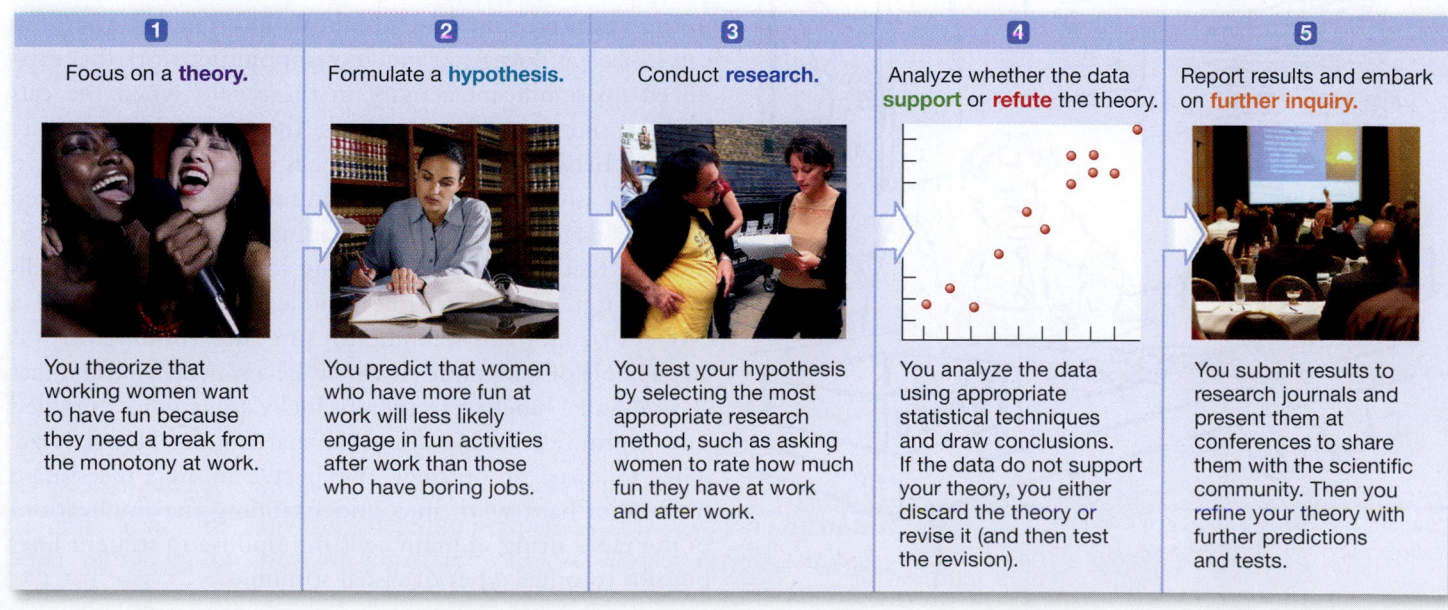

1	**2**	**3**	**4**	**5**
Focus on a **theory.**	Formulate a **hypothesis.**	Conduct **research.**	Analyze whether the data **support** or **refute** the theory.	Report results and embark on **further inquiry.**
You theorize that working women want to have fun because they need a break from the monotony at work.	You predict that women who have more fun at work will less likely engage in fun activities after work than those who have boring jobs.	You test your hypothesis by selecting the most appropriate research method, such as asking women to rate how much fun they have at work and after work.	You analyze the data using appropriate statistical techniques and draw conclusions. If the data do not support your theory, you either discard the theory or revise it (and then test the revision).	You submit results to research journals and present them at conferences to share them with the scientific community. Then you refine your theory with further predictions and tests.

THEORIES SHOULD GENERATE HYPOTHESES How can we decide whether a theory is good? When we talk about a good theory, we do not mean whether it is likely to be supported by research findings. Instead, a good theory produces a wide variety of *testable* hypotheses. For instance, in the early twentieth century, the developmental psychologist Jean Piaget proposed a theory of infant and child development that suggested that cognitive development occurs in a fixed series of "stages," from birth to adolescence. From a scientific standpoint, this was a good theory because it led to a number of hypotheses regarding the specific kinds of behaviors that should be observed at each stage of development. In the decades since its proposal, the theory has generated thousands of scientific papers (see Chapter 11, "Human Development"), and our understanding of child development has been enhanced both by studies that supported Piaget's stage theory and by those that failed to support it.

In contrast, Piaget's contemporary Sigmund Freud, in his famous treatise *The Interpretation of Dreams,* outlined the theory that all dreams represent the fulfillment of an unconscious wish. From a scientific perspective, Freud's theory was not a good one, because it generated few testable hypotheses regarding the actual function of dreams. Researchers were left with no way to evaluate whether the wish fulfillment theory was either reasonable or accurate, because unconscious wishes are, by definition, not known to anyone, including the person having the dreams. Indeed, on being presented with a patient's dream that clearly contained no hint of wish fulfillment, Freud went so far as to claim that the dreamer's unconscious wish was to prove his theory wrong!

Unexpected Findings Can Be Valuable

Research does not always proceed in a neat and orderly fashion. On the contrary, many significant findings are the result of *serendipity*—when researchers unexpectedly discover something important. For example, in the late 1950s, the physiologists Torsten Wiesel and David Hubel recorded the activity of cats' nerve cells in brain areas associated with vision. They were studying how information travels from the eye to the brain, and they had hypothesized that certain cells in the visual portion of the brain would respond when the cats looked at dots. After much disappointing work that produced no significant activity in these cells when the cats viewed slides of dot patterns, the projector suddenly jammed between slides, and the cells unexpectedly began to fire at an astonishing rate. The jammed slide had produced a visual "edge" on the screen, leading Wiesel and Hubel to discover that instead of responding to simple dots, the cells in question respond to lines and edges. They received a Nobel Prize for this serendipitous finding. Although this is an example of serendipity, it would be a mistake to think that Wiesel and Hubel were merely lucky folks who stumbled onto a groundbreaking discovery that led to a Nobel Prize. They followed up on their unexpected finding, investing a lifetime of hard work into understanding the implications of the rapid firing of brain cells in response to straight lines but not to other types of visual stimuli.

What Is Scientific Inquiry?

Our subjective beliefs, such as intuitions, can be useful in suggesting research questions, but they are often biased or based on limited information. To explain behavior, scientists must use objective, systematic procedures to measure it. The four goals of psychological science are to describe (what), predict (when), control (what causes), and explain (why) behavior and mental activity. The empirical process is based on the use of theories to generate hypotheses that can be tested by collecting objective data through research. Theories in turn must be adjusted and refined as new findings confirm or disconfirm the hypotheses. Good theories will generate several testable hypotheses. Unexpected findings can suggest new theories.

▶ **MEASURING UP**

1. How are theories, hypotheses, and research different?
   a. Theories ask questions about possible causes of thoughts, emotions, and behaviors; hypotheses provide the empirical answers; and research is used to prove that theories are correct.
   b. Theories are broad conceptual frameworks, hypotheses are derived from theories and are used to design research that will support or fail to support a theory, and research is a test of the hypotheses.
   c. Theories are assumed to be true, hypotheses need to be tested with appropriate experiments, and research is the final step.
   d. Theories do not require data for their verification because they are abstract, hypotheses depend on experimental findings, and research uses human participants to test theories and hypotheses.

2. How does psychological research differ from relying on personal experience or intuition as a way of understanding, thought, emotions, and behavior.
   a. Personal experience is the most objective method for understanding thoughts, emotions, and behaviors.
   b. Carefully designed research is the most objective method for understanding thoughts, emotions, and behaviors.
   c. Research provides theoretical answers that are best verified through individual experience.

What Are the Types of Studies in Psychological Research?

Once a researcher has defined a hypothesis, the next issue to be addressed is the type of study design to be used. There are three main types of designs: *descriptive*, *correlational*, and *experimental*. These designs differ in the extent to which the researcher has control over the variables in the study and therefore in the extent to which the researcher can make conclusions about causation. All research involves variables. A **variable** is anything that can be measured and that can vary; the term *variable* can refer to something that the experimenter either measures or manipulates. For instance, some of the variables a researcher might use in a study of whether women want to have fun after work include number of hours worked, how much fun the women have at work, what they say they want to do after work, what they actually do after work, whether they rate what they do as having fun, and so on.

LEARNING OBJECTIVES
List the advantages and disadvantages of different research methods.

Explain why random assignment is important when designing experiments.

variable Something in the world that can be measured and that can vary.

Researchers must define variables in precise ways that reflect the methods used to assess them. They do this by using *operational definitions,* which identify and quantify variables so they can be measured. For example, in studying whether women want to have fun after work, how would you define and quantify "wanting to have fun" to judge whether it is affected by how boring a woman's job is or how many hours a woman works? One option is to ask a group of women as they leave work to use a rating scale in which 1 equals "I do not want to have fun" and 10 equals "I want to have fun more than anything else in the world." In this example, the operational definition for how much a woman wants to have fun would be the number between 1 and 10 that she assigns in the after-work rating. This concrete definition would help other researchers know precisely what is being measured, so they could replicate the research. Alternatively, how much a woman wants to have fun could be inferred from her after-work behavior. For example, a researcher could have women rate different activities—such as grocery shopping, taking a class, or dancing—based on how much fun each activity is. Then, by asking a sample group of working women to choose from among these activities after work and keeping track of the women's choices, the researcher could infer how many women wanted to have fun after work.

Descriptive Studies Involve Observing and Classifing Behavior

Descriptive studies, sometimes called *observational studies* because of the manner in which the data typically are collected, involve observing and noting behavior to analyze it objectively (**FIGURE 2.3**). For instance, an observer might take notes on the types of foods that people eat in cafeterias, measure the time that people spend talking during an average conversation, count the number and type of mating behaviors that penguins engage in during their mating season, or tally the number of times poverty or mental illness is mentioned during a presidential debate. Some researchers observe behavior at regular time intervals, spanning durations from as short as seconds to as long as entire lifetimes and across generations. In this manner, the researchers can keep track of what research participants do at particular points in time, and behaviors can be studied that may take years to unfold, as in a study that tracks college graduates' job histories.

There are two basic types of descriptive studies. In **naturalistic observation,** the observer remains separated from and makes no attempt to change the situation. By contrast, in **participant observation,** the researcher is involved in the situation. An example of the latter was conducted by social psychologists who joined a doomsday cult to see how the cult members would respond when the world did not end on the date that was predicted by the cult (Festinger, Riecken, & Schachter, 1956). Some problems with participant observation are related to the observer's losing objectivity and the participants' changing their behavior if they know they are being observed. You can imagine, for example, how bar patrons would respond if researchers entered the bar and announced they were studying the behavior of people who go to bars to meet potential dates. Such an announcement would interfere with or might even eliminate the behavior being studied—in this case, the normal interactions that occur in bars. Thus observers need to keep their objectivity and minimize their impact on a situation.

naturalistic observation A passive descriptive study in which observers do not change or alter ongoing behavior.

participant observation A type of descriptive study in which the researcher is actively involved in the situation.

Descriptive studies involve observing and classifying behavior, either with no intervention by the observer (naturalistic observation) or with intervention by the observer (participant observation).

Advantages   Especially valuable in the early stages of research, when trying to determine whether a phenomenon exists. Takes place in a real-world setting.

Disadvantages   Errors in observation can occur because of an observer's expectations (observer bias). Observer's presence can change the behavior being witnessed (reactivity).

Naturalistic observation

Participant observation

FIGURE 2.3 Descriptive Studies (left) Employing naturalistic observation, the primatologist Jane Goodall observes a family of chimpanzees. Animals will more likely act naturally in their native habitats than in captivity. **(right)** The evolutionary psychologist and human behavioral ecologist Lawrence Sugiyama has conducted fieldwork in Ecuadorian Amazonia among the Shiwiar, Achuar, Shuar, and Zaparo peoples. Here, hunting with a bow and arrow, he is conducting a particularly active form of participant observation.

Descriptive techniques are especially valuable in the early stages of research, when researchers simply are trying to see whether a phenomenon exists. The value of even the simplest observations should not be underestimated. We can learn a great deal about behavior by just watching and taking careful notes about what we see. For example, if we observed seating patterns during lunch at two high schools and found that at one school the lunch tables were racially segregated but at the other school students sat in mixed-race groups, we would have learned something valuable about racial behaviors at these two schools. We would need different types of research designs to understand what causes student groups to be segregated or integrated, but description would have proved a good first step in documenting this phenomenon.

Some studies are designed specially to examine the developmental changes that occur over time—sometimes with the goal of watching changes unfold naturally as in a descriptive design, but other times to see how different interventions affect future development. **Longitudinal studies** are one type of developmental design (**FIGURE 2.4**). For example, if you wanted to know how intellectual abilities change over the adult years, you could assess the abilities of a group of young adults, then reassess them every five years, as they progressed toward old age. Alternatively, you could assess the intellectual abilities of young adults and old adults and compare their scores on various measures of intellectual ability. This latter sort of research design, comparing different groups to make inferences about both, is known as **cross-sectional studies** (**FIGURE 2.5**). Like all research design choices, each of these methods has advantages and disadvantages. Longitudinal designs provide information about the effects of age on the same people, but they are expensive, they take a long time, and they can be jeopardized when (not if) some participants drop out of the experiment over time. By contrast, cross-sectional designs are faster and less expensive, but they include the possibility that some unidentified variable is responsible for any difference

FIGURE 2.4 Longitudinal Studies The *Up* series of documentary films is an ongoing longitudinal study that since 1964 has traced the development of 14 British people from various socioeconomic backgrounds. New material has been collected every seven years starting when the participants were seven years old. Here, three participants—Jackie, Sue, and Lynn—are pictured from the latest film, *49 Up*.

Longitudinal studies involve observing and classifying developmental changes that occur in the same people over time, either with no intervention by the observer or with intervention by the observer.

Advantages Provide information about the effects of age on the same people, allowing researchers to see developmental changes.

Disadvantages Expensive, take a long time, and may lose participants over time.

Cross-sectional studies involve observing and classifying developmental changes that occur in different groups of people at the same time.

Advantages Faster and less expensive than longitudinal studies.

Disadvantages Unidentified variables may be involved (third variable problem, discussed below).

FIGURE 2.5 Cross-Sectional Studies Together, the young adults on the top and the older adults on the bottom might participate in a cross-sectional study.

observer bias Systematic errors in observation that occur because of an observer's expectations.

experimenter expectancy effect Actual change in the behavior of the people or animals being observed that is due to observer bias.

correlational study A research method that examines how variables are naturally related in the real world, without any attempt by the researcher to alter them.

between the groups. In the example above, the older people might not have received the same amount or type of education as the younger people, and this third variable might account for any differences between the groups.

OBSERVER BIAS In conducting observation research, scientists must guard against **observer bias**, systematic errors in observation that occur because of an observer's expectations. Observer bias can be especially problematic if cultural norms favor inhibiting or expressing certain behaviors. For instance, if observers are coding men's and women's facial expressions, they may be more likely to rate female expressions as indicating sadness because they believe that men are less likely to show sadness. Men's expressions of sadness might be rated as annoyance or some other emotion. Likewise, women might be rated as more assertive when exhibiting the same behavior as men, because in many societies women are generally expected to be less assertive. Cultural norms can affect both the participants' actions and the way observers perceive those actions.

Evidence indicates that observer bias can even change the behavior being observed, a phenomenon known as the **experimenter expectancy effect**. For example, in a classic study conducted in the 1960s by the social psychologist Robert Rosenthal, college students trained rats to run a maze. Half the students were told that their rats were bred to be very good at running mazes; the other half were not given this expectation. In reality, there were no genetic differences between the groups of rats. Nonetheless, the rats trained by the students who believed that their rats were bred to be fast maze learners did learn the task more quickly. Thus these students' expectations altered how they treated their rats, and this treatment in turn influenced the speed at which the rats learned. The students were not aware of their biased treatment, but it existed. Perhaps they supplied extra food when the rats reached the goal box, or they gave the rats inadvertent cues as to which way to turn in the maze, or they stroked the rats more often. This study exemplified the principle, introduced in the first chapter, that some aspects of our own behavior are not under our conscious control. We are not always consciously aware of the many factors that affect how we think, feel, and act. In this example, students' beliefs unconsciously affected their behavior (**FIGURE 2.6**).

To protect against experimenter expectancy effects, it is best if the person running the study is *blind* to, or unaware of, the study's hypotheses. The study above, which seemed to be about rats' speed in learning to run through a maze, was actually designed to study experimenter expectancy effects. Researchers studying two different groups of rats would want to protect against such effects by not telling students that the rats came from different groups or to which group each rat belonged.

Correlational Designs Examine How Variables Are Related

A **correlational study** examines how variables are naturally related in the real world, without any attempt by the researcher to alter them (**FIGURE 2.7**). For example, to study whether women who work longer than others want to have more fun after work, a researcher might sample a group of working women and compare the number of hours each woman worked to the way each woman rated her desire to have fun using the 1 to 10 scale suggested above. In this scenario, the goal would be to use the number of hours the women worked as a variable that the researcher did not control. This study would not tell the researcher, however, if the number of work hours directly *caused* the desire to have fun. Why not? A few potential problems prevent researchers from drawing causal conclusions from correlational studies.

As discussed extensively in this chapter, different types of research methods play important roles in the stories of psychological science. In each chapter of the book, **Scientific Method** features will lead you through the steps of some of the most interesting experiments and studies discussed in the text.

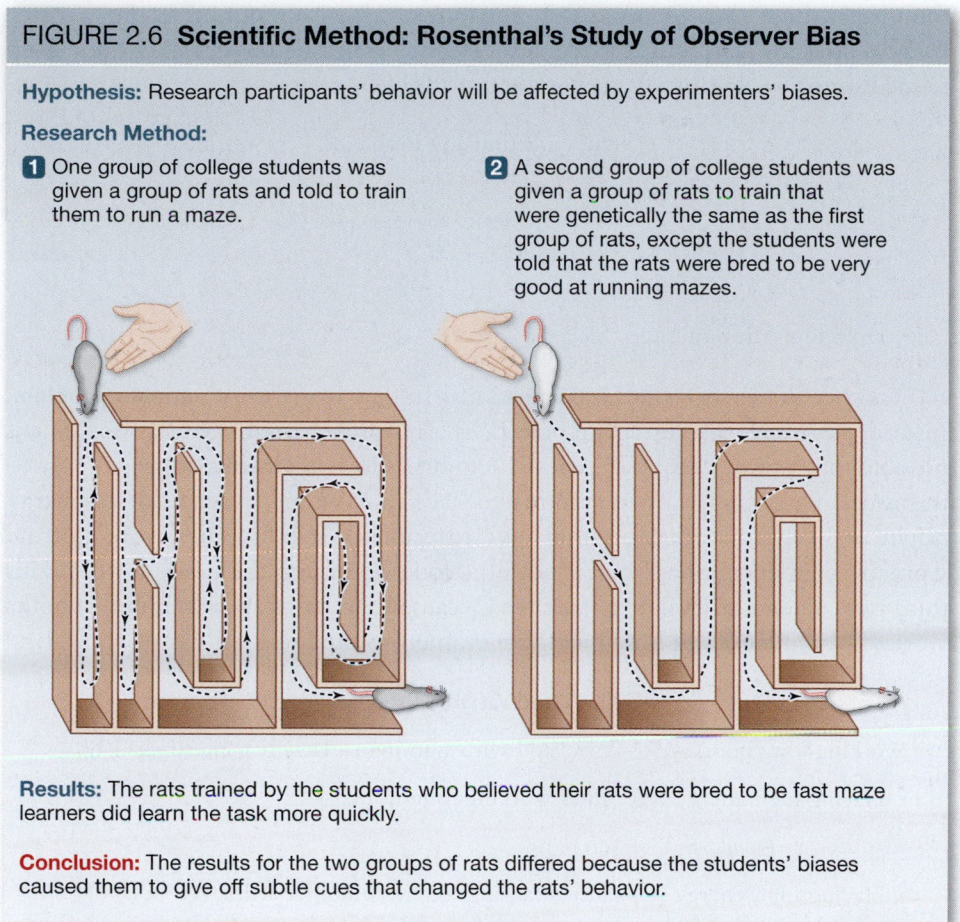

FIGURE 2.6 Scientific Method: Rosenthal's Study of Observer Bias

Hypothesis: Research participants' behavior will be affected by experimenters' biases.

Research Method:

1 One group of college students was given a group of rats and told to train them to run a maze.

2 A second group of college students was given a group of rats to train that were genetically the same as the first group of rats, except the students were told that the rats were bred to be very good at running mazes.

Results: The rats trained by the students who believed their rats were bred to be fast maze learners did learn the task more quickly.

Conclusion: The results for the two groups of rats differed because the students' biases caused them to give off subtle cues that changed the rats' behavior.

Correlational studies are popular research designs because they rely on naturally occurring relationships. Some research questions require correlational research designs for ethical reasons. For example, suppose you want to know if soldiers who experience the horrors of war have more difficulty learning new tasks after they return home than soldiers who did not experience traumatic combat. Even if you have a theory that traumatic combat experiences *cause* later problems with learning, it would be unethical to induce trauma in some soldiers so that you could compare those soldiers with others who were not traumatized. For this research question, you would need to study the soldiers' ability to learn a new task (e.g., computer programming) and see if those who experienced traumatic combat performed less well when learning this task (on average) than soldiers who did not experience traumatic combat. This sort of study can be used to determine that two variables are associated with each other (e.g., the horrors of war are associated with learning difficulties later in life), a connection that enables the researchers to make predictions. In this example, if you found the association you expected between combat experience and learning difficulties, you could predict that soldiers who go into combat will (again, on average) have more difficulty learning new tasks when they return than soldiers who do not experience combat. Because your study drew on but did not control the soldiers' wartime experiences, however, you have not established a causal connection.

Correlational studies examine how variables are related, with no intervention by the observer.

Advantages Rely on naturally occurring relationships. May take place in a real-world setting.

Disadvantages Cannot be used to support causal relationships (that one thing happened because of the other). Cannot show the direction of the cause/effect relationship between variables (directionality problem). An unidentified variable may be involved (third variable problem).

FIGURE 2.7 Correlational Studies There may be a correlation between the extent to which parents are overweight and the extent to which their children are overweight. A correlational study cannot demonstrate the cause of this relationship, such as including biological propensities to gain weight, lack of exercise, and high-fat diets.

Another problem with correlational studies is in knowing the direction of the cause-effect relation between variables. This sort of ambiguity is known as the **directionality problem.** Suppose some researchers surveyed a large group of people and found that those who reported sleeping a great deal also reported having a lower level of stress. Does reduced stress lead to longer and better sleep, or does sleep reduce stress levels? Both scenarios seem plausible:

The Directionality Problem

Sleep (A) and stress (B) are correlated.

- Does less sleep cause more stress? (A → B)

    or

- Does high stress cause less sleep? (B → A)

Another drawback with all correlational studies is the **third variable problem.** Instead of variable A causing variable B, as a researcher might have assumed, it is possible that a third variable, C, caused A and B. How might this concept apply to the issue of working women wanting to have fun? Women with a lot of energy might be likely to work long hours and to want to have fun after work, but the women's high energy level causes both the long hours and the desire for fun. This third variable, energy level (here, variable C) caused variations in the number of hours worked (variable A) and how much the women wanted to have fun (variable B):

The Third Variable Problem

Working long hours (A) is correlated with wanting to have fun after work (B).

- Having high energy (C) causes working long hours. (C → A)

    and

- Having high energy (C) causes wanting to have fun after work. (C → B)

Sometimes the third variable is obvious. For instance, if you were told that the more churches there are in a town, the greater the rate of crime, you would not conclude that churches cause crime, because obviously the population size of a city affects the number of churches and the frequency of crime. But sometimes third variables are not so obvious and may not even be identifiable. For instance, we have all heard that smoking causes cancer. Suppose some genetic defect makes people more likely to smoke and also more likely to get cancer. Indeed, recent evidence indicates that a particular gene predisposes some smokers to develop lung cancer (Paz-Elizur et al., 2003). Recent research supports the idea that, for at least some smokers, a genetic predisposition combines with environmental factors to increase the probability that someone will smoke *and* develop lung cancer (Thorgeirsson et al., 2008). This connection would exemplify a principle introduced in the first chapter, namely that nature and nurture work together in ways that are often inseparable. In this case, the combination of a genetic vulnerability and an action (smoking) may increase the likelihood of cancer.

In many other instances, people might erroneously believe there is a causal relationship between two variables when there is a correlation. Suppose the newspaper reports that children who attend preschool are better readers in first grade than those who do not. It is tempting to conclude that children are better readers in first grade *because* they learned prereading skills in preschool. This explanation of the data might be true, but so might another one: that children who attend preschool have parents who are concerned with their academic success, and that such parents probably read to their children and monitor their schoolwork more than parents who are less concerned with academic success (or less able to afford preschool). How would you design a study to determine if attending preschool, and not some other variable, caused higher reading scores?

The only way to know if attending preschool in itself makes children better readers in first grade would be to find a representative sample of preschool-age children and assign the children at random to either attend or not attend preschool. The researcher would then assess the reading skills of children from both groups at the end of first grade to see if the expected relationship was supported. This example shows how difficult it often can be to randomly assign participants to groups. Most parents want to decide if their children will attend preschool, and many parents would not participate in an experiment that might keep their children out of preschool. Furthermore, good data show that preschool is an important experience for young children, so it would be unethical to keep some children out of preschool. If we were unsure about the benefits of preschool, researchers could conduct a random assignment study (discussed below) to assess those benefits. Once the researchers had a good indication that preschool is beneficial, the experiment would need to end so that all the participating children could attend preschool.

Despite such potentially serious problems as these, correlational studies are widely used in psychological science because they provide important information about the natural relationships among variables, allowing researchers to make predictions. For example, correlational research has identified a strong relationship between depression and suicide, and therefore clinical psychologists often assess symptoms of depression to determine suicide risk. Most research on psychopathology uses the correlational method because it is unethical to induce mental disorders in people to study the effects. Typically, researchers who use the correlational method use other statistical procedures to rule out potential third variables and problems with the direction of the effect. By showing that a relationship between two variables holds even when potential third variables are taken into account, researchers can be more confident that the relationship is meaningful.

An Experiment Involves Manipulating Conditions

In experimental research, the investigator has maximal control over the situation. An **experiment** is a study in which the researcher manipulates one variable to examine that variable's effect on a second variable. In studying how the number of hours worked affects how much women want to have fun, you could manipulate whether participants work few or many hours, a variable that would require the cooperation of their employer (who might also want to know the answer to this research question); you would then ask all participants to rate how much they wanted to have fun after work. A **control** (or **comparison**) **group**, consisting of women who do not work at all, would allow you to compare two **experimental** (or **treatment**) **groups** (women who worked few hours, say 5 hours a day, and women who worked many hours, say 10 hours a day) to the control condition. Two experimental groups and one control group is just one possible research design for this question. The variable that is manipulated (the number of hours worked) is the **independent variable,** and the variable that is measured (how much women want to have fun after work) is the **dependent variable.**

The benefit of an experiment is that the researcher can study the *causal relationship* between the two variables. If the independent variable influences the dependent variable consistently (for example, higher ratings for the desire to have fun in the 10-hour group than in the 5-hour group, and higher ratings in the 5-hour group than in the control group), then the independent variable is assumed to cause the change in the dependent variable.

experiment A study that tests causal hypotheses by measuring and manipulating variables.

control (or comparison) group The participants in a study that receive no intervention or an intervention different from the one being studied.

experimental (or treatment) group The participants in a study that receive the intervention.

independent variable In an experiment, the condition that is manipulated by the experimenter to examine its impact on the dependent variable.

dependent variable In an experiment, the measure that is affected by manipulation of the independent variable.

Although experiments allow us to infer cause, they are often criticized for being artificial. In real life, for example, some people decide for themselves how many hours they will work each day. Depending on the type of workplace you study, assigning different numbers of working hours may be so artificial that you end up studying something you had not intended, such as how women react when they are told how many hours they must work. Alternatively, you could compare a group of women who work part-time to a group of women who work full-time, with the prediction that the women in the full-time group want to have fun more than those in the part-time group. But unless you have assigned participants randomly to the various conditions, the possibility always exists that any difference you find derived from preexisting differences among the groups. Research design often involves a series of choices: It means balancing the problems of taking people as they come with the problems of creating an artificial environment for the experiment.

CRITICAL THINKING SKILL

Identifying the Need for Control Groups

The two critical thinking skills for this chapter—recognizing the need for control groups and understanding why large samples provide more reliable data than small samples (see p. 47)—are essentially applications of research methods to everyday life. The idea that the principles of research methods can inform critical thinking was expressed by George (Pinky) Nelson, a leading U.S. astronaut who is deeply concerned with enhancing the critical thinking abilities of students as a way of preparing them for their future in the information age. Nelson said:

> Most people seem to believe that there is a difference between scientific thinking and everyday thinking. Clearly, most people haven't developed the capacity to think [scientifically]. Otherwise, they wouldn't buy lottery tickets that they can't afford. They wouldn't consistently fall for cheap promises and easy answers from politicians. They wouldn't become victims of medical quackery or misinformation from tobacco companies. They wouldn't keep employing the same failed strategies, both in their personal lives and in society at large, just because that's what they've always done. . . . But, the fact is, these same scientific thinking skills can be used to improve the chances of success in virtually any endeavor." (1998, April 29, p. A 14)

When designing an experiment, a researcher needs to include a control group that does not receive the treatment or experience being investigated. It is usually easy to recognize the need for such a comparison when planning a research project, but it can be difficult to spot the need for control groups when thinking about the many research results that we are bombarded with in newspapers, on the Web, in everyday conversation, and in advertisements. Suppose you read in the newspaper that 75 percent of couples who are going through a divorce argue about money. You might conclude that disputes about money are a major cause of divorce and perhaps even conclude that more marriages would be saved if couples learned how to handle financial disputes. Missing from this analysis is a comparison figure for couples who do not divorce. Suppose you learn that 80 percent of those couples argue about money. Such a result would mean that almost all married people argue about money and that arguing about money is not a predictor of which couples will divorce. It may still be a good idea for couples to learn how to handle financial disputes, but nothing in these data supports the conclusion that money woes cause couples to divorce. You need to consider appropriate control groups to evaluate research findings meaningfully, and when they are missing, you need to consider how they might alter your understanding of the research.

Here is another example that requires critical thinking to recognize the need for a control group. Parents of young children are bombarded with advertisements for educational products to enhance their children's intelligence. There are, for example, special (and expensive) DVDs for infants to watch immediately after birth. Suppose you learn that toddlers who have watched these DVDs are able to talk in two- and three-word phrases by the time they are 18 months old. You might infer that the toddlers are communicating at such a young age because of the DVDs. However, you are missing data about toddlers who do not watch this material. At what age do they talk in two- and three-word phrases? In fact, studies show that the age at which toddlers begin talking does not depend on the use of specific learning programs, and the National Academy of Pediatricians recommends that toddlers younger than two watch *no* DVDs, videos, or television. Without a control group, it would not be possible for you—as a researcher, a concerned citizen, or a parent—to know if particular programs had an effect on children's language development or any aspect of development.

ESTABLISHING CAUSALITY A properly performed experiment depends on rigorous control, the steps taken to minimize the possibility that anything other than the independent variable may affect the experiment's outcome. A **confound** is anything that affects a dependent variable and may unintentionally vary between the study's different experimental conditions. When conducting an experiment, a researcher needs to ensure that the only thing that varies is the independent variable. Control thus represents the foundation of the experimental approach, in that it allows the researcher to rule out *alternative explanations* for the observed data (**FIGURE 2.8**). For example, in an experiment about working women who want to have fun, if the participants who work 10 hours a day have more money than those who work 5 hours a day or those in the control group (who do not work at all), the differences among these groups in their ratings of how much they want to have fun might depend on the amount of

confound Anything that affects a dependent variable and may unintentionally vary between the experimental conditions of a study.

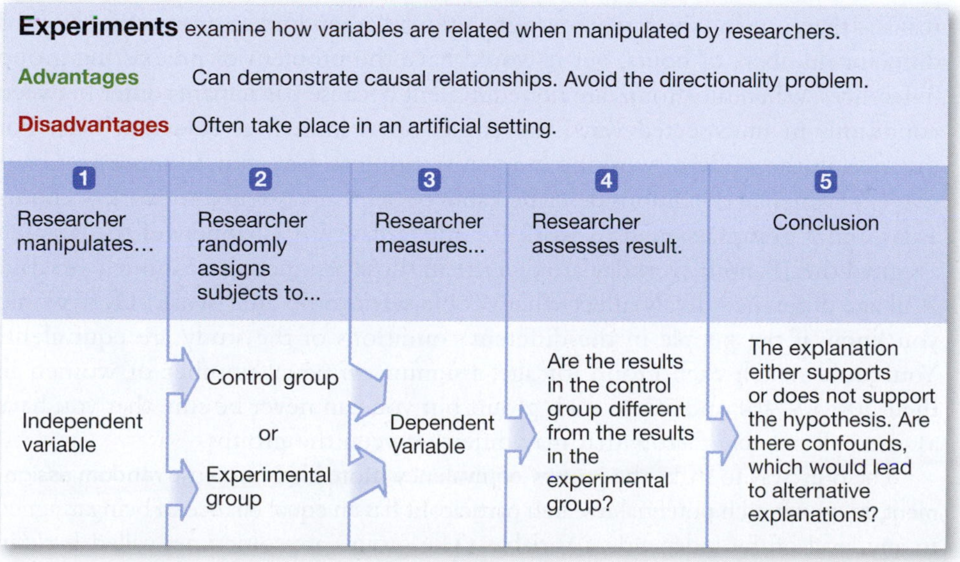

FIGURE 2.8 Experiments

Experiments examine how variables are related when manipulated by researchers.				
Advantages	Can demonstrate causal relationships. Avoid the directionality problem.			
Disadvantages	Often take place in an artificial setting.			
1	**2**	**3**	**4**	**5**
Researcher manipulates...	Researcher randomly assigns subjects to...	Researcher measures...	Researcher assesses result.	Conclusion
Independent variable	Control group or Experimental group	Dependent Variable	Are the results in the control group different from the results in the experimental group?	The explanation either supports or does not support the hypothesis. Are there confounds, which would lead to alternative explanations?

money available for fun activities and not the hours worked. In this example, the number of hours worked might be *confounded with* how much money the women in each group have to spend on fun activities, making it impossible to tell whether the number of hours worked or the amount of money is responsible for the ratings.

The more confounds and thus alternative explanations that can be eliminated, the more confident a researcher can be that the independent variable produced the change (or effect) in the dependent variable. For this reason, researchers have to watch vigilantly for potential confounds, and as consumers of research, we all need to think about confounds that could be causing particular results.

Random Assignment Is Used to Establish Equivalent Groups

An important issue to be considered for any research method is how to select people for inclusion in the study. Psychological scientists typically want to know that their findings *generalize,* or apply, to people beyond the individuals in the study. In studying working women's desire for fun, for example, researchers would not be interested in the behavior of the specific women participating in the study; they would want to discover general laws about human behavior so they could predict what women, in general, want to do after work. Such results would generalize to all women who work. Other results, depending on the nature of the study, might generalize to all college students, to students who belong to sororities and fraternities, to everyone in the world, and so on. The group you want to know about is the **population;** the subset of people who are studied is the **sample.** *Sampling* is the process by which people from the population are selected for the sample. The sample should represent the population, and the best method for making this happen is *random sampling,* in which each member of the population has an equal chance of being chosen to participate. Most of the time, a researcher will use a *convenience sample,* which, as the term implies, is a sample of people who are conveniently available for the study. Even if you wanted your results to generalize to all students in your country or in the world, you would, realistically, probably use a sample from your own college or university and hope that this sample represented all students in your country and beyond.

Even with random sampling, one likely confound is preexisting differences between groups that are assigned to different conditions. An example of this situation was presented above, with the possibility of studying women who work part-time and women who work full-time; such an experiment would be more realistic than one in which women were assigned at random to groups that worked different numbers of hours, but it would have the problem of preexisting group differences. When the groups are not equivalent because participants differ between conditions in unexpected ways, the condition is known as **selection bias.** For instance, in the study of working women wanting to have fun, suppose you have two experimental conditions described above—a group assigned to work 10 hours a day and a group assigned to work 5 hours a day. What happens if the women assigned the 10-hour workday are older than those assigned the 5-hour workday? Will age differences likely affect what people want to do after work? How would you know if the people in the different conditions of the study are equivalent? You could match each group for age, assigning an equal number of women in their 20s, 30s, 40s, and 50s to each group, but you can never be sure that you have assessed all possible factors that may differ between the groups.

The only way to make the groups' equivalency more likely is to use **random assignment,** in which each potential research participant has an equal chance of being assigned to any level of the independent variable. (The groups are sometimes called *levels*; in

population Everyone in the group the experimenter is interested in.

sample A subset of a population.

selection bias When participants in different groups in an experiment differ systematically.

random assignment The procedure for placing research participants into the conditions of an experiment in which each participant has an equal chance of being assigned to any level of the independent variable.

this case, the three levels would be not working, working 5 hours, and working 10 hours.) Perhaps you would have participants draw numbers from a hat to determine who was assigned to the control group (no-work group) and to each experimental group (5-hour workday group and 10-hour workday group). Of course, individual differences are bound to exist among participants. For example, any of your groups might include some women who have children and some women who do not—a variable likely to influence what women want to do after work—as well as women whose incomes and education vary. But these differences will tend to average out when participants are assigned to either the control or experimental groups randomly, so that the groups are equivalent *on average*. Random assignment balances out known and unknown factors (**FIGURE 2.9**).

Meta-analysis is a type of study that, as its name implies, is an analysis of multiple analyses, or studies that have already been conducted. (The plural of *meta-analysis* is *meta-analyses*.) With meta-analysis, many studies that addressed the same issue are combined and summarized in one "study of studies." Suppose, for example, that 10 studies had been conducted on men's and women's effectiveness as leaders. Among these 10 studies, 5 found no differences, 2 favored women, and 3 favored men. Researchers who conducted a meta-analysis would not just count up the numbers of different findings from the research literature. Rather, they would weight more heavily those studies that had larger samples, because large samples are more likely to provide more accurate reflections of what is true in populations. The researchers would also look at the size of each effect, that is, whether each study found a large difference, a small difference, or no difference between the groups being compared, in this case, women and men. (The researchers who conducted the meta-analysis on men's and women's effectiveness found no overall differences; Eagly, Karau, & Makhijani, 1995.) Because meta-analysis combines the results of separate studies, many researchers believe that meta-analysis provides stronger evidence than the results of any single study. As discussed earlier in this chapter, we can be more confident about results when the research findings are replicated. Meta-analysis has the concept of replication built into it.

meta-analysis A "study of studies" that combines the findings of multiple studies to arrive at a conclusion.

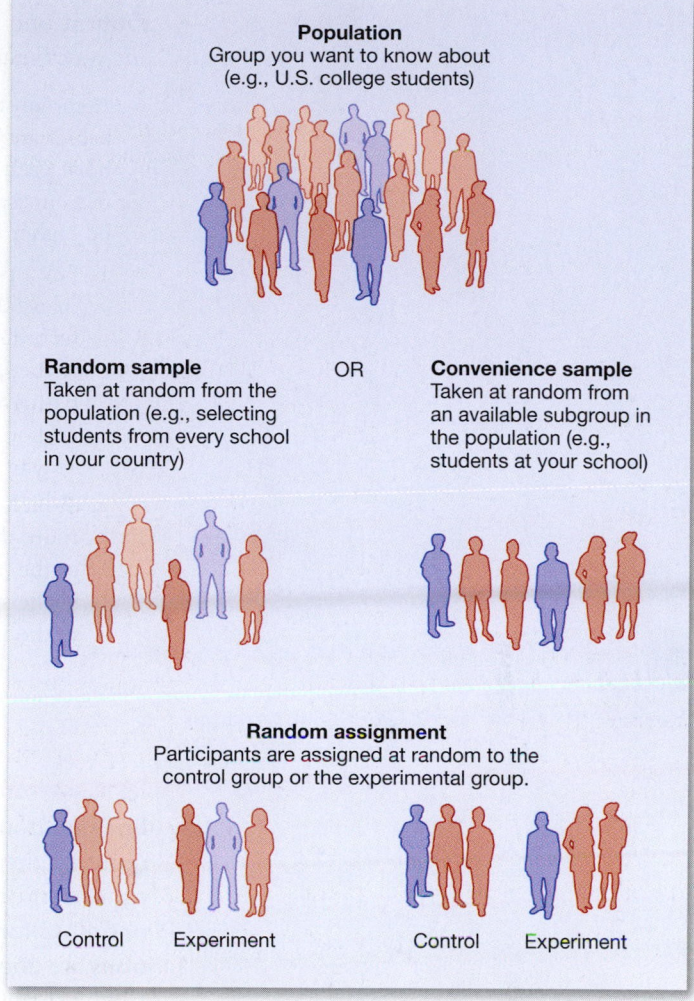

FIGURE 2.9 Sampling For the results of an experiment to be considered useful, the participants should be representative of the population. The best method for making this happen is random sampling, but most of the time researchers are forced to use a convenience sample. Random assignment is used when the experimenter wants to test a *causal* hypothesis.

Recognizing That Large Samples Generate More Reliable Results Than Small Samples

Given a thimbleful of facts, we rush to make generalizations as large as a tub.

—*Gordon Allport (1954, p. 8)*

A general critical thinking skill related to sampling from populations is considering the size of the sample, or the number of participants in the study. As consumers of research, we need to understand which studies provide strong evidence and which are junk science, and the number of participants in a sample is one critical difference between the two types of study. The importance of sample size can be difficult to understand when you think about it one way but easy to understand when you think about it a different way. First, read the following information and answer the questions:

A certain town is served by two hospitals. In the larger hospital, about 45 babies are born each day, and in the smaller hospital, about 15 babies are born each day. As you know, about 50% of all babies are boys. The exact percentage of baby boys, however, varies from day to day. Sometimes it may be higher than 50% and sometimes lower.

1. For a period of 1 year, each hospital recorded the days on which more than 60% of the babies born were boys. Which hospital do you think recorded more such days?
   a. the larger hospital
   b. the smaller hospital
   c. they would each record approximately the same number of days on which more than 60% of the babies born were boys.

2. Which hospital do you think is more likely to find on any one day that more than 60% of babies born were boys?
   a. the larger hospital
   b. the smaller hospital
   c. the probability of having more than 60% of babies born being boys on any day is the same for both hospitals

(Sedlmeier & Gigerenzer, 1997, p. 34; original problem posed by Kahneman & Tversky, 1972)

Look carefully at both questions and the way you answered them. The first question is about the number of days you would expect 60 percent or more of the births to be boys, and the second is about what you would expect on one specific day. If you answered like most people, you selected option C for the first question and B for the second question. Both questions are about sample sizes, however, and the answer to both questions is B. The smaller hospital has fewer births and therefore a smaller sample size, and small samples are more variable, as you will see below. It may help to think about a similar situation that you are more familiar with: tossing a coin. Suppose you want to know if a coin is fair—that is, heads will appear as often on the "up" side as tails when it is flipped. To demonstrate that the coin is fair, you would toss it a few times to show that heads and tails each come up about half the time. Suppose you flip it 4 times. Might you get 3 heads and 1 tail in 4 flips of a fair coin, when there is an equal chance of getting a head or tail on each flip? It is not hard to see how heads and tails might not appear equally if you flip a coin a few times. Now suppose you flip the same coin 100 times. You probably would not get exactly 50 heads and 50 tails, but just by chance you would get close to 50 for each. With only 4 flips, it is quite possible that 75 percent of the flips could be all heads or all tails just by chance. With 100 flips, that same 75 percent is very unlikely.

Can you see how this is the same problem as in the hospital scenario? The smaller hospital is more likely to have some days when the percentage of boys (or girls) is higher 60 percent of the time, even when the true number of girl and boy babies in the population is approximately equal. It is easier to understand this principle when thinking about any single day (question 2) than about the number of days (question 1), although the reasoning is the same. Variability is discussed in more detail later in this chapter, but for now, you need to understand that small samples are more variable than large samples.

The *law of large numbers* states that you get more accurate estimates of a population from a large sample than from a small one. To apply this law in everyday context, suppose you are deciding which of two colleges to attend. To help make this decision, you spend one day at each college and attend one class at each. You like the professor you meet at one of the colleges much better than the professor you meet at the other. Should this small sample of classes and professors influence your decision about which college to attend? Can you see how results from such a small sample could be very misleading? In planning a research project, as in deciding how you feel about a place, you must consider the size of the sample you are generalizing from (**FIGURE 2.10**).

FIGURE 2.10 **Think Critically: Large Samples Are More Accurate than Small Samples** If you wanted to compare how many women like going to the beach and how many men do, but you only considered this small inset sample of seven people, you might think that only women go to the beach! But looking at the big picture, you can see that is clearly not the case.

SUMMING UP

What Are the Types of Studies in Psychological Research?

There are three main types of studies in psychological research: descriptive, correlational, and experimental. In descriptive and correlational designs, researchers examine behavior as it naturally occurs. These types of studies are useful for describing and predicting behavior, but they do not allow researchers to assess causality. Correlational designs have limitations, including directionality problems (knowing whether variable A caused variable B or the reverse) and the third variable problem (the possibility that a third variable is responsible for variables A and B). In an experiment, a researcher manipulates the independent variable to study how it affects the dependent variable. An experiment allows a researcher to establish a causal relationship between the independent and dependent variables and to avoid the directionality problem when trying to understand how one variable might affect another. An experiment gives the researcher the greatest control, so that the only thing that changes is the independent variable. If the goal is to conclude that changes in one variable caused changes in another variable, the researcher must assign participants at random to different groups to make the groups as equal as possible (on average) on all variables except the one being studied. The researcher wants to know about a population, but because it is usually impossible for everyone in the population to be a research participant, the researcher uses a representative sample of the population and then generalizes the findings to the population. Random sampling, in which everyone in the population has an equal chance of being a research participant, is the best way to sample, but since this is usually not possible, most researchers use a convenience sample. Among the most important factors in whether the results from a particular sample can be generalized back to the population is sample size. In general, large samples provide more accurate results than small ones.

▶ MEASURING UP

1. The main reason researchers randomly assign participants to different groups in an experiment is that _____.
   a. it is easier to assign participants to different conditions than it is to find people who naturally fit into different conditions
   b. random assignment controls for any intuitions the participants may have at the start of the experiment
   c. random assignment is used when there are ethical reasons for not using observational or correlational research designs
   d. random assignment is the only way to ensure that the participants are (on average) equal and that any difference in the dependent variables must have been caused by their being in different groups

2. Match each of the main methods of conducting research with the advantages and disadvantages listed below. Write in "descriptive," "correlational," "experimental," "longitudinal," or "cross-sectional" next to its advantage or disadvantage.
   _____ a. Allows the researcher to conclude that one variable caused a change in another variable.
   _____ b. Allows for a detailed description in a real-world setting.
   _____ c. Allows the researcher to understand if two or more variables are related, without demonstrating a causal relationship.
   _____ d. Measures people of different ages to learn about developmental changes.
   _____ e. Data are most likely to be biased (reflect the thoughts and beliefs of the person collecting the data).
   _____ f. The same people are repeatedly measured over time to understand developmental changes.
   _____ g. The research conditions are most likely to be artificial (because this method is often used in a laboratory).
   _____ h. It is always possible that a third variable not considered by the researcher caused the results.

What Are the Data Collection Methods of Psychological Science?

Once the researcher has established the best design for a particular study, the next task is to choose a method for collecting the data. A fundamental principle of psychological research is that the question the researcher wants to answer dictates the appropriate method for collecting data. In short, as previously discussed, you start with an appropriate, theory-based question, and then ask yourself, "What sort of data will best answer my question?" Recall from Chapter 1 the four major research categories that span the levels of analysis: biological, individual, social, and cultural. The first step in selecting a data collection method is determining the level of analysis a particular question is addressing. The data collection method used in the study must be appropriate for questions at that level of analysis.

When the research question is aimed at the biological level, researchers measure such things as brain processes and differences in hormone levels. For instance, they might use brain imaging to examine how the brain responds when people look at pictures of scary faces, or they might measure whether men secrete more testosterone when their favorite team wins than when it loses. At the individual level, researchers are looking for individual differences among participants' responses. Researchers will therefore question participants or use indirect assessments, such as observing how quickly participants respond to a particular question or whether they accurately discriminate between stimuli. At the social level, researchers often collect data by observing people within a single culture and seeing how they interact. Most work at the cultural level compares groups of people from different cultures as a way of studying the effect of culture on some variable. For example, cross-cultural studies might examine beliefs about appropriate roles for women and men or attitudes toward pornography. The various methods for studying this latter topic might include attitudinal measures, such as noting cultural differences in defining pornography; behavioral measures, such as observing who buys pornographic materials in different countries; brain imaging, to see if arousal centers in the brain react differently when people in different countries view pornography; and even legislation summaries, collecting differences in the laws regarding pornography.

One difficulty in comparing people from different cultures is that some ideas and practices do not translate easily across cultures, just as some words do not translate easily into other languages. For example, in Turkey, there apparently is no word corresponding to *jerk;* and the title of the Disney movie *Lady and the Tramp* was translated into the equivalent of *Lady and the Street Dog,* because Turkish has no word with the same positive and negative connotations as *tramp.* Another such "untranslatable" word is *Schadenfreude,* German for taking pleasure in another person's misfortune. The experience of schadenfreude occurs around the world (as in the delight many people experienced in 2008 when Eliot Spitzer, the self-righteous and apparently straight-laced former prosecutor and New York State governor, had to resign because he was caught paying thousands of dollars to prostitutes), but some languages do not have a word for it. Thus a researcher studying the phenomenon of schadenfreude might have to explain the concept to participants whose language lacked a single word to describe it. Apparent differences among cultures may reflect such differences in language, or they may reflect participants' relative willingness to report negative things about themselves publicly (such as that they take pleasure in other

LEARNING OBJECTIVES
Provide examples of data collection methods that are appropriate for different research questions.

Identify ethical issues and explain their importance.

people's misfortunes). A central challenge for cross-cultural researchers is to refine their measurements to rule out these kinds of alternative explanations (**FIGURE 2.11**).

Culturally sensitive research practices take into account the significant role that culture plays in how we think, feel, and act (Adair & Kagitcibasi, 1995; Zebian, Alamuddin, Mallouf, & Chatila, 2007). The underlying idea of different cultural practices is that a culture has a "shared system of meaning" transmitted from one generation to the next (Betancourt & Lopez, 1993, p. 630). The worldviews that cultures share are adaptive; that is, they help ensure our species' survival. Adaptation is usually associated with the evolution of biological traits that are passed down through biological linkages, but here it refers to cultural traits, which include, in part, thoughts and behaviors. Some psychological traits are the same across all cultures (e.g., care for the young); others differ widely across cultures (e.g., behaviors expected of adolescents). In cities with diverse populations, such as Toronto, London, and Los Angeles, cultural differences exist among different groups of people living in the same neighborhoods and having close daily contact. Researchers therefore need to be sensitive to cultural differences even when they are studying people in the same neighborhood or the same school. Researchers must also guard against applying a psychological concept from one culture to another without considering whether the concept is the same in both cultures. For example, children's attachment to their parents may look very different among different cultural groups (Kappenberg & Halpern, 2006).

Observing Is an Unobtrusive Strategy

Observational techniques (see Figure 2.3) involve the systematic assessment and coding of overt behavior, as in watching and noting people's gestures during social interaction or coding the eating or sexual behavior of animals that have been injected with drugs that affect brain function. Using observational techniques to collect data requires researchers to make at least three decisions. First, should the study be conducted in the laboratory or in a natural environment? At issue are the extent to which the researchers are interested in behavior as it occurs in the real world and the possibility that the laboratory setting will lead to artificial behavior.

Second, how should the data be collected—as a written description of what was seen, or as a running tally of prespecified categories of behavior? For example, suppose you hypothesize that people greet friends and family more effusively at airports than at train stations (perhaps because people think of air travel as more dangerous than rail travel, or perhaps because travelers tend to make longer trips by air and so are likely to have been apart longer from the people greeting them). To begin your study, you would need to operationally define different categories of effusive greetings, rating hugging and kissing, for example, as more effusive than hand shaking or head nodding. While observing each episode of greeting at the airport gate or train platform, you could check off the appropriate category on a tally sheet. Researchers generally prefer preestablished categories as being more objective. However, badly chosen categories can lead observers to miss important behavior. For example, how would you classify the two-cheek air kiss, a more popular greeting in some countries than in others? The extent to which such a greeting is "effusive" depends on the cultural

culturally sensitive research Studies that take into account the ways culture affects thoughts, feelings, and actions.

observational technique A research method of careful and systematic assessment and coding of overt behavior.

Cross-cultural studies compare groups of people from different cultures.

Advantages Examine the effect of culture on some variable of interest, thereby making psychology more applicable around the world.

Disadvantages Some situations and some specific words do not convey the same meaning when translated across cultures and can leave room for alternative explanations (other than culture per se), such as misunderstanding during the research process.

FIGURE 2.11 Cross-Cultural Studies (top) The living space and treasured possessions of a family in Japan, for example, differ from **(bottom)** those of a family in Mali. Cross-cultural researchers might study how either family would react to crowding or to the loss of its possessions.

context. Likewise, a kiss on the mouth is a standard greeting between men in some parts of the world, but it suggests a romantic relationship in other parts of the world. Any greeting would need to be rated and interpreted in its cultural context.

Third, should the observer be visible? The concern here is that observation might alter the behavior being observed, an effect known as **reactivity.** People may feel compelled to make a positive impression on an observer, so they may act differently when they believe they are being observed. An example of this happened in a series of studies of the effects of workplace conditions, such as different levels of lighting, different pay incentives, and different break schedules, on productivity at the Hawthorne Works manufacturing plant of Western Electric in Cicero, Illinois, between 1924 and 1933 (Olson, Hogan, & Santos, 2006). This series of studies has become a classic in the psychological literature because the researchers were among the first to apply the principles of the scientific method to real-world questions in a workplace setting. The workers knew they were being observed, so they responded to changes in their working conditions by increasing productivity, regardless of the nature of the manipulation—including the lengthening or shortening of breaks and various changes to the pay system. The workers did not speed up continuously throughout the various studies—the main dependent variable was how long it took them to complete certain tasks—but they got faster at the start of a new type of manipulation. The *Hawthorne effect* refers to changes in behavior that occur when people know that others are observing them (**FIGURE 2.12**).

Can you think of ways the Hawthorne effect might operate in other studies? Consider, for example, a study of the effectiveness of a new reading program in elementary schools. Say that the teachers know they have been selected to try out a new program. They also know that their students' reading progress will be monitored closely and reported to the schools' superintendent. It is easy to see how

reactivity When the knowledge that one is being observed alters the behavior being observed.

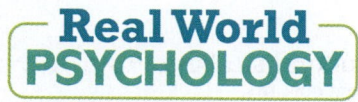

FIGURE 2.12 Scientific Method: The Hawthorne Effect

Hypothesis: Being observed can lead participants to change their behavior.

Research Method:

1 During studies of the effects of workplace conditions, the researchers manipulated several **independent variables,** such as the levels of lighting, pay incentives, and break schedules.

2 The researchers measured the **dependent variable,** the speed at which workers did their jobs.

Results: The workers' productivity increased when they knew they were being observed, regardless of the change to the independent variable.

Conclusion: Being observed can lead participants to change their behavior because people often act in particular ways to make positive impressions.

these teachers might teach more enthusiastically or pay more attention to each child's reading progress than would teachers using the old program. One likely outcome is that the students receiving the new program of instruction would show reading gains caused by the teachers' increased attention and not by the new program. In general, observation should be as unobtrusive as possible.

Case Studies Examine Individual Lives and Organizations

A **case study** involves the intensive examination of one person or a few individuals or one or a few organizations, typically people or organizations that are somehow unusual (**FIGURE 2.13**). For this reason, case studies are often considered a special type of observation or descriptive study, with a sample size equal to 1. An organization might be selected for intensive study because it is doing something very well (such as making a lot of money) or very poorly (such as losing a lot of money). The goal of an organizational case study is to determine which practices led to success or failure. Did the employees have flexible work schedules, or was an exercise program offered at work? Many psychologists work in organizations, studying the wide range of variables that influence human behavior at work. In psychology, case studies are frequently conducted with people who have brain injuries or psychological disorders. Case studies of people with brain injuries have provided a wealth of evidence about which parts of the brain are involved in various psychological processes. In one case, a man who was accidentally stabbed through the middle part of the brain with a fencing foil lost the ability to store new memories, and case histories of individuals with damage to the front portions of their brains reveal consistent difficulties with inhibiting impulsive behaviors (Squire & Moore, 1979; Chamberlain & Sahakian, 2007).

The major problem with clinical case studies, the ones used most frequently in psychology, is that it is difficult to know whether the researcher's theory about the cause of the psychological disorder is correct. The researcher has no control over the person's life and is forced to make assumptions about the effects of various life events. The same problem applies for organizational case studies. We cannot know why a certain life history may lead to a particular disorder for one

FIGURE 2.13 Case Studies The tragic story of Virginia Tech student Seung-Hui Cho provides a case study of a severely disturbed individual. Cho sent photos of himself to news organizations right before he went on a deadly campus shooting spree in April 2007, and he left in his wake a devastated campus that had lost 27 students and 5 teachers.

Case studies are a special type of observational/descriptive study that involves intensive examination of one person or a few individuals (clinical case studies) or one or a few organizations (organizational case studies).

Advantages   Can provide extensive data about one or a few individuals or organizations.

Disadvantages   Can be very subjective: If a researcher has a causal theory (for example, people who are loners are dangerous), this theory can bias what is observed and recorded. It is not possible to generalize the results from an individual to the population.

individual and not for others or why different work practices can have different outcomes for different organizations. Thus the interpretation of case studies is often very subjective.

In April 2007, Seung-Hui Cho, a student at Virginia Technical University, went on a campus shooting spree in which he killed 32 people, wounded many others, and then killed himself. The horror of this event led many people to ask what was known about his mental health prior to this tragedy. In fact, campus officials knew that Cho was deeply troubled, although no one could have predicted this violent outburst. His professors had been concerned about him because of the violent themes in his writing, especially a 10-page play that was filled with anger and extreme violence. On the day of the shooting, Cho first shot two students in their dorm and then returned to his room to write about his extreme loneliness and anger before going to a nearby classroom building, where he shot at everyone within his range.

This tragic story provides a snapshot into the mind of a severely disturbed individual. Psychologists and law enforcement officials cannot use the data from this unique case to identify other people who might erupt in similar ways because Cho is not representative of disturbed individuals in general. Professional writers, such as horror novelists and Hollywood scriptwriters, often detail anger and violence, and in that context, Cho's writing would not have been unusual. In hindsight, it is easy to see that Cho should have been put in a locked facility where he could not harm others and could get treatment. But before his rampage, there was not enough evidence to allow his involuntary commitment to an institution. Fortunately, murderous outbursts like this one are extremely rare, but that also means that they are almost impossible to predict. Some lonely people write violent stories, but very few of those people commit violent crimes. In this way, a case study can reveal a lot about the person being examined, but it does not allow generalization to all similar people (lonely ones, violent ones, what have you), and thus its use as a research tool is limited.

Asking Takes a More Active Approach

If observation is an unobtrusive approach for studying behavior, asking people about themselves—what they think, why they act the way they do, and how they feel— is a much more interactive way of collecting data. Methods of asking participants questions include surveys, interviews, questionnaires, and other self-reports. The type of information sought ranges from demographic facts (e.g., ethnicity, age, religious affiliation) to past behaviors, personal attitudes, beliefs, and so on. "Have you ever used an illegal drug?" "Should people who drink and drive be jailed for a first offense?" "Are you comfortable sending food back to the kitchen in a restaurant when there is a problem?" Questions such as these require people to recall certain events from their lives or reflect on their mental or emotional states to decide how they would react in different settings. A critical issue in asking research-based questions is how to frame the questions; there are several options. *Open-ended questions* allow respondents to provide any answer they think of and to answer in as much detail as they feel is appropriate. In contrast, *closed-ended questions* require respondents to select among a fixed number of options, as in a multiple-choice exam. Ultimately, the researcher decides what style of question will provide the most appropriate information for the hypothesis being investigated.

Like all methods of data collection, methods that require participants to answer questions have strengths and weaknesses. Consider, for example, the differences between asking respondents to fill out a survey and actually interviewing each person with open-ended questions. **Self-report methods**

self-report method A method of data collection in which people are asked to provide information about themselves, such as in questionnaires or surveys.

Surveys and questionnaires

Interviews

Experience sampling

FIGURE 2.14 **Interactive Methods**

such as questionnaires can be used to gather data from a large number of people (**FIGURE 2.14**). They can be mailed out to a sample drawn from the population of interest or handed out in appropriate locations. They are easy to administer and cost-efficient. Researchers who use questionnaires can collect a great deal of data in a relatively short time. Interviews can be used very successfully with groups that cannot be studied through surveys, such as young children. Furthermore, interviewing people gives the researcher the opportunity to explore new lines of questioning, if respondents' answers inspire avenues of inquiry that were not originally planned.

When researchers want to understand how thoughts, feelings, and behaviors vary throughout the day, week, or longer, they turn to a relatively new method of data collection, *experience sampling*. As the name implies, researchers take several samples of the participants' experiences over time. By repeatedly getting answers to set questions, researchers can determine how the responses vary over time. So, for example, if researchers wanted to know what a typical day is like for a high school student, they might give each student-participant a notebook with labeled categories in which to fill in what is happening and how the participant feels about it. Or each student-participant might be given a PDA (personal data assistant) to carry at all times. At random or predetermined times, the PDA would signal the participants to record what they are doing, thinking, or feeling at that moment. Studies with experience sampling have shown, by the way, that students are frequently bored in class; while teachers may believe that students are engaged in a learning activity, students are more likely not paying attention and are thinking about lunch, friends, or other topics unrelated to the course content (Schneider & Csikszentmihalyi, 2000).

SELF-REPORT BIAS A problem common to all asking-based methods of data collection is that people often introduce biases into their answers, making it difficult to discern an honest or true response. In particular, people may not reveal personal information that casts them in a negative light. Consider the question "How many times have you lied to get something you wanted?" Although most people have lied at some points in their lives to obtain desired outcomes or objects, few of us want to admit this, especially to strangers. At issue is the extent to which questions produce *socially desirable responding,* or *faking good,* in which the person responds in a way that is most socially acceptable. Imagine having an interviewer around your parents' age, or, if you are an older student, perhaps a twenty-something interviewer, ask you to describe intimate aspects of your sex life. Would you be embarrassed and therefore not very forthcoming? Might you even lie to the interviewer?

Even when respondents do not purposefully answer incorrectly, their answers may reflect less-than-accurate self-perceptions. Research has shown that, at least in some cultures, people tend to describe themselves in especially positive ways, often because people believe things about themselves that are not necessarily true. This is called the *better-than-average effect.* For instance, most people believe they are better-than-average drivers. The tendency to express positive things about oneself is especially common in Western cultures, such as those of North America and Europe, but is less pronounced in Eastern cultures, such as those in Korea and Japan (as you will learn in Chapter 13, "Personality"). A recent meta-analysis found that although East Asians tend to rate themselves as better than average on a wide range of variables, they do so less consistently than people from Canada and the United States (Heine & Hamamura, 2007).

One reason that researchers vary their data collection methods among different studies is that they can have more confidence in research findings when studies with different types of measures support the same conclusion. Recall the implicit association test described in the first chapter. In that test, participants respond as rapidly as possible to pictures and words, and researchers infer these people's thoughts and feelings based on the time it takes them to make different judgments. One cross-cultural study of self-esteem compared participants' reaction times to pleasant words (e.g., "good," "nice," "kind") with their reaction times when those words were applied to themselves. Researchers found no differences in the reaction times among people in Japan, China, and the United States and concluded that high self-esteem is culturally universal, though East Asians are less likely to express their self-esteem publicly (Yamaguchi et al., 2007). Studies like this one show why particular results can depend on the data collection method. Researchers would have come to a different conclusion about self-esteem across cultures if they had relied on self-report methods. These results also show why research methods are central to our understanding of psychological principles—because we can get different results when we use different methods.

Response Performance Measures Information Processing

As noted in Chapter 1, Wilhelm Wundt established the first psychology laboratory in 1879. Wundt and his students pioneered many of the methods for studying how the mind works, by examining, for example, how people responded to psychological tasks such as deciding whether two stimuli were the same or whether words flashed on a screen were the names of animals. **Response performance** can take three basic forms. First, the researcher can measure *reaction time,* the speed of a response. The interpretation of reaction times—the workhorse method of cognitive psychology—is based on the idea that the brain takes time to process information; the more processing a stimulus requires, the longer the reaction time to that stimulus. So research participants will make an easy decision, such as whether a figure flashed on a screen is red or blue, faster than a more difficult decision, such as whether that figure is red or blue *and* round or square. By manipulating what a subject must do with a stimulus and measuring reaction times, researchers can gain much information regarding the different operations involved in information processing.

A researcher can also measure *response accuracy.* For example, does paying attention to a stimulus improve a person's perception of that stimulus? One way to study this in the visual domain would be to ask participants to pay attention to one side of a computer screen while keeping their eyes focused on the center of the screen. The researcher would then present a stimulus requiring a discrimination response, such as by briefly flashing a shape on either side of the screen and then asking whether the shape was a hexagon or an octagon. If participants answered more accurately when the stimulus appeared on the side of the screen they were attending to than when it appeared on the side they were ignoring, the results would indicate that attention improves perception of the stimulus.

Finally, a researcher can measure response performance by asking people to make *stimulus judgments* regarding the different stimuli with which they are presented. Typical examples would be asking subjects whether they noticed a faint stimulus such as a very soft sound or light touch or asking them to

response performance A research method in which researchers quantify perceptual or cognitive processes in response to a specific stimulus.

FIGURE 2.15 **Response Performance
Methods**

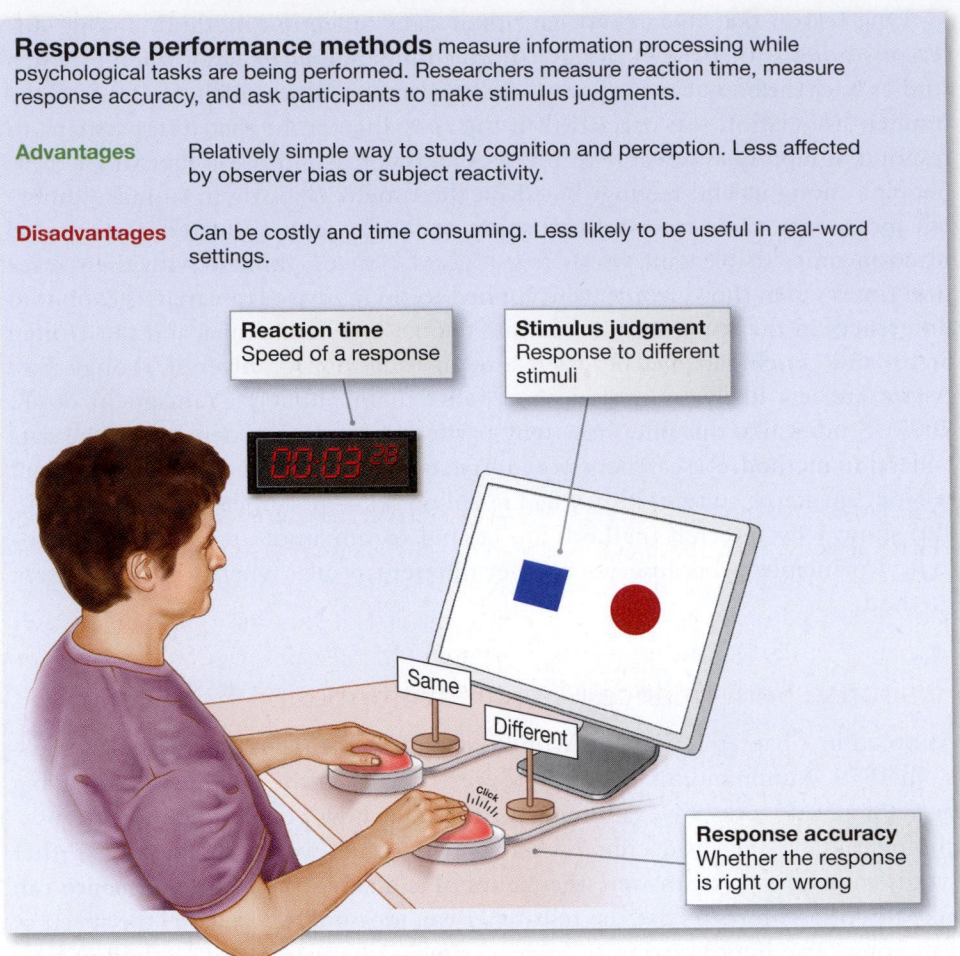

Response performance methods measure information processing while psychological tasks are being performed. Researchers measure reaction time, measure response accuracy, and ask participants to make stimulus judgments.

Advantages   Relatively simple way to study cognition and perception. Less affected by observer bias or subject reactivity.

Disadvantages   Can be costly and time consuming. Less likely to be useful in real-word settings.

Reaction time
Speed of a response

Stimulus judgment
Response to different stimuli

00:03 28

Same

Different

Response accuracy
Whether the response is right or wrong

Click

---

compare two objects and judge whether they are the same in some way, such as color, size, or shape (**FIGURE 2.15**).

Reaction times for responding to simple stimuli, such as the time it takes to press one key on a computer keyboard if a red shape appears and a different key if a blue shape appears, are often measured in hundredths or thousandths of a second. One reason psychological scientists use reaction times as dependent measures is that reaction times cannot be faked. If a participant tries to respond more slowly, for example, the reaction time will be much longer than what is expected (maybe two or three seconds instead of a fraction of a second), and the experimenter will know immediately that the response was not a measure of actual processing time.

Because people have very limited control over their reaction times, these measures again illustrate the idea that some psychological processes happen unconsciously. We have no conscious knowledge about what is happening in our brains as we use information, but reaction time measures indirectly reflect brain processing (**FIGURE 2.16**).

Body/Brain Activity Can Be Measured Directly

Researchers operate at the biological level of analysis when they collect data about the ways people's bodies and brains respond to particular tasks or events. Body/brain activity can be measured directly

---

FIGURE 2.16 **Try for Yourself: The Stroop Effect**

As quickly as you can, name the color of the ink each word is printed in. Do not read the words.

red	blue	green	red	blue	yellow	red	blue
blue	red	green	yellow	red	blue	green	red
yellow	blue	green	red	blue	yellow	red	green
green	yellow	red	yellow	blue	red	green	blue

If you are like most people, your reaction time for naming the ink colors in the bottom two rows was slower than your reaction time for naming the top two rows.

Explanation: The Stroop effect, named after the psychologist John Ridley Stroop, accounts for this phenomenon, in which it takes longer to name the colors of words for colors when they are printed in conflicting colors. The tendency to automatically read the words interferes with the process of naming the ink colors.

in different ways. For instance, certain emotional states influence the body in predictable ways. When people are frightened, their muscles become tense and their hearts beat faster. Other bodily systems influenced by mental states include blood pressure, blood temperature, perspiration rate, breathing rate, pupil size, and so on. Measurements of these systems are examples of *psychophysiological assessment,* in which researchers examine how bodily functions (physiology) change in association with behaviors or mental states (psychology). For example, police investigators often use *polygraphs*, popularly known as "lie detectors," to assess some of these bodily states, under the assumption that people who are lying experience more arousal and therefore more likely show physical signs of stress. Correspondence between mental state and bodily response is not perfect, however, and people who lie easily can show little or no emotional response when they lie during a polygraph recording, so lie detectors do not accurately measure whether someone is lying. (Brain activity methods—polygraphs and the techniques discussed below—are illustrated in **FIGURE 2.17**.)

ELECTROPHYSIOLOGY *Electrophysiology* is a data collection method that measures electrical activity in the brain. A researcher fits electrodes onto the participant's scalp. The electrodes act like small microphones that pick up the brain's electrical activity instead of sounds. The device that measures brain activity is an **electroencephalogram (EEG)**. This measurement is useful because different behavioral states produce different and predictable EEG patterns. As Chapter 4 discusses further, the EEG shows specific and consistent patterns as people fall asleep, and it reveals that the brain is very active even when the body is at rest, especially during dreams. As a measure of specific cognitive states, however, the EEG is limited because the recordings reflect all brain activity and therefore are too "noisy" or imprecise to isolate specific responses to particular stimuli.

electroencephalogram (EEG) A device that measures electrical activity in the brain.

BRAIN IMAGING The brain's electrical activity is associated with changes in the flow of blood carrying oxygen and nutrients to the active brain regions. **Brain imaging** methods measure changes in the rate, or speed, of blood flow, and by keeping track of these changes, researchers can monitor which brain areas are active when people perform particular tasks or experience particular events. Imaging is a powerful tool for uncovering where different systems reside in the brain and the manner in which different brain areas interact to process information. For example, research has shown that certain brain regions become active when people look at pictures of faces, whereas other brain regions become active when people try to understand what other people are thinking. The major imaging technologies are *positron emission tomography* and *magnetic resonance imaging*.

brain imaging A range of experimental techniques that make brain structures and brain activity visible.

Positron emission tomography (PET), is the computer-aided reconstruction of the brain's metabolic activity. When cells in the body, including brain cells, are active, they break down, or metabolize, glucose. After the injection of a relatively harmless radioactive substance into the bloodstream, a PET scan enables researchers to find the brain areas that are using glucose. The research participant lies in a special scanner that, by detecting the injected radiation, produces a three-dimensional map of the density of radioactivity inside the participant's brain. This map is useful because as the brain performs a mental task, blood flow increases to the most active regions, leading these regions to emit more radiation. By scanning participants as they perform some psychological task (for example, looking at pictures of faces expressing fear), and then by collating those scans, researchers obtain a map of the brain's metabolic activity during the task. However, since the entire brain is extremely metabolically active all the time, scans must also be made while the participants perform another, closely related task (for example, looking at pictures of faces with neutral expressions). In this way, brain regions can be correlated with specific mental activities.

positron emission tomography (PET) A method of brain imaging that assesses metabolic activity by using a radioactive substance injected into the bloodstream.

Brain activity methods measure body/brain responses to tasks or events.

Advantages Map the brain in various ways to show brain regions involved in different tasks.

Disadvantages Show only the brain regions active while tasks are performed or events occur—we do not know whether, for example, a particular brain region is necessary for a particular task because these data are correlational and thus have the disadvantage of the third variable problem; directionality problem.

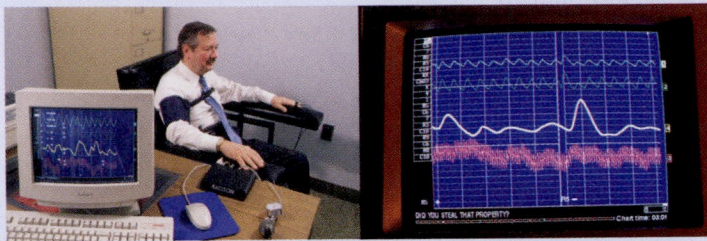

Polygraph (lie detector) measures changes in bodily functions related to behaviors or mental states. These are *not* reliable measures of lying.

Electroencephalogram (EEG) measures the brain's electrical activity.

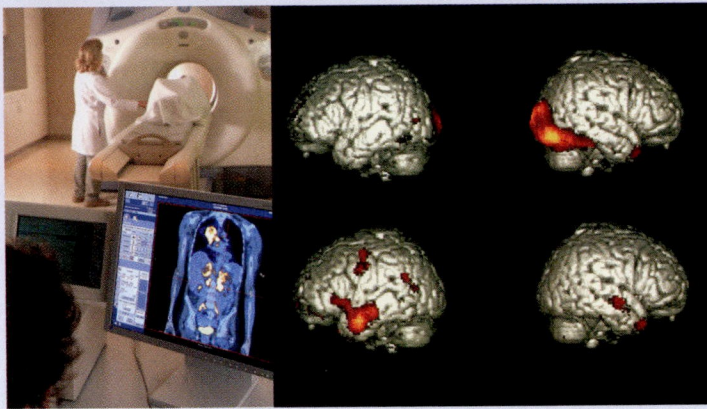

Positron emission tomography (PET) scans the brain's metabolic activity.

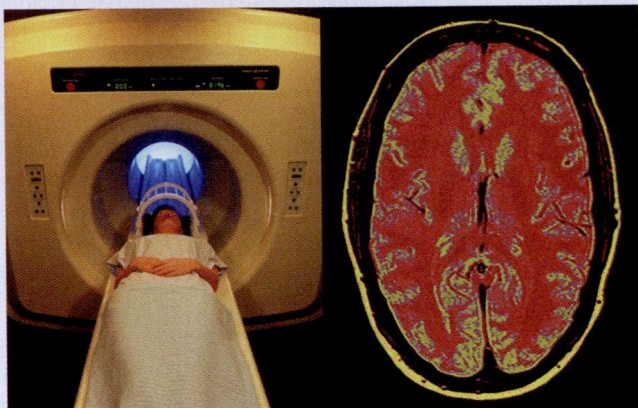

Magnetic resonance imaging (MRI) produces a high-resolution image of the brain.

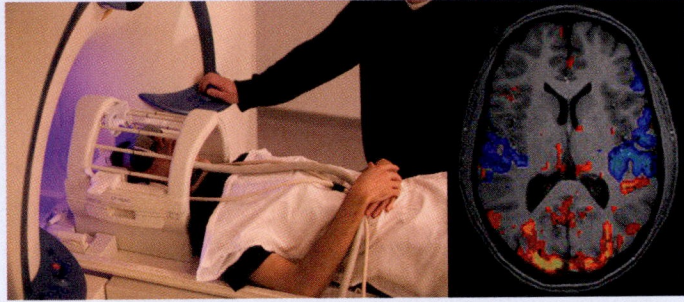

Functional magnetic resonance imaging (fMRI) maps mental activity by assessing the blood's oxygen level in the brain.

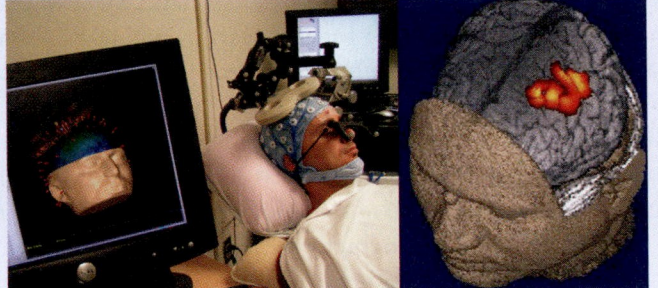

Transcranial magnetic stimulation (TMS) momentarily disrupts brain activity in a specific brain region.

FIGURE 2.17 Brain Activity Methods

magnetic resonance imaging (MRI) A method of brain imaging that produces high-quality images of the brain.

Magnetic resonance imaging (MRI) is the most powerful imaging technique. In MRI, a research participant lies in a scanner that produces a powerful magnetic field, as strong as that used to pick up scrap metal at junkyards. The researchers momentarily disrupt the magnetic forces, and during this process, energy is released from brain tissue in a form that can be measured by detectors surrounding the head. Because different types of brain tissue release energy differently, researchers can produce a high-resolution image of the brain. (The amount of energy released is very small, so having an MRI is not dangerous.)

MRI is extremely valuable for determining the location of, for example, brain damage, but it can also be used to create images of the working brain. Like a PET scan, **functional magnetic resonance imaging (fMRI)** makes use of the brain's blood flow to map mental activity, scanning the brains of participants as they perform tasks (e.g., deciding whether a face they are viewing is happy or sad). Whereas PET measures blood flow directly by tracking a harmless radioactive substance, fMRI measures blood flow indirectly by assessing changes in the blood's oxygen level. In all brain-imaging methods, including fMRI, participants are asked to perform tasks that differ in only one way, which reflects the particular mental function of interest. The researchers then compare images to examine differences in blood flow and therefore brain activity.

TRANSCRANIAL MAGNETIC STIMULATION One limitation of brain imaging is that the findings are necessarily correlational. We know that certain brain regions are active while a task is performed; we do not know whether each brain region is necessary for the task. As a correlational method, brain imaging has the conceptual problems, such as the third variable and directionality problems, discussed above. (If you are unsure what these terms mean, reread the section on correlational research designs; these important concepts will reappear throughout the book.) To see whether a brain region is important for a task, we ideally want to compare performance when that area is working effectively and when it is not. **Transcranial magnetic stimulation (TMS),** uses a very fast but powerful magnetic field to disrupt brain activity momentarily in a specific brain region. For example, placing the TMS coil over areas of the brain involved in language will disrupt a person's ability to speak. This technique has its limitations, particularly that it can be used only for short durations to examine brain areas close to the scalp, but when used along with imaging it is a powerful method for examining which brain regions are necessary for specific psychological functions.

Research with Animals Provides Important Data

Throughout the history of psychological science, many of the most important research findings have been obtained by studying nonhuman animals' behavior. For instance, watching animals—usually rats—run through mazes or press levers to earn rewards led to the development of many principles about learning. Indeed, Ivan Pavlov's observation of a salivating dog inspired John B. Watson to launch the behaviorist movement (see Chapter 6, "Learning"). One central assumption underlying Watson's behaviorism was that humans are subject to the same laws of nature as other animals. Although humans' behaviors might seem more complex than those of rats or dogs, the forces that control the behaviors of rats, dogs, and humans—indeed, of human and nonhuman animals—are in many ways the same.

As our knowledge of the human genome increases rapidly, interest increases in the way genes affect behaviors, mental and physical illnesses, and well-being. Psychological scientists working at the biological level of analysis manipulate genes directly to examine their effects on behavior. Of course, for ethical reasons, much of the genetic research cannot be conducted with humans, so researchers use other animals for this important work. (Government regulations require a careful monitoring of animals used in research.) As Chapter 3 discusses in greater detail, specific genes can be targeted for manipulation. Researchers can delete genes to eliminate their effects or move genes to other locations to enhance their effects. For research purposes, *transgenic mice* are produced by manipulating the genes in developing mouse embryos—for example, by inserting strands of foreign DNA. The new genes are integrated into every cell of each mouse's body. This sort of research is providing new hope for curing and preventing many diseases (**FIGURE 2.18**).

functional magnetic resonance imaging (fMRI) An imaging technique used to examine changes in the activity of the working human brain.

transcranial magnetic stimulation (TMS) The use of strong magnets to briefly interrupt normal brain activity as a way to study brain regions.

"WHAT IT COMES DOWN TO IS YOU HAVE TO FIND OUT WHAT REACTION THEY'RE LOOKING FOR, AND YOU GIVE THEM THAT REACTION."

There Are Ethical Issues to Consider

When scientists select a research method, they must make decisions with full knowledge of and strict adherence to the ethical issues involved. Are they asking the participants to do something unreasonable? Are the participants risking physical or emotional harm from the study? Some ethical concerns are specific to the kind of method used, while others apply across all methods. Therefore, to ensure the participants' well-being, all colleges, universities, and research institutes have strict guidelines in place regarding human- and animal-based research. **Institutional review boards (IRBs)** consisting of administrators, legal advisers, and trained scholars review all proposed research to ensure that it meets scientific standards and allays ethical concerns for the safety and well-being of participants.

One of the more prominent ethical concerns about research is participants' reasonable expectation of *privacy*. If behaviors are going to be observed, is it okay to observe people without their knowledge? This question obviously depends on what sorts of behaviors researchers might be observing. If the behaviors tend to occur in public rather than in private, researchers might be less concerned about observing people without their knowledge. For example, even without their knowledge it would be okay to observe couples saying good-bye in a public place such as an airport, but without their knowledge it would be inappropriate to observe those couples' private sexual behaviors. The concern over privacy is compounded by the ever-increasing technology for monitoring people remotely. Although it might be useful to compare men's and women's behaviors in public bathrooms, would it be acceptable to install discreet video cameras to monitor people in restrooms? No!

When people are asked for information, should some topics not be raised because they may be too personal or otherwise inappropriate? Say, for example, that researchers would like to understand how a physically and emotionally traumatic event affects people in the months and years after it occurs. Although such issues must be explored to develop strategies for overcoming physical and emotional anguish, researchers must consider how their line of questioning is affecting the individuals they are studying.

No matter what method is employed, researchers must also consider who will have access to the data they collect. Participant *confidentiality* should always be guarded carefully so that personal information is not linked publicly to the study's

institutional review boards (IRBs) Groups of people responsible for reviewing proposed research to ensure that it meets the accepted standards of science and provides for the physical and emotional well-being of research participants.

FIGURE 2.18 Animal Research
Researchers observe the behaviors of transgenic mice to understand how certain genes affect behavior.

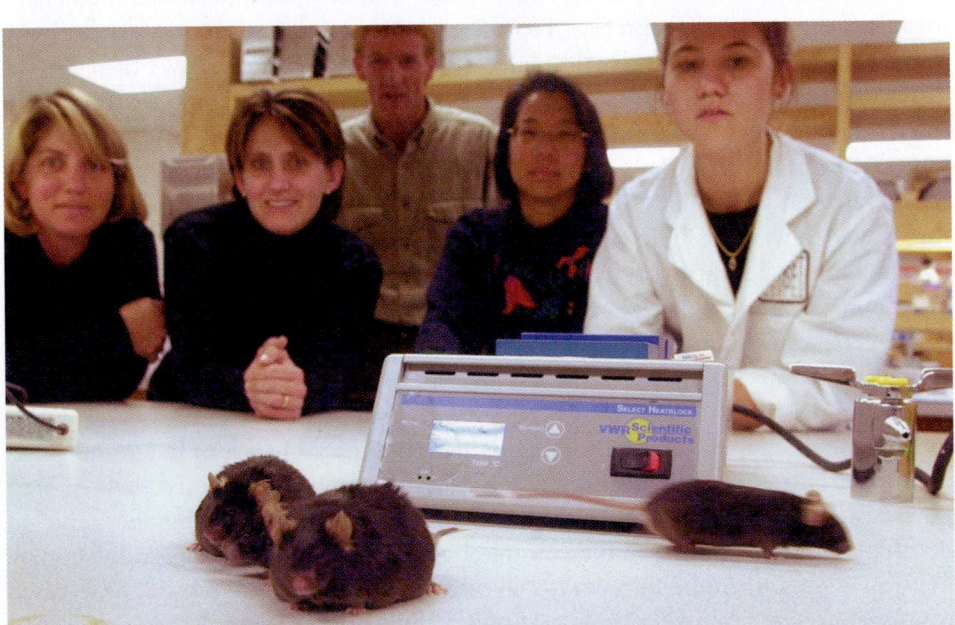

findings. When a study's participants are told that their information will remain confidential, the implicit promise is that their information will be kept secret or made available to only the few people who need to know it. Often the quality and accuracy of data depend on the participants' certainty that their responses will be kept confidential, especially when emotionally or legally sensitive topics are involved.

For studies concerning extremely sensitive topics, the participants' responses should remain anonymous. *Anonymity* is not the same as confidentiality, although these terms are often confused. Anonymity means that no personal information is collected, so responses can never be traced to any individual. For example, if you wanted to know how many college students in your sample had ever cheated on an exam, the students would have to be assured of anonymity so that they would be comfortable about responding honestly. An anonymous study might be conducted in the form of a written questionnaire that asked about cheating but did not ask for any identifying information; participants would return the completed questionnaires to a large box so that no questionnaire could be linked to any individual.

Sometimes psychologists will study an organization instead of individuals or animals. The organization could be a university department, a small business, a global corporation, a government, and so on. As with all research, the issue being investigated will determine the method or methods used. The methods for organizational research are most often questionnaires and interviews, but other methods, including experiments, such as those used in the studies at the Hawthorne Works plant described above, are also used. Privacy, confidentiality, and anonymity remain as important in organizational research as in research with individuals. Indeed, ethics is central to every aspect of psychological science.

INFORMED CONSENT Research involving human participants is a partnership based on mutual respect and trust. People who volunteer for psychological research have the right to know what will happen to them during the course of the study. Compensating people for their participation in research does not alter this fundamental right. Ethical standards require providing people with all relevant information that might affect their willingness to become participants. *Informed consent* means that participants make a knowledgeable decision to participate. Typically, informed consent is obtained in writing; in the case of observational studies of public behavior, to protect privacy, individuals are treated anonymously. Minors, the intellectually incapacitated, and the mentally ill cannot legally provide informed consent, and therefore the permission of a legal guardian is necessary.

It is not always possible to inform participants fully about a study's details. If knowing the study's specific goals may alter the participants' behavior, thereby rendering the results meaningless, researchers may need to use *deception*, which involves either misleading participants about the study's goals or not fully revealing what will take place. Researchers use deception only when other methods are not appropriate and when the deception does not involve situations that would strongly affect people's willingness to participate. If deception is used, a careful *debriefing*, or explanation of the study after its completion, must take place to inform participants of the study's goals and the need for deception and to eliminate or counteract any negative effects produced by the deception.

RELATIVE RISKS OF PARTICIPATION Another ethical issue is the relative risk to participants' mental or physical health. Researchers must always remain conscious of what they are asking of participants. They cannot ask people to endure unreasonable amounts of pain or of discomfort, either from stimuli or from the manner in which data measurements are taken. Fortunately, in the vast majority of research being

Deception and the Nuremberg Code

Institutional review boards (IRBs) were an outgrowth of the Nuremberg doctors' trial, during which 20 Nazi physicians were tried and convicted for contributing to the horrendous human experiments at the Auschwitz concentration camp (**FIGURE 2.19**). Among these men's moral justifications for their actions were that a few prisoners' deaths could save many German lives, to resist would be treasonous, and that medical ethics could be set aside by law or war.

In August 1947, the United States Counsel for War Crimes, concerned about the ethical issues raised by the Nazis' experiments, included in its verdict a section called "Permissible Medical Experiments," which later became known as the Nuremberg Code. It contained 10 directives. The first, the cornerstone of the code, was informed consent. In 1964, the World Medical Association drew up the Declaration of Helsinki, a set of ethical principles for the medical community regarding human experimentation and clinical research. The Declaration of Helsinki relaxed the conditions of consent. If a subject is unable to give consent, a proxy consent may be obtained from a legal guardian. The Nuremberg Code and the Declaration of Helsinki have not been incorporated directly into American law, but they are the foundation for the regulations issued by the U.S. Department of Health and Human Services governing federally funded research in the United States.

Particularly important to research in psychology, which differs from research in other fields, is the issue of deceit and informed consent. On the one hand, deceiving research participants is seen as inappropriate by many people, inside and especially outside the field of psychology, and it goes against the first tenet of the Nuremberg Code. On the other hand, individuals aware that they are being studied can modify many psychological processes. For instance, participants told that their responses will be used to determine how fast people read newspapers may try to read faster than their normal speeds to impress the researchers, whereas participants told that the point is to rate their interest in newspaper topics would most likely read at their normal speeds. Many of the processes now known to be taking place in the brain would not be understood if deceit had been eliminated from all psychological testing. The ethical guidelines of the American Psychological Association allow deception under certain circumstances. Determining what circumstances make it permissible is the ethical problem.

In the early 1960s, Stanley Milgram, who wanted to understand how ordinary German citizens could willingly obey orders to kill innocent citizens, used deceit to conduct one of the most controversial experiments on record. Milgram's results were unexpected and changed how people viewed the power of authority.

FIGURE 2.19 Informed Consent: The Nuremberg Trials

(They are discussed in Chapter 12, "Social Psychology.") Ironically, in performing the experiment that obtained these important results, Milgram violated the Nuremberg Code and deceived a group of individuals for the possible benefit to many, the same justification used by the Nuremberg defendants, although at a different level. But was the use of deceit inappropriate, as critics of his experiment charge? Today, this question would be addressed by an IRB; indeed, concern over the ethics of Milgram's research caused the rapid increase in IRBs. Along with ensuring research participants' rights and safety, IRBs have the tricky duties of assessing a study's scientific merit, evaluating the methods to be used, and balancing the benefits to society against the risks to the participants. However, because Milgram's results were so unexpected, an IRB reviewing a request for his experiment might not have foreseen the benefits to be gained from the work.

Without deception, many topics in psychology could not be studied, because participants' knowledge that they are being studied will often change how they behave. In thinking about this dilemma in psychological research, consider the risk/benefit ratio for any research. Is deception allowable when the research might yield a very important gain, such as a cure for a particular mental illness or a way to reduce prejudice? Can any form of deception be thought of as mild—for example, telling participants you are studying reading speed when you are really studying reading comprehension—or is any deception, no matter how seemingly harmless, unacceptable? Are there circumstances in which deception should be allowed? If so, what are they?

conducted, these types of concerns are not an issue. However, although risk is low, researchers have to think carefully about the potential for risk to specific participants. Again, any research conducted at a college, university, or research institute must be approved by an IRB familiar with the rules and regulations that protect participants from harm. Most IRBs look at the relative trade-off between risk and benefit. Potential gains from the scientific enterprise sometimes require asking participants to expose themselves to some risk to obtain important findings. The *risk/benefit ratio* is an analysis of whether the research is important enough to warrant placing participants at risk.

▶ SUMMING UP

What Are the Data Collection Methods of Psychological Science?

In psychological science, there are five basic data collection methods, which operate at different levels of analysis; the choice of which to use is generally dictated by the research question. First, researchers can observe behaviors as they take place and either write down general descriptions of the behaviors or check off a tally sheet of prespecified behavior categories. Second, researchers can ask people for information about their thoughts, feelings, and preferences by using surveys, questionnaires, interviews, and other self-reports. Third, researchers can measure how quickly and accurately people respond to a stimulus. Fourth, researchers can directly measure the brain's electrical activity and blood flow, and they can disrupt ongoing brain processes; these techniques are increasingly being combined with the other three methods. Finally, researchers can use animal models in which genes, chemicals involved in the way neurons function, or brain structures are altered to study the effects on behavior. Regardless of the method chosen, researchers must consider the ethical consequences of their data collection; they must weigh the study's relative risks against its potential benefits.

▶ MEASURING UP

For each example below, indicate which data collection method would work best. Fill in the blank with one of the following: description/observation, case study, survey, interview, experience sampling, response performance (which includes accuracy and reaction time), meta-analysis, EEG, brain imaging, or transcranial magnetic stimulation.

1. A researcher is investigating Adolf Hitler's childhood and teenage years to see if there are ways of recognizing the experiences that made Hitler evil as an adult. What data collection method is he using? _____

2. As discussed in Chapter 9, "Motivation and Emotion," Alfred Kinsey studied the sexual behaviors of large numbers of people from every walk of life. What data collection method or methods would you have suggested he use? _____

3. Fascinating new data reveal that the great apes' social lives are surprisingly similar to human social systems. What method was probably used to obtain these data? _____

4. In a study of families, the researchers want to know when children and their parents feel stressed, happy, relaxed, and bored throughout the day. What data collection method should the researchers use? _____

5. Many studies have addressed the question of whether self-esteem is related to school achievement. What method would you use to summarize these studies' results? _____

How Are Data Analyzed and Evaluated?

So far, this chapter has presented the essential elements of scientific inquiry in psychology: how to frame an empirical question using theories, hypotheses, and research; how to decide what type of study to run; and how to collect data. This section focuses on the data. Specifically, it examines the characteristics that make for good data and the statistical procedures that are used to analyze data.

Good Research Requires Valid, Reliable, and Accurate Data

validity The extent to which the data collected address the research hypothesis in the way intended.

If you collect data to answer a research question, the data must address that question. **Validity** refers to whether the data you collect address your question; valid data provide clear information researchers can use to evaluate the theory or hypothesis. Suppose your theory predicts that children who are physically abused by their parents are more likely than nonabused children to use drugs in high school. One way to test this hypothesis is to identify a sample of children who have been abused by their parents and another that was not abused. Court and medical records could be used to identify the abused children. Researchers could follow the children longitudinally until they are teens to determine if the children in the abused group are more likely to use drugs than those who were not abused as children. Regardless of the outcome of this research—whether or not the hypothesis is supported—the data from court and medical records would be a valid way to identify abused children.

The key here is that the data's validity depends on the question being studied. Data that is invalid for one question may be perfectly valid for a different question. Validity is essentially the extent to which the data really are measuring what you want to measure. If you wanted to assess an advertisement's effectiveness, for example, a valid measure would be whether people are more likely to purchase the advertised product after viewing the ad. Simply asking viewers how much they liked the advertisement would not validly measure the ad's effectiveness in persuading viewers to buy the product.

reliability The extent to which a measure is stable and consistent over time in similar conditions.

Another important aspect of data is **reliability,** or the stability and consistency of a measure over time. If the measurement is reliable, the data collected will not vary because of changes over time in the way they are measured. Suppose you hypothesize that people in their 20s are more likely to channel surf (rapidly switch among television channels) than are people in their 50s. To test your hypothesis, you would need to study television watching behavior and, in particular, the average length of time people stay tuned to each station they watch. One option for measuring the duration of each channel stay would be to have an observer use a stopwatch. However, there will likely be some variability in when the observer starts and stops the watch relative to when the surfer actually changes channels. As a consequence, the data in this scenario would be less reliable than data collected by a computer linked to each viewer's television remote.

The third and final characteristic of good data is **accuracy,** or the extent to which the measure is error free. A measure may be valid and reliable but still not *accurate.* Psychological scientists think about this problem by turning it on its head and asking, "How do errors creep into a measure?" There are two basic types of error, random and systematic (**FIGURE 2.20**). Take the channel surfing study. The problem with using a stopwatch to measure the duration of each channel stay is that each measurement will tend to overestimate or underestimate the duration (because of human error or variability in recording times). This is known as a *random error,* because although an error is introduced into each measurement, the value of the error differs each time. But suppose the stopwatch has a glitch, such that it always

accuracy The extent to which an experimental measure is free from error.

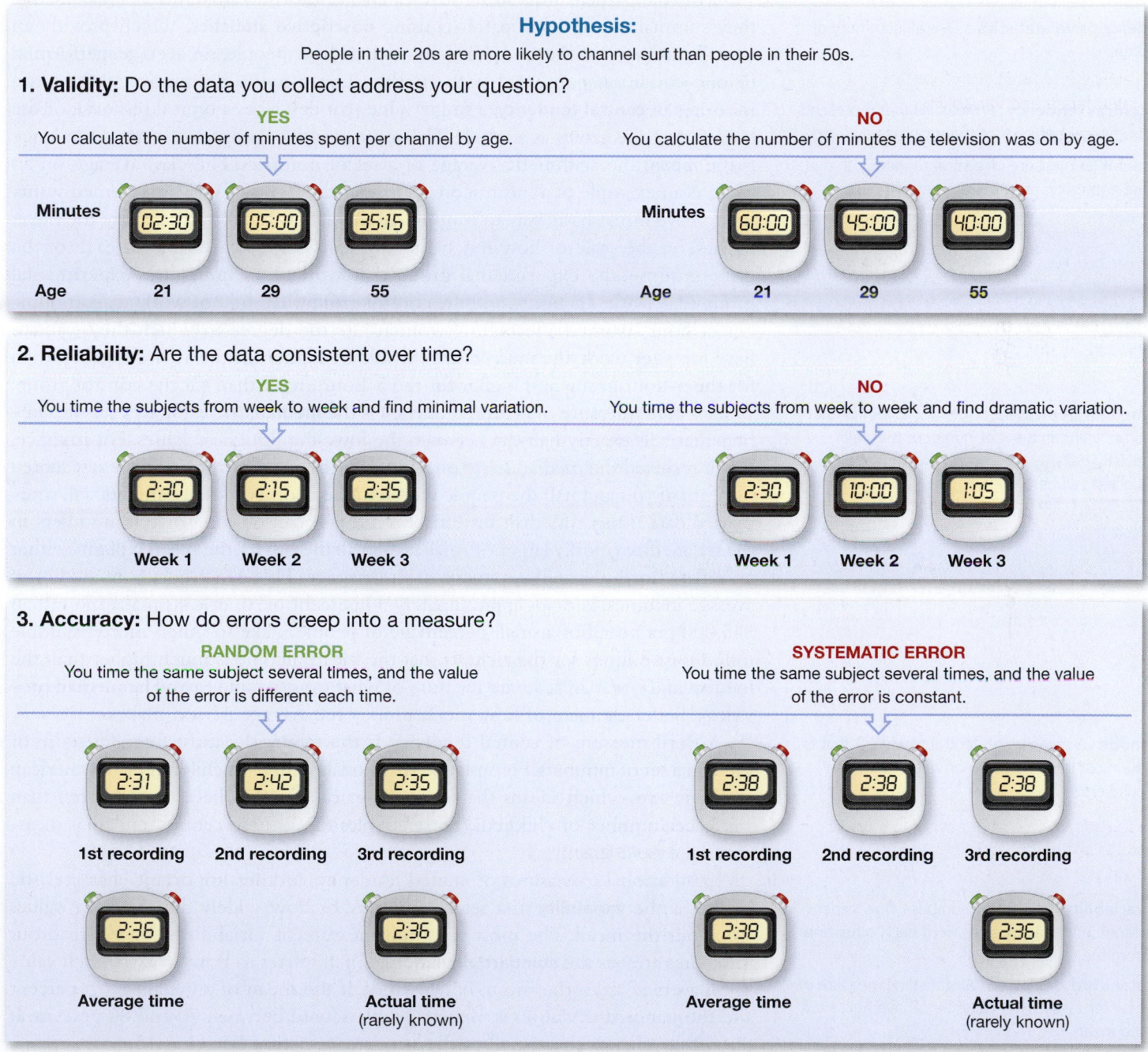

FIGURE 2.20 Validity, Reliability, and Accuracy Good data should be valid (addressing the research question), reliable (consistent over time, no matter when or how the data are collected), and accurate (free from error). Random error occurs when the degree of error varies each time; systematic error occurs when the measurement has the same degree of error each time.

overstates the time measured by two seconds. This is known as a *systematic error,* because the amount of error introduced into each measure is constant. Generally, systematic error is more problematic than random error because the latter tends to average out over time and therefore is less likely to produce inaccurate results.

Descriptive Statistics Provide a Summary of the Data

The first step in evaluating data is to inspect the *raw values*, data as close as possible to the form in which they were collected. In examining raw data, researchers look for errors in data recording. For instance, they assess whether any of the responses seem especially unlikely (e.g., blood alcohol content of 50 percent or a 113-year-old participant). Once the researchers are satisfied that the data make sense, they summarize the basic patterns using **descriptive statistics,** which provide an overall summary of the study's results, such as how people, on average, performed in one condition compared with another. The simplest descriptive statistics are measures of **central tendency,** a single value that describes a typical response or the behavior of the group as a whole. The most intuitive measure of central tendency is the **mean,** the arithmetic average of a set of numbers. The class average on an exam is an example of a mean score. Consider the study of working women wanting to have fun. A basic way to summarize the data would be to calculate the mean ratings, on the scale of how much the women want to have fun, for each of the three groups—the experimental group that worked 10 hours, the experimental group that worked 5 hours, and the control group that did not work at all. If number of hours worked affects how women rate the degree to which they want to have fun after work, the mean ratings would be higher for the 10-hour group than for the 5-hour group and higher for the 5-hour group than for the control group.

A second measure of central tendency is the **median,** the value in a set of numbers that falls exactly halfway between the lowest and highest values. For instance, if you received the median score on a test, half the people who took the test scored lower than you and half the people scored higher. Sometimes researchers will summarize data using a median instead of a mean because if one or two numbers in the set are dramatically larger or smaller than all the others, the mean will give either an inflated or a deflated summary of the average. This effect occurs in studies of average incomes. Perhaps approximately 50 percent of Americans make more than $45,000 per year, but a small percentage of people make so much more (multiple millions or billions for the richest) that the mean income is much higher than the median and is not an accurate measure of what most people earn. The median provides a better estimate of how much money the average person makes.

A third measure of central tendency is the **mode,** the most frequent score or value in a set of numbers. For instance, the modal number of children in an American family is two, which means that more American families have two children than any other number of children. (For examples of all three central tendency measures, see **FIGURE 2.21.**)

In addition to measures of central tendency, another important characteristic of data is the **variability** in a set of numbers, or how widely dispersed the values are about the mean. The most common measure of variability—how spread out the scores are—is the **standard deviation,** which relates to how far away each value is, on average, from the mean. For instance, if the mean of an exam is 75 percent and the standard deviation is 5, most people scored between 70 and 80 percent. If the mean remains the same but the standard deviation becomes 15, most people scored between 60 and 90—a much larger spread. Another measure of how spread out scores are is the *range,* the distance between the largest value and the smallest one; the range often is not of much use because it is based on only two scores.

descriptive statistics Overall summary of data.

central tendency A measure that represents the typical behavior of the group as a whole.

mean A measure of central tendency that is the arithmetic average of a set of numbers.

median A measure of central tendency that is the value in a set of numbers that falls exactly halfway between the lowest and highest values.

mode A measure of central tendency that is the most frequent score or value in a set of numbers.

variability In a set of numbers, how widely dispersed the values are from each other and from the mean.

standard deviation A statistical measure of how far away each value is, on average, from the mean.

You count the number of hours 11 women worked:

- One woman did not work
- Three women worked 1 hour
- Two women worked 2 hours
- One woman worked 3 hours
- Two women worked 4 hours
- One woman worked 6 hours
- One woman worked 9 hours

Written in ascending order, the number of hours per woman looks like this:

0 1 1 1 2 2 3 4 4 6 9

Mean
The arithmetic average of a set of numbers

$$\frac{\text{total \# of hours}}{\text{total \# of women}} = \frac{0+1+1+1+2+2+3+4+4+6+9}{11} = \frac{33}{11} = 3$$

Median
The value that falls exactly halfway between the lowest and highest values

01112 2 34469 = **2**

Mode
The most frequent score or value in a set of numbers

0 **1 1 1** 2 2 3 4 4 6 9 = **1**

Range
The distance between the largest and smallest values

0 1 1 1 2 2 3 4 4 6 **9** = 9 − 0 = **9**

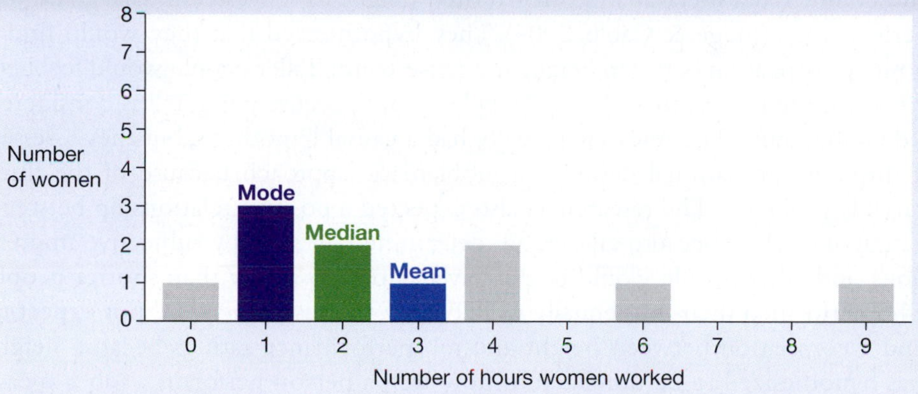

[bar chart: Number of women (y-axis, 0–8) vs Number of hours women worked (x-axis, 0–9), with bars labeled Mode (at 1), Median (at 2), Mean (at 3)]

Which measure of central tendency—mode, median, or mean—provides the best summary for these data?

FIGURE 2.21 Descriptive Statistics
Descriptive statistics are used to summarize a data set and to measure the central tendency and variability in a set of numbers.

FIGURE 2.22 Scatterplots Scatterplots are graphs that illustrates the relationship between two variables. In general, according to this scatter plot, the more women worked, the more they wanted to have fun.

Correlations Describe the Relationships between Variables

The descriptive statistics discussed so far are used for summarizing the central tendency and variability in a set of numbers. Descriptive statistics can also be used to summarize how two variables relate to each other. The first step in examining the relationship between two variables is to create a graph known as a **scatterplot,** which provides a convenient picture of the data (**FIGURE 2.22**).

In analyzing the relationship between two variables, researchers can compute a *correlation coefficient,* a descriptive statistic that provides a numerical value (between −1.0 and +1.0) indicating the strength of the relationship between the two variables. If the two variables have a strong relationship

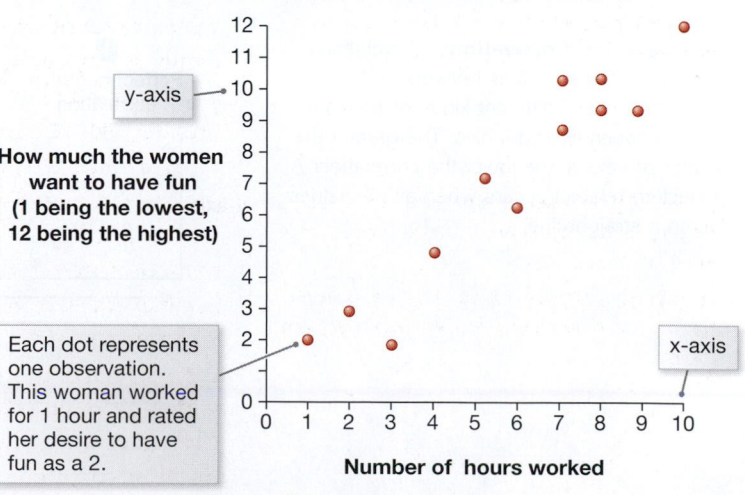

The relationship between how long women worked and how much they want to have fun

y-axis

How much the women want to have fun (1 being the lowest, 12 being the highest)

Each dot represents one observation. This woman worked for 1 hour and rated her desire to have fun as a 2.

x-axis

Number of hours worked

(we are considering only one type of relationship here—linear relationships, in which increases or decreases in one variable are associated with increases or decreases in the other variable), knowing how people measure on one variable enables you to predict how they will measure on the other variable. What signifies a strong relationship? Consider the different scatterplots in **FIGURE 2.23**. Two variables can have a *positive correlation,* in which the variables increase or decrease together. For example, taller people often weigh more than shorter people. A perfect positive correlation is indicated by a value of +1.0. Two variables can also have a *negative correlation:* As one increases in value, the other decreases in value. For example, if women who worked more hours rated their desire to have fun after work lower than did women who worked fewer hours, this finding would constitute a negative relationship. A perfect negative correlation is indicated by a value of −1.0. If two variables show no apparent relationship, the value of the correlation will be a number close to zero (assuming a linear relationship for the purposes of this discussion).

Have you ever wondered if height is correlated with success? There is a common belief that taller people, or at least taller men, are more successful than shorter ones because height is a desirable physical characteristic. The question about the relationship between height and success necessarily requires a correlational study because we cannot assign people at random to different heights and then see if height causes differences in their success. To answer the question about height and success, researchers reviewed all the studies published on this topic and conducted a meta-analysis that related height to self-esteem, salary, and job performance (Judge & Cable, 2004). They hypothesized that they would find a positive correlation between height and self-esteem: Taller people would feel better about themselves than shorter people would because being tall is considered a desirable trait. (The researchers really had a causal hypothesis, but they assessed it through correlational designs—a problematic approach because of the third variable problem.) The researchers also expected a positive relationship between height and salary because salaries are determined, in part, by subjective impressions, and taller people would be perceived more positively than shorter people who performed their jobs equally well. Finally, the researchers did not expect to find a correlation between height and job performance ratings because height was hypothesized to be unrelated to how well a person performs a job, a measure that is more objective (e.g., a good salesperson makes more sales, a skilled lawyer wins more legal cases) than self-esteem and how high a salary a person should be paid.

As hypothesized, the researchers found that height and self-esteem were positively correlated, as were height and salary, but contrary to expectations, height was also

FIGURE 2.23 Correlations Correlations can have different values between −1 and +1, which reveal different kinds of relationships between two variables. The greater the scatter of values, the lower the correlation. A perfect correlation occurs when all the values fall on a straight line.

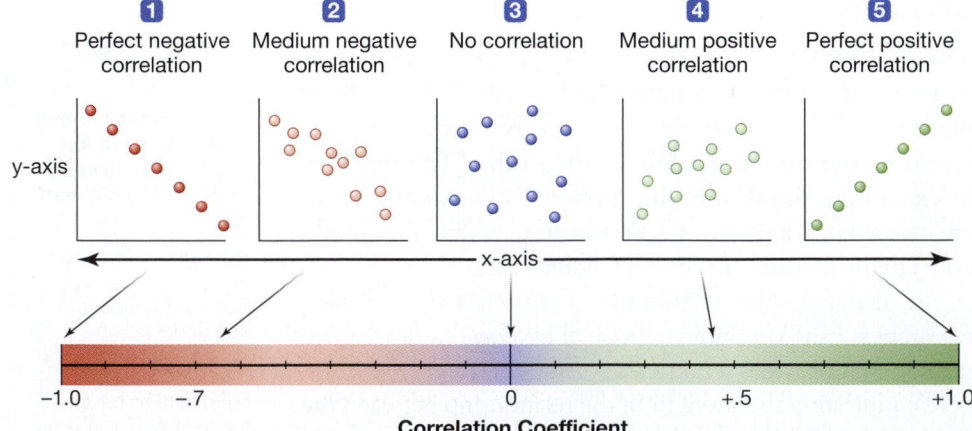

positively correlated with job performance. These three correlations were positive for men and women, but the relationship was not as strong for women as it was for men. Because the authors used a meta-analysis, a summary of the findings from many studies, we can have more confidence in these conclusions than in the results from any single study. Of course, the data are quite variable, and these are average effects. Some tall people are unsuccessful, and some short people are very successful!

This meta-analysis of height and success is a good example of a correlational study because it is not possible to use random assignment when studying the effects of height on some other variable. There is also no problem of understanding the direction of the effect because we have no reason to believe that high self-esteem or higher salaries cause people to grow taller. In theorizing about the way height might affect salary and job performance, the researchers suggested that taller people perform better (or at least have higher job performance ratings) because of expectancies created by their colleagues. (Remember the study, discussed above, in which some students were told they were training rats who would do well at maze learning; those students' rats performed better than the rats given to students who were not told anything special about their rats.) We may not be aware of our biases, but they affect our thinking and behavior—a theme emphasized throughout this book.

Inferential Statistics Permit Generalizations

While researchers use descriptive statistics to summarize data sets, they use **inferential statistics** to determine whether differences actually exist in the populations from which samples were drawn. For instance, suppose you find that the mean ratings of how much women want to have fun after work varied with the number of hours the women worked. How different do these means need to be between each experimental group and the control group for you to conclude that they reflect real differences in the larger population of women, all of whom work different numbers of hours? Recall that we use samples from a population when we conduct research; then, depending on what we find in our study, we generalize our findings back to the population from which we sampled. Researchers use inferential statistics to decide if the difference in sample means reflect differences in the populations from which they were drawn. How does this work? Assume for a moment that the number of hours women work does not influence their ratings of how much they want to have fun. Even so, if you measure the ratings made by women who work different numbers of hours, just by chance there will be some variability in the mean ratings made by the women in the different groups. We use statistical techniques to determine if the differences among the sample means are (probably) chance variations or whether they reflect differences in the populations.

The principle is the same as for how many heads appear when you flip a coin ten times: On average, the number will be five or close to it, but every now and then, just by chance, you will get no heads or ten heads. Therefore, when you are comparing two means, inferential statistics tell you how probable the outcome would be if there were no differences between the ratings made by participants in the two groups. This is the general logic researchers use to determine whether the differences between the groups represent real differences in the populations from which the groups were drawn.

When the results obtained from a study would be very unlikely to occur if there really were no differences among the groups of subjects, the researchers conclude that the results are *statistically significant*. How unusual do the results have to be for researchers to conclude that they are statistically significant? The coin-flipping example should help explain this concept. Suppose you and a friend stop for coffee every

inferential statistics A set of procedures used to make judgments about whether differences actually exist between sets of numbers.

"I think you should be more explicit here in step two."

day, and your friend suggests that he will flip a coin each day to decide who pays. Heads means you pay; tails means he pays. The first day, he flips heads; the second day, he flips heads again. How many coin flips would it take before you asked him if he was using a fair coin? Few people would be willing to accuse a friend of cheating after three heads in a row. But what about five or six heads in a row? Generally accepted standards determine how unusual a result must be before we say it is statistically significant: It would have to occur less than 5 percent of the time if no other factors affect the results. In this case, if the coin is fair, there is a greater than 5 percent chance of flipping three heads in a row (12.5%) but a less than 5 percent chance of flipping five heads in a row (3.125%). Similarly, in the example above, if the women in the no-work group rated their desire to have fun as a 2 (mean rating for the group) and those in the 10-hour work group rated their desire to have fun as a 9, we would use statistical methods to determine if this outcome would occur less than 5 percent of the time if the groups really were the same in all other respects. If the data meet this statistical test, we would say the results are statistically significant.

 ## SUMMING UP

How Are Data Analyzed and Evaluated?

Data analysis begins with descriptive statistics, which summarize the data. Measures of central tendency indicate statistical averages across sets of numbers, whereas the standard deviation indicates how widely numbers are distributed about an average. Correlations describe the relationship between two variables: positive, negative, or none. Inferential statistics show whether the results of a study were due to the effect of one variable on another or whether the results were more likely due to chance.

 ## MEASURING UP

1. When researchers want to summarize in a single number all the data they collect, they compute a measure of central tendency. Here are hypothetical data for a study in which 10 women in a sample indicated how many hours they worked that day and then used a rating scale to indicate how much they wanted to have fun. The rating scale ranged from 1 ("not at all") to 10 ("I want to have fun more than anything else in the world"). For each set of data, compute the mean, median, and mode.

Number of hours worked	Rating of how much they want to have fun
5	5
5	6
8	7
6	6
4	10
6	5
2	4
10	7
8	9
3	5
Mean =	Mean =
Median =	Median =
Mode =	Mode =

Now, using a grid like the one in Figure 2.22, draw a scatterplot of the data in question 1. When you are finished, look at the plot and decide if it represents a positive, a negative, or no (linear) relationship between these two variables. Explain what the scatterplot is showing, in your own words.

2. Which is an accurate description of the rationale for inferential statistics?
   a. When the means of two sample groups are significantly different, we still need to compute a mean value for each population before we can conclude that the groups really are different.
   b. When the means of two sample groups are significantly different, we can be fairly certain that we did not make any mistakes in our research.
   c. When the means of two sample groups are significantly different, we can be certain that the data are not correlated.
   d. When the means of two sample groups are significantly different, we can infer that the populations the groups were selected from are different.

CONCLUSION

This chapter has presented the major issues involved in designing and conducting research in psychological science. However, the ideas discussed here are most important when research is evaluated. The quality of research matters whether or not you have conducted the experiments yourself. Every day, the media report some new major finding, such as the link between height and self-esteem and salary discussed above. Should you believe a report and perhaps change your daily life as a result? Should you ignore new and potentially important data, because they came from a flawed study? To make educated decisions in this domain, as well as in your everyday experiences, requires understanding the way good psychological science is conducted, an understanding that in turn requires good critical thinking skills.

So what determines good science? Quality research stems from sound methodology *and* good questions. A number of factors need to be considered. Is a good theory guiding the design of the research? Were the method and level of analysis appropriate for the question of interest? Does the study have adequate operational definitions for the variables involved? Have the researchers presented their results as though the results show a causal relationship between two variables, even though an experiment was not performed? If an experiment was performed, was it carefully designed and well controlled, or might potential confounds have been overlooked? Did the researchers randomly assign participants to different experimental groups? How large was the sample, and were the participants representative of the population of interest? Was the research culturally sensitive, or did the researchers make the mistake of assuming that people in all cultures would respond the same way? These fundamental questions underscore the necessity of being a critical, well-informed research evaluator. If you cannot answer these questions when reading about a study, you cannot properly evaluate whether you should believe the results or the way those results have been interpreted.

■ CHAPTER SUMMARY

What Is Scientific Inquiry?

- **The Scientific Method Depends on Theories, Hypotheses, and Research:** Scientific inquiry relies on objective methods and empirical evidence to answer testable questions. Interconnected ideas or models of behavior (theories) yield testable predictions (hypotheses), which are tested in a systematic way (research) by collecting and evaluating evidence (data).

- **Unexpected Findings Can Be Valuable:** Unexpected (serendipitous) discoveries sometimes occur, but only researchers who are prepared to recognize their importance will benefit from them.

What Are the Types of Studies in Psychological Research?

- **Descriptive Studies Involve Observing and Classifying Behavior:** Researchers observe and describe naturally occurring behaviors to provide a systematic and objective analysis.

- **Correlational Designs Examine How Variables Are Related:** Correlational studies are used to examine how variables are naturally related in the real world, but cannot be used to establish causality or the direction of a relationship (which variable caused changes in another variable). Correlational reasoning occurs in many contexts, so readers need to be able to recognize correlational designs in everyday contexts, not just when reading research reports.

- **An Experiment Involves Manipulating Conditions:** In an experiment, researchers control the variations in the conditions that the participant experiences (independent variables) and measure the outcomes (dependent variables) to gain an understanding of causality. Researchers need a control group to know if the experiment had an effect.

- **Random Assignment Is Used to Establish Equivalent Groups:** Researchers sample participants from the population they want to study (e.g., all women who work). They use random sampling when everyone in the population is equally likely to participate in the study, a condition that rarely occurs. To establish causality between an intervention and an outcome, all participants must be equally likely to be in the experimental group or the control group, to control for preexisting group differences.

What Are the Data Collection Methods of Psychological Science?

- **Observing Is an Unobtrusive Strategy:** Data collected by observation must be defined clearly and collected systematically. Bias may occur in the data because the participants are aware they are being observed or because of the observer's expectations.

- **Case Studies Examine Individual Lives and Organizations:** A case study, one kind of descriptive study, examines an individual or an organization. An intensive study of an individual or organization can

be useful for examining an unusual participant or unusual research question. Interpretation of a case study, however, can be subjective.

- **Asking Takes a More Active Approach:** Surveys, questionnaires, and interviews can be used to directly ask people about their thoughts and behaviors. Self-report data may be biased by the respondents' desire to present themselves in a particular way (e.g., smart, honest). Culturally sensitive research recognizes the differences among people from different cultural groups and from different language backgrounds.

- **Response Performance Measures Information Processing:** Measuring reaction times and reaction accuracy and asking people to make stimulus judgments are methods used to examine how people respond to psychological tasks.

- **Body/Brain Activity Can Be Measured Directly:** Electrophysiology (often using an electroencephalograph, or EEG) measures the brain's electrical activity. Brain imaging is done using positron emission tomography (PET), magnetic resonance imaging (MRI), and functional magnetic resonance imaging (fMRI). Transcranial magnetic stimulation (TMS) disrupts normal brain activity, allowing researchers to infer the brain processing involved in particular thoughts, feelings, and behaviors.

- **Research with Animals Provides Important Data:** Research involving nonhuman animals provides useful, although simpler, models of behavior and of genetics. The purpose of such research may be to learn about animals' behavior or to make inferences about human behavior.

- **There Are Ethical Issues to Consider:** Ethical research is governed by a variety of principles that ensure fair and informed treatment of participants.

How Are Data Analyzed and Evaluated?

- **Good Research Requires Valid, Reliable, and Accurate Data:** Data must be meaningful (valid) and their measurement reliable (i.e., consistent and stable) and accurate.

- **Descriptive Statistics Provide a Summary of the Data:** Measures of central tendency and variability are used to describe data.

- **Correlations Describe the Relationships between Variables:** A correlation is a descriptive statistic that describes the strength and direction of the relationship between two variables. Correlations close to zero signify weak relationships; correlations near $+1$ or -1 signify strong relationships.

- **Inferential Statistics Permit Generalizations:** Inferential statistics allow us to decide whether differences between two or more groups are probably just chance variations (suggesting that the populations the groups were drawn from are the same) or whether they reflect true differences in the populations being compared.

■ KEY TERMS

accuracy, p. 67
brain imaging, p. 59
case study, p. 54
central tendency, p. 68
confound, p. 45
control (or comparison) group, p. 43
correlational study, p. 40

cross-sectional studies, p. 39
culturally sensitive research, p. 52
data, p. 35
dependent variable, p. 43
descriptive statistics, p. 68
descriptive studies, p. 38

directionality problem, p. 42
electroencephalogram (EEG), p. 59
experiment, p. 43
experimental (or treatment) group, p. 43

experimenter expectancy effect, p. 40
functional magnetic resonance imaging (fMRI), p. 61
hypothesis, p. 35
independent variable, p. 43

inferential statistics, p. 71
institutional review boards (IRBs), p. 62
longitudinal studies, p. 39
magnetic resonance imaging (MRI), p. 60
mean, p. 68

■ PRACTICE TEST

1. Which of the following is a technique that increases scientists' confidence in the findings from a given research study?
   a. amiable skepticism
   b. operationalization of variables
   c. replication
   d. serendipity

For the following five questions, imagine you are designing a study to investigate whether deep breathing causes students to feel less stressed. Because you are investigating a causal question, you will need to employ experimental research. For each step in the design process, indicate the most scientifically sound decision.

2. Which hypothesis is stronger? Why?
   a. Stress levels will differ between students who engage in deep breathing and those who do not.
   b. Students who engage in deep breathing will report less stress than those who do not engage in deep breathing.

3. Which sampling method is strongest? Why?
   a. Obtain an alphabetical list of all students enrolled at the college. Invite every fifth person on the list to participate in the study.
   b. Post a note to your Facebook and MySpace accounts letting friends know you would like their help with the study. Ask your friends to let their friends know about the study, too.
   c. Post fliers around local gyms and yoga studios inviting people to participate in your study.

4. Which set of conditions should be included in the study? Why?
   a. All participants should be given written directions for a deep breathing exercise.
   b. Some participants should be given written directions for a deep breathing exercise; some participants should be given a DVD with demonstrations of deep breathing exercises.
   c. Some participants should be given written directions for a deep breathing exercise; some participants should be given no instructions regarding their breathing.

5. How should participants be chosen for each condition? Why?
   a. Once people agree to participate in the study, flip a coin to decide if each will be in the experimental or control condition.
   b. Let participants select which condition they would like to be in.

6. Which operational definition of the dependent variable, stress, is stronger? Why?
   a. Stress is a pattern of behavioral and physiological responses that match or exceed a person's abilities to respond in a healthy way.
   b. Stress will be measured using five questions asking the participant to rate his or her stress level on a scale from 1 to 10, where 1 equals "not at all stressed" and 10 equals "as stressed as I've ever been."

For the following three questions, imagine you want to know whether students at your college talk about politics in their day-to-day lives. To investigate this issue, you would like to conduct an observational study and need to make three design decisions. For each decision, recommend the most appropriate choice.

7. Should you conduct the study in a lab or in a natural setting (e.g., in the campus dining hall)? Why?

8. Should you use written descriptions of what is heard or a running tally of prespecified categories of behavior? Why?

9. Should participants know you are observing them? Why?

10. Indicate which quality of good data is violated by each description. Response options are "accuracy," "reliability," "validity."
    a. A booth at the local carnival announces the discovery of a new way to assess intelligence. The assessment method involves interpreting the pattern of creases on one's left palm.
    b. At the end of a long night of grading, a professor reads what he believes to be the last essay in the pile. He assigns it a grade of 80%. When he goes to write the grade on the back of the paper, he realizes he has already graded this paper earlier in the evening—and only gave it a 70% the first time around.
    c. A five-year-old counts the jelly beans in a jar, often skipping over numbers ending in 8 (e.g., 8, 18, 28).

■ PSYCHOLOGY AND SOCIETY

1. Identify a song lyric that makes a claim about human behavior. Elaborate and/or refine this claim, focusing the question in a way that addresses a goal of empirical inquiry: description, prediction, identifying causes, or making explanations. Clearly label the goal most relevant to your question.

2. Locate a claim about human behavior in a newspaper or magazine or on the Internet. Evaluate the claim using at least three ideas from this chapter. Some ideas from the chapter that lend themselves to this sort of analysis are validity, reliability, accuracy, central tendency, variability, descriptive studies, correlational studies, experiments, random assignment, control group, ethics.

The answer key for all the Measuring Up exercises and the Practice Tests can be found at the back of the book.

Biological Foundations

WILLIAM (NOT HIS REAL NAME) HATES DRIVING because the sight of road signs tastes like a mixture of pistachio ice cream and ear wax (McNeil, 2006). This sort of cross-sensory experience—in which, for example, a visual image has a taste—is called **synesthesia.** There are many kinds of synesthesia. For another patient, M.M., any personal name has a specific taste; for example, the name *John* tastes like cornbread (Simner et al., 2006). For yet another *synesthete* (a person who experiences synesthesia), each day of the week is colored (Monday is red, Tuesday is indigo), as is each month of the year (December is yellow, January is red; Ramachandran, 2003). For others, colors evoke smells, sights evoke sounds, and numbers come in colors (e.g., 5 is always red, 2 is always green; FIGURE 3.1). Such experiences

---

What Is the Genetic Basis of Psychological Science?

- Heredity Involves Passing Along Genes through Reproduction
- Genotypic Variation Is Created by Sexual Reproduction
- Genes Affect Behavior
- Social and Environmental Contexts Influence Genetic Expression
- Genetic Expression Can Be Modified
- Critical Thinking Skill: Seeking Disconfirming Evidence

How Does the Nervous System Operate?

- Neurons Are Specialized for Communication
- Action Potentials Cause Neural Communication
- Neurotransmitters Bind to Receptors across the Synapse
- Neurotransmitters Influence Mind and Behavior

What Are the Basic Brain Structures and Their Functions?

- The Brainstem Houses the Basic Programs of Survival
- The Cerebellum Is Essential for Movement
- Subcortical Structures Control Emotions and Basic Drives
- The Cerebral Cortex Underlies Complex Mental Activity

How Are Neural Messages Integrated into Communication Systems?

- The Peripheral Nervous System Includes the Somatic and Autonomic Systems
- The Endocrine System Communicates through Hormones
- Actions of the Nervous System and Endocrine System Are Coordinated

How Does the Brain Change?

- The Interplay of Genes and Environment Wires the Brain
- Culture Affects the Brain
- The Brain Rewires Itself throughout Life
- Critical Thinking Skill: Recognizing Unstated Assumptions
- Females' and Males' Brains Are Similar and Different
- The Brain Can Recover from Injury

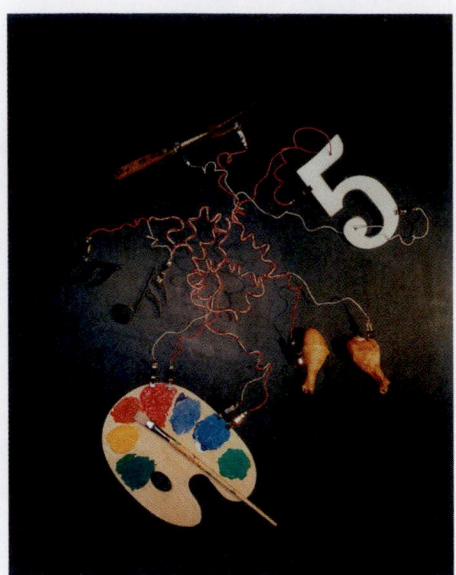

FIGURE 3.1 Synesthesia For synesthetes, sensory experiences are crossed. For example, colors may evoke smells, sights may evoke sounds, and numbers may come in colors.

are idiosyncratic—for one person, bread is always smooth in texture and silver in color, but for another person it sounds like a foghorn. For each person, the associations do not vary—if road signs have a taste, for example, they always taste the same. How can we understand such bizarre sensations? Can we just write these people off as crazy? Reports of people with synesthesia date as far back as ancient Greece (Ferry, 2002). Estimates of the percentage of the population that report these cross-sensory experiences range from 1 in 2,000 to 1 in 200.

Recent research into heredity and brain organization provides fascinating clues for understanding synesthesia; because synesthesia tends to run in families, it may help us understand how heredity affects the way we experience the world. Even more provocatively, brain research suggests that cross-sensory experiences could be related to creativity. Could the mixture of colors, words, and images by artists be the result of "special brain wiring" that they inherited (Blakeslee, 2001)? Can synesthesia explain why we call some smells "sharp" and some colors "loud"? Questions like these, and scientific research into answering them, are radically changing how we think about all human experience and behavior.

Over the past three decades, scientific understanding of the genetic and physiological foundations of psychological activity has increased dramatically. As technology has advanced, scientists have developed sophisticated tools to explore the biological bases of who we are. Researchers can now examine people's genetic make-up, their DNA (discussed below), to predict who will develop specific disorders and to understand how certain diseases are passed from one generation to the next. Researchers have also identified the gene or genes that predispose people to be outgoing, for example, or to be intelligent. Most recently, researchers have developed techniques that allow them to turn specific genes on and off. Changing the expression of a single gene can profoundly affect even a complex behavior such as social interaction (Insel & Young, 2001). Similarly, scientists have learned a great deal about brain activity's biological basis, such as why particular drugs affect thoughts and emotions in specific ways. As noted in the previous chapter, advances in the ability to watch the brain in action using imaging have enabled psychological scientists to better understand the functions of different brain regions. This chapter discusses psychological activity at the genetic and neurochemical levels, as well as the functions of various brain regions at the brain systems level of analysis.

What Is the Genetic Basis of Psychological Science?

Until the last few years, genetic research focused almost entirely on whether people possessed certain types of genes, such as genes for psychological disorders or for intelligence. Although it is important for us to discover the effects of individual genes, this approach misses the critical role of environmental factors in shaping who we are. While the term *genetics* is typically used to describe how characteristics such as height, hair color, and weight are passed along to offspring through inheritance, it also refers to the processes involved in turning genes "on" and "off." Hair this research reflects and reveals that environment affects our genes: how they are expressed and therefore how they influence our thoughts, feelings, and behavior. Genetic predispositions are often important in determining the environments we select for ourselves, so biology and environment mutually influence each other. To understand fully what makes us who we are, we need to understand how basic physiological processes—beginning with genetics—affect thoughts, feelings, and behavior. We also need to understand how those physiological processes interact with the environment—how nurture influences nature and the reverse. Indeed, the exciting new genetic research is reshaping the way psychologists think about these relationships.

One of the major developments in the new biological revolution occurred in February 2001, when two groups of scientists published separate articles detailing the results of the first phase of the *Human Genome Project,* an international research effort. This achievement represents the coordinated work of hundreds of scientists to map the entire structure of human genetic material. To understand the project's goals, you need a basic understanding of genetic processes.

Within nearly every cell in the body is the genome for making the entire organism. The genome is the master blueprint that provides detailed instructions for everything from how to grow a gall bladder to where the nose gets placed on a face. Whether a cell becomes part of a gall bladder or a nose is determined by which genes are turned on or off within that cell, and these actions are in turn determined by cues from outside the cell. The genome provides the option, and the environment determines which option is taken (Marcus, 2004).

Within each cell are **chromosomes,** structures made of genes. The typical human has 23 pairs of chromosomes, half of each pair coming from each parent. Genes are components of *DNA,* or deoxyribonucleic acid, a substance that consists of two intertwined strands of molecules (**FIGURE 3.2**). The sequence of these molecules along each DNA strand specifies an exact instruction to manufacture a distinct protein. Proteins, of which there are thousands of different types, are the basic chemicals that make up the structure of cells and direct their activities. A **gene,** then, is a segment of DNA, which is involved in producing a protein, which carries out a specific task. The environment determines which proteins are produced and when they are produced. For example, a certain species of butterfly becomes colorful or drab depending on the season in which it is born. The environment during its development probably causes a gene sensitive to temperature to be expressed (Marcus, 2004). Similarly, although each cell in the human body contains the same DNA, cells become specialized depending on which of their genes are expressed. Gene expression not only determines the body's basic physical makeup but also determines specific developments throughout life and is involved in all psychological activity. Gene expression allows us to sense, to learn, to fall in love, and so on.

The first step of the Human Genome Project was to map out the entire structure of DNA—in other words, to identify the precise order of molecules that

chromosomes Structures within the cell body that are made up of genes.

gene The unit of heredity that determines a particular characteristic in an organism.

FIGURE 3.2 The Human Body Down to Its Genes Each cell in the human body includes pairs of chromosomes, which consist of DNA strands. DNA has a double helix shape and is composed of genes. The 23rd chromosome pair determines sex: A female has two X chromosomes in that pair, whereas a male has one X and one Y.

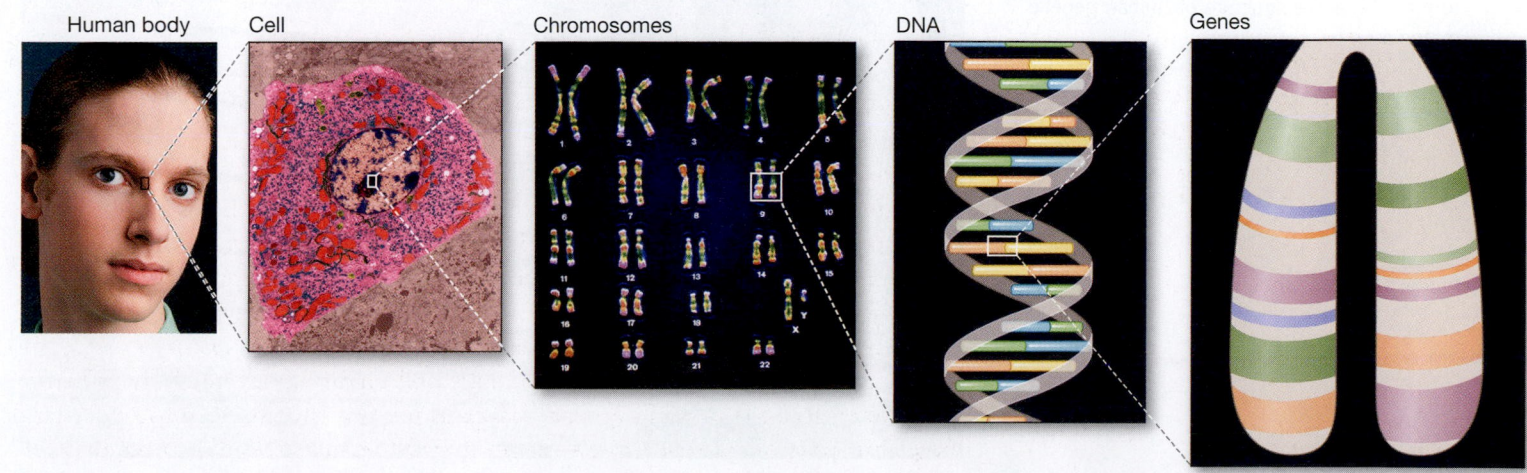

Human body   Cell   Chromosomes   DNA   Genes

make up each of the thousands of genes on each of the 23 pairs of human chromosomes (**FIGURE 3.3**). One of the most striking findings from the Human Genome Project is that we have fewer than 30,000 genes, only about twice as many as a fly (13,000) or a worm (18,000) does, and not much more than the number of genes found in some plants (26,000) and fewer than the number of genes estimated to be in an ear of corn (50,000). Indeed, more-recent estimates indicate that the human genome may consist of just over 20,000 genes (Pennisi, 2007). Thus humans' complexity may be due not simply to our possessing a large number of genes but to subtleties in how those genes are expressed and regulated (Baltimore, 2001). Now that the initial map of the human genome is complete, geneticists are mapping different individuals' genomes to see how they vary. That is, by comparing one person's genome to another, researchers hope to learn how variations in particular genes determine whether someone is likely to develop a specific disease or have some special ability. The project's eventual goal is to understand how genes and their variations interact to affect health as well as illness. Understanding how genes work should enable medical researchers, down the line, to cure various ailments by altering gene functions. Meanwhile, genetic research is giving psychological scientists a new understanding of the biological basis of psychological activity.

Heredity Involves Passing Along Genes through Reproduction

The first clues to the mechanisms responsible for heredity were discovered by the monk Gregor Mendel around 1866. At the monastery where Mendel lived, there was a long history of studying plants. For studying genetics, Mendel developed an experimental technique, *selective breeding,* that strictly controlled which plants bred with which other plants.

In one simple study, Mendel selected pea plants that had either only purple flowers or only white flowers. He then cross-pollinated the two types to see which color flowers the plants would produce. Mendel found that the first generation of pea

FIGURE 3.3 Human Genome Project
A map of human genes is presented by Celera Genomics president J. Craig Venter at a news conference in Washington on February 12, 2001. This map is but one part of the international effort by hundreds of scientists to map the entire structure of human genetic material.

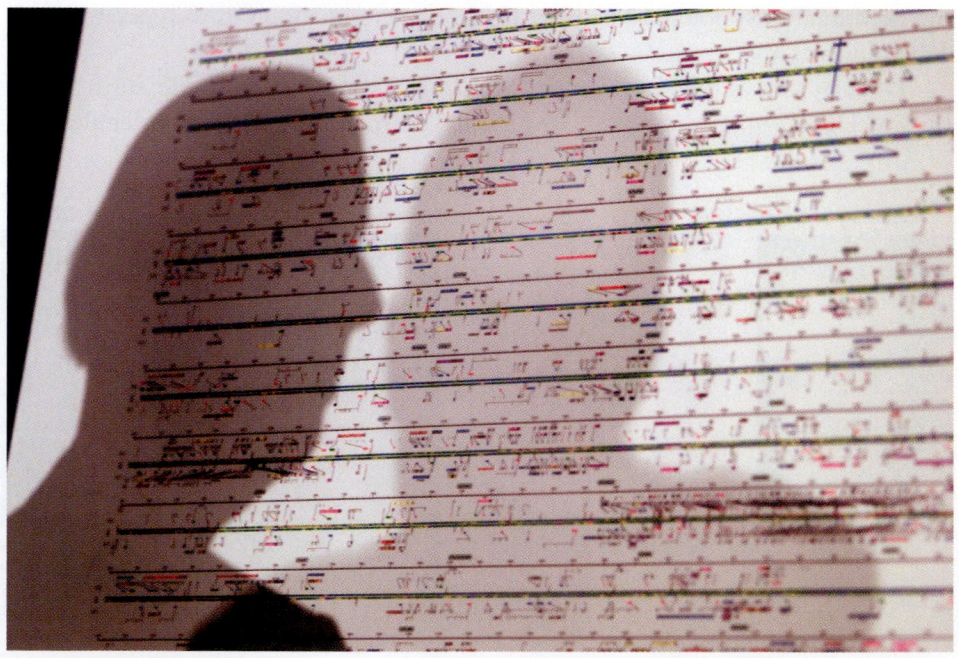

offspring tended to be completely white or completely purple. If he had stopped there, he would never have discovered the basis of heredity; however, he then allowed each plant to self-pollinate into a second generation. This second generation revealed a different pattern: Of the hundreds of pea plants, about 75 percent had purple flowers and 25 percent had white flowers. This three-to-one ratio repeated itself in additional studies, and it held true for other characteristics, such as pod shape. From this pattern, Mendel deduced that the plants contained separate units, now referred to as genes, that existed in different versions (e.g., white and purple). In determining offspring's features, some of these versions would be dominant and others would be recessive. We now know that a **dominant gene** from either parent is expressed (becomes apparent or physically visible) whenever it is present, whereas a **recessive gene** is expressed only when it is matched with a similar gene from the other parent. Thus because in pea plants white flowers were recessive, they occurred only when the gene for purple flowers was not present. All white genes and no purple ones were one of the four possible combinations of white and purple genes in Mendel's experiments (**FIGURE 3.4**).

GENOTYPE AND PHENOTYPE The existence of dominant and recessive genes means that not all genes are expressed. The **genotype** is an organism's genetic constitution, the genetic makeup determined at the moment of conception. The **phenotype** is that organism's observable physical characteristics, which result from

dominant gene A gene that is expressed in the offspring whenever it is present.

recessive gene A gene that is expressed only when it is matched with a similar gene from the other parent.

genotype The genetic constitution determined at the moment of conception.

phenotype Observable physical characteristics that result from both genetic and environmental influences.

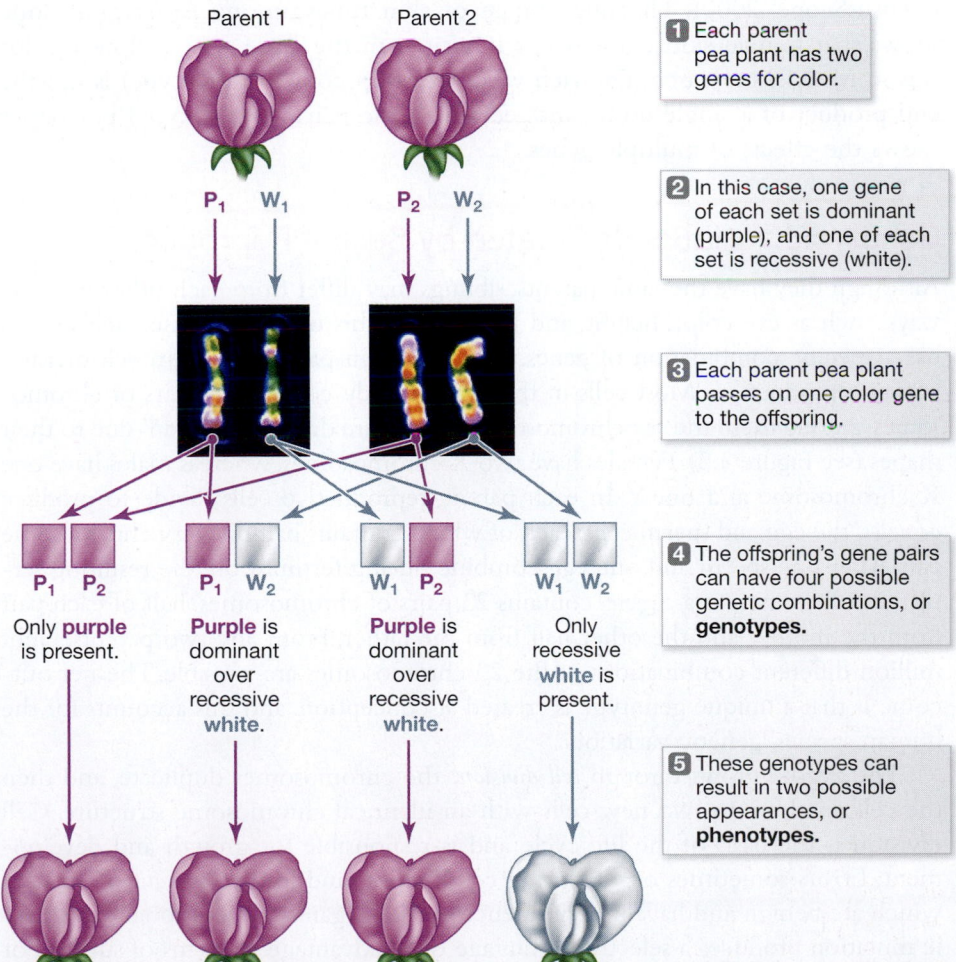

FIGURE 3.4 Genotypes and Phenotypes Mendel's experiments with cross-breeding pea blossoms resulted in purple flowers 75 percent of the time and white flowers 25 percent of the time.

Parent 1   Parent 2

P_1 W_1 P_2 W_2

1 Each parent pea plant has two genes for color.

2 In this case, one gene of each set is dominant (purple), and one of each set is recessive (white).

3 Each parent pea plant passes on one color gene to the offspring.

P_1 P_2 P_1 W_2 W_1 P_2 W_1 W_2

Only **purple** is present.

Purple is dominant over recessive **white**.

Purple is dominant over recessive **white**.

Only recessive **white** is present.

4 The offspring's gene pairs can have four possible genetic combinations, or **genotypes.**

5 These genotypes can result in two possible appearances, or **phenotypes.**

genetic and environmental influences. So, for instance, in Mendel's experiments two purple flowers had the same phenotype but might have differed in genotype, in that either one might have had two (dominant) genes for purple and either one might have had one (dominant) purple gene and one (recessive) white gene. Environment can also affect the phenotype. For instance, humans inherit their height and skin color, but good nutrition leads to increased size and sunlight changes skin color. Another example of environmental influence on the phenotype is *phenylketonuria (PKU)*, a disorder in which infants are unable to break down an enzyme, phenylalanine, contained in dairy and other products, such as aspartame, a sweetener in diet soft drinks. This rare genetic disorder can lead to severe brain damage. Fortunately, providing such children with a low-phenylalanine diet until they pass the critical stages of neural development greatly helps reduce brain damage. The phenotype, then, is modified by diet.

POLYGENIC EFFECTS Mendel's flower experiments dealt with single-gene characteristics, traits that appear to be determined by one gene each. But when a population displays a range of variability for a certain characteristic, such as height or intelligence, the characteristic is *polygenic,* influenced by many genes (as well as by environment). Think about human skin color, for example; there are not three or four separate skin colors but a spectrum. In the United States, the Census of 2000 allowed respondents to select more than one race for the first time. The data from that census showed that approximately 2.4 percent of the population (over 6.8 million people) identify themselves as multiracial (CensusScope, 2000). The huge range of skin tones among Americans alone shows that human skin color is not inherited in the same way as flower color was in Mendel's research. The rich variety of skin colors (phenotype) is not the end product of a single dominant/recessive gene pairing (genotype) but rather shows the effects of multiple genes.

Genotypic Variation Is Created by Sexual Reproduction

Although they have the same parents, siblings may differ from each other in many ways, such as eye color, height, and personality. This occurs because each person has a specific combination of genes, determined in part by random cell division before reproduction. Most cells in the human body contain 23 pairs of chromosomes, among them the sex chromosomes, which are denoted X and Y due to their shapes (see Figure 3.2). Females have two X chromosomes, whereas males have one X chromosome and one Y. In each parent, reproductive cells divide to produce *gametes,* the egg and sperm cells, each of which contains half of every chromosome pair. After one sperm and one egg combine during fertilization, the resulting fertilized cell, known as a *zygote,* contains 23 pairs of chromosomes, half of each pair from the mother and the other half from the father. From any two parents, eight million different combinations of the 23 chromosomes are possible. The net outcome is that a unique genotype is created at conception, and this accounts for the human species' genetic variation.

The zygote grows through *cell division:* the chromosomes duplicate, and then the cell divides into two new cells with an identical chromosome structure. Cell division is the basis of the life cycle and is responsible for growth and development. Errors sometimes occur during cell division and lead to *mutations,* most of which are benign and have little influence on the organism. Occasionally, a genetic mutation produces a selective advantage or disadvantage in terms of survival or reproduction—in other words, they are adaptive or maladaptive. The evolutionary significance of such a change in adaptiveness is complex, but a mutation that produces an ability or behavior may spread through the gene pool if the ability or behavior proves advantageous to the organism, because those who carry the gene are more likely to survive and reproduce. For instance, consider *industrial melanism,* a phenomenon in which areas of the world with heavy soot or smog tend to have moths, and butterflies, that are darker in color. Before industrialization, landscapes (trees, buildings, etc.) were lighter in color. Predators were more likely to spot darker insects against pale backgrounds, so any mutation that led to darker coloring in insects was eliminated quickly through natural selection. But with industrialization, pollution darkened the landscapes, and therefore darker insects became more adaptive because they were harder to see against the darker backgrounds.

Genetic mutations sometimes lead to disease, making them disadvantageous adaptively, and yet they remain in the gene pool. For instance, *sickle-cell disease* is a genetic disorder that alters the bloodstream's processing of oxygen; it can lead to pain, organ and bone damage, and anemia. The disease occurs mainly in African Americans, approximately 8 percent of whom are estimated to have the (recessive) gene for it (National Human Genome Research Institute, 2007). Because the sickle-cell gene is recessive, only those African Americans who receive it from both parents will develop the disease. Those who receive a recessive gene from only one parent will have healthy phenotypes in spite of genotypes that include the disease (**FIGURE 3.5**).

Recessive genes do not interfere with most people's health, so the recessive genes for diseases like sickle-cell can survive in the gene pool. This particular gene also has some benefit, in that it increases resistance to malaria, a parasitic disease prevalent in certain parts of Africa. People with only one sickle-cell gene enjoy this resistance without suffering from sickle-cell disease. In contrast to recessive gene disorders like this one, most dominant gene disorders are lethal for most of their carriers and therefore do not last in the gene pool.

Genes Affect Behavior

What determines the kind of person you are? What factors make you more or less bold, intelligent, or able to read a map? Your abilities and your psychological traits are influenced by the interaction of your genes and the environment in which you were raised or to which you are now exposed. The study of how genes and environment interact to influence psychological activity is known as *behavioral genetics.* Behavioral genetics has made important contributions to the biological revolution, providing information about the extent to which biology influences mind, brain, and behavior.

Any research suggesting that abilities to perform certain behaviors are biologically based is controversial. Most people do not want to be told that what they can achieve is limited by something beyond their control, such as their genes. It is easy to accept that genes control physical characteristics such as sex, race, eye color, and predisposition to diseases such as cancer and alcoholism. But can genes determine whether people will get divorced, how smart they are, or what careers they choose? Increasingly, science indicates that genes lay the groundwork for many human traits. From this perspective, people are born essentially like undeveloped photographs: The image is already captured, but the way it eventually appears can vary based on the development process. Psychological scientists study the ways in which characteristics are influenced by nature, nurture, and their combination—in other words, by the ways genes are expressed in environment.

(a) Moths displaying industrial melanism

(b) Red blood cells displaying sickle-cell disease

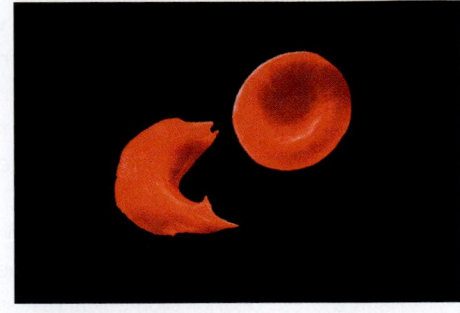

FIGURE 3.5 Mutations (a) Industrial melanism is caused by the fact that it is easier for predators to spot light-colored insects against dark backgrounds, so only darker moths and darker butterflies survive in more-polluted areas, where there are darker trees. **(b)** Sickle-cell disease occurs when people receive recessive genes for it from both parents, and it is most common among African Americans. It causes red blood cells to assume the distinctive "sickle" shape seen here in the left cell.

With our rapidly increasing knowledge about the human genome, we are being presented with new questions: Is it ethical to use (or not to use) genetic information, and to what extent should it be used? Today, if you know that you are a carrier of certain genetic diseases, you no longer need to risk passing your bad genes to your children. Current reproductive technology allows you to use in vitro fertilization (IVF), where several eggs are fertilized by sperm in a petri dish—that is, outside the body. After three days, when the resulting embryos are at the eight-cell stage, a single cell is removed, and the DNA is extracted. With an advanced procedure known as preimplantation genetic haplotyping (PGH), the DNA can be tested for thousands of genetic defects, and the healthiest embryos can be selected for implantation in the mother's uterus.

As in a great deal of biomedical research, the methods used to treat disease are being co-opted by the healthy population for other uses, and perhaps nowhere else are the ethical questions so rife as in the field of human reproduction. Using reproductive technologies to identify devastating genetic disease seems ethical and even laudable to many people, but the idea of using it to cater to personal preference is more debatable. One question is whether it is ethical to allow prospective parents to choose their offspring's sex. This practice has been going on since the 1970s, when *amniocentesis* (the analysis of amniotic fluid from the mother's uterus) made it possible to determine the sex of a fetus at 16–18 weeks of gestation. Amniocentesis originally was done for couples who were carriers of sex-linked genetic diseases, but both it and the less invasive *ultrasound* (creation of a two-dimensional image from vibrations in the uterus), developed in the 1980s, increasingly have been used for sex selection. Beginning in the 1990s, the sex of embryos used for IVF has been determined through genetic diagnosis, and many prospective parents choose the sex of the implanted embryos. More recently, Microsort, a private company, has developed a sperm-sorting sex determination technology that boasts a 73 percent success rate for males and a 90 percent success rate for females.

Advocates of sex determination argue that choosing the sex of one's child is a private decision that does not harm anyone. The most common objection to sex determination, however, is its discriminatory effect on women. In the few years that sex selection methods have been available, the male-to-female ratios in many countries have climbed dramatically. (The standard sex ratio is 105 baby boys born for every 100 baby girls, and any sex ratio over 106 is assumed to be evidence of sex control.) A report to the U.S. President's Council on Bioethics

FIGURE 3.6 China's "One Child Per Family" Policy

(2003b) found skewed sex ratios in regions around the world, including Venezuela (107.5); Yugoslavia (108.6); Egypt (108.7); Hong Kong (109.7); South Korea (110); Pakistan (110.9); Delhi, India (117); China (117); and Cuba (118). In Azerbaijan, Armenia, and Georgia, the sex ratio was as high as 120. In societies with such skewed male populations, each heterosexual male is less likely to find a mate, and the fear is that the society in general is likely to be more aggressive and suffer higher crime and greater social unrest. Certain cultures' strong preference for males has led to personal choices that have not just personal consequences but a societywide effect (**FIGURE 3.6**).

Controlling the sex of one's offspring is merely the beginning of what we may be able to control. Genes for traits such as eye color, skin color, height, temperament, personality, athleticism, and intelligence will be identified. When *germline therapy* becomes available (that is, changing the early embryonic genes, which are incorporated into all cells of the body and are passed on to future generations), scientists will be able to screen for particular genes and eventually to tinker with them. Eliminating genetic diseases is one thing, but in the future, children could be the specific results of their parents' desires: We may soon be able to order up our children just as we do burgers at fast-food restaurants. *Eugenics* (the science of attempting to improve a group's gene pool), whether it is in the hands of government or of individuals, raises a central question: By what standard are choices being made? In the case of sex determination, personal decisions appear to be based on cultural desires, religious beliefs, and so on. The consequences of such decisions are yet to be determined.

BEHAVIORAL GENETICS METHODS   Most of us, at one time or another, have marveled at how different siblings can be, even those raised around the same time and in the same household (**FIGURE 3.7**). The differences are to be expected, because most siblings share neither identical genes nor identical life experiences. Within and outside the household, environments differ subtly and not so subtly. Siblings have different birth orders, their mother may have consumed different foods and other substances during pregnancies, they may have different friends and teachers, and their parents may treat them differently. It is difficult to know what causes the similarities and differences between siblings, who always share some genes and often share much of their environments. Therefore, behavioral geneticists use two methods to assess the degree to which traits are inherited: twin studies and adoption studies.

Twin studies compare similarities between different types of twins to determine the genetic basis of specific traits. **Monozygotic twins,** or *identical twins,* result from one zygote (fertilized egg) dividing in two; each new zygote, and therefore each twin, has the same chromosomes and the same genes on each chromosome. Interesting research indicates, however, that monozygotic twins' DNA might not be as identical as long thought, due to subtle differences in how the mother's and father's genes are combined (Bruder et al., 2008). **Dizygotic twins,** sometimes called *fraternal* or *nonidentical twins,* result from two separately fertilized eggs developing in the mother's womb simultaneously; the resulting twins are no more similar genetically than any other pair of siblings. To the extent that monozygotic twins are more similar than dizygotic twins, the increased similarity is considered most likely due to genetic influence. Even identical twins do not have the exact same environment (and in rare circumstances might even have some different genes due to random mutations), and therefore they have different

monozygotic twins   Twin siblings who result from one zygote splitting in two and therefore share the same genes (i.e., identical twins).

dizygotic twins   Twin siblings who result from two separately fertilized eggs (i.e., fraternal twins).

FIGURE 3.7 **Try for Yourself: Genetic Matching**

Shown in the top row are two couples. Below are four children. Try to match which child comes from which parents.

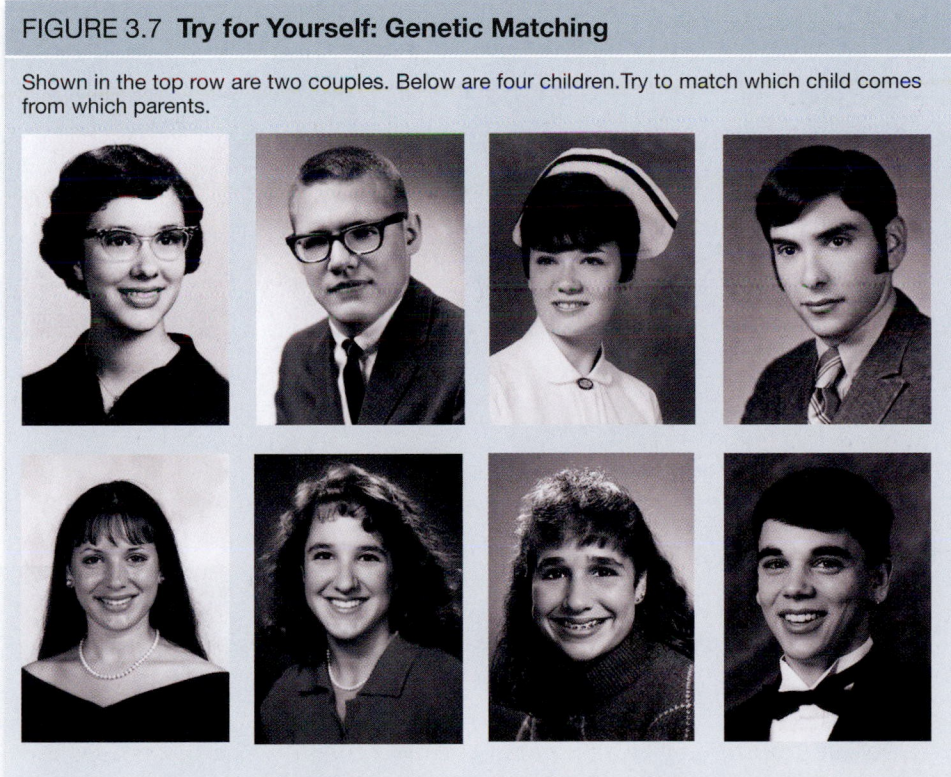

Answer: The boy and the girl at the ends of the bottom row are children of the parents at the top right. The two girls in the middle of the bottom row are children of the parents at the top left.

phenotypes, but they are typically much more similar than dizygotic twins, who differ in genotype and phenotype.

Adoption studies compare the similarities between biological relatives and adoptive relatives. Nonbiological adopted siblings may share similar home environments but will have different genes. Therefore, the assumption is that similarities among nonbiological adopted siblings have more to do with environment than with genes. Growing up in the same home turns out to have relatively little influence on many traits, such as personality. Indeed, after genetic similarity is controlled for, even biological siblings raised in the same home are no more similar than two strangers plucked at random off the street. (This point is examined in greater detail in Chapter 11, "Human Development," and Chapter 13, "Personality.")

One way to conduct a behavioral genetic study is to compare monozygotic twins who have been *raised together* with ones who were *raised apart*. Thomas Bouchard and his colleagues at the University of Minnesota identified more than 100 pairs of identical and nonidentical twins, some raised together and some raised apart (1990; **FIGURE 3.8**). The researchers examined a variety of these twins' characteristics, including intelligence, personality, well-being, achievement, alienation, and aggression. The general finding from the Minnesota Twin Project was that identical twins, raised together or not, were likely to be similar. The "Jim twins" were among the most famous case studies to emerge from this project. These twin brothers were separated at birth and raised by different families. It is easy to guess about how each one was given the same name, but how is it possible that each

FIGURE 3.8 Twins (a) Fraternal twins, such as this pair pictured during their 13th birthday party, result when two separate eggs are fertilized at the same time. **(b)** Identical twins result when one fertilized egg splits in two. Identical twins Gerald Levey and Mark Newman, participants in Dr. Bouchard's study, were separated at birth. Reunited at age 31, they discovered they were both firefighters and had similar personality traits.

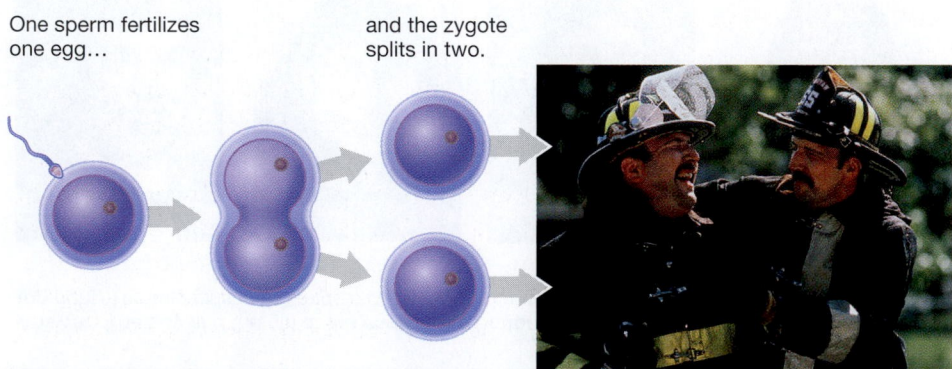

(a) Dizygotic (fraternal) twins

Two sperm fertilize two eggs...

which become two zygotes.

(b) Monozygotic (identical) twins

One sperm fertilizes one egg...

and the zygote splits in two.

James went on to marry a woman named Linda, divorce Linda and marry a woman named Betty, name a son James Alan (or James Allen), and name a dog Toy? In addition, both were part-time law-enforcement officers who drove Chevrolets and vacationed in Florida. Just to complete the circle, they were the same height and weight, chain-smoked the same brand of cigarettes, and drank the same brand of beer. Although no one would seriously suggest there are genes for naming dogs Toy or for marrying and divorcing women named Linda, the many similarities in the Jim twins' lives point to the strong genetic influences in shaping personality and behavior.

Some critics have argued that most of the adopted twins in the Minnesota study were raised in relatively similar environments, in part because adoption agencies try to match the child to the adoptive home. However, this argument does not explain the identical twins Oskar Stohr and Jack Yufe, who were born in Trinidad in 1933 (Bouchard et al., 1990). Oskar was raised a Catholic in Germany and eventually joined the Nazi Party. Jack was raised a Jew in Trinidad and lived for a while in Israel. Few twins have more different backgrounds. Yet when they met, at an interview for the study, they were wearing similar clothes, exhibited similar mannerisms, and shared odd habits such as flushing the toilet before using it, dipping toast in coffee, storing rubber bands on their wrists, and enjoying startling people by sneezing loudly in elevators. Some critics feel that nothing more than coincidence is at work in these case studies and that if a researcher randomly selected any two people of the same age, many surprising similarities would exist in those people and their lives, just by coincidence, even if the people and their lives differed in most other ways. But twins and other relatives share similarities beyond coincidental attributes and behavior quirks. For instance, intelligence and personality traits such as shyness tend to run in families due to strong genetic components.

Moreover, some evidence suggests that twins raised apart may be more similar than twins raised together. This phenomenon might occur if parents encouraged individuality in twins raised together by emphasizing different strengths and interests as a way of helping each twin develop as an individual. In effect, the parents would actively create a different environment for each twin.

UNDERSTANDING HERITABILITY *Heredity* is the transmission of characteristics from parents to offspring by means of genes. A term that is often confused with *heredity* but means something else altogether is **heritability,** which is a statistical estimate of the genetic portion of the variation in some specific trait. The heritability for a trait depends on the *variation,* the measure of the overall difference among a group of people for that particular trait. That is, within a group of people (e.g., American women), how much do members vary in some trait (e.g., height)? Once we know the typical amount of variation within the population, we can see whether people who are related show less variation. For instance, do sisters tend to be more similar in height than unrelated women chosen at random?

Heritability refers to populations, not to individuals. If within a certain population a trait such as height has a heritability of .60, that means 60 percent of height variation among individuals within that population is genetic, not that anyone necessarily gets 60 percent of his or her height from genetics and 40 percent from environment. For instance, almost everyone has two legs, and more people lose legs through accidents than are born without them. Thus the heritability value for having two legs is nearly zero, despite the obvious fact that the human genome includes instructions for growing two legs. Herein lies a key lesson: Estimates of heritability are concerned only with the extent that people differ in terms of their genetic makeup within the group.

heritability A statistical estimate of the variation, caused by differences in heredity, in a trait within a population.

Social and Environmental Contexts Influence Genetic Expression

In a longitudinal study of criminality, Avshalom Caspi and his colleagues (2002) followed a group of more than 1,000 New Zealanders from their births in 1972–1973 until adulthood, collecting enormous amounts of information about the participants and their lives each few years. When the participants were 26 years old, the investigators were able to examine which factors predicted who became a violent criminal. Prior research had demonstrated that children who are mistreated by their parents are more likely to become violent offenders. But not all mistreated children become violent, and these researchers wanted to know why not. They hypothesized that the enzyme monoamine oxidase (MAO) is important in determining susceptibility to the effects of maltreatment, because low levels of MAO have been implicated in aggressive behaviors (see Chapter 14, "Disorders of the Mind and Body"). The gene that controls MAO comes in two forms, one of which leads to higher levels of MAO and one of which leads to lower levels. Caspi and colleagues found that boys with the low-MAO gene appeared to be especially susceptible to early childhood maltreatment and were much more likely to be convicted of a violent crime than those with the high-MAO gene. Indeed, although only 1 in 8 boys *both* was mistreated *and* had the low–MAO gene, these boys were responsible for nearly half of all violent crimes committed by the group (**FIGURE 3.9**). The New Zealander study is a good example of how nature and nurture together affect behavior—in this case, unfortunately, violent behavior. Nature and nurture are inextricably entwined.

Many other studies have provided evidence that genes and social contexts interact to affect the phenotype. Sandra Scarr and her colleagues have proposed a theory of development that stresses the interactive nature of genes and environment (Scarr & McCarthy, 1983). According to Scarr, early environments influence young children, but children's genes also influence the experiences they receive. For instance,

FIGURE 3.9 Scientific Method: Caspi's Study of the Influence of Environment and Genes

Hypothesis: The enzyme monoamine oxidase (MAO) may be important in determining susceptibility to the effects of maltreatment, because low levels of MAO have been implicated in aggressive behaviors.

Research Method:

1 A group of more than 1,000 New Zealanders were followed from birth to adulthood.

2 Researchers measured which children were mistreated by their parents (**nurture**).

3 Researchers measured the presence of the MAO gene, which comes in two forms, one that leads to higher levels of MAO and one that leads to lower levels (**nature**).

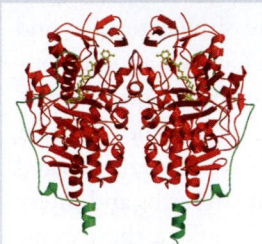

4 Researchers measured the tendency toward criminal behavior.

Results: Those who had the gene for low MAO activity were much more likely than others to have been convicted of violent crimes if they had been maltreated as children. The effects of maltreatment had less influence on those with the high-MAO gene.

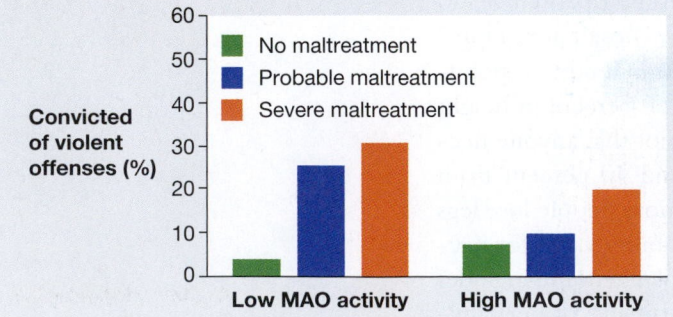

Conclusion: Nature and nuture can work together to affect human behavior.

children exposed to the same environment interpret and react to it in different ways. When teased, some children withdraw, others shrug it off without concern, and still others fight back. Because of differences in how they react to events, different children evoke different responses from others. A well-mannered, cuddly child cues more nurturing from parents and others than an irritable, fussy child does. Similarly, a child who seems to enjoy reading is likely to get more books and be read to more often than one who does not. And as children become older, they can choose their social situations. Some children prefer vigorous outdoor activities, others prefer quieter indoor activities, and so on. Thus genes predispose people to certain behaviors, those behaviors elicit particular responses, and those subsequent interactions then shape the phenotype. Because genes and social contexts interact, separating their independent effects can be very difficult—some would argue that it is impossible.

Genetic Expression Can Be Modified

Researchers can employ various gene manipulation techniques to enhance or reduce particular genes' expression or even to insert genes from one animal species into embryos of another. The researchers can then compare the genetically modified animals with unmodified ones to test theories about the affected genes' functions. Such techniques have dramatically increased our understanding of how gene expression influences thought, feeling, and behavior. For instance, among the transgenic mice discussed in Chapter 2 are *knockouts*, research mice from which genes have been "knocked out," or rendered inactive by being removed from or disrupted within the genome (**FIGURE 3.10**); if a gene is important for a specific function, knocking out that gene should interfere with the function. This experimental technique has revolutionized genetics, and in recognition the 2007 Nobel Prize in Medicine was awarded to the three scientists who developed it: Mario Capecchi, Oliver Smithies, and Sir Martin Evans.

One remarkable finding from genetic manipulation is that changing even a single gene can dramatically change behavior. Through various gene manipulations, researchers have created anxious mice, hyperactive mice, mice that cannot learn or remember, mice that groom themselves to the point of baldness, mice that fail to take care of their offspring, and even mice that progressively increase alcohol intake when stressed (Marcus, 2004; Ridley, 2003). In one study, a gene from the highly social prairie vole was inserted into the developing embryos of normally antisocial

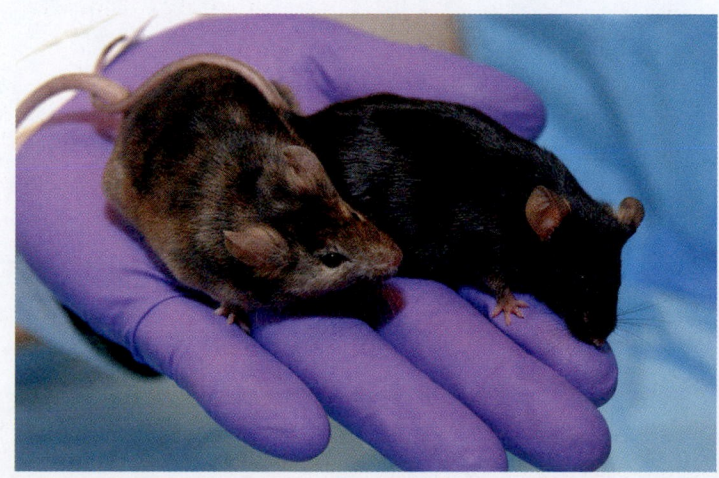

FIGURE 3.10 Genetic Modifications These mice look different because the gene affecting hair growth was "knocked out" of the mouse on the left but not the mouse on the right.

mice. The resulting transgenic mice exhibited social behavior more typical of prairie voles than of mice (Insel & Young, 2001). Another study found that knocking out specific genes led mice to forget mice they had previously encountered. These knockouts also failed to investigate new mice placed in their cages, though normal mice would do so readily. In essence, knocking out one gene led to multiple impairments in social recognition (Choleris et al., 2003). This finding indicates not that mice have a specific gene for being social, but that changing one gene's expression leads to the expression of a series of other genes, an effect that ultimately influences even complex behaviors. In other words, genes seldom work in isolation to influence mind and behavior; rather, complex interaction among thousands of genes gives rise to the complexity of human experience.

CRITICAL THINKING SKILL

Seeking Disconfirming Evidence

Most of us tend to focus on information that confirms what we already believe. This error occurs in various contexts and was even identified in a study of the way NASA scientists propose and test hypotheses—and they *are* rocket scientists! Suppose you believe that genetics plays only a small role in the way people think, feel, and act. How would you test this belief? If you are like most people, you would look for studies that show a small genetic effect and criticize studies that show a large one. But a better way to gather and study information would be to draw a 2 × 2 chart and fill in every cell (**FIGURE 3.11**).

On the left, you would list each position: your thesis (A) and its opposite, or antithesis (B). In the middle, you would supply at least one or two reasons supporting each position, provide evidence for each reason, and evaluate the relative strength of each piece of evidence. (For example, how reliable is your source for this information? If a study was conducted, did it use appropriate control groups?) On the right, you would supply at least one or two reasons contradicting each position, provide evidence for each of these reasons, and, as with the supporting evidence, evaluate the relative strength of each piece of

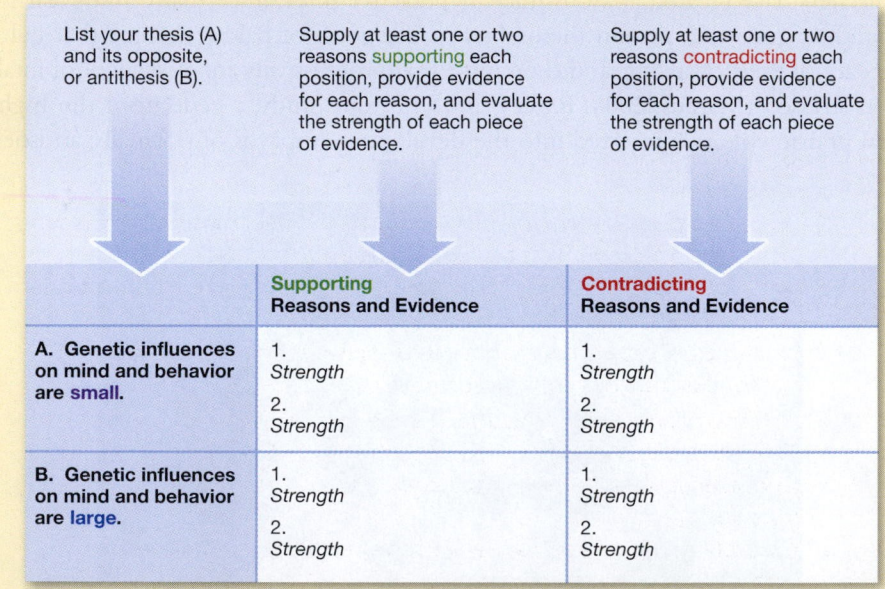

List your thesis (A) and its opposite, or antithesis (B).	**Supporting** Reasons and Evidence Supply at least one or two reasons supporting each position, provide evidence for each reason, and evaluate the strength of each piece of evidence.	**Contradicting** Reasons and Evidence Supply at least one or two reasons contradicting each position, provide evidence for each reason, and evaluate the strength of each piece of evidence.
A. Genetic influences on mind and behavior are small.	1. *Strength* 2. *Strength*	1. *Strength* 2. *Strength*
B. Genetic influences on mind and behavior are large.	1. *Strength* 2. *Strength*	1. *Strength* 2. *Strength*

FIGURE 3.11 Think Critically: Supporting and Contradictory Evidence

evidence. Thus the table would force you to consider not only information that supports your beliefs but also information that fails to support them.

Suppose you believe that vitamin C reduces your likelihood of getting a cold. If you acted on the natural tendency to consider only confirming information, you would look for studies in which people who took vitamin C had fewer colds. If you employed this table, you would also need to consider other possibilities, such as studies in which people took vitamin C and did not have fewer colds, or did not take vitamin C and had fewer colds, or did not take vitamin C and had more colds. To consider the subject thoroughly, you would include all four kinds of studies in your thinking. In many contexts, this critical thinking skill (or strategy) will not only guide you away from ignoring disconfirming evidence. It will also increase your ability to gather disconfirming evidence, evaluate it, and thereby strengthen your arguments—for and against.

SUMMING UP

What Is the Genetic Basis of Psychological Science?

Human behavior is influenced by genetic processes. People inherit both physical characteristics and personality traits from their parents. Only recently have scientists developed the tools to measure genetic processes and the roles that various genes play in psychological activity. The Human Genome Project has mapped DNA's basic sequence, information that eventually will be translated into medical treatments and a greater understanding of individual differences among people. Researchers increasingly are studying how and when genes are expressed, in addition to particular traits' heritability. Among the genetic research tools are methods that enhance or interrupt gene expression by selectively knocking out specific genes to reveal which behaviors are affected.

MEASURING UP

1. The difference between genotype and phenotype is that
   _____.
   a. genotype refers to an organism's genetic makeup; phenotype refers to observable characteristics that result from genetic and environmental influences
   b. genotype refers to monozygotic twins' (nearly) identical genetic makeup; phenotype refers to dizygotic twins' genetic makeup
   c. genotypes can be modified by experiences; phenotypes can be modified only if the underlying genes are knocked out
   d. genotypes direct the experiences organisms seek for themselves; phenotypes cannot affect environmental events

2. What is the principle behind knockout gene research?
   a. Aggressive behavior is inherited through so-called knockout genes.
   b. By rendering a single gene inactive, we can study that gene's effects on behavior.
   c. Knockout genes reveal the relative contributions of prenatal and postnatal experiences on offspring.
   d. Knockout genes reduce the need for using MRIs to study brain development.

How Does the Nervous System Operate?

Neurons Are Specialized for Communication

Neurons, the basic units of the nervous system, are cells that specialize in communication. Neurons differ from most other cells because they are excitable: They operate through electrical impulses and communicate with other neurons through chemical signals. They have three functions: taking in information from neighboring neurons (reception), integrating those signals (conduction), and passing signals to other neurons (transmission).

TYPES OF NEURONS The three basic types of neurons are *sensory neurons, motor neurons,* and *interneurons*. **Sensory neurons** detect information from the physical world and pass that information along to the brain, usually via the spinal cord. You know from hitting your funny bone that sensory neurons can transmit fast-acting signals that trigger a nearly instantaneous bodily response and sensory experience. Sensory neurons are often called *afferent* neurons, meaning they carry information to the brain. The sensory nerves that provide information from muscles are referred to as *somatosensory,* which is the general term for sensations experienced from within the body.

Motor neurons direct muscles to contract or relax, thereby producing movement. Motor neurons are therefore *efferent* neurons, neurons that transmit signals from the brain to the muscles throughout the body. **Interneurons** communicate within local or short-distance circuits. That is, interneurons integrate neural activity within a single area rather than transmitting information to other brain structures or to the body organs.

Together, sensory and motor neurons control movement (**FIGURE 3.12**). For instance, if you are using a pen to take notes as you read these words, you are contracting and relaxing your hand muscles and finger muscles to adjust your fingers' pressure on the pen. When you want to use the pen, your brain sends a message via motor neurons to your finger muscles so they move in specific ways. Receptors in both your skin and your muscles send back messages through sensory neurons to help determine how much pressure is needed to hold the pen. This symphony of neural communication for a task as simple as using a pen is remarkable, yet most of us employ motor control so easily that we rarely think about it.

neuron The basic unit of the nervous system; it operates through electrical impulses, which communicate with other neurons through chemical signals. Neurons receive, integrate, and transmit information in the nervous system.

sensory neurons One of the three types of neurons, these afferent neurons detect information from the physical world and pass that information along to the brain.

motor neurons One of the three types of neurons, these efferent neurons direct muscles to contract or relax, thereby producing movement.

interneurons One of the three types of neurons, these neurons communicate only with other neurons, typically within a specific brain region.

FIGURE 3.12 The Three Types of Neurons Receptors send afferent signals to the brain for processing. An efferent signal is then sent from the brain to the body via the spinal cord to produce a response.

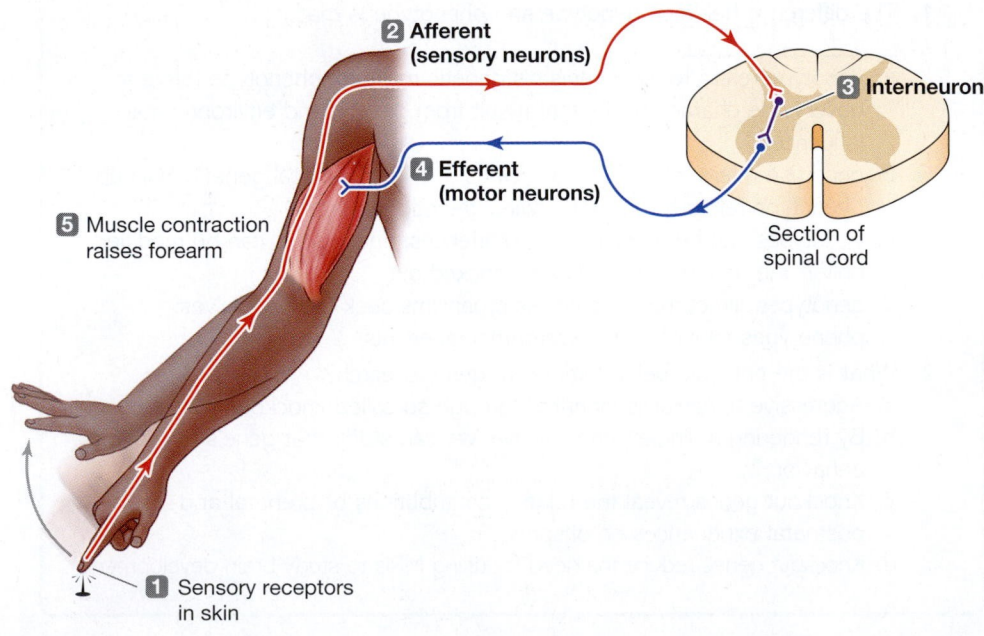

2 Afferent (sensory neurons)

3 Interneuron

4 Efferent (motor neurons)

Section of spinal cord

5 Muscle contraction raises forearm

1 Sensory receptors in skin

Complex networks of thousands of neurons sending and receiving signals are the functional basis of all psychological activity. In fact, they are the basis of your every thought, your every emotion, your every action. Essentially, you *are* your nervous system. Although single neurons' actions are simple to describe, human complexity results from billions of neurons, each making contact with tens of thousands of other neurons. Neurons do not communicate randomly or arbitrarily; they selectively communicate with other neurons to form circuits, or *neural networks*. These networks develop through maturation and experience, forming permanent alliances among groups of neurons.

NEURON STRUCTURE Neurons have different functions and come in a wide assortment of shapes and sizes, but all types usually share four structural regions that participate in the neuron's communication functions: the dendrites, the cell body, the axon, and the terminal buttons (**FIGURE 3.13**). The **dendrites** are short, branchlike appendages that increase the neuron's receptive field and detect chemical signals from neighboring neurons. In the **cell body,** the information received from thousands of other neurons is collected and integrated.

Once the incoming information from many other neurons has been integrated in the cell body, electrical impulses are transmitted along a long narrow outgrowth known as the **axon.** Axons vary tremendously in length, from a few millimeters to more than a meter. The longest axons stretch from the spinal cord to the big toe. You probably have heard the term *nerve,* as in a pinched nerve. Used in this context, a nerve refers to a bundle of axons that carry information between the brain and other places in the body.

Terminal buttons, small nodules at the axons' ends, receive the electrical impulses and release chemical signals from the neuron to an area called the **synapse,** or **synaptic cleft,** the site for chemical communication between neurons. Neurons do not touch each other; they communicate by sending chemicals into tiny gaps between the axon of the "sending" neuron and the dendrites of the "receiving" neuron. Chemicals leave one neuron, cross the synapse, and pass signals along to other neurons' dendrites.

The neuron's membrane serves as its boundary. The membrane also plays an important role in communication between neurons by regulating the concentration of electrically charged molecules that are the basis of the neuron's electrical activity (discussed further below). These electrical signals travel quickly down the axon because of the fatty **myelin sheath** that encases and insulates it like the plastic tubing around wires in an electrical cord. Made up of *glial cells* (Greek, "glue"), the myelin sheath grows along an axon in short segments. Between these segments are small gaps of exposed axon called the **nodes of Ranvier** (after Louis A. Ranvier, the researcher who first described them). At these gaps are ion channels, which allow negatively and positively charged ions to pass in and out of the cell when the neuron transmits signals down the axon.

dendrites Branchlike extensions of the neuron that detect information from other neurons.

cell body In the neuron, where information from thousands of other neurons is collected and processed.

axon A long narrow outgrowth of a neuron by which information is transmitted to other neurons.

terminal buttons Small nodules, at the ends of axons, that release chemical signals from the neuron to the synapse.

synapse, or synaptic cleft The site for chemical communication between neurons, which contains extracellular fluid.

myelin sheath A fatty material, made up of glial cells, that insulates the axon and allows for the rapid movement of electrical impulses along the axon.

nodes of Ranvier Small gaps of exposed axon, between the segments of myelin sheath, where action potentials are transmitted.

FIGURE 3.13 Neuron Structure
Messages are received by the dendrites, processed in the cell body, transmitted along the axon, and sent to other neurons via chemical substances released from the terminal buttons across the synapse.

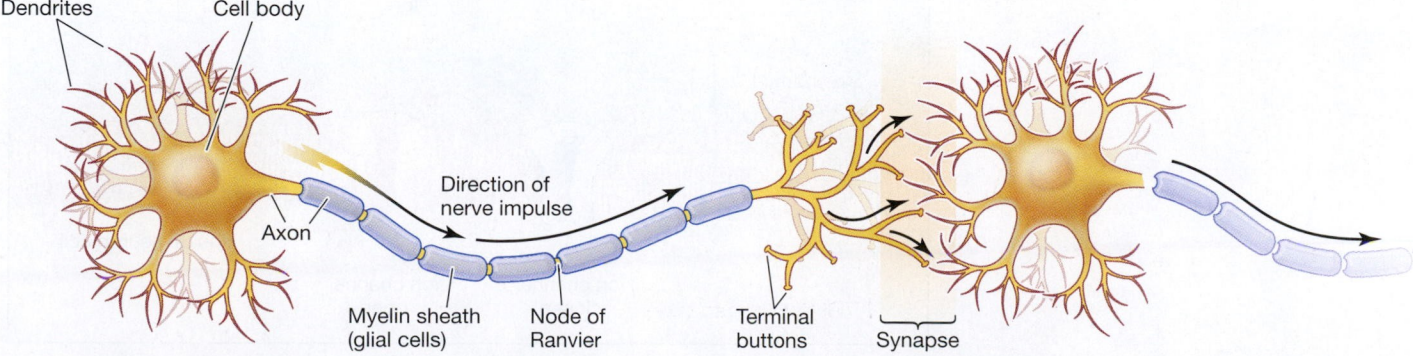

Dendrites · Cell body · Axon · Direction of nerve impulse · Myelin sheath (glial cells) · Node of Ranvier · Terminal buttons · Synapse

THE RESTING MEMBRANE POTENTIAL IS NEGATIVELY CHARGED When a
neuron is resting (not active) the inside and outside differ electrically, a phenomenon referred to as the **resting membrane potential** (FIGURE 3.14). This difference
occurs because the ratio of negative to positive ions is greater inside the neuron
than outside it. Therefore, the electrical charge inside the neuron is slightly more
negative than the one outside. Changing this differential electrical charge inside
and outside the neuron, *polarization,* creates the electrical energy necessary to
power the firing of the neuron.

THE ROLES OF SODIUM AND POTASSIUM IONS Two types of ions that contribute to a neuron's resting membrane potential are *sodium ions* and *potassium ions.*
Although other ions are involved in neural activity, sodium and potassium are most
important for this discussion. Ions pass through the cell membrane at *ion channels,*
specialized pores located at the nodes of Ranvier. Each channel matches a specific
type of ion (i.e., sodium channels allow sodium but not potassium and vice versa),
and the flow of ions through each channel is controlled by a gating mechanism.
When a gate is open, ions flow in and out of the cell membrane, but a closed gate
prevents their passage. Ion flow also is affected by the cell membrane's selective
permeability; the membrane allows some types of ions to cross more easily than

**FIGURE 3.14 Resting Membrane
Potential** A neuron at rest is polarized—it
has a different electrical charge inside and
outside. The passage of negative and positive
ions inside and outside the membrane is regulated by ion channels located at the nodes of
Ranvier.

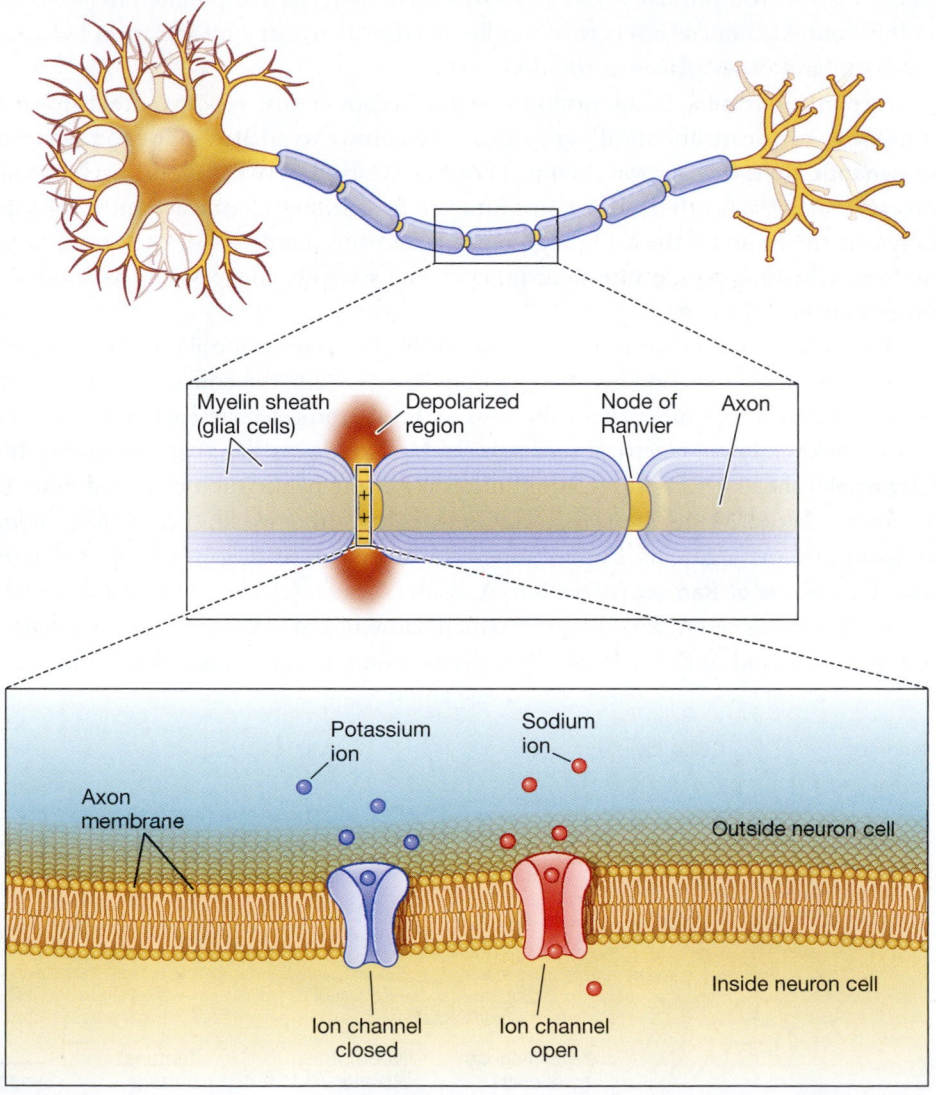

others, much like a bouncer at an exclusive nightclub. Partially as a result of this selective permeability of the cell membrane, more potassium is inside the neuron than sodium, an imbalance that contributes to polarization.

Action Potentials Cause Neural Communication

Neural communication depends on a neuron's ability to respond to incoming stimulation by changing electrically and then passing along signals to other neurons. An **action potential**, also called *neural firing*, is the electrical signal that passes along the axon and causes the release of chemicals that transmit signals to other neurons. The following sections examine some factors that contribute to an action potential's firing.

CHANGES IN ELECTRICAL POTENTIAL LEAD TO ACTION A neuron receives chemical signals from nearby neurons through its dendrites, and these signals tell the neuron whether to fire. The signals, which work by affecting polarization, arrive at the dendrites by the thousands and are of two types: *excitatory* and *inhibitory*. Excitatory signals depolarize the cell membrane, increasing the likelihood that the neuron will fire; inhibitory signals hyperpolarize the cell and decrease the likelihood that the neuron will fire. Excitatory and inhibitory signals received by the dendrites are integrated within the neuron. If the total amount of excitatory input from the other neurons surpasses the receiving neuron's threshold, an action potential is generated.

When a neuron fires, the sodium gates in the cell membrane open, allowing sodium ions to rush into the neuron. This influx of sodium causes the inside of the neuron to become slightly more positively charged than the outside. A fraction of a second later, potassium channels open to allow the potassium ions inside the cell membrane to rush out. This change from a negative charge to a positive one inside the neuron is the basis of the action potential. As the sodium ion channels close, the sodium ions stop entering the cell; similarly, as the potassium ion channels close, potassium ions stop exiting the cell. The electrical charge inside the cell during this process starts out slightly negative in its initial resting state, then becomes positive as it fires and allows more positive ions inside the cell, and then through natural restoration it goes back to its slightly negative resting state (**FIGURE 3.15**).

action potential The neural impulse that passes along the axon and subsequently causes the release of chemicals from the terminal buttons.

FIGURE 3.15 Action Potential The electrical charge inside the neuron starts out slightly negative (resting membrane potential). As the neuron fires, it allows more positive ions inside the cell (depolarization). Through natural restoration (repolarization), it then returns to its slightly negative resting state.

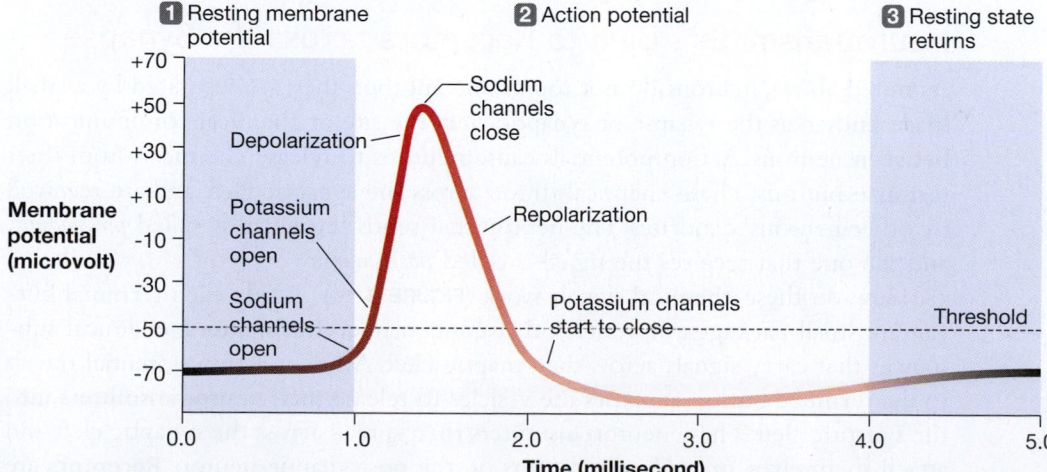

ACTION POTENTIALS SPREAD ALONG THE AXON When the neuron fires, the cell membrane's depolarization moves along the axon like a wave, an action called *propagation*. Sodium ions rush through their ion channels, causing adjacent sodium channels to open. Thus, like toppling dominoes, sodium ion channels open successively, always moving down the axon away from the cell body to the terminal buttons. Because of the insulation provided by the myelin sheath, the action potential skips quickly along the axon, pausing only briefly to be recharged at each node of Ranvier on the axon. The entire process takes only about 1/1,000 of a second, permitting the fast and frequent adjustments required for coordinating motor activity.

Deterioration of the myelin sheath leads to multiple sclerosis (MS), an especially tragic neurological disorder that begins in young adulthood. The earliest symptoms are often numbness in the limbs and blurry vision. Since the myelin insulation helps messages move quickly along axons, demyelination slows down neural impulses. The axons essentially short-circuit, and normal neural communication is interrupted. Motor actions become jerky, as those afflicted lose the ability to coordinate motor movements. Over time, movement, sensation, and coordination are severely impaired. As the myelin sheath disintegrates, axons are exposed and may start to break down.

ALL-OR-NONE PRINCIPLE Any one signal received by the neuron has little influence on whether it fires. Normally, the neuron is barraged by thousands of excitatory and inhibitory signals, and its firing is determined by the number and frequency of those signals. If the sum of excitatory and inhibitory signals leads to a positive change in voltage that exceeds the neuron's firing threshold, an action potential is generated.

A neuron either fires or it does not; it cannot partially fire. The **all-or-none principle** dictates that a neuron fires with the same potency each time (i.e., it does not fire in a way that can be described as weak or strong). How often the neuron fires depends on the strength of stimulation. For the sake of comparison, suppose you are playing a video game in which you fire missiles by pressing a button. Every time you press the button, a missile is launched at the same velocity as the previous one. It makes no difference how hard you press the button. But if you keep your finger on the button, additional missiles fire in rapid succession. Thus the strong stimulus—your finger holding down the button—controls the firing frequency. Likewise, if a neuron in the visual system, for example, receives information that a light is bright, it might respond by firing more rapidly and more often than when it receives information that the light is dim.

Neurotransmitters Bind to Receptors across the Synapse

As noted above, neurons do not touch one another; they are separated by a small space known as the synapse or synaptic cleft, the site of chemical communication between neurons. Action potentials cause neurons to release chemicals from their terminal buttons. These chemicals travel across the synaptic cleft and are received by other neurons' dendrites. The neuron that sends the signal is called *presynaptic,* and the one that receives the signal is called *postsynaptic.*

How do these chemical signals work (**FIGURE 3.16**)? Inside each terminal button are small packages, or vesicles, that contain **neurotransmitters,** chemical substances that carry signals across the synaptic cleft. After an action potential travels to the terminal button, it causes the vesicles to release their neurotransmitters into the synaptic cleft. These neurotransmitters then spread across the synaptic cleft and attach themselves, or *bind,* to receptors on the postsynaptic neuron. **Receptors** are

all-or-none principle The principle whereby a neuron fires with the same potency each time, although frequency can vary; it either fires or not—it cannot partially fire.

neurotransmitter A chemical substance that carries signals from one neuron to another.

receptors In neurons, specialized protein molecules, on the postsynaptic membrane, that neurotransmitters bind to after passing across the synaptic cleft.

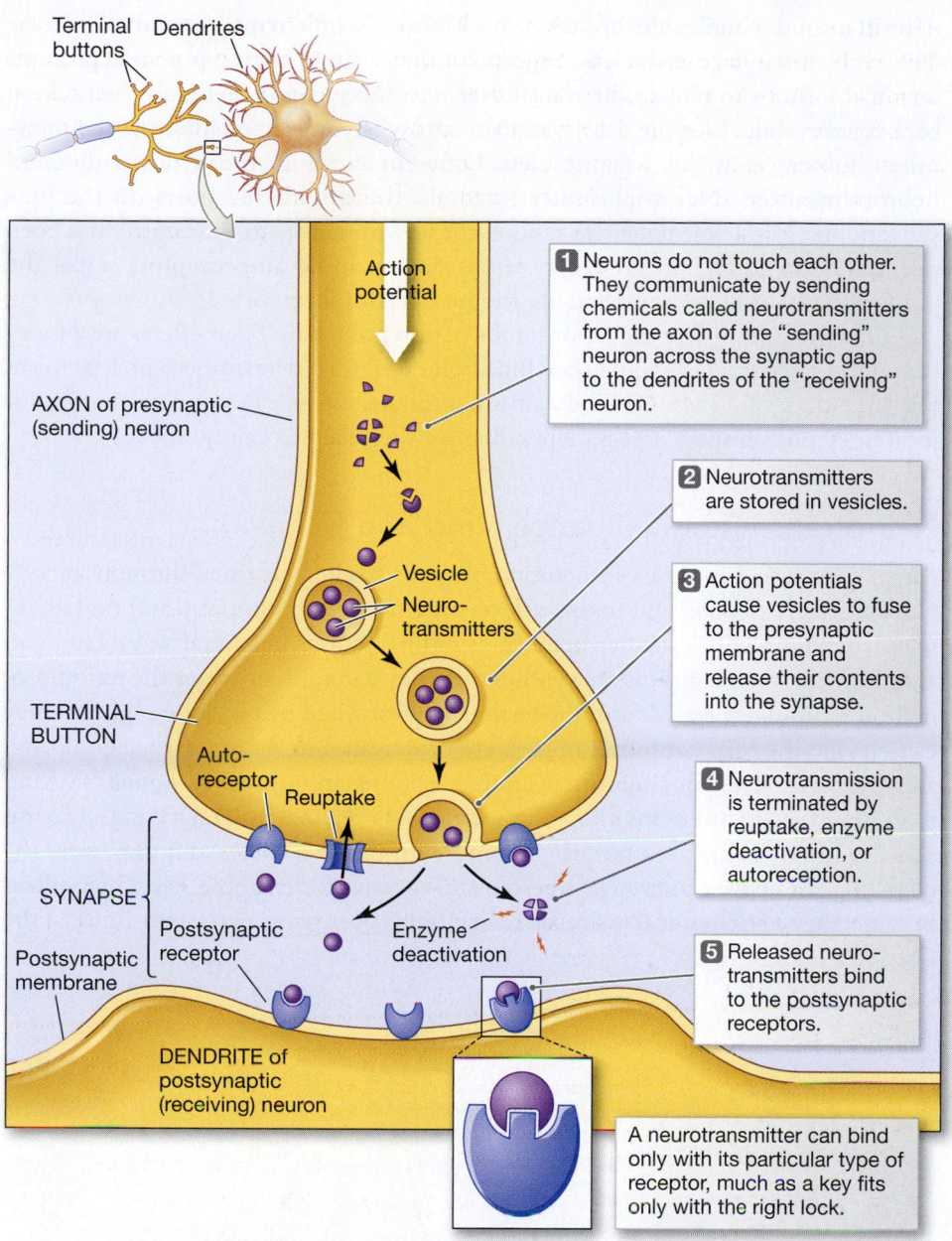

Terminal buttons   Dendrites

1 **Neurons do not touch each other.** They communicate by sending chemicals called neurotransmitters from the axon of the "sending" neuron across the synaptic gap to the dendrites of the "receiving" neuron.

Action potential

AXON of presynaptic (sending) neuron

2 Neurotransmitters are stored in vesicles.

Vesicle
Neuro-transmitters

3 Action potentials cause vesicles to fuse to the presynaptic membrane and release their contents into the synapse.

TERMINAL BUTTON

Auto-receptor   Reuptake

4 Neurotransmission is terminated by reuptake, enzyme deactivation, or autoreception.

SYNAPSE

Postsynaptic receptor   Enzyme deactivation

5 Released neuro-transmitters bind to the postsynaptic receptors.

Postsynaptic membrane

DENDRITE of postsynaptic (receiving) neuron

A neurotransmitter can bind only with its particular type of receptor, much as a key fits only with the right lock.

FIGURE 3.16 How Neurotransmitters Work

specialized protein molecules located on the postsynaptic membrane. The binding of a neurotransmitter with a receptor produces an excitatory or inhibitory signal for the postsynaptic neuron, thus encouraging or discouraging neural firing.

NEUROTRANSMITTERS BIND WITH SPECIFIC RECEPTORS Before the 1970s, most researchers believed that communication in the brain took place through the actions of just five or so neurotransmitters. Researchers now know that more than 60 chemicals transmit information in the brain and body. Different transmitters influence either emotion, thought, or behavior. In much the same way as a lock opens only with the correct key, each receptor can be influenced by only one type of neurotransmitter.

Once neurotransmitters are released into the synapse, they continue to fill and stimulate that receptor, and they block new signals until their influence is terminated. The three major events that terminate the transmitters' influence in the synaptic cleft are *reuptake, enzyme deactivation,* and *autoreception.* **Reuptake** occurs when the

reuptake The process whereby a neurotransmitter is taken back into the presynaptic terminal buttons, thereby stopping its activity.

neurotransmitter molecules are taken back into the presynaptic terminal buttons. The cycle of reuptake and release repeats continuously. An action potential prompts terminal buttons to release the transmitter into the synaptic cleft and then take it back for recycling. Enzyme deactivation occurs when an enzyme destroys the transmitter substance in the synaptic cleft. Different enzymes break down different neurotransmitters. Neurotransmitters can also bind with receptors on the presynaptic neuron. These *autoreceptors* monitor how much neurotransmitter has been released into the synapse. When excess is detected, the autoreceptors signal the presynaptic neuron to stop releasing the neurotransmitter.

All neurotransmitters trigger or inhibit action potentials. Their effects are a function of the receptors to which they bind, which in turn determine which neurons will fire or less likely fire. The same neurotransmitter can send excitatory or inhibitory postsynaptic signals, depending on the receptor's properties.

Neurotransmitters Influence Mind and Behavior

Much of what is known about neurotransmitters has been learned through the systematic study of drugs' and toxins' effects on emotion, on thought, and on behavior. Drugs and toxins can alter neurotransmitters' actions in several ways: They can alter how neurotransmitters are synthesized, they can raise or lower the amount of neurotransmitters released from the terminal buttons, and by blocking reuptake they can change the way neurotransmitters are deactivated in the synaptic cleft. Drugs and toxins that enhance neurotransmitters' actions are known as **agonists;** drugs inhibiting these actions are known as **antagonists** (FIGURE 3.17). Drugs and toxins can also mimic neurotransmitters and bind with their receptors as if they were the real thing. Addictive drugs such as heroin and cocaine, for example, have their effects because they are chemically similar to naturally occurring neurotransmitters; the

agonist Any drug that enhances the actions of a specific neurotransmitter.

antagonist Any drug that inhibits the action of a specific neurotransmitter.

FIGURE 3.17 How Drugs Work

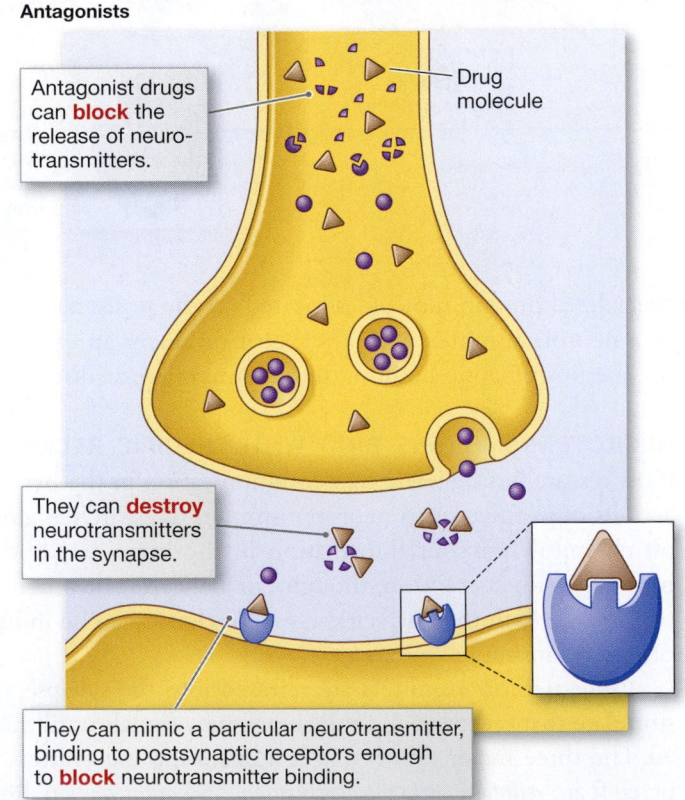

Agonists

Agonist drugs can **increase** the release of neurotransmitters.

Drug molecule

They can **block** the reuptake of neurotransmitters.

They can mimic a particular neurotransmitter, binding to postsynaptic receptors and either **activating** them or **increasing** the neurotransmitter's effects.

Antagonists

Antagonist drugs can **block** the release of neurotransmitters.

Drug molecule

They can **destroy** neurotransmitters in the synapse.

They can mimic a particular neurotransmitter, binding to postsynaptic receptors enough to **block** neurotransmitter binding.

receptors cannot differentiate between the ingested drug and the real neurotransmitter released from a presynaptic neuron. That is, although the relationship between a neurotransmitter and receptor is like a lock and key, the receptor cannot tell a real key from a forgery—either will open it.

Researchers often inject agonists or antagonists into animals' brains to assess a neurotransmitter's behavioral effects. In this way, they are working to develop drug treatments for many psychological and medical disorders. For instance, researchers can test the hypothesis that a certain neurotransmitter in a specific brain region leads to increased eating. Injecting an agonist into that brain region should increase eating while injecting an antagonist should decrease eating. Because obesity has become a major health problem in many industrialized countries, scientists are seeking the "magic pill" that will help decrease how much food a person eats (see Chapter 10, "Health and Well-Being").

TYPES OF NEUROTRANSMITTERS There are many kinds of neurotransmitters. Nine of them have been the focus of research in psychological science; these neurotransmitters are particularly important in understanding how we think, feel, and behave (**TABLE 3.1**).

The neurotransmitter **acetylcholine (ACh)** is responsible for motor control at the junctions between nerves and muscles. Terminal buttons release acetylcholine into synapses. After moving across the synapses, it binds with receptors on muscle cells, making the muscles contract or relax. For instance, ACh excites skeletal muscles and inhibits heart muscles. As is true of all neurotransmitters, whether ACh's effects will be excitatory or inhibitory depends on the receptors. Botulism, a form of food poisoning, inhibits the release of ACh from terminal buttons, leading to difficulty in breathing and chewing and often to death. Because of its ability to paralyze muscles, botulism is used in small, much less toxic doses for cosmetic surgery. Physicians inject botulism, popularly known as Botox, into the eyebrow region, paralyzing muscles that produce certain

acetylcholine (ACh) The neurotransmitter responsible for motor control at the junction between nerves and muscles; also involved in mental processes such as learning, memory, sleeping, and dreaming.

Table 3.1 Common Neurotransmitters and Their Major Functions

Neurotransmitter	Functions
acetylcholine	Motor control over muscles Learning, memory, sleeping, and dreaming
epinephrine	Energy
norepinephrine	Arousal and vigilance
serotonin	Emotional states and impulsiveness Dreaming
dopamine	Reward and motivation Motor control over voluntary movement
GABA (gamma-aminobutyric acid)	Inhibition of action potentials Anxiety and intoxication
glutamate	Enhances action potentials Learning and memory
endorphins	Pain reduction Reward
substance P	Pain perception Mood and anxiety

"I'LL HAVE TO GET DR. KENDRICK TO REDUCE HIS DOSAGE OF PROZAC."

epinephrine The neurotransmitter responsible for adrenaline rushes, bursts of energy caused by its release throughout the body.

noreinephrine The neurotransmitter involved in states of arousal and awareness.

serotonin A monoamine neurotransmitter important for a wide range of psychological activity, including emotional states, impulse control, and dreaming.

FIGURE 3.18 Acetylcholine and Botox Acetylcholine (ACh) is responsible for motor control between nerves and muscles. Botox inhibits the release of ACh, paralyzing muscles.

wrinkles (**FIGURE 3.18**). Because the effects wear off over time, a new dose of botulism needs to be injected every two to four months. If too much Botox is injected, however, the result can be an expressionless face, because Botox paralyzes the facial muscles we use to express emotions, as in smiling and frowning.

Acetylcholine is also involved in complex mental processes such as learning, memory, sleeping, and dreaming. Because ACh affects memory and attention, drugs that are ACh antagonists can cause temporary amnesia. In a similar way, Alzheimer's disease, a condition characterized primarily by severe memory deficits, is associated with diminished ACh functioning (Geula & Mesulam, 1994). Drugs that are ACh agonists may enhance memory and decrease other symptoms, but so far drug treatments for Alzheimer's have experienced only marginal success.

Four of these transmitters (epinephrine, norepinephrine, serotonin, and dopamine) are called *monoamines*. Their major functions are to regulate states of arousal and affect (feelings) and to motivate behavior. As discussed above, monoamine oxidase (MAO) is an enzyme that interrupts the activity of all monoamines. Men who have a gene that produces low levels of MAO and who have been mistreated as children are much more likely to be convicted of violent crimes.

The neurotransmitter **epinephrine** is found throughout the body, with small amounts in the brain. It was initially called *adrenaline* and is the basis for the phrase *adrenaline rush,* a burst of energy caused by its release in the body. **Noreinephrine** is involved in states of arousal and alertness. Norepinephrine is especially important for vigilance, a heightened sensitivity to what is going on around you. Norepinephrine appears useful for fine-tuning the clarity of attention; it inhibits responsiveness to weak synaptic inputs and strengthens or maintains responsiveness to strong synaptic inputs.

Serotonin is involved in many diverse behaviors; it is especially important for emotional states, impulse control, and dreaming. Low levels of serotonin are associated with sad and anxious moods, food cravings, and aggressive behavior. Drugs that block serotonin reuptake and thus leave more serotonin in the synapse to bind with the postsynaptic neurons are now used to treat a wide array of

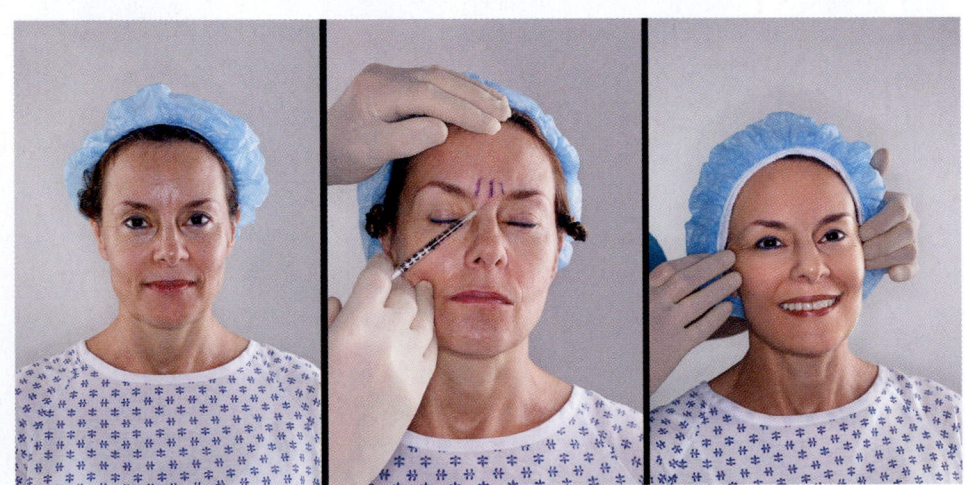

mental and behavioral disorders, including depression, obsessive-compulsive disorders, eating disorders, and obesity (Tollesfson, 1995). One class of drugs that specifically target serotonin is prescribed widely to treat depression; these drugs, which include Prozac, are referred to as *selective serotonin reuptake inhibitors,* or *SSRIs.*

Dopamine serves many significant brain functions, especially motivation and motor control. Many theorists believe dopamine is the primary neurotransmitter that communicates which activities may be rewarding. Eating when hungry, drinking when thirsty, and having sex when aroused, for example, activate dopamine receptors and therefore are experienced as pleasurable. At the same time, dopamine activation is involved in motor control and planning, thereby guiding behavior toward things—objects and experiences—that will lead to additional reward. Dopamine also is involved in controlling voluntary muscle movements. Research in the past few decades implicates dopamine depletion in **Parkinson's disease,** a degenerative and fatal neurological disorder marked by muscular rigidity, tremors, and difficulty initiating voluntary action. With Parkinson's disease, the dopamine-producing neurons slowly die off. In the later stages of the disorder, people suffer from cognitive and mood disturbances. Injections of one of the chief building blocks of dopamine, *L-DOPA,* help the surviving neurons produce more dopamine. When used to treat Parkinson's disease, L-DOPA often produces a remarkable, though temporary, recovery.

A promising development in Parkinson's research is the transplanting of fetal tissue into human brains in the hope that the new fetal cells will produce dopamine. The first American to undergo fetal neural transplantation, Donald Wilson, regained the ability to walk and returned to his hobby of woodworking. Brain scans showed an increased release of dopamine one year following implantation (**FIGURE 3.19**). Although case studies indicate that fetal transplants have promise for treating Parkinson's disease, clinical studies using random assignment have not found large differences between patients receiving fetal cell transplants and those undergoing sham surgery, which mimics the real surgery but does not involve transplantation (Olanow et al., 2003). These methods are still being developed, though, and researchers continue to explore how fetal cell transplants might be used to treat brain disorders.

GABA (gamma-aminobutyric acid) is the primary inhibitory transmitter in the nervous system and works throughout the brain. Without the inhibitory effect of GABA, synaptic excitation might get out of control and spread through the brain chaotically. Epileptic seizures may happen because of low levels of GABA (Upton, 1994). Drugs that are GABA agonists are also widely used to treat anxiety disorders. For instance, people with nervous disorders commonly use benzodiazepines, which include drugs such as Valium, to relax. Ethyl alcohol—the type people drink—has similar effects on GABA receptors, which is why alcohol typically is experienced as relaxing. GABA reception also may be the primary mechanism by which alcohol interferes with motor coordination (**FIGURE 3.20**).

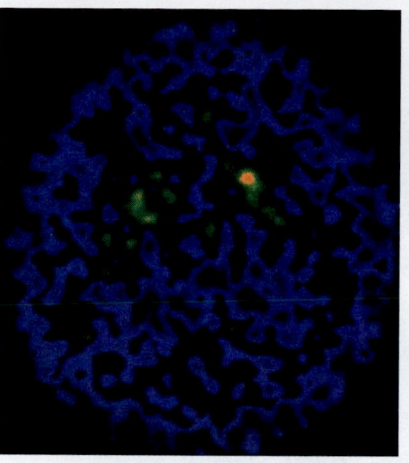
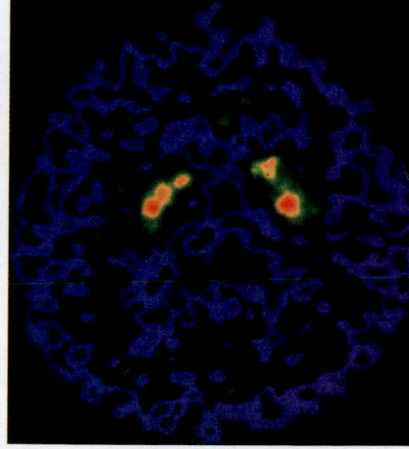

FIGURE 3.19 Dopamine Activity These PET scans show dopamine activity before **(left)** and after fetal transplant surgery **(right)**. The visible increase suggests that the transplant was successful and that the new neurons are producing dopamine.

dopamine A monoamine neurotransmitter involved in reward, motivation, and motor control.

Parkinson's disease A neurological disorder that seems to be caused by dopamine depletion, marked by muscular rigidity, tremors, and difficulty initiating voluntary action.

GABA (gamma-aminobutyric acid) The primary inhibitory transmitter in the nervous system.

FIGURE 3.20 GABA and Alcohol Consumption GABA (gamma-aminobutyric acid) is the primary inhibitory transmitter in the nervous system. By affecting GABA receptors, alcohol produces a relaxed feeling and interferes with motor coordination.

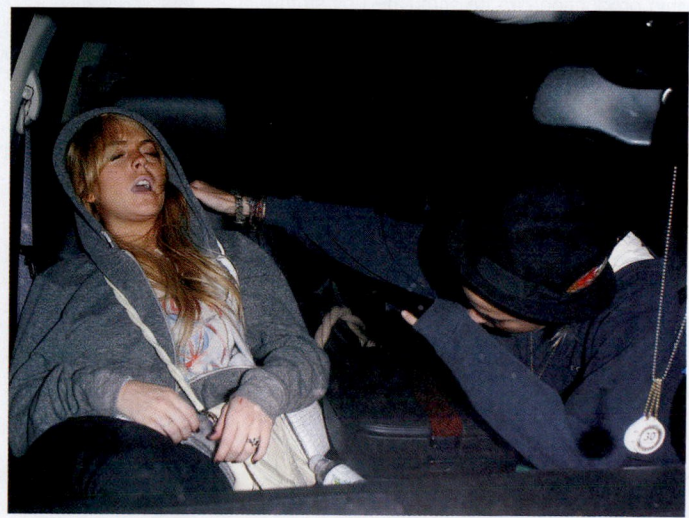

FIGURE 3.21 Glutamate and MSG
Glutamate is the primary excitatory transmitter in the nervous system. Monosodium glutamate is a sodium salt of glutamic acid, commonly used as a flavor enhancer in foods.

FIGURE 3.22 Endorphins and Runner's High Endorphins are involved in both pain reduction and reward. It is thought that endorphin production can be stimulated by strenuous exercise, such as running a marathon. Here, David Mandago of Kenya celebrates after winning the Hamburg Marathon in 2008.

glutamate The primary excitatory transmitter in the nervous system.

endorphins A neurotransmitter involved in natural pain reduction and reward.

substance P A neurotransmitter involved in pain perception.

In contrast, **glutamate** is the primary excitatory transmitter in the nervous system, opening sodium gates in postsynaptic membranes, and is involved in fast-acting neural transmission throughout the brain. Glutamate receptors aid learning and memory by strengthening synaptic connections (**FIGURE 3.21**).

Endorphins are involved in both natural pain reduction and reward (**FIGURE 3.22**). In the early 1970s, the pharmacology researchers Candace Pert and Solomon Snyder established that opiate drugs such as heroin and morphine bind to receptors in the brain, and this finding led to the discovery of naturally occurring substances that bind to those sites. Called *endorphins* (short for *endogenous morphine*), these substances are part of the body's natural defense against pain. Pain is useful because it signals to animals, human and nonhuman, that they are hurt or in danger and therefore should try to escape or withdraw, but pain can also interfere with adaptive functioning. If pain prevented animals from engaging in behaviors such as eating, competing, and mating, they would fail to pass along their genes. Endorphins' painkilling, or analgesic, effects help animals perform these behaviors even when they are in pain. In humans, administration of drugs, such as morphine, that bind with endorphin receptors reduces the subjective experience of pain. Apparently, morphine alters the way pain is experienced rather than blocking the nerves that transmit pain signals: People still feel pain, but report detachment and do not experience the pain as aversive (Foley, 1993).

Substance P is another neurotransmitter involved in pain perception as well as mood states and anxiety. This mysterious-sounding substance was first identified in 1931 by the pharmacology researchers Ulf von Euler and John Gaddum, who referred to it in their notes simply by the initial "P." Substance P helps transmit signals about pain to the brain. Probably the best evidence for it can be found

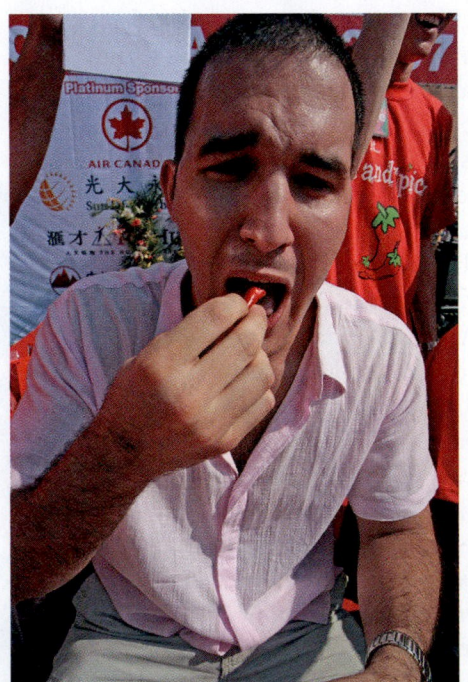

at your local Mexican restaurant, where you can conduct your own experiment. Chili peppers, such as jalapeños, contain the substance capsaicin, which activates sensory neurons and leads to the release of substance P in the brain. This neural activity makes your tongue and mouth burn, your eyes water, and your hand reach for the nearest pitcher of water—though water spreads capsaicin around and causes the release of more substance P, which only intensifies the pain (**FIGURE 3.23**).

FIGURE 3.23 Substance P and Chili Peppers The burning that comes from eating chili peppers is due to the release of substance P, a neurotransmitter involved in pain perception.

How Does the Nervous System Operate?

Neurons are the nervous system's basic units. Their primary task is to take in information, integrate that information, and pass signals to other neurons. A neuron receives information at the dendrites and processes that information in its cell body. It passes signals down its axon and then to other neurons' dendrites by firing. The insulating myelin sheath surrounding the axon allows the firing, or action potential, to travel, or propagate, rapidly. When a neuron is in a resting state, it is (slightly) negatively charged. Whether a neuron fires depends on the combination of excitatory and inhibitory signals the dendrites receive. Excitatory neurotransmitters make the postsynaptic neuron more likely to fire, and inhibitory neurotransmitters make the postsynaptic neuron less likely to fire. This firing results from the changes in the electrical charge across the cell membrane: sodium ions rush in when the sodium channels open, and potassium ions rush out when the potassium channels open. When the channels close, sodium ions stop entering and potassium ions stop exiting, allowing the neuron to return to its resting state. The intensity of the excitatory signal affects the frequency of neural firing but not its strength—neurons fire on an all-or-none basis.

Action potentials cause vesicles to release neurotransmitters into the synaptic cleft. Neurotransmitters diffuse across the synaptic cleft and bind with specific postsynaptic receptors. These signals are terminated through reuptake, enzyme deactivation, or the actions of autoreceptors. Substances that enhance neurotransmitters' actions are agonists; those that inhibit action are antagonists. The number of known substances that act as neurotransmitters is now more than 60 and growing, but certain neurotransmitters are especially important for psychological research: Acetycholine is involved in motor movement as well as complex thought, dopamine is involved in emotion and motor movement, serotonin is important in mood regulation and dreaming, GABA and glutamate are related to general inhibition and excitation, endorphins are important in pain reduction, and substance P is important in pain perception.

▶ MEASURING UP

1. Neurons communicate by firing. Put the following steps in the correct order so they describe this process.
   a. The presynaptic neuron "reuptakes" the neurotransmitter from the synapse.
   b. If the receptors allow a sufficient excess of excitatory neurotransmitters into the cell, the postsynaptic neuron will respond by opening its sodium and potassium gates.
   c. Neurotransmitters bind with receptors on the postsynaptic neuron's dendrites.
   d. Excitatory and inhibitory messages are compared in the cell body of the postsynaptic neuron.
   e. Neurotransmitters are released into the synapse by a presynaptic neuron.
   f. The charge inside the cell goes from negative to positive.
   g. The gates open in succession as the information is passed along the axon away from the cell body and toward the terminal buttons.
   h. The sodium and potassium gates close, and the neuron returns to its resting potential.

2. Match each major neurotransmitter with its major functions.

The neurotransmitters are	The major functions are
a. substance P	1. emotional states, dreaming
b. glutamate	2. reward, motivation, voluntary muscle control
c. acetylcholine	3. enhancing action potentials, facilitating learning and memory
d. serotonin	4. pain perception, mood and anxiety
e. endorphins	5. motor control, learning, memory, dreaming
f. dopamine	6. reward, pain reduction
g. GABA	7. inhibiting action potentials, reducing anxiety, producing intoxication

What Are the Basic Brain Structures and Their Functions?

LEARNING OBJECTIVE
Identify the basic structures in the brain and their primary functions.

central nervous system (CNS) The brain and spinal cord.

peripheral nervous system (PNS) All nerve cells in the body that are not part of the central nervous system. The PNS includes the somatic and autonomic nervous systems.

The nervous system is an amazing network, responsible for everything we think, feel, or do. It is divided into two functional units: the **central nervous system (CNS)**, which consists of the spinal cord and brain, and the **peripheral nervous system (PNS)**, which consists of all the other nerve cells in the body. The two systems are anatomically separate, but their functions are highly interdependent. The PNS transmits a variety of information to the CNS, which organizes and evaluates that information and then directs the PNS to perform specific behaviors or make bodily adjustments. The discussion below first considers the CNS, focusing on the relation between the brain and psychological function.

Consider the human brain's complexity. The first animals' nervous systems were probably little more than a few specialized cells with the capacity for electrical signaling. An adult human brain today weighs approximately 3 pounds (1.4 kilograms) and has the consistency of a soft-boiled egg. The brain is best viewed as a collection of interacting neural circuits that have accumulated and developed throughout human evolution. Through the process of adapting to the environment, the brain has evolved specialized mechanisms to regulate breathing, food intake, sexual behavior, and bodily fluids, as well as sensory systems to aid in navigation and assist in recognizing friends and foes. Everything we are and do is accomplished by the brain and, for more rudimentary actions, the spinal cord. Early in life, overabundant connections form among the brain's neurons; subsequently, life experiences help "prune" some of these connections to strengthen the rest.

The brain's basic structures and their functions enable us to accomplish feats such as seeing, hearing, remembering, and interacting with others. Understanding these relationships also helps us understand psychological disorders. As we learn more about the brain, however, we must avoid jumping to conclusions about brain/behavior relationships that are not warranted by the data.

THE BRAIN: A BRIEF HISTORY OF UNDERSTANDING ITS FUNCTIONS

Psychological scientists have learned a great deal of what they know about the functioning of different brain regions through the careful study of people whose brains have been damaged by disease or injury. Perhaps the most famous historical example of brain damage is the case of Phineas Gage. In 1848, Gage was a 25-year-old foreman on the construction of Vermont's Rutland and Burlington Railroad. One day, he dropped his tamping iron on a rock, igniting some blasting powder. The resulting explosion drove the iron rod—over a yard long and an inch in diameter—into his cheek, through his frontal lobes, and clear out through the top of his head (**FIGURE 3.24**). Gage was still conscious as he was hurried back to town on a cart. Able to walk, with assistance, upstairs to his hotel bed, he wryly remarked to the awaiting physician, "Doctor, here is business enough for you," and said he expected to return to work in a few days. In fact, Gage lapsed into unconsciousness and remained unconscious for two weeks. Afterward, his condition steadily improved, and he recovered remarkably well, at least physically.

Unfortunately, Gage's accident led to major personality changes. Whereas the old Gage had been regarded by his employers as "the most efficient and capable" of workers, the new Gage was not. As one of his doctors later wrote, "The equilibrium or balance, so to speak, between his intellectual faculties and animal propensities seems to have been destroyed. He is fitful, irreverent, indulging at times in the grossest profanity, . . . impatient of restraint or advice when it conflicts with his desires. . . . A child in his intellectual capacity and manifestations, he has the animal passions of a strong man." In summary, Gage was "no longer Gage."

Unable to get his foreman's job back, Gage exhibited himself in various New England towns and at the New York Museum (owned by P. T. Barnum), worked at the stables of the Hanover Inn at Dartmouth College, and drove coaches and tended horses in Chile. After a decade, his health began to decline, and in 1860 he started having epileptic seizures and died within a few months. Gage's recovery was initially used to argue that the entire brain works uniformly and that the healthy parts of Gage's brain had taken over the damaged parts' work. However, the medical community eventually recognized that Gage's psychological impairments had been severe and that some areas of the brain in fact have specific functions. Gage's case provided the basis for the first modern theories of the role of a part of the brain called the prefrontal cortex in personality and self-control. Reconstruction of Gage's injury through examination of his skull has made it

FIGURE 3.24 Phineas Gage As discussed below, analysis of Gage's damaged skull provided the basis for the first modern theories of the prefrontal cortex's role in both personality and self-control. **(a)** This photo shows Gage's death mask next to his skull. **(b)** This computer-generated image reconstructs the rod's probable path into the skull.

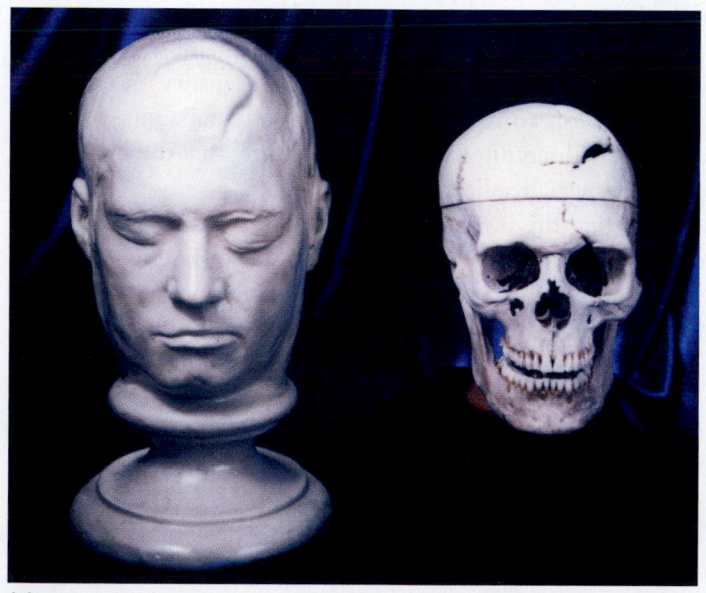

(a)

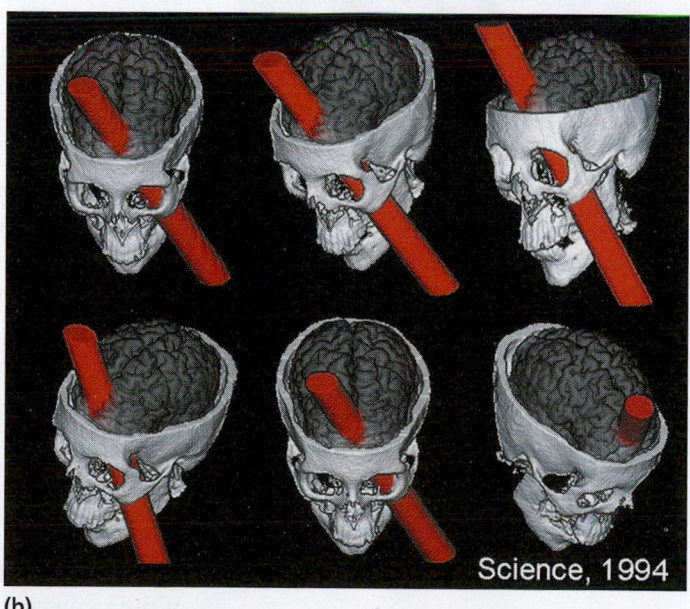

Science, 1994

(b)

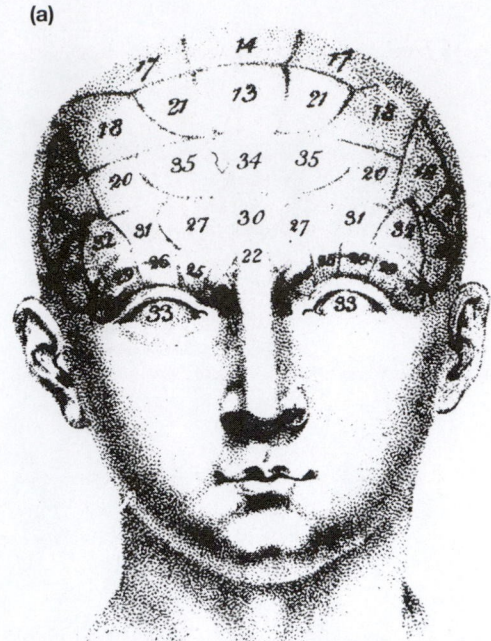

(a)

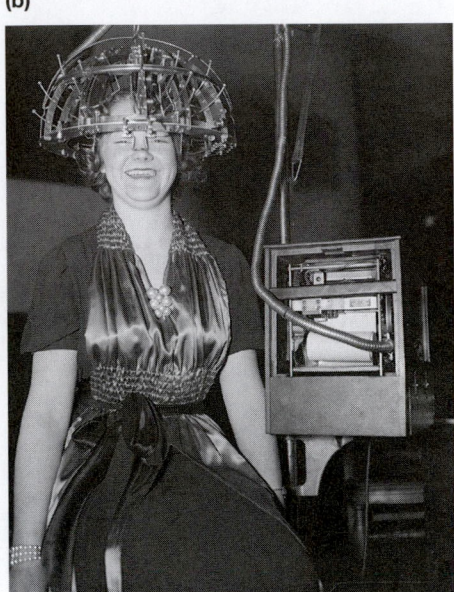

(b)

FIGURE 3.25 Phrenology and the Psychograph (a) In the early nineteenth century, Johann Spurzheim created phrenological maps of the skull, including this one, where each numbered region corresponds to a different characteristic. **(b)** Psychographs, such as the one depicted here, were marketed as being able to "do the work of a psychoanalyst" by showing "your talents, abilities, strong and weak traits, without prejudice or flattery."

Broca's area The left frontal region of the brain, crucial for the production of language.

clear that the prefrontal cortex was the area most damaged by the tamping rod (Damasio, Grabowski, Frank, Galaburda, & Damasio, 1994). Recent studies of patients with similar injuries reveal that this brain region is particularly concerned with social phenomena, such as following social norms, understanding what other people are thinking, and feeling emotionally connected to others. People with damage to this region do not typically have problems with memory or general knowledge, but they often have profound disturbances in their ability to get along with others.

The brain was not always recognized as the mind's home. The ancient Egyptians, for example, viewed the heart as more important; they elaborately embalmed each dead person's heart, which was to be weighed in the afterlife to determine the deceased's fate. The person's brain, however, they simply threw away. But in the following centuries, especially among the Greeks and Romans, recognition grew that the brain was essential for normal mental functioning. Much of this change came from observing people with brain injuries. At least since the time of the Roman gladiators, it was clear that a blow to the head often produced disturbances in mental activity, such as unconsciousness or the loss of speech.

By the beginning of the nineteenth century, anatomists understood the brain's basic structure reasonably well. But debates raged over how the brain produced mental activity. Did different parts do different things? Or were all areas of the brain equally important in cognitive activities such as problem solving and memory (an idea called *equipotentiality*)? In the early nineteenth century, the neuroscientist Franz Gall and his assistant, the physician Johann Spurzheim, proposed their theory of *phrenology*, based on the idea that the brain operates through functional localization. *Phrenology* is the practice of assessing personality traits and mental abilities by measuring bumps on the human skull. The theory of phrenology was so popular that in the 1930s an enterprising company manufactured 33 Psychographs. Psychographs were devices used to tell about participants' personalities based on the locations and sizes of bumps on their heads. That these machines were popular at state fairs and amusement parks suggests few people, if any, took the personality readings seriously (**FIGURE 3.25**).

Although phrenology was an influential theory in its day because it was based on the seemingly scientific principle that brain functions were localized, its validity could not be tested scientifically. Taking this general idea of localization, the behavioral psychologist Karl Lashley set out to identify the places in the brain where learning occurred. Lashley believed that specific brain regions (namely, parts of the cortex—discussed below) were involved in motor control and sensory experiences, but that all other parts of the brain contributed equally to mental abilities. Today, Lashley's theory has been largely discredited, and we now know that the brain consists of a patchwork of highly specialized areas.

The first strong evidence that the brain regions perform specialized functions came from the work of the physician and anatomist Paul Broca (Finger, 1994). In 1861, Broca performed an autopsy on his patient Monsieur Leborgne. Before his death, Leborgne had lost the ability to say anything other than the word *tan* but could still understand language. When he examined Leborgne's brain, Broca found substantial damage to the front left side, caused by a large lesion. This observation led him to conclude that this particular region was important for speech. Broca's theory has survived the test of time. This left frontal region became known as **Broca's area,** and it has since been repeatedly confirmed to be crucial for the production of language (**FIGURE 3.26**).

The debate over whether psychological processes are located in specific parts of the brain or distributed throughout the brain continued so long, in part, because

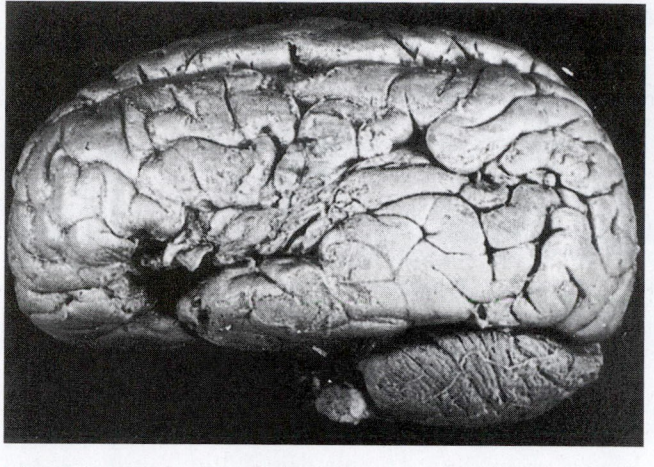

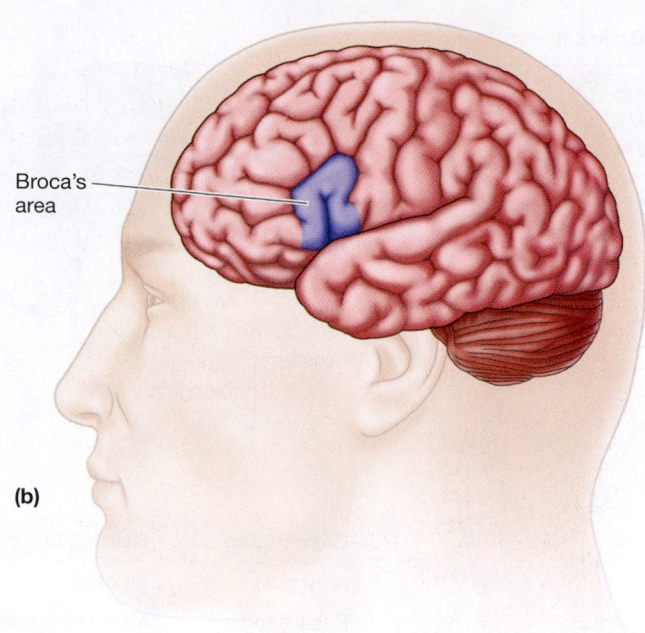

(a)

(b)

FIGURE 3.26 **Broca's Area** **(a)** Paul Broca studied Monsieur Leborgne's brain and identified the lesioned area as crucial for speech production. **(b)** This illustration shows the location of Broca's area.

until fairly recently researchers have not had methods for studying ongoing mental activity in the working brain. The invention of brain imaging methods in the late 1980s changed that situation swiftly and dramatically. Since then, research has exploded, cutting across various levels of analysis, linking specific brain areas with particular behaviors and mental processes. The new imaging techniques have advanced our understanding of the human brain the way the development of telescopes advanced our understanding of astronomy—and the brain's structures and functions may be as complex as distant galaxies. Although philosophers have long debated what it means to be conscious of something, psychological scientists now examine, even measure, consciousness and other mental states that were previously viewed as too subjective to be studied.

The following sections consider the question of how brain and mind are connected. These sections also explore how the mind is adaptive, one of this text's seven major themes.

The Brainstem Houses the Basic Programs of Survival

The spinal cord is a rope of neural tissue that runs inside the hollows of the vertebrae from just above the pelvis up into the base of the skull (**FIGURE 3.27**). The spinal cord coordinates each reflex—a handful of neurons' simple conversion of sensation into action—but its most important function is to carry sensory information up to the brain and carry signals from the brain to the body parts below. In cross section, the cord is seen to be composed of two distinct tissue types: the *gray matter,* which is dominated by neurons' cell bodies, and the *white matter,* which consists mostly of axons and the fatty sheaths that surround them. Gray and white matter are clearly distinguishable throughout the brain as well.

In the base of the skull, the spinal cord thickens and becomes more complex as it transforms into the **brainstem.** Consisting of the *medulla oblongata,* the *pons,* and the *midbrain,* the brainstem houses the nerves that control the most basic functions of survival, such as breathing, swallowing, vomiting, urination, and orgasm. As a continuous extension of the spinal cord, the brainstem performs functions for the head

brainstem A section of the bottom of the brain, housing the most basic programs of survival, such as breathing, swallowing, vomiting, urination, and orgasm.

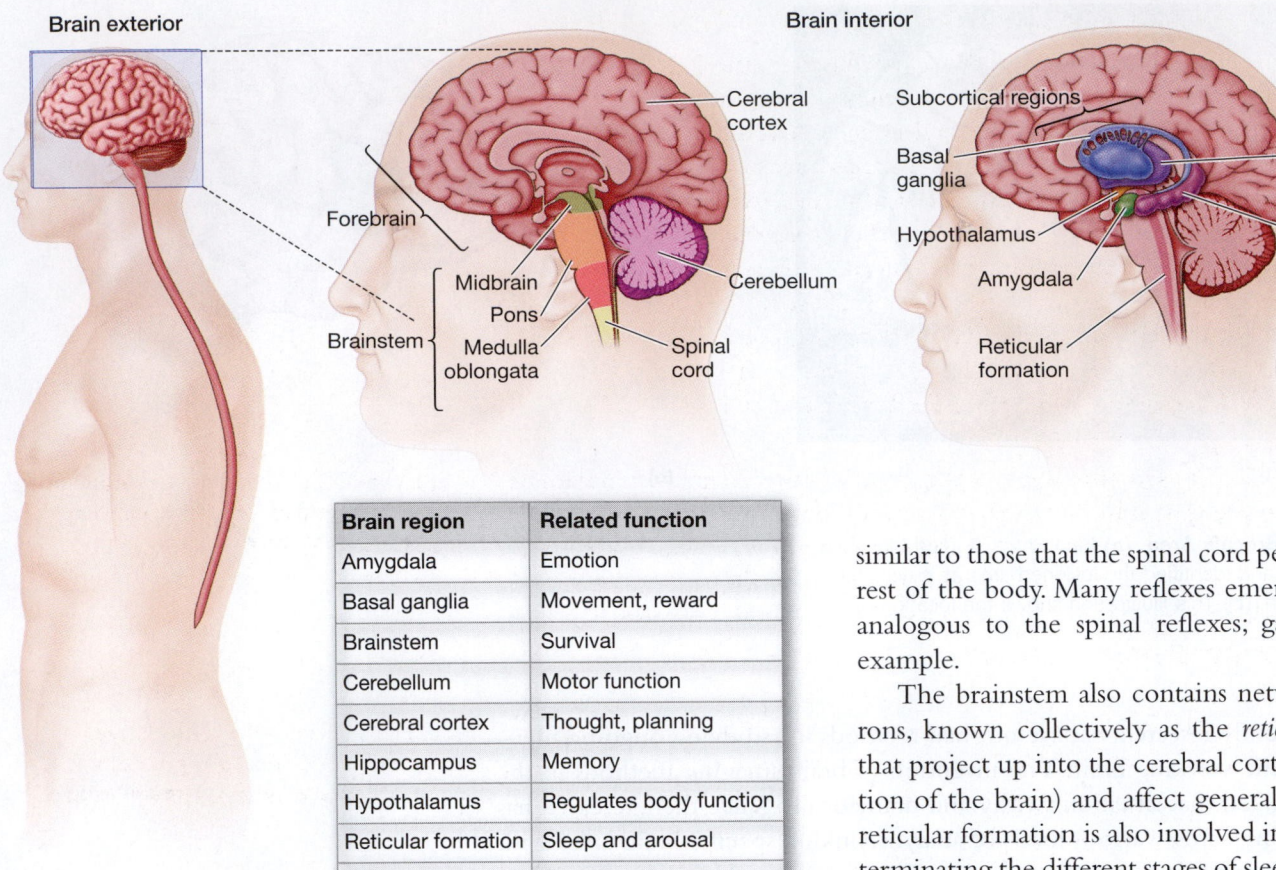

Brain region	Related function
Amygdala	Emotion
Basal ganglia	Movement, reward
Brainstem	Survival
Cerebellum	Motor function
Cerebral cortex	Thought, planning
Hippocampus	Memory
Hypothalamus	Regulates body function
Reticular formation	Sleep and arousal
Thalamus	Sensory gateway

FIGURE 3.27 The Structures of the Brain

cerebellum A large, convoluted protuberance at the back of the brainstem, essential for coordinated movement and balance.

similar to those that the spinal cord performs for the rest of the body. Many reflexes emerge from here, analogous to the spinal reflexes; gagging is one example.

The brainstem also contains networks of neurons, known collectively as the *reticular formation,* that project up into the cerebral cortex (outer portion of the brain) and affect general alertness. The reticular formation is also involved in inducing and terminating the different stages of sleep (as discussed in Chapter 4, "The Mind and Consciousness").

The Cerebellum Is Essential for Movement

The **cerebellum** (Latin, "little brain") is a large protuberance connected to the back of the brainstem (see Figure 3.27). Its size and convoluted surface make it look like an extra brain. The cerebellum is extremely important for proper motor function, and lesions to its different parts produce very different effects. Damage to the little nodes at the very bottom causes head tilt, balance problems, and a loss of smooth compensation of eye position for head movement. Try turning your head while looking at this book and notice that your eyes remain focused on the material. Your eyes would not be able to do that if an injury affected the bottom of your cerebellum. Damage to the ridge that runs up its back would affect your walking. Damage to the bulging lobes on either side would cause a loss of limb coordination, so you would not be able to perform tasks such as reaching smoothly to pick up a pen.

The cerebellum's most obvious role is in motor learning. It seems to be "trained" by the rest of the nervous system and operates independently and unconsciously. The cerebellum allows you, for example, to ride a bicycle effortlessly while thinking about what you will eat for lunch. Functional imaging studies indicate an even broader role for the cerebellum, suggesting it is involved in various cognitive processes, including making plans, remembering events, using language, and experiencing emotion. Researchers have observed the cerebellum's activation when a person experiences a painful stimulus or observes a loved one receiving that stimulus, so the cerebellum may be involved in the experience of empathy (Lamm, Batson, & Decety, 2007; Singer et al., 2004).

Subcortical Structures Control Emotions and Basic Drives

Above the brainstem and cerebellum is the *forebrain* (see Figure 3.27), which consists of the two cerebral hemispheres (left and right). From the outside, the most noticeable feature of the forebrain is the *cerebral cortex* (discussed in the next section). Below this are the *subcortical* regions, so named because they lie under the cortex. Subcortical structures that are important for understanding psychological functions include the *hypothalamus,* the *thalamus,* the *hippocampus,* the *amygdala,* and the *basal ganglia.* Some of these structures belong to the *limbic system; limbic* means "border" and separates the evolutionarily older (brainstem and cerebellum) and newer (cerebral cortex) parts of the brain. The brain structures in the limbic system are especially important for controlling basic drives, such as eating and drinking, and emotions (as discussed in Chapter 9, "Motivation and Emotion").

HYPOTHALAMUS The **hypothalamus** is the brain's master regulatory structure. Indispensable to the organism's survival, it receives input from almost everywhere in the body and brain and projects its influence to almost everywhere in the body and brain. It affects many internal organs' functions, regulating body temperature, body rhythms, blood pressure, and blood glucose levels. It is also involved in many basic drives, including thirst, hunger, aggression, and lust.

hypothalamus A small brain structure that is vital for temperature regulation, emotion, sexual behavior, and motivation.

THALAMUS The **thalamus** is the gateway to the cortex: Almost all incoming sensory information must go through the thalamus before reaching the cortex. The only exception to this rule is the sense of smell, the oldest and most fundamental sense; it has a direct route to the cortex. During sleep, the thalamus shuts the gate on incoming sensations while the brain rests. (The thalamus is discussed further in Chapter 5, "Sensation and Perception.")

thalamus The gateway to the brain; it receives almost all incoming sensory information before that information reaches the cortex.

HIPPOCAMPUS AND AMYGDALA The **hippocampus** (Greek, "sea horse," for its sea horse shape) plays an important role in the storage of new memories. It seems to do this important work by creating new interconnections within the cerebral cortex with each new experience. Karl Lashley, in his research discussed above, failed to find the location of memory by removing parts of rats' cerebral cortices (plural of *cortex*). Had he damaged their hippocampal formations as well, his results would have been quite different.

hippocampus A brain structure important for the formation of certain types of memory.

Consistent with its role in memory formation, the hippocampus has recently been shown to grow larger with increased use. One hypothesis suggests that the hippocampus may be involved in how we remember the arrangements of both places and objects in space, such as how streets are laid out in a city or how furniture is positioned in a room. The best study to support this theory focused on London taxi drivers. Maguire and colleagues (2003) found that one region of the hippocampus was much larger in London taxi drivers' brains than in most other London drivers' brains. Is a person with a large hippocampus more likely to drive a taxi? Or does the hippocampus grow as the result of navigational experience? London taxi drivers are, after all, well known for their expertise; to acquire a commercial license a London taxi driver must take an exam testing knowledge of the city's streets. That the volume of gray matter in the hippocampal region was highly correlated with the number of years of experience as a taxi driver suggests that the hippocampus increases its volume to store more accurate and larger representations of the spatial world. Thus it changes with experience. This phenomenon is just one of many examples of the way the brain's size and structure change in response to experiences.

amygdala A brain structure that serves a vital role in our learning to associate things with emotional responses and in processing emotional information.

The **amygdala** (Latin, "almond," for its almond shape), located immediately in front of the hippocampus, serves a vital role in our learning to associate things in the world with emotional responses: an unpleasant food with disgust, for example. The amygdala thus enables the organism to overrule instinctive responses by connecting memories of things to the emotions engendered by those things. The amygdala also intensifies memory's function during times of emotional arousal. For example, a frightening experience can be seared into your memory for life, although (as discussed further in Chapter 7, "Attention and Memory") your memory of the event may not be completely accurate.

The amygdala plays a special role in our responding to stimuli that elicit fear. Affective processing of frightening stimuli in the amygdala is a hard-wired circuit that has developed over the course of evolution to protect animals from danger. The amygdala is also involved in evaluating a facial expression's emotional significance (Adolphs et al., 2005). Imaging studies have found that the amygdala activates especially strongly in response to a fearful face (Whalen et al., 2005).

Recent neuroimaging investigations have also implicated the amygdala in the processing of more positive emotions, including sexual arousal. Hamann and colleagues (2004) have found that activity within the amygdala increases when people view sexually arousing stimuli, such as nude photos or videos of sexual activity, and that the amygdala activates markedly higher in men. It has long been observed that males are more responsive than females to visual sexual stimuli; this study suggests that the amygdala may play a role in that greater responsiveness.

basal ganglia A system of subcortical structures that are important for the initiation of planned movement.

THE BASAL GANGLIA The **basal ganglia** are a system of subcortical structures crucial for planning and producing movement. They receive input from the entire cerebral cortex and project to the motor centers of the brainstem and, via the thalamus, back to the cortex's motor planning area. Evidence indicates that damage to the basal ganglia can impair the learning of movements and of habits, such as automatically looking for cars before you cross the street.

One structure in the basal ganglia, the *nucleus accumbens,* provides a good example of how environment interacts with the brain. Research has shown that the nucleus accumbens is important for experiencing reward. As discussed in Chapter 6, nearly every pleasurable experience, from eating chocolate (if you like chocolate) to looking at a person you find attractive, activates dopamine neurons in the nucleus accumbens. One brain imaging study found that viewing expensive sports cars led to greater activation of the nucleus accumbens in men than did viewing less expensive economy cars. Society generally values expensive objects, so this study and others indicate that cultural beliefs help make particular objects desirable and that the more desirable objects are, the more they activate basic reward circuitry in our brains (Erk, Spitzer, Wunderlich, Galley, & Walter, 2002).

The Cerebral Cortex Underlies Complex Mental Activity

cerebral cortex The outer layer of brain tissue, which forms the convoluted surface of the brain.

The **cerebral cortex** is the outer layer of the cerebral hemispheres and gives the brain its distinctive, wrinkled appearance. (*Cortex* is Latin for "bark"—the kind on trees.) In humans, the cortex is relatively enormous—the size of a large sheet of newspaper—and folded in against itself many times so as to fit within the skull. It is the site of all thoughts, detailed perceptions, and consciousness—in short, of everything that makes us human. It is also the source of culture and communication, allowing us to learn fine distinctions and intricate details of the outside world, to understand other people, to follow rules, to perform complex behaviors, and to *think* before we act. Each cerebral hemisphere has four "lobes": the *occipital, parietal,* *temporal,* and *frontal* (**FIGURE 3.28**). The *corpus callosum,* a massive bridge of millions of axons, connects the hemispheres and allows information to flow between them.

The **occipital lobe,** at the back portion of the head, is devoted almost exclusively to vision. It consists of many visual areas, of which the *primary visual cortex* is by far the largest and is the major destination for visual information. As discussed further in Chapter 5, visual information is typically organized for the cerebral cortex in a way that preserves spatial relationships: that is, the image, relayed from the eye, is "projected" more or less faithfully onto the primary visual cortex. Two objects near one another in a visual image, then, will activate neurons near one another in the primary visual cortex. Surrounding the primary visual cortex is a patchwork of secondary visual areas that process various attributes of the visual image, such as its colors, forms, and motions.

The **parietal lobe** is devoted partially to touch: It includes the *primary somatosensory* (Greek, "bodily sense") *cortex,* a strip running from the top of the brain down the side. The labor is divided between the left and right cerebral hemispheres: The left hemisphere receives touch information from the right side of the body; the right hemisphere receives touch information from the left side of the body. This information is represented along the primary somatosensory cortex in a way that groups nearby sensations: Sensations on the fingers are near sensations on the palm, for example. The result, covering the primary somatosensory area, is a distorted representation of the entire body: the *somatosensory homunculus* (Greek, "little man"; **FIGURE 3.29**). The homunculus is distorted because more cortical area is devoted to the body's more sensitive areas, such as the face and fingers.

One of the most interesting neurological disorders can result from a stroke or other damage to the right parietal region. In this syndrome, *hemineglect,* patients fail to notice anything on their left sides. Looking in a mirror, they will shave or put makeup on only the right sides of their faces. If two objects are held up before

occipital lobe A region of the cerebral cortex, at the back of the brain, important for vision.

parietal lobe A region of the cerebral cortex, in front of the occipital lobes and behind the frontal lobes, important for the sense of touch and of the spatial layout of an environment.

FIGURE 3.28 The Lobes and Hemispheres of the Cerebral Cortex

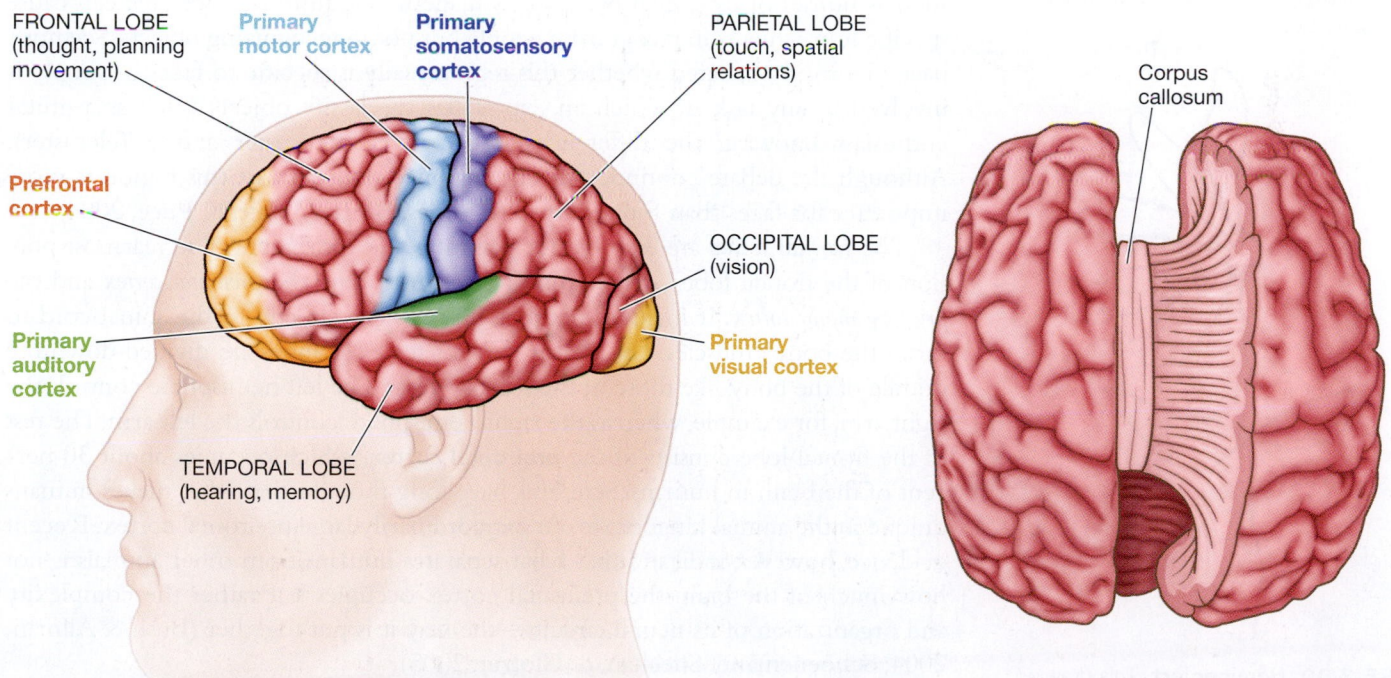

FRONTAL LOBE (thought, planning movement)

Primary motor cortex

Primary somatosensory cortex

PARIETAL LOBE (touch, spatial relations)

Corpus callosum

Prefrontal cortex

OCCIPITAL LOBE (vision)

Primary auditory cortex

Primary visual cortex

TEMPORAL LOBE (hearing, memory)

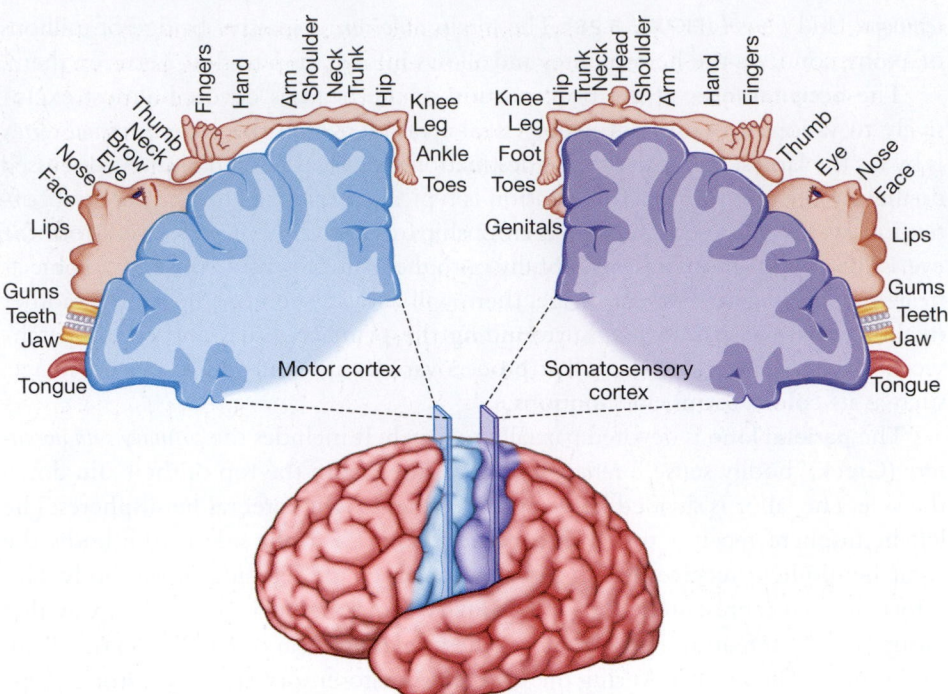

FIGURE 3.29 The Somatosensory and Motor "Homunculus" The cortical representation of the body surface is organized in strips that run down the side of the brain. Connected areas of the body tend to be represented next to each other in the cortex, and more sensitive skin regions have more cortical area devoted to them.

temporal lobes The lower region of the cerebral cortex, important for processing auditory information and for memory.

frontal lobes The region at the front of the cerebral cortex concerned with planning and movement.

prefrontal cortex A region of the frontal lobes, especially prominent in humans, important for attention, working memory, decision making, appropriate social behavior, and personality.

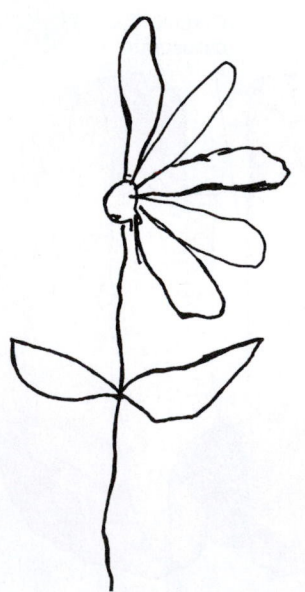

FIGURE 3.30 Hemineglect This drawing, made by a hemineglect patient, omits much of the flower's left side.

them, they will see only the one on the right. Asked to draw a simple object, they will draw only its right half (**FIGURE 3.30**).

The **temporal lobes** hold the *primary auditory cortex,* the brain region responsible for hearing. Also within the temporal lobes are specialized visual areas (for recognizing detailed objects such as faces), plus the hippocampus and amygdala (both critical for memory, as discussed above). At the intersection of the temporal and occipital cortices is the *fusiform face area.* Its name comes from the fact that this area is much more active when people look at faces than when they look at other things. In contrast, other regions of the temporal cortex are more activated by objects, such as houses or cars, than by faces. Damage to the fusiform face area can cause specific impairments in recognizing people but not in recognizing objects. Scientists have vigorously debated whether this region really is specific to faces or simply is involved in any task in which an expert has to classify objects (such as a guitar enthusiast knowing the differences between a Stratocaster and a Telecaster). Although the debate continues, recent evidence suggests that this region is more important for faces than for expertise (Rhodes, Byatt, Michie, & Puce, 2004).

The **frontal lobes** are essential for planning and movement. The rearmost portion of the frontal lobes are the motor areas, including the *premotor cortex* and the *primary motor cortex.* It includes neurons that project directly to the spinal cord to move the body's muscles. The motor cortex's responsibilities are divided down the middle of the body, like those of the sensory areas: The left hemisphere controls the right arm, for example, whereas the right hemisphere controls the left arm. The rest of the frontal lobe consists of the **prefrontal cortex,** which occupies about 30 percent of the brain in humans. Scientists have long thought that what makes humans unique in the animal kingdom is our extraordinarily large prefrontal cortex. Recent evidence, however, indicates that what separates humans from other animals is not how much of the brain the prefrontal cortex occupies but rather the complexity and organization of its neural circuits—the way it is put together (Bush & Allman, 2004; Schoenemann, Sheehan, & Glotzer, 2005).

Parts of the prefrontal cortex are responsible for directing and maintaining attention, keeping ideas in mind while distractions bombard us from the outside world, and developing and acting on plans. Indispensable for rational activity, the prefrontal cortex is especially important for many aspects of human social life, such as understanding what other people are thinking, behaving according to cultural norms, and even contemplating our own existence. It provides both our sense of self and our capacity to empathize with others or feel guilty about harming them.

In the early twentieth century, mental health professionals employed a procedure called *lobotomy,* deliberately damaging the prefrontal cortex, to treat many mental patients (**FIGURE 3.31**). This form of brain surgery generally left patients lethargic and emotionally flat, and therefore much easier to manage in mental hospitals, but it also left them disconnected from their social surroundings. Most lobotomies were performed in the late 1940s and early 1950s.

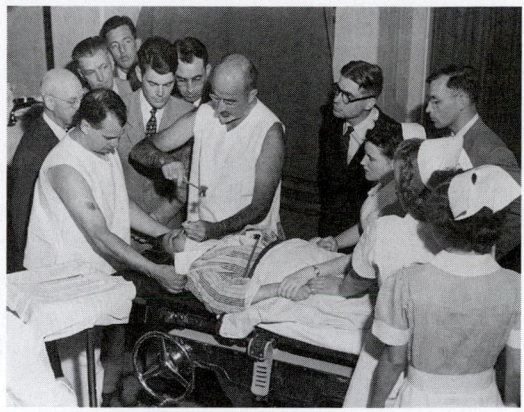

FIGURE 3.31 Lobotomy Dr. Walter Freeman performs a lobotomy by inserting an ice pick–like instrument under the upper eyelid of his patient to cut the nerve connections in the front part of the brain, 1949.

> ## SUMMING UP

What Are the Basic Brain Structures and Their Functions?

The nervous system's different parts all have essential roles. The spinal cord is involved in basic movement and reflexes. The brainstem serves survival functions, controlling breathing and heart rate. At the back of the brainstem is the cerebellum, a workhorse that learns routine habits of movement and possibly of thought. Beneath the cortex, the thalamus serves as a way station through which sensory information travels, the hypothalamus regulates bodily systems and controls the hormonal system, the hippocampus is involved in memory, and the amygdala influences emotional states, especially fear. Finally, the cerebral cortex is the outer surface of the brain, divided into occipital, parietal, temporal, and frontal lobes. Each lobe serves specific functions; the frontal lobe is essential for both higher-level thought and social behavior.

> ## MEASURING UP

1. Match each lobe of the brain with its functions.

   The lobes are
   a. frontal
   b. occipital
   c. parietal
   d. temporal

   The functions are
   1. hearing
   2. thought
   3. touch
   4. vision

2. Match each of the following brain structures with its role or function. (You will need to remember these terms and facts to understand later discussions of learning, memory, loving, mental illness, anxiety, and other aspects of mind and behavior.)

   The brain structures are
   a. brainstem
   b. cerebellum
   c. basal ganglia
   d. hypothalamus
   e. thalamus
   f. hippocampus
   g. amygdala
   h. cerebral cortex

   The roles and functions are
   1. primary structure for memory
   2. sensory relay station
   3. important for emotions
   4. divided into four lobes
   5. regulates vital functions such as body temperature
   6. regulate planned movement and reward
   7. regulates breathing and swallowing
   8. "little brain," involved in movement

How Are Neural Messages Integrated into Communication Systems?

LEARNING OBJECTIVE
Describe the key structures in the endocrine system and how they communicate to affect behavior.

As noted in the section above, the nervous system consists of two functional units: the central nervous system (CNS), just discussed, and the peripheral nervous system (PNS), which transmits a variety of information to the CNS and responds to messages from the CNS to perform specific behaviors or make bodily adjustments. This section describes the interaction of the nervous system and a different mode of communication, the *endocrine system,* in the production of psychological activity.

The Peripheral Nervous System Includes the Somatic and Autonomic Systems

The PNS has two primary components, which themselves are referred to as nervous systems: the *somatic nervous system* and the *autonomic nervous system* (**FIGURE 3.32**). The **somatic nervous system** transmits sensory signals to the CNS via nerves (bundles of axons). Specialized receptors in the skin, muscles, and joints send sensory information to the spinal cord, which relays it to the brain. In addition, the CNS sends signals through the somatic nervous system to muscles, joints, and skin to initiate, modulate, or inhibit movement. The second major component of the PNS, the **autonomic nervous system (ANS)** regulates the body's internal environment by stimulating glands (such as sweat glands) and by maintaining internal organs (such as the heart). Nerves in the ANS carry *somatosensory* signals to the CNS, providing information about, for example, the fullness of your stomach or how anxious you feel.

somatic nervous system A major component of the peripheral nervous system; it transmits sensory signals to the CNS via nerves.

autonomic nervous system (ANS) A major component of the peripheral nervous system; it regulates the body's internal environment by stimulating glands and by maintaining internal organs such as the heart, gall bladder, and stomach.

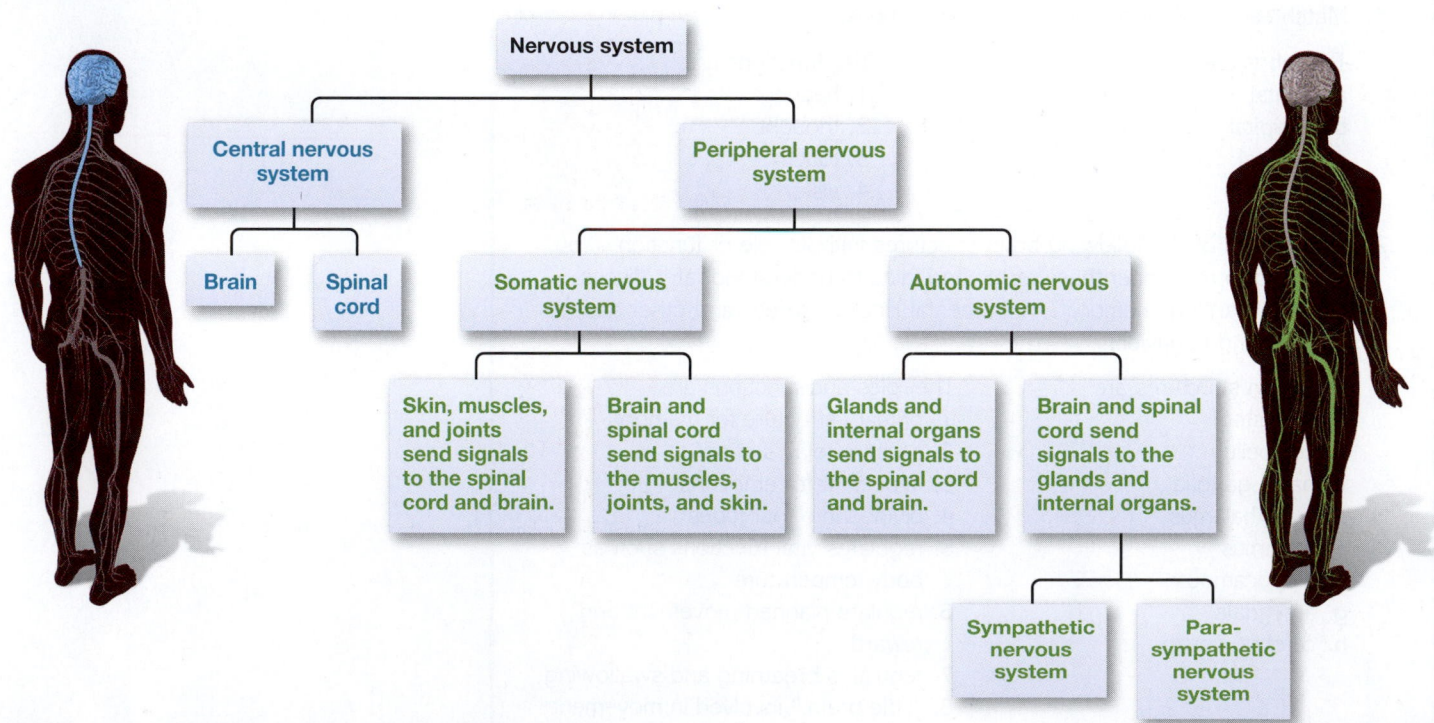

FIGURE 3.32 **The Major Divisions of the Nervous System**

SYMPATHETIC AND PARASYMPATHETIC DIVISIONS Two types of signals, sympathetic and parasympathetic, travel from the CNS to organs and glands in the PNS (**FIGURE 3.33**). To understand them, imagine you hear a fire alarm. In the second after you hear the alarm, signals go out to parts of your body that tell those parts to prepare for action. As a result, blood flows to skeletal muscles, epinephrine is released to increase heart rate and blood sugar, your lungs take in more oxygen, your digestive system suspends activity as a way of conserving energy, your pupils dilate to maximize visual sensitivity, and you perspire to keep cool. These preparatory actions are prompted by the autonomic nervous system's **sympathetic division.** Should there be a fire, you will be physically prepared to flee. If the alarm turns out to be false, your heart will return to its normal steady beat, your breathing will slow, you will resume digesting food, and you will stop perspiring. This return to a normal state will be prompted by the ANS's **parasympathetic division.** Most of your internal organs are controlled by inputs from sympathetic and parasympathetic systems. The more aroused you are, the greater the sympathetic system's dominance.

It does not take a fire alarm to activate your sympathetic nervous system. When you meet someone you find attractive, for example, your heart beats quickly, you

sympathetic division of ANS A division of the autonomic nervous system; it prepares the body for action.

parasympathetic division of ANS A division of the autonomic nervous system; it returns the body to its resting state.

The **sympathetic** division of the nervous system prepares the body for action.

The **parasympathetic** system returns the body to a resting state.

FIGURE 3.33 The Sympathetic and Parasympathetic Systems

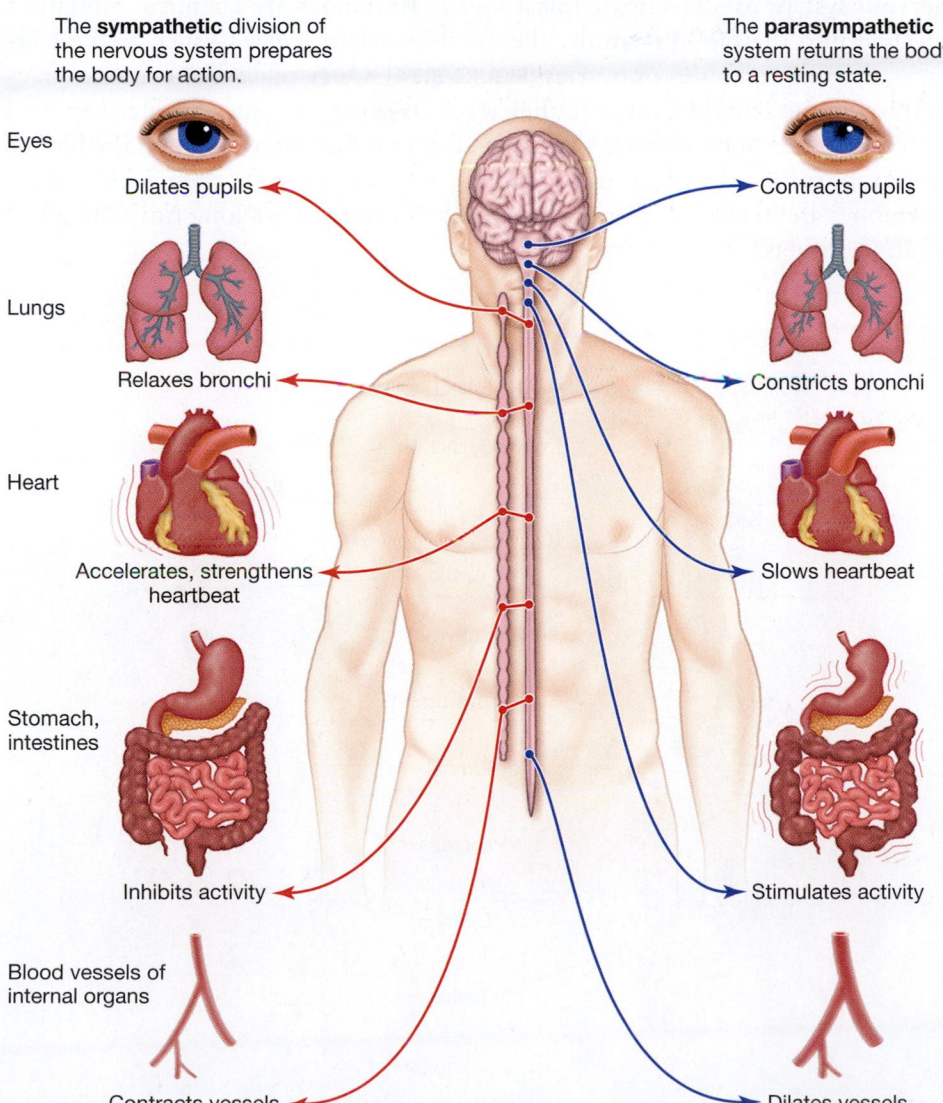

Eyes — Dilates pupils / Contracts pupils

Lungs — Relaxes bronchi / Constricts bronchi

Heart — Accelerates, strengthens heartbeat / Slows heartbeat

Stomach, intestines — Inhibits activity / Stimulates activity

Blood vessels of internal organs — Contracts vessels / Dilates vessels

perspire, you might start breathing heavily, and your pupils widen. Such signs of sexual arousal, which happens when the ANS's sympathetic division is activated provide nonverbal cues during social interaction. The sympathetic nervous system is also activated by psychological states such as anxiety or unhappiness. Certain people worry a great deal or do not cope well with stress; their bodies are in a constant state of arousal. Chronic activation of the sympathetic nervous system is associated with medical problems that include ulcers, heart disease, and asthma (Davison & Pennebaker, 1996).

The Endocrine System Communicates through Hormones

endocrine system A communication system that uses hormones to influence thoughts, behaviors, and actions.

Like the nervous system, the **endocrine system** is a communication network that influences thoughts, behaviors, and actions. Both systems work together to regulate psychological activity. For instance, from the nervous system the brain receives information about potential threats to the organism, and through the endocrine system it prepares the organism to deal with those threats. (The threats could involve physical injury or be mental, such as nervousness at having to talk in front of a group.) The main difference between the two systems is in their modes of communication: The endocrine system uses hormones, whereas the nervous system uses electrochemical signals. **Hormones** are chemical substances released into the bloodstream by the ductless *endocrine glands,* such as the pancreas, thyroid, and testes or ovaries (**FIGURE 3.34**). Once released, hormones travel through the bloodstream until they reach their target tissues, where they bind to receptor sites and influence the tissues. Because they travel through the bloodstream, hormones can take from seconds to hours to exert their effects; once hormones are in the bloodstream, their effects can last for a long time and affect multiple targets.

hormones Chemical substances, typically released from endocrine glands, that travel through the bloodstream to targeted tissues, which are subsequently influenced by the hormones.

FIGURE 3.34 The Major Endocrine Glands

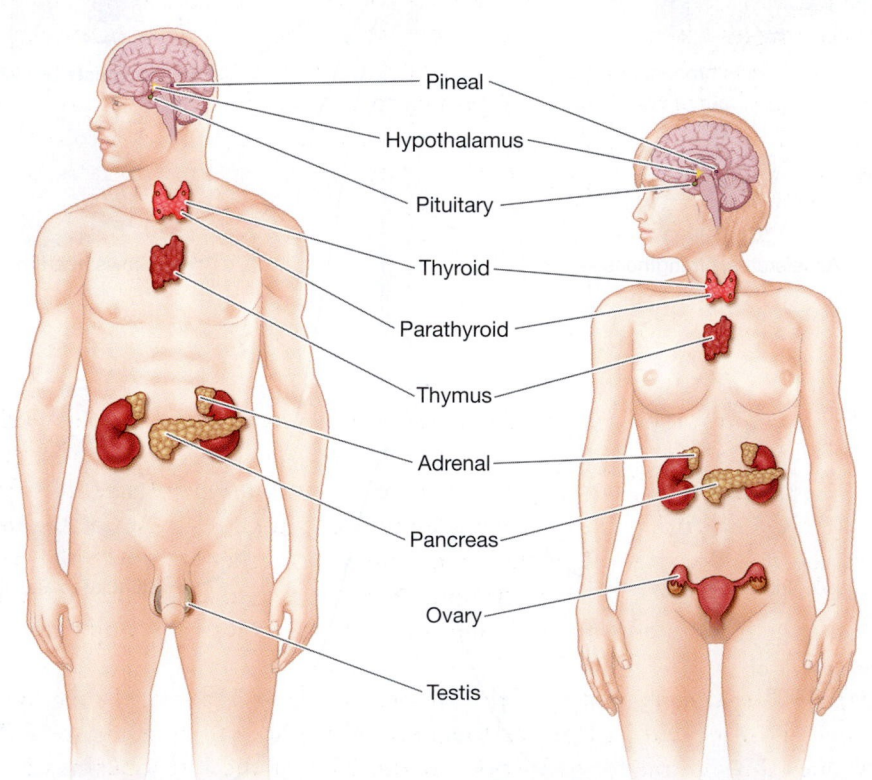

Pineal

Hypothalamus

Pituitary

Thyroid

Parathyroid

Thymus

Adrenal

Pancreas

Ovary

Testis

HORMONES' EFFECTS ON SEXUAL BEHAVIOR An example of hormonal influence is in sexual behavior. The main endocrine glands influencing sexual behavior are the **gonads**—the testes in males and the ovaries in females. Although many people talk about "male" and "female" hormones, the two major gonadal hormones are identical in males and females, but the quantity differs: *androgens* such as testosterone are more prevalent in males, whereas *estrogens* such as estradiol and progesterone are more prevalent in females. Gonadal hormones influence both the development of secondary sex characteristics and adult sexual behavior.

For males, successful sexual behavior depends on having at least a minimum amount of testosterone. Prior to puberty, surgical removal of the testes, or *castration,* diminishes the capacity for developing an erection and lowers sexual interest. Yet a man castrated after puberty will be able to perform sexually if he receives an injection of testosterone. That testosterone injections do not increase sexual behavior in healthy men implies that a healthy man needs only a minimum amount of testosterone to perform sexually (Sherwin, 1988).

Gonadal hormones' influence on females is much more complex. Many nonhuman female animals experience a finite period, *estrus,* when the female is sexually receptive and fertile. During estrus, the female displays behaviors designed to attract the male. Surgical removal of the ovaries terminates estrus: no longer receptive, the female ends her sexual behavior. However, injections of estrogen reinstate estrus. Women's sexual behavior, by contrast, is not particularly linked to the menstrual cycle, and surgical removal of the ovaries has a minimal or no effect on women's sexual interest or behavior (Dennerstein & Burrows, 1982). In fact, many women's sexual desire increases after the removal of their ovaries, because they no longer worry about becoming pregnant. Moreover, women's sexual behavior may have more to do with androgens than estrogens (Morris, Udry, Khan-Dawood, & Dawood, 1987). Women with higher levels of testosterone report greater interest in sex, and testosterone injections increase women's sexual interest after surgical removal of the uterus (Sherwin, 1994).

"You've been charged with driving under the influence of testosterone."

gonads The main endocrine glands involved in sexual behavior: in males, the testes; in females, the ovaries.

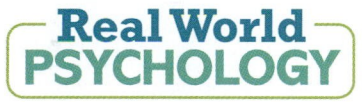

Real World PSYCHOLOGY

Actions of the Nervous System and Endocrine System Are Coordinated

All the communication systems described in this chapter link neurochemical and physiological processes to behaviors, thoughts, and feelings. These systems are fully integrated and interact to facilitate survival, using information from the organism's environment to direct adaptive behavioral responses. Ultimately, the endocrine system is under the central nervous system's control. The brain interprets external and internal stimuli, then sends signals to the endocrine system, which responds by initiating various effects on the body and on behavior.

Most of the central control of the endocrine system is accomplished by the hypothalamus, located just above the roof of the mouth (see Figure 3.27). How does this central control work? At the base of the hypothalamus is the

pituitary gland Located at the base of the hypothalamus; the gland that sends hormonal signals controlling the release of hormones from endocrine glands.

pituitary gland, which governs the release of hormones from the rest of the endocrine glands. Neural activation causes the hypothalamus to secrete a particular *releasing factor*. The releasing factor causes the pituitary to release a hormone specific to that factor, and the hormone then travels through the bloodstream to endocrine sites throughout the body. Once the hormone reaches the target sites, it touches off the release of other hormones, which subsequently affect bodily reactions or behavior. The pituitary is often referred to as the "master gland" of the body: By releasing hormones into the bloodstream, it controls all other glands and governs major processes such as development, ovulation, and lactation.

This integration can be extremely finely tuned. For example, consider physical growth. *Growth hormone (GH),* an extract from the pituitary gland, prompts bone, cartilage, and muscle tissue to grow or helps them regenerate after injury. Since the 1930s, many people have administered or self-administered GH to increase body size and strength. The legendary baseball pitcher Roger Clemens, for example, has been accused of injecting GH to improve his performance. Clemens has denied the accusation, but many athletes have sought a competitive advantage through GH (**FIGURE 3.35**).

Similarly, GH has helped make the current generation of young adults in Japan considerably taller than their parents' generation (Murata, 2000). This increase has come about thanks to the increased availability and consumption of dietary protein in Japan after World War II. How is GH related to protein intake? *Growth hormone releasing factor (GRF)* stimulates the release of GH, which relies on protein to build bones and muscles. GRF also selectively stimulates the eating of protein but not of fats or carbohydrates, perhaps by making protein especially enjoyable (Dickson & Vaccarino, 1994). The area of the hypothalamus connected to GRF neurons is involved in sleep/wake cycles, and thus the bursts of GH, the need for protein, and the consumption of protein are controlled by the body's

FIGURE 3.35 Growth Hormone and Baseball Growth hormone (GH) helps bone, cartilage, and muscle tissues to grow or to regenerate after injury. In February 2008, the U.S. Congress held hearings on the use of performance-enhancing drugs in Major League baseball, addressing in particular accusations that legendary pitcher Roger Clemens had injected GH and steroids to improve his competitive advantage.

internal clock. All these connections illustrate how the CNS, the PNS, and the endocrine system work together to ensure the organism's survival: These systems prompt the behaviors that provide the body with the substances it needs when it needs them.

SUMMING UP

How Are Neural Messages Integrated into Communication Systems?

The central nervous system, consisting of the brain and spinal cord, attends to the body and the environment, initiates actions, and directs the peripheral nervous system and endocrine system to respond appropriately. All three systems use chemicals to transmit their signals, but transmission in the nervous system occurs across synapses whereas transmission in the endocrine system uses hormones that travel through the bloodstream. Gonadal hormones (estrogen, progesterone, and testosterone) are important in the development of secondary sex characteristics and in the sex drive. The hypothalamus controls the endocrine system by directing the pituitary to release specific hormones. The various communication systems are integrated and promote behavior that is adaptive to the environment.

MEASURING UP

1. Match each statement with one or more of the following terms: peripheral nervous system (PNS); somatic nervous system; autonomic nervous system (ANS); sympathetic division; parasympathetic division.

   a. You are studying quietly in the library when a friend jumps out from behind a partition and scares you, making your heart race. your _____ has been affected.

   b. When you calm down and return to your former (not scared) state, your _____ is affected.

   c. Michael Phelps, winner of a record eight gold medals at the 2008 Olympics, must have a remarkable _____.

   d. _____ works directly with the central nervous system (CNS) to coordinate behavior.

   e. _____ consists of two main parts, which maintain homeostasis.

2. Which of the following statements are true? Mark as many as apply.

   a. Only gays and lesbians secrete testosterone and estrogen.

   b. All (normal) people of both sexes secrete testosterone and estrogen.

   c. Men have gonads, and women have ovaries.

   d. The endocrine system acts more slowly than the nervous system.

   e. Hormones are secreted from several places in the body, including the brain.

   f. The pituitary gland is called the master gland.

   g. The central nervous system and the peripheral nervous system work together, whereas the endocrine system works independently.

   h. Women's sexual responsiveness is related more to androgens (such as testosterone) than to estrogen.

How Does the Brain Change?

Despite the great precision and the specificity of its connections, the brain is extremely malleable. Over the course of development, after injury, and throughout our constant stream of experience, the brain continually changes, a property known as **plasticity.** The brain can reorganize itself based on which parts of it are used lightly and which are used heavily. Research into the way the brain changes is providing major insights into the mind. The latest brain research techniques and the knowledge derived from them are direct outgrowths of science's biological revolution.

The brain follows a predictable development pattern, with different structures and abilities progressing at different rates and maturing at different points in life. Reptiles hatch from their leathery eggs ready to go; in contrast, human infants require lots of both sleep and high-quality nutrition before they can function independently. As children's bodies grow and develop, their brains grow and develop, actively rewiring in major ways for many years. In addition, every life experience refines and retunes an individual brain's connections. Thus brain plasticity reflects the interactive nature of our biological and psychological influences.

The Interplay of Genes and Environment Wires the Brain

The brain's development follows set sequences programmed in the genes: Babies' general vision develops before their ability to see depth, for example, and the prefrontal cortex is not anatomically fully mature until early adulthood. But even with these meticulously specified genetic instructions, environment plays a major role. Gene expression depends utterly on environment. Which cells express which genes, and to what extent, is determined by environment. Through the constant interplay between nature and nurture, environment affects our DNA's activity and the products of that activity.

CELL IDENTITY BECOMES FIXED OVER TIME In the developing embryo, each new cell receives signals, from its surroundings, that determine what type of cell it will become. If cells from one part of an embryo are surgically transplanted to another part, the transplant's success depends on how developed the cells' identity is. Tissue transplanted early enough completely transforms into whatever type is appropriate for its new location. As an embryo develops, each cell becomes more and more committed to its identity, so transplanting cells too late may disfigure the organism. Many people are therefore excited about the possibility of transplanting fetal cells, which are undeveloped enough to become any type of tissue, to cure diseases and even restore mobility to people who have lost some motor abilities. This work is in its infancy, so to speak, but it promises breakthroughs in how mental illness and other psychological conditions are treated. Neural cells transplanted early enough take on the identity appropriate to their new location, and the organism develops normally.

EXPERIENCE FINE-TUNES NEURAL CONNECTIONS Connections form between brain structures when growing axons are directed by certain chemicals that tell them where to go and where not to go. The major connections are established by chemical messengers, but the detailed connections are governed by experience. If a cat's eyes are sewn shut at birth, depriving the animal of visual

LEARNING OBJECTIVES

Explain how culture and other environmental factors change the brain.

Describe the similarities and differences in females' and males' brains and explain the limitations on what we can infer from sex differences in the brain.

plasticity A property of the brain that allows it to change as a result of experience, drugs, or injury.

input, the visual cortex fails to develop properly; if the sutures are removed weeks later, the cat is permanently blind, even though its eyes function normally. Adult cats that are similarly deprived do not lose their sight (Wiesel & Hubel, 1963). Evidently, ongoing activity is necessary in the visual pathways to refine the visual cortex enough for it to be useful. In general, such plasticity has *critical periods*, times in which certain experiences must occur for development to proceed normally.

To study experience's effects on development, researchers reared rats in two different laboratory environments. One group was raised in a normal environment for laboratory rats: featureless boxes with bedding at the bottom, plus dishes for food and water. The other group was raised in an enriched environment, with many interesting things to look at, puzzles to solve, obstacles to run, toys to play with, running wheels to exercise on, and even balance beams to hone athletic skills on. This second group's "luxury" items might simply have approximated rat life in the wild, allowing normal rat development, while the mental deprivation of the first group's environment caused the unused portions of those rats' brains to atrophy. As a result, the second group developed bigger, heavier brains than the first group (Rosenzweig, Bennett, & Diamond, 1972). Thus experience is important for normal development and maybe even for superior development.

Culture Affects the Brain

Humans are social animals, and our daily social interactions, which vary among cultures (and subcultures and individuals), are reflected in the ways our brains are organized. *Cultural neuroscience* studies cultural variables' effects on the brain, the mind, genes, and behavior. This subdiscipline is necessarily multidisciplinary, bringing together information about brain functions (i.e., methods and data from brain imaging), analyses of social and emotional processes (e.g., recognizing faces, deciding whom to trust), and examinations of perceptual processes. It exemplifies the way that psychological science works across multiple levels of analysis.

Growing evidence indicates that cultural experiences shape perception and cognition to the extent that cultural differences contribute to different patterns of brain activity. For instance, as discussed in Chapter 1, people from Eastern cultures tend to focus on background (i.e., context) whereas people from Western cultures tend to focus on foreground. Measurements of eye movements have shown that American participants spend more time looking at objects than do Chinese participants, who are much more likely to look at those objects' surroundings (Chua, Boland, & Nisbett, 2005). In recent brain imaging studies comparing participants in the United States and Singapore, researchers presented images whose backgrounds and foregrounds varied in complexity and found differences in brain activity in a number of visual brain regions, supporting the general conclusion that Westerners focus more on objects than do Easterners (Goh et al., 2007; Gutchess et al., 2006).

Does this mean that people from different cultures see the world in fundamentally different ways? One way to address this question is to examine whether the cultural groups differ in early or late stages of visual processing. If they differ in early stages, such as those in the primary visual cortex, their visual systems most likely process the raw information differently. If the groups differ in later visual processing, they might be employing learned preferences for attending to different aspects of the visual world. In one recent brain imaging study (Hedden, Ketay, Aron, Markus, & Gabrieli, 2008), investigators asked participants to judge whether lines were absolute (i.e., did the line match the line shown on a previous trial?) or relative (i.e., did the line match the proportional scaling of the previous line to its surrounding?). On some trials, the absolute and relative judgments were at odds with each other (i.e., the line was the same length, but differed in proportional scaling). As the researchers had hypothesized, the European American participants found the relative task most difficult and the Asian participants, who preferred to make relative judgments, found the absolute task most difficult. For both kinds of participants, performing the most difficult task led to increased activity in brain regions involved in focusing attention on that task. These findings indicate no cultural differences in how the participants understood the tasks but cultural differences in how the participants paid attention to the tasks. Such differences suggest that within cultural contexts people learn which features in the environment, being more important, merit more attention.

A similar pattern governs people's responses to facial expressions of emotion. Cultures differ slightly in how they express emotions, and as discussed further in Chapter 9, evidence indicates that people are better at identifying emotional expressions from members of their own cultures than from members of other cultures. This occurs in part, it seems, because people have more experience in interpreting emotional expressions among those with whom they interact regularly. If so, the greater recognition should mean that people's brain responses are enhanced when they are interpreting emotional expressions within their own cultural groups than within other cultural groups. In a recent brain imaging study, investigators showed pictures of neutral facial expressions and fearful facial expressions, both kinds on Japanese and American faces, to participants in Japan and the United States (Chiao et al., 2008). As noted earlier in this chapter, the amygdala shows increased activity when people view fearful expressions, and in this study amygdala activity was greatest when participants viewed fearful expressions within their own cultural group. Thus cultural experience appears to fine-tune the brain's responses to such important environmental cues (**FIGURE 3.36**).

The Brain Rewires Itself throughout Life

Although an organism's plasticity decreases with age, the human brain retains the ability to rewire itself throughout life, and into very old age it can grow new connections among neurons and even grow new neurons. The rewiring and growth within the brain represents learning's biological basis. Because the laws of learning and of brain development are as certain as the laws of gravity, it is impossible for a person with a normally developing brain not to learn. One of this book's seven themes is that we are often unaware of what we can and cannot control in our lives, and frequently we cannot control what we learn in any particular situation.

CHANGE IN THE STRENGTH OF CONNECTIONS UNDERLIES LEARNING In every moment of life, we gain memories: experiences and knowledge that are acquired instantaneously and may be recalled later, as well as habits that form gradually. All these memories are reflected in the brain's physical changes.

Psychological scientists widely accept that changes in the brain are most likely not in its larger wiring or general arrangement but mainly in the strength of existing connections. One possibility is that when two neurons fire simultaneously, the synaptic connection between them strengthens, making them more likely to fire together in the future; conversely, *not* firing simultaneously tends to weaken two neurons' connection. This theory, summarized by the catchphrase "Fire together, wire together," is consistent with a great deal of experimental evidence and many theoretical models. It accounts for both the "burning in" of an experience (a pattern of neural firing becomes more likely to recur, and its recurrence leads the mind to recall an event) and the ingraining of habits (repeating a behavior makes the repeater tend to perform that behavior automatically).

Until very recently, scientists believed that, uniquely among bodily organs, adult brains produced no new cells—presumably to avoid obliterating the connections already established in response to experience. But even as the existing neural connections get strengthened, plasticity enables the brain to grow new neurons (Eriksson et al., 1998); this process, *neurogenesis,* appears

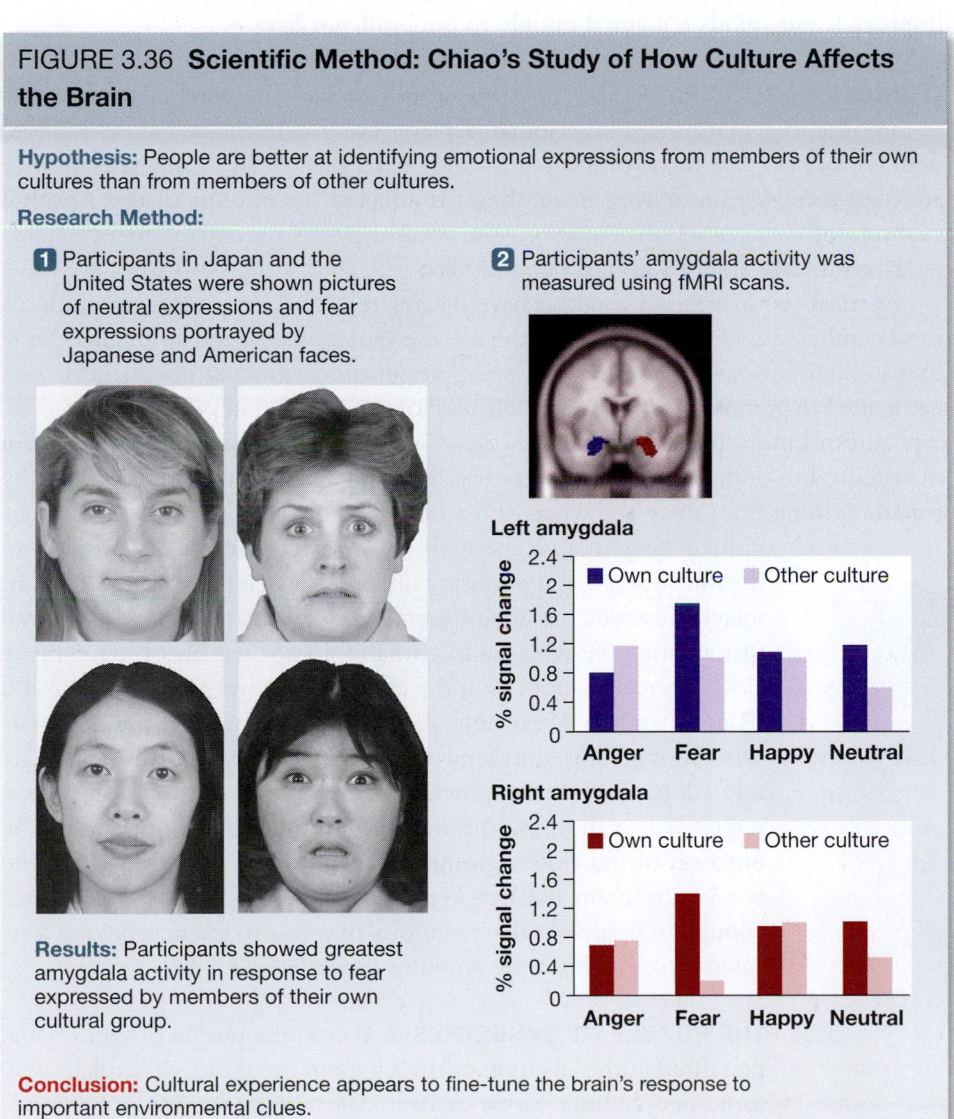

FIGURE 3.36 Scientific Method: Chiao's Study of How Culture Affects the Brain

Hypothesis: People are better at identifying emotional expressions from members of their own cultures than from members of other cultures.

Research Method:

1 Participants in Japan and the United States were shown pictures of neutral expressions and fear expressions portrayed by Japanese and American faces.

2 Participants' amygdala activity was measured using fMRI scans.

Left amygdala

Own culture / Other culture

Right amygdala

Own culture / Other culture

Results: Participants showed greatest amygdala activity in response to fear expressed by members of their own cultural group.

Conclusion: Cultural experience appears to fine-tune the brain's response to important environmental clues.

to be a major factor in recovery from brain injury. A fair amount of neurogenesis apparently occurs in the hippocampus. Recall from earlier in this chapter that memories are retained within (or at least require) the hippocampus initially but are eventually transferred to the cortex, so the hippocampus is continuously overwritten. Perhaps, without disrupting memory, neurons in the hippocampus can be lost and replaced.

Elizabeth Gould and her colleagues have demonstrated that environmental conditions can play an important role in neurogenesis. For example, they have found that for rats, shrews, and marmosets, stressful experiences, such as being confronted by strange males in their home cages, interfere with neurogenesis during development and adulthood (Gould & Tanapat, 1999). When animals are housed together, they typically form dominance hierarchies that reflect social status. Dominant animals—those who possess the highest social status—show greater increases in new neurons than do subordinate animals (Kozorovitskiy & Gould, 2004). Thus social environment can strongly affect brain plasticity, a dynamic process we are only beginning to understand. Neurogenesis may underlie neural plasticity. If so, further research might enable us, through neurogenesis, to reverse the brain's natural loss of neurons and slow down age-based mental decline. Imagine how humans' quality of life would improve if our minds remained nimble throughout our lives.

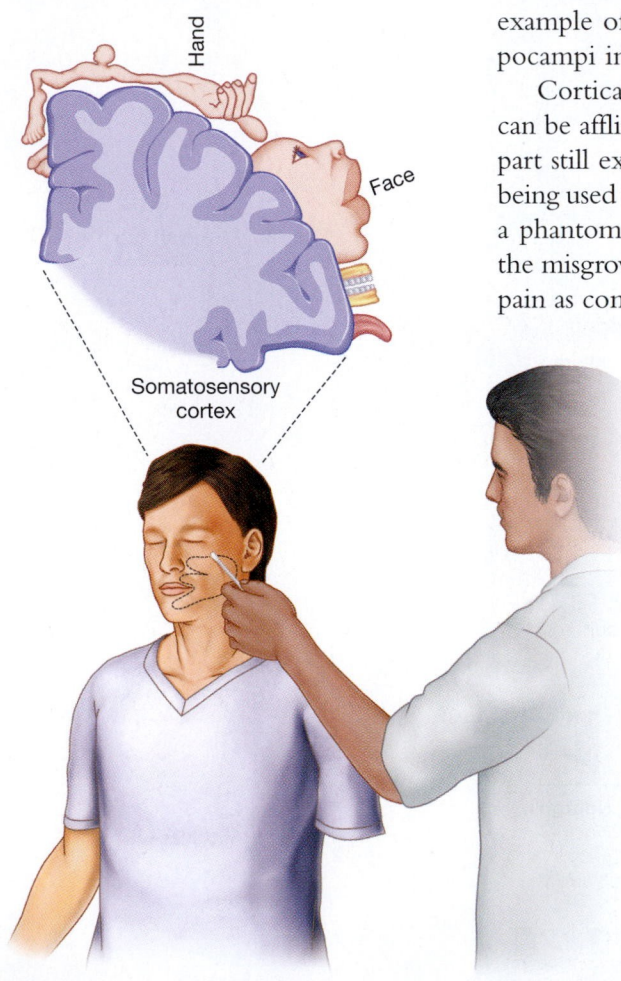

FIGURE 3.37 Cortical Remapping Following Amputation The participant felt a cotton swab touching his cheek as touching his missing hand. This effect may occur because the hand and face are near each other in somatosensory space.

Hand

Face

Somatosensory cortex

CHANGES IN THE BRAIN The functions of portions of the cerebral cortex shift in response to activity. Recall the somatosensory homunculus (see Figure 3.29), in which more cortical tissue is devoted to body parts that receive more sensation or are used more. Again, wiring in the brain is affected by amount of use. Another example of changes in cortical maps, discussed above, is the enlargement of hippocampi in experienced London taxi drivers.

Cortical reorganization can also have bizarre results. For example, an amputee can be afflicted with a *phantom limb,* the intense sensation that the amputated body part still exists. Some phantom limbs are experienced as moving normally, such as being used to gesture in conversation, whereas some are frozen in position. Moreover, a phantom limb often is accompanied by pain sensations, which may result from the misgrowth of the severed pain nerves at the stump; the cortex misinterprets the pain as coming from the place where those nerves originally came from. This phenomen suggests that the brain has not reorganized in response to the injury and that the missing limb's cortical representation remains intact. However, the neurologist V. S. Ramachandran has discovered that an amputee who has lost a hand may, when his or her eyes are closed, perceive a touch on the cheek as if it were the missing hand (Ramachandran & Hirstein, 1998). Apparently, on the somatosensory homunculus the hand is represented next to the face. The unused part of the amputee's cortex (the part that would have responded to the now-missing limb) assumes to some degree the function of the closest group, representing the face. Somehow, the rest of the brain has not kept pace with the somatosensory area enough to figure out these neurons' new job, so the neurons are activated by a touch on the amputee's face (**FIGURE 3.37**).

THE PUZZLE OF SYNESTHESIA Recall the puzzle of synesthesia, presented at the opening of this chapter. How can we explain why some people taste words or hear colors? Can we use our knowledge of the structure and organization of the brain to create a brain based model of synesthesia?

V. S. Ramachandran, the neurologist who conducted many of the studies on phantom limbs (discussed in the previous section), has also conducted a series of experiments to better understand what is happening when someone reports, for example, that a sound is lime-green or that chicken tastes pointy (Ramachandran & Hubbard, 2001). Synesthesia tends to run in families and thus must have a genetic basis, and Ramachandran inferred that the genes involved were related to brain formation. Because the brain area involved in seeing colors is physically close to the brain area involved in understanding numbers, he theorized that in people with color/number synesthesia, these two brain areas have some connections or cross-wiring. The process of linking these areas would have resembled the process of linking areas of an amputee's brain (again, discussed just above): One portion of the brain would have adopted another portion's role.

To test his hypothesis, Ramachandran examined MRIs taken of synesthetes when they looked at black numbers on a white background. He found evidence of neural activity in the brain area responsible for color vision. Control participants without synesthesia did not experience activity in this brain area when they looked at the same numbers (**FIGURE 3.38**).

One major difference between a phantom limb and synesthesia, however, is that the phantom limb is caused primarily by environment (the loss of the limb) while synesthesia is caused primarily by genetics. Why has this sensory anomaly remained in the gene pool? Ramachandran suggests that it confers an adaptive advantage: Synesthete's brains are wired to connect seemingly disparate topics, and the ability to make remote associations is an important part of creativity. As an example, Ramachandran and his collaborator E. M. Hubbard ask us to consider Shakespeare's line "It is the East and Juliet is the sun." The likening of Juliet to the sun is a metaphor, but where did it come from? Its association of a woman and a bright light resembles a synesthetic experience. In fact, these authors conclude that creative people experience a higher incidence of synesthesia than do noncreative people (2003).

FIGURE 3.38 **Try for Yourself: Synesthesia Test**

Two stimuli used by Ramachandra and Hubbard (2003) to study synesthesia:

Look first at the square on the left, and as quickly as possible count the number of 2s.

Now do the same task with the square on the right

Explanation: Unless you have synesthesia and it causes you to see particular numbers in particular colors, you were much faster at counting the 2s on the right. They "popped out" at you because they are a different color from the 5s. Some synesthetes are equally fast at both tasks because they see the numbers in different colors. This test is one of many used to determine if someone has color-related synesthesia.

Recognizing Unstated Assumptions

All human interactions are based partly on assumptions. All conversations assume the parties have some knowledge in common but not all knowledge. When you enter a classroom, you assume the instructor will act differently than your fellow students. In writing this textbook, the authors explained information they assumed would be new for most readers, but they did not define words they assumed most readers would know.

When you are trying to understand a complex topic, begin by recognizing your and other people's unstated assumptions about that topic. Once you make those assumptions explicit, you can apply reason to them.

Consider for example, common assumptions about genetic influences and the brain. Many people assume that if a trait or tendency is passed along genetically, then those who inherit that trait or tendency cannot change it in themselves. By this thinking, those who inherit shyness, intelligence, or boldness cannot change how shy, intelligent, or bold they are.

When people learn about sex differences in the brain, they often assume that the brain does not change and that it "causes" sex differences in behaviors. In reality, the brain reflects genetic inheritance and experience, and together these variables determine the size, function, and structure of the brain.

In fact, because nature is inextricably intertwined with nurture, no biological effects can occur independently from environment. Just as all learning is influenced by assumptions, all choices are influenced by past learning and its influence on both thoughts and feelings.

Females' and Males' Brains Are Similar and Different

The interplay of biological and environmental effects on the brain is reflected in the similarities and differences between females' and males' brains. Everything that influences a person is reflected in his or her brain, of course, and females and males differ in their life experiences and hormonal makeups.

The study of the brain's *sexual dimorphism*—that is, sex differences in anatomical structures—has a long history. Many comparisons of males' and females' brains, especially the earliest comparisons, were pseudoscience used to show that female brains were inferior (for a review, see Halpern, 2000). The unstated assumption was always that if two groups (in this case, females and males) were different, one had to be inferior. But people do not have to be the same to be equal. In fact, evidence suggests that men and women may perform a task, such as remembering a recent occurrence, equally well but using different parts of the brain. For example, Richard Haier and colleagues (2005) have found that females and males may solve some complex problems, such as items on IQ tests, differently: Females show greater use of language-related brain regions, and males show greater use of spatial-related brain regions, even when participants are matched for intelligence.

Among the several intriguing differences between males' and females' brains are in brain size and in the distribution of language functions in the two hemispheres. Males generally have larger brains than females, but larger is not necessarily better. In fact, one developmental process in the brain involves disconnecting neurons so that only the most useful connections remain. Jay Giedd and his colleagues (1997) at the U.S. National Institutes of Health concluded that, among both sexes, brain structures' sizes are highly variable. They reported that boys' brains are approximately 9 percent larger than girls' brains, with some differences in the rate of maturation for different parts of the brain for girls and boys.

As discussed in Chapter 4, to some extent the brain's two hemispheres are lateralized, meaning that each is dominant for different cognitive functions. A considerable body of evidence says that female brains are more bilaterally organized for language. In other words, the brain areas important in processing language are more likely to be found in both halves of females' brains, whereas the equivalent language areas are more likely to be in only one hemisphere, usually the left, in males' brains (**FIGURE 3.39**). One source of data that supports this distinction is people's experiences following strokes. Even when patients are matched on the location and severity of the brain damage caused by a stroke, men and women are affected differently. For example, some studies have found that women are less impaired in language than men are following a stroke (Jiang, Sheikh, & Bullock, 2006). A possible reason for women's better outcomes is that, because language is represented in both halves of women's brains, damage to half of a woman's brain will have less effect on that woman's ability to process language than it would if most of the language areas were in the damaged half of the brain. A related hypothesis, in accord with the idea that women's brains are more bilaterally organized, is that the halves of women's brains are connected by more neural fibers than men's are. Remember that a thick band of neurons, the corpus callosum, connects the brain's two halves (see Figure 3.28), and some researchers have found that a portion of this connective tissue is larger in women (Gur & Gur, 2004).

Before we can be confident about recent findings of sex differences in the brain, much more research is needed. We need to better understand normal, healthy brain development. We also need to better understand brain and behavior relationships before we can reason about human sex differences from our knowledge of brain structures (Halpern et al., 2007). Finally, although we tend to focus on the ways in which males and females are different, we need to keep in mind that their brains are similar in many (perhaps most) ways.

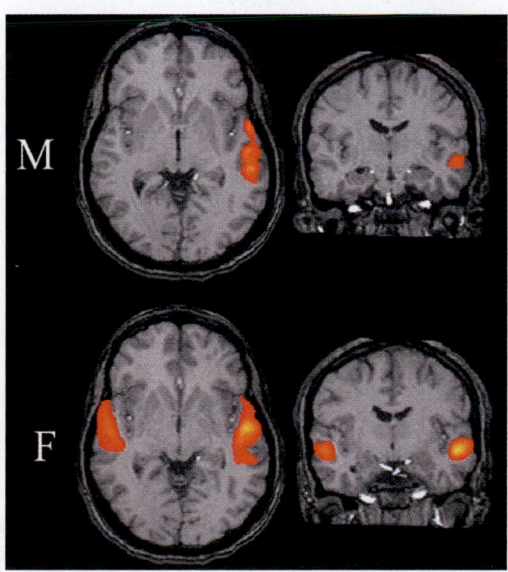

FIGURE 3.39 Male versus Female Brains A considerable body of evidence indicates that female brains are more bilaterally organized for language. For example, researchers at Indiana University studied men and women listening to someone reading aloud. As these fMRI images show, the men listened with one side of their brains, whereas the women tended to listen with both sides.

The Brain Can Recover from Injury

Just as the brain reorganizes in response to amount of use, it also reorganizes in response to brain damage. Following an injury in the cortex, the surrounding gray matter assumes the function of the damaged area, like a local business scrambling to pick up the customers of a newly closed competitor. This remapping seems to begin immediately, and it continues for years. Such plasticity involves all levels of the nervous system, from the cortex down to the spinal cord.

Reorganization is much more prevalent in children than adults, in accord with the critical periods of normal development. Young children afflicted with severe and uncontrollable epilepsy that has paralyzed one or more limbs sometimes undergo *radical hemispherectomy,* the surgical removal of an entire cerebral hemisphere. The remaining hemisphere eventually takes on most of the lost hemisphere's functions, and the children regain almost complete use of their limbs. This procedure is not possible in adults, in whom the lack of neural reorganization would lead to inevitable and permanent paralysis and loss of function.

As discussed earlier in this chapter, one of the most exciting areas of current neurological research is the transplantation of human fetal tissue into the brain to repair damage. The transplanted tissue consists specifically of *stem cells,* "master" cells that not only can regenerate themselves but also can develop into any type of tissue, such as muscle or nerve cells. This relatively new procedure is being explored as a possible treatment for strokes and degenerative diseases such as Parkinson's and Huntington's. The significant challenge is to get the newly introduced cells to make the proper connections so that the damaged circuits regrow. Many people oppose the use of fetal tissue for any research purposes, however, on religious or other philosophical grounds. Fortunately, many new methods are emerging that allow researchers to create stem cells by reprogramming adult cells (Kim et al., 2008).

 SUMMING UP

How Does the Brain Change?

Although neural connections are intricate and precise, they are malleable. The human genome, the blueprint for normal development, is affected by environmental factors, such as injury, sensory stimulation, sensory deprivation, and life experiences. During development and throughout our lifetimes of learning, the circuitry is reworked and updated. Culture, as context for experience, affects the organization and structure of the brain. The brain can reorganize after a brain injury, though children's recovery ability is far greater than adults'. An understanding of genetic transmission and of brain organization, along with the knowledge that brain regions are specialized for different perceptions, has allowed researchers to unravel the puzzle of synesthesia. Females' and males' brains differ in several ways, although the similarities are more obvious. Males' brains tend to be larger, and evidence suggests that females' brains are organized more bilaterally.

MEASURING UP

1. A person's brain changes in response to environment, including all of that person's experiences. Place an X next to the statements below that support this idea.
   _____ **a.** Males' brains generally are larger than females' because males have more-stimulating environments.
   _____ **b.** The sizes of London taxi drivers' hippocampi were correlated with how long the participants had been London taxi drivers.

_____ c. Some amputees can feel sensations in their amputated limbs when their eyes are closed and their faces are touched.

_____ d. Many drugs can mimic neurotransmitters' actions.

_____ e. Laboratory rats raised in enriched environments developed heavier brains than laboratory rats raised in standard environments.

_____ f. Phineas Gage's personality changed profoundly after his frontal cortex was damaged.

_____ g. Some brain responses to selected stimuli vary due to cultural influence.

2. Indicate whether the following statements, about the ways in which females' and males' brains differ, are true or false.

_____ a. Males' brains generally are larger than females' brains.

_____ b. Males' and females' brains have no differences.

_____ c. Researchers have found that sex differences in the brain explain why males tend to hold executive positions more than females do.

_____ d. Sex differences in the brain prove that males and females have essentially different abilities.

_____ e. A larger brain is a better brain—more advanced, plus more complex in its organization.

CONCLUSION

The human body is a biological machine, produced by a genome that has been shaped by millions of years of evolution. Some 30,000 genes provide instructions for producing proteins, and this modest process builds a brain that thinks, feels, and acts. In psychological science, the biological revolution has revealed that these genes not only build the common structures of the human body but also are partly responsible for differences in the personalities, mental abilities, and physical appearances of individuals. At the genetic level of analysis, so far we have only a minimal understanding of our mental lives' complexity. We are beginning to understand the relationship between our environments and our genes, but we do not know how environment causes our genes to turn on and off. Understanding genetic expression's inner workings may lead to profound insights into what makes us human and how our minds work.

Evolution has bestowed on humans a marvelous three-pound organ called the brain. This complex assemblage of cells coordinates messages about environment and bodily state using systems of neurons and of hormones, and these systems determine the ways in which we are all similar and all different. There are more neural connections in the human brain than there are stars in our galaxy (Kandel, Schwartz, & Jessell, 1995), and the messages transmitted across those connections are modulated by subtle variations in the actions of dozens of chemicals in the synapses. Psychological scientists are quickly developing methods to better understand how the brain works and the different brain regions' functions. We know that the brain changes dramatically through experiences (with culture as the context for those experiences) and that the brain's plasticity allows for recovery from certain injuries. More and more, psychological scientists are looking to the workings of the brain to understand the rich complexity of human experience. As discussed throughout this book, contemporary research is helping us understand the biological underpinnings of human mental life.

■ CHAPTER SUMMARY

What Is the Genetic Basis of Psychological Science?

- **Heredity Involves Passing Along Genes through Reproduction:** The Human Genome Project has mapped the genes that make up humans' 23 chromosomal pairs. Genes' variations are either dominant or recessive. The genome represents the genotype, and the observable characteristics are the phenotype. Many characteristics are polygenic.

- **Genotypic Variation Is Created by Sexual Reproduction:** Because half of each chromosome comes from each parent and the two halves are joined randomly, there is enormous potential variation in the resulting zygote's genome. Mutations also give rise to variations.

- **Genes Affect Behavior:** Behavioral geneticists can quantify the similarity and variation in a population's shared characteristics. Twin studies, research on adoptees, and other investigations of hereditary and genetic influence provide insight into heritability.

- **Social and Environmental Contexts Influence Genetic Expression:** Gene expression is a complex interaction between genetic makeup and environmental context.

- **Genetic Expression Can Be Modified:** Genetic manipulation has been achieved in mammals such as mice, but has proved difficult in humans. However, animal studies using the technique of "knocking out" genes to determine their effects on behaviors and on disease are a valuable tool for understanding genetic influences.

How Does the Nervous System Operate?

- **Neurons Are Specialized for Communication:** Neurons are the basic building blocks of the nervous system. They receive and send chemical messages. All neurons have the same basic structure, but neurons vary by function and by location in the nervous system.

- **Action Potentials Cause Neural Communication:** Changes in a neuron's electrical charge are the basis of an action potential, or neural firing. Firing is the means of communication within networks of neurons.

- **Neurotransmitters Bind to Receptors across the Synapse:** Neurons do not touch; they release chemicals (neurotransmitters) into the synapse, a small gap between the neurons. Neurotransmitters bind with the receptors of postsynaptic neurons, thus changing the charge in those neurons. Neurotransmitters' effects are halted by reuptake of the neurotransmitters into the presynaptic neurons, enzyme deactivation, or autoreception.

- **Neurotransmitters Influence Mind and Behavior:** Neurotransmitters have been identified that influence aspects of the mind and of behavior in humans, including emotions, motor skills, sleep, learning and memory, pain control, and pain perception. Drugs and toxins mimic neurotransmitters' actions or reduce neurotransmitters' availability.

What Are the Basic Brain Structures and Their Functions?

- **The Brainstem Houses the Basic Programs of Survival:** The top of the spinal cord forms the brainstem, which is involved in basic functions such as breathing and walking as well as general arousal.

- **The Cerebellum Is Essential for Movement:** The cerebellum ("little brain"), the bulging structure connected to the back of the brainstem, controls balance and is essential for movement.

- **Subcortical Structures Control Emotions and Basic Drives:** The subcortical structures play a key part in psychological functions because they control vital functions (the hypothalamus), sensory relay (the thalamus), memories (the hippocampus), emotions (the amygdala), and the planning and producing of movement (the basal ganglia).

- **The Cerebral Cortex Underlies Complex Mental Activity:** The lobes of the cortex play specific roles in controlling vision (occipital), touch (parietal), hearing and speech comprehension (temporal), and planning and movement (frontal).

How Are Neural Messages Integrated into Communication Systems?

- **The Peripheral Nervous System Includes the Somatic and Autonomic Systems:** The body's internal environment is regulated by the autonomic system, which is divided into the alarm response (sympathetic) and the return-to-normal response (parasympathetic). The somatic system relays sensory information.

- **The Endocrine System Communicates through Hormones:** Both endocrine glands and organs produce and release chemical substances, which travel to body tissues through the bloodstream and influence a variety of processes, including sexual behavior.

- **Actions of the Nervous System and Endocrine System Are Coordinated:** Most of the central control of the endocrine system occurs through the actions of both the hypothalamus and the pituitary gland; the latter controls the release of hormones from the rest of the endocrine glands.

How Does the Brain Change?

- **The Interplay of Genes and the Environment Wires the Brain:** Chemical signals influence cells' growth and function. Environmental experiences, especially during critical periods, are necessary for cells to develop properly and for them to make more detailed connections.

- **Culture Affects the Brain:** Daily social interactions, which vary among cultures (and subcultures and individuals), are reflected in each brain's unique organization.

- **The Brain Rewires Itself throughout Life:** Although plasticity decreases with age, the brain retains the ability to rewire itself throughout life. This ability is learning's biological basis.

- **Females' and Males' Brains Are Similar and Different:** Although males' and females' brains are predominantly similar, males' brains are larger than females' (on average), and females' verbal abilities are organized more bilaterally (more equally in both hemispheres). There are sex differences in the rate of development for some areas of the brain.

- **The Brain Can Recover from Injury:** The brain can reorganize its functions in response to brain damage, although this capacity decreases with age. Anomalies in sensation and in perception, such as synesthesia, are attributed to cross-wiring connections in the brain.

■ KEY TERMS

■ PRACTICE TEST

1. Complete the following analogy: Genes are to chromosomes as _____ are to _____.
   a. recipes, ingredients
   b. seeds, vegetables
   c. bricks, walls
   d. feet, shoes

2. Which of the following statements are true regarding the relationship between genetic makeup and environment?
   a. Environmental factors can influence gene expression.
   b. The presence of certain genes can influence an organism's susceptibility to environmental stressors.
   c. Genes and environment can interact to effect phenotype.

3. Which *two* labels accurately describe neurons that detect information from the physical world and pass that information along to the brain?
   a. motor neuron
   b. sensory neuron
   c. interneuron
   d. efferent neuron
   e. afferent neuron

4. You witness a major car accident on your way to school. You pull over and rush to help one of the victims, who has severe cuts across his forehead and legs. When you ask if he is in any pain, he says no. Which neurochemical is likely keeping the man pain free despite his obvious injuries?
   a. dopamine
   b. GABA
   c. glutamate
   d. endorphins
   e. substance P

5. Who do you predict would have a larger hippocampus?
   a. someone who plays computer games requiring the exploration of complex virtual worlds
   b. someone who plays computer games requiring extraordinarily quick reflexes and body awareness

6. Someone suffers a stroke that causes damage to the left motor cortex. Which of the following impairments will the person most likely exhibit?
   a. an inability to comprehend spoken language
   b. an inability to recognize faces
   c. paralysis of the left side of the body
   d. paralysis of the right side of the body

7. Because it determines other glands' activities, the _____ is sometimes called "the master gland."
   a. pituitary
   b. pancreas
   c. thyroid
   d. gonad

8. The adage *You can't teach an old dog new tricks* is consistent with which phenomenon?
   a. plasticity
   b. critical periods
   c. cortical reorganization
   d. synesthesia

9. True or false: Differences in the brains of people from different cultures necessarily reveal underlying differences in biology.

■ PSYCHOLOGY AND SOCIETY

1. A relative who suffers from arthritic pain finds a Web site on the benefits of magnet therapy. The Web site claims that magnets can bring relief to arthritic joints by increasing blood flow and oxygen levels. Using the critical thinking skills discussed in this chapter, write a letter helping your relative evaluate the Web site's claims.

2. Scan the news for a story that mentions a particular brain area. For example, check newspapers' science sections or look for sports stories involving head injuries. Then use this textbook and other reputable sources of information to research this brain area. Imagine you are charged with teaching fellow introductory psychology students about this area, and prepare a short lecture explaining its location and key functions (you may wish to include a drawing or diagram to help explain the location). In your lecture, describe how an understanding of this brain area contributes to your understanding of the news story.

The answer key for all the Measuring Up exercises and the Practice Tests can be found at the back of the book.

 Find more review materials online at www.wwnorton.com/psychologicalscience.

Test Preparation   ■   131

The Mind and Consciousness

THE MOVIE *THE DIVING BELL AND THE BUTTERFLY* (2007) tells the story of Jean-Dominique Bauby, a French fashion magazine editor who suffered a devastating stroke at age 43. Twenty days later, Bauby woke up to a nightmare: Nearly all his voluntary muscles were paralyzed. Even though he was awake and alert, he could not communicate with those around him. This rare condition, *locked-in syndrome,* occurs when part of the brain stem gets damaged. As a psychological state, it has been compared to being buried alive: Imagine seeing all the sights around you and hearing every noise, but being unable to respond physically to your sensations. Imagine feeling every itch, but being unable to scratch yourself or move to gain relief. Bauby proved able to blink his left eye, and eventually a speech therapist taught him to use that eye to communicate. As she sat beside him pointing to letters of the alphabet, Bauby blinked to select the letter he wanted. Letter by letter, he formed words, sentences, and so on. In fact, through this painstakingly slow process, Bauby wrote a memoir, blinking to an assistant one letter at a time. Although Bauby died of heart failure only days after the

How Is the Conscious Mind Experienced?
- Consciousness Is a Subjective Experience
- There Are Variations in Conscious Experience
- Splitting the Brain Splits the Conscious Mind
- Unconscious Processing Influences Behavior
- Brain Activity Produces Consciousness

What Is Sleep?
- Sleep Is an Altered State of Consciousness
- Sleep Is an Adaptive Behavior
- Sleep and Wakefulness Are Regulated by Multiple Neural Mechanisms
- People Dream while Sleeping

What Is Altered Consciousness?
- Hypnosis Is Induced through Suggestion
- Meditation Produces Relaxation
- People Can Lose Themselves in Activities

How Do Drugs Affect Consciousness?
- People Use—and Abuse—Many Psychoactive Drugs
- Critical Thinking Skill: Providing Examples of Slippery Slope Thinking
- Alcohol Is the Most Widely Abused Drug
- Critical Thinking Skill: Showing How Circular Reasoning Is a Misuse of Operational Definitions
- Addiction Has Psychological and Physical Aspects

book was published in 1997, his memoir, *The Diving Bell and the Butterfly,* received critical acclaim. The movie based on it, by the artist and filmmaker Julian Schnabel, received a prize at the 2007 Cannes Film Festival.

Bauby's use of blinking to communicate was triumphant in part because it was so slow and difficult. Recent scientific advances have raised the possibility that patients like Bauby will be able to communicate much more quickly and easily: We might be able to "read" their thoughts by imaging brain activity in real time. Communication of this kind is the goal of scientists working with Erik Ramsay, an American with locked-in syndrome (FIGURE 4.1A). In 2000, at age 16, Ramsay suffered a brain stem injury in a car accident. Four years later, researchers planted electrodes in the speech region of his left hemisphere, and for the past several years Ramsay has been listening to recordings of vowel sounds and mentally simulating those sounds. His simulation of each vowel sound should produce its own pattern of brain activity. Ultimately, the researchers hope to use this brain activity to create a voice synthesizer that will translate Ramsay's neural patterns into understandable speech. Their initial results have been promising. Within a few years, they speculate, Erik might be able to communicate through his voice synthesizer (Bartels et al., 2008).

Other researchers have obtained similarly promising results. British researchers have used brain imaging to demonstrate that a 23-year-old woman who was in an apparent coma could respond to requests to imagine either playing tennis or walking through her house (Owen et al., 2006). This woman's pattern of brain activity was quite similar to those of control subjects who also imagined playing tennis or walking through a house (FIGURE 4.1B). The researchers believe that although the woman could not give outward signs of awareness, she was able to understand language and respond to the experimenters' requests. This finding's implications are extraordinary. Could the researchers' method be used to reach other people who are in comas, aware of their surroundings, but unable to communicate? Such potential communicators would not include people in vegetative states, among them the much-discussed patient Terri Schiavo. As discussed later in this chapter, people such as Schiavo are effectively brain dead; whatever brain activity they show does not indicate any sort of awareness.

How do you know you are conscious? You know this only because you are experiencing the outside world (through seeing, hearing, touching) and you are aware that you are thinking. But what gives rise to consciousness? Is it the many neurons firing in your brain? If so, how do these brain circuits' actions give rise to your experiences? An iPod's circuits produce sound when they are energized, but gadgets like iPods are not conscious in the same way humans are. Is the difference biological? Not entirely.

FIGURE 4.1 Challenging the Definition of Consciousness (a) Erik Ramsay (right, with his father, Eddie) suffers from locked-in syndrome, with total awareness but no way of expressing himself other than blinking. Researchers hope to create a voice synthesizer that will translate his neural patterns into speech. **(b)** Brain imaging has shown that a young woman in a coma, with no outward signs of awareness, responded to directions to visualize playing tennis and walking around with neural activity similar to that of healthy volunteers.

(a)

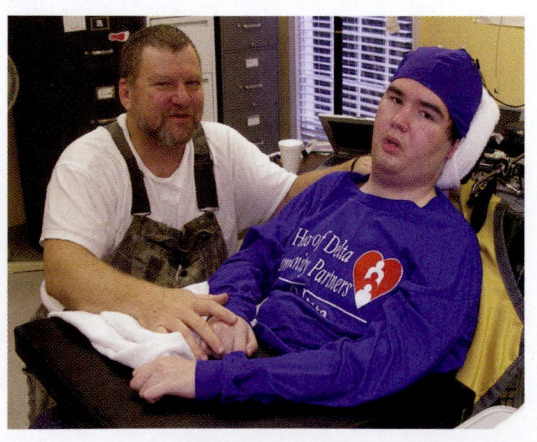

(b)

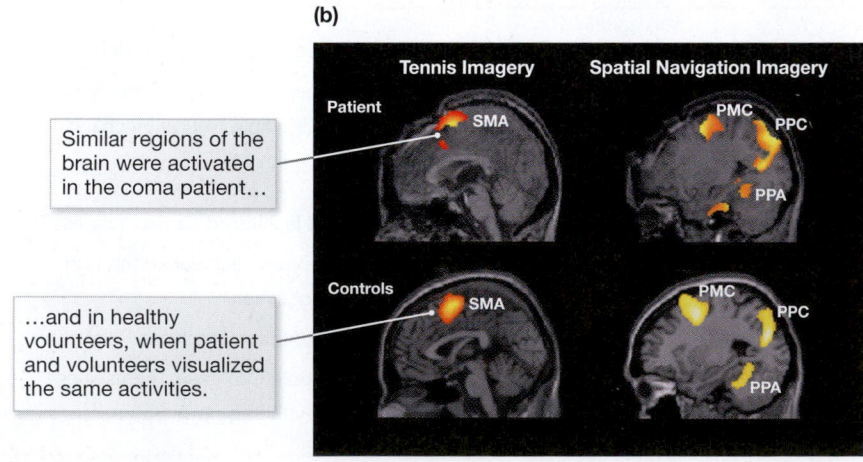

Similar regions of the brain were activated in the coma patient...

...and in healthy volunteers, when patient and volunteers visualized the same activities.

Your body includes many highly active biological systems, such as your immune system, that do not produce the sort of consciousness you are experiencing right now, for example, as you contemplate these questions.

In considering consciousness and its variations, this chapter has two main points, which are highlighted in the examples above. First, people can be conscious of their surroundings even when they do not appear to be. Indeed, as noted below, people who are deeply asleep still show awareness of their surroundings; they generally do not roll off the bed, for example. Second, conscious experiences are associated with brain activity, and understanding this brain activity might help us better understand consciousness, the nature of which has been one of psychology's most vexing mysteries.

How Is the Conscious Mind Experienced?

What's on your mind? Having a conscious mind that thinks, feels, daydreams, and so on is one defining aspect of being human. Despite the fact that each normally functioning human has some degree of self-awareness, consciousness is difficult to study scientifically. On the one hand, consciousness is very real; scientists can differentiate between being "conscious" and being "unconscious." On the other hand, one of the biological sciences' greatest unanswered questions is how neural activity in the brain gives rise to a person's subjective experience of the world—the state of being conscious. At every minute, our brains are regulating our body temperatures, controlling our breathing, calling up memories as necessary, and so on, but we are not conscious of the brain operations that do these things. Similarly, our brains are extremely active during sleep, even though we are not conscious at the time. Why are we conscious only of certain experiences? What is consciousness?

Consciousness refers to moment-by-moment subjective experiences, such as reflecting on one's current thoughts or paying attention to one's immediate surroundings. Psychological scientists study two components of consciousness: the *contents* of consciousness (the things we are conscious of) and the *level* of consciousness (such as coma, sleep, and wakefulness). In addition to considering consciousness in terms of content and level, psychological scientists differentiate between doing things consciously (e.g., choosing to wear one outfit over another) and doing things unconsciously (e.g., automatically scratching an itch). In discussing actions, we refer to conscious intentions rather than conscious awareness. So, throughout this chapter, *consciousness* refers to awareness, to experiences. The chapter will take up the issue, however, of which behaviors are under conscious control and which seem to occur more automatically, without conscious intent.

Philosophers have long debated the nature of consciousness. In the seventeenth century, the philosopher René Descartes stated that the mind is physically distinct from the brain, a view of consciousness called *dualism*. Most psychological scientists now reject dualism, instead believing that the brain and mind are inseparable. According to this view, the activity of neurons in the brain produces the contents of consciousness: the sight of a face, the smell of a rose. More specifically, each type of content—each sight, each smell—has an associated pattern of brain activity. The activation of this particular group of neurons in the brain somehow gives rise to the conscious experience. Likewise, when people drink too much, their conscious experience is changed (i.e., they become drunk) because alcohol affects how the brain works. Therefore, studying the brain helps psychological scientists study consciousness, and advances in the ability to image the working brain have provided new insights into conscious experience. After considering how the brain gives rise to conscious experience, this chapter discusses how these experiences differ because of natural variation (e.g., sleep), natural manipulation (e.g., meditation), and artificial manipulation (e.g., drugs).

consciousness   The subjective experience of the world and of mental activity.

THE BIRTH OF SELF-CONSCIOUSNESS

HOLY SMOKE—I'M STANDING HERE!

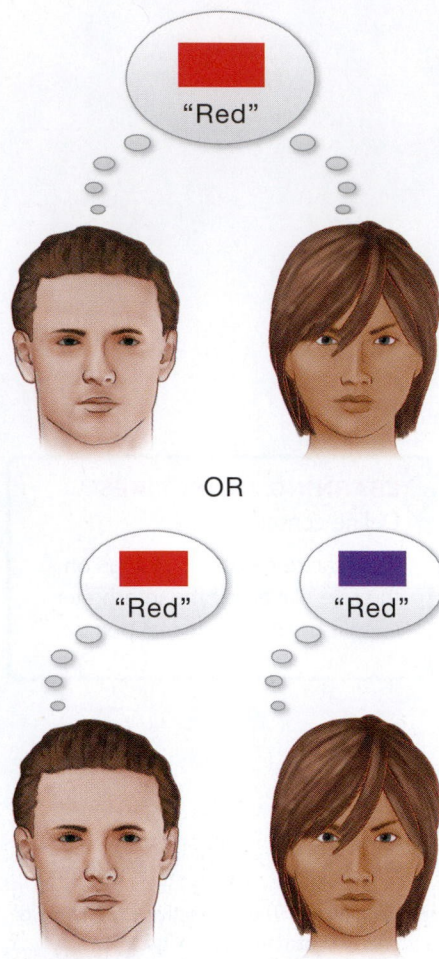

FIGURE 4.2 Qualia: Seeing Red One difficult question related to consciousness is how people experience qualia, the phenomenological percepts of the world. For instance, does red look the same to everyone who has normal color vision?

Consciousness Is a Subjective Experience

Because each of us experiences consciousness personally—that is, subjectively—we cannot know if any two people experience the world in exactly the same way. What does the color red look like to you? How does an apple taste? In the 1920s, philosophers coined the term *qualia* to describe the properties of our subjective experiences, such as our perceptions of things (**FIGURE 4.2**). As discussed in Chapter 1, early pioneers in psychology attempted to understand consciousness through introspection, but psychologists largely abandoned this method because of its subjective nature. Qualia exist, but their subjective nature makes them difficult to study empirically. So, when as children we played the game "I spy, with my little eye," players might have been looking at the same thing—say, "something that is red"—but they might have been experiencing that thing differently. In other words, there is no way to know whether each player's experience of the thing and its color was the same or whether each player was using the same words to describe a different experience. The labels applied to experience do not necessarily do justice to the experience. When you experience heartbreak and a friend consoles you by saying "I know how you feel," does your friend definitely know?

Despite scientists' difficulty in understanding experiences of qualia, growing evidence indicates that imaging methods can help identify commonalities in brain activity across experiences. Scientists cannot (yet) read your mind by looking at your brain activity, but they can identify objects you are looking at by looking at your brain activity (Kay, Naselaris, Prenger, & Gallant, 2008). For instance, researchers can use fMRI (see Chapter 2, "Research Methodology") to determine, based on your pattern of brain activity at that moment, whether the picture you are looking at is of a house, a shoe, a bottle, or a face (O'Toole et al., 2005). Similarly, brain imaging can reveal whether a person is looking at a striped pattern that is moving up and down or one moving side to side, whether a person is looking at a picture or a sentence, and so on (Norman et al., 2006). Frank Tong and colleagues (1998) studied the relationship between consciousness and neural responses in the brain. Participants were shown images in which houses were superimposed on faces. Neural activity increased within the temporal lobe's fusiform face area when participants reported seeing a face, but neural activity increased within temporal lobe regions associated with object recognition when participants reported seeing a house (on brain regions, see Chapter 3, "Biological Foundations"). This finding suggests that different types of sensory information are processed by different brain regions: The particular type of neural activity determines the particular type of awareness (**FIGURE 4.3**). As psychological science is beginning to reveal, common brain activity may give rise to people's subjective experiences.

How might reading brain activity allow researchers to improve the lives of those with spinal injuries? In our daily interactions with the world, we use our arms and hands to manipulate objects around us, such as when we type on keyboards, play computer games with joysticks, change television channels with remotes, and control cars with steering wheels. Imaging being able to manipulate such objects simply by thinking about using them. In groundbreaking research that provides hope for those with paralysis, neuroscientists have taught monkeys how to control a robot arm using only their thoughts (Carmena et al., 2003). As the media have quipped, "Monkey see, robot do."

How did the researchers accomplish this remarkable feat? The first step was to implant small electrodes in the frontal and parietal lobes of two rhesus monkeys and then record impulses from those electrodes while the monkeys learned to play a simple computer game. These brain areas were chosen because they are known to be involved in controlling complex movement. In the computer game, the monkeys

FIGURE 4.3 Scientific Method: The Relationship between Consciousness and Neural Responses in the Brain

Hypothesis: Specific patterns of brain activity can predict what a person is seeing.

Research Method:

1. Participants were shown images with houses superimposed on faces.

2. Participants were asked to report whether they saw a house or a face.

3. Researchers used fMRIs to measure neural responses in participants' brains.

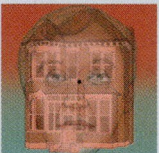

Results: Activity increased in the fusiform face area when participants reported seeing a face, but temporal cortex regions associated with object recognition became active when participants reported seeing a house.

Conclusion: Type of awareness is related to which brain region processes the particular sensory information.

---

used a joystick that allowed them to perform actions—such as steering a cursor and squeezing a trigger to achieve a goal—that involved moving a robotic arm they could see but not touch. By examining the recordings from the various brain regions, the researchers determined which patterns of brain activity led to specific motor actions. They then unplugged the joystick so that it no longer controlled the movement of the robotic arm, and they made movements of the robotic arm directly dependent on the pattern of neuronal firing from the monkeys' motor cortices. At first, the monkeys moved their arms wildly as if controlling the joystick, but it was not their arm movements that controlled the robot; it was their thoughts. "The most amazing result, though, was that after only a few days of playing with the robot in this way, the monkey suddenly realized that she didn't need to move her arm at all," says the lead neuroscientist, Miguel Nicolelis, describing one of the experiment's subjects (**FIGURE 4.4**). "Her arm muscles went completely quiet, she kept the arm at her side and she controlled the robot arm using only her brain and visual feedback. Our analyses of the brain signals showed that the animal learned to assimilate the robot arm into her brain as if it were her own arm" ("Gazette: Monkeys Move Matter, Mentally," 2004).

How soon might this research help those who are paralyzed? A team of researchers led by John Donoghue, in collaboration with a private company, received permission from the U.S. Food and Drug Administration to implant a small computer chip into five quadriplegic individuals. The chip reads signals from hundreds of neurons in the motor cortex. The first human to benefit from this technology was 25-year-old Matthew Nagle, who had been paralyzed from the neck down following a knife attack in 2001. The implanted device, called BrainGate, has allowed him to use a remote control to perform physical actions—such as changing television channels and opening and closing curtains—entirely with his thoughts. As in the rhesus monkey research, the brain's firing pattern is translated into signals that control the movement of a robotic arm. The goal of this research is to allow paralyzed individuals, through brain activity, to control prosthetic devices that will assist them in all aspects of daily living.

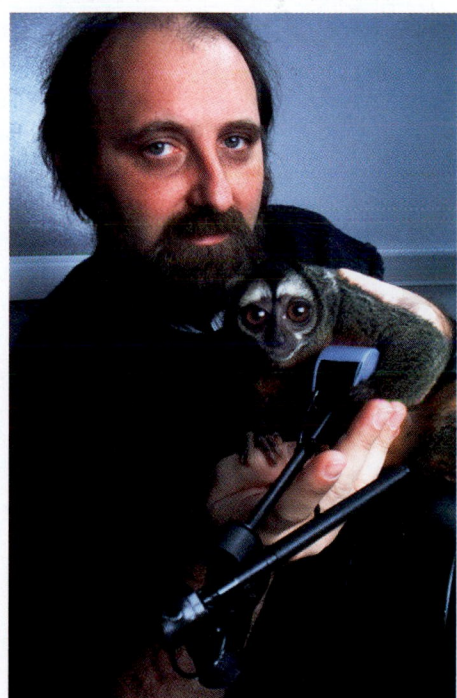

FIGURE 4.4 Advances in Motor Control Neurobiologist Miguel Nicolelis with one of the monkeys used in his study of the brain's motor command signals. Dr. Nicolelis's research has revealed new information on how reading brain activity may be used to improve the lives of people who are paralyzed.

There Are Variations in Conscious Experience

As you read this chapter, what are you conscious of, and how conscious are you? Is your mind wandering, occasionally or often? Is your stomach rumbling? Are you sitting comfortably? Are you drowsy? Is your mental state artificially pepped up thanks to coffee, soda, an energy drink? As you go through any day, you experience variations in consciousness. Your level of consciousness varies naturally through the day in your sleep/wake cycle. It will also, as discussed below, be affected by your actions (such as meditating to relax) and by consciousness-altering substances you consume (such as caffeine and alcohol).

As William James, one of the first American psychologists, described it, conscious experience is a continuous stream of thoughts that often floats from one thought to another. It is a unified and coherent experience—there is a limit to how many things you can be conscious of at the same time. You cannot pay attention to reading while also watching a television show, doing your calculus homework, and instant messaging with several friends. As you focus on developments in the show, you might realize you have no idea what you just read or what your friend just replied. Likewise, all at the same time you cannot think about what you will do tomorrow, what kind of car you would like to own, and where you most recently went on vacation. While driving to a familiar destination, have you ever begun to think about something other than your driving? Before you knew it, you had arrived. But how did you get there? You knew you had driven, but you could not remember details of the drive, such as whether you stopped at traffic lights or passed other vehicles. In general, we can execute routine or *automatic* tasks (such as driving, walking, or catching a baseball) that are so well learned that we do them without much conscious effort. Indeed, paying too much attention can interfere with these automatic behaviors. By contrast, difficult or unfamiliar tasks require greater conscious effort. Such *controlled* processing is slower than automatic processing, but it helps us perform in complex or novel situations. Thus if a rainstorm starts while you are driving, you will need to pay more attention to your driving and be very conscious of the road conditions.

CONSCIOUSNESS AND COMA As the cognitive neuroscientist Steven Laureys (2007) notes, medical advances mean that a greater number of people are surviving traumatic brain injuries; doctors now save the lives of many people who previously would have died from injuries sustained in car accidents or on battlefields, for example. However, surviving is just the first step toward recovery, and many of those who sustain serious brain injuries fall into comas. Most people who regain consciousness after such injuries do so within a few days, but some people do not regain consciousness for weeks. In this state, they have sleep/wake cycles—they open their eyes and appear to be awake, close their eyes and appear to be asleep—but they do not seem to respond to their surroundings. When this condition lasts longer than a month, it is known as a *persistent vegetative state*. The longer the persistent vegetative state lasts, the less likely the person is to ever recover consciousness or show normal brain activity. As you might recall, Terri Schiavo, an American woman living in Florida, spent more than 15 years in a persistent vegetative state. Eventually, her husband wanted to terminate her life support, but her parents wanted to continue it. Both sides waged a legal battle. Her parents believed that although Schiavo was in a coma, she was aware and occasionally had even responded to their presence. Schiavo's husband and doctors disputed these claims, believing her to be in an irreversible vegetative state with no hope of recovery. Indeed, an EEG of Schiavo's brain showed no activity.

A court ruled in the husband's favor, and life support was terminated. After Schiavo's death, an autopsy revealed substantial and irreversible damage throughout her brain and especially in cortical regions known to be important for consciousness (**FIGURE 4.5A**).

Between the vegetative state and full consciousness is the *minimally conscious state,* in which people make some deliberate movements, such as following an object with their eyes, and may try to communicate. The prognosis for those in a minimally conscious state is much better than for those in a persistent vegetative state. Consider the case of the Polish railroad worker Jan Grzebski, who in June 2007 woke up from a 19-year coma (**FIGURE 4.5B**). Grzebski remembers events that were going on around him for those 19 years, including his children's marriages. There is some indication that he tried to speak on occasion but was not understood. He now spends much of his time watching television or going out in his wheelchair, and he finds the world prettier than it was under communism (Scislowska, 2007, AP). In 2003, Terry Wallis, an American man living in Arkansas, began to talk with family members 19 years after an auto accident placed him in a minimally conscious state similar to Grzebski's. During his 19-year coma, Wallis had shown hints of awareness and occasionally seemed responsive to visitors. Recall as well the young woman, discussed above, who appeared to be in a coma but, at researchers' requests, mentally imagined walking through her house or playing tennis and thus showed signs of being minimally conscious rather than in a persistent vegetative state. Although differentiating between states of consciousness by behavior alone is difficult, brain imaging may prove useful for identifying the extent of a patient's brain injury and likelihood of recovery.

As discussed throughout this book, science often creates ethical issues. One such issue is whether brain evidence should be used to make end-of-life decisions. The outcome of Terry Schiavo's case, for example, remains highly controversial. Examining the brain of a person in an apparent coma, however, increases the chances of making well-informed medical decisions. Emerging evidence indicates that stimulating the thalamus (using a device something like a heart pacemaker) increases awareness among those in minimally conscious states, but when is this procedure advisable? A 38-year-old man, unable to communicate for more than six years following brain injury but still showing fMRI evidence of brain activity, was able to interact meaningfully and consistently with others, using vocalizations and social movements, after six months of thalamic stimulation (Schiff et al., 2007). That a similar procedure was ineffective for Terri Schiavo further reinforces the evidence that her cortex had deteriorated beyond recovering. Thus brain imaging might be useful for determining which patients are good candidates for treatment.

Splitting the Brain Splits the Conscious Mind

Studying people who have undergone brain surgery to treat disorders has given researchers a better understanding of the conscious mind. Often this surgery has attempted to treat epilepsy by removing the part of the brain in which the seizures began. Another strategy, pioneered in the 1940s and still practiced on occasion when other interventions have failed, is to cut connections within the brain to try to isolate the site of seizure initiation, so a seizure that begins at that site will less likely spread throughout the cortex. (Chapter 7, "Attention and Memory," includes a discussion of H.M., one of psychology's most famous case studies because of the memory loss he suffered as a result of brain surgery conducted to stop his severe seizures.)

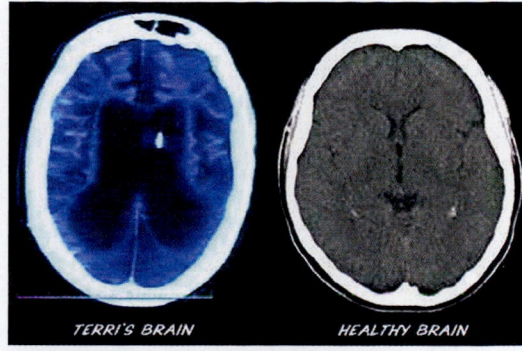

(a)

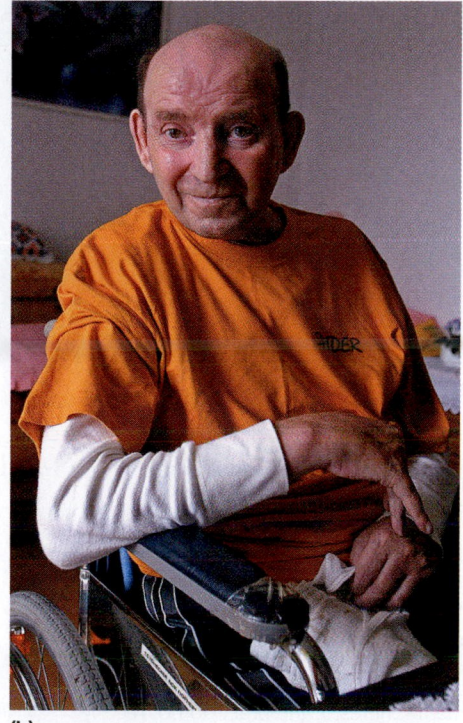

(b)

FIGURE 4.5 The Range of Consciousness (a) Terry Schiavo spent more than 15 years in a persistent vegetative state before she was taken off life support. Her parents and their supporters believed she showed some awareness, despite brain scans that showed no brain activity. **(b)** Jan Grzebski was in a minimally conscious state for 19 years before he awoke and reported that he had in fact been aware of events around him.

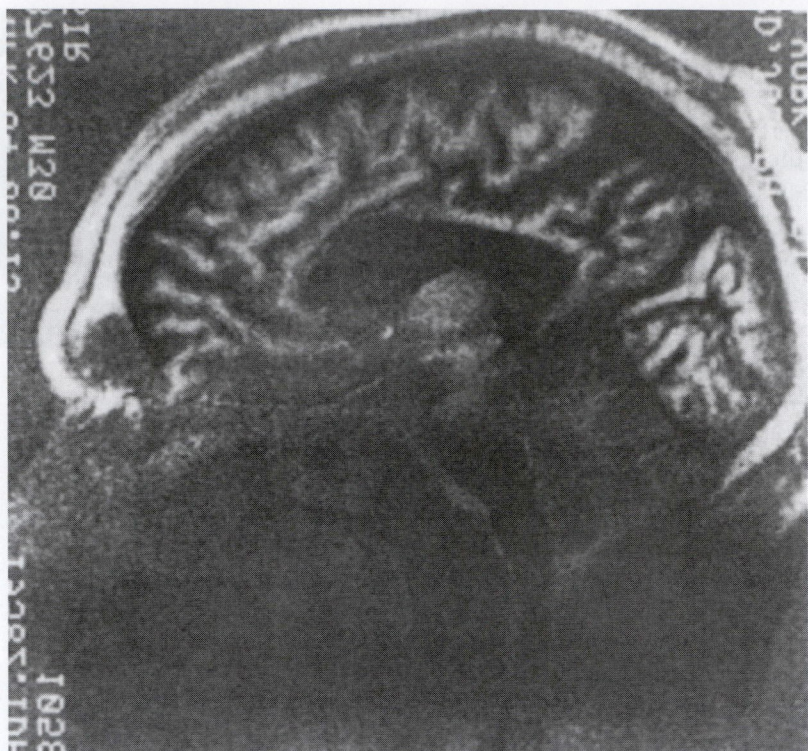

FIGURE 4.6 The Corpus Callosum
This MRI shows a patient's brain after the corpus callosum was completely sectioned.

split brain A condition in which the corpus callosum is surgically cut and the two hemispheres of the brain do not receive information directly from each other.

The major connection between the hemispheres that may readily be cut without damaging the gray matter is the massive fiber bundle called the *corpus callosum* (**FIGURE 4.6**). Most epilepsy responds to treatment with modern medications, but in rare, extreme cases that do not respond to medications, the corpus callosum may be cut completely as a means of treatment. When the corpus callosum is severed, the brain's halves are almost completely isolated from each other, a condition called **split brain.** This surgical procedure has provided many important insights into the basic organization and specialized functions of each brain hemisphere. But this procedure also raises an interesting question: "If you split the brain, do you split the mind?"

What is it like to have your brain split in half? Although you might think it would lead to dramatic personality changes, perhaps the most obvious thing about the split-brain patients after their operations is how normal they are. Unlike patients following other types of brain surgery, split-brain patients have no immediately apparent major problems. In fact, some early investigations suggested the surgery had not affected the patients in any discernible way. They could walk normally, talk normally, think clearly, and interact socially. In the 1960s, this book's coauthor Michael Gazzaniga, working with the Nobel laureate Roger Sperry, conducted a series of tests on the first split-brain participants. The results were stunning: Just as the brain had been split in two, so had the mind!

As discussed in Chapter 5, images from the visual field's left side (left half of what you are looking at) go to the right hemisphere, and those from the right side go to the left; the left hemisphere also controls the right hand, and the right hemisphere controls the left hand. With a split-brain patient, these divisions allow researchers to provide information to and get information from a single hemisphere at a time (**FIGURE 4.7**).

Psychologists have long known that in most people the left hemisphere is dominant for language. If a split-brain patient sees two pictures flashed on a screen briefly and simultaneously—one to the visual field's right side and one to the left side—the patient will report that only the picture on the right was shown. Why is this? Because the left hemisphere, with its control over speech, sees only the picture on the right side, so it is the only picture a person with a split brain can talk about. The mute right hemisphere (or "right brain"), having seen the picture on the left, is unable to articulate a response. The right brain can act on its perception, however: If the picture on the left was, for example, of a spoon, the right hemisphere can easily pick out an actual spoon from a selection of objects, using the left hand (which is controlled by the right hemisphere). Still, the left hemisphere does not know what the right one saw. Splitting the brain, then, produces two half brains, each with its own perceptions, thoughts, and consciousness (**FIGURE 4.8**).

Further explorations have revealed much more about the division of labor within the brain. In all the split-brain patients studied, the left hemisphere was far more competent at language than the right, so much so that in many patients the right hemisphere had no discernable language capacity. In some patients, though, the right

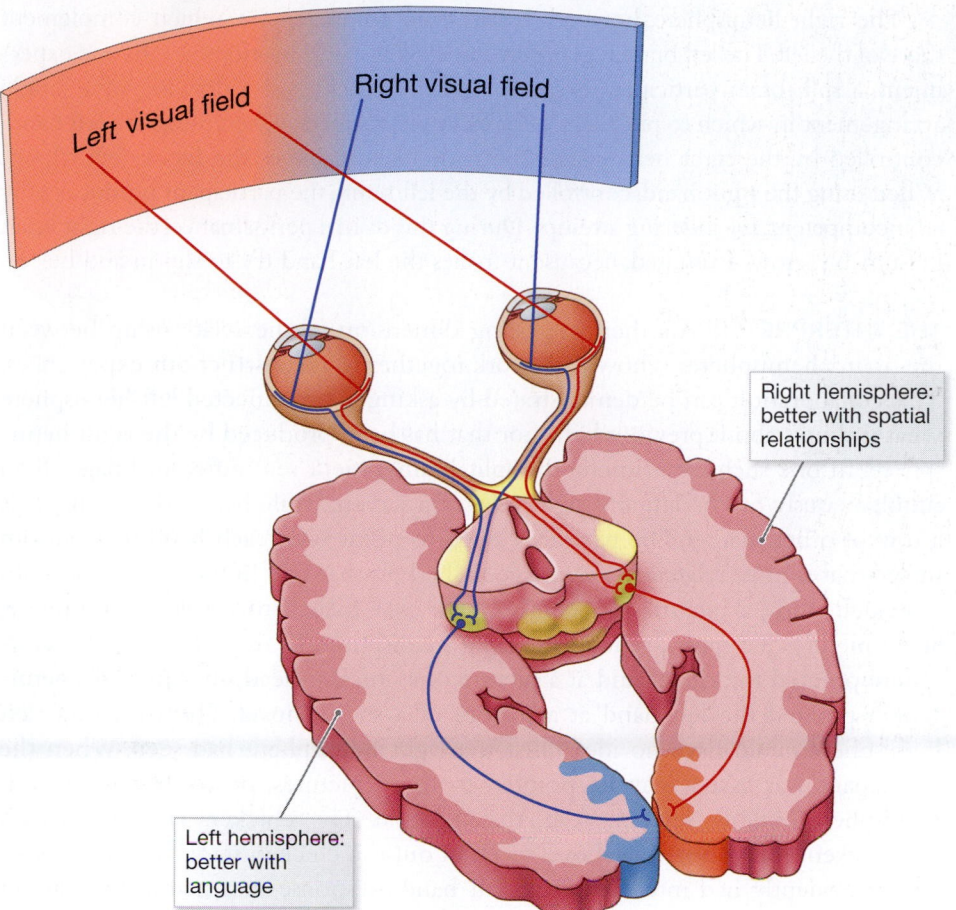

FIGURE 4.7 Visual Input Images from the left side go to the brain's right hemisphere, and images from the right side go to the left hemisphere.

Right hemisphere: better with spatial relationships

Left visual field

Right visual field

Left hemisphere: better with language

hemisphere displayed some rudimentary language comprehension, such as being able to read simple words. Interestingly, such right hemisphere language capabilities tend to improve in the years following the split-brain operation, presumably as the right hemisphere attains communication skills unnecessary when that hemisphere was connected to the fluent left brain.

FIGURE 4.8 Split-Brain Experiment: The Left Hemisphere versus the Right Hemisphere

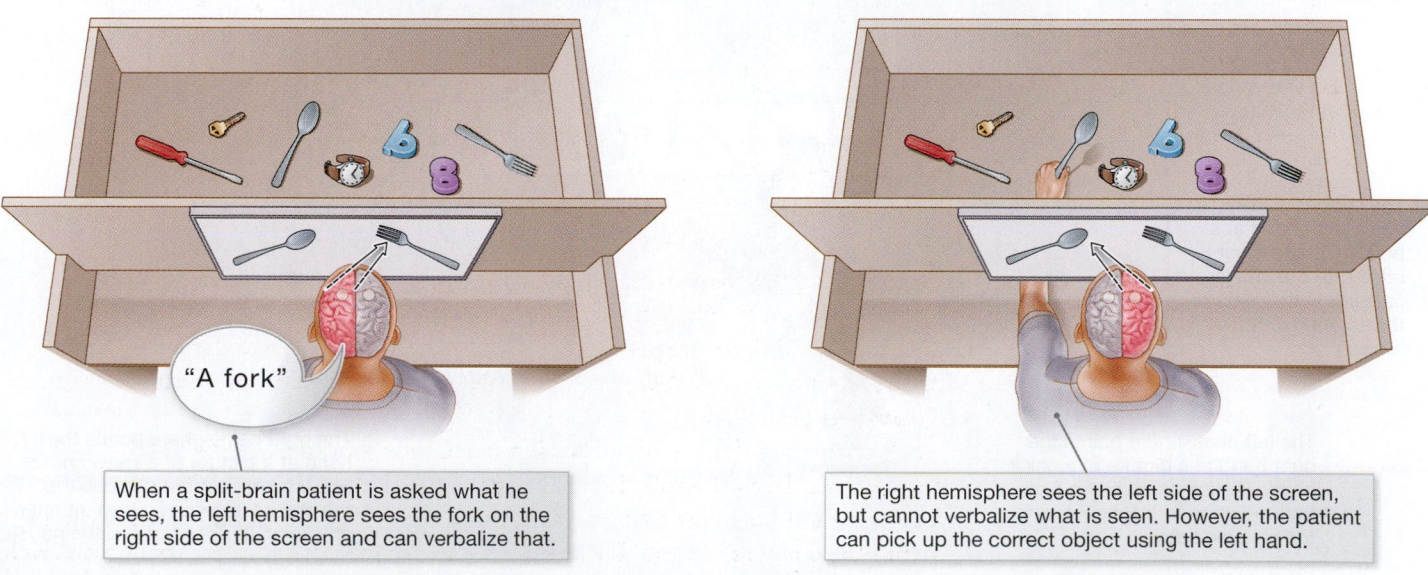

"A fork"

When a split-brain patient is asked what he sees, the left hemisphere sees the fork on the right side of the screen and can verbalize that.

The right hemisphere sees the left side of the screen, but cannot verbalize what is seen. However, the patient can pick up the correct object using the left hand.

The right hemisphere, however, has its own competencies, which complement those of the left. The left brain is generally hopeless at spatial relationships. In one experiment, a split-brain participant is given a pile of blocks and a drawing of a simple arrangement in which to put them—for example, a square. When using the left hand, controlled by the right hemisphere, the participant arranges the blocks effortlessly. When using the right hand, controlled by the left brain, the participant produces only an incompetent, meandering attempt. During this dismal performance, the right brain presumably grows frustrated, because it makes the left hand try to slip in and help!

THE INTERPRETER Another interesting dimension to the relationship between the brain's hemispheres is how they work together to reconstruct our experiences. This collaboration can be demonstrated by asking a disconnected left hemisphere what it thinks about previous behavior that has been produced by the right hemisphere. In one such experiment, the split-brain patient sees different images flash simultaneously on the left and right sides of a screen, while below those images is a row of other images. The patient is asked to point with each hand to a bottom image that is most related to the image flashed on that side of the screen above. In one such study, a picture of a chicken claw was flashed to the left hemisphere, and a picture of a snow scene to the right hemisphere. In response, the left hemisphere pointed the right hand at a picture of a chicken head, and the right hemisphere pointed the left hand at a picture of a snow shovel. The (speaking) left hemisphere could have no idea what the right hemisphere had seen. When the participant was asked why he pointed to those pictures, he (or, rather, his left hemisphere) calmly replied, "Oh, that's simple. The chicken claw goes with the chicken, and you need a shovel to clean out the chicken shed." The left hemisphere evidently had interpreted the left hand's response in a manner consistent with the left brain's knowledge (**FIGURE 4.9**).

FIGURE 4.9 The Left Hemisphere Interpreter On the basis of limited information, the left hemisphere attempts to explain behavior governed by the right hemisphere.

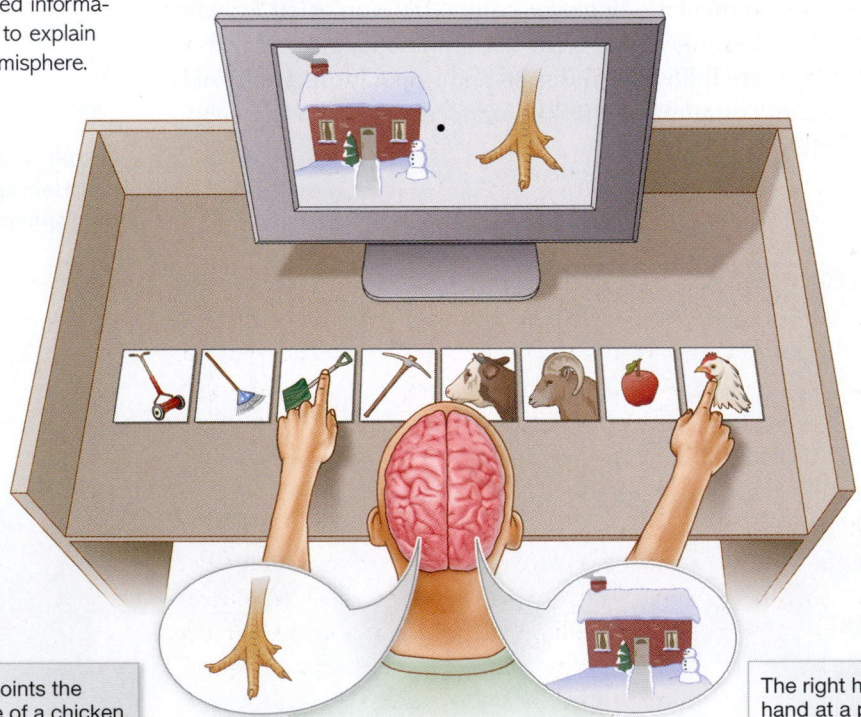

1 A split-brain participant watches as different images flash simultaneously on the left and right.

2 Below the screen is a row of other images.

3 The patient is asked to point each hand at a bottom image most related to the image flashed on that side of the screen.

The left hemisphere points the right hand at a picture of a chicken head. The left hemisphere says that the chicken claw goes with the chicken head.

The right hemisphere points the left hand at a picture of a snow shovel. The left hemisphere decides that the shovel is used to clean up after chickens. (It does not see the house.)

The left hemisphere's propensity to construct a world that makes sense is called the **interpreter,** because the left hemisphere is interpreting what the right hemisphere has done (Gazzaniga, 2000). In this last example, the left hemisphere interpreter created a ready way to explain the left hand's action, which was controlled by the disconnected right hemisphere. The explanation was unrelated to the right hemisphere's real reason for commanding that action. Yet to the patient, the movement seemed perfectly plausible once the action had been interpreted. Usually, the interpreter's explanations come readily. To give another example: If the command *Stand up* is flashed to a split-brain patient's right hemisphere, the patient will stand up. But when asked why he has stood up, the patient will not reply, "You just told me to," because the command is not available to his (speaking) left hemisphere. Instead, unaware of the command, he will say something like, "I just felt like getting a soda." His left hemisphere is compelled to concoct a story that explains, or interprets, his action after it has occurred.

Such interpretation does not always happen instantly. Sometimes it takes the patient's left hemisphere as long to figure out why the left hand is acting as it would take an outside observer. In one session, Gazzaniga and his colleagues presented the word *phone* to the right hemisphere of patient J.W. and asked him to verbalize what he saw. J.W replied that he did not see anything. Of course, J.W. was speaking from his left hemisphere, which did not see the word *phone,* and his right hemisphere was mute. However, when a pen was placed in his left hand and he was asked to draw what he saw, J.W. immediately started drawing a phone. Outside observers who had not seen the word *phone* took some time to make out what J.W. was drawing. J.W.'s left hemisphere was in the same boat. Fortunately, J.W. tended to articulate what he was thinking (a helpful trait in a research subject). He was initially confused by what he was drawing and started guessing about what it was. Not until the picture was almost complete did the outside observers, including J.W.'s left hemisphere, understand what his left hand was drawing. At that point, J.W. exclaimed, "Duh, it's a phone!" The communication between the hemispheres occurred on the paper and not within his head. J.W.'s right hemisphere drew what it saw; after viewing the drawing, his left hemisphere identified it as a phone. In the meantime, his interpreter struggled to guess what his hand was drawing.

THE INTERPRETER SPECULATES The interpreter strongly influences the way we view and remember the world. Shown a series of pictures that form a story and asked later to choose which of another group of pictures they had seen previously, normal participants have a strong tendency to falsely "recognize" pictures consistent with the theme of the original series and to reject those inconsistent with the theme. The left brain, then, tends to "compress" its experiences into a comprehensible story and to reconstruct remembered details based on the gist of that story. The right brain seems simply to experience the world and remember things in a manner less distorted by narrative interpretation.

Sometimes the left brain interpreter makes life more difficult than it needs to be. In one experiment, human or (nonhuman) animal participants must predict, on each trial, whether a red light or a green light will flash. A correct prediction produces some small reward. Both lights flash in a random sequence, but overall the red light flashes 70 percent of the time. Participants pretty quickly notice that the red light comes on more often. So to receive the most reward, what strategy do they follow? After doing this task a number of times, most animals simply choose the red light—the most probable response—100 percent of the time; by doing so, they receive rewards on 70 percent of the trials. This

interpreter A left hemisphere process that attempts to make sense of events.

strategy makes great sense in terms of adaptiveness, in that it guarantees the animals receive the maximum rewards, yet humans do something much different. They try to figure out patterns in the way the lights flash, and they choose the red light about 70 percent of the time. That is, overall their choices match the frequency of how often red flashes, but because the lights flash randomly, on any given trial humans may choose incorrectly. Indeed, when humans choose the red light 70 percent of the time, they generally receive rewards on only 58 percent of the trials.

Why do humans not follow the optimal strategy, which even rats can figure out? According to George Wolford and colleagues (2000), the left hemisphere interpreter leads people to search for patterns that might not even exist. To test this idea, the researchers had two split-brain patients perform a version of the task described above. The patients' right hemispheres tended to respond in the optimal way that animals did (choosing the same thing 100 percent of the time), whereas the patients' left hemispheres chose red only 70 percent of the time. The left hemisphere interpreter's tendency to seek relationships between things may be adaptive in some contexts, but it can produce less-than-optimal outcomes when such relationships (e.g., patterns) do not exist.

subliminal perception Information processed without conscious awareness.

The split brain is a rare condition, of course, and nearly all people have two hemispheres that communicate and cooperate on the tasks of daily living. The popular media have sometimes exaggerated this research's findings, suggesting that certain people are "left brain" logical types and others are "right brain" artistic types. In reality, although the hemispheres are specialized for certain functions, such as language or spatial navigation, most cognitive processes involve both hemispheres' coordinated efforts. Split-brain research provides a unique opportunity to study each hemisphere's capacities.

Unconscious Processing Influences Behavior

Before reading further, think of your phone number. If you are familiar enough with the number, you probably remembered it quickly. Yet you have no idea how your brain worked this magic. That is, you do not have direct access to the neural or cognitive processes that lead to your thoughts and behavior. You thought about your phone number, and (if the magic worked) the number popped into your consciousness.

This brief exercise illustrates a central property of consciousness: We are aware of some mental processes and not aware of others. Over the last several decades, many researchers have explored different ways in which unconscious cues, or **subliminal perception,** can influence cognition. Subliminal perception refers to stimuli that get processed by sensory systems but, because of their short durations or subtle forms, do not reach consciousness. Advertisers have long been accused of using subliminal cues to persuade people to purchase products (**FIGURE 4.10**). The evidence suggests that subliminal messages have quite small effects on purchasing behavior (Greenwald, 1992), but material presented subliminally can influence how people think even if it has little or no effect on complex actions. (Buying something you did not intend to buy would count as a complex action.) That

FIGURE 4.10 **Try for Yourself: Subliminal Perception**

Try to pick out the subliminal message in the advertisement below.

Answer: The ice cubes spell out S-E-X.

is, considerable evidence indicates that people are affected by events—stimuli—they are not aware of (Gladwell, 2005). In one recent study, participants exerted greater physical effort when large images of money were flashed at them, even though the flashes were so brief the participants did not report seeing the money (Pessiglione et al., 2007). The subliminal images of money also produced brain activity in areas of the limbic system, which is involved in emotion and motivation.

Other events can influence our thoughts without our awareness. In a classic experiment by the social psychologists Richard Nisbett and Timothy Wilson (1977), the participants were asked to examine word pairs, such as *ocean-moon,* that had obvious semantic associations between the words. They were then asked to free-associate on other, single words, such as *detergent.* Nisbett and Wilson wanted to find out the degree, if any, to which the word pairs would influence the free associations—and, if the influence occurred, whether the participants would be aware of it. When given the word *detergent* after the word pair *ocean-moon,* participants typically free-associated the word *tide.* However, when asked why they said "tide," they usually gave reasons citing the detergent's brand-name, such as "My mom used Tide when I was a kid"; they were not aware that the word pair had influenced their thoughts. Here again, the left hemisphere interpreter was at work, making sense of a situation and providing a plausible explanation for cognitive events when complete information was not available. We are, of course, frequently unaware of the many different influences on our thoughts, feelings, and behavior. Similar effects underlie the classic mistake called a *Freudian slip,* in which an unconscious thought is suddenly expressed at an inappropriate time and/or in an inappropriate social context.

Another example of unconscious influences' power comes from the work of John Bargh and his colleagues (1996), who asked participants to make sentences out of groups of words. Some of these words were associated with the elderly, such as *old, Florida,* and *wrinkles.* After the participants had made up a number of sentences, they were told the experiment was over. But the researchers continued observing the participants, interested in whether the unconscious activation of beliefs about the elderly would influence the participants' behavior. Indeed, participants primed with stereotypes about old people walked much more slowly than did those who had been given words unrelated to the elderly. When questioned later, the slow-walking participants were not aware that the concept of "elderly" had been activated or that it had changed their behavior. Other researchers have obtained similar findings. For instance, Ap Dijksterhuis and Ad van Knippenberg (1998) found that people at Nijmegen University, in the Netherlands, better answered trivial questions when they were subtly presented with information about "professors" than when they were subtly presented with information about "soccer hooligans," although they were unaware that their behavior was influenced by the information. Such findings indicate that much of our behavior occurs without our awareness or intention (Bargh & Morsella, 2008).

THE SMART UNCONSCIOUS Common sense tells us that consciously thinking about a problem or deliberating about the options is the best strategy for making a decision. Consider the possibility that *not* consciously thinking can produce an outcome superior to that of consciously thinking.

In a study by Ap Dijksterhuis (2004), participants evaluated complex information regarding real-world choices—for example, selecting an apartment. In each case, the participants chose between alternatives that had negative features (e.g., high rent, bad location) and positive features (e.g., nice landlord, good view), but objectively, one apartment was the best choice. Some participants were required to make an immediate choice (no thought); some to think for three minutes and then choose (conscious thought); and some to work for three minutes on a difficult, distracting task and then choose (unconscious thought). Across three separate trials, those in the unconscious thought condition made the best decisions. According to Dijksterhuis and Nordgren (2006), unconscious processing is especially valuable for complex decisions in which it is difficult to weigh the pros and cons consciously. A similar phenomenon has also been reported in the creativity literature: Anecdotal reports suggest that allowing an idea to incubate over time helps in problem solving. Perhaps this is why, for very important decisions, people often choose to "sleep on it." (Chapter 8, "Thinking and Intelligence," will return to this idea in discussing problem-solving strategies.)

Consider also the possibility that consciously thinking can undermine good decision making. Tim Wilson and Jonathan Schooler (1991) asked research participants to rate jams. When the participants simply tasted the jams, their ratings were very similar to experts' ratings. However, when the participants had to explain their ratings jam by jam, their ratings differed substantially from the experts'. Unless the experts were wrong, the participants had made poorer judgments: Having to reflect consciously about their reasons apparently altered their perceptions of the jams. The cognitive psychologist Jonathan Schooler has introduced the concept of *verbal overshadowing* to describe the performance impairment that occurs when people try to explain verbally their perceptual experiences that are not easy to describe (Schooler & Engslter-Schooler, 1990; Schooler, 2002). For example, participants who had to describe the perpetrator they saw in a simulated bank robbery were less able to pick the person out of a lineup than were participants who did not have to provide a description. The descriptive labels used by the first group altered those participants' memories of the robber. In another study, participants who had to describe a wine's taste were later less able to detect that wine's taste than were participants who simply tasted the wine and did not describe the taste (Melcher & Schooler, 1996). Consciously reflecting on the wine's qualities impaired performance. The take-home message of these studies is that we are not very good at describing perceptual experiences; when we are forced to do so, the act of verbally labeling alters our memories. Although it is unclear exactly why thinking too much can impair judgment and memory, some things appear to be best left unsaid (**FIGURE 4.11**).

FIGURE 4.11 Try for Yourself: Verbal Overshadowing

Pick the image below that is by a famous painter.

Now explain why you chose the image you did.

If you are like most people, you found it difficult to verbalize your perceptual experience.

Answer: *Untitled XX*, on the right, is by Willem de Kooning (1904–1997), considered a master of abstract expressionism. The painting on the left, *Lollipop House*, was painted by Marla Olmstead (b. 2000), the subject of the 2007 documentary *My Kid Could Paint That*.

Brain Activity Produces Consciousness

Except in research situations, we can know that a particular person is aware of a certain something only when that person reports the awareness. Because a person cannot be aware of having perceived subliminal stimuli, for example, the person cannot report on them or their effects. As discussed above, though, subliminal information can influence behavior, and brain imaging reveals that subliminal stimuli are processed in the brain despite their perceivers' lack of conscious awareness. Only research can reveal such processing, and during the past few decades, researchers have worked to identify the brain regions most important to different forms of awareness. By studying awareness in individuals with damage to specific regions of the brain, for example, researchers hope to link selective losses of awareness—that is, losses of awareness for specific forms of information—to the damaged brain areas.

BLINDSIGHT Some research on visual awareness has examined **blindsight,** a condition in which a person who experiences some blindness because of damage to the visual system continues to show evidence of some sight, but is unaware of being able to see at all. Typically, a blindsighted patient loses vision in only a portion of the visual field. For example, when looking forward the person might not be able to see anything on his or her left. Researchers have discovered that when a stimulus is presented in this blind field, the patient can respond unconsciously to that stimulus. For example, a moving dot might be presented to the blind spot, and the patient must indicate in which direction the dot is moving. Typically, the patient reports having seen nothing. However, when pressed to guess the direction of motion, more often than by chance the patient will guess correctly.

One example of blindsight was recently found in a 52-year-old physician who had become blind following two consecutive strokes that destroyed the primary visual cortices in both brain hemispheres (Pegna, Khateb, Lazeyras, & Seghier, 2005). Nothing was wrong with his eyes, but the visual regions of his brain could not process any information they received from them. Although alert and aware of his surroundings, the patient reported being unable to see anything, not even the presence of intense light. Visual information also goes to other brain regions, such as the amygdala, however. As discussed in Chapter 9, one theory suggests that the amygdala processes visual information very crudely and quickly, to help identify potential threats. For example, the amygdala becomes activated in imaging studies when people observe subliminal presentations of faces expressing fear (Whalen et al., 2005). When the blind physician was shown a series of faces and was asked to guess their emotional expression, he had no sense of having seen anything but was able to identify the expression at a level much better than chance. He did not respond to other stimuli (such as shapes, animal faces, or scary stimuli). A brain scanner showed that his amygdala became activated when he was presented with emotional faces but not with faces showing neutral expressions. Thus his amygdala might have processed the faces' emotional content despite his lack of awareness. This raises the intriguing question of whether the patient was "seeing" the faces; it also may help illuminate how visual information reaches the amygdala when primary visual areas are damaged.

GLOBAL WORKSPACE The *global workspace model* posits that consciousness arises as a function of which brain circuits are active (Baars, 1988; Dehaene et al., 2006). That is, you experience your brain regions' output as conscious awareness. Studying people with brain injuries, who are sometimes unaware of their deficits,

blindsight A condition in which people who are blind have some spared visual capacities in the absence of any visual awareness.

supports this idea. For instance, a person who has vision problems caused by an eye injury will know about those problems because the brain's visual areas will notice something is wrong. But if that same person then suffers damage to the brain's visual areas so that they stop delivering output, the person may have no visual information to consider and thus will not be aware of vision problems. Of course, if the person suddenly becomes blind, as did the doctor described above, that person will know he or she cannot see. But a person who loses part of the visual field because of a brain injury tends not to notice the gap in visual experience. This tendency appears with hemineglect, for example (see Figure 3.30). A hemineglect patient is not aware of missing part of the visual world. In one patient's words, "I knew the word 'neglect' was a sort of medical term for whatever was wrong but the word bothered me because you only neglect something that is actually there, don't you? If it's not there, how can you neglect it?" (Halligan & Marshall, 1998). Jeffrey Cooney and Michael Gazzaniga (2003) explain this phenomenon by arguing that the left hemisphere interpreter can make sense only of available information, so even though normally sighted people might find the hemineglect patients' attitude bizarre, the hemineglect patients see their particular limited visual states as perfectly normal. The hemineglect patients' unawareness of their visual deficits supports the idea that consciousness arises through the brain processes active at any point in time.

Most importantly, the global workspace model presents no single area of the brain as responsible for general "awareness." Rather, different areas of the brain deal with different types of information, and each of these systems in turn is responsible for conscious awareness of its type of information (**FIGURE 4.12**). From this perspective, consciousness is the mechanism that is actively aware of information and that prioritizes what information we need or want to deal with at any moment.

FIGURE 4.12 Areas of Awareness A central theme emerging from cognitive neuroscience is that awareness of different aspects of the world is associated with functioning in different parts of the brain. This simplified diagram indicates major areas of awareness.

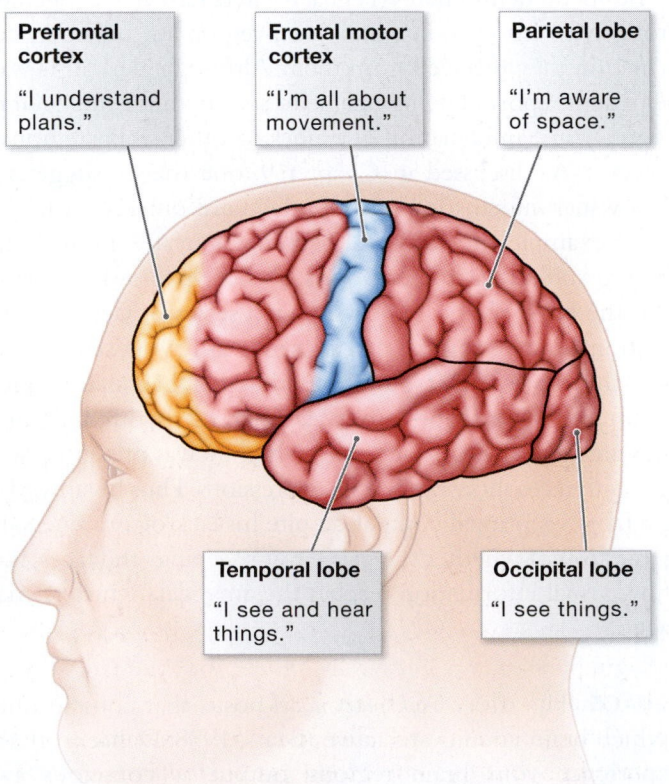

Prefrontal cortex
"I understand plans."

Frontal motor cortex
"I'm all about movement."

Parietal lobe
"I'm aware of space."

Temporal lobe
"I see and hear things."

Occipital lobe
"I see things."

⊙ **SUMMING UP**

How Is the Conscious Mind Experienced?

Although the relationship between the physical brain and consciousness has been debated at least since Descartes' time, psychological scientists have developed methods of assessing both the contents and the variations of consciousness. Consciousness refers to a person's experience of the world, including thoughts and feelings. The brain gives rise to consciousness by bringing multiple systems' activities together in a global workspace. Most brain activities do not rise to the level of consciousness, but these unconscious processes influence behavior.

⊙ **MEASURING UP**

1. Which of the following statements are correct, according to our understanding of consciousness? Choose as many as apply.
   a. The presence of consciousness is one of the main ways we can distinguish between humans' thoughts and nonhuman animals' thoughts.
   b. Brain research shows that some people in comas have higher brain activity levels than others.
   c. The contents of consciousness cannot be labeled.
   d. Any biological process can be made conscious through effortful processing.
   e. Our behaviors and thoughts are affected by some events about which we have no conscious knowledge.
   f. Consciousness is subjective.
   g. Without brain activity, there is no consciousness.
   h. People in comas may differ in levels of consciousness.
   i. People are either conscious or unconscious; there is no middle ground.

2. In a split-brain patient, the left hemisphere interpreter _____.
   a. explains what to do when the patient does not understand instructions
   b. translates from one language to another until the patient understands what is being said
   c. makes sense of actions directed by the right hemisphere
   d. uses language to direct the right hemisphere's activities.

What Is Sleep?

At regular intervals, the brain does a strange thing—it goes to sleep. A common misperception is that the brain shuts itself down during sleep and no longer processes information from the external world; nothing could be further from the truth. Many brain regions are more active during sleep than during wakefulness. It is even possible that some complex thinking, such as working on difficult problems, occurs in the sleeping brain (Walker & Stickgold, 2006). In one study, people had to learn a task at which they would slowly get better with practice. Unbeknownst to the participants, a hidden rule existed that, once discovered, would lead to much better performance. The participants proved more likely to figure out the rule after sleep than after a comparable period of wakefulness, independent of the time of day (Wagner, Gals, Haider, Verleger, & Born, 2004).

During sleep, the brain is still active. The conscious experience of the outside world is largely turned off, but to some extent people remain aware of their surroundings, as when sleeping parents sense their baby rustling in the crib. Given that

LEARNING OBJECTIVES
List and describe the stages of sleep.

Explain why we sleep and dream.

most animals sleep and that humans cannot go without sleep for more than a few days, most researchers believe sleep serves some important (but so far unknown) biological purpose.

The average person sleeps around eight hours per night, but individuals differ tremendously in the number of hours they sleep. Infants sleep most of the day, and people tend to sleep less as they age. Some adults report needing 9 or 10 hours of sleep a night to feel rested, whereas others report needing only an hour or two a night. When a 70-year-old retired nurse, Miss M., reported sleeping only an hour a night, researchers were skeptical. On her first two nights in a research laboratory, Miss M. was unable to sleep, apparently because of the excitement. But on her third night, she slept for only 99 minutes, then awoke refreshed, cheerful, and full of energy (Meddis, 1977). You might like the idea of sleeping so little and having all those extra hours of spare time, but most of us do not function well on so little sleep. And as discussed in later chapters, sufficient sleep is important for memory and good health.

Sleep Is an Altered State of Consciousness

The difference between being awake and being asleep has as much to do with conscious experience as with biological processes. When you sleep, you are not conscious, but your brain still processes information and, to some extent, remains aware of your environment. Your mind is at work, analyzing potential dangers, controlling bodily movements, and shifting body parts to maximize comfort. For this reason, people who sleep next to children or to pets tend not to roll over onto them. Nor do most people fall out of bed while sleeping—in this case, the brain is aware of at least the edges of the bed. (Because the ability to not fall out of bed when asleep is learned or perhaps develops with age, infant cribs have side rails and young children may need bed rails when they transition from crib to bed.)

Before the development of objective methods to assess brain activity, most people believed the brain went to sleep along with the rest of the body. Invented in the 1920s, the *electroencephalogram,* or *EEG,* a machine that measures the brain's electrical activity (see Chapter 2, "Research Methods"), revealed that a lot goes on in the brain during sleep. That different psychophysiological states occur during sleep has been called one of neuroscience's first major discoveries (Hobson, 1995). When people are awake, their brains' neurons are extremely active, as evidenced by short, frequent, desynchronized brain signals known as *beta waves* (shown in **FIGURE 4.13**). When people close their eyes and relax, brain activity slows and becomes more synchronized, a pattern that produces *alpha waves.*

STAGES OF SLEEP Sleep occurs in stages, as evidenced by changes in EEG readings (see Figure 4.14). As you drift off to sleep, you enter stage 1, characterized by *theta waves,* from which you can be aroused easily. Indeed, if awakened you will probably deny that you were sleeping. In this light sleep, you might see fantastical images or geometric shapes; you might have the sensation that you are falling or that your limbs are jerking.

FIGURE 4.13 Brain Activity during Sleep Using an EEG, researchers measured these examples of the patterns of electrical brain activity during different stages of normal sleep.

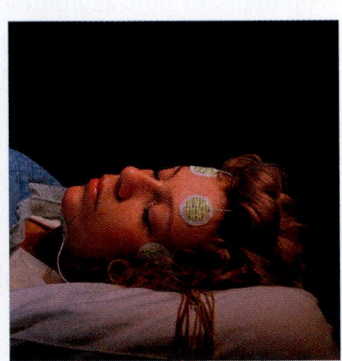

Alert wakefulness
Beta waves

Just before sleep
Alpha waves

Stage 1
Theta waves

Stage 2
Sleep spindle   K complex

Stage 3
Delta waves

Stage 4

As you progress to stage 2, your breathing becomes more regular, and you become less sensitive to external stimulation. You are now really asleep. Although the EEG would continue to show theta waves, it would also show occasional bursts of activity called *sleep spindles* and large waves called *k-complexes*. Some researchers believe that these are signals from brain mechanisms involved with shutting out the external world and keeping people asleep (Steriade, 1992). Two findings—that abrupt noise can trigger k-complexes; and that as people age and sleep lighter, their EEGs show fewer sleep spindles—indicate that the brain must work to maintain sleep.

The progression to deep sleep occurs through stages 3 and 4, which are marked by large, regular brain patterns called *delta waves*. This period is often referred to as *slow-wave sleep*. People in slow-wave sleep are very hard to wake and often very disoriented when they do wake up. However, people still process some information in stage 4, as the mind continues to evaluate the environment for potential danger. Parents in stage 4 can be aroused by their children's cries, for example, but blissfully ignore sounds, such as sirens or traffic noise, louder than the crying children.

REM SLEEP After about 90 minutes of sleep, a peculiar thing happens. The sleep cycle reverses, returning to stage 3 and then to stage 2. At this point, the EEG suddenly shows a flurry of beta wave activity that usually indicates an awake, alert mind. The eyes dart back and forth rapidly beneath closed eyelids, and for these *rapid eye movements* this stage is called **REM sleep.** It is sometimes called *paradoxical sleep* because of the paradox of a sleeping body with an active brain. Indeed, some neurons in the brain, especially in the occipital cortex and brainstem regions, are more active during REM sleep than during waking hours. But while the brain is active during REM episodes, most of the body's muscles are paralyzed. At the same time, the body shows signs of genital arousal: Most males of all ages develop erections, and most females of all ages experience clitoral engorgement.

REM sleep is psychologically significant because about 80 percent of the time when people are awakened during REM sleep, they report dreaming, compared with less than half of the time during non-REM sleep (Solms, 2000). As discussed further below, the dreams differ between these two types of sleep.

Over the course of a typical night's sleep, the cycle repeats, as the sleeper progresses from slow-wave sleep through to REM sleep, then back to slow-wave sleep and through to REM sleep (**FIGURE 4.14**). As morning approaches, the sleep cycle becomes shorter, and the sleeper spends relatively more time in REM sleep. People briefly awaken many times during the night but do not remember these awakenings in the morning. As people age, they sometimes have more difficulty going back to sleep after awakening.

REM sleep The stage of sleep marked by rapid eye movements, dreaming, and paralysis of motor systems.

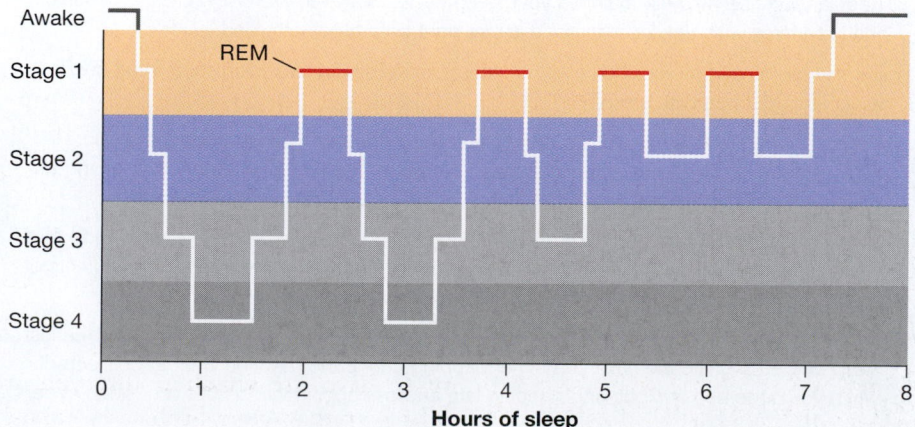

FIGURE 4.14 Stages of Sleep This chart illustrates the normal stages of sleep over the course of the night.

insomnia A disorder characterized by an inability to sleep.

SLEEP DISORDERS According to an old joke, when someone says, "I slept like a baby," it must mean waking up every few hours feeling miserable and unable to get back to sleep. Sleep problems are relatively common throughout life; about half the population reports difficulty getting to sleep or staying asleep. Even though nearly everyone has occasional sleep difficulties, for some people the inability to sleep causes significant problems in their daily lives. **Insomnia** is a sleep disorder in which people's mental health and ability to function are compromised by their inability to sleep. Indeed, chronic insomnia is associated with diminished psychological well-being, including feelings of depression (Hamilton et al., 2007). An estimated 12 percent to 20 percent of adults have persistent insomnia; it is more common in women than in men and more common in older adults than in younger adults (Espie, 2002). One factor that complicates the estimation of how many people have insomnia is that many people who believe they are poor sleepers overestimate how long it takes them to fall sleep and often underestimate how much sleep they get on a typical night. For instance, some people experience *pseudoinsomnia,* in which they basically dream they are not sleeping. Their EEGs would indicate sleep, though if you roused them they would claim to have been awake.

In an odd twist, a major cause of insomnia is worrying about sleep. People may be tired, but when they lie down they worry about whether they will get to sleep and may even panic about how a lack of sleep will affect them the next day. This anxiety leads to heightened arousal, which interferes with normal sleep patterns. To overcome these effects, many people take sleeping pills, which may work in the short run but can cause significant problems down the road. People may come to depend on the pills to help them sleep. If so and if they do not take the pills, they may lie awake wondering whether they can get to sleep on their own. The preferred psychological treatment for insomnia is *cognitive-behavioral therapy* (discussed in Chapter 15, "Treating Disorders of the Mind and Body"), which helps patients overcome their worries about sleeping (Smith & Perlis, 2006). Other factors that contribute to insomnia include poor sleeping habits (ways to improve sleeping habits are listed in **TABLE 4.1**).

Table 4.1 How to Develop Good Sleeping Habits

1. Establish a routine to help set your biological clock: Every day, including weekends, go to bed at the same time and wake up at the same time. Changing the time you go to bed or wake up each day can alter your regular nightly sleep cycle and/or disrupt other physiological systems.

2. Never consume alcohol or caffeine just before going to bed. Alcohol might help you get to sleep more quickly, but it will interfere with your sleep cycle and most likely cause you to wake up early the next day.

3. Regular exercise will help maintain your sleep cycle. However, exercising creates arousal that interferes with sleep, so do not exercise right before going to bed.

4. Do not spend time in your bed reading, eating, or watching television. Your mind needs to associate your bed with sleeping.

5. Relax. Do not worry about the future. Have a warm bath or listen to soothing music. Relaxation techniques—such as imagining you are on the beach, with the sun shining on your back and radiating down your hands—may help you deal with chronic stress.

6. When you cannot fall asleep, get up and do something else. Do not lie there trying to force sleep. One sleepless night will not affect you very much, and worrying about the effects of not sleeping will only make it more difficult to sleep.

7. When you have trouble falling asleep on a particular night, do not try to make up for the lost sleep by sleeping late the next morning or napping during the day. You want to be sleepy when you go to bed at night, and sleeping late and/or napping will disrupt your sleep cycle.

Another fairly common sleeping problem is **sleep apnea,** a disorder in which a person stops breathing for temporary periods while asleep, resulting in a loss of oxygen and sleep disruption. Sleep apnea is most common among middle-aged men and is often associated with obesity (Spurr, Graven, & Gilbert, 2008). People with sleep apnea are often unaware of their condition since the main symptom is loud snoring and they do not remember their frequent awakenings during the night. Yet chronic apnea causes people to have poor sleep, which is associated with daytime fatigue and even problems such as inability to concentrate while driving. For serious cases, physicians often prescribe a breathing device that, during sleep, blows air into the person's nose or nose and mouth (**FIGURE 4.15**).

A student who falls asleep during a lecture is likely sleep deprived, but a professor who falls asleep while lecturing is probably experiencing an episode of **narcolepsy,** a disorder in which excessive sleepiness occurs during normal waking hours. During an episode of narcolepsy, a person may experience the muscle paralysis that accompanies REM sleep, perhaps causing him or her to go limp and collapse. Obviously, people with narcolepsy—an estimated 1 in 2,000 people—have to be very careful about the activities they engage in during the day, as unexpectedly falling asleep can be dangerous or fatal depending on the surroundings. Evidence suggests that narcolepsy is a genetic condition that affects the neural transmission of a specific neurotransmitter in the hypothalamus (Chabas, Taheri, Renier, & Mignot, 2003; Nishino, 2007). The most effective treatments for this condition are drugs such as the stimulant modafinil, which has fewer side effects than traditional stimulants (such as amphetamines, discussed later in this chapter) and is much less likely to be addictive (Roth, 2007).

A sleep disorder that is roughly the opposite of narcolepsy is *REM behavior disorder,* in which the normal paralysis that accompanies REM sleep is disabled so that people act out their dreams while sleeping, often striking their sleeping partners. This rare disorder is caused by a neurological deficit and is most often seen in elderly males.

Unlike REM behavior disorder, sleepwalking is a relatively common behavior that occurs during stage 4 sleep. Technically called *somnambulism,* sleepwalking is most common among young children and typically occurs within the first hour or two after falling asleep. During an episode, the person is glassy-eyed and seems disconnected from other people and/or the surroundings. No harm is done if the sleepwalker wakes up during the episode. Being gently walked back to bed is safer for the sleepwalker than being left to wander around and potentially get hurt.

Sleep Is an Adaptive Behavior

In terms of adaptiveness, sleep might seem illogical. Tuning out the external world during sleep can be dangerous and thus a threat to survival. Beyond that, humans might have advanced themselves in countless ways if they had used all their time productively rather than wasting it by sleeping. But people cannot override indefinitely the desire to sleep; the body shuts down whether we like it or not. Why do we sleep? Sleep must do something important, because many animals sleep, even if they have peculiar sleeping styles. (For example, some dolphin species have *unihemispherical sleep,* in which the cerebral hemispheres take turns sleeping. Although it used to be assumed that all animals sleep, evidence indicates that some animals, such as some frogs, never exhibit a state that can be considered sleep [Siegel, 2008].) Researchers have proposed three general explanations for sleep's adaptiveness: *restoration, circadian cycles,* and *facilitation of learning.*

RESTORATION AND SLEEP DEPRIVATION According to the *restorative theory,* sleep allows the brain and body to rest and to repair themselves. Various kinds of evidence support this theory: Released during deep sleep, growth hormone

sleep apnea A disorder in which a person stops breathing while asleep.

narcolepsy A sleep disorder in which people fall asleep during normal waking hours.

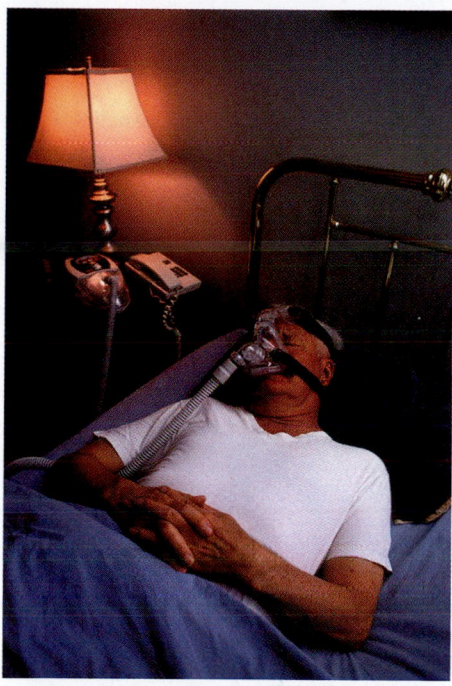

FIGURE 4.15 Sleep Apnea A continuous positive airway pressure (CPAP) device blows air to keep a sleep apnea patient's throat open.

facilitates the repair of damaged tissue. After people engage in vigorous physical activity, such as running a marathon, they generally sleep longer than usual. Sleep apparently allows the brain to replenish glycogen stores and strengthen the immune system (Hobson, 1999).

Numerous laboratory studies have examined sleep deprivation's effects on physical and cognitive performance. Surprisingly, most studies find that two or three days of sleep deprivation have little effect on strength, athletic ability, or the performance of complex tasks. In a brain imaging study, sleep deprived people showed increased activation of the prefrontal cortex, a finding that suggests some brain regions may compensate for sleep deprivation's effects (Drummond et al., 2000). However, sleep deprived people find it difficult to perform quiet tasks (such as reading) and nearly impossible to perform boring or mundane tasks.

Eventually, over a long period, sleep deprivation causes mood problems and decreases cognitive performance. People who suffer from chronic sleep deprivation—including many college students!—may experience attention lapses and reduced short-term memory. Studies using rats have found that extended sleep deprivation compromises the immune system and leads to death. Sleep deprivation is also dangerous and potentially disastrous because it makes people prone to **microsleeps,** in which they fall asleep during the day for periods ranging from a few seconds to a minute.

Sleep deprivation might serve one very useful purpose, however: helping people overcome depression. Consistent evidence has emerged over the past decade demonstrating that depriving depressed people of sleep sometimes alleviates their depression. This effect appears to occur because sleep deprivation leads to increased activation of serotonin receptors, as do drugs used to treat depression (Benedetti et al., 1999). For people who are not depressed, however, sleep deprivation is more likely to produce negative moods than positive ones.

CIRCADIAN RHYTHMS Brain and other physiological processes are regulated into patterns known as **circadian rhythms** (*circadian* roughly translates to "about a day"). For example, body temperature, hormone levels, and sleep/wake cycles operate according to circadian rhythms. A kind of biological clockwork, circadian rhythms are controlled by the cycles of light and dark, although human and nonhuman animals continue to show these rhythms when light cues are removed.

The *circadian rhythm theory* proposes that sleep has evolved to keep animals quiet and inactive during times of the day when there is greatest danger, usually when it is dark. According to this theory, animals need only a limited amount of time each day to accomplish the necessities of survival, and it is adaptive for them to spend the remainder of the time inactive, preferably hidden. Accordingly, an animal's typical amount of sleep depends on how much time that particular animal needs to obtain food, how easily it can hide, and how vulnerable it is to attack. Small animals tend to sleep a lot. Large animals vulnerable to attack, such as cows and deer, sleep little. Large predatory animals that are not vulnerable sleep a lot (**FIGURE 4.16**). Humans depend greatly on vision for survival, and they adapted to sleeping at night because the lack of light increased the dangers around them.

FACILITATION OF LEARNING Scientists have also proposed that sleep is important because it is involved in the strengthening of neural connections that serve as the basis of learning. The general idea is that circuits wired together during the waking period are consolidated, or strengthened, during sleep (Wilson & McNaughton, 1994). Robert Stickgold and colleagues (2000) conducted a study

microsleeps Brief, unintended sleep episodes, ranging from a few seconds to a minute, caused by chronic sleep deprivation.

circadian rhythms The regulation of biological cycles into regular patterns.

FIGURE 4.16 Sleeping Predator After a fresh kill, a lion may sleep for days.

in which participants had to learn a complex task. After finding that participants improved at the task only if they had slept for at least six hours following training, the researchers argued that learning the task required neural changes that normally occur only during sleep. Both slow-wave sleep and REM sleep appeared to be important for learning to take place. Indeed, some evidence indicates that students experience more REM sleep during exam periods, when a greater mental consolidation of information might be expected to take place (Smith & Lapp, 1991). The argument that sleep, especially REM sleep, promotes development of brain circuits for learning is also supported by the changes in sleep patterns that occur over the life course. Infants and the very young, who learn an incredible amount in a few years, sleep the most and also spend the most time in REM sleep.

Findings linking sleep to learning should give caution to students whose main style of studying is the all-nighter. In one recent study, students who were sleep deprived for one night showed reduced activity the next day in the hippocampus, a brain area essential for memory (Yoo et al., 2007; see Figure 3.27). These sleep-deprived students also showed poorer memory at subsequent testing. According to the investigators, substantial evidence shows that sleep not only is essential for consolidating memories but also seems to prepare the brain for its memory needs for the next day. (For a further discussion of why the all-nighter is an inefficient way to learn, see Chapter 7, "Attention and Memory.")

Sleep and Wakefulness Are Regulated by Multiple Neural Mechanisms

Multiple neural mechanisms are involved in producing and maintaining circadian rhythms and sleep. A tiny structure in the brain called the *pineal gland* (FIGURE 4.17) secretes *melatonin,* a hormone that travels through the bloodstream and affects various receptors in both the body and the brain. Bright light suppresses the production of melatonin, whereas darkness triggers its release. Researchers recently have noted that taking melatonin can help people cope with jet lag and shift work, both of which interfere with circadian rhythms. Taking melatonin also appears to help people fall asleep, although it is unclear why this happens.

Researchers have identified a gene that influences sleep (Koh et al., 2008). Called SLEEPLESS, this gene regulates a protein that, like many anesthetics, reduces action potentials in the brain. Loss of the protein leads to an 80 percent reduction in sleep.

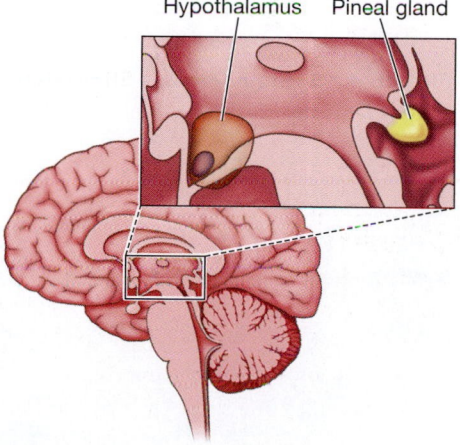

Hypothalamus   Pineal gland

FIGURE 4.17 The Pineal Gland The biological clock signals the pineal gland to secrete melatonin, which affects bodily states related to being tired.

BRAINSTEM AND AROUSAL Sleep is controlled by brain mechanisms that produce alterations in states of arousal. In 1949, Giuseppe Moruzzi and Horace Magoun found that stimulating the *reticular formation* in the brainstem leads to increased arousal in the cerebral cortex. If you cut the fibers from the reticular formation to the cortex, animals fall asleep and stay asleep until they die. Accordingly, Moruzzi and Magoun proposed that low levels of activity in the reticular formation produce sleep, and high levels lead to awakening.

If the reticular formation triggers arousal, what triggers sleep? Some evidence suggests that the basal forebrain, a small area just in front of the hypothalamus, is involved in inducing non-REM sleep. Neurons in this area become more active during non-REM sleep, and any lesion in the area will lead to insomnia. Once activated, the region sends inhibitory signals to the reticular formation, thereby reducing arousal and triggering sleep.

People Dream while Sleeping

dreams The product of an altered state of consciousness in which images and fantasies are confused with reality.

Because **dreams** are the products of an altered state of consciousness, dreaming is one of life's great mysteries. Why does the sleeper's mind conjure up images, fantasies, stories that make little sense, scenes that ignore physical laws and rules of both time and space? Why does it confuse these conjurings with reality? Why does it sometimes allow them to scare the dreamer awake? Usually, only when people wake up do they realize they have been dreaming. Some people claim not to remember their dreams, but everyone dreams unless a particular kind of brain injury or a particular kind of medication gets in the way. Indeed, the average person spends six years of his or her life dreaming. If you want to remember your dreams better, you can teach yourself to do so: Keep a pen and paper or a voice recorder next to your bed so you can record your dreams as soon as you wake up. If you wait, you likely will forget most of them.

Dreams occur in REM and non-REM sleep, although the dreams' contents differ in the two types of sleep. Activation of different brain regions during REM and non-REM sleep may be responsible for the different types of dreams. REM dreams are more likely to be bizarre, involving intense emotions, visual and auditory hallucinations (but rarely taste, smell, or pain), illogical contents, and an uncritical acceptance of events. Non-REM dreams are often very dull, about mundane activities such as deciding what clothes to wear or taking notes in class (**FIGURE 4.18**).

"Look, don't try to weasel out of this. It was my dream, but you had the affair in it."

FIGURE 4.18 Brain Regions Stimulated during Dreams

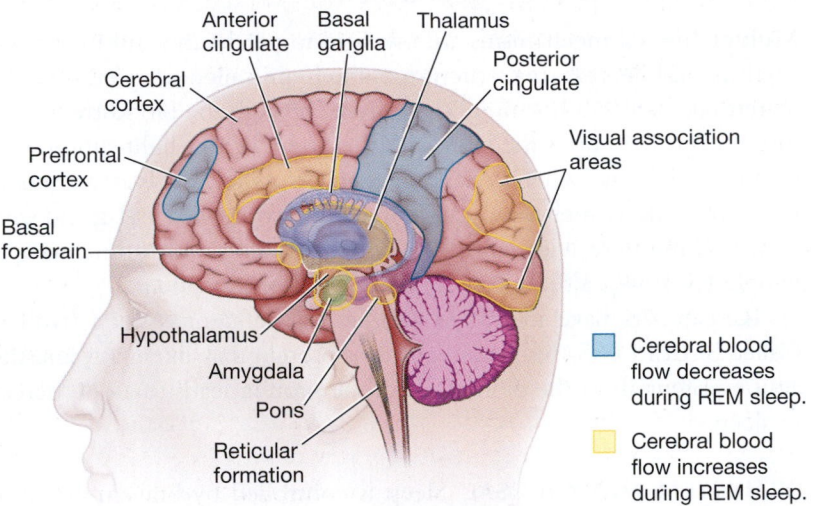

Anterior cingulate
Basal ganglia
Thalamus
Cerebral cortex
Posterior cingulate
Prefrontal cortex
Visual association areas
Basal forebrain
Hypothalamus
Amygdala
Pons
Reticular formation

▮ Cerebral blood flow decreases during REM sleep.

▮ Cerebral blood flow increases during REM sleep.

REM dreams are often bizarre and full of intense emotion

Non-REM dreams are often dull and about mundane activities

When researchers first noticed rapid eye movements, in the 1950s, they believed dreams were mainly a product of REM sleep. Initially, they dismissed non-REM dreams as trivial or as based on faulty recollection. We now know that REM sleep can occur without dreaming and that dreams can occur without REM sleep. Moreover, REM and dreaming appear to be controlled by different neural signals (Solms, 2000), so REM might be linked with dreams' contents rather than producing the dream state. REM dreams' contents result from activation of brain structures associated with motivation, emotion, and reward along with activation of visual association areas. The brain's emotion centers and visual association areas interact without self-awareness, reflective thought, or conscious input from the external world. Of course, dreams sometimes incorporate external sounds or other sensory experiences, but this happens without the type of consciousness experienced during wakefulness.

WHAT DO DREAMS MEAN? Sigmund Freud, in one of the first major theories of dreams, argued that dreams contain hidden content that represents unconscious conflicts. According to Freud, the **manifest content** is the dream the way the dreamer remembers it, whereas the **latent content** is what the dream symbolizes, or the material disguised to protect the dreamer. Virtually no support exists for Freud's ideas that dreams represent hidden conflicts and that objects in dreams have special symbolic meanings. However, daily life experiences do influence dreams' contents. For example, you may be especially likely to have anxiety dreams while studying for exams.

Some dreams have thematic structures, in that they unfold as events or stories rather than as jumbles of disconnected images, but such structures apparently hold no secret meanings. Most people think their dreams are uniquely their own, but many common themes occur in dreams. Have you ever dreamed about showing up for an exam and being unprepared or finding that you are taking the wrong test? Many people in college have dreams like these. Even after you graduate and no longer take exams routinely, you likely will have similar dreams about being unprepared. Retired professors sometimes dream about being unprepared to teach classes!

ACTIVATION-SYNTHESIS HYPOTHESIS In the 1980s, the sleep researcher Alan Hobson proposed a model that has dominated scientific thinking about dreaming. According to Hobson's **activation-synthesis hypothesis**, random neural stimulation can activate mechanisms that normally interpret visual input. The sleeping mind tries to make sense of the resulting activity in visual and motor neurons by synthesizing it with stored memories. From this perspective, dreams are *epiphenomenal*—the side effects of mental processes. In 2000, Hobson and his colleagues revised the activation-synthesis model to take into account recent findings in cognitive neuroscience. For instance, they included amygdala activation as the source of dreams' emotional content, and they proposed that deactivation of the frontal cortices contributes to dreams' delusional and illogical aspects. By its nature, the activation-synthesis hypothesis is concerned more with REM dreams than with non-REM ones. Critics of Hobson's theory argue that dreams are seldom as chaotic as might be expected if they were based on random eye movements (Domhoff, 2003). Indeed, most dreams are fairly similar to waking life, albeit with some strange features as described earlier.

EVOLVED THREAT-REHEARSAL STRATEGIES The cognitive neuroscientist Antti Revonsuo (2000) has proposed an evolutionary account wherein dreams sometimes simulate threatening events to allow people to rehearse coping strategies. In providing individuals with solutions to adaptive problems, dreaming would help

manifest content The plot of a dream; the way a dream is remembered.

latent content What a dream symbolizes, or the material that is disguised in a dream to protect the dreamer.

activation-synthesis hypothesis A theory of dreaming that proposes that neural stimulation from the pons activates mechanisms that normally interpret visual input.

the human species survive and reproduce and thus might be the result of evolution. That the majority of dreams reported by people involve negative emotions, such as fear and anxiety, supports the evolved threat-rehearsal theory. In addition, people tend to dream about threats in their lives and to have nightmares about even long-past traumas. Moreover, dreaming is associated with the activation of limbic structures, such as the amygdala, that are activated by real dangers.

SUMMING UP

What Is Sleep?

Almost all animals experience sleep, an altered state of consciousness in which the sleeper loses most contact with the external world. Sleep's several stages can be identified through different patterns on EEG recordings. REM sleep and non-REM sleep differ, and different neural mechanisms produce each type, although the brainstem figures prominently in the regulation of sleep/wake cycles. Dreams occur in REM sleep and non-REM sleep, but the dreams' contents differ between the types. This variation may be due to differential activation of brain structures associated with both emotion and cognition. Theories have been proposed to explain why sleeping and dreaming happen, but the biological functions of both sleeping and dreaming are unknown.

MEASURING UP

1. When people sleep, _____.
   a. the brain shuts down so it can rest
   b. brain activity goes through several cycles of different stages, and each stage has its own characteristic pattern of brain waves
   c. the brain goes into a random pattern of firing that causes dreaming—dreaming is the left hemisphere interpreter making sense of brain activity
   d. REM sleep occurs continuously throughout the sleep period as different types of brain waves determine how deeply we sleep
2. Select the hypothesized reasons why we dream. Select as many as apply.
   a. Dreams get rid of excessive energy that accumulates throughout the day.
   b. Dreams are a way of making sense of neural firing patterns.
   c. Dreams allow us to rehearse coping strategies for anxiety producing events.
   d. Dreams help us forget information we no longer need to remember.
   e. Dreams restore natural brain waves to their original state.

What Is Altered Consciousness?

A person's consciousness varies naturally over the course of the day. Often this variation is due to the person's actions. Watching television might encourage the person's mind to zone out, whereas learning to play a piece on the piano might focus the person's attention. Unusual subjective experiences, diminished or enhanced levels of self-awareness, and disturbances in a person's sense of control over physical actions are associated with **altered states of consciousness**. Discussed below are altered states of consciousness such as *hypnosis, meditation,* and *immersion in an action.*

Hypnosis Is Induced through Suggestion

As part of an act, a stage performer or magician might hypnotize audience members and instruct them to perform silly behaviors, such as making animal noises. Has this hypnotist presented a real change in mental state or just good theater? The essential question regarding hypnosis is: *What exactly is hypnosis?* **Hypnosis** involves a social interaction during which a person, responding to suggestions, experiences changes in memory, perception, and/or voluntary action (Kihlstrom, 1985; Kihlstrom & Eich, 1994). Psychological scientists generally agree that hypnosis affects some people, but they do not agree on whether it produces a genuinely altered state of consciousness. During a hypnotic induction, the hypnotist makes a series of suggestions to at least one person, such as "You are becoming sleepy," "Your eyelids are drooping," "Your arms and legs feel very heavy." As the person falls more deeply into the hypnotic state, the hypnotist makes more suggestions, such as "You cannot move your right arm," "You feel warm," "You want to bark like a dog." If everything goes according to plan, the person follows all the suggestions as though they are true (so the person really barks like a dog, for example).

Sometimes the hypnotist suggests that, after the hypnosis session, the person will experience a change in memory, perception, or voluntary action. Such a *posthypnotic suggestion* is usually accompanied by the instruction to not remember the suggestion. For example, a stage performer or magician serving as a hypnotist might suggest, much to the delight of the audience, "When I say the word *dog,* you will stand up and bark like a dog. You will not remember this suggestion." Therapists sometimes hypnotize patients and give them posthypnotic suggestions to help them diet or quit smoking, but evidence suggests that hypnosis has quite modest effects on these behaviors. Evidence clearly indicates, however, that like unconscious stimuli, posthypnotic suggestions can at least subtly influence behaviors.

Consider a study of moral judgment conducted by Thalia Wheatley and Jonathan Haidt (2005), in which subjects received a posthypnotic suggestion to feel a pang of disgust whenever they read a certain word, which itself was neutral (e.g., the word *often*). Subsequently, subjects made more-severe moral judgments when reading stories that contained the word, even when the story was innocuous. Like split-brain patients, the subjects were surprised by their reactions and sometimes made up justifications for their harsh ratings, such as saying that the lead character seemed "up to something." This behavior suggests that the left hemisphere interpreter might be involved in people's understanding their own behavior, when that behavior results from posthypnotic suggestion or other unconscious influence.

To the extent that hypnosis works, it relies mostly on the person being hypnotized rather than the hypnotist: Most of us could learn to hypnotize other people, but most of us cannot be hypnotized. Why not? Hypnosis works primarily for people who are highly suggestible; in fact, standardized tests exist for hypnotic suggestibility (Kallio & Revonsuo, 2003). What does it mean to be the approximately 1 in 5 people who is highly suggestible? Researchers have a hard time identifying the personality characteristics of people who can or cannot be hypnotized. Suggestibility seems related less to obvious traits such as intelligence and gullibility than to the tendencies to get absorbed in activities easily, to not be distracted easily, and to have a rich imagination (Baltharzard & Woody, 1992; Crawford et al., 1996; Silva & Kirsch, 1992). Furthermore, a person who dislikes or finds frightening the idea of being hypnotized would likely not be hypnotized easily. To be hypnotized, a person must go along with the hypnotist's suggestions willingly. No reliable evidence indicates that people will do things under hypnosis that they find immoral or otherwise objectionable.

hypnosis A social interaction during which a person, responding to suggestions, experiences changes in memory, perception, and/or voluntary action.

Real World
PSYCHOLOGY

THEORIES OF HYPNOSIS As mentioned above, considerable controversy exists over whether hypnosis is an altered state of consciousness (Jamieson, 2007). Some psychological scientists believe that a person under hypnosis essentially plays the role of a hypnotized person. That person is not faking hypnosis; rather, he or she acts the part as if in a play—willing to perform actions called for by the "director," the hypnotist. According to this *sociocognitive theory of hypnosis,* hypnotized people behave as they expect hypnotized people to behave, even if those expectations are faulty (Kirsch & Lynn, 1995; Spanos & Coe, 1992). Alternatively, although it acknowledges social context's importance to hypnosis, the *dissociation theory of hypnosis* views the hypnotic state as an altered state, namely a trancelike one in which conscious awareness is separated, or dissociated, from other aspects of consciousness (Gruzelier, 2000).

It seems unlikely that a person could alter his or her brain activity to please a hypnotist, even if that hypnotist is a psychological researcher, and numerous brain imaging studies have supported the dissociation theory of hypnosis (Rainville et al., 2002). In one of the earliest such studies, Stephen Kosslyn and colleagues (2000) demonstrated that when hypnotized participants were asked to imagine black-and-white objects as containing color, they showed activity in visual cortex regions involved in color perception, whereas subjects asked to drain color from colored images showed diminished activity in those same brain regions (**FIGURE 4.19**). This activity pattern did not occur when participants were not hypnotized.

Another study used the Stroop test, which involves naming the color in which a color's name is printed; recall from Figure 2.16 that, for example, it takes longer to name the color of the word *red* when that word is printed in blue ink than when it is printed in red ink. Participants took the test having received the posthypnotic suggestion that they would be looking at meaningless symbols instead of words. The participants apparently followed that suggestion and therefore did not show the standard Stroop interference effect, which is believed to result from automatic cognitive processes that cannot be controlled (Raz et al., 2002). In a subsequent

FIGURE 4.19 The Brain Hypnotized (a) Are hypnotized people merely playing the part? **(b)** This PET image from one of Stephen Kosslyn's studies shows that areas in the visual cortex associated with color perception are activated more when hypnotized participants are told to imagine color—a finding that suggests the brain follows hypnotic suggestions.

(a)

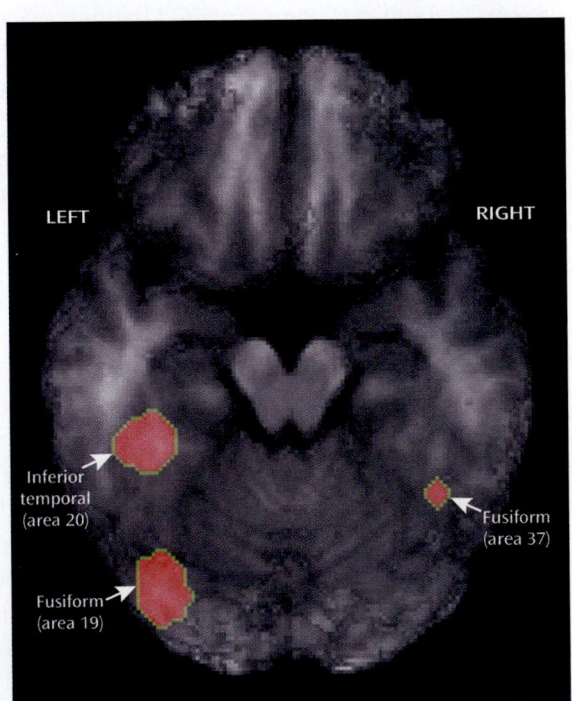

(b)

imaging study, the same researchers found that their suggestion to view the words as meaningless were associated with less activity in brain regions typically activated when people read or perform the Stroop test. Thus these participants seem to have perceived the stimuli as nonwords, an alteration of brain activity that would be hard for people to accomplish just to please a hypnotist—or a researcher (Raz et al., 2005).

HYPNOSIS FOR PAIN One of the most powerful uses of hypnosis is *hypnotic analgesia,* a form of pain reduction. Laboratory research has demonstrated that this technique works reliably (Hilgard & Hilgard, 1975; Nash & Barnier, 2008). For instance, a person who plunges one of his or her arms into extremely cold water will feel great pain, and the pain will intensify over time. On average, a person can leave the arm in the water for only about 30 seconds, but a person given hypnotic analgesia can hold out longer. As you might expect, people high in suggestibility who are given hypnotic analgesia can tolerate the cold water the longest (Montgomery et al., 2000).

Overwhelming evidence indicates that, in clinical settings, hypnosis is effective in dealing with immediate pain (e.g., from surgery, dental work, burns) and chronic pain (e.g., from arthritis, cancer, diabetes; Patterson & Jensen, 2003). Patients can also be taught aspects of self-hypnosis to improve recovery from surgery (**FIGURE 4.20**). Hypnosis may work more by changing people's interpretations of pain than by diminishing pain; that is, people feel the sensations associated with pain, but they feel detached from those sensations (Price, Harkins, & Baker, 1987). An imaging study confirmed this pattern by showing that while hypnosis does not affect the sensory processing of pain, it reduces brain activity in regions that process the emotional aspects of pain (Rainville et al., 1997). Findings such as these provide considerable support for the dissociation theory of hypnosis. It seems implausible that either expectations about hypnosis or social pressure not to feel pain could explain, first, how people given hypnotic analgesia are able to undergo painful surgery and not feel it, and, second, why hypnosis leads to differential brain activation during the experience of pain.

FIGURE 4.20 Self-Hypnosis Advertisements promote the idea that people can use self-hypnosis to recover from surgery.

Meditation Produces Relaxation

With a growing awareness of different cultural and religious practices and alternative approaches to medicine, people in the West have become more interested in examining Eastern techniques, including acupuncture and meditation. Different forms of meditation are popular in many Eastern religions, including Hinduism, Buddhism, and Sikhism. **Meditation** is a mental procedure that focuses attention on an external object or on a sense of awareness. Through intense contemplation, the meditator develops a deep sense of calm tranquility. Mark Leary (2004) notes that one goal of meditation is to quiet the internal voices we experience as we go through the day or as we try to sleep. Do you ever find that while you are trying to concentrate on a lecture or carry on a conversation an inner voice keeps interrupting you, perhaps reminding you of things you need to do or wondering what the other person thinks of you? A common cause of sleeplessness is that this inner voice chatters about worries and concerns that the person would prefer to forget so that he or she can sleep. During meditation, people learn to calm this inner voice, sometimes by simply letting it continue without paying attention to it.

There are two general forms of mediation. In *concentrative meditation,* you focus attention on one thing, such as your breathing pattern, a mental image, or a specific phrase (sometimes called a *mantra*). In *mindfulness meditation,* you let your thoughts flow freely, paying attention to them but trying not to react to them. You hear the contents of your inner voice, but you allow them to flow from one topic to the next without examining their meaning or reacting to them in any way. Why not take a break from reading and try one of these methods (**FIGURE 4.21**)?

Do you feel more relaxed? Meditation aims to help people achieve a deep state of relaxation so they can deal with the tensions and stresses in their lives. Although religious forms of meditation are meant to bring spiritual enlightenment, most forms of meditation popular in the West are meant to expand the mind and bring about feelings of inner peace. These methods include *Zen, yoga,* and *transcendental meditation,* or *TM,* the third of which is perhaps the best known meditation procedure. TM involves meditating with great concentration for 20 minutes twice a day. Many early studies found benefits from TM, such as reduced blood pressure, decreased reports of stress, and changes in the hormonal responses underlying stress. However, these studies have been criticized because they had small samples and lacked appropriate control groups. In a more rigorous recent study, a large number of heart patients were randomly assigned to TM or an educational program. After 16 weeks, the patients performing TM improved more than the control group on a number of health measures, such as blood pressure, blood lipids, and insulin resistance (Paul-Labrador et al., 2006). Unfortunately, this study does not show which aspects of TM produced the health benefits. Was it simply relaxing, or was it the altered state of consciousness? If you were a heart patient, of course, you would not care which aspect of TM helped you improve. (As discussed in Chapter 10, reducing stress, no matter how it is done, yields substantial health benefits.)

Psychological scientists also study how meditation affects cognitive processing and brain function (Cahn & Polich, 2006). After only five days of intensive meditation training, randomly assigned subjects showed both significant improvements in attention and stress reductions, compared with a group completing relaxation training (Tang et al., 2007). Long-term practitioners of Buddhist meditation show differential patterns of brain activity in the face of distracting sounds, a finding that supports the idea that such meditators are better at ignoring distractions (Brefczynski-Lewis, Lutz, Schaefer, Levinson & Davidson, 2007). Some researchers argue that long-term meditation brings about structural changes in the brain that help maintain brain function

meditation A mental procedure that focuses attention on an external object or on a sense of awareness.

FIGURE 4.21 Try for Yourself: Meditation

For 20 minutes, try focusing your attention on your breathing pattern, in and out (*concentrative meditation*), or let your thoughts flow freely without reacting to them (*mindfulness meditation*).

Result: The goal of meditation is to help people achieve a deep state of relaxation.

over the life span. For instance, one study found that the volume of gray matter (the section of the brain containing neurons' cell bodies; see Chapter 3, "Biological Foundations") did not diminish in older adults who practiced Zen meditation as it typically does with age (Pagnoni & Cekic, 2007), a finding that suggests Zen meditation might help preserve cognitive functioning as people age. A review of this literature notes that despite advances in psychological science, the reasons that meditation seems to improve health and cognitive functions remain unclear (Doraiswamy & Xiong, in press). People who meditate may differ substantially from people who do not, especially in terms of lifestyle choices such as diet and a willingness to take care of their health. As Chapter 2 notes, correlational data such as these do not prove causation. Careful empirical research using the methods of psychological science should contribute significantly to our understanding of meditation's effects.

People Can Lose Themselves in Activities

Hypnosis and meditation involve doing something to alter consciousness. As noted throughout this chapter, however, a person's level of conscious awareness changes as a result of the time of day as well as the person's activities. For instance, when a person performs an automatic task, such as driving, that person's conscious thoughts might not include the driving experience. There can be a negative side to this lack of attention: In the United States over the past decade, more than 300 children have died because they were left unattended in hot cars, often because a parent forgot to drop the child off at day care on his or her way to work. It is easy to imagine forgetting your lunch in the car, but your child? Fortunately, such incidents are rare, but they seem to be especially likely when the parent's typical routine does not include daycare drop-off duty. While the parent is driving, his or her brain shifts to "autopilot" and automatically goes through the process of driving to the workplace instead of stopping at day care first. During most of our daily activities, of course, we are consciously aware of only a small portion of both our thoughts and our behaviors.

EXERCISE, RELIGIOUS PRAYER, AND FLOW Have you ever had the experience, during exercise, of one minute being in pain and feeling fatigued and the next minute being euphoric and feeling a glorious release of energy? Commonly known as *runner's high,* this state is partially mediated by physiological processes (especially endorphin release; see Chapter 3, "Biological Foundations"), but it also occurs in part because of a shift in consciousness. For example, many people cannot exercise without music, which offers a distraction from physical exertions and, in doing so, may energize an exerciser to keep going for another mile. In fact, many runners were dismayed when, in 2007, the association USA Track and Field banned them from using audio players and headphones in organized races. No more cranking up "Gonna Fly Now," the theme song from *Rocky,* to get down the last stretch in a marathon.

Shifts in consciousness that are similar to runner's high occur at other moments in our lives. Religious ceremonies often decrease awareness of the external world and create feelings of euphoria. Indeed, such rituals often involve chanting, dancing, and/or other behaviors as a way for people to lose themselves in *religious ecstasy.* Like meditation, religious ecstasy directs attention away from the self; in this way, it allows a person to focus on his or her spiritual awareness (**FIGURE 4.22**).

One psychological theory about such peak experiences is based on the concept of *flow,* "a particular kind of experience that is so engrossing and enjoyable [that it is] worth doing for its own sake even though it may have no consequence outside

FIGURE 4.22 Shifts of Consciousness
During certain religious festivals, such as this Christian Orthodox rite in Greece, people walk on smoldering embers as an act of faith. The embers' top layer is not as hot as the bottom layer, so walking on the burning embers, while always risky, is not as difficult as it appears.

itself" (Csikszentmihalyi, 1999, p. 824). That is, a person might perform a particular task out of fascination with it rather than out of a desire for a reward. Flow is an optimal experience, in that the activity is completely absorbing and completely satisfying. The person experiencing flow loses track of time, forgets about his or her problems, and fails to notice other things going on (Csikszentmihalyi, 1990). The person's skills are well matched with the task's demands; the situation is less like driving, where much of the work happens automatically, than like rock climbing, where every thought is on the next step and is concrete, not deep and abstract (Leary, 2004). Flow experiences have been reported during many activities, including playing music (O'Neil, 1999) or a moderately challenging version of the computer game *Tetris* (Keller & Bless, 2008), participating in sports (Jackson et al., 2001), and simply doing satisfying jobs (Demerouti, 2006). According to Csikszentmihalyi (1999), flow experiences bring personal fulfillment and make life worth living.

ESCAPING THE SELF Our conscious thoughts can be dominated by worries, frustrations, and feelings of personal failure. Sometimes people get tired of dealing with life's problems and try to make themselves feel better through escapist pursuits. Potential flow activities such as sports or work may help people escape thinking about their problems, but people engage in such activities mainly to feel personally fulfilled. The difference is between escaping and engaging. Sometimes people choose to escape the self rather than engage with life: To forget their troubles, they drink alcohol, take drugs, play video games, watch television, and so on. The selective appeal of escapist entertainment is that it distracts people from reflecting on their problems or their failures, thereby helping them avoid feeling bad about themselves. Some escapist activities—such as running or reading—tend to have positive effects, some tend to be relatively harmless distractions, and some tend to come at great personal expense. For example, people obsessively playing online games such as *World of Warcraft* have lost their jobs and even their marriages (**FIGURE 4.23**). Moreover, evidence suggests that some ways of escaping the self can be associated with self-destructive behaviors such as binge eating, unsafe sex, and, at an extreme, suicide. According to the social psychologist Roy Baumeister (1991), people engage in such behaviors because they have low self-awareness when they escape the self. Chapter 12 further discusses the connections between behavior and self-awareness; the next section of this chapter looks at a common way people try to escape their problems, namely using drugs or alcohol to alter consciousness.

FIGURE 4.23 Escapist Entertainment Simple entertainment can veer toward obsession. Some have reported spending as many as 50 hours a week playing video games such as *World of Warcraft*.

> ### SUMMING UP
> #### What Is Altered Consciousness?
> An altered state of consciousness is a change in subjective experience, such as through hypnosis or meditation. Some people are susceptible to hypnosis, such that a posthypnotic suggestion can alter how they think, feel, or behave, though they are not conscious that a suggestion was given. Hypnosis can also be used to control pain. Patterns of brain activation show neural correlates of hypnosis that suggest that it is not a faked performance or some other theatrical trick. People can experience altered states of consciousness during profound religious experiences, during extreme physical exertion, or when they are deeply absorbed in tasks matched to both their interests and their abilities.
>
> ### MEASURING UP
> Mark each statement below with an "S" if it supports the conclusion that hypnosis is a real phenomenon. Put an "F" next to any false statement.
>   a. Participants under hypnosis who were told that they would not see real words did not show the Stroop effect. (For a reminder on the Stroop effect, see Figure 2.16.)
>   b. Brain imaging showed that hypnotized subjects really were asleep.
>   c. Brain imaging showed that hypnosis changes brain activity in ways inconsistent with the idea that people are simply role-playing.
>   d. Some people cannot be hypnotized.
>   e. People who are hypnotized will do anything the hypnotist tells them to.
>   f. Hypnosis is not useful in reducing pain.
>   g. Hypnotized people are aware of the hypnotist's suggestions, so they just go along with what they are asked to do.

How Do Drugs Affect Consciousness?

Throughout history, people have discovered that ingesting certain substances can alter their mental states in various ways. Some of those altered states, however momentary, can be pleasant. Some, especially over the long term, can have negative consequences including injury or death. Societal problems stemming from drug abuse are well known. Most people probably know and care about someone addicted to a commonly abused drug, such as alcohol, an illegal substance, or a prescription medication. If we include nicotine and caffeine on that list, most people probably *are* drug addicts. To investigate drug addiction, psychological science asks various questions across multiple levels, from the biological to the individual to the social: Why do people use drugs? Why do some people become addicted to drugs? Why do drug addicts continue to abuse drugs when doing so causes turmoil and suffering?

> **LEARNING OBJECTIVE**
> Describe the effects of marijuana, of stimulants, of MDMA, and of opiates.

People Use—and Abuse—Many Psychoactive Drugs

Drugs are a mixed blessing. The right ones can provide soothing relief—from severe pain or a moderate headache. Other right ones can lift depressed people's moods and help them lead more satisfying lives. Still others can help children who have attention deficits or hyperactivity disorders settle down and learn better. But many of these same drugs can be used for "recreational" purposes—to alter physical sensations, levels of consciousness, thoughts, moods, and behaviors in ways that users believe are desirable—and this recreational use sometimes can have negative consequences.

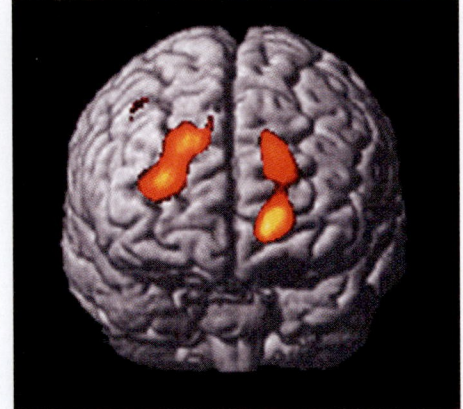

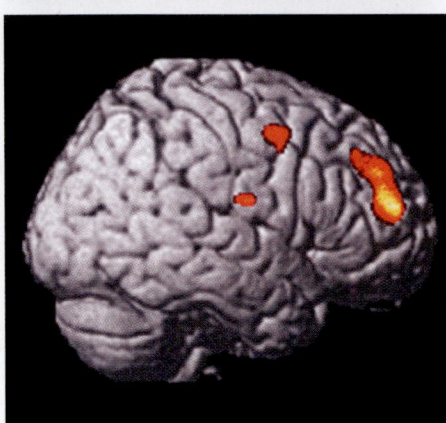

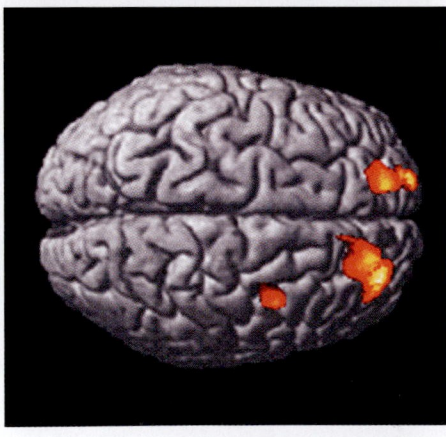

FIGURE 4.24 Drugs' Effects on the Brain Brain scans from three views show the areas in this brain that have been affected by methamphetamine use. Specifically, the yellow and red areas show reduced gray matter density in the frontal cortexes (Kim et al., 2006).

Psychoactive drugs are mind-altering substances that change the brain's neurochemistry by activating neurotransmitter systems. The effects of a particular psychoactive drug depend on which systems it activates (**FIGURE 4.24**). Common psychoactive drugs include *stimulants, depressants, narcotics,* and *hallucinogens.* This section considers drugs that often have legitimate medical uses but sometimes are abused outside of treatment.

MARIJUANA The most widely used illegal drug in North America is marijuana, the dried leaves and flower buds of the hemp plant. The psychoactive ingredient in marijuana is the chemical *THC,* or *tetrahydrocannabinol,* which produces a relaxed mental state, uplifted or contented mood, and some perceptual and cognitive distortions. Marijuana users report that THC also makes perceptions more vivid, and some say it especially affects taste. Most first-time users do not experience the "high" obtained by more experienced users. Novice smokers might use inefficient techniques and/or might have trouble inhaling, but users apparently must learn how to *appreciate* the drug's effects (Kuhn, Swartzwelder, & Wilson, 2003). In this way, marijuana differs from most other drugs, whose first-time uses have stronger effects and subsequent uses lead to tolerance in which a person has to use more of the drug to get the same effect.

Although the brain mechanisms that marijuana affects remain somewhat mysterious, investigators have recently discovered a class of receptors that are activated by naturally occurring THC-like substances. Activation of these cannabinoid receptors appears to adjust and enhance mental activity and perhaps alter pain perception. The large concentration of these receptors in the hippocampus may partly explain why marijuana impairs memory (Ilan, Smith, & Gevins, 2004). Marijuana is also used for its medicinal properties. For instance, cancer patients undergoing chemotherapy report that marijuana is effective for overcoming nausea. Nearly 1 in 4 AIDS patients reports using marijuana to relieve both nausea and pain (Prentiss et al., 2004). The medical use of marijuana is controversial because of the possibility that chronic use can cause health problems or lead to abuse of the drug.

STIMULANTS *Stimulants* are drugs that increase behavioral and mental activity. They include caffeine and nicotine as well as cocaine and amphetamines. These substances activate the sympathetic nervous system (increasing heart rate and blood pressure), improve mood, cause people to become restless, and disrupt sleep. Stimulants generally work by interfering with the normal reuptake of dopamine by the releasing neuron, allowing dopamine to remain in the synapse and thus prolonging its effects, although sometimes stimulants also increase the release of dopamine. Drugs that block dopamine's action reduce stimulants' rewarding properties.

Cocaine is derived from the leaves of the coca bush, which grows primarily in South America. After inhaling (snorting) cocaine as a powder or smoking it in the form of *crack cocaine,* users experience a wave of confidence. They feel good, alert, energetic, sociable, and wide awake. These short-term effects are especially intense for crack cocaine users. In contrast, habitual use of cocaine in large quantities can lead to paranoia, psychotic behavior, and violence (Ottieger, Tressell, Inciardi, & Rosales, 1992).

Cocaine has a long history of use in America. John Pemberton, a pharmacist from Georgia, was so impressed with cocaine's effects that in 1886 he added the drug to soda water for easy ingestion, thus creating Coca-Cola (see Figure 4.26a). In 1906, the U.S. government outlawed cocaine, so it was removed from the drink.

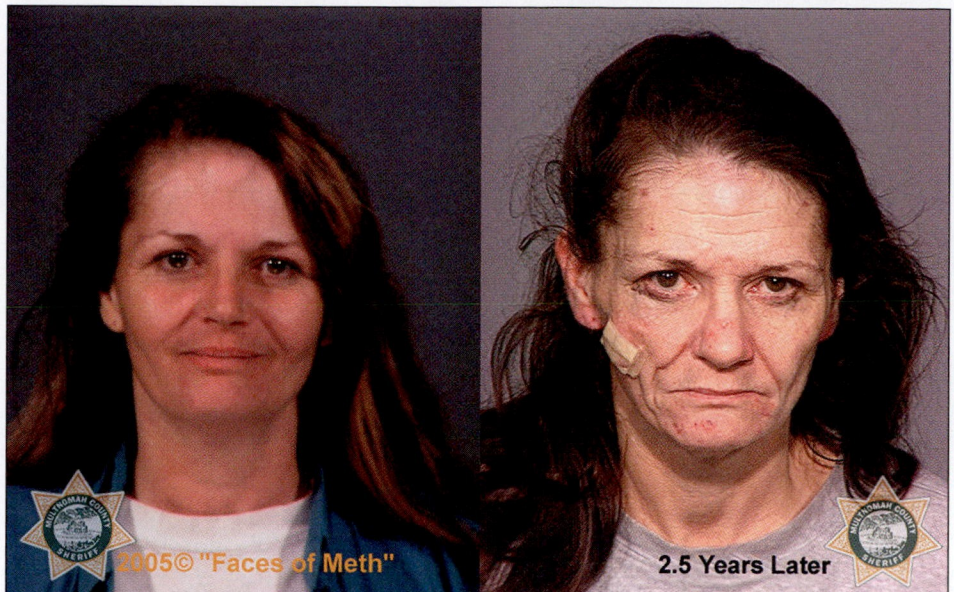

FIGURE 4.25 Methamphetamine's Effects These before-and-after photos dramatically illustrate how the physical damage from metamphetamine can affect appearance.

To this day, however, coca leaves from which the cocaine has been removed are used in the making of Coke.

Amphetamines are synthesized using simple lab methods. They go by street names such as *speed, meth* (for *methamphetamine*), *ice,* and *crystal*. Amphetamines have a long history of use for weight loss and staying awake. However, their numerous negative side effects include insomnia, anxiety, and heart problems; people quickly become addicted to them; and they are seldom used for legitimate medical purposes.

Methamphetamine is the world's second most commonly used illicit drug, after marijuana (Barr et al., 2006). Although it was first developed in the early twentieth century as a nasal decongestant, its recreational use became popular in the 1980s. The National Institute of Drug Abuse (2006) estimates that just over 4 percent of the U.S. population has tried methamphetamine at some point in life. One factor that encourages its use, and may explain its surge in popularity over the past decade, is that methamphetamine is easy to make from common over-the-counter drugs.

Methamphetamine not only blocks reuptake of dopamine, it also increases the release of dopamine and thus yields much higher levels of dopamine in the synapse. In addition, methamphetamine stays in the body and brain much longer than, say, cocaine, so its effects are prolonged. Methamphetamine abuse damages various brain structures and ultimately depletes dopamine levels. Its damage to the temporal lobe and the limbic system, for example, may explain its effects on memory and emotion in long-term users (Kim et al., 2006; Thompson et al., 2004). It also causes considerable physical damage (**FIGURE 4.25**).

MDMA One drug that has become popular since the 1990s is *MDMA,* or *ecstasy,* which produces an energizing effect similar to that of stimulants but also causes slight hallucinations. According to the National Institute of Drug Abuse, MDMA use by high school students increased from 2004 to 2007: In one study, just under 5 percent of high school seniors reported using MDMA in the previous year (2007). The drug first became popular among young adults in nightclubs and at all-night parties known as raves. Compared with amphetamines, MDMA is associated with less dopamine release and more serotonin release. The serotonin release may explain ecstasy's hallucinogenic properties. Although many users believe it to be relatively safe, researchers have documented a number of impairments from long-term ecstasy use, especially memory problems and a diminished ability to perform complex tasks (Kalechstein et al., 2007). Because ecstasy also depletes serotonin, users often feel depressed when the drug's rewarding properties wear off.

OPIATES Heroin, morphine, and codeine belong to the family of drugs known as *opiates.* These drugs provide enormous reward value by increasing dopamine activation in the nucleus accumbens and binding with opiate receptors, producing feelings of relaxation, analgesia, and euphoria. Heroin provides a rush of intense pleasure that most addicts describe as similar to orgasm, which then evolves into a pleasant, relaxed stupor. The dual activation of opiate receptors and dopamine receptors may explain why heroin and morphine are so highly addictive (Kuhn et al., 2003).

Opiates have been used to relieve pain and suffering for hundreds of years. Indeed, before the twentieth century, heroin was widely available without prescription and was marketed by the Bayer aspirin company (**FIGURE 4.26**). The benefits of short-term opiate use to relieve severe pain seem clear, but long-term opiate use to relieve chronic pain will much more likely lead to abuse or addiction than will short-term use (Ballantyne & LaForge, 2007). Moreover, long-term use of opiates is associated with a number of neurological and cognitive deficits, such as attention and memory problems (Gruber, Silveri, & Yurgelin-Todd, 2007). Therefore, clinicians need to be cautious in prescribing opiates, especially when the drugs will be used over extended periods.

FIGURE 4.26 Drugs through History
(a) This early advertisement's claim that Coca-Cola is "a valuable Brain Tonic" may have been inspired by the incorporation of cocaine into the drink before 1906.
(b) Before 1904, Bayer advertised heroin as "the sedative for coughs."

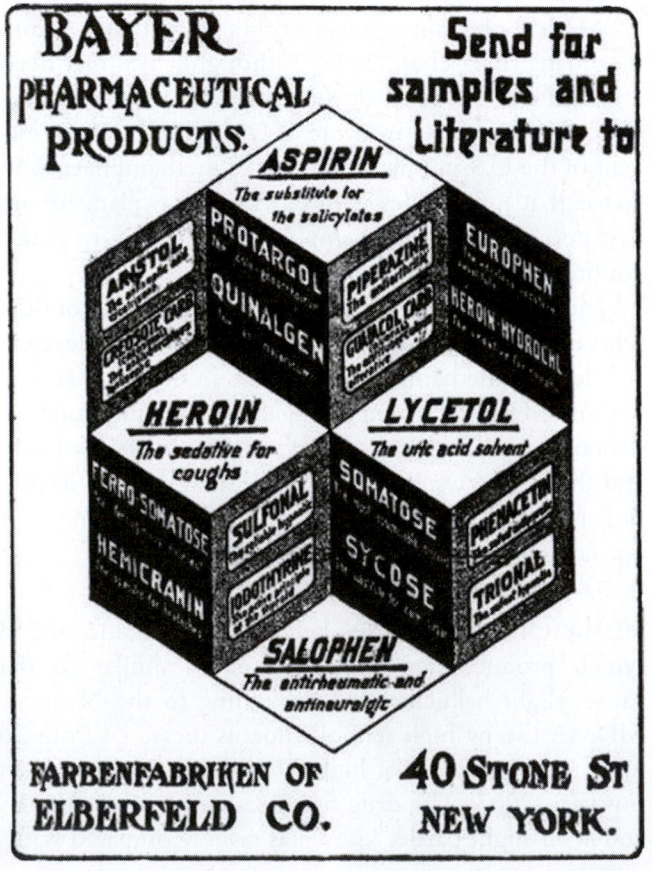

Providing Examples of Slippery Slope Thinking

What happens when you slip while walking down a slope? Might you fall to the bottom? A person making a *slippery slope argument* reasons that some first slippery step must lead down to a larger, more slippery step or even a large fall. For example, a slippery slope argument against all "recreational" drug use proposes that if you start using a drug that is not likely to have lasting or harmful effects (say, marijuana), this behavior will lead you to take "harder" drugs (say, cocaine), and soon you will be robbing to support your heroin habit. The "starter," less powerful drug is referred to as a *gateway drug,* because it supposedly opens the gate to more regular and more dangerous drug use. The data on whether using something like marijuana is associated with later use of drugs like heroin is mixed, but even if it were a strong relationship, what might be wrong with these data? The conclusion that taking marijuana *causes* people to take harder drugs cannot be inferred from these data. There are many other possible explanations for this relationship, including the more likely one that people apt to get addicted could start with any drug and generally do start with the cheapest and most available one, marijuana. It might or might not be true that a minor action will lead to a more serious one, but there is no reason to assume that it is always or even usually true.

Alcohol Is the Most Widely Abused Drug

Americans have a love/hate relationship with alcohol. On the one hand, moderate drinking is an accepted aspect of normal social interaction and may even be good for health. On the other hand, alcohol is a major contributor to many of our societal problems, such as spousal abuse and other forms of violence. Alcohol factors in more than half of all fatal car accidents, killing more than 20,000 Americans each year. Moreover, one-quarter of suicide victims and one-third of homicide victims have blood alcohol levels that meet legal criteria for impairment. One study found that approximately one-third of college students reported having had sex during a drinking binge, and the heaviest drinkers were likely to have had sex with a new or casual partner (Leigh & Schafer, 1993), thus increasing their risk for exposure to AIDS and other sexually transmitted diseases. The overall cost of problem drinking in the United States—from lost productivity due to employee absence, from health care expenses, and so on—is estimated to be more than $100 billion annually.

GENDER DIFFERENCES IN ALCOHOL CONSUMPTION ACROSS CULTURES The World Health Organization is conducting a massive international study of gender-related and culture-related differences in alcohol consumption (Obot & Room, 2005). This study is expected to continue over the coming decade; however, many findings are already available. The study's main premise is that to understand alcohol consumption worldwide, we need to study the various ways alcohol is used, by men and by women, across cultural and social contexts. The authors call the gender gap in alcohol consumption "one of the few universal gender differences in human social behavior" (Wilsnack, Wilsnack, & Obot, 2005, p. 1). Can you guess whether men or women consume more alcohol? In every region of the world, across a wide variety of measures (e.g., drinking versus abstinence, heavy drinking versus occasional drinking, alcohol-related disorders), men drink a lot more. Men are twice as likely to report binge drinking (drinking five or more servings in one evening), chronic drinking, and recent alcohol intoxication. However, gender gaps in binge drinking may be smaller among university students.

Real World PSYCHOLOGY

An estimated of 8 percent Americans are addicted to alcohol or controlled substances. Addiction and substance abuse affect not only the addicts and abusers but also their families, their friends, their coworkers, and victims of crimes that result from their altered mental states (e.g., drunk driving) or their desperation when funds run low (e.g., mugging). Society also shoulders the financial burden of these problems through the criminal justice system, drug trafficking prevention, health care, and lost productivity.

The rate of addicts and substance abusers is much higher in the prison population. In 2005, 37 percent of prisoners on probation in the northeastern United States suffered from addiction or substance abuse (Law and Neuroscience Project, 2007). When drug addicts end up in the criminal justice system, punishment by prison sentence does not deter their drug use. Approximately 70 percent to 85 percent of drug abusing offenders resume regular drug use within a year of release from prison, and more than 95 percent resume drug use within three years (Nurco, Hanlon, & Kinlock, 1991; Martin, Butzin, Saum, & Inciardi, 1999; Marlowe, 2006).

Among the biological treatments for addiction is a drug called naltrexone. This opiate antagonist occupies opiate receptors but does not activate them; rather, it prevents other opiates or opioids from activating opiate receptors, and it dislodges any opiate already bound to the receptor. It is available in an injectable form that lasts about 30 days and in an implant form that lasts six months. Naltrexone is very safe, is nonaddictive, and causes only minor side effects, such as nausea and headache, in a few users. It has been successful in treating opiate addicts and some alcoholics, particularly, in the latter case, ones with a family history of alcoholism (Volpicelli, Alterman, Hayashida, & O'Brien, 1999). Despite this and other promising treatments, the problem remains that most addicts are not as motivated to overcome addiction as they are motivated by their pleasure centers to seek more drugs or alcohol.

Is it ethical to force prisoners to use naltrexone even if they do not want to? The fundamental principles for all medical ethics involve patient autonomy and self-determination. Even though an intervention may overwhelmingly benefit the patient, his or her family, or society, if the patient refuses, the physician's hands are tied. However, a physician is allowed to intervene for the protection of one or more third parties who cannot protect themselves (such as a near-term fetus) or when the patient does not have the capacity to consent and is not capable of autonomy.

Although the question of whether addiction's costs to society justify mandatory treatment raises its own ethical questions, the thornier issue is whether addictive substances affect free will and autonomous decision-making ability. The medical ethicist Arthur Kaplan (2006) writes, "People who are addicted really do not have the full capacity to be self-determining or autonomous because their addiction literally coerces their behavior. They cannot be autonomous agents precisely because they are caught up in the behavioral vice that is addiction." Kaplan continues, "If a drug can break the power of addiction sufficiently to restore or reestablish personal autonomy or to markedly increase the capacity for autonomy, then mandating its use might be justifiable." In other words, Kaplan argues, drugs and alcohol rob addicts of their autonomy, so forcing addicts to overcome their addictions does not deny their free will but rather restores it to them.

Others have suggested that prisoners could be motivated, instead of forced, to use naltrexone or other therapies to quit. The criminal justice system is the major source of addiction treatment referral in the United States (O'Brien & Cornish, 2006), and it has a unique opportunity to supply motivation in the form of a plea bargain: Take naltrexone and seek counseling or go to jail. No force is used—rather, a choice is given—and a plea bargain expands the defendant's available options rather than restricts them. Would it work? Controlled trials of naltrexone use in probationers and parolees are few, but the results are promising (Cornish et al., 1997; Foster, Brewer, & Steele, 2003).

Does an addiction negate a person's free will and autonomous decision-making ability? And should the criminal justice system have the authority to make such medical decisions? Alternatively, is it ethical to offer naltrexone or other medications instead of prison time or as a conditional part of either probation or parole (**FIGURE 4.27**)?

	Supporting Reasons and Evidence	Contradicting Reasons and Evidence
A. Addicted prisoners should be forced to use naltrexone.	1. *Strength* 2. *Strength*	1. *Strength* 2. *Strength*
B. Addicted prisoners should not be forced to use naltrexone.	1. *Strength* 2. *Strength*	1. *Strength* 2. *Strength*

FIGURE 4.27 Think Critically: Examining Evidence For and Against Naltrexone Use To consider whether it is ethical to force an addicted prisoner to use a drug such as naltrexone, fill out a matrix like the one introduced in Figure 3.11.

Several factors may explain this large and universal gender difference. One is that women do not metabolize alcohol as quickly as men and generally have smaller body volumes, so they consume less alcohol than men to achieve the same effects. Another explanation is that women's drinking may be more hidden because it is less socially accepted than men's drinking. According to this theory, women's alcohol consumption may be underreported, especially in cultures where it is frowned upon or forbidden. In some cultures, "real men" are expected to drink a lot and prove they can "hold" their liquor, whereas women who do the same are seen as abnormal.

Psychosocial researchers have studied four factors that might affect the gender-related differences in a specific culture's alcohol consumption: (1) *Power*. Drinking alcohol in large quantities is a symbol of male power (i.e., privilege). As women gain more power through paid employment in jobs that traditionally were held by men, will they increase their alcohol consumption? So far, the answer is no. In Europe and North America, where this hypothesis was tested, the increased autonomy that women now have has not increased the amount of alcohol they drink. (2) *Sex*. Men and women may drink because they expect doing so to enhance their sexual performance or enjoyment of sex, though in fact alcohol, especially in large quantities, is more likely to lead to impotence for men. It can also increase women's vulnerability to men's sexual aggression; knowing this, some women may limit their own drinking. (3) *Risks*. Men enjoy taking risks more than women do, so men may be more likely to engage in heavy drinking, which is known to be hazardous. (4) *Responsibilities*. Men may drink more than women because drinking allows them to ignore their social responsibilities. In some social contexts, "domestic role obligations"—for men, usually, supporting a family and having responsibilities around the house—may magnify the gender gap in drinking.

EXPECTATIONS One reason people consume alcohol is that they anticipate alcohol will have certain effects on their emotions and behavior. Light and heavy drinkers believe alcohol reduces anxiety, so many people have a drink or two after a difficult day. The available evidence does not support this belief: Although moderate doses of alcohol are associated with a more positive mood, larger doses are associated with a more negative mood. Also, although alcohol can interfere with the cognitive processing of threat cues, such that anxiety-provoking events are less troubling when people are intoxicated, this effect occurs only if people drink *before* the anxiety-provoking events. According to this research, drinking after a hard day can increase people's focus on and obsession with their problems (Sayette, 1993).

Alan Marlatt (1999), a leading substance abuse researcher, has noted that people view alcohol as the "magic elixir," capable of increasing social skills, sexual pleasure, confidence, and power. Expectations about alcohol's effects are learned very early in life, through observation; children may see that people who drink have a lot of fun and that drinking is an important aspect of many celebrations. Teenagers may view drinkers as sociable and grown up, two things they desperately want to be. Studies have shown that children who have very positive expectations about alcohol are more likely to start drinking and to be heavy drinkers than children who do not share those expectations (Leigh & Stacy, 2004).

According to the social psychologists Jay Hull and Charles Bond (1986), expectations about alcohol profoundly affect behavior. To study alcohol's true effects on behavior, these researchers gave participants tonic water with or without alcohol and, regardless of the drinks' actual contents, told some participants they were getting just tonic water and some they were getting tonic water with alcohol. This balanced-placebo design allowed for a comparison of those who thought they were drinking tonic water but were actually drinking alcohol with those who thought they were drinking alcohol but were actually drinking tonic water. In thus separating drug effects from beliefs, the researchers demonstrated that alcohol impairs motor processes, information processing, and mood, independent of whether the person thinks he or she has consumed it. In contrast, the belief that one has consumed alcohol leads to disinhibition regarding various social behaviors, such as sexual arousal and aggression, whether or not the person has consumed alcohol. Thus some behaviors generally associated with drunkenness are accounted for by learned beliefs about intoxication rather than by alcohol's pharmacological properties. Sometimes the learned expectations and the pharmacology work in opposite ways. As mentioned above, for instance, alcohol tends to increase sexual arousal, but it interferes with sexual performance.

PHYSICAL EFFECTS Alcohol triggers a number of neurotransmitter systems and activates receptors for GABA, opiates, and dopamine (for all these terms, see Chapter 3, "Biological Foundations"). Evidence suggests that alcohol's rewarding aspects stem from its activation of dopamine receptors, as is the case with other addictive drugs. Alcohol also interferes with the neurochemical processes involved in memory; for this reason, memory loss can follow excessive alcohol intake. Heavy long-term alcohol intake can cause extensive brain damage. *Korsakoff's syndrome* is an alcohol-related disorder characterized by both severe memory loss and intellectual deterioration.

CRITICAL THINKING SKILL

Showing How Circular Reasoning Is a Misuse of Operational Definitions

Have you ever seen a cat chase its tail? It can be a pretty funny sight, as the cat never gets closer to its "prey." Similarly, in a circular argument, the reason for believing the conclusion is just a restatement of the conclusion, so the argument ends up where it started. Here is an example: "We need to raise the legal drinking age from 21 to 25 because 21-year-olds are too young to drink." Can you see what is wrong with this argument? Saying that 21-year-olds are too young to drink is just another way of saying "We need to raise the legal drinking age from 21." The argument does not explain *why* 21 is too young. If the speaker had said, "We need to raise the legal drinking age from 21 to 25 because research shows that 25-year-olds have half the number of traffic accidents that 21-year-olds do" or ". . . because the frontal areas of the brain mature between ages 21 and 25" or ". . . because 25-year-olds are more responsible," he or she would have provided a reason to support the conclusion.

Addiction Has Psychological and Physical Aspects

The term *physical dependence* is synonymous with *addiction,* a physiological state in which failing to ingest a substance leads to symptoms of *withdrawal,* a state characterized by anxiety, tension, and craving. Physical dependence is associated with *tolerance,* so that a person needs to consume more of the substance to achieve the same subjective effect. Addiction researchers now widely accept that dopamine activity in the limbic system underlies the rewarding properties of taking drugs and is central to addiction (Baler & Volkow, 2006; Chapter 9 further discusses dopamine's role in reward). A brain region called the *insula* seems to be important for craving and addiction, since this region becomes active when addicts view images of drug use. A recent study compared the experience of quitting smoking for patients with insula damage to the experiences for patients with other types of brain damage. The patients with insula damage reported that immediately after being injured they quit smoking easily and that they no longer experienced conscious urges to smoke. One patient who had a stroke to his left insula commented that he quit smoking because his "body forgot the urge to smoke" (Naqvi et al., 2007).

In contrast to physical dependence, *psychological dependence* refers to habitual and compulsive substance use despite the consequences. People can be psychologically dependent without showing tolerance or withdrawal. This section focuses on addiction to substances that alter consciousness, but people can also become psychologically dependent on behaviors, such as gambling or shopping (**FIGURE 4.28**).

How do people become addicted? Many theories related to the initiation of drug or alcohol use among either children or adolescents focus on the social level of analysis. They explore social learning processes that emphasize the roles of parents, peers, and mass media. One example of media's influence is the Joe Camel advertising campaign of the early 1990s, as a result of which Camel cigarettes experienced a tenfold increase in market share; at one point, more young children could identify Joe Camel than could identify Mickey Mouse (Mizerski, 1995). Social learning theories also emphasize self-identification with high-risk groups (e.g., "stoners" or "druggies") as central to the initiation of drug or alcohol use. Teenagers want to fit in somewhere, even with groups that society perceives as deviant. And as discussed further in Chapter 6, children imitate the behavior of role models, especially those they admire or with whom they identify. For children whose parents smoke, the modeling of the behavior may be continuous through early childhood and elementary school. Unsurprisingly, then, multiple studies show that when parents smoke, their children tend to have positive attitudes about smoking and to begin smoking early (Rowe, Chassin, Presson, & Sherman, 1996).

As individuals, some adolescents are especially likely to experiment with illegal drugs and to abuse alcohol. Children high in sensation seeking (a personality trait that involves attraction to novelty and risk taking) are more likely to associate with deviant peer groups and to use alcohol, tobacco, and drugs (Wills, DuHamel, & Vaccaro, 1995). These children and their parents tend to have poor relationships, which in turn promote the children's association with deviant peer groups. Does the family environment determine alcohol and drug use, then? Some theorists, operating at the biological level of analysis, suggest that an inherited predisposition to sensation seeking may predict behaviors, such as affiliating with drug users, that increase the possibility of substance abuse. Indeed, some evidence points to genetic components of addiction, especially for alcoholism, but little direct evidence points to a *single* "alcoholism" or "addiction" gene. Rather, what might be inherited is a cluster of characteristics, including certain personality traits, a reduced concern about personal harm, a nervous system chronically low in arousal, or a predisposition to finding chemical substances pleasurable. In turn, such factors may make some people more likely to explore drugs and enjoy them.

One of the most fascinating aspects of addiction is that only about 5 percent to 10 percent of those who use drugs become addicted. Indeed, more than 90 million Americans have experimented with illicit drugs, yet most of them use drugs only occasionally or try them for a while and then give them up. In a longitudinal study, Jonathan Shedler and Jack Block (1990) found that those who had experimented with drugs as adolescents were better adjusted in adulthood than those who had never tried them. Complete abstainers and heavy drug users had adjustment problems compared with those who had experimented. However, this finding does not suggest that everyone should try drugs or that parents should encourage drug experimentation. After all, no one can predict just who will become addicted or know who is prepared to handle drugs' effects on behavior.

(a)

(b)

FIGURE 4.28 Physical Dependence versus Psychological Dependence Both types of dependence can force people to go to extremes. **(a)** A savvy restaurant owner in Germany figured out how to accommodate his patrons who are physically addicted to smoking but do not want to step outside—he made padded holes in the wall. **(b)** With their enclosed spaces, bright lights, and stimulating sounds, casinos, such as this one in Las Vegas, encourage patrons' psychological addiction to gambling.

ADDICTION'S CONTEXT Some evidence suggests that context is important for understanding addiction. For example, in the late 1960s, estimates suggested that drug abuse among U.S. soldiers, including the use of narcotics such as heroin and opium, had become epidemic. The widespread drug use was not surprising—it was a time of youthful drug experimentation, soldiers in Vietnam had easy access to various drugs, and drugs helped the soldiers cope temporarily with fear, depression, homesickness, boredom, and the repressiveness of army regulations. The military commanders mostly ignored drug use among soldiers, viewing it as "blowing off steam."

Beginning in 1971, the military began mandatory drug testing of soldiers to identify and detoxify drug users before they returned to the United States. Amid speculation that a flood of addicted soldiers returning from Vietnam would swamp treatment facilities back home, the White House asked a team of behavioral scientists to study a group of returning soldiers and assess the extent of the addiction problem. Led by the behavioral epidemiologist Lee Robins, the research team examined a random sample of 898 soldiers who were leaving Vietnam in September 1971. Robins and her colleagues found extremely high levels of drug use among them (Robins, Helzer, & Davis, 1975). Over 90 percent reported drinking alcohol, nearly three-quarters smoked marijuana, and nearly half used narcotics such as heroin, morphine, and opium. About half the soldiers who used narcotics either had symptoms of addiction or reported believing they would be unable to give up their drug habits. Their findings suggested that approximately 1 soldier in 5 returning from Vietnam was a drug addict. Given the prevailing view that addiction was a biological disorder with a low rate of recovery, these results indicated that tens of thousands of heroin addicts would soon be inundating the United States. But this did not happen.

Robins and her colleagues examined drug use among the soldiers after they returned to the United States. Of those who were apparently addicted to narcotics in Vietnam, only half sought out drugs when they returned to the States, and fewer still maintained their narcotic addictions. Approximately 95 percent of the addicts no longer used drugs within months of their return—an astonishing quit rate considering that the success rate of the best treatments is typically only 20 percent to 30 percent. A long-term follow-up study conducted in the early 1990s confirmed that only a handful of those who were addicts in Vietnam remained addicts.

Why did coming home help the addicts recover? In the United States, they likely did not have the same motivations for taking the drugs as they did in Vietnam. No longer needing the drugs to escape combat's horrors, they focused on other needs and goals, such as careers and family obligations. An important lesson from this case study is that we cannot ignore environment when we try to understand addiction. Knowing drugs' physical actions in the brain may give us insights into addiction's biology, but that information fails to account for how these biological impulses can be overcome by other motivations.

 SUMMING UP

How Do Drugs Affect Consciousness?

People have long ingested drugs that alter the way they think, feel, and act. The use and abuse of drugs has enormous societal costs, including impaired driving, illness, and crime. Although moderate use of drugs such as alcohol and caffeine may have few consequences, excessive use can lead to physical or psychological dependence. The term *addiction* refers to physical dependence, in which not using the drug produces withdrawal and more of the drug is needed to obtain its effects.

Psychoactive drugs affect a variety of neurotransmitter systems, but the user's beliefs about a particular drug also affect the experience and behavior of that user.

MEASURING UP

1. All drugs work by _____.
   a. increasing neural firing in the cerebellum
   b. decreasing the amount of neurotransmitter affected by reuptake
   c. creating dizziness, which the interpreter translates as a drug state
   d. activating neurotransmitter systems

2. Match each of the following drugs or drug categories with as many true statements as apply: stimulants, MDMA, opiates, marijuana, alcohol.
   a. involved in over half of all fatal car accidents
   b. the only drug that does not have its strongest effect on first-time users
   c. include heroin, morphine, and codeine
   d. increase(s) dopamine action in a brain structure called the nucleus accumbens
   e. include cocaine, nicotine, caffeine, and amphetamines
   f. known as ecstasy
   g. according to their reports, one-third of college students had sex while under its influence
   h. include a drug used in Coca-Cola's original recipe
   i. has negative long-term effects on memory

CONCLUSION

Try to imagine human life without consciousness. How could you live without experiencing the world around you? Conscious experience is an essential aspect of the human condition, one that psychologists and philosophers have long wanted to understand the nature of. Over the past century, the topic has largely been philosophers' domain, because psychologists' increasing emphasis on empiricism has cast doubt on the scientific study of subjective states, such as consciousness. The qualia of consciousness are inaccessible to direct observation, but psychologists have not ignored consciousness. They have examined the ways that people alter levels of consciousness, such as by creating subjectively pleasant or spiritually meaningful mental states. Mind-altering substances play prominent roles in many religious ceremonies, and some religious practices purposely alter conscious states through prayer and meditation.

What has eluded the scientific world is how our thoughts and behaviors alter the conscious experience. Brain imaging has allowed researchers to examine consciousness objectively, and we now know that conscious experience reflects the brain's ongoing activity. For instance, emotional dreams are experienced as such because emotional brain regions are active at that time and brain regions involved in rational thought and self-awareness are not. Although many philosophical questions remain, psychological scientists are making considerable progress in understanding the biological foundations of consciousness. Perhaps more so than in any other area of inquiry, brain imaging and other physiological methods have opened up the subjective world to scientific examination, allowing for a much better appreciation and understanding of the human experience.

■ CHAPTER SUMMARY

How Is the Conscious Mind Experienced?

- **Consciousness Is a Subjective Experience:** Consciousness is difficult to study because of the subjective nature of our experience of the world. Brain imaging research has shown that particular brain regions are activated by particular types of sensory information.

- **There Are Variations in Conscious Experience:** Consciousness is each person's unified and coherent experience of the world around him or her. At any one time, each person can be conscious of a limited number of things. A person's level of consciousness varies throughout the day and depends on the task at hand. Whereas some people in comas show no brain activity (a persistent vegetative state), people in minimally conscious states show brain activity indicating some awareness of external stimuli.

- **Splitting the Brain Splits the Conscious Mind:** The corpus callosum connects the brain's two sides; cutting it in half results in two independently functioning hemispheres. The left hemisphere is responsible primarily for language, and the right hemisphere is responsible primarily for images and spatial relations. The left hemisphere strives to make sense of experiences, and its interpretations influence the way a person views and remembers the world.

- **Unconscious Processing Influences Behavior:** Research findings indicate that much of a person's behavior occurs automatically, without that person's constant awareness. Thought and behavior can be influenced by stimuli that are not experienced consciously.

- **Brain Activity Produces Consciousness:** Blindsight demonstrates visual ability without awareness. The global workspace model of consciousness demonstrates how awareness depends on activity in various different cortical areas.

What Is Sleep?

- **Sleep Is an Altered State of Consciousness:** Sleep occurs in stages, which vary according to levels of brain activity and of respiration. REM sleep activates the brain and produces both body paralysis and genital stimulation. Sleep disorders include insomnia, sleep apnea, and narcolepsy.

- **Sleep Is an Adaptive Behavior:** Sleep restores the body, and circadian rhythms control changes in body function and in sleep. Learning is consolidated during sleep.

- **Sleep and Wakefulness Are Regulated by Multiple Neural Mechanisms:** Brainstem structures are involved in arousal and REM sleep.

- **People Dream while Sleeping:** REM dreams activate different brain areas than do non-REM dreams. Sigmund Freud thought dreams revealed unconscious conflicts. The activation-synthesis hypothesis posits that dreams are side effects of brain activity. Antti Revonsuo has theorized that dreaming is adaptive.

What Is Altered Consciousness?

- **Hypnosis Is Induced through Suggestion:** Scientists debate whether hypnosis is an altered state of consciousness or whether hypnotized people merely play the role they expect (and are expected) to play. Brain imaging research suggests that hypnotized subjects undergo changes in their brain activity.

- **Meditation Produces Relaxation:** The goal of meditation, especially as practiced in the West, is to bring about a state of deep relaxation. Studies have shown that meditation can have multiple benefits for people's physical and mental health.

- **People Can Lose Themselves in Activities:** Exercise, certain religious practices, and other engaging activities can produce a state of altered consciousness called flow, in which people become completely absorbed in what they are doing. Flow is a positive experience, but escapist activities can be harmful if people use them for avoidance rather than for fulfillment.

How Do Drugs Affect Consciousness?

- **People Use—and Abuse—Many Psychoactive Drugs:** Stimulants increase behavioral and mental activity. MDMA (ecstasy) produces energizing and hallucinogenic effects. THC (the active ingredient in marijuana) alters perception. All drugs, including opiates, provide high reward value by increasing dopamine activation.

- **Alcohol Is the Most Widely Abused Drug:** Though believed to reduce anxiety, alcohol consumption can increase anxiety and negative mood. A drinker's expectation can significantly affect his or her behavior while under the influence of alcohol.

- **Addiction Has Psychological and Physical Aspects:** Physical addiction involves the body's responses to and tolerance toward a substance. Psychological dependence involves both habitual use and compulsion to use, despite consequences.

■ KEY TERMS

activation-synthesis hypothesis, p. 157

blindsight, p. 147

circadian rhythms, p. 154

consciousness, p. 135

dreams, p. 156

hypnosis, p. 159

insomnia, p. 152

interpreter, p. 143

latent content, p. 157

manifest content, p. 157

meditation, p. 162

microsleeps, p. 154

narcolepsy, p. 153

REM sleep, p. 151

sleep apnea, p. 153

split brain, p. 140

subliminal perception, p. 144

The answer key for all the Measuring Up exercises and the Practice Tests can be found at the back of the book.

■ PRACTICE TEST

1. What is a key distinction between a person in a persistent vegetative state and a person in a minimally conscious state?
   a. The person in the minimally conscious state is less responsive to her or his surroundings.
   b. The person in the persistent vegetative state is more likely to regain full consciousness at some point in the future.
   c. The person in the minimally conscious state shows some degree of brain activity, whereas the person in the persistent vegetative state shows no brain activity.
   d. The person in the minimally conscious state is dreaming, whereas the person in the persistent vegetative state is in a coma.

2. A researcher asks study participants to play a word game in which they unscramble letters to form words. In Condition A, the unscrambled words are *outgoing, talkative,* and *smile.* In Condition B, the unscrambled words are *standoffish, silent,* and *frown.* After participants complete the word game, they meet and interact with a stranger. What do you predict participants' behavior during that interaction will reveal?
   a. Participants in Conditions A and B will behave nearly identically.
   b. Participants in Condition A will be more friendly toward the stranger than will participants in Condition B.
   c. Participants in Condition B will be more friendly toward the stranger than will participants in Condition A.

3. A study participant who has a severed corpus callosum is asked to focus on a dot in the middle of a computer screen. After a few seconds, a car appears on the left half of the screen while an automobile tire appears on the right half of the screen. How will the participant most likely respond if asked to describe the objects in the pictures?
   a. The participant will say he saw a tire and will draw a car.
   b. The participant will say he saw a car and will draw a tire.
   c. The participant will say he saw a car and a tire, but he will not be able to draw either object.
   d. The participant will draw a car and a tire, but he will not be able to name either object.

4. For each description below, name the sleep disorder: insomnia, apnea, narcolepsy, or somnambulism.
   _____ a. Despite feeling well-rested, Marcus falls asleep suddenly while practicing piano.
   _____ b. Emma walks through the living room in the middle of the night, seemingly oblivious to those around her.
   _____ c. Sophia spends most of the night trying to fall asleep.
   _____ d. Ivan's roommate regularly complains that Ivan's snoring wakes him multiple times throughout the night.

5. Which of the following pieces of evidence suggest sleep is an adaptive behavior? Check all that apply.
   a. A few days of sleep deprivation do not impair physical strength.
   b. All animals sleep.
   c. It is impossible to resist indefinitely the urge to sleep.

d. Sleep deprivation helps people feel less depressed.
   e. Animals die when deprived of sleep for extended periods.

6. Four students discuss a hypnotist's performance on campus. Which student's claim about hypnotism is most consistent with current evidence?
   a. "We just witnessed a bunch of people acting goofy solely because they thought they were supposed to act goofy."
   b. "I can't believe the hypnotist was able to make those people do things they would usually be so opposed to!"
   c. "What worries me is that someone could hypnotize me without my even knowing about it."
   d. "It's pretty cool that a hypnotist could help those people enter an altered state of consciousness."

7. Which of the following instruction sets would a yoga teacher trained in concentrative meditation be most likely to give?
   a. "Close your eyes while sitting in a comfortable position. Let your thoughts move freely through your mind, like clouds passing through the sky. Acknowledge them, but do not react to them."
   b. "Lying on your back, rest your hands gently on your abdomen. As you breathe in and out, focus attention on your breath. Notice the rhythmic rise and fall of your abdomen and the slow, deep movement of your chest."

8. Match each of the following drugs with the appropriate description of a user's typical response: alcohol, marijuana, MDMA, opiates, stimulants.
   _____ a. increased heart rate, elevated mood, restlessness
   _____ b. relaxation, contentment, vivid perceptual experiences
   _____ c. impaired motor skills, decreased sexual performance
   _____ d. energy, slight hallucinations
   _____ e. lack of pain, euphoria, intense pleasure

9. A group of people are talking about their weekend plans. Which of the following statements suggest the most understanding regarding alcohol's effects? Multiple responses may be correct.
   a. "I've been in a crummy mood all week. I'm heading to the bar tonight to chase my blues away with beer."
   b. "I've been really stressed out all week. I just need a few beers to help me unwind and get my mind off all this work."
   c. "I won't drink tonight because I really need a good night's sleep and I always wake up insanely early after I drink."
   d. "I think a beer or two will give me the liquid courage I need to ask Jordan out on a date."

10. Which of the following phenomena are best described as symptoms of physical dependence?
   a. strong cravings for the substance
   b. elevated tolerance for the substance
   c. habitually reaching for the substance when in certain environments (e.g., lighting a cigarette each time you get into your car)
   d. using the substance as prescribed by a physician

■ PSYCHOLOGY AND SOCIETY

1. Consider the critical thinking skills highlighted in this chapter: circular reasoning and slippery slope thinking. To find examples of lapses in either or both of these critical thinking skills, search through newspapers, blogs, and other sources for articles related to the use of medical devices to maintain the lives of people in persistent vegetative states, the medical use of marijuana or other psychoactive drugs, or the practice of mandating treatment for persons addicted to drugs.

Write a paragraph explaining the lapses you find and how the writers (or thinkers being written about) might have avoided them.

2. Evidence suggests the gender gap in alcohol use is nearly nonexistent among college students. That is, women in college seem to drink just as much and just as often as men in college. Think of at least two possible explanations for why this is so. Then briefly describe a study design that would allow you to investigate the validity of each hypothesized cause.

Sensation and Perception

WHEN HELEN KELLER WAS 19 MONTHS OLD, she completely lost the senses of sight and hearing. Her life became dark and silent, and for her the world existed only through touch, smell, and taste. She recognized her parents, and determined her location, by touch and by smell. But otherwise she was completely isolated in a mental prison. Realizing that others could communicate but she could not, she became so enraged and frustrated that she threw daily tantrums. She later wrote, "Sometimes, I stood between two persons who were conversing and touched their lips. I could not understand, and was vexed. I moved my lips and gesticulated frantically without result. This made me so angry at times that I kicked and screamed until I was exhausted" (quoted in *Time Magazine*, June 14, 1999, paragraph 1).

When Keller was six years old, her parents sought assistance from Alexander Graham Bell, who invented devices such as the telephone but also taught a system called "Visible Speech" to deaf children. Bell put them in touch with the Perkins School for the Blind, in Watertown,

How Do We Sense Our Worlds?
- Stimuli Must Be Coded to Be Understood by the Brain
- Psychophysics Relates Stimulus to Response
- Critical Thinking Skill: Recognizing the Effects of Context on Judgments

What Are the Basic Sensory Processes?
- In Taste, Taste Buds Detect Chemicals
- In Smell, the Nasal Cavity Gathers Odorants

- In Touch, Sensors in the Skin Detect Pressure, Temperature, and Pain
- In Hearing, the Ear Detects Sound Waves
- In Vision, the Eye Detects Light Waves
- Humans and Animals Have Other Sensory Systems
- The Evidence for Extrasensory Perception (ESP) Is Weak or Nonexistent
- Critical Thinking Skill: Understanding That Perception Can Be Deceiving

What Are the Basic Perceptual Processes?
- Perception Occurs in the Brain
- Object Perception Requires Construction
- Depth Perception Is Important for Locating Objects
- Culture Influences Perception
- Size Perception Depends on Distance Perception
- Motion Perception Has Internal and External Cues
- Perceptual Constancies Are Based on Ratio Relationships

FIGURE 5.1 Keller and Sullivan Eight-year-old Helen Keller **(left)** sits with her teacher, Anne Sullivan, in Cape Cod in 1888.

Massachusetts. Through the school, the Kellers hired a teacher, Anne Sullivan, to teach Helen to communicate with signs. At first, Helen simply mimicked Sullivan's strange hand motions, making no sense. One day, Sullivan ran water over one of Helen's hands while spelling *w-a-t-e-r* in the other, and Helen made the connection. She grabbed some dirt and asked Sullivan to spell its name. By evening, Helen had memorized her first 30 words in sign language and had begun a life of both passionate learning and social activism (**FIGURE 5.1**).

Try to imagine what it would be like to go through most of your life, as Helen Keller did, without being able to see or hear. Further, try to imagine what it would be like to be not only blind and deaf but also unable to smell, unable to taste, and unable to feel pain or temperature. You would still feel hunger and other bodily sensations, such as fatigue, but you would know no world beyond your body's boundaries. You would have no way of knowing about other people or an environment outside your body. You would be completely alone: No one could communicate with you, and you could communicate with no one. What would you do without sensation, your windows to the world, and perception, your ability to make sense of your sensory experiences?

sensation The sense organs' responses to external stimuli and the transmission of these responses to the brain.

perception The processing, organization, and interpretation of sensory signals; it results in an internal representation of the stimulus.

How Do We Sense Our Worlds?

Psychological scientists often divide the way we experience the world into two distinct phases: *sensation* and *perception*. **Sensation** is our sense organs' detection of and responses to external stimulus energy (light, air vibrations, odors, and so on) and how those responses are transmitted to the brain. It is an elementary experience such as color or motion without the more complex perceptual experience of what is being seen or what is moving. **Perception** is the brain's further processing of these detected signals that results in internal representations of the stimuli—representations that form a conscious experience of the world. Whereas the essence of sensation is detection, the essence of perception is construction of useful and meaningful information about a particular environment. For example, a green light emits photons that are detected by specialized neurons in the eyes, which transmit signals to the brain (sensation). The brain processes those neural signals, and the observer experiences a green light (perception; **FIGURE 5.2**).

The study of sensation and perception is the study of the bodily systems that convert stimulus energy into useful information. This chapter will discuss how the sense organs detect various types of stimulus energy, how the brain constructs

FIGURE 5.2 From Sensation to Perception

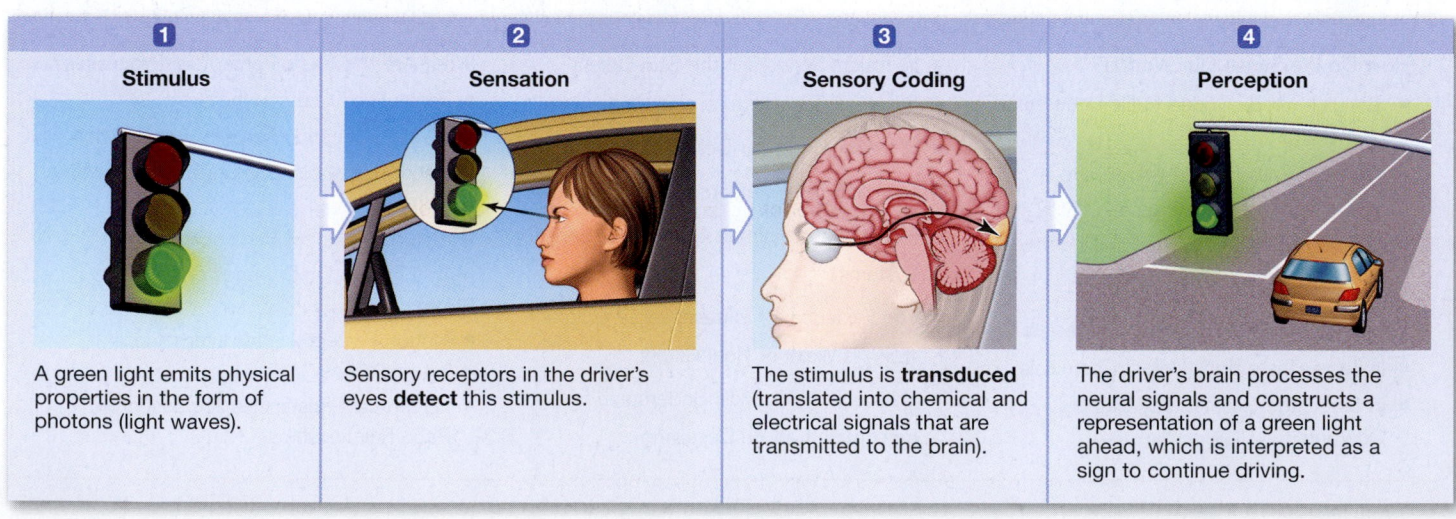

1 Stimulus	**2** Sensation	**3** Sensory Coding	**4** Perception
A green light emits physical properties in the form of photons (light waves).	Sensory receptors in the driver's eyes **detect** this stimulus.	The stimulus is **transduced** (translated into chemical and electrical signals that are transmitted to the brain).	The driver's brain processes the neural signals and constructs a representation of a green light ahead, which is interpreted as a sign to continue driving.

information about the world on the basis of what has been detected, and how we use this constructed information to guide ourselves through the world around us. Perception is often based on our prior experiences, which shape our expectations about new sensory experiences. You are unlikely to see a blue, apple-shaped object as a real apple, for example, because you know from past experience that apples are not blue. An important lesson in this chapter is that our perception of the world does not work like a camera or tape recorder, faithfully and passively capturing the physical properties of stimuli we encounter. Rather, what we *sense* (what we see, hear, taste, touch, or smell) is the result of brain processes that actively construct perceptual experiences and, as a result, allow us to adapt to our environments' details. This system can get the details wrong, sometimes by filling in information that has not been provided, but it does so in an intelligent and efficient way that still produces a meaningful understanding of what is and what happens. Because of the different adaptive challenges that humans and the various nonhuman animals have faced, humans are sensitive to different types of physical energy than nonhuman animals are, and so this chapter focuses on sensation and perception as they operate in humans.

Stimuli Must Be Coded to Be Understood by the Brain

Our sensory organs' translations of stimuli's physical properties into neural impulses is called *sensory coding*. The different features of the physical environment are coded by different neural impulse patterns. Thus a green stoplight will be coded by a particular neural response pattern in the eye's retina before being read by the brain; when the hand touches a hot skillet, other neurons, in the hand and in the brain, will signal pain. The brain cannot process raw stimuli, so the stimuli must be translated into chemical and electrical signals the brain can interpret. Sensory coding therefore begins with **transduction,** in which *receptors,* specialized neurons in the sense organs, pass impulses to connecting neurons when the receptors receive physical or chemical stimulation. Connecting neurons then transmit information to the brain in the form of neural impulses. Most sensory information first goes to the thalamus, a structure in the middle of the brain. Neurons in the thalamus then send information to the cortex, where incoming neural impulses are interpreted as sight, smell, sound, touch, or taste. (For the brain regions, see Figure 3.27. **TABLE 5.1** lists the stimuli and receptors for each major sensory system. The brain's interpretation of these impulses—perception—is discussed later in this chapter.)

transduction A process by which sensory receptors produce neural impulses when they receive physical or chemical stimulation.

Table 5.1 The Stimuli, Receptors, and Pathways for Each Sense

Sense	Stimuli	Receptors	Pathway to the Brain
Taste	Molecules dissolved in fluid on the tongue	Taste cells in taste buds on the tongue	Portions of facial, glossopharyngeal, and vagus nerves
Smell	Molecules dissolved in fluid on mucous membranes in the nose	Sensitive ends of olfactory neurons in the mucous membranes	Olfactory nerve
Touch	Pressure on the skin	Sensitive ends of touch neurons in skin	Trigeminal nerve for touch above the neck, spinal nerves for touch elsewhere
Hearing	Sound waves	Pressure-sensitive hair cells in cochlea of inner ear	Auditory nerve
Vision	Light waves	Light-sensitive rods and cones in retina of eye	Optic nerve

To function effectively, our brains need *qualitative* and *quantitative* information about a stimulus. If you were waiting to cross a city street, qualitative information would include knowing whether the nearby traffic light is red or green. The difference between sounds—say, a tuba's honk versus a flute's toot—is qualitative. The difference between a salty taste and a sweet one is qualitative. We can identify qualitative differences because different sensory receptors respond to qualitatively different stimuli. In contrast, quantitative differences in stimuli are coded by the speed of a particular neurons' firing—a more rapidly firing neuron is responding at a higher frequency to, for example, a brighter light, a louder sound, or a heavier weight (**FIGURE 5.3**).

In most sensory systems, receptors provide *coarse coding,* in which sensory qualities are coded by only a few different types of receptors, each of which responds to a broad range of stimuli. The combined responses by different receptors firing at different rates allow us to tell the difference between, for example, lime green and forest green or between a pinch on the arm and a shove. Sensation and perception are a symphony of sensory receptors and the neurons those receptors communicate with, each firing in different combinations and at different rates; as discussed in Chapter 4, the sum of this activity is consciousness, the huge range of perceptions that make up our experience of the world.

Psychophysics Relates Stimulus to Response

Humans have long understood that perceptual experience is constructed from information detected by the sense organs. For more than a century, psychological scientists have tried to understand the relationship between the world's physical properties and how we sense and perceive them. *Psychophysics,* a subfield developed during the nineteenth century by the researchers Ernst Weber and Gustav Fechner, examines our psychological experiences of physical stimuli. It assesses how much physical energy is required for our sense organs to detect a stimulus, for example, and how much change is required before we notice that change. To test such things, researchers present very subtle changes in stimuli and observe how participants respond. They study the limits of humans' sensory systems, which are remarkably sensitive.

SENSORY THRESHOLDS As noted throughout Chapter 4, your sensory organs constantly acquire information from your environment, much of which you do not notice. The *absolute threshold* is the minimum intensity of stimulation that must occur before you experience a sensation, or the stimulus intensity detected above

FIGURE 5.3 Qualitative versus Quantitative Sensory Information

Qualitative Information
Sensory receptors respond to qualitative differences by firing in different combinations.

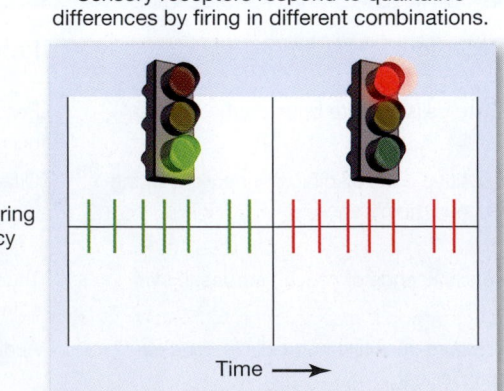

A green light is coded by different receptors than a red light.

Quantitative Information
Sensory receptors respond to quantitative differences by firing at different rates.

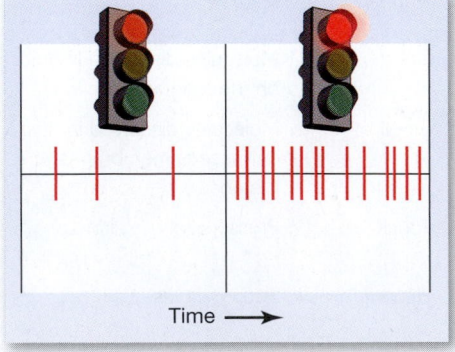

A bright light causes receptors to fire more rapidly (at a higher frequency) than a dim light.

Neural firing frequency

Time →

Time →

chance. The absolute threshold for hearing is the faintest sound a person can detect 50 percent of the time (**FIGURE 5.4**). For instance, how loudly must someone in the next room whisper for you to hear it? In this case, the absolute threshold for auditory stimuli would be the quietest whisper you could hear half the time. (**TABLE 5.2** lists some approximate minimum stimuli for each sense.)

A *difference threshold* is the just noticeable difference between two stimuli—the minimum amount of change required for a person to detect a difference. If your friend is watching a television show while you are reading and a commercial comes on that is louder than the show, you might look up, noticing that something has changed. The difference threshold is the minimum change in volume required for you to detect a difference. The difference threshold increases as the stimulus becomes more intense. Pick up a one-ounce letter and a two-ounce letter, and you will easily detect the difference. But pick up a five-pound package and a package weighing one ounce more, and the difference will be harder, maybe impossible, to discern. This principle, *Weber's law*, states

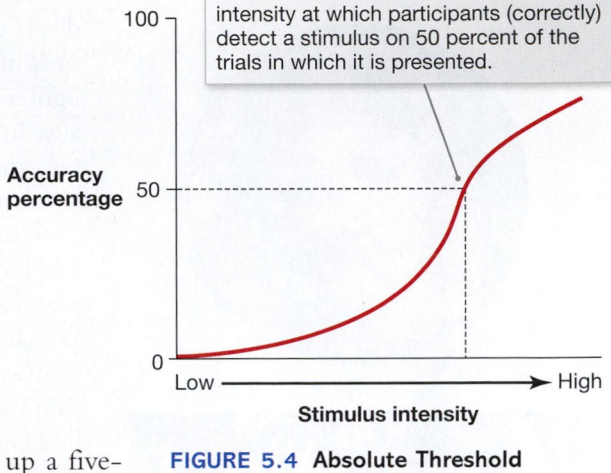

Absolute threshold is the level of intensity at which participants (correctly) detect a stimulus on 50 percent of the trials in which it is presented.

FIGURE 5.4 **Absolute Threshold**

Table 5.2 Approximate Absolute Sensory Threshold (Minimum Stimulus) for Each Sense

Sense	Minimum Stimulus
Taste	One teaspoon of sugar in 2 gallons of water
Smell	One drop of perfume diffused into the entire volume of six rooms
Touch	A fly's wing falling on your cheek from a distance of 1 centimeter
Hearing	The tick of a clock at 20 feet under quiet conditions
Vision	A candle flame seen at 30 miles on a dark, clear night

that the just noticeable difference between two stimuli is based on a proportion of the original stimulus rather than on a fixed amount of difference. The formula for Weber's law is $\Delta I/I$ = a constant, so if you can detect a single candle when you have 10 candles (1/10 = .1), you will need 10 candles to detect a difference in brightness when you have 100 candles (10/100 = .1). This key psychological principle about difference applies in many different contexts and not just to perception.

Recognizing the Effects of Context on Judgments

Are you smart? Are you beautiful? Are you good in math? Any judgment you make about yourself will be affected to a large extent by the context in which you make it. For example, to what or whom are you comparing yourself? In fact, context affects any judgment (Is that person trustworthy? Is that sunburn painful? Who is rich?), although we often make comparisons automatically and usually without being conscious that we are relying on some comparator.

FIGURE 5.5 Think Critically: Context Matters If you had seen just the detail, would you have guessed the bigger picture? The girl turns out to be crying because she is at the studio for *MTV Total Request Live,* seated between Nick Jonas **(left)** and Joe Jonas, of the Jonas Brothers.

Imagine sitting in a windowless room illuminated with one small candle. If you light a second candle, the room will appear much brighter. Now imagine sitting in a room lit brightly by several 200-watt lightbulbs. If you light a small candle here, the room's brightness might not differ perceptually. In other words, the subtle effects of context within a situation can become obvious when that situation is viewed from afar or later or in the abstract (**FIGURE 5.5**).

Context effects also extend beyond immediate perceptions, across a wide range of events. For example, people generally define their own social and physical characteristics by comparing themselves with others (Alicke, LoSchiavo, Zerbst, & Zhang, 1997). Often without realizing they are doing it, many women compare themselves with the highly attractive and ultra-thin models in advertising. Since the viewers cannot match the perfect, air-brushed images they encounter, they experience negative feelings (e.g., Bower, 2001). If the viewers are prone to making immediate comparisons, their moods become more negative, and they feel more dissatisfied with their own bodies (Tiggermann & McGill, 2004). One study found that when male and female college students viewed beautiful models, they rated photos of more average-looking people as less attractive than did a similar group of college students who did not see the models' photos (Kenrick, Montello, Gutierres, & Trost, 1993).

Research has shown that we do not completely control comparisons we make unconsciously. However, Gilbert, Giesler, and Morris (1995) have found that we can control comparisons by either avoiding some encounters or rejecting conclusions we have come to in the past. Thus women prone to feeling bad about themselves after seeing advertisements with seemingly perfect models could stop reading magazines that carry such advertisements, or they could continue to read the magazines but remind themselves that these models set unattainable standards that do not apply to real people. Women can define themselves as students, writers, scientists, mothers, and so on, and reject fashion models as their standards for comparison. Understanding the basis for any comparison is the key to making a sound judgment related—positively or negatively—to that comparison.

SIGNAL DETECTION THEORY Classical psychophysics was based on the idea of a sensory *threshold;* either you saw something or you did not, depending on whether the intensity of the stimulus was above or below the sensory threshold. As research progressed, however, it became clear that early psychophysicists had ignored an important variable: human judgment. Imagine you are a participant in a study of sensory thresholds. You are sitting in a dark room, and an experimenter asks if you detect a faint light, hear a faint sound, or feel a very light touch on your arm. Even if you do not detect this stimulus, you might ask yourself if you do—or if you should, since someone has asked about it. You might convince yourself you had sensed a weak stimulus that had not been presented, or you might fail to detect a weak stimulus that had been presented. After realizing that their methods of testing absolute thresholds were flawed, researchers formulated **signal detection theory (SDT),** which states that detecting a stimulus requires making a judgment about its presence or absence, based on a subjective interpretation of ambiguous information.

SDT applies, for example, to the work of radiologists, who scan medical images to detect early signs of disease. A radiologist might be looking for the kind of faint

signal detection theory (SDT) A theory of perception based on the idea that the detection of a faint stimulus requires a judgment—it is not an all-or-none process.

shadow that signals an early-stage cancer and, even after years of training and experience, have difficulty judging whether an abnormality in the image is likely cancerous. The radiologist's knowledge of the patient (e.g., age, sex, family medical history) will likely affect this judgment; so, of course, will factors such as the radiologist's levels of both motivation and attention. Moreover, the knowledge of the consequences can influence a radiologist's judgment: Being wrong could mean missing a fatal cancer or, conversely, causing unnecessary and potentially dangerous treatment. Because stimulus-based judgment is critical in radiologists' work and so many other areas, signal detection is a central topic in psychology.

Research on signal detection involves a series of trials in which a stimulus is presented in only some trials. In each trial, participants must state whether they sensed the stimulus. Any trial in which participants judge whether an event occurs can have one of four outcomes (**FIGURE 5.6**). If the signal is presented and the observer detects it, the outcome is a *hit*. If the participant fails to detect the signal, the outcome is a *miss*. If the participant "detects" a signal that was not presented, the outcome is a *false alarm*. If the signal is not presented and the observer does not detect it, the outcome is a *correct rejection*. The participant's sensitivity to the signal is usually computed by comparing the hit rate with the false-alarm rate—thus correcting for any bias the participant might bring to the testing situation.

Response bias refers to a participant's tendency to report detecting the signal in an ambiguous trial. The participant might be strongly biased against responding and need a great deal of evidence that the signal is present. Under other conditions, that same participant might need only a small amount of evidence. For example, a radiologist checking a CAT scan for signs of a brain tumor might be extra cautious about accepting any abnormality as a signal (i.e., a tumor), since a positive response could lead to drastic and dangerous neurosurgery. A doctor checking an X-ray for signs of a broken bone might be more willing to make a positive diagnosis, since treatment, although uncomfortable, will most likely not endanger the life of the patient. People's expectations often influence the extent to which they are biased. For instance, a soldier expecting an imminent attack will likely err on the side of responding, such as by mistaking a dim shape as an enemy when in fact no one is there. Higher-level processes in the brain, such as beliefs and expectancies, influence how sensations from the environment are perceived.

There are four possible outcomes when a subject is asked whether something occurred during a trial.

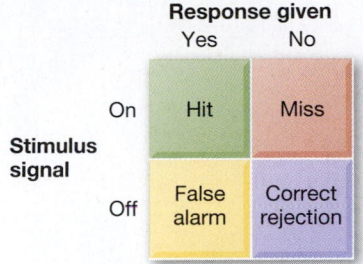

Those who are biased toward reporting a signal tend to be "yea-sayers."

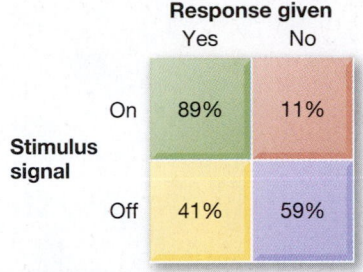

Those who are biased toward denying that a signal occurred tend to be "nay-sayers."

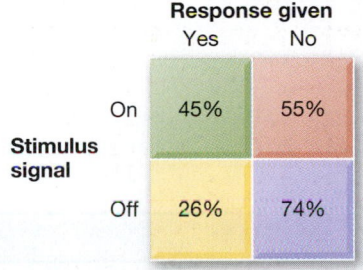

FIGURE 5.6 Payoff Matrices for Signal Detection Theory

SENSORY ADAPTATION Sensory systems are tuned to detect environmental changes: It is important for us to be able to detect such changes, because they might require responses, while it is less critical to keep responding to unchanging stimuli. **Sensory adaptation** is a decrease in sensivity to a constant level of stimulation (**FIGURE 5.7**). As such, it exemplifies this book's theme that the mind is adaptive. Imagine, for example, you are studying in the library when work begins at a nearby construction site. When the equipment starts up, the sound seems particularly loud and disturbing. After a few minutes, however, you hardly notice the noise; it seems to have faded into the background. Researchers have often noticed that if a stimulus is presented continuously, the responses of the sensory systems that detect it tend to diminish over time. Similarly, when a continuous stimulus stops, the sensory systems usually respond strongly as well. If the construction noise suddenly halted, you would likely notice the silence. As discussed later in this chapter, focusing on such adaptations helps researchers explore the nature of sensory systems.

FIGURE 5.7 Sensory Adaptation Because of sensory adaptation, people who live near constant noise, such as those (pictured here) who live near London's Heathrow Airport, eventually become less aware of the noise.

▶ SUMMING UP

How Do We Sense Our Worlds?

The study of sensation focuses on the way our sense organs respond to and detect external stimulus energy. Stimuli need to be transduced for the brain to use their information. Qualitative aspects of stimuli, such as color and bitterness, are coded by the combination of the specific receptors each activates. Sensory coding for quantitative factors, such as intensity and loudness, depends on the number of neurons firing and how frequently they fire. The development of psychophysical methods has allowed scientists to study psychological reactions to physical events. Psychophysical methods can be used to determine thresholds for detecting events and for noticing change. These thresholds can be influenced by situational factors and by biases in human judgment.

▶ MEASURING UP

1. Suppose you are designing an experiment to determine the absolute threshold for detecting a salty taste. You plan to give participants plain water that _____.
   a. always has a small amount of salt in it
   b. sometimes has a small amount of salt in it and sometimes has no salt

   You plan to have them sip a small amount of water and tell you _____.
   a. whether they taste salt or no salt
   b. how much salt is in each sip from different glasses of water

   You will use the participants' responses to calculate an absolute threshold for tasting salt by _____.
   a. comparing hits and false alarms
   b. calculating the amount of salt used in each sip of water

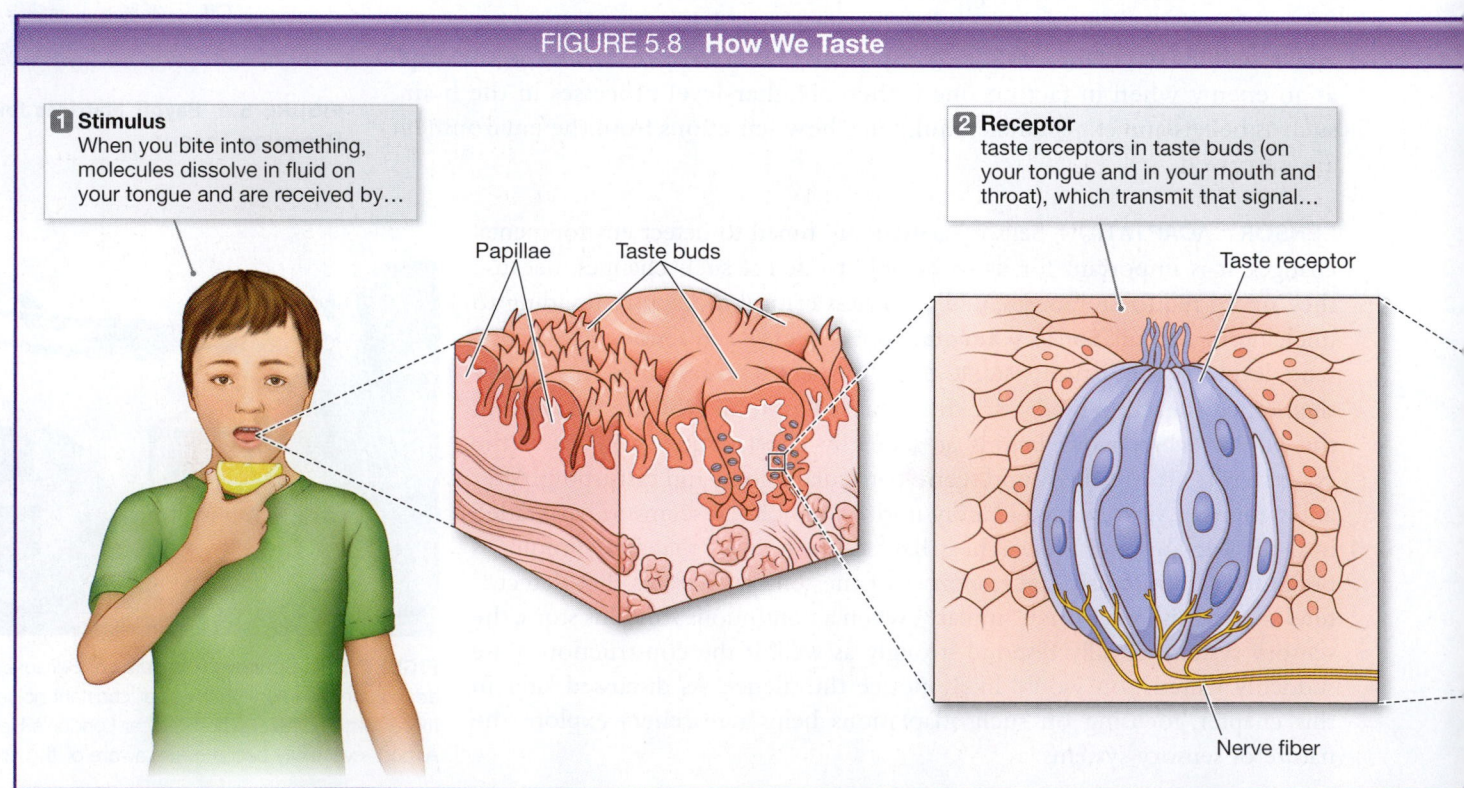

FIGURE 5.8 **How We Taste**

1 Stimulus
When you bite into something, molecules dissolve in fluid on your tongue and are received by…

2 Receptor
taste receptors in taste buds (on your tongue and in your mouth and throat), which transmit that signal…

Papillae   Taste buds

Taste receptor

Nerve fiber

2. What is Weber's law?
   a. When participants are unsure whether they can detect a stimulus, they will guess about it.
   b. Some people are biased toward saying they detected something, and others are biased toward saying they detected nothing.
   c. We are especially tuned to detect changes in stimulation.
   d. The amount of physical energy needed to detect a change in sensation depends on the proportional change from the original stimulus.

What Are the Basic Sensory Processes?

As discussed above, Helen Keller was blind and deaf. In scientific terms, her perceptual experience was restricted because her visual and auditory systems were damaged so that the neurons in her brain that constructed visual and auditory perceptions did not receive any sensory signals. Keller's situation helps illustrate how information about the world gets into the brain: Only the neurons in the sensory organs respond directly to events in the world. The neurons in the brain do not respond to events in the world; they respond only to input from other neurons. This section discusses how each sense organ detects stimuli and how the resulting information is then sent to the brain.

LEARNING OBJECTIVES
Trace the neural processes from the receptor to the brain for taste, smell, touch, hearing, and vision.

Describe the process of pain perception and how the perception of pain can be reduced.

In Taste, Taste Buds Detect Chemicals

The job of **gustation,** our sense of taste, is to keep poisons out of our digestive systems while allowing good food in. The stimuli for taste are chemical substances from food that dissolve in saliva, though how these stimuli work is still largely a mystery. The taste receptors are part of the **taste buds,** which are mostly on the tongue (in the tiny, mushroom-shaped structures called *papillae*) but are also spread throughout the mouth and throat. An individual has anywhere from 500 to 10,000 taste buds. When food stimulates them, the taste buds send signals to the brain, which then produces the experience of taste (**FIGURE 5.8**).

gustation The sense of taste.

taste buds Sensory receptors that transduce taste information.

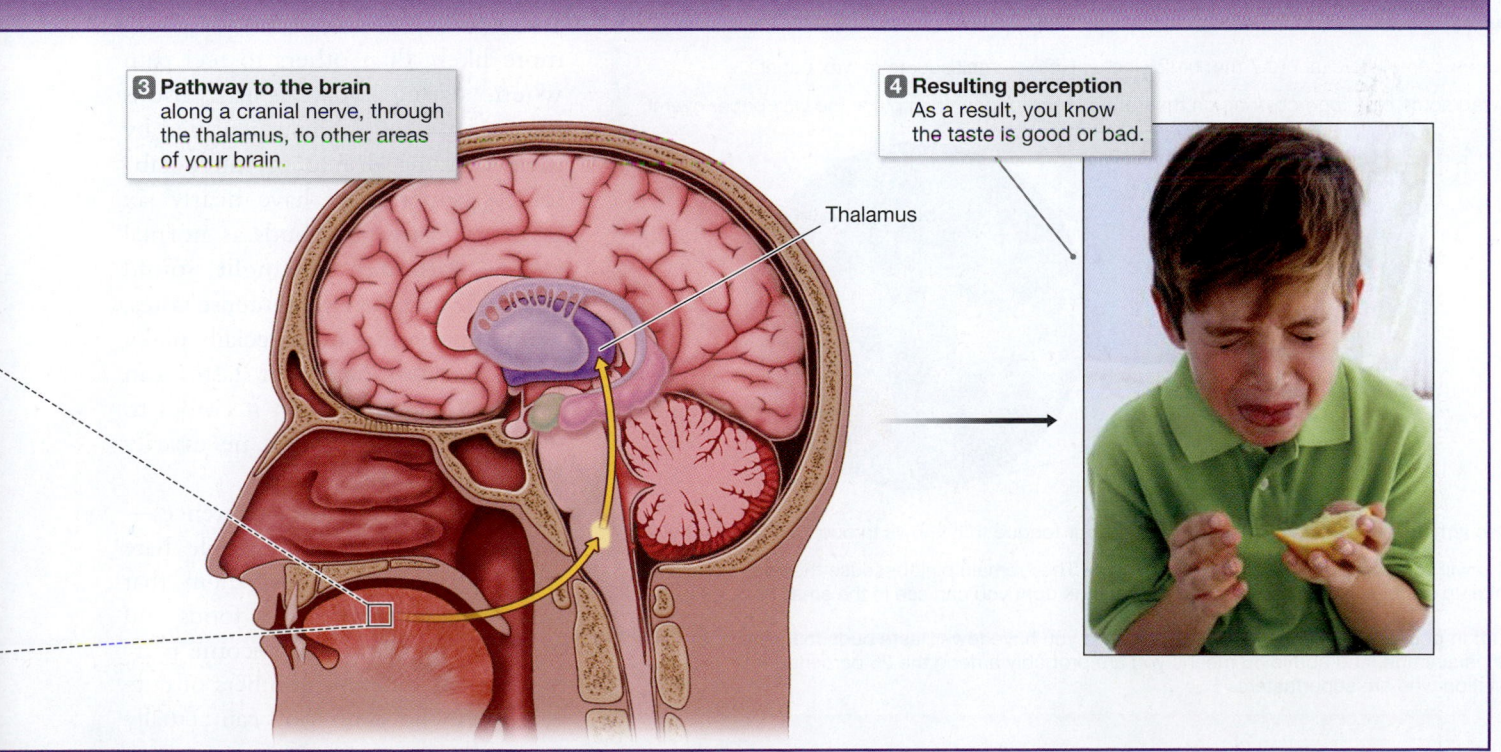

3 Pathway to the brain along a cranial nerve, through the thalamus, to other areas of your brain.

4 Resulting perception As a result, you know the taste is good or bad.

Thalamus

In all the senses, a near-infinite variety of perceptual experiences arises from the activation of unique combinations of receptors. Scientists once believed that different regions of the tongue are more sensitive to certain tastes, but they now know that the different taste buds are spread relatively uniformly throughout the tongue and mouth (Lindemann, 2001). Every taste experience is composed of a mixture of five basic qualities: sweet, sour, salty, bitter, and umami. *Umami* (Japanese for "savory" or "yummy") has only recently, within the last decade, been recognized by scientists as a fifth taste sensation (Krulwich, 2007). This delicious taste was perhaps first created intentionally in the late 1800s, when the famous French chef Auguste Escoffier invented a veal stock that did not taste sweet, sour, salty, or bitter. Independently of Escoffier, in 1908, the Japanese cook and chemist Kikunae Ikeda identified it as arising from the detection of glutamate, an excitatory neurotransmitter that occurs naturally in foods such as meat, some cheese, and mushrooms. Glutamate is the sodium salt in glutamic acid, and as *monosodium glutamate,* or *MSG,* which is commercially available under the brand name Accent, it can be added to various foods as a "flavor enhancer." To identify the flavor of umami, you might taste a food that does not include Accent, add Accent to it, and then taste it again. But beware: Some people experience odd sensory effects and/or headaches after consuming MSG.

Taste alone does not affect how much you like a certain type of food. As you might know from having had colds, food seems tasteless if your nasal passages are blocked—taste relies heavily on the sense of smell. A food's texture also matters: Whether a food is soft or crunchy, creamy or granular, tender or tough affects the sensory experience, as does the extent to which the food causes discomfort, as can happen with spicy chilies. The entire taste experience occurs not in your mouth but in your brain, which integrates these various sensory signals.

Some people experience especially intense taste sensations, a trait largely determined by genetics. These individuals, known as *supertasters,* are highly aware of flavors and textures and are more likely than others to feel pain when eating very spicy foods (Bartoshuk, 2000). First identified by their extreme dislike of bitter substances, supertasters have nearly six times as many taste buds as normal tasters. Although it might sound enjoyable to experience intense tastes, many supertasters are especially picky eaters because particular tastes can overwhelm them. When it comes to sensation, more is not necessarily better (**FIGURE 5.9**).

Our individual taste preferences—for example, that some people hate anchovies and others love them, that some people prefer spicy foods and others prefer bland ones—come partly from our different numbers of taste receptors. The same food can actually

FIGURE 5.9 Try for Yourself: Are You a Supertaster?

Do you wonder if you are a supertaster? Supertasters tend to be thin and to dislike vegetables that can be bitter, such as broccoli. Women are more likely to be supertasters than men are. Supertasters are born with more taste buds and are more likely to become professional chefs or wine tasters. To determine if you are a supertaster, Linda Bartoshuk, a psychologist at University of Florida's School of Dentistry, suggests the following test:

1 Punch a small hole (about 7 mm or .25 inches) into a small square of wax paper.

2 Swab some blue food coloring on the front of your tongue, then place the wax paper over it.

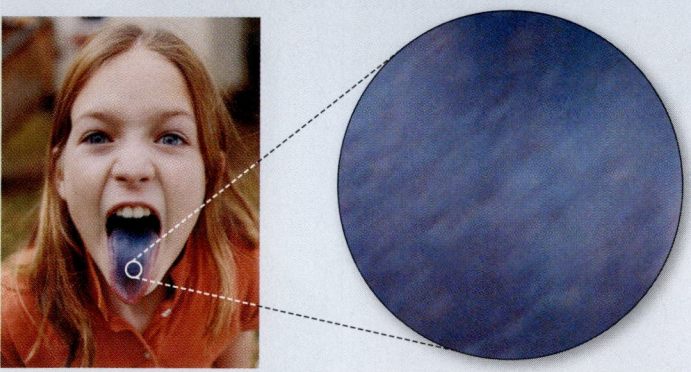

3 Use a magnifying glass to view the part of your tongue that shows through the small hole.

4 You will see pink dots, which are the papillae. They remain pink because they do not take up the blue dye. Count the number of pink dots you can see in the small hole.

Result: In general, fewer than 15 papillae means you have fewer taste buds than average, 15–35 is average, and above 35 means you are probably among the 25 percent of the population who are supertasters.

taste different, because the sensation associated with that food differs in different people's mouths. But cultural factors influence taste preferences as well.

Cultural influences on food preferences—for example, whether people eat croissants or bagels for breakfast—begin in the womb. In a study of infant food preferences, pregnant women were assigned to four groups: Some drank carrot juice every day during the last two months of pregnancy, while some drank a comparable amount of water every day during those months; some drank the juice every day during the first few months after childbirth, while some drank the water every day during those months (Mennella, Jagnow, & Beaucamp, 2006). All the mothers breast-fed their babies, so the taste of what each mother ate was in the breast milk that constituted each newborn's sole food source during the first few months of life. When the babies were several months old, they were all fed carrot juice (either alone or mixed with their cereal). The infants whose mothers drank carrot juice either during the two months before or the first few months after childbirth showed a preference for carrot juice compared with the infants whose mothers drank water during those same months. Thus, through their own eating behaviors before and immediately following birth, mothers apparently pass their eating preferences on to their offspring. Once again, as noted throughout this book, nature and nurture are inextricably entwined (**FIGURE 5.10**).

In Smell, the Nasal Cavity Gathers Odorants

Lacking vision and hearing, Helen Keller relied on her other senses. She called her sense of smell a "potent wizard" that guided her through life. In general, however, humans' sense of smell is vastly inferior to that of many animals, such as dogs, in

---

FIGURE 5.10 Scientific Method: Infant Taste Preferences Affected by Mother's Diet

Hypothesis: Taste preferences in newborns are influenced by their mothers' food preferences during the months immediately before and after birth.

Research Method:

1. Pregnant women were assigned at random to one of four groups instructed to drink a certain beverage every day for two months before the baby's birth and two months after the baby's birth:

	Before birth	After birth
Group 1:	carrot juice	water
Group 2:	carrot juice	carrot juice
Group 3:	water	carrot juice
Group 4:	water	water

Results: Babies whose mothers were in Groups 1, 2, or 3 preferred the taste of carrot juice more than did babies whose mothers were in Group 4 and did not drink carrot juice.

Conclusion: Babies become familiar with the taste of foods their mothers consume around the time of their birth, and they prefer familiar tastes.

part because we rely mainly on vision. Dogs have 40 times more olfactory receptors than humans do, and thus they are 100,000 to 1,000,000 times more sensitive to odors than humans are. Yet smell's importance to us in our daily lives is evidenced by the vast sums of money we spend on both deodorants and mouthwash, at least in Western cultures.

Of all the senses, smell, or **olfaction,** has the most direct route to the brain, but it may be the least understood. Like taste, it involves the sensing of chemicals that come from outside the body. We smell something when chemical particles, or *odorants,* pass into the nose and, when we sniff, into the nasal cavity's upper and back portions. In the nose and the nasal cavity, the odorants come into contact with the **olfactory epithelium,** a thin layer of tissue embedded with smell receptors; these receptors transmit information to the **olfactory bulb,** the brain center for smell, just below the frontal lobes. From here, smell information goes direct to other brain areas. Unlike other sensory information, smell signals bypass the thalamus, the early relay station. A recent imaging study found that areas in the brain's prefrontal cortex process information about whether a smell is pleasant or aversive, whereas the smell's intensity is processed in another brain region, the amygdala (Anderson et al., 2003). The prefrontal cortex is also involved in emotion and memory, so it is not surprising that olfactory stimuli can evoke feelings and memories (**FIGURE 5.11**). For example, many people find that the aromas of certain holiday foods cooking, the smell of bread baking, and/or the fragrance of particular perfumes generate fond childhood memories. When a perfume commercial on television claimed that the object of your desire would not be able to forget you if you wore the advertised perfume, the advertisers were linking scent with memory—and counting on the object of your desire finding the scent (and thus the memory of you) pleasant!

olfaction The sense of smell, which occurs when receptors in the nose respond to chemicals.

olfactory epithelium The thin layer of tissue, within the nasal cavity, that is embedded with smell receptors.

olfactory bulb The brain center for smell, located below the frontal lobes.

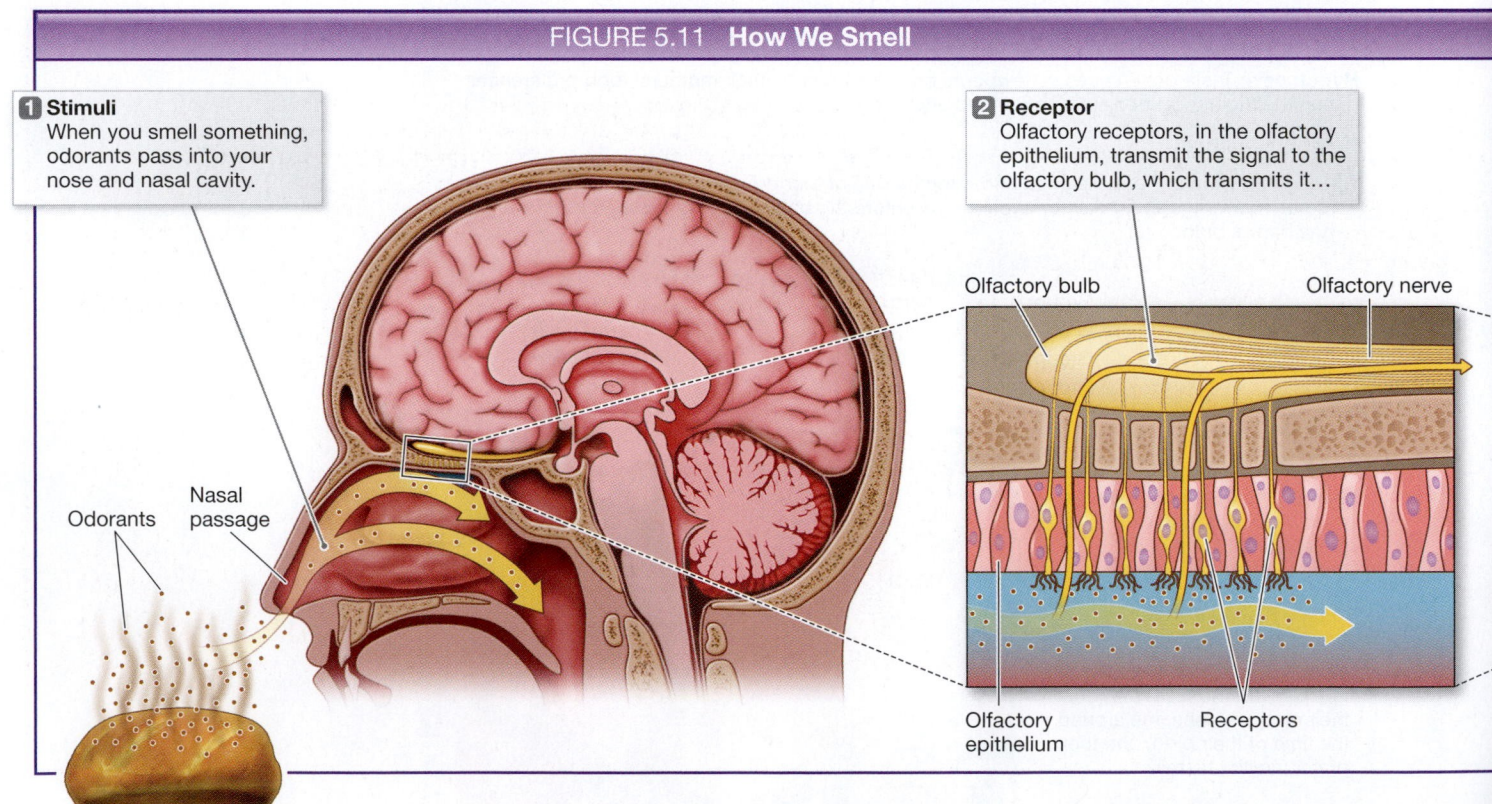

FIGURE 5.11 **How We Smell**

1 Stimuli
When you smell something, odorants pass into your nose and nasal cavity.

2 Receptor
Olfactory receptors, in the olfactory epithelium, transmit the signal to the olfactory bulb, which transmits it…

Olfactory bulb

Olfactory nerve

Odorants

Nasal passage

Olfactory epithelium

Receptors

Researchers have identified thousands of receptors in the olfactory epithelium, each responsive to a different chemical group. It remains unclear exactly how these receptors encode distinct smells. One possibility is that each receptor type is uniquely associated with a specific odor (one type would encode, for example, only the scent of roses); this explanation is unlikely, however, given the huge number of scents we can detect. Another possibility, more likely to be correct, is that each odor stimulates several receptors and that the activation pattern across several receptor types determines the olfactory perception (Lledo, Gheusi, & Vincent, 2005).

Several researchers (Bromley & Doty, 1995; Lehrner, 1993; Schab, 1991) have investigated sex differences in odor perception. All have found that females are better able to perceive and identify odors than males are: From ages 5 to 99, females perform better at odor identification tasks (Doty et al., 1984). Females also have better memory for odors than males do. One of several theories about why females are better at odor identification is related to their tendency to excel at certain verbal tasks. Females are more likely to label each smell, and doing so would give them handy mnemonic devices for retrieving particular smells. Another theory is related to women's evolutionary roles. Women are more likely to feed infants and young children and thus need to be able to identify spoiled food. (Adults may get ill from eating bad food, but they are less likely to die from eating it than infants and young children are.)

As we age, our sensory and perceptual systems become less acute. But a deteriorating sense of smell can signal problems beyond the normal changes that occur with aging. A series of recent studies has found that an impaired sense of smell is associated with an increased risk of mental decline and of Alzheimer's disease, a

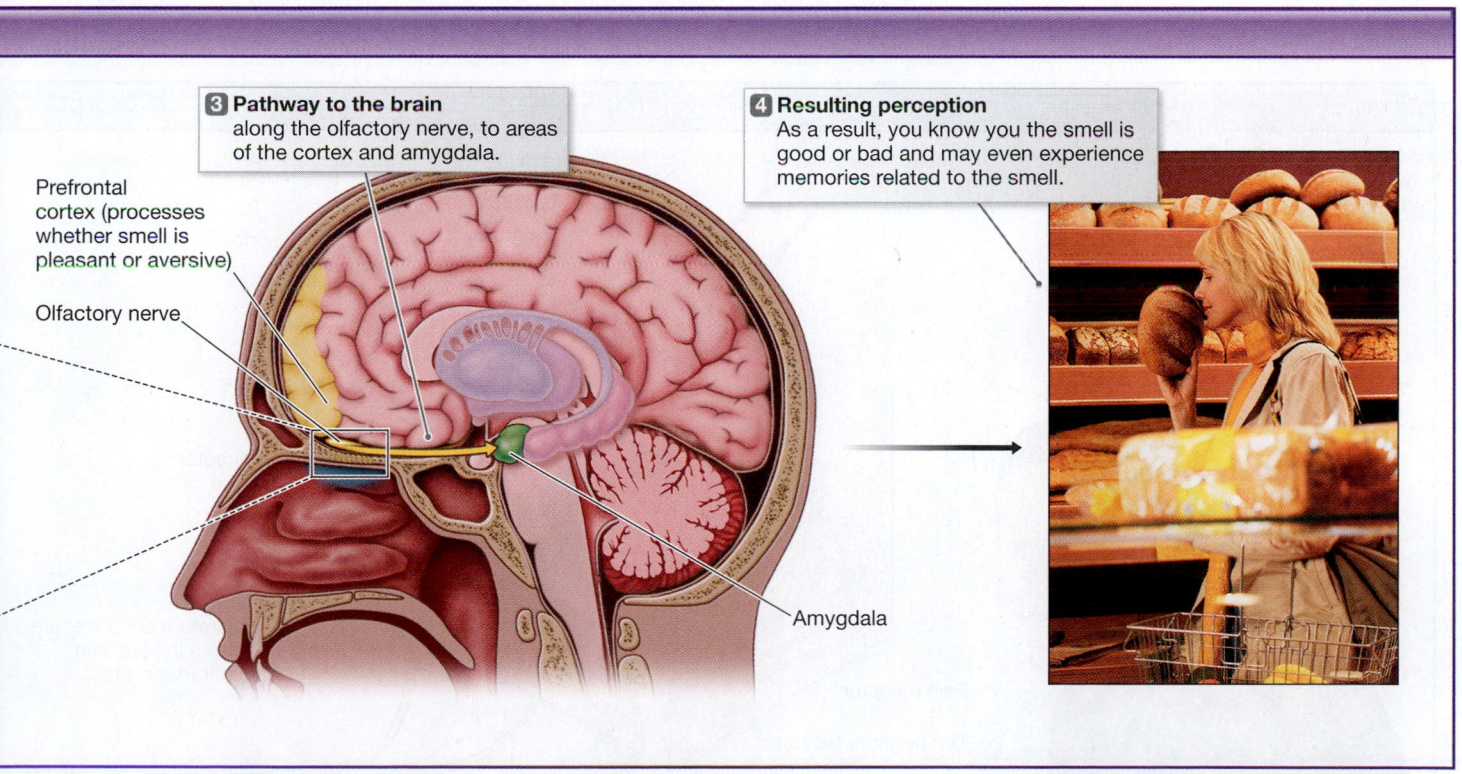

3 Pathway to the brain along the olfactory nerve, to areas of the cortex and amygdala.

4 Resulting perception As a result, you know you the smell is good or bad and may even experience memories related to the smell.

Prefrontal cortex (processes whether smell is pleasant or aversive)

Olfactory nerve

Amygdala

devastating condition more prevalent in older adults. Alzheimer's disease causes a rapid decline in cognition, such that in its most advanced states, people with this disease are unable to recognize family members or care for themselves. In one study, older adults with an average age of 80, who were well enough to be living in the community, were given a smell identification test (Wilson et al., 2007). These older adults were followed for five years after the testing. Participants who scored in the lowest 25th percentile on the smell identification test had a 50 percent higher incidence of cognitive impairment five years later than those who scored in the top 25th percentile.

In Touch, Sensors in the Skin Detect Pressure, Temperature, and Pain

haptic sense The sense of touch.

Touch, the **haptic sense,** conveys sensations of temperature, of pressure, and of pain and a sense of where our limbs are in space. Thus, although we commonly refer to the five senses, humans really have eight, when the haptic sense's four parts—hot, cold, pressure, and pain—are counted separately. Anything that makes contact with our skin provides *tactile stimulation,* which gives rise to an integrated experience of touch. The haptic receptors for both temperature and pressure are sensory neurons that terminate in the skin's outer layer. Their long axons enter the central nervous system by way of spinal or cranial nerves. For sensing temperature, there appear to be separate hot receptors and cold ones, although both can be triggered at the same time by intense stimuli (**FIGURE 5.12**). The simultaneous activation of hot and cold receptors can produce strange sensory experiences, such as a false feeling of wetness. Some receptors for pressure are nerve fibers at the bases of hair follicles that respond to movement in the hair. Other pressure receptors are capsules in the skin that respond to continued

FIGURE 5.12 How We Experience Touch: The Haptic Sense

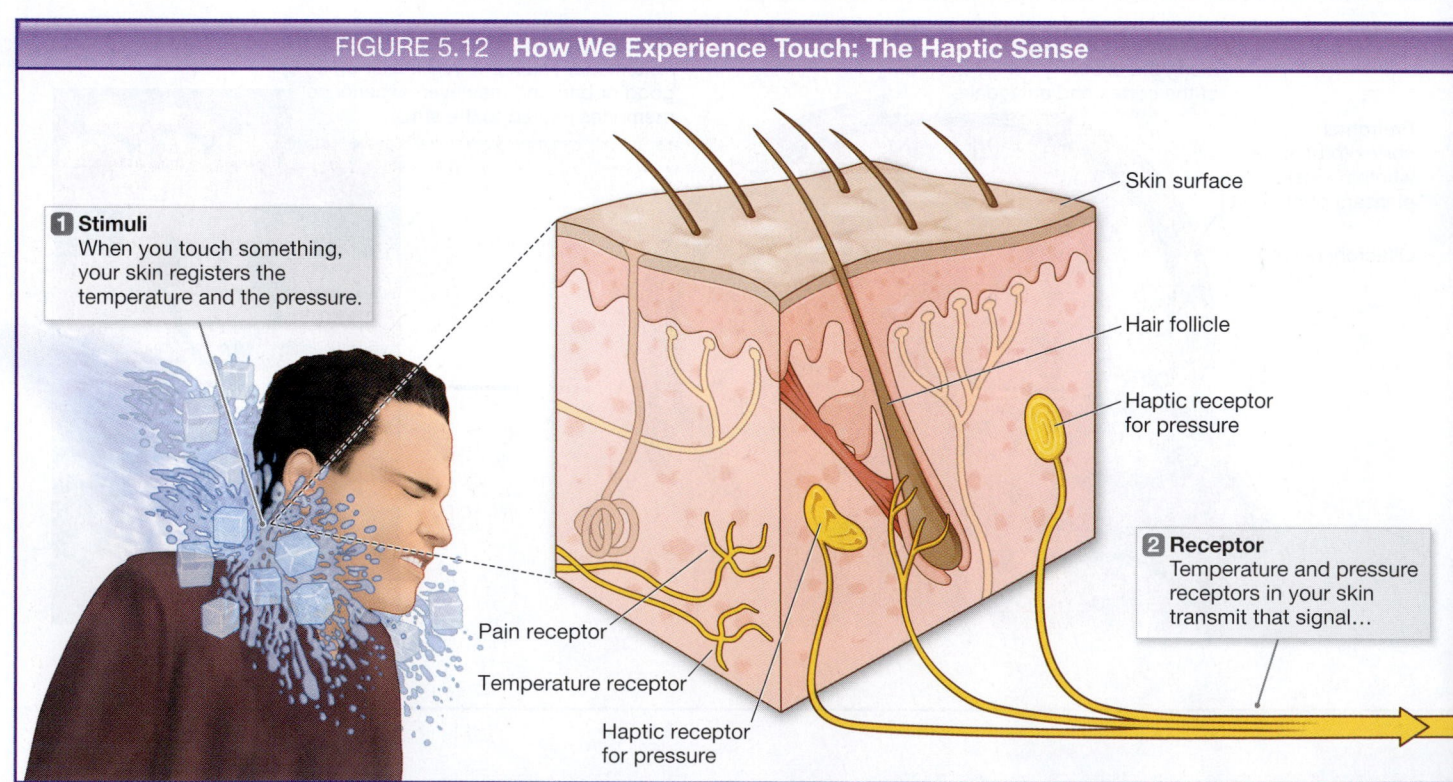

1 Stimuli
When you touch something, your skin registers the temperature and the pressure.

Skin surface

Hair follicle

Haptic receptor for pressure

2 Receptor
Temperature and pressure receptors in your skin transmit that signal...

Pain receptor

Temperature receptor

Haptic receptor for pressure

vibration, to sudden movements, and to steady pressure. Pain receptors, discussed in greater detail below, are found throughout the body, not just in the skin. The integration of various signals and higher-level mental processes produces haptic experiences. For instance, stroking multiple pressure points can produce a tickling sensation, which can be pleasant or unpleasant depending on the mental state of the person being tickled. An age-old question asks why you cannot tickle yourself, and imaging research has found that the brain areas involved in touch sensation respond less to self-produced tactile stimulation than to external tactile stimulation (Blakemore, Wolpert, & Frith, 1998; the relationship between the brain and touch is discussed further in Chapter 3, "Biological Foundations").

TWO TYPES OF PAIN Pain is part of a warning system that stops you from continuing activities that may harm you. Whether the message is to remove your hand from a hot burner or to stop running when you have damaged a tendon, pain signals that you should quit doing whatever you are doing. Children born with a rare genetic disorder that leaves them insensitive to pain usually die young, no matter how carefully they are supervised. They simply do not know how to avoid activities that harm them or to report when they are feeling ill (Melzack & Wall, 1982). Like other sensory experiences, the actual experience of pain is created by the brain. For instance, as discussed in Chapter 3, a person whose limb has been amputated may sometimes feel phantom pain in the nonexistent limb. The person really feels pain, but the pain occurs because the brain misinterprets neural activity.

Most experiences of pain result when damage to the skin activates haptic receptors. The nerve fibers that convey pain information are thinner than those for temperature and for pressure and are found in all body tissues that sense pain: skin,

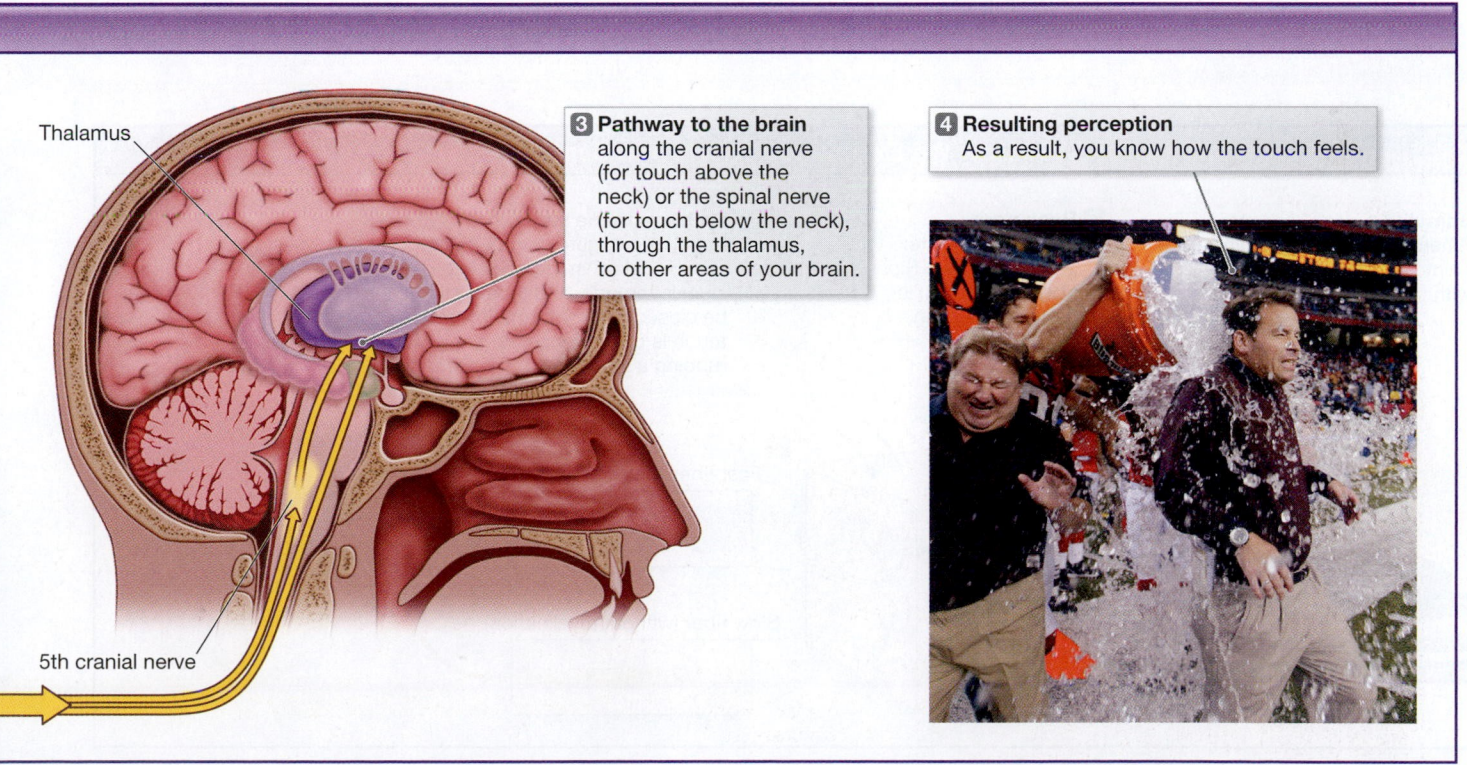

Thalamus

5th cranial nerve

3 Pathway to the brain along the cranial nerve (for touch above the neck) or the spinal nerve (for touch below the neck), through the thalamus, to other areas of your brain.

4 Resulting perception As a result, you know how the touch feels.

muscles, membranes around both bones and joints, organs, and so on. Two kinds of nerve fibers have been identified for pain: fast fibers for sharp, immediate pain and slow fibers for chronic, dull, steady pain. An important distinction between these fibers is the myelination or nonmyelination of their axons, which travel from the pain receptors to the spinal cord. Recall from Chapter 3 that myelination speeds up neural signals. Myelinated axons, like heavily insulated wire, can respond quickly; nonmyelinated axons respond more slowly. Think of a time when you touched a hot pan. You probably can recall feeling two kinds of pain: a sharp, fast, localized pain at the moment your skin touched the pan, followed by a slow, dull, more diffuse burning pain. The fast-action receptors are activated by strong physical pressure and temperature extremes, whereas the slow-acting receptors are activated by chemical changes in tissue when skin is damaged. From an adaptive perspective, fast pain leads us to recoil from harmful objects and therefore is protective, whereas slow pain keeps us from using the affected body parts and therefore helps in recuperation (**FIGURE 5.13**).

GATE CONTROL THEORY The brain regulates the experience of pain, sometimes producing it, sometimes suppressing it. The *gate control theory of pain,* formulated by Ronald Melzack and Patrick Wall (1982), states that for us to experience pain, pain receptors must be activated and a neural "gate" in the spinal cord must allow the signals through to the brain. According to this theory, pain signals are transmitted by small-diameter nerve fibers, which can be blocked at the level of the spinal cord (prevented from reaching the brain) by the firing of larger sensory nerve fibers. Thus sensory nerve fibers can "close a gate" and prevent or reduce the perception of pain. This is why scratching an itch is so satisfying, why rubbing an aching muscle helps reduce the ache, and why vigorously rubbing the skin where an injection is about to be given reduces the needle's sting. A number of cognitive states, such as distraction, can also close the gate. Athletes sometimes play through pain because of their intense focus on the game; wounded soldiers sometimes continue to fight during

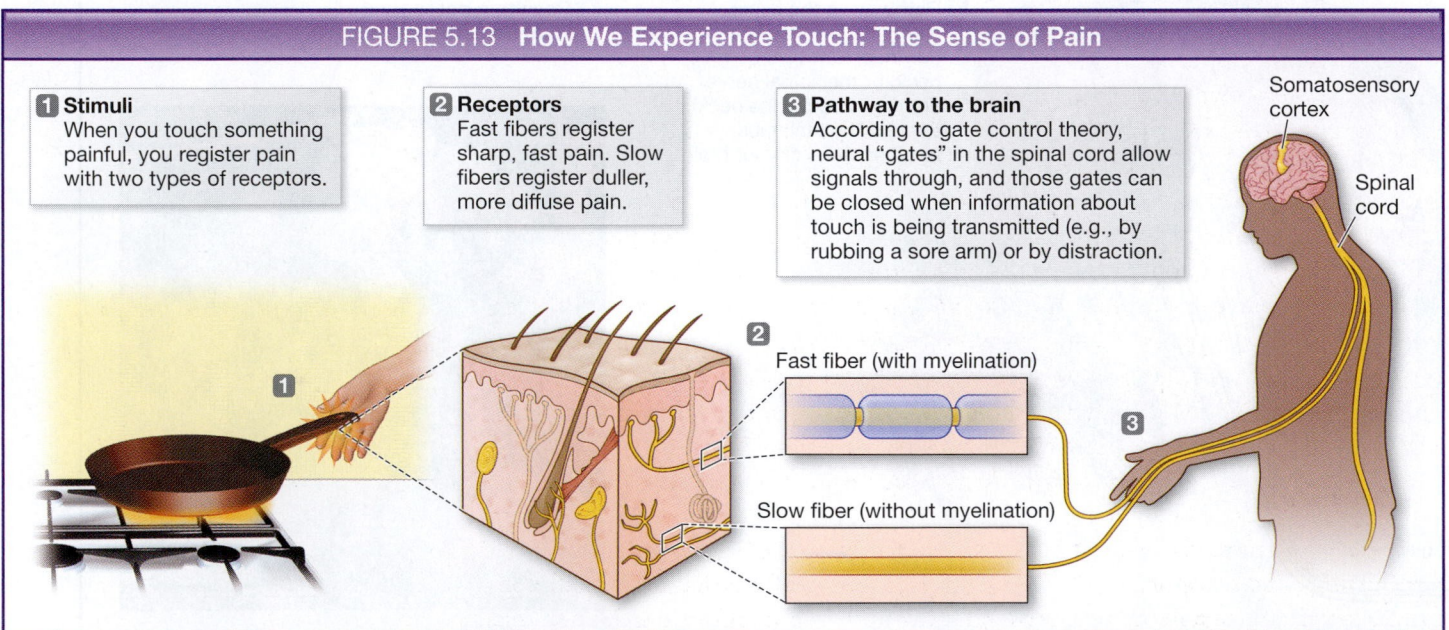

FIGURE 5.13 **How We Experience Touch: The Sense of Pain**

1 Stimuli
When you touch something painful, you register pain with two types of receptors.

2 Receptors
Fast fibers register sharp, fast pain. Slow fibers register duller, more diffuse pain.

3 Pathway to the brain
According to gate control theory, neural "gates" in the spinal cord allow signals through, and those gates can be closed when information about touch is being transmitted (e.g., by rubbing a sore arm) or by distraction.

Somatosensory cortex

Spinal cord

Fast fiber (with myelination)

Slow fiber (without myelination)

combat, often failing to recognize a level of pain that would render them inactive at other times. An insect bite bothers us more when we are trying to sleep and have few distractions than when we are wide awake and active.

Conversely, some mental processes, such as worrying about or focusing on the painful stimulus, seem to open the pain gates wider. Research participants who are well-rested rate the same level of a painful stimulus as less painful than do participants who are fearful, anxious, or depressed. Because pain is processed in the same areas of the brain as stress, fear, and anxiety, it is a sensory experience and an emotional response.

Pain perception is complex, depending on biological, psychological, and cultural factors. Numerous studies have found that females generally are more sensitive to pain than males are (Fillingim, 2003). That females have lower pain thresholds has been shown both in controlled laboratory studies and in clinical studies. According to the theory of men's "macho" responses to pain, both sexes may feel the same amount of pain, but men will not admit they are in pain because to do so is not consistent with the male sex role. Evidence against this explanation comes from studies of autonomic responses—that is, responses not under voluntary control. For example, women exhibit greater pupil dilation in response to pain than men do (Ellermeir & Westphal, 1995). Females also have more complex pain management systems. For example, women are able to experience pregnancy-induced analgesia, which reduces the perception of pain during childbirth (Gintzler & Liu, 2000). For women who menstruate, normal monthly fluctuations in hormones alter pain perception, so that pain thresholds are lowest during the high-estrogen stages of the menstrual cycle. Estrogen replacement therapy, which increases estrogen levels in menopausal women, is also associated with increased risk of pain (Musgrave, Vogt, Nevitt, & Cauley, 2001). These findings have important implications for the clinical treatment of pain and may lead to pain treatments tailored to take sex differences into account.

One new method for treating pain takes advantage of advances in brain imaging that allow us to see which parts of the brain are active when we feel pain. Pain researchers divide the perception of pain into two large areas in the brain. One area responds to the sensory input from the part of the body that is in pain—the dull pain of a chronic backache, the stabbing pain of a cut on the arm, and so on. The other part of the brain that is involved when we feel pain registers the emotional aspect of pain, which includes how unpleasant it is. When we feel pain, both brain areas are active. Researchers have studied whether, by engaging in activities that reduce the activity in brain areas that underlie pain perception, people can learn to reduce pain perception. DeCharms and colleagues (2005) have pioneered techniques that offer great hope for people who suffer from painful conditions. The researchers sought to teach people in pain, many of these people in chronic pain, to visualize their pain more positively. For example, participants were taught to think about a burning sensation as soothing, like the feeling of being in a sauna. As they tried to learn such techniques, they viewed fMRI images that showed which regions of their brains were active as they performed the tasks. (On fMRI, see Chapter 2, "Research Methodology.") Many participants learned techniques that altered their brain activity and reduced their pain.

Of course, more-traditional ways exist to control pain. Most of us have taken legal drugs, usually aspirin, to reduce pain perception. If you have ever suffered from a severe toothache or needed surgery, you have probably experienced the benefits of pain medication. When a dentist administers Novocain to sensory neurons in the mouth, pain messages are not transmitted to the brain, so the mouth feels numb. General anesthesia slows down the firing of neurons throughout the nervous system, and the patient becomes unresponsive to stimulation (Perkins, 2007).

You can use your knowledge of pain perception anytime you need to reduce your own pain or to help others in pain. Distraction is usually the easiest way to reduce pain, so if you are preparing for a painful procedure or suffering after one, watching an entertaining movie can help, especially if it is funny enough to elevate your mood. Rapid rubbing can benefit a stubbed toe, for example, or a finger that was caught in a closing drawer. Various drugs can help block severe pain caused by illness, surgery, or injury. You will also feel less pain if you are rested, not fearful, and not anxious. If you are undergoing a procedure, learn what to expect and focus on the positive aspects, such as how much better you will feel in the future, perhaps after a health problem has been corrected. Finally, try to visualize your pain as something more pleasant. Of course, severe pain is a warning system and should be treated by a medical professional.

In Hearing, the Ear Detects Sound Waves

audition The sense of sound perception.

For humans, hearing, or **audition,** is second only to vision as a source of information about the world. It not only is a mechanism for determining what is happening in an environment but also provides a medium for spoken language. Hearing results when the movements and vibrations of objects cause the displacement of air molecules. Displaced air molecules produce a change in air pressure, and that change travels through the air. The pattern of the changes in air pressure through time is called a **sound wave.** The wave's *amplitude* determines its loudness; higher amplitude is perceived as louder. The wave's *frequency* determines its pitch; higher frequencies are perceived as higher in pitch. Sound's frequency is measured in vibrations per second, called *hertz* (abbreviated *Hz*). Most humans can detect sound waves with frequencies from about 20 Hz to about 20,000 Hz. Like (again) all other sensory experiences, the sensory experience of hearing occurs within the brain, as the brain integrates the different signals provided by various sound waves. Therefore, we finally have an answer to an age-old question: If a tree falls and no one hears it, air pressure will change, but there will be no sound unless that change is registered in a brain.

sound wave The pattern of the changes in air pressure through time that results in the percept of a sound.

Our ability to hear is based on the intricate interactions of various regions of the ear, which convert sound waves into brain activity, producing the sensation of meaningful sound. Changes in air pressure produce sound waves that arrive at the *outer ear* and travel down the auditory canal to the **eardrum,** a membrane stretched tightly across the canal and marking the beginning of the *middle ear.* The sound waves make the eardrum vibrate. These vibrations are transferred to *ossicles,* three tiny bones commonly called the hammer, anvil, and stirrup. The ossicles transfer the eardrum's vibrations to the *oval window,* a membrane of the *cochlea,* or *inner ear,* a fluid-filled tube that curls into a snaillike shape. Running through the center of the cochlea is the thin *basilar membrane.* The oval window's vibrations create pressure waves in the inner ear's fluid; these waves prompt the *hair cells* to bend and cause neurons on the basilar membrane to fire. These hair cells are the primary

eardrum (tympanic membrane) A thin membrane, which sound waves vibrate, that marks the beginning of the middle ear.

auditory receptors. Thus the mechanical signal of a sound wave hitting the eardrum is converted into a neural signal that travels to the brain via the auditory nerve (**FIGURE 5.14**).

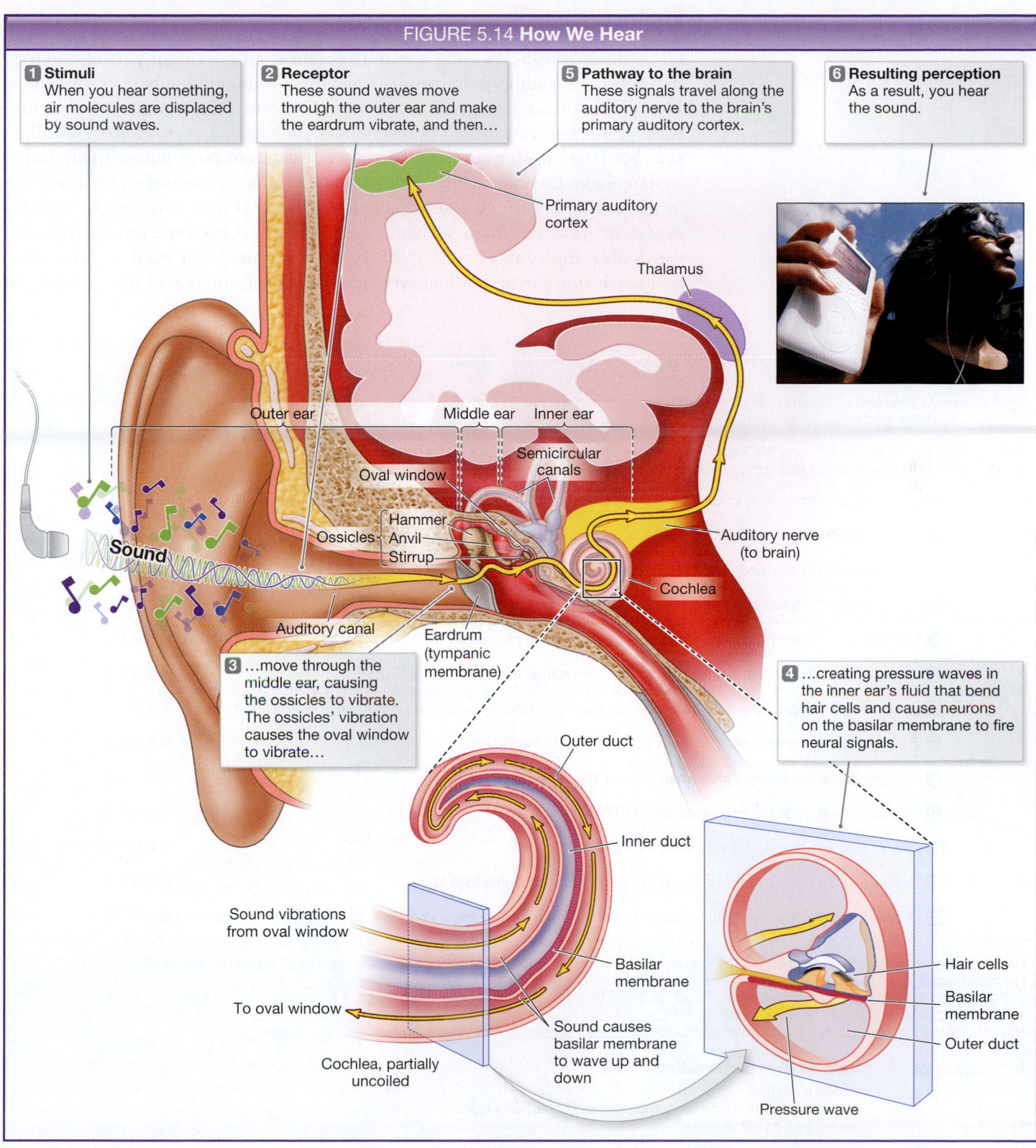

FIGURE 5.14 **How We Hear**

1 Stimuli
When you hear something, air molecules are displaced by sound waves.

2 Receptor
These sound waves move through the outer ear and make the eardrum vibrate, and then...

5 Pathway to the brain
These signals travel along the auditory nerve to the brain's primary auditory cortex.

6 Resulting perception
As a result, you hear the sound.

Primary auditory cortex

Thalamus

Outer ear

Middle ear   Inner ear

Semicircular canals

Oval window

Hammer
Anvil
Stirrup

Ossicles

Sound

Auditory nerve (to brain)

Cochlea

Auditory canal

Eardrum (tympanic membrane)

3 ...move through the middle ear, causing the ossicles to vibrate. The ossicles' vibration causes the oval window to vibrate...

4 ...creating pressure waves in the inner ear's fluid that bend hair cells and cause neurons on the basilar membrane to fire neural signals.

Outer duct

Inner duct

Sound vibrations from oval window

Basilar membrane

To oval window

Cochlea, partially uncoiled

Sound causes basilar membrane to wave up and down

Hair cells

Basilar membrane

Outer duct

Pressure wave

What Are the Basic Sensory Processes?   ■   **197**

To get an estimate of whether your hearing is in the normal range, try the *Hearing Screening Inventory* (**FIGURE 5.15**). Although this inventory correlates well with hearing tests, it is not a medical diagnosis, so if you score in the range of hearing loss, you should have your hearing checked by an audiologist or other hearing professional.

LOCATING SOUNDS Locating a sound's origin is an important part of auditory perception. In audition, the sensory receptors do not code where events occur. Instead, the brain integrates the different sensory information coming from each of our two ears. Much of researchers' understanding of auditory localization has come from examining barn owls, nocturnal birds whose finely tuned hearing helps them locate their prey. In fact, in a dark laboratory a barn owl can locate a mouse through hearing alone. A barn owl uses two cues to locate a sound: the time the sound arrives in each ear, and the sound's intensity in each ear. Unless the sound comes from exactly in front or in back of the owl, it will reach one ear first. Whichever side it comes from, it will sound softer on

---

FIGURE 5.15 Try for Yourself: Hearing Screening Inventory (HSI)

Developed by Coren and Hakstian (1992), this questionnaire deals with some common hearing situations. For each question, select the response that best describes you and your behaviors.

For 1–8, you can select from among the following response alternatives: **N**ever (or almost never), **S**eldom, **O**ccasionally, **F**requently, **A**lways (or almost always). For 9–12: **G**ood, **A**verage, **S**o-So, **P**oor, **V**ery poor.

Circle the letter corresponding to the first letter of your choice.

1 Are you ever bothered by feelings that your hearing is poor?	N S O F A
2 Is your reading or studying easily interrupted by noises in nearby rooms?	N S O F A
3 Can you hear the telephone ring when you are in the same room in which it is located?	N S O F A
4 Can you hear the telephone ring when you are in the room next door?	N S O F A
5 Do you find it difficult to make out the words in recordings of popular songs?	N S O F A
6 When several people are talking in a room, do you have difficulty hearing an individual conversation?	N S O F A
7 Can you hear the water boiling in a pot when you are in the kitchen?	N S O F A
8 Can you follow the conversation when you are at a large dinner table?	N S O F A
9 Overall I would judge my hearing in my RIGHT ear to be	G A S P V
10 Overall I would judge my hearing in my LEFT ear to be	G A S P V
11 Overall I would judge my ability to make out speech or conversations to be	G A S P V
12 Overall I would judge my ability to judge the location of things by the sound they are making alone to be	G A S P V

Result: For questions 1, 5, and 6, score 1 for "Never," 2 for "Seldom," 3 for "Occasionally," 4 for "Frequently," and 5 for "Always."
For questions 2, 3, 4, 7, and 8, reverse the scoring from 1 for "Always" up to 5 for "Never."
For questions 9 through 12, score from 1 for "Good" to 5 for "Very Poor."
Your hearing score is the sum of these 12 items.
Now check the following table for your predicted best-ear hearing sensitivity (this prediction is 92 percent accurate).

HSI Scale Total	Predicted Best-Ear Sensitivity
12 to 27	Hearing is normal
28 to 37	Hearing loss 25 dB or more (some conversational hearing loss)
38 or more	Hearing loss 55 dB or more

The *Hearing Screening Inventory* is copyrighted by SC Psychological Enterprises Ltd. and is reprinted here with permission.

the other side because the owl's head acts as a barrier. These differences in timing and magnitude are minute—but not too small for the owl's brain to detect and act on. Although humans' ears are not as finely tuned to the location of sounds as owls' are, human brains use information from the two ears similarly (**FIGURE 5.16**).

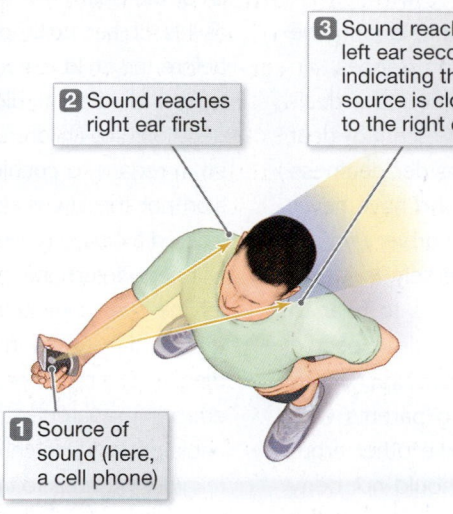

3 Sound reaches left ear second, indicating the source is closer to the right ear.

2 Sound reaches right ear first.

1 Source of sound (here, a cell phone)

FIGURE 5.16 Auditory Localization Like barn owls, humans draw on the intensity and timing of sounds to locate where the sounds are coming from.

ON **Ethics**   The Cochlear Implant

The cochlear implant was the first neural implant used successfully in humans; over 100,000 of these devices have been implanted worldwide since 1984, when the U.S. Food and Drug Administration, or FDA, approved them for adults. (In 1990, the FDA approved them for two-year-olds, and it has since approved them for one-year-olds.)

The cochlear implant has helped people with severe hearing problems due to the loss of hair cells in the inner ear, which are responsible for transmitting auditory stimuli. Unlike a hearing aid, the implant does not amplify sound; rather, it directly stimulates the auditory nerve. The downside is that after the implant is put in place, the person who received it loses all residual normal hearing in that ear, because sound no longer travels via the ear canal and middle ear. Instead, sound is picked up by a tiny microphone behind the ear, sent through a computer processor, and then transmitted to the implant's electrodes inside the cochlea. If the devices are implanted at a young enough age (younger than two years being optimal) in a child born deaf, the child's hearing will be quite functional, and he or she will learn to speak normally (**FIGURE 5.17**).

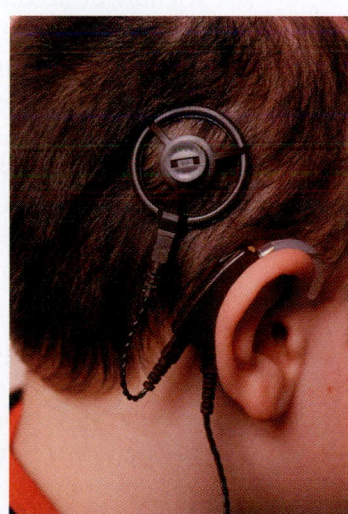

FIGURE 5.17 Cochlear Implants and Deaf Culture Cochlear implants, such as the one fitted on the side of this 10-year-old girl's head, consist of a microphone around the ear and a transmitter fitted to the scalp, linked to electrodes that directly stimulate the auditory nerve. When implanted at a young age, these devices can enable people with hearing loss to learn to speak and hear.

Although the benefits of cochlear implants might seem indisputable to many people with normal hearing, in the 1990s, deaf people who do not consider deafness a disability voiced concerns that the implants might adversely affect deaf culture.

continued

In fact, some deaf people believe that cochlear implants are a weapon being wielded by the medical community to commit cultural genocide. They argue that the cochlear implants disrupt the deaf community's cohesiveness. While deaf people with cochlear implants can still use sign language, apparently they are not always welcome in the signing community (Chase, 2006). This attitude has slowly been changing, but is still held by many deaf signers.

There are specific ethical concerns about implanting the devices in deaf children. Under normal circumstances, an adult can decide whether to get the implants, but the decision is made for a child by the parents. Ninety percent of deaf children are born to hearing parents who consider deafness a disability. Is it ethical for hearing parents, who have never experienced being deaf, to decide that a baby or very young child should receive cochlear implants? Conversely, is it ethical for deaf parents who have never been able to hear to decide against implanting the devices? Some deaf people believe the decision should be informed by their experiences of living deaf, not the experiences of hearing parents who know nothing of the deaf world. But of course other arguments can be made: Perhaps deaf parents should not deny hearing to their children.

Some people believe the decision should be made by the child when he or she is mature enough. However, postponing the decision denies the child the language benefits of an early implant. In fact, by adolescence the brain loses the ability to use auditory information in the building of spoken-language skills. If a child is to benefit fully from implants, the parents must decide before the child is capable of making a decision, and if the goal is for the deaf child to use spoken language at the same level as his or her hearing peers, the device should be implanted before the child is two years old (Nicholas & Geers, 2006).

According to medical ethics and the legal system, medical decisions for children are made by their parents or guardians, so in regard to cochlear implants, neither the medical profession nor the law is concerned with whether deafness is considered a disability. However, society's attitude toward deafness will help determine how the implants are paid for. Is it ethical for the deaf community to deny that deafness is a disability if that denial results in cochlear implants not being covered by medical insurance or funded by government programs? If it is ethical for parents to refuse on cultural grounds to obtain implants for deaf children, is it ethical to refuse on cultural or religious grounds to treat children for any other condition, handicap, injury, or disease?

In Vision, the Eye Detects Light Waves

If we acquire knowledge through our senses, then vision is by far our most important source of knowledge. Does a place look safe or dangerous? Does a person look friendly or hostile? Even our metaphors for knowledge and for understanding are often visual: "I see," "The answer is clear," "I'm fuzzy on that point." Unsurprisingly, then, most scientific study of sensation and of perception is concerned with vision.

Sight seems so effortless, so automatic, that we take it for granted. Every time a person opens his or her eyes, though, nearly half of that person's brain springs into action to make sense of the energy arriving in the eyes. Of course, the brain can do so only based on sensory signals from the eyes. If the eyes are damaged, the sensory system fails to process new information. This section focuses on how energy is transduced in the visual system, but what we commonly call *seeing* is much more than transducing energy. As the psychologist James Enns notes in his book *The Thinking Eye, the Seeing Brain* (2005), very little of what we call seeing takes place in the eyes; rather, what we see results from constructive processes that occur throughout much of the brain to produce our visual experiences. Seeing is therefore an intelligent process that produces useful information about our environments.

Although some people have suggested that the human eye works like a crude camera, focusing light to form an image on the retina, this analogy does not do justice to the intricate processes that take place in the eye. Light first passes through the **cornea,** the eye's thick, transparent outer layer. The cornea focuses incoming light in a process called *refraction*. Light rays then enter and are bent farther inward by the *lens,* which focuses the light to form an image on the **retina,** the inner surface of the back of the eyeball.

cornea The clear outer covering of the eye.

retina The thin inner surface of the back of the eyeball. The retina contains the photoreceptors that transduce light into neural signals.

Although more refraction (bending of light) happens at the cornea than at the lens, the lens is adjustable, whereas the cornea is not. The **pupil,** the dark circle at the center of the eye, is a small opening in the front of the lens, and to determine how much light enters the eye it either contracts or dilates (opens). The **iris,** an opaque, circular muscle, determines the eye's color and controls the pupil's size. The pupil enlarges in dim light but also when we see something we like, such as an attractive person or a cute baby (Tombs & Silverman, 2004).

Behind the iris, muscles change the shape of the lens—flattening it to focus on distant objects and thickening it to focus on closer objects. This process is called *accommodation*. The lens and cornea work together to collect and focus light rays reflected from an object, to form on the retina an upside-down image of the object. The world looks right-side up to us even though the image of the world projected on the retina is upside down; the information that travels from our eyes to the brain is very different from how we "see" the world. The eye sends visual images to the brain not as a complete "picture" but in bits of information transmitted through neural signals. Just as the dots and dashes of Morse code transmit information that does not physically resemble the letters represented, so the visual system uses patterns of neurons that fire at different rates and in different combinations to represent the external world (Ramachandran, 2003; **FIGURE 5.18**).

RODS AND CONES The retina has two types of receptor cells: **rods** and **cones,** each type so called because of its distinctive shape. Rods respond at extremely low levels of illumination and are responsible primarily for night vision; they do not support color vision, and they resolve fine detail poorly. Many people do not realize that humans cannot see colors in dim illumination, but go outside on the next moonless night and you will see gray colors instead of any bright ones you would have seen during the day. In contrast to rods, cones are less sensitive to low levels of light; they are responsible primarily for vision under high illumination and for seeing both color and detail. Within the rods and cones, light-sensitive chemicals called *photopigments* initiate the transduction of light waves into electrical neural impulses.

Each retina holds approximately 120 million rods and 6 million cones. Near the retina's center, cones are densely packed in a small region called the **fovea.** Although cones are spread throughout the remainder of the retina (except in the blind spot, as you will see shortly), they become increasingly scarce near the outside edge. Rods are all located at the retina's edges; none are in the fovea. If you look directly at a very dim star on a moonless night, the star will appear to vanish, because its light will fall on the fovea, where there are no rods. However, if you look just to the side of the star, the star will be visible, because its light will fall just outside the fovea, where there are rods.

TRANSMISSION FROM THE EYE TO THE BRAIN The generation of electrical signals by the photoreceptors in the retina begins the visual process. Immediately after light is transduced into neural impulses by the rods and cones, other cells in the retina—*bipolar, amacrine,* and *horizontal cells* (see Figure 5.18)—perform on those impulses a series of sophisticated computations that help the visual system process the incoming information. The outputs from these cells converge on about one million retinal *ganglion cells,* the first cells in the visual pathway to generate action potentials.

The ganglion cells send their signals along their axons from inside the eye to the thalamus. These axons are gathered into a bundle, the *optic nerve,* which exits

pupil The small opening in the eye; it lets in light waves.

iris The colored muscular circle on the surface of the eye; it changes shape to let in more or less light.

rods Retinal cells that respond to low levels of illumination and result in black-and-white perception.

cones Retinal cells that respond to higher levels of illumination and result in color perception.

fovea The center of the retina, where cones are densely packed.

FIGURE 5.18 **How We See**

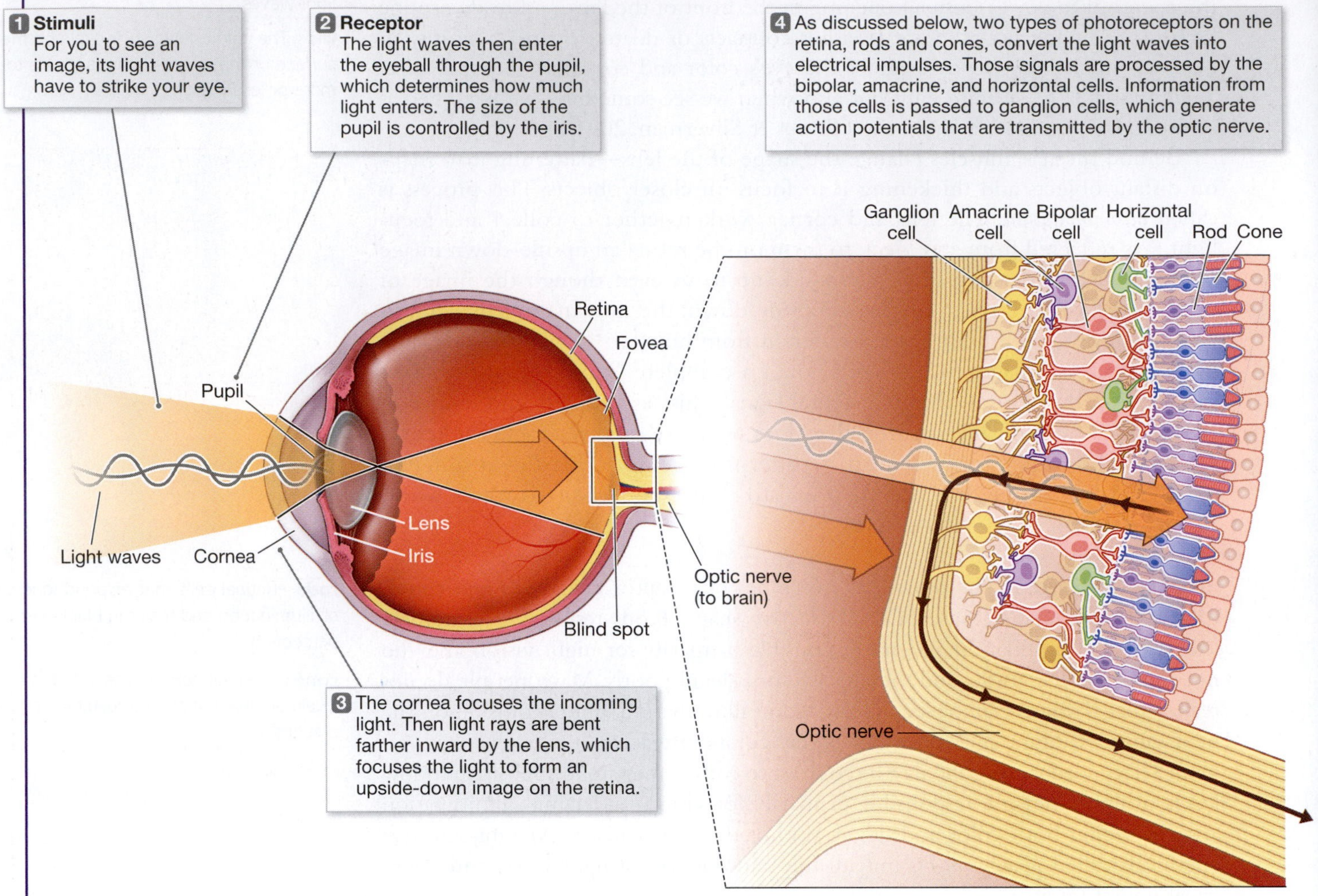

1 Stimuli
For you to see an image, its light waves have to strike your eye.

2 Receptor
The light waves then enter the eyeball through the pupil, which determines how much light enters. The size of the pupil is controlled by the iris.

4 As discussed below, two types of photoreceptors on the retina, rods and cones, convert the light waves into electrical impulses. Those signals are processed by the bipolar, amacrine, and horizontal cells. Information from those cells is passed to ganglion cells, which generate action potentials that are transmitted by the optic nerve.

Ganglion cell   Amacrine cell   Bipolar cell   Horizontal cell   Rod   Cone

Retina
Fovea

Pupil

Light waves   Cornea

Lens
Iris

Optic nerve (to brain)

Blind spot

Optic nerve

3 The cornea focuses the incoming light. Then light rays are bent farther inward by the lens, which focuses the light to form an upside-down image on the retina.

FIGURE 5.19 **Try for Yourself: Find Your Blind Spot**

To find your blind spot, hold this book in front of you and look at the dot, closing your left eye. Move the book toward and away from your face until the rabbit disappears.

You can repeat this for your right eye by turning the book upside down.

Result: The optic nerve creates the blind spot—a small point at the back of the retina. There are no receptors at this spot because it is where the nerves leave the eye.

---

the eye at the back of the retina. The point at which the optic nerve exits the retina has no rods or cones, resulting in a blind spot in each eye: If you look at one of your fists as you hold it out at arm's length, the size it appears to you is about the size of your blind spot. The brain normally fills in this gap automatically, so you assume the world continues and are not aware that a blind spot exists in the middle of your field of vision. However, you can isolate your blind spot (**FIGURE 5.19**).

Each optic nerve carries information to the central nervous system. At the *optic chiasm,* half of the axons in the optic nerves cross (those that project from the portion of the retina nearest the nose). Information from the left side of visual space (i.e., everything visible to the left of the point of gaze) is projected to the brain's right hemisphere and vice versa. The first synapse of the majority of ganglion cells lies within the visual areas of the thalamus, and visual information is transmitted from there to the *primary visual cortex,*

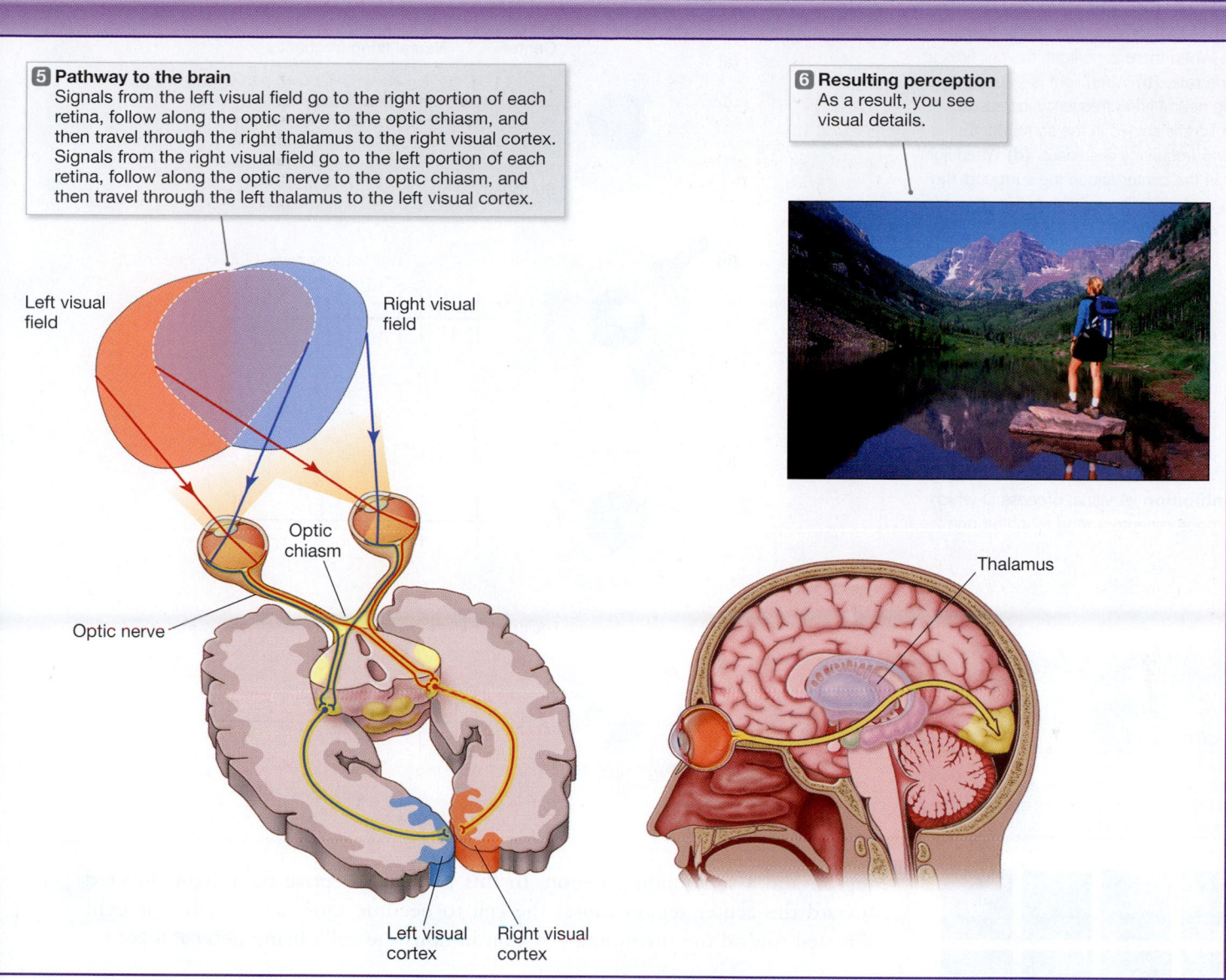

5 **Pathway to the brain**
Signals from the left visual field go to the right portion of each retina, follow along the optic nerve to the optic chiasm, and then travel through the right thalamus to the right visual cortex. Signals from the right visual field go to the left portion of each retina, follow along the optic nerve to the optic chiasm, and then travel through the left thalamus to the left visual cortex.

6 **Resulting perception**
As a result, you see visual details.

Left visual field

Right visual field

Optic chiasm

Optic nerve

Thalamus

Left visual cortex

Right visual cortex

cortical areas in the occipital lobe, at the back of the head. The pathway from the retina to this region carries all the information that we consciously experience as seeing.

THE DETECTION OF VISUAL INFORMATION Sensory neurons are generally picky about what they respond to in the world—each has a particular "tuning." To understand how this works, think of a tuning fork tuned to, say, middle C. If the air around this tuning fork vibrates at the frequency of middle C, those vibrations will make the tuning fork vibrate—that is, the fork will resonate with the energy around it. However, if the air vibrates at a different frequency, the tuning fork will not resonate. Similarly, particular visual neurons respond best to particular colors, particular shape orientations, or particular directions of motion. A given visual neuron's tuning specifies its **receptive field,** the population of sensory receptors that influences activity in a sensory neuron. (Receptive fields have been identified for neurons of the visual system, of the auditory system, and of the somatosensory system, which provides information from muscles.) One of the most common types of visual receptive fields is a circle that consists of a center

receptive field The region of visual space to which neurons in the primary visual cortex are sensitive.

FIGURE 5.20 Receptive Fields (a) A typical receptive field consists of a center and a surround. When there is no light, the cell fires at its baseline rate. **(b)** When light is shined in the center, the neural firing frequency increases. **(c)** When light is shined in the surround, the neural firing frequency decreases. **(d)** When light is shined in the center and in the surround, the cell's firing rate is balanced out and is similar to its baseline rate.

lateral inhibition A visual process in which adjacent photoreceptors tend to inhibit one another.

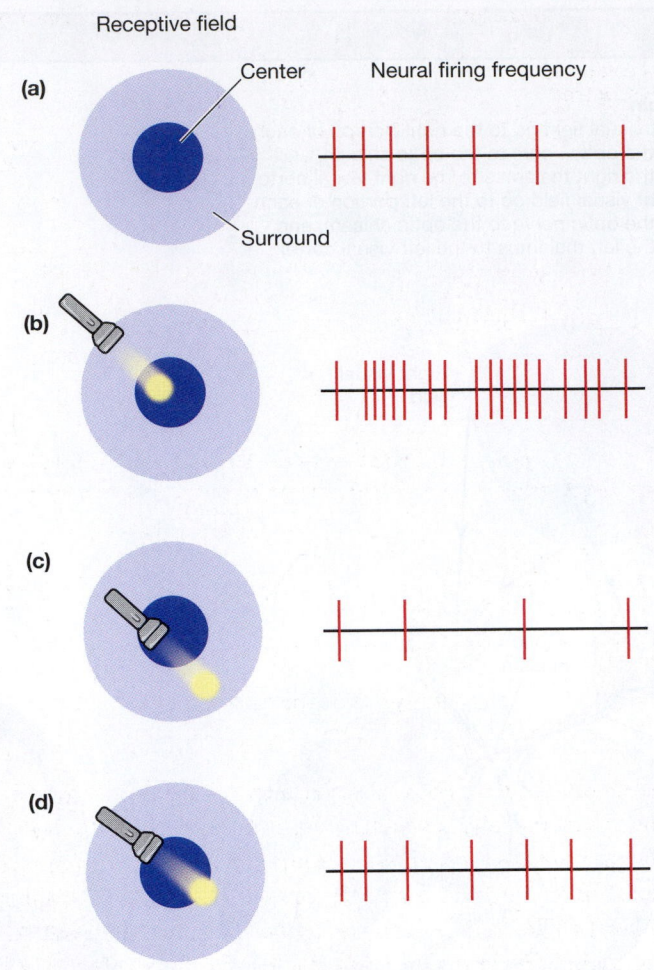

FIGURE 5.21 Try for Yourself: Lateral Inhibition with the Hermann Grid

Look at the figure as a whole and you immediately will see darkened spots at the intersections of the white lines.

However, if you look directly at the intersections, or cover all but one row of squares, you will see that the dark spots are illusory.

Result: The Hermann grid demonstrates lateral inhibition. Receptors coding information from the white lines are inhibited by their neighbors on two sides. Receptors coding information from the intersections, however, are inhibited from four sides, so they respond less vigorously. Thus the intersections appear to be darker than the lines.

region and a surrounding region. In this type of receptive field, light directed toward the center region causes the cell to become more active, whereas light directed toward the surrounding region inhibits the cell's firing (**FIGURE 5.20**).

LATERAL INHIBITION Our visual systems are especially sensitive to edges because edges tell us where objects end. If a rod or cone is stimulated, it sends information to the brain, but it also sends information to its neighboring receptors, inhibiting their activity. The physiological mechanism causing this effect, **lateral inhibition,** emphasizes changes in visual stimuli. (**FIGURE 5.21** shows one result of lateral inhibition: the illusion of gray dots appearing at the intersections of white lines against a dark background. Another result, simultaneous contrast, is that an object will look lighter against a black background than against a white one; see also Figure 5.28.) The visual system is especially sensitive to edges and contours. From a very early stage of processing, then, the visual system's circuitry is "wired" to make finding objects' boundaries easier.

THE COLOR OF LIGHT IS DETERMINED BY ITS WAVELENGTH Humans can distinguish among millions of shades of color. But when we look at colors—whether we are choosing which crayons to color with, matching paint samples with already painted walls, finding the right color thread for tightening a button on a shirt—we are not seeing the actual shades. We are seeing the light waves that objects (crayons, paint, walls, thread, you name it) reflect to our eyes. Visible light consists of electromagnetic waves ranging in length from about 400 to 700 nanometers (abbreviated *nm;* this length

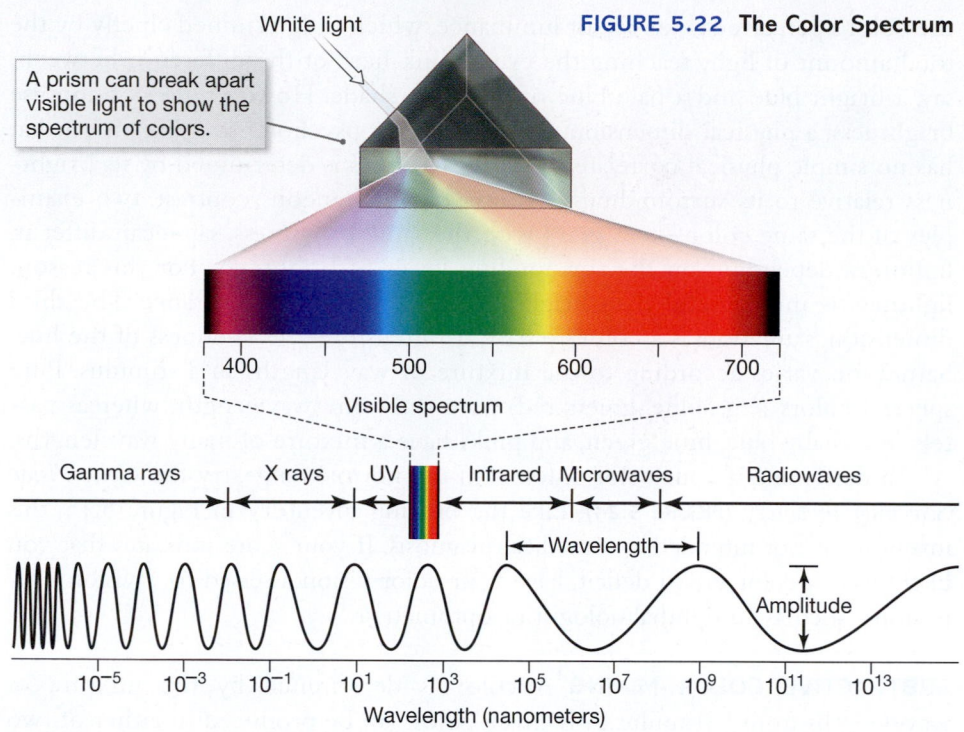

White light

A prism can break apart visible light to show the spectrum of colors.

FIGURE 5.22 **The Color Spectrum**

400   500   600   700

Visible spectrum

Gamma rays   X rays   UV   Infrared   Microwaves   Radiowaves

|← Wavelength →|

Amplitude

10^{-5} 10^{-3} 10^{-1} 10^{1} 10^{3} 10^{5} 10^{7} 10^{9} 10^{11} 10^{13}

Wavelength (nanometers)

is about one billionth of a meter). In simplest terms, the color of light is determined by the wavelengths of the electromagnetic waves that reach the eye (**FIGURE 5.22**). It would be wrong, however, to equate specific physical wavelengths with specific perceived colors. There are three kinds of cones, and each kind is most sensitive to different wavelengths. This differential sensitivity is illustrated in **FIGURE 5.23**, which shows the percentage of light at different wavelengths that is absorbed by each kind of cone. How the brain converts physical energy into the experience of color is quite complex and can be understood only by considering the response of the visual system to different wavelengths at the same time. When we see white light, for example, our eyes are receiving the entire range of wavelengths in the visible spectrum.

We categorize color along three dimensions: *hue, brightness,* and *saturation.* Hue consists of the distinctive characteristics that place a particular color in the spectrum: a particular color's greenness or orangeness, for example, which will depend primarily on the light's dominant wavelength when it reaches the eye. Brightness is

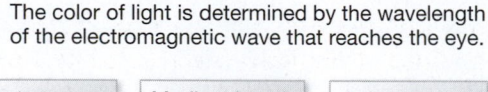

The color of light is determined by the wavelength of the electromagnetic wave that reaches the eye.

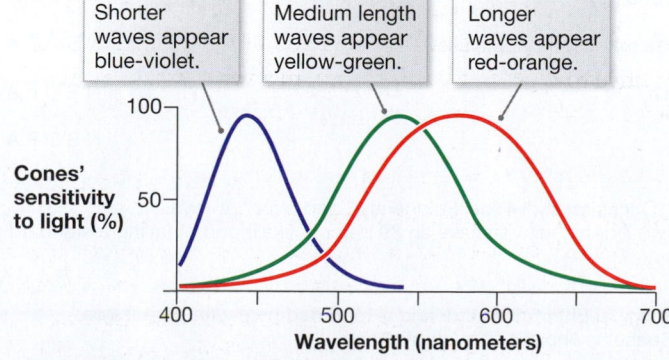

Shorter waves appear blue-violet.

Medium length waves appear yellow-green.

Longer waves appear red-orange.

Cones' sensitivity to light (%)

100
50

400   500   600   700

Wavelength (nanometers)

FIGURE 5.23 **The Experience of Color**

the color's perceived intensity, or luminance, which is determined chiefly by the total amount of light reaching the eye—think here of the difference between, say, a bright blue and a pale blue of the same shade. However, do not confuse brightness, a physical dimension, with *lightness,* a psychological dimension that has no simple physical correlate. An area's lightness is determined by its brightness relative to its surroundings. Because of simultaneous contrast, two examples of the same color—two grays with the same brightness, say—can differ in lightness, depending on the surrounding levels of brightness. For this reason, lightness is more useful than brightness for describing appearance. The third dimension, saturation, is a color's purity, or intensity—the vividness of the hue. Saturation varies according to the mixture of wavelengths in a stimulus. Pure spectral colors (e.g., blue, green, red) have only one wavelength, whereas pastels (e.g., baby blue, lime green, and pink) have a mixture of many wavelengths.

To determine if your color vision is in the normal range, try the *Color Vision Screening Inventory* (**FIGURE 5.24**). Like the hearing inventory in Figure 5.15, this inventory is not intended as a medical diagnosis. If your score indicates that you likely have a color vision deficit, have your color vision assessed by a vision professional such as an ophthalmologist or optometrist.

SUBTRACTIVE COLOR MIXING A color is determined by the mixture of wavelengths from a stimulus. Any given color can be produced in either of two ways, depending on the stimuli: *subtractive* and *additive* mixture of wavelengths

---

FIGURE 5.24 **Try for Yourself: Color Vision Screening Inventory (CVSI)**

Developed by Coren and Hakstian (1987, 1988), this questionnaire assesses color perception. For each question, select the response that best describes you and your behaviors.

You can select from among the following response alternatives: **N**ever (or almost never), **S**eldom, **O**ccasionally, **F**requently, **A**lways (or almost always).

Circle the letter corresponding to the first letter of your choice.

1	Do you have difficulty discriminating between yellow and orange?	N S O F A
2	Do you have difficulty discriminating between yellow and green?	N S O F A
3	Do you have difficulty discriminating between gray and blue-green?	N S O F A
4	Do you have difficulty discriminating between red and brown?	N S O F A
5	Do you have difficulty discriminating between green and brown?	N S O F A
6	Do you have difficulty discriminating between pale green and pale red?	N S O F A
7	Do you have difficulty discriminating between blue and purple?	N S O F A
8	Do the color names that you use disagree with those that other people use?	N S O F A
9	Are the colors of traffic lights difficult to distinguish?	N S O F A
10	Do you tend to confuse colors?	N S O F A

Result: Score your responses 1 for "Never," 2 for "Seldom," 3 for "Occasionally," 4 for "Frequently," and 5 for "Always." Then add together your scores for the 10 questions. If your score is 17 or higher, you have an 89 percent likelihood of failing a standard screening test for color vision.

The *Color Vision Screening Inventory* is copyrighted by SC Psychological Enterprises Ltd. and is reprinted here with permission. Additional vision screening questionnaires are available on StudySpace: wwnorton.com/studyspace.

(**FIGURE 5.25**). Mixing paints, for example, is one form of **subtractive color mixing,** because the mixture occurs within the stimulus and is a physical process. Paint colors are determined by pigments—chemicals on objects' surfaces that absorb different wavelengths of light and prevent them from being reflected to the eye. The color of a pigment is determined by the wavelengths that are reflected and enter the eye. When pigments are mixed, they absorb (subtract) each other's wavelengths, and the resulting color—the color we see—corresponds to the wavelengths that are "left over." If we mix blue and yellow paints, we get green, because the yellow pigment absorbs the blue wavelengths and the blue pigment absorbs the red and yellow wavelengths. What remains to be reflected is the wavelength corresponding to green, because these wavelengths are not absorbed. When we see a blue shirt, it is blue because the material the shirt is made from has absorbed medium and long wavelengths (yellow and red) and is reflecting only short wavelengths that are perceived as blue. Yellow pigments absorb shorter (blue) and longer (red) wavelengths, but they reflect wavelengths in the central yellow region of the visible spectrum. Red, yellow, and blue are the *subtractive primary colors.* Mix all three together and you get black, because together these pigments absorb nearly all the colors of the visible spectrum.

ADDITIVE COLOR MIXING When lights of different wavelengths are mixed, what you see is determined by the interaction of these wavelengths within the eye's receptors. This process is called **additive color mixing.** Stage lighting designers employ additive color mixing, for example, when they aim red and green lights at the same point on a stage to create a yellow light. In fact, as laid out by the *three primaries law of color,* almost any color can be created by combining just three wavelengths, so long as one is from the long-wave end of the spectrum (red), one is from the middle (green-yellow), and one is from the short end of the spectrum (blue-violet). For reasons that will become clear soon, most psychologists consider the *additive primary colors* to be red, green, and blue. Whereas mixing red, green, and blue paint yields black paint, mixing red, green, and blue light yields white light. The mathematician and physicist Isaac Newton discovered that white light is made up of many colors of light. You can see this for yourself with a prism (see Figure 5.22). Because different wavelengths of light bend (refract) at different angles when they pass through a prism, white light entering a prism leaves it with all the colors of a rainbow. Indeed, rainbows form in the sky because tiny water droplets in the air function as prisms, refracting sunlight in different directions.

EXPLAINING COLOR VISION An object appears to be a particular color because of the wavelengths it reflects. Thus color is a property of our visual system; there is no color in the physical world. The colors that always look so tantalizing in a new box of crayons are the products of your visual system and not properties of the crayons!

Color vision begins in the retina's center, where the cone cells transduce light into neural impulses. (Remember: **C**olor vision is **C**aused by **C**ones in the **C**enter of the retina.) There are three types of cones in the retina, and each responds best to a different wavelength of light. One type of cone is most sensitive to blue light (short wavelength), another is most sensitive to green light (medium wavelength), and the remaining cones are most sensitive to red light (long wavelength). The three cone populations are therefore called "S," "M," and "L" cones because they respond maximally to short, medium, and long wavelengths, respectively.

subtractive color mixing A way to produce a given spectral pattern in which the mixture occurs within the stimulus itself and is actually a physical, not psychological, process.

additive color mixing A way to produce a given spectral pattern in which different wavelengths of lights are mixed. The percept is determined by the interaction of these wavelengths with receptors in the eye and is a psychological process.

Subtractive Color Mixing
Physical process of color mixing that happens within the stimulus

Subtractive primary colors: red, yellow, blue

Additive Color Mixing
Mixing that happens when lights of different wavelengths are perceived by the eye

Additive primary colors: red, green, blue

FIGURE 5.25 Subtractive and Additive Color Mixing

FIGURE 5.26 Try for Yourself: Afterimage

For at least 30 seconds, stare at this version of the Union Jack, flag of the United Kingdom. Then look at the blank space to the right.

Result: Because your receptors have adapted to the green and orange in the first image, the afterimage appears in the complementary colors red and blue. You can tell that afterimages are caused by events in the retina, because the afterimage moves with you as you move your eyes, as though it is "painted" on the retina.

Yellow light looks yellow because it stimulates the L and M cones about equally and hardly stimulates the S cones at all. Ultimately, our perception of different colors is determined by the ratio of activity among the three types of cone receptors.

The initial coding of color information by just three types of retinal cone cells is one of the most important discoveries in the scientific study of visual perception. It illustrates how an essentially limitless variety of colors can be encoded by a small number of receptors. Some aspects of color vision, however, are not predicted by the existence of three types of cones in the retina. For example, some colors seem to be "opposites" (Hering, 1878/1964). When we stare at a red image for some time, we see a green afterimage when we look away (and vice versa). Likewise, when we stare at a blue image for some time, we see a yellow afterimage when we look away (and vice versa; **FIGURE 5.26**). We also have trouble visualizing certain color mixtures. For instance, it is easier to imagine reddish yellow or bluish green than reddish green or bluish yellow.

That some colors seem to be opposites cannot be explained by the responses of the different cones in the retina. To account for opposites, we must turn to the second stage in visual processing, which occurs in the ganglion cells—the cells that make up the optic nerve, which carries information to the brain. Different combinations of cones converge on the ganglion cells in the retina. One type of ganglion cells may receive excitatory input from L cones (the ones that respond to long wavelengths, which we see as red) but may be inhibited by M cones (medium wavelengths, which we see as green). These cells create the perception that red and green are "opposites." Other ganglion cells are excited by input from S cones (short wavelengths, which we see as blue) but are inhibited by both L- and M-cone activity (or vice versa). These different types of ganglion cells that work in opposing pairs create the perception that blue and yellow are opposites. (Opposite colors are involved in the McCollough effect, named for the vision researcher Celeste McCollough, who first described it. For a demonstration of this visual phenomenon, which is among many that we do not fully understand, see **FIGURE 5.27**.)

FIGURE 5.27 Try for Yourself: The McCollough Effect

Alternate your gaze from the green stimulus with vertical lines to the magenta stimulus with horizontal lines, changing from one to the other approximately every second for 40 seconds.

Then look at the black-and-white stimulus, composed of vertical and horizontal lines.

What do you see?

Result: You should see magenta vertical lines and green horizontal lines. Because the McCollough Effect can last for hours or even a day, it cannot be explained by simple neural fatigue. For this reason, the effect more likely occurs in higher brain regions, not in the eye. As noted in the text, the visual system is especially primed to process information about edges, and color-related edge perception may be involved.

SIMULTANEOUS CONTRAST *Simultaneous contrast* is an optical illusion in which identical stimuli appear different when presented against different backgrounds. Even if we know that these stimuli are identical, we cannot make ourselves see them as the same (**FIGURE 5.28**). One theory to explain this effect is that lateral inhibition in the retina emphasizes the difference between an object and its background. Whatever its cause, simultaneous contrast again illustrates the theme that we often are unaware of factors affecting our perception of the world. (Other color effects created by the visual system are shown in **FIGURE 5.29**.)

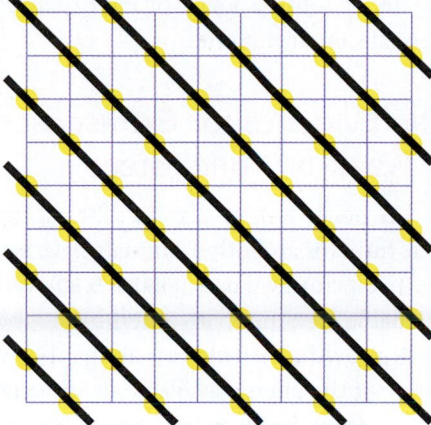

(a) The Colored Ray Illusion

(b) Illusory Yellow Lines

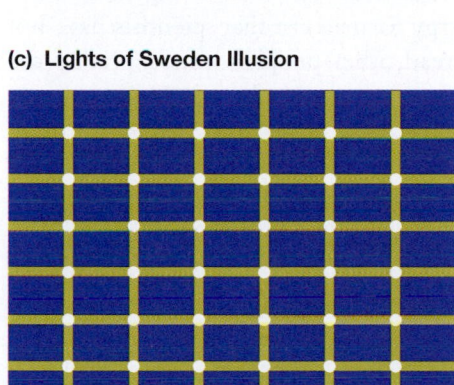

(c) Lights of Sweden Illusion

FIGURE 5.29 Color Illusions
(a) Look closely at this figure. Do red lines appear to run on the diagonal between the red intersections? These lines do not physically exist—your visual system is filling them in. **(b)** Illusory yellow lines appear to run obliquely over the grid. **(c)** Do you see a blue light that appears to scintillate in white circles? Scientists believe that visual illusions such as the three illustrated here are due to lateral inhibition and the size and shape of receptive fields.

FIGURE 5.28 **Try for Yourself: Simultaneous Contrast**

Look at the colors of the central squares in each pair. Do they look the same or different?

Result: The central squares in each pair are identical, but they look different because of the different background colors. For example, most people see the gray square that is surrounded with red as lighter than the gray square surrounded with green. If you doubt that the central squares are identical, cover the surrounding portions of each square.

Humans and Animals Have Other Sensory Systems

Humans have several internal sensory systems in addition to the five primary ones. Subtle sensory systems send messages to the brain about things such as blood glucose level and blood pressure. The **kinesthetic sense,** which some researchers group with the touch senses, refers to sensations we gather from receptors, in muscles, tendons, and joints, that pinpoint the position in space and the movements of both our body and our limbs. This information helps us coordinate voluntary movement and is invaluable in avoiding injury. The **vestibular senses** use data from receptors in the semicircular canals of the inner ear. These canals contain a liquid that moves when the head moves, bending hair cells at the ends of the canal. The bending generates nerve impulses that inform us of the head's rotation and is thus responsible for a sense of balance. It explains why inner-ear infections or

kinesthetic sense Perception of our limbs in space.

vestibular sense Perception of balance.

standing up quickly can make us dizzy. The experience of being seasick or carsick results in part from conflicting signals arriving from the vestibular system and the visual system.

Researchers are studying nonhuman animals' more-exotic sensory systems, such as *sonar senses* and *electroreception* (senses based on electrical fields). Our understanding of sensory systems that use sonar for navigation comes primarily from the study of both bats and dolphins. These animals produce calls and then respond to the echoes of those calls; the system is biosonar because the sound waves emanate from the animal. Electroreception operates in a similar way: Some fish emit an electrical field and then analyze disruptions in the field to avoid predators or find prey. Others respond to the electrical fields emitted by other fish. In each case, evolution has produced an adaptive solution that allows an animal to create or sense a form of energy and use that information to interact with the animal's environment.

The Evidence for Extrasensory Perception (ESP) Is Weak or Nonexistent

In his book *Sensory Exotica* (2000), the psychologist Howard Hughes points out that humans and other animals have several internal sensory systems in addition to the five primary senses (**FIGURE 5.30**). What about the so-called *sixth sense,* the "unexplainable" feeling that something is about to happen? Humans' many sensory systems provide information about the world, but they are sensitive to only a small range of the energy available in any environment. For instance, dogs can hear much higher frequencies than humans can, and many insects can sense energy forms that we cannot detect. Might frequencies or energy forms exist that scientists have not discovered but that allow some people to read other people's minds, predict the future by examining the stars, or communicate with ghosts? Might people be able to perceive information beyond ordinary sensory information through *extrasensory perception,* or *ESP?*

Many reports of ESP are based on anecdotal cases. Anecdotes are not science, even if people tell stories in ways that sound scientific. Psychological scientists reject claims supported only by anecdotes because such evidence is difficult to disprove and because ordinary thought processes can explain many of the claims. For instance, if you see a couple fighting all the time, you might predict accurately that they will break up, but that does not make you a psychic. Much of our social perception requires us to be sensitive to the subtle cues that guide behavior in a situation. But the information we glean from social situations does not arrive from some "extra" sensory system.

Perhaps the best evidence for ESP was obtained by the social psychologist Daryl Bem and his collaborator Charles Honorton (1994). In their studies, a "sender" in a soundproof booth focused on a randomly generated image, and a receiver in another room tried to sense the sender's imagery. The receiver was then asked to choose among four alternatives, one of them correct. By chance, the receivers should have been correct 25 percent of the time, but across 11 studies, Bem and Honorton found that receivers were right about 33 percent of the time. Is this evidence of ESP? Many psychological scientists say that other factors in the experiments might have affected the results; after all, receivers were wrong 67 percent of the time. A statistical review of many such studies found little support for ESP (Milton & Wiseman, 2001). Moreover, numerous scientific organizations and government agencies have reviewed decades of research and have concluded that no such phenomenon exists.

FIGURE 5.30 Howard Hughes Hughes describes several sensory systems that humans and other animals have in addition to the five primary systems of touch, taste, smell, sight, and hearing.

The Amazing Randi, also known as James Randi, is a well-known magician and escape artist devoted to disabusing people of their beliefs in the supernatural. In 1996, he established a $1,000,000 prize for anyone who could demonstrate psychic powers under controlled conditions. No one has won this prize. He has produced video clips of psychics wearing earphones that enabled them to receive information from others in the room and using other clever tricks that make them appear to have extrasensory powers. Psychics draw on social factors, for example, to *read* information from their clients and their audiences.

But does any of this prove that ESP does not exist? An important quality of critical thinking is to keep an open mind and not conclude that something does not exist just because it has not yet been demonstrated. The only reasonable conclusion is that the evidence for ESP is currently weak and that healthy skepticism demands better evidence. Psychology is an empirical science, of course, and further psychological research on ESP would require empirical methods of science. What kinds of studies and what kinds of evidence would prove or disprove ESP's existence?

CRITICAL THINKING SKILL

Understanding That Perception Can Be Deceiving

As a result of the McCollough effect (see Figure 5.27), you can look at a black-and-white grid and see colored lines. Such optical effects have inspired perception psychologists to modify the expression "Seeing is believing" to "Seeing is deceiving, at least some of the time." Perhaps you believe in psychic powers because you have seen a stage performer accomplish amazing feats. Be warned: Most magic tricks are designed to fool your basic senses; they are elaborate examples of visual illusions like those presented in this chapter. They rely on the fact that our sensory systems are far from perfect and that our expectations shape much of what we perceive. In short, they are *tricks,* not evidence of psychic abilities. Magic's allure may be strong, but given all the laboratory studies showing that we often perceive the world the way we expect it to be rather than the way it is, why do people still believe in magic—in fact, claim to have seen it with their own eyes?

Good magicians know we are easily distracted by movement, so to perform their illusions they first capture our attention. Have you ever wondered why people who get "sawed in half" have to go inside a box first or why people who levitate need to be covered or why the magician needs a cloth to cover the disappearing rabbit? The box, the covering, or the cloth is used to conceal the trick that gives rise to the perception that something supernatural is happening (**FIGURE 5.31**).

Do you want to be sawed in half while you are in a box? No problem—as you step into the box, fold your legs so that

FIGURE 5.31 Think Critically: Are Magic Tricks Real? Are there ways to explain what is going on in these pictures without believing in magic?

you take up only half the box (all of you above the saw line). Let fake legs that look like yours and shoes identical to ones you are wearing dangle out the other end of the box. A variation on this trick is to have someone small in the bottom half of the box wearing shoes identical to yours, so when you are "sawed in half," your entire body is in the top box and someone else is in the bottom box waving what appears to be your disconnected feet. This trick can be a lot of fun, but it does not represent magic.

To bend a spoon with your bare hands before an audience, the trick is to have bent the spoon beforehand and kept it concealed in your hand. Proudly show the spoon to your audience with the bowl or flat side facing out. From that angle, the spoon will look straight. Talk to the audience to distract them while you rub the spoon. In a short while, while the audience is watching, allow the spoon's bent part to just peek out from between your fingers so that it appears to be bending. Anyone can get quite good at this, with a little practice.

Levitating is more difficult than bending a spoon. Wear shoes that you can easily slip out of, and attach the shoes to each other so that when one rises, the other will too. Place a curtain or blanket in front of yourself, allow-ing your shoes to show beneath it. Surreptitiously slip one foot out of its shoe and step onto a small box or platform, keeping your knees bent. As you straighten your knees, you will appear to be slowly rising. Your shoes will appear to rise together as you support yourself on the foot that is on the box or platform. Wave your arms, arch your chest, chant, or use other techniques that will draw the audience's attention from your feet. As you rise onto the foot that is on the box or platform, keep your dangling shoes just visible so you will appear to be levitating. With some practice, you too can levitate like a pro.

SUMMING UP

What Are the Basic Sensory Processes?

All the senses share similar processes. Each has receptors that respond to differ-ent physical or chemical stimuli by transducing them into some pattern of brain activity. Typically, different receptors respond to different types of stimuli, and most sensory systems integrate signals from these different receptors into an overall sen-sation. This system allows a relatively small number of receptors to code a wide variety of stimuli. For example, the visual system can interpret the entire range of colors with only three cone types, and all the taste sensations are made up of five primary taste receptors. These various sensory receptors help the perceptual sys-tem receive important information that assists in solving adaptive problems. Sensory information, although obtained from the outside world, is processed entirely in the brain to produce sensory experience through perception.

MEASURING UP

1. The sensory systems _____.
   a. use all the available energy in their environment to create a true repre-sentation of both objects and events
   b. use only a small portion of the available energy in their environment

2. A general principle regarding sensation is that _____.
   a. the combined firing of many different receptors and the neurons they connect with creates our sensations
   b. each sensation (for example, seeing a blue color or hearing a high-pitch tone) is coded by one type of receptor, which is sensitive to only one type of stimulus
3. An intense stimulus such as a loud sound or a heavy touch, is coded by _____.
   a. different sensory receptors that project to different areas of the brain
   b. an increase in the number of neurons that respond to the stimulation

What Are the Basic Perceptual Processes?

The perceptual system is stunningly intelligent in its ability to guide each of us around. Right this minute, for example, your brain is making millions of calculations—all in milliseconds—to produce a coherent experience of your environment. As a result, your experience is a construction of your brain and resides inside your skull, despite the illusion that the object and events you are experiencing exist in the space around you. Neurons inside your brain do not directly experience the outside world, but they communicate with other neurons inside and outside your brain, and your conscious experience of the world emerges from this communication. For instance, as you stare at a computer screen, you are aware of one image, not the thousands that dance across your retina to create that constant, static scene. What you perceive, then, is vastly different from the pattern of stimulation your retina is taking in. If you were aware of what your brain was doing every moment, you would be paralyzed by information overload. Most of the computations the brain performs never reach your consciousness—only important new outcomes do. How does the brain extract a stable representation of the world from the information the senses provide? Perception research seeks to answer that question.

Perceptual psychologists have drawn on many disciplines, crossing the levels of analysis, to understand how humans represent (or misrepresent) the world. Areas as diverse as art, computer science, philosophy, anatomy, and physiology have informed the understanding of perception. As discussed in Chapter 1, for example, music has been used to explore various aspects of perception, from how genes predispose perfect pitch to how sound can affect mood. In addition, researchers have worked backward from cases where brain injuries have disrupted perception, inferring how the intact brain processes information.

Perception Occurs in the Brain

So far, you have seen how sensory stimuli are transduced into electrical impulses by sensory receptors and transmitted to the brain by nerves. These electrical impulses are all that the brain works with to create a person's rich variety of perceptual experiences. With the exception of olfaction, all sensory information is relayed to cortical and other areas of the brain from the thalamus. From the thalamus, information from each sense is projected to a specific region of the cerebral cortex. In these *primary sensory areas* (**FIGURE 5.32**), the perceptual process begins in earnest. The following section considers perceptual processing in hearing, touch, and vision. The brain regions involved in taste and smell are less well understood and therefore will not be discussed here.

HEARING Auditory neurons in the thalamus extend their axons to the *primary auditory cortex* (called *A1,* for the *first* auditory area), which is in the temporal lobe. Neurons in this region code the frequency (or pitch) of auditory stimuli. Neurons toward the rear of A1 respond best to lower frequencies, such as that of a foghorn, whereas those toward the front of A1 respond best to higher frequencies, such as that of a train whistle.

TOUCH Touch information from the thalamus is projected to the *primary somatosensory cortex* (called *S1*), which is in the parietal lobe. In the 1940s, in a classic series of studies of patients undergoing brain surgery, the neurosurgeon Wilder Penfield (Penfield & Jasper, 1954) discovered that electrical stimulation of S1 could evoke the sensation of touch in different regions of the body. Penfield found that neighboring body parts tended to be represented next to one another in S1, so that the body is effectively mapped out there according to physical proximity. As shown in Chapter 3's drawing of the homunculus (see Figure 3.29), more-sensitive body parts have relatively larger amounts of cortical tissue dedicated to them. The most sensitive regions of the body, such as lips and fingers, have a great deal of S1 devoted to them. Other areas, such as the back and the calves, have very little.

VISION The study of perception has focused to a large extent on the visual cortex and the multiple areas in which the retinal image is processed. The complexity of visual perception is underscored by the amount of cortical real estate dedicated to processing visual information. Some estimates suggest that up to half the cerebral cortex may participate in visual perception in some way. As noted above, the *primary visual cortex* (*V1*) is in the occipital lobe. The neural pathway from the retina to the occipital lobe preserves spatial relationships, so that adjacent areas of the retina correspond to adjacent areas in V1.

In the 1960s, the neurophysiologists David Hubel and Torsten Wiesel (1962) began exploring the properties of neurons in VI by recording activity from single

FIGURE 5.32 Primary Sense Regions These are the primary sense areas where information about taste, touch, hearing, smell, and vision are projected. Note that separate "streams" of visual information—what you see and where it is—are sent from the occipital lobe (visual cortex) to different parts of the brain for further processing.

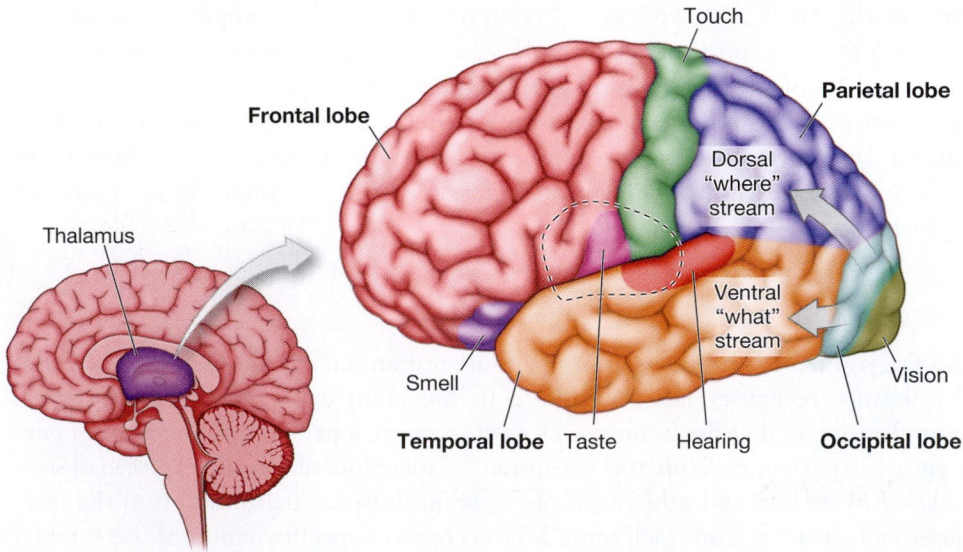

cells—work for which they were awarded a Nobel Prize. They discovered that some neurons in the primary visual cortex respond more to lines of particular orientations than to any other type of stimulus, including lines tilted at a different angle; for example, some neurons increase their firing rate when a vertical line segment is presented in their receptive field (**FIGURE 5.33**). The firing rate of these cells, termed *simple cells* by Hubel and Wiesel, decreases as the orientation of the line segment is rotated away from the preferred orientation. Further studies by Hubel and Wiesel and others have also found neurons that specialize in detecting either corners, colors, the ends of lines, or more complex visual features.

WHAT VERSUS WHERE One core discovery of the past few decades has been that neurons in different parts of the brain tend to have different types of receptive fields. These areas appear to process specific aspects of a visual stimulus, such as color or motion. (As noted above, other sensory systems also have receptive fields.) One important theory proposes that visual areas beyond V1 form two parallel processing streams: The lower, *ventral stream,* pathway appears to be specialized for the perception and recognition of objects, such as determining their colors and shapes, whereas the upper, *dorsal stream,* pathway seems to be specialized for spatial perception—determining where an object is and relating it to other objects in a scene. (Both pathways are shown in Figure 5.32.) These two processing streams therefore are known as the *"what" pathway* and the *"where" pathway* (Ungerleider & Mishkin, 1982). Subsequent brain imaging studies have confirmed that brain regions in the upper pathway are activated by tasks that require decisions about

P. BYRNES.

"Great! O.K., this time I want you to sound taller, and let me hear a little more hair."

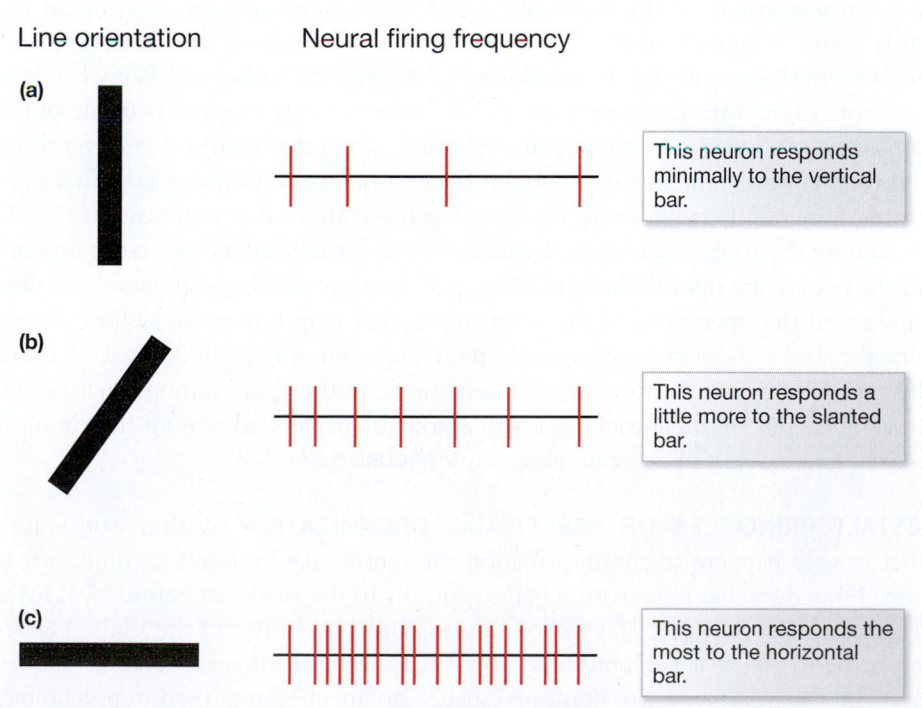

Line orientation   Neural firing frequency

(a)

This neuron responds minimally to the vertical bar.

(b)

This neuron responds a little more to the slanted bar.

(c)

This neuron responds the most to the horizontal bar.

FIGURE 5.33 Simple Cells Some neurons, called simple cells, respond more to lines of particular orientations.

spatial relationships between objects, whereas regions in the lower pathway are activated by tasks that require identifying objects.

Damage to certain regions of the visual cortex provides evidence for distinguishing between these two streams of information. Consider the case of D.F. (Goodale & Milner, 1992), who at age 34 suffered carbon monoxide poisoning that damaged her visual system, particularly regions involved in the "what" pathway. She was no longer able to recognize the faces of her friends and family members, common objects, or even drawings of squares or of circles. She could recognize people by their voices, however, and objects if they were placed in her hands. Her condition—*object agnosia,* the inability to recognize objects—is striking in what she could and could not do. When presented with a drawing of, say, an apple, she could not identify or reproduce it. But if asked to draw an apple, she could do so from memory. Despite major deficits in object perception, she could use visual information about the size, shape, and orientation of objects to control visually guided movements—her "where" pathway appeared to be intact. For instance, she could walk across a room and step around things adeptly. She could reach out and shake a person's hand. Most confounding, in laboratory tests, she could reach out and grasp a block, with the exactly right distance between her fingers, even though she could not tell you what she was going to pick up or how large it was. Thus her conscious visual perception of objects was impaired— she was not aware of taking in any visual information about objects she saw. However, other aspects of her visual processing were unaffected. The intact regions of her visual cortex allowed her to use information about the size and location of objects despite her lack of awareness. As illustrated by D.F.'s case, these systems operate independently to help us understand the world around us. Here again, the biological revolution has helped change scientists' understanding of psychological processes.

Object Perception Requires Construction

The neural computations required for object perception begin in the early stages of visual processing. As discussed above, lateral inhibition among neurons in the retina helps accentuate areas of changing stimulation—which are likely to correspond to the edges of objects. In addition, the work of Hubel and Wiesel on the properties of neurons in the primary visual cortex strongly suggests that one of the most important roles for V1 (the primary visual area in the brain) is to extract those edges and contours that define the boundaries of objects. Thus one of the first steps in processing a form appears to be encoding the features that compose it.

Among the tools psychological scientists have for understanding the brain's use of information are optical illusions. Many perceptual psychologists believe that illusions reveal the operations of the mechanisms that help our visual systems determine the sizes and distances of objects in the visual environment. In doing so, illusions illustrate how we form accurate representations of the three-dimensional world. Researchers rely on these tricks to reveal automatic perceptual systems that, in most circumstances, result in accurate perception (**FIGURE 5.34**).

GESTALT PRINCIPLES OF PERCEPTUAL ORGANIZATION Within our brains, what exactly happens to the information the senses take in about an object's features? How does that information get organized? In the years just before World War I (as discussed in Chapter 1), psychologists in both Germany and the United States began theorizing that perception is more than the result of accumulating sensory data. The German word *Gestalt* means "shape" or "form," but as used in psychology

(a)

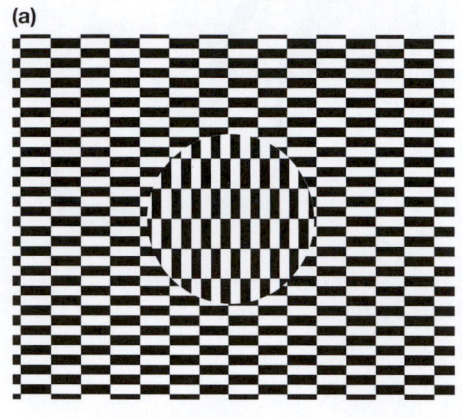

(b)

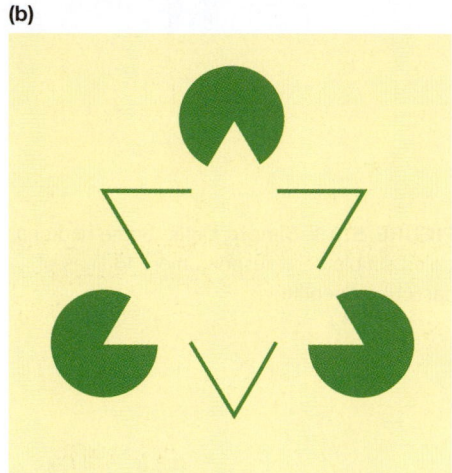

FIGURE 5.34 Optical Illusions (a) The Ouchi illusion—named for the Japanese artist Hajime Ouchi, who invented it—shows how we separate a figure from its background. Here, the object is a circle made of lines offset from the rest of the display. Scrolling the image horizontally or vertically gives a much stronger effect. Some people report seeing colors and movement in this illusion. **(b)** The illusory triangle in front of the circles is not physically present—it is an illusion created by your visual system. It also appears brighter than the surrounding area, as would be expected if it were closer to the observer.

it means "organized whole." The founders of Gestalt psychology postulated a series of laws to explain how perceived features of a visual scene are grouped into organized wholes. Gestalt psychology holds that our brains use innate (that is, built-in) principles to organize sensory information (**FIGURE 5.35**).

PROXIMITY AND SIMILARITY Two of the most important Gestalt laws concern proximity and similarity. The *principle of proximity* states that the closer two figures are to each other, the more likely we are to group them and see them as part of the same object (Figure 5.35a). You might already be familiar with the *principle of similarity* as illustrated by the *Sesame Street* song and game "One of These Things Is Not like the Others." We tend to group figures according to how closely they resemble each other, whether in shape, color, or orientation (Figure 5.35b). According to both of these principles, we tend to cluster elements of the visual scene, enabling us to consider them as wholes rather than as individual parts. For example, we often perceive a flock of birds as a single entity because all the elements, the birds, are similar and in close proximity.

THE "BEST" FORMS Other Gestalt laws describe how we perceive a form's features. *Good continuation* is the tendency to interpret intersecting lines as continuous rather than as changing direction radically. Good contour continuation appears to play a role in completing an object behind an *occluder,* which can be anything that hides a portion of an object or an entire object from view. For example, in Figure 5.35c the bar in the left-hand illustration appears to be completely behind the occluder. However, good continuation may operate over more complex representations than contour information. For example, in the right-hand illustration (by the vision scientist Peter Tse), two cats appear to be one extremely long cat wrapped around the pole, yet no continuous contours permit this completion. *Closure* refers to the tendency to complete figures that have gaps, as in Figure 5.35d.

A phenomenon that illustrates several Gestalt principles is *illusory contours,* which refers to the fact that we perceive contours (boundary lines) even though they do not exist. Illusory contours appear when stimulus configurations suggest that contours ought to be present—for example, when cues to depth are implied or useful in interpreting a pattern (Figure 5.35e).

FIGURE 5.35 Gestalt Principles Gestalt psychology describes how perceived features of a visual scene are grouped into organized wholes.

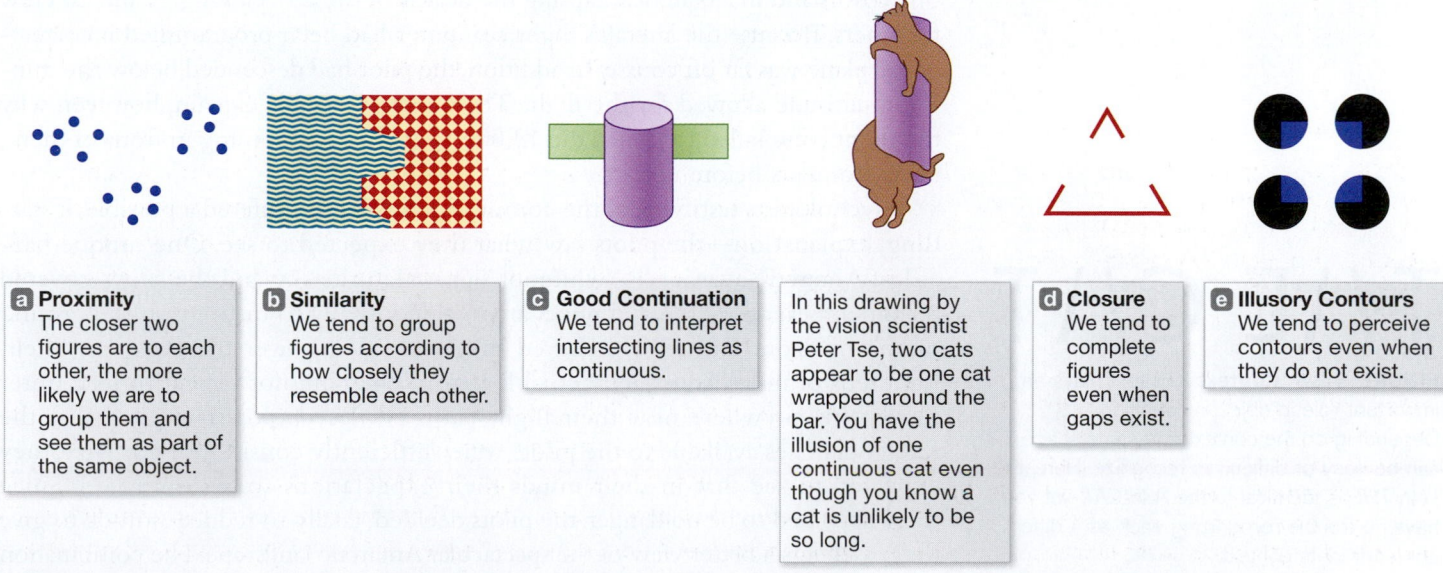

a Proximity The closer two figures are to each other, the more likely we are to group them and see them as part of the same object.

b Similarity We tend to group figures according to how closely they resemble each other.

c Good Continuation We tend to interpret intersecting lines as continuous.

In this drawing by the vision scientist Peter Tse, two cats appear to be one cat wrapped around the bar. You have the illusion of one continuous cat even though you know a cat is unlikely to be so long.

d Closure We tend to complete figures even when gaps exist.

e Illusory Contours We tend to perceive contours even when they do not exist.

FIGURE AND GROUND One of the visual perception system's most basic organizing principles is distinguishing between figure and ground. A classic illustration of this is the *reversible figure illusion* (see Figure 1.16), in which we see either a full face or two faces looking at each other—but not both at the same time. In identifying either figure—indeed, *any* figure—the brain assigns the rest of the scene to the background. In this illusion, the "correct" assignment of figure and ground is ambiguous, so the figures periodically reverse (switch back and forth) as the visual system strives to make sense of the stimulation. In ways like this, visual perception is dynamic and ongoing.

As discussed in Chapter 1, Richard Nisbett and his colleagues (2001) have demonstrated cultural differences between Eastern people's perceptions and Western people's. Easterners focus on a scene holistically, whereas Westerners focus on single elements in the forefront. Thus Easterners will more likely be influenced by the (back)ground of a figure, and Westerners will more likely extract the figure from its (back)ground.

In Figure 1.15, it is hard to see the Dalmatian standing among the many black spots scattered on the white background because the part of the image corresponding to the dog lacks contours that define the dog's edges and because the dog's spotted texture resembles that of the background. Many observers find that they first recognize one part of the dog—say, the head—and from that are able to discern the dog's shape. Once you perceive the dog, it becomes very difficult to *not* see it the next time you look at the figure. Thus memories of particular shapes can inform shape processing.

BOTTOM-UP AND TOP-DOWN INFORMATION PROCESSING How do we assemble the information about parts into a perception of a whole object? According to most models of the process, pattern recognition is hierarchical, using **bottom-up processing.** This means data are relayed from lower to higher levels of processing. But perception is actually a combination of bottom-up and **top-down processing,** in which information at higher levels of processing can influence lower, "earlier" levels in the processing hierarchy. For this reason, context affects perception: What we expect to see influences what we perceive, as in the Dalmatian illustration discussed just above. Also consider the incomplete letter in **FIGURE 5.36**, where the two lines in the center of each word are perceived as either "H" or "A" depending on which interpretation would make sense in the context of the word.

Faulty expectations can lead to faulty perceptions. For example: On November 28, 1979, Air New Zealand Flight 901 crashed into the slopes of Mount Erebus, on Ross Island in Antarctica, causing the deaths of the 237 passengers and 20 crew members. Because the aircraft's flight computer had been programmed incorrectly, the plane was far off course. In addition, the pilot had descended below the minimum altitude allowed for the flight. These factors do not explain, however, why the flight crew failed to notice the 12,000-foot volcano looming in front of them, until moments before impact.

Psychologists testifying at the commission of inquiry offered a possible, if startling, explanation—the pilots saw what they expected to see. One unique hazard of Antarctic aviation is "whiteout," in which the sky and the snow-covered terrain appear to merge and pilots are unable visually to distinguish the ground or the horizon. The pilots believed they were flying over the Ross Ice Shelf, hundreds of miles from their actual location. They did not expect to encounter mountains anywhere near their flight path. The psychologists argued that the few visual cues available to the pilots were sufficiently consistent with what they expected to see that in their minds their expectations were confirmed. Since there appeared to be no danger, the pilots decided, fatally, to reduce altitude to give the passengers a better view of the spectacular Antarctic landscape. The combination

bottom-up processing A hierarchical model of pattern recognition in which data are relayed from one processing level to the next, always moving to a higher level of processing.

top-down processing A hierarchical model of pattern recognition in which information at higher levels of processing can also influence lower, "earlier" levels in the processing hierarchy.

THE CAT

FIGURE 5.36 Context Context plays an important role in object recognition. Depending on the context, the same shape can be easy or difficult to recognize. Here, the *H* in *THE* is identical to the *A* in *CAT,* yet you have no trouble recognizing each as a different letter in its context.

of an unusually sparse visual environment and the pilots' beliefs conspired to fool their visual systems into seeing terrain that was not there—and failing to see the mountain that was.

FACE PERCEPTION One special class of object that the visual system cares about is faces, and psychological scientists have studied face perception across multiple levels of analysis, from how different brain regions seem to be especially responsive to anything that resembles a face, to how people determine whose face they are looking at, to how a face's various characteristics determine whether we find that face attractive. As highly social animals, humans are well able to perceive and interpret facial expressions. Several studies support the idea that human faces reveal "special" information that is not available in any other way. For example, we can more readily discern information about a person's mood, attentiveness, gender, race, age, and so on by looking at that person's face than by listening to the person talk, watching the person walk, or studying his or her clothing (Bruce & Young, 1986). Some people have selected deficits in the ability to recognize faces (a condition known as *prosopagnosia*) but not in the ability to recognize other objects (Farah, 1996).

At the biological level of analysis, faces are so important that certain brain regions appear to be dedicated solely to perceiving them. As part of the "what" stream discussed above, certain cortical regions, and even specific neurons, seem to be specialized to perceive faces. A number of separate brain imaging studies have found that a region of the *fusiform gyrus,* in the right hemisphere, may be specialized for perceiving faces (Grill-Spector, Knouf, & Kanwisher, 2004; McCarthy, Puce, Gore, & Allison, 1997; **FIGURE 5.37**). Indeed, this brain area responds most strongly to upright faces, as we would perceive them in the normal environment (Kanwisher, Tong, & Nakayama, 1998). Other brain areas are sensitive to changes in faces, such as in facial expression and gaze direction. A face's emotional significance appears to activate the amygdala, which is involved in calculating potential danger (Adams, Gordon, Baird, Ambady, & Kleck, 2003; Adolphs, 2003).

In a series of studies, researchers found that people more quickly and accurately recognize angry facial expressions than happy ones (Becker, Kenrick, Neuberg, Blackwell, & Smith, 2007). In addition, the researchers found that most people recognize anger more quickly on a man's face than on a woman's, and they found the reverse for happiness. The researchers think these results are due partly to people's beliefs that men express anger more often than women do and that women express happiness more often than men do, but they also think that female and male facial features drive the effect. Bushy eyebrows low on the face, for example, will more likely be perceived as an expression of anger, and men typically have bushier and lower eyebrows than women. Evolutionary psychology posits an advantage to the detection of angry faces, and given that men in every society commit most violent crimes, it is adaptive to be especially fast and accurate at recognizing angry male faces. Thus facial recognition supports the idea that the mind is adaptive.

Men and women also differ in their abilities to recognize the faces of people they have previously encountered. Females of all ages more accurately recognize faces (e.g., Lewin & Herlitz, 2002). Perhaps the most surprising finding is that girls and women are most accurate when recognizing female faces, an example of the *own-sex bias.* Females' ability to recognize female faces better than male faces, like their better performance than males on all measures of face recognition, has been replicated cross-culturally with both participants and face stimuli from Sweden and Bangladesh (Herlitz & Kabir, 2006; Rehman & Herlitz, 2006).

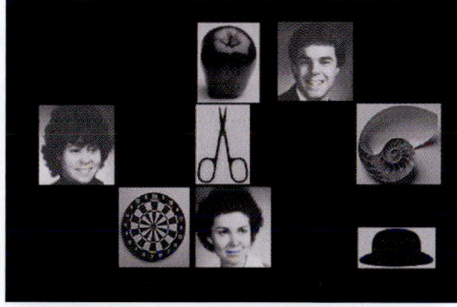

Participants were presented with an array of nonobjects or objects.

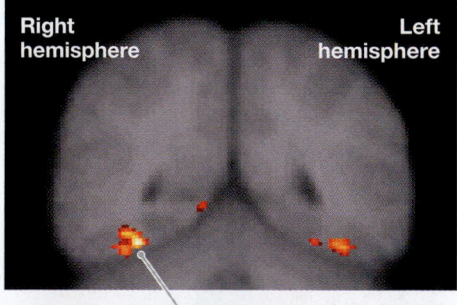

Right hemisphere   Left hemisphere

The visual perception of faces activated an area of the brain known as the fusiform gyrus. The right hemisphere responded more strongly than the left, especially when faces were presented among objects.

FIGURE 5.37 Perceiving Faces Brain imaging shows increased activity in the right hemisphere when faces are viewed.

FIGURE 5.38 Try for Yourself: The Thatcher Illusion

These two inverted pictures of Margaret Thatcher look normal. Turn your book upside down to reveal a different perspective.

Result: Inversion of the whole face interferes with the perception of the individual components. This effect implies that we pay most attention to the eyes and mouth; as long as they are oriented correctly, the rest of the face appears normal even if it is not.

FIGURE 5.39 Scientific Method: Face Recognition

Hypothesis: People are better at recognizing faces from their own racial or ethnic group than from other racial or ethnic groups.

Research Method:

1 Black and white participants were shown a series of photographs of black and white faces, and the neural activity in their fusiform facial areas was recorded.

2 The participants were then shown those faces again, mixed in with a larger set of photographs to determine which faces they could remember seeing, and the neural activity in their fusiform facial areas was recorded.

Results: Black and white participants were better at recognizing same-race faces, but this finding was significantly greater in the white participants. There was significantly greater activation in the fusiform gyrus when viewing same-race faces.

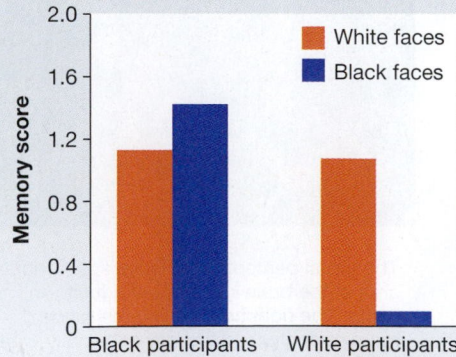 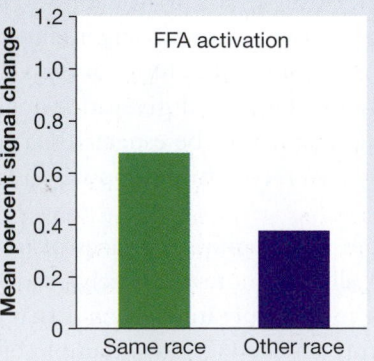

Conclusion: We attend to and more accurately encode information about the faces of people whose race is the same as our own. Brain imaging supports the behavioral results, showing more activity in the fusiform face area when people view same-race faces.

People of both sexes have a surprisingly hard time recognizing faces, especially unknown faces, that are upside down. We are much worse at this task than we are at recognizing other inverted objects. The inversion interferes with the way people perceive the relations among facial features (Hancock, Bruce, & Burton, 2000). For instance, if the eyebrows are bushier than usual, this facial characteristic is obvious if the face is upright but not detectable when the face is inverted. One interesting example of the perceptual difficulties associated with inverted faces is evident in the Thatcher illusion, so called because the effect was first studied using photos of the former British prime minister Margaret Thatcher (Thompson, 1980; **FIGURE 5.38**).

At the social level, people are better at recognizing members of their own race or ethnic group than members of other races or ethnic groups. This tendency may occur because people have more exposure to people with their own race or ethnicity. Indeed, in the United States, where whites greatly outnumber blacks, whites are much better at recognizing white faces than black faces (Brigham & Malpass, 1985). An interdisciplinary team of social and cognitive psychologists sought to examine the neural correlates of this same-race effect (Golby, Gabrieli, Chiao, & Eberhardt, 2001). They asked white and black participants to remember pictures of faces from both racial groups along with pictures of objects (e.g., antique radios) as a control comparison. They found significantly greater activation in a region of the fusiform gyrus when people viewed same-race faces compared with other-race faces, especially for whites, and such activation was associated with better recognition of same-race faces (**FIGURE 5.39**). One reason this effect appears to be smaller for blacks might be that, as minorities in the United States, they have more exposure to white faces than whites have to black faces. Thus cultural context may affect the perception of faces

Table 5.3 Research on Face Perception and Face Identification

Level of Analysis	Researchers	Findings
Biological	Grill-Spector, Knouf, & Kanwisher, 2004; McCarthy, Puce, Gore, & Allison, 1997	Fusiform gyrus shows more activity in perceiving own-race faces than in perceiving other-race faces.
Individual	Lewin & Herlitz, 2002	Generally, females recognize faces better than males do, and females recognize female faces better than male faces.
Social	Becker, Kenrick, Neuberg, Blackwell, & Smith, 2007	Most people are faster at recognizing anger than happiness and are faster at recognizing anger on men's faces and happiness on women's faces.
Cultural	Herlitz & Kabir, 2006; Rehman & Herlitz, 2006	Swedes and Bangledeshis better identified faces from their own races/cultures (*own-race bias*).

as well as other objects. (For a review of research on face perception and face identification, see **TABLE 5.3**.)

REGAINING VISION BY FIXING THE EYES People see with their brains, not with their eyes (Enns, 2005). Most people who become blind later in life have lost sensory input from the retina, yet they still remember what objects look like and can visualize them. What happens when we repair the visual system after someone has lost his or her sight? Does perception return to the way it was before? With advances in medical treatment, many people who have become blind because of illness or injury are now regaining their sight. For instance, Nogaye Gueye, a 58-year-old woman from Senegal, lost her sight because of cataracts (**FIGURE 5.40A**). Volunteer surgeons from Sight Savers International performed a 20-minute procedure that restored her vision. In a BBC interview, Gueye said she had not wanted to get too excited, in case the surgery did not work. Indeed, when the doctors first took the bandage off, she could see only blue. While traveling home, she made out objects such as palm trees and cars. But then her sight slowly returned: "During the day, I gradually began to see all the other colors again. I was very excited now. The first thing I wanted to look at was my nieces and nephews, and to see their small children for the first time." Gueye's vision returned to normal, but she had been blind for only 2 of her 58 years. What would restored sight be like for a person who had been blind much longer?

Michael May lost his eyesight in a chemical explosion when he was three and a half years old. In March 2000, at age 43, he underwent an experimental procedure: a cornea and stem cell transplant on his right eye (the other eye was lost entirely in the explosion). Prior studies had found that people whose sight was restored after many years had great difficulty using visual information. The psychological scientists Ione Fine, Donald MacLeod, and their colleagues followed May's progress and tested his visual capacities (Fine et al., 2003). Two years after the surgery, May was able to detect color and motion, but he still had great difficulty with other visual tasks, especially those that required higher-level constructive processes, such as using depth cues and identifying objects (**FIGURE 5.40B**). Indeed, he had special difficulty recognizing faces; he could not recognize his wife or children by sight alone, and he had a hard time judging if someone was male or female by looking at the person's face. A brain imaging study showed that brain areas that normally react robustly to both faces and objects were not at all active for May. But the brain regions that process motion reacted similarly to the same brain regions in typical research participants. Motion, however, is still a strange experience for him.

(a)

(b)

FIGURE 5.40 Advances in Treatment
(a) Nogaye Gueye, who had been blind for two years, regained her vision following 20-minute cataract-removal surgery. (b) Michael May, pictured here playing soccer with his son, became blind at age three; his vision in one eye was partially restored by corneal and stem cell implants.

May had been an expert skier, having learned through verbal instructions. After the surgery, he skied with his eyes closed because the overwhelming sensation of motion gave him a frightening sense that he was going to crash. He also became more nervous about crossing roads, which he used to do without much thought. So was having his sight restored a good or bad experience for May? According to May, not a day goes by that he does not appreciate the return of his sight.

May's case provides some interesting insights into visual perception. The brain is fine-tuned through experience: If a cortical region is not used in perception, it ceases to develop normally. Perhaps most interesting is how May's brain had adapted to his loss of vision, so that he was highly successful in navigating his environment using his other senses. Regaining his sight added new joys, but his way of interacting with the world was thrown into turmoil by the novel experience of vision. Even though his progress is slow, May continues to develop better vision with hard work. This outcome demonstrates that brain plasticity continues well into adulthood. It will be interesting to observe May's progress over the coming years as his brain continues to learn how to use sensory cues effectively.

Can someone who has been totally blind since birth create art that resembles the visual experiences of sighted people? Most congenitally blind people cannot render things realistically, but one exceptional individual has never had vision but has received acclaim for his realistic paintings. Born in a poor Turkish family, Esref Armagan received no formal education or art training, yet he taught himself to write and draw. Instead of using a brush, he paints with his hands. To paint a portrait, he asks a sighted person to outline the contours of the person he is painting from a photograph of that person. He then turns the paper over to feel the outlines of the tracing and transfers what he feels to another paper, which he then paints. The psychologist John Kennedy has studied Armagan's unusual techniques and verified his artistic abilities (**FIGURE 5.41**).

FIGURE 5.41 Painting by a Uniquely Talented Blind Artist Born totally blind, Esref Armagan is able to paint scenes, such as this landscape, that he has never seen.

Depth Perception Is Important for Locating Objects

One of the visual system's most important tasks is to locate objects in space. Without this capacity, we would find it difficult to navigate in and interact with the world. One of the most enduring questions in psychological research is how we are able to construct a three-dimensional mental representation of the visual world from two-dimensional retinal input. That we can see depth in a photograph illustrates this point. A three-dimensional array of objects creates exactly the same image on the retina that a photograph of the same array of objects does. Despite this inherent ambiguity, we do not confuse pictures with the scenes they depict. We use the ambiguous nature of depth perception when we look at photographs, movies, and television images. We are able to perceive depth in these two-dimensional patterns because the brain applies the same rules or mechanisms that it uses to work out the spatial relations between objects in the three-dimensional world. To do this, the brain rapidly and automatically exploits certain prior assumptions it has about the nature of the relationship between two-dimensional image cues and three-dimensional world structure. Among these assumptions are cues that help the visual system perceive depth. These depth cues can be divided into those available from both eyes together, called **binocular depth cues,** and those available from each eye alone, called **monocular depth cues.**

BINOCULAR DEPTH PERCEPTION One of the most important cues to depth perception is the **binocular disparity** (or *retinal disparity*) caused by the distance between humans' two eyes. Because each eye has a slightly different view of the

binocular depth cues Cues of depth perception that arise from the fact that people have two eyes.

monocular depth cues Cues of depth perception that are available to each eye alone.

binocular disparity A cue of depth perception that is caused by the distance between a person's eyes, which provides each eye with a slightly different image.

world, the brain has access to two different but overlapping retinal images. The brain uses the disparity between these two retinal images to compute distances to nearby objects (**FIGURE 5.42**).

The ability to determine an object's depth based on that object's projections to each eye is called *stereoscopic vision*. In 1838, the physicist and inventor Charles Wheatstone created the stereoscope, a device that enables a viewer to perceive depth in a pair of two-dimensional pictures, each taken from a slightly different perspective. The resulting three-dimensional image is due to the brain's reconciling the disparate image received by each eye. Wheatstone used the stereoscope to demonstrate that depth perception is influenced by binocular disparity and thus that stereoscopic vision is an important cue for an object's depth. The stereoscope became a popular parlor amusement. In 1849, David Brewster, the physicist who invented the kaleidoscope, created the autostereogram—an optical illusion that turns specially designed pairs of two-dimensional images into three-dimensional images by presenting them in an unfocused manner (thus delivering a slightly different image to each eye; see **FIGURE 5.43**).

MONOCULAR DEPTH PERCEPTION Although binocular disparity is an important cue for depth perception, it is useful only for objects relatively close to us. Furthermore, we can perceive depth even with one eye closed, because of monocular depth cues. Artists routinely use these cues to create a sense of depth, so they are also called *pictorial depth cues*. The Renaissance painter, sculptor, architect, and engineer Leonardo da Vinci first identified many of these cues, which include:

- *Occlusion:* A near object occludes (blocks) an object that is farther away.

- *Relative size:* Far-off objects project a smaller retinal image than close objects do.

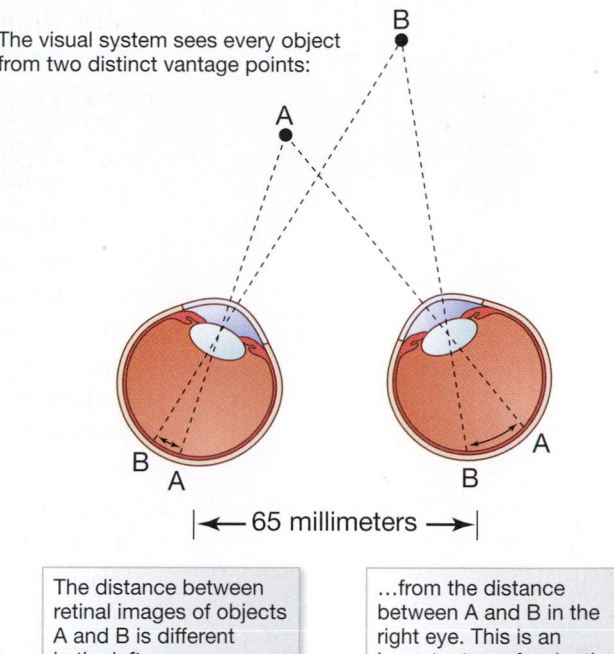

The visual system sees every object from two distinct vantage points:

|← 65 millimeters →|

The distance between retinal images of objects A and B is different in the left eye…

…from the distance between A and B in the right eye. This is an important cue for depth.

FIGURE 5.42 Binocular Disparity To demonstrate your own binocular disparity, hold one of your index fingers out in front of you and close first one eye and then the other. Your finger appears to move because each eye, due to its position relative to the object in question (i.e., the finger), has a unique retinal image.

FIGURE 5.43 Try for Yourself: Autostereogram

Hold the picture on the left close to your eyes and stare straight ahead. Try to relax your eyes and let them look through the book to an imaginary point in the distance. Slowly move the book away from you, still fixating on that imaginary point. Try to allow the doubled images to fall on top of each other and keep them there.

 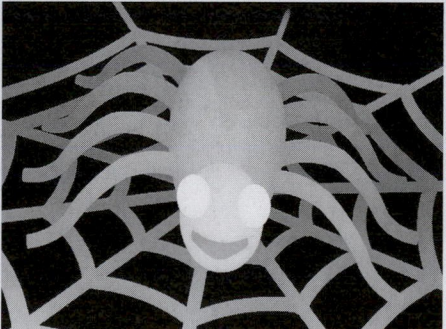

Result: The result of superimposing the images should be a three-dimensional effect. The picture on the right is the embedded image. If you do not see it in a few minutes, stop and try again later. Each eye is focusing at a different depth plane, so when the images are superimposed they appear to "pop out" in depth.

- *Familiar size:* We know how large familiar objects are, so we can tell how far away they are by the size of their retinal images.
- *Linear perspective:* Parallel lines appear to converge in the distance.
- *Texture gradient:* As a uniformly textured surface recedes, its texture continuously becomes denser.
- *Position relative to horizon:* All else being equal, objects below the horizon that appear higher in the visual field are perceived as being farther away. Objects above the horizon that appear lower in the visual field are perceived as being farther away.

Can you identify these cues to depth in **FIGURE 5.44**, Edvard Munch's painting *Evening on Karl Johan Street* (circa 1892)?

Culture Influences Perception

It may seem obvious that cues to depth can give rise to the perception of three dimensions on a flat canvas. But psychologists have wondered if these cues have to be learned or whether they emerge automatically as a by-product of normal three-dimensional perception. One problem in investigating questions like this one is that researchers need to find people who from young ages have not had the sort of experiences that would teach them how to interpret pictorial depth. Most people have regular access to pictures and live in a "carpentered world," where buildings and other structures have straight edges and parallel lines. If you grew up in a carpentered world, as most readers of this book probably did, you have had a lifetime of experience learning that, for example, parallel lines seem to converge in the distance. The *Mueller-Lyer illusion,* one of the visual illusions most frequently employed in psychological research, provides a way of answering

FIGURE 5.44 Pictorial Depth Cues

Occlusion
The tree blocks the building behind it.

Relative size
The people at the front of the picture are larger than the people toward the middle and back of the picture.

Familiar size
We know about how tall the man in the middle is, so we can guess how far away he must be.

Linear perspective
The lines of the street and of the buildings converge toward the horizon.

Texture gradient
The texture of the buildings gets denser as the buildings recede into the distance.

Position relative to horizon
The figures get higher toward the horizon line—that is, the farther away they are.

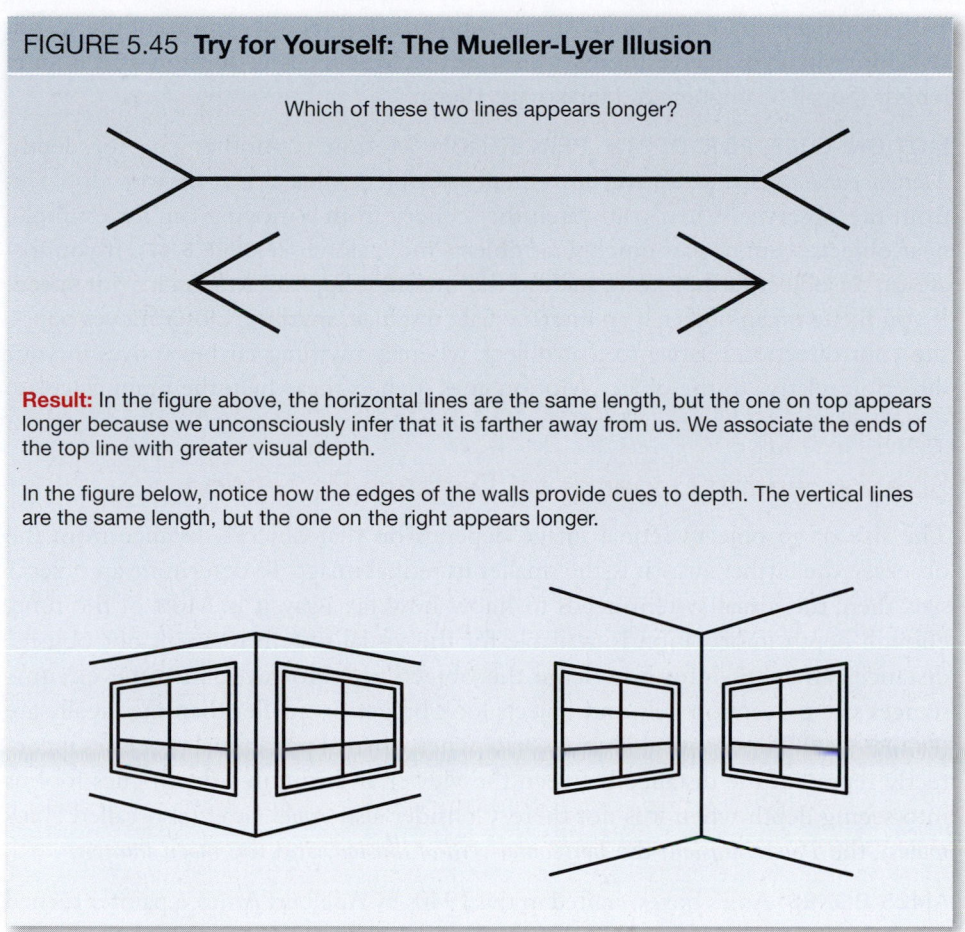

FIGURE 5.45 **Try for Yourself: The Mueller-Lyer Illusion**

Which of these two lines appears longer?

Result: In the figure above, the horizontal lines are the same length, but the one on top appears longer because we unconsciously infer that it is farther away from us. We associate the ends of the top line with greater visual depth.

In the figure below, notice how the edges of the walls provide cues to depth. The vertical lines are the same length, but the one on the right appears longer.

the question of whether people automatically use pictures' depth cues or whether they learn how to use them (**FIGURE 5.45**).

Do people who live in areas of the world where there are few or no buildings with straight edges, and who have little or no experience with pictures, recognize pictorial depth cues? Do they see the Mueller-Lyer illusion the same way that people who live in carpentered worlds do? To find out, William Hudson (1967) drew a series of stimuli with different depth cues (**FIGURE 5.46**), and then presented these stimuli to schooled and unschooled black and white South Africans. The participants who had attended school were better at identifying the objects in the pictures than those who never attended school, and the findings were the same for both races. This investigation was repeated with the Baganda people of Uganda (Kilbride & Robbins, 1969). The researchers found that Bagandas who lived in urban areas correctly identified more of the objects and animals in the drawings than those who lived in rural areas; among those who lived in rural areas, those who were more acculturated to the larger society identified more elements in the pictures correctly than those who were less acculturated. The researchers concluded that cultural experiences are important factors in the acquisition and development of visual-perceptual skills.

Given the finding that people in different cultures were not equally good at identifying the objects in the pictures drawn by Hudson (1967), what would you predict about cultural differences in susceptibility to the Mueller-Lyer illusion? Cross-cultural studies have shown that people who grew up in and live in uncarpentered worlds, and who have had little experience

FIGURE 5.46 **Drawings Used to Investigate Depth Cues** These are two of the drawings used by Hudson (1967) and Kilbride and Robbins (1969) to study if depth cues are learned and therefore dependent on cultural experiences. The converging lines in the right-hand drawings provide pictorial cues to depth that are missing from the drawings on the left.

FIGURE 5.47 Motion Parallax Near objects seem to pass us more quickly in the opposite direction of our movement. Objects farther away seem to move more slowly.

FIGURE 5.48 Distance Perception This picture, by Rebecca Robinson, captures what appears to be a tiny Sarah Heatherton standing on James Heatherton's head. This illusion occurs because the photo does not convey the hill on which Sarah is standing and so fails to present depth information.

FIGURE 5.49 The Ames Box Ames played with depth cues to create size illusions. For example, as illustrated here, he made a diagonally cut room appear rectangular by using crooked windows and floor tiles. When one child stands in a near corner and another (of similar height) stands in a far corner, the room creates the illusion that they are equidistant from the viewer; therefore, the closer child looks like a giant compared to the child farther away.

with modern technologies and with two-dimensional representations of the world, will more likely perceive the two lines in the Mueller-Lyer illusion as the same length (Segall, Campbell, & Herskovits, 1966).

MOTION CUES FOR DEPTH PERCEPTION Motion is another cue for depth. *Motion parallax* is the relative movements of objects that are at various distances from the observer. When you watch the scenery from a moving car, for example, near objects seem to pass quickly, far objects more slowly (**FIGURE 5.47**). If you fixate on an object farther away, such as the moon, it appears to match your speed. If you fixate on an object at an intermediate distance, anything closer moves opposite your direction relative to that object, whereas anything farther moves in your direction relative to the object. Motion cues such as these help the brain calculate which objects are closer and which are farther away.

Size Perception Depends on Distance Perception

The size of an object's retinal image depends on that object's distance from the observer; the farther away it is, the smaller its retinal image. To determine an object's size, then, the visual system needs to know how far away it is. Most of the time, enough depth information is available for the visual system to work out objects' distances and thus infer how large the objects are. However, in some circumstances size perception fails, and objects look bigger or smaller than they really are (**FIGURE 5.48**). These optical illusions arise when normal perceptual processes incorrectly represent the distance between the viewer and stimuli—depth cues fool us into seeing depth when it is not there. Consider also *Ames boxes* (also called *Ames rooms*), the *Ponzo illusion,* the *horizontal-vertical illusion,* and the *moon illusion.*

AMES BOXES Ames boxes, crafted in the 1940s by Adelbert Ames, a painter turned psychologist, present powerful depth illusions. These boxes elaborate on the Victorian trick in which a person looking through a peephole would see a furnished room and then open the door to find the room empty—with a dollhouse room nailed to the door. Inside the Ames boxes, rooms play with linear perspective and other distance cues. One such room makes a far corner appear the same distance away as a near corner. Normally, a nearby child projects a larger retinal image than a child farther away, but does not appear larger because the perceptual system takes depth into account when assessing size. If the depth cues are wrong, so the child appears farther away than he is—as in one Ames box—the disproportionate size of his image on your retina makes the child look huge (**FIGURE 5.49**).

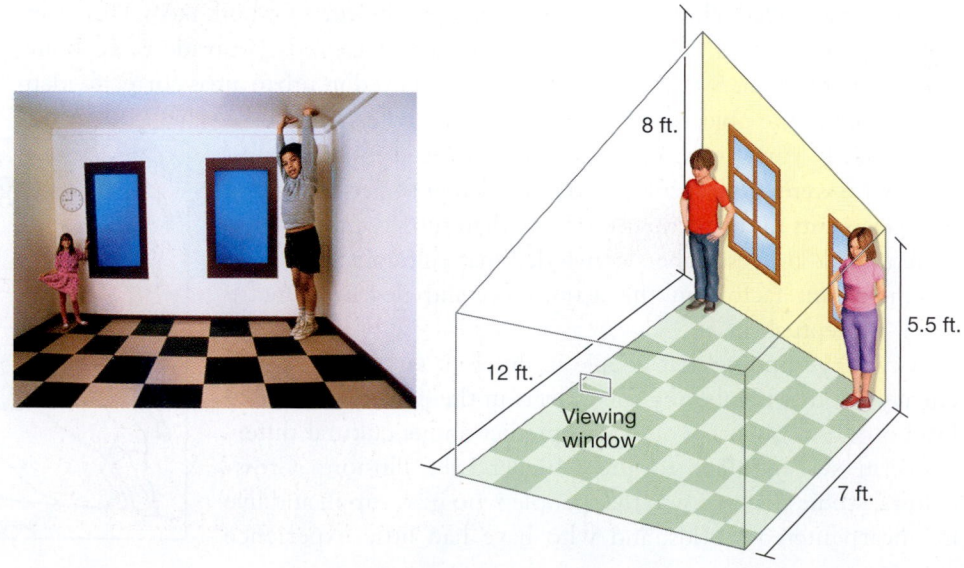

THE PONZO ILLUSION The Ponzo illusion (**FIGURE 5.50**), first described by Mario Ponzo in 1913, is another classic example of a size/distance illusion. The common explanation for this effect is that monocular depth cues make the two-dimensional figure seem three-dimensional (Rock, 1984). As noted above, parallel lines appear to converge in the distance. Here, the two lines drawn to look like railroad tracks receding in the distance trick your brain into thinking they are parallel. Therefore, you perceive the two parallel lines in the center as if they are at different distances and thus different in size when they actually are the same size. This illusion shows how much we rely on depth perception to gauge size—the brain defaults to using depth cues even when depth is absent.

HORIZONTAL/VERTICAL ILLUSION The horizontal/vertical illusion also demonstrates how our perceptions of the world may be inaccurate. In **FIGURE 5.51**, does the top hat appear taller than it is wide or wider than it is tall? The exact cause of this well-known illusion has been debated. According to one theory, the horizontal line looks relatively shorter because our visual field is wider than it is tall. Another theory suggests that we unconsciously interpret the vertical dimension as receding in the distance and thus being longer than it actually is. A third theory states that we judge vertical distances as longer than equal horizontal ones because our eyes rest in horizontal sockets, so looking up and down is more effortful than looking side to side.

THE MOON ILLUSION A full moon looks much larger when it is near the horizon than when it is overhead (**FIGURE 5.52**). This effect is an illusion—the moon remains the same size and distance from the earth, and the image on your retina is the same size whether the moon is on the horizon or overhead. The most common explanation for this illusion is that when the moon is near the horizon, several depth cues indicate that it is really very far away. When the moon is overhead, no such cues are available, so the moon looks as if it is closer to the earth. The logic of this explanation is similar to that offered for the Ponzo illusion: The horizon moon looks farther away than the overhead moon, yet since they are really the same distance away, they create identical images on the retina. The brain can reconcile this discrepancy only by assuming that the horizon moon is larger than the overhead moon. Another theory says that since we unconsciously believe the sky is like an inverted soup bowl, we judge the moon to be larger at the horizon because we unconsciously assume it is farther away. All the many possible explanations agree that perceived distance is the source of the moon illusion.

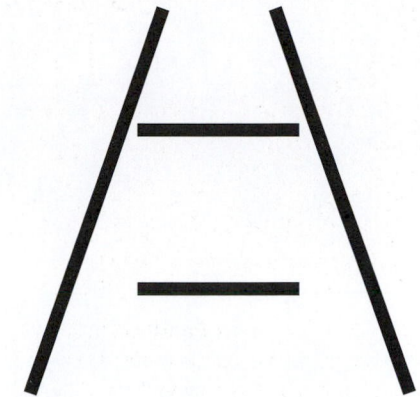

FIGURE 5.50 The Ponzo Illusion The two horizontal lines appear to be different sizes but are the same length.

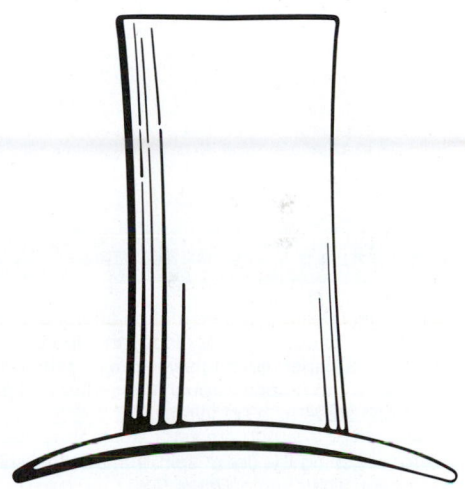

FIGURE 5.51 The Horizontal/Vertical Illusion This top hat appears much taller than it is wide, yet its height and width are the same length.

(b)

(a)

FIGURE 5.52 The Moon Illusion In these paintings, the artist Henri Daumier emphasized how the moon looks larger **(a)** when it is near the horizon than **(b)** when it is overhead. We infer the position of the moon in these paintings from its size.

Motion Perception Has Internal and External Cues

We know how motion can cue depth perception, but how does the brain perceive motion? One answer is that we have neurons specialized for detecting movement—they fire when movement occurs. But how does the brain know what is moving? If you look out a window and see a car driving past a house, how does your brain know the car is moving and not the house? Consider the dramatic case of M.P., a German woman who developed selective loss of motion perception following damage to secondary visual areas of the brain—areas critical for motion perception. M.P. saw the world as a series of snapshots rather than as a moving image (Zihl, von Cramon, & Mai, 1983). Pouring tea, she would see the liquid frozen in air and be surprised when her cup overflowed. Before crossing a street, she might spot a car far away, but when she tried to cross, that car would be right in front of her. M.P. had a unique deficit—she could perceive objects and colors but not continuous movement. This section considers three phenomena that offer insights into how the visual system perceives motion; *motion aftereffects, compensation for head and eye motion,* and *stroboscopic motion perception.*

MOTION AFTEREFFECTS Motion aftereffects occur when you gaze at a moving image for a prolonged period and then look at a stationary scene. You experience a momentary impression that the new scene is moving in the opposite direction from the moving image. This illusion is also called the *waterfall effect,* because if you stare at a waterfall and then turn away, the scenery you are now looking at will seem to move upward for a moment. Aftereffects are strong evidence that motion-sensitive neurons exist in the brain. The theory behind this illusion combines sensory adaptation with neural specificity. The visual cortex has neurons that respond to movement in a given direction. When you stare at a moving stimulus long enough, these direction-specific neurons begin to adapt to the motion, becoming fatigued and therefore less sensitive. If the stimulus is suddenly removed, the motion detectors that respond to all the other directions are more active than the fatigued motion detectors. Thus you see the new scene moving in the other direction. (You can experience this illusion by following the instructions in **FIGURE 5.53**.)

COMPENSATORY FACTORS The existence of motion-sensitive neurons does not completely explain motion perception. How do you know, for instance, whether an object is moving or whether you, or your eyes, are moving? Images move across your retina all the time and you do not always perceive them as moving. Each

FIGURE 5.53 Try for Yourself: Spiral Aftereffects

This spiral design creates motion aftereffects when you view it spinning for approximately 30 seconds. To see the effect, copy the figure and cut out the copy along the outermost curve. Unbend a paper clip and stick one end through the middle of the figure so that you can spin it, or stick a thumbtack through the center and put the sharp end into the eraser end of a pencil that can serve as a spinning stick.

After watching the figure spin, immediately shift your gaze to a photo, such as the one of Margaret Thatcher in Figure 5.38.

Result: If the spiral appeared to expand as it spun, the photo will appear to shrink. These effects will be created totally by your visual system.

The visual system detects movement in two ways:

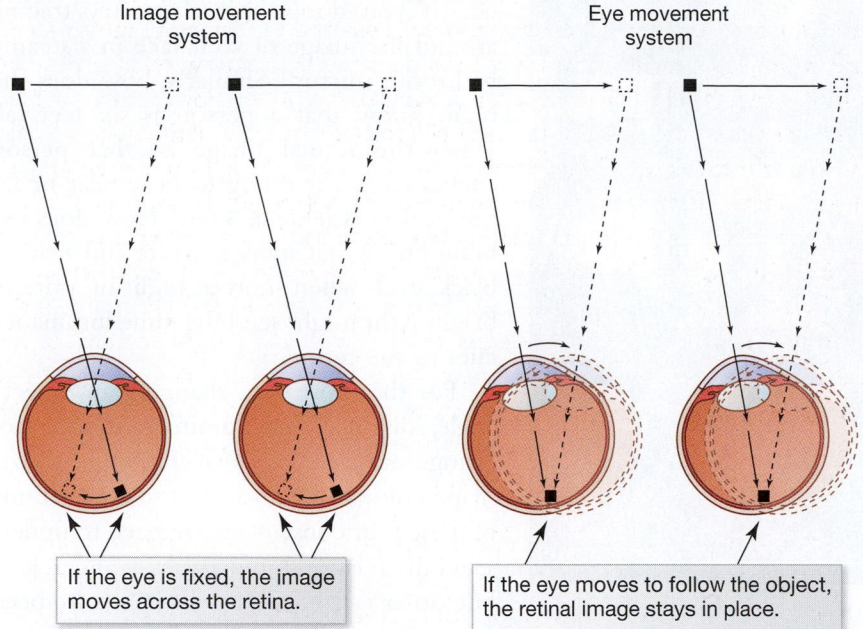

FIGURE 5.54 **Perceiving Movement**

Image movement system

Eye movement system

If the eye is fixed, the image moves across the retina.

If the eye moves to follow the object, the retinal image stays in place.

slight blink or eye movement creates a new image on the retina. Why is it that every time you move your eye, or your head, the images you see do not jump around? One explanation is that the brain calculates an object's perceived movements by monitoring the movement of the eyes, and perhaps also of the head, as they track a moving object. In addition, motion detectors track an image's motion across the retina, as the receptors in the retina fire one after the other (**FIGURE 5.54**).

STROBOSCOPIC MOVEMENT Movies are made up of still-frame images, presented one after the other to create the illusion of motion pictures. This phenomenon is based on stroboscopic movement, a perceptual illusion that occurs when two or more slightly different images are presented in rapid succession. The Gestalt psychologist Max Wertheimer conducted experiments in 1912 by flashing, at different intervals, two vertical lines placed close together. He discovered that when the interval was less than 30 milliseconds, subjects thought the two lines were flashed simultaneously. When the interval was greater than 200 milliseconds, they saw two lines being flashed at different times. Between those times, movement illusions occurred: When the interval was about 60 milliseconds, the line appeared to jump from one place to another; at slightly longer intervals, the line appeared to move continuously—a phenomenon called *phi movement*. (You can create stroboscopic movement by using **FIGURE 5.55**.)

Perceptual Constancies Are Based on Ratio Relationships

As discussed above, illusions occur when the brain creates inaccurate representations of stimuli. In the opposite situation, **perceptual constancy,** the brain correctly perceives objects as constant despite sensory data that could lead it to think otherwise. Consider your image in the mirror. What you see in the mirror might look like

perceptual constancy People correctly perceive objects as constant in their shape, size, color, and lightness, despite raw sensory data that could mislead perception.

FIGURE 5.55 **How Moving Pictures Work** This static series would appear transformed if you spun the wheel. When the slightly different images were presented in rapid succession, stroboscopic movement would tell your brain that you were watching a moving horse.

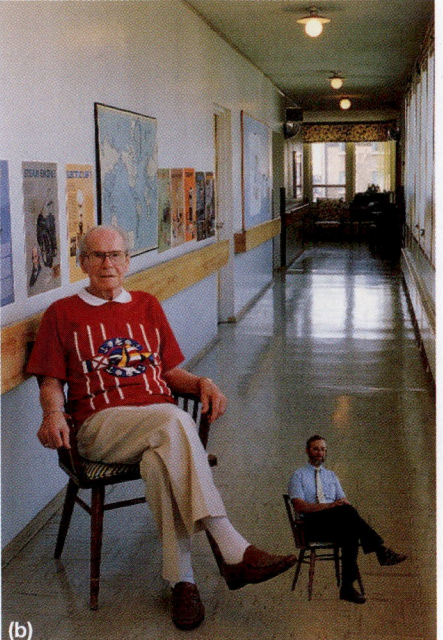

FIGURE 5.56 Perceptual Constancy
When you look at each of these photos, your retinal image of the bearded man is the same. In **(a),** depth cues make him look farther away. In **(b),** the absence of depth cues make him look smaller.

it is your actual size, but the image is much smaller than the parts of you being reflected. (If you doubt this claim, try tracing around the image of your face in a steamy bathroom mirror.) Similarly, how does the brain know that a person is six feet tall when the retinal image of that person changes size according to how near or far the person is (**FIGURE 5.56**)? How does the brain know that snow is white and a tire is black, even when snow at night or a tire in bright light might send the same luminance cues to the retina?

For the most part, changing an object's angle, distance, or illumination does not change our perception of that object's size, shape, color, or lightness. But to perceive any of these four constancies, we need to understand the relationship between it and at least one other factor. For *size constancy,* we need to know how far away the object is from us. For *shape constancy,* we need to know from what angle we are seeing the object. For *color constancy,* we need to compare the wavelengths of light reflected from the object with those reflected from its background. Likewise, for *lightness constancy,* we need to know how much light is being reflected from the object and from its background. In each case, the brain computes a ratio based on the relative magnitude rather than relying on each sensation's absolute magnitude. The perceptual system's ability to make relative judgments allows it to maintain constancy across various perceptual contexts. Although their precise mechanisms are unknown, these constancies illustrate that perceptual systems are tuned to detect changes from baseline conditions, not just to respond to sensory inputs.

By studying how illusions work, many perceptual psychologists have come to believe that the brain has built-in assumptions that influence perceptions. The vast majority of visual illusions appear to be beyond our conscious control—we cannot make ourselves not see illusions, even when we know they are not true representations of objects or events (**FIGURE 5.57**). Thus the visual system is a complex interplay of constancies, which allow us to see both a stable world and perceptual illusions that we cannot control.

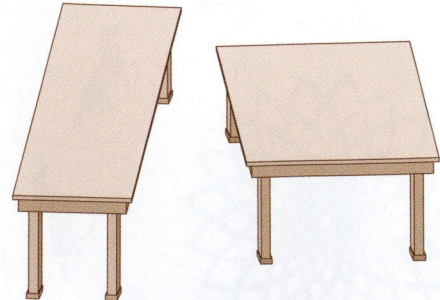

FIGURE 5.57 The Tabletop Illusion
Created by the psychologist Roger Shepard, this illusion demonstrates the brain's automatic perceptual processes. Even when we know the two tabletops are the same size and shape—even if we have traced one image and placed it on top of the other—perspective cues make us see them as different.

> ## SUMMING UP
>
> ### What Are the Basic Perceptual Processes?
>
> The perceptual system is stunningly intelligent. It takes ambiguous sensory information and constructs rich and meaningful experiences that allow us to navigate the world around us. All perception occurs in the brain, where various perceptual processes take incoming sensations and construct them into meaningful perceptions. Information first arrives in primary sensory regions, such as V1 for vision and A1 for audition, but multiple brain regions contribute to our unified perceptual experience. The perceptual system uses cues from the person's environment to help interpret sensory information. For instance, visual cues help provide information

about what objects are and where they are located, as well as information about depth and motion. Contemporary theorists emphasize that perceptions are not faithful reproductions of the physical world but rather are constructed through multiple processes that allow us to taste, smell, touch, hear, and see.

▶ MEASURING UP

1. Match each of the following monocular depth cues with its description: familiar size, linear perspective, occlusion, position relative to horizon, relative size, texture gradient.
   a. Parallel lines appear to converge in the distance.
   b. Near objects block those that are farther away.
   c. We use our knowledge of an object's size to judge the object's distance.
   d. Smaller objects are judged to be farther away.
   e. Uniform surfaces appear denser in the distance.
   f. Objects near the horizon are judged to be farther away.

2. What is binocular disparity?
   a. a disorder in which a person loses depth perception
   b. a cue to depth caused by the formation of a slightly different image in each eye
   c. the distance between our eyes
   d. the ability to see depth in a two-dimensional stimulus by defocusing our vision

3. Perceptual constancy _____.
   a. allows us to see objects as stable even when there are large fluctuations in the sensory information we receive
   b. allows us to understand how physical energy is transduced into neural activity
   c. is a misnomer because our perceptions are not constant
   d. was based on the idea that different parts of the brain underlie different perceptual experiences

CONCLUSION

Perceptual psychologists seek to understand how the brain translates elementary sensations into conscious perception. Our entire experience of the world relies on this translation process. Although perceiving seems effortless, it relies on numerous active processes that work together to construct our experience. Our senses gather information from relatively limited sources of physical energy. We hear few of the available sound waves, for example, and see only a small portion of the electromagnetic spectrum. But our experience does not feel limited, because our perceptual systems allow us to perform the tasks necessary for both survival and reproduction. After more than a century of research, scientists still cannot state definitely how perception works. No single theory or model successfully accounts for more than a fraction of perceptual phenomena. The workings of our perceptual systems have begun to yield to the concerted efforts of psychological scientists working at many levels of analysis, however. With the advent of new technologies for studying the brain, the urgency of these efforts has increased. Perhaps the twenty-first century will yield answers to two of humankind's most enduring questions: How do we know our world? And how are mental events realized in the brain's physical events?

■ CHAPTER SUMMARY

How Do We Sense Our Worlds?

- **Stimuli Must Be Coded to Be Understood by the Brain:** Stimuli reaching the receptors are converted to neural impulses through the process of transduction.

- **Psychophysics Relates Stimulus to Response:** By studying how people respond to different sensory levels, scientists can determine thresholds and perceived change (based on signal detection theory). Our sensory systems are tuned to both adapt to constant levels of stimulation and detect changes in our environment.

What Are the Basic Sensory Processes?

- **In Taste, Taste Buds Detect Chemicals:** The gustatory sense uses taste buds to respond to the chemical substances that produce at least five basic sensations: sweet, sour, salty, bitter, and umami (savory). The number and distribution of taste buds vary among individuals. Cultural taste preferences begin in the womb.

- **In Smell, the Nasal Cavity Gathers Odorants:** Receptors in the olfactory epithelium respond to chemicals and send signals to the olfactory bulb, in the brain. Females are much more accurate than males at detecting and identifying odors.

- **In Touch, Sensors in the Skin Detect Pressure, Temperature, and Pain:** The haptic sense relies on tactile stimulation to activate receptors for temperature, for sharp and dull pain, and for other sensations. Neural "gates" in the spinal cord also control pain. We can reduce pain perception by distraction, visualizing pain as more pleasant, being rested and relaxed, learning how to change brain activity that underlies pain perception, and taking drugs that interfere with the neural transmission of pain or render us unconscious.

- **In Hearing, the Ear Detects Sound Waves:** The size and shape of sound waves activate different hair cells in the inner ear. The receptors' responses depend on the sound waves' frequency and timing and on the activated receptors' location along the basilar membrane. Having two ears allows us to locate the source of a sound.

- **In Vision, the Eye Detects Light Waves:** Receptors (rods and cones) in the retina detect different forms of light waves. The lens helps the eye focus the stimulation on the retina for near versus far objects. Color is determined by wavelengths of light, which activate certain types of cones; by the absorption of wavelengths by objects; or by the mixing of wavelengths of light.

- **Humans and Animals Have Other Sensory Systems:** In addition to the five "basic" senses, humans and other animals have a kinesthetic sense (ability to judge where one's limbs are in space) and a vestibular sense (ability to compare one's bodily position to the upright position).

Some animals can use sound waves or disruptions in an electrical field to navigate.

- **The Evidence for Extrasensory Perception (ESP) Is Weak or Nonexistent:** Little or no good evidence supports the intriguing idea that some people have additional sensory systems that allow them to know what other people are thinking, for example, or to see through objects.

What Are the Basic Perceptual Processes?

- **Perception Occurs in the Brain:** Neural activity in the primary auditory cortex gives rise to hearing. Touch is mediated by neural activity in the primary somatosensory cortex. Vision results from a complex series of events in various areas of the brain but primarily in the occipital lobe.

- **Object Perception Requires Construction:** The Gestalt principles of stimulus organization account for some of the brain's perceptions of the world. Those perceptions involve cues about similarity, proximity, form, figure and background properties, and shading. Perception involves dual processes: bottom-up (sensory information) and top-down (expectations about what we will perceive).

- **Depth Perception Is Important for Locating Objects:** An object's pattern of stimulation on each of the two retinas (binocular) informs the brain about depth. The brain uses pictorial (monocular) cues—information about the object's appearance relative to the surroundings—to perceive depth and relative motion.

- **Culture Influences Perception:** People raised in a carpentered world—who have interacted with carpentered structures—are more prone to illusions based on cues such as linear perspective than are people raised in a noncarpentered world.

- **Size Perception Depends on Distance Perception:** Illusions of size can be created when the retinal size conflicts with the known size of objects in the visual field, as in the Ames, Ponzo, and moon illusions.

- **Motion Perception Has Internal and External Cues:** Motion detectors in the cortex respond to stimulation. The perceptual system establishes a stable frame of reference and relates object movement to it. Intervals of stimulation of repeated objects give the impression of continuous movement. Motion aftereffects, which are opposite in motion from things that have been observed, tell us about the fatigue of neural receptors that fire in response to motion in certain directions.

- **Perceptual Constancies Are Based on Ratio Relationships:** We create expectancies about the world that allow us to use information about the shape, size, color, and lightness of objects in their surroundings to achieve constancy.

■ KEY TERMS

1. Which answer accurately lists the order in which these structures participate in sensation and perception (except for smell)?
   a. specialized receptors, thalamus, cortex
   b. specialized receptors, cortex, thalamus
   c. cortex, specialized receptors, thalamus
   d. thalamus, specialized receptors, cortex

2. While listening to a string quartet, you find you can easily decipher the notes played by the violins, by the viola, and by the cello. When you focus on the viola, you find some of the notes especially loud and others barely discernable. Which of the following statements best describes your sensations of the quartet?
   a. You can decipher qualitative differences among the instruments because of the rate of firing of your sensory neurons, whereas you can make quantitative distinctions—recognizing variations in the notes' intensity—due to the involvement of specific sensory receptors.
   b. You can decipher quantitative differences among the instruments because of the rate of firing of your sensory neurons, whereas you can make qualitative distinctions—recognizing variations in the notes' intensity—due to the involvement of specific sensory receptors.
   c. You can decipher qualitative differences among the instruments because of the involvement of specific sensory receptors, whereas you can make quantitative distinctions—recognizing variations in the notes' intensity—due to the rate of firing of your sensory neurons.
   d. You can decipher quantitative differences among the instruments because of the involvement of specific sensory receptors, whereas you can make qualitative distinctions—recognizing variations in the notes' intensity—due to the rate of firing of your sensory neurons.

3. When the violist plays a solo, you cannot hear it. Which of the following statements is the most likely explanation?
   a. The differences in intensity between the notes of the solo are too small to be noticeable.
   b. The intensity of the auditory stimulation does not exceed the minimum threshold needed for you to detect a sensation.
   c. The quartet's playing has left your hearing receptors overstimulated and thus unable to process less intense stimuli.

4. Imagine you have a steady, radiating pain across your lower back. No matter how you position yourself, you cannot make the pain go away. Select the answer choices most relevant to this type of pain. More than one choice may be correct.
   a. activated by chemical changes in tissue
   b. activated by strong physical pressure of temperature extremes
   c. fast fibers
   d. myelinated axons
   e. nonmyelinated axons
   f. slow fibers

5. A one-year-old girl skins her knees on a rough sidewalk. The girl cries in pain. Which of the following interventions will most likely calm her?
   a. Promising to give her a piece of candy if she stops crying.
   b. Quickly cleaning and bandaging the skinned knees.
   c. Looking intently into her eyes and saying, "Let's take some deep breaths together. Ready. . . . Breathe in. . . . Now breathe out."
   d. Directing the girl's hand on a quick touching tour of the nearby environment and saying things such as "Feel this tree's rough bark. Touch the grass; it tickles. Feel how smooth this rock is!"

6. After hours of waiting, a bird watcher hears the call of rare bird species. The bird watcher instinctively turns his head about 45 degrees to the left and sees the bird. Which of the following statements best describes how the bird watcher knew where to turn his head?
   a. The call reached the bird watcher's left ear before it reached his right ear; the call was less intense in the bird watcher's right ear than in his left ear.
   b. The call reached the bird watcher's left ear before it reached his right ear; the call was less intense in the bird watcher's left ear than in his right ear.
   c. The call reached the bird watcher's right ear before it reached his left ear; the call was less intense in the bird watcher's right ear than in his left ear.
   d. The call reached the bird watcher's right ear before it reached his left ear; the call was less intense in the bird watcher's left ear than in his right ear.

7. In which lobe of the brain (frontal, occipital, parietal, temporal) does each of the following sensory cortices reside?
   a. primary auditory cortex
   b. primary somatosensory cortex
   c. primary visual cortex

8. Imagine you are preparing to conduct a brain imaging study of visual processing. Which pathway—dorsal or ventral—do you hypothesize will be activated by each of the following experimental tasks?
   a. Deciding which of two objects is farther away.
   b. Describing an object's color.
   c. Describing a silhouette's shape.
   d. Naming an object.
   e. Selecting which two of three objects are closest together.

PSYCHOLOGY AND SOCIETY

1. Spend a few minutes reviewing "Critical Thinking Skill: Seeking Disconfirming Evidence" (Chapter 3), and then create a 2 × 2 chart for the question *Does ESP exist?* Use information from the chapter, from Internet searches, and/or from peer-reviewed psychology literature to complete the cells of the chart. Based on your analysis of the evidence, write a brief justification for your position.

2. Which sense do you think it would be most difficult to live without? Why? Do you think it would be more or less challenging to lose that sense at birth, at a young age, or later in life? Why? If it were possible to regain that sense at some point in the future, what would be the arguments for or against doing so? Your response should reflect an understanding of how each of the senses helps people navigate the physical world. To start thinking about these questions, revisit the sections in this chapter that discuss the uses of cochlear implants and of surgery to restore partial or full vision.

The answer key for all the Measuring Up exercises and the Practice Tests can be found at the back of the book.

Learning

THE PERSON WHO ARGUABLY HAD THE GREATEST INFLUENCE on contemporary psychological science started out as a novelist. Burrhus Frederick (B. F.) Skinner was inspired to pursue writing during his senior year in college after the poet Robert Frost read some of Skinner's work and provided encouraging comments. After many months spent toiling away in his parents' attic, with measly results, Skinner began to contemplate alternative careers. He had wanted to be a novelist so that he could explore large questions about the human condition, but Skinner had always been a bit socially awkward and aloof and did not have the insight into other people's emotions that we associate with great novelists. As a novelist, he could describe people's actions, but this did not help him gain the true understanding he sought into why people act the ways they do. To pursue his intellectual interests in the human condition, particularly in human behavior, Skinner considered a career in

How Did the Behavioral Study of Learning Develop?
- Behavioral Responses Are Conditioned
- Phobias and Addictions Have Learned Components
- Classical Conditioning Involves More Than Events Occurring at the Same Time
- Critical Thinking Skill: Recognizing and Avoiding Inappropriate Association Effects in Reasoning

How Does Operant Conditioning Differ from Classical Conditioning?
- Reinforcement Increases Behavior

- Both Reinforcement and Punishment Can Be Positive or Negative
- Operant Conditioning Is Influenced by Schedules of Reinforcement
- Biology and Cognition Influence Operant Conditioning
- The Value of Reinforcement Follows Economic Principles

How Does Watching Others Affect Learning?
- Learning Can Be Passed On through Cultural Transmission
- Learning Can Occur through Observation

- Animals and Humans Imitate Others
- Critical Thinking Skill: Avoiding the Association of Events with Other Events That Occur at the Same Time

What Is the Biological Basis of Learning?
- Dopamine Activity Underlies Reinforcement
- Habituation and Sensitization Are Simple Models of Learning
- Long-Term Potentiation Is a Candidate for the Neural Basis of Learning

psychology, though he had not taken a single psychology course in college. He became convinced that psychology was his calling after reading the psychologist John B. Watson's book *Behaviorism* (1924) and the novelist H. G. Wells's 1927 *New York Times Magazine* article expressing admiration for the work of the physiologist Ivan Pavlov. Increasingly, the behaviorists' perspective made sense to Skinner.

In graduate school at Harvard University, Skinner came into his own. He received his Ph.D. from Harvard in 1931, but he differed with his professors about what psychologists should study. Many faculty members were concerned about his apparent disdain for their efforts to analyze the mind through *introspection*, an approach then common at Harvard. As discussed in Chapter 1, introspection is the process of thinking about one's own thoughts and feelings and then talking about them as a way of making them public and available for others to study. The main objection to using introspection as a research method is that it is not very reliable. By contrast, behaviorists such as Skinner believed that, to be scientists, psychologists had to study observable actions—the behaviors that people and animals display.

Inspired by the work of Watson and of Pavlov, Skinner believed that he could dramatically change an animal's behavior by providing incentives to the animal for performing particular acts. For the next half century, he conducted systematic studies of animals, often pigeons or rats, to discover the basic rules of learning. In the process, he outlined many of the most important principles that shape animal and human behavior, principles as relevant today as they were more than 50 years ago.

His groundbreaking work led Skinner to form radical ideas about behaviorism. Dismissing the importance of mental states and questioning philosophical concepts such as free will, he believed that the application of basic learning principles could create a better, more humane world, one free of poverty and violence. In *Walden Two* (1948), a best-selling novel, he depicts a utopia in which children are raised only with praise and incentives, never with punishment. *Walden Two* has inspired many people; entire communities, such as northern Mexico's Los Horcones and rural Virginia's Twin Oaks, live according to the principles in it.

Skinner also raised his own children—two daughters—according to the ideas established through his research, especially in emphasizing reward over punishment. The media has sometimes misinterpreted Skinner's parenting as the work of a cold, mad scientist. In the "Baby in a Box" incident, for example, Skinner developed a glassed-in sleeping chamber for his infant daughter Deborah that maintained an optimal temperature and provided a continuous supply of fresh linens (FIGURE 6.1). Contrary to rumors, however, he did not lock his daughter in the box, nor did she grow up to be depressed, sue her father, or commit suicide. In fact, Deborah, an artist, has denounced such rumors. She and her sister, Julie, an author and educator, had excellent relationships with their father until his death, in 1990.

B. F. Skinner's work has been enormously influential throughout society, from classrooms to clinics and beyond. This chapter focuses on what Skinner and a number of other learning theorists have discovered about how learning takes place. This material represents some of psychology's central contributions to our understanding of human and animal behavior. A cornerstone for a number of the foundational principles of psychological science, learning theories have also affected the other major areas of psychology. This chapter shows how these findings have been used to improve quality of life and to train humans and animals to learn new tasks, how contemporary psychological scientists are discovering the brain mechanisms that support this learning, and what new theories are emerging to explain how we learn.

FIGURE 6.1 **"Baby in a Box"** B. F. Skinner developed this crib for his daughter in 1945.

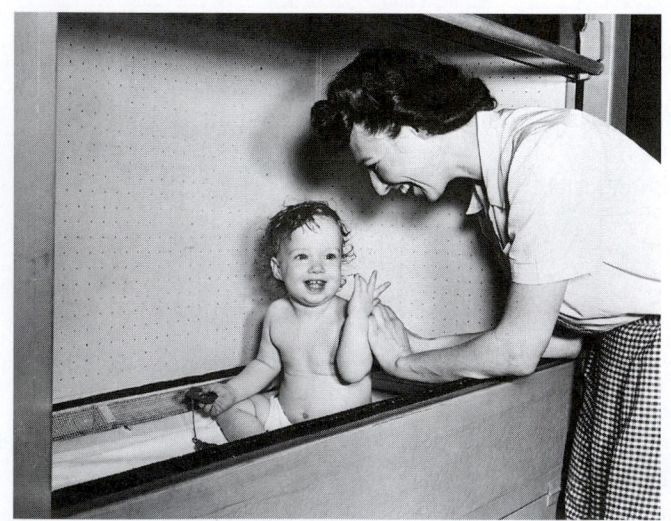

How Did the Behavioral Study of Learning Develop?

Learning is a relatively enduring change in behavior, one that results from experience. It occurs when animals benefit from experience so that their behavior is better adapted to the environment. The ability to learn is crucial for all animals. To survive, animals need to learn such things as which types of foods are dangerous, when it is safe to sleep, and which sounds indicate potential dangers. Learning is central to almost all aspects of human existence, from basic abilities, such as walking and speaking, to much more complex ones, such as flying airplanes, performing surgery, or maintaining intimate relationships. Learning also shapes many aspects of daily life, from clothing choices and musical tastes to social rules about how close we stand to each other, cultural values about either exploiting or preserving the environment, and so on.

The essence of learning is understanding how events are related; for example, you might associate going to the dentist with being in pain, and you might associate working with getting paid. Associations develop through *conditioning,* a process in which environmental stimuli and behavioral responses become connected. Psychologists study two types of conditioning. The first, **classical conditioning,** or *Pavlovian conditioning,* occurs when we learn that two types of events go together—for example, when we watch a scary movie and our hearts beat faster. The second, **operant conditioning,** or *instrumental conditioning,* occurs when we learn that a behavior leads to a particular outcome, such as that studying leads to better grades. This latter type of learning was of greatest interest to B. F. Skinner. Other types include learning by observing others—for example, learning about new fashions by paying attention to what celebrities are wearing.

The rise of learning theory in the early twentieth century was due partly to the dissatisfaction among some psychologists with the widespread use of introspection, in which verbal reports are used to assess mental states. At the time, Freudian ideas were at the heart of psychological theorizing. Freud and his followers used verbal report techniques such as dream analysis and free association to assess the unconscious mental processes they believed were behavior's primary determinants. In contrast, John B. Watson, arguing that Freudian theory was unscientific and ultimately meaningless, scorned any psychological enterprise that focused on things that could not be observed directly, such as people's mental experiences. According to Watson, observable behavior was the only valid indicator of psychological activity. Although he acknowledged that thoughts and beliefs existed, he believed they could not be studied using scientific methods.

As discussed in Chapter 1, Watson founded behaviorism, a school of thought based on the belief that animals and humans are born with the potential to learn just about anything. Based on the seventeenth-century philosopher John Locke's idea of *tabula rasa* (Latin, "blank slate"), which states that infants are born knowing nothing and that all knowledge is acquired through sensory experiences, behaviorism stated that environment and its associated effects on animals were the sole determinants of learning. Watson felt so strongly about the preeminence of environment that he issued the following bold challenge: "Give me a dozen healthy infants, well formed, and my own specified world to bring them up in and I'll guarantee to take any one at random and train him to become any type of specialist I might select—doctor, lawyer, artist, merchant-chief, and yes, even beggar-man and thief, regardless of his talents, penchants, tendencies, abilities, vocations and race of his ancestors" (Watson, 1924, p. 82). In America, Watson enormously influenced the study of psychology. Behaviorism was the dominant psychological paradigm there well into the 1960s; it affected the methods and theories of every area within psychology.

LEARNING OBJECTIVES

Explain the types of learning that occur through conditioning.

Differentiate among UR, US, CS, and CR.

Describe the "Little Albert" experiment and explain how it is used as a model for understanding phobias.

learning   An enduring change in behavior, resulting from experience.

classical conditioning, or Pavlovian conditioning   A type of learned response that occurs when a neutral object comes to elicit a reflexive response when it is associated with a stimulus that already produces that response.

operant conditioning, or instrumental conditioning   A learning process in which the consequences of an action determine the likelihood that it will be performed in the future.

Behavioral Responses Are Conditioned

Watson developed his ideas about behaviorism after reading the work of Ivan Pavlov, who had won a Nobel Prize in 1904 for his work on the digestive system. Pavlov was interested in the *salivary reflex,* the automatic and unlearned response that occurs when a food stimulus is presented to a hungry animal, including a human. For his work on the digestive system, Pavlov had created an apparatus that collected saliva from dogs so that he could measure differences in salivary output when he placed various types of food into a dog's mouth (**FIGURE 6.2**). Like so many major scientific advances, Pavlov's contribution to psychology started with a simple observation. One day he realized that the laboratory dogs were salivating before they tasted the food. Indeed, the dogs started salivating the moment a lab technician walked into the room or whenever they saw the bowls that usually contained food. Pavlov's genius was in recognizing that this behavioral response was a window to the working mind. Unlike inborn reflexes, salivation at the sight of a person or of a bowl is not automatic and therefore must have been acquired through experience. This insight led Pavlov to devote the rest of his life to studying the basic principles of learning.

PAVLOV'S EXPERIMENTS In a typical Pavlovian experiment, a *neutral stimulus* unrelated to the salivary reflex, such as a ringing bell, is presented along with a stimulus that reliably produces the reflex, such as food. This pairing, a *conditioning trial,* is repeated a number of times; then, on *critical trials,* the bell sound is presented alone and the salivary reflex is measured. Pavlov found that under these conditions, the sound of the bell on its own produced salivation. This type of learning, when a neutral stimulus elicits a reflexive response because it has become associated with a stimulus that already produces that response, is now referred to as *classical conditioning* or *Pavlovian conditioning.*

Pavlov called the salivation elicited by food the **unconditioned response (UR),** because it occurred without prior training. An unconditioned response is an unlearned, automatic behavior, such as any simple reflex. Similarly, the food is the **unconditioned stimulus (US).** In the normal reflex response, the food (US) leads to salivation (UR). Because the ringing bell produces salivation only after training, it is the **conditioned stimulus (CS);** it stimulates salivation only after learning takes place. The salivary reflex that occurs when only the conditioned stimulus is presented is the **conditioned response (CR);** it is an acquired, learned response. Both the unconditioned and the conditioned responses

---

unconditioned response (UR) A response that does not have to be learned, such as a reflex.

unconditioned stimulus (US) A stimulus that elicits a response, such as a reflex, without any prior learning.

conditioned stimulus (CS) A stimulus that elicits a response only after learning has taken place.

conditioned response (CR) A response that has been learned.

FIGURE 6.2 Pavlov's Apparatus and Classical Conditioning (a) Ivan Pavlov, pictured here with his colleagues and one of his canine subjects, conducted groundbreaking work on classical conditioning. **(b)** Pavlov's apparatus collected and measured a dog's saliva.

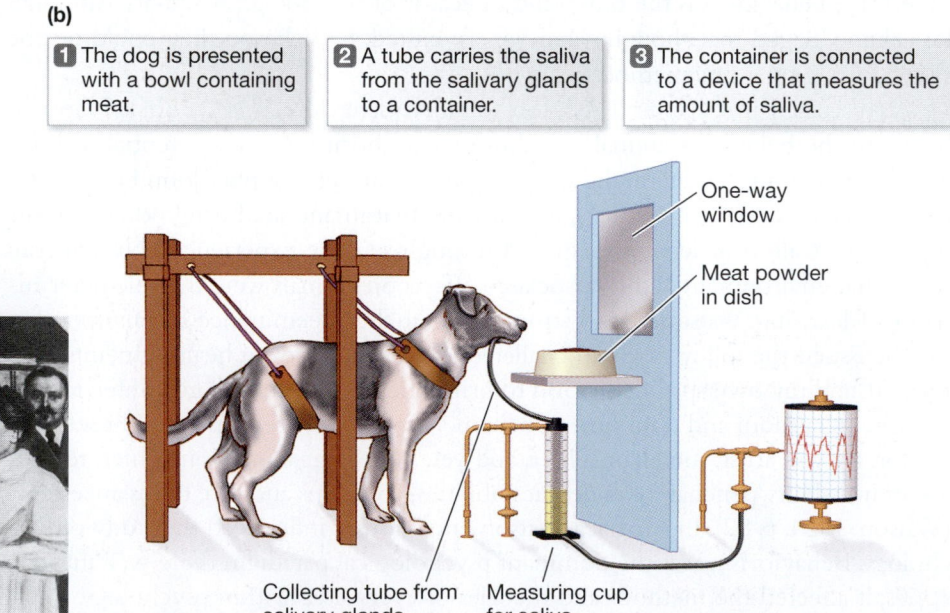

(b)

1 The dog is presented with a bowl containing meat.

2 A tube carries the saliva from the salivary glands to a container.

3 The container is connected to a device that measures the amount of saliva.

One-way window

Meat powder in dish

Collecting tube from salivary glands

Measuring cup for saliva

(a)

are salivation, but they are not identical: The conditioned response usually is weaker than the unconditioned response, such that the bell produces less saliva than the food does. (The process of conditioning is outlined in **FIGURE 6.3**.)

Consider this common reaction. Watching a frightening scene in a movie, such as one in which someone is attacked, makes you feel tense, anxious, and perhaps even disgusted. In this scenario, the frightening scene (the stimulus) and your response to it are unconditioned—they occur naturally. Now imagine a piece of music that does not initially have much effect on you but that you hear in the movie just before each frightening scene. (A good example is the musical theme from *Jaws.*) Eventually you will begin to feel tense and anxious as soon as you hear the music. You have learned that the music, the conditioned stimulus, predicts scary scenes, and therefore you feel the tension and anxiety, the conditioned response. As in Pavlov's studies, the CS (music) produces a somewhat different emotional response than the US (the scary scene)—it may be less intense, more a feeling of apprehension than of fear or disgust. If you later hear this music in a different context, such as on the radio, you will

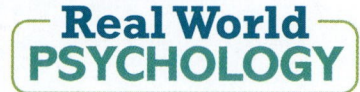

FIGURE 6.3 Scientific Method: Pavlov's Classical Conditioning

Hypothesis: A dog can learn that a bell predicts food.

Research Method:

1 Food (**unconditioned stimulus**) causes the dog to salivate (**unconditioned response**).

Before conditioning

US

UR

A bell (**neutral stimulus**) does not cause the dog to salivate.

Neutral stimulus

UR

2 During conditioning trials, the ringing bell is presented to a dog along with the food.

Conditioning

Neutral stimulus

+

US

3 During critical trials, the ringing bell (**conditioned stimulus**) is presented without the food, and the dog's response is measured.

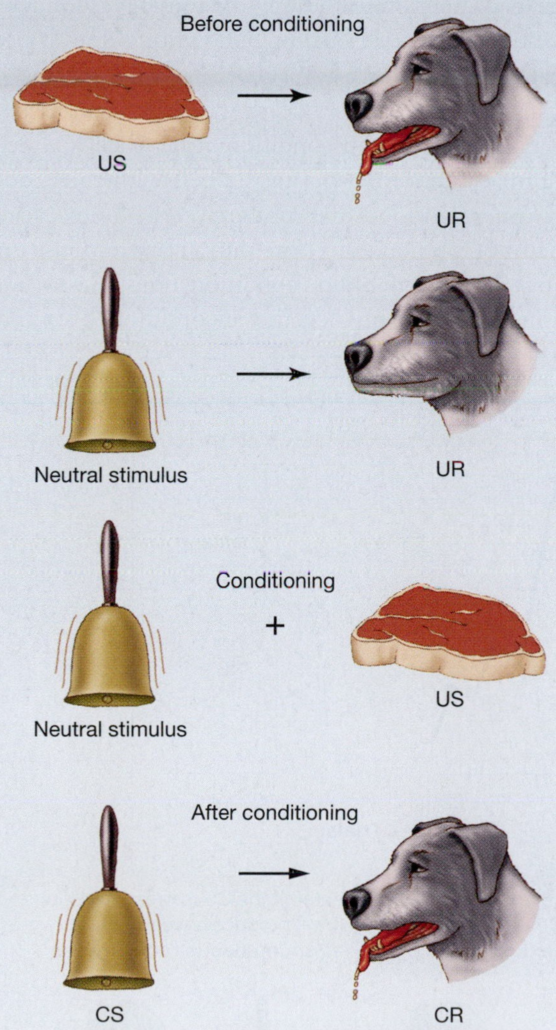

After conditioning

CS

CR

Result: After conditioning, the ringing bell causes the dog to salivate (**conditioned response**).

Conclusion: The dog was conditioned to associate the bell with food.

again feel tense and anxious even though you are not watching the movie. You have been classically conditioned to be anxious when you hear the music.

ACQUISITION, EXTINCTION, AND SPONTANEOUS RECOVERY Like many other scientists (of his time and subsequently), Pavlov was greatly influenced by Darwin's *On the Origin of Species.* Pavlov believed that conditioning is the basis for how animals learn to adapt to their environments. By learning to predict what objects bring pleasure or pain, animals acquire new adaptive behaviors. For instance, suppose that each time it rains, a delicious and nutritious plant blooms. An animal that learns this association will seek out this plant each time it rains. In this example, **acquisition,** the initial learning of a behavior, is the gradual formation of an association between stimuli, one conditioned (rain) and one unconditioned (plant bloom). From his research, Pavlov concluded that the critical element in the acquisition of a learned association is that the stimuli occur together in time, a bond referred to as *contiguity.* Subsequent research has shown that the strongest conditioning actually occurs when there is a very brief delay between the CS and the US. Thus you will develop a stronger conditioned response to a piece of music if it comes just before a scary scene than if it occurs during the scary scene: The music's role in predicting the frightening scene is an important part of the classical conditioning. The next time you watch a horror movie, pay attention to the way the music gets louder just before a scary part begins.

Once a behavior is acquired, how long does it persist? For instance, what if the animal seeks out the tasty plants every time it rains, but the plants stop appearing? Animals sometimes have to learn when associations are no longer adaptive. Normally, after standard Pavlovian conditioning, the bell (CS) leads to salivation (CR) because the animal learns to associate the bell with the food (US). If the bell is presented many times and food does not arrive, the animal learns that the bell is not a good predictor of food, and therefore the salivary response gradually disappears. This process is known as **extinction.** The conditioned response is *extinguished* when the conditioned stimulus no longer predicts the unconditioned stimulus (**FIGURE 6.4**).

acquisition The gradual formation of an association between the conditioned and unconditioned stimuli.

extinction A process in which the conditioned response is weakened when the conditioned stimulus is repeated without the unconditioned stimulus.

FIGURE 6.4 Extinction and Spontaneous Recovery

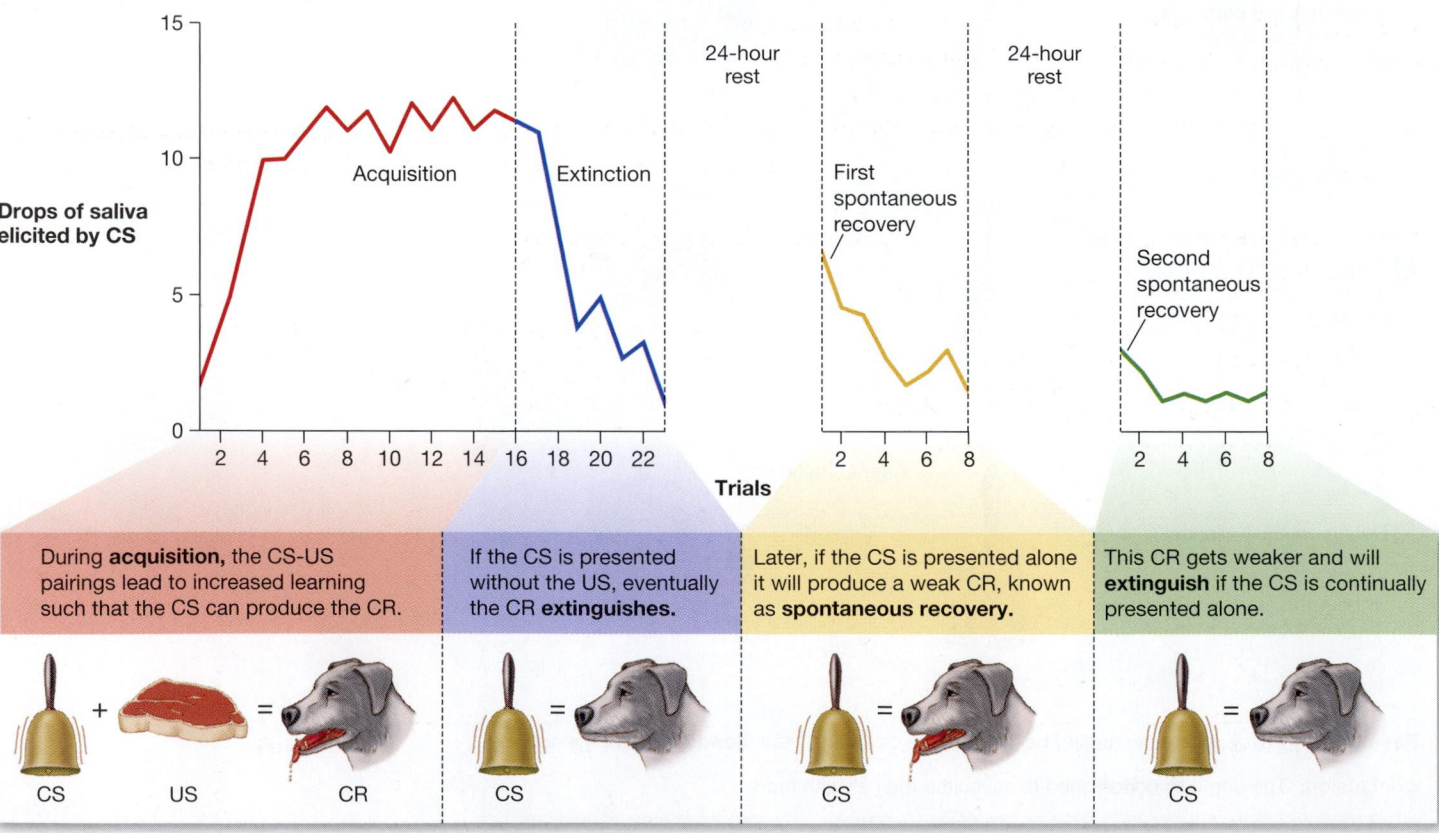

But suppose the delicious plant blooms only during a certain time of year. The adaptive response is to check back once in a while to see if the plant blooms after rain. In the lab, an analogous situation occurs when the conditioned stimulus is presented a long time after extinction. Sounding the bell will once again produce the conditioned response of salivation (see Figure 6.4). Such **spontaneous recovery,** in which the extinguished CS again produces a CR, is temporary and will fade quickly unless the CS is again paired with the US. Even a single pairing of the CS with the US will reestablish the CR, which will then again diminish if CS–US pairings do not continue. Thus extinction inhibits (reduces the strength of) the associative bond but does not eliminate it. Extinction is a form of learning that overwrites the previous association; what is learned is that the original association no longer holds true (i.e., the bell no longer signals that it will be followed by meat; Bouton, 1994; Bouton, Westbrook, Corcoran, & Maren, 2006).

GENERALIZATION, DISCRIMINATION, AND SECOND-ORDER CONDITIONING
In any learning situation, hundreds of possible stimuli can be associated with the unconditioned stimulus to produce the conditioned response. How does the brain determine which stimulus is—or which stimuli are—relevant? For instance, suppose we classically condition a dog so that it salivates (CR) when it hears a 1,000- hertz (Hz) tone (CS). After the CR is established, tones similar to 1,000 Hz will also produce salivation, but the farther the tones are from 1,000 Hz, the less the dog will salivate. **Stimulus generalization** occurs when stimuli similar but not identical to the CS produce the CR. Generalization is adaptive because in nature the CS is seldom experienced repeatedly in an identical fashion. Slight differences in variables, such as background noise, temperature, and lighting, lead to slightly different perceptions of the CS, so animals learn to respond to variations in the CS.

Of course, generalization has limits. Sometimes it is important for animals to distinguish among similar stimuli. For instance, two plant species might look similar, but one might be poisonous. In **stimulus discrimination,** animals learn to differentiate between two similar stimuli if one is consistently associated with the unconditioned stimulus and the other is not (**FIGURE 6.5**). Pavlov and his students

spontaneous recovery A process in which a previously extinguished response reemerges following presentation of the conditioned stimulus.

stimulus generalization Occurs when stimuli that are similar but not identical to the conditioned stimulus produce the conditioned response.

stimulus discrimination A differentiation between two similar stimuli when only one of them is consistently associated with the unconditioned stimulus.

FIGURE 6.5 Stimulus Generalization and Stimulus Discrimination

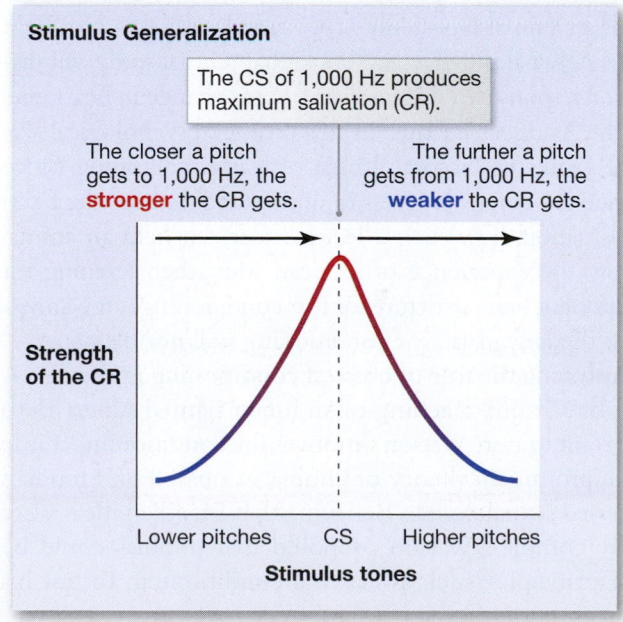

Stimulus Generalization

The CS of 1,000 Hz produces maximum salivation (CR).

The closer a pitch gets to 1,000 Hz, the **stronger** the CR gets.

The further a pitch gets from 1,000 Hz, the **weaker** the CR gets.

Strength of the CR

Lower pitches   CS   Higher pitches

Stimulus tones

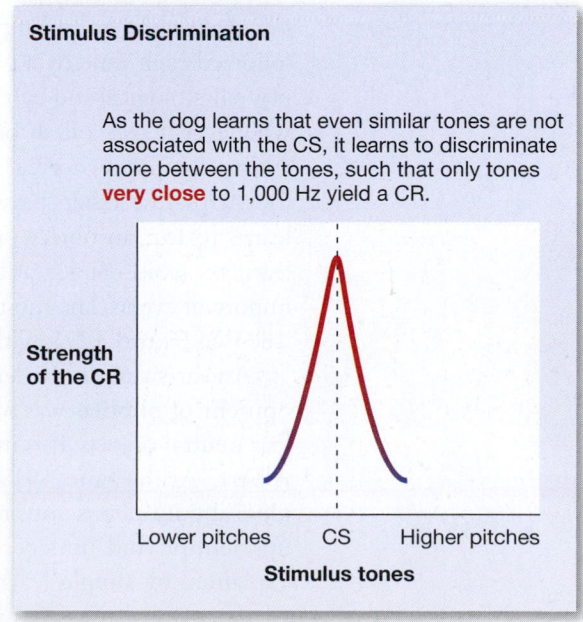

Stimulus Discrimination

As the dog learns that even similar tones are not associated with the CS, it learns to discriminate more between the tones, such that only tones **very close** to 1,000 Hz yield a CR.

Strength of the CR

Lower pitches   CS   Higher pitches

Stimulus tones

demonstrated, for example, that dogs can learn to make very fine distinctions between similar stimuli, such as subtle differences in shades of gray.

Sometimes a conditioned stimulus becomes directly associated not with an unconditioned stimulus but rather with other stimuli associated with the US, a phenomenon known as *second-order conditioning*. In one of Pavlov's early studies, a CS–US bond was formed between a tone and food so that the tone (CS) led to salivation (CR). In a second training session, a black square was repeatedly presented at the same time as the tone. There was no US (no presentation of the meat) during this phase of the study. After a few trials, the black square was presented alone, and it also produced salivation. Second-order conditioning helps account for the complexity of learned associations, especially in people. For instance, money is usually just paper or cheap metal, but it means something entirely different. People's association between that paper or that metal and what it can buy makes them want to have the money. As discussed below, second-order conditioning makes money feel rewarding for those who receive it or wish to receive it. Similarly, advertisers often hire popular celebrities to endorse products, because when people associate familiar, famous, and/or powerful figures with particular brands, they generally develop positive attitudes about those brands (**FIGURE 6.6**). Even though second-order conditioning powerfully influences many of our beliefs and attitudes, most of it occurs implicitly, without our awareness or intention.

FIGURE 6.6 Second-Order Conditioning Advertisers hope to influence attitudes and behavior by pairing popular celebrities with products, such as the singer Victoria Beckham with this handbag.

Phobias and Addictions Have Learned Components

Classical conditioning helps explain many behavioral phenomena, including phobias and addictions.

phobia An acquired fear that is out of proportion to the real threat of an object or of a situation.

PHOBIAS AND THEIR TREATMENT A **phobia** is an acquired fear out of proportion to the real threat (phobias are discussed further in Chapter 14, "Disorders of the Mind and Body"). Common phobias include the fears of heights, of dogs, of insects, of snakes, and of the dark. According to classical-conditioning theory, phobias develop through the generalization of a fear experience, as when a person stung by a wasp develops a fear of all flying insects.

Animals can be classically conditioned to fear neutral objects, a process known as *fear conditioning*. For example, if an animal repeatedly is presented with a flash of light followed each time by a moderately painful electric shock, that animal soon will display physiological and behavioral responses indicating fear, such as change in heart rate, whenever it sees a flash of light. As discussed later in this chapter, psychological scientists now know a great deal about the biological basis of fear conditioning. Since the 1990s, researchers have made enormous progress in understanding how the brain learns to fear an object or a situation, how such a learned fear can help an animal learn to avoid danger, and how the experience of fear can strengthen learning for important events. The most important brain structure for fear conditioning is the amygdala (see Figure 3.27); without the amygdala, fear conditioning will not happen.

An early case study demonstrating the role of classical conditioning in the development of phobias was John B. Watson's teaching of an infant named Albert B. to fear neutral objects. It is important to note Watson's motives for conditioning "Little Albert." At the time, 1919, the prominent theory of phobia was based on Freudian ideas about unconscious repressed sexual desires. Believing that Freudian ideas were unscientific and unnecessarily complex, Watson proposed that phobias could be explained by simple learning principles, such as classical conditioning. To test his hypothesis, Watson devised a learning study. He asked a woman he knew to let him use her son, Albert B., in the study. Because this child was emotionally stable, Watson believed the experiment would cause him little harm. When Albert was nine months old, Watson and his lab assistant, Rosalie Rayner, presented him with various neutral objects, including a white rat, a rabbit, a dog, a monkey, costume masks, and a ball of white wool. Albert showed a natural curiosity regarding these items, but displayed no overt emotional responses.

When Albert was eleven months old, Watson and Rayner began the conditioning trials. This time, as they presented the white rat and Albert reached for it, Watson smashed a hammer into an iron bar, producing a loud clanging sound. The sound scared the child, who immediately withdrew and hid his face. Watson did this a few more times at intervals of five days until Albert would whimper and cringe when the rat was presented alone. Thus the US (smashing sound) led to a UR (fear), and eventually the pairing of the CS (rat) and US (smashing sound) led to the rat producing fear (CR) on its own. The fear response generalized to other stimuli that Watson had presented along with the rat at the initial meeting, and Albert eventually became frightened of them all, including the rabbit and the ball of wool. Even a Santa Claus with a white beard produced a fear response. Thus classical conditioning was shown to be an effective method of inducing phobia (**FIGURE 6.7**).

Watson had planned to conduct extinction trials to remove the learned phobias, but Albert's mother removed him from the study before Watson could conduct those trials. No one knows what became of Albert. Watson's conditioning of

FIGURE 6.7 Scientific Method: Watson's "Little Albert" Experiment

Hypothesis: Phobias can be explained by classical conditioning.

Research Method:

1 Little Albert was presented with neutral objects, such as a white rat and costume masks, that provoked a neutral response.

2 During conditioning trials, when Albert reached for the white rat (CS) a loud clanging sound (US) scared him (UR).

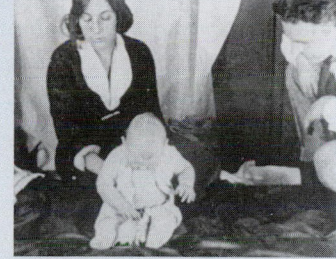

Results: Eventually, the pairing of the rat (CS) and the clanging sound (US) led to the rat producing fear (CR) on its own. The fear response generalized to other stimuli presented with the rat initially, such as the costume masks.

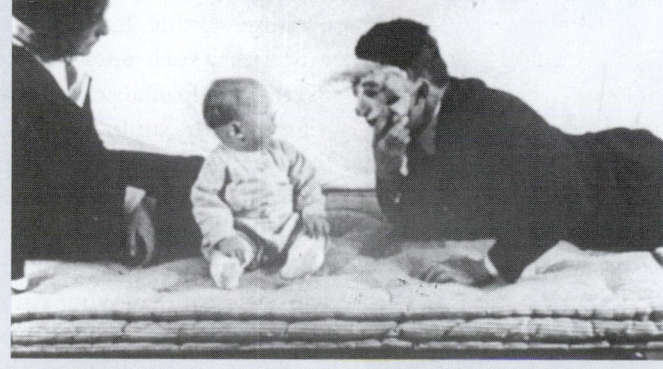

Conclusion: Classical conditioning can cause participants to fear neutral objects.

Albert has long been criticized as unethical, and nowadays an ethics committee likely would not approve such a study. In his detailed plans for the reconditioning, however, Watson described a method of continually presenting the feared items to Albert paired with more pleasant things, such as candy. Such classical-conditioning techniques have since proven valuable for developing very effective behavioral therapies to treat phobias. For instance, exposing people to small doses of the feared stimulus while having them engage in a pleasurable task, a technique called *counterconditioning,* can help people overcome a fear. The behavioral therapist Joseph Wolpe has developed a formal treatment based on counterconditioning, *systematic desensitization* (Wolpe, 1997): After patients are taught how to relax their muscles, they are asked to imagine the feared object or situation while continuing to use the relaxation exercises. Eventually, the patients are exposed to the feared stimulus while they are relaxing. The general idea is that the $CS \rightarrow CR_1$ (fear) connection can be broken by developing a $CS \rightarrow CR_2$ (relaxation) connection. As discussed in Chapter 15, it is now believed that repeated exposure to the feared stimulus is more important than relaxation in breaking the fear connection.

DRUG ADDICTION Classical conditioning also plays an important role in drug addiction. Conditioned drug effects are common and demonstrate conditioning's power. For example, the smell of coffee can become a conditioned stimulus, one that leads coffee drinkers to feel activated and aroused as though they have actually consumed caffeine. Likewise, for heroin addicts, the sight of the needle and the feeling when it is inserted into the skin become a CS, so addicts sometimes inject themselves with water to reduce their cravings when heroin is unavailable. Sometimes, the sight of a straight-edge razor blade, which is often used to "cut" heroin, can briefly increase drug addicts' cravings. When former heroin addicts are exposed to environmental cues associated with their drug use, they often experience cravings. Not satisfying these cravings can lead the addict to experience *withdrawal,* the unpleasant state of tension and anxiety that occurs when addicts stop using drugs. Addicts who quit using drugs in treatment centers often relapse when they return to their old environments because they experience conditioned craving.

In the laboratory, presenting heroin addicts or cocaine addicts with cues associated with drug ingestion leads to cravings and various physiological responses associated with withdrawal, such as changes in heart rate and blood pressure. Brain imaging studies have found that such cues lead to activation of the prefrontal cortex and various regions of the limbic system, areas of the brain involved in the experience of reward (Volkow et al., 2008). Seeing a tantalizing food item when you are hungry activates these same brain regions, as you anticipate enjoying your tasty meal. In the same way, the sight of drug cues produces an expectation that the drug high will follow (**FIGURE 6.8**). (On the limbic system's involvement in both

FIGURE 6.8 PET Scans Showing Activation of Limbic System Structures Cocaine addicts were shown videos of nature scenes and of cocaine cues. The cocaine-related videos sparked activation in brain regions associated with reward, such as the anterior cingulate and the amygdala. These areas would not have been activated by nature scenes alone. (Areas with greatest activation are shown in red.)

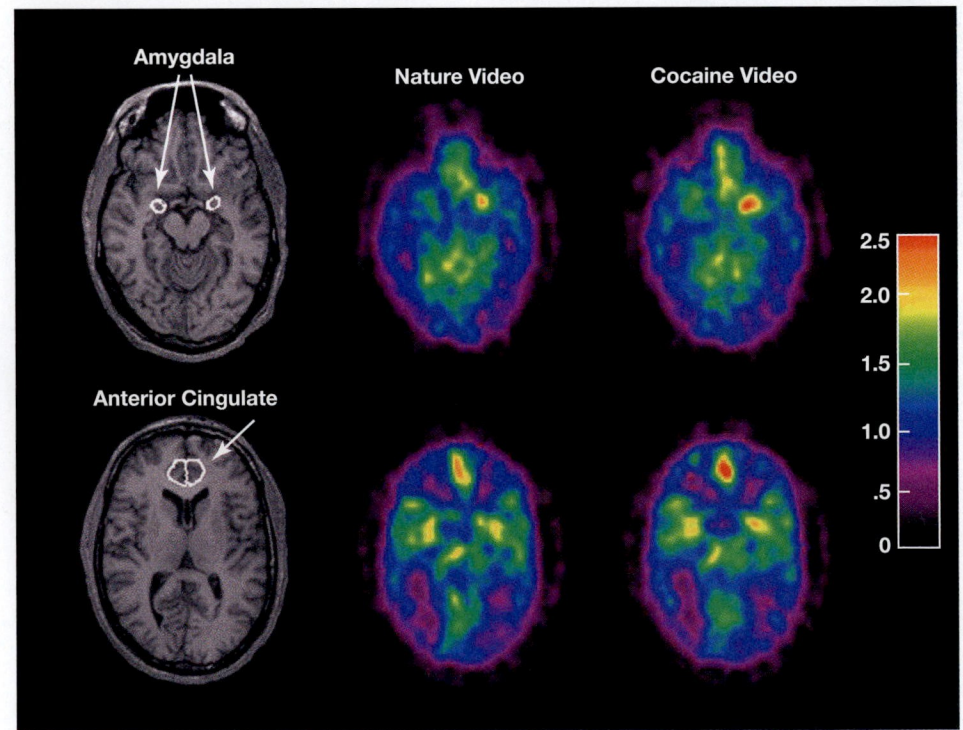

emotion and motivation, see Chapter 3, "Biological Foundations." On the limbic system's role in addiction, see Chapter 9, "Motivation and Emotion.")

The learning theorist Shepard Siegel has conducted research showing that drug tolerance effects are specific to certain situations. As discussed in Chapter 4, tolerance is a process by which addicts need more and more of a drug to experience the same effects. Tolerance can be so great that addicts regularly use drug doses that would be fatal for the inexperienced user. Siegel's research has shown that tolerance effects are greatest when the drug is taken in the same location as previous drug use, presumably because the body has learned to expect the drug in that location and then to compensate for the drug, such as by altering neurochemistry or physiology to metabolize it. Conversely, Siegel's findings imply that if addicts take their usual large doses in novel settings, they are more likely to overdose, because their bodies will not respond sufficiently to compensate for the drugs (Siegel, 1984; Siegel, Hinson, Krank, & McCully, 1982).

Classical Conditioning Involves More Than Events Occurring at the Same Time

Pavlov's original explanation for classical conditioning was that any two events presented in contiguity would produce a learned association. Pavlov and his followers believed that the association's strength was determined by factors such as the intensity of the conditioned and unconditioned stimuli, such that greater intensity would increase learning. (A louder bell or larger piece of meat would produce stronger associations than a softer bell or smaller piece of meat.) In the mid-1960s, a number of challenges to Pavlov's theory suggested that some conditioned stimuli would more likely produce learning than others and that contiguity was not sufficient to create CS–US associations.

EVOLUTIONARY SIGNIFICANCE According to Pavlov, any object or phenomenon could be converted into a conditioned stimulus during conditioning trials. Thus, for example, any light, tone, color, or odor could be associated with any unconditioned stimulus (e.g., a piece of meat or a loud sound). Apparently, however, not all stimuli are equally effective in producing learning. Research conducted by the psychologist John Garcia and his colleagues showed that certain pairings of stimuli are more likely to become associated than others. For instance, when animals receive nonlethal amounts of poison in their food that make them ill, they quickly learn to avoid the tastes or smells associated with the food (Garcia & Koelling, 1966).

Likewise, most people can recall a time when they ate a particular food and then became ill with nausea, stomach upset, and vomiting. Whether or not the food caused the illness, even if the illness clearly was caused by a virus or some other condition, most people respond to this sequence of events with a *conditioned food aversion,* especially if the food was not part of the person's usual diet. The association between eating a novel food and getting sick, even when the illness occurs hours after eating, is so strong that a food aversion can be formed in one trial (**FIGURE 6.9**). Some people cannot stand even the smell of a food they associate with a stomach-related illness.

Conditioned food aversions are easy to produce with smell or taste, but they are very difficult to produce with light or sound. This difference makes sense, since smell and taste are the main cues that guide animals' eating behaviors. From an evolutionary viewpoint, animals that quickly associate a certain flavor with illness, and therefore avoid that flavor, will be more successful—that is, likely to survive and pass along their genes.

Research has shown that monkeys can more easily be conditioned to fear snakes than to fear objects such as flowers or rabbits (Cook & Mineka, 1989).

(a)

(b)

FIGURE 6.9 Conditioned Food Aversion in Animals (a) After eating a monarch butterfly, **(b)** this blue jay vomited and thus learned to avoid eating anything that looks like the butterfly.

The psychologist Martin Seligman (1970) has argued that animals are genetically programmed to fear specific objects; he refers to this programming as *biological preparedness.* Preparedness helps explain why animals tend to fear potentially dangerous things (e.g., snakes, fire, heights) rather than objects that pose little threat (e.g., flowers, shoes, babies). Also, when people participate in conditioning experiments in which aversive stimuli are paired with members of their own racial group or members of a different racial group, they more easily associate the negative stimuli with out-group members (Olsson, Ebert, Banaji, & Phelps, 2005). This finding indicates that people might be predisposed to wariness of out-group members, presumably since out-group members have been more dangerous over the course of human evolution. This tendency has sometimes been exploited to create or enhance prejudice toward out-groups during wars and other intergroup conflicts. For example, as the Nazis prepared for and conducted their extermination of Jews during World War II, they created films in which Jews' faces morphed into those of rats crawling in filth. By showing these images to the German population, the Nazis aimed to condition a national repulsion response to facial features associated with being Jewish. (Videos of these films are available for viewing at the Museum of Tolerance, in Los Angeles, California.)

At the most general level, contemporary researchers are interested in how classical conditioning helps animals learn adaptive responses (Hollis, 1997; Shettleworth, 2001). The adaptive value of a particular response varies according to the animal's evolutionary history. For example, taste aversions are easy to condition in rats but difficult to condition in birds because in selecting food, rats rely more on taste and birds rely more on vision. Accordingly, birds quickly learn to avoid a visual cue they associate with illness. Different types of stimuli cause different reactions even within a species. Rats freeze and startle if a CS is auditory, but rise on their hind legs if the CS is visual (Holland, 1977). Such differences in learned adaptive responses may reflect the meanings of, and potential dangers associated with, auditory and visual stimuli in particular environments.

GENDER DIFFERENCES IN LEARNING Psychologists differ in the extent to which they emphasize an evolutionary perspective on learning. It has been clearly established that the behaviors we learn most easily are adaptive in an evolutionary sense, but how important are the principles of evolution in understanding everyday aspects of human behavior? One area that has generated considerable research and controversy is how differently men and women learn their ways around a given environment. The argument for expecting differences is that for most of human history people lived in hunter–gatherer societies, in which women gathered edible vegetation, usually returning home each day, and men traveled longer distances as they hunted for the animals that made up the protein portion of the societies' diets. In addition, the argument goes, since women spent much of their adult lives pregnant or nursing, they did not travel as much as men, and thus women generally did not develop the ability to learn their way through an environment as well as men did.

Researchers have revealed some differences in how females and males learn to navigate. Earlier research with rats and other nonhuman animals reported large sex differences in maze performance (reviewed in Halpern & Collaer, 2005). In what seems like a modern-day variation of the earlier methods that used rats running through mazes, researchers are now using virtual mazes to study human way-finding (Moffat, Hampson, & Hatzipantelis, 1998). Many studies suggest that when females learn a route, either from a map or from direct experience, they tend to rely on landmarks to find the way, whereas males more likely will attend to and keep track of the compass direction in which they are traveling (Lawton, 1994). Similarly, when adults learn a route from a map, males make fewer errors in getting to the destination, but females better recall landmarks along the way (Galea & Kimura, 1993). Research that compared maze route learning found that female college students were more likely to use a learning strategy that consisted of a series of turns (e.g., right, right, left, right) and male college students were more likely to use a "place" strategy that required keeping track of the general direction of a goal (Schmitzer-Torbert, 2007). Thus women will more likely use landmarks and memorize a series of terms when navigating through space; males will more likely keep track of cardinal directions (north, south, etc.). When the participants could use either strategy, the men learned the task more quickly, but with additional trials, the women's performances were identical to the men's.

CRITICAL THINKING SKILL

Recognizing and Avoiding Inappropriate Association Effects in Reasoning

(a)

One basic principle in psychology is that if two events occur close together in time and/or space, people will form an association between them. This idea underlies conditioning—a person or animal is conditioned to expect that when one event occurs, the associated event will occur. Sometimes, this expectation is perfectly reasonable, but other times, a person's thinking is biased because someone else has deliberately exploited the natural tendency to make associations. Association techniques are widely used in the political arena, for example, especially to create *guilt by association*. A typical approach is to associate Person A, usually a friend or relative of a political candidate, with something bad. Person B, the candidate, is then associated with Person A. The inference is that Person B shares the same bad characteristics associated with Person A. Suppose you read in the newspaper that a mass murderer endorsed a presidential candidate. This endorsement could be detrimental to the candidate, even if he or she did not desire it and did nothing to promote it. Once you are aware of the deliberate use of guilt by association, you will find examples in every election. Read over the various charges leveled against political candidates, and you will find exactly this sort of (generally) faulty reasoning.

Guilt by association occurs in a wide range of contexts. If you have a friend or relative who belongs to a terrorist group, the negative associations of belonging to a terrorist group may be associated with you. The association may be logical—perhaps you went to group meetings with your friend but did not join the group. Without additional evidence, however, the association will more likely be misleading.

Similarly, people can perceive virtue by association. If your brother or sister volunteers to build homes for the homeless, some of this virtue will likely be associated with you. Virtue by association is one reason political dynasties exist in many countries throughout the world. For example, Benazir Bhutto was twice elected prime minister of Pakistan, her popularity enhanced by her father's success as prime minister. Indira Gandhi served as prime minister of India for three consecutive terms, her popularity enhanced by the success of her political family, especially that of her father, Jawaharlal Nehru. In the United States, the Kennedy, Bush, and perhaps Clinton families represent political dynasties. In thinking about political candidates—or even the people we meet in our everyday lives—we need to consider their individual characteristics and not assume they are similar to people they are related to or know (**FIGURE 6.10**).

(b)

FIGURE 6.10 Positive Associations and Political Gains (a) Indira Gandhi, **right,** enjoyed great popularity as prime minister of India, partly because of her association with family members such as her father, Jawaharlal Nehru, a former prime minister and powerful figure in the Indian independence movement. **(b)** The Bush dynasty includes two U.S. presidents: George W. Bush and his father, George H. W. Bush.

THE COGNITIVE PERSPECTIVE Until the 1970s, most learning theorists were concerned only with observable stimuli and observable responses. Since then, learning theorists have placed a greater emphasis on trying to understand the mental processes that underlie conditioning. An important principle that has emerged from this work is that classical conditioning is a means by which animals come to *predict* the occurrence of events. Psychological scientists' increasing consideration of mental processes such as prediction and expectancy is called the *cognitive perspective* on learning (Hollis, 1997).

The psychologist Robert Rescorla (1966) conducted one of the first studies highlighting cognition's role in learning. He argued that for learning to take place, the conditioned stimulus must accurately predict the unconditioned stimulus. For instance, a stimulus that occurs *before* the US is more easily conditioned than one that comes *after* it. Even though the two are both contiguous presentations with the US (close to it in time), the first stimulus is more easily learned because it predicts the US. Indeed, as mentioned above, across all conditioning situations, some delay between the CS and the US is optimal for learning. The length of delay varies depending on the natures of the conditioned and unconditioned stimuli. For instance, eyeblink conditioning occurs when a sound (CS) is associated with a puff of air blown into the eye (US), which leads to a blink. Optimal learning for eyeblink conditioning is measured in milliseconds. By contrast, conditioned food aversions often take many hours, since the ill effects of consuming poisons or food that has gone bad may not be felt for hours after eating.

> **Rescorla-Wagner model** A cognitive model of classical conditioning; it states that the strength of the CS-US association is determined by the extent to which the unconditioned stimulus is unexpected.

The cognitive model of classical learning, published by Rescorla and his colleague Allan Wagner, profoundly changed our understanding of learning (Rescorla & Wagner, 1972). The **Rescorla-Wagner model** states that the strength of the CS–US association is determined by the extent to which the US is unexpected or surprising. The greater the surprise of the US, the more effort an organism puts into trying to understand its occurrence so that it can predict future occurrences. The result is greater classical conditioning of the event (CS) that predicted the US. Say you always use an electric can opener to open a can of dog food. Your dog associates the sound of the can opener (CS) with the appearance of food (US), so it wags its tail and runs around in circles when it hears that sound. Now say the electric can opener breaks and you replace it with a manual one. Without hearing the sound of the electric can opener, your dog receives food. According to Rescorla and Wagner, the unexpected appearance of the food (US) will cause your dog to attend to events in the environment that might have produced the food. Your dog soon will learn to associate being fed with your use of the new opener.

Consistent with the Rescorla-Wagner model, novel stimuli are more easily associated with the unconditioned stimulus than are familiar stimuli. For example, dogs can be conditioned more easily with smells novel to them (such as that of almonds) than with smells they know (that of dog biscuits, perhaps). Once learned, a conditioned stimulus can prevent the acquisition of a new conditioned stimulus, a phenomenon known as the *blocking effect*. For example, a dog that has learned that the smell of almonds (CS) is a good predictor of food (US) does not need to look for other predictors. Furthermore, a stimulus associated with a CS can act as an *occasion setter*, or trigger, for the CS (Schmajuk, Lamoureaux, & Holland, 1998). For example, a dog might learn that the smell of almonds predicts food when the smell is preceded by a sound or by a flash of light and not at other times. The sound or light indicates whether the association between the smell of almonds and food is active.

SUMMING UP

How Did the Behavioral Study of Learning Develop?

Behaviorism, founded by John B. Watson, focuses on observable aspects of learning. Ivan Pavlov developed the classical-conditioning theory to account for the learned association between neutral stimuli and reflexive behaviors. Conditioning occurs when the conditioned stimulus becomes associated with the unconditioned stimulus. For learning to occur, the conditioned stimulus needs to reliably predict the unconditioned stimulus, not simply be contiguous with it. The cognitive model that accounts for most conditioning phenomena is the Rescorla-Wagner model, which states that the amount of conditioning is determined by the extent to which the US is unexpected or surprising, with stronger effects when a novel or unusual CS is used in conditioning.

MEASURING UP

1. Which of the following are true statements about conditioning? Check as many as apply.
   a. Conditioning is one kind of learning.
   b. Only nonhuman animals can be conditioned.
   c. B. F. Skinner used rats and pigeons in most of his research because he was not concerned with human learning.
   d. Conditioning usually involves the association of two events that occur close in time.
   e. Conditioning does not meet the definitional criteria for learning because the association can be extinguished, or unlearned.
   f. Learning results only from experiences.
   g. Learning involves short-term changes in behavior.
   h. Classical and operant conditioning are the same.
   i. Skinner came to appreciate the introspection methods used by his professors.
   j. Differences between females' and males' strategies in virtual maze tasks have been used to argue for evolutionary influences on learning.

2. John B. Watson had planned to extinguish Little Albert's conditioned response to, for example, the rat. Which of the following techniques would have achieved that goal?
   a. Repeatedly showing Little Albert the rat without making a loud sound.
   b. Making a loud sound every time a different and unrelated object was presented.
   c. Teaching Little Albert to strike the bar so he could make the loud sound.
   d. Repeatedly making a loud sound when related objects, such as the ball of wool, were presented.

How Does Operant Conditioning Differ from Classical Conditioning?

Classical conditioning is a relatively passive process in which a person or animal associates events that occur together in time, regardless of what the person or animal does beyond that. This form of conditioning does not account for the many times that one of the events occurs because the person or animal has taken some action. Our behaviors often represent means to particular ends. We buy food to eat it, we study to get good grades, we work to receive money, and so on. Thus many of our actions are *instrumental*—done for a purpose. We learn that behaving in certain ways leads to

LEARNING OBJECTIVES

List the similarities and differences between operant and classical conditioning.

Explain how variable and ratio schedules of reinforcement combine with positive reinforcement, negative reinforcement, and punishment, to affect behavior.

rewards, and we learn that not behaving in other ways keeps us from punishment; these processes are called *instrumental conditioning* or *operant conditioning.* B. F. Skinner, the psychologist most closely associated with this type of learning, selected the term *operant* to express the idea that animals operate on their environments to produce effects. Operant conditioning is the learning process in which an action's consequences determine the likelihood that the action will be performed in the future.

The study of operant conditioning began in the basement of the Harvard psychologist William James's house in Cambridge, Massachusetts, in the late nineteenth century. A young graduate student working with James, Edward Thorndike, had been influenced by Darwin and was studying whether nonhuman animals showed signs of intelligence. As part of his research, Thorndike built a *puzzle box,* a small cage with a trapdoor (**FIGURE 6.11A**). The trapdoor would open if the animal inside performed a specific action, such as pulling a string. Thorndike placed food-deprived animals, initially chickens, inside the puzzle box to see if they could figure out how to escape. When Thorndike moved to Columbia University to complete his PhD, he switched from using chickens to using cats in his studies. To motivate the cats, he would place

(a)

(b)

1 The cat is placed in the box, and food is placed outside where the cat can see it.

2 After several attempts to get out, the cat accidentally presses the lever, the door opens, and the cat eats.

3 The cat is put back in the box and more quickly presses the lever to get out.

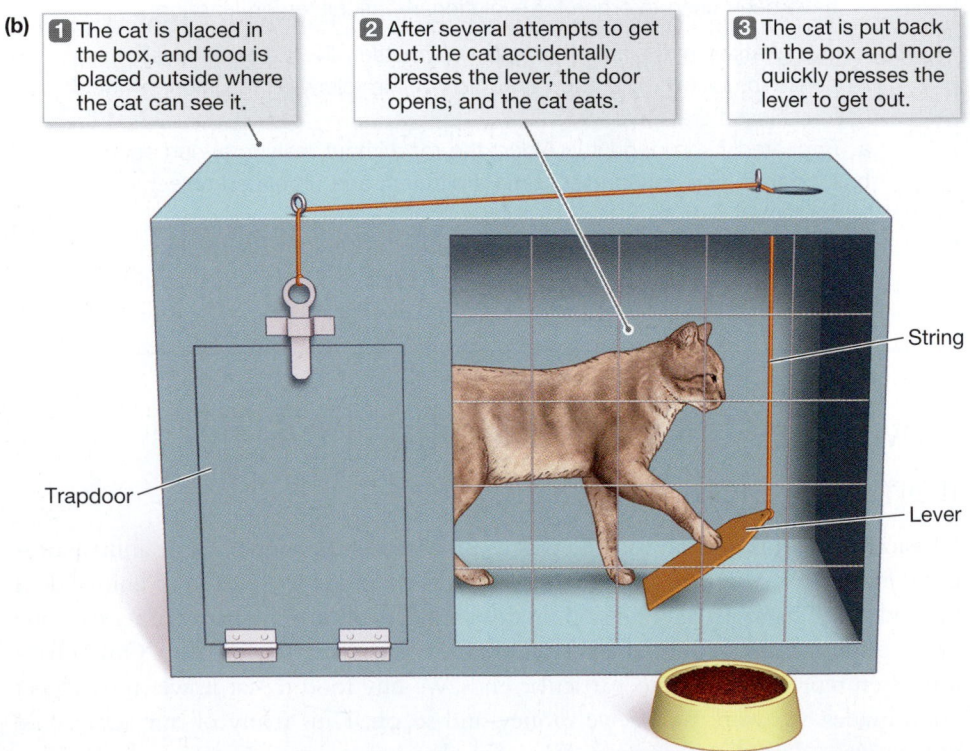

String

Trapdoor

Lever

FIGURE 6.11 Thorndike's Puzzle Box
Thorndike used a primitive puzzle box, such as the one depicted here, to assess learning in animals.

food just outside the box. When a cat was first placed in the box, it usually attempted to escape through numerous nonproductive behaviors. After 5 to 10 minutes of struggling, the cat would *accidentally* pull the string, and the door would open. Thorndike would then return the cat to the box and repeat the trial. Thorndike found that the cat would pull the string more quickly on each subsequent trial, until it soon learned to escape from the puzzle box within seconds (**FIGURE 6.11B**). From this line of research, Thorndike developed a general theory of learning, the **law of effect**, which states that any behavior leading to a "satisfying state of affairs" will more likely occur again, while any behavior leading to an "annoying state of affairs" will less likely occur again (**FIGURE 6.12**).

Reinforcement Increases Behavior

Thirty years after Thorndike, another Harvard graduate student in psychology, B. F. Skinner, developed a more formal learning theory based on the law of effect. As discussed at the beginning of this chapter, Skinner had been greatly influenced by John B. Watson and shared his philosophy of behaviorism. He therefore objected to the subjective aspects of Thorndike's law of effect: States of "satisfaction" are not observable empirically. Skinner coined the term *reinforcer* to describe an event that produces a learned response. A **reinforcer** is a stimulus that occurs after a response and increases the likelihood that the response will be repeated. Skinner believed that behavior—studying, eating, driving on the proper side of the road, and so on—occurs because it has been reinforced.

THE SKINNER BOX To assess operant conditioning, Skinner developed a simple device, a small chamber or cage in which one lever or response key is connected to a food supply, another to a water supply. An animal, usually a rat or pigeon, is placed in the chamber or cage; it learns to press one lever or key to receive food, the other lever or key to receive water. In his earlier research, Skinner had used a maze in which a rat had to take a specific turn to get access to the reinforcer, usually a small piece of food in the goal box. After the rat completed a trial, Skinner had to return the rat to the maze's beginning. He developed the *operant chamber,* as he called it, basically because he got tired of fetching rats. With the device—which came to be known as the *Skinner box,* although he never used that term—he could expose rats or pigeons to repeated conditioning trials without having to do anything but observe (**FIGURE 6.13**). Skinner later built

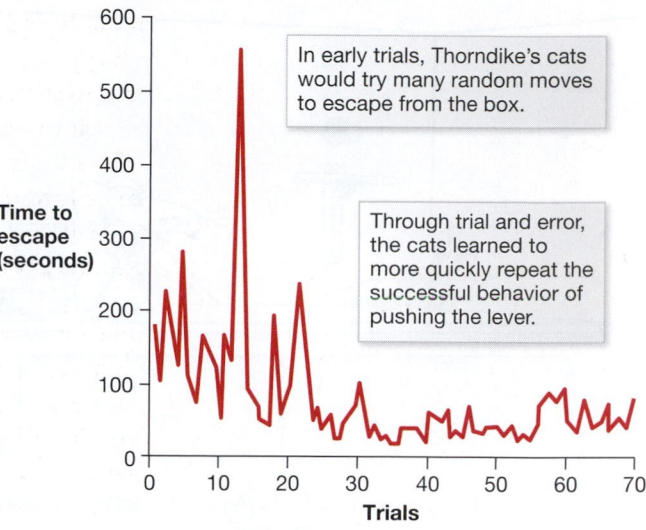

FIGURE 6.12 **Law of Effect** By studying cats' attempts to escape from a puzzle box, Thorndike was able to formulate his general theory of learning.

law of effect Thorndike's general theory of learning: Any behavior that leads to a "satisfying state of affairs" will more likely occur again, and any behavior that leads to an "annoying state of affairs" will less likely recur.

reinforcer A stimulus that follows a response and increases the likelihood that the response will be repeated.

(a)

(b)

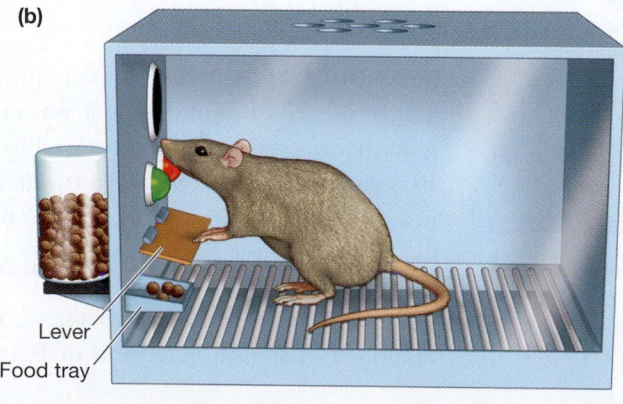

FIGURE 6.13 **Skinner Box**
(a) B. F. Skinner and one of his subjects demonstrate (b) the Skinner box.

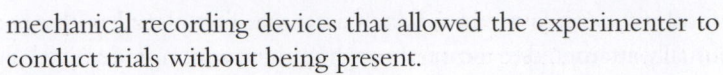

"Oh, not bad. The light comes on, I press the bar, they write me a check. How about you?"

shaping A process of operant conditioning; it involves reinforcing behaviors that are increasingly similar to the desired behavior.

FIGURE 6.14 Shaping Shaping can be used to train animals to perform extraordinary behaviors. Here, a trained dog water skis for a boat show.

mechanical recording devices that allowed the experimenter to conduct trials without being present.

SHAPING When performing operant conditioning, you cannot provide the reinforcer until the person or animal displays the appropriate response. An animal inside the Skinner box has so little to do that it typically presses the lever or key sooner rather than later. One major problem with operant conditioning outside the Skinner box is that the same animal might take a while to perform the action you are looking for. Rather than wait for the animal to spontaneously perform the action, you can use an operant-conditioning technique to teach the animal to do so. This powerful process, **shaping**, involves reinforcing behaviors that are increasingly similar to the desired behavior. Suppose you are trying to teach your dog to roll over. You initially reward your dog for any behavior that even slightly resembles rolling over, such as lying down. Once this behavior is established, you reinforce behaviors more selectively. Reinforcing *successive approximations* eventually produces the desired behavior by teaching the animal to discriminate which behavior is being reinforced. Shaping has been used to condition animals to perform amazing feats: pigeons playing table tennis, dogs playing the piano, pigs doing housework such as picking up clothes and vacuuming, and so on (**FIGURE 6.14**). Shaping has also been used to teach mentally ill people appropriate social skills, to teach autistic children language, and to teach mentally retarded individuals basic skills such as dressing themselves. More generally, parents and educators often use shaping to encourage appropriate behavior in children, such as praising children for their initial—often illegible—attempts at handwriting.

REINFORCERS CAN BE CONDITIONED The most obvious reinforcers are those necessary for survival, such as food or water. Those that satisfy biological needs are called *primary reinforcers*. From an evolutionary standpoint, the learning value of primary reinforcers makes a great deal of sense, since organisms that repeatedly perform behaviors reinforced by food and water are more likely to survive and pass along their genes. But many apparent reinforcers do not directly satisfy biological needs. For example, a compliment, money, or an *A* on a paper can be reinforcing. Events or objects that serve as reinforcers but do not satisfy biological needs are called *secondary reinforcers*. These reinforcers are established through classical conditioning, as described earlier in this chapter: We learn to associate a neutral stimulus, such as money (CS), with rewards such as food, security, and power (US). Money is really only pieces of metal or of paper, but these and other neutral objects become meaningful through their associations with unconditioned stimuli.

REINFORCER POTENCY Some reinforcers are more powerful than others. An integrative theory of reinforcement was proposed by the psychologist David Premack, who theorized that a reinforcer's value could be determined by the amount of time an organism engages in a specific associated behavior when free to do anything. For instance, most children would choose to spend more time eating ice cream than eating spinach, so ice cream appears to be more reinforcing for children. One great advantage of Premack's theory is that it can account for differences in individuals' values. For people who prefer spinach to ice cream, spinach serves as a more potent reinforcer. A logical extension of Premack's theory, the *Premack principle,* is that a more valued activity can be used to reinforce the performance of a less valued activity. Parents use the Premack principle all the time: "Eat your spinach and then you'll get dessert," "Finish your homework and then you can go out," and so on.

Both Reinforcement and Punishment Can Be Positive or Negative

Reinforcement and punishment have the opposite effects on behavior. Whereas reinforcement increases a behavior's probability, punishment decreases its probability. For example, feeding a rat after it presses a lever will increase the probability that the rat will press the lever; giving a rat an electric shock after it presses a lever will decrease that action's probability. Both reinforcement and punishment can be positive or negative, depending on whether something is given or removed, not on whether any part of the process is good or bad.

POSITIVE AND NEGATIVE REINFORCEMENT Through the administration of a stimulus, **positive reinforcement** increases the probability that a behavior will be repeated. Positive reinforcement sometimes involves *reward*. Rewarded behaviors increase in frequency, as when people work harder in response to praise or increased pay. In contrast, **negative reinforcement** increases behavior through the *removal* of a stimulus. For instance, a rat is negatively reinforced when required to press a lever to turn off an electric shock. Negative reinforcement differs from punishment. If the rat were being punished, it would receive a shock *for* pressing the lever. The key point is that reinforcement—positive or negative—*increases* the likelihood of a behavior, whereas punishment *decreases* the likelihood of a behavior. Negative reinforcement is quite common in everyday life. You close the door to your room to shut out noise. You change the channel to avoid watching an awful program. In each case, you are trying to avoid or escape an unwanted stimulus, the negative reinforcer.

POSITIVE AND NEGATIVE PUNISHMENT Punishment reduces the probability that a behavior will recur, but it can do so through positive or negative means. **Positive punishment** decreases the behavior's probability through the administration of a stimulus. A rat's getting a shock for pressing a lever is an example of positive punishment. **Negative punishment** decreases the behavior's probability through the removal of a pleasurable stimulus. Teens whose driving privileges are revoked for speeding may be less likely to speed the next time they get behind the wheel. However, although losing driving privileges is a form of negative punishment, getting a speeding ticket is a form of positive punishment. In thinking about these terms, which can be confusing, consider whether the behavior is more likely to occur (reinforcement) or less likely to occur (punishment). A reinforcer or punisher is positive if something is applied and negative if something is removed or terminated. (For an overview of positive and negative kinds of both reinforcement and punishment, see **FIGURE 6.15**.)

positive reinforcement The increase in the probability of a behavior's being repeated following the administration of a stimulus.

negative reinforcement The increase in the probability of a behavior's being repeated through the removal of a stimulus.

positive punishment Punishment that occurs with the administration of a stimulus and thus decreases the probability of a behavior's recurring.

negative punishment Punishment that occurs with the removal of a stimulus and thus decreases the probability of a behavior's recurring.

FIGURE 6.15 Negative and Positive Reinforcement, Negative and Positive Punishment

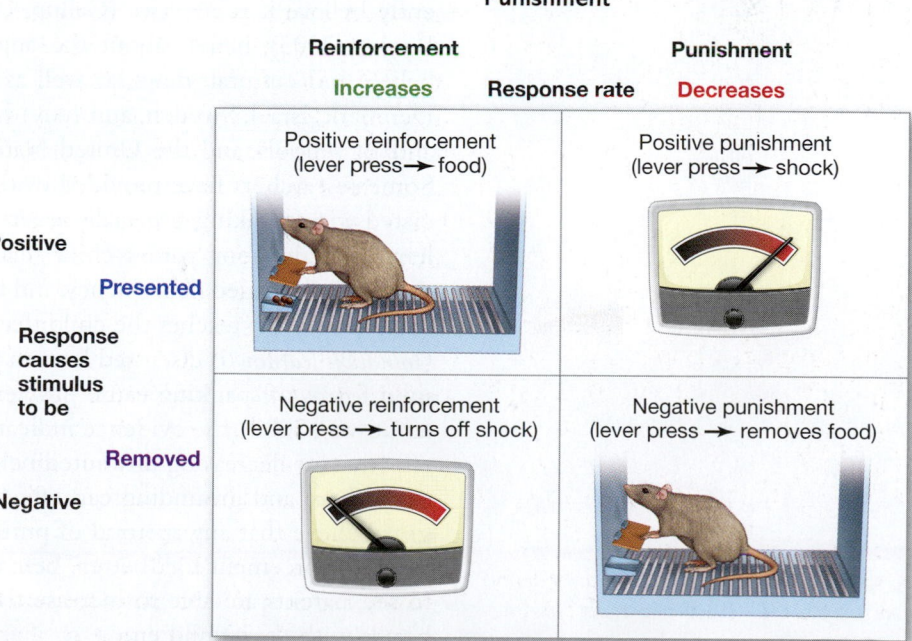

	Reinforcement	Punishment
	Increases	Response rate **Decreases**
Positive / Presented	Positive reinforcement (lever press → food)	Positive punishment (lever press → shock)
Response causes stimulus to be		
Removed / Negative	Negative reinforcement (lever press → turns off shock)	Negative punishment (lever press → removes food)

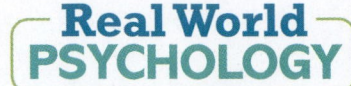
Real World PSYCHOLOGY

EFFECTIVENESS OF PARENTAL PUNISHMENT To make their children behave, parents sometimes use punishment as a means of discipline. But many contemporary psychologists believe that punishment is often applied ineffectively and that it may have unintended and unwanted consequences. Research has shown that for punishment to be effective, it must be reasonable, unpleasant, and applied immediately so that the relationship between the unwanted behavior and the punishment is clear (Goodall, 1984; O'Leary, 1995). But considerable potential exists for confusion. For example, sometimes punishment is applied after a desired action. If a student is punished after admitting to cheating on an exam, for example, the student may then associate the punishment with being honest rather than with the original offense, with the result that he or she learns not to tell the truth. As Skinner once pointed out, one thing people learn from punishment is how to avoid it; they learn not to get caught rather than how to behave appropriately.

Punishment can also lead to negative emotions, such as fear and anxiety, which may become associated, through classical conditioning, with the person who administers the punishment. A child may learn to fear a parent or teacher rather than stop the undesired behavior, and this result may damage the long-term relationship between adult and child (Gershoff, 2002). In addition, punishment often fails to offset the behavior's reinforcing aspects. In real life, any behavior can be reinforced in multiple ways. For instance, thumb sucking may be reinforced because it makes a child feel good and provides relief from negative emotions and hunger. The threat of punishment may not be sufficient to offset such rewards, but it may reinforce the child's secrecy about thumb sucking. For these and other reasons, most psychologists agree with Skinner's recommendation that reinforcement be used rather than punishment. A child complimented for being a good student will likely perform better academically than one punished for doing poorly. After all, reinforcing good behavior tells the child what to do, whereas punishing the child for bad behavior does not provide information about what the child should do to improve.

One form of punishment that most psychologists believe is especially ineffective is physical punishment, such as spanking. However, spanking is very common; nearly three-quarters of American parents spank their children and thus apparently believe it is effective (Gallup, 1995). As noted by Alan Kazdin and Corina Benjet (2003), beliefs about the appropriateness of spanking involve religious beliefs and cultural views, as well as legal issues. Many countries (e.g., Austria, Denmark, Israel, Sweden, and Italy) have banned corporal punishment in homes and/or schools, and the United Nations has passed resolutions discouraging it. Some researchers have provided evidence of numerous negative outcomes associated with spanking, especially severe spanking (Bender et al., 2007). These problems include poor parent-child relations, weaker moral values, mental health problems, increased delinquency, and future child abuse. One concern is that physical punishment teaches the child that violence is appropriate behavior for adults. (*Imitation learning* is discussed later in this chapter.) Although the extent to which mild forms of spanking cause problems is open to debate (Baumrind, Larzelere, & Cowan, 2002), the evidence indicates that other forms of punishment are more effective for decreasing unwanted behaviors (Kazdin & Benjet, 2003). Time-outs, small fines, and grounding can effectively modify behavior. Yet many psychologists believe that any method of punishment is less effective than providing positive reinforcement for "better" behaviors. By rewarding the behaviors they wish to see, parents are able to increase those behaviors while building more positive bonds with their children.

Operant Conditioning Is Influenced by Schedules of Reinforcement

How often should a reinforcer be given? For fast learning, behavior might be reinforced each time it occurs, a process known as **continuous reinforcement.** In the real world, behavior is seldom reinforced continuously. Animals do not find food each time they look for it, and people do not receive praise each time they behave acceptably. Reinforcing behavior intermittently, or **partial reinforcement,** is used more commonly. Partial reinforcement's effect on conditioning depends on the reinforcement schedule.

RATIO AND INTERVAL SCHEDULES Partial reinforcement can be administered according to either the number of behavioral responses or the passage of time. For instance, factory workers can be paid by the piece (behavioral responses) or by the hour (passage of time). A **ratio schedule** is based on the number of times the behavior occurs, as when a behavior is reinforced on every third or tenth occurrence. An **interval schedule** is based on a specific unit of time, as when a behavior is reinforced when it is performed every minute or hour. Ratio reinforcement generally leads to greater responding than does interval reinforcement. For example, factory workers paid by the piece are usually more productive than those paid by the hour, especially if the workers receive incentives for higher productivity.

FIXED AND VARIABLE SCHEDULES Partial reinforcement also can be given on a *fixed* or *variable* schedule. In a **fixed schedule,** the reinforcer consistently is given after a specific number of occurrences or after a specific amount of time. For example, whether factory workers are paid by the piece or by the hour, they usually are paid according to a fixed rate, earning the same for each piece or for each hour. The rate of reinforcement is entirely predictable. In a **variable schedule,** the reinforcer is given at different rates or at different times. The responder does not know how many behaviors need to be performed or how much time needs to pass before reinforcement will occur. One example of variable reinforcement is when a salesperson receives a commission only when a customer agrees to purchase a product. (The patterns of behavior typically observed under different schedules of reinforcement are illustrated in **FIGURE 6.16.**)

BEHAVIORAL PERSISTENCE The schedule of reinforcement also affects the persistence of behavior. Continuous reinforcement is highly effective for teaching a behavior, but if the reinforcement is stopped, the behavior extinguishes quickly.

continuous reinforcement A type of learning in which the desired behavior is reinforced each time it occurs.

partial reinforcement A type of learning in which behavior is reinforced intermittently.

ratio schedule A schedule in which reinforcement is based on the number of times the behavior occurs.

interval schedule A schedule in which reinforcement is available after a specific unit of time.

fixed schedule A schedule in which reinforcement is consistently provided upon each occurrence.

variable schedule A schedule in which reinforcement is applied at different rates or at different times.

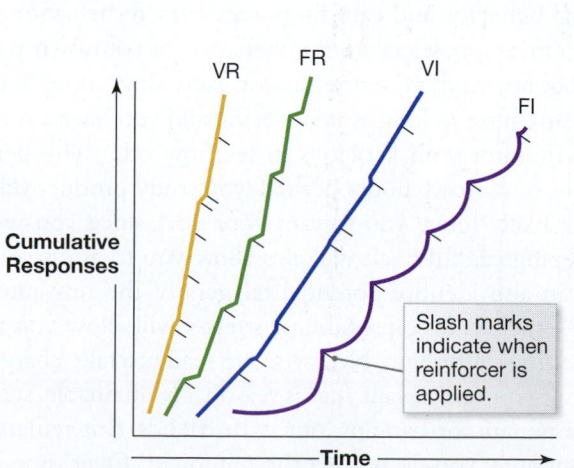

VR FR VI FI

Cumulative Responses

Slash marks indicate when reinforcer is applied.

Time

Variable ratio: A slot machine pays off on average every few pulls, but you never know which pull will pay.

Fixed ratio: You are paid each time you complete a chore.

Variable interval: You listen to the radio to hear your favorite song. You do not know when you will hear it.

Fixed interval: When quizzes are scheduled at fixed intervals, students study only when the quiz is to be administered (the grade is the reinforcer).

FIGURE 6.16 Behavior and Reinforcement The curves on this graph show a relative comparison of cumulative responses under different schedules of reinforcement over time. The steeper the line, the higher the response rate. Ratio reinforcement leads to the highest rate of response.

For instance, normally when you put money in a vending machine it gives you a product. If it fails to do so, you quickly will stop putting your money into it. By contrast, at a casino you might drop a lot of money into a slot machine that rarely rewards you with a "win." Such behavior is not simply the result of an addiction to gambling. Rather, people put money in slot machines because the machines *sometimes* provide monetary rewards. Psychologists explain this persistent behavior as the effect of a *variable-ratio schedule* of reinforcement.

The **partial-reinforcement extinction effect** refers to the greater persistence of behavior under partial reinforcement than under continuous reinforcement. During continuous reinforcement, the learner easily can detect when reinforcement has stopped. But when the behavior is reinforced only some of the time, the learner needs to repeat the behavior comparatively more times to detect the absence of reinforcement. Thus the less frequent the reinforcement during training, the greater the resistance to extinction. Conditioning a behavior so that it persists involves reinforcing it continuously during early acquisition and then slowly changing to partial reinforcement. Parents naturally follow this strategy in teaching behaviors to their children, as in toilet training.

BEHAVIOR MODIFICATION **Behavior modification** is the use of operant-conditioning techniques to eliminate unwanted behaviors and replace them with desirable ones. The general rationale behind behavior modification is that most unwanted behaviors are learned and therefore can be unlearned. Parents, teachers, and animal trainers use conditioning strategies widely. People can be taught, for example, to be more productive at work, to save energy, and to drive more safely. Children with profound learning disabilities can be trained to communicate and to interact. As discussed in Chapter 15, operant techniques are also effective for treating many psychological conditions, such as depression and anxiety disorders.

Another widespread behavior modification method draws on the principles of secondary reinforcement. Chimpanzees can be trained to perform tasks in exchange for tokens, which they can later trade for food. The tokens thus reinforce behavior, and the chimps work as hard to obtain the tokens as they work to obtain food. Using similar principles, prisons, mental hospitals, schools, and classrooms often use *token economies*, in which people earn tokens for completing tasks and lose tokens for behaving badly. The people can later trade their tokens for objects or privileges, rewards that not only reinforce good behavior but also give participants a sense of control over their environment. So, for instance, teachers can provide tokens to students for obeying class rules, turning in homework on time, and helping others. At some future point, the tokens can be exchanged for rewards, such as fun activities or extra recess time. In mental hospitals, token economies can encourage good grooming and appropriate social behavior and can discourage bizarre behavior.

To see behavior modification in action, select a target behavior of your own you wish to change, such as swearing, not studying enough, not exercising enough, or watching too much television—anything, as long as it is specific and you have a realistic goal for changing it. Then monitor your activities to see how often you perform this behavior—for example, how many hours per day you study productively. Simply noting the behavior will likely move you toward your goal, since you will be more conscious of it, but keeping careful track will also allow you to assess your progress. By monitoring, you can also identify potential triggers of the unwanted behavior. Knowing the triggers—such as time pressure or stress—will allow you to develop plans or strategies for dealing with them. Now you are ready to take charge. Pick a good reinforcer, something you really want that is reasonably attainable, such as seeing a movie, eating at a restaurant, or hanging out with friends. But remember: If you do not behave appropriately, you do not get the reinforcer! Over time, as

partial-reinforcement extinction effect The greater persistence of behavior under partial reinforcement than under continuous reinforcement.

behavior modification The use of operant-conditioning techniques to eliminate unwanted behaviors and replace them with desirable ones.

you successfully change the behavior, phase out the reinforcer so you are performing the behavior out of habit. Once you are used to exercising regularly, for example, you will do it regularly, and it may even become reinforcing on its own. Give it a try—you might amaze yourself with the power of behavior modification.

Biology and Cognition Influence Operant Conditioning

Behaviorists such as B. F. Skinner believed that all behavior could be explained by straightforward conditioning principles. Recall from the opening of this chapter that Skinner's *Walden Two* describes a utopia in which all of society's problems are solved through operant conditioning. In reality, however, reinforcement schedules explain only a certain amount of human behavior. Biology constrains learning, and reinforcement does not always have to be present for learning to take place.

BIOLOGICAL CONSTRAINTS Although behaviorists believed that any behavior could be shaped through reinforcement, we now know that animals have a hard time learning behaviors that run counter to their evolutionary adaptation. A good example of biological constraints was obtained by Marian and Keller Breland, a husband-and-wife team of psychologists who used operant-conditioning techniques to train animals for commercials (Breland & Breland, 1961). Many of their animals refused to perform certain tasks they had been taught. For instance, a raccoon learned to place coins in a piggy bank, but eventually refused to perform this task, instead standing over the bank and briskly rubbing the coins in its paws. The rubbing behavior was not reinforced; it actually delayed reinforcement. One explanation for the raccoon's behavior is that the task was incompatible with innate adaptive behaviors. The raccoon associated the coin with food and treated it the same way: Rubbing food between the paws is hardwired for raccoons (**FIGURE 6.17**). Along similar lines, pigeons can be trained to peck at keys to obtain food or secondary reinforcers, but it is difficult to get them to peck at keys to avoid electric shock. However, they can learn to avoid shock by flapping their wings because wing flapping is their natural means of escape. The psychologist Robert Bolles has argued that animals have built-in defense reactions to threatening stimuli (Bolles, 1970). Conditioning is most effective when the association between the behavioral response and the reinforcement is similar to the animal's built-in predispositions.

From the evolutionary perspective, the brain is a compilation of domain specific modules, each responsible for different cognitive functions. Thus learning results not from general learning mechanisms but from many unique mechanisms that solve individual adaptive problems (Rozin & Kalat, 1971; Shettleworth, 2001). As the evolutionary psychologist Randy Gallistel (2000) argues, just as lungs are adapted for breathing and ears are adapted for hearing—no one would argue that lungs can be used to hear or ears can be used to breathe—so various learning mechanisms have evolved to solve specific problems. Consider, says Gallistel, an ant that leaves its nest to forage for food. Typically, the ant takes a circuitous path until it finds food, at which point it takes a direct path back to the nest, even over unfamiliar territory. No traditional model of learning accounts for how the ant calculates that direct path. The ant has never been rewarded for following this path, nor does it have a classically conditioned association between environmental objects and the path. Instead, the ant is guided by mental processes that compute small changes in distance and direction. These mental processes occur because, through adaptation, the ant's ancestors "learned" (became hardwired) to find that direct path and thus not risk losing the food on a circuitous journey home. Gallistel's point is that learning consists of specialized mechanisms (rather than universal mechanisms) that solve the adaptive problems animals face in their environments.

FIGURE 6.17 Biological Constraints
Animals have a hard time learning behaviors that run counter to their evolutionary adaptation. For example, raccoons are hardwired to rub food between their paws, as this raccoon is doing; they have trouble learning *not* to rub objects.

ACQUISITION/PERFORMANCE DISTINCTION Another challenge to the idea that reinforcement is responsible for all behavior is that learning can take place without reinforcement. Edward Tolman, an early cognitive theorist, argued that reinforcement has more impact on performance than on learning. At the time, Tolman was conducting experiments in which rats had to learn to run through complex mazes to obtain food. Tolman believed that the rats developed **cognitive maps,** in this case spatial representations of the mazes, that helped them learn to find the food quickly. To test his theory, Tolman and his students studied three groups of rats whose task was to travel through a maze to a "goal box" containing the reinforcer, usually food. The first group received no reinforcement—they found no food in the box—and simply wandered through the maze on each trial. The second group received reinforcement on every trial and learned to find the goal box quickly. The third group, critically, started receiving reinforcement only after the first 10 trials, at which point it showed an amazingly fast learning curve and immediately caught up to the group that had been continuously reinforced. This result implies that the rats had learned a cognitive map of the maze and used it when the reinforcement began. Tolman's term **latent learning** refers to learning that takes place without reinforcement (**FIGURE 6.18**).

cognitive map A visual/spatial mental representation of an environment.

latent learning Learning that takes place in the absence of reinforcement.

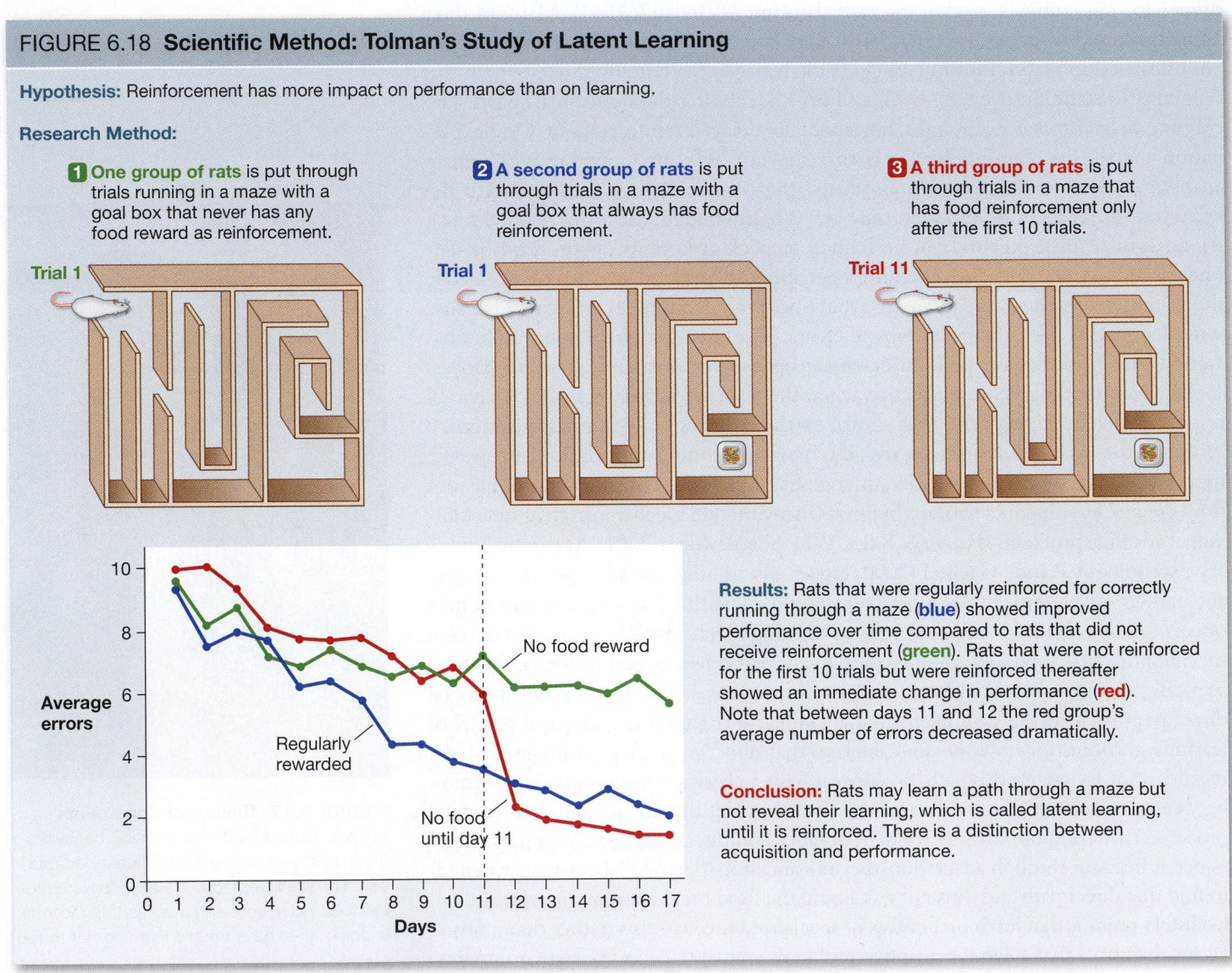

FIGURE 6.18 Scientific Method: Tolman's Study of Latent Learning

Hypothesis: Reinforcement has more impact on performance than on learning.

Research Method:

1 **One group of rats** is put through trials running in a maze with a goal box that never has any food reward as reinforcement.

Trial 1

2 **A second group of rats** is put through trials in a maze with a goal box that always has food reinforcement.

Trial 1

3 **A third group of rats** is put through trials in a maze that has food reinforcement only after the first 10 trials.

Trial 11

Average errors

No food reward

Regularly rewarded

No food until day 11

Days

Results: Rats that were regularly reinforced for correctly running through a maze (**blue**) showed improved performance over time compared to rats that did not receive reinforcement (**green**). Rats that were not reinforced for the first 10 trials but were reinforced thereafter showed an immediate change in performance (**red**). Note that between days 11 and 12 the red group's average number of errors decreased dramatically.

Conclusion: Rats may learn a path through a maze but not reveal their learning, which is called latent learning, until it is reinforced. There is a distinction between acquisition and performance.

Another form of learning that takes place without reinforcement is *insight learning*—a form of problem solving in which a solution suddenly emerges after either a period of inaction or contemplation of the problem. (On problem solving, see Chapter 8, "Thinking and Intelligence.") You probably have had this sort of experience, in which you mull over a problem for a while and then suddenly know the answer. The presence of reinforcement does not adequately explain insight learning, but it predicts whether the behavior is subsequently repeated.

The Value of Reinforcement Follows Economic Principles

A relatively new approach to understanding operant conditioning considers reinforcement's value in the context of basic economic principles, such as supply and demand. That which is in short supply typically is valued more and therefore is a more potent reinforcer. Sometimes the economic considerations are more complicated. Which would you prefer, $100 today or $1,000 next year? Although the larger payment might appear to be more reinforcing, its value is discounted because of the significant delay before you receive it. But if you really need money right now, waiting has additional costs. Indeed, adults with lower incomes discount future payments more steeply than do those with higher incomes (Green, Myerson, Lichtman, Rosen, & Fry, 1996). At the heart of the behavioral economics approach are two ideas: that people and other animals often need to choose between reinforcers, and that a particular reinforcer's worth is affected by the likelihood of its payoff and how long that payoff might take. This approach has provided insights into various behaviors, especially those associated with addiction. Warren Bickel and his colleagues (1999; Madden, Petry, Badger, & Bickel, 1997) found that smokers and heroin addicts discounted future rewards more greatly than did nonaddicts, a tendency that may contribute to their problems with impulsivity and self-control (Bickel et al., 2007). (The issue of delaying immediate gratification to obtain long-term rewards is discussed more fully in Chapter 9, "Motivation and Emotion.")

Behavioral choice is also implicated in studies of animal foraging. Where animals choose to eat depends on the likelihood that food will be present, the energy costs associated with obtaining the food, and the risks associated with predators (Shettleworth, 2001). Should an animal eat all the berries in one patch and then search for a new patch, or should it save some berries for later while it searches (since the new patch might take a while to find)? Researchers who study animals in their natural habitats find that animals are highly sensitive to the relative rates of reinforcement among different patches and will sometimes take risks in finding food. The time an animal spends eating in one patch will be influenced by the rate of reinforcement, the relative rate of reinforcement in other patches, and the time it might take to travel to those other patches. *Optimal foraging theory* describes how animals in the wild choose their own reinforcement schedules.

Consider an animal faced with the choice of feeding from two locations: Both have the same average amount of food, but one is much more variable, sometimes having no food and sometimes having a lot. If the animal is facing starvation, its best chance for survival is to follow the apparently risky strategy of foraging in the more highly variable location, because if the consistent site has no food on one day it is likely not to have food the next day. Animals also learn to vary how they eat according to the likelihood of being attacked by predators. Researchers have found that rats, especially when food deprived, eat especially quickly in the dark (Wishaw, Drigenberg, & Comery, 1992). Although eating quickly is optimal for consuming large amounts of food, it is not optimal for digestion. When in the light, where they are better able to detect predators, rats eat more slowly, but they frequently scan the environment to check for danger. Such variations reflect the fact that even a simple behavior such as eating requires a number of calculations to detect the costs and benefits associated with different behavioral options. Animals' choices reflect specialized learning capacities adaptive to their environments.

 SUMMING UP

How Does Operant Conditioning Differ from Classical Conditioning?

Whereas classical conditioning involves the learned association between two events, operant conditioning involves the learned association between a behavior and its consequences. B. F. Skinner developed the concept of operant conditioning to explain why some behaviors are repeated and others are not. Reinforcement increases a behavior's likelihood of being repeated, whereas punishment reduces that likelihood. If a reinforcer increases a behavior when presented, it is a positive reinforcer; if it increases the behavior when removed, it is a negative reinforcer. Although Skinner was confident that operant conditioning could ultimately explain all behavior, his theories have faced a number of challenges. Chief among these are that it is difficult to change instinctive behaviors and that learning can take place without reinforcement. Modern learning theorists recognize cognitive processes' influence on behavior and biology's constraints on it. Models based on economic theory have become increasingly useful for understanding how animals choose among reinforcers.

MEASURING UP

1. Indicate whether each of the following people and phenomena is related to operant conditioning or classical conditioning.
   a. Ivan Pavlov
   b. B. F. Skinner
   c. behavior modification
   d. A behavior is associated with its consequences.
   e. Two events that occur close together in time are associated.
   f. used to train animals to perform tricks and useful tasks
   g. Premack principle
   h. Punishment's effects are explained by this type of conditioning.

2. Suppose a mother is trying to get her eight-year-old to stop cursing. Each time the child curses, the mother waits until the child's father is present before spanking the child. Select the better answers:
   a. The time interval between the cursing and the punishment is
      _____ too long for optimal learning.
      _____ fine as long as the punishment is administered on the same day as the cursing.
   b. One likely outcome to the continued use of this punishment is
      _____ the child will curse at times he or she is unlikely to be caught.
      _____ the child will gradually extinguish the cursing response.
   c. Generalization is likely to occur such that
      _____ the child curses only when the father is at work.
      _____ the child comes to fear the father and mother.
   d. What is the child likely to learn?
      _____ Do not get caught cursing.
      _____ Cursing is a nasty behavior that must be stopped.
   e. A more effective approach would be to
      _____ spank the child as soon as the cursing occurs.
      _____ provide rewards for not cursing.

How Does Watching Others Affect Learning?

Suppose you were teaching someone to fly an airplane. How might you apply the learning principles discussed in this chapter to accomplish your goal? Obviously, reinforcing arbitrary correct behaviors would be a disastrous way to train an aspiring pilot. Similarly, teaching someone to play football, eat with chopsticks, or perform complex dance steps requires more than simple reinforcement. We learn many behaviors not by doing them but by observing others doing them. We learn social etiquette through observation, for example. We sometimes learn to be anxious in particular situations by seeing that other people are anxious. We often acquire attitudes about politics, religion, people, objects, and so on, from outside sources, such as parents, peers, teachers, and the media.

LEARNING OBJECTIVES

Provide an example of culture's effect on learning.

Describe Bandura's Bobo doll study and explain its significance.

Discuss mirror neurons' role in learning.

Learning Can Be Passed On through Cultural Transmission

Although all humans belong to the same species and share the vast majority of genes, around the world there is enormous cultural diversity in what people think and how they behave. Would you be the same person if you had been raised in a small village in China, or in the jungles of South America, or in the mountains of Afghanistan? Probably not, since your religious beliefs, your values, and even your musical tastes are shaped by the culture in which you are raised. The term that evolutionary psychologists use for transmitted cultural knowledge is *meme*. **Memes** are analogous to genes, in that they are selectively passed on from one generation to the next, though some, such as fads, die out quite quickly.

meme A unit of knowledge transferred within a culture.

One good example of the cultural transmission of knowledge is the case of Imo the monkey. In the 1950s, researchers who were studying monkeys in Japan threw some sweet potatoes onto a sandy beach for the monkeys there to eat. Imo developed the habit of washing her sweet potatoes in the ocean to get the sand off. Within a short time, other monkeys copied Imo, and soon all the monkeys were washing their potatoes before eating them. Through social learning, this behavior has continued to be passed along from one generation to the next, and monkeys there still wash their potatoes (Dugatkin, 2004; **FIGURE 6.19**). Unlike natural selection, which typically occurs slowly over thousands of years, memes can spread quickly, as in the worldwide adoption of the Internet. Although memes can be conditioned through association or reinforcement, many memes are learned by watching others' behavior.

CULTURAL BELIEFS ABOUT LEARNING Children's levels of achievement sometimes differ widely across cultures. For example, Asian children often perform better in school than their North American and European peers, especially in math and science (Stevenson & Stigler, 1992). Many explanations of this "learning gap" have been proposed (some of which will be considered in more detail in the next chapter). One prominent theory is that Asians and Westerners have somewhat different understandings of learning and that these differences affect the motivation to learn and learning behaviors. According to Li (2003), the Chinese regard knowledge as "something that is indispensable to their personal lives," a notion rooted in the Confucian understanding of learning. By contrast, Li found that samples of Western learners view the ability to learn as something relatively enduring that exists within the learner—some people can learn well, and others cannot. The Asian view is seen as more adaptive because it is consistent with the notion that we can all learn if we work hard. For Asians, learning is an incremental process, and a good foundation makes later learning easier.

FIGURE 6.19 Memes In the 1950s, Imo developed and unwittingly passed along to her fellow monkeys the meme, or cultural knowledge, of washing sweet potatoes in the ocean. The descendants of these sweet potato–washing macaques continue the behavior, as shown here.

Learning Can Occur through Observation

observational learning Learning that occurs when behaviors are acquired or modified following exposure to others performing the behavior.

Observational learning, the acquiring or modifying of a behavior after exposure to at least one performance of that behavior, is a powerful adaptive tool for humans and other animals. Offspring can learn basic skills by watching adults perform those skills, they can learn which things are safe to eat by watching what adults eat, and they can learn to fear dangerous objects and dangerous situations by watching adults avoid those objects and situations. Children even acquire beliefs through observation. Young children are sponges, absorbing everything that goes on around them. They learn by watching as much as by doing.

BANDURA'S OBSERVATIONAL STUDIES The most thorough work on observational learning was conducted in the 1960s by the psychologist Albert Bandura. In a now-classic series of studies, Bandura showed preschool children a film of an adult playing with a large inflatable doll called Bobo. In the film, the adult either played quietly with Bobo or attacked the doll furiously, whacking it with a mallet, punching it in the nose, and kicking it around the room. When the children were later allowed to play with a number of toys, including the Bobo doll, those who had seen the more aggressive display were more than twice as likely to act aggressively toward the doll (Bandura, Ross, & Ross, 1961). These results suggest that exposing children to media violence may encourage them to act aggressively (**FIGURE 6.20**).

FIGURE 6.20 Scientific Method: The Bobo Doll Studies

Hypothesis: Children can acquire behaviors through observation.

Research Method:

1 Two groups of preschool children were shown a film of an adult playing with a large inflatable doll called Bobo.

2 One group saw the adult play quietly with the doll (activity not shown below).

3 The other group saw the adult attack the doll (activity shown in top row below).

Result: When children were allowed to play with the doll later, those who had seen the aggressive display were more than twice as likely to act aggressively toward the doll.

Conclusion: Exposing children to media violence may encourage them to act aggressively.

SOCIAL LEARNING OF FEAR The psychologist Susan Mineka noticed that monkeys raised in laboraties do not fear snakes, whereas monkeys raised in the wild fear snakes intensely. She set out to explore whether monkeys, by observing other monkeys reacting fearfully to snakes, could develop a phobia of snakes. Mineka and her colleagues set up an experiment with two groups of rhesus monkeys, one group reared in the laboratory and one group reared in the wild. To obtain food, the monkeys were required to reach beyond a clear box that contained either a snake or a neutral object. When a snake was in the box, the wild-reared monkeys not only did not touch the food but also showed signs of distress, such as clinging to their cages and making threatening faces. The laboratory-raised monkeys reached past the box even if it contained a snake, and they showed no overt signs of fear. The researchers then showed the laboratory-raised monkeys the wild monkeys' fearful response, to see if it would affect the laboratory monkeys' reactions to the snake. The laboratory monkeys quickly developed a fear of the snakes, and this fear was maintained over a three-month period (Mineka, Davidson, Cook, & Keir, 1984; **FIGURE 6.21**). Humans too can learn to fear particular stimuli by observing others, as when people become afraid of traveling to a specific neighborhood after watching news video of a person being assaulted there. In fact, people can learn to fear particular things simply by hearing that the things are dangerous. Thus social forces play an important role in the learning of fear (Olsson & Phelps, 2007).

TEACHING THROUGH DEMONSTRATION Because humans can learn through observation, they can be taught many complex skills through demonstration. For instance, parents use slow and exaggerated motions to show their children how to tie their shoes. Although the idea is somewhat controversial, some nonhuman animals appear to teach their offspring certain skills through demonstration (Caro & Hauser, 1992). For instance, cheetah mothers appear to facilitate the stages in which their young learn to hunt. At first, the mothers kill their prey. Later, they simply knock down the prey and let their cubs kill it, or they injure the prey to make it easier for the cubs to knock down and kill.

Animals and Humans Imitate Others

Human and nonhuman animals readily imitate others' actions. In one study, pigeons observed other pigeons receiving reinforcement, namely food, for stepping on a bar attached to a feeder or pecking at the feeder. When the observing pigeons were placed before the feeder, they tended to use whichever technique they had seen (Zentall, Sutton, & Sherburne, 1996). Within a few days (or even hours) of birth, human newborns will imitate facial expressions, and they will continue to imitate gestures and other actions as they mature (**FIGURE 6.22**)—just like the monkeys, discussed above, who copied Imo the monkey's potato washing.

The imitation of observed behavior is commonly called **modeling,** in that humans or other animals reproduce the behaviors of *models*—those being observed. Modeling in humans is influenced by numerous factors. Generally, we will more likely imitate the actions of models who are attractive, have high status, and are somewhat similar to ourselves. In addition, modeling will be effective only if the observer is physically capable of imitating the behavior. Simply watching Tiger Woods blast 300-yard drives does not mean we could do so if handed a golf club.

Models' influences on behavior often occur implicitly, without our being aware that our behaviors are being altered. People might not want to admit that they have changed their ways of speaking or dressing to resemble those of celebrities, but

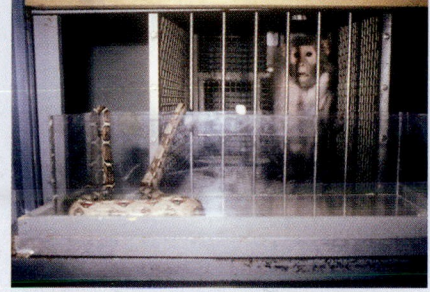

FIGURE 6.21 Scientific Method: Fear Response in Rhesus Monkeys

Hypothesis: Monkeys can develop phobias about snakes by observing other monkeys reacting fearfully to snakes.

Research Method:

1 Two sets of monkeys, one reared in the laboratory and one reared in the wild, had to reach past a clear box to get food.

2 When the clear box contained a snake, the laboratory-reared monkeys reached across the box, but the wild-reared monkeys refused to reach across the box.

Results: After watching wild-reared monkeys react, laboratory-reared monkeys no longer reached across the box.

Conclusion: Fears can be learned through observation.

modeling The imitation of behavior through observational learning.

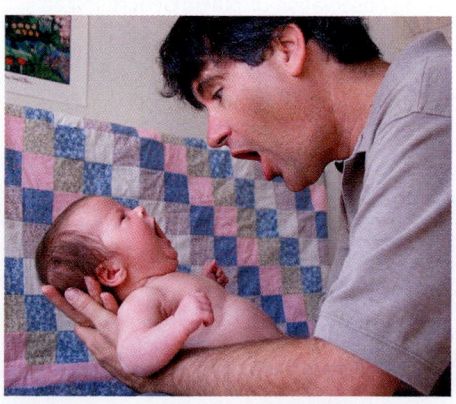

FIGURE 6.22 Modeling Babies frequently imitate expressions and behaviors.

overwhelming evidence says that we imitate what we see in others, especially those we admire. Adolescents whose favorite actors smoke in movies are much more likely to smoke (Tickle, Sargent, Dalton, Beach, & Heatherton, 2001), and the more smoking that adolescents observe in movies, the more positive their attitudes about smoking become and the more likely they are to begin smoking (Sargent et al., 2005). These effects are strongest among children whose parents do not smoke, perhaps because what such children learn about smoking comes completely through the media, which tend to glamorize the habit. Movies, for example, often present smokers as attractive, healthy, and wealthy, not like the typical smoker. Adolescents do not generally decide to smoke after watching one movie's glamorous depiction of smoking. Rather, images of smokers as mature, cool, sexy—things adolescents want to be—shape adolescents' attitudes about smoking and subsequently lead to imitation. As adolescent viewers learn to associate smoking with people they admire, they incorporate the general message that smoking is desirable.

VICARIOUS REINFORCEMENT Another factor that determines whether observers imitate a model is whether the model is reinforced for performing the behavior. In one study, Bandura and his colleagues showed children a film of an adult aggressively playing with a Bobo doll, but this time the film ended in one of three different ways (Bandura, Ross, & Ross, 1963). In the first version, a control condition, the adult experienced no consequences for the aggressive behavior. In the second version, the adult was rewarded for the behavior with candy and praise. In the third version, the adult was punished for the behavior by being both spanked and verbally reprimanded. When subsequently allowed to play with the Bobo doll, the children who observed the model being rewarded were much more likely to be aggressive toward the doll than was the control group. In contrast, those who saw the model being punished were less likely to be aggressive than was the control group. These findings do not mean that the less aggressive children did not learn the behavior. Later, all the children were offered small gifts to perform the model's actions and performed them reliably. A key distinction in learning is between the *acquisition* of a behavior and its *performance*. Here, all the children learned the behavior, but only those who saw the model being rewarded performed the behavior. **Vicarious learning** occurs when people learn about an action's consequences by observing others being rewarded or punished for performing the action.

MIRROR NEURONS What happens in the brain during imitation learning? An intriguing study found that, when a monkey observes another monkey reaching for an object, **mirror neurons** in the observing monkey's brain become activated (Rizzolatti, Fadiga, Gallese, & Fogassi, 1996). These same (mirror) neurons would be activated if the observing monkey performed the behavior. Mirror neurons are especially likely to become activated when a monkey observes the target monkey engaging in movement that has some goal, such as reaching to grasp an object. Neither the sight of the object alone nor the sight of the target monkey at rest leads to activation of these mirror neurons.

Brain imaging techniques have identified similar mirror neurons in humans (Rizzolatti & Craighero, 2004). Thus every time you observe another person engaging in an action, similar neural circuits are firing both in your brain and in the other person's. Mirror neurons' function is currently open to debate. This system may serve as the basis of imitation learning, but mirror neurons' firing in the observer's brain does not always lead to imitative behavior in the observer. Therefore, some theorists speculate, mirror neurons may help us explain and predict others' behavior. In other words, mirror neurons may allow us to step into the shoes of people we

vicarious learning Learning that occurs when people learn the consequences of an action by observing others being rewarded or punished for performing the action.

mirror neurons Neurons that are activated during observation of others performing an action.

observe so we can better understand those people's actions. One speculation is that mirror neurons are the neural basis for empathy, the emotional response of feeling what other people are experiencing.

Humans also have mirror neurons for mouth movements, and these are stimulated when observers see a mouth move in a way typical of chewing or speaking (Ferrari, Gallese, Rizzolatti, & Fogassi, 2003). This phenomenon has led to speculation that mirror neurons are important not only for imitation learning but also for humans' ability to communicate through language. Mirror neurons may be a brain system that creates a link between the sender and receiver of a message. Rizzolatti and Arbib (1998) have proposed that the mirror neuron system evolved to allow language. Their theory relies on the idea that speech evolved mainly from gestures, and indeed people readily understand many nonverbal behaviors, such as waving or thrusting a fist in the air. If their theory is true, speech sounds came to represent gestures. Indeed, evidence indicates that listening to sentences that describe actions activates the same brain regions active when those actions are observed (Tettamanti et al., 2005). Even reading words that represent actions leads to brain activity in relevant motor regions, as when the word *lick* activates brain regions that control tongue movements (Hauk, Johnsrude, & Pulvermüller, 2004).

MEDIA AND VIOLENCE On average, a television in the United States is on for five or six hours per day, and young children often spend more time watching television than doing any other activity, including schoolwork (Roberts, 2000). Worldwide, children consume an average of three hours per day of screen media—television, movies, and video games (Groebel, 1998). The most popular media contain considerable amounts of violence (Carnagey, Anderson, & Bartholow, 2007). Saturday morning cartoons, watched by 60 percent of American children, average 20 aggressively violent acts per hour, whereas prime-time TV shows average only five (National Television Violence Study, 1997, 1998).

Media violence has been found to increase the likelihood of short- and long-term aggressive and violent behavior (Anderson et al., 2003). In one study, after children played a violent video game for only 20 minutes, they were less physiologically aroused by scenes of real violence; in other words, they had become desensitized to violence, showing fewer helping behaviors and increased aggression (Carnagey, Anderson, & Bushman, 2007). In another study, Leonard Eron and his colleagues found that TV viewing habits at age 8 predicted, for age 30, amounts of both violent behavior and criminal activity (Eron, 1987). Adolescents who played certain types of violent video games showed decreased activation in the prefrontal brain regions (involved in inhibition, concentration, and self-control) and more activation in the amygdala (involved in emotional arousal) than those who played a nonviolent game (Radiological Society of North America, 2006). A 2002 meta-analysis of studies involving media violence effects—taking into account laboratory experiments, field experiments, cross-sectional correlational studies, and longitudinal studies showed that exposure to violent media increases the likelihood of aggression (Gentile, Saleem, & Anderson, 2007). The average effect size (the magnitude of the association between independent and dependent variables), determined by statistically averaging across the hundreds of studies, is nearly as large as that linking smoking and cancer, and is larger than the effect size for condom nonuse and HIV transmission or for children's lead exposure and their IQs (Bushman & Anderson, 2001).

A number of problems exist, however, with the studies on this topic. The social psychologist Jonathan Freedman (1984) notes that many of the so-called aggressive behaviors displayed by children could be interpreted as playful rather than aggressive. A more serious concern is whether the studies generalize to the real world.

Do people learn violent behavior through the media? As discussed above, the research says yes, but the evidence remains controversial (**FIGURE 6.23**). The neuroscience philosopher Susan Hurley (2004) calls attention to current work, in the cognitive sciences, about imitation and mirror neurons. This research shows that in addition to learning through conscious imitative behavior, humans imitate behavior automatically and unconsciously—they are not always aware of the cues that influence their actions. Violent behavior is subject to these unconscious imitative tendencies. Hurley suggests that the importance for individuals and the social significance of imitative behavior are greatly underappreciated. People have difficulty recognizing that they are ruled to a large extent by unconscious and automatic behavior because this notion threatens their beliefs about personal autonomy and conscious control. The less aware people are of the influences on their behavior, including their violent behavior, the less they are able to control the extent of these influences.

Given these findings, should the United States have a public policy limiting violent media? Opponents to such regulation argue that it would tamper with freedom of speech, one of the fundamental beliefs of a liberal society. Even speech that can harm others is protected on the basis of truth, democracy, and autonomy. But as Hurley points out, not all speech is protected: You are not allowed to shout "Fire!" in a theater or make loud noises where there is avalanche danger. Hurley argues that violent entertainment does not deserve protection under freedom of speech, since its effects feed unconscious, automatic responses. It therefore cannot be rationalized by audience autonomy—or even by speaker autonomy because of the producers' primarily commercial motives. If "violent entertainment produces through automatic processes significant harm to others as a result of increased levels of violent behavior across the popu-

FIGURE 6.23 Media and Violent Behavior Many scientists see a direct correlation between exposure to violent media (such as this video game) and aggressive behavior. Still, correlation does not prove causation (see Chapter 2, "Research Methodology").

lation of viewers," Hurley argues, "prevention of such harm to third parties provides a strong reason (or 'compelling interest') for liberal government to interfere with violent entertainment."

Should depictions of violence be banned even if they affect only some people? What might parents do if they are concerned about what their children watch? Are we obligated to protect people from the results of violent media? If so, what is the best way to do so? Who should rate the violent content of television shows, of films, and of video games? How should citizens be informed so they can make informed choices about consuming media violence and letting their children consume it? Should the news media have guidelines to ensure the accurate reporting of scientific findings about media violence's effects? Should the government require medical personnel to discuss media violence with parents or guardians, such as during children's immunization visits?

Viewing a violent film clip in a lab is unlike watching TV in one's living room. The film clips used in studies are often brief and extremely violent, and the child watches them alone. In the real world, violent episodes are interspersed with nonviolent material, and children often watch them with others, who may buffer the effect.

Even the longitudinal studies that assess childhood TV watching and later violent behavior fail to prove satisfactorily that TV caused the behavior. Extraneous variables, such as personality, poverty, or parental negligence, could have affected both TV viewing habits and violent tendencies. After all, not all of those who view violence on TV become aggressive later in life. Perhaps those who watch excessive amounts of TV, and therefore have fewer opportunities to develop social skills, act aggressively. Correlation does not prove causation (as discussed in Chapter 2, "Research Methodology"; see, for example, "Critical Thinking Skill: Identifying the Need for Control Groups"). Only through careful laboratory studies in which participants are randomly assigned to experimental conditions can we determine causality. Obviously, it is not practical to assign children randomly to experience different types of media, and it is ethically questionable to expose any children to violence if it might make them more aggressive.

Despite the problems with specific studies, most scientists see a direct relation between exposure to violence and aggressive behavior. Indeed, a recent joint statement by professional groups representing psychologists and pediatricians concluded that a plethora of studies "point overwhelmingly to a causal connection between media violence and aggressive behavior in some children" (Joint Statement, 2000, p. 1).

How might media violence promote aggression in children? One possibility is that exposure to massive amounts of violence in movies, which misrepresent the prevalence of violence in real life, leads children to believe that violence is common and inevitable. Because in movies few people are punished for acting violently, children may come to believe that such behaviors are justified (Bushman & Huesmann, 2001). That is, the portrayal of violence in movies teaches children questionable social scripts for solving personal problems. By mentally rehearsing a violent scenario or observing the same violent scenario enacted many times and perhaps in different movies, a child might come to believe that engaging in brutality is an effective way to both solve problems and dispense with annoying people (Huesmann, 1998).

CRITICAL THINKING SKILL

Avoiding the Association of Events with Other Events That Occur at the Same Time

Do you have a lucky charm? Do you wear your "good luck" socks every time you take an exam? Do you try to blow out the candles on your birthday cake in just one breath so that your silent wish will come true? The list of people's superstitions is virtually endless. In North America and Europe, people avoid the number 13. In China, Japan, Korea, and Hawaii, they avoid 4. The basketball player Michael Jordan, a graduate from the University of North Carolina, always wore shorts with the North Carolina logo under his uniform for good luck; the baseball player Wade Boggs ate only chicken on the day of a game (Morrison, n.d.). Even pigeons *might* be superstitious. In conditioning pigeons' pecking behavior, Skinner found that, during each trial, a particular pigeon would swing its head in the same way before responding, while another would do a half turn before responding. The tendency to associate events that occur together in time is so strong that human and nonhuman animals sometimes associate chance events unrelated to reinforcements or punishments, if those events happen to occur close in time to reinforcers or punishers. People, and apparently other animals, have a strong need to understand what causes or predicts events. Their resulting associations can lead people, at least, to cling to superstitions. Most superstitions are harmless, but some can interfere with daily living, as when people stay in bed on the 4th or 13th of every month or refuse to get off on the 4th or 13th floor of a building. As a critical thinker, be aware of the tendency to associate events with other events that occur, perhaps simply by chance, at the same time (**FIGURE 6.24**).

FIGURE 6.24 Think Critically: Superstitions Common superstitions include the fear of black cats crossing your path and the prohibition against walking under ladders. But what could actually go wrong in the situations shown here?

SUMMING UP

How Does Watching Others Affect Learning?

Thanks to psychological research, we know that humans learn much of our behavior by observing the behavior of others. Children can learn language, social skills, and political attitudes from observing their parents, peers, and teachers, and adults teach complex skills, such as surgery and driving, by demonstration. Nonhuman animals also learn through observation—for example, which food is safe to eat and which objects should be feared. People imitate models that are attractive, high in status, and somewhat similar to themselves. Modeling is more likely to occur when the model has been rewarded for the behavior and less likely to occur when the model has been punished. Vicarious conditioning influences whether a behavior is performed but not whether it is learned. Mirror neurons, which fire when a behavior is observed, may be the neural basis of imitation learning.

MEASURING UP

1. How do cultural beliefs about learning affect human performance?
   a. Cultures with the realistic view that some people do not have the ability to learn in some areas, such as math, produce happier students, who are realistic about their career choices.
   b. Students from cultures that view learning as the result of persistence work harder and therefore achieve more than students from cultures with other beliefs.
   c. Because all people are biologically prepared to learn some behaviors and concepts better than others, culture has very little effect on learning outcomes.
   d. All cultures that use mild punishments to regulate behaviors produce anxious adults.

2. The critical finding from Bandura's Bobo doll research was that _____.
   a. children exhibited more aggressive behaviors toward the doll after viewing an actor being rewarded for acting aggressively toward the doll than did children in the control condition
   b. using a control group is vital
   c. children learned to exhibit aggression toward the Bobo doll, behavior later generalized to their own dolls
   d. it allowed researchers to prove that watching violence on television causes children to become more violent

3. Mirror neurons _____.
   a. fire when we are watching motor activity in other people
   b. connect to sensory neurons, except in olfaction because little or no motion occurs when people smell an odor
   c. are probably more important in learning a second language than in learning a first language
   d. are among the smallest neurons in the human body

What Is the Biological Basis of Learning?

LEARNING OBJECTIVE
Describe the neural basis of learning.

Scientists have long believed that learning involves relatively permanent changes in the brain that result from exposure to environmental events. That is, your experience of the world changes your brain, and these changes reflect learning. Over the past few decades, psychological scientists have made numerous discoveries about the biological basis of learning. For instance, researchers have explored the brain processes that underlie reinforcement, demonstrating that similar brain activity occurs for most rewarding experiences. Likewise, we now understand considerably more about how learning occurs at the neuronal level. The following section discusses the findings regarding learning's biological basis that have emerged through the methods of psychological science.

Dopamine Activity Underlies Reinforcement

Although people often use the term *reward* as a synonym for positive reinforcement, Skinner and other traditional behaviorists defined reinforcement strictly in terms of *whether* it increased behavior. They were relatively uninterested in *why* it increased behavior. Indeed, they carefully avoided any speculation about whether subjective experiences had anything to do with behavior, since they believed mental states were impossible to study empirically. Although the behaviorists avoided any reference to internal mental states, generally positive reinforcement works because it provides the subjective experience of pleasure. The neural basis of this reinforcement is the release of the neurotransmitter dopamine. As discussed in Chapter 3, dopamine is involved in motivation and emotion. Research over the past 50 years has shown that dopamine plays an important role in the experience of reward and is thus crucial for positive reinforcement (Wise & Rompre, 1989).

PLEASURE CENTERS   One of the earliest discoveries pointing to neural mechanisms' role in reinforcement came about because of a small surgical error. In the early 1950s, the brain researchers Peter Milner and James Olds were testing whether electrical stimulation to a specific brain region would facilitate learning. To see whether the learning they observed was caused by brain activity or by the aversive qualities of the electrical stimulus, Olds and Milner administered electrical stimulation to rats' brains only while the rats were in one specific location in the cage. The logic was that if the application of electricity was aversive, the rats would selectively avoid that location. Fortunately for science, Milner and Olds administered each shock to the wrong part of the brain, and instead of avoiding the area of the cage associated with electrical stimulation, the rats quickly came back, apparently looking for more stimulation.

Olds and Milner then set up an experiment to see whether rats would press a lever to self-administer shock to specific sites in their brains, a procedure subsequently referred to as *intracranial self-stimulation* (ICSS; FIGURE 6.25). The rats

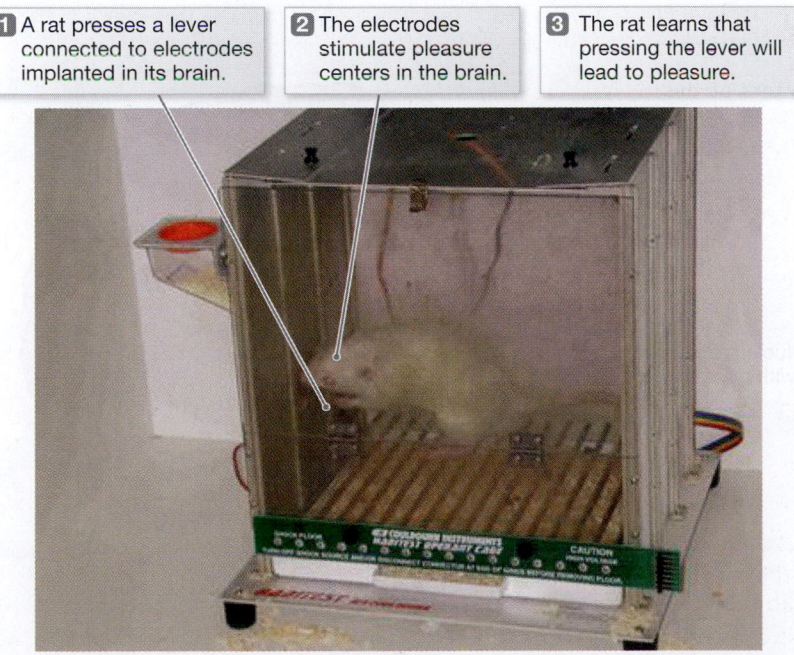

1 A rat presses a lever connected to electrodes implanted in its brain.

2 The electrodes stimulate pleasure centers in the brain.

3 The rat learns that pressing the lever will lead to pleasure.

FIGURE 6.25 Intracranial Self-Stimulation (ICSS)

self-administered electricity to their brains with gusto, pressing the lever hundreds of times per hour (Olds & Milner, 1954). Olds and Milner referred to brain regions that support ICSS as *pleasure centers*. Although behaviorists objected to the term *pleasure,* ICSS was a powerful reinforcer. In one experiment, rats that had been on a near-starvation diet for ten days were given a choice between food and the opportunity to administer ICSS. They chose the electrical stimulation more than 80 percent of the time! Deprived rats also chose electrical stimulation over water or receptive sexual partners; they even crossed a painful electrified grid to receive ICSS. Rats will continue intracranial self-stimulation until they collapse from exhaustion. Monkeys tested in similar studies have been found to press a bar for electrical stimulation up to 8,000 times per hour (Olds, 1962).

Most psychologists believe that ICSS acts on the same brain regions as those activated by natural reinforcers, such as food, water, and sex. In rats, applying electrical stimulation to pleasure centers and then turning it off elicits naturally motivated behaviors, such as feeding, drinking, and copulating with an available partner. Also, depriving an animal of food or of water leads to increased ICSS, a finding taken to indicate that the animal is trying to obtain the same reward experience it would obtain from drinking water or eating. Finally, the neural mechanisms underlying both ICSS and natural reward appear to use the same neurotransmitter system, namely, dopamine. This evidence suggests that dopamine serves as the neurochemical basis of positive reinforcement in operant conditioning. For instance, ICSS activates dopamine receptors; interfering with dopamine eliminates self-stimulation as well as naturally motivated behaviors, such as feeding, drinking, and copulating.

NUCLEUS ACCUMBENS ACTIVATION The *nucleus accumbens* is a subcortical brain region that is part of the limbic system. The experience of pleasure usually results from activation of dopamine neurons in the nucleus accumbens (**FIGURE 6.26**). For example, enjoying food depends on dopamine activity. Hungry rats given food experience an increased dopamine release in the nucleus accumbens, and the greater the hunger, the greater the dopamine release (Rolls, Burton, & Mora, 1980). Food tastes better when you are hungry, and water is more rewarding when you are thirsty, because more dopamine is

FIGURE 6.26 Pleasure Centers of the Brain

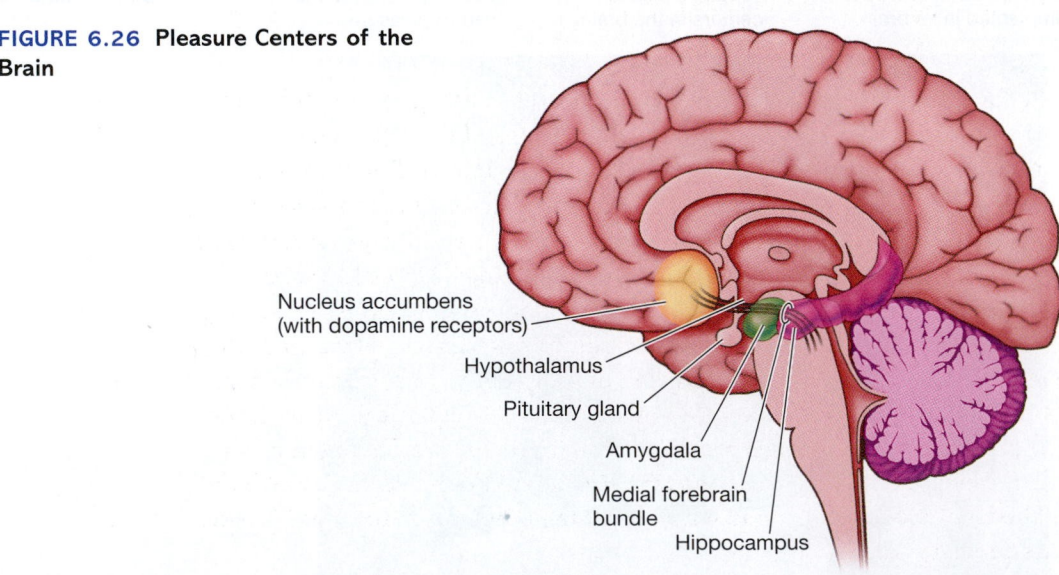

Nucleus accumbens (with dopamine receptors)

Hypothalamus

Pituitary gland

Amygdala

Medial forebrain bundle

Hippocampus

released under deprived than nondeprived conditions. Even looking at funny cartoons activates the nucleus accumbens (Mobbs, Greicius, Abdel-Azim, Menon, & Reiss, 2003).

In operant conditioning, dopamine release sets a reinforcer's value. Drugs that block dopamine's effects disrupt operant conditioning. In one study, rats were taught to run a maze to receive electrical stimulation, but after being injected with a dopamine blocker, the rats would not run the maze until the electrical current was turned up (Stellar, Kelley, & Corbett, 1983). The blocker decreased the value of the reinforcement. Dopamine blockers are often given to individuals with *Tourette's syndrome,* a motor control disorder, to help them regulate their involuntary body movements. These individuals often have trouble staying on their drug regimens, however, because they feel the drugs prevent them from enjoying life. Conversely, as you might expect, drugs that enhance dopamine activation, such as cocaine and amphetamines, increase stimuli's reward value.

SECONDARY REINFORCERS ALSO RELY ON DOPAMINE Natural reinforcers appear to signal reward directly through the activation of dopamine receptors in the nucleus accumbens. But what about secondary reinforcers, such as money or good grades? Through a classical-conditioning process, neutral stimuli that at first fail to stimulate a dopamine release do so readily after being paired with unconditioned stimuli. In one study, monkeys were presented with a trapdoor that opened occasionally. The door opening did not activate dopamine activity. The experimenters then placed apples in the doorway, such that the monkeys associated the door opening with the unconditioned stimulus of eating a tasty food. After many conditioning trials, the door opening led on its own to increased activation of dopamine (Ljungberg, Apicella, & Schultz, 1992). Similarly, seeing a loved one, getting a good grade, or receiving a paycheck may be conditioned to produce dopamine activation. Money is an excellent example of a secondary reinforcer, as mentioned earlier, and anticipated monetary rewards have been found to activate dopamine systems (Knutson, Fong, Adams, Varner, & Hommer, 2001).

Habituation and Sensitization Are Simple Models of Learning

As noted above, learning involves relatively permanent changes in the brain that result from exposure to environmental events. The roots of this idea can be traced back to numerous scientists, including the researcher Richard Semon, who in 1904 proposed that memories are stored through changes in the nervous system. Semon called the storage of learned material an *engram,* a term later popularized by the psychologist Karl Lashley. In 1948, the psychologist Donald Hebb proposed that learning results from alterations in synaptic connections. According to Hebb, when one neuron excites another, some change takes place such that the synapse between the two strengthens. Subsequently, one neuron's firing becomes increasingly likely to cause the other's firing. Most of the many interpretations of Hebb's postulate can be summed up as "cells that fire together wire together" (a concept discussed in Chapter 3, "Biological Foundations"). Hebb did not have the technology to examine whether his hypothesis was true, but his basic theory has proven correct.

What activity at the synapse leads to learning? One answer is found in research using simple invertebrates such as the *aplysia,* a small marine snail that eats seaweed (**FIGURE 6.27**). The aplysia is an excellent species to use to study learning because it has relatively few neurons, some of which are large enough to be seen without a microscope (Kandel, Schwartz, & Jessell, 1995). The neurobiologist Eric Kandel and his colleagues have used the aplysia to study the neural basis of two types of simple learning: *habituation* and *sensitization.* As a result of this research, Kandel received a Nobel Prize for medicine in 2000.

Habituation is a decrease in behavioral response following repeated exposure to nonthreatening stimuli. When an animal encounters a novel stimulus, it pays attention to it, behavior known as an *orienting response.* If the stimulus is neither harmful nor rewarding, the animal learns to ignore it. We constantly habituate to meaningless events around us. For instance, sit back and listen to the background sounds wherever you are. Perhaps you can hear a clock, or a computer fan, or your roommates playing music in the next room, but had you really noticed this noise before being directed to or had you habituated to it? Habituation can be demonstrated quite easily by repeatedly touching an aplysia. The first few touches cause it to withdraw its gills, but after about 10 touches it stops responding, and this lack of response lasts about two to three hours. Repeated habituation trials can lead to a state of habituation that lasts several weeks.

Sensitization is an increase in behavioral response following exposure to a threatening stimulus. For instance, imagine that while studying you smell burning. You will not likely habituate to this smell. You might focus even greater attention on your sense of smell to assess the possible threat of fire, and you will be highly vigilant for any indication of smoke or of flames. In general, sensitization leads to heightened responsiveness to other stimuli. Giving a strong electrical shock to an aplysia's tail leads to sensitization. Following the shock, a mild touch anywhere on the body will cause the aplysia to withdraw its gills.

Kandel's research on aplysia has shown that alterations in the functioning of the synapse lead to habituation and sensitization. For both types of simple learning, presynaptic neurons alter their neurotransmitter release. A reduction in neurotransmitter release leads to habituation; an increase in neurotransmitter release leads to sensitization. Knowing the neural basis of simple learning gives us the building blocks to understand more complex learning processes.

habituation A decrease in behavioral response following repeated exposure to nonthreatening stimuli.

sensitization An increase in behavioral response following exposure to a threatening stimulus.

FIGURE 6.27 Simple Model of Learning The aplysia, a marine invertebrate, is used to study the neurochemical basis of learning.

Long-Term Potentiation Is a Candidate for the Neural Basis of Learning

To understand learning in the brain, researchers have investigated *long-term potentiation,* a phenomenon first described in 1973. The word *potentiate* means to strengthen, to make something more potent. **Long-term potentiation (LTP)** is the strengthening of the synaptic connection so that postsynaptic neurons are more easily activated. To demonstrate LTP, researchers first establish the extent to which electrically stimulating one neuron leads to an action potential (the level of stimulation needed to activate or "fire," discussed in Chapter 3, "Biological Foundations") in a second neuron. They then provide intense electrical stimulation to the first neuron, perhaps giving it a hundred pulses of electricity in five seconds. Finally, a single electrical pulse is readministered to measure the extent of the second neuron's activation. LTP occurs when the intense electrical stimulation increases the likelihood that stimulating one neuron leads to an action potential in the second neuron (**FIGURE 6.28**). In aplysia, whereas habituation and sensitization are due to changes in neurotransmitter release from the presynaptic neuron, LTP results from changes in the postsynaptic neuron that make it more easily activated.

Numerous lines of evidence support the idea that LTP is the cellular basis for learning and memory (Beggs et al., 1999; Cooke & Bliss, 2006). For instance, LTP effects are most easily observed in brain sites known to be involved in learning and memory, such as the hippocampus. Moreover, the same drugs that improve memory also lead to increased LTP, and those that block memory also block LTP. Finally, behavioral conditioning produces neurochemical effects nearly identical to LTP.

The process of long-term potentiation also supports Hebb's contention that learning results from a strengthening of synaptic connections between neurons that fire together. Hebb's rule can be used to explain a variety of learning phenomena, including classical conditioning. Neurons that signal the unconditioned stimulus are active at the same time as those that signal the conditioned stimulus. Over repeated trials, the synapses that connect these two events become strengthened, so that when one fires, the other fires automatically, producing the conditioned response.

LTP AND THE NMDA RECEPTOR Over the last decade, researchers have made considerable progress in understanding how LTP works. The *NMDA receptor* (a

long-term potentiation (LTP) The strengthening of a synaptic connection so that postsynaptic neurons are more easily activated.

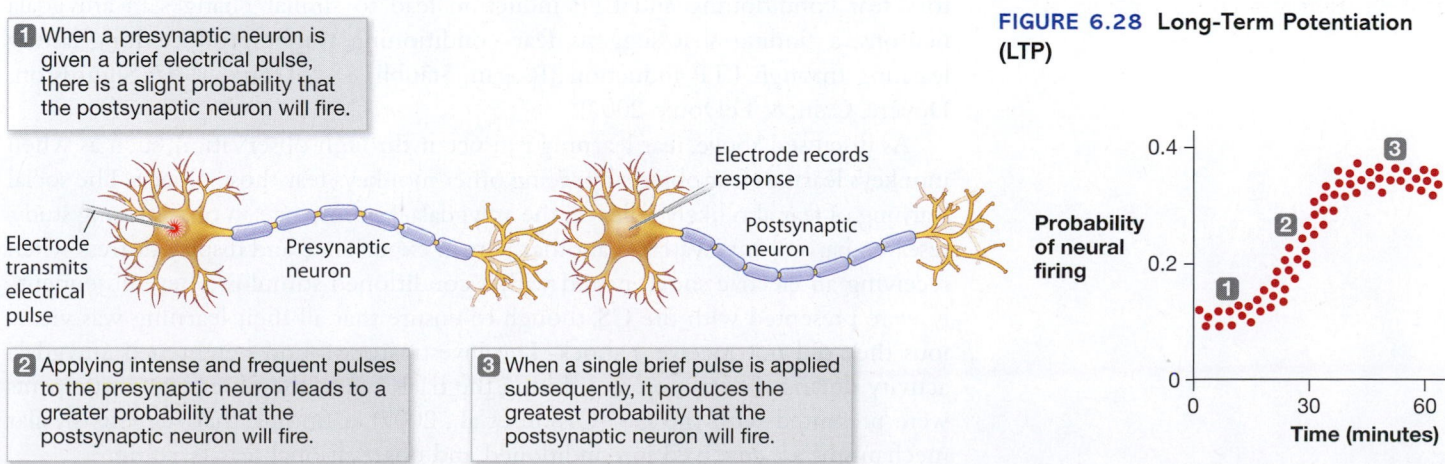

FIGURE 6.28 Long-Term Potentiation (LTP)

1 When a presynaptic neuron is given a brief electrical pulse, there is a slight probability that the postsynaptic neuron will fire.

Electrode transmits electrical pulse

Presynaptic neuron

Electrode records response

Postsynaptic neuron

2 Applying intense and frequent pulses to the presynaptic neuron leads to a greater probability that the postsynaptic neuron will fire.

3 When a single brief pulse is applied subsequently, it produces the greatest probability that the postsynaptic neuron will fire.

Probability of neural firing

Time (minutes)

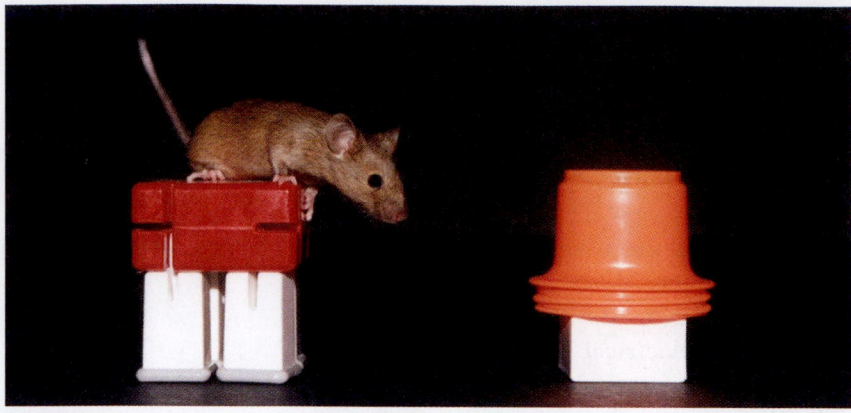

FIGURE 6.29 Doogie Mice In this learning and memory test, Doogie mice (such as the one pictured here) and regular mice were given the chance to familiarize themselves with two objects. One of the objects was then replaced with a novel object. This change was quickly recognized by the Doogie mice but not by the normal mice.

type of glutamate receptor) is required for it and has a special property: It opens only if a nearby neuron fires at the same time, a phenomenon supporting Hebb's rule ("cells that fire together wire together"). The finding that the NMDA receptor is involved in LTP led researchers to examine genetic processes that might influence learning. For instance, the neuroscientist Joseph Tsien modified genes in mice to make the genes' NMDA receptors more efficient. When tested in standard learning tasks, these transgenic mice performed amazingly well, learning novel tasks more quickly and showing increased fear conditioning (Tsien, 2000). The mice were such great learners that Tsien named them "Doogie mice," after the prime-time television character Doogie Howser, a boy doctor (**FIGURE 6.29**). Might we be able to modify human genes so that people learn more quickly? This fascinating question raises all sorts of ethical issues, but various pharmaceutical companies are exploring drugs that might enhance the learning process by manipulating gene expression or activating NMDA receptors. If successful, such treatments might prove valuable for treating patients with diseases such as Alzheimer's. This especially active area of research is increasing our understanding of how genes, neurotransmitters, and the environment interact to produce learning.

FEAR CONDITIONING Although LTP originally was observed in the hippocampus, recent evidence indicates that fear conditioning may induce LTP in the amygdala (Kim & Jung, 2006). In a typical fear conditioning study, a rat is classically conditioned to produce a fear response to an auditory tone: Electric shock follows the tone, and eventually the tone produces fear responses on its own, including specific physiological and behavioral reactions. One interesting response, *freezing*—standing still—is observed in many species, including humans. For example, as captured in video footage, for the first few seconds after the bomb exploded at the Atlanta Summer Olympics in 1996, most people froze in a crouch. Immediately keeping still might be a hardwired response that helps animals deal with predators, which often are attracted by movement (LeDoux, 2002). Substantial evidence indicates that the amygdala is crucial for fear conditioning. If one particular part of the amygdala is removed, an animal is unable to learn that shock follows the tone (Davis, 1997). Joseph LeDoux and his students have demonstrated that auditory fear conditioning and LTP induction lead to similar changes in amygdala neurons, a finding that suggests fear conditioning might produce long-lasting learning through LTP induction (Rogan, Stäubli, & LeDoux, 1997; Sigurdsson, Doyère, Cain, & LeDoux, 2007).

As discussed above, fear learning can occur through observation, such as when monkeys learn to fear objects by seeing other monkeys fear those objects. The social learning of fear also likely relies on the amygdala. For instance, in one imaging study, research participants watched another person experience and display distress when receiving an electric shock paired with a conditioned stimulus. They subsequently were presented with the CS, though to ensure that all their learning was vicarious they did not receive a shock. The investigators found heightened amygdala activity during observation and during the trials when the observing participants were presented with the CS (Olsson et al., 2007), a finding that suggests similar mechanisms are involved in conditioned and observational fear learning.

SUMMING UP

What Is the Biological Basis of Learning?

Researchers are rapidly identifying the neurophysiological basis of learning. Much of what has been learned supports Hebb's theory that neurons that fire together wire together. Kandel's work on aplysia has shown that habituation and sensitization, two simple forms of learning, occur through alteration in neurotransmitter release. The discovery of long-term potentiation shows that intense stimulation of neurons can strengthen synapses, increasing the likelihood that one neuron's activation will increase the firing of other neurons in the network. LTP occurs when NMDA receptors are stimulated by two nearby neurons. LTP in the amygdala appears to be important for fear learning.

MEASURING UP

1. What can we learn from the superlearner Doogie mice?
   a. NMDA receptors are important in producing learning.
   b. A breed of extremely smart mice provides a good model for understanding how some people are able to become doctors at a young age.
   c. Neurons that fire together wire together.
   d. Animal models of human learning cannot account for mirror neurons' action.

2. What is the evidence that dopamine is a critical neurotransmitter for reinforcers' effects on behavior?
   a. The increased administration of self-stimulation suppresses dopamine release.
   b. Rats will work continuously to deliver electrical stimulation to a portion of the brain that uses dopamine in its neural processes.
   c. When rats press a lever to self-administer dopamine directly into the brain, they stop eating and drinking.
   d. When rats receive dopamine, they increase the rate at which they deliver intracranial self-stimulation.

CONCLUSION

Behaviorism has been a powerful force in psychological science since early in the twentieth century, when a shift from subjective to empirical methods established psychology as a science. A renewed interest in mental processes eventually led many to abandon strict behavioral principles, but basic conditioning and learning processes remain foundational to our understanding of both mind and behavior. Psychological scientists use learning principles in studies across all levels of analysis, from synaptic connections in aplysia (biological) to the cultural transmission of morals and of values (cultural). With all its competing theories and its sharing of ideas, the field of learning also serves as an excellent example of how psychological research is based on cumulative principles. We still see that dynamic in operation. The principles of classical and operant conditioning are basic methodologies used by all neuroscientists to study brain mechanisms. In turn, recent advances in neuroscience techniques resulting from the biological revolution have allowed for a more complete understanding of learning processes.

■ CHAPTER SUMMARY

How Did the Behavioral Study of Learning Develop?

- **Behavioral Responses Are Conditioned:** Pavlov established the principles of classical conditioning, a process that occurs when associations are made between two stimuli, such as the sound of a bell and a piece of meat. This type of learning is based on reflexes, such as the salivation that occurs in response to the meat. Acquisition, discrimination, generalization, and extinction are measured in classical conditioning. Some emotional responses are learned through conditioning.

- **Phobias and Addictions Have Learned Components:** Phobias are learned fear associations. Similarly, addiction involves a conditioned response, which can result in withdrawal symptoms at the mere sight of drug paraphernalia, and tolerance, the need for more of the particular drug, when that drug is administered in a familiar context, to get a high comparable to the one obtained earlier.

- **Classical Conditioning Involves More Than Events Occuring at the Same Time:** Not all stimuli are equally potent in producing conditioning. Animals are biologically prepared to make connections between stimuli that are potentially dangerous, such as learning to freeze when shock is administered. Animals are also predisposed to form predictions that enhance survival, such as judging the likelihood that food will continue to be available at one location.

How Does Operant Conditioning Differ from Classical Conditioning?

- **Reinforcement Increases Behavior:** A behavior's positive consequences will likely strengthen it or make it more likely to occur. Shaping is a procedure in which successive approximations of a behavior are reinforced, leading to the desired behavior. Reinforcers may be primary (those that satisfy biological needs) or secondary (those that do not directly satisfy biological needs).

- **Both Reinforcement and Punishment Can Be Positive or Negative:** In either positive reinforcement or positive punishment, a stimulus is delivered after the animal responds. In negative reinforcement or negative punishment, a stimulus is removed after the animal responds. Positive and negative reinforcements increase a behavior's likelihood; positive and negative punishments decrease a behavior's likelihood.

- **Operant Conditioning Is Influenced by Schedules of Reinforcement:** Reinforcement can be delivered at either a fixed rate or a variable rate that depends on the number (ratio) or time (interval) of responses. A variable rate of reinforcement leads to resistance to extinction.

- **Biology and Cognition Influence Operant Conditioning:** An organism's biological makeup restricts the types of behaviors the organism can learn. Latent learning takes place without reinforcement. Such learning often is not performed until a reinforcer is introduced.

- **The Value of Reinforcement Follows Economic Principles:** In choosing between reinforcers, human and nonhuman animals consider the likelihood of obtaining each reward and the amount of time it might take to receive each one.

How Does Watching Others Affect Learning?

- **Learning Can Be Passed On through Cultural Transmission:** Memes (knowledge transferred within a culture) are analogous to genes, in that behaviors are selectively passed on from generation to generation.

- **Learning Can Occur through Observation:** Observational learning is a powerful adaptive tool. Humans and other animals learn by watching others' behaviors and the consequences of those behaviors.

- **Animals and Humans Imitate Others:** Modeling occurs when one individual reproduces another individual's behavior. Vicarious learning occurs as the result of one individual seeing another individual's behavior reinforced or punished. Mirror neurons are activated when we watch a behavior, just as when we actually perform the behavior.

What Is the Biological Basis of Learning?

- **Dopamine Activity Underlies Reinforcement:** The brain has specialized centers that produce pleasure when stimulated. Behaviors that activate these centers are reinforced. The nucleus accumbens (a part of the limbic system) has dopamine receptors, which are activated by pleasurable behaviors. Through conditioning, secondary reinforcers can also activate dopamine receptors. Drugs also increase activation, which can lead to addiction.

- **Habituation and Sensitization Are Simple Models of Learning:** Repeated exposure to a stimulus results in habituation, a decrease in behavioral response. Sensitization is an increase in behavioral response to a new threatening stimulus.

- **Long-Term Potentiation Is a Candidate for the Neural Basis of Learning:** Synaptic connections are strengthened when neurons fire together. This occurs in the hippocampus and, in fear responses, in the amygdala. The receptor NMDA is required for long-term potentiation. Genetically altered mice that had more efficient NMDA receptors were superlearners. LTP is also important for fear conditioning.

■ KEY TERMS

■ PRACTICE TEST

1. Every night for a few weeks, you feed your pet rat while watching the evening news. Eventually, the rat learns to sit by its food dish when the news program's opening theme song plays. In this example of classical conditioning, what are the US, UR, CS, and CR?

2. At a psychology lecture, each student receives 10 lemon wedges. The professor instructs the students to bite into a lemon wedge anytime a large blue dot appears within her slide presentation. Nearly every time the students bite into lemons, their mouths pucker. The 11th time a blue dot appears on the screen, many students' mouths pucker visibly. In this case, what are the US, UR, CS and CR?

3. A few minutes later in that same psychology lecture, the professor projects the image of a turquoise dot. How will the students likely respond to this image?
   a. The students will not experience puckering responses, because the conditioned association has been extinguished.
   b. The students will not experience puckering responses, because they are able to discriminate between the two dot colors.
   c. The students will experience puckering responses, because of stimulus generalization.

4. Which pairing of stimuli will most quickly create a learned association?
   a. Eating a box of raisins and experiencing extreme nausea at the same time.
   b. Eating a box of raisins and experiencing extreme nausea a few hours later.
   c. Seeing clouds in the sky and experiencing a severe rain shower a few minutes later.
   d. Seeing clouds in the sky and experiencing a severe rain shower a few hours later.

5. Identify each statement as an example of negative punishment, positive punishment, negative reinforcement, or positive reinforcement.
   a. Whenever a puppy barks, it gets its belly rubbed, so it barks more.
   b. A professor directs all questions to the student who arrives late to class.
   c. A person with a clean driving record receives a reduced insurance premium.
   d. Your date arrives an hour late, and you refuse to speak for the rest of the evening.

6. Match each scenario with one of the following reinforcement schedules: fixed ratio, variable ratio, fixed interval, variable interval.

   a. You check your mailbox for mail at the same time every day.
   b. Every once in a while, you receive exciting mail.
   c. Every seventh newspaper you receive is loaded with coupons you want to use.
   d. Every week, a boy buys packets of baseball cards. Sometimes none of the packets includes a valuable card, but sometimes multiple packets hold valuable cards.

7. Recently, Albert Bandura has employed serial television dramas to address global social issues such as illiteracy and overpopulation. He believes principles of social learning should apply when viewers observe fictional characters engaging in behaviors relevant to a particular issue. Based on what you have read about social learning, which of the following factors do Bandura and his collaborators likely consider when creating these shows? Select all that apply.
   a. The culture's commonly held beliefs that might facilitate or impede social change.
   b. Employing role models whom viewers likely will see as very different from themselves.
   c. Demonstrating the positive outcomes associated with engaging in the desirable behavior.
   d. Employing positive role models (people engaged in the desirable behavior).
   e. Encouraging viewers to engage in behaviors they are not capable of imitating.
   f. Demonstrating the costs associated with not engaging in the desirable behavior.
   g. Employing negative role models (people not engaged in the desirable behavior).

8. Hebb's postulate states that _____.
   a. primary and secondary reinforcers rely on dopamine
   b. cells that fire together wire together
   c. orienting responses protect organisms
   d. long-term potentiation is the basis for neural learning

9. _____ is more closely associated with long-term potentiation than with reinforcement. Select as many as apply.
   a. Dopamine
   b. The hippocampus
   c. NMDA
   d. The nucleus accumbens

■ PSYCHOLOGY AND SOCIETY

1. A relative e-mails you about a reality show in which nannies help families modify the behaviors of out-of-control kids. He is amazed by the effectiveness of strategies such as time-outs and sticker charts (e.g., placing a smiley face sticker on a poster each time a child clears his or her place after a meal). Your relative knows you are enrolled in a psychology course and wonders if you can explain why these strategies work. Drawing on your knowledge from this class, compose an e-mail to your relative explaining the behavioral learning principles at work in these behavior modification strategies.

2. Create a public service announcement, in either print or video format, that could be used to inform parents about the consequences of exposure to media violence. Communicate to your audience why they should care about this issue, what psychological science tells us about the effects of exposure to violent media, and at least two concrete ways parents can reduce the impact on their children of exposure to media violence.

The answer key for all the Measuring Up exercises and the Practice Tests can be found at the back of the book.

Attention and Memory

IMAGINE WHAT YOUR WORLD WOULD BE LIKE if you lost the ability to remember new experiences. You would not be able to remember meeting people, or what you did last night, or even what you had for breakfast this morning. In a few minutes, you would not even remember having contemplated this problem. Such was the fate of H.M. He was one of the most famous people in memory research, yet until his death in 2008, we did not know his real name (Henry Molaison)

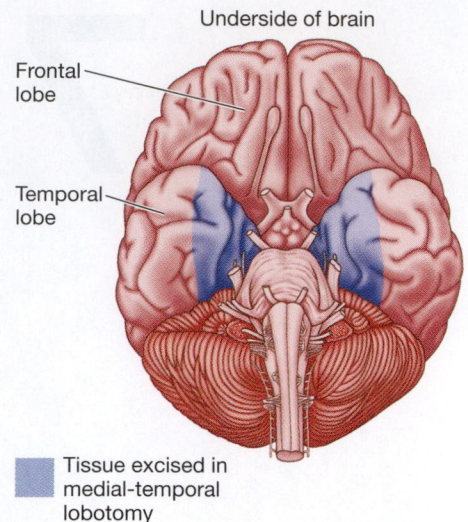

Underside of brain

Frontal lobe

Temporal lobe

Tissue excised in medial-temporal lobotomy

FIGURE 7.1 A Drawing of H.M.'s Brain
The portions of the medial temporal lobe that were removed from H.M.'s brain are indicated by the shaded regions.

FIGURE 7.2 Tracing Task

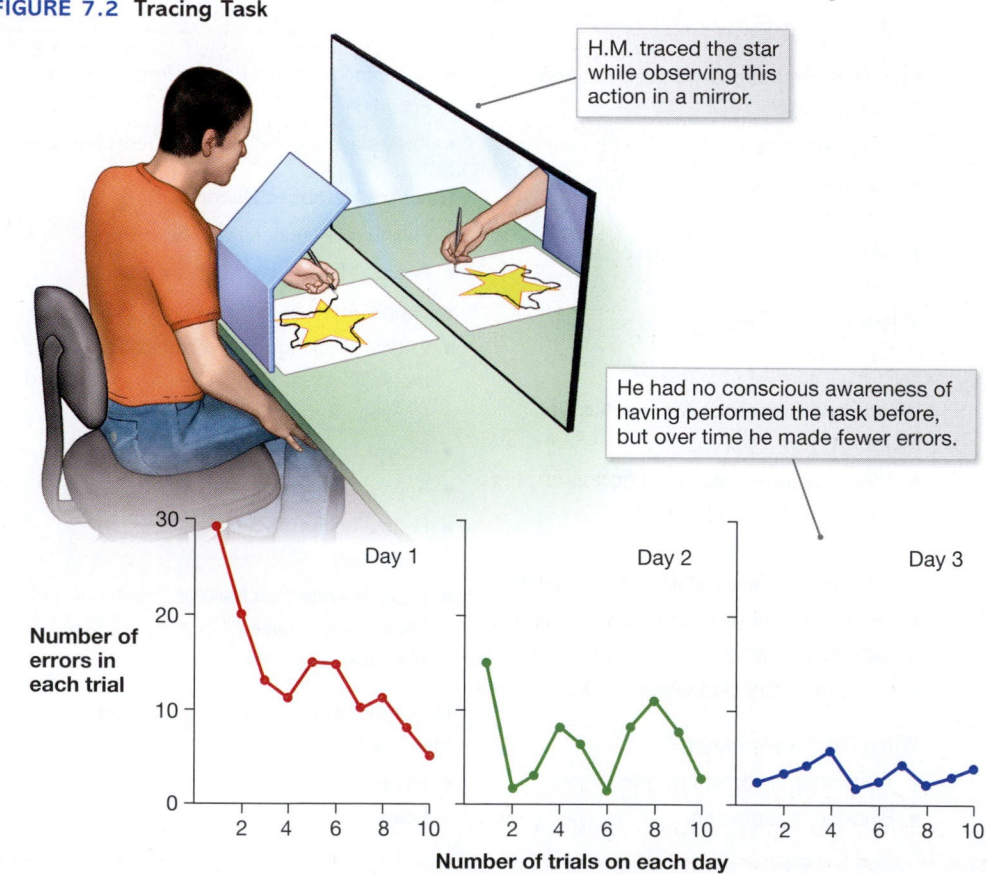

H.M. traced the star while observing this action in a mirror.

He had no conscious awareness of having performed the task before, but over time he made fewer errors.

Number of errors in each trial

Day 1

Day 2

Day 3

Number of trials on each day

or what he looked like, because his privacy was guarded by the researchers who studied his memory. When H.M. was a young man, over 50 years ago, he suffered from severe epilepsy. Every day, he had several grand mal seizures, an affliction that made it impossible for him to lead a normal life. Seizures are uncontrolled random firing of groups of neurons, and they can spread across the brain; H.M.'s seizures originated in the temporal lobes and would spread from there. Because the anticonvulsive drugs available at that time could not control H.M.'s seizures, surgery was the only choice for treatment. The reasoning behind this surgery was that if the seizure-causing portion of his brain was removed, he would stop having seizures. In September 1953, H.M.'s doctors removed parts of his medial temporal lobes, including the hippocampus (FIGURE 7.1). The surgery quieted H.M.'s seizures, but had an unexpected and unfortunate side effect: H.M. lost the ability to form new long-term memories.

H.M.'s memory problems were profound. His world stopped in September 1953, when he was 27. He never knew the day of the week, what year it was, or his own age. However, he could tell you about his childhood, explain the rules of baseball, and describe members of his family, things he knew at the time of the surgery. According to the psychologists who tested him, his IQ was slightly above average, so his thinking abilities were fine. He could also hold a normal conversation as long as he was not distracted, but he forgot the conversation in a minute or less. That he could hold a conversation at all showed that his short-term memory was intact, since to make meaning from spoken language a person needs to remember the words recently spoken (e.g., a sentence's beginning and end). But he lost every new memory he acquired through conversation, before that new memory could be transformed into a long-term memory. People who worked with H.M., such as the psychologist Brenda Milner, who has followed his case for over 40 years, had to introduce themselves to him every time they met. As H.M. put it, "Every day is alone in itself"; the quotation makes sense when you understand that H.M. remembered nothing from minute to minute but knew that he remembered nothing.

Although he did not know it, H.M. learned some new things, most impressively new motor tasks. In one series of tests, he was required to trace the outline of a star while watching his hand in a mirror. Most people do poorly the first few times they try this difficult task. On each of three consecutive days, H.M. was asked to trace the star 10 times. His performance improved over the three days, an indication that he had retained some information about the task; on each day, however, H.M. could not recall ever performing the task previously (FIGURE 7.2). His ability to learn new motor skills allowed him to get a job at a factory, where he mounted cigarette lighters on cardboard cases. But his condition left him unable to describe the job or the workplace. Studies of H.M.'s profound memory loss have contributed many clues to how memories are stored—normally and abnormally—in the brain, and references to his case will appear throughout this chapter.

Memory is the nervous system's capacity to acquire and retain usable skills and knowledge, allowing organisms to benefit from experience. We remember millions of pieces of information, from the trivial to the vital. Each person's entire sense of self, or self-identity, is made up of what that person knows from memories, from his or her recollections of personal experiences and of things learned from others. Yet memory does not work like a digital video camera that faithfully captures and just as faithfully retrieves the events its operator experiences; instead, memories are often incomplete, biased, and distorted. It is often surprising how vastly two people's memories for the same event can differ; each person stores and retrieves memories of the event distinctively. We tend to remember personally relevant information and filter our memories through our various perceptions and our knowledge of related events. Memories are stories that can be altered subtly through tellings and retellings.

This chapter explores the mental processes involved in acquiring and retaining knowledge. We have multiple memory systems, each with its own "rules." The processes that underlie memory for something we will need to retrieve in 10 seconds, for example, operate differently from the processes that underlie memory for information we will need to retrieve in 10 years. In recent years, psychologists and neuroscientists have made great strides in their knowledge of how to improve memory and what happens in the brain when we remember. Researchers also examine how people's memories of past events are selectively distorted.

memory The nervous system's capacity to acquire and retain usable skills and knowledge.

How Does Attention Determine What Is Remembered?

Your elementary school teachers probably had a basic understanding of the way memory works and so they demanded that you and your fellow students "pay attention." Good teachers know that to get information into memory, a person needs to attend. Think about the difference between the words *see* and *look, hear* and *listen. Look* and *listen* are commands that tell you where to direct your attention. Each of us has the ability to direct something in ourselves, called *attention,* to some information, at the cost of paying less attention to other information—the word *pay* indicates that costs are associated with attending to some forms of information and not others. Attention is limited, and when it is divided among too many tasks or the tasks are difficult, performance suffers. Of course, people have always been able to multitask (that is, attend to more than one thing): Parents monitor their children while cooking dinner, we carry on conversations while walking, students do homework while listening to music, and so on. But those who overload their systems by, for example, studying while checking e-mail, instant messaging, and watching television will do worse at all these tasks than they would if they focused on one at a time (Manhart, 2004).

Attention is important to your ability to function in your daily life, as you try to focus attention on the tasks at hand and ignore other things that might distract you. A task as simple as having a conversation requires paying focused attention. If the other speaker has unusual facial features or has food hanging from his or her chin, the unusual features or hanging food might capture your attention and make it difficult to comprehend what the person is saying. If the other speaker is boring, your mind might wander and find its own thoughts or even a quiet conversation nearby more interesting to attend to than the long-winded companion. The following section presents the basic principles of how human attention works.

LEARNING OBJECTIVES

Explain how attention is adaptive.

Explain why we can be blind to many changes in our environments.

(a)

Visual Attention Is Selective and Serial

The psychologist Anne Treisman has made great advances in the study of attention. According to her theory about attention and recognition, we automatically identify "primitive" features, such as color, shape, orientation, and movement, within an environment. Treisman has proposed that separate systems analyze objects' different visual features. Through **parallel processing,** these systems all process information at the same time, and we can attend selectively to one feature by effectively blocking the further processing of the others (Treisman & Gelade, 1980). In studies employing Treisman's *visual search tasks* (also called *feature search tasks*), participants look at a display of different objects on a computer screen, searching for ones, called *targets,* that differ from the others in only one feature. The other objects in the display are called *distractors.* Thus a typical display might consists of a few red As (targets) among many black ones (distractors; **FIGURE 7.3**). In these conditions, the targets seem to pop out immediately, regardless of the number of distractors. Some features that seem to pop out when the targets differ from the distractors are color, motion, orientation, and size (Wolfe & Horowitz, 2004). So if you are trying to find a friend in a large crowd of people, it will be fairly easy if your friend is wearing red and everyone else is wearing black, or if your friend is the only one waving, the only one standing up, or much larger or smaller than everyone else. As discussed in Chapter 3, a similar research paradigm was used to identify synesthetes, some of whom see particular numbers as printed in particular colors even when all the numbers are black. If you are not a synesthete, it might take you a while to find, for example, all the 2s in an array of 2s and 5s if all the numbers are black. A synesthete who sees 2s in one color and 5s in another color will be able to find the 2s very quickly.

Although searching for a single feature, such as a red stimulus, is fast and automatic, searching for two features is *serial* (you need to look at the stimuli one at a time) and *effortful* (takes longer and requires more attention). For example, imagine trying to find all the red Xs in a display of differently colored Xs and Ys; this would be called a *conjunction task* because the stimulus you are looking for is made up of two simple features (**FIGURE 7.4**).

(b)

FIGURE 7.3 Parallel Processing
(a) Parallel processing allows us to process information from different visual features at the same time by focusing on targets (here, the red objects) over distractors. **(b)** In this photo, the woman's red jacket, upward gaze, and smile serve as targets.

Auditory Attention Allows Selective Listening

Because attention is limited, it is hard to perform two tasks at the same time, especially if they rely on the same mechanisms. We easily can listen to music and drive at the same time, but it is hard to listen to two conversations at once. Think about driving along an open road, singing along with a song on the radio, and perhaps even talking with a passenger. What happens when you suddenly see the brake lights of the cars ahead of you? You need to stop talking and singing and direct your attention to the task of driving, which suddenly becomes more difficult and requires additional attention. Driving and listening to the radio at the same time can even be hazardous, depending on what you are listening to—for example, a sports broadcast might engage your visual system if it inspires you to imagine a game in progress, diverting attention from the visual cues on the road ahead. Recent research has shown that talking on a cell phone while driving is more hazardous than talking with a passenger in the car while driving. A cell phone conversation will not vary naturally with the driving conditions, because the person talking with the driver will not know what is happening—that, for example, traffic has gotten heavy or the car ahead has suddenly braked. A driver talking with a passenger can signal in many ways that the conversation needs to pause as situations demand (Strayer & Drews, 2007). Hands-free cell phones do not solve the attention problem when drivers have to divide their attentional resources among multiple tasks.

FIGURE 7.4 Try for Yourself: Conjunction Tasks

Count the blue squares as quickly as you can.

Result: This task is relatively difficult because you are searching for two features. You need to slow down and determine if each stimulus is blue *and* square.

In 1953, the psychologist E. C. Cherry described what he called the *cocktail party phenomenon:* You can focus on a single conversation in the midst of a chaotic cocktail party, yet a particularly pertinent stimulus, such as hearing your name mentioned in another conversation or hearing a juicy piece of gossip, can capture your attention. While proximity and loudness influence what you will attend to, your selective attention can also determine which conversation you hear. Imagine you are having dinner with a friend at a crowded restaurant. Suddenly the conversation at the next table piques your interest. If you really want to hear that conversation, you can focus your attention on it rather than on what your closer (and therefore probably louder) friend is saying. When your friend notices the blank look on your face and protests, "You're not listening to me!" chances are you will not be able to tell your friend what he or she said—but you will be able to relate the drama at the next table.

Cherry developed selective-listening studies to examine what people's minds do with unattended information when people pay attention to one task. He used a technique called *shadowing,* in which a participant wears headphones that deliver one message to one ear and a different message to the other. The person is asked to attend to one of the two messages and "shadow" it by repeating it aloud. In this situation, the subject usually notices the unattended sound (the message given to the other ear) but will have no knowledge about its content (**FIGURE 7.5**).

Imagine you are participating in an experiment about what happens to unattended messages, and you are repeating whatever is spoken into one ear (shadowing) and ignoring the message spoken into the other ear. What would happen if your own name were spoken into the unattended ear? You would probably hear your own name but know nothing about the rest of the message. Some important information gets through the filter of attention, but it needs to be personally relevant information, such as your name or the name of someone close to you, or it has to be particularly loud or different in some obvious physical way.

Selective Attention Can Operate at Multiple Stages of Processing

In 1958, the psychologist Donald Broadbent developed the *filter theory* to explain the selective nature of attention. He assumed that people have a limited capacity for sensory information and thus screen incoming information, letting in only the most important. In this model, attention is like a gate that opens for important information and closes for irrelevant information. But can we really close the gate to ignore some information? When and how is the gate closed?

Some stimuli demand attention and virtually shut off the ability to attend to anything else. Imagine you are focusing all your attention on reading this book, and suddenly you develop a muscle cramp. What will happen to your attention? The sharp jab of the cramp will demand your attention, and whatever you are reading will leave your consciousness until you attend to the muscle. Similarly, certain sounds, especially high-pitched ones, are harder to ignore than others. For example, a baby's high-pitched cry signals sharp pain, whereas a low-pitched cry signals that the baby is merely wet, bored, or mildly hungry. If you have ever spent much time with a baby who had colic (the little-understood condition in which infants cry excessively) or was sick in some other way, you can probably still recall the infant's high-pitched wail.

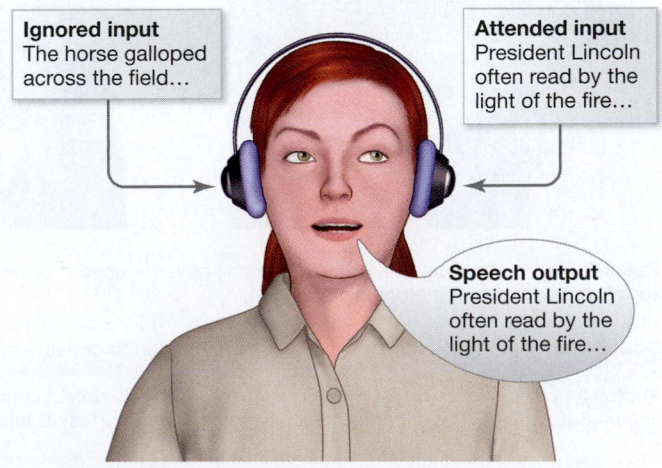

FIGURE 7.5 Shadowing The participant receives a different auditory messages in each ear, but is required to repeat ("shadow") only one.

Ignored input
The horse galloped across the field...

Attended input
President Lincoln often read by the light of the fire...

Speech output
President Lincoln often read by the light of the fire...

The higher-pitched sound signals the greater need and is more likely to get a caregiver's attention. Similarly, adults' screams, which generally signal great distress, such as pain or fear, tend to be much higher pitched than normal speaking voices.

Some evidence says that decisions about what to attend to are made early in the perceptual process, but studies also reveal that unattended information is processed at least to some extent. (As discussed in Chapter 4, people are often influenced by information delivered subliminally or incidentally.) Several selective-listening studies have found that even when participantts cannot repeat an unattended message, they still have processed its contents. In one experiment, participants were told to attend to the message coming in one ear: "They threw stones at the bank yesterday." At the same time, the unattended ear was presented with one of two words: either "river" or "money." Afterward, participants could not report the unattended words; however, those presented with "river" interpreted the sentence to mean someone had thrown stones at a riverbank, while those presented with "money" interpreted the sentence to mean someone had thrown stones at a financial institution (MacKay, 1973). Thus they extracted meaning from the word even though they did not process the word consciously.

change blindness The common failure to notice large changes in environments.

One striking demonstration of how inattentive we can be is the phenomenon known as **change blindness,** the fact that we are often "blind" to large changes in our environments because we cannot attend to everything in the vast array of visual information available. For example, would you notice if the person you were talking to suddenly changed into another person? In a series of studies in which subjects gave directions to a stranger who was momentarily blocked by a large object and was then replaced with another person, 50 percent of the people giving directions never noticed they were talking to a different person, as long as the replacement was of the same race and sex as the first stranger (Simons & Levin, 1998; **FIGURE 7.6**).

FIGURE 7.6 Scientific Method: Change Blindness Studies

Hypothesis: People can be "blind" to large changes around them.

Research Method:

1 A participant is approached by a stranger asking for directions.

2 The stranger is momentarily blocked by a larger object.

3 While being blocked, the original stranger is replaced by another person.

Results: Half the participants giving directions never noticed they were talking to a different person (as long as the replacement was of the same race and sex as the original stranger).

Conclusion: Change blindness results from inattention to certain visual information.

Photos from Simons, D. J., & Levin, D. T. (1998). Failure to detect changes to people during a real-word interaction. *Psychonomic Bulletin and Review,* 5, 644–649. © 1998 Psychonomic Society, Inc. Figure courtesy Daniel J. Simons.

Change blindness shows that we can attend to a limited amount of information and that large discrepancies exist between what most people believe they see and what they actually see. Change blindness also shows how attention influences memory. When giving directions to a stranger, we normally do not attend to the distinctive features of the stranger's face or clothing, so we are unable to recall them later—not because we forgot them, but more likely because we never encoded these features. After all, how often do we need to recall this information? Thus our perceptions of the world are often inaccurate, and we have little awareness of our perceptual failures; we simply do not know how much information we miss in the world around us.

Recognizing When "Change Blindness Blindness" May Be Occurring

The main message from studies of change blindness is that people can miss obvious changes in what they see and hear. Despite this possibility, most people believe they will always notice large changes, that important events automatically draw their attention. This erroneous belief persists because people often do not find out about the things they fail to perceive (Simons & Ambinder, 2005). In addition, the phenomenon of change blindness is so counterintuitive that few people believe how much they do not see. *Change blindness blindness* is people's unawareness that they often do not notice apparently obvious changes in their environments.

Imagine you are driving up a hill. At the top of the hill, there is an intersection. When you reach the top, you see another car heading straight into your lane, and in a flash you swerve to avoid a collision. The other car hits yours, but your last-minute swerve convinces eyewitnesses that you caused the accident by driving erratically. Change blindness blindness could be a factor in their reports: Perhaps out of a desire to help, the eyewitnesses believe they saw the whole accident, but they may have missed the critical moments because they were attending to their own activities.

Being aware of change blindness blindness is a critical thinking skill. Thinking that we always notice large changes in our visual field may lead us to perceive things incorrectly, such as in erroneously believing something did or did not happen. Recognizing the limitations of attention may help prevent us from misleading ourselves about our perceptions. Knowledge about change blindness should make us more humble about what we really see and what we remember.

▶ SUMMING UP

How Does Attention Determine What Is Remembered?

Attention is the ability to focus on certain stimuli, which are passed along to be encoded into a neural code that can be retrieved later. It is an adaptation that enables a person to handle the huge amounts of information in an environment without becoming overloaded. Still, a person can fail to notice major changes in an environment because his or her attention is focused on something else.

Visual search tasks indicate that we process visual information about basic features (e.g., color, motion, orientation, and size) quickly, automatically, and effortlessly. Searching for stimuli that are the conjunction of two basic features (e.g., trying to find large, red numbers) is slow, serial, and effortful. A key aspect of attention is that it is selective; we can choose the stimuli to which we attend, as when we ignore a nearby conversation in favor of a more interesting one farther away. However, to an extent we can process some information contained in sensory stimuli to which we are not consciously attending. Attention can operate in multiple stages of perceptual processing, and unattended stimuli are reduced rather than eliminated from further processing. Because of change blindness, people have difficulty remembering events to which they did not attend.

▶ MEASURING UP

1. Which statement correctly describes the two stages of attention?
   a. Attention can be captured by stimuli that vary along multiple dimensions (e.g., red, tilted squares) and stimuli that are important for survival (e.g., high-pitched screams).
   b. Attention has a rapid process that searches for one feature and a slower, serial process that searches for multiple features one at a time.
   c. Attention first segregates stimuli and then uses a binding process to build perceptions.
   d. Attention is first narrow in focus and then broadens to include all items in the visual field.
2. What happens to information when we are not paying attention?
   a. Some of the unattended information is passed on for further processing, but it is weaker than attended information.
   b. It is always lost because attention filters out unattended information.
   c. Unattended information is always available in some form; we just need to design experiments to demonstrate that it is available.
   d. Loud unattended messages will be lost because we can block information from our auditory channels.

What Are the Basic Stages of Memory?

Memory allows us to take information from our experiences and store it for retrieval later. However, all experiences are not equally likely to be remembered. Some life events pass swiftly, leaving no lasting memory; others remain for a lifetime. The following section considers experiences that are never learned and leave no trace, others that create memories that will last into very old age, and others that are remembered but later forgotten.

Since the late 1960s, most psychologists have viewed memory as a form of information processing, with processes analogous to the ways through which computers process information: A computer receives information through the keyboard or modem, and software determines how the information is processed; the information may then be stored in some altered format on the hard drive; and the information may be retrieved when it is needed. Likewise, memory's multiple processes can be thought of as operating over time in three distinct phases: (1) The **encoding** phase, which occurs at the time of learning, as information is acquired/encoded, or changed into a neural code that the brain can use (on acquisition, see Chapter 6, "Learning"); (2) the **storage** phase, which can last a fraction of a second or as long as a lifetime (there are at least three storage systems, which

encoding The processing of information so that it can be stored.

storage The retention of encoded representations over time that corresponds to some change in the nervous system that registers the event.

differ in how long they store information); and (3) **retrieval,** which we usually think of as reaching into our memory storage to find or retrieve a previously encoded and stored memory when we need it.

Psychological scientists often describe memory differently—as a three-part system that involves *sensory memory, short-term* or *working memory,* and *long-term memory.* This framework, the **modal memory model,** was proposed by the psychologists Richard Atkinson and Richard Shiffrin in 1968. Since then, although it is somewhat inaccurate and incomplete, the modal model has dominated psychological thinking about memory, and vocabulary from it remains widely used in memory research (**FIGURE 7.7**).

Sensory Memory Is Brief

Sensory memory is a temporary memory system, lasting only a fraction of a second and closely tied to the sensory systems. It is not what we usually think of when we think about memory, because it is so short and, under most circumstances, we are not aware that it is operating.

As discussed in Chapter 5, we obtain all our information about the world through our senses. Our sensory systems transduce, or change, that information into neural impulses, and everything we remember is the result of neurons firing in the brain. A memory of a sight or of a sound, for example, is created by intricate patterns of neural activity in the brain. A sensory memory occurs when a light, a sound, an odor, a taste, or a tactile impression leaves a vanishing trace on the nervous system for a fraction of a second. When you look at something and quickly glance away, you can briefly picture the image and recall some of its details. When someone angrily proclaims, "You're not paying attention to me," you can often repeat back the last few words the person spoke, even if you were thinking about something else.

retrieval The act of recalling or remembering stored information to use it.

modal memory model The three-stage memory system that involves sensory memory, short-term memory, and long-term memory.

sensory memory Memory for sensory information that is stored briefly close to its original sensory form.

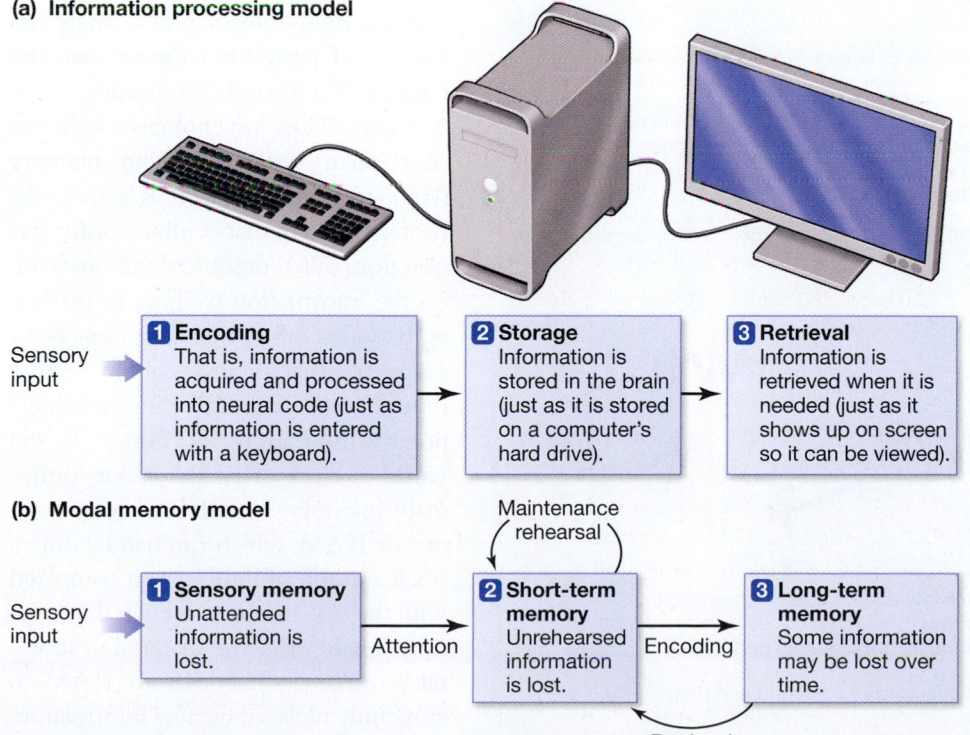

(a) Information processing model

Sensory input →

1 Encoding	**2** Storage	**3** Retrieval
That is, information is acquired and processed into neural code (just as information is entered with a keyboard).	Information is stored in the brain (just as it is stored on a computer's hard drive).	Information is retrieved when it is needed (just as it shows up on screen so it can be viewed).

(b) Modal memory model

Maintenance rehearsal

Sensory input →

1 Sensory memory	**2** Short-term memory	**3** Long-term memory
Unattended information is lost.	Unrehearsed information is lost.	Some information may be lost over time.

Attention · Encoding

Retrieval

FIGURE 7.7 Memory Systems
(a) The information processing model compares the working of memory to the actions of a computer. **(b)** The modal memory model serves as a useful framework for thinking about the basic stages of memory.

In 1960, the cognitive psychologist George Sperling provided the initial empirical support for sensory memory. In this classic experiment, three rows of letters were flashed on a screen for one-twentieth of a second. Participants were asked to recall all the letters. Most people believed they had seen all the letters, but they could recall only three or four. That is, in the time it took them to name the first three or four, they forgot the other letters. These reports suggested the participants had very quickly lost their memories of exactly what they had seen. Sperling tested this hypothesis by showing all the letters exactly as he had done before, but signaling with a high-, medium-, or low-pitched sound as soon as the letters disappeared. A high pitch meant the participants should recall the letters in the top row, a medium pitch meant they should recall the letters in the middle row, and a low pitch meant they should recall the letters in the bottom row. When the sound occurred very shortly after the letters disappeared, the participants correctly remembered almost all the letters in the signaled row. But the longer the delay between the letters' disappearance and the sound, the worse the participants performed. Sperling concluded that the visual memory persisted for about one-third of a second, after which the sensory memory trace faded progressively until it was no longer accessible (**FIGURE 7.8**).

Our sensory memories allow us to experience the world as a continuous stream rather than in discrete sensations, much the way a movie projector plays a series of still pictures that follow each other closely enough in time to look like continuous action. In everyday vision, when you turn your head, the scene passes smoothly in front of you rather than in jerky bits, thanks to visual memory, which keeps information just long enough for you to connect one image with the next in a smooth way that corresponds to the way objects move in the real world.

short-term memory (STM) A limited-capacity memory system that holds information in awareness for a brief period.

working memory (WM) An active processing system that keeps different types of information available for current use.

FIGURE 7.8 Scientific Method: Sperling's Sensory Memory Experiment

Hypothesis: Information in sensory memories is lost very quickly if it is not transferred for further processing.

Research Method:

1 Participants looked at a screen on which three rows of letters flashed for one-twentieth of a second.

2 When a high-pitched tone followed the letters, it meant the participants should recall the letters on the top row. When a medium-pitched tone followed the letters, it meant the participants should recall the middle row. And when a low-pitched tone followed the letters, it meant the participants should recall the bottom row.

3 The tones sounded at various intervals: .15, .30, .50, or 1 second after the display of the letters.

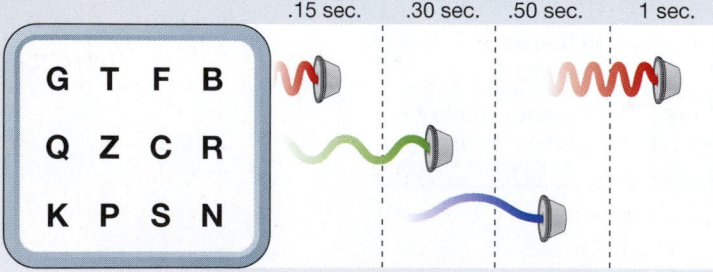

Results: When the tone sounded very shortly after the letters appeared, participants remembered almost all the letters in the signaled row. The longer the delay between the disappearance of the letters and the tone, the worse the participants performed.

Conclusion: Sensory memory persists for about one-third of a second and then progressively fades.

Working Memory Is Active

Information attended to is passed from sensory stores to **short-term memory (STM)**, a limited-capacity memory system that holds information in awareness for a brief period but longer than the fraction of a second that sensory memory lasts. Most psychologists call this short-term system **working memory (WM)**, to indicate that it is a memory (storage) system that combines information from different sources and can work on the information we have in memory. It is also called *immediate memory*, to emphasize that it consists of our fleeting thoughts, ever-shifting feelings, and temporary impressions of things in the world. A computer analogy for immediate memory is random-access memory, or RAM, which can handle only a small amount of information compared with the vast amount stored in the computer's hard disk. The material in short-term memory, like that in RAM, is constantly replaced by new information, and it is lost forever if not saved.

Information remains in working memory for about 20 to 30 seconds, then disappears unless you actively prevent that from happening by thinking about or rehearsing the information. For instance, when you look up a telephone number and walk across the room to the phone, you repeat the number over and over until you dial it. If the number is busy, or if you trip over the cat on the way to phone, you probably will forget the number even though only a few seconds have passed since you looked it up.

As an example, try to remember some new information: the three-letter string of consonants X C J. As long as you keep repeating the string over and over, you will keep it in working memory. But if you stop rehearsing, you probably will soon forget the letters, because you are bombarded with other events that compete for your attention, and you may not be able to stay focused. Try again to remember X C J, but this time count backward in threes from the number 309. Most people find it difficult to remember the consonants after a few seconds of backward counting, and the longer they spend counting, the less able they are to remember the consonant string. After only 18 seconds of counting, most people recall the consonants extremely poorly—an indication that working memory lasts less than a half a minute without continuous rehearsing as a way to remember.

MEMORY SPAN AND CHUNKING Why do new items in working memory interfere with the recall of older items? WM can hold a limited amount of information. The cognitive psychologist George Miller has noted that the limit is generally seven items (plus or minus two), a figure referred to as *memory span*. More-recent research suggests that Miller's estimate may be too high (Conway, Kane, Hambrick, Wilhelm, & Engle, 2005). Memory span also varies among individuals. Indeed, some intelligence tests use memory span as part of the measure of IQ.

Because WM is limited, you might expect almost everyone to have great difficulty remembering a string of letters such as

UTPHDNYUMAUCLABAMIT.

These 20 letters would tax even the largest memory span. But what if we organized the information into smaller, meaningful units? For instance,

UT PHD NYU MA UCLA BA MIT.

Here the letters are separated to produce acronyms for universities and academic degrees. This organization makes them much easier to recall, for two reasons. First, memory span is limited to seven items, probably fewer, but the items can be letters or groups of letters, numbers or groups of numbers, words, or even concepts. Second, meaningful units are easier to remember than nonsense units. This process of organizing information into meaningful units is known as **chunking,** as in breaking down the information into chunks. The more efficiently you chunk information, the more you can remember. Master chess players who glance at a scenario on a chessboard, even for a few seconds, later can reproduce the exact arrangement of pieces (Chase & Simon, 1973). They can do so because they instantly chunk the board into a number of meaningful subunits based on their past experiences with the game. However, if the pieces are arranged on the board in ways that make no sense in terms of chess, experts are no better than novices at reproducing the board. In general, the greater your expertise with the material, the more efficiently you can chunk information, and therefore the more you can remember.

Over the last several years, the World Memory Championship, or Memory Olympics, has grown rapidly in popularity. Contestants compete by showing how much they can remember in several events (**FIGURE 7.9**). For example, they may be given a deck of shuffled cards and told to turn over each card just once; then they have to

chunking Organizing information into meaningful units to make it easier to remember.

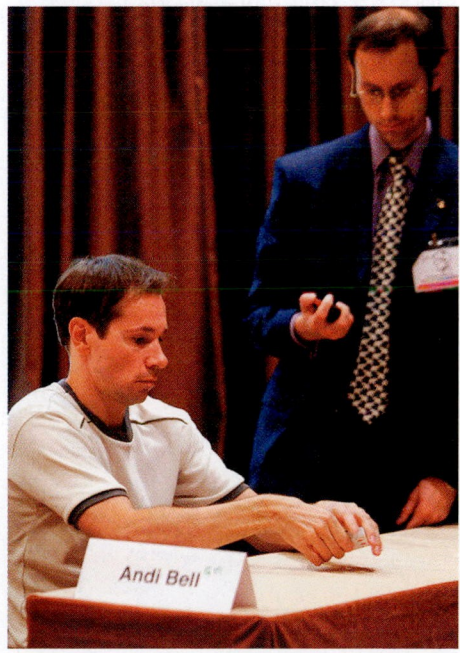

FIGURE 7.9 Memory Olympics
Contestants in the Memory Olympics memorize names, faces, and even decks of cards, as shown here at the meet in Kuala Lumpur, October 2003. Almost all participants in such memory contests use strategies involving chunking.

recall as many cards as they can in the correct order. The contestants rely on various strategies to improve recall, but virtually all of them use some form of chunking. They need to remember not 52 cards in order but fewer chunks of information. A sequence of the queen of hearts, the 7 of spades, and the 2 of diamonds might be encoded as a single chunk consisting of a queen with a heart shaped face digging up 2 diamonds with her 7 spades. Thus the three separate cards become a single chunk. (The use of a visual image also helps with remembering, as discussed later in this chapter.)

You can apply chunking in your everyday life when you need to remember many separate pieces of information. For example, suppose you were trying to memorize the historian Michael Hart's list of the 14 most influential men in history: Aristotle, Augustus, Buddha, Columbus, Confucius, Einstein, Galileo, Gutenberg, Jesus, Mohammed, Newton, St. Paul, Shi Huang-ti, and T'sai lung (World History: HyperHistory, http://www.hyperhistory.com/online_n2/History_n2/a.html). You might chunk these names by imagining Aristotle sitting on Buddha's belly as a picture on a calendar for the month of August, Columbus looking confused while Einstein is pointing the way, and so on. (Other ways of improving memory are discussed later in this chapter.)

WORKING MEMORY'S FOUR PARTS Researchers initially saw short-term memory as simply a buffer, or holding place, in which verbal information was rehearsed until it was stored or forgotten. They learned, however, that WM is not a single storage system but rather an active processing unit that deals with multiple types of information, such as sounds, images, and ideas. Alan Baddeley and his colleagues (2002) developed an influential model of an active memory system that they called working memory. The three components of working memory are the *central executive,* the *phonological loop,* the *visuospatial sketchpad,* and the *episodic buffer* (**FIGURE 7.10**).

FIGURE 7.10 Baddeley's Working Memory System The working memory system details the components and processes of short-term memory.

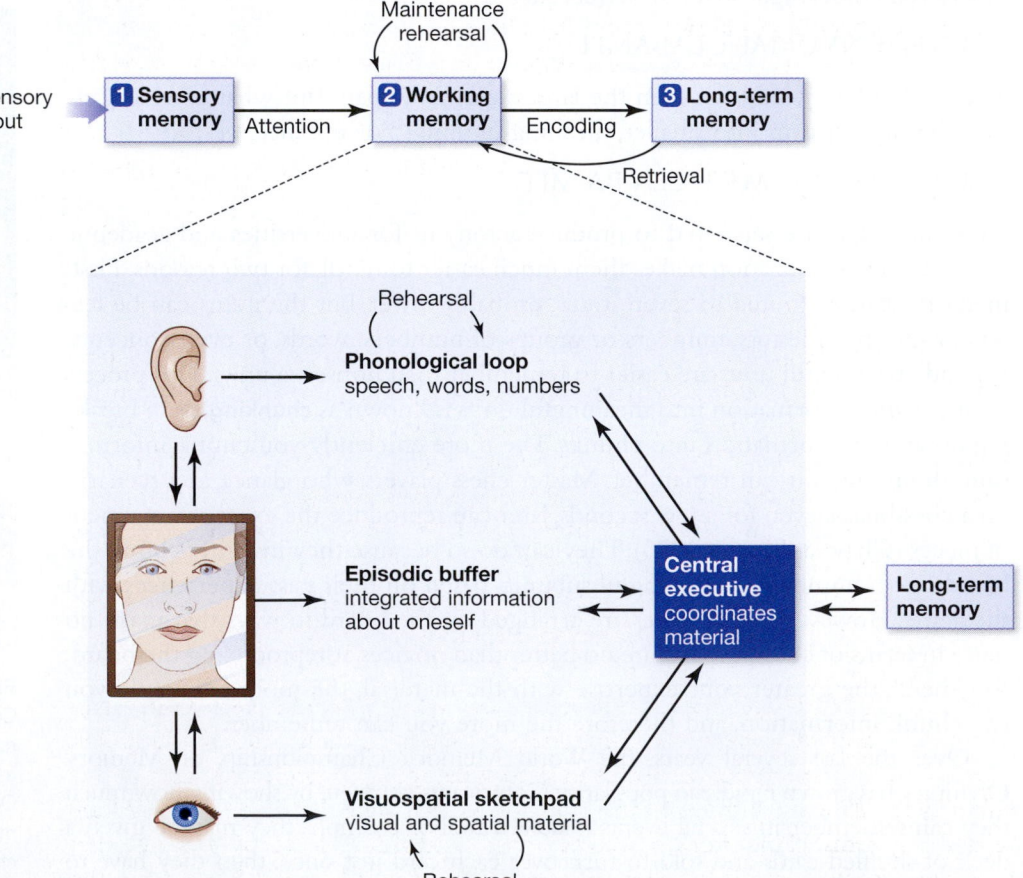

The central executive presides over the interactions among the phonological loop, the visuospatial sketchpad, the episodic buffer, and long-term memory (discussed in the next section); as its name suggests, it is the boss. It encodes information from the sensory systems and then filters information that is sufficiently important to be stored in long-term memory. It also retrieves information from long-term memory as needed. The central executive relies on the other three subcomponents, which temporarily hold auditory or visuospatial information or personally relevant information.

The phonological loop encodes auditory information and is active whenever a person tries to remember words by reading them, speaking them, or repeating them. You probably have noticed your "inner voice," which reads along as your eyes process written material—it is difficult to absorb meaning simply by scanning your eyes across the text. If you are not familiar with your inner voice, try to read the rest of this sentence while reciting the alphabet, a task that interferes with your ability to "speak" the words of the sentence in your head. (Give up?) Evidence for the phonological loop comes from studies in which participants are shown lists of consonants and asked to remember them. People tend to make errors with consonants that sound alike rather than those that look alike—for instance, misremembering a D as a T rather than as a Q, which is visually similar to D but does not sound like it. Recall is also poorer when many words on a list sound the same than when they sound dissimilar but are related in meaning. These examples suggest that words are processed in WM by how they sound rather than by how they look or what they mean.

The visuospatial sketchpad processes visual information, such as objects' features and where they are located. Suppose you are walking and see a dog. The visuospatial sketchpad allows you to keep track of both where the dog is located and whether it is the sort of dog you need to be aware of. Researchers have distinguished between phonological loop and visuospatial sketchpad by studying patients with specific kinds of brain damage. Patients with some types of brain injury have great difficulty remembering spatial layouts but have little difficulty remembering words, for example, whereas others show the opposite pattern. Such findings demonstrate that WM consists of much more than an all-inclusive storage system.

Recently added to Baddeley's model of working memory, the episodic buffer holds temporary information about oneself, drawing heavily on long-term episodic memory.

Long-Term Memory Is Relatively Permanent

When people talk about memory, they usually are referring to the relatively permanent storage of information: **long-term memory (LTM)**. In the computer analogy presented above, LTM is the storage of information on a hard drive. In thinking about LTM's capacity, try to imagine counting everything you know and everything you are likely to know in your lifetime. It is hard to imagine what that number might be—you can always learn more. Unlike computer storage, human LTM is nearly limitless. Long-term memory allows you to remember nursery rhymes from childhood, the meanings and spellings of words you rarely use (say, *aardvark*), what you had for lunch yesterday, and so on, and so on.

long-term memory (LTM) The relatively permanent storage of information.

DISTINGUISHING LONG-TERM MEMORY FROM WORKING MEMORY Long-term memory is distinct from working memory in two important ways, duration and capacity. A controversy exists, however, as to whether LTM represents a truly different type of memory storage from WM. Initial evidence that LTM and WM are separate systems came from research, at the individual level of analysis, that required people to recall long lists of words. The ability to recall items from the

serial position effect The ability to recall items from a list depends on order of presentation, with items presented early or late in the list remembered better than those in the middle.

list depended on order of presentation: Items presented early or late in the list were remembered better than those in the middle. Better recall of early and late items in a list relative to items in the middle of the list is known as the **serial position effect,** which involves two separate effects: The *primacy effect* refers to the better memory people have for items presented at the beginning of the list, whereas the *recency effect* refers to people's better memory for the most recent items, the items at the end of the list (**FIGURE 7.11**).

One explanation for the serial position effect relies on a distinction between WM and LTM. When research participants study a long list of words, they rehearse the earliest items the most, so that information is transferred into LTM. The last few items, by contrast, are still in WM when the participants have to recall the words immediately after reading them. The idea that primacy effects are due to LTM whereas recency effects are due to WM is supported by studies in which there is a delay between the presentation of the list and the recall task. Such delays interfere with the recency effect but not the primacy effect, just as you would expect if the former involves WM and the latter LTM. However, it is questionable whether the recency effect can be attributed entirely to WM. After all, you probably remember your most recent class better than the classes you had earlier, even though you are not holding that material in WM. If you had to recall the past presidents or past prime ministers of your country, you would probably recall the early ones and most recent ones best and have poorer recall for those in between, but it is unlikely that you maintain the information about presidents or prime ministers in WM.

Perhaps the best support for the distinction between WM and LTM exists at the biological level of analysis, in case studies such as that of H.M., the patient described at the beginning of this chapter. His WM system is perfectly normal, as shown by his ability to keep track of a conversation as long as he stays actively involved in it, and much of his LTM system is intact, since he remembers events that occurred before his surgery, but he is unable to transfer new information from WM into LTM. In another case, a 28-year-old accident victim with damage to the left temporal lobe had extremely poor WM, with a span of only one or two items. However, he had perfectly normal LTM—he had a fine memory for day-to-day happenings and reasonable knowledge of events that occurred before his surgery (Shallice & Warrington, 1969). Somehow, despite the bottleneck in his WM, he was relatively good at

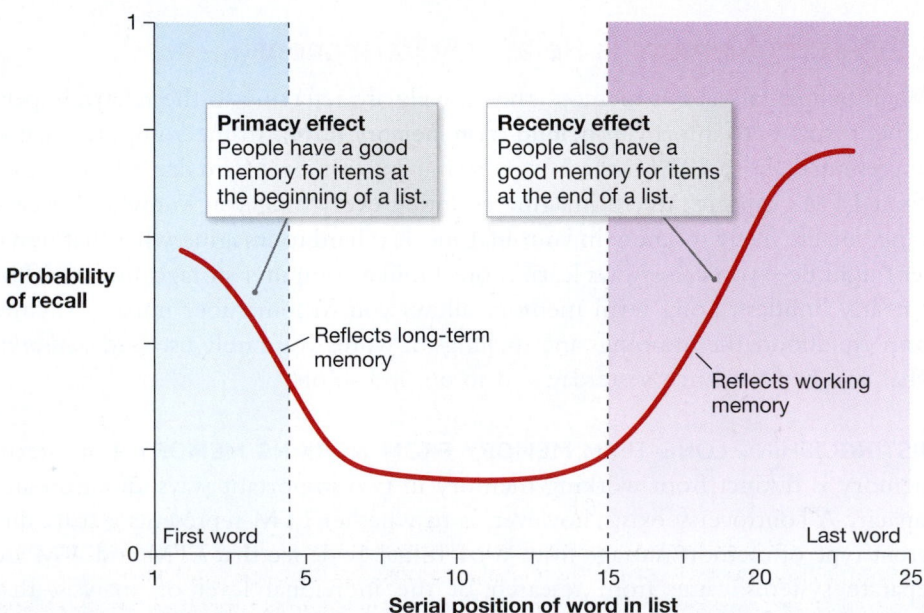

FIGURE 7.11 The Serial Position Effect

retrieving information from LTM. These case studies demonstrate that LTM can be dissociated (separated) from WM. However, the two memory systems are highly interdependent, at least for most of us. For instance, to chunk information in WM, people need to form meaningful connections based on information stored in LTM.

WHAT GETS INTO LONG-TERM MEMORY Considering that we are bombarded with so much information and engage in so many activities, it seems obvious that some type of filtering system or series of rules must constrain what goes into our LTM. Researchers have provided several possible explanations for this process. One possibility is that information enters permanent storage through rehearsal. When you study for exams, you often go over the material many times to be sure you have learned it. Memory researchers have also shown that *overlearning,* in which you keep rehearsing material you already know pretty well, leads to improved memory, especially over longer periods of time. For this reason, material studied in multiple sessions over time,—that is, through *distributed practice*—is remembered better than material studied in a brief period, through *massed practice,* or cramming. The conclusion from many years of research is that the most efficient way to learn is to study for shorter periods (in time blocks long enough to get a meaningful amount of information into memory) but to spread those study sessions out over several days or weeks. Unless you plan to "regurgitate" the information on an exam and never use it again, cramming is an ineffective way to acquire information. In later sections, this chapter will discuss ways to improve learning and memory. In the meantime, remember that "cramming is crummy" for long-term retention and recall.

Although rehearsal is a way to get some information into LTM, simply repeating something many times is not a good method for making information memorable. After all, sometimes we have extremely poor memory for objects that are highly familiar (**FIGURE 7.12**). Merely seeing something countless times does not

FIGURE 7.12 **Try for Yourself: The Penny Quiz**

Can you tell which drawing of the U.S. penny is correct?

(a) (b) (c) (d) (e)

(f) (g) (h) (i) (j)

(k) (l) (m) (n) (o)

Answer: Even if you live in the United States and see pennies all the time, you might have had trouble identifying "(a)" as the accurate version. In any country, most people do not pay much attention to the specific details of their currency.

enable people to recall its details. You can try this with your friends: Cover their watches, and ask each friend to describe his or her watch face. A surprising number of people will not know, for example, if all of the numbers are on the face, even if they look at the watch many times a day. This loss of information in memory really shows how well attention and memory function: We attend just enough for the task at hand and lose information that seems irrelevant.

Only information that helps us adapt to the environment is typically transformed into a long-term memory. Of the billions of both sensory experiences and thoughts we have each day, we want to store only useful information so as to benefit from experience. Remembering that a penny is money and being able to recognize one when we see it are much more useful than being able to recall its specific features, unless you receive counterfeit pennies and have to separate them from real ones.

Evolutionary theory helps explain how we decide in advance what information will be useful. Memory allows us to use information in ways that assist in reproduction and survival. For instance, animals that can use past experiences to increase their chances of survival have a selective advantage over animals that fail to learn from past experiences. Recognizing a predator and remembering an escape route will help an animal avoid being eaten. Accordingly, remembering which objects are edible, which people are friends and which are enemies, and how to get home are typically not challenging for people with intact memory systems, but they are critical for survival.

 ## SUMMING UP

What Are the Basic Stages of Memory?

From the somewhat dated perspective of information processing, memory has three basic parts: sensory memory, short-term memory, and long-term memory. Sensory memory consists of brief traces on the nervous system that reflect perceptual processes. Material is passed from sensory memory to short-term memory, a limited system that briefly holds information in awareness. More recently, psychologists have come to think about STM as working memory, which involves a central executive, a phonological loop, an episodic buffer, and a visuospatial sketchpad. WM is limited to approximately seven (five to nine) chunks of information. The rules for chunking are determined by the meaning provided from LTM, a virtually limitless, relatively permanent store. The distinction between WM and LTM is best established by case studies of people with impairments to one but not to the other.

 ## MEASURING UP

1. Indicate how long each of the three stages of memory holds information, and indicate its capacity.

   Stage:
   a. sensory memory
   b. short-term (or working) memory
   c. long-term memory

   Duration:
   i. one week
   ii. a fraction of a second
   iii. about one day
   iv. between 20 and 30 seconds
   v. potentially as long as a person lives
   vi. until middle age

Capacity:
  i. 20 chunks, plus or minus 10
  ii. five to nine chunks
  iii. much of the visual world
  iv. almost limitless
  v. about 100,000 pieces of information
  vi. equal to the number of neurons in the brain

2. Which memory system is responsible for your ability to remember the first word in this question?
  a. sensory memory
  b. working memory
  c. long-term memory

What Are the Different Long-Term Memory Systems?

Only in the last few decades have most psychologists begun to think about long-term memory as composed of several systems. The older view was that memories differed in terms of their strength (how likely something would be recalled) and their accessibility (context in which something would be recalled), but generally all memories were considered to be of the same type. In the late 1970s and early 1980s, cognitive psychologists such as Endel Tulving, Daniel Schacter, and Larry Squire began to challenge this view. They argued that memory is not just one entity but rather a process that involves several interacting systems. Although the systems share a common function—to retain and use information—they encode and store different types of information in different ways. For instance, several obvious differences exist between your remembering how to ride a bicycle and your recalling what you ate for dinner last night or that the capital of Canada is Ottawa. These are long-term memories, but they differ in how they were acquired (learned) and in how they are stored and retrieved. Remembering how to ride a bike requires a behavioral component, an integration of specific motor and perceptual skills that you acquired over time. You are not consciously aware of your efforts to maintain balance or follow the basic rules of the road. By contrast, recalling a specific event you experienced or knowledge you learned from someone else sometimes requires a conscious effort to retrieve the information from LTM.

Scientists do not agree on the number of human memory systems. For instance, some researchers have distinguished among memory systems based on how information is stored in memory, such as whether the storage occurs with or without deliberate effort. Other researchers have focused on the types of information stored, such as words and meaning versus particular muscle movements versus information about a city's spatial layout. Understanding how different memory systems work has provided tremendous insight into memory, such as why it sometimes fails.

Explicit Memory Involves Conscious Effort

The most basic distinction between memory systems is the division of memories we are consciously aware of from memories we acquire without conscious effort or intention and do not know we know. Remember that H.M., the memory loss sufferer described at the beginning of this chapter, improved at mirror tracing (tracing a pattern when only its mirror image is visible), so he must have learned this motor task

LEARNING OBJECTIVES
Explain the differences among episodic, semantic, implicit, explicit, and prospective memories.

Provide an example of each of these types of memory.

implicit memory The system underlying unconscious memories.

explicit memory The processes involved when people remember specific information.

declarative memory The cognitive information retrieved from explicit memory; knowledge that can be declared.

episodic memory Memory for one's personal past experiences.

semantic memory Memory for knowledge about the world.

FIGURE 7.13 **Explicit Memory** Explicit memory involves information that individuals are aware of knowing. **(a)** When these World War II veterans assembled aboard the USS *Intrepid* to reminisce on Memorial Day, they were drawing on episodic memory, which is based on past experiences. **(b)** Game shows such as *Jeopardy* test semantic memory—the memory of facts independent of personal experience. In 2004, Ken Jennings (pictured here) became the longest-defending champion on *Jeopardy* when he won 75 games in a row.

even without knowing that he had. We all have memories about which we have no conscious knowledge. Such unconscious memory is called **implicit memory**. **Explicit memory** involves the processes we use to remember information we can say we know. The cognitive information retrieved in explicit memory is **declarative memory,** knowledge that can be declared (consciously brought to mind).

You use explicit memory when you recall what you had for dinner last night, for example, or what the word *aardvark* means. Declarative memories can involve words or concepts, visual images, or both. For instance, when you imagine the earth's orbit around the sun, you might also retrieve the images and names of the other planets. You could describe this knowledge in words, so it is in declarative memory. Most of the examples presented in this chapter so far are of explicit memories. Every exam you ever took in school likely tested declarative memory.

In 1972, Endel Tulving found that explicit memory can be divided into *episodic* and *semantic memory*. **Episodic memory** refers to a person's past experiences and includes information about the time and place the experiences occurred (**FIGURE 7.13A**). If you can remember aspects of your 14th birthday, for example, such as where you were and what you did there, this information is part of your episodic memory. **Semantic memory** represents the knowledge of facts independent of personal experience. We might not remember where or when we learned it, but we know it (**FIGURE 7.13B**). For instance, people know what Jell-O is, they know the capitals of countries they have never visited, and even those who have never played baseball know that three strikes mean you are out.

Scientists have learned a great deal about normal memory by studying people like H.M. and others who have abnormal memories. Evidence that episodic and semantic systems of explicit memory are separate can be found in cases of brain injury in which semantic memory is intact even though episodic memory is impaired. Researchers found this pattern of abnormal memory in a group of British children who experienced brain damage during infancy or early childhood and developed poor memory for episodic information (Vargha-Khadem et al., 1997). The children had trouble reporting what they had for lunch, what they were watching on television five minutes earlier, what they did during summer vacation. Their parents reported that the children had to be constantly monitored to make sure they remembered things such as going to school. Remarkably, these children attended mainstream schools and did reasonably well. Moreover, their IQs fell within the normal range. They learned to speak and read, and they could remember many facts. For instance, when asked "Who is Martin Luther King Jr.?"

(a)

(b)

one of the children responded, "An American; fought for Black rights, Black rights leader in the 1970s; got assassinated." These children, then, were able to encode and retrieve semantic information.

Implicit Memory Occurs without Deliberate Effort

Implicit memory consists of memories without awareness of them, so you are not able to put the memories into words. If you ran to catch a ball that had been thrown high in the air, you would not be able to say just how you knew where the ball would be when you could reach it; if you came reasonably close to catching the ball, how to be in position to do so is information you know and can use. Classical conditioning, described in Chapter 6, employs implicit memory: If you always experience fear at the sight of a person in a white lab coat, for example, you might have past associations (implicit memories) between a person in a white lab coat and pain. In addition, implicit memory does not require conscious attention, but happens automatically, without deliberate effort. Suppose that while driving you realize you have been daydreaming and have no episodic memory of the past few minutes. During that time, you employed implicit memories of how to drive and where you were going—you did not crash the car or go in the wrong direction.

Implicit memory influences our lives in subtle ways, as when our attitudes are influenced by implicit learning. For example, you might like someone because he or she reminds you of another person you like, even if you are unaware of the connection. Advertisers rely on implicit memory to influence our purchasing decisions. Constant exposure to brand names makes us more likely to think of them when we buy products. If you find yourself wanting a particular brand of jeans, for example, you might be "remembering" advertisements for that brand, even if you cannot recall the specifics. This effect is another example of one of the seven main themes in this book: We often are unaware of influences on how we think or feel.

At the social level of analysis, implicit attitude formation can affect our beliefs about people, such as whether particular people are famous. Ask yourself: Is Richard Shiffrin famous? Try to think for a second how you know him. If you thought he was famous, you might have recalled that Shiffrin was one of the psychologists who introduced the modal memory model (an accomplishment that might make him famous in scientific circles), or you might have remembered reading his name before even if you could not remember where. In studying what he called the *false fame effect,* the psychologist Larry Jacoby had research participants read aloud a list of made-up names (Jacoby, Kelley, Brown, & Jasechko, 1989). The participants were told that the research project was about pronunciation. The next day, Jacoby had the same people participate in an apparently unrelated study, in which they were asked to read a list of names and decide whether each person was famous or not. The participants misjudged some of the made-up names from the previous day as being those of famous people. Because the participants knew they had heard the names before but could not remember where, implicit memory led them to assume the familiar names were those of famous people. The saying *There is no such thing as bad publicity* may be an exaggeration, but if all you remember about a name is that you have heard it before (it feels familiar), you will likely assume it belongs to a famous person.

Implicit memory is also involved in *repetition priming,* the improvement in identifying or processing a stimulus that has been experienced previously. In a typical priming experiment, participants are exposed to a list of words and asked to do something, such as count the number of letters in the words. Following some brief delay, the participants are shown word fragments and asked to complete them with

FIGURE 7.14 Implicit Memory The innate muscle memory for knowing how to ride a bicycle (procedural or motor memory) is an example of implicit memory, or memory without the awareness of having the memory. Once people learn how to ride a bike, they usually can remember how to do it again, unconsciously, at any age.

procedural memory A type of implicit memory that involves motor skills and behavioral habits.

prospective memory Remembering to do something at some time in the future.

the first word that comes to mind. For example, participants might be asked to count the letters in the words *appearance, chestnut, patent*. Then they would be asked to complete the stems app____, che____, and pat____ with the first word that comes to mind. Typically, participants will much more likely complete the fragments with the words they previously encountered, which were primed (activated in memory) and therefore more easily accessible. In this example, they would more likely complete the stems as *appearance, chestnut,* and *patent* than as, say, *application, cheese,* and *paternal*. This effect occurs even when participants cannot explicitly recall the words in the first task. Even many hours after viewing the primes, participants show implicit memory without explicit recall of the words.

Another example of implicit memory is **procedural memory,** or *motor memory,* which involves motor skills, habits, and other behaviors employed to achieve goals, such as coordinating muscle movements to ride a bicycle or following the rules of the road while driving (**FIGURE 7.14**). You remember to stop when you see a red light because you have learned to do so, and you might drive home on a specific route without even thinking about it. Procedural memories have an automatic, unconscious aspect, so much so that most people find that consciously thinking about automatic behaviors interferes with the smooth production of those behaviors. The next time you are riding a bicycle, for instance, try to think about each step involved in the process.

Prospective Memory Is Remembering to Do Something

"When you see Pablo, tell him to call me, and don't forget to stop for milk on your way home from school." Unlike the other types of remembering discussed so far in this chapter, **prospective memory** is future oriented, in that it means an individual remembers to do something at some future time. As noted earlier in this chapter, paying attention has a "cost": The cognitive effort involved in attending to certain information makes us unable to attend closely to other information. Likewise, remembering to do something takes up valuable cognitive resources, either by reducing the number of items we can deal with in working memory or by reducing the number of things we can attend to (Einstein & McDaniel, 2005). In one laboratory study of prospective memory's effects, participants were given a list of words to learn, but in one condition they also had to remember to do something (such as press a key when they saw a certain word). The group that had to remember to do something took longer to learn the list than the control group that learned the same list of words but did not have to remember to do something (Cook, Marsh, Clark-Foos, & Meeks, 2007).

Prospective memory involves both automatic and controlled processes. As discussed in Chapter 4, automatic processes happen without conscious awareness or intent (McDaniel & Einstein, 2000). Sometimes the retrieval cues occur in a particular environment—for example, seeing Pablo might automatically trigger your memory, so you effortlessly remember to give him the message. Sometimes particular environments do not have obvious retrieval cues for particular prospective memories—for example, you might not encounter a retrieval cue for remembering to buy milk, unless on your way home you drive past a market that has a large dairy display outside. Remembering to stop for milk might require some ongoing remembering as you travel home and perhaps earlier, even if you are not aware of that remembering.

Prospective memory for events without retrieval cues are the reason sticky notes are so popular—by sticking one that says "Milk" on the steering wheel of your car, for example, you will ensure that you see it before heading home. By jogging your memory, the note helps you avoid the effort of remembering (**FIGURE 7.15**).

FIGURE 7.15 Prospective Memory
Prospective memory involves remembering to do something in the future. When you use a device, such as this personal digital assistant (PDA), to remember appointments and deadlines, you are assisting your prospective memory.

 SUMMING UP

What Are the Different Long-Term Memory Systems?

Memory is not a single process or brain system. Fundamental differences exist among episodic and semantic memory, explicit and implicit memory, and prospective memory. Explicit memory involves the conscious storage and retrieval of declarative memories, such as personal experiences or meanings of words; explicit memories can be episodic or semantic. Episodic memory is of personally experienced events, such as where and when the events occurred—for example, you might remember that you had eggs for breakfast at home this morning. Semantic memory is of information that does not include the memory for where and when it was learned. Implicit memory is enhancement of memory without effort or awareness. Examples of implicit memory include procedural (or motor) memory, attitude formation, and repetition priming. Prospective memories involve a person's remembering to do things. If the cue to remember is available in the person's environment, prospective memory can operate automatically, but without a retrieval cue, remembering requires conscious effort.

MEASURING UP

Indicate whether each of the following examples of memory is prospective, implicit, or explicit; if it is explicit, also indicate whether it is episodic or semantic.

    a. walking (for an adult)
    b. the value of pi to six decimal places
    c. writing a computer program
    d. the fact that working memory has three basic components
    e. the fact that you need to drive your sister home from school
    f. that the smell of eggs makes you sick and you do not know why

How Is Information Organized in Long-Term Memory?

Events important enough to be remembered permanently need to be stored in a way that allows for later retrieval. Imagine if a video store put each video or DVD wherever there was empty space on a shelf. How would you find a certain movie? You would have to go through the inventory film by film until you encountered the movie. Just as this random storage would not work well for movies, it would not work well for memories. The following section examines the temporal (time-based) and organizational principles of long-term memory.

 LEARNING OBJECTIVES
Illustrate the organization of long-term memory.

Show how retrieval cues can determine what we remember.

Long-Term Storage Is Based on Meaning

As viewed through the computer analogy presented a few sections above, memory is a process of storing new information so that the information is available when the rememberer needs it. And as discussed in Chapter 5, our perceptual experiences

are transformed into representations, or *codes,* which are then stored. For instance, when your visual system senses a shaggy, four-legged animal and your auditory system senses barking, you perceive a dog. The concept of "dog" is a *mental representation* for a category of animals that share certain features, such as barking and fur. You do not have a tiny picture of a dog stored in your head; rather, you have a mental representation. The mental representation for "dog" differs from that for "cat," even though the two are similar in many ways. You also have mental representations for complex and abstract ideas, including beliefs and feelings such as love.

All of this information is stored in networks of neurons in the brain. Memories, then, are stored representations. As discussed above, memories represent many different kinds of information, such as visual images, facts, ideas, tastes, or even muscle movements, such as the memories for riding a bicycle. Retrieval often involves an explicit effort to access the contents of memory storage, as when you try to remember your fifth birthday or something you learned in the previous chapter. But often you retrieve information without any effort, as when you instantly remember the name of an acquaintance you encounter. Thus retrieval is involved in explicit and implicit memory systems.

There are many ways to organize a large collection of things. For example, public libraries generally store books by Library of Congress numbers, telephone books list names alphabetically, and video stores tend to organize movies by type *and* alphabetically. Memories are stored by meaning. In the early 1970s, the psychologists Fergus Craik and Robert Lockhart developed an influential theory of memory based on depth of elaboration. According to their *levels of processing* model, the more deeply an item is encoded, the more meaning it has and the better it is remembered. Craik and Lockhart proposed that different types of rehearsal lead to differential encoding. *Maintenance rehearsal* is simply repeating the item over and over. *Elaborative rehearsal* encodes the information in more meaningful ways, such as thinking about the item conceptually or deciding whether it refers to oneself. In other words, in this type of rehearsal we elaborate on basic information by linking it to knowledge from long-term memory.

How does the levels of processing model work? Suppose you showed research participants a list of words and then asked them to do one of three things. You might ask them to make simple perceptual judgments, such as whether each word is printed in capital or lowercase letters. You might ask them to judge the sound of each word, as in whether the word rhymes with *boat.* Or you might ask them about each word's semantic meaning, as in "Does this word fit the sentence *They had to cross the _____ to reach the castle?*" Once participants had completed the task (that is, processed the information), you might ask them to recall as many words as possible. You would find that words processed at the deepest level, based on semantic meaning, were remembered the best (**FIGURE 7.16**). At the biological (brain systems) level of analysis, brain imaging studies have shown that semantic encoding activates more brain regions than shallow encoding (Kapur et al., 1994). This greater brain activity is associated with better memory.

FIGURE 7.16 Encoding Participants are asked to consider a list of words according to how the words are printed, how they sound, or what they mean.

The more deeply the material is processed, the better it is remembered.

Percentage who recognized word

Visual: what the word looks like

Acoustic: how the word sounds

Semantic: what the word means

Type of encoding

Schemas Provide an Organizational Framework

If people store memories by meaning, how is that meaning determined? Chunking, discussed above, is a good way to encode groups of items for memorization. The more meaningful the chunks, the better they will be remembered. Decisions about how to chunk information depend on **schemas:** structures in long-term memory that help us perceive, organize, process, and use information. Schemas help us sort out incoming information, and they guide our attention to an environment's relevant features. Thanks to schemas, we construct new memories by filling in holes within existing memories, overlooking inconsistent information, and interpreting meaning based on past experiences.

While helping us make sense of the world, schemas can lead to biased encoding. Specifically and heavily, culture influences schemas. In a classic demonstration conducted in the early 1930s, the psychologist Frederic Bartlett asked British participants to listen to a Native American folktale, which involved supernatural experiences and was difficult to understand for non–Native Americans unfamiliar with such tales. Fifteen minutes later, Bartlett asked the participants to repeat the story exactly as they had heard it. The participants altered the story greatly—and consistently, so that it made sense from their own cultural standpoint. Sometimes they simply forgot the supernatural parts they could not understand.

To understand schemas' influence on which information is stored in memory, consider a study in which students read a story about an unruly girl. Some participants were told the girl was Helen Keller, whereas others were told it was Carol Harris, a made-up name (Sulin & Dooling, 1974). One week later, the participants who had been told the girl was Helen Keller were more likely to mistakenly report having read the sentence *She was deaf, mute, and blind* in the story than those who thought the story was about Carol Harris. The students' cultural schema for Helen Keller included her disabilities, and when they retrieved information about Keller from memory, everything they knew about her was retrieved along with the story they were trying to remember.

To see how schemas affect your ability to recall information, read the following paragraph carefully:

> The procedure is actually quite simple. First arrange things into different bundles depending on makeup. Don't do too much at once. In the short run this may not seem important, however, complications easily arise. A mistake can be costly. Next, find facilities. Some people must go elsewhere for them. Manipulation of appropriate mechanisms should be self-explanatory. Remember to include all other necessary supplies. Initially the routine will overwhelm you, but soon it will become just another facet of life. Finally, rearrange everything into their initial groups. Return these to their usual places. Eventually they will be used again. Then the whole cycle will have to be repeated. (Bransford & Johnson, 1972, p. 722)

How easy did you find this paragraph to understand? Could you now recall specific sentences from it? It might surprise you to know that in a research setting, college students who read this paragraph found it easy to understand and relatively straightforward to recall. How is that possible? It was easy when the participants knew that the paragraph described washing clothes. Go back and reread the paragraph. Notice how your schema for doing laundry helps you understand and remember how the words and sentences are connected to one another.

schema A hypothetical cognitive structure that helps us perceive, organize, process, and use information.

Information Is Stored in Association Networks

One highly influential set of theories about memory organization is based on *networks of associations*. We can trace back to the ancient Greek philosopher Aristotle the idea that our knowledge of the world is organized so that things related in meaning are linked in storage. In a network model proposed by the psychologists Allan Collins and Elizabeth Loftus, an item's distinctive features are linked so as to identify the item. Each unit of information in the network is a *node*. Each node is connected to many other nodes. When you look at a fire engine, for example, all the nodes that represent a fire engine's features are activated, and the resulting activation pattern gives rise to the knowledge that the object is a fire engine rather than, say, a cat. An important feature of network models is that activating one node increases the likelihood that closely associated nodes will also be activated. As shown in **FIGURE 7.17**, the closer the nodes, the stronger the association between them and therefore the more likely that activating one will activate the other. Seeing a fire engine activates nodes that indicate other vehicles, so that once your fire engine nodes are activated, you are much quicker to recognize other vehicles than, for instance, fruits or animals. A central tenet of *spreading activation* models of memory is the idea that activating one node increases the likelihood of associated nodes becoming active. According to these views, stimuli in working memory activate specific nodes in long-term memory, and this activation increases the ease of access to that material, thereby facilitating retrieval.

Associative networks' overall organization is based on hierarchically structured categories, which provide a clear and explicit blueprint for where to look for needed information. Given the vast amount of material in memory, it is amazing how quickly we can search for and obtain needed memories from storage. Each time you hear a sentence, you not only have to remember what all the words mean but also have to recall all relevant information that helps you understand the sentence's overall meaning. For this process to occur, the information needs to be organized logically. Imagine trying to find a specific file on a full 40-gigabyte hard disk by opening one file at a time. Such a method would be hopelessly slow. Instead, most computer disks are organized into folders, within each folder are more-specialized folders, and so on. Associative networks in the brain work similarly, and this hierarchical storage system allows us to find needed information quickly.

retrieval cue Anything that helps a person (or other animal) recall information from memory.

FIGURE 7.17 A Network of Associations In this semantic network, similar concepts are connected through their associations.

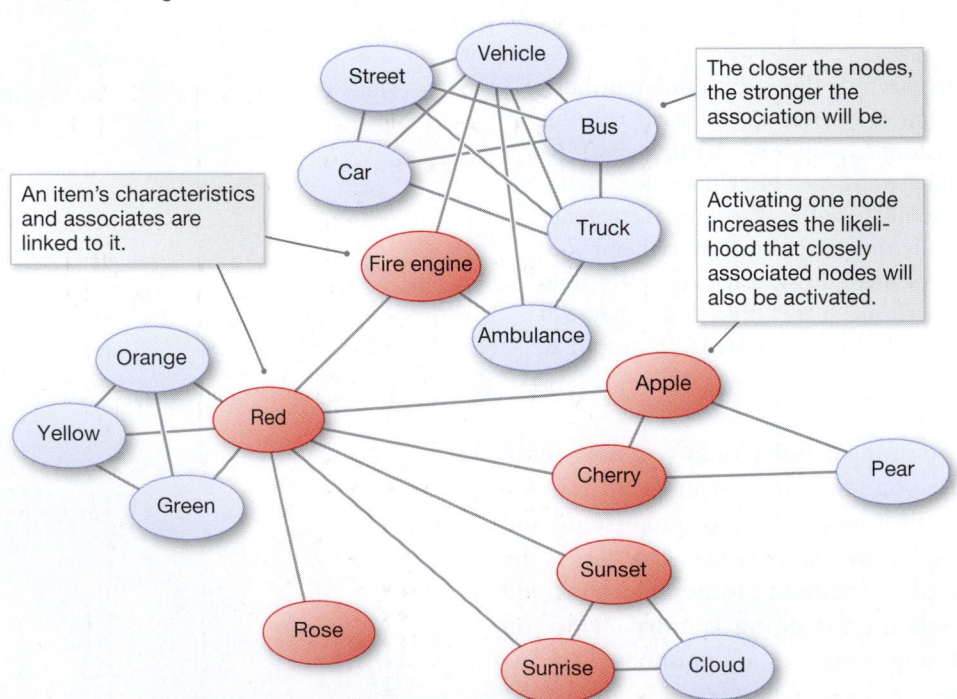

An item's characteristics and associates are linked to it.

The closer the nodes, the stronger the association will be.

Activating one node increases the likelihood that closely associated nodes will also be activated.

Retrieval Cues Provide Access to Long-Term Storage

A **retrieval cue** can be anything that helps a person sort through the vast data in long-term memory to access the right information. Say, for example, you remember the name of your French teacher in your senior year of high school. The activation of this memory node makes it more likely that you will remember the name of the person who sat next to you in French class than if you cannot recall your French teacher's name. In this case, your French teacher's name serves as a retrieval cue for your classmate's name. Retrieval cues' power explains why it is easier to *recognize* than to *recall* information. For example, if you were asked to name the capital of Australia and are not very knowledgeable about that country, for a moment or two you probably would have to think about whether you could retrieve the correct answer. If, however, you were asked whether Australia's capital is Canberra, London, or Pierre, you probably would find it easier to remember that Canberra is the correct answer. The word would help you retrieve information, such as that London is England's capital and Pierre is South Dakota's capital, that allows you to answer the question. However, if Sydney were among the options, you might have selected Sydney, remembering that it is a major city in Australia. Because it is easier to recognize a correct answer than to recall it, many students prefer multiple-choice exams over essay exams. After all, a multiple-choice exam provides all the correct answers—you only have to recognize them.

ENCODING SPECIFICITY Almost anything can be a retrieval cue. Encountering stimuli such as the smell of turkey, a favorite song from years past, a familiar building, and so on, can trigger unintended memories. According to Endel Tulving's **encoding specificity principle,** any stimulus encoded along with an experience can later trigger a memory of the experience. In one study of encoding, participants studied 80 words in either of two rooms. The rooms differed in ways such as location, size, and scent. The participants were then tested for recall in the room in which they studied or in the other room. When they studied and were tested in the same room, participants recalled an average of 49 words correctly. In contrast, when they were tested in the room in which they did not study, participants recalled an average of 35 words correctly (Smith, Glenberg, & Bjork, 1978). This kind of memory enhancement, when the recall situation is similar to the encoding situation, is known as *context dependent memory.* Context dependent memory can be based on things such as physical location, odors, and background music. In the most dramatic research demonstration of context dependent memory, scuba divers who learned information underwater later tested better underwater than on land (Godden & Baddeley, 1975; **FIGURE 7.18**).

encoding specificity principle Any stimulus that is encoded along with an experience can later trigger memory for the experience.

FIGURE 7.18 Scientific Method: Godden and Baddeley's Study of Context-Dependent Memory

Hypothesis: When the recall situation is similar to the encoding situation, memory is enhanced.

Research Method:

1 One group of scuba divers learned a list of words on land.

2 Another group of scuba divers learned a list of words underwater.

Results: The scuba divers who learned information underwater tested better underwater than on land, and those who studied on land tested better on land than underwater.

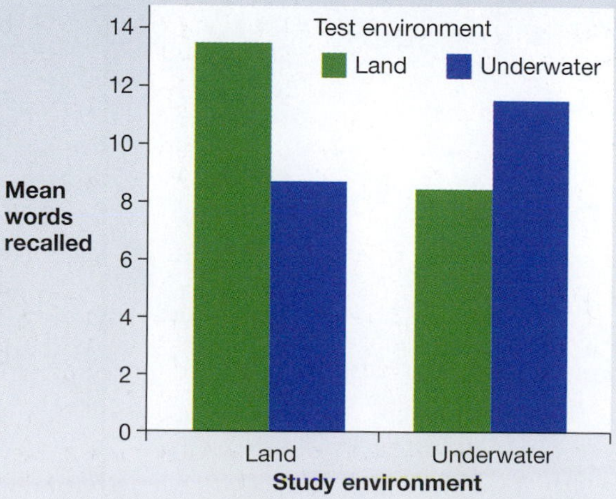

Conclusion: Information is best recalled in the same environment where it is learned.

Just as physical context can affect memory, so internal cues such as mood state or inebriation can facilitate the recovery of information from long-term memory. Enhancement of memory when internal states match during encoding and recall is known as *state dependent memory*. Research on this topic was inspired by the observation that alcoholics often misplace important objects, such as paychecks, because they store them in safe places while they are drinking but cannot remember where when they are sober. The next time they are drinking, however, they may remember where they hid the objects. Eric Eich and his colleagues (1975) conducted a study of state-dependent memory and marijuana use. Participants best remembered items on a list when tested in the same state in which they had studied the list, either sober or high. Overall, however, they recalled the information best when they were sober during studying and testing. In a study involving alcohol, participants performed worst when they studied intoxicated and took the test sober. They did worse than participants who studied sober and took the test intoxicated. Participants who studied intoxicated and took the test intoxicated did much worse than those who were sober during study and test (Goodwin, Powell, Bremer, Hoine, & Stern, 1969). So, if you were thinking about taking your next exam high or intoxicated, think again. You will do far better if you study sober and take the test sober.

SUMMING UP

How Is Information Organized in Long-Term Memory?

Human memory is stored according to meaning. The more a meaning is elaborated at the time of storage, the richer the later memory will be because more connections can serve as retrieval cues for additional aspects. Schemas help people perceive, organize, and process information, which is then stored if processed deeply. Culture influences our schemas and thus can affect what and how we remember. Hierarchical networks of associated nodes provide semantic links between related items. Activation of a node spreads throughout the rest of its network. Retrieval cues, including contextual cues and internal states, help us access stored information.

MEASURING UP

1. Which is the best way to teach scuba divers how to surface safely?
   a. Teach them in a classroom so they can use their declarative knowledge on a written test.
   b. Teach them underwater because the situation will provide retrieval cues for when they need to use the knowledge.
   c. Teach them when they are on land and better able to pay attention.
   d. Have them learn from experience so the method becomes part of their implicit and explicit memory systems.

2. One strategy for improving memory is to relate something you are learning to information you already know. Why would that strategy be effective?
   a. Because the known information can act as a retrieval cue to help you remember the new information when you need it.
   b. Because the known information will create a feeling of familiarity, which will make the new information similar to what you already know.
   c. Because new information is easier to remember than known information and can help you remember older memories by making them more distinct and exciting.
   d. Because old and new information need to mingle in memory so you are not confused when you implicitly try to retrieve information.

What Brain Processes Are Involved in Memory?

What role does biology play in the formulation of our memories? This question is fundamental for memory researchers. As an outgrowth of the biological revolution, researchers have made tremendous progress over the past two decades in understanding what happens in the brain when we store and retrieve memories. Brain imaging has revealed memory processes in the healthy brain, and studies of patients with brain injuries have uncovered the basic foundations of memory's neural basis. The following section focuses on the biological level of analysis, presenting first the brain structures involved in memory, then some of the neurochemical processes that affect what and when we remember.

LEARNING OBJECTIVE
Describe the underlying changes in the brain when something is learned.

There Has Been Intensive Effort to Identify Memory's Physical Location

One of memory researchers' central goals during the twentieth century was to figure out where in the brain memories are stored. As discussed in Chapter 3, Karl Lashley spent much of his career trying to localize memory; his term *engram* refers to the physical site of memory storage. As part of his research, Lashley trained rats to run a maze, then removed different areas of their cortices. (On the cortex, and on brain regions discussed below such as the cerebellum and the amygdala, see **FIGURE 7.19**.) In testing how much of the maze learning the rats retained after the surgery, Lashley found that the size of the area removed rather than its location was most important in predicting retention. From these findings, he concluded that memory is distributed throughout the brain rather than confined to any specific location, an idea known as *equipotentiality*. Lashley was partially right—memories are not stored in any one brain location—but in other ways he was quite wrong.

Memories are stored in multiple regions of the brain and linked through memory circuits, as proposed by the psychologist Donald Hebb, who suggested that neurons that "fire together wire together" (see Chapter 6, "Learning"). Not all brain areas are equally involved in memory, however. A great deal of neural specialization occurs, such that different brain regions are responsible for storing different aspects of information. Indeed, different memory systems, such as declarative memory and procedural memory, use different brain regions. Lashley's failure to find critical brain regions for memory is due to at least two factors. First, the maze task he used to study memory involved multiple sensory systems (such as vision and smell), so the rats could compensate for the loss of one by using other senses. Second, Lashley did not examine subcortical areas, which are now known to be important for memory retention.

Over the past three decades, researchers have identified many brain regions that contribute to learning and memory. For instance, we know from studies of H.M. (discussed in this chapter's opening section) that regions within the temporal lobes are important for the ability to encode new memories. The temporal lobes are important for declarative memory (being able to say what you remember) but less important for implicit memory (such as motor learning and classical conditioning). As noted in Chapter 3, the cerebellum plays a role in how motor actions are learned and remembered. The amygdala, in contrast, is responsible for one type of classical conditioning,

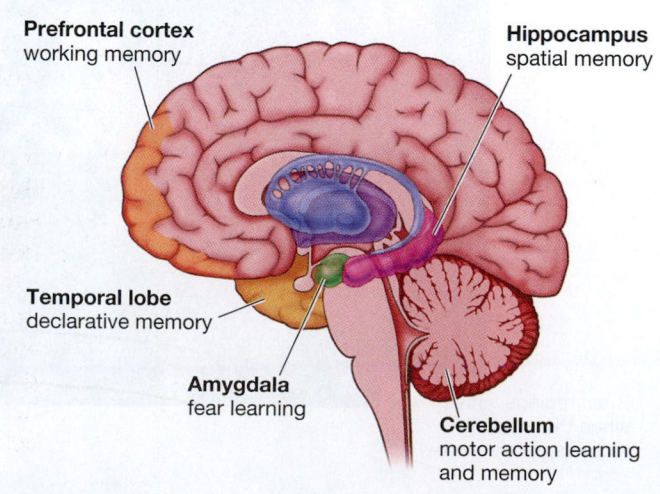

FIGURE 7.19 Brain Regions Associated with Memory

Prefrontal cortex
working memory

Hippocampus
spatial memory

Temporal lobe
declarative memory

Amygdala
fear learning

Cerebellum
motor action learning and memory

fear learning. As noted in Chapter 6, an animal without an amygdala cannot learn to fear objects that signal danger. Other important sites for memory are discussed in the following sections.

The Medial Temporal Lobes Are Important for Consolidation of Declarative Memories

The brain area repeatedly identified as important for declarative memory is the middle section (called the *medial* section) of the temporal lobes. The medial temporal lobes consist of numerous structures relevant to memory, including the amygdala and the hippocampus. As described earlier, H.M.'s brain surgery rendered him unable to form new memories. Brain imaging revealed that a large portion of H.M.'s hippocampus had been removed (Corkin, Amaral, Gonzalez, Johnson, & Hyman, 1997). We now know that damage to this region causes *anterograde amnesia,* the inability to store new explicit memories (discussed further below). However, this finding does not mean that the medial temporal lobes are the final repository of memory. After all, H.M. remembered things from before his surgery. Thus damage to the medial temporal lobes interrupts storage of new material without impairing access to old material.

Immediate memories become lasting memories through **consolidation.** All learning leaves a biological trail in the brain. This process results from changes in the strength of neural connections that support memory and from the construction of new synapses (Miller, 2005). For example, reading this chapter should be making some of your neural connections stronger and creating new ones, especially in your hippocampus. Your brain is different than it was before you began reading the chapter.

The current thinking is that the medial temporal lobes are responsible for coordinating and strengthening the connections among neurons when something is learned, but that the actual storage most likely occurs in the particular brain regions engaged during the perception, processing, and analysis of the material being learned. For instance, visual information is stored in the cortical areas involved in visual perception, whereas sound is stored in the areas involved in auditory perception. Thus memory for sensory experiences, such as remembering something seen or heard, involves reactivating the cortical circuits involved in perceiving them (**FIGURE 7.20**). The medial temporal lobes form links, or pointers, between the different storage sites and direct the gradual strengthening of the connections between these links (Squire, Stark, & Clark, 2004).

It has been proposed that once memories are activated they need to be consolidated again to be stored back in memory (LeDoux, 2002). This process, **reconsolidation,** would be like taking a book out of the library—once you return it, a librarian puts it back on the shelf for storage until it is needed again. Researchers have found evidence for reconsolidation by administering drugs that interfere with memory storage after a memory has been activated (Debiec, LeDoux, & Nader, 2002). Their findings suggest that when memories for past events are retrieved, those memories can be affected by new circumstances, so

consolidation A hypothetical process involving the transfer of contents from immediate memory into long-term memory.

reconsolidation Neural processes involved when memories are recalled and then stored again for later retrieval.

FIGURE 7.20 Brain Activation from Various Stimuli Four horizontally sliced brain images acquired using magnetic resonance imaging indicate that regions of the sensory cortex are reactivated when we remember sensory-specific information.

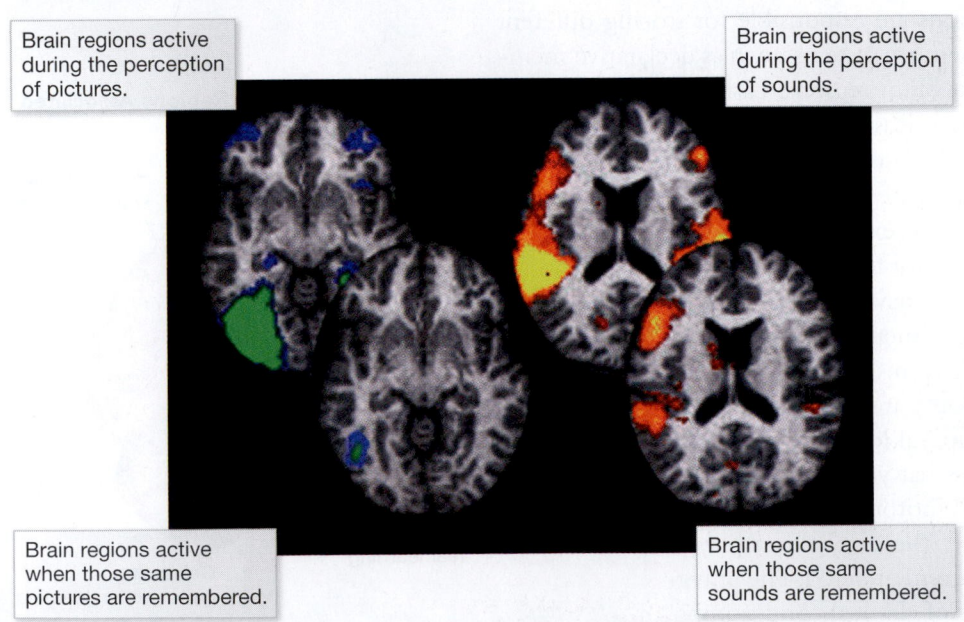

Brain regions active during the perception of pictures.

Brain regions active during the perception of sounds.

Brain regions active when those same pictures are remembered.

Brain regions active when those same sounds are remembered.

that the newly reconsolidated memories may differ from their original versions. This explanation suggests that our memories change when we use them and are not accurate reproductions of what was experienced. In the library book analogy, this change would be like tearing pages out of the book or adding new pages before returning it. The book placed on the shelf differs, however slightly, from the one taken out; the information in the torn-out pages is no longer available for retrieval, and the new pages that were inserted alter the memory the next time it is retrieved. The reconsolidation process repeats itself each time a memory is activated and placed back in storage, and it may explain why our memories for events can change over time. As you might imagine, this theory has received considerable attention: It not only has implications for what it means to remember something but also opens up the intriguing possibility that bad memories could be erased by activating them and then interfering with reconsolidation.

SPATIAL MEMORY Another important memory function of the hippocampus is **spatial memory,** memory for the physical environment, including information such as directions, locations of objects, and cognitive maps. A laboratory example of this type of learning is the *Morris water maze test,* in which a rat is placed into a circular pool of murky water and learns to swim to an invisible platform just below the surface. Although they do not like to swim, rats are good swimmers, and they can quite readily use environmental cues to remember where to find the platform. Rats with hippocampal damage are severely impaired at this learning task, however. The role of the hippocampus in spatial memory is supported by *place cells,* neurons that, in lab tests with rats, fire only when a rat returns to a specific location, such as one part of a maze. When a rat is placed in a novel environment, none of the hippocampal place cells fire. But as the rat becomes familiar with the environment, its place cells acquire links to aspects of the surroundings. This finding suggests that the hippocampus helps an animal orient itself and find its way (**FIGURE 7.21**). Indeed, birds that store food and thus rely on memory to find it, such as chickadees, have larger hippocampal regions than birds that do not

spatial memory Memory for the physical environment; it includes things such as location of objects, direction, and cognitive maps.

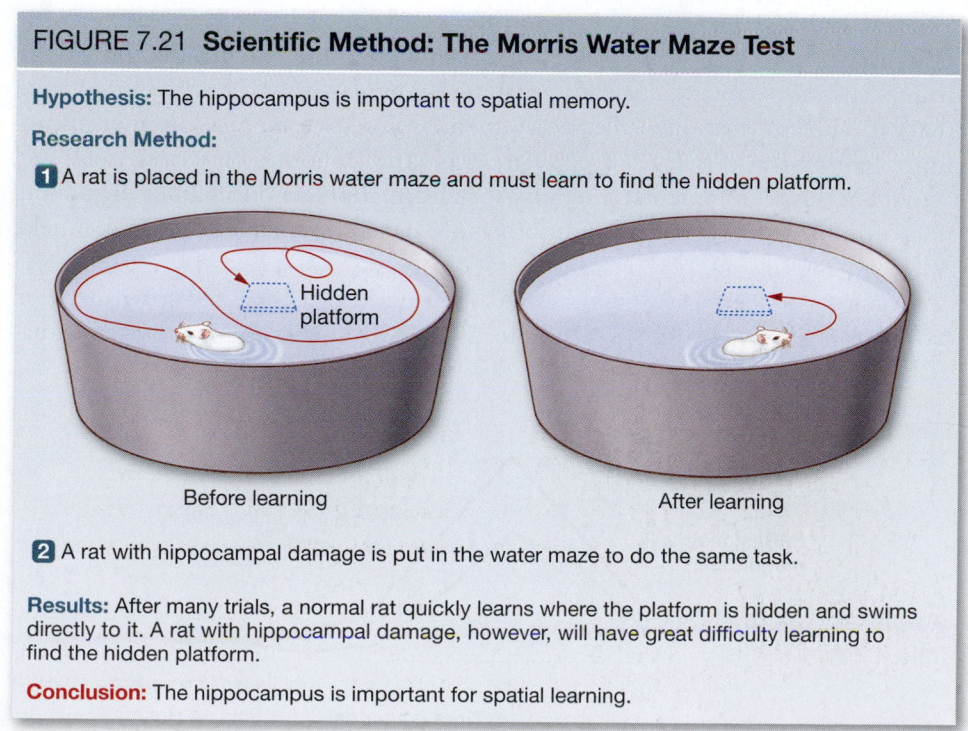

FIGURE 7.21 **Scientific Method: The Morris Water Maze Test**

Hypothesis: The hippocampus is important to spatial memory.

Research Method:

1 A rat is placed in the Morris water maze and must learn to find the hidden platform.

Hidden platform

Before learning

After learning

2 A rat with hippocampal damage is put in the water maze to do the same task.

Results: After many trials, a normal rat quickly learns where the platform is hidden and swims directly to it. A rat with hippocampal damage, however, will have great difficulty learning to find the hidden platform.

Conclusion: The hippocampus is important for spatial learning.

store food. And as discussed in Chapter 3, a study showed that the sizes of London taxi drivers' hippocampi (plural of hippocampus) were positively correlated with the number of years the drivers had driven taxis in London, a finding that suggests the hippocampus is also important for humans' spatial memory (Maguire, Frackowiak, & Frith, 1997; Maguire et al., 2000).

In a study of rats' hippocampal place cells, the researchers found that the place cells that fired when rats were learning a maze fired again during the rats' REM sleep, a finding that suggests the rats were dreaming about the maze they had just learned (Wilson & McNaughton, 1994). Similarly, when research participants sleep after learning, their recall is better than in control conditions where participants remain awake (Drosopoulos, Schulze, Fischer, & Born, 2007). In both humans and rodents, it seems, one important role of sleep is to consolidate memories. The next time you dream—about driving to work, finding your way through the halls at school, or what have you—the neurons in your hippocampus will be firing.

The Frontal Lobes Are Involved in Many Aspects of Memory

Researchers have long known that the frontal lobes are important to many aspects of memory, including episodic memory, working memory, spatial memory, time sequences, and various aspects of encoding and retrieval (Wager & Smith, 2003). Extensive neural networks connect the prefrontal cortex with other brain regions involved in memory, such as the medial temporal areas. Thus the frontal lobes work together and with other brain regions to coordinate the encoding, storage, and retrieval of memory.

Brain imaging studies have provided compelling evidence that the frontal lobes are crucial for encoding (Buckner, Kelley, & Petersen, 1999). Moreover, deep encoding tasks (learning about a text's meaning, for example) will more likely lead to frontal activation than will shallow encoding tasks (such as learning which typeface that text is printed in). Frontal activation is also a particularly good predictor for which events will later be remembered or forgotten (Brewer, Zhao, Glover, & Gabrieli, 1998). Researchers have found, for instance, that remembered words are associated with stronger activation of the frontal lobes than are forgotten words (Wagner et al., 1998; **FIGURE 7.22**). Further, activity in frontal brain regions involved in processing specific types of information is associated with better memory for that type of information (Paller & Wagner, 2002). For example, the medial prefrontal cortex is selectively active when people think about themselves. As a result, activity in this region predicts memory for information encoded about the self but not for information encoded about others (Macrae, Moran, Heatherton, Banfield, & Kelley, 2004).

Some researchers have hypothesized that the frontal lobes also play a role in working memory (Curtis & D'Esposito, 2003). Working memory holds informa-

FIGURE 7.22 Brain Activation in Memory Tasks The amount of brain activation and the areas activated in the brain depend on the type and timing of the material being remembered.

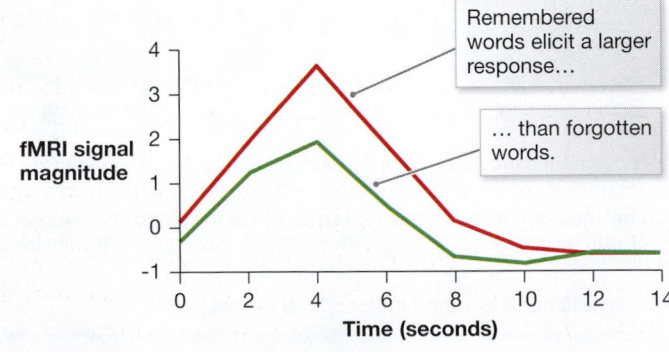

tion temporarily so that it can be used to solve problems, understand conversations, and follow plans. Patients with damage to the frontal areas often have difficulty following plans and goals, and monkeys given frontal lesions show impaired working memory (Goldman-Rakic, Scalaidhe, & Chafee, 2000). In one research task, a monkey watches the experimenter hide a reward under one of two objects. After a delay, the monkey is allowed to reach for the object covering the reward. A monkey with a frontal lesion has difficulty with this task, as will a human infant when presented with a similar task. These results further implicate the frontal lobes in working memory, since a human's frontal lobes do not fully mature until much later in development (Diamond & Doar, 1989).

Frontal regions become active when information is being retrieved from long-term memory into working memory or encoded from working memory into long-term memory. For example, when you enter a college classroom, your frontal lobes oversee the retrieval of stored knowledge about college classrooms from neural networks that are spread throughout your cortical and subcortical locations. This information helps you remember what to do when you enter the room (sit down), who the person is at the front of the class (the instructor), and the meaning of the sounds that will emanate from the instructor's mouth (words that form a lecture). The frontal lobes and medial temporal lobes then work together to consolidate storage of the lecture in your long-term declarative memory.

Neurochemistry Underlies Memory

Memory involves alterations in connections across synapses. As memories are consolidated, neurons link into distributed networks, and those networks become linked. Research has shown that various of neurotransmitters can weaken or enhance memory. Collectively, these neurotransmitters are known as *memory modulators,* because they modulate, or modify, memory storage.

NEUROCHEMISTRY INDICATES THE MEANINGFULNESS OF STIMULI As discussed in the sections above, we store meaningful information. Important events, for example, lead to neurochemical changes that produce emotional reactions, which in turn make those events especially likely to be stored in memory. An animal that outruns a predator experiences a fear reaction that will help the animal remember to avoid that predator and perhaps other predators. A child that eats and enjoys a particular food experiences an easily remembered rewarding sensation (as parents who have watched their preverbal children point at cookie jars can readily attest).

What neurochemical signals indicate that an experience is meaningful? After animals engage in minimally arousing tasks, they retain little memory of those tasks. When injected with epinephrine, the hormone secreted when a person or animal is excited or scared, those same animals show significant memory enhancement even for trivial events. It is as if the jolt of epinephrine gives the message *Remember!*

Epinephrine is secreted not within the brain but into the bloodstream from the adrenal glands, which are near the kidneys. Thus it does not affect memory directly. Researchers initially believed that epinephrine affected memory because it causes a release of glucose, which then enters the brain and influences memory storage. As discussed in previous chapters, brain neurons use glucose when we perform particular tasks. When we learn something new, for example, we drain glucose from key parts of the brain (e.g., the hippocampus) that are associated with memory and learning. Glucose's role as a memory enhancer was

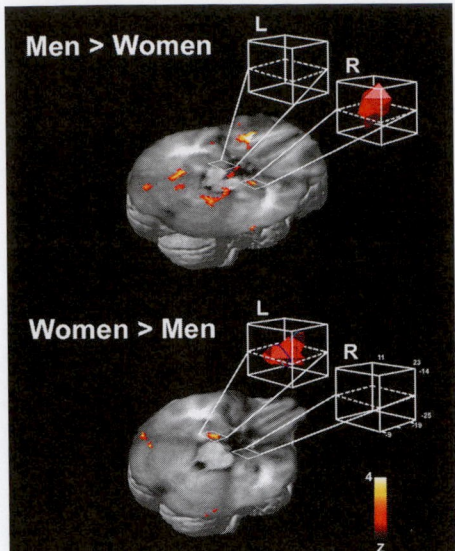

FIGURE 7.23 Sex Differences in Brain Activity Related to Memory Studies have shown that men's and women's brains respond differently to emotional experiences and to the memories of those experiences. **(Top)** This image shows the greater activity in the right amygdala of a man's brain while the man is viewing emotionally arousing images. **(Bottom)** This image shows the greater activity in the left amygdala of a woman's brain while the woman is viewing emotionally arousing images.

posttraumatic stress disorder (PTSD)
A mental disorder that involves frequent nightmares, intrusive thoughts, and flashbacks related to an earlier trauma.

implicated in a study in which elderly participants were given a memory test after consuming lemonade sweetened with glucose (sugar) or saccharine (a sugar substitute). Those who drank the lemonade with glucose better remembered the items they studied, even when the recall test was given a day later (Gold, McIntyre, McNay, Stefani, & Korol, 2001). These results do not mean that you should eat candy to enhance your learning and memory, because other studies show that complex carbohydrates (fruits, vegetables, whole grains) improve the brain's available glucose; simple carbohydrates (e.g., soda and other simple sugars) elevate blood sugars and contribute to diabetes and other diseases that cause learning deficits in the long run.

THE AMYGDALA AND THE NEUROCHEMISTRY OF EMOTION Any arousing event causes greater activity of norepinephrine receptors, which strengthens the memory of that event. The amygdala, that almond-shaped brain structure discussed so frequently in this book, has norephinephrine receptors and is involved in the memory of fearful events. For example, in humans, the amygdala is activated when people are asked to recall an emotional film clip but not during recall of neutral film clips (Cahill et al., 1996). There appears to be a gender difference in this effect, however: Emotional memory activates the right but not the left amygdala in men, and it activates the left but not the right amygdala in women (Cahill et al., 2001; **FIGURE 7.23**). Moreover, women have better memory than men for emotional events. For instance, when Turhan Canli and colleagues (2002) showed men and women neutral and negative pictures, women not only reported greater emotional reactions to the negative pictures but also remembered those pictures better. Women may process emotional information differently than men, perhaps rehearsing it and thinking about it more, or they may focus on different aspects of stimuli (Cahill, 2003). On average, women are more likely to suffer from depression than men are. Thus sex differences in responses to emotional situations have important implications for what and how we remember, for the role of the brain in memory for emotional events, and for mental health. A recent review, "Why Sex Matters for Neuroscience," lists many reasons for studying sex differences in brain structure and function to understand brain disorders and normal brain functioning (Cahill, 2006). The review provides many examples of tasks that reveal significant differences in the patterns of women's and men's brain activity, though men and women perform equally well on memory tests related to those tasks.

When people experience severe stress or emotional trauma—such as having a serious accident, being raped, fighting in active combat, or surviving a natural disaster—they often have negative reactions long after the danger has passed. In severe cases, people develop **posttraumatic stress disorder (PTSD),** a serious mental health disorder that involves frequent and recurring unwanted thoughts related to the trauma, including nightmares, intrusive thoughts, and flashbacks. Those with PTSD often have chronic tension, anxiety, and health problems, and they may experience memory and attention problems in their daily lives. PTSD involves an unusual problem in memory—the inability to forget. PTSD is associated with an attentional bias, such that people with PTSD are hypervigilant to stimuli associated with their traumatic events. For instance, soldiers with combat-induced PTSD show increased physiological responsiveness to pictures of troops, sounds of gunfire, and even words associated with combat. Exposure to stimuli associated with past trauma leads to activation of the amygdala (Rauch, van der Kolk, Fisler, & Alpert, 1996). It is as if the severe emotional event is "overconsolidated," burned into memory.

SUMMING UP

What Brain Processes Are Involved in Memory?

Research during the past thirty years has demonstrated that memories are encoded in distributed networks of neurons in relatively specific brain regions. We now know that damage to the medial temporal lobes, especially to the hippocampus, causes significant memory disturbances. These medial temporal regions are important for the consolidation of declarative memories into storage. The sites of memory storage are the brain structures involved in perception. Fear causes activation of the amygdala, which is associated with the strengthening of memories. There are sex differences in which of the brain regions underlie emotional memories and perhaps in the processing of emotional memories. Memories for highly traumatic events can result in posttraumatic stress disorder, a clinical disorder diagnosed when the traumatic memories intrude into everyday life.

MEASURING UP

1. What changes occur at the synapses when people learn and remember? Choose as many as apply.
   a. Neuronal connections are strengthened.
   b. Reuptake is enhanced.
   c. Neurons make more synaptic connections.
   d. Brain regions associated with learning and remembering become more sensitive to glucose.
   e. The amygdala grows larger.
2. One difference between females' and males' underlying brain mechanisms for memory is found in _____.
   a. motor memory
   b. emotional memory
   c. childhood memory
   d. explicit memory

When Do People Forget?

In addition to remembering information, people fail to remember it. **Forgetting,** the inability to retrieve memory from long-term storage, is a perfectly normal, everyday experience. Ten minutes after you see a movie, you probably remember plenty of its details, but the next day you might remember mostly the plot and the main characters. Years later, you might remember the gist of the story, or you might not remember having seen the movie at all. We forget far more than we remember.

Most people bemoan forgetting, wishing they could better recall the information they study for exams, the names of childhood friends, the names of all seven dwarfs who lived with Snow White, what have you. But imagine what life would be like if you could not forget. Imagine, for example, walking up to your locker and recalling not just its combination but the 10 or 20 combinations from all of the locks you have ever used. Consider the case of a Russian newspaper reporter who had nearly perfect memory. If someone read him a tremendously long list of items and he visualized the items for a few moments, he could recite the list, even many years later. But his memory was so cluttered with information that he

LEARNING OBJECTIVE
List and explain the basic processes used to understand forgetting.

forgetting The inability to retrieve memory from long-term storage.

ON Ethics Altering Memory

Posttraumatic stress disorder (PTSD) is a serious public health problem, with an estimated prevalence of 7.8 percent in the United States alone (Kessler et al., 1995). The trauma that triggers it may be something that threatened the sufferer's life or the life of someone close to the sufferer—a serious illness, a car accident, a natural disaster, a personal assault, a terrorist attack. Post-traumatic stress disorder is an occupational hazard for police officers, firefighters, soldiers, butchers, rescue workers, and so on.

Consider train crews. According to Edward Dubroski (2000), international president of the Brotherhood of Locomotive Engineers and Trainmen (BLET), a train strikes a motor vehicle every two hours. No doubt such an event gets seared into the crew's memory, with the help of an epinephrine rush. BLET's Timothy L. Smith (2007) testified to the U.S. House of Representatives: "You cannot imagine the terror a train's crew experience when their train comes roaring around a curve at full speed and a truck, car, or pedestrian is just ahead. You can't blow the whistle long enough or loud enough, and your heart creeps up further in your throat with each passing yard as your closing distance races to zero. . . . The emotional toll that is exacted on our members—who are unable to stop these incidents—is often life-altering." Why should these workers suffer such agonizing memories, which may result from another person's carelessness? If it were possible, would it be more humane to give the sufferers drugs that could erase or lessen the emotional memories of these events?

Much research is under way to produce drugs that will alter memory, not only to increase the ability to remember things but also to erase unwanted memories. One drug, propranolol, blocks the postsynaptic norepinephrine receptors. If it is given before or right after a traumatic experience, the hormonally enhanced memories and fear response for that event are reduced, and the effect lasts for months (Cahill et al., 1994; Pitman et al., 2002). Using propranolol in such situations is equivalent to treating a possible future disease, since there is no way to know whether the person who has just had the difficult experience (or is about to have it) will develop PTSD.

Is tampering with memory formation ethical? Like many medications, treatments for PTSD could also be used for other purposes. Such drugs could be used to prepare soldiers to kill (or kill again), to blunt the memory of one's own shameful or embarrassing acts, to dull the pain of the loss of a loved one,

FIGURE 7.24 Altering Memories In the 2004 film *Eternal Sunshine of the Spotless Mind,* Joel Barish (played by Jim Carrey) undergoes a procedure that eliminates memories of his former girlfriend. In real life, researchers struggle with the ethical implications of developing drugs that can alter memory.

or to allow criminals to numb their consciences. Who should determine which uses are appropriate and which are not (**FIGURE 7.24**)? Some memories are so traumatic that they destroy the life of the individual who suffers them. If we could erase such traumatic memories, should only those of traumas that were beyond the sufferer's control be relieved? Or should a person be treated for suffering a guilty conscience after an intentional malicious act?

Humans are social animals with intricate societal structures honed by evolution. Many of those societal structures are based on reciprocity and on detecting people who cheat. Although it may benefit an individual to have a blunted memory of a traumatic assault, will society survive if individuals no longer have the moral outrage to pursue their perpetrators, thus undermining cheater detection? Victims of the Holocaust have suffered greatly from traumatic memories but also have contributed greatly to society by increasing our vigilance against regimes like the Nazis. Would memory alteration put truth (remembering events as they really happened) in opposition to compassion or well-being (President's Council on Bioethics, 2003a)? Our senses of ourselves, of who we are, come from the amalgamation of memories that we each possess. Would we be better or worse off if we could cherrypick those memories? And finally, do we really understand memory well enough to start tinkering with it?

had great difficulty functioning in normal society. Tortured by this condition, he eventually was institutionalized. Paradoxically, not being able to forget is as maladaptive as not being able to remember. It is therefore not surprising that we tend to best remember meaningful points. We remember the forest rather than the individual trees. Normal forgetting helps us remember and use important information (**FIGURE 7.25**).

The study of forgetting has a long history in psychological science. The late-nineteenth-century psychologist Hermann Ebbinghaus, working at the individual level of analysis, provided compelling evidence that forgetting occurs rapidly over the first few days but then levels off. Ebbinghaus used the so-called *methods of savings* to examine how long it took people to relearn lists of nonsense syllables (e.g., vut, bik, kuh). Most of us do not need to memorize nonsense syllables, but Ebbinghaus's general findings apply to meaningful material as well. You may remember very little of the Spanish or calculus you took in high school, but relearning these subjects would take you less time and effort than it took the first time. The difference between the original learning and relearning is "savings"—time and effort saved because of what you remember.

Daniel Schacter (1999) has identified what he calls *the seven sins of memory* (**TABLE 7.1**). The first three sins, *transience, absentmindedness,* and *blocking,* are

FIGURE 7.25 Forgetting and Remembering In the 2000 film *Memento,* Leonard Shelby (played by Guy Pearce) suffers from severe memory loss. In search of his wife's killer, he tattoos words onto his body to remind himself of information he has discovered. People can suffer from an excess of remembering as much as from an excess of forgetting.

Table 7.1 Seven Sins of Memory

ERROR	TYPE	DEFINITION	EXAMPLE
Transience	Forgetting	Reduced memory over time	Forgetting the plot of a movie
Absentmindedness	Forgetting	Reduced memory due to failing to pay attention	Losing your keys or forgetting a lunch date
Blocking	Forgetting	Inability to remember needed information	Failing to recall the name of a person you meet on the street
Misattribution	Distortion	Assigning a memory to the wrong source	Falsely thinking that Richard Shiffrin is famous because his name is well known
Suggestibility	Distortion	Altering a memory because of misleading information	Developing false memories for events that did not happen
Bias	Distortion	Influence of current knowledge on our memory for past events	Remembering past attitudes as similar to current attitudes even though they have changed
Persistence	Undesirable	The resurgence of unwanted or disturbing memories that we would like to forget	Remembering an embarrassing faux pas

SOURCE: Based on Schacter (2001).

related to forgetting and discussed below. The next three, *misattribution, suggestibility,* and *bias,* are discussed later in this chapter. *Persistence* is discussed above as posttraumatic stress disorder. These so-called sins are very familiar to most people, and Schacter argues that they are useful or perhaps even necessary characteristics for survival, by-products of otherwise desirable aspects of human memory.

Transience Is Caused by Interference

transience The pattern of forgetting over time.

Memory **transience** is the pattern of forgetting over time, such as the one Ebbinghaus observed in his studies of nonsense syllables. What causes transience? Many early theorists argued that forgetting results from the memory trace's *decay* in a person's nervous system. Indeed, some evidence indicates that unused memories are forgotten. However, research over the last few decades has established that most forgetting occurs because of *interference* from other information. Additional information can lead to forgetting through *proactive interference* or *retroactive interference*. In both cases, competing information displaces the information we are trying to retrieve (**FIGURE 7.26**). In **proactive interference,** old information inhibits the ability to remember new information. For instance, if you receive a new locker combination each year, you may have difficulty remembering the current one because you keep recalling the previous one. Indeed, because the physical context provides retrieval cues for that earlier combination, you might find it especially difficult to remember the current one while standing in front of your locker! In **retroactive interference,** new information inhibits the ability to remember old information. So once you finally memorize your new locker combination, you might forget the old one.

proactive interference When prior information inhibits the ability to remember new information.

retroactive interference When new information inhibits the ability to remember old information.

Blocking Is Temporary

blocking The temporary inability to remember something that is known.

Blocking occurs when a person temporarily is unable to remember something: You can't recall the name of a favorite CD, you forget the name of someone you're introducing, you "blank" on some lines when acting in a play, and so on. Such temporary blockages are common and frustrating. Another good example of blocking is the *tip-of-the-tongue phenomenon,* first described by the psychologists Roger Brown and David MacNeill, in which people experience great frustration as they try to recall specific, somewhat obscure words. The researcher Alan Brown (no relation to Roger) has shown that the tip-of-the-tongue phenomenon can be produced reliably in the laboratory (Brown, 1991). For instance, when

FIGURE 7.26 Proactive and Retroactive Interference Proactive interference occurs when information already known (here, psychology material) interferes with the ability to remember new information (here, anthropology material). Retroactive interference occurs when new information (anthropology material) interferes with memory for old information (psychology material).

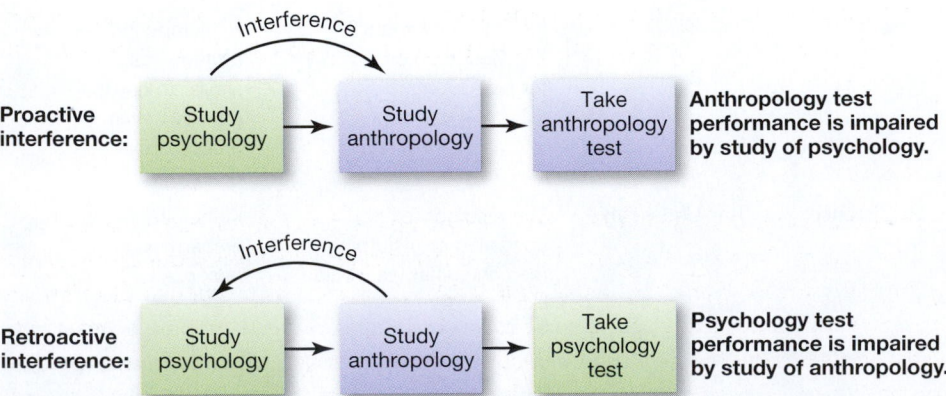

asked to provide a word that means "patronage bestowed on a relative, in business or politics" or "an astronomical instrument for finding position," people often struggle. Sometimes they know which letter the word begins with, how many syllables it has, and even what it sounds like, but even with these partial retrieval cues they cannot pull the precise word into working memory. (Did you know the words were *nepotism* and *sextant*?) Blocking often occurs because of interference from words that are similar in some way, such as in sound or meaning, and that keep recurring, as when you keep calling an acquaintance Margaret though her name is Melanie.

Absentmindedness Results from Shallow Encoding

Absentmindedness is the inattentive or shallow encoding of events—for instance, forgetting where you left your keys, the name of a person you met five minutes before, or whether you took your vitamins this morning (**FIGURE 7.27**). As discussed earlier in this chapter, the phenomenon of change blindness is demonstrated when people fail to notice that a person they have been talking with is replaced by someone else. In the original study, older people were especially likely not to notice a change in the person asking them for directions; college students were pretty good at noticing the change. Are older people especially inattentive? Or do they tend to process a situation's broad outlines rather than its details? Perhaps the older people encoded the stranger as simply "a college student" and did not look for more-individual characteristics. To test this idea, Simons and Levin (1998) conducted an additional study in which a construction worker asked college students for directions. Sure enough, the college students failed to notice the replacement of one construction worker with another, a finding that supports the idea that the students encoded the person as belonging to a broad category of "construction workers" without looking more closely at him. For these students, construction workers are pretty much all alike and interchangeable.

A recent study examined whether cultural differences exist in change blindness. The underlying idea behind this study was that East Asians live in highly interdependent societies, so they are more likely to attend to an event's context than are U.S. citizens and Canadians, who live in more-individualistic societies and thus are more likely to attend to a salient object. To test this hypothesis, Takahiko Masuda and Richard Nisbett (2006) had American and East Asian college students view pairs of images in which either the object in the foreground changed or an object in the background changed. As predicted, the East Asian students recognized changes in the picture's background faster than the American students did, whereas Americans and Canadians better recognized changes in the foreground object. The researchers verified these results across several studies, concluded that there are cultural variations in patterns of attention, and attributed these differences to early socialization practices, when children learn what to attend to.

Amnesia Is a Deficit in Long-Term Memory

Sometimes we lose the ability to retrieve vast quantities of information from long-term memory. **Amnesia** is a deficit in long-term memory, resulting from disease, brain injury, or psychological trauma (**FIGURE 7.28**). The two basic types of amnesia are *retrograde* and *anterograde*. In **retrograde amnesia,** people lose past memories for events, facts, people, or even personal information. Most portrayals of amnesia in the media are of retrograde amnesia, as when a character in a soap opera awakens from a coma

FIGURE 7.27 Absentmindedness The major cause of absentmindedness is failing to pay sufficient attention when encoding memories. The celebrated musician Yo-Yo Ma is pictured here with his $2.5 million eighteenth-century cello, which was returned to him after he absentmindedly left it in a cab.

absentmindedness The inattentive or shallow encoding of events.

amnesia Deficits in long-term memory that result from disease, brain injury, or psychological trauma.

retrograde amnesia The condition in which people lose past memories, such as memories for events, facts, people, or even personal information.

FIGURE 7.28 Amnesia Jeff Ingram, pictured here, developed amnesia after leaving his home, in Washington state. When he arrived in Denver, Colorado, four days later, he had no memory of his previous life. He was recognized two months later, when he appeared on the news pleading for help from anyone who knew who he was. Though he did not remember his three-year relationship with his fiancée (here seated next to him), the two eventually married.

anterograde amnesia An inability to form new memories.

and does not know who he or she is. By contrast, in **anterograde amnesia,** people lose the ability to form new memories. As discussed at the beginning of this chapter, H.M. had a classic case of anterograde amnesia. He could remember old information about his past, but after his surgery he lost the ability to form new memories. However, evidence suggests that H.M. acquired some new semantic knowledge about things that occurred after 1953. For instance, when given a list of people who became famous after 1953, H.M. was able to provide some information about them (O'Kane, Kensinger, & Corkin, 2004). Given the name Lee Harvey Oswald, H.M. described him as the man who "assassinated the president." This new learning may have occured through extensive repetition of materials over a long time.

Many cases of amnesia result from damage to the medial temporal lobes. Damage to other subcortical areas, such as around the thalamus, can also lead to amnesia. A common cause of this type of amnesia is *Korsakoff's syndrome,* a severe form of memory disturbance linked to chronic alcoholism. Long-term alcohol abuse can lead to vitamin deficiency that results in thalamic damage and, subsequently, amnesia.

 SUMMING UP

When Do People Forget?

Forgetting is the inability to retrieve memory from long-term storage. The ability to forget is just as important as the ability to remember. Forgetting that occurs over time is often due to interference from competing stimuli. Blocking—a temporary inability to retrieve specific information, as exemplified by the tip-of-the-tongue phenomenon—also is caused by interference during retrieval. Absentmindedness results from shallow encoding, which occurs when people fail to pay sufficient attention to details. There are cultural differences in what people attend to (for example, East Asians attend more carefully to changes in the background, and North Americans attend more carefully to changes in a central figure), and these attention differences necessarily imply differences in what people remember. Amnesia is a deficit in long-term memory, causing people to forget past information (retrograde amnesia) or making them unable to store new information (anterograde amnesia). Most amnesia is caused by brain injury.

 MEASURING UP

1. Indicate whether each of the following is an example of retroactive interference or proactive interference or neither.
   a. You learned Russian as a teenager, but now you speak Hungarian. You have forgotten much of the Russian you used to know.
   b. According to an old saying in Yiddish, a language spoken by Eastern Europeans a generation or two ago, you should never marry someone with a name similar to that of your last spouse. Although the expression loses a lot in translation, the idea is that you will forget and call your new spouse by the old spouse's name.
   c. For years you took a bus home from work, and then you got a new car. One night after work, you take the bus home, forgetting that you drove your new car to work.

2. Which of the following examples reflects an accurate understanding of cultural differences in change blindness?
   a. East Asians are more self-centered, so they tend to pay attention to changes important to self-image or self-esteem. North Americans are less concerned with "saving face," so they are free to make more errors.
   b. North Americans tend to be more individualistic and therefore tend to notice changes to a central figure faster than East Asians do, whereas East Asians notice changes in background information faster.

c. Students from Canada and the U.S. are faster at noticing changes because they are more familiar with research paradigms than are students from East Asia.

d. East Asian students are more competitive than American students and thus notice changes in visual displays faster.

How Are Memories Distorted?

Most people believe that human memory is permanent storage, from which even minute and apparently forgotten details can be retrieved through hypnosis, truth drugs, or other techniques (Magnussen et al., 2006). Research has shown clearly, however, that human memory is biased, flawed, and distorted. In the following section, you will learn how the human memory systems provide less-than-accurate portrayals of past events. Keep in mind that a thing is not necessarily faulty because it does not work the way we think it works. As Daniel Schacter has argued, many of the seemingly flawed aspects of memory may be by-products of beneficial mechanisms.

Flashbulb Memories Can Be Wrong

Do you remember where you were when you found out about the terrorist attacks on the World Trade Center and the Pentagon? Roger Brown and James Kulik (1977) have found that people vividly remember the death of U.S. president John F. Kennedy, in 1963. In recalling when they heard about the assassination, people generally can provide details such as who they were with, what they were doing or thinking, who told them or how they found out, and what their emotional reaction was. Brown and Kulik's term **flashbulb memories** refers to vivid memories for the circumstances in which one first learned of a surprising and consequential or emotionally arousing event.

DO YOU REMEMBER WHERE YOU WERE WHEN YOU HEARD...? An obvious problem affects research into the accuracy of flashbulb memories, namely that researchers have to wait for a "flash" to go off and then immediately conduct their study. The explosion of the space shuttle *Challenger,* at 11:38 AM Eastern Standard Time on January 28, 1986, provided a unique opportunity for research on this topic. Ulric Neisser and Nicole Harsch (1993) had 44 psychology students fill out a questionnaire the day the shuttle exploded. When they tested the students' memories three years later, only three students had perfect recall, and the rest were incorrect about multiple aspects of the situation (**FIGURE 7.29A**). However, other researchers have documented better memory for flashbulb experiences, such as where British participants were when they heard about Prime Minister Margaret Thatcher's resignation. Martin Conway and his colleagues (1994) have shown that better memory for the flashbulb experience occurs among those who found the news surprising and felt the event was important. Thus students in the United Kingdom experienced stronger flashbulb memories for the Thatcher resignation than did students in the United States (**FIGURE 7.29B**).

STRESS AND MEMORY REVISITED Flashbulb memories are not perfectly accurate, but they are just as accurate as any other type of memory. Indeed, it is possible that flashbulb experiences are recalled more accurately than inconsequential or unsurprising events (Christianson, 1992). Any event that produces a strong emotional response will likely produce a vivid, though not necessarily accurate, memory. Or a distinctive event might simply be recalled more easily than trivial events, however inaccurate the result. This latter phenomenon is known as the *von Restorff effect,* named after Hedwig von Restorff, the researcher who first described it in 1933.

flashbulb memories Vivid memories for the circumstances in which one first learned of a surprising, consequential, and emotionally arousing event.

LEARNING OBJECTIVE
Describe how memories can be distorted.

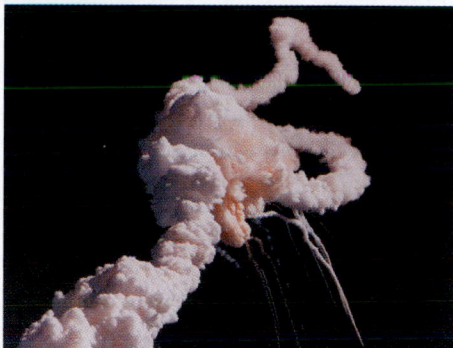
(a)

(b)

FIGURE 7.29 Flashbulb Memories Surprising and consequential or emotionally arousing events can produce flashbulb memories. For example, **(a)** the explosion of the *Challenger* in 1986 and **(b)** the resignation of Margaret Thatcher in 1990 have left flashbulb memories of different kinds, depending on how consequential the events were to the people remembering them.

People Make Source Misattributions

As discussed above, Daniel Schacter has identified **source misattribution**—the mis-remembering of the time, place, person, or circumstances involved with a memory—as one of memory's seven sins. A good example of this is the *false fame effect,* also discussed above, in which people mistakenly believe that someone is famous simply because they have encountered the person's name before. Another example, long known about by social psychologists, is the *sleeper effect,* in which arguments that initially not very persuasive because they come from questionable sources become more persuasive over time. For example, you probably would disbelieve a weekly tabloid's claim that scientists had discovered a way for people to learn calculus while sleeping. Yet over time you might remember the argument but fail to remember the source; hence you might come to believe that people can learn calculus while sleeping, or you might at least wonder if they can.

CRYPTOMNESIA An intriguing example of source misattribution is **cryptomnesia,** when a person thinks he or she has come up with a new idea, but really has retrieved an old idea from memory and failed to attribute the idea to its proper source (Macrae, Bodenhausen, & Calvini, 1999). Students who take verbatim notes while conducting library research sometimes experience the illusion that they have written the sentences, a mistake that can later lead to an accusation of plagiarism. (Be especially vigilant about indicating verbatim notes while you are taking them; **FIGURE 7.30**.) George Harrison, the former Beatle, was sued because his 1970 song "My Sweet Lord" is strikingly similar to the song "He's So Fine," recorded in 1962 by the Chiffons. Harrison acknowledged having known "He's So Fine," but vigorously denied having plagiarized it. He argued that with a limited number of musical notes available to all musicians, and an even smaller number of chord sequences appropriate for rock and roll, some compositional overlap was inevitable. In a controversial verdict, the judge ruled against Harrison, who later wrote "This Song" as a wryly bitter response to the trial: The opening lyrics are "This song has nothing tricky about it / This song ain't black or white and as far as I know / Don't infringe on anyone's copyright . . ." (Harrison, 1976).

People Are Bad Eyewitnesses

One of the most powerful forms of evidence is the eyewitness account. Research has demonstrated that very few jurors are willing to convict an accused individual on the basis of circumstantial evidence alone. But add one person who says, "That's the one!" and conviction rates shoot up, even if it is shown that the witness had poor eyesight or some other condition that raises questions about the testimony's accuracy. Eyewitness testimony's power is troubling because witnesses are so often in error. When Gary Wells and his colleagues (1998) studied 40 cases in which DNA evidence indicated that a person had been falsely convicted of a crime, they found that in 36 of these cases the person had been misidentified by one or more eyewitnesses (**FIGURE 7.31**).

CROSS-ETHNIC IDENTIFICATION At the social level of analysis, people are particularly bad at accurately identifying individuals of other ethnicities or races. This effect occurs among Caucasians, Asians, African Americans, and Hispanics. In brain imaging studies discussed in Chapter 5, African

FIGURE 7.30 Cryptomnesia In a possible case of cryptomnesia—thinking she had come up with new material, but really having retrieved other people's material from memory—the Harvard student Kaavya Viswanathan wrote a novel, *How Opal Mehta Got Kissed, Got Wild, and Got a Life,* that had to be recalled from bookstores. Several passages in the novel were taken from books that Viswanathan admitted having read in high school.

source misattribution Memory distortion that occurs when people misremember the time, place, person, or circumstances involved with a memory.

cryptomnesia A type of misattribution that occurs when a person thinks he or she has come up with a new idea, yet has only retrieved a stored idea and failed to attribute the idea to its proper source.

FIGURE 7.31 Eyewitness Accounts Can Be Unreliable William Jackson **(left)** served five years in prison because he was wrongly convicted of a crime based on the testimony of two eyewitnesses. How much does Jackson look like the man on the right, the real perpetrator?

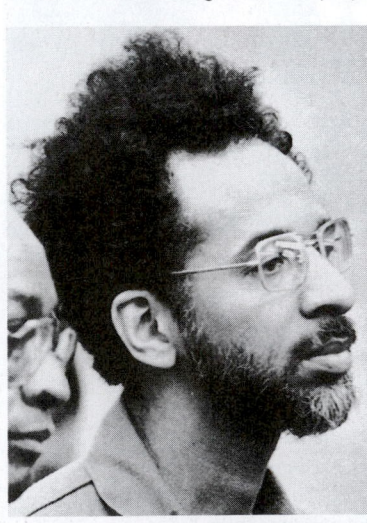

Americans and Caucasian Americans showed better memory for same-race faces. The difference in participants' performances were associated with the degrees of activity in the fusiform face area (Golby, Gabrieli, Chiao, & Eberhardt, 2001), which, as discussed in Chapter 3, responds more strongly to faces than to other objects. Apparently, the greater activation of this area to same-race faces accounts for people's superior memory for members of their own racial group. One explanation for this effect is that people tend to have less frequent contact with members of other races and ethnicities; another is that people encode race and ethnicity according to rules of categorization and do not notice much about the individual person beyond this group description—a phenomenon similar to the way, discussed above, that in the change blindness experiments older people saw "a college student," students saw "a construction worker," and neither old people nor students noticed individual characteristics.

SUGGESTIBILITY AND MISINFORMATION During the early 1970s, Elizabeth Loftus and her colleagues conducted a series of important studies demonstrating that people can develop biased memories when provided with misleading information—the "sin" of **suggestibility.** The general methodology of this research involved showing research participants an event and then asking them specific questions about it; the questions' wording altered the participants' memories for the event. In one experiment (Loftus, Miller, & Burns, 1978), one group of participants viewed a videotape of a car—a red Datsun—approaching a stop sign. A second group viewed a videotape of that same scene but with a yield sign instead of a stop sign. Each group was then asked, "Did another car pass the red Datsun while it was stopped at the stop sign?" Some participants in the second group, even though they had seen the red Datsun approaching a yield sign, claimed to have seen it stop at the stop sign (**FIGURE 7.32**).

In another experiment, Loftus and John Palmer (1974) found that participants, when asked about a videotape of a car accident, estimated the cars to be traveling faster when they heard the word *smashed* than when they heard the words *contacted, hit, bumped,* or *collided.* In a related study, participants saw a videotape of a car accident and then were asked about seeing the cars either *smash into* or *hit* each other. One week later, they were asked if they had seen broken glass on the ground in the video. No glass broke in the video, but nearly one-third of those who heard *smashed* falsely recalled having seen broken glass, whereas very few of those who heard *hit* did.

Are these sorts of laboratory analogues appropriate for studying eyewitness accuracy? After all, the sights and sounds of a traffic accident, for example, impress the event on the witness's awareness. Some evidence supports the idea such memories are better in the real world than in the laboratory. A study in Vancouver examined reports of those who had witnessed a fatal shooting (Yuille & Cutshall, 1986). All observers had been interviewed by the police within two days of the incident. Months afterward, the researchers found the eyewitness reports, including

suggestibility The development of biased memories when people are provided with misleading information.

FIGURE 7.32 Scientific Method: Loftus's Studies on Suggestibility

Hypothesis: People can develop biased memories when provided with misleading information.

Research Method:

1 One group of participants was shown a videotape of a red Datsun approaching a stop sign.

2 Another group of participants was shown a videotape of a red Datsun approaching a yield sign.

3 Immediately after viewing the tapes, the participants were asked, "Did another car pass the red Datsun while it was stopped at the stop sign?"

Results: Some participants who had seen the yield sign responded to the question by claiming they had seen the car at the stop sign.

Conclusion: People can "remember" seeing nonexistent objects.

FIGURE 7.33 Fallibility of Memory For "The Innocents Project," Taryn Simon collaborated with members of the Innocence Project, an organization devoted to correcting errors in the criminal justice system. Here John Stickels **(right)**, a member of the Innocence Project's board of directors, congratulates the exultant Patrick Waller on July 3, 2008, in a Dallas courthouse. Waller has just been told that, thanks to the revisiting of DNA evidence, he has been exonerated of a crime for which he had been wrongly convicted and sent to prison for 15 years.

the details, highly stable. Given the memory modulation effect of stress hormones, it makes sense for eyewitnesses' accounts to be more vivid than laboratory research participants', but it remains unclear how accurate those stable memories were in the first place. And by retelling their stories over and over again—to the police, to friends and relatives, to researchers, and so on—eyewitnesses might inadvertently develop stronger memories for inaccurate details.

EYEWITNESS CONFIDENCE How good are observers, such as jurors, at judging eyewitnesses' accuracy? The general finding from a number of studies was that people cannot differentiate accurate eyewitnesses from inaccurate ones (Clark & Wells, 2008; Wells, 2008). The problem is that eyewitnesses who are wrong are just as confident, often more confident, than eyewitnesses who are right. Eyewitnesses who report vivid details of all the scene's aspects are probably less credible than those with poor memories for trivial details. After all, eyewitnesses to real crimes tend to be focused on the weapons or on the action—they fail to pay attention to minor details. Thus strong confidence for minor details may be a cue that the memory is likely inaccurate or even false. However, some people are just particularly confident, and jurors find them convincing. Taryn Simon, a photographer for the *New York Times,* created "The Innocents Project," a photo essay of people who were wrongfully convicted of crimes they did not commit, most because of faulty eyewitness testimony (**FIGURE 7.33**). Simon explained, "Police officers and prosecutors influence memory—both unintentionally and intentionally—through the ways in which they conduct the identification process. They can shape, and even generate, what comes to be known as eyewitness testimony." Simon described many cases—many compelling examples of memory's malleability—including one in which a victim, Jennifer Thompson, misidentified her attacker. According to Thompson, who was shown multiple images of possible assailants, "All the images became enmeshed to one image that became Ron, and Ron became my attacker" (Quoted in Simon, 2003).

CRITICAL THINKING SKILL

Recognizing How the Fallibility of Human Memory Can Lead to Faulty Conclusions

Brooke Patterson (2004) refers to the "tyranny of the eyewitness," meaning that people generally believe an eyewitness even though memory researchers know that eyewitnesses are frequently wrong. Of course, beliefs often remain strong despite data showing those beliefs are unjustified. When a person confidently reports what he or she heard or saw, other people tend to assume the report reflects an accurate memory. For the most part, however, there is little or no relationship between a person's confidence about a memory and the probability of that memory's accuracy (Weber & Brewer, 2004). An unknown number of innocent people have been imprisoned or even put to death because of memory errors. No doubt, guilty people have gone free because of either faulty memories or failure to believe valid memories. Most people do not like to have their memories questioned, and unless an independent party can verify the information, it is difficult to distinguish between a valid memory and a faulty one. As a critical thinker with an understanding of psychological science, you must recognize the fallibility of memories—including your own, even when you believe your memories are accurate. When a memory is important to some outcome, consider that memory's likely accuracy. Whenever possible, check the memory against related objective facts, such as video or audio recordings.

People Have False Memories

Source amnesia occurs when a person has a memory for an event but cannot remember where he or she encountered the information. What is your earliest childhood memory? How vivid is it? Are you actually recalling the event or some retelling of the event? How do you know you are not remembering something you saw in a photograph, or a story related to you by family members? Most people cannot remember specific memories from before age three. The absence of early memories, *childhood amnesia,* may be due to the early lack of linguistic capacity as well as to immature frontal lobes. The social psychologist Dana Dunn tells the following story about his own first memory, from the day John F. Kennedy was killed (discussed above): He recalls his mother and grandfather being upset and putting him outside on a swing while all the adults sat glued to the television as the events of that fateful day unfolded. But he was only three and a half years old at the time, so it is unlikely that anyone would have left him alone outside, especially given that the assassination occurred late in November, when it was already very cold. He cannot recall anything else from such a young age, and his memory cannot be accurate, yet the account seems so real in his memory. Memories for events when we were very young may seem real, but they are more likely constructed from information learned later in life.

CREATING FALSE RECOGNITION Read the following list out loud: sour, candy, sugar, bitter, good, taste, tooth, nice, honey, soda, chocolate, heart, cake, tart, pie. Now put your book aside and write down as many of the words as you remember.

Researchers have devised tests such as this for investigating whether people can be misled into recalling or recognizing events that did not happen (Roediger & McDermott, 1995). For instance, without looking back, which of the following words did you recall? *Candy, honey, tooth, sweet, pie.* If you recalled *sweet* (or think you did), you have experienced a false memory, because *sweet* was not on the original list. All the words on that list are related to sweetness, though. This basic paradigm produces false recollections extremely reliably. Moreover, people are often extremely confident in saying they have seen or heard the words they recollect falsely.

CONFABULATION Some types of brain injury are associated with **confabulation,** the false recollection of episodic memory. Morris Moscovitch, a memory research pioneer, has described confabulating as "honest lying," because the person does not intend to deceive and is unaware that his or her story is false. Moscovitch (1995) provides a striking example of confabulation in a patient he refers to as H.W., a 61-year-old man who was the biological father of four children, all of them grown. H.W. experienced severe frontal lobe damage following a cerebral hemorrhage. Here is part of the clinical interview:

Q. Are you married or single?
H.W. Married.
Q. How long have you been married?
H.W. About four months.
Q. How many children do you have?
H.W. Four. (He laughs.) Not bad for four months!
Q. How old are your children?
H.W. The eldest is 32, his name is Bob, and the youngest is 22, his name is Joe.
Q. How did you get those children in four months?
H.W. They're adopted.
Q. Does this all sound strange to you, what you are saying?
H.W. (He laughs.) I think it is a little strange.

Patients such as H.W. confabulate for no apparent purpose. They simply recall mistaken facts and, when questioned, try to make sense of their recollections by

source amnesia A type of amnesia that occurs when a person shows memory for an event but cannot remember where he or she encountered the information.

confabulation The false recollection of episodic memory.

adding facts that make the story more coherent. (Chapter 4 discusses Michael Gazzaniga's theory of the interpreter and how split-brain patients confabulate to make sense of conflicting information fed to each cerebral hemisphere.) A dramatic example of confabulation occurs in *Capgras syndrome,* where patients delusionally believe their family members have been replaced by impostors; even when confronted with contradictory evidence, they persist in inventing facts that support their delusions. In fact, no amount of evidence can convince them that their siblings, parents, spouses, children, and so on, are real. This bizarre syndrome is devastating to the family members accused of being imposters. Patients with Capgras often have damage to the frontal lobes and the limbic brain regions. The most likely cause is that the brain region involved in emotions is separated from the visual input, so the images of family members are no longer associated with warm feelings. The visual image is the same, but the feeling is not, leading the sufferer to conclude that the people are not their real relatives. Once we understand the underlying brain mechanisms, bizarre behaviors such as this become more understandable.

Repressed Memories Are Controversial

Over the past few decades, one of the most heated debates in psychological science has centered on repressed memories. On one side, some psychotherapists and patients claim that long-repressed memories for traumatic events can resurface during therapy. Recovered memories of sexual abuse are the most commonly reported repressed memories, and in the early 1990s there was a rash of reports about celebrities who had recovered memories of early childhood sexual abuse. On the other side, memory researchers such as Elizabeth Loftus point out that little credible evidence indicates that recovered memories are genuine or at least sufficiently accurate to be believable. Part of the problem is best summarized by a leading memory researcher, Daniel Schacter: "I am convinced that child abuse is a major problem in our society. I have no reason to question the memories of people who have always remembered their abuse, or who have spontaneously recalled previously forgotten abuse on their own. Yet I am deeply concerned by some of the suggestive techniques that have been recommended to recover repressed memories" (Schacter, 1996, p. 251).

Schacter alludes to the frightening possibility that false memories for traumatic events have been implanted by well-meaning but misguided therapists. Convincing evidence indicates that methods such as hypnosis, age regression, and guided recall can implant false memories. Likewise, a growing body of evidence from carefully controlled laboratory studies has demonstrated that children can be induced to remember events that did not occur (Ceci & Bruck, 1995). In a few infamous examples, adults have accused their parents of abuse based on memories that the accusers later realized were not reality but the products of therapy. For instance, Diana Halbrook came to believe not only that she had been abused but that she had been involved in satanic ritualistic abuse, as part of which she had killed a baby. When she expressed doubts to her therapist and her "support" group about these events' veracity, they told her she was in denial and not listening to "the little girl" within. After all, the other members of the support group had recovered memories of being involved in satanic ritualistic abuse. After Halbrook left her therapy group, she came to believe she had not been abused and had not killed. Tellingly, "though thousands of patients have 'remembered' ritual acts, not a single such case has ever been documented in the United States despite extensive investigative efforts by state and federal law enforcement" (Schacter, 1996, p. 269).

Understandably, people on both sides of the debate about repressed memories hold strong and passionate beliefs. While research shows that some therapeutic techniques seem especially likely to foster false memories, it would be a mistake simply to dismiss all adult reports of early abuse. Some abuse certainly could have occurred and been forgotten until later, and we cannot ignore the memories of actual victims. In the latter half of the 1990s, the incidence of recovered memories fell dramatically, but we do not know whether this decline happened because of less media attention to reports or because fewer people sought therapy to uncover their past memories. The unhappy truth is that some error will always occur when memory is on trial. Some abusers may go free because their victims are not believed, and some innocent people may be imprisoned for crimes they did not commit.

People Reconstruct Events to Be Consistent

A final example of memory distortion is **memory bias,** in which people's memories for events change over time to be consistent with current beliefs or attitudes. As one of psychology's greatest thinkers, Leon Festinger (1987, p. 1), put it: "I prefer to rely on my memory. I have lived with that memory a long time, I am used to it, and if I have rearranged or distorted anything, surely that was done for my own benefit."

Consider people who take study skills courses. Students often fail to heed the advice they receive in such courses, and only modest evidence indicates that the courses are beneficial, yet most students who take them describe them as extremely helpful. How can something that generally produces unimpressive outcomes be endorsed so positively? To understand this phenomenon, researchers randomly assigned students to either a genuine study skills course or a control group that received no special training. Students who took the real course showed few signs of improvement; in fact, their final-exam performances were slightly poorer than the control group's. Still, they reported the study skills program as helpful. The experiment had one feature that helps explain why. At the beginning of the course, participants were asked to rate their studying skills. At the end of the course, they again rated themselves and were asked to recall how they had originally rated themselves. In describing their earlier ratings, students in the study skills course recalled themselves as having been significantly worse than they had rated themselves at the beginning, thereby "getting what they want by revising what they had" (Conway & Ross, 1984).

People tend to recall their past attitudes and past beliefs as being consistent with their current ones, often revising their memories when they change attitudes and beliefs. People also tend to remember events as casting them in prominent roles or favorable lights. As discussed further in Chapter 12, people also tend to exaggerate their contributions to group efforts, take credit for successes and blame failures on others, and remember their successes more than their failures. Societies, too, bias their recollections of past events. Groups' collective memories can seriously distort the past, as expressed in George Orwell's observation that we can change only the past, not the future. Most societies' official histories tend to downplay their past unsavory, immoral, and even murderous behaviors; perpetrators' memories are generally shorter than victims'.

Neuroscience May Make It Possible to Distinguish between "True" and "False" Memories

With so many advances in the neuroscience of how we learn and remember, you might wonder if any neuroscientific techniques can help us distinguish between "true" memories (memories for events that really happened) and "false" memories (memories for events that people believe really happened but that happened differently than remembered or not at all). It is important to distinguish between

memory bias The changing of memories over time in ways consistent with prior beliefs.

two very different situations: when a person tells a lie, reporting something he or she knows is not true, and when a person experiences a false or faulty memory but honestly believes it is true.

Recall that when we remember something, the brain areas activated are the same ones that were active when we first learned it—auditory memories activate auditory areas of the brain, for example. Retrieving a memory seems to require the same neural activity that was involved in the initial encoding. Given this information, how might researchers try to answer the question about whether we can determine if someone is having a "true" memory or a "false," illusory one? If the memory is "true" (psychologists use the term *veridical*), the brain areas activated should be the same as those active when the event occurred, but if the memory is "false," unrelated brain areas would be activated (Garoff-Eaton, Slotnick, & Schacter, 2006). In fact, some preliminary data suggest we can make this distinction, but this emerging area of research needs a great deal of further testing. One problem with this method is that false memories tend to be similar in many ways to true memories; for example, you might correctly recall an event that occurred in high school gym class but have a false memory about the teacher involved. In a case like this one, the area of the brain involved in true memory for similar events in high school would probably also be involved in the retrieval of the false memory. A totally unrelated memory, such as about what you ate for lunch today, would involve different brain regions.

Some evidence indicates that brain imaging one day may be used as a lie detector (**FIGURE 7.34**), as has been suggested in a case that involves a mother who served a three-year prison term for attempting to poison her child. The mother has maintained her innocence and believes brain imaging will support her case. Investigators have published a scholarly paper stating that her brain activation differed when she told the truth and when she repeated the allegations that she attempted to poison her daughter, which she claims is a lie (Spence, Kaylor-Hughes, Brook, Lankappa, & Wilkinson, 2007). Many movies and television shows depict older versions of lie detectors, machines designed to pick up subtle physical cues that might indicate someone is lying. However, these detectors are so inaccurate that their findings are not allowed in court, and this defendant's attempt to use her fMRI data to show her innocence most likely will not be allowed in court either. Over the next several years, scientists likely will debate whether fMRI is reliable and acceptable for distinguishing among true memories, false memories, and lies. The courts must decide if fMRI data on this topic are admissible as evidence. As studies with fMRIs of false memories that are similar to true memories have shown, it is difficult, perhaps impossible, to tell these two types of memories apart.

FIGURE 7.34 Brain Activity as a Lie Detector The fMRIs below come from a study in which the investigators examined brain activity while the subjects engaged in deception. T-score is a statistical estimate of the size of the difference in neural activity between truth and deception conditions; on the scale here, bright yellow indicates the strongest brain activity. As the images show, various brain regions were involved in deceptive answers. The investigators were particularly interested in their theory linking memory and language processes to deception, and activity in areas indicated by arrows most strongly supported their theory.

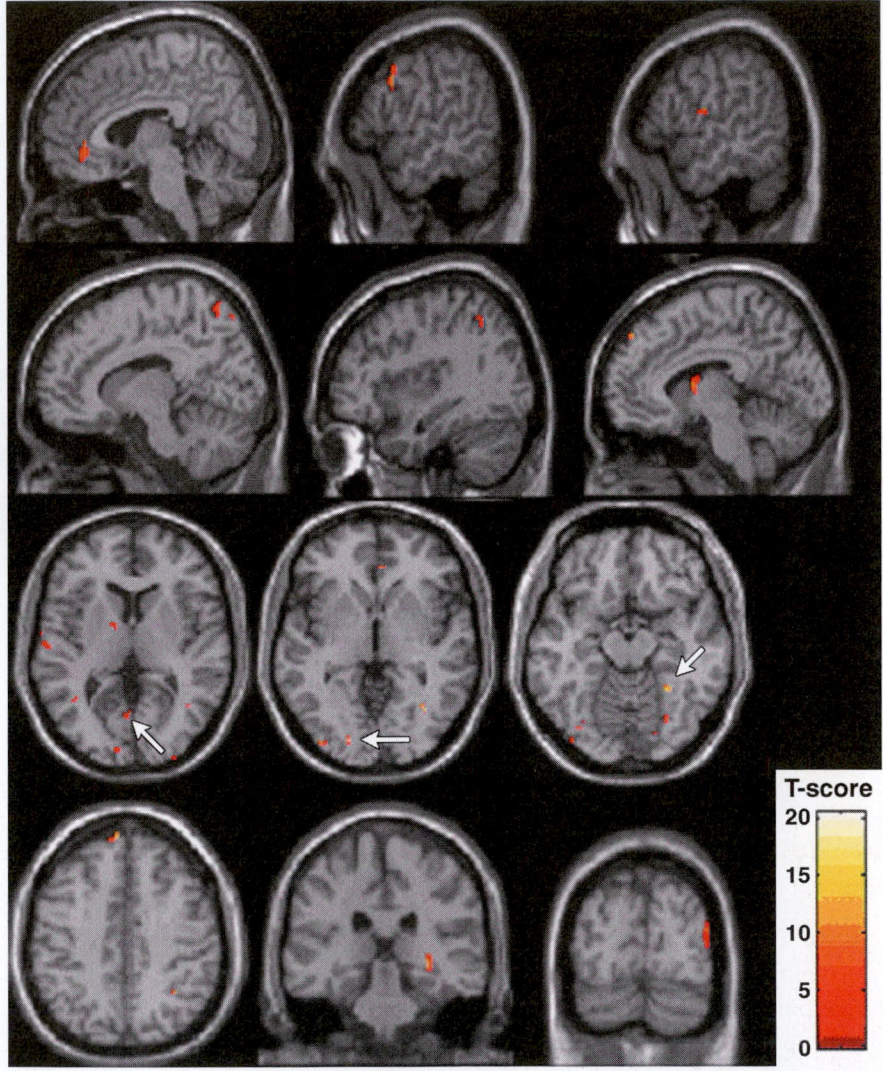

How Are Memories Distorted?

Memory is far from a faithful, objective recorder of facts and events. Rather, memory often includes biases and distortions. People tend to make poor eyewitnesses because human memory is better for broad outlines than for details. Yet people maintain unjustified confidence in their personal memories, such as flashbulb memories. Memories can be distorted, or even implanted, by false information, and the mind has a general bias toward maintaining consistency in our memories. Exciting new work uses fMRIs to distinguish between true and false memories, but thus far the technique may not be sensitive enough to make this critical distinction reliably.

MEASURING UP

1. Which principles must be balanced in a court of law when considering memories' accuracy?
   a. Does the witness have a motive for lying, and is the witness trustworthy?
   b. What activity patterns does an fMRI show for true memories, and what patterns does it show for false memories?
   c. What body language does the witness use, and do the lawyers ask leading questions?
   d. What are the costs of letting a possible felon go free, and what are the costs of incarcerating someone who may be innocent?

2. Flashbulb memories _____.
   a. are almost always true memories because they involve emotional events
   b. are likely to be wrong because people misattribute the source of information
   c. are often distorted in the same way as other memories, but "feel" true to the people whose memories they are
   d. are less important for men than for women because, on average, men are less emotional and have less need to remember emotional events

3. Suppose a teacher accuses you of plagiarizing a term paper. To back up his accusation, he shows you a published passage similar to one you wrote in your paper. Of course, you did not commit plagiarism—you would never do that. Which of the following phenomena might be cited in your defense?
   a. cryptomnesia
   b. social comparison
   c. absentmindedness
   d. temporary blocking

How Can We Improve Learning and Memory?

Mnemonics Are Useful Strategies for Learning

This chapter has described research indicating how and when people are more likely to remember or forget information. One central question in psychological science is how people learn, and research over the past century has provided a wealth of information directly relevant to education. Many findings from psychological laboratories make their way into classrooms, as teachers apply new techniques that enhance both learning and memory. Through research, psychological scientists have also developed specific strategies, called **mnemonics,** for improving memory. By using mnemonic strategies, most people can study and remember the information

LEARNING OBJECTIVE
Explain how we can use scientific knowledge about memory to improve memory.

mnemonics Strategies for improving memory.

on long lists. The following section examines some of the ways that findings from psychological science can help you study more effectively.

PRACTICE To become proficient in any activity, you need to practice. The more times you repeat an action, the easier it is to perform that action. Motor skills, such as those used to play the piano, play golf, and drive, become easier with practice. Memories are strengthened with retrieval, so one way to make durable memories is to practice retrieval. Recent research in classrooms has shown that repeated testing is a good way to strengthen memories. In fact, it is even better than spending the same amount of time reviewing information you have already read (Roediger & Karpicke, 2006). When you study—retrieving information by remembering it or rehearsing it—you are strengthening existing synaptic connections and making new ones. So, for example, after reading a section in this or any other book, look back at the main section heading and, if it is not already a question, rephrase it as a question; then be sure that you can answer the heading's question without looking at the text. (Also note that there are test questions at the end of every section in this book except the one you are now reading. There is a practice test at the end of each chapter. And on the book's Web site additional tests provide feedback and explanations of the additional tests' correct answers.)

ELABORATE THE MATERIAL The deeper the level of processing, the more likely you are to remember the material later. This is another reason that critical thinking skills are important. Rather than just reading the material, think about its meaning and how it is related to other concepts. Try to organize the material in a way that makes sense to you, putting the concepts into your own words. Indeed, making the material relevant to you is an especially good way to process material deeply and therefore to remember it easily.

OVERLEARN With material in front of them, people are often overly confident that they will remember it later. But recognition is easier than recall, and information in a book might not be as accessible when the book is closed and you have to answer questions about what you read. Rehearse material even after you think you have learned it. Test yourself by trying to recall the material a few hours after studying. Keep rehearsing until you can recall the material easily. Distributing your study over time rather than cramming will help you retain the information for longer periods of time (Cepeda, Pashler, Vul, Wixted, & Rohrer, 2006). Three sessions of two hours each are much better for learning than one six-hour marathon.

GET ADEQUATE SLEEP Many students underestimate the importance of getting a good night's sleep. Some compelling evidence indicates that sleep may help with the consolidation of memories and that disturbing sleep interferes with learning. Chronic sleep deprivation certainly will interfere with learning.

USE VERBAL MNEMONICS How many days are there in September? In the Western world at least, most people can readily answer this question thanks to the old saying that begins, "Thirty days hath September." Children also learn "i before e except after c" and "*weird* is weird." By memorizing such phrases, we more easily remember things that are difficult to remember. Advertisers, of course, often create slogans or jingles that rely on *verbal mnemonics* so that consumers cannot help but remember them. Students have long used acronyms to remember information, such as HOMES to remember the great lakes (Huron, Ontario, Michigan, Erie, and Superior). In studying Chapter 13, the acronym OCEAN will help you remember the major personality traits: openness to experience, conscientiousness, extraversion, agreeableness, and neuroticism. Even complex ideas can be understood through simple mnemonics, such as "cells that fire together wire together" as a way to remember long-term potentiation, the brain mechanism responsible for learning, discussed in Chapter 6.

USE VISUAL IMAGERY Creating a mental image of material is an especially good way to remember. Recall that working memory has a verbal component called the phonological loop and a visuospatial component, sometimes called a sketchpad. When you use visual imagery, you are engaging both systems in working memory and creating a more lasting memory. Memory researchers have developed specific strategies that rely on imagery to help people remember long lists of information. One, the *method of loci,* involves visualizing yourself placing objects in familiar locations so that when you have to retrieve the material you simply imagine going back to that location. A similar technique involves learning a list of key words, or *pegs,* then hanging new words on those pegs by visualizing the new words together with the pegs. Although useful for remembering long lists, these strategies typically are not widely used. Most of us find it just as easy to keep lists of things we need on our computers, our PDAs, or even pieces of paper. (We simply have to remember where we put the lists!)

 SUMMING UP

How Can We Improve Learning and Memory?

Memory is strengthened with repeated retrieval, so frequent testing and active responding spaced out over time is a strategy to enhance memory. When you relate new information to information you already know, you create more retrieval cues, which make you more likely to recall the new information later. Overlearning also creates stronger memory traces, probably because of repeated retrieval. Because memories undergo consolidation during sleep, it is important to get adequate sleep. Catchy verbal associations can help you remember information because the phrases can act as retrieval cues. Imagery requires you to pay attention, and it uses both the verbal and visuospatial components in working memory, thus creating stronger memory traces. Finally, many external aids, including paper and pencil, can be helpful when you need to remember something.

CONCLUSION

The brain has allowed humans to develop language, build civilizations, and visit the moon. However, even this wonderfully evolved organ cannot guarantee that people will remember where they left their keys, that the witnesses or victims of crimes will remember the criminals' faces, that readers will recall details from books they read last year, or that anyone will recognize a name and know for sure whether the person is famous. As a system, memory has evolved to solve certain problems related to survival, such as remembering our friends and foes. It did not evolve to remember phone numbers, textbook definitions, how to drive a car, and so on, but it does a pretty good job at tasks like these, considering the amount of information that bombards the nervous system. Finally, as one of the most dynamic areas of research in psychological science, memory highlights our four fundamental themes, in particular the way that researchers are working at various levels of analysis to unwrap the mystery of the mind.

■ CHAPTER SUMMARY

How Does Attention Determine What Is Remembered?

- **Visual Attention Is Selective and Serial:** Simple searches for stimuli that differ in only one primary factor (e.g., size, color, orientation) occur automatically and rapidly, but searches for objects that are the conjunction of two or more properties (e.g., red and large) occur slowly and serially.

- **Auditory Attention Allows Selective Listening:** We can attend to more than one message at a time but not well. Evidence indicates that we weakly process some unattended information.

- **Selective Attention Can Operate at Multiple Stages of Processing:** We often miss large objects in our visual field when we are attending to something else, a phenomenon known as change blindness.

What Are the Basic Stages of Memory?

- **Sensory Memory Is Brief:** Visual and auditory memories are maintained long enough to ensure a continuous sensory experience.

- **Working Memory Is Active:** Immediate active memory is limited. Chunking reduces information into units that are easier to remember. The four components of working memory are the central executive, the phonological loop, the visuospatial sketchpad, and the episodic buffer.

- **Long-Term Memory Is Relatively Permanent:** Long-term memory (LTM) is the potentially indefinite storage of all memories. Meaningful memories are stored in LTM in networklike structures.

What Are the Different Long-Term Memory Systems?

- **Explicit Memory Involves Conscious Effort:** Explicit, declarative memories that we consciously remember include personal events (episodic memory) and general knowledge (semantic memory).

- **Implicit Memory Occurs without Deliberate Effort:** Procedural (motor) memories of how to do things automatically are implicit.

- **Prospective Memory Is Remembering to Do Something:** Prospective memory has "costs" in terms of reducing attention and reducing working memory capacity.

How Is Information Organized in Long-Term Memory?

- **Long-Term Memory Is Based on Meaning:** Memory processes include encoding, storage, and retrieval. Elaborative rehearsal involves encoding information in more meaningful ways and results in better memory than maintenance (repetition) rehearsal.

- **Schemas Provide an Organizational Framework:** Schemas, cognitive structures of meaning, aid the organization of memories. Cultural variations in schemas produce differences in what and how information is remembered.

- **Information Is Stored in Association Networks:** Networks of associations are formed by nodes of information, which are linked together and are activated by spreading activation.

- **Retrieval Cues Provide Access to Long-Term Storage:** According to the encoding specificity principle, any stimulus encoded along with an experience can later trigger the memory of the experience. The memory's context is also activated.

What Brain Processes Are Involved in Memory?

- **There Has Been Intensive Effort to Identify Memory's Physical Location:** Research has revealed that a number of specific brain regions contribute to learning and memory.

- **The Medial Temporal Lobes Are Important for Consolidation of Declarative Memories:** The process of consolidation of new memories involves changes in neural connections. The hippocampus, a structure in the medial temporal lobe, is important for declarative memories. Place cells in the hippocampus aid spatial memory.

- **The Frontal Lobes Are Involved in Many Aspects of Memory:** Extensive neural networks connect the frontal lobes with other memory regions of the brain. Activation of neurons in the frontal lobe is associated with deeper meaning.

- **Neurochemistry Underlies Memory:** Neurochemicals modulate the storage of memories. Epinephrine enhances memory. The amygdala is probably responsible for memory modulation through activity in its norepinephrine receptors.

When Do People Forget?

- **Transience Is Caused by Interference:** Forgetting over time occurs because of interference from both old and new information.

- **Blocking Is Temporary:** The tip-of-the-tongue phenomenon is a person's temporary trouble retrieving the right word, usually due to interference from a similar word.

- **Absentmindedness Results from Shallow Encoding:** Inattentive or shallow processing causes memory failure.

- **Amnesia Is a Deficit in Long-Term Memory:** Both injury and disease can result in amnesia, either the inability to recall past memories (retrograde) or the inability to form new memories (anterograde).

How Are Memories Distorted?

- **Flashbulb Memories Can Be Wrong:** The strong emotional response that attends a flashbulb memory may affect the memory's strength and accuracy.

- **People Make Source Misattributions:** A person can misremember the source of a memory (source misattribution). In cryptomnesia, a person thinks he or she has come up with a new idea, but has only retrieved a memory.

- **People Are Bad Eyewitnesses:** Poor eyewitness recall occurs, particularly when people try to identify those of other ethnicities. Suggestibility leads to misinformation.

- **People Have False Memories:** Immature frontal lobes cause childhood amnesia. False memories can be implanted. Confabulation can occur because of brain damage.

- **Repressed Memories Are Controversial:** Some therapeutic techniques can result in false repressed memories.

- **People Reconstruct Events to Be Consistent:** People tend to maintain consistency between their past memories, their current knowledge, and their current attitudes.

- **Neuroscience May Make It Possible to Distinguish between "True" and "False" Memories:** By examining brain activity at encoding and retrieval, researchers hope to distinguish true from false memories. The current research has many flaws, but the techniques may be improved.

How Can We Improve Learning and Memory?

- **Mnemonics Are Useful Strategies for Learning:** Mnemonics include practicing at retrieval through frequent testing, overlearning, getting enough sleep, spacing study sessions, and using imagery.

The answer key for all the Measuring Up exercises and the Practice Tests can be found at the back of the book.

absentmindedness, p. 315
amnesia, p. 315
anterograde amnesia,
    p. 316
blocking, p. 314
change blindness, p. 284
chunking, p. 289
confabulation, p. 321
consolidation, p. 306
cryptomnesia, p. 318
declarative memory,
    p. 296
encoding, p. 286

encoding specificity
    principle, p. 303
episodic memory, p. 296
explicit memory, p. 296
flashbulb memories,
    p. 317
forgetting, p. 311
implicit memory, p. 296
long-term memory
    (LTM), p. 291
memory, p. 281
memory bias, p. 323
mnemonics, p.325

modal memory model,
    p. 287
parallel processing,
    p. 282
posttraumatic stress
    disorder (PTSD),
    p. 310
proactive interference,
    p. 314
procedural memory,
    p. 298
prospective memory,
    p. 298

reconsolidation, p. 306
retrieval, p. 287
retrieval cue, p. 302
retroactive interference,
    p. 314
retrograde amnesia,
    p. 315
schema, p. 301
semantic memory, p. 296
sensory memory, p. 287
serial position effect,
    p. 292

short-term memory
    (STM), p. 288
source amnesia, p. 321
source misattribution,
    p. 318
spatial memory, p. 307
storage, p. 286
suggestibility, p. 319
transience, p. 314
working memory
    (WM), p. 288

■ PRACTICE TEST

1. The card game Set requires players to attend to four features (shape, color, shading, and number) across 12 cards in an effort to identify a "Set." A player has identified a Set when "any feature in the 'Set' of three cards is either common to all three cards or is different on each card" (directions from Set Enterprises, Inc.). Playing this game requires participants to engage in a _____, which is _____.
   a. conjunction task; effortful
   b. conjunction task; fast and automatic
   c. primitive features task; effortful
   d. primitive features task; fast and automatic

2. Sarah and Anna are chatting at a coffee shop. Anna notices that Sarah does not seem to be paying attention to what she, Anna, is saying. Which strategy could Anna use to effectively pull Sarah's attention back to the conversation?
   a. Anna should buy Sarah a fresh cup of coffee; more caffeine will help her pay attention.
   b. Anna should covertly modify something about her own appearance (for example, remove her earrings); even subtle changes in a person's visual field draw attention.
   c. Anna should lower her voice to a near-whisper.
   d. Anna should use Sarah's name in a sentence.

3. Imagine you are a manager seeking to hire a new employee. Before leaving work Monday afternoon, you look through a stack of 30 resumes organized alphabetically by last name. When you return to work Tuesday morning, which job applicant are you most likely to remember?
   a. Alvarado
   b. Martonosi
   c. Russo

4. You are asked to memorize a list of words. Which encoding strategy will likely result in the best recall performance?
   a. As you read each word, repeat it five times.
   b. As you read each word, count the number of letters in it.

   c. As you read each word, think of a word that rhymes with it.
   d. As you read each word, think of a synonym for it.

5. You ask a friend to memorize the following list: bed, rest, night, tired, blanket, pillow, relaxed. Later, you ask your friend to tell you as many words from the list as he or she can remember. In addition to remembering some of the words, your friend lists the word *sleep,* which did not appear on the original list. Which of the following phenomena is most related to your friend's error in recall?
   a. context-dependent encoding
   b. culturally relevant schemas
   c. networks of associations
   d. state-dependent encoding

6. Damage to which area of the brain (amygdala, frontal lobe, hippocampus) would most likely lead to each of the following impairments?
   a. In spite of having lived in the same city all her life, Kate is unable to describe the route from her home to the market.
   b. Moses rates a list of adjectives on the extent to which each describes him. He is later asked to recall the words on the list, but is unable to do so.
   c. Meriam claims to have no emotional understanding of fear.

7. Which "sin of memory" is demonstrated in each of the following examples?
   a. A friend introduces you to her brother; five minutes later, you find you cannot remember the brother's name.
   b. A friend introduces you to her brother. Later, you ask your friend, "How's your brother . . . ah, what's his name? Jake? John? Oh, James! How is James?"

8. Fill in the blanks. People experiencing _____ amnesia are unable to recall memories from the past, whereas people experiencing _____ amnesia are unable to form new memories.

■ PSYCHOLOGY AND SOCIETY

1. Write a letter to a newspaper editor that articulates your position on whether using a cell phone while driving should be legal. Support your position with scientific evidence and statistics from reputable sources. Be sure your letter will make sense to someone not already familiar with the concepts and methodologies of psychology.

2. Imagine you have been asked to serve as the director of your school's academic advising program for first-year students. Prepare a study skills brochure to be distributed to new students. An effective brochure will explain why the study skills work and will reflect your awareness of particular issues on your campus and resources available there.

Thinking and Intelligence

ON SEPTEMBER 11, 2001, AND FOR DAYS AFTERWARD, footage of the two jets striking the World Trade Center was broadcast repeatedly throughout the world (FIGURE 8.1A). Most of us who were near televisions and computers at the time will never forget those vivid images, which made it impossible not to think of the passengers in the hijacked planes and of the office workers in the World Trade Center and the Pentagon who died as a result of the hijackings. Another tragic consequence of 9/11 has rarely been discussed: the hundreds of people who died in automobile accidents because they chose to drive rather than fly in the months following the tragedy. These additional deaths were caused not by terrorists' actions but by the way people commonly think about risks.

The psychologist Gerd Gigerenzer (2004) has proposed that low-probability events that are highly publicized and have dire consequences, such as the deaths associated with the hijackings of 9/11, can result in fears he calls *dread risks*. Dread risks can profoundly affect reasoning and decision making. After 9/11, for example, even in countries that were not

How Does the Mind Represent Information?
- Mental Images Are Analogical Representations
- Concepts Are Symbolic Representations
- Schemas Organize Useful Information about Environments

How Do We Make Decisions and Solve Problems?
- People Use Deductive and Inductive Reasoning

- Decision Making Often Involves Heuristics
- Critical Thinking Skill: Understanding How the Availability and Representativeness Heuristics Can Affect Thinking
- Problem Solving Achieves Goals

How Do We Understand Intelligence?
- Intelligence Is Assessed with Psychometric Tests
- Critical Thinking Skill: Recognizing and Avoiding Reification

- General Intelligence Involves Multiple Components
- Intelligence Is Associated with Cognitive Performance
- Genes and Environment Influence Intelligence
- Group Differences in Intelligence Have Multiple Determinants

(a)

(b)

FIGURE 8.1 **Dread Risks** **(a)** The second plane strikes the World Trade Center on September 11, 2001. **(b)** For months after the attacks, airports around the United States were practically deserted. Here, Reagan National Airport in Washington, D.C., is pictured on November 1, 2001.

likely targets for terrorists, many more people feared flying than normally do (FIGURE 8.1B). In fact, in October, November, and December 2001, airline revenues dropped by 20 percent, 17 percent, and 12 percent compared with those same months in 2000. As fewer people were flying, estimates for miles driven in the United States during those months increased by almost 3 percent; the largest increase (5.3 percent) was on interstate rural highways. But while hijacked planes may prompt people to avoid airline travel, the number of people who die in car accidents every year far exceeds the number who die in airline disasters, much less in hijackings. The number of traffic fatalities in the three months following 9/11 was significantly above average: An estimated 350 Americans died during those months because they avoided flying—more than the 266 airplane passengers and crew members who died in all four hijackings on 9/11.

When reasoning about the right choice to make, humans do not always weigh the actual probabilities of different actions. In fact, we can be influenced heavily by numerous factors that might not be considered rational, such as the prominence of events or of images in our minds. Psychologists have identified some of the typical biases that enter into reasoning and decision making. Gigerenzer believes the biases that typically affect decision making after highly unlikely tragic events should be publicized, so that education about dread risks might prompt people to reconsider choices that could result in additional negative consequences. As Gigerenzer suggests, the way we think about information makes important differences in the quality of our lives—both individually and collectively. This chapter therefore considers the nature of thought: How we represent ideas in our minds, how we use these ideas to solve problems and to make decisions, and how we can explain differences in intelligence among people.

How Does the Mind Represent Information?

What is the nature of thought, and how can exploring the nature of thought help us improve our thinking? To begin answering these questions, consider your thinking processes as you respond to a few more questions:

What does your mother look like? In answering this question, were you consciously aware of a mental image, similar to an internal picture, of your mother's face?

In the alphabet, what letter comes after N? Did you find yourself singing "l, m, n, o, p?" Most people do.

How much is 2 + 2? Did "4" immediately pop into your mind?

In your home when you were 10 years old, how many windows did the living room have? Answering this question might have required at least two sorts of mental processes. If you moved many times as a child, you might have put some pieces of information together to recall where you lived when you were 10 and if that place even had a living room; then you might have created a mental image of the living room, so you could "look around" as you counted the windows. If you have lived in the same home at least since you were 10, you would have skipped the first step and gone directly to generating an image. You also might have recalled the number of windows without imagery—for example, if you recently bought curtains for all the windows in that room.

What is Julia Roberts's phone number? Unless you hobnob with celebrities, you immediately realized that you do not know this movie star's phone number and never did. You most likely did not search through your memory and decide the number was not there. You know you did not forget the number, but how did you know so quickly what you do not know?

The preceding two chapters discussed how we learn and remember information. But once we have acquired information, how do we use it? This chapter is concerned with how we use information when we think and what it means to think intelligently. Our thoughts guide much of our behavior as we solve problems, make decisions, and try to make sense of events going on around us. Sometimes our thought processes lead to great ideas and creative discoveries, but sometimes they lead to bad decisions and regret. Yet even in the face of all these thought processes and biases, some people seem to be better at using information than others; we describe this ability as intelligence.

For the most part, our thinking is adaptive. We develop rules for making fast decisions, for example, because daily life demands we do so. In his 2005 book, *Blink: The Power of Thinking without Thinking,* the science writer Malcolm Gladwell makes the case that the ability to use information rapidly is a critical human skill. When you encounter a person on the street who might pose a threat, you might change your route to avoid that person. Being able to size up whether a person is trustworthy allows you to avoid harm, and you do this sizing up instantly and without conscious awareness. Unconscious cognitive processes not only influence thought and behavior (as discussed in Chapter 4) but also affect decision making and problem solving.

In illustrating how snap judgments can have important consequences, Gladwell describes a firefighter who led his colleagues in an effort to put out a kitchen fire. When they sprayed water on it, the fire did not respond in the expected way. Sensing that something was wrong, the firefighter quickly ordered everyone to leave the building; his decision turned out to be a good one because the fire was in the basement, under the kitchen, and the kitchen floor collapsed moments after the building was evacuated. The firefighter had known something was wrong but not what it was, and if he had stopped to figure out the problem, he and his colleagues might have been killed. His decision saved him and the others, but it was based on an intuition developed over years of experience in fighting fires.

Sometimes, however, snap decisions can be disastrous—as in the case (described in Chapter 1) of the police shooting of Amadou Diallo, an unarmed African man in New York City. After a high-profile police shooting of an unarmed black person, a community generally feels victimized and mistrustful toward the police (Correll et al., 2007). The tragedy of Diallo's death has led to research on ways of understanding and reducing the effects of personal characteristics, including race, on police officers' split-second decisions regarding whether to shoot. (Chapter 12, "Social Psychology," considers the Diallo shooting in light of how stereotypes influence both perception and judgment.)

Some thoughts, as when we are describing someone or counting the windows in a room we remember, generate images in our heads. Others are like words spoken in our heads. Still others are difficult to describe because we seem to pull them up fully formed without any conscious awareness of where they came from. The field of cognitive psychology was originally based on the notions that the brain *represents* information and that the act of thinking—that is, **cognition**—is directly associated with manipulating these representations.

cognition Mental activity such as thinking or representing information.

In this way, we use representations to understand objects we encounter in our environments. Representations are all around us. A road map represents streets, a menu represents food options, a photograph represents part of the world, as might a verbal description. The challenge for cognitive psychologists is to understand the nature of our everyday *mental* representations. You do not need a map if you have a mental representation of the local streets, and although you might like to have a picture of your mother on your desk, you most likely can describe what she looks like without referring to it. But what are the characteristics of mental representations? When are such representations like maps or pictures, ones that happen to be in your mind? And when are they more abstract, like language?

We use two basic types of representations, *analogical and symbolic,* which usually correspond to images and words, respectively. Both types of representations are useful in understanding how we think because they form the basis of human thought, intelligence, and the ability to solve everyday life's complex problems. **Analogical representations**—which have some characteristics of (and are therefore *analogous* to) actual objects—include maps, which correspond to geographical layouts, and family trees, which depict relationships between relatives. By contrast, **symbolic representations,** usually words or ideas, are abstract and do not have relationships to physcial qualitites of objects in the world. For example, the world *violin* stands for a musical instrument. There are no correspondences between what a violin looks or sounds like and the letters or sounds that make up the word *violin.* In Chinese, the world for violin is

小提琴

In Mandarin, it is pronounced *xiǎotíqín,* or *shiaw ti chin*. Like the English word *violin,* it is a symbolic representation because it bears no systematic relationship to the object it names. The individual characters that make up the word stand for different parts of what makes a violin, but they are arbitrary—you cannot "see" any part of a violin in their shapes (**FIGURE 8.2**).

Mental Images Are Analogical Representations

In the mind's eye, we often *see* images without trying. For example, pause while reading this sentence and think about a lemon. What form did your "lemon" thought take? Did you pull up an image that resembled an actual lemon, with its yellow and waxy, dimpled skin? Did your mouth water (a different sort of mental image)? Not surprisingly, several lines of evidence support the notion that representations take on picturelike qualities.

In a famous set of studies in the early 1970s, participants were shown letters and numbers and asked to determine whether each object was in its normal orientation (e.g., R) or was a mirror image (Я). The objects were rotated and presented in various positions, sometimes upright, sometimes upside down, sometimes somewhere in between. The time a participant took to determine whether an object was in its normal orientation or a mirror image depended on its degree of rotation (Cooper & Shepard, 1973). The farther the object was rotated from the upright position, the longer the discrimination took; the longest reaction time occurred when the object was fully upside down. Based on the reaction times, the researchers concluded that the participants had mentally rotated representations of the objects to "view" the objects in their upright positions.

analogical representation A mental representation that has some of the physical characteristics of an object; it is analogous to the object.

symbolic representation An abstract mental representation that does not correspond to the physical features of an object or idea.

(a)   **(b)**

Violin

FIGURE 8.2 Analogical Representations and Symbolic Representations
(a) Analogical representations, such as this picture of a violin, have some characteristics of the objects they represent. **(b)** Symbolic representations, such as the word *violin,* are abstract and do not have relationships to the objects.

Presumably, the farther an object was from upright, the longer the task took because the representation needed to be rotated more (**FIGURE 8.3**).

But are all representations of objects analogical? Could they instead be simple representations based on factual knowledge about the world: Lemons (1) are yellow and (2) have dimpled, waxy skin, so perhaps instead of visualizing a lemon you recalled its attributes without a visual image (Pylyshyn, 1984)? Researchers have used the tools of cognitive neuroscience to demonstrate that at least some thoughts take the form of mental images. In analyzing mental representations at the biological level, Stephen Kosslyn and his colleagues (1995) have shown that visual imagery is associated with activity in visual perception–related areas of the brain (that is, the primary visual cortex). In other words, the same brain areas activated when we view something are active when we think in images.

Such studies have shown that when you retrieve information from memory, as when you recall a picture you recently saw in a newspaper, the representation of that picture in your mind's eye parallels the representation in your brain the first time you saw the picture. This process is like having an eye that faces into the brain instead of outside to the world. Of course, no "picture" exists inside your head; neural activity consists of electrical impulses that cause groups of neurons to fire (as explained in Chapter 3, "Biological Foundations"), but the experience seems like viewing a picture inside your head. The mental image is not perfectly accurate; rather, it corresponds generally to the physical object it represents. By using mental images, you can answer questions about objects not in your presence, as when you visualize a lemon and describe its color. Manipulating mental images also allows you to think about your environment in novel and creative ways, helping you solve problems.

LIMITS OF ANALOGICAL REPRESENTATIONS We can represent only a limited range of knowledge analogically. If something cannot be perceived wholly by our perceptual system, we cannot form a complete analogical representation of it. Maps are an interesting case. For example, most of us can pull up a visual image, a map, of Africa's contours even if we have never seen the actual contours with our own eyes. Mental maps therefore involve a mixture of analogical and symbolic representations.

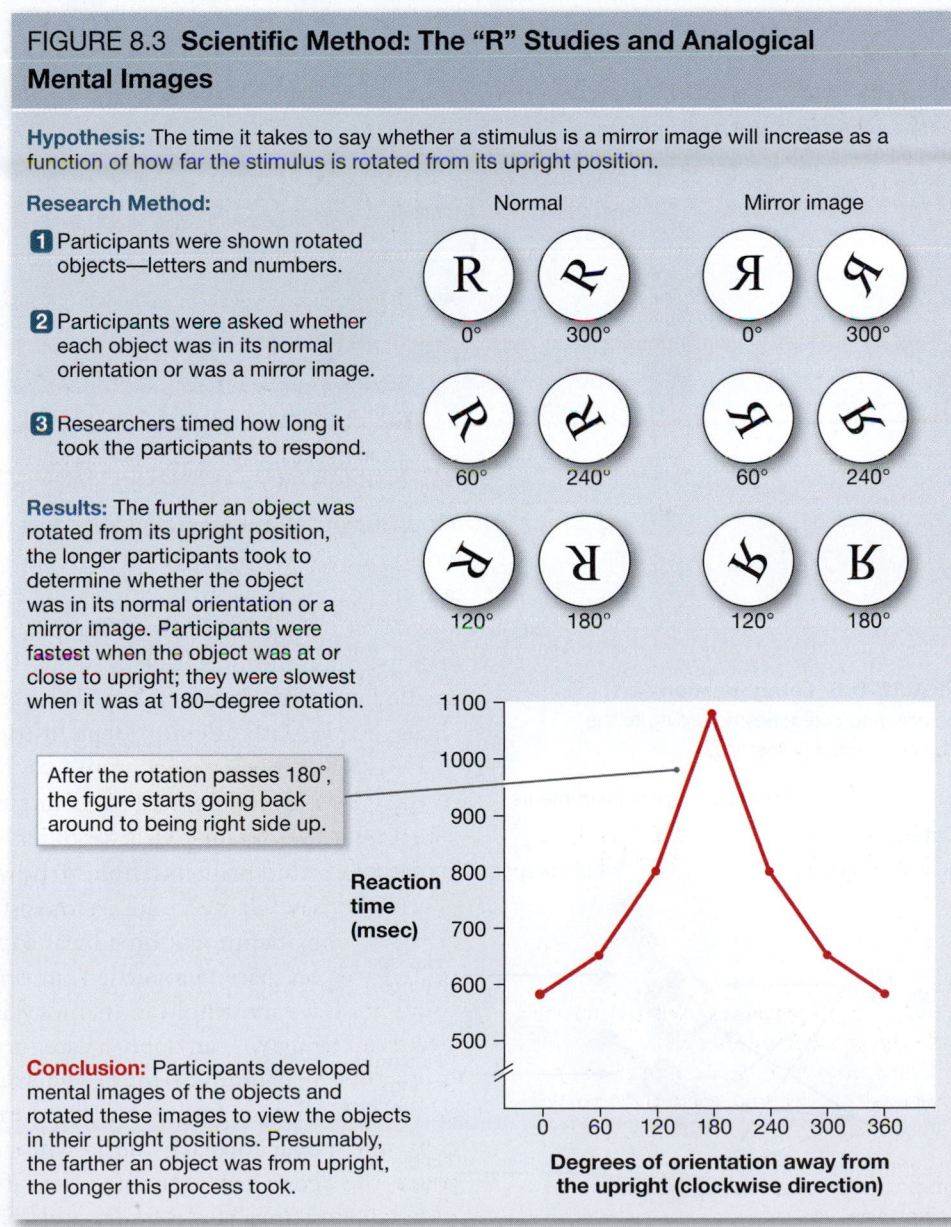

FIGURE 8.3 **Scientific Method: The "R" Studies and Analogical Mental Images**

Hypothesis: The time it takes to say whether a stimulus is a mirror image will increase as a function of how far the stimulus is rotated from its upright position.

Research Method:

1. Participants were shown rotated objects—letters and numbers.

2. Participants were asked whether each object was in its normal orientation or was a mirror image.

3. Researchers timed how long it took the participants to respond.

Results: The further an object was rotated from its upright position, the longer participants took to determine whether the object was in its normal orientation or a mirror image. Participants were fastest when the object was at or close to upright; they were slowest when it was at 180–degree rotation.

After the rotation passes 180°, the figure starts going back around to being right side up.

Conclusion: Participants developed mental images of the objects and rotated these images to view the objects in their upright positions. Presumably, the farther an object was from upright, the longer this process took.

Normal | Mirror image

R 0° R 300° | Я 0° Я 300°

R 60° R 240° | Я 60° Я 240°

R 120° R 180° | Я 120° Я 180°

Reaction time (msec)

Degrees of orientation away from the upright (clockwise direction)

FIGURE 8.4 **Try for Yourself: Conceptual Mental Maps**

When asked whether San Diego or Reno is farther east, your symbolic knowledge probably informed you that California is farther west than Nevada.

So your conceptual mental map made you think that San Diego was west of Reno.

But this real map, showing location relative to uniform lines of longitude, shows that symbolic knowledge was inadequate in this case.

Explanation: Symbolic representations can lead to errors, because we can represent only a limited range of knowledge analogically and thus use memory shortcuts unconsciously. In this case, you probably were not taking into account the way northern Nevada juts west and southern California juts east.

Try for Yourself: Which is farther north, Seattle, Washington, or Montreal, Canada? You probably are picturing a mental map that looks like this, but be careful—consider the lines of latitude on a real map.

Answer: Seattle (47° north latitude) is north of Montreal (45° north latitude).

Consider the following question about two U.S. cities: *Which is farther east, San Diego, California, or Reno, Nevada?* If you are like most people (at least most Americans), you answered that Reno is farther east than San Diego, though in fact, San Diego is farther east than Reno. Even if you formed an analogical representation of a map of the southeastern United States, your symbolic knowledge probably told that a city on the Pacific Coast is always farther west than a city in a state that does not border the Pacific Ocean. However, a symbolic representation can yield a wrong answer in this instance, because while our general knowledge is correct, it does not take into account the way Nevada juts west and the Pacific Coast near Mexico juts east. The regularization of irregular shapes in memory is a shortcut we use unconsciously for keeping information in memory; while generally useful, such shortcuts can lead to errors (**FIGURE 8.4**).

Concepts Are Symbolic Representations

Much of our thinking reflects not only visual representations of objects in the world but also our general knowledge about the world. Our symbolic representations consist of words, which can represent abstract ideas in a succinct verbal form. Picturing a lemon, for example, does not tell you what to do with a lemon or how a lemon tastes. But knowing that parts of a lemon are edible helps you decide how to use the fruit—such as squeezing its juice onto a piece of fish. Thus what you do with a lemon depends on how you think about it. One question of interest to cognitive psychologists is how we use knowledge about objects efficiently. As discussed in Chapter 7, our memory systems are organized so we quickly can call up information as needed. The same principle holds true when we think about objects. If asked to say what a violin is, for instance, most people probably would begin by defining it broadly as a musical instrument. Grouping things based on shared properties, *categorization,* reduces the amount of knowledge we must hold in memory and is therefore an efficient way of thinking. We can apply a category such as "musical instruments"—objects that produce music when played—automatically to all members of the category rather than storing this same bit of knowledge over and over for each musical instrument. We have to store unique knowledge for each member of a category, however, such as "has four strings" for a violin and "has six strings" for a guitar (**FIGURE 8.5**).

FIGURE 8.5 Categorization We group objects into categories according to the objects' shared properties.

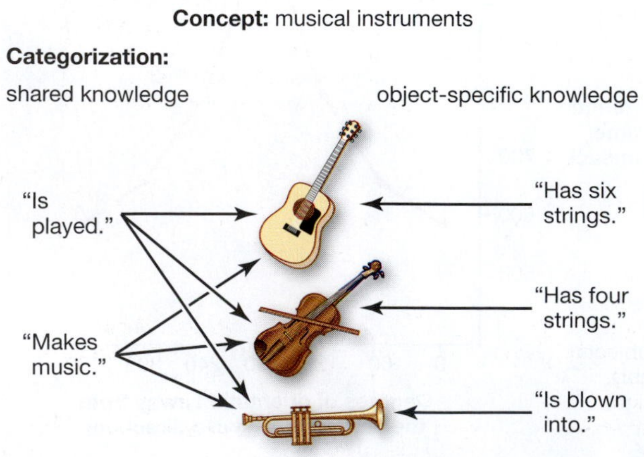

Concept: musical instruments

Categorization:

shared knowledge   object-specific knowledge

"Is played."   "Has six strings."

          "Has four strings."

"Makes music."

          "Is blown into."

A **concept** is a category, or class, that includes subtypes and/or individual items. A concept can consist of mental representations (musical instruments, fruits, bachelors, what have you), of a relation between representations (e.g., "violins are smaller than violas," "elephants are heavier than mice"), or of a quality or dimension, such as brightness or width. By allowing us to organize mental representations around a common theme, a concept ensures that we do not have to store every instance of an object, a relation, or a quality or dimension individually. Instead, we store an abstract representation based on the properties that particular items or particular ideas share.

Consider the concept of a bachelor. If asked to, you probably could indicate whether each of your male acquaintances is a bachelor. According to the **defining attribute model** of concepts, each concept is characterized by a list of features that are necessary to determine if an object is a member of the category. The dictionary defines a bachelor as a male who has not married, so this concept's defining attributes would be *male* and *unmarried;* for a musical instrument, attributes would include *is a device that produces sound* (**FIGURE 8.6**).

Although the defining attribute model is intuitively appealing, it fails to capture many key aspects of how we organize things in our heads. First, the model suggests that membership within a category is on an all-or-none basis, but in reality we often make exceptions in our categorizations, allowing members into groups even if they do not have all the attributes or excluding them even if they have all the attributes. For instance, most people would include *can fly* as an attribute of *bird.* However, some birds, such as penguins, cannot fly. In addition, some people use spoons and even saws to play music, yet we do not usually categorize a spoon or saw as a musical instrument.

Second, the defining attribute model suggests that all of a given category's attributes are equally salient in terms of defining that category. However, research demonstrates not only that some attributes are more important for defining membership than others but that the boundaries between categories are much fuzzier than the defining attribute model suggests. For example, *has wings* is generally considered a clear attribute of *bird,* whereas *is warm-blooded* does not as readily come

concept A mental representation that groups or categorizes objects, events, or relations around common themes.

defining attribute model The idea that a concept is characterized by a list of features that are necessary to determine if an object is a member of the category.

FIGURE 8.6 The Defining Attribute Model In the defining attribute model, concepts are organized hierarchically, such that they can be superordinate or subordinate to each other. For example, horns and stringed instruments are subordinate categories of the superordinate category of musical instruments.

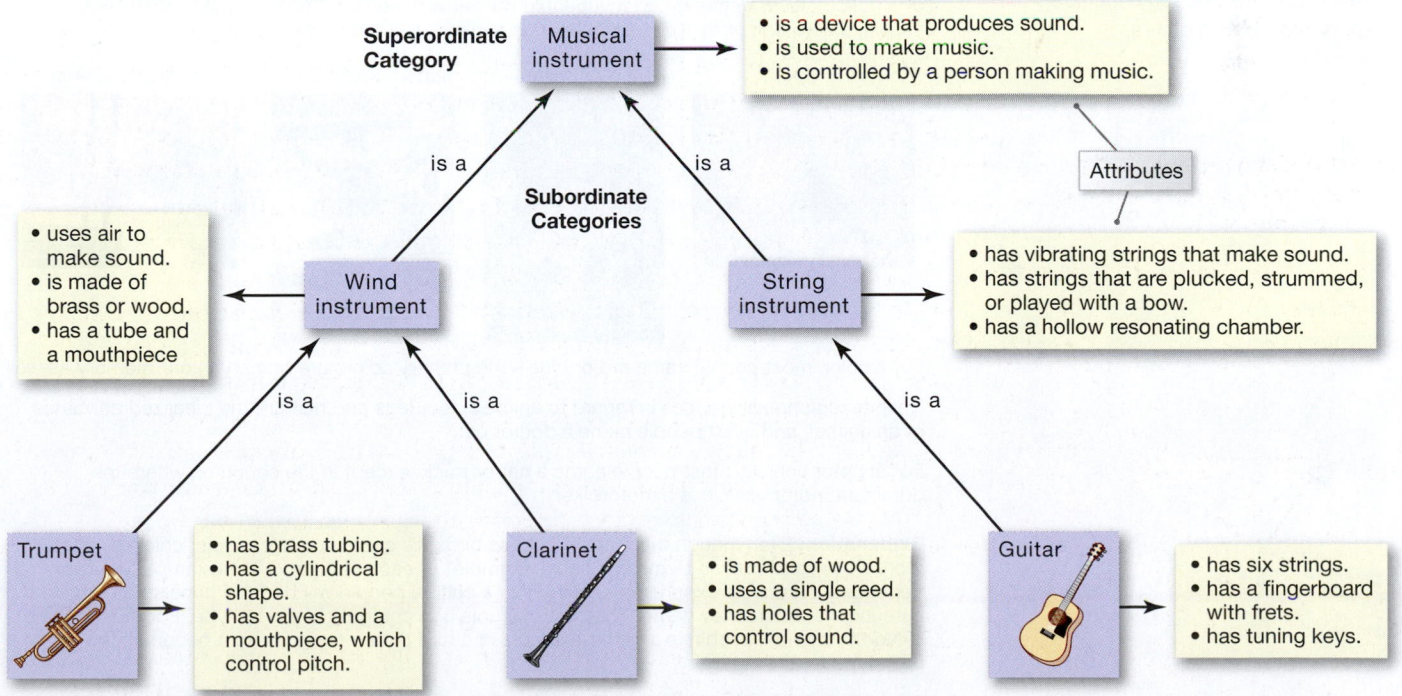

Category: instruments

Prototypical ──────────────▶ Nonprototypical

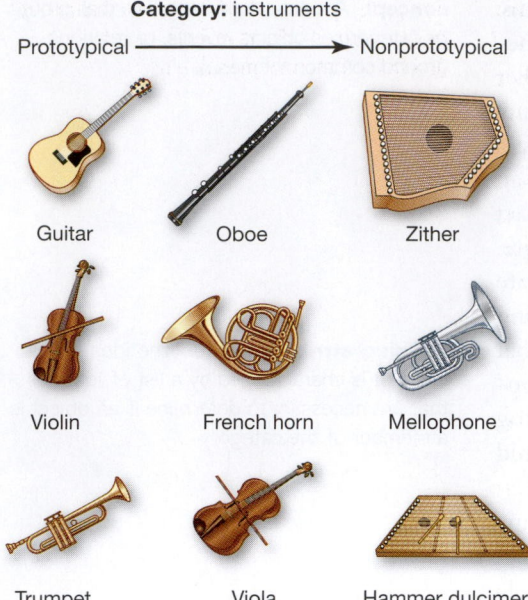

Guitar   Oboe   Zither

Violin   French horn   Mellophone

Trumpet   Viola   Hammer dulcimer

FIGURE 8.7 The Prototype Model
According to the prototype model, some items within a group or class are more representative (or prototypical) of that category than are other items within that group or class.

prototype model An approach to object categorization that is based on the premise that within each category, some members are more representative than others.

to mind when we think of birds, so being warm blooded is not salient in how we think about birds.

Third, the model posits that all members of a category are equal in category membership—no one item is a better fit than any other. Consider again the concept of a bachelor. According to the definition, a 16-year-old boy, a man who has been in a committed relationship for 25 years but never married, and a man in his 30s who goes on dates a few nights a week would equally exemplify the category *bachelor.* Do they seem the same to you?

Among the alternatives to the defining attribute model is the **prototype model** of concepts (**FIGURE 8.7**). In thinking about a category, we tend to think of terms of a "best example," or *prototype,* for that category (**FIGURE 8.8**).

One positive feature of the prototype model is that it allows for flexibility in the representation of concepts. One drawback related to that flexibility is that a particular prototype can be chosen for different reasons: Is it the most common example of that particular category? Is it a representation that all category members most resemble?

FIGURE 8.8 Try for Yourself: The Prototype Model of Concepts

For each of the following categories, name the first member that comes into your mind (based on demonstration from Decyk, 1994):

a bird _____
a hero _____
a color _____
an animal _____
a motor vehicle _____

Result: For a bird, you likely named a robin or sparrow if you live in North America. If you live in Australia, you might have named a kiwi. Wherever you live, you probably named a common bird in your country—a bird that seems to represent an idealized version of all birds.

For a hero, most people name a superhero such as Superman, Spiderman, or Mighty Mouse, or a police officer or firefighter; few people will name a woman, child, or real animal (such as Lassie, a hero dog from a popular television series), all of whom can be heroes.

   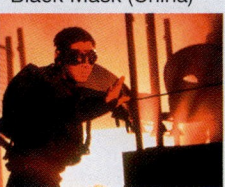

Robin (Europe)   Kiwi (Australia)   Superman (U.S.)   Black Mask (China)

For a color, most people name red or blue—the primary colors are primary in our memory as well.

Despite regional differences in regard to animals, four legs and hair are the idealized attributes of an animal, and most people name a dog or cat.

For a motor vehicle, most people name a car or truck, except in the countries where the dominant motor vehicle is a motorbike.

Explanation: Even though there are countless birds we could name (penguin, chicken, dodo, etc.), we tend to think in terms of a "best example" of each category. The example will vary depending on our life experiences, but within a culture people will be fairly consistent in the category members they name. The best example of a category is a prototype. For most people in North America, a robin is a better example of a bird than a penguin, so it becomes the prototype for the category.

Or does it represent a combination of typical attributes? The **exemplar model** addresses this concern, proposing that any concept has no single best representation—instead, all the examples, or *exemplars,* of category members form the concept (**FIGURE 8.9**). For instance, your representation of dogs is made up of all the dogs you have encountered in your life. If you see an animal in your yard, you compare this animal with your memories of other animals you have encountered. If it most closely resembles the dogs you have encountered (as opposed to the cats, squirrels, rats, and other animals), you conclude it is a dog. How would you explain the difference between a dog and a cat to someone who has never seen either? Dogs bark, but a dog is still a dog if it does not bark. It is still a dog if it loses its tail or a leg. The exemplar model assumes that through experience people form a fuzzy representation of a concept because there is no single representation of any concept. And the exemplar model accounts for the observation that some category members are more prototypical than others: The prototypes are simply members we have encountered more often.

If you have spent much time with a preschool child who is forming concepts, you probably know how fascinating it can be to see these cognitive processes develop. Many years ago, this book's coauthor Diane Halpern was standing in line at the supermarket with her toddler son in the cart. When her son saw a man standing in line in front them, he began to yell out, "Daddy, Daddy!" The man in front of them became red-faced and stammered in an equally loud voice that he was not the daddy of this child, while other people in line laughed. For the toddler, all men with certain characteristics belonged in the category *Daddy.* Similarly, children may categorize cats as dogs or all soft brown foods as dog food. As young children develop, they refine and narrow their categories.

The defining attribute and prototype models explain how we classify objects we encounter and how we represent those objects in our minds. The following section considers how in our daily lives we use classifications and representations.

Schemas Organize Useful Information about Environments

How we think about the world extends well beyond a simple list of facts about the specific items we encounter every day. Rather, a different class of knowledge, called *schemas,* enables us to interact with the complex realities of our daily environments. As discussed in Chapter 7, schemas help us perceive, organize, and process information. As we move through various real-world settings, we act appropriately by drawing on knowledge of what objects, behaviors, and events apply to each setting. For example, at a casino blackjack table it is appropriate to squeeze in between the people already sitting down. However, if a stranger tried to squeeze into a group of people dining together in a restaurant, the group's reaction would likely be quite negative. This kind of knowledge regarding situations and social contexts differs greatly from the knowledge associated with object classification.

Basically, researchers believe we develop schemas about the different types of real-life situations we encounter. One prominent theory in this domain has focused on schemas about the sequences of events in certain situations. Roger Schank and Robert Abelson (1977) have referred to these schemas about

exemplar model Information stored about the members of a category is used to determine category membership.

FIGURE 8.9 The Exemplar Model The exemplar model holds that all members of a category are exemplars. For example, even this strange-looking feline—a brown tortie white and tabby sphinx—is an exemplar of the category *cats.*

(a)

(b)

(c)

FIGURE 8.10 Script Theory of Schemas
According to this theory, we tend to follow general scripts of how to behave in particular settings. **(a)** At the movies, for example, we expect to buy a ticket, the cost of which might depend on the moviegoer's age and the time of day. **(b)** Next, we might opt to buy a snack before selecting a seat. **(c)** Although quiet talking might be appropriate before the movie, most of us expect talking to cease once the feature begins.

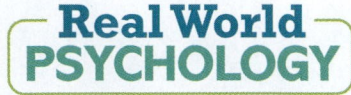
Real World PSYCHOLOGY

sequences as *scripts.* For example, *going to the movies* is a script most of us are familiar with (**FIGURE 8.10**).

Gender roles, the prescribed behaviors for females and males, are one type of schema. These scripts operate at the unconscious level: We follow them without consciously knowing we are doing so. One reason we need to become aware of the way schemas and scripts direct our thinking is that they may unconsciously cause us to think, for example, that women are generally unsuited for positions of leadership because they lack assertiveness. A recent study found that both men and women believe male leaders "take charge" but that female leaders "take care." These beliefs reflect a fundamental fallacy: The underlying assumption is that these traits are mutually exclusive, that leaders cannot take charge *and* take care. By dichotomizing leadership behaviors as either feminine or masculine, we limit women and men to narrow ranges of behaviors instead of encouraging both take-charge and take-care behaviors from our leaders (Catalyst, 2006). In a recent cross-cultural study of female leaders who made it to the tops of their professions while taking on family responsibilities such as child care, Halpern and Cheung (2008) found that these women had redefined the schemas of *good leader* and *good mother* in ways that make them compatible. Being leaders helped these women be better mothers, just as being mothers helped make them better leaders.

We can employ schemas because (a) common situations have consistent attributes (e.g., libraries are quiet and contain books), and (b) people have specific roles within situational contexts (e.g., a librarian behaves differently in a library than a reader does). Unfortunately, schemas and scripts, like prototypes, sometimes have unintended consequences, such as reinforcing sexist or racist beliefs (**FIGURE 8.11**). For example, when children and teens are asked to draw a scientist, very few draw women as scientists, because they unconsciously associate being a scientist with being male (Chambers, 1983). You could try this experiment with your family members and friends and see how many of them assume that scientists are men. (Stereotypes are discussed extensively in Chapter 12, "Social Psychology.")

Scripts dictate appropriate behaviors, and what we view as appropriate is shaped by culture. The script for a heterosexual date, perhaps "dating" back to the automobile's invention, traditionally has involved the male driving and paying for dinner. In the 1950s, a black person's script for getting on a bus in the southern United States involved going to the back of the bus. The schemas and scripts that children learn will likely affect their behavior when they are older. In one recent study, children aged two to six were asked to use props and dolls to act out a social evening for adults (Dalton et al., 2005). As part of the role play, each child selected items from a miniature grocery store stocked with 73 products, including beer, wine, and cigarettes. Two of the most common items purchased were alcohol (by 62 percent) and cigarettes (by 28 percent). Children whose parents smoked or consumed alcohol were four times more likely to select them. When the children were asked about the items they chose, alcohol and cigarettes were clearly included in most children's scripts for adult social life. One four-year-old girl who selected cigarettes explained, "I need this for my man. A man needs cigarettes."

If scripts and schemas are potentially problematic, why do they persist? Their adaptive value is that they minimize the amounts of attention required to navigate familiar environments. They also allow us to recognize and avoid unusual or dangerous situations. Mental representations in all forms assist us in using information about objects and events in adaptive ways. Manipulating our mental representations—that is, thinking about objects, events, and circumstances—allows us to take appropriate actions, make intelligent decisions, and function efficiently in our daily lives.

(a)

(b)

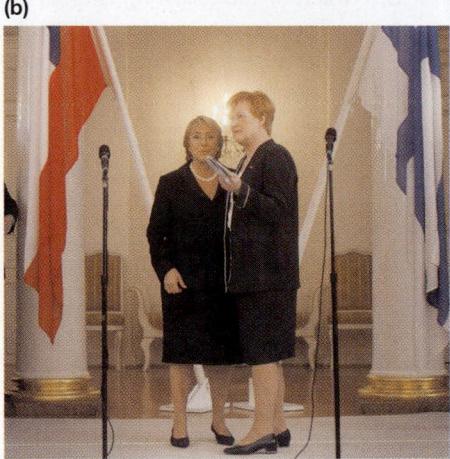

FIGURE 8.11 Scripts Distorted by Stereotypes (a) Many reactions to the presidential candidacies of Hillary Clinton and Barack Obama reflected stereotypical scripts that exist in the United States. **(b)** Different countries have different scripts concerning gender, race, leadership, and many other issues; here, Chilean President Michelle Bachelet **(left)** meets with Finnish President Tarja Halonen **(right)** in May 2007.

⊳ SUMMING UP

How Does the Mind Represent Information?

Our thoughts consist of mental representations of the objects and events we learn about in our environments. When we think of an object, we often bring to mind a visual image, or analogical representation, of the object. By contrast, a symbolic representation will correspond not to the object's physical features but to our knowledge of the object. Much of our knowledge of the world is based on concepts, which are ways of classifying objects. Concepts are based on either defining attributes, prototypes, or exemplars. Schemas assist us in organizing information so that it is useful in our daily lives, such as in understanding what script to follow in a restaurant. Scripts allow us to make quick judgments with little effort, but they can also lead to thinking in stereotypical ways.

⊳ MEASURING UP

1. Indicate whether each of the following examples is an analogical or symbolic representation.

   _____ **a.** a watch with a standard watch face
   _____ **b.** a digital watch
   _____ **c.** a drawing of the information in a math problem
   _____ **d.** the word *rouge,* meaning "red" in French
   _____ **e.** a photograph of your best friend
   _____ **f.** a mental image of your best friend
   _____ **g.** a sketch of a football play

How Do We Make Decisions and Solve Problems?

The previous sections discussed how we represent and organize knowledge of the world. But how do we use knowledge to guide our daily actions? Throughout each day we make decisions: what to eat for breakfast, which clothes to wear, which route to take to work or school, and so on. We scarcely notice making many of these decisions. Some decisions, such as about which college to attend, whether to buy a house, and if it is time to commit to one's relationship partner, are much more consequential and require greater reflection. We also solve problems, as in figuring out how to break bad news or identifying the best way to study for a particular exam. Thinking enables us to do these things.

Sometimes the terms *reasoning, decision making,* and *problem solving* are used interchangeably, but there are differences among them. In **reasoning,** you determine if a conclusion is valid, using information you believe is true. In **decision making,** you select among alternatives, usually by identifying important criteria and determining how well each alternative satisfies these criteria. If you can go to Paris or Cancún for your spring break, for example, you need to choose either one. If you need to solve a calculus problem and know several ways to do it, you might want to select the fastest method. In **problem solving,** you overcome obstacles to move from a present state to a desired goal state. For example, if you decide to go to Paris but do not have enough money for a plane ticket, or if you cannot figure out a solution on a calculus test, you have a problem. In general, you have a problem when a barrier or a gap exists between where you are and where you want to be.

reasoning Using information to determine if a conclusion is valid or reasonable.

decision making Attempting to select the best alternative among several options.

problem solving Finding a way around an obstacle to reach a goal.

People Use Deductive and Inductive Reasoning

How do we evaluate evidence to draw conclusions? A police detective sifts through all the clues and tries to identify the right suspect. A parent listens to two children's conflicting stories and tries to figure out the truth. A scientist analyzes data to see if they support or refute a given hypothesis. Each situation requires reasoning, or evaluating information, arguments, and beliefs to draw a conclusion. Psychological scientists generally distinguish between *deductive* and *inductive reasoning,* although in real life, people switch back and forth between the two classes. In **deductive reasoning,** you reason from the general to the specific, as in expecting a person from Vancouver to be friendly because you have heard the people there are friendly. In **inductive reasoning,** you reason from the

deductive reasoning Using a belief or rule to determine if a conclusion is valid (follows logically from the belief or rule).

inductive reasoning Using examples or instances to determine if a rule or conclusion is likely to be true.

specific to the general, as in deciding the people in Vancouver are friendly because the five people you have met from there are friendly. (The differences among deductive reasoning, inductive reasoning, decision making, and problem solving are presented in **FIGURE 8.12.**)

DEDUCTIVE REASONING In deductive reasoning, you use logic to draw specific conclusions under certain assumptions, or *premises*. For example, imagine you are deciding on a place to go for dinner and your friend Bonnie tells you the new Thai restaurant is excellent. If you like Thai food and think Bonnie has good taste, then choosing the place Bonnie has recommended might be an excellent decision. Deductive reasoning tasks are often presented as syllogisms, logical arguments containing premises (statements) and a conclusion. Syllogisms can be *conditional* or *categorical*. In a conditional syllogism, the argument takes the form *If A is true, then B is true.* The argument's conclusion is conditioned on whether the premise—the part that follows *If*—is true. If you can assume the premise is true, you can be certain about the conclusion. If Bonnie has good taste, then the Thai restaurant she recommends will have delicious food. If you like Thai cuisine, then you will enjoy your meal. These conclusions are deductively valid, because they follow the rules of "if, then" reasoning. The conclusion may or may not be true.

FIGURE 8.12 Deductive Reasoning, Inductive Reasoning, Decision Making, and Problem Solving

You use **deductive reasoning** to move from general to specific—you might expect your Parisian pen pal to be fashion conscious, because you have read that Parisians are.

You use **inductive reasoning** to move from specific to general—you might expect people from France to be friendly because you have met several people from there who are friendly.

You use **decision making** to select among options—if you prefer cityscapes to beaches, you might visit Paris instead of Cancún.

You use **problem solving** to overcome obstacles such as getting lost or a delayed flight.

In a categorical syllogism, the logical argument contains two premises and a conclusion, which can be determined to be either valid or invalid. Categorical syllogisms take the following form:

All A are B.   All chimpanzees are primates.
All B are C.   All primates are mammals.
Therefore, all A are C.   Therefore, all chimpanzees are mammals.

This conclusion is valid in that it follows logically from the premises. Now consider this syllogism:

All people from Vancouver are friendly.
Some friendly people like Thai food.
Therefore, some people from Vancouver like Thai food.

In this case, the conclusion is invalid. After all, since some friendly people might not like Thai food, it is possible that no one in Vancouver likes Thai food, so it is impossible to determine from the information provided if some people from Vancouver like Thai food. Knowing a person is from Vancouver, even accepting the unlikely premise that all people from Vancouver are friendly, does not help us deduce that person's culinary preferences when we reason with categorical syllogisms.

Deductive reasoning allows the reasoner to determine a statement's validity given the premises. However, the reasoner can come up with a valid but incorrect conclusion if the premises use terms inconsistently or ambiguously. Consider the following:

Nothing is better than a piece of warm apple pie.
A few crumbs of bread are better than nothing.
Therefore, a few crumbs of bread are better than warm apple pie.

The ambiguity of the word *nothing* causes a logical error in this syllogism.

Categorical syllogisms can have other problems. Although we often assume that deductive reasoning principles should apply equally in all circumstances, research indicates that our prior beliefs (schemas) about typical events and typical situations can influence our performances on reasoning tasks (Klauer, Musch, & Naumer, 2000). For instance, if you were told that *all foods made with spinach are delicious* and that *the cake is made with spinach,* the valid conclusion would be that *the cake is delicious,* but you might have certain ideas about what cakes should be made of, and—in the real world, as opposed to the world of abstract reasoning—those ideas will influence what conclusions you are willing to accept as valid. Even though this conclusion is deductively valid, in the real world a spinach cake is unlikely to be delicious for many people. It is important to understand the difference between a valid conclusion and truth. In deductive reasoning, a conclusion follows logically from its premises, it is valid, but it may or may not be true.

INDUCTIVE REASONING In some situations, we can determine the validity of a conclusion about a specific instance based on general premises, or statements we assume to be true. There are few everyday instances, however, in which we can use deductive reasoning. A more common reasoning problem is to determine general principles from specific instances. For example, suppose you have arranged to meet a new friend for lunch, and your friend is late. In this instance, you might conclude that special circumstances resulted in your new friend's tardiness. After a number of such instances, however, you might *induce* the general conclusion that your friend is usually tardy. In this way, you would make a conclusion about your friend's behavior based on several separate instances.

The use of the scientific method to discover general principles is one example of inductive reasoning. If a group of researchers hypothesize that students involved in school clubs perform better academically, they might select a random sample of students, half of whom participate in school clubs and half of whom do not, and compare their grade point averages. Finding that the students in school clubs have significantly higher GPAs would lead to the general conclusion that, overall, students who participate in school clubs perform better academically. In other words, the researchers would induce a general principle from the specific instances of the students in the experiment.

As discussed in Chapter 2, the scientific method dictates that scientists meet certain standards when inducing general principles from several specific instances. These standards are designed to guard against biases in inductive reasoning. For example, researchers need an adequately large sample size to infer that a hypothesis is likely true. In day-to-day life, however, we may be more likely to reach inappropriate conclusions when reasoning about general principles from everyday circumstances. Say, for instance, you are considering buying a car that was highly rated by a consumer magazine, but a friend tells you that when his uncle had that type of car, it broke down all the time. Because it is based on a very small sample (one person's experience), this report should have little weight on your purchasing decision. However, using stories as a way of understanding may be hardwired in us as a result of our evolutionary history (Gardner, 2008). We often are strongly influenced by anecdotal reports, especially when an anecdote comes from someone close to us—even from someone we know remotely, such as a friend's uncle—more than a conclusion drawn from a faceless mass of research participants. Indeed, physicians often lament that their patients reject therapies supported by science but gladly accept ones supported by testimonials (Diotallevi, 2008).

Decision Making Often Involves Heuristics

Research on decision making has been influenced by *normative models* and *descriptive models*. Historically speaking, normative models of decision making have viewed humans as optimal decision makers, who always select the choice that yields the largest gain, which usually means the most money because these theories were developed from traditional economics. More recently, descriptive models have tried to account for humans' tendencies to misinterpret and misrepresent the probabilities underlying many decision making scenarios and to act irrationally even when they understand the probabilities. Psychologists focus on understanding how humans make decisions in everyday life—especially when those decisions fail to comply with the predictions of "rational" behavior. Because we often need to make decisions without taking time to consider all the possible pros and cons, processes that allow us to make decisions quickly are useful for dealing with many real-world challenges.

Expected utility theory is one normative model of how humans should make decisions (von Neumann & Morgenstern, 1947). The theory views decision making as a computation of *utility,* the overall value for each possible outcome in a decision making scenario. Thus, according to this theory, we make decisions by considering the possible alternatives and choosing the most desirable one. To arrive at the most desirable alternative, we first rank the alternatives in order of preference, determining whether each is more desirable, less desirable, or equally desirable compared with each competing alternative. For example, if you were deciding what to do after graduation, you would list the alternatives, which might include getting a job as a ski instructor, going to law school, or trying to make a living as a musician. The rational way to decide would be to rank order these alternatives and select the one with the most utility, or value, to you. But do we always choose the most desirable alternative?

In the 1970s, Amos Tversky and Daniel Kahneman spearheaded descriptive research on both reasoning and decision making. Because of the importance of both reasoning and decision making in economic theory, Kahneman received the Nobel Prize in economics for their research. (Tversky was deceased when the prize was awarded.) In examining how people make everyday decisions, Tversky and Kahneman identified several common **heuristics,** the mental shortcuts or rules of thumb that people typically use to make decisions.

Psychologists distinguish between heuristics and algorithms. An *algorithm* is a procedure that, if followed correctly, will always yield the correct answer. If you wanted to know the area of a circle, for example, you could get the right answer by multiplying pi (3.1416) by the radius squared. This formula is an algorithm because it will always work. Similarly, if you follow a recipe exactly, it should always yield pretty much the same outcome. If you substitute one ingredient for another (say, using honey instead of the sugar the recipe calls for, estimating the sweetness), you are using a heuristic—an informed guide. Your result will likely be fine, but there is no guarantee. Heuristic thinking often occurs unconsciously; we are not aware of taking these mental shortcuts. Indeed, heuristic processing is useful partly because it allows us to focus our attention on other things, since the conscious mind's processing capacity is limited. Heuristics require minimal cognitive resources.

Heuristic thinking can be adaptive in that it allows us to decide quickly rather than weighing all the evidence each time we have to decide. People might always buy the second-cheapest item, no matter what they are buying, because they believe that by using this strategy they save money but avoid purchasing the worst products. Other people might buy only brand names. Such quick rules of thumb often provide reasonably good decisions. However, as Tversky and Kahneman have demonstrated, heuristics can also result in biases, which may lead to errors or faulty decisions. Consider the commonly believed heuristic that a high price equals high quality. Although laboratory studies show that one type of soap is basically as good as any other, high prices have convinced many consumers that "fancy" soaps are superior.

heuristics In problem solving, shortcuts (rules of thumb or informal guidelines) used to reduce the amount of thinking that is needed to move from an initial state to a goal state.

availability heuristic Making a decision based on the answer that most easily comes to mind.

CRITICAL THINKING SKILL

Understanding How the Availability and Representativeness Heuristics Can Affect Thinking

The **availability heuristic** is the tendency, when we think about events or make judgments (especially judgments regarding frequency), to rely on information that is easy to retrieve. For example, in the study on false fame—discussed in Chapter 7, "Attention and Memory"—the made-up names were available in memory for the participants who had read them aloud the day before, even if the participants could not have said where they heard the names. Based on their familiarity with the names, these participants decided the people were famous. The demonstration, earlier in this chapter, that prototypes come to mind when we think about certain categories shows that prototypes are readily available in memory.

Consider this question: In most industrialized countries, are there more farmers or more librarians? If you do not live in an agricultural area, you probably said librarians; if you live in an agricultural area, you probably said farmers. Most people who answer this question think of the librarians they know (or know about) and the farmers they know (or know about), and if they can retrieve many more instances in one category, they assume it is the larger category. In fact, there are many more farmers than librarians, but people who live in cities and suburbs and may never have met a farmer will likely believe the opposite.

Consider this example: You supervise two people, one introverted and one extroverted, both of whom do comparably outstanding work. If you can promote only one of them, which employee is more likely to come to mind first? For most of us, the extroverted person would come to mind first. However, through more careful analysis we would be able to overcome the availability heuristic and systematically consider the merits of each employee.

We use the **representativeness heuristic** when we base a decision on the extent to which each option reflects what we already believe about a situation. For example, say that Helena is intelligent, ambitious, and scientific-minded. She enjoys working on mathematical puzzles, talking with other people, reading, and gardening. Would you guess that she is a cognitive psychologist or a postal worker? Most people would employ the representativeness heuristic; that is, they would guess that Helena is a cognitive psychologist, because these characteristics seem more representative of psychologists than of postal workers.

But the representativeness heuristic can lead to faulty reasoning if you fail to take other information into account, such as the *base rate,* or the frequency of an event's occurring. People pay insufficient attention to base rates in reasoning and instead focus on whether the information presented is representative of one conclusion or another. For example, there are many more postal workers than cognitive psychologists, so the base rate for postal workers is higher than that for cognitive psychologists. Therefore, any given person, including Helena, is much more likely to be a postal worker. Although Helena's traits may be more representative of cognitive psychologists overall, they also likely apply to a large number of postal workers.

We cannot be aware of every heuristic we rely on. Being aware of frequently used ones such as the availability and representativeness heuristics, however, and knowing they can lead us to make faulty judgments, can help us make more rational decisions (**FIGURE 8.13**).

representativeness heuristic A rule for categorization based on how similar the person or object is to our prototypes for that category.

Is *r* more commonly the first letter in a word or the third letter?

r _ _ _ _ ?   _ _ *r* _ _ ?

How would you determine the answer?

Result: If you are like most people, you have concluded that *r* is more often the first letter of a word. You might have tried to think of as many words as you could with *r* as the first letter (e.g., *right* or *read*) or *r* as the third letter (e.g., *care* or *sir*) and decided that *r* is more common at the beginning because those words came most easily to mind. However, *r* is much more likely to be the third letter in a word.

FIGURE 8.13 Think Critically: Availability Heuristic

FRAMING EFFECTS How information is presented can alter how people perceive it, and that effect is known as **framing.** Framing a decision to emphasize the potential losses or potential gains of at least one alternative can significantly influence the decision making. Consider the following problem:

> Imagine that the United States is preparing for the outbreak of a disease that is projected to kill about 600 people. Two alternative programs are proposed to combat the disease. According to scientific estimates, if Program A is chosen, 200 of the 600 people will be saved; if Program B is chosen, there is a one-third probability that all 600 people will be saved and a two-thirds probability that nobody will be saved. (p. 343)

framing The effect of presentation on how information is perceived.

Which would you choose? When asked this question, 72 percent of respondents chose program A (Kahneman & Tversky, 1984). Each program potentially could save 200 people, but respondents clearly preferred Program A's sure gain, as opposed to Program B's chance of a larger gain and additional chance of no gain.

Now consider these alternatives:

> If Program A is chosen, 400 people will die. If Program B is chosen, there is a one-third probability that nobody will die and a two-thirds probability that 600 people will die. (p. 343)

When asked this question, 78 percent of respondents chose program B. In this case, most people felt Program A's certain death of 400 people was a worse alternative than Program B's likely but uncertain death of 600 people. A sure loss was less appealing than an uncertain but possibly greater loss. However, the probabilities and outcomes in this second scenario are identical to those in the first, except that the gains are emphasized in the first and the losses are emphasized in the second. Clearly, framing the decision to emphasize gains or losses affects the decision making.

To account for framing's effects, Daniel Kahneman (2007) and Amos Tversky came up with *prospect theory,* a major theory in decision making. Their theory has two main components: (a) the need to take into account people's wealth in predicting their choices, and (b) the fact that because losses feel much worse than gains feel good, people try to avoid situations that involve losses.

In most traditional studies of decision making, participants were presented with two choices. One choice was a "sure thing," such as winning $200; the other choice was associated with a probability, such as having a .20 probability of winning $1,000. These choices had the same "expected utility"; that is, after numerous trials the first choice would have yielded $200 each time, while after numerous trials the second choice would have yielded an average of $200 each time (thanks to the .20 probability of winning $1,000). On those grounds, participants should have "preferred" the choices equally, since each choice would likely have yielded the same payoff. Because this choice was a one-time opportunity, however, participants who selected the second option would not win an average amount from numerous trials—they would win either $1,000 or $0. Given that reality, would you expect poorer people to have made the same selection as richer ones? A student struggling to pay bills and working for $10 an hour, for example, would likely pick the sure $200. A student with a high income, or with a rich and generous parent, would likely pick the gamble, because $200 would have less utility for that student. In other words, all money does not have the same subjective value.

According to the principle of *loss aversion,* the second component of Kahneman and Tversky's prospect theory, losing is much worse than gaining is good. Think how happy you would feel if someone walked over to you right now and handed you $1,000. Now think how bad you would feel if someone took $1,000 from your checking account (**FIGURE 8.14**).

Advertisers exploit this tendency to view costs and benefits differently. Suppose a gallon (roughly 3.75 liters) of gasoline costs U.S. $4.05. You get a discount of $.05 a gallon if you pay with cash. Sound good? Now suppose gasoline is $3.95 a gallon and you pay a surcharge of $.05 per gallon for using a credit card. Does the additional charge for using a credit card seem worse than the discount for using cash? The cost would prove identical in these two scenarios ($4.05 − $.05 = $4.00; $3.95 + $.05 = $4.00), but fewer people would be willing to pay the surcharge than to get the discount. Aware of framing's powerful effects and borrowing from Kahneman and Tversky's work, advertisers would frame the decision in terms of a discount (money gained) instead of a surcharge (money lost). The lure of saving money profoundly affects how we think.

AFFECTIVE FORECASTING Daniel Gilbert and Timothy Wilson (2007) have found that people are not good at knowing how they will feel about something

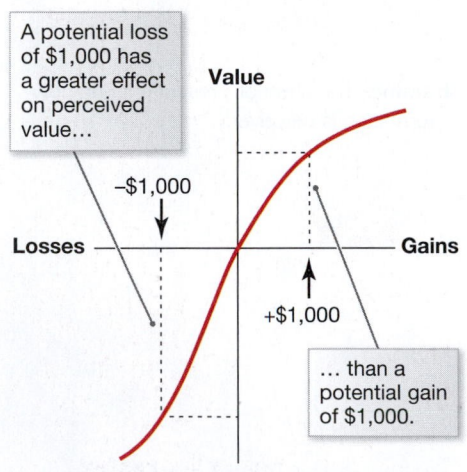

A potential loss of $1,000 has a greater effect on perceived value...

Value

−$1,000

Losses

Gains

+$1,000

... than a potential gain of $1,000.

FIGURE 8.14 Loss Aversion Potential losses affect decision making more than potential gains do.

in the future; even more important, people generally do not realize how poor they are at predicting their future feelings. Compelling evidence indicates that people overestimate the extent to which negative events, such as breaking up with a romantic partner, losing a job, or being diagnosed with a serious medical illness, will affect them in the future (Gilbert, Pinel, Wilson, Blumberg, & Wheatley, 1998; Wilson & Gilbert, 2003). It seems that when we think about the death of a loved one or the loss of a limb or some other tragic loss, we consider only the immediate, intense pain. Over time, however, life continues, with its daily joys and sorrows, so the pain of the loss becomes less salient against the backdrop of everyday events.

According to Gilbert and Wilson (2007), after a negative event, people engage in strategies that help them feel better, such as rationalizing why it happened and minimizing the event's importance. These strategies are generally adaptive in that they protect the sufferers' mental health—making sense of an event helps reduce its negative emotional consequences. Humans have an amazing capacity for manufacturing happiness, and even after suffering anguish because of a negative event, most people will adapt and return to their typical positive outlook. Consider, for example, a woman who had polio, a crippling disease that has virtually disappeared in most places in the world thanks to the polio vaccine, who is glad that she had polio because it has taught her how to persevere and overcome adversity. Generally, however, people seem unaware that they can find positive outcomes from tragic events, so when asked to predict how they will feel following an aversive event, they overestimate their pain and underestimate how well they will cope with the event (Gilbert, Morewedge, Risen, & Wilson, 2004).

Affective forecasting can also influence our perceptions of positive events. How would you feel if you won an Olympic medal? Just about anyone would feel very good, right? Consider, however, the American tennis player Mardy Fish. As he prepared for his final match at the 2004 Athens Olympics, he fantasized about standing on the podium listening to "The Star-Spangled Banner" and having a gold medal placed around his neck. Fish's Olympic performance was amazing. He was an unseeded player who made it to the medal stand, but instead of a gold medal he won a silver medal, and he cried tears of sadness rather than joy as he listened to the national anthem of Chile. The experience was bittersweet as he reflected on what he might have done differently to win the gold (**FIGURE 8.15**).

Perhaps ironically, Fish might have been happier if he had won a bronze medal instead of a silver one. According to research by the social psychologists Victoria Medvec, Scott Madey, and Thomas Gilovich, the subjective outcome of winning a silver medal can be more negative than that of winning a bronze. To test their hypothesis, Medvec and her colleagues (1995) studied videotapes of Olympic athletes' crucial moments. Observers watched, for instance, Jackie Joyner-Kersee complete her last long jump to win the bronze medal, Matt Biondi receive the silver medal for the 50-meter freestyle, and the Lithuanian men's basketball team receive bronze medals, and they rated the athletes' facial expressions on a 10-point emotional scale, "from agony to ecstasy." The researchers found consistent evidence that, both at the moment of finding out how they did and when they were on the podium, bronze medal winners were happier than those who won silver.

When asked how you would feel if you won an Olympic medal, you probably compared winning a medal to winning no medal. But as discussed in Chapter 5, recognizing the context is crucial to determining the sort of comparison being made. Winning silver or bronze seems like quite an achievement next to winning no medal, but for Olympic athletes winning silver does not measure up to winning gold.

FIGURE 8.15 Affective Forecasting
Mardy Fish **(left)** was disappointed when he won the silver medal for tennis at the 2004 Olympics.

Do any data support the idea that people who make good decisions have better lives? This question is difficult to answer because of the complexity of measuring the success of a life outcome. However, de Bruin, Parker, and Fischoff (2007), three leading researchers in the area of decision making, have studied this difficult question, and their answer is a resounding "Yes!" These researchers recruited a large sample of adults to take a series of tests. One test posed questions that drew on seven thinking skills like the ones in this book's critical thinking sections. (Among the skills drawn on was recognition of the framing effect, discussed just above. The researchers' underlying idea regarding the framing effect is that a good thinker should be less affected by a situation's framing than a poor thinker would be.)

The measurement of good life outcomes was based on a list of activities. In the past year, for example, had participants rented a movie but never watched it? Doing so represented poor decision making, especially if it happened several times in one year. Questions like this tested whether participants generally made good or bad decisions. Participants who performed better on the decision making test reported fewer negative life events than those who performed poorly on the test. In other words, applying critical thinking skills can positively affect multiple areas of a person's life. Learning and using the critical thinking skills presented in this book, for example, can pay off in a lifetime of better decisions.

Problem Solving Achieves Goals

Our thoughts are often focused on our goals and how to achieve them: How do you get into your car when you have locked the keys inside? How can you make enough money to spend your spring break somewhere nice? What do you have to do to get an *A* in this course? and so on. The following section examines some of the best ways to solve problems. For the purposes of this discussion, a person has a problem when he or she has no simple and direct means of attaining a particular goal. To solve the problem, the person must use knowledge to determine how to move from the current state to the goal state, often by devising strategies to overcome obstacles. How the person thinks about the problem can help or hinder that person's ability to find solutions.

ORGANIZATION OF SUBGOALS One approach to the study of problem solving is to identify people's steps in solving particular problems. Researchers examine how people proceed from one step to the next, the typical errors people make in negotiating tricky or unintuitive steps, and how people decide on more efficient (or, in some cases, less efficient) solutions. For example, in the classic "Tower of Hanoi" problem, participants are given a board that has a row of three pegs on it; the peg on one end has three discs stacked on it in a descending order of size, such that the largest disc is on the bottom. The task is to move the ordered stack of discs to the peg on the other end. Solving the problem requires breaking the task down into *subgoals* (**FIGURE 8.16**).

Using subgoals is important for many problems. Imagine a high school senior has decided she would like to become a doctor. To achieve this goal, she needs first to attain the more immediate subgoal of being admitted to a good college. To get into a good college, she needs to earn good grades in high school. This additional subgoal would require developing good study skills and paying attention in class. Breaking down a problem into subgoals is an important component of problem solving, although identifying the appropriate steps or subgoals and their order can be challenging for complex problems in which there is no obvious next step.

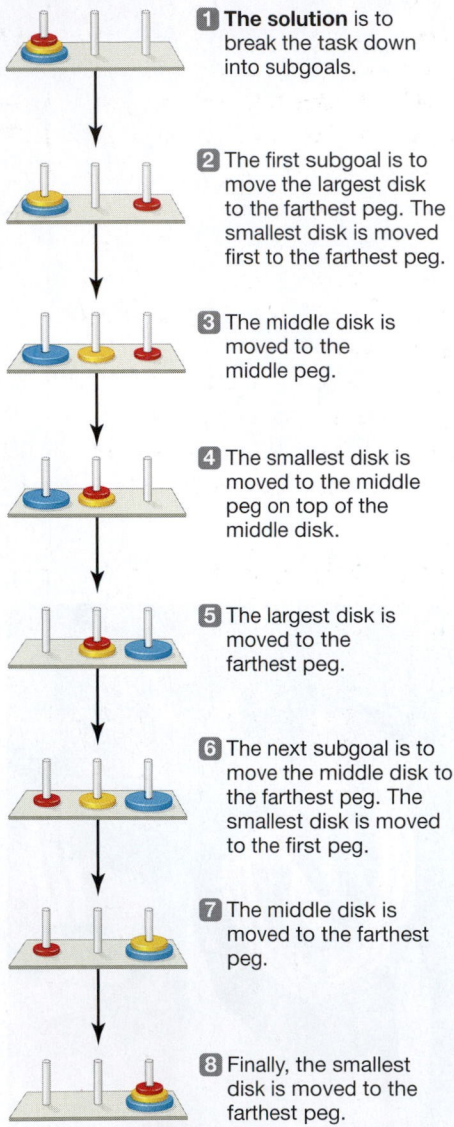

The task is to move the disks to the peg on the other end, moving only one disc at a time, and never placing a larger disc on top of a small disk.

1 **The solution** is to break the task down into subgoals.

2 The first subgoal is to move the largest disk to the farthest peg. The smallest disk is moved first to the farthest peg.

3 The middle disk is moved to the middle peg.

4 The smallest disk is moved to the middle peg on top of the middle disk.

5 The largest disk is moved to the farthest peg.

6 The next subgoal is to move the middle disk to the farthest peg. The smallest disk is moved to the first peg.

7 The middle disk is moved to the farthest peg.

8 Finally, the smallest disk is moved to the farthest peg.

You can simulate this problem by stacking a quarter, a nickel, and a penny.

FIGURE 8.16 **The Tower of Hanoi Problem**

SUDDEN INSIGHT Problems often are not identified as problems until they seem unsolvable and the problem solver is, more or less, stuck. Only when you spot the keys in the ignition of the locked car, for example, do you know you have a problem. Sometimes, as you stand there pondering the problem, a solution will pop into your head. How does this happen? **Insight** is the metaphorical mental light-bulb that goes on in someone's head when he or she suddenly realizes the solution to a problem.

insight The sudden realization of a solution to a problem.

In 1925, the Gestalt psychologist Wolfgang Köhler conducted one of psychology's most famous examples of research on insight. Convinced that some nonhuman animals could behave intelligently, Köhler studied whether chimpanzees could solve problems. He would place a banana outside a chimp's cage, just beyond the chimp's reach, and provide several sticks that the chimp could use. Could the chimp figure out how to move the banana within grabbing distance? In one situation, neither of two sticks was long enough to reach the banana. One chimpanzee, who sat looking at the sticks for some time, suddenly grabbed the sticks and joined them together by placing one stick inside an opening in the other stick. With this longer stick the chimp obtained the banana. Köhler argued that, after pondering the problem, the chimp had the insight to join the sticks into a tool long enough to reach the banana. Having solved that problem, the chimp transferred this solution to other, similar problems and solved them quickly.

In another classic study of insight, Norman Maier (1931) brought participants, one at a time, into a room that had two strings hanging from the ceiling and a table in the corner. On the table were several random objects, including a pair of pliers. Each participant was asked to tie the strings together. However, it was impossible to grab both strings at once—if a participant was holding one string, the other was too far away to grab. The solution was to tie the pliers onto one string and use that string as a pendulum; the participant could then hold the other string and grab the pendulum string as it swung by. Although a few participants eventually figured out this solution on their own, most people were stumped by the problem. After letting these people ponder the problem for ten minutes, Maier casually crossed the room and brushed up against the string, causing it to swing back and forth. Once the participants saw the brushed string swinging, most immediately solved the problem, as if they had experienced a new insight. However, these participants did not report that Maier had given them the solution. They all believed they had come up with it independently.

Maier's study also provides an example of how insight can be achieved when a problem initially seems unsolvable. In this case, most people had failed to see the pliers as a pendulum weight. To solve the problem, these people needed to reconsider the possible functions of the pliers and string. Thus how we view or represent a problem can significantly affect how easily we solve it. When a standard view does not work, the problem might be structured in other, less obvious ways. Often, for example, a student will ponder a problem or listen attentively to a lecture, then suddenly grin and exclaim, "Now I understand!" One successful lawyer reports that she spent the first three-fourths of her first year in law school in an intellectual fog, understanding little about the basic concepts. Then, something "clicked," and she suddenly understood the reasoning that lay behind legal principles. Although sayings such as "think outside the box" and "think different" have become clichés (at least in Western culture), the ideas they embody about insight have been around for a long time and continue to be of great value. Unfortunately, advice such as "think different"—or, to be grammatically correct, "think differently"—may not be very useful without guidelines for how to get started.

"Never, ever, think outside the box."

restructuring A new way of thinking about a problem that aids its solution.

mental set A problem solving strategy that has worked in the past.

CHANGING REPRESENTATIONS TO OVERCOME OBSTACLES *Have you heard about the new restaurant that opened on the moon? It has great food but no atmosphere!* The premise of this joke is that *atmosphere* means one thing when interpreted in light of the restaurant schema but means something else in the context of the moon. Humor often violates an expectation, so "getting" the humor means rethinking some common representation. In problem solving, too, we often need to revise a mental representation to overcome an obstacle.

Among the strategies that problem solvers commonly use to overcome obstacles is **restructuring** the problem—representing it in a novel way. This technique can yield a solution not available under the old problem structure, leading to the sudden "Aha!" moment characteristic of insight. In one now-famous study, Scheerer (1963) gave each participant a sheet of paper that had a square of nine dots on it. The task was to connect all nine dots using at most four straight lines, without lifting the pencil off the page (**FIGURE 8.17A**). As shown in **FIGURE 8.17B**, one solution is to see that keeping the lines within the box is not a requirement, although people tend to think the problem includes that restriction. Another solution is to use one *very* fat line that covers all nine dots. Solving the problem requires restructuring the representation by eliminating assumed constraints.

In trying to solve a problem, we commonly think back to how we have solved similar problems. We tend to persist with previous strategies, **mental sets,** which often are useful but sometimes make it difficult to find the best solution. In 1942, the Gestalt psychologist Abraham Luchins demonstrated a classic example of a mental set. He asked participants to measure out specified amounts of water, such as 100 cups, using three jars of different sizes. Say, for example, that jar A held 21 cups, jar B held 127 cups, and jar C held 3 cups. The solution to this problem was to fill jar B, use jar A to remove 21 cups from jar B's 127 cups, then use jar C to remove 3 cups of water twice, leaving 100 cups in jar B. The structure to the solution is $B - A - 2(C)$. Participants were given many of these problems, in each of which the jar sizes and goal measurements differed but the same formula applied. Then participants were given another problem: They were given jar A, which held 23 cups, jar B, which held 49 cups, and jar C, which held 3 cups, and were asked to measure out 20 cups. Even though the simplest solution was to fill jar A and use jar C to remove 3 cups from jar A's 23, participants usually came up with a much more complicated solution using all three jars. Having developed a mental set of using three jars in combination to solve this type of problem, they had trouble settling on the simpler solution of using only two jars. Surprisingly, when given a

FIGURE 8.17 **Scheerer's Nine-Dot Problem**

(a) **The task** is to connect the dots using at most four straight lines. Most participants consider only solutions that fit within the square formed by the dots.

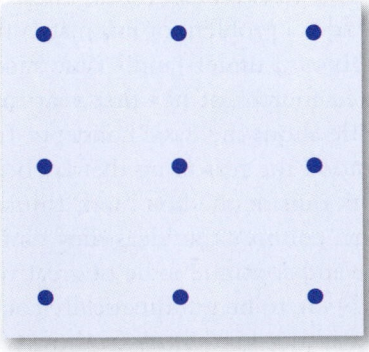

(b) **One solution** is to extend the lines beyond the boundary formed by the dots.

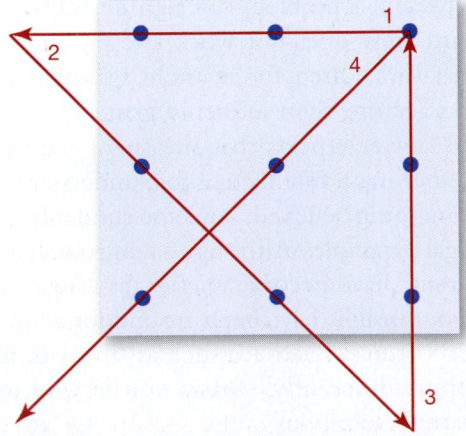

problem with a simple solution for which the original formula did not work, many participants failed to solve the problem most efficiently (**FIGURE 8.18**).

As demonstrated by Maier's experiment with the strings and pliers, discussed above, our mental representations about objects' typical functions can also create difficulties in problem solving. Overcoming *functional fixedness* requires the problem solver to reinterpret an object's potential function. One research example involves the candle problem, developed in 1945 by Karl Duncker. Participants are given a candle, a box of matches, a bulletin board, a box of tacks, and the following challenge: *Using only these objects, attach the candle to the bulletin board in such a way that the candle can be lit and burn properly* (**FIGURE 8.19**). Most people have difficulty in coming up with an adequate solution. However, if they reinterpret the function of the box, a solution emerges. The side of the box is tacked to the bulletin board so that it creates a stand; the candle is then placed on the box and lit. In general, subjects have difficulty viewing the box as a possible stand when it is being used as a container for the matches. When participants are shown representations of this problem with an empty box and the matches on the table next to it, they solve it somewhat more easily.

CONSCIOUS STRATEGIES Although restructuring mental representations is a valuable way to develop insight into solving a problem, we often find it difficult to enact this strategy consciously when we are stuck. However, we can always apply other strategies that may help lead to a solution.

One common heuristic strategy for overcoming obstacles is *working backward*. When the appropriate steps for solving a problem are not clear, proceeding from the goal state to the initial state can generate helpful strategies. Consider the "water lily" problem (Fixx, 1978, p. 50):

> Water lilies double in area every 24 hours. On the first day of summer there is only one water lily on the lake. It takes 60 days for the lake to be completely covered in water lilies. How many days does it take for half of the lake to be covered in water lilies?

One way to solve this problem is to work from the initial state to the goal state: You figure that on day 1 there is one water lily, so on day 2 there are two water lilies, on day 3 there will be four water lilies, and so on, until you discover how many water lilies there are on day 60 and see which day had half that many. But if you work backward, from the goal state to the initial state, you realize that if on day 60 the lake is covered in water lilies and that *water lilies double every 24 hours,* then on day 59 half of the lake must have been covered in water lilies.

Another common strategy for overcoming a problem solving obstacle is *finding an appropriate analogy* (Reeves & Weisberg, 1994). Say, for example, that a surgeon needs to use a laser at high intensity to destroy a patient's tumor. The surgeon must aim that laser so as to avoid destroying the surrounding living tissue. From his reading, the surgeon remembers a story about a general who wanted to capture a fortress. The general needed to move a large number of soldiers up to the fortress, but all the roads to the fortress were planted with mines. A large group of soldiers would have set off the mines, but a small group could travel safely, so the general divided the soldiers into small groups and had each group take a different road to the fortress, where the groups converged and attacked together. Because his problem had constraints analogous to the general's problem, the doctor got the idea to aim several lasers at the tumor from different angles. By itself, each laser was weak enough to avoid destroying the living tissue in its path, but the combined intensity of all the converging lasers was strong enough to destroy the tumor.

FIGURE 8.18 Luchins's Mental Set

The task is to measure out specified amounts of water using the three jars.

A B C

	Desired water	Jar A	Jar B	Jar C
Trial 1	100	21	127	3
Trial 2	8	18	48	11
Trial 3	62	10	80	4
Trial 4	31	20	59	4
Trial 5	29	20	57	4
Trial 6	20	23	49	3
Trial 7	25	28	76	3

In trials 1–6, **the solution** to getting the desired amount of water is to fill jar B, use jar A to remove water from jar B, and then use jar C to remove water twice. In the first trial, $127 - 21 - 2(3) = 100$; in the second trial, $48 - 18 - 2(11) = 8$; and so on.

In trial 6, **an easier solution** would be to fill jar A and remove water with jar C once to get the desired amount. Only this solution will work in trial 7.

FIGURE 8.19 Overcoming Functional Fixedness

The task is to attach a candle to the bulletin board using only a box of matches and a box of tacks.

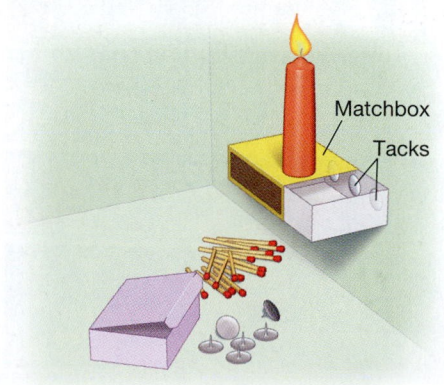

Matchbox

Tacks

The solution requires restructuring our concept of the matchbox by using it as a stand for the candle.

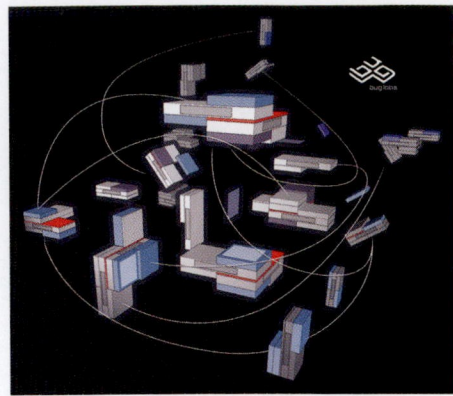
(a)

(b)

FIGURE 8.20 Analogies (a) Peter Semmelhack got the idea for his computer modules **(b)** while playing with Legos.

FIGURE 8.21 Paradox of Choice Having too many possibilities can make it difficult to choose one option.

Transferring a problem solving strategy—that is, using a strategy that works in one context to solve a structurally similar problem—requires paying attention to each problem's structure. Analogous problems enhance our ability to solve each one. Some researchers have found that participants who solve two or more analogous problems develop a schema that helps them solve similar problems (Gick & Holyoak, 1983). However, analogous solutions work only if people recognize the similarities between the problem they face and those they have solved (Keane, 1987; Reeves & Weisberg, 1994).

Consider a recent example of someone finding a creative solution to a problem by using an analogy from a different context. Peter Semmelhack (Bug Labs, n.d.), a software designer, was playing with Legos with his son when he had an idea for a new product. As Semmelhack assembled Lego pieces into a toy building, he imagined a new type of computer hardware. He thought: Suppose that users could decide what they wanted their computers to do and then could buy separate modules that snapped together into new machines and performed the desired functions. As easily as clicking a few Legos together, the consumers could design the computers of their dreams, with one module that downloaded music, one that turned the lights on at home, one that sent reminders about upcoming events, and so on. Semmelhack went on to build module units that could perform countless combinations of tasks and to start a company that sells those units. It will be interesting to see if his analogical thinking will yield big gains (**FIGURE 8.20**).

THE PARADOX OF CHOICE In modern society, many people believe the more options they have, the better. But daily life presents an ever-widening array of choices, from major ones concerning careers and health care plans to minor ones concerning breakfast cereals and beverages (Will that cup of coffee be a latte, a cappuccino, or a mocha? hot or cold? caffeinated or not? with skim or soy or regular milk? and so on). Although some choice is better than none, some scholars note that too much choice can be frustrating, unsatisfying, and ultimately debilitating (Schwartz, 2004).

Imagine if you were told which car to drive, which kind of food to eat, or what brand of shoes to wear. At least in Western cultures, not being able to choose violates our sense of freedom. As discussed in Chapter 9, psychological reactance is people's tendency to respond to being told what to do and not to do by wanting to do exactly what is forbidden to them, even if they had no strong preference before their choices were restricted. Feeling free to make our own choices generally gives us a sense of having control over our lives—and these states are generally viewed as beneficial to mental health. But when too many options are available, especially when all of them are attractive, people experience conflict and indecision (**FIGURE 8.21**). In one study, Iyengar and Lepper (2000) presented shoppers at a grocery store with a display of either 6 or 24 varieties of jam to sample. They also gave each shopper a discount coupon for any variety of jam. The greater variety attracted more shoppers, but it failed to produce more sales; 30 percent of those with the limited choice bought jam, whereas only 3 percent with the greater variety did so. In a subsequent study, the same investigators found that people choosing among a small number of chocolates were more satisfied with the ones they selected than were people who chose from a wider variety.

According to the psychologist Barry Schwartz, having too much choice makes some people miserable. He divides the world into *satisficers* and *maximizers*. Satisficers live according to a philosophy of "good enough." Schwartz borrowed the term *satisficing* from the late Nobel laureate psychologist Herbert Simon, who described it as choosing an option that sufficiently satisfies needs. Satisficers do not lack standards; rather, they look around until they find something that most closely matches what they want and then buy it, without worrying about whether better or cheaper products are available. They like good things, but they do not care if those things are not the best. They are the people at supermarkets who readily select their produce without going through every apple and tomato to find the very best ones.

By contrast, maximizers always seek to make the best possible choices. They devote time and effort to reading labels, checking consumer magazines, reading Internet reviews, considering alternatives, and comparing prices. They often are frustrated by the countless options available to them and feel paralyzed by indecision when they have to select between equally attractive choices. For maximizers, making the wrong choice can have enormous consequences. Ordering the fish special for dinner means they will not have the pleasure of tasting the chicken special. What if the chicken is better than the fish? Not only do maximizers hesitate in making decisions, but they continue to analyze and question their choices even after they have made their selections, often ruminating about those selections' negative features. As a result, they generally are more disappointed with their decisions and more likely to experience regret.

The paradox of choice might also be responsible for a cultural shift in the average age at which people are settling into jobs and marriage. Historically, well before age 25 people were set in their career paths and often married and having children. A pattern emerging in industrialized nations is for young adults to delay decisions about these life stages for many years, as they explore their vast career options and seek mates who match their ideals (Grossman, 2005). In countries such as Canada, England, France, Germany, Italy, the United States, and Japan, the average age for marriage is now approaching 30. One possible explanation for this phenomenon is that young adults are trying to maximize their life choices. They want just the right job and just the right marriage, to avoid the serious consequences of picking badly in either area.

According to Schwartz, the consequence of nearly unlimited choice may help explain the increase in clinical depression in modern countries: "If virtually every choice you make fails to live up to expectations and aspirations, and if you consistently take personal responsibility for the disappointments, the trivial looms larger and larger, and the conclusion that you can't do anything right becomes devastating" (2004, p. 215). Schwartz believes that when decisions are not crucial people should restrict their options and settle for choices that meet their needs even if those choices might not be the absolute best. He also encourages people not to dwell on their choices but instead to focus on the positive aspects of their decisions. Is Schwartz advising people to strive for mediocrity? If he is, perhaps picking mediocre produce is fine, especially if it saves an hour at the supermarket every time you shop.

SUMMING UP

How Do We Make Decisions and Solve Problems?

People use deductive and inductive reasoning to draw valid conclusions. In decision making, they use rules to choose among alternatives. When solving problems, people find ways to achieve their goals. Although normative models, such as the expected utility theory, were assumed to be accurate because they describe how humans make decisions when performing optimally, it is increasingly clear that humans are not completely rational in reasoning, decision making, and problem solving.

The descriptive approach to these areas shows that people often use heuristics, which can lead to faulty outcomes. Framing defines how an issue is described, highlighting positive or negative information about particular options, and thus it affects a person's choice regarding that issue. To solve a problem, a person often needs to restructure the problem, reconsidering it by breaking out of a mental set. Working backward from the goal and finding an appropriate analogy are useful conscious strategies. Unconscious processes also play an important role in problem solving and decision making. Insight, the sudden recognition of a solution, is one example of the unconscious processing of problems.

▶ MEASURING UP

1. For each of the following terms, identify the appropriate definition(s). Each term might have more than one definition, and some definitions might not apply to any term.

   _____ reasoning
   _____ decision making
   _____ problem solving

   a. There are multiple alternatives to select from.
   b. There is a barrier between the present state and the desired goal.
   c. Conclusions are deductively valid if they follow from the premises.
   d. Conclusions are true if they follow from the premises.
   e. There may be multiple ways to get around a barrier.
   f. If a premise is assumed to be correct, certain conclusions will follow.
   g. There is always only one solution.

2. In performing affective forecasting, _____.
   a. most people are poor judges of how they will feel about something in the future
   b. forecasters predict phenomena such as the weather and the stock market's performance
   c. most people underestimate the negative emotions they will experience as a result of their decisions
   d. scientists are more accurate in predicting their future emotions because they work with scientific principles

How Do We Understand Intelligence?

So far, this chapter has considered the ways knowledge is represented in the mind and how we use knowledge to reason, make decisions, and solve problems. Among the most hotly debated topics in psychological science are the way knowledge and its application in everyday life translate into intelligence and the degree to which intelligence is determined by genes and by environment (Neisser et al., 1996). **Intelligence** is the human ability to use knowledge to reason, make decisions, solve problems, understand complex ideas, learn quickly, and adapt to environmental challenges. As modern society becomes more complex, with greater amounts of information available and greater demands on people to understand it all, being able to adapt to change and deal with increasing complexity is becoming more and more important (Gottfredson, 2004a; Lubinski, 2004). To succeed, people need to be innovative and "stay ahead of the curve." We are all intelligent beings, but individuals differ in terms of intelligence, just as we differ physically and psychologically. We observe physical differences and even psychological ones, such as in how shy people are or how much they worry. How do we know someone's level of intelligence?

LEARNING OBJECTIVES ▶

List various ways of assessing intelligence, along with the strengths and weaknesses of each.

Explain the nature/nurture controversy, and cite evidence for both sides.

Describe stereotype threat and explain how it may be a threat to validity.

intelligence The human ability to use knowledge, solve problems, understand complex ideas, learn quickly, and adapt to environmental challenges.

ON Ethics Cognition-Enhancing Drugs

Is it ethical to enhance your brain function through drugs (**FIGURE 8.22**)?

Sam is middle-aged and starting to notice age-related memory loss. Sometimes he cannot remember where he puts his keys. Sometimes, in the middle of a presentation at work, he cannot think of the word he is looking for. Would it be acceptable for Sam to take medication that prevents the normal slow loss of brain function? Few people would say no.

The development of most cognition-enhancing drugs has been driven by research on treating Alzheimer's disease and age related memory loss, but such drugs might be co-opted for other uses as well. What if Sam were a college student with a normal memory who was taking this medication to improve his memory? What if he popped a pill, went to his physics lecture, and came out with the lecture locked in his brain? He would not have to study, use flash cards, practice, expend real effort apart from paying attention to the lecture. Some people would view that process as cheating—gain without pain. But we all know people who were born able to encode memories faster and better than most of us can. Is that fair? In a sense, the rest of us were cheated by Mother Nature. If we can create a pill to cheat her back, why not take it?

Objections to these drugs center on concerns about safety and side effects, on the personal and societal levels. Such concerns increase when medications are given to the healthy for enhancement, especially when the full ramifications are unknown. Another objection is that if learning does not involve hard work, virtues such as perseverance will fall by the wayside, but this objection confuses a personality trait with memory function. A person can be perseverant with or without a good memory, or can have a great memory but not the perseverance to apply it. Others foresee decreased admiration for achievement and decreased senses of accomplishment.

However, we admire not simply feats of memory but how memory is used. We admire actors for their delivery of the lines they have memorized, mathematicians for applying the formulae they know. A good memory is just one capacity that may increase a person's achievement; intelligence, personality, and temperament also come into play. A lazy genius can be as unaccomplished as a lazy person with far less brain power.

Another concern is that cognitive enhancements may provide such an advantage that people will be coerced into taking them: Parents will want their children to have every advantage, teachers will find it much easier to teach "enhanced" students, employers will want to hire employees who require less training, and so on. Eventually, anyone who wants to compete for the best schools and best jobs will need to take them. This proliferation would present problems of distribution and affordability. Would cognition-enhancing medications be expensive? Would insurance companies pay for them? Would government provide them, perhaps to offset its savings in education and in unemployment insurance?

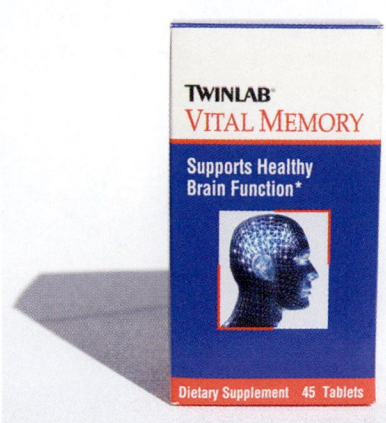

FIGURE 8.22 Memory Pills

Many of us already use caffeine and sugar, chemicals that enhance memory and performance. Many elementary school children take Ritalin to treat attention deficit hyperactivity disorder (ADHD) and attention deficit disorder (ADD), but in some school districts the proportion of boys taking it is greater than the highest estimates of the prevalence of ADHD (Diller, Tanner, & Weil, 1996). In other words, children within the range of normal behavior are being given a drug whose long-term side effects are still unknown to change their cognitive states. Among high school and college students who do not have ADHD or ADD, 16 percent take prescription stimulants (such as Ritalin and dextroamphetamine) as study aids.

Perhaps the memory drugs being developed will appeal only to those suffering from Alzheimer's and age-related memory loss. The side effects of an improved memory might not be so appealing. After all, our brains' capacity to forget, as well as their capacity to remember, may have been honed through millions of years of evolution and thus may serve vital purposes. Time may no longer heal all wounds if memories stay as fresh as the day they are forged. The memory of every embarrassing moment, rejection, and faux pas may linger, affecting people's senses of self.

The rich have many advantages the poor do not have. What if rich people could pay for cognition-enhancing drugs but poor people could not? Would a drug-enhanced advantage differ from other learning advantages, such as books, that money can buy? Are there times when cognition-enhancing drugs should always be used, such as when someone has Alzheimer's, and times when they should never be used, such as at the request of a healthy person with a moderately high IQ?

The earliest efforts to study intelligence were led by the scientist Sir Francis Galton in the late 1800s. Galton believed that intelligence was related to the speed of neural responses and the sensitivity of the sensory/perceptual systems—the quicker our responses and the keener our perceptions, the smarter Galton believed us to be. Today, most intelligence tests are timed, so we still believe quick processing of information suggests higher intelligence. Since Galton's time, researchers have taken numerous approaches to defining and studying intelligence. Three general approaches to understanding intelligence cross the major levels of analysis: The *psychometric* approach focuses on how people perform on standardized achievement tests, examining what people know and their problem solving skills. The *cognitive* approach examines the particular mental abilities that allow people to operate intelligently: how they process information, the speed at which they react, the amount of information they can hold in memory, and the extent to which they can stay focused on tasks. The *biological* approach is concerned with how the brain processes information and the extent to which differences in brain activity are affected by genes and environment.

Intelligence Is Assessed with Psychometric Tests

For much of the past century, the psychometric approach to intelligence has been the most dominant and influential, especially in terms of how intelligence is viewed in everyday life. Tests that focus on *achievement* assess current levels of skill and of knowledge. In the United States, millions of schoolchildren now take these kinds of exams every three years as mandated by the federal government as part of the No Child Left Behind Act (2001). *Aptitude* tests examine whether people will be good at various tasks in the future and may predict what jobs people might be good at—for example, accounting, piloting planes, or even spying. Their performances on these tests can hugely affect people's lives. How were these high-stakes tests developed?

Although testing people to match them with jobs they might excel in dates back to ancient China, the measurement of intelligence began in earnest just over a century ago. At the encouragement of the French government, the psychologist Alfred Binet developed the first method of assessing intelligence (**FIGURE 8.23**), to identify children in the French school system who needed extra attention and special instruction. Binet proposed that intelligence is best understood as a collection of high-level mental processes—in today's terms, attributes such as verbal, mathematical, and analytical abilities. Accordingly, with the help of his assistant Théodore Simon, Binet developed a test for measuring each child's vocabulary, memory, skill with numbers, and other mental abilities, the *Binet-Simon Intelligence Scale*. One assumption underlying the test was that although a child might do better on some specific components by chance, how he or she performed on average across the different components would indicate the child's overall level of intelligence. Indeed, Binet found that scores on his tests were consistent with both teachers' beliefs about children's abilities and the children's grades.

A number of other intelligence tests have been developed. In 1919, the psychologist Lewis Terman, at Stanford University, modified the Binet-Simon test and established normative scores for American children (average scores for each age). This test—the *Stanford Revision of the Binet-Simon Scale,* known colloquially as the "Stanford–Binet" test and revised for the fifth time in 2003—remains among the most widely used for children in the United States. In 1939, the psychologist David

FIGURE 8.23 Alfred Binet and Intelligence Assessments Binet launched the psychometric approach to intelligence.

Wechsler developed a test for use among adults. The Wechsler Adult Intelligence Scale (WAIS), the most current version being the WAIS-III, has two parts, each consisting of several tasks. The *verbal* part measures aspects such as comprehension, vocabulary, and general knowledge. The *performance* part involves nonverbal tasks, such as arranging pictures in proper order, assembling parts to make a whole object, and identifying a picture's missing features.

INTELLIGENCE QUOTIENT Binet introduced the important concept of **mental age,** an assessment of a child's intellectual standing compared with that of same-age peers. Binet noticed that some children seem to think like younger or older normal children. For instance, an eight-year-old who reads Shakespeare and knows calculus might score as well as an average 16-year-old and thus would have a mental age of 16. The **intelligence quotient (IQ),** developed by the psychologist Wilhelm Stern, is computed by dividing a child's estimated mental age by the child's chronological age and multiplying the result by 100. Today, the average IQ is set at 100. The eight-year-old with a mental age of 16 would have an IQ of 200 (16/8 × 100), an extraordinarily high score!

The term *IQ* continues to be used, but the measure is conceptualized differently, because the formula breaks down when used with adults. According to the formula, a 60-year-old would need to get twice as many test items correct as a 30-year-old to have the same IQ. Intelligence in the adult range is better conceptualized as what someone knows relative to the average adult and not to adults at different ages. Across large groups of people, the distribution of IQ scores forms a bell curve, or *normal distribution*. Most people are close to the average, and fewer and fewer people score at the tails of the distribution (**FIGURE 8.24**).

VALIDITY Are intelligence tests valid? That is, do they really measure what they claim to measure? To evaluate the tests, we need to consider what it means to be intelligent. If the word means doing well at school or at a complex career, intelligence tests perform reasonably well: The overall evidence indicates that IQ is a fairly good predictor of such life outcomes (Gottfredson, 2004b). *IQ* here means a score on a normed test of intelligence—that is, a score relative to those of the large number of people who already took the test. To explore intelligence tests' validity, researchers analyzed data about more than 20,000 people who took the *Miller's Analogy Test,* which requires test takers to complete analogies such as "Fingers are to hands as toes are to _____." The researchers found that Miller's Analogy Test scores predicted not only graduate students' academic performances but also their productivity, creativity, and job performances (Kuncel, Hezlett, & Ones, 2004). Similarly, people in professional careers, such as attorneys, accountants, and physicians, tend to have high IQs, while those who work as miners, farmers, lumberjacks, barbers, and so on, tend to have lower IQs (Jencks, 1979; Schmidt & Hunter, 2004). While these statistics refer to averages rather than individuals, the data suggest modest correlations between IQ and work performance, IQ and income, IQ and jobs requiring complex skills. Although higher IQ does not predict who will be a better truck driver, it predicts who will be a better computer programmer (Schmidt & Hunter, 2004).

When considering these findings, note that IQ scores typically predict only about 25 percent of the variation in performance at either school or work, so additional factors contribute to individuals' success (Neisser et al., 1996). People from privileged backgrounds

mental age An assessment of a child's intellectual standing relative to that of his or her peers; determined by a comparison of the child's test score with the average score for children of each chronological age.

intelligence quotient (IQ) The number computed by dividing a child's estimated mental age by the child's chronological age, and then multiplying this number by 100.

FIGURE 8.24 The Distribution of IQ Scores As discussed in Chapter 2, the statistical concept of standard deviation indicates how far people are from an average. The standard deviation for most IQ tests is 15, such that approximately 68 percent of all people fall within 1 standard deviation (they score from 85 to 115) and just over 95 percent of people fall within 2 standard deviations (they score from 70 to 130).

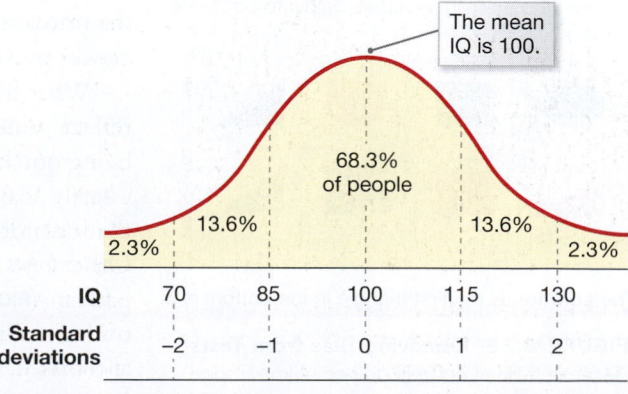

How Do We Understand Intelligence? ■ **359**

SIPRESS

"I don't have to be smart, because someday I'll just hire lots of smart people to work for me."

tend to have higher IQs, but other advantages—such as family contacts, access to internships, and acceptance to schools that can cater to their needs—also help determine their success. Moreover, people have greatly different amounts of motivation and differ greatly in how much time they are willing to spend to get ahead. One 20-year follow-up study of nearly 2,000 gifted 13-year-olds (those with IQs in the top 1 percent of their age group) revealed huge differences in how much people reported working as well as how much they were willing to work. At age 33, some individuals refused to work more than 40 hours per week, whereas others reported regularly working more than 70 (Lubinski & Benbow, 2000). Even with factors such as IQ and social background being more or less equal, a person working twice as many hours per week may have that much more chance of accomplishing his or her goals (Lubinski, 2004). In other words, IQ may be important, but it is among several factors that contribute to success in the classroom, the workplace, and life generally.

CULTURAL BIAS One important criticism of intelligence tests is that they may penalize people for belonging to particular cultures or particular groups. That is, doing well on intelligence tests often requires knowing the language and culture of the mainstream. For instance, consider this analogy:

STRING is to GUITAR as REED is to

a. TRUMPET

b. OBOE

c. VIOLIN

d. TROMBONE

Being able to solve this analogy requires specific knowledge of these instruments, in particular knowing that an oboe uses a reed to make music. But unless you were exposed to this information and had an opportunity to learn it, you could not answer the question. Moreover, some words mean different things to different groups, and how a person answers a test item is determined by its meaning in his or her culture. When Randy Jackson on *American Idol* describes someone's performance as "da bomb," he does not mean she or he "bombed," or did badly. He means it was "cool," which does not mean it was cold. And so on. A person's exposure to mainstream language and mainstream culture affects which meaning of a word comes most quickly to mind, if the person knows the meaning at all.

What it means to be intelligent also varies across cultures. Most measures of IQ reflect values of what is considered important in modern Western culture, such as being quick witted or speaking well. But what is adaptive in one society is not necessarily adaptive in others. One approach to dealing with cultural bias is to use items that do not depend on language, such as the performance measures on the WAIS. Other tests show a series of patterns and ask the test taker to identify the missing pattern (**FIGURE 8.25**). Although these tests may be fairer than those that rely on understanding language, most of the proposed substitutes for intelligence tests are also biased. For example, interviews and ratings of job performance are subject to bias in ways difficult to detect and quantify and may exacerbate the problem of cultural

The task is to identify the missing shape in this sequence.

Choose from the eight shapes below to complete the sequence:

The solution is the first triangle in the bottom row.

FIGURE 8.25 Removing Bias from Tests
Because it does not rely on verbal knowledge, this test is not culturally biased—or is it?

bias in intelligence assessments. It is difficult to remove all forms of bias from testing situations; doing well on tests, among them IQ tests, simply matters more to some groups than to others, and tests generally favor those who wish to do well.

Recognizing and Avoiding Reification

Reification is the tendency to think about complex traits as though they have a single cause and an objective reality. A good example of reification is the complex concept of intelligence. Because we measure intelligence with IQ scores, people tend to think intelligence can be understood with these numbers. As discussed above, IQ is a number derived from a normed intelligence test. If you score near the mean, your IQ is close to 100. If you score in the top 2 percent, your score is higher than 130. The number conveys how you scored relative to the people who were in the sample used to norm the test. It is not synonymous with intelligence. For example, if English is your native language but you speak enough Spanish to take an intelligence test in Spanish, you probably would not expect the resulting IQ to reflect your intelligence accurately. Intelligence is a multifaceted concept defined within a context, not just by a score in isolation.

Compare the concept of intelligence with that of weight. We can measure, gain, and lose weight, which makes it seem similar to intelligence, but weight's physical reality makes it unlike intelligence. When we think about intelligence as having physical reality, we are reifying the concept. Once we think about IQ as though it explains intelligence, we ignore all the problems with intelligence tests, including possible cultural biases. Critical thinkers avoid treating an abstract concept as though it has a tangible reality and recognize the complexity in complex concepts.

General Intelligence Involves Multiple Components

Binet viewed intelligence as a general ability. However, we all know people who are especially talented in some areas but weak in others. Some people write great poems, for example, but cannot solve difficult calculus problems—or at least feel more confident doing one than doing the other. The question then is whether intelligence reflects one overall talent or many individual ones. An early line of research examined the correlations among all items using *factor analysis,* a statistical technique that clusters items similar to one another; the clusters are referred to as factors. Using this method, Charles Spearman (1904) found that most intelligence test items tended to cluster as one factor and that people who scored highly on one type of item also tended to score highly on other types of items: In general, people who are very good at math are also good at writing, problem solving, and other mental challenges. Spearman viewed **general intelligence,** or **g,** as a factor that contributes to performance on any intellectual task. In a sense, providing a single IQ score reflects the idea that one general factor underlies intelligence. Although most psychological scientists agree that some form of g exists, they also recognize that intelligence comes in various forms.

general intelligence (g) The idea that one general factor underlies all mental abilities.

FLUID VERSUS CRYSTALLIZED INTELLIGENCE Raymond Cattell (1971) proposed that g consists of two types of intelligence. **Fluid intelligence** involves information processing, especially in novel or complex circumstances, such as

fluid intelligence Information processing in novel or complex circumstances.

crystallized intelligence Knowledge acquired through experience and the ability to use that knowledge.

multiple intelligences The idea that people can show different skills in a variety of different domains.

reasoning, drawing analogies, and thinking quickly and flexibly. It is often assessed in nonverbal, more culture-fair intelligence tests (such as the one in Figure 8.25). In contrast, **crystallized intelligence** involves knowledge we acquire through experience, such as vocabulary and cultural information, and the ability to use this knowledge to solve problems (Horn, 1968; Horn & McArdle, 2007). Distinguishing between fluid intelligence and crystallized intelligence is somewhat analogous to distinguishing between working memory (which is more like fluid intelligence) and long-term memory (which is more like crystallized intelligence). As would be expected because both intelligences are components of g, people who score highly on one factor also tend to score highly on the other, a finding that suggests a strong crystallized intelligence is likely aided by a strong fluid intelligence. As discussed in Chapter 11, throughout the adult years crystallized intelligence grows steadily, while fluid intelligence declines steadily.

MULTIPLE INTELLIGENCES Whereas Cattell argued that two types of intelligence contribute to g, Howard Gardner (1983) proposed a theory of **multiple intelligences,** in which he identified different types of intellectual talents that are independent from one another. For example, he proposed that musical intelligence enables some people to discriminate subtle variations in pitch or in timbre and therefore to have an above average appreciation of music. Among the other intelligences Gardner proposed are bodily-kinesthetic (such as the forms that make athletes and dancers highly attuned to their bodies and able to control their motions with exquisite skill), linguistic (excellent verbal skills), mathematical/logical, spatial (thinking in terms of images and pictures), intrapersonal (or self-understanding), and interpersonal (or social understanding; **FIGURE 8.26**).

FIGURE 8.26 Multiple Intelligences Howard Gardner suggested that intelligence can take many different forms. Here, four different types of intelligence are represented by **(a)** the athlete Mia Hamm, **(b)** the musician Yo-Yo Ma, **(c)** the scientist Shirley Jackson, and **(d)** the artist Diego Rivera.

Gardner's theory is important partly because it recognizes that people can be average or even deficient in some domains and outstanding in others. Consider the Juilliard School student Jay Greenberg, a typical boy in all regards—except that he has been described as perhaps the greatest prodigy in the last two hundred years; his composing skills are said to rival those of historical greats such as Mozart and Beethoven. Greenberg does not know where the music comes from, but he hears it fully written, as if it were being played by an orchestra in his head (*60 Minutes,* November 28, 2004).

According to Gardner, each person has a unique pattern of intelligences and no one should be viewed as smarter than others, just differently talented, a view that strikes some psychologists as a feel-good philosophy with little basis in fact. These critics have questioned whether being able to control body movements or compose music is truly a form of intelligence or should instead be considered a specialized talent. Is clumsiness or tone deafness a form of unintelligence? There are still no standardized ways to assess many of Gardner's intelligences, in part because Gardner believes the existing tests fail to capture the true essence of intelligence. Instead, Gardner provides exemplars, such as the artist Pablo Picasso, the dancer Martha Graham, the physicist Albert Einstein, and the poet T. S. Eliot. Each of these figures was especially talented in his or her field, but they were also talented in many respects, and all were high in general intelligence (Gottfredson, 2004b).

Robert Sternberg (1999) proposed a theory of three intelligences: *Analytical intelligence* is similar to that measured by psychometric tests, as in being good at problem solving, completing analogies, figuring out puzzles, and other academic challenges. *Creative intelligence* involves the ability to gain insight and solve novel problems—to think in new and interesting ways. *Practical intelligence* refers to dealing with everyday tasks, such as knowing whether a parking space is large enough for your vehicle, being a good judge of people, being an effective leader, and so on. Evidence for the existence of such multiple intelligences is that many phenomenally successful public figures did not excel academically. Bill Gates dropped out of college, yet he developed one of the world's largest companies and became the world's richest person. Former U.S. President George W. Bush was a mediocre student. Neither the flamboyant billionaire Richard Branson nor the cosmetic giant Estée Lauder attended college. Each of these individuals clearly has talents that might not be measured on standardized intelligence tests.

EMOTIONAL INTELLIGENCE Conceived by the psychological scientists Peter Salovey and John Mayer and subsequently popularized by the science writer Daniel Goleman, **emotional intelligence (EQ)** is a form of social intelligence that emphasizes the ability to perceive, understand, manage, and use emotions to guide thoughts and actions (Salovey & Mayer, 1990). Emotional intelligence consists of four abilities: to manage one's own emotions, to use one's own emotions to facilitate activities, to recognize other people's emotions, and to understand emotional language (Salovey & Grewel, 2005). People high in EQ recognize emotional experiences in themselves and others, then respond to those emotions productively. As discussed in Chapter 9, emotions sometimes overwhelm cognition and undermine motivation. For instance, when people are upset, they sometimes act impulsively and thoughtlessly, by lashing out at others, eating a pound of chocolate, or doing other things they later regret. Regulating one's mood, resisting both impulses and temptations as appropriate, and controlling one's behavior are all important components of EQ.

Emotional intelligence is correlated with the quality of social relationships (Reis et al., 2007). The idea of emotional intelligence has had a large impact in schools and industry, and programs have been designed to increase students' and

emotional intelligence (EQ) A form of social intelligence that emphasizes the ability to perceive, understand, manage, and use emotions to guide thoughts and actions.

workers' emotional intelligence. At the same time, some critics have questioned whether EQ really is a type of intelligence or whether it stretches the definition of intelligence too far. The concept highlights the idea that many human qualities are important; whether or not EQ is a type of intelligence, it is advantageous for those who have it.

IMPORTANCE OF G Intelligence may be defined in different ways, but a general capacity likely lies behind it, namely g. Some scholars have viewed g as a statistical anomaly that has no factual basis. Within the last few years, however, a growing number of psychological scientists have concluded that g exists and that it exerts an important influence over life's outcomes (Conway, Kane, & Engle, 2003; Deary, 2001; Garlick, 2002; Gray & Thompson, 2004; Haier, Jung, Yeo, Head, & Alkire, 2005). Research has shown that g predicts not only performance in school and at work but also longevity. Low g is related to early death from causes including heart disease, diabetes, stroke, Alzheimer's disease, traffic accidents, and drownings (Gottfredson, 2004a; Gottfredson & Deary, 2004). These patterns might result from the different environmental forces at work on each of us, such that people who do not perform well in academic settings end up with dangerous jobs, people with less dangerous and/or better-paying jobs have better access to health care, and so on.

According to Linda Gottfredson (2004a), however, g may directly affect health. People who score higher on intelligence tests may generally be more literate about health issues: accumulating greater health knowledge, better able to follow medical advice, better able to understand the link between behavior and health. As medical knowledge rapidly advances and becomes more complex, trying to keep up with and process all this new information is a challenge, and people who are higher in g have an advantage in doing so. This provocative idea warrants further investigation. If it is true, it has a number of important implications for the medical system and the way doctors communicate medical advice.

As mentioned above, general intelligence, especially fluid intelligence, seems to predict performance in jobs that require fast and creative thinking. A number of theorists have proposed that g's main value is in allowing people to adapt quickly to environmental challenges, and that the more complex the challenge, the greater g's importance. Satoshi Kanazawa (2004) suggests general intelligence is relevant only in novel situations. He notes that for most of human evolution, our ancestors were hunter-gatherers who experienced few changes in their daily routines. Indeed, the lives of prehistoric hunter-gatherers remained pretty much the same as their ancestors' lives going back thousands of years. Only during the occasional novel event, such as a drought or other natural disaster, did those high in general intelligence have an advantage.

According to Kanazawa, one's level of intelligence does not matter for recurring adaptive challenges, so it has little influence over many aspects of daily human life, such as figuring out what to eat, finding mates, recognizing friends, and raising children. Indeed, people with high levels of intelligence have no advantage in these domains. For instance, there is no evidence that people with high g make better parents (Herrnstein & Murray, 1994). But today we encounter a multitude of phenomena that scarcely could be imagined even a century or two ago, such as automobiles, airplanes, electric appliances, high-rise buildings, televisions, computers, wireless telephones, and international conglomerates. Such inventions and institutions increase the value of adapting to novel challenges and of thinking creatively. The overall evidence is consistent with the idea that general intelligence is most valuable for tasks that require understanding novel, complex information (Lubinski, 2004). But what aspects of g provide these abilities?

Intelligence Is Associated with Cognitive Performance

What cognitive processes are involved in producing intelligence? Being able to take a three-hour exam requires us to stay focused and pay attention, for example, whereas recalling the definition of the word *heraldry* requires us to remember information about the Middle Ages. According to the scientist Francis Galton (1822–1911), intelligence is related to our brains' efficiency as well as to keen perceptual skills. He has speculated that intelligent people have larger, more efficient brains. Other psychological scientists believe intelligence is supported by low-level cognitive processes, such as mental processing, working memory, and attention. But can we equate these types of brain performance with intelligence?

SPEED OF MENTAL PROCESSING People who are not very intelligent are sometimes described as "a bit slow." That description might be accurate, because people who score higher on intelligence tests respond more quickly and consistently on reaction time tests than those who score lower on intelligence tests (Deary, 2000). A test of *simple reaction time* might require a person to press a computer key as quickly as possible whenever a stimulus (e.g., an X) appears on the screen. A more difficult test might require a person to choose, again as quickly as possible, the right response for the stimulus presented (e.g., press the X key when an X appears, press the A key when an A appears, and so on). Scores on intelligence tests are related even more strongly to this *choice reaction time* (Jensen, 1998). (See the discussion of reaction time measures in Chapter 2, "Research Methodology.")

Another line of evidence supporting a relation between general intelligence and speed of mental processing comes from *inspection time* tests. If a stimulus is presented and then covered up, how much viewing time does a particular person require to determine which side, A or B, is longer (**FIGURE 8.27**)? According to research, people who need very little time for this task tend to score higher on psychometric tests of intelligence (Deary, 2001). Additional evidence that highly intelligent people's brains work faster has been found by measuring brains' electrical activity in response to stimuli presentation.

The relation between intelligence and mental speed appears to be involved in the greater longevity of people with high IQs. In a recent longitudinal study, those higher in intelligence and those who had faster reaction times at age 56 were much less likely to die in the next 14 years, even after factors such as smoking, social class, and education were controlled for. The relationship between reaction time and longevity was somewhat stronger than that between scores on standardized intelligence tests and longevity (Deary & Der, 2005). Although the various response time measures lead to the conclusion that intelligence is associated with speed of mental processing, researchers are far from knowing what this finding means. Perhaps being able to process information quickly is just one of the many talents possessed by people high in general intelligence. This ability may allow them to solve problems, or make decisions, quickly when doing so is advantageous. The adaptive value of quick reaction time is obvious when you consider that lives hang on the snap judgments of firefighters (as in an example above), police officers, medical personnel in emergency rooms, soldiers in combat, and so on.

WORKING MEMORY Over the past decade, a growing number of researchers have noted that general intelligence scores are closely related to working memory (Conway et al., 2003), although the two are not identical (Ackerman, Beier, & Boyle, 2005). As discussed in Chapter 7, working memory is the active processing system that holds information for use in activities such as reasoning, comprehension, and problem solving. In that capacity, working memory might be related to

The task is to determine whether side A or side B of the stimulus is longer. The stimulus is presented and then quickly followed by a mask.

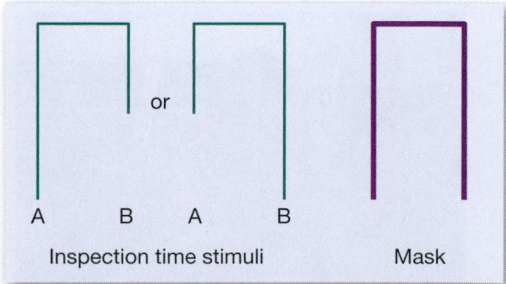

Inspection time stimuli | Mask

Judging the lengths is easy when you have enough time to view the stimulus but difficult when the mask decreases viewing time severely.

FIGURE 8.27 Inspection Time Tasks

For a simple *word span task,* a participant listens to a short list of words and then repeats them in order.

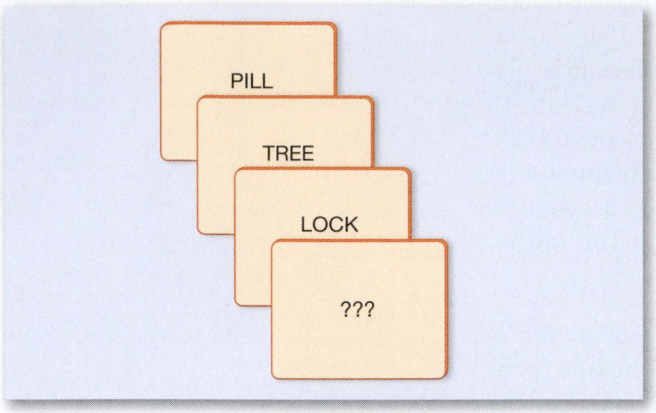

For a more difficult *secondary processing task,* a participant has to solve simple mathematical operations at the same time the words are presented. Once again, the person has to repeat the words in the order they are presented (adapted from Conway et al., 2003).

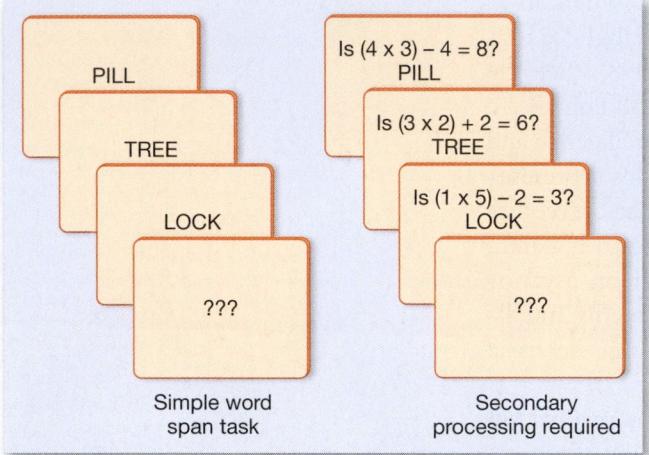

Simple word span task

Secondary processing required

FIGURE 8.28 Memory Span Tasks

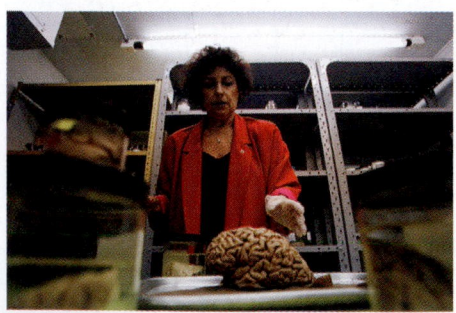

FIGURE 8.29 Extraordinary Brain
Sandra Witelson with Einstein's brain in her lab at McMaster University.

intelligence (Kyllonen & Christal, 1990; Süß, Oberauer, Wittman, Wilhelm, & Schulze, 2002). Many studies of the relationship between working memory and intelligence differentiate between simple tests of memory span and memory tests that require some form of secondary processing (**FIGURE 8.28**). Performance on a simpler test of memory, as in listening to a list of words and then repeating the list in the same order, is related weakly to general intelligence (Engle, Tuholski, Laughlin, & Conway, 1999). Memory tests that have dual components, however, show a strong relation between working memory and general intelligence (Gray & Thompson, 2004; Kane, Hambrick, & Conway, 2005; Oberauer, Schulze, Wilhelm, & Süß, 2005).

The link between working memory and intelligence may be attention. In particular, being able to pay attention, especially while being bombarded with competing information or other distractions, allows a person to stick to a task until successfully completing it (Engle & Kane, 2004). The importance of staying focused makes great sense in light of the relationship, discussed above, between general intelligence and the accomplishment of novel, complex tasks. The question, then, is whether brain regions that support working memory are involved in intelligence.

BRAIN STRUCTURE AND FUNCTION Intelligent people are sometimes called "brainy," but how are the brain and intelligence related? Many studies have documented a relationship between head circumference, which researchers use to estimate brain size, and scores on intelligence tests (Vernon, Wickett, Bazana, Stelmack, & Sternberg, 2000). Head circumference also predicts school performance, although the correlation is quite small (Ivanovic et al., 2004). Studies using magnetic resonance imaging have found a small but significant correlation between the size of selected brain structures and scores on intelligence tests (Johnson, Jung, Colom, & Haier, 2008; on MRI, see Chapter 2, "Research Methodology"). A meta-analysis of 37 samples totaling more than 1,500 people found that brain volume, as assessed by MRI, explained about 10 percent of the differences in people's general intelligence (McDaniel, 2005). However, these findings are correlations, so we cannot infer that brain size necessarily causes differences in intelligence. In fact, people with autism also tend to have larger brains (Piven et al., 1995).

Is intelligence related to the brain's overall size or to the sizes of certain brain regions (such as those associated with working memory, planning, reasoning, and problem solving)? Studies have found that the volume of neuronal cell bodies (gray matter) in the frontal lobes and in other brain regions that support attentional control is related to fluid intelligence (Frangou, Chitins, & Williams, 2004; Haier et al., 2005; Wilke, Sohn, Byars, & Holland, 2003) but not to crystallized intelligence (Gong et al., 2005). These findings are consistent with evidence that injury to the frontal lobes causes impairments in fluid intelligence but not to crystallized intelligence (Duncan, Burgess, & Emslie, 1995).

Sandra Witelson, a Canadian neuroscientist at McMaster University, has her own personal collection of brains—125 of them, all from Canadians. She also has an enviable specimen from outside Canada—she is the official keeper of Albert Einstein's brain (**FIGURE 8.29**). (A pathologist at Princeton Hospital, where

Einstein died, stole Einstein's brain and later gave it to Witelson to study. Although the pathologist lost his job for this famous theft, he reports not regretting his actions [Roberts, 2006].) Einstein's brain is rather unremarkable in overall size and weight, but Witelson has found some remarkable features that support a relationship between brain size and intelligence. The parietal lobe of Einstein's brain, the portion used in visual thinking and spatial reasoning, is 15 percent larger than average.

SAVANTS How would you like to be able to read a page of this textbook in 8 to 10 seconds? Perhaps less useful but even more impressive would be the ability to recite all the zip codes and area codes in the United States by the region to which they are assigned, or to name hundreds of classical-music pieces just by hearing only a few notes of each? These amazing abilities are just a few of the extraordinary memory feats demonstrated by Kim Peek (Treffert & Christensen, 2006). Mr. Peek, a savant who was the inspiration for the character played by Dustin Hoffman in the movie *Rain Man* (1988), has also memorized the content of over 9,000 books, but he cannot button his own clothes or manage any of the usual chores of daily living, such as making change. He scored an 87 on an intelligence test, but this number does not adequately describe his intelligence. Mr. Peek was born, in 1951, with an enlarged head and many brain anomalies, including a missing corpus callosum, the thick band of nerves that connect the brain's two halves. He also has abnormalities in several other parts of his brain, especially the left hemisphere.

We know very little about *savants,* people who have minimal intellectual capacities in most domains but at a very early age show an exceptional ability in some "intelligent" process, such as related to math, music, or art. Savants are very rare, and while the combination of prodigious memory and the inability to learn seemingly basic tasks is a great mystery, this combination should cause us to rethink the nature of intelligence. Oliver Sacks (1995) recounts the story of Stephen Wiltshire, an artistic savant who could reproduce highly accurate drawings of buildings and of places years after having only glanced at the original pictures. However, Wiltshire has autism, a developmental disorder (discussed further in Chapter 14), and only with the utmost effort did he acquire language sufficient for even the simplest verbal communication (**FIGURE 8.30**).

Genes and Environment Influence Intelligence

One of the most contentious battles in psychological science has been over genes' role in determining intelligence. This battle exemplifies the nature/nurture debate in action: To what extent are individual differences in intelligence due to genes, and to what extent are they due to environment? As emphasized throughout this book, nature and nurture are important for all development, and they are especially so for the development of intelligence. Consider an example that combines a key point from Chapter 3 (that gene expression is strongly influenced by external factors) with a key point from the section just above (that head circumference is correlated with general intelligence). The size of parents' and their children's heads is correlated, yet childhood nutritional status is closely related to head size, such that malnourished children have smaller than expected head circumference and brain growth. Moreover, all the findings linking intelligence to the size and structure of the brain are correlational, so perhaps more education and frequent exposure to intellectual challenges lead to selective increases in some brain regions. (As discussed in Chapter 3, for example, driving a taxi in London seems to enlarge the

FIGURE 8.30 Stephen Wiltshire Despite his autism, Stephen Wiltshire had published a book of his remarkably accurate, memory-based drawings by the time he was a young teenager. This example is Wiltshire's *Big Ben on a Rainy Day.*

hippocampus, the portion of the brain linked to spatial cognition.) Perhaps more intelligent individuals seek out mental challenges, which in turn increase their frontal lobes' volume (Gray & Thompson, 2004).

Consider an even more familiar example of the way nature and nurture are inextricably entwined in the development of intelligence: The size of someone's vocabulary is considerably heritable, but every word in it is learned in an environment (Neisser et al., 1996). Moreover, which words are learned is affected by the culture in which an individual is raised and the amount of schooling he or she receives. Thus even if intelligence has a genetic component, the way intelligence becomes expressed is affected by various situational circumstances. Instead of seeking to demonstrate whether nature or nurture is the more important factor, psychological scientists try to identify how each of these crucial factors contributes to intelligence.

BEHAVIORAL GENETICS As discussed in Chapter 3, behavioral geneticists study the genetic basis of behaviors and traits like intelligence. They use twin and adoption studies to estimate the extent to which particular traits are heritable, that is, the portion of particular traits' variance that can be attributed to genes. Numerous behavioral genetics studies have made clear that genes help determine intelligence—but the extent to which genes do so is difficult to determine (**FIGURE 8.31**). For example, studies show that twins raised apart are highly similar in intelligence, and this finding seems to support the importance of genetics in the development of intelligence, but that hasty conclusion fails to consider the way people interact with and alter their environments. Even when raised apart, twins who have inherited an advantage might receive some *social multiplier,* an environmental factor or an entire environment, that increases what might have started as a small advantage (Flynn, 2007). If the twins have inherited a higher than average verbal ability, for example, adults who notice this ability might read to them more often and give them more books.

The "intelligence gene" has eluded researchers, probably because thousands of genes contribute to intelligence and each has only a small effect (Plomin & Spinath, 2004). One way the behavioral genetics of intelligence has been studied is by selectively destroying specific genes (knockout genes) or replacing selected genes with other ones (knockin genes). A great deal of media hype resulted when behavioral

FIGURE 8.31 Genes and Intelligence Shown are average IQ correlations for family, adoption, and twin study designs. Siblings raised together show more similarity than siblings raised apart. Parent and child are more similar when the parent raises the child than when the child is raised by someone else. The highest correlations are found among monozygotic twins, whether they are raised in the same household or not. Overall, the greater the degree of genetic relation, the greater the correlation in intelligence.

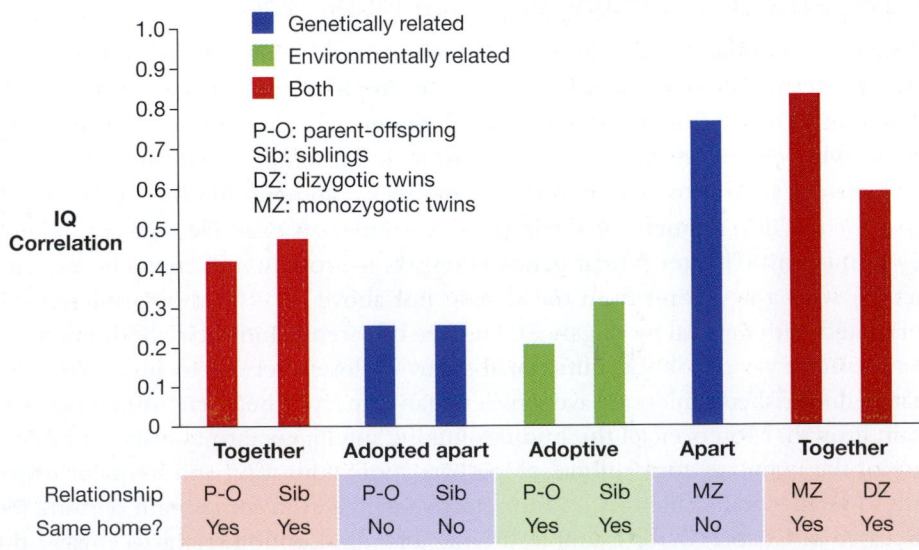

geneticists altered the expression of a particular gene in mice to produce mice who were "superlearners." After news outlets touted the discovery of the "learning gene," or "smart gene," the general public began considering the possibility of designer babies genetically engineered, in utero, to be smarter. However, the hype was largely unfounded, because the enhanced learning ability lasted from a few hours to a few days. The paths from genes to the proteins they manufacture and those proteins' effects on intelligence are largely unknown.

ENVIRONMENTAL FACTORS It is well established that the environments people are raised in profoundly affect those people's intelligence (Neisser et al., 1996). As mentioned above, poor nutrition can affect brain development and decrease intelligence. Other environmental influences on human intelligence include prenatal factors (e.g., the mother's intake of substances, including toxins) and postnatal factors (e.g., family, social class, education, cultural beliefs about the value of intelligence, and the person's intake of substances, including toxins). Each factor likely exerts an independent influence during development.

There is a long history of research suggesting that firstborns tend to have slightly higher IQs than later-born children, but psychologists have disagreed about these findings. Researchers have finally established a negative relationship between birth order and intelligence, meaning that later-born siblings, on average, have slightly lower IQs than firstborns (Kristensen & Bjerkedal, 2007). The data suggest that environment is responsible for this effect (**FIGURE 8.32**).

One hypothesized link between birth order and intelligence is that adults in a family devote more time and more attention to older siblings, who grow up with fewer other children around. If you are the third-born child, for example, you share parental attention with your two older siblings, unless they have died. The advantage to the firstborn is very small, but even a small effect could mean the difference between achieving or not achieving a particular goal in life. The more important lesson from these data is that parental and adult care is important for cognitive development.

Marinus Van IJzendoorn and Femmie Juffer (2005) conducted a meta-analysis of adoption studies to determine if adopted children show IQs and school achievement more like those of the nonadopted siblings in their adopted homes or more like those of their biological siblings who either remain with their birth family or are placed in institutions. In data from more than 17,000 children in 62 separate studies, the researchers found that adopted children had higher IQs and better school performances than their biological siblings who had not been adopted. Their IQs were similar to their adoptive siblings', but school performances lagged somewhat behind, possibly because of early traumas prior to adoption. These data are strong because they are based on many studies, and they show that environment powerfully affects the development of intelligence. The authors conclude that "adoption is a natural intervention with great success" (p. 329). Thus the repeated theme that biology and environment are equally important is seen again in studies of the intelligence of adopted children.

As noted in Chapter 3, rats raised in enriched environments show more synaptic connections and larger neurons than those raised in impoverished environments. Research from numerous laboratories has shown that enriched environments enhance learning and memory as well (Lambert, Fernandez, & Frick, 2005; Tang, Wang, Feng, Kyin, & Tsien, 2001). The implication is that environment influences how genes involved in brain development are expressed. In one study, genetically identical mice were split into groups, which were then exposed to different levels of an enriched environment—given toys, tunnels, and the like. These researchers

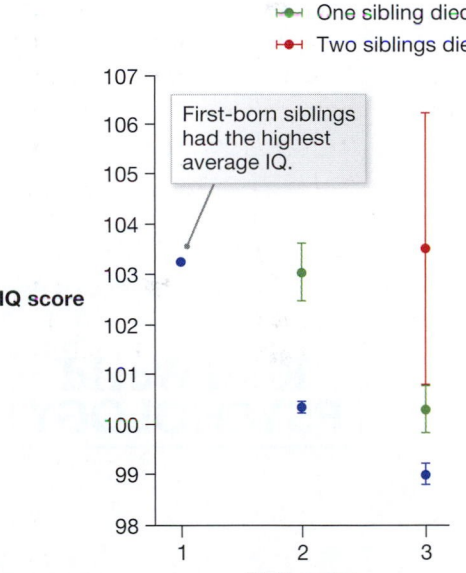

FIGURE 8.32 Birth Order and IQ There is a clear correlation between birth order and IQ: Firstborns have an average IQ of 103. Second-born children have an average IQ very close to 100, except if the firstborn child has died, in which case the average IQ for second-born children is 103. Third-born children have an average IQ of 99, except if one of the older siblings has died (the third-borns' average is 100) or if both older siblings have died (the third-borns' average is 103). Apparently, having two older siblings grow up in the same household lowers the third child's IQ.

found that enrichment was associated with the activation of genes involved in a number of brain functions, including forming new synapses (Rampon et al., 2000). These results present clear evidence that our environments can affect properties associated with intelligence by influencing the expression of our genes. Research has shown that humans as well as mice gain clear advantages from living in stimulating environments and that these environmental effects can be seen in the brain.

The intellectual opportunities a child receives also affect intelligence. Stephen Ceci (1999) notes that schooling, for instance, makes an important contribution to intelligence. The longer children remain in school, the higher their IQs will be. Students who start school early because of where their birth dates fall on the calendar have higher test scores than their same-age peers who start school a year later. Schooling not only builds knowledge but also teaches critical thinking skills such as being able to think abstractly and learn strategies for solving problems (Neisser et al., 1996).

Taken together, the evidence is considerable that environmental factors contribute to intelligence. For example, IQ scores have risen dramatically during the last century of intelligence testing; this rise has been called the *Flynn effect* after James R. Flynn, the researcher who first described it (Flynn, 1981, 1987). (The various intelligence tests have been restandardized on numerous occasions over time so that the mean IQ score remains 100.) Since genes cannot have changed much during this period, the increase must be due to environmental factors. One possible explanation for the increase in IQ scores across generations is that, since every generation needs more education than the preceding one, and since work and leisure activities require more complex cognitive processing than in earlier years, cognitive abilities escalate within the span of one generation (Flynn, 2007). Other explanations include better nutrition, better health care, the refinement of education methods, longer school years, and smaller families with more intensive parenting, as well as exposure to technology such as computers.

Group Differences in Intelligence Have Multiple Determinants

GENDER Which is the smarter sex—males or females? A great deal of research literature has addressed this commonly asked question. It might seem that the simplest way to answer this question is to determine whether females or males have the higher average IQ score, but this solution does not work because most of the commonly used intelligence tests were written in ways that would avoid creating an overall sex difference in IQ (Brody, 1992). Arthur Jensen (1998) weighed in on the question of sex differences in intelligence, analyzing tests that "load heavily on g." In his study, Jensen used only tests that had not deliberately eliminated sex differences, thus making it more likely that he would find evidence for sex differences in intelligence, if they existed. Based on this analysis, Jensen concluded, "No evidence was found for sex differences in the mean level of g or in the variability of g. . . . Males, on average, excel on some factors; females on others" (pp. 531–32). There are differences between females and males, on average, on some measures that presumably reflect intelligence. Females get better grades in school and tend to have the advantage on measures of writing and of language usage; by contrast, males tend to get higher scores on some standardized tests of math aptitude and of visuospatial processing (Halpern et al., 2007). Therefore, neither sex is "smarter."

Cross-national data from 18 countries show consistently, however, that females tend to estimate their own intelligence as lower than males' estimates of their own (Furnham, Wytykowska, & Petrides, 2005). In a commentary about these findings, one researcher concluded that females receive modesty training, which emphasizes humility for girls and thus leads them to underestimate their intelligence (Beloff, cited in Furnham, Wytykowska, & Petrides, 2005). Even if this explanation is true, we still do not know if the females' lower self-estimates reflect genuine beliefs about their intelligence. One reason to think so is that females and males tend to attribute higher IQs to their fathers than to their mothers (Furnham et al., 2005). Modesty training most likely would not affect women's estimates of their parents' intelligence, although it is possible that females generalize their modesty to other females.

RACE The most controversial aspect of intelligence testing over the last century has been the idea that genetics can explain overall differences in intelligence scores between racial groups. In particular, the debate continues about differences in African Americans' and white Americans' scores on measures of intelligence. In a 1969 paper, Arthur Jensen created a firestorm of controversy by asserting that African Americans are, on average, less intelligent than European Americans. Multiple studies over the past 30 years have found that, while many African Americans have higher intelligence scores than most white Americans, whites score about 10 to 15 points higher on average than African Americans on most measures of intelligence. At issue is what causes the group difference, not whether the difference exists. Given the importance of intelligence to educational and career attainment, claims that some groups are superior to others require close scrutiny, and it is important to discuss controversial and sensitive topics with an eye to being as fair to all sides as possible.

What is the meaning of such differences, and why can it be so uncomfortable to talk about them? A finding that two or more groups differ with respect to some variable, such as scores on intelligence tests, does not mean the differences are inevitable or immutable. (Recall the discussion of reification, earlier in this chapter, and do not be tempted to think of intelligence as though it had the same physical reality as height or weight.) The first issue to be considered is whether "race" is a biologically meaningful concept. Many psychologists and anthropologists believe it is not. Indeed, a special issue of the flagship journal of the American Psychological Association, *American Psychologist* (January 2005), was devoted to the validity of race, and in it various authors noted that the vast majority of genes (perhaps as many as 99.9 percent) are identical among people. We differ in physical attributes such as hair color and skin color to varying degrees depending on our entire ancestry, which raises troublesome issues of classification. Is Tiger Woods, for example, black or Asian? He has ancestors from both groups. Most methods of classifying race depend on self-report, in which people group themselves into categories. The rise in interracial families is making it harder for some people to select only one category, and an increasing number of people are identifying themselves as biracial and multiracial. Some genetically based biological differences exist between people who identify themselves as black and those who identify themselves as white. But are differences in biological attributes such as skin color related to the mental capacities that underlie intelligence?

Whether the effects of race are real or not, it is not scientifically appropriate to conclude that genes cause differences among groups, if there are any environmental differences among those groups. Richard Lewontin (1976) has provided

Field 1 is an impoverished environment.

Field 2 is an enriched environment.

FIGURE 8.33 Environmental Impacts

stereotype threat Apprehension about confirming negative stereotypes related to one's own group.

an excellent example of the difficulties of contrasting groups of people who differ in their circumstances. Consider seeds planted in two separate containers (**FIGURE 8.33**). In one container, the soil is rich, and the seeds receive regular watering, all the necessary nutrients, and abundant sunlight. In the other container, the soil is poor, and the seeds receive restricted water, few nutrients, and intermittent sunlight. Within each planter, differences between individual plants' growth can be attributed to the seeds' genetic differences. After all, the environment is identical, so only genes can explain the differences. But in addition, as groups, the plants in one container will differ from those in the other container because of their different environments. The enriched environment will help the seeds reach their potential, whereas the impoverished environment will stunt growth.

On average, African Americans have very different life circumstances than do white Americans. On average, African Americans make less money and more likely live in poverty. On average, they have fewer years of education and lower-quality health care, and they more likely face prejudice and discrimination. Around the world, minority groups that are the targets of discrimination, such as the Maori in New Zealand, the burakumin in Japan, and the Dalits, or "untouchables," in India, have lower intelligence scores on average. John Ogbu (1994) argues that poor treatment of minority-group members can make them pessimistic about their chances of success within their cultures, potentially making them less likely to believe that hard work will pay off for them; such attitudes may lower their motivational levels and therefore their performances. This explanation is plausible, but it is not a clear-cut basis—indeed, at this time there is no clear-cut basis—for understanding the differences in test scores between African Americans and white Americans (Neisser et al., 1996).

One interesting line of work shows it is relatively easy to reduce at least some of the between-group difference in performance for different racial groups. A research report in the journal *Science* showed that negative stereotypes about the intelligence of African American children can make school stressful for these students and result in reduced performance (Cohen, Garcia, Apfel, & Master, 2006). This conclusion came from a study in which students were assigned randomly to either a minimal-intervention group or a control group. The teachers did not know which children were in either group. Students who received the intervention were told to write about the most important value(s) of their own lives, specifically as members of their race; control students wrote about the least important value(s) of their own lives. African American students who wrote about the most important value(s) showed a 40 percent reduction in the racial gap in grades (from .75 grade points to .3 grade points). The intervention did not affect the performances of the white American children, presumably because these children did not feel a race-related psychological threat associated with their performances in school. The authors of this study believe that by encouraging the children to focus on positive aspects of their lives and their race, the intervention buffered African American students against **stereotype threat,** the apprehension or fear that they would confirm negative stereotypes about their racial group. This study is part of a large and growing literature on stereotype threat, which causes distraction and anxiety, interfering with performance by reducing the capacity of short-term memory and undermining confidence and motivation.

Stereotype threat applies to any group about which there is a negative stereotype, including women, who tend to perform less well on some, but not all, standardized tests (such as the SATs) than men. Women tend to do more poorly than men when taking an exam on which they believe men typically outscore women, but they often perform as well as men on the same test if they do not hold such a belief (Schmader, Johns, & Forbes, 2008). In an especially intriguing example of stereotype threat, Asian American women did well on a math test when the "Asians are good at math" stereotype was primed by having them respond to questions about racial identity, but they did poorly when the "women are bad at math" stereotype was primed by having them respond to questions about gender (Shih, Pittinsky, & Ambady, 1999).

Because stereotype threat affects the scores of test takers from stigmatized groups, it has been studied using the SAT, a standardized assessment used for college admissions (**FIGURE 8.34**). When their membership in groups stereotyped as scoring low on the SAT is made prominent (e.g., "You are a woman," "You are not a native English-language speaker") immediately before testing, test takers achieve lower scores than when their membership in such groups is not made prominent. The possible inaccuracy of these scores undermines the SAT's goal, which is to provide a standardized assessment of all students taking the test. This topic is hotly debated among psychologists, some of whom cite data showing that stereotype threat has effects too small to be meaningful (Stricker & Ward, 2004), whereas others come to opposite conclusions using the same data (Danaher and Crandall, 2008). Stricker and Ward (2008) maintain that "inquiring about gender and ethnicity did not affect test performance of women or Black students" (p. 1656). Still, it may be decades before research resolves this acrimonious debate.

(a)

(b)

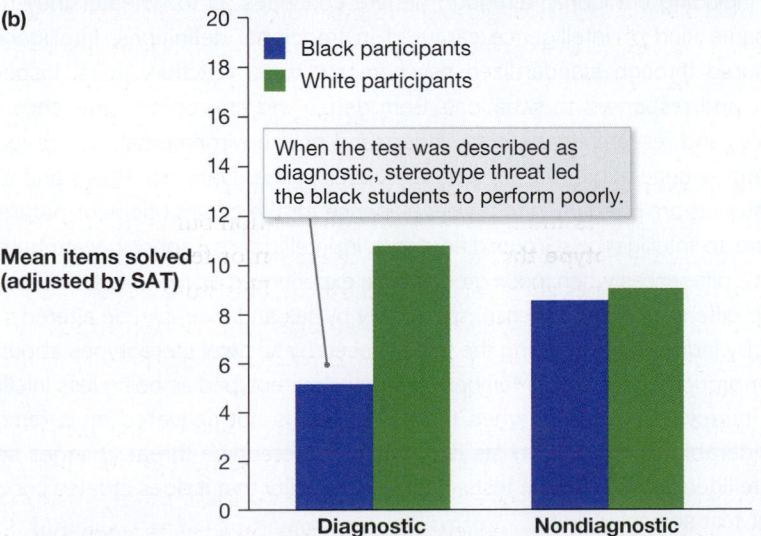

Mean items solved (adjusted by SAT)

When the test was described as diagnostic, stereotype threat led the black students to perform poorly.

FIGURE 8.34 Stereotype Threat
(a) Students face considerable pressure to perform well on the SAT, a standard component of the college application process.
(b) Stereotype threat may lead black students to perform poorly.

A recent study used brain imaging techniques to settle the controversy. Earlier studies had found that when stereotype threat is aroused, test takers' resulting anxiety reduces the capacity of their working memories (Schmader & Johns, 2003). Krendl, Richeson, Kelley, and Heatherton (2008) recruited a group of women who believed it was important to do well in math. Half the women were assigned to a stereotype threat condition in which they were reminded of the stereotype that women perform poorly in math, and half the women served as a control group and were not given these reminders. All the women were placed in a brain scanner that identified which brain areas were active while the women solved complex arithmetic problems. The women who had been reminded about the negative stereotypes concerning women's abilities to do math solved fewer math problems correctly and responded more slowly; most important, they showed neural activity in different brain areas than did women in the control group. The stereotype threat group had more activation in the brain regions involved in social and emotional processing, a result that suggests they were anxious about their performances and the anxiety led to poorer performances. By contrast, the women in the control group showed greater activation in neural networks associated with mathematical learning. This new knowledge about the brain basis of stereotype threat expands our understanding of the way negative stereotypes decrease performance, even for talented members of negatively stereotyped groups.

 SUMMING UP

How Do We Understand Intelligence?

Intelligence is the ability of humans to reason, solve problems, think quickly and efficiently, and adapt to environmental challenges. The psychometric approach reveals multiple components to intelligence but also a central dimension that has been called general intelligence, or g. Fluid intelligence is the type of intelligence we use when faced with novel problems that do not have solutions we can simply pull from memory; it is related to cognitive measures, such as working memory and speed of mental processing. By contrast, crystallized intelligence reflects knowledge we have already acquired, as in finding the area of a triangle after having been taught the formula. Multiple forms of intelligence have been identified, including emotional, although debate continues as to whether they reflect the same kind of intelligence captured in traditional definitions. Intelligence is measured through standardized psychometric tests, reaction times, inspection times, and responses to situations. Both genes and environment influence intelligence, and researchers seek to understand how environmental factors lead to differential gene expression in regard to intelligence. Data from twin and adoption studies are often used to garner evidence for the contributions of nature and nurture to intelligence. Group differences in intelligence cannot be attributed to genetic differences when those groups have experienced environmental differences. Group differences in intelligence, specifically by sex and race, can be altered somewhat by inducing or removing the threat posed by societal stereotypes about particular groups' intelligence. Members of groups stereotyped as being less intelligent may improve their scores when the stereotype is not activated or is removed. Considerable controversy exists over whether stereotype threat changes scores on intelligence and aptitude tests, but the possibility that it does creates concerns about test scores' validity.

1. While discussing with his grandmother what he has been studying at college, Dave was impressed by how much she knows. When he showed her his new cell phone, she quickly understood its complexities. His grandmother's general knowledge exemplifies her _____ intelligence, whereas her ability to figure out the cell phone exemplifies her _____ intelligence.

    _____ **a.** verbal, spatial

    _____ **b.** crystallized, fluid

    _____ **c.** fluid, spatial

    _____ **d.** g, multiple

2. If you wanted to reduce the effects of stereotype threat, you could _____.

    a. make the assessment as difficult as possible to create a threat for all test takers.

    b. include only information not taught in school.

    c. use members of groups with which no negative stereotypes are associated.

    d. tell test takers the upcoming test will not reflect group differences.

CONCLUSION

Thought has allowed humans to all but eradicate dread diseases such as polio, create technologies that simplify our lives, travel to the moon and beyond. By thinking, humans can take in and use vast quantities of information. Our cognitive talents include reasoning, thinking critically, solving problems, and making important decisions, but our thought processes often draw on biases that compromise the quality of our conclusions. Using knowledge effectively, to solve problems and achieve goals, is not always easy, and even very smart people can act irrationally.

How do we make people more intelligent? Apparently, we are doing it already. By emphasizing the importance in early childhood of both nutrition and education, by building good schools that stimulate and challenge, and by developing new technologies, society makes possible considerable gains in intelligence. An important but as yet unfulfilled goal is ensuring that each person can benefit from these circumstances, irrespective of sex, race, ethnicity, or social group.

■ CHAPTER SUMMARY

How Does the Mind Represent Information?

- **Mental Images Are Analogical Representations:** Thoughts can take the form of visual images. The primary visual cortex is activated proportionally to the size of an image in the mind's eye; therefore, mental visual imagery involves the same underlying brain processes involved in seeing the external world. Symbolic knowledge affects the ways we use visual imagery.

- **Concepts Are Symbolic Representations:** Concepts are mental representations of subtypes of broad knowledge categories; the concept of *cat,* for example, is a subcategory of *animals.* Concepts may be formed by defining attributes, prototypes, or exemplars. Many categories have fuzzy boundaries; we have no simple way of telling a cat from a dog or a rat, for example, since conceptually they are similar (*four-legged, hairy animals*).

- **Schemas Organize Useful Information about Environments:** We develop schemas based on our real-life experiences. Scripts are schemas that allow us to form expectations about the sequence of events in a given context.

How Do We Make Decisions and Solve Problems?

- **People Use Deductive and Inductive Reasoning:** Deductive reasoning proceeds from a general statement to specific applications. Syllogisms are formal structures of deduction. For example: If all psychology textbooks are fun to read and this is a psychology textbook, then this textbook will be fun to read. Inductive reasoning proceeds from specific instances to general conclusions. For example: If you read many psychology textbooks and find them interesting, you can infer that psychology books generally are interesting.

- **Decision Making Often Involves Heuristics:** Expected utility models assume people behave according to logical processes, such as always selecting the outcome that will yield the greatest reward. Descriptive models highlight reasoning shortcomings, specifically the use of mental shortcuts (i.e., heuristics) that sometimes lead to faulty decisions. We select information to confirm our conclusions, to avoid loss or regret or both, and to be consistent with a problem's framing.

- **Problem Solving Achieves Goals:** Problem solving involves reaching a goal, which usually is broken down into subgoals. Insights come suddenly, when we see elements of a problem in new ways. Restructuring aids solutions; mental sets and functional fixedness inhibit solutions.

How Do We Understand Intelligence?

- **Intelligence Is Assessed with Psychometric Tests:** The *Binet-Simon Intelligence Test* was the first modern test of mental ability and led to the concept of IQ as a ratio of mental age and chronological age. This test was later normed to a distribution with a mean of 100 and standard deviation of 15; therefore, average ability is between 85 and 115. The question of the validity of intelligence tests persists, and one significant criticism is cultural bias. Other ways of assessing intelligence also have the potential for bias, as when interview questions are ambiguous.

- **General Intelligence Involves Multiple Components:** Charles Spearman concluded that a general intelligence component exists, known as g. Fluid intelligence is involved when people solve novel problems, whereas crystallized intelligence is accumulated knowledge retrieved from memory. Howard Gardner has proposed a theory of multiple intelligences that include linguistic, mathematical/logical, spatial, bodily-kinesthetic, intrapersonal, and interpersonal abilities. Robert Sternberg has proposed that there are three types of intelligence: analytical, creative, and practical. Emotional intelligence is the ability to understand emotions and use them appropriately.

- **Intelligence Is Associated with Cognitive Performance:** Speed of mental processing (e.g., reaction time, inspection time) is part of intelligence. The relationship of working memory to intelligence seems to involve attention. The size and activity of the brain's frontal lobes are related to qualities of intelligence, but since brain size is altered by experience, we cannot infer cause from this correlation.

- **Genes and Environment Influence intelligence:** Behavioral genetics has revealed genes' substantial influence in setting the limits of the expression of intelligence. Environmental factors, including nutrition, parenting, schooling, and intellectual opportunities generally, seem to establish where IQ falls within the genetic limits.

- **Group Differences in Intelligence Have Multiple Determinants:** One of the most contentious areas in psychology concerns group differences in intelligence. Females and males score differently, on average, on different measures of intelligence, with some measures favoring males and others favoring females. Thus there is no overall sex difference in intelligence. Race differences in intelligence are confounded with a multitude of environmental differences, including income, discrimination, and health care. Additionally, many scientists question the idea of race as referring to anything more than a small number of human differences, such as skin color.

■ KEY TERMS

The answer key for all the Measuring Up exercises and the Practice Tests can be found at the back of the book.

■ PRACTICE TEST

1. Which of the following statements reflect incorrect assumptions in the *defining attribute model* of concepts? Select all that apply.
   a. All attributes of a category are equally salient.
   b. All members of a category fit equally well into that category.
   c. An understanding of the category requires knowing a list of typical attributes of members of that category.
   d. An understanding of the category requires knowing the most common example of a member of that category.
   e. Membership within a category is on an all-or-none basis.

2. Which of the following fruits will most likely be considered prototypical? Which will least likely be considered prototypical?
   a. apple
   b. pineapple
   c. tomato
   d. strawberry

3. On the first day of the semester, students enter a new class. On each desk is a handout that lists a couple of thought-provoking questions with the instruction "Discuss in groups of 3 to 4 people." It is time for class to begin, yet the teacher is not there. Based on our script for the first day of class, what will students most likely do?
   a. Students will settle into their seats and perhaps glance over the handout. People who already know each other might converse, but they most likely will not discuss the questions.
   b. Students will settle into their seats, quietly read the handout, and jot some ideas in their notebooks to prepare for the discussion they imagine will happen once class begins.
   c. Students will settle into their seats, read the handout, organize themselves into groups, and begin discussing the questions.

4. Label each of the following statements as an example of deductive reasoning or inductive reasoning.
   a. "I love my new pen! From now on, I'm going to buy all my pens from this company."
   b. "I'm not sure I'm in the mood for a concert. It's a ska band? Well, I do like ska. I'm sure I'll like the band."
   c. "She must be at least 18 years old, since she's in the club and the club only admits people who are over 18."
   d. "This restaurant is horrible. There's not a healthy item on this entire menu. Actually, we probably won't be able to find a decent meal in this entire town."
   e. "Yeah, I took a class from her last semester. It was pretty brutal. I bet all of her classes are tough."

5. Label each of the following scenarios as an example of affective forecasting, the availability heuristic, a framing effect, or the representativeness heuristic.

   a. Two candidates are running for office. One claims, "My administration will promote international trade and commerce." The other claims, "My opponent wants to send U.S. jobs—your jobs—overseas."
   b. Two friends come up with a hypothesis that married couples in their town seem much more likely to get divorced than couples in the United States in general. Their hypothesis seems bolstered when they quickly name five or six couples they know who got divorced over the past year.
   c. Jason, a sophomore at a state college in Nebraska, is tan and has blonde, shaggy hair. He spends a lot of time hanging out at the beach. When people meet him, they typically assume he is from California, although few Californians attend college in Nebraska.

6. _____ is an indicator of current levels of skill or knowledge, whereas _____ is an indicator of future potential.
   a. achievement, aptitude
   b. achievement, intelligence
   c. aptitude, achievement
   d. aptitude, intelligence

7. Casey is very empathic. It is as if he can read the minds of the people around him, knowing instantly if someone is uncomfortable with a topic of conversation, interested in garnering someone's affections, stressed out, and so on. We would expect Casey to score well on which indicators of intelligence? Check all that apply.
   a. creative intelligence
   b. EQ
   c. fluid intelligence
   d. g
   e. interpersonal intelligence
   f. IQ

8. Which one of the following comments most accurately reflects the facts about the roles of nature and of nurture in intelligence?
   a. "There's overwhelming evidence that genes are the most important predictor of intelligence."
   b. "Give any child a stimulating environment, early schooling, and good health care, and he or she can evidence genius."
   c. "About 50 percent of intelligence is a function of what you're born with, and 50 percent is a function of the environment in which you're raised."
   d. "Group differences in intelligence cannot be attributed to genetic differences if there are environmental differences between the groups."

■ PSYCHOLOGY AND SOCIETY

1. Write a script for a daily task such as ordering lunch at a restaurant or getting onto an elevator. Then carry out the task, but violate the culturally expected norms in some way (make sure the violation is safe and legal). For example, invite the server at the restaurant to sit down with you; stand in the elevator facing the rear wall or sit on the elevator's floor. Write an essay describing the cultural script for the task you engaged in, explain how you violated that script, and analyze the reactions of yourself and others to this violation. How

did it feel to go against the grain? How did other people respond to you, whether explicitly or through their body language?

2. Imagine you see the following post on a blog: "Let's face it, whites simply aren't as good at math as Asians, and girls simply aren't as good at math as boys. End of story." Compose a comment to post on the blog, using ideas from this chapter to address the author's claims.

Find more review materials online at www.wwnorton.com/psychologicalscience.

Test Preparation ■ 377

Motivation and Emotion

IN HIS EARLY THIRTIES, ELLIOT BEGAN SUFFERING from severe headaches. He was happily married, a good father, and doing well professionally. His headaches increased until he could no longer concentrate, so he went to see his doctor. Sadly, as it turned out, a tumor the size of a small orange was growing behind Elliot's eyes (FIGURE 9.1). The tumor grew, forcing his frontal lobes upward into the top of his skull. When a group of skilled surgeons removed the noncancerous tumor, they could not avoid removing some of the surrounding frontal lobe tissue. At first, the surgery appeared to be a great success—Elliot's physical recovery was quick, and he continued to be an intelligent man with a superb memory. But Elliot changed in a way that baffled his friends and family: He no longer experienced emotion.

The neurologist Antonio Damasio was asked to examine Elliot to find out whether his emotional problems were caused by the surgery. Damasio noted that Elliot displayed few emotional responses: "I never saw a tinge of emotion in my many hours of conversation

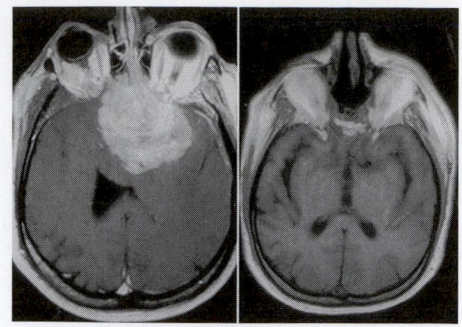

FIGURE 9.1 Orbitofrontal Tumor
Elliot suffered from a brain tumor in the frontal lobe, behind his eye. The brain scan on the left shows a similarly placed tumor (the light-gray mass is the tumor). On the right is a follow-up brain scan, taken two years after the tumor was removed.

with him: no sadness, no impatience, no frustration with my incessant and repetitious questioning" (Damasio, 1994, p. 45). Damasio's research team showed Elliot a series of disturbing pictures, such as severely injured bodies, and observed no emotional reaction from him. Elliot was not oblivious to his loss of emotion. He knew the pictures were disturbing and believed that before the surgery he would have had an emotional response, but now he had none.

On the surface, Elliot seemed a reasonable, intelligent, charming man—and yet his life fell apart. The absence of emotions also sabotaged Elliot's ability to make rational decisions. He lost his job; entered a doomed business venture with a sleazy character against his family's advice and lost all his savings; divorced, remarried, and then quickly divorced again; and so on. He was incapable of making even trivial decisions, and he failed to learn from his mistakes. Once he was a caring and compassionate man; now, he was detached from his problems and reacted to them as if they were happening to someone he did not care that much about. Elliot's brain surgery left his intellect intact, but it robbed him of his ability to function as a member of society.

Elliot apparently suffered impairments in motivation and emotion: He just did not care. Imagine living without feelings or aspirations to make something of yourself. What sort of life would that be? Emotions are a primary source of motivation, as we seek objects and activities that make us feel good and avoid doing things that make us feel bad. Together, motivation and emotion make things happen (both words are from the Latin *movere,* "to move").

Emotions permeate human life, as we fall in love, achieve success, feel inspired to work out at the gym, and so on. They also underlie the painful episodes most of us try to avoid—and, when they happen, try to forget. As Chapter 8 emphasizes, everyday cognition is far from cold and rational. Our decisions and judgments are affected by how we feel. Psychological science increasingly focuses on understanding how emotion influences our daily lives and how it motivates certain types of behavior. Psychological researchers are studying motivation and emotion across all levels of analysis, and the biological revolution in psychological science is producing exciting new findings about how neural and cognitive processes are involved. Case studies of people such as Elliot provide ample evidence about how various brain regions produce and regulate emotional responses as well as how emotions affect daily lives.

How Does Motivation Activate, Direct, and Sustain Behavior?

LEARNING OBJECTIVES
Describe Maslow's need hierarchy and give an example of a motivated behavior for each level of the hierarchy.

Explain how intrinsic motivation and extrinsic motivation affect behavior.

Motivation is the area of psychological science concerned with the factors that energize, or stimulate, behavior. It focuses on what produces behavior—for instance, what makes you get up in the morning and go to class. Theories of motivation seek to answer questions such as *Where do needs come from? How are goals established? How are motives converted into action?* More concrete questions are *Why do you choose to eat what you do? Does being involved in a sexual relationship interest you, or do you not think about it very much? What grade do you want in this course?* Most of the general theories of motivation emphasize four essential qualities of motivational states. First, motivational states are *energizing*. They activate or arouse behaviors—they cause animals to do something. For instance, the desire for fitness might motivate you to get up and go for a run on a cold morning. Second, motivational states are *directive*—they guide behaviors toward satisfying specific goals or specific needs.

motivation Factors that energize, direct, or sustain behavior.

Hunger motivates eating; thirst motivates drinking; pride (or fear, or many other feelings) motivates studying hard for exams. Third, motivational states help people *persist* in their behavior until goals are achieved or needs are satisfied. Hunger gnaws at you until you find something to eat; a desire to win drives you to practice foul shots until you succeed. Fourth, most theories agree that motives differ in *strength,* depending on internal and external factors. The next section looks at a wider range of forces that motivate people's behaviors.

Multiple Factors Motivate Behavior

What do we really need to do to stay alive? For one, we have to satisfy our biological needs. We all *need* air and food to survive. But satisfying our basic biological needs is not enough to live a fully satisfying life. We also have social needs, including the need for achievement and the need to be with others. People *need* other people, although our preferences to be solitary or social vary. A **need**, then, is a state of deficiency, which can be either biological (e.g., water) or social (e.g., to be with other people). Either way, needs lead to goal-directed behaviors. Failure to satisfy a particular need leads to psychosocial or physical impairment.

In the 1940s, Abraham Maslow proposed an influential "need theory" of motivation. Maslow believed that humans are driven by many needs, which he arranged into a **need hierarchy** (**FIGURE 9.2**). He placed survival needs (such as hunger and thirst) at the base of the hierarchy, believing they had to be satisfied first, and personal growth needs at the pinnacle. Maslow believed that to experience personal growth, people must fulfill their biological needs, feel safe and secure, feel loved, and have a good opinion of themselves. Maslow's theory is an example of *humanistic psychology,* viewing people as striving toward personal fulfillment. Humanists focus on the *person* in motivation—it is you who desires food, not your stomach. From the humanist perspective, human beings are unique among animals because we continually try to improve ourselves. A state of **self-actualization** occurs when someone achieves his or her personal dreams and aspirations. A self-actualized person is living up to his or her potential and therefore is truly happy. Maslow

need State of biological or social deficiencies.

need hierarchy Maslow's arrangement of needs, in which basic survival needs are lowest priority and personal growth needs are highest priority.

self-actualization A state that is achieved when one's personal dreams and aspirations have been attained.

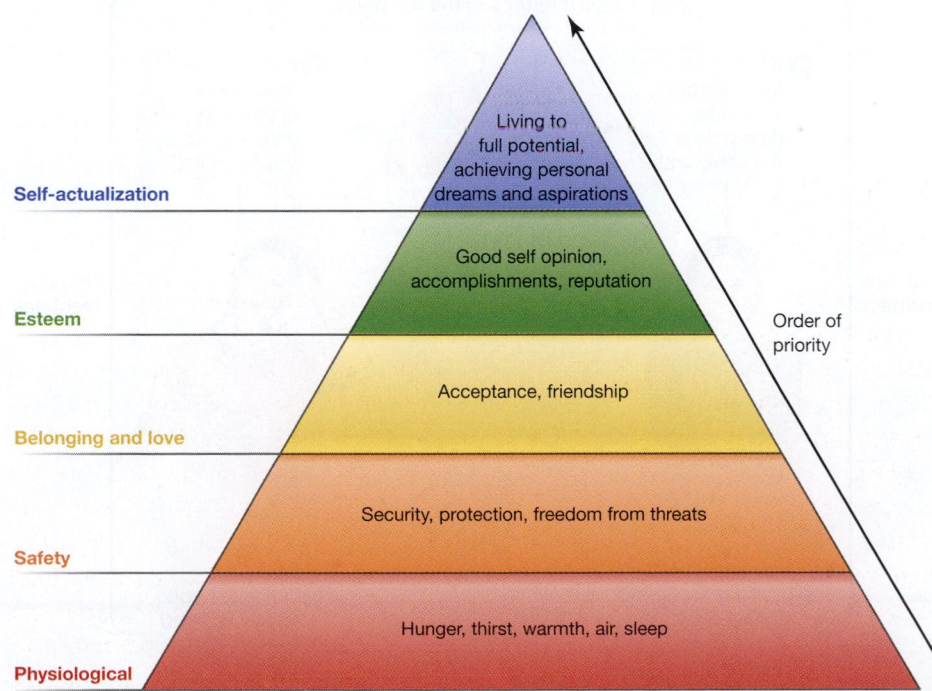

Self-actualization — Living to full potential, achieving personal dreams and aspirations

Esteem — Good self opinion, accomplishments, reputation

Belonging and love — Acceptance, friendship

Safety — Security, protection, freedom from threats

Physiological — Hunger, thirst, warmth, air, sleep

Order of priority

FIGURE 9.2 Need Hierarchy Maslow's hierarchy of needs indicates that basic needs, such as for food and water, are satisfied before higher needs, such as for achievement.

FIGURE 9.3 **Try for Yourself: Needs and Drives**

FIGURE 9.3 **Try for Yourself: Needs and Drives**

Hold your breath as long as you can.

Results: Eventually you will breathe, satisfying your need for oxygen. Before that, after a minute or so of not breathing, you probably will start feeling a strong sense of urgency, even anxiety. This state of arousal is a drive. Needs create drives that motivate specific behaviors, as diagrammed below with other examples.

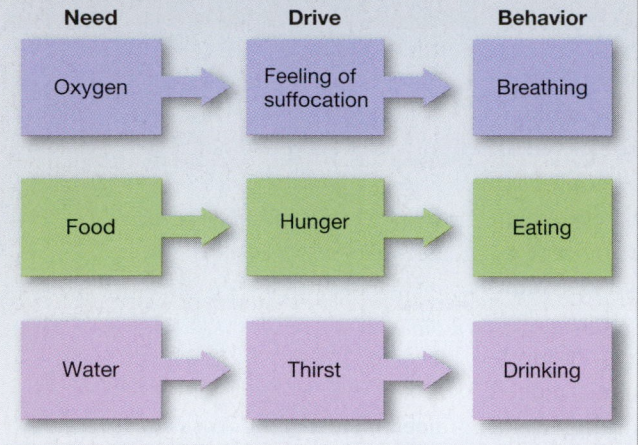

Need	Drive	Behavior
Oxygen	Feeling of suffocation	Breathing
Food	Hunger	Eating
Water	Thirst	Drinking

arousal Psychological activation, such as increased brain activity, autonomic responses, sweating, or muscle tension.

drive Psychological state that motivates an organism to satisfy its needs.

homeostasis The tendency for bodily functions to maintain equilibrium.

writes, "A musician must make music, an artist must paint, a poet must write, if he is ultimately to be at peace with himself. What a man *can* be, he *must* be" (Maslow, 1968, p. 46).

Maslow's need hierarchy has long been embraced in education and business, but it generally lacks empirical support. Independent of whether self-actualization is a requirement for being happy, the ranking of needs is not as simple as Maslow suggests. For instance, some people starve themselves in hunger strikes to demonstrate the importance of their personal beliefs, whereas others who have satisfied physiological and security needs prefer to be left alone. Maslow's hierarchy, therefore, is more useful as an indicator of what might be true about people's behaviors than of what actually is true about them.

DRIVES AND INCENTIVES What motivates us to satisfy our needs? Needs create *arousal,* which motivates behavior. **Arousal** is a generic term used to describe physiological activation (such as increased brain activity) or increased autonomic responses (such as quickened heart rate, increased sweating, or muscle tension). **Drives** are psychological states that encourage behaviors that satisfy needs. To experience one of your own needs and a drive in response to it, see **FIGURE 9.3**.

For biological states such as thirst or hunger, basic drives help animals maintain steadiness, or *equilibrium.* In the 1920s, the physiologist Walter B. Cannon coined the term **homeostasis** to describe the tendency for body functions to maintain equilibrium. A good analogy is a home heating and cooling system controlled by a thermostat set to some optimal level, or *set-point,* a hypothetical state that indicates homeostasis. If the actual temperature is different from the set-point, the furnace or air conditioner operates to adjust the temperature (**FIGURE 9.4**).

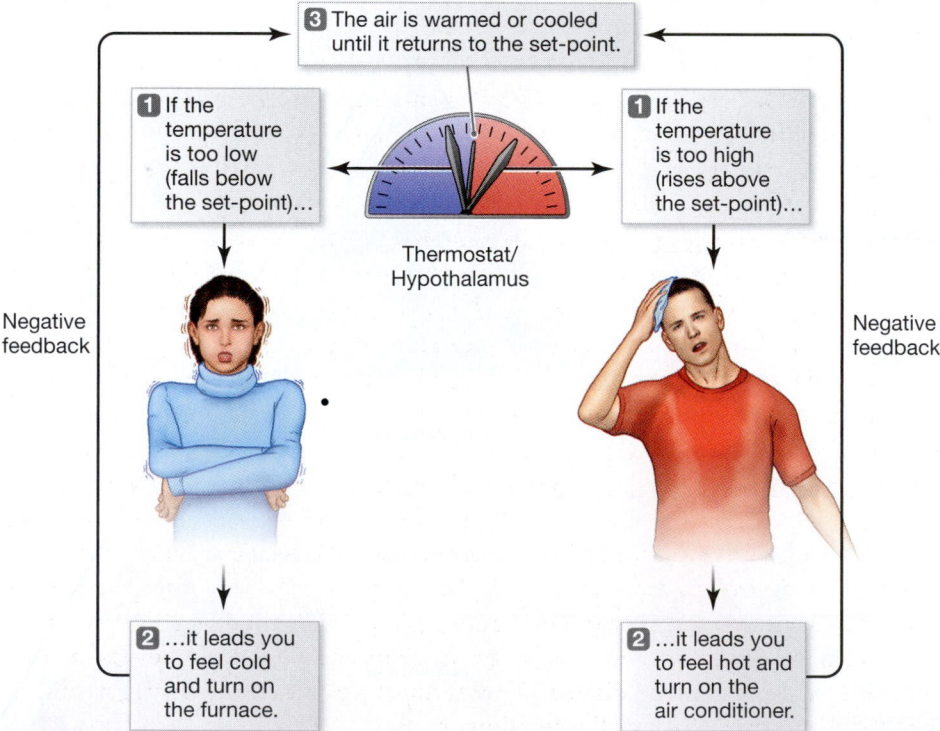

FIGURE 9.4 A Negative Feedback Model of Homeostasis

3 The air is warmed or cooled until it returns to the set-point.

1 If the temperature is too low (falls below the set-point)...

1 If the temperature is too high (rises above the set-point)...

Thermostat/ Hypothalamus

Negative feedback

Negative feedback

2 ...it leads you to feel cold and turn on the furnace.

2 ...it leads you to feel hot and turn on the air conditioner.

Similarly, the human body regulates a set-point of around 37° Celsius (98.6°F). When people are too warm or too cold, brain mechanisms, particularly the hypothalamus, initiate responses such as sweating (to cool the body) or shivering (to warm the body). At the same time, behaviors such as taking off or putting on clothes are motivated. Negative feedback models such as these are useful for describing various basic biological processes, among them eating, fluid regulation, and sleep.

Building on Cannon's work, Clark Hull proposed that when an animal is deprived of some need (such as water, sleep, or sex), a drive increases in proportion to the amount of deprivation (**FIGURE 9.5**). The hungrier you are, the more driven you are to find food. The drive state creates arousal, which encourages you to do something to reduce the drive, such as having a late-night snack. Although the initial behaviors the animal engages in are arbitrary, any behavior that satisfies a need is reinforced and therefore is more likely to reoccur. Over time, if a behavior consistently reduces a drive, it becomes a *habit;* the likelihood that a behavior will occur is due to drive and habit. For example, you might find that watching television makes you forget your troubles—an outcome that reinforces further television viewing. Over time, you might develop the habit of watching television, especially when you are stressed. Think for a second about your bad habits. What does engaging in those behaviors do for you? What keeps the habit going?

In some situations, people choose to engage in actions that do not satisfy biological needs. Why, for instance, does a person stay up all night studying for an exam? Why does a person have a second piece of pumpkin pie at Thanksgiving dinner, even if that person was not hungry when eating the first piece? Drive states push us to reduce arousal, but we are also pulled toward certain things in our environments. **Incentives** are external objects or external goals, rather than internal drives, that motivate behaviors. Getting a good grade on the exam is an incentive for studying hard; the comforting, sweet taste of the pumpkin pie is an incentive for eating two pieces; having money to buy a car or help pay your tuition is an incentive for working during summer vacation; and so on. Some things are more valuable to us than others, and we are more highly motivated to obtain them. What we value, in turn, is determined largely by our cultures and our personal histories.

AROUSAL AND PERFORMANCE

If drives create arousal and motivate behavior, it seems to follow that more arousal will lead to more motivation and thus to better performance. However, the **Yerkes-Dodson law** (a psychological principle named after the two researchers who formulated it in 1908) dictates that performance increases with arousal up to an optimal point and then decreases with increasing arousal. A graph of this relationship is shaped like an *inverted U* (**FIGURE 9.6**). The Yerkes-Dodson law predicts, for instance, that students perform best on exams when feeling moderate anxiety. Too little anxiety can make them inattentive or unmotivated; too much anxiety can interfere with their thinking ability. Likewise, athletes have to "get up" for the game, but they can fall apart under too much stress.

All of us, athletes included, function better with some arousal. That we prefer to be somewhat aroused goes against the idea that motivation always lowers tension and arousal. Instead, we are motivated to seek an *optimal level of arousal,* the level of arousal we most prefer. Too little, and we are bored; too much, and we are overwhelmed. Arousal theories help explain why we choose exciting activities—those that arouse us and absorb our attention. Thus we might dance, listen to music, read exciting books, watch horror or adventure movies, and so on, but (as discussed further in Chapter 13) we differ in how stimulating or exciting or frightening we like these and other forms of entertainment.

FIGURE 9.5 Clark Hull Hull was one of the pioneers of behavioral models of drive reduction. His drive theory of motivation is among the most influential theories in the history of psychological science.

incentives External stimuli that motivate behaviors (as opposed to internal drives).

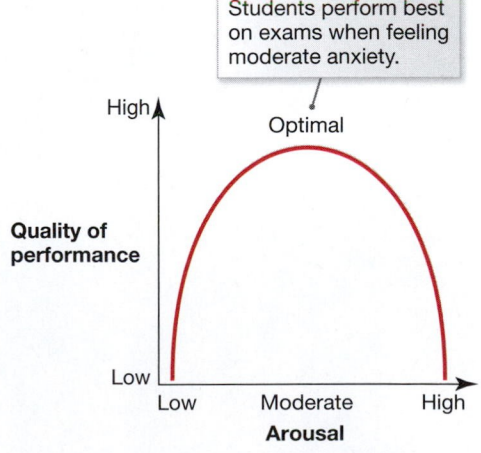

FIGURE 9.6 The Yerkes-Dodson Law According to this law, performance increases with arousal until an optimal point, after which arousal interferes with performance.

PLEASURE Sigmund Freud proposed that drives are satisfied according to the *pleasure principle,* which drives people to seek pleasure and avoid pain. This idea is central to many theories of motivation. Originating with the ancient Greeks, the concept of *hedonism* refers to humans' desire for pleasantness. We do things that feel good; and if something feels good, we do it again. Sexual activity often can be a good example of hedonism, in that many people engage in it simply for enjoyment and not because it is essential to survival of the species.

The idea that pleasure motivates behavior helps us understand a criticism of biological drive theories (such as Clark Hull's)—that animals engage in behaviors that do not necessarily satisfy biological needs. These behaviors, such as eating dessert when you are not hungry, commonly occur because they are pleasurable. From an evolutionary perspective, behaviors associated with pleasure often promote the animals' survival and reproduction, whereas behaviors associated with pain interfere with survival and reproduction. A good example of this principle is the finding that animals prefer to eat sweets. Infants given sweet solutions seem to find them pleasurable, as revealed by their facial expressions (Steiner, 1977; **FIGURE 9.7**). Sweetness usually indicates that food is safe to eat. By contrast, most poisons and toxins taste bitter, so it is not surprising that animals avoid bitter tastes.

Some Behaviors Are Motivated for Their Own Sake

The discussion so far has centered on the pleasure associated with reducing drive and sustaining biological needs. However, many of the activities people find most satisfying, such as reading a good novel, seem to fulfill no obvious purpose other than enjoyment. **Extrinsic motivation** emphasizes the external goals an activity is directed toward, such as reducing drive or obtaining a reward—for example, working to earn a paycheck. **Intrinsic motivation** refers to the value or pleasure that is associated with an activity that has no apparent external goal—for example, playing, solving crossword puzzles, or listening to music. Intrinsically motivated behaviors are performed for their own sake. They simply are enjoyable.

Some intrinsically motivated activities may satisfy our natural curiosity and creativity. After playing with a new toy for a long time, children start to lose interest and will seek out something new. Playful exploration is characteristic of all mammals

extrinsic motivation Motivation to perform an activity because of the external goals toward which that activity is directed.

intrinsic motivation Motivation to perform an activity because of the value or pleasure associated with that activity, rather than for an apparent external goal or purpose.

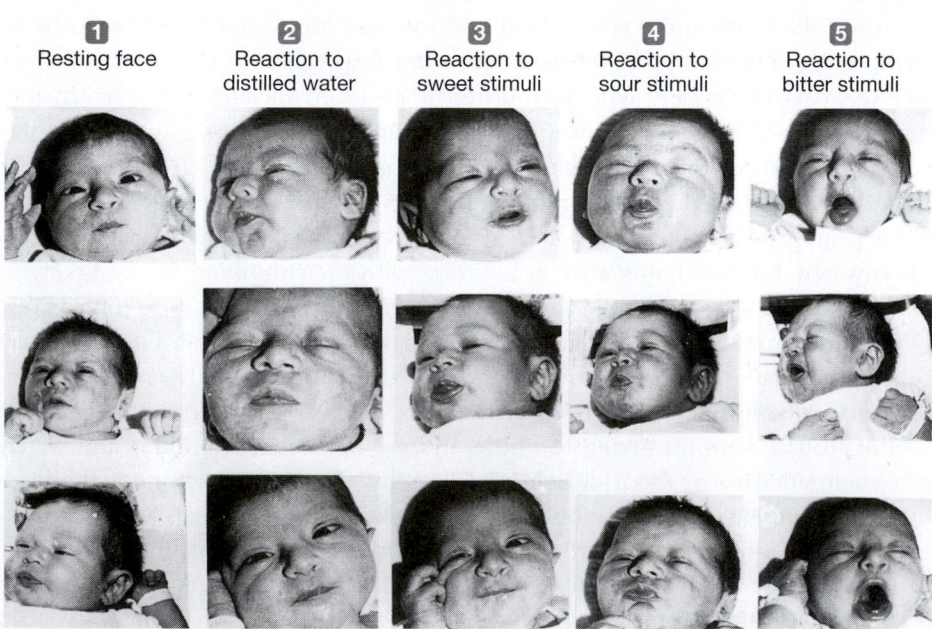

| 1 Resting face | 2 Reaction to distilled water | 3 Reaction to sweet stimuli | 4 Reaction to sour stimuli | 5 Reaction to bitter stimuli |

FIGURE 9.7 Early Motivation Even newborns prefer sweet tastes to bitter ones.

and especially primates. As the psychologist Harry Harlow and his colleagues have shown, for example, monkeys have a strong exploratory drive; they will work hard, without an external reward, to solve relatively complex puzzles (Harlow, Harlow, & Meyer, 1950). One function of play is that it helps us learn about the objects in an environment. This outcome clearly has survival value, since knowing how things work allows us to use those objects for more serious tasks.

Similarly, many of us are driven toward creative pursuits: Whether we are visiting an art museum or creating artwork ourselves, we may do so simply because we enjoy activities that allow us to express our creativity. *Creativity* is the tendency to generate ideas or alternatives that may be useful in solving problems, communicating, and entertaining ourselves and others (Franken, 1988). People are motivated to make sense of the world, and they do so in various ways—by constructing new images, synthesizing two or more ideas, and consolidating information into coherent stories. Although many creative pursuits are not adaptive solutions, creativity is an important factor in solving adaptive problems.

REWARDING INTRINSIC MOTIVES As discussed in Chapter 6, a basic principle of learning theory is that rewarded behaviors increase in frequency. You might expect that rewarding intrinsically motivated behaviors would reinforce them. Surprisingly, consistent evidence suggests that extrinsic rewards can undermine intrinsic motivation. In a classic study, Mark Lepper and his colleagues allowed children to draw with colored marking pens—an activity most children find intrinsically motivating (Lepper, Greene, & Nisbett, 1973). One group of children was extrinsically motivated to draw by being led to expect a "good player award." Another group of children was rewarded unexpectedly following the task. A third group was neither rewarded nor led to expect a reward. During a subsequent free-play period, children who were expecting an extrinsic reward spent much less time playing with the pens than did the children who were never rewarded or the children who received an unexpected reward. The first group of children responded as though it was their job to draw with the colored pens: Why would they play with them for free when they were used to being paid?

CONTROL THEORY AND SELF-PERCEPTION Another theory argues that extrinsic rewards may reduce intrinsic value because such rewards undermine people's feeling that they are choosing to do something for themselves. In contrast, feelings of *personal control* and competence make people feel good about themselves and inspire them to do their most creative work (Deci & Ryan, 1987). Another explanation is based on Daryl Bem's (1967) *self-perception theory,* which states that people seldom are aware of their specific motives and instead draw inferences about their motivations according to what seems to make the most sense. Imagine, for example, somebody gives you a big glass of water; after drinking the whole thing, you exclaim, "Wow, I must have been thirsty." You believe you were thirsty because you drank the whole glass, even though you were unaware of any physical sensations of thirst. When people cannot come up with obvious external explanations for their behaviors—such as that they acted with the expectation of being rewarded or to satisfy a biological drive—they conclude that they simply like the behaviors. Rewarding people for engaging in an intrinsic activity, however, gives them an alternative explanation for engaging in it: not because the behavior is fun, but because of the reward. Therefore, without the reward, they have no reason to engage in the behavior. The reward has replaced the goal of pure pleasure.

"What do you think . . . should we get started on that motivation research or not?"

FIGURE 9.8 Think Critically: Reverse Psychology Which of these promotional offers conveys more urgency?

Recognizing When Psychological Reactance May Be Influencing Your Thinking

Imagine you are thinking about declaring your college major. You have enjoyed your classes in English and computer science, and you cannot decide which field to choose. You discuss the decision with your parents, who insist that you major in computer science because it will lead to better job opportunities after college. They even hint that they are not willing to help pay your tuition if you do not major in the field they prefer. How would this conversation make you feel about the two majors? Would it make the English major seem more attractive? In general, when another person tells you not to do or have something, does that very something become more desirable? Scientific studies and daily experience show that, for most of us, it does.

Psychological reactance is a motivational state aroused when our feelings of personal freedom are threatened (Woller, Buboltz, & Loveland, 2007). Often, we act in ways to regain that freedom, trying to obtain whatever is being withheld. You may be familiar with the common notion of reverse psychology, which is based on psychological reactance. For example, you might play hard to get if you want someone to be romantically interested in you. Similarly, a company might advertise a product as available only to a select few, thus making consumers eager to buy it so they are not left out (**FIGURE 9.8**).

Why is recognizing psychological reactance a critical thinking skill? This motivational state often affects how we make choices—even when, in fact, there is no reason to prefer an alternative just because it has been denied. By noticing if your thinking has been influenced by this potentially irrelevant variable, you will find it easier to make better-informed and more-rational choices.

People Set Goals to Achieve

A *goal* is a desired outcome, usually associated with some specific object (such as tasty food) or some future behavioral intention (such as getting into medical school). So far, this chapter has focused on motivation to fulfill short-term goals, such as satisfying our hunger or spending a pleasurable afternoon. But we have long-term aspirations as well. What motivates us to fulfill those goals? For instance, what would you like to be doing in 10 years? What things about yourself would you change? In the 1930s, the personality psychologist Henry Murray proposed 27 basic *psychosocial needs,* including the needs for power, autonomy, achievement, and play. The study of psychosocial needs has yielded important insights into what motivates human behavior. A key insight is that people are especially motivated to achieve personal goals. *Self-regulation* of behavior is the process by which people alter or change their behavior to attain personal goals.

Good goals motivate people to work hard. But what is a good goal? According to an influential theory developed by the organizational psychologists Edwin Locke and Gary Latham (1990), *challenging*—but not overly *difficult*—and *specific* goals are best. Challenging goals encourage effort, persistence, and concentration. In contrast, goals that are too easy or too hard can undermine motivation and therefore lead to failure. Dividing specific goals into concrete steps also leads to success. If you are interested in running the Boston Marathon, for instance, your first goal might be gaining the stamina to run one mile. When you can run a mile, you can set another goal and thus build up to running the 26-mile marathon. Focusing on concrete, short-term goals facilitates achieving long-term goals.

SELF-EFFICACY AND ACHIEVEMENT MOTIVATION Albert Bandura argued that people's personal expectations for success play an important role in motivation. For instance, if you believe studying hard will lead to a good grade on an exam, you will be motivated to study. *Self-efficacy* is the expectancy that your efforts will lead to success; this belief helps mobilize your energies. If you have low self-efficacy—that is, if you do not believe your efforts will pay off—you may be too discouraged even to study. People with high self-efficacy often set challenging goals that lead to success. However, sometimes people whose self-views are inflated set goals they cannot possibly achieve. Goals that are challenging but not overwhelming usually are most conducive to success.

People differ in how insistently they pursue challenging goals. The *achievement motive* is the desire to do well relative to standards of excellence. Compared with those low in achievement need, students high in achievement need sit closer to the front of classrooms, score higher on exams, and obtain better grades in courses relevant to their career goals (McClelland, 1987). Students with high achievement need are more realistic in their career aspirations than are students low in achievement need. Those high in achievement need set challenging but attainable personal goals; those low in achievement need often set extremely easy or impossibly high goals.

DELAYED GRATIFICATION One common challenge in self-regulation is postponing immediate gratification in the pursuit of long-term goals. Students who want to be accepted to medical school often have to stay home and study while their friends are out having fun. Delay of gratification is the process of transcending immediate temptations to achieve long-term goals. In a series of now-classic studies, the developmental psychologist Walter Mischel gave children the choice of waiting to receive a preferred toy or food item or having a less preferred toy or food item right away. Mischel found that some children are better at delaying gratification than others are, and that the ability to do so is predictive of success in life. Children able to delay gratification at age four were rated 10 years later as being more socially competent and better able to handle frustration. The ability to delay gratification in childhood has been found to predict higher SAT scores and better school grades (Mischel, Shoda, & Rodriguez, 1989).

How did some children manage to delay gratification? Given the choice between eating one marshmallow right away or two after several minutes, some four-year-olds waited and engaged in strategies to help them not eat the marshmallow while they waited. One strategy was simply ignoring the tempting item rather than looking at it. Older children, who on average were better at delaying gratification, covered their eyes or looked away. Very young children tended to look directly at the item they were trying to resist, making the delay especially difficult. A related strategy was self-distraction, through singing, playing games, or pretending to sleep. The most successful strategy involved what Mischel and his colleague Janet Metcalfe refer to as turning *hot cognitions* into *cold cognitions*. This strategy involves mentally transforming the desired object into something undesired; children reported imagining a tempting pretzel as a brown log or imagining marshmallows as clouds (**FIGURE 9.9**). Hot cognitions focus on the rewarding, pleasurable

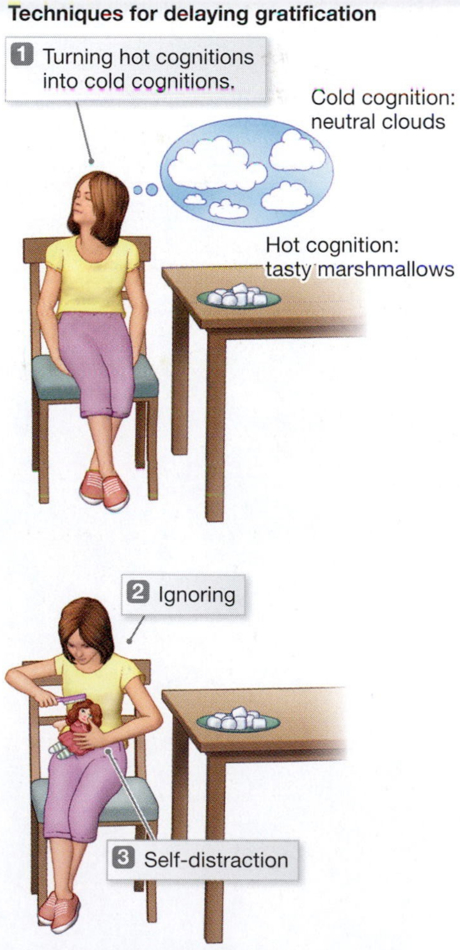

Techniques for delaying gratification

FIGURE 9.9 Delaying Gratification
Ignoring, self-distraction, and turning hot cognitions into cold cognitions are among the techniques children use to delay gratification.

aspects of objects, whereas cold cognitions focus on conceptual or symbolic meanings. Metcalfe and Mischel (1999) proposed that this hot/cold distinction is based on how the brain processes the information. As discussed in Chapter 3, subcortical brain regions such as the amygdala and nucleus accumbens are important for motivating behavior, whereas the prefrontal cortex performs cold cognitive processes, such as the control of thought and of behavior.

People Have a Need to Belong

Over the course of human evolution, those who lived with others were more likely to survive and pass along their genes. Children who stayed with adults (and resisted being left alone) were more likely to survive until their reproductive years because the adults would protect and nurture them (see Chapter 11, "Human Development"). Similarly, adults capable of developing long-term, committed relationships were more likely to reproduce and to have offspring who survived to reproduce. Effective groups shared food, provided mates, and helped care for offspring (including orphans). Some survival tasks (such as hunting large mammals or looking out for predatory enemies) were best accomplished by group cooperation. It therefore makes great sense that, over the millennia, humans have committed to living in groups. Roy Baumeister and Mark Leary (1995) formulated the **need to belong theory,** which states that the need for interpersonal attachments is a fundamental motive that has evolved for adaptive purposes.

need to belong theory The need for interpersonal attachments is a fundamental motive that has evolved for adaptive purposes.

MAKING AND KEEPING FRIENDS The need to belong theory explains how easily most people make friends (**FIGURE 9.10**). College students often make lifelong friendships within days of arriving on campus. Societies differ in their types of groups, but all societies have some form of group membership (Brewer & Caporael, 1990). Not belonging to a group increases a person's risk for various adverse consequences, such as illnesses and premature death (Cacioppo et al., 2006). Such ill effects suggest that the need to belong is a basic motive driving behavior, just as hunger drives people to seek food and avoid dying from starvation.

If humans have a fundamental need to belong, they ought to have mechanisms for detecting whether they are included in particular groups (MacDonald & Leary, 2005). In other words, given the importance of being a group member, humans need to be sensitive to signs that the group might kick them out. Indeed, evidence indicates that people feel anxious when facing exclusion from their social groups. Further,

FIGURE 9.10 Making Friends

people who are shy and lonely tend to worry most about social evaluation and pay much more attention to social information (Gardner, Pickett, Jefferis, & Knowles, 2005). The take-home message is that just as a lack of food causes hunger, a lack of social contact causes emptiness and despair. In the movie *Cast Away,* Tom Hanks's character becomes stranded on a deserted island and has such a strong need for companionship that he begins carrying on a friendship with a volleyball he calls Wilson (named for the manufacturer, whose name is on the ball). As noted by the film reviewer Susan Stark (2000), this volleyball convinces us that "human company, as much as shelter, water, food and fire, is essential to life as most of us understand it."

ANXIETY AND AFFILIATION Do you like to be around other people when you are anxious, or do you prefer to avoid them? When the terrorists struck the World Trade Center in 2001, for instance, did you seek out other people or did you want to be left alone? In a classic study, Stanley Schachter and his colleagues (1959) manipulated anxiety levels and then measured how much the participants, all female, preferred to be around others. The participants in these studies thought they were taking part in a routine psychological study. "Dr. Zilstein," a serious- and cold-looking man with a vaguely European accent, greeted them at the lab. After explaining that he was from the neurology and psychiatric school, the doctor said the study involved measuring "the physiological effects of electric shock." Zilstein told the participants he would hook them up to some electrical equipment and then administer electric current to their skin. Those in the low-anxiety condition were told the shocks would be painless—no more than a tickle. Those in the high-anxiety condition were told, "These shocks will hurt; they will be painful. As you can guess, if we're to learn anything that will really help humanity, it is necessary that our shocks be intense. These shocks will be quite painful, but, of course, they will do no permanent damage." As you might imagine, the participants who heard this speech were quite fearful and anxious.

Zilstein then said he needed time to set up his equipment, so there would be a 10-minute period before the shocks began. At that point, the participants were offered a choice: They could spend the waiting time alone or with others. This choice was the critical dependent measure, and after the choice was made, the experiment was over. Schachter found that increased anxiety led to increased affiliative motivations: Those in the high-anxiety condition were much more likely to want to wait with other people (**FIGURE 9.11**). Thus misery appears to love company. But does misery love just any company? A further study revealed that high-anxiety participants wanted to wait only with other high-anxiety participants, not with people who supposedly were waiting just to see their research supervisors. So misery loves miserable company, not just any company.

Why do people in a stressful situation prefer to be around other people in the same situation? According to Schachter, other people provide information that helps us evaluate whether we are acting appropriately. According to Leon Festinger's *social comparison theory* (1954), we are motivated to have accurate information about ourselves and others. We compare ourselves with those around us to test and validate personal beliefs and emotional responses, especially when the situation is ambiguous and we can compare ourselves with people relatively similar to us.

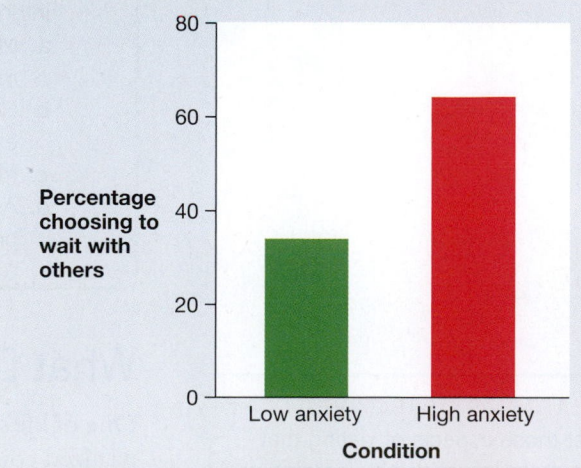

FIGURE 9.11 **Scientific Method: Schachter's Study on Anxiety and Affiliation**

Hypothesis: Feeling anxious makes people want to be with others.

Research Method:

❶ The participants, all female, were told they would be hooked up to equipment that would administer electric current to their skin.

❷ Some participants were told the shocks would be painless. Others were told the shocks would be quite painful.

❸ All participants were then asked if, while the experiment was being set up, they wanted to wait alone or with others.

Results: The participants who were told the shocks would be painful (the high-anxiety condition) were much more likely to want to wait with others.

Conclusion: Increased anxiety led to increased motivation to be with others, at least for females.

SUMMING UP

How Does Motivation Activate, Direct, and Sustain Behavior?

Researchers study motivation to understand how people set goals for themselves and how they achieve those goals. Maslow described an idealized need hierarchy, in which people first must satisfy lower needs, such as hunger and thirst, then turn to safety needs, which are followed by social needs, esteem, and self-actualization. Needs arise from states of deficiency, such as not having enough food or enough human contact; drives are the physiological states that lead us to engage in behaviors that satisfy needs. Our bodies tend toward homeostasis, a balanced state. Each of us prefers an optimal level of arousal, and people's optimal levels vary widely. If we are underaroused or overaroused, our performance will suffer. When we do something for the sheer joy of it, such as listening to music or drawing, we are intrinsically motivated. People with high self-efficacy, the belief that with hard work they will achieve their goals, set reasonably high goals for themselves because they are confident in their ability to succeed. Social motives are also important: People have a need to belong. For example, when they are anxious, females tend to prefer being with others.

MEASURING UP

1. Arrange the levels of Maslow's need hierarchy in the correct order, with lowest needs at the bottom, and then match each example with the correct level.

   Needs:
   a. belonging and love
   b. self-actualization
   c. physiological
   d. esteem
   e. safety

   Examples:
   1. You are in a mine shaft with low levels of oxygen.
   2. You are being bullied at school.
   3. You are about to take an exam in a class you are failing.
   4. You have just moved to a new city, where you know few people.
   5. You are an accomplished poet engaged in writing a new book of poems.

2. Indicate whether the motivation in each of the following scenarios is intrinsic or extrinsic.
   a. Mary enjoys reading her psychology textbook so much that she is even reading the chapters her teacher did not assign.
   b. Natasha is reading her psychology textbook to get a good grade on the exam and would never read an unassigned chapter.
   c. Most children love to read and will do so for the sheer joy of reading.
   d. As part of a plan to increase children's reading, a librarian will award prizes to the children who read the most books over the summer.

What Determines How We Eat?

LEARNING OBJECTIVE
List those aspects of eating that are more influenced by learning or culture and those that are more influenced by biology.

One of life's greatest pleasures is eating, and we do a lot of it: Most people in industrialized countries consume between 80,000 and 90,000 meals during their lives—more than 40 tons of food! Everyone needs to eat to survive, but eating involves much more than simply survival. Around the globe, special occasions often involve elaborate feasts, and much of the social world revolves around eating. Common sense dictates that most eating is controlled by hunger and *satiety*. People eat when they feel hungry and stop eating when they are full. However, some people eat a lot even when they are not hungry, whereas others avoid eating even though they are not full. What complex interactions between biology, cultural influences, and cognition determine human eating behavior?

Time and Taste Play Roles

Eating is greatly affected by learning. Have you ever noticed that most people eat lunch at approximately the same time—somewhere between noon and 2:00 PM? On a physiological level, this practice makes little sense because people differ greatly in their metabolic rates, the amounts they eat for breakfast, and the amounts of fat they have stored for long-term energy needs. We eat not because we have deficient energy stores but because we have been classically conditioned to associate eating with regular mealtimes. The clock indicating mealtime is much like Pavlov's bell—it leads to various anticipatory responses that motivate eating behavior and prepare the body for digestion. For instance, an increase in insulin promotes glucose use and increases short-term hunger signals. The sight and smell of tasty foods can have the same effect, and simply thinking about treats—freshly baked bread, pizza, a decadent dessert—may initiate bodily reactions that induce hunger.

A main factor that motivates eating is flavor—not just good-tasting food but variety. Animals presented with a variety of foods tend to eat much more than animals presented with only one food type. For instance, rats that normally maintain a steady body weight when eating one type of food eat huge amounts and become obese when presented with a variety of high-calorie foods, such as chocolate bars, crackers, and potato chips (Sclafani & Springer, 1976; **FIGURE 9.12**). Humans show the same effect, eating much more when various foods are available than when only one or two types of food are available. People also eat more when portions are larger (B. Rolls, Roe, & Meengs, 2007), a finding that suggests the large portions served by many restaurants may help explain the increase in obesity in industrialized nations over the past few decades.

One reason rats and people eat more when presented with a variety of foods is that they quickly grow tired of any one flavor. *Sensory-specific satiety* is a phenomenon in which animals will stop eating relatively quickly if they have just one type of food to eat, but they will eat more if presented with a different type of food. Apparently, the frontal lobe regions involved in assessing food's reward value exhibit decreased activity when the same food is eaten over and over but increased activity when a new food is presented (E. Rolls, 2007). This increased activity, in encouraging people to continue eating, may explain people's behavior during celebration feasts: As discussed above, even though we cannot imagine eating another bite of turkey, we often can find room for a piece—or two—of pumpkin pie to finish the meal. From an evolutionary perspective, sensory-specific satiety may be advantageous because animals that eat many types of food are more likely to satisfy nutritional requirements and thus to survive than are those that rely on a small number of foods. In addition, eating large meals may have been adaptive when the food supply was scarce or unpredictable.

FIGURE 9.12 The Impact of Variety on Eating Behavior
(a) Rats will become obese if given ample opportunity. **(b)** This trend appears to be true for humans as well.

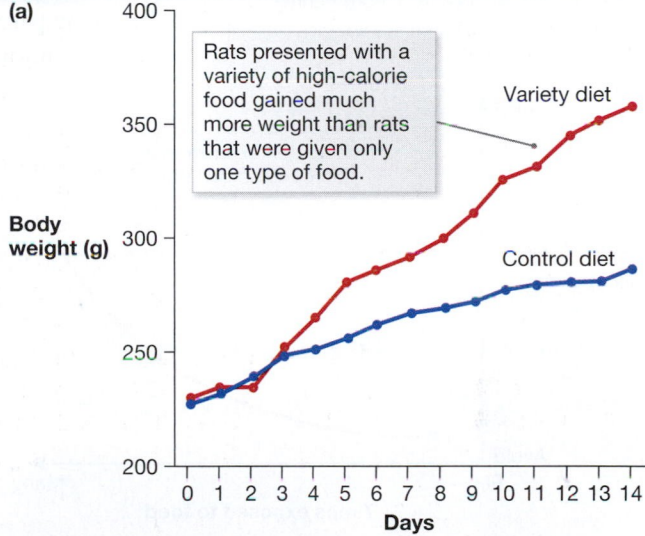

(a)

Rats presented with a variety of high-calorie food gained much more weight than rats that were given only one type of food.

Variety diet

Control diet

Body weight (g)

Days

(b)

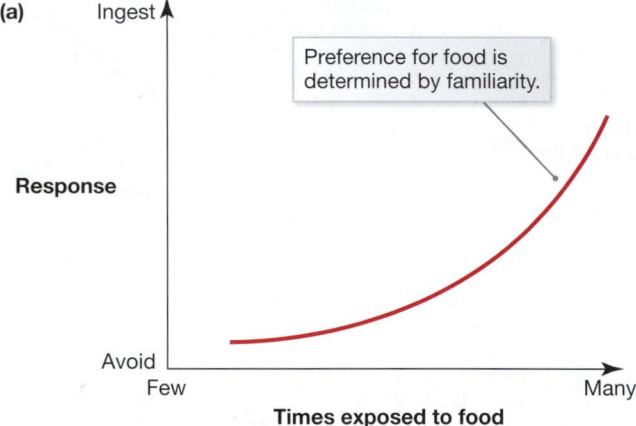

Culture Determines What We Eat

Would you eat a bat? In the Seychelles Islands, bat is a delicacy—it tastes something like chicken. What we will eat has little to do with logic and everything to do with what we believe is food. Some of the most nutritious foods are not eaten in North America because they are viewed as disgusting. For instance, fried termites, a favorite in Zaire, have more protein than beef does; spiders are nutritious and in many countries are eaten as tasty treats. At the same time, people from other cultures might be nauseated by some of North America's favorite foods, such as pizza and ice cream. Even when people are starving to death, they will refuse to eat perfectly nutritious substances. People died in Naples in 1770 because they were suspicious of the potatoes sent to relieve their famine; in Ireland, many of those who died in the potato famine refused to eat corn sent from America. Three million people died in Bengal in 1943 despite being supplied with wheat, which they rejected because it was not familiar as food.

What people will eat is determined by a combination of personal experience and cultural beliefs. Infants have an inborn preference for sweets, but they can learn to like just about anything. Generally, familiarity determines food preferences (**FIGURE 9.13**). The avoidance of unfamiliar foods is an example of *neophobia*, the fear of novel things. This behavior makes great sense because unfamiliar foods may be dangerous or poisonous, so avoiding them is adaptive for survival. Getting children to like new foods often involves exposing them to small amounts at a time, until they get used to the taste. Infants and toddlers also learn to try foods by observing their parents and siblings—if Mom eats something, it must be okay. Children will much more likely eat a new food offered by their mothers than the same food offered by a friendly stranger. This behavior, too, makes great sense from an evolutionary standpoint.

Of course, what a mother or father prefers to eat is determined by his or her own upbringing and experiences, and therefore families tend to like specific types of food. Ethnic differences in food preference often continue when a family moves to a new country. Although people often enjoy novel ethnic foods, in their regular diets most people prefer the foods of their own culture. Moreover, as Paul Rozin (1996) has pointed out, cultural rules govern which foods are appropriate in different contexts. For example, most people in North America like chocolate and french fries, but few people like them combined. Local norms for what to eat and how to prepare it—guidelines that Rozin calls *cuisine*—reinforce many food preferences. Moreover, religious and cultural values often tell people which foods to avoid: Kosher Jews eat beef but not pork, and Hindus eat pork but not beef. Taboos on certain types of food may have been adaptive because those foods were likely to contain harmful bacteria. However, many food taboos and preferences are idiosyncratic and have nothing to do with avoiding harm. They simply reflect an evolved group preference for specific foods, prepared and eaten in certain ways. Culturally transmitted food preferences powerfully affect what foods people eat.

Multiple Neural Processes Control Eating

The hypothalamus (see Figure 3.27) is the brain structure that most influences eating. Although it does not act alone to elicit eating, the hypothalamus integrates the various inhibitory and excitatory feeding messages and organizes behaviors involved in eating. In the

---

FIGURE 9.13 The Impact of Culture on Eating Behavior (a) As this graph illustrates, animals like the food they know, and they tend to avoid unfamiliar food. **(b)** How eagerly would you eat the fried cricket being offered by this vendor in Phnom Penh? Crickets are a popular snack among Cambodians.

first half of the twentieth century, research revealed that, depending on the specific area injured, damage to the hypothalamus dramatically changes eating behavior and body weight. One of the first observations occurred in 1939, when researchers discovered that patients with tumors of the hypothalamus became obese. To examine whether obesity could be induced in animals of normal weight, researchers selectively damaged specific hypothalamic regions. Damaging the middle, or *ventromedial,* region of the hypothalamus (*VMH*) causes rats to eat great quantities of food—a condition called *hyperphagia.* Rats with VMH damage grow extremely obese. In contrast, damaging the outer, or *lateral,* area of the hypothalamus (*LH*) is associated with a condition called *aphagia,* in which diminished eating behavior leads to weight loss and eventual death unless the animal is force-fed (**FIGURE 9.14**).

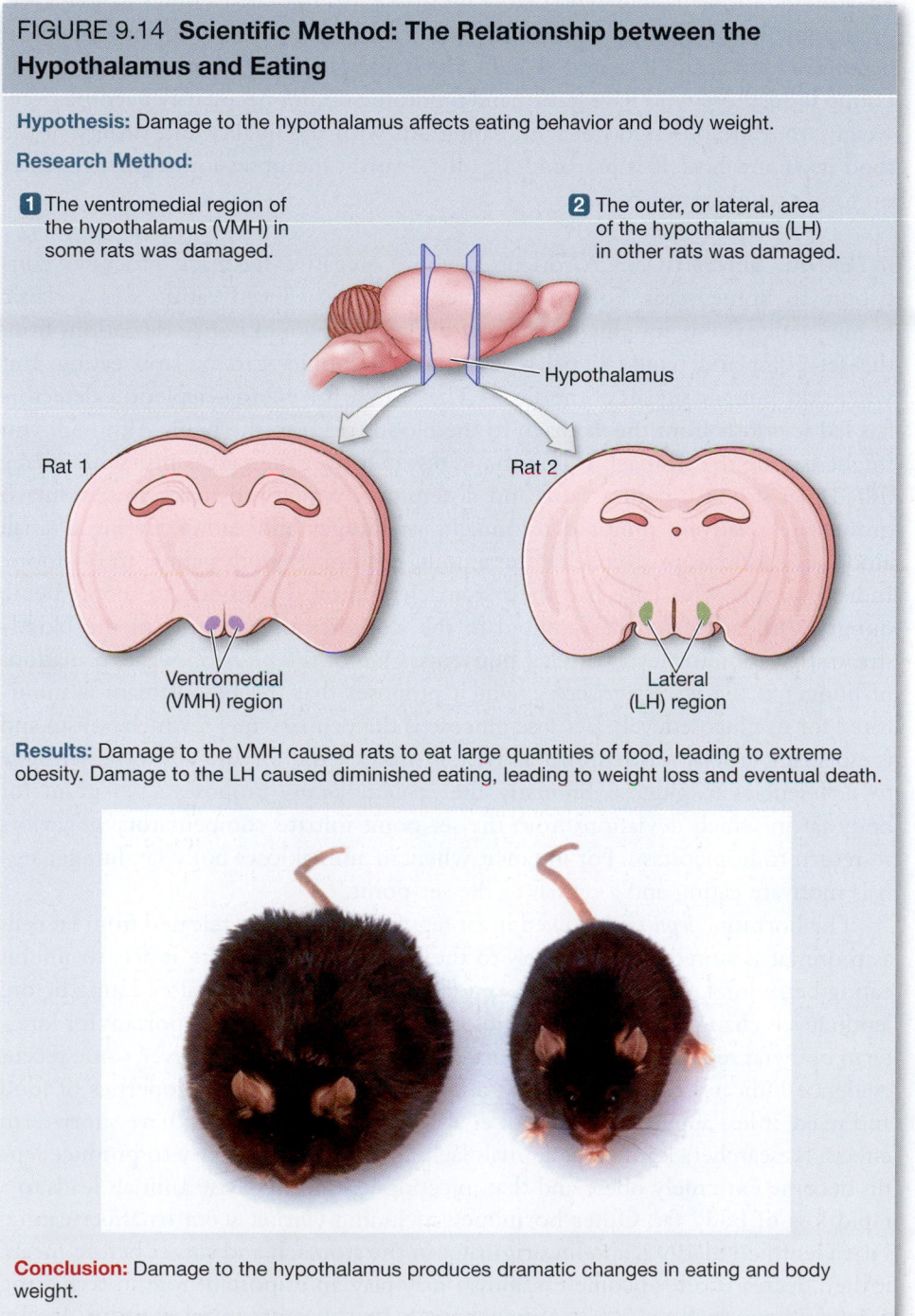

FIGURE 9.14 Scientific Method: The Relationship between the Hypothalamus and Eating

Hypothesis: Damage to the hypothalamus affects eating behavior and body weight.

Research Method:

1 The ventromedial region of the hypothalamus (VMH) in some rats was damaged.

2 The outer, or lateral, area of the hypothalamus (LH) in other rats was damaged.

Hypothalamus

Rat 1

Rat 2

Ventromedial (VMH) region

Lateral (LH) region

Results: Damage to the VMH caused rats to eat large quantities of food, leading to extreme obesity. Damage to the LH caused diminished eating, leading to weight loss and eventual death.

Conclusion: Damage to the hypothalamus produces dramatic changes in eating and body weight.

Brain structures other than the hypothalamus are involved in eating behavior. For instance, a region of the prefrontal cortex processes taste cues such as sweetness and saltiness (E. Rolls, 2007). This prefrontal region appears to process information about the potential reward value of food. Recent brain imaging studies have found that the craving triggered by seeing good-tasting food is associated with activity in the limbic system (Volkow, 2007), which (as discussed in Chapter 3) is the main brain region involved in reward. Indeed, overweight people show more activity in reward regions of the brain when they look at good-tasting foods than do normal-weight individuals (Rothemund et al., 2007). Damage to the limbic system or the right frontal lobes sometimes produces *gourmand syndrome,* in which people become obsessed with fine food and food preparation (**FIGURE 9.15**). One 48-year-old stroke patient, who before his stroke had not been a finicky eater, grew preoccupied with food and eventually left his job as a political correspondent to become a food critic (Regard & Landis, 1997). Despite their fascination with good-tasting food, those who have gourmand syndrome do not necessarily become overweight; they are obsessed not with eating but with the quality and variety of the food itself and how it is prepared. In other words, the obsession seems to center on food's reward properties.

INTERNAL SENSATIONS As discussed above, negative feedback processes contribute to homeostasis. For a long time, scientists believed eating was a classic homeostatic system, in which some sort of detector would notice deviations from the set-point and would signal that an animal should start or stop eating. But where do hunger signals come from? The search for energy-depletion detectors has led scientists from the stomach to the bloodstream to the brain. Although you might assume the stomach is important, research over the past century has established that stomach contractions and distensions (which can make your stomach growl) are relatively minor determinants of hunger and eating. Eating a small amount of food stops stomach contractions, but usually leads people to eat more. Indeed, people who have had their stomachs removed continue to report being hungry. Other research has pointed to the existence of receptors in the bloodstream that monitor levels of vital nutrients. One of the best-known explanations of hunger is the *glucostatic theory,* which proposes that the bloodstream is monitored for its glucose levels. Because glucose is the primary fuel for metabolism and is especially crucial for neuronal activity, it makes sense for animals to be sensitive to deficiencies in glucose. Similarly, the *lipostatic theory* proposes a set-point for body fat in which deviations from the set-point initiate compensatory behaviors to return to homeostasis. For instance, when an animal loses body fat, hunger signals motivate eating and a return to the set-point.

The hormone *leptin* is involved in fat regulation. Leptin is released from fat cells as more fat is stored. Leptin travels to the hypothalamus, where it acts to inhibit eating behavior. Leptin acts slowly, so it takes considerable time after eating before leptin levels change in the body. Therefore, leptin may be more important for long-term body fat regulation than for short-term eating control. However, some recent evidence indicates that leptin might also influence the reward properties of food and make it less appetizing (Farooqi et al., 2007), so leptin might have short-term effects. Researchers know that animals lacking the gene necessary to produce leptin become extremely obese and that injecting leptin into these animals leads to a rapid loss of body fat. Other hormones, including *ghrelin,* seem to affect eating. First identified in 1999, ghrelin originates in the stomach and surges before meals; it then decreases after people eat and so may play an important role in triggering eating (Higgins et al., 2007). When people lose weight, an increase in ghrelin

FIGURE 9.15 Gourmand Syndrome At what point does a healthy interest in fine food become an obsession?

motivates additional eating in a homeostatic fashion (Zorrilla et al., 2006). How much any of these hormones contribute to human obesity is unclear, but considerable research is under way to find out whether manipulating them can help prevent or treat obesity. As you will learn in Chapter 10, many factors—from genes to culture to bad eating habits—contribute to obesity. You will also learn why most people who diet have trouble losing weight and keeping it off.

> ## SUMMING UP
>
> **What Determines How We Eat?**
>
> To survive, animals need to eat. A number of redundant physiological systems motivate eating behavior to satisfy nutritional requirements. The motivation for variety helps animals achieve nutritious diets, whereas fear of new foods and acquired aversions to certain tastes help animals avoid potential harm. People consume a great variety of substances as food and learn from those around them to like certain flavors. Different brain mechanisms are involved in determining how much we eat, but glucose in our blood and hormones released from our stomachs and from fat cells are also involved.
>
> ## MEASURING UP
>
> Imagine you are asked to design a program for people who need to lose weight. Based on the information in this chapter about the processes that regulate eating, what suggestions would you make in each of the following areas?
>
> 1. Time effects on eating
>   a. To make late-night snacking less likely, create a cultural expectation about eating meals further apart during the day, perhaps by serving meals at 8 AM, 2 PM, and 8 PM.
>   b. Vary meal times so people eat at different times every day.
> 2. Cultural effects on eating
>   a. Teach cultural and ethnic groups how to prepare lower-calorie versions of their usual foods.
>   b. Teach cultural and ethnic groups how to prepare low-calorie foods from a range of cuisines.
> 3. Sensory-specific satiety
>   a. Do not present much variety in the foods you serve.
>   b. Be sure that every meal includes a variety of foods.
> 4. What research would you recommend based on findings with leptin?
>   a. Study ways to get the body to produce more leptin.
>   b. Study ways to get the body to produce less leptin.

What Factors Motivate Sexual Behavior?

Sexual desire has long been recognized as one of humanity's most durable and powerful motivators. Most human beings have a significant desire for sex, but sex drives vary substantially among individuals and across circumstances. Variation in sexual frequency can be explained by individual differences and by society's dominating influence over how and when individuals engage in sexual activity.

For much of the history of psychological science, the study of sex was taboo. The idea that women were motivated to have sex was almost unthinkable; many

LEARNING OBJECTIVES

Compare biological, cultural, and evolutionary perspectives on sexual behavior.

Describe the human sexual response cycle.

theorists even believed women were incapable of enjoying sex. In the 1940s, the pioneering work of Alfred Kinsey and his colleagues provided—for the times—shocking evidence that women's sexual attitudes and behaviors were in many ways similar to those of men. In Kinsey's surveys of thousands of Americans, he found that more than half of both men and women reported premarital sexual behavior, that masturbation was common in both sexes, that women enjoyed orgasms, and that homosexuality was much more common than most people believed. Very little was known about human sexuality when Kinsey began his work, and Kinsey's approach exemplified psychology's empirical nature. His surveys were controversial, but Kinsey showed a deep respect for collecting data as a way of answering a research question. More than 50 years later, we know a great deal more about sexual behavior, but the topic still makes many people uncomfortable. Public discussion of sexual activity is rare, except perhaps on talk radio and daytime television shows. This section examines what psychological science has learned about the motivation for sex.

Biological Factors Influence Sexual Behavior

Kinsey's research during the 1940s demonstrated how little most people knew about human sexual behavior. Despite his eye-opening contributions, ignorance about the physiology of sex persisted into the 1960s, when William Masters and Virginia Johnson began laboratory studies of sexual behavior. Their sample was somewhat biased, in that only people willing to be filmed while having intercourse or masturbating served as research participants. Nonetheless, Masters and Johnson gained considerable insight into the physiology of human sexual behavior. The most enduring contribution of their research was the identification of the **sexual response cycle**—a predictable pattern of physical and psychological responses that occur in four stages (**FIGURE 9.16**). The *excitement phase* occurs when people contemplate sexual activity or begin engaging in behaviors such as kissing and touching in a sensual manner. During this stage, blood flows to the genitals, and people report feelings of arousal. For men, the penis begins to become erect. For women, the clitoris becomes swollen, the vagina expands and secretes fluids, and the nipples enlarge.

As excitement continues into the *plateau phase,* pulse rate, breathing, and blood pressure increase, as do the various other signs of arousal. For many people, this stage is the frenzied phase of sexual activity, in which inhibitions are lifted and passion takes control. The plateau phase culminates in the *orgasm phase,* consisting of involuntary muscle contractions throughout the body, dramatic increases in breathing and heart rate, rhythmic contractions of the vagina for women, and ejaculation of semen for men. For healthy males, orgasm nearly always occurs; for females, orgasm is more variable. When it occurs, however, women and men report nearly identical pleasurable sensations. Following orgasm, there is a dramatic release of sexual tension and a slow return to a normal state of arousal. In this *resolution phase,* the male enters a refractory period, during which he is temporarily unable to maintain an erection or have an orgasm. The female does not have such a refractory period and may experience multiple orgasms with short resolution phases between each one. Again, the female response is more variable than the male response.

HORMONES As discussed in Chapter 3, hormones are involved in producing and terminating sexual behaviors. In nonhuman animals,

sexual response cycle A pattern of physiological responses during sexual activity.

FIGURE 9.16 Sexual Response Cycle

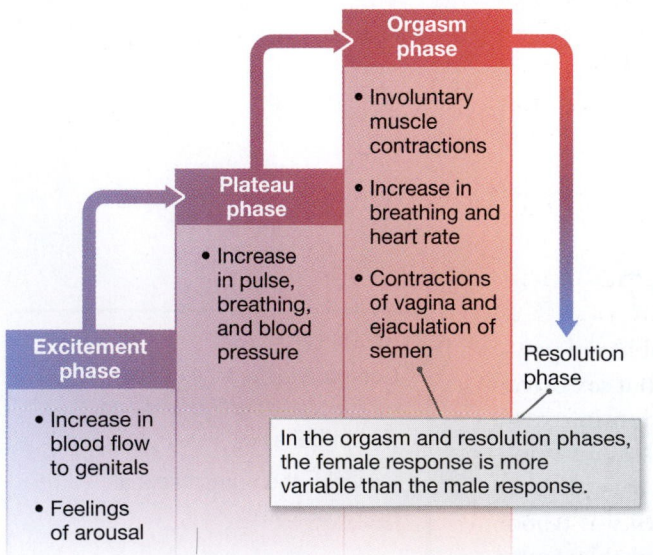

In the orgasm and resolution phases, the female response is more variable than the male response.

hormones profoundly influence sexual activity. In many species, females are sexually receptive only when fertile, and estrogen is believed to control reproductive behaviors. Estrogen appears to play only a small role in human female sexuality, but hormones affect human sexual behavior in two ways. First, they influence physical development of the brain and body. In the developmental phase of *puberty,* hormone levels increase throughout the body and stimulate physical changes—the development of *secondary sexual characteristics,* including pubic hair, body hair, and, for females, breasts. Puberty typically begins around age 11 or 12 for most males and often earlier for females.

The second way hormones influence sexual behavior is through motivation; they activate reproductive behavior. As noted in Chapter 3, sex hormones are released from the gonads (testes and ovaries), and females and males have some amount of all the sex hormones. But males have a greater quantity of androgens than females do, and females have a greater quantity of estrogens and progesterone. Androgens are apparently much more important for reproductive behavior than estrogens are, at least for humans. In men and women, testosterone—a type of androgen—is involved in sexual functioning. Males need a certain amount of testosterone to be able to engage in sex, although they do not perform better if they have more testosterone. The availability of testosterone, not large quantities of it, apparently drives male sexual behavior. The more testosterone women have, the more likely they are to have sexual thoughts and desires—although normal females have relatively low levels of testosterone (Meston & Frohlich, 2000). Adolescent females with higher than average testosterone levels for their age are more likely to engage in sexual intercourse (Halpern, Udry, & Suchindran, 1997). Another important hormone in men and women is *oxytocin,* which is released during sexual arousal and orgasm. (As discussed in Chapter 10, oxytocin also is associated with trust.) Some researchers believe oxytocin may promote feelings of love and attachment between partners; it also seems to be involved in social behavior more generally (Bartels & Zeki, 2004). Given the important role of the hypothalamus in controlling the release of hormones into the bloodstream, it is no surprise that the hypothalamus is the brain region considered most important for stimulating sexual behavior. Studies have shown that damaging the hypothalamus in rats interrupts sexual behavior, although which damaged brain area has the greatest effect differs slightly for males and females.

NEUROTRANSMITTERS Neurotransmitters can affect various aspects of the sexual response. For instance, dopamine receptors in the limbic system are involved in the physical experience of pleasure. Serotonin also is implicated in sexual behavior. The most common pharmacological treatments for depression enhance serotonin function, but they seriously reduce sexual interest, especially for women. Small doses of drugs that enhance serotonin are also useful for treating premature ejaculation. Researchers currently do not know why these effects occur.

One chemical that acts as a neurotransmitter in the brain and is critical for sexual behavior is *nitric oxide.* Sexual stimulation leads to nitric oxide production, which then promotes blood flow to both the penis and the clitoris and subsequently plays an important role in sexual arousal, especially penile erections. When this system fails, males cannot maintain an erection. Various drugs that enhance this system, such as Viagra, have been developed to treat erectile disorders. It is not clear whether such drugs can be used to treat women's sexual disorders, but they appear to enhance the sexual experience for healthy women (Caruso, Intelisano, Farina, Di Mari, & Agnello, 2003).

FIGURE 9.17 Sexual Scripts Sexual scripts influence behaviors such as flirting, pursuing romantic interest, and dating.

VARIATIONS ACROSS THE MENSTRUAL CYCLE Women differ from men in how the hypothalamus controls the release of sex hormones. Whereas in men hormones are released at the same rate over time, in women the release of hormones varies according to a cycle that repeats itself approximately every 28 days—the menstrual cycle. Although research has found only minimal evidence that women's sexual behavior varies across the menstrual cycle, recent evidence indicates that women may process social information differently depending on whether they are in a fertile phase of the cycle. For instance, when researchers used a computer program to alter masculinity and femininity in male faces, they found that compared with preferences expressed in other phases of the menstrual cycle, during ovulation women preferred the more masculine faces (Penton-Voak et al., 1999). In another study, in which women watched videotapes of men, women who were ovulating rated self-assured men as more desirable potential sex partners, but women who were not ovulating did not (Gangestad, Simpson, Cousins, Garver-Apgar, & Christensen, 2004). These studies add to a growing literature suggesting that women evaluate men differently across the menstrual cycle, although the everyday effects of these differences on women, and on the men they interact with, are unknown.

NEURAL CORRELATES OF VIEWING EROTICA Some brain imaging studies indicate that viewing erotica activates reward regions in the brain, such as various limbic structures. This effect is greatest for men who have higher blood levels of testosterone (Stoleru et al., 1999). As noted in Chapter 4, Hamann and colleagues (2004) found that when men and women viewed sexually arousing stimuli, such as film clips of sexual activity or pictures of opposite-sex nudes, men showed more activation of the amygdala—activation that, the authors suggest, increases the arousal caused by the stimulus. Men are more likely than women to report visual erotic stimulation as pleasurable (Herz & Cahill, 1997), but this finding might simply mean that more erotica is produced for men than for women. Research has shown that women prefer erotica produced specifically for women, which tends to emphasize more of the emotional factors of sexual interaction. A recent study found that although both sexes prefer viewing erotic movies aimed at their own sex, men were aroused by both types of movies (Janssen, Carpenter, & Graham, 2003). Finally, one brain imaging study found that women's reactions to viewing erotica varied according to the phases of their menstrual cycles, indicating once again that women's responses will likely be more variable (Gizewski et al., 2006).

Cultural Scripts and Cultural Rules Shape Sexual Interactions

In the movies, sexual relationships often start when one attractive young person meets another by chance, they spend some exciting time together, an attraction develops, and sexual behavior ensues—often within a day or two. In real life, however, the course of action is often quite different. For one thing, most people rely on social networks to meet their sex partners. In addition, people generally do not fall into bed together as fast as they do in the movies; most people know someone a long time before having sex. But the depiction of sexual behavior in movies and other media shapes beliefs and expectancies about what sexual behaviors are appropriate and when they are appropriate. *Sexual scripts* are cognitive beliefs about how a sexual episode should be enacted (on scripts, see Chapter 8, "Thinking and Intelligence"). For instance, the sexual script indicates who should make the first move, whether the other person should resist, the sequence of sexual acts, and even how the partners should act afterward (**FIGURE 9.17**).

In Westernized societies, the sexual script involves initial flirtation through non-verbal actions, the male initiating physical contact, the female controlling whether sexual activity takes place, and refusals typically being verbal and direct (Berscheid & Regan, 2005). The scripts differ in many places in the world, such as in countries where arranged marriages are common.

DOUBLE STANDARDS At the social level, the double standard is a well-known pattern of cultural influence. It stipulates that certain activities (such as premarital or casual sex) are morally and socially acceptable for men but not for women. The sexual revolution of the late twentieth century significantly changed sexual behaviors in many, but not all, countries. Most of these behaviors must be attributed to changing cultural pressures and expectations. Although sexual customs and norms vary across cultures, all known cultures have some form of sexual morality—indicating the importance to society of regulating sexual behavior. Cultures may seek to restrain and control sex for various reasons, including maintaining control over the birth rate, establishing paternity, and reducing conflicts.

SEX DIFFERENCES IN SEXUAL MOTIVES A noticeable and consistent finding in nearly all measures of sexual desire is that men, on average, have a higher level of sexual motivation than women do—allowing for many individual exceptions. Research studies have found that in general men masturbate more frequently than women, want sex earlier in the relationship, think and fantasize about sex more often, spend more time and money (and other resources) in the effort to obtain sex, desire more different sexual activities, initiate sex more and refuse sex less, and rate their own sex drives as stronger than women's (Baumeister, Catanese, & Vohs, 2001). In one study, researchers asked college-age men and women how many sex partners they ideally would like to have in their lives, if they were unconstrained by fears about disease, social pressures, and the like (Miller & Fishkin, 1997). Most women wanted one or two partners, whereas men's average answer was several dozen. A study of more than 16,000 people from 10 major regions around the world found that the greater male motivation for sexual activity and sexual variety occurs in all cultures (Schmitt et al., 2003).

The relative influence of nature and culture on sexual motivation may vary with gender. Roy Baumeister's (2000) term *erotic plasticity* refers to the extent that sex drive can be shaped by social, cultural, and situational factors. Evidence suggests that women have higher erotic plasticity than men. A woman's sexuality may evolve and change throughout her adult life; a man's desires remain relatively constant (except for a gradual decline with age). Women's sexual desires and behaviors depend significantly on social factors such as education and religion, whereas men's sexuality shows minimal relationships to such influences.

According to the **sexual strategies theory** of the evolutionary psychologist David Buss, these differences are due to the different adaptive problems faced throughout human history by men and by women (Buss & Schmitt, 1993). From this perspective, women differ from men in how they maximize the passing along of their genes to future generations. Women's basic strategy is intensive care of a relatively small number of infants. Their commitment is to nurture offspring rather than simply maximize production. Once a woman is pregnant, additional matings are of no reproductive use; and once she has a small child, an additional pregnancy can put her current offspring at risk. Thus biological mechanisms—for example, nursing typically makes ovulation less likely to occur—ensure spacing between children. On purely reproductive grounds, men have no such sexual interludes. For them, all matings may have a reproductive payoff; they bear few of the personal costs of pregnancy, and their fertility is unaffected by getting a woman pregnant.

sexual strategies theory Evolutionary theory that suggests men and women look for different qualities in their relationship partners because of gender-specific adaptive problems.

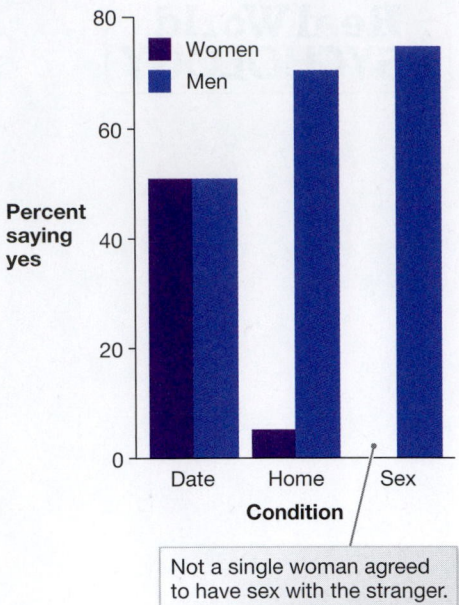

Not a single woman agreed to have sex with the stranger.

FIGURE 9.18 Sexual Motives and Responses When men and women were propositioned by an attractive stranger of the opposite sex, both sexes were equally likely to accept a date. Men were much more willing than women to agree to have sex or to go home with the stranger.

"I'm rich, you're thin. Together, we're perfect."

According to the sexual strategies theory, because having offspring is a much more intensive commitment for women, they likely are more cautious about having sex. Indeed, evidence indicates that women are much less willing than men to have sex with someone they do not know well. In one study of 96 university students, an attractive stranger approached people of the opposite sex and said, "I have been noticing you around campus. I find you attractive. Would you go to bed with me tonight?" Not one woman said yes, but three-quarters of the men agreed to the request (**FIGURE 9.18**). Indeed, the men were less likely to agree to go on a date with the attractive woman than they were to agree to have sex with her (Clark & Hatfield, 1989). In another study, people were asked how long a couple should be together before it would be acceptable for them to have sexual intercourse, given mutual desire. Women tend to think couples should be together for at least a month or more before sex is appropriate; men believe that even after relatively short periods of acquaintanceship, such as on the first or second date, sex is acceptable (Buss & Schmitt, 1993).

Mating Strategies Differ between the Sexes

Humans generally desire to enter into romantic relationships, and for the most part they want the same things in their mates. Men and women seek mates who are attractive, kind, honest, and good-natured. In addition to wanting the same basic qualities in potential mates, both sexes avoid certain characteristics, such as insensitivity, bad manners, loudness or shrillness, and the tendency to brag about sexual conquests (Cunningham, Barbee, & Druen, 1996). Despite these similarities, males and females differ in the relative emphases they place on physical appearance and social status, at least for long-term relationships. Men are more concerned with appearance, and women are more concerned with status. How does psychological science explain these differences? Women's preference for status over attractiveness depends on several factors, such as whether the relationship is short or long term (looks are more important in the short term) and whether the woman perceives herself as attractive. Women who view themselves as very attractive appear to want it all—status and good looks (Buss & Schackelford, 2008). In one study, men and women reported kindness and intelligence as necessary in their selection of mates, but their views of status and attractiveness differed. For the average woman seeking a long-term mate, status was a necessity and good looks were a luxury. In contrast, men viewed physical attractiveness as a necessity rather than a luxury in mate selection—looks matter most when men are searching for mates (Li, Bailey, Kenrick, & Linsenmeier, 2002).

In one study, Buss asked 92 married couples which characteristics they valued in their spouses. Women generally preferred men who were considerate, honest, dependable, kind, understanding, fond of children, well liked by others, good earners, ambitious, career oriented, from a good family, and fairly tall. Men tended to value good looks, cooking skills, and sexual faithfulness. Across some 37 cultures studied, females valued a good financial prospect more than did men (Buss, 1989). In addition, women in all 37 cultures tended to marry older men, who often are more settled and financially stable. In general, men and women value physical attractiveness highly, but their relative emphases conform to evolutionary predictions.

The evolutionary account of human mating is controversial. Some researchers believe that behaviors shaped by evolution have little impact on contemporary relationships. We must consider two important factors. First, the modern era is a tiny fraction of human evolutionary history, and the modern mind resides in a Stone Age brain, solving adaptive problems that have faced our species for thousands of years. Thus remnants of behaviors that were adaptive in prehistoric times may linger even if they are not adaptive in contemporary society. More important, however, natural selection bestows biological urges as well as a strong sensitivity to cultural and group norms, so instinctive behaviors are constrained by social context. The frontal lobes work to inhibit people from breaking social rules, which are determined largely by culture. The current social context differs greatly from that of millions of years ago, and human mating strategies are influenced by these contemporary norms. For example, from a biological view, it might seem advantageous for humans to reproduce as soon as they are able. But many contemporary cultures discourage sexual behavior until people are older and better able to care for their offspring. The critical point is that human behavior emerges to solve adaptive problems, and to some degree the modern era introduces new adaptive challenges based on societal standards of conduct. These standards shape the context in which men and women view sexual behavior as desirable and appropriate.

People Differ in Sexual Orientation

Why are some people homosexual and others heterosexual? Homosexual behavior, more commonly known as lesbian (for women) and gay (for men) behavior, has been noted in various forms throughout recorded history. From an evolutionary perspective, homosexuality appears to make little sense; exclusive homosexuality would not lead to reproduction and therefore would not survive in the gene pool. Many theories of homosexuality have emerged, but none has received conclusive support. One evolutionary theory is that lesbians and gays often act as "spare" parents to their siblings' offspring, and anecdotal evidence suggests they are sensitive and caring aunts and uncles; in this way, they might ensure the continuation of family genes. Of course, many gays and lesbians are parents—sometimes from earlier marriages and sometimes through artificial insemination or adoption. In the nineteenth and much of the twentieth century, homosexuality was regarded as deviant and abnormal, a psychological disorder. Until 1973, psychiatrists officially viewed homosexuality as a mental illness. Classic psychoanalytic theories of homosexuality emphasized the importance of parenting practices. Families with a domineering mother and a submissive father were thought to cause the children to identify with the opposite-sex parent (e.g., a boy with his mother). Such identification translated into a sexual attraction toward the gender opposite of their identification—that is, a same-sex attraction. However, the overwhelming majority of studies have found little or no evidence that how parents treat their children has anything to do with sexual orientation. Likewise, no other environmental factor has been found to account for homosexuality. Does biology determine sexual orientation?

Remember that when we ask whether something is biological, we really are talking about the relative contributions of biological factors compared with those of environmental factors. Every behavior results from biological processes, such as gene expression, that are themselves influenced by events in environment. One approach to examining the extent to which biological factors contribute to sexual orientation explores the effect of hormones. For instance, early theorists speculated that lesbians had higher levels of testosterone and gay males had higher levels of estrogen, but those speculations were wrong; the levels of circulating hormones do not differ between heterosexual and homosexual same-sex individuals. Rather, the best available evidence suggests that exposure to hormones, especially androgens, in the prenatal environment

might play some role in sexual orientation (Mustanski, Chivers, & Bailey, 2002). For example, because of a mother's medical condition, some females are exposed to higher than normal levels of androgens during prenatal development. These girls often have masculine characteristics, at birth and throughout life, and later in life are more likely to report being lesbians. Girls who were exposed to abnormally high levels of testosterone in utero are more likely to report being lesbians later in adulthood. An intriguing finding is that compared to heterosexual males, gay males are more likely to have older male siblings. One explanation is that the mother's body responds in some way to being pregnant with a boy, and this response alters the level of hormones in the prenatal environment when the mother becomes pregnant with another boy (Blanchard & Ellis, 2001, Bogaert, 2006). But most males with older brothers are not homosexual, so why would this response affect only some males?

A second approach to understanding the biological contribution to sexual orientation is through behavioral genetics. The idea that gene expression might be involved in sexual orientation is supported by a recent study using fruit flies. Researchers found that altering the expression of a single "master" gene reversed the sexual orientations of male and female flies (Demir & Dickson, 2005). But what about in humans? In 1993, the biologist Dean Hamer reported finding a link between a marker on the X chromosome and sexual orientation in males, and the media quickly dubbed the marker "the gay gene." Other researchers have failed to find any specific genes for sexual orientation. Is homosexuality inherited? Twin studies have provided some support for the idea of a genetic component to homosexuality, particularly for males. As discussed in Chapter 3, identical twins are most similar in genetic makeup, but they also are likely to have had similar environments, and it is difficult to pull apart these two types of contributions. In a review of previous studies, Mustanski and colleagues (2002) report the heritability of homosexuality as being greater for males than for females but with a significant genetic component for both. It remains unclear how human sexual orientation might be encoded in the genes.

Some research suggests the hypothalamus may be related to sexual orientation. In postmortem examinations, the neuroscientist Simon LeVay (1991) found that an area of the hypothalamus that typically differs between men and women was only half as large in homosexual men as in heterosexual men. In fact, the size of this area in homosexual men was comparable to its size in heterosexual women. Likewise, in a recent brain imaging study, heterosexual males showed greater activation of the hypothalamus when they sniffed a female pheromone substance (a hormonal secretion that travels through the air) than they did when they sniffed a male pheromone substance, whereas females showed greater activation when they sniffed a male rather than female pheromone substance (Savic, Berglund, & Lindström, 2005). Male homosexuals showed a pattern more similar to that of women than of heterosexual men—greater activation of the hypothalamus in response to the male pheromone substance.

Although intriguing, both of these studies can be criticized on the grounds that correlation does not equal causation. That is, a size difference or activation difference in any one part of the brain cannot establish whether this area determines sexual orientation, whether being heterosexual or homosexual results in changes to brain structure or function, or whether a third variable is responsible for all these effects. For instance, some researchers believe that the size of the hypothalamus is determined by prenatal exposure to androgens. Thus although these studies' findings are suggestive, evidence currently is insufficient to establish a causal connection between brain regions and sexual orientation. Considered together, the evidence is consistent that biological processes play some role in sexual orientation. The question is how and when biology contributes, and to what degree. Many psychological scientists believe it likely that multiple processes affect a person's sexual orientation in subtle ways (**FIGURE 9.19**).

In determining sexual orientation, biology might interact in various ways with aspects of environment. Daryl Bem (1996) has proposed that feeling different from opposite- or same-sex peers predicts later sexual orientation. A notable finding in the literature is that homosexuals report preferring the leisure activities of their opposite-sex peers—a tendency Bem believes may be due to biological differences in temperament. Children tend to play in same-sex groups, so boys and girls often are segregated. Regarding sexual orientation, Bem believes people are attracted to what is different. The difference creates arousal, and this arousal is the essence of sexual attraction—in Bem's words, "the exotic becomes erotic." Because the opposite sex is different, it becomes attractive; so most girls are attracted to boys, and vice versa. However, to some children, peers of their own sex seem different, so members of the same sex ultimately become erotic. Bem's model is interesting because it is based on the idea of initial biological differences in temperament but then proposes that the social environment shapes what is sexually attractive. Although the theory is supported by anecdotal evidence, so far no concrete evidence supports it. But how can researchers ever really test such theories in humans? What evidence is needed to conclude whether sexual orientation is determined or chosen?

Sexual orientation is not easy to change. Indeed, although there are Web reports of effective homosexual conversion therapies, there is little empirical evidence that these programs do any more than suppress behavior. No good evidence exists that sexual orientation can be changed through therapy. Moreover, being with people whose sexual orientation differs from yours does not change your sexual orientation. In some cultures and subcultures, people may engage in same-sex behaviors for a period and then revert to heterosexual behaviors, as in jail, where men and women often engage in same-sex relationships but do not consider themselves homosexuals. For reasons such as these, few psychologists or physicians believe sexual orientation—as opposed simply to sexual activity—is a choice or that it can be changed. Modern society, too, is increasingly acknowledging homosexuals' rights to express their sexuality: Canada, Spain, and some states in the United States allow homosexuals to marry, and other places around the world recognize same-sex relationships in varying ways. The Catholic Church has allowed gay priests to continue their calling as long as they do not commit sexual acts—the same requirement that holds for heterosexual priests. In some ways, the contemporary world is catching up with human history, within which homosexuals have always existed, whether or not they were free to be themselves.

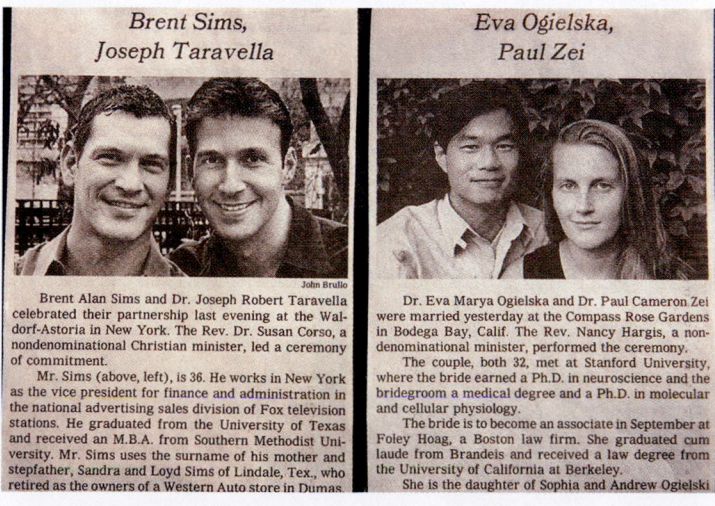

Brent Sims,
Joseph Taravella

John Brullo

Brent Alan Sims and Dr. Joseph Robert Taravella celebrated their partnership last evening at the Waldorf-Astoria in New York. The Rev. Dr. Susan Corso, a nondenominational Christian minister, led a ceremony of commitment.
Mr. Sims (above, left), is 36. He works in New York as the vice president for finance and administration in the national advertising sales division of Fox television stations. He graduated from the University of Texas and received an M.B.A. from Southern Methodist University. Mr. Sims uses the surname of his mother and stepfather, Sandra and Loyd Sims of Lindale, Tex., who retired as the owners of a Western Auto store in Dumas.

Eva Ogielska,
Paul Zei

Dr. Eva Marya Ogielska and Dr. Paul Cameron Zei were married yesterday at the Compass Rose Gardens in Bodega Bay, Calif. The Rev. Nancy Hargis, a nondenominational minister, performed the ceremony.
The couple, both 32, met at Stanford University, where the bride earned a Ph.D. in neuroscience and the bridegroom a medical degree and a Ph.D. in molecular and cellular physiology.
The bride is to become an associate in September at Foley Hoag, a Boston law firm. She graduated cum laude from Brandeis and received a law degree from the University of California at Berkeley.
She is the daughter of Sophia and Andrew Ogielski

FIGURE 9.19 Sexual Orientation The complexity of contemporary society—as illustrated by these gay and straight wedding announcements—mirrors the complexity of factors underlying humans' sexual orientation.

SUMMING UP

What Factors Motivate Sexual Behavior?

Pioneering research by Alfred Kinsey launched the study of human sexual behavior and shattered many myths regarding men's and women's sexual lives. Masters and Johnson identified four stages in the sexual response cycle that are very similar for men and women: excitement, plateau, orgasm, and resolution. Sexual behavior involves physiological and psychological factors. Hormones influence the development of secondary sex characteristics as well as motivate sexual behavior. However, behaviors are constrained by sexual scripts, which dictate appropriate actions for men and women. Men and women look for similar qualities in potential partners, but men are more concerned about a potential partner's attractiveness, and women are more concerned with a potential partner's status. These differences in relative importance may be due partly to the different adaptive problems the sexes faced over the course of human evolution. On average, and across nearly all measures, men have a higher level of sexual motivation and engage in more sexual activity, especially masturbation, than women do. Many theories have been devised to explain sexual orientation. Leading among them is the possibility that hormones during the individual's development while still in utero have important effects on the brain and subsequent sexual orientation, but these data are correlational and cannot be used to make causal inferences. Other theories, such as the psychoanalytic perspective (that sexual orientation is caused by parental behaviors) or that sexual orientation is carried on a specific gene, have not been supported.

MEASURING UP

1. Identify whether each of the following statements about human sexual behavior best describes a biological, cultural, or evolutionary perspective. Some statements may describe more than one perspective.
   a. Researchers have found that women prefer masculine-looking faces more during ovulation than in other phases of the menstrual cycle.
   b. Across 37 cultures, women preferred men who could earn a good living, and men rated a future mate's physical attractiveness as more important than women did.
   c. Across religious groups and in different countries, there are differences in women's willingness to engage in premarital sex.
   d. Women tend to prefer erotica that is more relationship oriented than men do.
   e. Many drugs used for depression also reduce sex drive, especially in women.
   f. Male sex function requires a minimal level of androgens.
   g. In general, men have higher levels of sexual motivation than women do.
2. Arrange the stages of the human sexual response cycle in order, and match each stage with its description.
   Stages: plateau, excitement, resolution, orgasm, refractory.
   a. occurs only in men
   b. increasing signs of arousal, including blood pressure and breathing rate
   c. contractions of the vagina for women and ejaculation of semen for men
   d. swelling of genitals in response to blood flow
   e. return to prestimulation state

How Are Emotions Adaptive?

How we feel about things profoundly affects what we think and do. Almost everyone has an intuitive sense of what *emotion* means, but the term is difficult to define precisely. For psychological scientists, **emotion** (or *affect*) refers to feelings that involve subjective evaluation, physiological processes, and cognitive beliefs. Emotions are immediate responses to environmental events, such as being cut off in traffic or getting a nice gift. It is useful to distinguish *emotion* from *mood,* since the two often are used equivalently in everyday language. Moods are diffuse, long-lasting emotional states that influence rather than interrupt thought and behavior. Often people who are in good or bad moods have no idea why they feel the way they do. Some researchers believe moods reflect people's perceptions of whether they have the personal resources necessary to meet environmental demands (Morris, 1992). Thus emotions tend to be specific, in response to events in the particular environment, and they typically interrupt whatever is happening or trigger changes in behavior. Moods, by contrast, refer to a vague sense that people feel certain ways. So people feel irritated (emotion) for particular reasons (e.g., getting cut off in traffic), but they sometimes feel irritable (mood) for no apparent reasons.

Research on emotions clearly illustrates that the mind helps solve adaptive problems. Negative and positive experiences guide behavior that increases the probability of surviving and reproducing. Emotions are adaptive because they prepare and guide behaviors, such as running when you encounter dangerous animals. Emotions provide information about the importance of stimuli to personal goals and then prepare people for actions aimed at achieving those goals (Frijda, 1994). Because humans are social animals, many emotions involve interpersonal dynamics. People feel hurt when teased, angry when insulted, happy when loved, proud when complimented, and so on. Moreover, people interpret facial expressions of emotion to predict other people's behavior. Facial expressions provide many clues about whether our behavior is pleasing to others or whether it is likely to make them reject, attack, or cheat us. Thus both emotions and emotional expressions provide adaptive information.

Facial Expressions Communicate Emotion

In his 1872 book *Expression of Emotion in Man and Animals,* Charles Darwin argued that expressive characteristics were adaptive in all forms of life, from the dog's hard stare and exposed teeth when defending territory to the human's red face when preparing to fight. Being able to tell when other people or other species are threatening has obvious survival value.

Emotional expressions are powerful nonverbal communications. English alone includes over 550 words that refer to emotions (Averill, 1980), but humans can communicate emotions quite well without verbal language. Consider human infants. Because infants cannot talk, they must communicate their needs largely through nonverbal action and emotional expressions. At birth, infants are capable of expressing joy, interest, disgust, and pain. By two months of age, infants can express anger and sadness. By six months, they can express fear (Izard & Malatesta, 1987). The social importance of emotional expressions can be seen even in 10-month-old infants, who have been found to smile more while their mothers are watching (Jones, Collins, & Hong, 1991). Thus, in the absence of verbal expression, nonverbal displays of emotions signal inner states, moods, and needs. The lower half of the face may be more important than the upper half in communicating emotion.

LEARNING OBJECTIVES

Summarize the ways culture and gender affect the expression of emotions.

Provide examples of emotional states and explain how they might have an adaptive function.

emotion Feelings that involve subjective evaluation, physiological processes, and cognitive beliefs.

In a classic study, Knight Dunlap (1927) demonstrated that the mouth better conveys emotion than the eyes, especially for positive affect (**FIGURE 9.20**). However, the eyes are extremely important in communicating emotion. If people are presented with pictures of just eyes or just mouths and asked to identify the emotion expressed, they are more accurate when using the eyes (Baron-Cohen, Wheelwright, & Jolliffe, 1997). But if the whole face is presented at once, the mouth appears to be most important in determining how people perceive the emotional expression (Kontsevich & Tyler, 2004).

FACIAL EXPRESSIONS ACROSS CULTURES Darwin argued that the face innately communicates emotions to others and that these communications are understandable by all people, regardless of culture. To test this hypothesis, Paul Ekman and colleagues (1969) went to Argentina, Brazil, Chile, Japan, and the United States and asked people to identify the emotional responses displayed in photographs of posed emotional expressions. They found that people from all these countries recognized the expressions as anger, fear, disgust, happiness, sadness, and surprise. However, critics could argue that, because people in these countries have extensive exposure to each other's cultures, learning and not biology is responsible for the cross-cultural agreement. The researchers then traveled to a remote area in New Guinea that had little exposure to outside cultures and where the people

FIGURE 9.20 How Faces Convey Emotion Based on Dunlap's classic study of the effects of facial expression, these photos show that the mouth conveys emotion better than the eyes. In **(a),** the face is expressing pleasure. In **(b),** it is expressing sadness. In **(c)** and **(d),** the lower halves of (a) and (b) have been interchanged. The downturned mouth and upturned mouth continue to carry emotional weight.

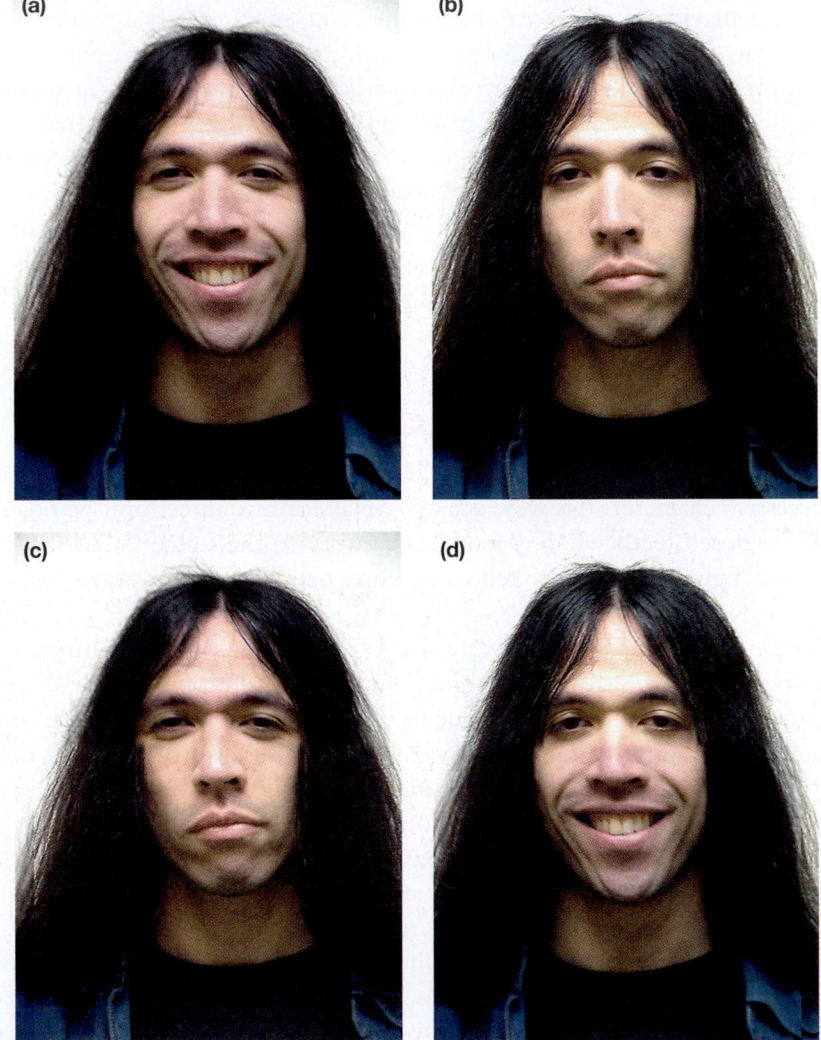

received only minimal formal education. The New Guinea natives were able to identify the emotions seen in the photos fairly well, although agreement was not quite as high as in other cultures. The researchers also asked participants in New Guinea to display certain facial expressions and found that evaluators from other countries identified the expressions at a level better than chance (Ekman & Friesen, 1971, **FIGURE 9.21**). Subsequent research finds general support for cross-cultural congruence in identifying some facial expressions; support is strongest for happiness and weakest for fear and disgust (Elfenbein & Ambady, 2002). Some scholars believe the cross-cultural consistency results may be biased by cultural differences in the use of emotion words and by the way people are asked to identify emotions (Russell, 1994). Overall, however, the evidence is sufficiently consistent to indicate that some facial expressions are universal and therefore likely biologically based.

DISPLAY RULES AND GENDER Although basic emotions seem to be expressed similarly across cultures, the situations in which they are displayed differ substantially. **Display rules** govern how and when emotions are exhibited. These rules are learned through socialization and dictate which emotions are suitable to given situations. Differences in display rules help explain cultural stereotypes, such as the loud and obnoxious Americans, the cold and bland British, and the warm and emotional Italians. Display rules also may explain why the identification of facial expressions is much better within cultures than between cultures (Elfenbein & Ambady, 2002).

display rules Rules learned through socialization that dictate which emotions are suitable to given situations.

FIGURE 9.21 Scientific Method: Ekman's Study of Facial Expressions across Cultures

Hypothesis: The face innately communicates emotions to others, and these communications are understandable by all people, regardless of culture.

Research Method:

1 In the second part of this study, participants in New Guinea were photgraphed displaying certain facial expressions, such as if they had come across a rotting pig or one of their children had died.

2 Participants from other countries were asked to identify the emotions being expressed by the New Guineans.

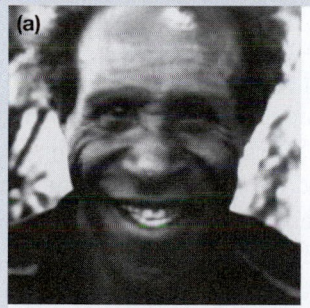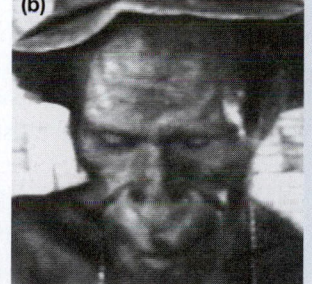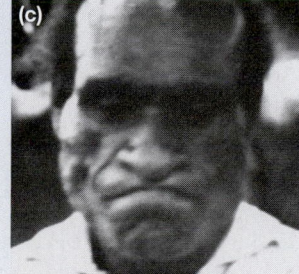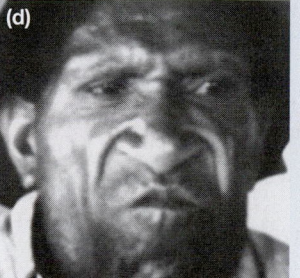

Results: People across cultures largely agreed on the meaning of different facial expressions, such as **(a)** happiness, **(b)** sadness, **(c)** anger, and **(d)** disgust.

Conclusion: Recognition of facial expressions may be universal and therefore biologically based.

Gender differences in display rules also guide emotional expression, particularly for smiling and crying. It is generally believed that women more readily, frequently, easily, and intensely display emotions (Plant, Hyde, Keltner, & Devine, 2000), and the current evidence suggests they do—except perhaps for emotions related to dominance, such as anger (LaFrance & Banaji, 1992). Men and women may vary in their emotional expressiveness for evolutionary reasons: The emotions most closely associated with women are related to caregiving, nurturance, and interpersonal relationships, whereas emotions associated with men are related to competitiveness, dominance, and defensiveness. Women may be more likely to display emotions, but they do not necessarily experience them more intensely. Although the evidence generally indicates that women report more intense emotions, this finding might reflect societal norms about how women are supposed to feel (Grossman & Wood, 1993). Moreover, perhaps because of differences in upbringing, in modern Western society, women tend to be better than men at articulating their emotions (Feldman Barrett, Lane, Sechrest, & Schwartz, 2000), and this ability might account for their more intense descriptions.

Emotions Serve Cognitive Functions

For a long time, psychological scientists studied cognitive processes without considering emotional processes. Studies on decision making, memory, and so on were conducted as if people were evaluating the information from a purely rational perspective. Yet our immediate affective responses arise quickly and automatically, coloring our perceptions at the very instant we notice an object. As Robert Zajonc pointed out, "We do not just see 'a house': We see a *handsome* house, an *ugly* house, or a *pretentious* house" (1980, p. 154). These instantaneous evaluations subsequently guide decision making, memory, and behavior. Therefore, psychological scientists now generally acknowledge that it is unrealistic to try to separate emotion from cognition (Phelps, 2006).

Clearly, people's moods can alter ongoing mental processes. When people are in good moods, they tend to use heuristic thinking (see Chapter 8, "Thinking and Intelligence"), which allows them to make decisions more quickly and more efficiently. Positive moods also facilitate creative, elaborate responses to challenging problems and motivate persistence (Isen, 1993). During the pursuit of goals, positive feelings signal that satisfactory progress is being made, thereby encouraging additional effort. One recent theory proposes that increased dopamine levels mediate the effects of positive affect on cognitive tasks (Ashby, Isen, & Turken, 1999). According to this view, positive affect leads to higher levels of dopamine production, which subsequently lead to heightened activation of dopamine receptors in other brain areas; this activation of dopamine receptors appears crucial for the advantageous cognitive effects of positive affect.

CRITICAL THINKING SKILL

Recognizing and Correcting for Belief Persistence in Your Own Thinking and in That of Others

A primary reason the United States declared war on Iraq in March 2003 was the suspicion that the Iraqi government had active programs for developing weapons of mass destruction (WMDs). The assertion that Iraq had WMDs was immediately controversial and sparked a 15-month investigation by the Iraq Survey Group, organized by the Pentagon and the U.S. Central Intelligence Agency (CIA). On September 30, 2004, Charles Duelfer of the CIA submitted a much publicized report (often referred to as the Duelfer Report) concluding that Iraq had neither WMDs nor significant programs for developing them. However, despite the Duelfer Report findings and previous statements expressing similar conclusions, an October 2004 survey found that among supporters of President George W. Bush, many "continued to believe that Iraq had actual WMD (47%) or a major program for developing them (25%)" (PIPA, 2004, p. 1). According to that same survey, supporters of John Kerry, the 2004 Democratic presidential candidate, believed that Iraq had neither the weapons nor the program.

How might we explain the difference in perceptions between Bush and Kerry supporters in the face of information such as that presented in the Duelfer Report? Bush supporters in the survey likely were demonstrating *belief persistence,* the tendency to hold onto previous ideas even when presented with evidence that the belief is questionable or just plain wrong. Belief persistence is sometimes called "my side bias" to denote that regardless of the evidence, people tend to believe information consistent with the side of an issue they already believe true. One study of belief persistence found that once participants had generated their own explanations for their beliefs, they were resistant to information discrediting the beliefs they had just explained (Davies, 1997).

With practice and the desire to make the most-informed decisions possible, however, you can become aware of this pervasive bias. You can be more open to examining all sides of an issue fairly and altering your beliefs when the evidence supports the change. In fact, deliberately seeking evidence that disconfirms a belief is a good way to reduce the effects of belief persistence bias (**FIGURE 9.22**).

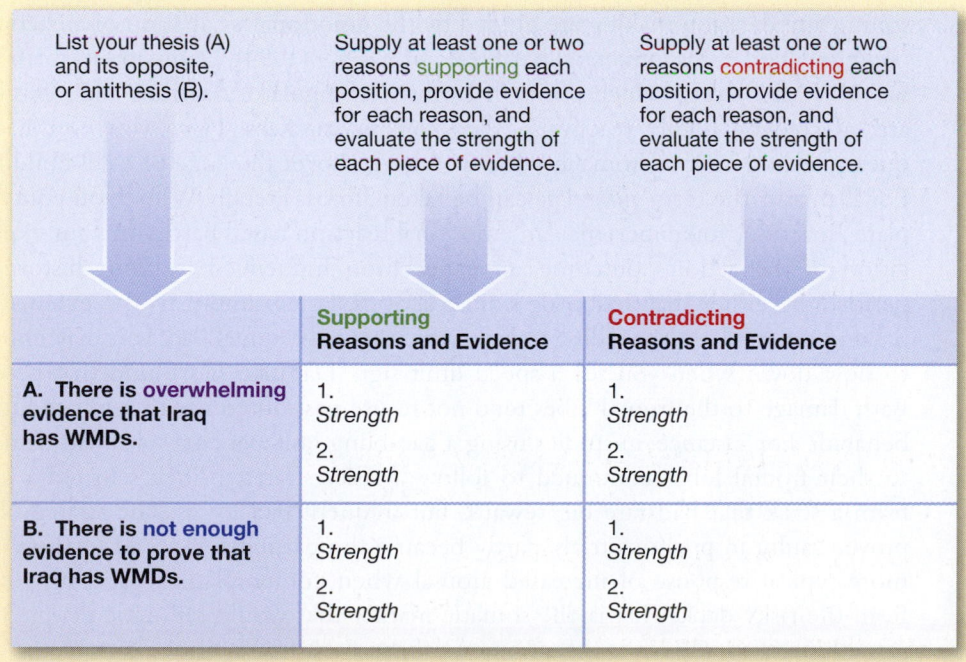

FIGURE 9.22 Think Critically: Examining Evidence

DECISION MAKING In the face of complex, multifaceted situations, emotions are heuristic guides that provide feedback for making quick decisions (Slovic, Finucane, Peters, & MacGregor, 2002). Would you rather go rock climbing in the Alps or attend a performance by a small dance troupe in Paris? Anticipated emotional states are an important source of information and a guide in decision making (see Chapter 8, "Thinking and Intelligence"). Moreover, emotion appears to have a direct effect that does not depend on cognitive processes. For instance, people might decide to cancel air travel shortly after hearing about a plane crash, even if the news does not change their outward belief about the likelihood that their own plane will crash. Recent or particularly vivid events have an especially strong influence on behavior. Thus risk judgments are strongly influenced by current feelings, and when cognitions and emotions are in conflict, emotions typically have more impact on decisions (Loewenstein, Weber, Hsee, & Welch, 2001).

According to the *affect-as-information* theory, posited by Norbert Schwarz and Gerald L. Clore (1983), people use their current mood states to make judgments and appraisals, even if they do not know the sources of their moods. For instance, Schwarz and Clore asked people to rate their overall life satisfaction—a question that potentially involves considering a multitude of factors from a lifetime, including situations, expectations, personal goals, and accomplishments. As the researchers noted, however, in arriving at their answers people did not labor through all these elements but instead seemed to rely on their current moods. People in good moods rated their lives as satisfactory, whereas people in bad moods gave lower overall ratings. Likewise, people's evaluations of plays, of lectures, of politicians, and even of strangers are influenced by their moods, which are influenced by day of the week, weather, health, and the like. However, if people are made aware of the sources of their moods (as when the researcher suggests that a good mood might be caused by the bright sunshine), their feelings no longer influence their judgments.

somatic markers Bodily reactions that arise from the emotional evaluation of an action's consequences.

SOMATIC MARKERS The neuroscientist Antonio Damasio has suggested that reasoning and decision making are guided by the emotional evaluation of an action's consequences. In his influential book *Descartes' Error* (1994), Damasio sets forth the *somatic marker theory,* which posits that most self-regulatory actions and decisions are affected by bodily reactions called **somatic markers.** Have you ever had a queasy feeling in your stomach when you looked over the edge of a tall building? For Damasio, the term *gut feeling* can be taken almost literally. When you contemplate an action, you experience an emotional reaction based partly on your expectation of the action's outcome, an expectation influenced by your history of performing either that action or similar actions. For example, to the extent that driving fast has led to speeding tickets, which made you feel bad, you may choose to slow down when you see a speed limit sign. Damasio has found that people with damage to the frontal lobes tend not to use past outcomes to regulate future behavior. For instance, in studies using a gambling task, patients who had damage to their frontal lobes continued to follow a risky strategy: They selected a card from a stack that had rare big rewards but frequent bad losses. The strategy had proven faulty in previous trials, partly because the participants failed to show the more typical response of increased arousal when contemplating selecting a card from the risky deck. That is, the somatic marker that would tell most people that something is a bad idea is absent among those with frontal lobe damage.

In terms of adaptiveness, emotional reactions help us select responses likely to promote survival and reproduction. Thus if we anticipate that an event, action, or object will produce a pleasurable emotional state, we will be motivated to approach it; conversely, anticipation of negative emotions motivates us to avoid other situations. Hence somatic markers may guide us to engage in adaptive behaviors.

Emotions Strengthen Interpersonal Relations

For most of the twentieth century, psychologists paid little attention to interpersonal emotions. Guilt, embarrassment, and the like were associated with Freudian thinking and therefore not studied in mainstream psychological science. However, recent theories have reconsidered interpersonal emotions in view of humans' evolutionary need to belong to social groups. Given that survival was enhanced for those who lived in groups, those who were expelled would have been less likely to survive and pass along their genes. According to this view, people were rejected primarily because they drained group resources or threatened group stability. The fundamental need to belong, described earlier, indicates that people will be sensitive to anything that might lead them to be kicked out of the group, and social emotions may reflect reactions to this possibility. Thus social emotions may be important for maintaining social bonds.

GUILT STRENGTHENS SOCIAL BONDS Guilt is a negative emotional state associated with anxiety, tension, and agitation. The experience of guilt rarely makes sense outside the context of interpersonal interaction. For instance, the typical guilt experience occurs when someone feels responsible for another person's negative affective state. Thus when people believe something they did directly or indirectly harmed another person, they experience feelings of anxiety, tension, and remorse, feelings that can be labeled as guilt. Guilt occasionally can arise even when individuals do not feel personally responsible for others' negative situations (for example, survivor guilt).

Although excessive feelings of guilt may have negative consequences, guilt is not entirely negative. One theoretical model of guilt outlines its benefits to close relationships. Roy Baumeister and colleagues (1994) contend that guilt protects and strengthens interpersonal relationships in three ways. First, feelings of guilt keep people from doing things that would harm their relationships—such as cheating on their partners—while encouraging behaviors that strengthen relationships, such as phoning their parents regularly. Second, displays of guilt demonstrate that people care about their relationship partners, thereby affirming social bonds. Third, guilt is an influence tactic that can be used to manipulate others. Guilt is especially effective when people hold power over us and it is difficult to get them to do what we want. For instance, you might try to make your boss feel guilty so you do not have to work overtime. Children may use guilt to get adults to buy them presents or grant them privileges.

Evidence indicates that socialization is more important than biology in determining specifically how children experience guilt. One longitudinal study examined socialization's impact on the development of various negative emotions, including guilt, in identical and dizygotic (fraternal) twins at 14, 20, and 24 months (Zahn-Waxler & Robinson, 1995). The study found that all the negative emotions showed considerable genetic influence (as evidenced by higher concordance rates for identical twins), but guilt was unique in being highly influenced by social environment. With age, the influence on guilt of a shared environment became stronger, whereas the evidence for genetic influences disappeared. These findings support the hypothesis that socialization is the predominant influence on moral emotions such as guilt. Perhaps surprisingly, parental

ON Ethics — Lie Detection Technology

Using physiological evidence to determine whether someone is lying is not a new phenomenon in the U.S. criminal justice system; the polygraph, or lie detector test, has been used in police departments since the 1920s, although it is not considered reliable enough to be allowed in most legal cases. As discussed in Chapter 2, a polygraph is used during questioning to measure physiological responses that indicate emotional arousal, such as heart and breathing rate. The theory behind polygraphs is that lying is stressful and that when people are stressed they are aroused. To determine a person's nonaroused physiological responses, the polygrapher asks the participant control questions designed not to be arousing, such as "Are you a student?" interspersed with critical questions pertinent to the investigation, such as "Did you steal the necklace?" The difference between the responses to the control and critical questions is the measure used to determine if the subject is lying (**FIGURE 9.23**). The problem is, people may also be aroused if they have been falsely accused or framed, if they are afraid, if they are attracted to the person administering the test, or for any number of other reasons. Also, participants can increase their arousal states for control questions by tensing up, biting their tongues, or tightening their anal sphincter muscles; they then can make an effort to relax for critical questions. College students who were taught these methods could avoid detection by experienced polygraphers 50 percent of the time. One study has shown that polygraphy identifies guilty subjects 76 percent of the time and wrongly accuses someone of lying 37 percent of the time (Kleinmuntz & Szucko, 1984).

Because polygraphs can be unreliable, more-sophisticated methods are being pursued. One such technology, computerized knowledge assessment (CKA), measures the increases and decreases in an EEG brain wave response called P300. The P300 wave has greater amplitude when a person recognizes a familiar sound, smell, or sight. Hypothetically, a suspected terrorist could be shown pictures of a terrorist training camp, or a suspected criminal could be shown pictures of a crime scene, and the suspect's P300 response would indicate either familiarity or unfamiliarity with the scene. CKA was developed by Lawrence Farwell, who calls his method *brain fingerprinting* (Farwell & Donchin, 1991; Farwell & Smith, 2001) and has formed a company to market it. In 2000, brain fingerprinting was ruled admissible evidence by one Iowa court. However, opponents of its use point out that it has not received adequate and objective testing (Wolpe, Foster, & Langleben, 2005). The case of CKA raises the question whether judges

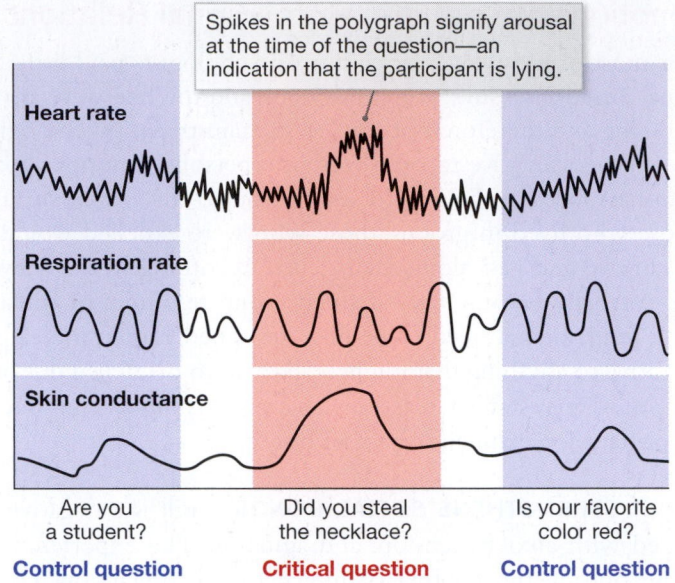

Spikes in the polygraph signify arousal at the time of the question—an indication that the participant is lying.

Heart rate

Respiration rate

Skin conductance

Are you a student?	Did you steal the necklace?	Is your favorite color red?
Control question	**Critical question**	**Control question**

FIGURE 9.23 Polygraph Questioning

are qualified to decide when scientific research has been adequately verified and peer-reviewed. The court relies on expert witnesses, but who decides which of these so-called experts are qualified? Should there also be specific criteria or a peer-reviewed process to approve expert witnesses?

Another lie detection technology uses fMRI to compare the brain activity of liars with that of truth tellers. Daniel Langleben and colleagues (2002) have found cognitive differences between deception and truth telling that have neural correlates detectable by fMRI. Two companies, No Lie MRI and Cephos, are working on improving the accuracy of fMRI lie detection so the technology can be admitted in court.

Lie detecting technology has huge potential, ranging from local law enforcement and courts to screening for terrorists. Private industries would be interested in screening future employees. Scout troops, schools, and day care centers would be interested in screening applicants for child molesters. Are these uses of the technology legitimate and justified? Where do we draw the line?

If accurate lie detection comes about, it will raise civil rights issues as well. Is using lie detection technologies equivalent to search and seizure that violates the Fourth Amendment? Would compelling a witness to unwittingly testify against himself or herself violate the Fifth Amendment? On the flip side, what if an innocent defendant wanted to be tested to prove he or she was not lying? Does saving an innocent person from prosecution justify any method of doing so?

warmth is associated with greater guilt in children, suggesting that feelings of guilt arise in healthy and happy relationships. As children become citizens in a social world, they develop the capacity to empathize, and they subsequently experience feelings of guilt when they transgress against others.

EMBARRASSMENT AND BLUSHING Embarrassment usually occurs following violations of cultural norms, loss of physical poise, teasing, and self-image threats (Miller, 1996). Some theories of embarrassment suggest that it rectifies interpersonal awkwardness and restores social bonds after a transgression. Embarrassment represents submission to and affiliation with the social group and a recognition of the unintentional social error. Research supports these propositions in showing that individuals who look embarrassed after a transgression elicit from onlookers more sympathy, more forgiveness, more amusement, and more laughter (Cupach & Metts, 1990). Like guilt, embarrassment may reaffirm close relationships after a transgression.

The writer Mark Twain once said, "Man is the only animal that blushes. Or needs to." Darwin, in his 1872 book, called blushing the "most peculiar and the most human of all expressions," thereby separating it from emotional responses he deemed necessary for survival (**FIGURE 9.24**). Recent theory and research suggests that blushing occurs when people believe others view them negatively and that blushing communicates a realization of interpersonal errors. This nonverbal apology is an appeasement that elicits forgiveness in others, thereby repairing and maintaining relationships (Keltner & Anderson, 2000).

FIGURE 9.24 Blushing The United Kingdom's Prince William is blushing, but his straightforward gaze and sly grin do not tell us why.

SUMMING UP

How Are Emotions Adaptive?

Emotions are adaptive because they bring about states of behavioral readiness. The evolutionary basis for emotions is supported by research on the cross-cultural recognition of emotional displays. Facial expressions communicate meaning to others and enhance emotional states. Emotions aid in memory processes by garnering increased attention and deeper encoding of emotionally relevant events. Positive and negative emotions serve as guides for action. Emotions also repair and maintain close interpersonal relationships.

MEASURING UP

1. A display rule is _____.
   a. a term that refers to displays of aggression among animals in the wild
   b. a rule that specifies when and how certain people can express an emotion
   c. a way of measuring the extent of people's emotions
   d. an interacting system of guidelines for interpreting various motivations
2. What is a likely explanation for blushing?
   a. It is a nonverbal way of admitting a mistake.
   b. It has no adaptive function, although in earlier times it probably signaled lower social status.
   c. It shows a disregard for others and thus can maintain social status for the blushing person.
   d. It signals weakness, which is important in human evolution.

How Do People Experience Emotions?

Psychologists generally agree that emotions have three components: the *subjective experience,* or the feelings that accompany the emotions; the *physical changes,* such as increases in heart rate, in skin temperature, and/or in brain activation; and the *cognitive appraisal,* people's beliefs and understandings about why they feel the way they do.

Emotions Have a Subjective Component

Emotions are *phenomenological,* meaning we experience them subjectively. We know we are experiencing emotions, in other words, because we *feel* them. The intensity of emotional reactions varies; some people report many distinct emotions every day, whereas others report only infrequent and minor emotional reactions. People who are over- or underemotional tend to have psychological problems. Among the former are people with *mood disorders* such as depression or panic attacks. People with mood disorders experience such strong emotions that they can become immobilized.

At the other extreme are those who suffer from *alexithymia,* a disorder in which people do not experience emotions' subjective component. Elliot, discussed at the beginning of this chapter, had alexithymia as a result of his brain surgery. One cause of the disorder is that the physiological messages associated with emotions do not reach the brain centers that interpret emotion. Damage to certain brain regions, especially the prefrontal cortex, is associated with a loss of mood's subjective component. Since a person with alexithymia does not experience (or express) many emotions, does it surprise you to learn that recent studies have found symptoms of alexithymia are more common in men than in women (Levant et al., 2006)? The question of whether women generally experience more emotions—or experience them more deeply—than men do has proved difficult to answer because the display rules are different for women and men. As discussed in Chapter 14, women are more likely to be depressed than men are. On the other hand, men are more likely to report an absence of emotions. Do these findings reflect learned patterns of behaviors or biologically based sex differences? Because nature and nurture work together, it is difficult—often impossible—to distinguish their effects.

DISTINGUISHING AMONG TYPES OF EMOTIONS How many emotions does a person experience, and how are different emotions related to one another? Many emotion theorists distinguish between primary and secondary emotions, an approach conceptually similar to viewing color as consisting of primary and secondary hues. Basic or **primary emotions** are evolutionarily adaptive, shared across cultures, and associated with specific biological and physical states. They include anger, fear, sadness, disgust, and happiness—and possibly surprise and contempt. **Secondary emotions** are blends of primary emotions; they include remorse, guilt, submission, and anticipation.

One approach to understanding the experience of emotion is the *circumplex model,* in which emotions are arranged in a circle around the intersections of two core dimensions of affect (Russell, 1980). The circumplex maps emotions according to their *valence,* indicating how negative or positive they are, and their *activation,* indicating how arousing they are (**FIGURE 9.25**). Psychologists have

LEARNING OBJECTIVES

Differentiate between primary and secondary emotions.

Compare the three main theories of emotion—James-Lange, Cannon-Bard, and two-factor—and provide an example of each.

Describe the major physiological components of emotion.

primary emotions Evolutionarily adaptive emotions that humans share across cultures; they are associated with specific biological and physical states.

secondary emotions Blends of primary emotions, including states such as remorse, guilt, submission, and anticipation.

FIGURE 9.25 Circumplex Map of Emotion

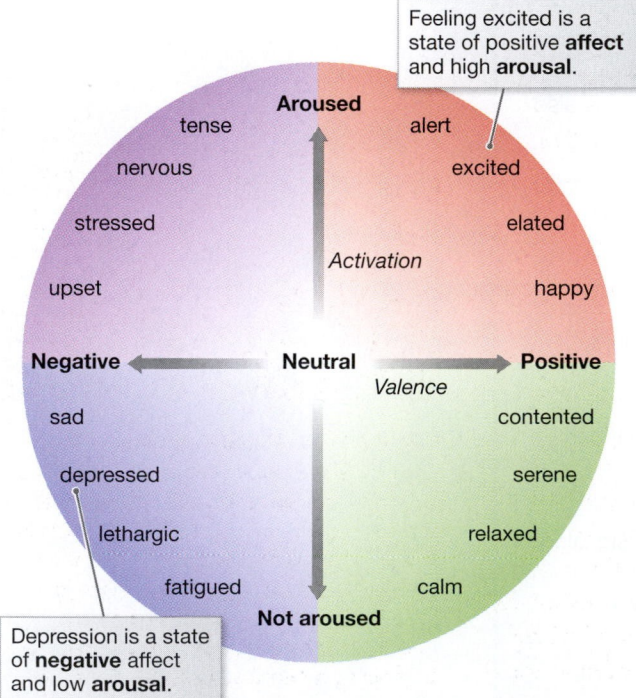

Feeling excited is a state of positive **affect** and high **arousal**.

Depression is a state of **negative** affect and low **arousal**.

debated the names of dimensions and the whole idea of naming dimensions, but circumplex models have proved useful as a basic taxonomy, or classification system, of mood states (Barrett, Mesquita, Ochsner, & Gross, 2007).

As David Watson and his colleagues (1999) have pointed out, negative and positive affect are independent—people can even experience both kinds of emotions simultaneously. For example, consider the bittersweet feeling of being both happy and sad, as you might feel when remembering good times with someone who has died. In one study, research participants surveyed just after seeing the movie *Life Is Beautiful* (in which a good-natured father tries to protect his son in a Nazi prison camp), moving out of their dormitories, or graduating from college felt happy and sad at the same time (Larsen, McGraw, & Cacioppo, 2001). Neurochemical evidence supports the idea that positive and negative affect are independent, suggesting that positive activation states are associated with an increase in dopamine and negative activation states are associated with an increase in norepinephrine (on neurochemistry, see Chapter 3, "Biological Foundations"). Further, Watson and colleagues argue that positive and negative activations are adaptive. For instance, the motivation to seek out food, sex, and companionship is typically associated with pleasure, whereas the motivation to avoid dangerous animals is associated with pain (Watson, Wiese, Vaidya, & Tellegen, 1999).

Emotions Have a Physiological Component

Emotions are associated with physical changes. Common sense suggests the emotions lead to the physical changes—we feel angry or sad or embarrassed, and our bodies respond. But in 1884, William James argued that it was just the opposite. In a proposal similar to one Descartes made in the 1600s concerning the split between mind and body (see Chapter 1, "Introduction"), James asserted that a person's interpretation of the physical changes in a situation leads that person to feel an emotion. In James's words, "we feel sorry because we cry, angry because we strike, afraid because we tremble, [it is] not that we cry, strike, or tremble because we are sorry, angry, or fearful." James believed that physical changes occur in distinct patterns that translate directly into specific emotions. Around the same time, a similar theory was independently proposed by the physician and psychologist Carl Lange, so the idea that felt emotion is the result of perceiving specific patterns of bodily responses is called the *James-Lange theory of emotion*.

One implication of the James-Lange theory is that if you mold your facial muscles to mimic an emotional state, you activate the associated emotion. According to the *facial feedback hypothesis,* first proposed by Silvan Tomkins in 1963, facial expressions trigger the experience of emotions, not the other way around. James Laird tested this idea in 1974 by having people hold a pencil between their teeth or with their mouths in a way that produced a smile or a frown (**FIGURE 9.26**). When participants rated cartoons, those in a posed smile found the cartoons funniest. Further support comes from the results of studies by Paul Ekman and colleagues (1983), who asked professional actors to portray anger, distress, fear, disgust, joy, and surprise. Physiological changes recorded during the actors' portrayals differed for various emotions. Heart rate changed little with surprise, joy, and disgust, but it increased with distress, fear, and anger. Anger was also associated with higher skin temperature, whereas the other emotions resulted in little change in skin temperature. Thus these results give some support to James's theory that specific patterns of physical changes are the basis for emotional states. However, subsequent evidence suggests that physical reactions are not specific enough to fully explain the subjective experience of emotions. We experience more emotions than there are distinct bodily reactions.

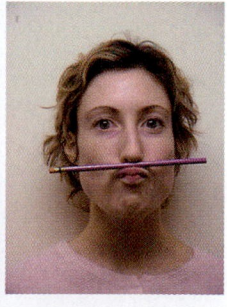

FIGURE 9.26 Facial Feedback Hypothesis Even the forced alteration of a person's facial expression can change that person's experience of emotion. The woman on the left ("smiling" because of the pen in her mouth) will more likely report feeling happy than will the woman on the right ("frowning" because of the pencil on her lip). Try holding a pencil in these positions and reflecting on your feelings.

The counterintuitive James–Lange theory quickly attracted criticism. In 1927, Walter Cannon, who had developed the idea of homeostasis, noted that although the human mind is quick to experience emotions, the body is much slower, taking at least a second or two to respond. Cannon also noted that many emotions produced similar visceral responses, making it too difficult for people to determine quickly which emotion they were experiencing. For instance, anger, excitement, and sexual interest all produce similar changes in heart rate and blood pressure. Cannon, along with Philip Bard, proposed instead that the mind and body operate independently in experiencing emotions. According to the *Cannon-Bard theory of emotion*, the information from an emotion-producing stimulus is processed independently in cortical and in subcortical structures, causing the experience of two separate things at roughly the same time: an emotion (from cortex) and a physical reaction (from subcortex). When a grizzly bear threatens you, for example, you simultaneously feel afraid, begin to sweat, experience a pounding heart, and—if you can—run (**FIGURE 9.27**). Everything happens together.

THE AMYGDALA In 1937, James Papez proposed that many subcortical brain regions were involved in emotion. Fifteen years later, Paul MacLean expanded this list and called it the *limbic system*. (As discussed in Chapter 3, the limbic system consists of brain structures that border the cerebral cortex.) We now know that many brain structures outside the limbic system are involved in emotion and that many limbic structures are not central to emotion per se. For instance, the hippocampus is important mostly for memory and the hypothalamus mostly for motivation. Thus the term *limbic system* is

James-Lange Theory

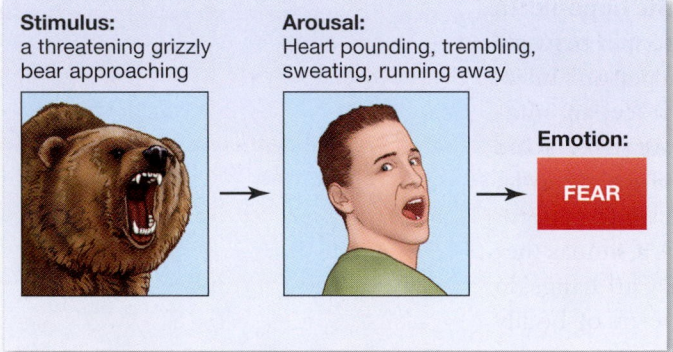

Cannon-Bard Theory

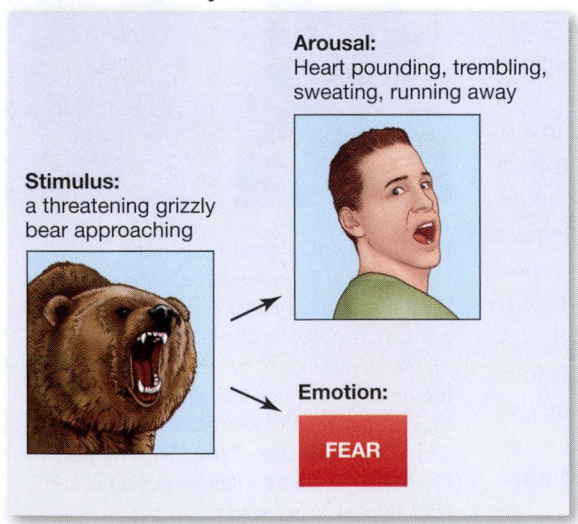

Schachter-Singer Two-Factor Theory

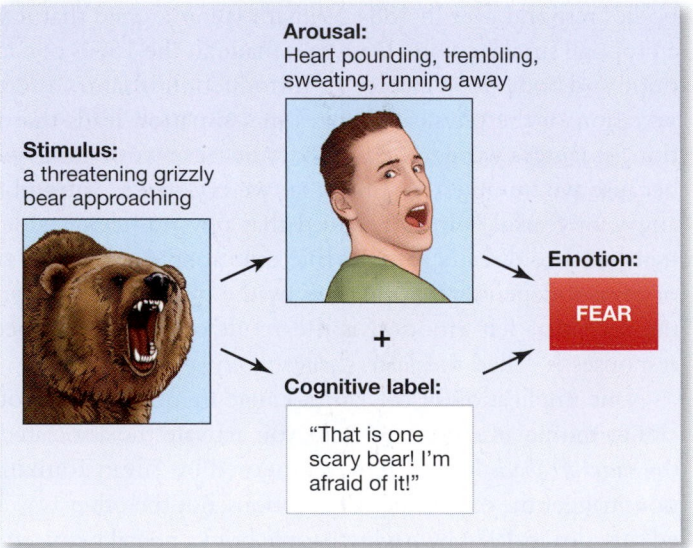

FIGURE 9.27 Three Major Theories of Emotion The theories differ not only in their relative emphases on physiology and on cognition but also in terms of when an emotional state is determined. (The two-factor theory is discussed below.)

used mainly in a rough, descriptive way rather than as a means of directly linking brain areas to specific emotional functions. For understanding emotion, the two most important brain regions are the amygdala and the prefrontal cortex (**FIGURE 9.28**).

The amygdala processes the emotional significance of stimuli and generates immediate emotional and behavioral reactions (Phelps, 2006). According to Joseph LeDoux (2007), affective processing in the amygdala is a circuit that has developed over the course of evolution to protect animals from danger. LeDoux (1996; 2007) has established the amygdala as the brain structure most important for emotional learning, as in the development of classically conditioned fear responses. Humans with damage to the amygdala show fear when confronted with dangerous objects, but they do not develop conditioned fear responses to objects associated with dangerous objects (see Chapter 6, "Learning"). For instance, if people receive an electric shock each time they see a picture of a blue square, they normally will develop a conditioned response, evidenced by greater physiological arousal, when they see the blue square. But people with damage to the amygdala do not show classical conditioning of these fear associations. Consider patient S.P., who first showed signs of neurological impairment around age three and later was diagnosed with epilepsy (Anderson & Phelps, 2000). At age 48, her right amygdala was removed to reduce the seizures' frequency. The surgery was reasonably successful, and S.P. retained most of her intellectual faculties. She has a normal IQ, has taken college courses, and performs well on standardized tasks of visual attention. However, she does not show fear conditioning. Strangely, S.P. can tell you that the blue square is associated with shock, but her body shows no physiological evidence of having acquired the fear response.

Information reaches the amygdala along two separate pathways. The first path is a "quick and dirty" system that processes sensory information nearly instantaneously. Sensory information travels quickly through the thalamus to the amygdala for priority processing. (As discussed in Chapter 5, "Sensation and Perception," all sensory information except smell travels to the thalamus before going on to other brain structures and the related portion of the cortex.) The second pathway is somewhat slower, but it leads to more deliberate and thorough evaluations. Sensory material travels from the thalamus to the sensory cortex, where the information is scrutinized in greater depth before it is passed along to the amygdala. Contemporary thinking is that the fast system prepares animals to respond should the slower pathway confirm the threat.

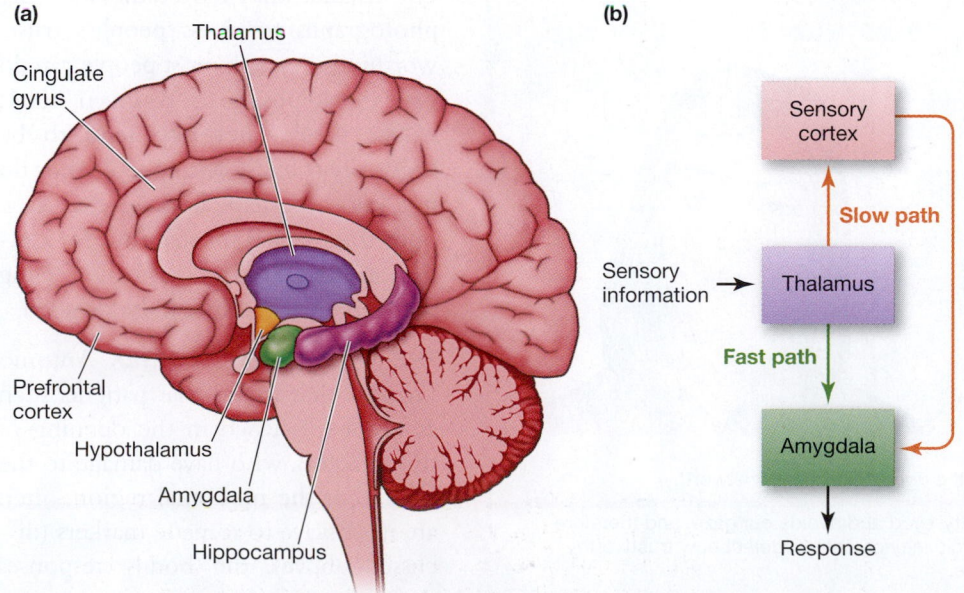

FIGURE 9.28 The Emotional Brain
(a) The two most important brain structures for processing emotion are the amygdala and prefrontal cortex. (b) There are two pathways for assessing and responding to emotion-producing stimuli.

As noted in Chapter 7, emotional events are especially likely to be stored in memory. Indeed, brain imaging studies demonstrate that increased activity in the amygdala during an emotional event is associated with improved long-term memory for that event (Cahill et al., 2001; Hamann, Ely, Grafton, & Kilts, 1999). Researchers believe the amygdala modifies how the hippocampus consolidates memory, especially memory for fearful events (Phelps, 2004; 2006). That is, emotions such as fear strengthen memories. Other emotions activate the amygdala; and the more they do so, the more they influence memory. Thus if you want to be remembered, research has shown, express an emotion such as happiness or fear (Armony, Chochol, Fecteau, & Belin, 2007). We tend to remember people we associate with intense emotions.

Another role of the amygdala in processing emotions is its involvement in the perception of social stimuli, as in deciphering facial expressions' affective meanings. For instance, fMRI studies demonstrate that the amygdala is especially sensitive to the intensity of fearful faces (Dolan, 2000). This effect occurs even if a face is flashed so quickly on a screen that participants are unaware they have seen it (Whalen et al., 1998). Perhaps surprisingly, the amygdala reacts more when a person observes a face displaying fear than when the person observes a face displaying anger. On the surface this difference makes little sense, because a person looking at you angrily is likely to be more dangerous. According to some researchers, the greater activity of the amygdala when a person looks at a frightened face is due to the ambiguity of the situation (Whalen et al., 2001)—that is, to the perceiver's not being sure what the person fears. The amygdala also responds to other emotional expressions, even happiness, but generally the effect is greatest for fear. One recent study showed that the amygdala can be activated even by neutral facial expressions, but only in chronically anxious people (Somerville, Kim, Johnstone, Alexander, & Whalen, 2004).

Given that the amygdala is involved in processing the emotional content of facial expressions, it is not surprising that social impairments result when the amygdala is damaged. Those with damage to the amygdala often have difficulty evaluating the intensity of fearful faces—but they do not show impairments in judging the intensity of other facial expressions, such as happiness. One study suggests that those with damage to the amygdala can tell a smile from a frown but that they fail to use information within facial expressions to make accurate interpersonal judgments (Adolphs, Tranel, & Damasio, 1998). For instance, they have difficulty using photographs to assess people's trustworthiness—a task most people can do easily (Adolphs, Sears, & Piven, 2001; **FIGURE 9.29**). They also tend to be unusually friendly with people they do not know, perhaps because they lack both the normal mechanisms for caution around strangers and the feeling that some people should be avoided.

THE PREFRONTAL CORTEX Antonio Damasio has found that patients such as Elliot (discussed in the opening of this chapter), who have damage to the middle of the prefrontal region, often are insensitive to somatic markers (discussed above), the bodily responses that usually accompany emotions.

FIGURE 9.29 Try for Yourself: Evaluate Facial Expressions

Which of these people would you trust?

 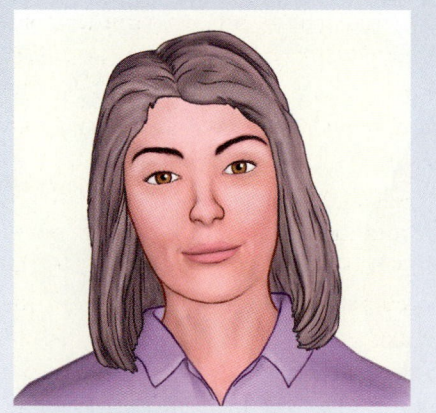

Results: Most people would say the person on the right looks more trustworthy.

Conclusion: The person on the left appears shifty-eyed and avoids our gaze, and therefore he looks less trustworthy. People with certain brain injuries cannot detect how trustworthy people are from facial expressions such as these.

When these regions are damaged, people still can recall information, but it has lost most of its affective meaning. They might be able to describe their current problems or talk about the death of a loved one, but they do so without experiencing any of the emotional pain that normally accompanies such thoughts.

Some evidence suggests that the left and right frontal lobes are affected by different emotions. The psychological scientist Richard Davidson has shown that unequal activation of the left and right hemispheres of the prefrontal cortex is associated with specific emotional states, a pattern known as *cerebral asymmetry*. In a series of studies, Davidson and his colleagues (2000) found that greater activation of the right prefrontal cortex is associated with negative affect, whereas greater activation of the left hemisphere is associated with positive affect. People also can be dominant in one hemisphere, and that hemisphere can bias emotion. Hemispherical dominance is assessed through a series of questions that ask participants how they might feel in an emotional situation (such as being anxious). Those who tend to move their eyes to the right are left-hemisphere dominant, and those who move theirs to the left are right-hemisphere dominant. A study of responses to film clips found that people who were left-hemisphere dominant showed the most positive response to pleasant scenes, whereas those who were right-hemisphere dominant showed the most negative response to unpleasant scenes. As you might expect from this pattern, people who tend to be depressed show greater right than left hemisphere activity, mainly because the left hemisphere does not seem to respond normally (Davidson et al., 2002).

Emotions Have a Cognitive Component

According to Stanley Schachter's *two-factor theory of emotion,* a situation evokes a physiological response, such as arousal, and a cognitive interpretation, or *emotion label*. When people experience arousal, they initiate a search for its source. According to Schachter, a person searches for an explanation when, for instance, his or her heart starts to race and his or her blood pressure rises. So the person might, for example, see a grizzly bear approaching and immediately label bodily responses such as racing heart and rising blood pressure as fear. Although the search for a cognitive explanation is often quick and straightforward, since we generally recognize the event that led to our emotional state, sometimes the situation is more ambiguous. What happens then? According to the two-factor theory, whatever the person believes caused the emotion will determine how the person labels the emotion.

Schachter and Jerome Singer (1962) devised an ingenious experiment to test the two-factor theory. First, participants were injected with either a stimulant or a placebo. The stimulant was adrenaline, which produced symptoms such as sweaty palms, increased heart rate, and shaking. Then participants either were told that the drug they took would make them feel aroused or were not told anything about the drug's effects. Finally, each participant was left to wait with a confederate of the experimenter, someone who was working with the experimenter and behaved according to the research plan. In the euphoric condition, participants were exposed to a confederate who played with a hula hoop and made paper airplanes. In the angry condition, they were exposed to a confederate who asked them very intimate, personal questions, such as "With how many men (other than your father) has your mother had extramarital relationships?" (To make the question even more insulting, the choices were four or fewer, five to nine, or ten or more.) Participants who received the adrenaline but were told how their bodies would respond to the drug had an easy explanation for their arousal and attributed it to the adrenaline, not to the situation. In contrast, the participants who received adrenaline but were not given information about its effects, who were just as aroused as the informed group but did not know why, looked to the environment to explain or label their body's response—sweating palms, increased heart rate, and shaking. Participants in the no-explanation group reported that they felt happy when they waited with the euphoric confederate and that they felt less happy when they waited with the angry confederate. They attributed their feelings to what was happening in the environment; participants in the informed group did not (**FIGURE 9.30**).

PEOPLE CAN MISATTRIBUTE THE SOURCE OF EMOTIONAL STATES One interesting implication of the Schachter theory is that physical states caused by a situation can be attributed to the wrong emotion. When people misidentify the source of their arousal, it is called *misattribution of arousal*. In one exploration of this phenomenon, researchers tried to see whether people could fall in love through misattribution (Dutton & Aron, 1974). Male participants were met by an interviewer on one of two bridges over the Capilano River in British Columbia. One was a narrow suspension bridge with a low rail that swayed 230 feet above raging, rocky rapids; the

---

FIGURE 9.30 Scientific Method: Testing the Two-Factor Theory

Hypothesis: Whatever a person believes caused an emotion will determine how the person labels the emotion.

Research Method:

1 Participants were injected with a stimulant (adrenaline) or a placebo.

2 Participants were told the drug they were given would make them feel aroused or were not told anything about the drug's effects.

3 In the euphoric condition, participants were exposed to a confederate who played with a hula hoop and made paper airplanes. In the angry condition, they were exposed to a confederate who asked them very intimate, personal questions, such as "With how many men (other than your father) has your mother had extramarital relationships?"

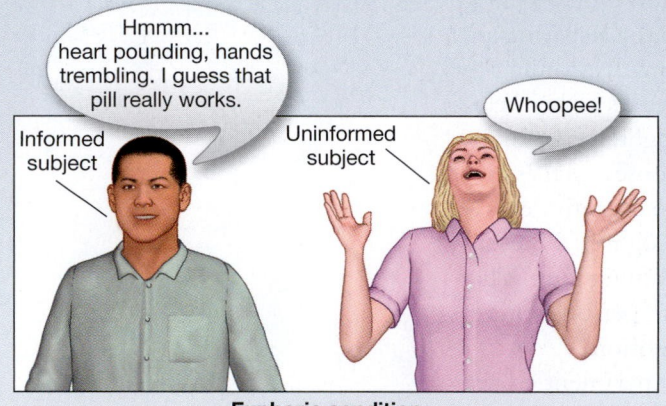

Euphoric condition

Angry condition

Results: Participants who received the adrenaline but were told how their bodies would respond to the drug had an easy explanation for their arousal and attributed it to the adrenaline, not to the situation. In contrast, the participants who received adrenaline but were not given information about its effects looked to the environment to explain or label their bodies' responses.

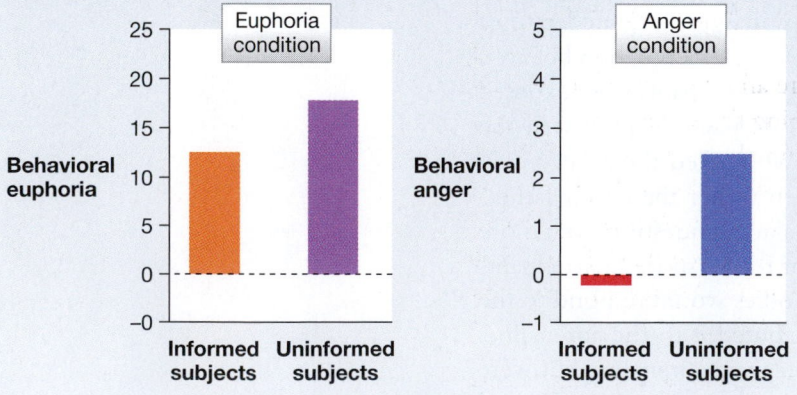

Participants in the no-explanation group reported that they felt happy when they waited with the euphoric confederate and that they felt angry when they waited with the confederate who asked insulting questions. They attributed their feelings to what was happening in the environment; participants in the informed group did not.

Conclusion: Physiological states caused by a situation can be attributed to the wrong emotion.

---

other was a sturdy modern bridge just above the river. An attractive female research assistant approached the men and interviewed them in the middle of the bridge. She gave them her phone number and offered to explain the results of the study to them at a later date if they were interested. According to the two-factor theory of emotion, the less stable bridge would produce arousal (sweaty palms, increased heart rate), which could be misattributed as attraction to the interviewer. Indeed, men interviewed on the less stable bridge were more likely to call the interviewer and ask her for a date (**FIGURE 9.31**). A possible confound is that there could have been initial differences among the men who chose to cross the less stable bridge and those who chose the safer bridge—perhaps men who were more likely to take risks were more likely to take a scary bridge and to call for a date. However, the general idea that people can misattribute arousal for affection has been supported in other studies.

During a similar form of misattribution, *excitation transfer*, residual physiological arousal caused by one event is transferred to a new stimulus. In the period after exercise, for example, there is a slow return to baseline during which the body continues to have residual arousal symptoms, such as an elevated heart rate. However, after a few minutes, most people will have caught their breath and may not realize their bodies are still aroused. During this interim period, they likely will transfer the residual excitation from the exercise to any event that occurs. This response has a practical application: You might want to take a date to a movie that produces arousal—a tearjerker or an action film—in the hope that residual arousal will be misattributed to you.

FIGURE 9.31 Excitation Transfer Men who walked across this narrow and scary bridge over the Capilano River displayed more attraction to a female experimenter on the bridge than did men who walked across a safer bridge.

People Regulate Their Moods

As discussed extensively above, emotions are adaptive, helping us respond to environmental challenges in ways that have proved successful over the course of human evolution. At the same time, emotions can be disruptive and troublesome—as when people feel so anxious that they cannot study for exams, or when they are so angry at someone who raced ahead of them at an intersection that they want to run the other car off the road. In our daily lives, circumstances often require us to harness our emotional responses, but doing so is not easy. Consider how difficult it is to mask your expression of disgust when you are obligated by politeness to eat something you dislike—or when you have to be nice about losing a competition that really matters to you.

Successfully regulating our emotional states depends on several strategies. Some of these strategies help us prevent or prepare for bad events, and some of them help us deal with those events after they occur. James Gross (1999) outlined various strategies people use to regulate their emotions. For instance, they try to put themselves in certain situations and to avoid other situations. If you want to feel romantic when proposing to your girlfriend, you are better off doing so in a quiet, intimate bistro than in a fast-food joint; if you want to avoid feeling jealous of your sister's athletic skill, you could choose not to attend her soccer, basketball, and softball games; and so on. People also can help manage their emotional states by focusing their attention on certain aspects of situations. If you are afraid of flying, for example, you can distract yourself from your anxiety by helping the woman next to you entertain her restless toddler. People also can try to directly alter their emotional reactions to events by reappraising those events in more neutral terms. So, if you get scared while watching a movie, you can remind yourself that the whole spectacle has been staged and no one is actually being hurt. Recent studies have found that engaging in reappraisal changes the activity of brain regions involved in the experience of emotion (Ochsner, Bunge, Gross, & Gabrieli, 2002).

HUMOR Humor is a simple, effective method of regulating negative emotions and has many mental and physical health benefits. Most obviously, humor increases positive affect. When we find something humorous, we smile, laugh, and enter a state of pleasurable, relaxed excitation. Research shows that laughter stimulates endocrine secretion, improves the immune system, and stimulates the release of hormones, catecholamines, and endorphins. When people laugh, they experience rises in circulation, blood pressure, skin temperature, and heart rate, along with a decrease in pain perception. All these responses are similar to those resulting from physical exercise, and they are considered beneficial to short-term and long-term health.

People sometimes laugh in situations that do not seem very funny, such as funerals or wakes. According to one theory, laughing in these situations helps people distance themselves from their negative emotions and strengthens their connections to other people. In one study on the topic, Dacher Keltner and George Bonanno (1997) interviewed 40 people who had recently lost a spouse. The researchers found that genuine laughter during the interview was associated with positive mental health and fewer negative feelings, such as grief. It was a way of coping with a difficult situation.

SUPPRESSION AND RUMINATION People make two common mistakes when trying to regulate mood. The first is *thought suppression,* in which they attempt not to feel or respond to the emotion at all. Research by Daniel Wegner and his colleagues (1990) has demonstrated that trying to suppress negative thoughts is extremely difficult and often leads to a *rebound effect,* in which people think more about something after suppression than before. Thus, for example, people who are dieting and try to not think about tasty foods end up thinking about them more than if they had tried to engage in another activity as a way of not thinking about food. *Rumination,* the second mistake, involves thinking about, elaborating, and focusing on undesired thoughts or feelings. This response prolongs the mood and impedes successful mood regulation strategies, such as distracting oneself or focusing on solutions for the problem (Lyubomirsky & Nolen-Hoeksema, 1995).

Overall, distraction is the best way to avoid the problems that come with thought suppression or with rumination, since distraction absorbs attention and temporarily helps people stop thinking about their problems. But some distractions backfire, such as thinking about other problems or engaging in maladaptive behaviors. As noted in Chapter 4, for example, when people escape self-awareness, they sometimes overeat or binge drink. Moreover, watching a movie that captures your attention helps you escape your problems, but watching a movie that reminds you of your troubled situation may lead you to wallow in mental anguish.

 SUMMING UP

How Do People Experience Emotions?

Emotions are often classified as primary emotions, which are similar across cultures and have an evolutionarily adaptive purpose, or secondary emotions, which are blends of primary emotions. Emotions have a valence (positive or negative) and a level of activation (level of arousal). The three main theories of emotion differ in their relative emphases on subjective experience, physiological changes, and cognitive interpretation. The James-Lange theory states that specific patterns of physical changes give rise to the perception of associated emotions. The Cannon-Bard theory proposes that two separate pathways, physical changes and subjective experience, occur at the same time. Schachter's two-factor theory emphasizes the combination of generalized physiological arousal and cognitive appraisals in determining specific emotions. We often misattribute the causes of our emotions, seeking environmental explanations for our feelings. People also use various strategies to alter their moods. The best methods for regulating negative affect include humor and distraction.

For each of the three main theories of emotions—James-Lange, Cannon-Bard, and two-factor—select all the descriptive statements and examples that apply. Some answers may apply to more than one theory.

Descriptive statements:
1. Our emotions follow from our bodily responses.
2. Our cognitive responses to situations are important in determining our emotions.
3. Bodily responses are an important part of how we label emotions.
4. Excitation transfer is incompatible with this theory of emotion.

Examples:
a. If you sing a happy song, you will feel happy.
b. If you want someone to fall in love (not necessarily stay in love) with you, you should choose an exciting activity, such as snowboarding or rock climbing.
c. Smiling during a painful procedure, such as a painful injection, will put you in a better mood.
d. You feel angry and then notice your heart is beating fast.

CONCLUSION

The study of motivation and emotion helps explain a wide array of thoughts and behaviors, from composing poetry to working late while finishing an important project to overcoming embarrassment about singing in front of friends. Motivation and emotion are linked in determining behavior; we are motivated to engage in behaviors that improve our moods, and we avoid behaviors that cause us distress. Motivation is concerned not only with immediate survival but also with our efforts to achieve our loftiest goals. Many motivations arise to satisfy our bodies' basic biological needs, such as drinking to quench our thirst or eating when we are hungry. But other needs are also important in our lives, such as the need for other people and the need to feel competent.

An important principle in motivation is that over the course of human evolution, the activities that brought pleasure or positive emotions were often adaptive. Doing them increased survival and reproduction; sexual behavior is perhaps the most obvious example. However, evolution merely leads to adaptive changes being passed along through generations; it does not guarantee that those changes will be advantageous indefinitely. Contemporary society, unlike the worlds of our hunter-gatherer ancestors, often requires us to override the urge to seek pleasure, as in restricting our consumption of tasty foods or not using drugs. Humans differ from other animals because we can set personal goals and try to achieve them. Studying motivation helps us understand why people desire to do certain things—and why sometimes they need to inhibit those desires.

At the same time, people react to environmental input with physiological reactions and cognitions, which together produce mental states perceived to be positive or negative, or shades in between. This response, emotion, is a primary force in motivating adaptive behaviors and discouraging maladaptive behaviors. For instance, when we look at the sun dipping below the horizon, we see not an astronomical event but a beautiful sunset that evokes all sorts of feelings. Emotions, even negative ones, are central to the human experience. Among their most important functions are supporting people's social bonds. Without emotions, would life be worth living?

■ CHAPTER SUMMARY

How Does Motivation Activate, Direct, and Sustain Behavior?

- **Multiple Factors Motivate Behavior:** Motives activate, direct, and sustain behaviors that will satisfy a need. Needs create arousal, and the response to being aroused is a drive to satisfy the need. *Homeostasis* refers to the body's attempts to maintain a state of equilibrium. The Yerkes-Dodson Law states that a person performs best when his or her level of arousal is neither too low nor too high.

- **Some Behaviors Are Motivated for Their Own Sake:** Behaviors such as playing games are unrelated to needs. People are intrinsically motivated by the joy of engaging in these behaviors.

- **People Set Goals to Achieve:** People with a high need to achieve set reasonably high goals and believe that with hard work, they can achieve their goals. These people are high in self-efficacy. They are able to delay gratification as they work toward difficult goals.

- **People Have a Need to Belong:** For most people, social motivation is very strong. Evolutionary theorists point out the survival advantage of having others to share dangerous tasks and care for one another. When people were made anxious in an experimental setting, they preferred to be with other people in a similar situation, most likely because they could interpret their own situation by comparing themselves to similar others.

What Determines How We Eat?

- **Time and Taste Play Roles:** Customs and local norms strongly determine the foods we find appetizing and the times of day when we have our meals. Sensory-specific satiety is people's tendency to eat less when there is little variety in their food choices.

- **Culture Determines What We Eat:** Culture determines what a person considers edible. Neophobia is the reluctance to eat unfamiliar foods. Researchers have found that infants are more likely to try a new food when a family member offers it.

- **Multiple Neural Processes Control Eating:** The hypothalamus is the brain structure most closely identified with eating. Rats whose ventromedial hypothalamus was damaged experienced hyperphagia—they consumed huge quantities of food. By contrast, rats whose lateral hypothalamus was damaged exhibited aphagia—they stopped eating to the point of death. The limbic system, which is involved in reward, shows more activity when overweight people look at food than when people of normal weight do. Set-point sensors for body fat, blood glucose monitors, and hormones also play important roles in how much we eat.

What Factors Motivate Sexual Behavior?

- **Biological Factors Influence Sexual Behavior:** The four stages of the human sexual response cycle are excitement, plateau, orgasm, and resolution. Men have a refractory period following orgasm, during which time they cannot become sexually aroused; women do not have a refractory period. Both men's and women's sexual responsiveness depends on their having a minimal amount of testosterone available. Some data show that heterosexual women's preferences for masculine-looking men vary over the menstrual cycle.

- **Cultural Scripts and Cultural Rules Shape Sexual Interactions:** Our beliefs about how we should behave sexually are influenced by cultural scripts defining sexual behavior for men and women. The double standard allows men greater sexual latitude than it allows women.

- **Mating Strategies Differ between the Sexes:** According to the evolutionary view, women want men to be faithful and be good providers for their children because women's investments in pregnancy and child care are intensive. By contrast, men want—at least subconsciously—to impregnate many women as a strategy to promote the survival of as many of the men's offspring as possible.

- **People Differ in Sexual Orientation:** Evolutionary theorists have difficulty explaining homosexuality because same-sex relations do not result in offspring. A portion of the hypothalamus was found to be smaller in gay men than in heterosexual men, but as with any correlational data, the casual relation is unclear. Research suggests that prenatal hormones may be important in determining sexual orientation.

How Are Emotions Adaptive?

- **Facial Expressions Communicate Emotion:** People from multiple cultures interpret a particular facial expression as representing the same emotion. Men appear to be less emotional than women, possibly because of societal display rules.

- **Emotions Serve Cognitive Functions:** We use our emotions as a guide when making decisions. One theory is that we use emotions as somatic markers informing our behaviors—meaning we interpret our body's responses and use that information to help make decisions.

- **Emotions Strengthen Interpersonal Relations:** Social bonds are strengthened when we can read other people's emotions accurately.

How Do People Experience Emotions?

- **Emotions Have a Subjective Component:** Primary emotions are adaptive across cultures. They include anger, fear, sadness, disgust, happiness, surprise, and content. Secondary emotions are blends of the primary emotions.

- **Emotions Have a Physiological Component:** Emotions are associated with changes in bodily states. Research points to important roles of the amygdala and the prefrontal cortex in the production and experience of emotion.

- **Emotions Have a Cognitive Component:** According to the two-factor theory, emotions have an arousal component and a cognitive or interpretive component. The interpretation determines which emotion is felt.

- **People Regulate Their Moods:** When experiencing intense moods, we can use strategies such as distraction to manage them. Thought suppression and ruminating are not effective strategies.

■ KEY TERMS

■ PRACTICE TEST

1. Students enrolled in a difficult class are preparing to give end-of-term presentations, which will count 50 percent toward final grades. Which student below is likely to perform the best?
   a. Ahn is not at all stressed about the presentation. He has done well all semester and is confident he will do just fine this time around, too. He puts together his slides a week before the due date and then reviews the talk a few hours before giving the presentation.
   b. Sonya is somewhat anxious about this presentation. She knows her stuff but recognizes how much is riding on the quality of this presentation. This anxious energy motivates her to polish her slides and practice her talk.
   c. Marcus is very stressed about this presentation. A bad evaluation on the presentation will ruin his grade for the class, which in turn will ruin his strong GPA. He decides to spend every waking moment preparing the talk, working late into the night and sometimes dreaming about the presentation.

2. A classmate tells you he is having a hard time remembering which eating outcomes are associated with damage to different parts of the hypothalamus. Which of the following verbal mnemonics would be most helpful to your classmate? Select all that apply.
   a. Organisms with damage to the **hyp**othalamus have **hyp**erphagia.
   b. Organisms with damage to the lateral area of the hypothalamus (**L**H) eat **l**ittle.
   c. Organisms with damage to the preoptic area of the hypothalamus (**P**H) **p**ut on the **p**ounds.
   d. Organisms with damage to the ventromedial region of the hypothalamus (**VM**H) eat **v**ery **m**uch.

3. Which statement below is backed by empirical findings?
   a. Parental treatment of a child gives rise to the child's sexual orientation.
   b. High levels of androgens in women lead them to become lesbian, and high levels of estrogens in men lead them to become gay.
   c. Prenatal exposure to hormones is associated with sexual orientation.

   d. People are attracted to what is different: "the exotic becomes erotic."

4. Which neurotransmitter is *not* implicated in the sexual response?
   a. dopamine
   b. GABA
   c. nitric oxide
   d. serotonin

5. Which of these statements likely describe somatic markers? Select all that apply.
   a. "My mind is wandering."
   b. "I have butterflies in my stomach."
   c. "My heart is pounding so hard it is going to jump out of my chest."
   d. "My leg just fell asleep."

6. People [can / cannot] experience positive and negative affect simultaneously.

7. Positive affective states are associated with increased levels of [GABA / dopamine].

8. Negative affective states are associated with increased levels of [dopamine / norepinephrine].

9. Which of these statements are true regarding involvement of the amygdala in emotion?
   a. Information reaches the amygdala along two separate pathways.
   b. Increased activity in the amygdala during an emotional event is associated with improved long-term memory for that event.
   c. The amygdala helps process the emotional content of facial expressions.

10. Would you expect activity in the left or right prefrontal cortex in response to pictures of dead and decomposing livestock?
   a. left
   b. right

■ PSYCHOLOGY AND SOCIETY

1. Write down a goal you have for yourself. Provide a one-paragraph written analysis of whether this articulation of the goal has the qualities of a "good goal," meaning challenging (but not overly difficult) and specific. If your articulation of the goal falls short on any of these qualities, revise it to make it stronger. Finally, list the subgoals you will need to complete to reach this goal.

2. A friend asks you for advice on how to get over a recent relationship breakup. Compose an e-mail to your friend, drawing insight from the portion of this chapter that deals with regulation; describe effective strategies your friend should try as well as ineffective strategies your friend should avoid. Be sure to give specific and concrete advice.

The answer key for all the Measuring Up exercises and the Practice Tests can be found at the back of the book.

Find more review materials online at www.wwnorton.com/psychologicalscience.

Test Preparation ■ **425**

Health and Well-Being

WHEN IS DISCRIMINATION LEGAL IN THE UNITED STATES? The answer seems to be when it is against fat people. By all accounts, Gary Stocklaufer is an ideal father. He is a happily married man, a state-certified foster parent, and the adoptive father of a great son. When his cousin was unable to raise Max, the cousin's baby son, Mr. Stocklaufer and his wife stepped in as the child's foster parents. After three months, they filed the paperwork to adopt their cherished foster son. A judge in Missouri, who also presided over Stocklaufer's earlier adoption, said no. The judge cited Stocklaufer's weight—at the time, between 500 and 600 pounds—as the reason for the denial. The Stocklaufers are healthy, but the judge reasoned that Mr. Stocklaufer would likely develop a serious disease and die at a young age because he was obese (FIGURE 10.1). When asked about the case, the judge responded that he was required to consider the welfare and best interests of the child. The National Association to Advance Fat Acceptance (NAAFA),

FIGURE 10.1 Gary Stocklaufer
Stocklaufer is shown here weighing over 500 pounds. Shortly after this photograph was taken, he underwent surgery to lose weight.

LEARNING OBJECTIVES

Describe the biopsychosocial model of health.

Provide examples of the ways behavior contributes to the leading causes of death.

Explain how placebos can affect health.

health psychology The field of psychological science concerned with the events that affect physical well-being.

well-being A positive state that includes striving for optimal health.

asking whether "fat = poor parenting," established a legal defense fund for Stocklaufer. Ultimately, the case was appealed, and the judge reversed his earlier ruling because Stocklaufer had lost over 200 pounds following gastric bypass surgery (Associated Press, 2008).

Stocklaufer's case is only one of many similar stories in which fat people were denied the right to adopt. Is it reasonable to consider someone's weight when deciding something as important as a possible adoption? Since body weight has a substantial genetic component, should a Mr. Stocklaufer be held accountable for his weight? Would it make a difference if we could show that his obesity is caused by factors beyond his control? Would a judge be acting in the children's best interests if he ruled that people who smoke cannot adopt children? What about people with diabetes or other conditions associated with reduced life spans? In considering health and well-being, this chapter will relate these factors to individual differences and individuals' rights.

Can Psychosocial Factors Affect Health?

People often think about health and wellness in biological and medical terms. They are therefore surprised to learn that their behaviors and attitudes affect their health. The traditional medical model emphasizes disease states and the treatments and drugs designed to rid us of disease. According to this model, people are passive recipients of disease and the medical treatments designed to return them to health after illness. The underlying idea in the traditional medical model is that health professionals know best and thus maintain control over what happens to the patient. Psychologists—and, increasingly, many medical professionals—take a more holistic and active approach to health and well-being. They believe our behaviors and attitudes are critical in keeping us healthy, helping us regain health following illness, and helping us achieve well-being. As you will learn in this chapter, a healthy lifestyle goes a long way toward promoting health and preventing disease.

Health psychology, one of psychology's many subdisciplines, is an area of study that integrates research on health and on psychology. This field was launched nearly three decades ago, when psychologists, physicians, and other health professionals came to appreciate the importance of lifestyle factors to physical health. Health psychologists apply their knowledge of psychological principles to promote health and well-being, instead of thinking about health merely as the absence of disease. **Well-being** is a positive state in which we feel our best; it includes a striving for optimal health. To achieve optimal health, each of us needs to actively participate in maintaining wellness through health-enhancing behaviors. Health and well-being is a growing area of psychology, and there are now psychologists who provide health services and conduct research on the health outcomes of different behaviors and emotions. Some psychologists, recognizing the importance of behavioral and psychological variables in health, practice along with physicians in a wide range of contexts, such as diabetes management, cardiac specialties, and general medical settings.

Psychologists who study health and well-being rely on the experimental and statistical methods of psychology to understand the interrelationship among thoughts (health-related cognitions), actions, and physical and mental health. Researchers address issues such as ways to help people lead healthier lives. They study the ways in which our behavior and social systems affect our health, and how ethnic and gender differences in healthy behaviors influence health outcomes.

Health psychologists also study the inverse of these relationships: how health behaviors and health outcomes affect behavior, cognition, and emotions. Health psychology is necessarily an interdisciplinary field that combines theories and research from the various areas of health studies and of psychology.

The Biopsychosocial Model of Health Incorporates Multiple Perspectives for Understanding and Improving Health

How can someone's personality or thoughts or behaviors affect his or her health? To answer this question, you need to understand the **biopsychosocial model,** which "views health and illness as the product of a combination of factors including biological characteristics (e.g., genetic predisposition), behavioral factors (e.g., lifestyle, stress, health beliefs), and social conditions (e.g., cultural influences, family relationships, social support)" (American Psychological Association Health Psychology, 2008). Research that integrates these levels of analysis helps scientists identify strategies that prevent disease by helping people lead healthier lives.

As shown in **FIGURE 10.2,** the biopsychosocial model is circular: Our thoughts and actions affect the environments we choose to interact with, and those environments, in turn, affect the biological underpinnings of our thoughts and actions. To understand how this continuous loop operates in real life, suppose you are genetically predisposed to be anxious, and you learn that one way to reduce your anxiety is to eat comfort foods such as mashed potatoes, oatmeal, and ice cream. If you consume these foods in excess, you will gain weight and eventually become overweight. Overweight people often find that exercise is not very pleasant. If their extra weight makes even moderate exercise difficult, they may decrease physical activity, that decrease would slow down their metabolism, and so on. Additional examples of the interplay between biological, social, and psychological factors are presented in several places throughout this chapter. The biopsychosocial model is central to understanding the difference between the traditional medical model, in which the individual is passive, and the approach taken by health psychologists, in which the individual's thoughts, feelings, and behaviors are central to understanding and improving health.

biopsychosocial model A model of health that integrates the effects of biological, behavioral, and social factors on health and illness.

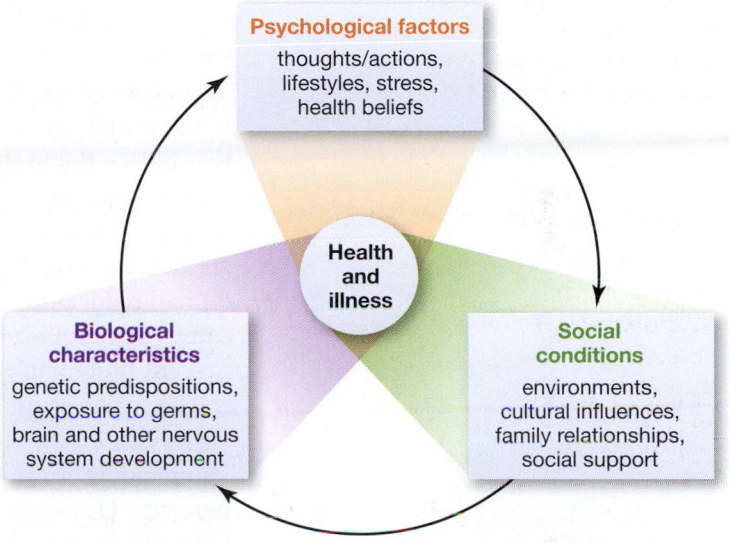

FIGURE 10.2 **The Biopsychosocial Model** This model illustrates how health and illness result from a combination of factors.

Behavior Contributes to the Leading Causes of Death

Are you an anxious flyer? Are you afraid of being killed in a shark attack? Does the thought of eating a hamburger terrorize you? Like many people, you may be at least somewhat anxious about flying. You may (surreptitiously) look around for nearby sharks whenever you wade into the ocean—or even a swimming pool, if you are very afraid of sharks. Most likely you do not find a hamburger terrifying; but given the actual leading causes of death, most people clearly fear the wrong things. A statistical expert in the field of aviation who is also a professor at MIT explained the risk of death from flying this way: "It's once every 19,000 years— and that is only provided the person flew on an airplane once a day for 19,000 years!" (Barnett, 2007). Other researchers have estimated that 1 in 13 million passengers die in airplane crashes. If you have read Chapter 8, you know that in the

months following the September 11, 2001, terrorist attack in the United States, many people avoided flying—preferring instead what they believed to be the safety of driving. Yet, as described more fully in Chapter 8, the number of people who died in automobile accidents because they chose to drive instead of fly in the three months following the attacks far exceeded the number of people who were killed in the attacks.

What about death by shark attack? You can be confident that it just is not going to happen. According to the International Shark Attack Files (and who knew there were such things?), 1,909 shark attacks were confirmed worldwide between the years 1580 and 2003. In the same time period, in what is now the United States, there have been 38 confirmed deaths from shark attacks. In other words, the real odds of being attacked by a shark are approximately 1 in 250 million (SixWise.com, n.d.).

According to data from the U.S. National Center for Health Statistics (Miniño, Heron, & Smith, 2006), people are most likely to die from causes that stem from their own behaviors, which they can learn to modify. For example, the most common cause of death in the United States in 2004 was heart disease. Obesity, lack of exercise, smoking, high fat diets, and, as you will learn later in this chapter, some personality traits contribute to this cause of death. Those who suffer from heart disease are not always to blame for their conditions, because heart disease also occurs in easy-going people who lead healthy lives. But all of us can change our behaviors in ways that reduce the likelihood of heart disease or postpone it until late in life.

Accidents are another leading cause of death. Most of us think about accidents as being beyond our control. But many accidents are avoidable, and for those that are not, we can reduce the probability of an accident (for example, by driving safely) and reduce the resulting injury (for example, by wearing seat belts). Additional causes of death—accidental or not—include risky sexual behavior (AIDS is 100 percent preventable), the use of illegal drugs or the illegal use of legal drugs, and the use of firearms. It is easy to understand how our behaviors literally can kill us.

Even more sobering are the data regarding behaviors of both teenagers and young adults. In this age group, almost half of all deaths are due to accidents (49 percent). Homicides are the second leading cause of death (12 percent), closely followed by suicide (10 percent; Centers for Disease Control and Prevention, 2006). It is a paradox of modern life that in the transition period between childhood and young adulthood, when most people are at their strongest and in their best health, they tend to make bad decisions that often have disastrous outcomes. Lifestyle behaviors that begin in childhood and the teen years may decrease health or even lead to death. For example, although relatively few teens die from heart disease, poor eating habits ("You want fries with that burger?") contribute to heart disease later in life. Violence, accidents, obesity, lack of exercise, risky sexual behaviors, the use and abuse of drugs—all these negative factors are associated strongly with young people.

In your great-grandparents' generation, and even more so in their parents' generation, the leading causes of death were childbirth, infectious diseases, and accidents. Thanks to medical and financial advances, the first two items on this list are rarely fatal in modern societies. And while hunger and malnutrition, like disease, remain tragic realities in developing countries, most industrialized countries have made great progress in feeding their populations. The abundance of cheap, tasty food has brought new health problems to the developed world, however. As the circular biopsychosocial model makes clear, good and bad behaviors influence environments, and environments in turn influence the good and bad biological bases of behaviors.

Identifying Regression to the Mean

Think about a time when you had a cold or flu. Did you wait until you felt very bad before you started taking medicine or before you made an appointment to see a physician? If so, you are like most people, who seek medical help only when their symptoms are bad. Usually when you are sick, you will get better no matter what you do; that is, eventually you will return to your usual state of not feeling sick. If you wait until you are very sick to get medical help, then almost anything you do, including nothing at all, will be followed with feeling better. However, because you went to the doctor, you might credit him or her with making you feel better.

For any range of events, a more extreme event (in this case, feeling very sick) will tend to be followed by an event closer to the average or mean (in this case, feeling better). This principle is true for statistical reasons, and it operates in almost every situation. The phenomenon being described is called *regression to the mean*. It can be a difficult concept to understand and recognize because most of us usually have other explanations for why we returned to more normal states. As presented in the biopsychosocial model, our thoughts—in this case, the ways we explain both why we get sick and how we get well—are a critical determinant of how we take care of our health. Such thoughts often direct our behaviors, which in turn affect the biological underpinnings of health and well-being.

Remember: An extreme event will most likely be followed by a less extreme event. If you are aware of this principle, regression to the mean, you are less likely to believe an unrelated factor is responsible for the return to a more normal state (**FIGURE 10.3**).

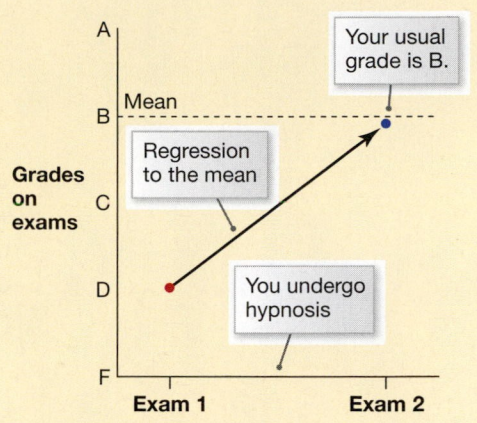

FIGURE 10.3 Think Critically: Identifying Regression to the Mean Suppose you study as usual for an exam, but just by bad luck, the professor asks questions you cannot answer, so you get a very low grade. If you study as usual for the next exam, you are likely (but not guaranteed) to get a grade closer to your usual high grades. If you study as usual but also go to a hypnotist to help calm your anxiety for the next exam, what will most likely happen? You probably will score closer to the way you usually do. Other than the hypnosis (on the realities of which, see Chapter 4, "The Mind and Consciousness"), what factors would explain the improvement?

Placebos Can Be Powerful Medicine

Suppose you feel sick and go to a doctor, but the doctor does not take your complaint very seriously. To keep you happy, the doctor prescribes "sugar pills." You, believing the pills will work because the doctor said they would, quickly feel better. Stories like this one usually end with a good laugh about how gullible and foolish the patient is. In this story, the pills act as placebos—they have no apparent physiological effect on the health condition for which they are prescribed. Often a drug or treatment will be studied by being compared with a placebo. As described in Chapter 2, research participants typically are assigned at random to either the drug/treatment group or the placebo group. Ideally, everything about the two groups is as similar as possible. If the treatment consists of a large blue pill or weekly injections or dietary restrictions, the placebo group would take a large blue pill or receive weekly injections or follow different dietary restrictions; but for the placebo group, the pill might be made of sugar, the injections might deliver only water, and the diet might restrict foods believed to be unrelated to the treatment. Would you guess that some participants get well with only placebos? In fact, they do. This improvement in health, attributed to the inert drug or bogus treatment, is called the **placebo effect.** Its validity is complicated. After all, statistically speaking, most people's illnesses will improve even without treatment (see "Critical Thinking Skill: Identifying Regression to the Mean"). Even a few people with presumably terminal illnesses seem to beat the odds. Please do not take these points to mean that

placebo effect A drug or treatment, unrelated to the particular problem of the person who receives it, may make the recipient feel better because the person believes the drug or treatment is effective.

when you are ill you will always have statistics on your side. You cannot determine, for example, how long a minor illness might take to improve, or what complications it might produce if left untreated, or whether it is in fact the beginning of a major illness. When you are suffering, seek appropriate treatment. When you are well, take preventative measures.

For a placebo to improve health, the participant must believe it will. The person who receives the placebo must not know that, for example, the pills are chemically inert. Have you ever gone to a doctor's office feeling very sick—and noticed that as soon as the doctor said your problems were not serious, you immediately felt so relieved that you started feeling better? Some portion of the placebo effect is attributable to decreased anxiety, which can reduce pain and help recovery from an illness. But the placebo effect clearly is more than a reduction in anxiety. We cannot separate the effects of our minds from those of our bodies; they are seamlessly the same. The placebo effect is "all in the head," but the effect is real—all of our thoughts and feelings are in our heads. Thus the placebo effect is gaining new respect now that psychological scientists have a better understanding of its biological bases.

As discussed in Chapter 5, pain is more than just a sensory experience. How much pain people feel depends on many variables, including context (e.g., being on a battlefield versus being at home), expectations (i.e., feeling anxious or calm about a potentially painful experience), and thoughts about the pain (e.g., imagining it as less unpleasant). When people are calmer, their pain is less intense, so an important part of getting well lies in finding ways to reduce anxiety. Placebos can reduce pain perception when people believe they will (Wager, 2005). One placebo's ability to reduce pain was reduced when naloxone, a drug known to reduce the analgesic (pain-relieving) effects of several drugs, was administered after the placebo (Amanzio & Benedetti, 1999). In other words, a drug that makes pain relievers ineffective also made the placebo ineffective. The functional MRI, a type of brain imaging that allows researchers to see which areas of the brain are active while participants are engaged in specific tasks (discussed fully in Chapter 2, "Research Methodology"), shows that when patients have positive expectations about a placebo, the neural processes involved in responding to it are the same ones activated in response to a biologically active treatment (Benedetti, Mayberg, Wagner, Stohler, & Zubieta, 2005).

The placebo effect is an experimental control that some researchers see as a nuisance when they want to determine if a new drug or other treatment is effective. But placebos reveal a great deal about the power of the brain and body to produce healing effects. The placebo effect is a good example of the biopsychosocial model at work. The belief that a medication will work (psychological) affects the body in ways similar to those of medications, or treatments, with known biological effects (biological). These effects occur within a context that determines when, if, and how much the body will respond to the placebo (social). In the study of health and well-being, it sometimes can be difficult to separate these influences.

CRITICAL THINKING SKILL

Recognizing Placebo Effects When Evaluating Treatment Claims

Placebo effects can occur in many contexts, not just for health, so critical thinkers need to watch out for them in various settings. Suppose you are participating in a study and the researchers tell you your room is being infused with an odorless substance that will make you feel better. Each day, the researchers ask you to write in a journal how you feel that day and whether you feel better than you did the previous day. If you believe their claim about the odorless substance, you probably will feel a little better each day, and you might attribute this subjective judgment about how you feel to the odorless chemical you supposedly are breathing.

In fact, we fall for such false claims all the time. Consider this advertisement for copper bracelets, which is paraphrased only slightly:

> For hundreds of years people have worn copper bracelets to relieve pain from arthritis. This folklore belief has persisted, and copper bracelets continue to be popular. These bracelets promote close contact between the copper and your wrist.

The advertisement does not say that copper bracelets relieve arthritis pain. They do not have this effect, and explicitly saying they do could lead to legal problems. But what do people remember after reading this advertisement? They remember reading that copper bracelets are good for arthritis. Many people wear copper bracelets and believe the bracelets provide some relief for their arthritis pain (**FIGURE 10.4**). You might ask if it matters as long as people feel less pain. Yes, it matters, because people who fall for phony treatments often avoid medical care, which can provide greater pain relief than they are getting from these placebo bracelets. They also are paying for treatments that do not really treat their health problem. A believer in copper bracelets might ask, If it really does not work, then why do I feel better? No one believes he or she will fall for a placebo, so it can be difficult to acknowledge that much of how we feel (but by no means all of it) is influenced by our beliefs.

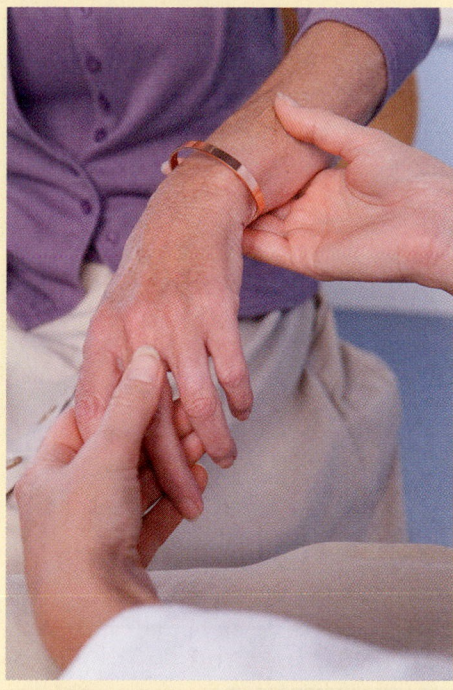

FIGURE 10.4 Think Critically:
Recognizing Placebo Effects Many people believe copper and zinc increase circulation. The idea appeals to those suffering from conditions such as athritis, but any relief people feel from such "treatments" might be only a placebo effect.

 SUMMING UP

Can Psychosocial Factors Affect Health?

The biopsychosocial model of health and illness posits the interaction of biological variables (such as genetic predispositions), psychological variables (such as personality types and health behaviors), and social variables (such as social support and cultural beliefs about diseases). The leading causes of serious illness and death are, at least in part, behavioral. Behaviors such as overeating, lack of exercise, and smoking contribute in large measure to the development of coronary heart disease and other illnesses. For teens and young adults, accidents, homicides, and suicides are the leading causes of death; almost half of all deaths in this age range are due to accidents, many of them preventable. Placebos can powerfully affect health, so it not surprising that they activate the same areas of the brain and respond to other drugs in ways that are similar to validated treatments.

MEASURING UP

1. Of the following possibilities, select one way that our behaviors contribute to reduced health.
   a. We can make unhealthy choices such as eating a poor diet and smoking.
   b. We can have genetic predispositions to obesity.
   c. We can refuse to be in any research that has a placebo control group.

d. Our beliefs in a placebo can result in neural activity similar to the neural activity that results from validated treatments.
e. Our personalities cannot be controlled, so they cannot affect our health behaviors.
f. By being too passive, we allow other people to take advantage of us, often to the detriment of our health.

2. Which of the following statements exemplifies the biopsychosocial model?
a. The heart is a biological organ that we cannot control directly, so we rely on other people to affect the health of our hearts.
b. By engaging in healthy behaviors, we can strengthen our immune systems.
c. Reckless people exist in every society in the world, so behaviors related to accidents are not likely to be affected by culture.
d. That hostile people cannot change their personalities proves that biology influences health.

How Do People Cope with Stress?

stress A pattern of behavioral and physiological responses to events that match or exceed an organism's abilities to respond.

stressor An environmental event or stimulus that threatens an organism.

coping response Any response an organism makes to avoid, escape from, or minimize an aversive stimulus.

Stress is a basic component of our daily lives (**FIGURE 10.5**). Luckily, a small amount of it may be beneficial (Segerstrom & Miller, 2004). Stress does not exist objectively, out in the world, but rather results directly from the ways we think about events in our lives. Some students respond to final exams as extremely stressful events, for example, and often get sick at exam time, while others perceive the same finals as mere inconveniences. **Stress** is a pattern of behavioral and physiological responses to events that match or exceed an organism's ability to respond in a healthy way. A **stressor** is an environmental event or stimulus that threatens an organism by seeming overwhelming; it elicits a **coping response,** which is any response an organism makes to avoid, escape from, or minimize an aversive stimulus. When too much is expected of us or when events are worrisome or scary, we

FIGURE 10.5 Stress in Everyday Life
Stress is part of life. How do you cope with the stress in your life?

perceive a discrepancy, real or not, between the demands of the situation and the resources of our biological, psychological, and social systems. In general, positive and negative life changes are stressful—going to college, getting a job, marrying, being fired, losing a parent, winning a major award, and so on. The greater the number of changes, the greater the stress, and the more likely the stress will affect our physiological state. Stress is often divided into two types: *eustress*, the stress of positive events (e.g., being admitted to the college you really want to attend or preparing for a party you are looking forward to) and *distress* (or duress), the stress of negative events (e.g., being trapped in traffic when you are late for an important meeting or dealing with an ongoing and serious illness of a loved one).

Most people use the term *stress* only in referring to negative events, but both distress and eustress put strains on our bodies. Different levels of stress are optimal for different people; learning how much stress you can handle is essential for recognizing its effects on your mental, physical, and emotional well-being and for making life choices such as the type of career to pursue. Extreme distress, like the stress of war or of a natural disaster (e.g., a flood or an earthquake) can lead to serious health problems. Combat soldiers and others in prolonged stressful situations often must use combinations of strategies to cope with the stress of their situations.

Daily hassles are small, day-to-day irritations and annoyances, such as driving in heavy traffic, dealing with difficult people, or waiting in line. Daily hassles are stressful, and their combined effects can be comparable to the effects of major life changes. Because these low-level irritations are ubiquitous, they pose a threat to coping responses by slowly wearing down personal resources. Studies that ask people to keep diaries of their daily activities find consistently that the more intense and frequent the hassles, the poorer the physical and mental health of the participant. People may habituate to some hassles but not to others, such as interpersonal difficulties, which appear to have a cumulative effect on health. Living in poverty or in a crowded, noisy, or polluted place also can have detrimental effects on emotional well-being.

Stress Has Physiological Components

Researchers have a good understanding of the biological mechanisms that underlie the stress response. A stressor activates a complex chain of events, in what is known as the **hypothalamic-pituitary-adrenal (HPA) axis.** As shown in **FIGURE 10.6**, stress begins in the brain with the perception of some stressful event. For our very distant ancestors, the event might have been the sight of a predator approaching at a rapid clip; more likely for us, it is an approaching deadline, a stack of unpaid bills, a fight, an illness, and so on. In the HPA axis, the hypothalamus sends a chemical message to the pituitary gland (a major gland located just below the brain), which in turn secretes hormones that travel through the bloodstream until they reach the adrenal glands (located near the kidneys), which in turn secrete cortisol. Cortisol is responsible for many of the feelings we have when we are stressed.

The HPA axis was an efficient system for our ancestors because it results in increased energy, and energy is necessary for either outrunning a charging predator or standing your ground and fighting it. (Either response will cause you

hypothalamic-pituitary-adrenal (HPA) axis The biological system responsible for the stress response.

FIGURE 10.6 Hypothalamic-Pituitary-Adrenal (HPA) Axis Stress sets off a complex chain of events in the body.

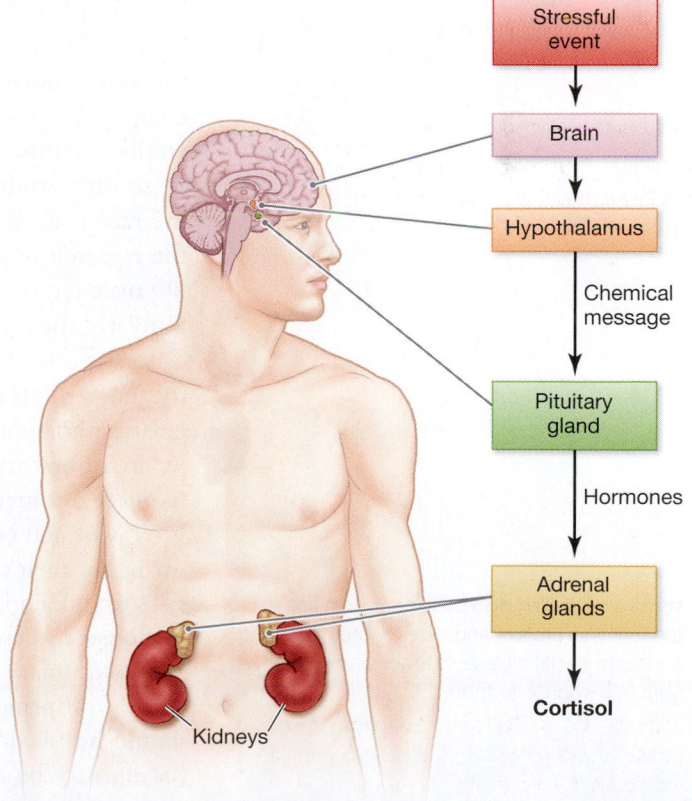

stress.) Because hormones travel relatively slowly through the bloodstream, stress affects organs much longer than stressors do. Scientific studies of stress (with human and nonhuman models) show that excessive stress disrupts working memory, especially when the demands on working memory are high (Oei, Everaerd, Elzinga, Van Well, & Bermond, 2006). Chronic stress has also been associated with memory impairments caused when cortisol damages neurons in brain areas including the hippocampus, which is a primary structure for memory (Sapolsky, 1994). Using brain imaging techniques, researchers can see the effect of stress on the brain. Neural-level effects of stress have been studied with strong experimental designs (experiments with random assignment to conditions) in rats and other nonhuman mammals, and this research provides clear evidence that stress interferes with the ability to recall previously learned information (Diamond, Fleshner, Ingersoll, & Rose, 1996).

There Are Sex Differences in Responses to Stressors

From an evolutionary perspective, people's ability to deal effectively with stressors is important to survival and reproduction. The physiological and behavioral responses that accompany stress help mobilize resources to deal with danger. The physiologist Walter Cannon coined the term **fight-or-flight response** to describe the physiological preparation of animals to deal with an attack. Within seconds or minutes, this response to a stressor allows the organism to direct all energy to dealing with the threat at hand. The physical reaction includes increased heart rate, redistribution of the blood supply from skin and viscera (digestive organs) to muscles and brain, deepening of respiration, dilation of the pupils, inhibition of gastric secretions, and an increase in glucose released from the liver. At the same time, less critical autonomic activities such as food digestion, which can occur after the stressor is removed, are postponed. (The autonomic system is described in more detail in Chapter 3.)

The generalizability of the fight-or-flight response has been questioned by Shelley Taylor and her colleagues (2006; Taylor et al., 2002). They argue that because the vast majority of human and nonhuman animal research has been conducted using males (women represent fewer than 1 in 5 of the participants), it has distorted the scientific understanding of responses to stress. The exclusion of women from these early studies has many possible explanations. For example, researchers often use rats in studies of heart disease that cannot be conducted with humans because the research might increase participants' risk of heart disease, and most rat studies use male rats to avoid complications that may be caused by female hormonal cycles. Similarly, most researchers have avoided using women in their studies of responses to stress because female menstrual patterns might make women more difficult to study—their responses could be mediated by (influenced by) fluctuations in circulating hormones that vary over the menstrual cycle. The result is a sex inequality in laboratory stress studies, a research bias that can blind us to the fact that women and men often respond differently to social or biological stressors.

Taylor and her colleagues argue that females respond to stress by protecting and caring for their offspring, as well as by forming alliances with social groups to reduce risks to individuals, including themselves. They coined the phrase **tend-and-befriend response** to describe this pattern. Tend-and-befriend responses make sense from an evolutionary perspective. Females typically bear a greater responsibility for the care of offspring, and responses that protect their offspring as well as themselves would be maximally adaptive. When a threat appears, quieting the offspring and hiding may be more effective means of avoiding harm than trying to flee while

fight-or-flight response The physiological preparedness of animals to deal with danger.

tend-and-befriend response Females' tendency to protect and care for their offspring and form social alliances rather than flee or fight in response to threat.

pregnant or with a clinging infant. Furthermore, females who selectively affiliate with others, especially other females, might acquire additional protection and support. The tend-and-befriend stress response is an excellent example of how thinking about psychological mechanisms in view of their evolutionary significance may lead us to question long-standing assumptions about how the mind works. Females who respond to stress by nurturing and protecting their young and by forming alliances with other females apparently have a selective advantage over those who fight or flee, and thus these behaviors would pass to future generations.

As is true for any theory of human behavior, Taylor's theory about stress responses cannot be applied universally to all women and all men. There is almost always overlap between the behaviors of males and of females: Some males exhibit behaviors more typical of females, and some females exhibit behaviors more typical of males. Geary and Flinn (2002) note that males often engage in "tending behavior," for example, such as caring for their children; thus the concept of tend-and-befriend should apply to men as well as women. Taylor and her colleagues (2002) reply that men are often caring and nurturing fathers but that such behavior is not a typical male response to the stress of a threat—and their theory specifically describes the typical response of each sex.

Consider once again the HPA axis model of stress and how it can be applied to tend-and-befriend responses to stress. **Oxytocin,** a hormone important for mothers in bonding to newborns, is produced in the hypothalamus and released into the bloodstream through the pituitary gland. Recent research with human and non-human models has shown that oxytocin levels tend to be high during socially stressful situations. Although oxytocin exists naturally in men and women, it seems especially important in women's stress response; thus it provides a possible biological basis for the tend-and-befriend response to stress exhibited (mainly) by women (Taylor, 2006). A great deal of research currently is being conducted on the role of oxytocin during stress responses and should lead to a better understanding of its role in maternal bonding. Recent research suggests that estrogen is important in understanding the differences in how women and men respond to stress (Kajantie, 2008). When estrogen levels are high for women (between menarche—the onset of menstruation—and menopause), they have reduced responses to stress, relative to men and to women in later life. Researchers have suggested that sex differences in response to stress are one of the reasons women live an average of five to eight years longer than men.

oxytocin A hormone that is important for mothers in bonding to newborns.

The General Adaptation Syndrome Is a Bodily Response to Stress

In the early 1930s, Hans Selye began studying the physiological effects of sex hormones by injecting rats with hormones from other animals. When he examined the rats, he found enlarged adrenal glands, decreased levels of **lymphocytes** (specialized white blood cells) in the blood, and stomach ulcers. Surmising that the foreign hormones must have caused these changes, Selye conducted further tests, using different types of chemicals and even physically restraining the animals to create stressful situations. He found slight variations in some physiological effects; but each manipulation produced a pattern of bloated adrenal glands, damaged lymphatic structures (part of the **immune system**), and stomach ulcers. He concluded that these three responses, which reduce the organism's potential ability to resist additional stressors, were the hallmarks of a *nonspecific stress response.*

lymphocytes Specialized white blood cells known as B cells, T cells, and natural killer cells that make up the immune system.

immune system The body's mechanism for dealing with invading microorganisms, such as allergens, bacteria, and viruses.

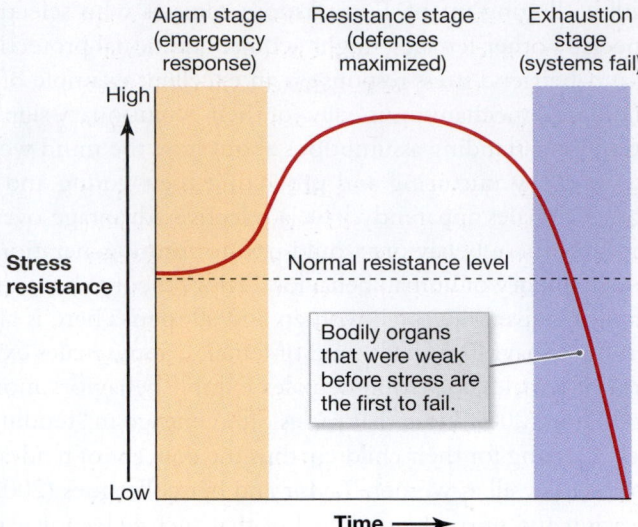

High

Stress
resistance

Normal resistance level

Bodily organs
that were weak
before stress are
the first to fail.

Low

Time ⟶

**FIGURE 10.7 The General Adaptation
Syndrome** Selye described the three stages
of physiological response to stress.

The consistent pattern of responses that Selye identified, the **general adaptation
syndrome,** consists of three stages: alarm, resistance, and exhaustion (**FIGURE 10.7**). This
syndrome occurs in addition to specific physiological responses to particular stressors. In the *alarm stage,* an emergency reaction that prepares the body to fight or flee,
physiological responses are aimed at boosting physical abilities while reducing activities that make the organism vulnerable to infection after injury. In this stage, the body
is most likely to be exposed to infection and disease, so the immune system kicks in
and the body begins fighting back. During the *resistance stage,* the defenses prepare
for a longer, sustained attack against the stressor; immunity to infection and disease
increases somewhat as the body maximizes its defenses. When the body reaches the
exhaustion stage, a variety of physiological and immune systems fail. Bodily organs
that were already weak before the stress are the first to fail.

Stress Affects Health

One of Selye's central points was that the prolonged action of stress hormones, such
as cortisol, negatively affects health. Indeed, although stress hormones are essential to
normal health, over the long term they are associated with problems such as increased
blood pressure, cardiac disease, diabetes, declining sexual interest, and dwarfism (caused
by the suppression of growth hormones). People who have very stressful jobs—such
as air traffic controllers, combat soldiers, and firefighters—tend to have many health
problems that presumably are due partly to the effects of chronic stress. According
to Robert Sapolsky (1994), overwhelming evidence indicates that chronic stress, especially psychosocial stress, is associated with the initiation and progression of a wide
variety of diseases, from cancer to AIDS to cardiac disease. Stress leads to specific
physiological responses that affect health, and many people cope with stress by engaging in damaging behaviors. For instance, the number one reason problem drinkers give
for abusing alcohol is to cope with negative stress in their lives. When people are stressed,
they drink, smoke cigarettes, eat junk food, use drugs, and so on. As discussed later in
this chapter, most of the major health problems in industrialized societies are partly
attributable to unhealthful behaviors, many of which occur when people feel stressed.

THE IMMUNE SYSTEM Stress alters the functions of the immune system. When
foreign substances such as viruses, bacteria, or allergens enter the body, the
immune system launches into action to destroy the invaders. Stress interferes with
this natural process. The field of *psychoneuroimmunology* studies the response of the

body's immune system to psychological variables. Over the last 30 years, more than 300 studies have demonstrated that short-term stress boosts the immune system, whereas chronic stress weakens it, leaving the body less able to deal with infection (Segerstrom & Miller, 2004).

The detrimental effects of immediate and long-term stress on physical health are due partly to decreased lymphocyte production, which renders the body less capable of warding off foreign substances. In a particularly clear demonstration that stress affects health, Sheldon Cohen and his colleagues (1991) paid healthy volunteers to have cold viruses swabbed into their noses. Those who reported the highest levels of stress before being exposed to the cold viruses developed worse cold symptoms and higher viral counts than those who reported being less stressed (**FIGURE 10.8**). (Surprisingly, behaviors such as smoking, maintaining a poor diet, and not exercising had very small effects on the incidence of colds.) Apparently, when the underlying physiological basis of the stress response is activated too often or too intensely, the function of the immune system is impaired, and the probability and severity of ill health increases (Herbert & Cohen, 1993; McEwen, 2007).

In a study that looked specifically at the effects of desirable and undesirable events on the immune system, participants kept daily diaries for up to 12 weeks. In the diaries, they recorded their moods and the events in their lives and rated the events as desirable or undesirable. Each day, the participants took an antigen, a substance their immune systems recognized as a threat and therefore formed antibodies to protect against it. Then they provided saliva samples so that researchers could examine their antibody responses. The more desirable events a participant reported, the greater the antibody production. Similarly, the more undesirable events reported, the weaker the antibody production. The effect of a desirable event on antibodies lasted for two days (Stone, Neale, Cox, & Napoli, 1994). These and subsequent findings provide substantial evidence that perceived stress influences the immune system. Chronic stress, especially when associated with changes in social roles or identity (such as becoming a refugee, losing a job, or getting divorced), has the greatest impact on the immune system (Segerstrom & Miller, 2004).

HEART DISEASE Coronary heart disease is the leading cause of death for adults in the industrialized world. According to a World Health Organization report in 2002, each year more than 30 million people around the globe have heart attacks, and more than 12 million people die from them (**FIGURE 10.9**). Even though the rate of heart disease is lower in women than in men, heart disease is the number one killer of women. Genetics is among the many factors that determine heart disease, but two extremely important determinants are health behaviors and a small number of personality traits related to the way people respond to stress. Later, this chapter will discuss three major risk factors for heart disease: lack of exercise, obesity, and smoking. This section is concerned with the way personality traits can affect the heart.

The heart pumps nearly 2,000 gallons of blood each day, on average beating more than 100,000 times. A vast network of blood vessels carries oxygen and nutrients throughout the body.

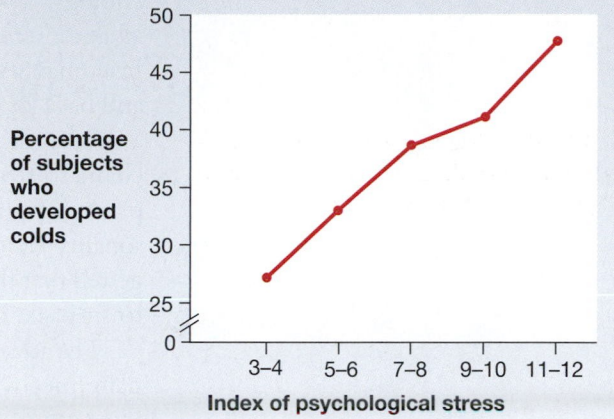

FIGURE 10.8 **Scientific Method: Cohen's Study of Stress and the Immune System**

Hypothesis: Stress affects health.

Research Method: Researchers swabbed the noses of healthy volunteers with cold viruses.

Results: Participants who reported higher levels of stress before being exposed to the cold viruses developed worse cold symptoms.

Percentage of subjects who developed colds (y-axis: 25, 30, 35, 40, 45, 50)

Index of psychological stress (x-axis: 3–4, 5–6, 7–8, 9–10, 11–12)

Conclusion: The functioning of the immune system can be impaired when a stress response is activated.

Over 270,000 people suffer a heart attack each year

FIGURE 10.9 **Heart Disease** To increase people's awareness of this growing problem, countries, cities, and local agencies employ public service campaigns like this one.

As people age, the arteries leading from the heart become narrow due to the buildup of fatty deposits, known as plaque. This narrowing makes it more difficult for the heart to pump blood and leads to coronary heart disease. When pieces of plaque break off from the wall of a blood vessel, blood clots form around the plaque and interrupt blood flow. If a clot blocks a blood vessel feeding the heart, it causes a heart attack; if it blocks a vessel that feeds the brain, it causes a stroke.

The idea that some personality traits could cause or worsen heart disease was first put forward in the 1950s. Surprisingly, this concept began with an upholstered chair. The cardiac specialist Meyer Friedman, a pioneer in the field of health psychology, was having the chairs in his waiting room reupholstered. The upholsterer commented that he had never seen chairs that wore out the way they did in Friedman's waiting room: The front edge of each seat was frayed, but the armrests and back of the chair were still in good condition. This observation gave Friedman a sudden insight. Can you guess how he used the frayed front of his waiting room chairs to hypothesize a link between personality and heart disease? Friedman had plenty of time to get to know his patients, and they seemed to share certain personality traits: They were impatient and driven. The upholsterer's comment suggested that they literally were sitting on the edges of their chairs, unable or unwilling to sit back, like racehorses pacing nervously at the starting gate.

The idea that personality could influence the development of heart disease initially met with considerable resistance. The idea just did not fit with the prevailing notion—since proven false—that biology existed separately from psychology. In the decades since Friedman recognized that some people might have personality traits that cause or worsen heart disease, hundreds of studies have been conducted to test this relationship. The results clearly show that negative emotions increase the risk of coronary heart disease (Booth-Kewley & Friedman, 1987; Sirois & Burg, 2003).

One of the earliest tests of the hypothesis that personality affects coronary heart disease was conducted in 1960, when the Western Collaborative Group began what was to be an eight-and-a-half-year study. Physicians recruited 3,500 men from northern California who were free of heart disease at the start of the study and screened them annually for symptoms such as high blood pressure, accelerated heart rate, and high cholesterol. Their overall health practices—and personal details such as education level, medical and family history, income, and personality traits—also were assessed.

The results indicated that, adjusting for the presence of established risk factors (such as high blood pressure, accelerated heart rate, or high cholesterol), a set of personality traits predicted heart disease. This set, the **Type A behavior pattern,** describes competitive, achievement-oriented, aggressive, hostile, time-pressed (feeling hurried, restless, unable to relax), impatient, confrontational people. Men who exhibited these traits were much more likely to develop coronary heart disease than were those who exhibited the **Type B behavior pattern,** which describes relaxed, noncompetitive, easygoing, accommodating people. In fact, this study found that a Type A personality was as strong a predictor of heart disease as was high blood pressure, high cholesterol, or smoking (Rosenman et al., 1975). Although the initial work was done only with men, more-recent research shows that these conclusions apply to women as well (Knox, Weidner, Adelman, Stoney, & Ellison, 2004; Krantz & McCeney, 2002).

Over the past 50 years, research has found that the original list of traits was too broad and that only certain components of the Type A behavior pattern are related to heart disease. Researchers at Duke University found that the most toxic factor was hostility (Williams, 1987). Hot-tempered people who are frequently angry, cynical, and combative are much more likely to die at an early age from heart

Type A behavior pattern A pattern of behavior characterized by competitiveness, achievement orientation, aggressiveness, hostility, restlessness, inability to relax, and impatience with others.

Type B behavior pattern A pattern of behavior characterized by relaxed, noncompetitive, easygoing, and accommodating behavior.

disease (Eaker, Sullivan, Kelly-Hayes, D'Agostino, & Benjamin, 2004). Indeed, having a high level of hostility while in college predicts greater risk for heart disease later in life (Siegler et al., 2003). Considerable evidence indicates that other negative emotional states, especially depression, also predict heart disease (Miller, Freedland, Carney, Stetler, & Banks, 2003). Of course, having a heart condition might make people hostile and depressed; but having a hostile personality and being depressed also predicted the worsening of heart disease, so causes and effects might be connected in a vicious cycle. In contrast, optimistic people tend to be at lower risk for heart disease (Maruta, Colligan, Malinchoc, & Offord, 2002). Learning to manage both stress and anger improves outcomes for those who have heart disease (Sirois & Burg, 2003). (Later in this chapter, you will find many suggestions for managing stress.)

TYPE Z BEHAVIOR

How might negative personality traits combine to promote coronary heart disease? Being hostile, angry, or depressed can cause heart problems in two ways. First, as noted above, people often cope with their problems through behavioral strategies that are bad for health, and negative personality traits can increase people's problems—another vicious cycle. But negative personality traits also can produce direct physiological effects on the heart. Think back to a time when you were very angry at someone. How did it feel to be so angry? Your body responded by increasing your heart rate, shutting down digestion, moving more blood to your muscles—in short, acting as though you were preparing to fight or to run away. You may have seen someone turn red with anger or start to shake. People with hostile personalities frequently experience such physiological responses, which take a toll on the heart. Chronic hostility can lead to overstimulation of the sympathetic nervous system, causing higher blood pressure, constriction of blood vessels, elevated levels of cortisol (recall that cortisol is a stress hormone), increased release of fatty acids into the bloodstream, and greater buildup of plaque on arteries—all these events contribute to heart disease. Over time, then, being hostile or angry causes wear and tear on the heart, making it more likely to fail.

Numerous studies have identified the biological pathways that lead from being angry and hostile to developing heart disease. As you might expect, the repeated cascade of bodily responses in hostile and angry individuals affects more than just the health of their hearts. Other bodily organs suffer as well. Researchers investigated whether an association existed between hostility and chronic pulmonary disease or early indicators that pulmonary disease was developing (Jackson, Kubzansky, Cohen, Jacobs, & Wright, 2007). Chronic pulmonary disease, a progressive condition in which airflow to the lungs is reduced, is a serious health risk in itself and a contributor to coronary heart disease. Even among the young, healthy participants in this study, higher levels of hostility were related to several measures of reduced pulmonary functioning.

Stress researchers discuss their findings using the framework of the **allostatic load theory of illness.** Allostatic load is similar to *homeostasis,* the body's ability to maintain a steady state, or constancy. As discussed in Chapter 9, the body works like a room regulated by a thermostat, registering when it gets too warm or too cold. To cool itself, the body employs physiological mechanisms such as sweating; to warm itself, it shivers and constricts the blood vessels. Likewise, allostatic systems regulate the body's response to excessive stress. After responding to a stressful event, the body needs to return to a steady state. When people are continually stressed, the allostatic loads on their bodies are too great for the bodies to return to their normal resting states and recover from the effects of stress. Thus the bodies of people who have more-positive emotions should return to their normal resting states more quickly and more frequently.

allostatic load theory of illness When people are continually stressed, they are unable to return to bodily states that characterize normal stress levels.

The evidence across multiple studies with different indices of disease and markers for the early development of disease is clear: Hostile, angry people are at greater risk for serious diseases and earlier death than are those with more optimistic and happier personalities. This conclusion appears to be universal. For example, a cross-cultural comparative study conducted with Japanese and non–Japanese college students replicated the association of anger and impatience with a wide range of health symptoms for students from all ethnic and cultural groups (Nakano & Kitamura, 2001).

Coping Is a Process

We all experience stressful events. To deal effectively with the stressors in our lives, we use cognitive appraisals that link feelings with thoughts, so we can think about and manage our feelings more objectively. Richard Lazarus (1993) conceptualized a two-part appraisal process: People use **primary appraisals** to decide whether stimuli are stressful, benign, or irrelevant. When they deem stimuli as stressful, people use **secondary appraisals** to evaluate response options and choose coping behaviors. Such cognitive appraisals also affect people's perceptions of and reactions to potential stressors in the future and help people prepare for stressful events. Coping that occurs before the onset of a future stressor is *anticipatory coping*—for example, when parents rehearse how they will tell their children they are planning to divorce.

TYPES OF COPING A taxonomy of coping strategies, developed by Susan Folkman and Richard Lazarus (1988), outlines two general categories of coping: In **emotion-focused coping**, a person tries to prevent an emotional response to the stressor, adopting strategies, often passive, to numb the pain. Such strategies include avoidance, minimizing the problem, trying to distance oneself from the outcomes of the problem, or engaging in behaviors such as eating or drinking. For example, if you are having difficulty at school, you might avoid the problem by skipping class, minimize the problem by telling yourself school is not all that important, distance yourself from the outcome by saying you can always get a job if college does not work out, or overeat and drink alcohol to dull the pain of the problem. These strategies do not solve the problem or prevent it from recurring in the future. By contrast, **problem-focused coping** involves taking direct steps to solve the problem: generating alternative solutions, weighing their costs and benefits, and choosing between them. In this case, if you are having academic trouble, you might think about ways to alleviate the problem, such as getting tutoring or asking for an extension for a paper. Given these alternatives, you could consider how likely a tutor is to be helpful, discuss the problem with your professors, and so on. People adopt problem-focused behaviors when they perceive stressors as controllable and are experiencing only moderate levels of stress. Conversely, emotion-focused behaviors may enable people to continue functioning in the face of uncontrollable stressors or high levels of stress.

The best way to cope with stress depends on personal resources and on the situation. Most people report using problem- and emotion-focused coping. Usually, emotion-based strategies are effective only in the short run. For example, if your partner is in a bad mood and is giving you a hard time, just ignoring him or her can be the best option. In contrast, ignoring your partner's drinking problem will not make it go away, and eventually you will need a better coping strategy. However, problem-focused coping strategies work only if the person can do something about the situation. In one study that tested the best way to cope with an extremely threatening situation (Strentz & Auerbach, 1988), 57 airline workers were held hostage for four

primary appraisal Part of the coping process that involves making decisions about whether a stimulus is stressful, benign, or irrelevant.

secondary appraisal Part of the coping process during which people evaluate their options and choose coping behaviors.

emotion-focused coping A type of coping in which people try to prevent having an emotional response to a stressor.

problem-focused coping A type of coping in which people take direct steps to confront or minimize a stressor.

Real World PSYCHOLOGY

days by five "terrorists." Even though the participants volunteered to be hostages and knew their captors were actually FBI agents, the situation was very realistic and extremely stressful. Half the participants had been trained to use emotion-based coping, and half had been trained to use problem-based coping. Can you predict which strategy worked better? The emotion-based participants experienced less stress because they assumed any resistence they offered would just put them in greater danger. In other words, their best coping strategy was to remain calm. In contrast, on September 11, 2001, the passengers on the hijacked United Airlines Flight 93 knew that three other planes had been crashed by terrorists that morning (see the opening of Chapter 8, "Thinking and Intelligence"). Assuming their hijackers also planned to crash Flight 93, these passengers knew they had an equal or better chance of surviving if they resisted. Some of them decided they had nothing to lose, chose a problem-based coping strategy, and fought back against the hijackers (**FIGURE 10.10**).

FIGURE 10.10 Flight 93 This film still is from *United 93* (2006), a dramatic re-creation of events on the fourth hijacked plane on 9/11. Here, passengers discuss their options after learning about the crashes of the three other planes.

Susan Folkman and Judith Moskowitz (2000) have demonstrated that two strategies in addition to problem-focused coping can help people use positive thoughts to deal with stress. Both strategies involve *positive reappraisal,* a cognitive process in which a person focuses on possible good things in his or her current situation, looking for the proverbial silver lining. One strategy is to make *downward comparisons,* comparing oneself to those who are worse off; doing so has been shown to help people cope with serious illnesses. *Creation of positive events* is a strategy of infusing ordinary events with positive meaning. If you were diagnosed with diabetes, for example, you could focus on how having diabetes will force you to eat a healthy diet and exercise regularly (positive reappraisal), recognize that it is not as serious as having heart disease (downward comparisons), and take joy in everyday activities such as riding a bike. Positive events might include such things as enjoying a beautiful sunset, finding humor in a situation, savoring a recent compliment—all of which might help you focus on the positive aspects of your life and deal with your negative stress.

INDIVIDUAL DIFFERENCES IN COPING People differ widely in their perceptions of how stressful life events are. Some people could be termed *stress-resistant* for their ability to adapt to life changes by viewing events constructively. This personality trait has been characterized as *hardiness* by Suzanne Kobasa (1979), who lists three components: *commitment, challenge,* and *control.* People high in hardiness are committed to their daily activities, view threats as challenges or as opportunities for growth, and see themselves as being in control of their lives. People low in hardiness typically are alienated, fear or resist change, and view events as being under external control. Numerous studies have found that people high in hardiness report fewer negative responses to stressful events. In a laboratory experiment in which participants were given difficult cognitive tasks, people high in hardiness exhibited higher blood pressure during the tasks—a physiological indicator of active coping. Moreover, a questionnaire completed immediately after the tasks revealed that participants high in hardiness increased the number of positive thoughts they had about themselves in response to the stressor.

FAMILY-FOCUSED INTERVENTIONS One of the most stressful events in life is dealing with a chronic illness—such as cancer, asthma, heart disease, AIDS—or chronic pain, whether the illness or pain is our own or that of a loved one. Many, perhaps all, readers of this chapter likely have provided care for an ill person or will need to do so sometime in the future. Although including family members in the treatment plan for a chronically ill person might seem important, a review of the research literature shows that including family members in a treatment plan is often not effective (Martire & Schulz, 2007). A major problem in enlisting family members is that the patient may feel as though family members are controlling his or her life rather than providing assistance. A common theme in the psychological literature is that being in control of essential decisions in one's life reduces stress and promotes well-being (Karasek & Theorell, 1990); it is also a central component of hardiness.

Family interventions can be beneficial, however, when family members promote the patient's autonomy. Some behaviors that seem to help when a family member has a chronic illness include (1) motivating the patient to make his or her own health and life choices and to carry out the activities of everyday living, (2) modeling healthy behaviors, (3) providing rewards, and (4) pointing out the positive consequences of caring for one's illness (Martire & Schulz, 2007). For example, family members might prepare food for the patient or help the patient practice relaxation techniques. By providing motivation, encouragement, and emotional support, families can also assist the patient in adjusting to life with the illness.

 SUMMING UP

How Do People Cope with Stress?

Stress occurs when people feel overwhelmed by the challenges they face, as when major change happens in their lives. Hans Selye's general adaptation theory conceptualizes the stages of physiological coping. Stresses include major life changes as well as daily hassles. Females' responses to stress include the tendency to affiliate with a group in which members care for each other, whereas males tend to have a fight-or-flight response in which their bodies prepare them for combat or fast escape. Cognitive appraisals, such as determining the relevance of the stressor and adopting a problem-focused versus emotion-focused approach, can alleviate stress or minimize its harmful effects. Hardy people handle stress well because they believe they can control events in their lives, are committed to and actively engaged in what they do, and see obstacles as challenges to be overcome. A positive appraisal of events is also a good way to regulate emotions. When providing care for an ill person, it is important to allow the patient to maintain control over his or her life. Maintaining such control is a trait of hardy people.

 MEASURING UP

1. Match each stage in the general adaptation syndrome—alarm, resistance, and exhaustion—with one of the following examples.
   a. After years of responding to tight deadlines at work, the executive developed several medical problems that required hospitalization.
   b. When Myrtle returned home and found a stranger in her living room, her heart began pounding rapidly.
   c. As the hurricane lashed the shore, nearby residents struggled to keep themselves safe.

2. How does long-term stress affect health?
   a. The extended physiological response damages organs such as the heart.
   b. Long-term stress sharpens a person's awareness of potentially harmful events and increases the person's attention span.
   c. Repeated stress tunes the immune system so that the body is better able to fight disease.
   d. Long-term stress provides an evolutionary advantage in modern societies.

What Behaviors Affect Mental and Physical Health?

The previous sections looked at how stress affects the body, and how people cope with stress. This section looks at the effects of stress on people's behavior. Before the twentieth century, most people died from infections and from diseases transmitted person to person. But the last century saw a dramatic shift in the leading causes of mortality. People now are most likely to die from heart disease, cancer, accidents, diabetes, liver disease, and so on—all of which are at least partially outcomes of lifestyle. Our daily habits—such as smoking, poor eating, alcohol use, and lack of exercise—contribute to nearly every major cause of death in developed nations (Smith, Orleans, & Jenkins, 2004). And stress plays an important role in motivating each of these health-threatening behaviors. A study of more than 12,000 people from Minnesota found that high stress was associated with greater intake of fat, less-frequent exercise, and heavier smoking (Ng & Jeffrey, 2003).

Obesity Results from a Genetic Predisposition and Overeating

Obesity is a major health problem with physical and psychological consequences. One factor that contributes to obesity is overeating, which some people are especially likely to do when stressed (Heatherton & Baumeister, 1991). Why some people can control how much they eat and others cannot remains unclear. Some people believe that those who overeat are lazy or unmotivated. In fact, obese people typically try multiple diets and other "cures" for fat—and even when they lose weight, they likely will gain it all back.

Society's negative attitudes toward overweight people provide plenty of motivation for those who suffer from prejudice against the obese. Bettye Travis (cited in Stewart, 2007), the former president of the National Association to Advance Fat Acceptance (NAAFA), described societal reactions to obesity this way: Fat people are "one of the last marginal groups that are still targeted. . . . [I]t is still OK to make fun of fat people" (p. B7). After a lifetime of both shame and failed attempts to lose weight, she learned to say "the f word": *fat.* NAAFA exists to help fat people fight "size discrimination," as in being denied the right to be an adoptive parent (see the opening of this chapter). NAAFA members do not oppose attempts to lose weight, nor do they dispute the research indicating serious health risks for people who are obese. But after experiencing repeated disappointments with diets, they realize they will likely always be fat and that they must learn to accept themselves and to educate society about obesity. Given the rise in obesity in industrialized countries around the world, especially in the United States, the organization may see its membership grow. However, even many obese people stigmatize obese people and may not want to join a group that advocates "fat acceptance."

There is no precise definition of obesity, but people are considered obese if they are approximately 20 percent over ideal body weight, as indicated by various mortality studies. One measure of obesity widely used in research is **body mass index (BMI),** a ratio of body weight to height. (**FIGURE 10.11** shows how to calculate BMI and how to interpret the value obtained.) According to standard BMI cutoffs, more than one-third of Americans currently are medically obese. Over the last 60 years, researchers have learned a great deal about the causes of obesity—a multifaceted problem influenced, like so many physical and psychological phenomena discussed in this book, by genes and environment. Thus understanding obesity requires a

body mass index (BMI) A ratio of body weight to height, used to measure obesity.

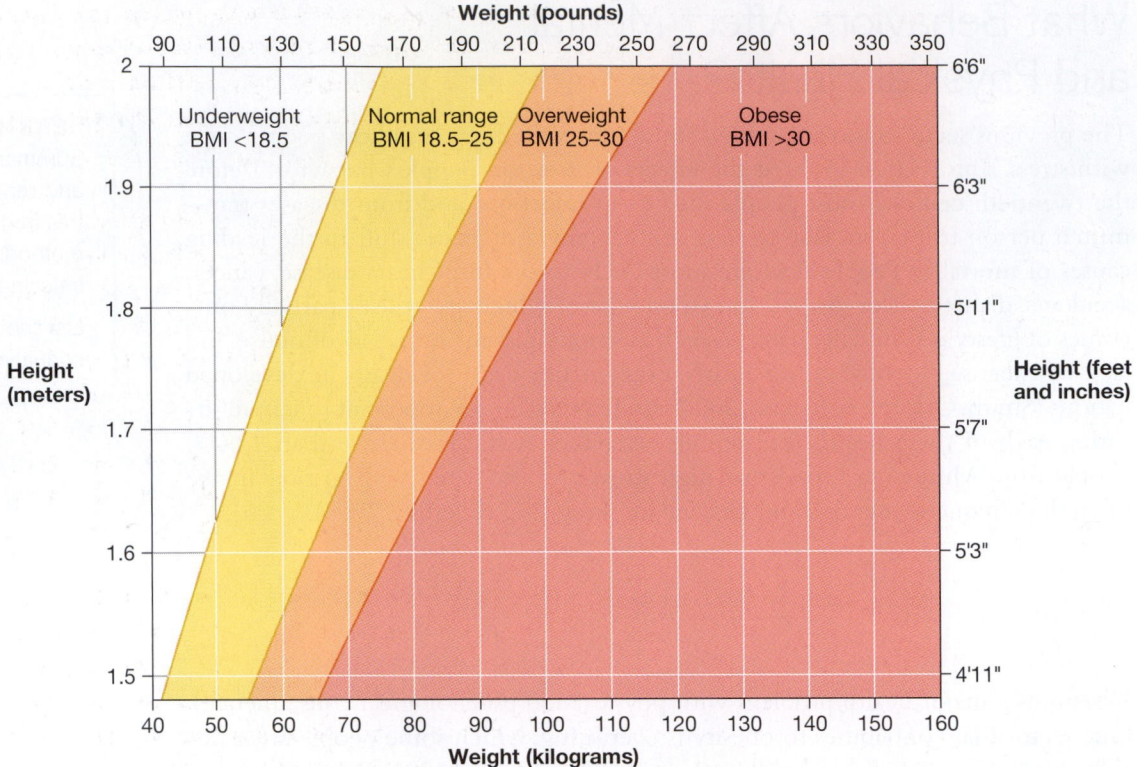

FIGURE 10.11 Determining Body Mass Index You can find your own BMI by finding the point at which your weight and height meet on the graph. Beyond or below the optimal normal range, you are at greater risk for health problems.

multilevel approach that examines behavior, underlying biology, cognition (how we think about food and obesity), and the societal context that makes cheap and tasty food readily available. Obesity is an ideal example of the biopsychosocial model of health presented earlier in the chapter. As you read about obesity, keep in mind the linkages among genetic predispositions, thoughts, feelings, and behaviors as well as the continuous loop through which these variables cycle.

GENETIC INFLUENCE A trip to the local mall or anyplace families gather reveals one obvious fact about body weight: Obesity tends to run in families. Indeed, various family and adoption studies indicate that approximately half the variability in body weight can be considered the result of genetics (Klump & Culbert, 2007). One of the best and largest studies, carried out in Denmark during the 1980s, found that the BMI of adopted children was strongly related to the BMI of their biological parents and not at all to the BMI of their adoptive parents (Sorensen, Holst, Stunkard, & Skovgaard, 1992). Studies of identical and fraternal twins provide even stronger evidence of genetic control of body weight, finding heritability estimates ranging from 60 percent to 80 percent. (As discussed in Chapter 3, heritability refers to the proportion of variability, in a population, attributed to genetic transmission of a trait from parents to their offspring.) Moreover, the similarity between the body weights of identical twins does not differ for twins raised together versus twins raised apart, a finding that suggests environment has far less effect on body weight than genetics has.

If genes primarily determine body weight, why has the percentage of Americans who are obese doubled over the past few decades? Albert Stunkard, a leading researcher on human obesity, points out that genetics determines whether a person can become obese, but environment determines whether that person *will* become obese (Stunkard, 1996). In an important study conducted by the geneticist Claude Bouchard, identical twins were overfed by approximately 1,000 calories each day for 100 days. Most of the twins gained some weight, but there was great variability among pairs in how much they gained (ranging from 4.3 kg to 13.3 kg, or 9.5 lbs to 29.3 lbs; Bouchard et al., 1990). Further, within the twin pairs there was a striking degree of similarity in how much weight they gained and in which parts of the body they stored the fat. Some of the twin pairs were especially likely to put on weight. Thus genetics determines sensitivity to environmental influences. Genes predispose some people to obesity in environments that promote overfeeding, such as contemporary industrialized societies. Many genes are involved in obesity, as might be expected for such a complex condition: More than 300 genetic markers or genes have been identified as playing some role (Snyder et al., 2004).

THE STIGMA OF OBESITY Obesity is associated with a significant number of medical problems, including heart disease, high blood pressure, and gastric ailments. It also can give rise to various psychological problems, primarily because of the extreme stigma associated with being overweight. In most Western cultures, obese individuals are viewed as less attractive, less socially adept, less intelligent, and less productive than their normal-weight peers (Dejong & Kleck, 1986). Moreover, perceiving oneself as overweight is linked to depression, anxiety, and low self-esteem. (As noted in Chapter 2, we cannot randomly assign people to different weight conditions or different levels of self-esteem, so most of the obesity research with humans is correlational.)

It might be tempting to infer that being overweight causes these problems, but a recent study suggests that low self-esteem might cause weight gain (Lemeshow et al., 2008). Almost 6,000 girls aged 12 to 18 rated their social status at school, using a scale of 1 to 10, with 10 being the most admired and popular. The girls who rated themselves as 4 or less on this scale were much more likely—after a control for other relevant variables (e.g., age, television viewing, height growth, household income)—to show a gain of 2 BMI points two years after rating their self-esteem than were girls who rated themselves higher. Many possible explanations exist for this correlation, however, so we cannot claim any causal relationships between low self-esteem and weight gain.

Not all cultures stigmatize obesity (Hebl & Heatherton, 1998). In some developing countries, such as many African nations, being obese is a sign of being upper class. Obesity may be desirable in developing countries because it helps prevent some infectious diseases, reduces the likelihood of starvation, and is associated with having more successful births. It may also serve as a status symbol in developing countries, an indication that one can afford to eat luxuriously. In Pacific Island countries such as Tonga and Fiji, being obese is a source of personal pride, and dieting is uncommon (**FIGURE 10.12A**).

In most industrialized cultures, where food is generally abundant, being overweight is associated with lower socioeconomic status, especially for women. The upper classes in Western cultures have a clear preference for very thin body types, as exemplified in fashion magazines. The typical woman depicted by the fashion industry is 5 feet, 11 inches tall and weighs approximately 110 pounds—7 inches taller and 30 pounds lighter than the average woman in the United States. Such an extreme standard of thinness represents a body weight ideal that is difficult, if not impossible, for most people to achieve. Indeed, women report holding body weight ideals that are not only lower than average weight but also lower than what men find attractive (Fallon & Rozin, 1985).

(a)

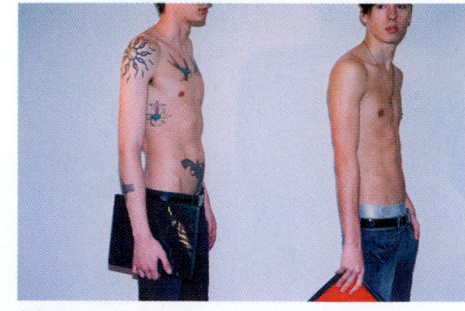

(b)

FIGURE 10.12 Variations in Body Image
(a) In some places, larger shapes are more desirable, as embodied by these welcoming women on the island of Fatu Hiva, in French Polynesia. (b) In other places, such as the United States, skinniness is prized, as epitomized by these male models.

Ultrathin has long been "in" for female models. More recently, male models have joined their skinny female peers, and men as well as women are faced with unrealistically thin images when they peruse the fashion pages (**FIGURE 10.12B**). This comment by a *New York Times* fashion editor says it all: "Skinny, skinny, skinny. Everybody's shrinking themselves" (Trebay, 2008). Stas Svetlichnyy, a typical male model, is 6 feet tall and has a 28-inch waist; his highest weight is about 145 pounds. This new, skinnier male model is increasingly at odds with most men's bodies. American men are taller and weigh more today than they did 40 years ago. The average height has gone from 5 feet, 8 inches in 1960 to 5 feet, 9.5 inches in 2002. At the same time, average weight has risen from 166.3 pounds to 191 pounds (Centers for Disease Control and Prevention, 2004).

RESTRICTIVE DIETING DOES NOT WORK Dieting is a notoriously ineffective means of achieving permanent weight loss. Most individuals who lose weight through dieting eventually regain the weight; often, they gain back more than they lost. Most diets fail primarily because of the body's natural defense against weight loss (Kaplan, 2007). Body weight is regulated around a set-point determined primarily by genetic influence. Consider two examples. In 1966, several inmates at a Vermont prison were challenged to increase their body weight by 25 percent (Sims et al., 1968). For six months, these inmates consumed more than 7,000 calories per day, nearly double their usual intake. If each inmate was eating about 3,500 extra calories a day (the equivalent of seven large cheeseburgers), simple math suggests that each should have gained approximately 170 pounds over the six months. In reality, few inmates gained more than 40 pounds, and most lost the weight when they went back to normal eating. Those who did not lose the weight had family histories of obesity, a finding that supports the view that genetics predisposes some people to obesity.

At the other end of the spectrum, more than 100 men volunteered to take part in a scientific study as an alternative to military service during World War II (Keys, Brozek, Henschel, Mickelsen, & Taylor, 1950). The researchers were investigating the short- and long-term effects of semistarvation, and over six months the participants lost an average of 25 percent of their body weight. Most found this weight reduction very hard to accomplish, and some had great difficulty losing more than 10 pounds. The men underwent dramatic changes in emotions, motivation, and attitudes toward food. They became anxious, depressed, and listless; they lost interest in sex and other activities; and they became obsessed with eating. Many of these outcomes are similar to those experienced by people with eating disorders.

Although it is possible to alter body weight, the body responds to weight loss by slowing down the metabolism and using less energy. Therefore, after the body has been deprived of food, it needs less food to maintain a given body weight. Likewise, weight gain occurs much faster in previously starved animals than would be expected by caloric intake alone. In addition, repeated alterations between caloric deprivation and overfeeding have been shown to have cumulative metabolic effects, so that weight loss and metabolic functioning are slowed more each time the animal is placed on caloric deprivation, and weight gain occurs more rapidly with each resumption of feeding. Such patterns might explain why "yo-yo dieters" tend to become heavier over time.

Recent research has yielded the surprising finding that body weight is also socially contagious (Christakis & Fowler, 2007). One study found that close friends of the same sex tend to be similar in body weight. Even when close friends live far apart from each other, if one friend is obese, the other one is likely to be obese as well. Studies of the social transmission of obesity tell us that it is not eating the same meals or cooking together that is critical; rather, it is the implicit agreement on what body weight is acceptable or normal. If many of your close friends are obese, implicitly you learn that obesity is normal. Thus subtle communications can affect how we think and act when we eat. Such findings highlight a main theme of this book: We are not aware of many of the psychological influences on our thoughts, behaviors, and attitudes.

RESTRAINED EATING Diets may also fail because people engage in occasional, or not so occasional, bouts of overeating. Janet Polivy and Peter Herman (1985) have demonstrated that chronic dieters, whom they call *restrained eaters,* are prone to excessive eating in certain situations. For instance, if restrained eaters believe they have eaten high-calorie foods, they abandon their diets. Their mind-set becomes "I've blown my diet, so I might as well just keep eating." Many restrained eaters diet all week and then lose control on the weekend, when they are faced with increased food temptations and at the same time are in less structured environments. Being under stress also leads restrained eaters to break their diets (Heatherton, Herman, & Polivy, 1991).

Binge eating by restrained eaters depends on their *perceptions* of whether they have broken their diets. Dieters can eat 1,000-calorie Caesar salads and believe their diets are fine; but if they eat 200-calorie chocolate bars, they feel their diets are ruined and become disinhibited (first they inhibit their eating, and then they lose the inhibition—that is, they become *disinhibited*). The problem for restrained eaters is that they rely on cognitive control of food intake: Rather than eating according to internal states of hunger and satiety, restrained eaters eat according to rules, such as time of day, number of calories, and type of food. Such patterns will likely break down when dieters eat high-calorie foods or feel distressed. Getting restrained eaters back in touch with internal motivational states is one goal of sensible approaches to dieting.

DISORDERED EATING When dieters fail to lose weight, they often blame their lack of willpower, vowing to redouble their efforts on the next diet. Repeated dietary failures may have harmful and permanent physiological and psychological consequences. In physiological terms, weight-loss and weight-gain cycles alter the dieter's metabolism and may make future weight loss more difficult. Psychologically, repeated failures diminish satisfaction with body image and damage self-esteem. Over time, chronic dieters tend to feel helpless and depressed. Some eventually engage in more extreme behaviors to lose weight, such as taking drugs, fasting, exercising excessively, or purging. For a vulnerable individual, chronic dieting may promote the development of a clinical eating disorder.

The two most common eating disorders are *anorexia nervosa* and *bulimia nervosa* (Wiseman, Harris, & Halmi, 1998). Individuals with **anorexia nervosa** have an excessive fear of becoming fat; as a result, they refuse to eat. Anorexia most often begins in early adolescence and mainly affects upper-middle- and upper-class Caucasian girls. Although many adolescent girls strive to be thin, fewer than 1 in 100 meet the clinical criteria of anorexia nervosa (**TABLE 10.1**). These criteria include both objective measures of thinness and psychological characteristics that indicate an abnormal obsession with food and body weight. Those who have anorexia view themselves as fat despite being at least 15 percent to 25 percent underweight. Issues of food and weight pervade their lives, controlling how they view themselves and how they view the world. Initially, the results of self-imposed starvation may draw favorable comments from others. But as the anorexic

anorexia nervosa An eating disorder characterized by an excessive fear of becoming fat and thus a refusal to eat.

Table 10.1 Diagnostic Criteria for Anorexia Nervosa and Bulimia Nervosa

CRITERIA FOR ANOREXIA NERVOSA

A. Refusal to maintain body weight at or above a minimum normal for age and height (e.g., weight loss leading to maintenance of body weight less than 85 percent of that expected; or failure to make expected weight gain during period of growth, leading to body weight less than 85 percent of that expected).

B. Intense fear of gaining weight or becoming fat, even though underweight.

C. Disturbance in the way in which one's body weight or shape is experienced, undue influence of body weight or shape on self-evaluation, or denial of the seriousness of the current low body weight.

D. In postmenarcheal females, amenorrhea (the absence of at least three consecutive menstrual cycles).

CRITERIA FOR BULIMIA NERVOSA

A. Recurrent episodes of binge eating. An episode of binge eating is characterized by both of the following:

  (1) Eating, in a discrete period (e.g., within any 2-hour period), an amount of food that is definitely larger than most people would eat during a similar period of time and under similar circumstances.

  (2) A sense of lack of control over eating during the episode (e.g., a feeling that one cannot stop eating or control what or how much one is eating).

B. Recurrent inappropriate compensatory behavior in order to prevent weight gain, such as self-induced vomiting; misuse of laxatives, diuretics, enemas, or other medications; fasting; or excessive exercise.

C. The binge eating and inappropriate compensatory behaviors both occur, on average, at least twice a week for 3 months.

D. Self-evaluation is unduly influenced by body shape and weight.

SOURCE: *Diagnostic and Statistical Manual of the American Psychiatric Association,* 1994.

---

approaches her emaciated ideal, family and friends usually become concerned. In many cases, medical attention is required to prevent death from starvation. Anorexia is difficult to treat, since patients maintain the belief that they are overweight or not as thin as they would like to be, even when they are severely emaciated. This dangerous disorder causes a number of serious health problems, in particular a loss of bone density, and about 15 percent to 20 percent of those with anorexia eventually die from the disorder—they literally starve themselves to death (American Psychiatric Association, 2000).

bulimia nervosa An eating disorder characterized by dieting, binge eating, and purging.

Individuals with **bulimia nervosa** alternate between dieting and binge eating. Bulimia often develops during late adolescence. Like anorexia, bulimia is most common among upper-middle- and upper-class Caucasian women, but it is more common among minorities and men than anorexia is. Approximately 1 percent to 2 percent of women in high school and college meet the definitional criteria for bulimia nervosa. These women tend to be of average weight or slightly overweight. They regularly binge eat, feel their eating is out of control, worry excessively about body weight issues, and engage in one or more compensatory behaviors, such as self-induced vomiting, excessive exercise, or the abuse of laxatives. Whereas anorexics cannot easily hide their self-starvation, binge-eating behavior tends to occur secretly. When ordering large quantities of food, bulimics pretend they are ordering for a group, and they often hide the massive quantities of food they buy for binges. They try to vomit quietly or seek out little-used bathrooms to avoid being heard while they vomit. Although bulimia is associated with serious health problems, such as dental and cardiac disorders, it is seldom fatal (Keel & Mitchell, 1997). A variant of bulimia is *binge-eating disorder,* wherein individuals engage in binge eating but do not purge. Many people with binge-eating disorder are obese.

If a fairly close relative or friend needed a kidney transplant because of renal failure and you were a perfect or very good match, would you donate one of your kidneys to that person? What if the person's renal failure was due to her obesity, a condition that increases the risk of kidney failure sevenfold? Imagine further that maintaining a healthy weight has been difficult for you; you jog four miles a day and are vigilant about what you eat, while your relative or friend has not been so careful. Would you still feel a moral obligation to donate your kidney?

The increasing incidence of obesity is no secret, and concern is growing rapidly in the United States, Britain, Australia, and various European countries. The Centers for Disease Control and Prevention reports that about one-third of American adults are obese and more are overweight. Obesity is a well-recognized cause of chronic health problems such as cancer, diabetes, hypertension, and heart disease—some of the leading causes of health care spending, disability, and death. The economist Roland Sturm (2002) has found that obesity helps increase the number of chronic conditions at a rate similar to that of twenty years' aging and significantly greater than current or past smoking or problem drinking. But unlike smokers and drunk drivers, fat people do not compromise the well-being of others. Or do they? What about the costs of treating obesity-related disease? In 2002, obesity and obesity-related complications accounted for 9.1 percent of U.S. health care expenditures (more than $92 billion), and those numbers continue to rise (Finkelstein, Fiebelkorn, & Wang, 2003).

Explanations for the rise in obesity are numerous: increasingly sedentary lifestyles because of television, videogames, computers, and car travel; a decrease in physical activity programs in schools; increased portion sizes; more fast food and fewer healthy, home-cooked meals (Vanchieri, 1998); even high fructose corn syrup. Jeffrey M. Friedman (2003), however, argues that we cannot discuss obesity meaningfully until we resist the impulse to assign blame. Nor, he argues, can we hold to the simple belief that through willpower alone, people consciously can resist food's allure and precisely control their weight. Friedman emphasizes that there is more to the equation and that the answers seem to reside in our genes and their interactions with environmental factors. Epidemiological, experimental, and twin studies have found major differences in individuals' sensitivity and resistance to obesity. In fact, in the United States, morbid obesity is increasing more rapidly than moderate obesity (Sturm, 2003), and the BMI of adults in the lowest percentiles has not changed nearly as much as has the BMI of those in the highest percentiles. Some people appear susceptible to obesity in what is essentially a toxic environment of high-fat diets and decreased physical activity, and others are relatively resistant. To most of us, these facts are no surprise. We all know people who eat like horses and never gain weight and people who eat very little and are always fighting to keep their weight down.

Some antiobesity researchers suggest that because no good medical treatment exists for obesity and most dieters fail at their attempts to maintain weight loss, the best hope for dealing with the "obesity epidemic" might be political. Suggestions have been made to restrict the marketing of junk foods, especially to children in schools and on television; to impose taxes (known as "the fat tax") and put calorie labels on junk food and fast food; to reinvigorate physical education and healthy cooking classes in schools; to change farm subsidies to encourage production and consumption of grains, fruits, and vegetables; and to form a government agency with a clear responsibility for matters pertaining to food, nutrition, and health.

Although the Center for Science in the Public Interest has mounted antiobesity campaigns, other public interest groups, such as NAAFA, argue that fatness is a form of body diversity, is not a disease, and should be tolerated and respected. Is obesity a public health issue that needs to be addressed, as the antiobesity researchers preach? Or is it a form of body diversity that should be accepted as a variation of normal, as NAAFA believes? Is it ethical for the government to interfere in our personal lives regarding food choice, or do people have a right to live their lives the way they choose? Are the added costs to the health care system of an unhealthy diet and lack of exercise different from the strain put on it by people who make other unhealthy lifestyle choices, such as smoking and not using condoms?

Eating disorders tend to run in families and, like obesity, are due partly to genetics. The incidence of eating disorders in the United States increased into the 1980s (Keel, Baxter, Heatherton, & Joiner, 2007), so a genetic predisposition for them appears to be manifested in societies with an abundance of food. Bulimia seems to be more culture bound, meaning there are large cultural variations in its incidence, whereas anorexia is prevalent in all societies that have abundant food.

Smoking Is a Leading Cause of Death

Despite overwhelming evidence that smoking cigarettes leads to premature death, millions around the globe continue to light up (Carmody, 1993). According to a recent report from the World Health Organization, increasing numbers of people are smoking in low-income countries, and 5.4 million deaths are caused by tobacco every year. Thirty percent of all smokers worldwide are in China; 10 percent are in India; and an additional 25 percent come from Indonesia, Russia, the United States, Japan, Brazil, Bangladesh, Germany, and Turkey combined (World Health Organization [WHO] Report on Global Tobacco Epidemic, 2008; **FIGURE 10.13**). It is estimated that more than one billion people will die from smoking in this century. The Centers for Disease Control reported that in 2002, about 1 in 4 American adults was a current smoker. Smoking is blamed for more than 440,000 deaths per year in the United States and decreases the typical smoker's life by more than 12 years (USDHHS, 2001).

Most smokers begin in childhood or early adolescence, and every day nearly 5,000 Americans aged 11 to 17 have their first cigarette (Gilpin, Choi, Berry, & Pierce, 1999). About half of these young smokers will likely continue smoking into adulthood, and one-third of those will die from smoking (USDHHS, 2001).

Among the numerous health problems smoking causes are heart disease, respiratory ailments, and various cancers. Cigarette smoke also causes health problems for nonsmoking bystanders—a finding that has led to bans on smoking in many public and private places. Smokers also endure scoldings from physicians, and loved ones, concerned for their health and welfare. Besides spending money on cigarettes, smokers pay significantly more for life insurance and health insurance. Why do they continue to smoke? Why does anyone start?

STARTING SMOKING It is hard to imagine any good reason to start smoking. First attempts at smoking often involve a great deal of coughing, watering eyes, a terrible taste in the mouth, and feelings of nausea. So why do kids persist? Most researchers point to powerful social influences as the leading cause of adolescent smoking (Chassin, Presson, & Sherman, 1990; **FIGURE 10.14**). Research has demonstrated that adolescents will more likely smoke if their parents or friends smoke (Hansen et al., 1987). They often smoke their first cigarettes in the company of other smokers, or at least with the encouragement of their peers. Moreover, many adolescent smokers appear to show a false-consensus effect—they overestimate the number of adolescent and adult smokers (Sherman, Presson, Chassin, Corty, & Olshavsky, 1983). Adolescents who incorrectly believe that smoking is common may take it up to fit in with the crowd.

Other studies have pointed to the potential meaning of "being a smoker" as having a powerful influence. For instance, research has shown that smokers are viewed as having positive qualities such as being tough, sociable, and good with members of the opposite sex. Children take up smoking partially to look "tough, cool, and independent of authority" (Leventhal & Cleary, 1980, p. 384). Thus smoking may be one way for adolescents to enhance their self-images as well as their public images (Chassin

(a)

(b)

FIGURE 10.13 Smoking Is a Global Phenomenon (a) These men are smoking in Tiananmen Square, in Beijing, China. **(b)** These smokers belong to the Mentawi people, a seminomadic hunter-gatherer tribe in the coastal and rain forest regions of Indonesia.

et al., 1990). By the 12th grade, 70 percent of adolescents have had some experience with tobacco products (Mowery, Brick, & Farrelly, 2000). Of course, it is hard to look tough while gasping and retching; so while most adolescents try one or two cigarettes, most do not become regular smokers. Even so, approximately 30 percent of 12th graders in the United States smoke on a regular basis (Baker, Brandon, & Chassin, 2004).

Over time, casual smokers become addicted. It is now widely acknowledged that the drug nicotine, in tobacco, is of primary importance in motivating and maintaining smoking behavior (Fagerström & Schneider, 1989; USDHHS, 2004). Once the smoker becomes "hooked" on nicotine, going without cigarettes will lead to unpleasant withdrawal symptoms, including distress and heightened anxiety (Russell, 1990). Some people appear especially susceptible to nicotine addiction, perhaps because of genetics (Sabol et al., 1999). Nicotine may lead to increased activation of dopamine neurons, which can have a rewarding effect. (On the role of dopamine neurons, see Chapter 3, "Biological Foundations.")

MAINTAINING A HEALTHY WEIGHT OR QUITTING SMOKING

For weight loss programs to be successful, individuals need to make permanent lifestyle changes that include altering eating habits, increasing exercise, eliminating food cues, enlisting family members to help, and, for some, taking prescription drugs and undergoing surgery. Although it is far from easy, some people manage to lose excess weight and maintain healthy weights.

Gary Stocklaufer, discussed at the opening of this chapter, is one of the many obese people who have had surgery to reduce their stomachs and prevent them from overeating because they could not lose weight with diet and exercise. Many other obese people have turned to drugs to help them lose weight, but there are no get-thin-quick medications, and all the available medications require exercise and healthy eating to bring about weight loss. People who are not obese but want to shed extra pounds can join support groups to help them exercise more and eat better. In fact, many people have lost weight and kept it off by adopting healthy lifelong habits.

Cigarette smokers similarly need orchestrated efforts for their best chances at stopping smoking. These efforts often include nicotine patches to assist with the withdrawal symptoms, avoiding places where other people smoke, and substituting behaviors that are healthier than smoking. However, like other addicts, smokers may need to "hit rock bottom" before realizing they have to do something about their behavior. The psychologist David Premack provides an example of a man who quit smoking because of something that happened as he was picking up his children at the city library:

> A thunderstorm greeted him as he arrived there; and at the same time a search of his pockets disclosed a familiar problem: he was out of cigarettes. Glancing back at the library, he caught a glimpse of his children stepping out in the rain, but he continued around the corner, certain that he could find a parking space, rush in, buy the cigarettes and be back before the children got seriously wet. (Premack, 1970)

For the smoker, it was a shocking vision of himself "as a father who would actually leave the kids in the rain while he ran after cigarettes." The man quit smoking on the spot.

FIGURE 10.14 Social Influence and Smoking As this 1950s advertisement illustrates, cigarette companies have employed "authorities" and other role models to encourage smoking, even touting the fact that doctors use particular brands.

Exercise Has Physical, Emotional, and Cognitive Benefits

Forget the dumb-jock jokes. Research clearly shows the benefits of physical exercise on almost every aspect of our lives, including reduced depression, enhanced memory, and enhanced cognition (Harburger, Nzerem, & Frick, 2007). Exercise has been described as "Miracle-Gro for our brains" because we now know that aerobic exercise (the kind that temporarily increases breathing and heart rates) promotes neurogenesis, the growth of new neurons and neural connections (Carmichael, 2007; "Miracle-Gro" is the brand name for a line of plant food products). The additional neurons created through exercise result in a larger brain—affecting especially the hippocampus, an area of the brain important in memory and cognition (see Chapter 3, "Biological Foundations").

Unlike societies throughout most of human history, modern society allows people to exert little physical energy. People drive to work, take elevators, spend hours watching remote-controlled television, use various labor-saving devices, and complain about not having time to exercise. Once people are out of shape, it is difficult for them to start exercising regularly.

Fortunately, it is never too late to start exercising and getting its positive benefits. In one study, sedentary adults between the ages of 60 and 79 were randomly assigned to either six months of aerobic training (such as running or fast dancing) or a nonaerobic control group. Participants in aerobic training significantly increased their brain volume, including both white (myelinated) and gray matter. The nonaerobic control group experienced no comparable changes. In another study, older adults were assigned randomly to either three months of aerobic exercise or a nonaerobic control group. All the participants agreed to have small cuts made on their bodies so the researchers could study whether aerobic exercise hastened the time it took for the wounds to heal (Emery, Kiecolt-Glaser, Glaser, Malarkey, & Frid, 2005). The wounds of the aerobic group took an average of 29.2 days to heal, while those of the nonaerobic group took an average of 38.9 days to heal. Besides faster healing time, the aerobic group had better cardiorespiratory (heart and lung) fitness. Another recent study randomly assigned older adults with memory problems to an exercise group (three hours a week for two weeks) or to a control group (Lautenschlager et al., 2008). The participants in the exercise group improved in their overall cognition, including memory; the control group showed no changes. The researchers concluded that exercise reduces cognitive decline in older adults with moderate memory problems. The data are abundantly clear: Exercise is as close to a fountain of youth and fitness as we will get.

In general, the more people exercise, the better their physical and mental health. Aerobic exercise is especially good for cardiovascular health; it lowers blood pressure and strengthens the heart and lungs (Lesniak & Dubbert, 2001). Other recent evidence indicates that exercise might help prevent certain cancers and improve the immune system. Because exercise helps control appetite and metabolism, in addition to burning calories, it is an essential element of any weight control program.

Exercise is also good for mental health because it can reduce stress and improve mood. Indeed, as little as 10 minutes of exercise can improve feelings of vigor and enhance mood, although at least 30 minutes of daily exercise is associated with the most positive mental state (Hansen, Stevens, & Coast, 2001). The evidence is compelling that exercise can contribute to positive outcomes for the clinical treatment of depression (Craft & Perna, 2004) as well as addiction and alcoholism (Read & Brown, 2003). How exercise exerts these positive effects is not known. It may simply make people feel good because they know the exercise is good for them, or it may build self-confidence and help people cope with stress. It may affect neurotransmitter systems involved in reward, motivation, and emotion. It may also enhance neurogenesis, the production of neurons, and synaptogenesis, the production of synaptic connections in the brain.

There Are Ethnic Differences in Health Behaviors

Worldwide, racial and ethnic groups exhibit large disparities in health. For example, in the United States, the life expectancy for children born in 2005 varies as follows: 77.5 years for white males, 82.8 years for white females, 71.5 years for African American males, and 78.5 years for African American females (Centers for Disease Control and Prevention, 2007, Table 27). The reasons that racial and ethnic groups experience differences in their health include genetics, access to affordable health care, and cultural factors. For example, compared with European Americans, Hispanic Americans and African Americans have twice the obesity rate and higher rates of sedentary behavior (Center for Disease Control and Prevention, 2002). *Acculturation*— the extent to which individuals assimilate the customs, values, beliefs, and behaviors of the mainstream culture—is an important variable in understanding why different groups have disparate health behaviors and health outcomes.

In a study of health behaviors and ethnicity, a sample of college students who were similar in their educational backgrounds but came from a range of ethnic backgrounds filled out both a survey of their health behaviors (for example, how often they got medical checkups, went to the dentist, exercised, and ate fruits) and an acculturation scale that assessed the extent to which they listened to mainstream music, watched mainstream television shows, followed mainstream fashion, and so on (Despues & Friedman, 2007). African Americans and Hispanic Americans were less likely to smoke or drink alcohol than European Americans and Asian Americans. However, African Americans, Hispanic Americans, and Asian Americans were all less likely to exercise, eat fruit, or go to a dentist than were members of the mainstream culture—European Americans. Additionally, in each group, those who were more acculturated tended to be more like the European Americans in their health behaviors.

Such important differences in health behaviors among ethnic groups will have long-term consequences for people's health and expected life spans (**FIGURE 10.15**). Thus, by assuming a biopsychosocial perspective, researchers can see how cultural-level variables influence behaviors and how behaviors alter underlying biology. Each level of analysis provides a piece of the intricate puzzle that determines health and well-being. Not all healthy behaviors are associated with acculturation to the mainstream society, however, so people might want to keep the healthy behaviors associated with their own ethnic groups while adopting the healthy behaviors of other groups.

FIGURE 10.15 The Longest-Living People The Japanese tend to live very long lives. Pictured here are 99-year-old Matsu and 91-year-old Taido, both of Ogimi Village.

 SUMMING UP

What Behaviors Affect Mental and Physical Health?

How people behave in their daily lives profoundly affects their physical and mental health. People engage in many unhealthy behaviors when they are stressed, such as eating fatty foods and smoking. Other behaviors that directly affect health include suicides, homicides, and accidents. People who eat too much may become obese, especially if they have a genetic predisposition to put on weight, and obesity poses some serious health risks. Smoking is especially bad for health and is a leading cause of death. Unfortunately, smoking typically starts in adolescence, when people give little thought to long-term consequences. Exercise is one of the best things people can do for their health. Regular physical activity enhances emotional experiences, improves memory and cognition, and builds a strong, healthy body. Racial and ethnic groups exhibit health disparities, some of which can be attributed to differences in their health behaviors. Interventions may work best if they are grounded in an understanding of the health behaviors of different races and different ethnicities.

▶ MEASURING UP

1. How does exercise affect the brain?
   a. Exercise improves muscles and lungs, but does not affect the brain.
   b. As revealed in MRI brain scans, excessive exercise can cause an aversion to physical activity.
   c. People already in good physical shape show no brain effects, and those in poor physical shape show an enlargement in the areas corresponding to motor control.
   d. Exercise causes the growth of new neurons and new neural connections, especially in brain areas associated with memory and cognition.

2. Why do restrictive diets rarely work in reducing obesity?
   a. Obese people usually cheat when they are on restrictive diets.
   b. The body learns to conserve calories, so restrictive dieting may lead ultimately to greater weight gain.
   c. We do not know enough about foods' caloric contents to determine good diets.
   d. The obese tend to lose less weight with restrictive diets than other people do.

Can a Positive Attitude Keep Us Healthy?

LEARNING OBJECTIVE
Discuss research showing that optimism, social support, trust, and spirituality are good for our health.

It seems more like a trite remark than objective science to say that people feel better when they "put on a happy face," but there just might be something to the advice to "Keep your sunny side up." Did the lyricists of old musicals know more about human nature and health than have most psychologists and physicians in the last 50 years? Regardless of the inspiration for these happy songs, the message is a good one—you can collect handsome health dividends if you "Smile, smile, smile" (**FIGURE 10.16**).

Being Positive Has Health Benefits

Psychologists from the humanist school of thought focused on what is positive in the human experience. Abraham Maslow, Carl Rogers, and Erik Erikson were among the early pioneers in the field of positive psychology, although it was not known by that title then. These early humanist psychologists enjoyed the greatest success in the decades from 1950 to 1970. Other schools of thought, especially cognitive perspectives, then took the leading roles in psychology. Since the 1990s, positive psychology has enjoyed a tremendous comeback. The new *positive psychology* emphasizes the strengths and virtues that help people thrive. Its primary aim is an understanding of what makes people happy. If you have read Chapter 2, then you might be wondering how the term *happy* is operationalized, or identified and measured. According to positive psychologists, it has three components: (1) positive emotion and pleasure, (2) engagement in life, and (3) a meaningful life (Seligman, Steen,

FIGURE 10.16 Positivity Laughing clubs, such as this one in India, believe in laughter as therapy and a way to keep in shape.

Park, & Peterson, 2005). For example, a happy college professor might experience pleasure when interacting with students and colleagues (component 1), might be actively engaged in teaching and research (component 2), and might find meaning in contributing to the success of students and of colleagues (component 3). Such variables affect each other: When any one increases, the others increase as well; although, as with most of the data on health variables, we can conclude that they are correlated and can only speculate about causal linkages.

ARE HAPPIER PEOPLE HEALTHIER? Earlier in this chapter, you read about the negative health consequences of negative emotions, especially hostility and stress. You may have wondered about the flip side of this relationship: Are positive emotions associated with health and well-being (**FIGURE 10.17**)? This question was addressed in a study in which more than 1,000 patients in a large medical practice returned questionnaires about their emotional traits (Richman et al., 2005). The questionnaires included scales measuring the positive emotions hope and curiosity and the negative emotions anxiety and anger. Two years after receiving the questionnaires, the patients' medical files were used to determine if relationships existed among these emotions and three broad types of diseases: hypertension, diabetes mellitus, and respiratory tract infections. Higher levels of hope were associated with reduced risk of these medical diseases, and higher levels of curiosity were associated with reduced risk of hypertension and diabetes. Therefore, the answer is, in general, yes: Positive emotions can predict better health.

A great deal of research literature focuses on the health effects of positive emotions. Having a positive affect, or being generally positive, has been shown to have multiple beneficial effects on the immune system (Marsland, Pressman, & Cohen, 2007). People with a positive affect show enhanced immune system functioning and greater longevity than their less positive peers. They have fewer illnesses after exposure to cold germs and flu viruses (Cohen, Alper, Doyle, Treanor, & Turner, 2006). Thus, across multiple studies and types of measures, optimistic people are found to be healthier.

FIGURE 10.17 Try for Yourself: How to Be Happier

Research shows that with relatively short interventions, people can become happier, at least in the short run; the long-term effects are unknown.

Here are some suggestions based on research findings about happiness. You can try these activities for yourself to test their effects.

1. In the next week, write a letter of gratitude and deliver it in person to someone who has been kind to you but whom you have never thanked.

2. Every night, write down three things that went well that day and explain why they went well.

3. Write about a time when you did your very best, and then think about the strengths you displayed. Review this story every night for the next week.

4. Imagine yourself 10 years in the future as your best possible self, as having achieved all your most important goals. Describe in writing what your life is like and how you got there.

5. Keep a journal in which you write about the positive aspects of your life. Reflect on your health, freedom, friends, and so on.

6. Act like a happy person. Sometimes just going through the motions of being happy will create happiness.

Result: Data suggest that each of these activities can enhance a person's happiness (Lyubomirsky, King, & Diener, 2005). Activities such as these are called "shotgun interventions" because they are fast acting, cover a broad range of behaviors, have relatively large effects for such a small investment, and pose little risk.

Social Support and Social Integration Are Associated with Good Health

There is a Broadway song about people who need people being the luckiest people in the world. Perhaps the songwriters again got it right. Happy people tend to have strong social networks and are more socially integrated than are less happy people (Smith, Langa, Kabeto, & Ubel, 2005).

Social interaction is beneficial for physical and mental health. People with larger social networks (more people they interact with regularly) will less likely get colds (Cohen, Doyle, Skoner, Rabin, & Gwaltney, 1997). Apparently, people who have more friends also live longer than those who have fewer friends. A study that used a random sample of almost 7,000 adults found that people with smaller social networks were more likely to die during the 9-year period between assessments than were those with more friends. Men with fewer friends were 2.3 times more likely to die than comparable men with more friends; women with fewer friends were 2.8 times more likely to die than comparable women with more friends (Berkman & Syme, 1979). These risk factors for social support were independent of other common risks such as stated health at the time of the first contact, obesity, smoking, socioeconomic status, and physical activity. In addition, ill people who are socially isolated will likely die sooner than those who are well connected to others (House, Landis, & Umberson, 1988), in part because isolation is associated with many health problems.

social integration The quality of a person's social relationships.

The positive benefits of social interaction depend on more than just the size of a person's social network, however. **Social integration** refers to the quality of the social relationships a person has. Having social support is an essential component of positive mental and physical health. A review of more than 80 studies found strong evidence linking social support to fewer health problems (Uchino, Cacioppo, & Kiecolt-Glaser, 1996).

Social support helps people cope and maintain good health in two basic ways. First, people with social support experience less stress overall. Consider single parents who have to juggle job and family demands. The lack of a partner places more demands on them, thus increasing their likelihood of feeling stressed. Therefore, social support can take tangible forms, such as providing material help or assisting with daily chores. To be most effective, however, social support needs to imply that people care about the recipient of the support. Knowing that other people care can lessen the negative effects of stress. The **buffering hypothesis** (Cohen & Wills, 1985) proposes that when others provide emotional support, such as expressions of caring and willingness to listen to another person's problems, the recipient is better able to cope with stressful events.

buffering hypothesis The idea that other people can provide direct support in helping individuals cope with stressful events.

EMOTIONAL DISCLOSURE HAS POSITIVE HEALTH EFFECTS Can expressing your emotions improve your health? A large body of evidence supports the conclusion that writing about or talking about emotional events can yield substantial health benefits. James Pennebaker and his colleagues conducted a series of studies in which the emotional events disclosed ranged from childhood incest and the horrors of the Holocaust to less traumatic events, such as not being included in a social event. Repeatedly, they found positive health effects for people who wrote about or talked about these emotional events (Pennebaker, Mayne, & Francis, 1997; Pennebaker, Barger, & Tiebout, 1989; **FIGURE 10.18**). The linkage between writing about the emotional events in one's life and health was seen in several measures. In one study, college students randomly assigned to write about an emotional event visited the university health center fewer times than students assigned to write about other topics, even though there were no group differences in how often the students visited the health center before participating in the writing study (Pennebaker & Beall, 1986).

In their review of the literature, Anderson and Anderson (2003) show multiple benefits of disclosure and explain how it works best. Writing about emotional events can help the writers understand the causes of those events. As people write in this way, they construct meaningful stories out of experiences so they can better understand the experiences and can move on from them. (Talking into a recording device may work similarly for people who have difficulty writing.) Anderson and Anderson suggest that when trying this technique people should anticipate some negative feelings, at least in the short run, but that over time these feelings will dissipate. They suggest starting with something that needs a resolution—a topic that might be difficult to disclose to other people. Write about it or talk about it for at least 15 minutes without stopping, they advise, both describing the troubling situation and expressing feelings about it. (If you are suffering from a traumatic event that needs resolution, consider seeing a professionally trained psychotherapist—a topic discussed in Chapter 15, "Treating Disorders of the Mind and Body.")

MARRIAGE CAN BE GOOD FOR YOUR HEALTH The research on social support shows clearly that positive relationships are good for health. Marriage is generally people's most intimate and long-lasting supportive relationship, but being married has health benefits only if the marriage is a good one, and the positive effects of marriage are stronger for husbands than for wives (Kiecolt-Glaser & Newton, 2001). Single women have 50 percent greater mortality than married women; single men have 250 percent greater mortality than married men. (Recent data on the relationship between marital status and health are shown in **FIGURE 10.19**.) Comparable data are not available for homosexuals who are married or in long-term, marriagelike relationships, but it is reasonable to expect that they would receive the same beneficial effects as heterosexuals. A recent study compared heterosexual and gay and lesbian couples, all of whom were in long-term, committed relationships, and found them indistinguishable on measures including self and partner reports of the quality of the relationship as well as a variety of physiological measures that are indicators of health. The one exception was that the lesbian couples worked more cooperatively on laboratory tasks than did the heterosexual or gay couples (Roisman, Clausell, Holland, Fortuna, & Elieff, 2008).

Marriage is not a panacea for ill health, however. Troubled marriages are associated with increased stress, and unmarried people are happier than those in bad marriages. In a study categorizing newlyweds based on observed interactions,

FIGURE 10.18 Emotional Disclosure Holocaust survivors may find comfort in talking with others about their experiences. The survivors above, siblings Hilda Shlick and Simon Glasberg, are holding a picture of their parents.

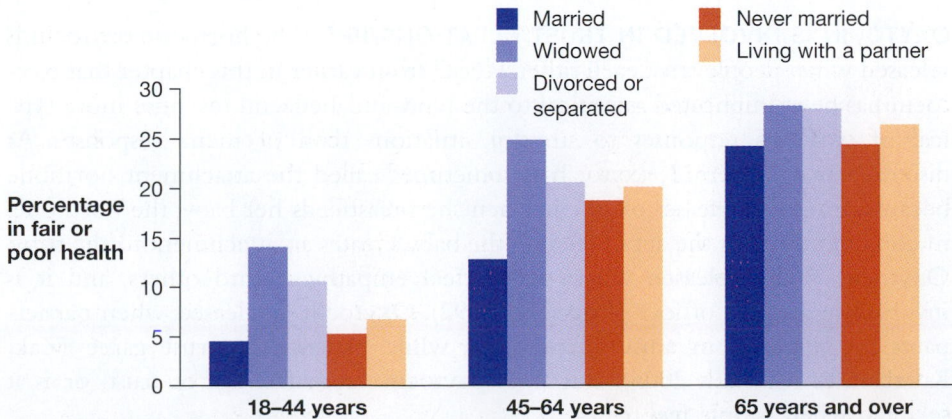

FIGURE 10.19 Relationship between Marriage and Health These data come from the National Health Interview Surveys in the United States from 1999 to 2002. The greatest benefit from marriage can be seen in the age range 45–64 years.

couples who fought more and showed more hostility toward each other exhibited decreased immune system activity in the 24 hours after conflict (Kiecolt-Glaser, Malarkey, Chee, & Newton, 1993). Janice Kiecolt-Glaser and Ronald Glaser (1988) found that people with troubled marriages and people going through a divorce or bereavement all had compromised immune systems.

Marital conflict has more negative health outcomes for wives than for husbands. In a review of 64 studies of the relationship between marriage and health, Kiecolt-Glaser and Newton (2001) drew linkages among marital discord, sex-related differences in response to stress, and effects on health. They found that women, who generally are more attuned to the emotional quality of their marriages than men are, are also more responsive physiologically. Given that women initiate fully two-thirds to three-quarters of divorces in the United States, Kiecolt-Glaser and Newton (2001) argue that women's greater responsiveness to conflict and the higher premium they place on emotional closeness makes them more likely than men to seek divorce when there is high conflict.

Trust and Health Are Related across Cultures

How would you respond in the following research situation? Suppose you are in a laboratory to play a "trust game" over the computer network with another participant whom you do not know and will never meet in person. At the start of the game, each of you receives $10 with which to play. At random, one of you is selected to go first. The first player transfers some amount of his or her $10 to the other player; the player who receives the money gets four times the amount sent and then transfers some amount of money back to the first player. The game proceeds for several rounds, after which each player takes home the money he or she has. If you go first, you have to decide how much to transfer to the other player. If you transfer all $10, you will have $0 left and the other person will have $50 (original $10 plus four times the amount you transferred). The best strategy is to cooperate and transfer the maximum amount of money at each round. But what if you send the other player $10 and you get back $1 or even $0, so you end up with little or nothing and the other player has a much bigger win than you do? How would you behave in this situation?

As you might expect, when people receive a generous proportion of the money available from the other player, they send more money to that player on the next round, and the reverse is true when little money is received. Can you see why this game is based on "trust"? How you behave and how much money you end up with depends on whether you and the other player trust each other. Earlier in this chapter, we talked about hostility as a personality trait bad for your health. Although trust is not exactly the opposite of hostility, it is at least close. Is trust good for your health?

OXYTOCIN IS INVOLVED IN TRUST RELATIONSHIPS The hormone oxytocin is released when people trust each other. Recall from earlier in this chapter that oxytocin has been implicated as critical to the tend-and-befriend response more typical of women's responses to stressful situations than of men's responses. As discussed in Chapter 11, oxytocin is sometimes called the attachment hormone because a mother releases oxytocin when she breastfeeds her baby; the hormone, in conjunction with the act of feeding the baby, creates an attachment to the baby. Oxytocin is also released when people feel empathy toward others, and it is involved in feelings of love (Panksepp, 1992). Oxytocin is released when participants are engaged in trust relationships while playing the trust game (Zak, Kurzban, & Matzner, 2005). But does oxytocin cause feelings of trust, or is it secreted when people feel trust?

In an experimental study, oxytocin was sprayed into the players' noses while they were playing the trust game. (Receptors for oxytocin exist throughout the brain but especially along the olfactory passages.) Players who had oxytocin sprayed in their noses gave the other players more money—in other words, they behaved as though they trusted the other players more than did players who had placebos sprayed in their noses. These results suggest that having more oxytocin caused people to be more trusting. Kerstin Uvnas-Moberg (1998, p. 155) commented that "a causal relationship may exist between oxytocin and personality." According to this theory, people who secrete more oxytocin have more trusting personalities and form attachments more readily than do those who secrete less oxytocin.

Now, consider how people respond when they distrust someone. Suppose that while playing the trust game you send $9 to the other player, who responds by sending you $1. You are unlikely to send a large amount of money on the next trial, because you probably will not trust the other player to reciprocate. Paul Zak and his colleagues have conducted a series of studies on the connection between distrust and the secretion of testosterone, the male hormone implicated in physically aggressive behaviors such as fighting predators or rivals. Males secrete testosterone in response to environmental events, whereas females generally have low levels of testosterone. The researchers therefore hypothesized that men would secrete more testosterone when they distrusted someone, but that women would not show changes in their levels of testosterone or any of the sex hormones. As predicted, men showed large increases in testosterone levels within a few minutes after responding to a player they did not trust, but women showed no change in their testosterone levels. Other hormones, monitored as controls, showed no response to levels of trust (Zak, Kurzban, & Matzner, 2005). Thus women and men respond differently when they distrust someone, although there seems to be more similarity between the sexes in other measures. For example, women and men secrete increased amounts of oxytocin when they are in trusting relationships.

Like hostility, trust is an important factor for health because it determines how many people we affiliate with and how closely attached we are to other people. Given that social relationships are critical for health, it should be clear that trust is essential for psychological and physical health. In fact, various sources of data suggest that trust is associated with better health and a longer life. This relationship was supported in a study of more than 160,000 people from every state in the United States, who responded to the question *Most people can't be trusted. Do you agree or disagree with this statement?* In each state, as the percentage of respondents who believed most people cannot be trusted increased, so did the percentage who reported that their health was fair to poor (Kawachi, Kennedy, & Glass, 1999; **FIGURE 10.20**).

Taken alone, this correlational study can only support hypotheses that have been tested with more rigorous research designs (see Chapter 2, "Research Methodology"). The study cannot prove that being distrustful causes poorer health, because a third factor could be causing an association

FIGURE 10.20 **Relationship between Trust and Health**

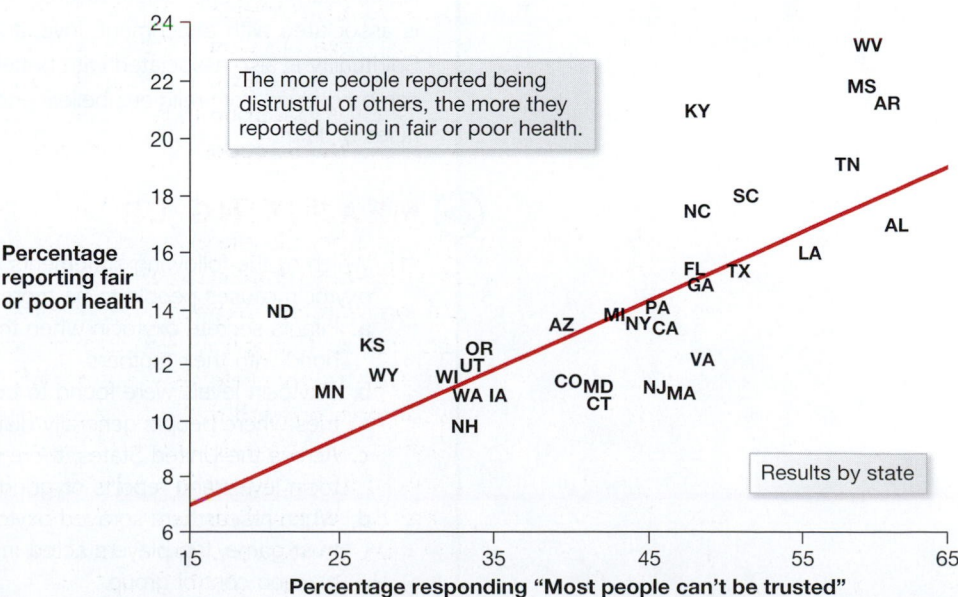

FIGURE 10.21 Spirituality and Well-Being A sense of spirituality can have positive effects on health and on well-being, but that sense does not have to be connected with a particular religion.

between distrust and poorer health. But when we consider this study in conjunction with strong experiments such as the one in which oxytocin or a placebo was sprayed into participants' noses, we can be more confident that the relationship is causal.

Spirituality Contributes to Well-Being

In many studies, people who are religious report greater feelings of well-being than do those who are not religious. The positive effects are associated not with any single religion but with a sense of spirituality that occurs across religions (Myers, 2000; **FIGURE 10.21**). David Myers and his colleagues found that religious people are better at coping with crises in their lives. Their religious beliefs serve as a buffer against hard knocks, such as having a child with a serious disability, getting divorced, experiencing the death of a loved one, and having a serious illness. From their faith, people also derive meaning and purpose in their lives. The theme of needing to find meaning in life appears repeatedly in the writing and reflections of Holocaust survivors (Frankel, 1959). Myers (2000) describes the effect of spirituality by quoting Rabbi Harold Kushner, who writes that people need to feel they are "something more than just a momentary blip in the universe" (p. 64). On a daily basis, religious beliefs can help people achieve and maintain well-being through the social and physical support provided by faith communities. Religions support healthy behaviors, such as avoiding alcohol and tobacco; and some religions place eating restrictions on less healthful foods such as pork, fatty meats, or caffeine.

 SUMMING UP

Can a Positive Attitude Keep Us Healthy?

A variety of evidence shows that optimistic people are healthier and live longer than their more negative counterparts. These findings show the flip side of the negative health consequences associated with hostile personalities. Social support and being socially integrated in a group are also protective health factors, because concerned others provide material and psychological support. Marriages low in conflict have a positive association with health, though these effects are greater for men than for women. Women are more likely than men to feel the stress of conflictual marriages and initiate divorce when marriages are troubled. Similarly, trust is associated with attachment, love, and better health across the United States. Spirituality is also associated with better health due to the sense of meaning that can be derived from religious beliefs and the support people receive from communities of faith.

 MEASURING UP

1. Which of the following statements explains how researchers concluded that oxytocin causes people to be more trusting?
   a. Infants secrete oxytocin when they are being nursed, causing them to bond with their mothers.
   b. Oxytocin levels were found to be highest among people living in countries where people generally distrust each other.
   c. Across the United States, there was a linear relationship between oxytocin levels and reports of good health.
   d. When researchers sprayed oxytocin in the noses of people playing the trust game, the players acted in a more trusting way than did the placebo control group.

2. What aspects of social support are most important in creating a positive effect on health?
   a. The support needs to come from family members because of the genetic basis of this effect.
   b. It is more important to know many people than it is to interact with them regularly.
   c. It is most important that people around you genuinely care about your well-being.
   d. It is most important that the people providing social support be religious because they can share in your spirituality.

Action Plan for Health and Well-Being

Taking Care of Mind and Body

Over the last 25 years, psychological science has learned much about the complex relations among stress, behavior, and health. Fifty years ago, people did not know that smoking is so unhealthy, that saturated fats and other dietary factors contribute to cardiovascular disease, or that being under prolonged stress can damage the body. We now know that to live healthy lives people need to cope with stress, regulate their emotions, and control their daily habits. The following strategies will enhance your health and well-being. Are you willing to adopt them and take control of your life?

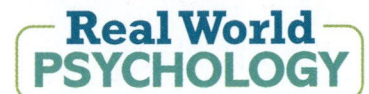

- **Eat natural foods** Food fads come and go, but the basic rules never change: Eat a varied diet that emphasizes natural foods (e.g., whole grains, fruits, and vegetables) and avoid processed and fast foods. Various animal products can also be part of a natural, healthy diet. Avoid foods containing trans-fatty acids and other artificial types of fat that prolong store shelf life. Some studies have found that natural oils, such as olive oil, can benefit the heart.

- **Watch portion size** Eat a varied diet in moderation—and eat only when you are hungry. Many prepared foods are sold in large portions, which encourage overeating. Over time, the extra calories from large portions contribute to obesity. Eating small snacks between meals can prevent people from becoming too hungry and overeating at their next meal.

- **Drink alcohol in moderation, if at all** Some research indicates that one glass of wine per day, or similar quantities of other alcohol-containing drinks, may have cardiovascular benefits. But excessive alcohol consumption can cause serious health problems, including alcoholism, liver problems, some cancers, heart disease, immune system deficiencies, and so on.

- **Keep active** Engage in moderate physical activity at least four times a week for at least 30 minutes. Ignore the saying *no pain, no gain*— research shows it is inaccurate, because pain deters people from exercising over the long run. Start with moderate exercise that will not leave you breathless, and gradually increase your exercise intensity. Look for other ways to be active, such as taking the stairs or walking to work or school.

- **Do not smoke** This recommendation may seem obvious, yet many college students and other adults begin smoking each year. Smoking eventually produces undesirable physical effects for all smokers, such as a hacking cough, unpleasant odor, bad breath, some cancers, and death at a younger age.

- **Practice safe sex** Sexually transmitted diseases (STDs) affect millions of people worldwide—including college students. Many new HIV cases are occurring among those under age 25, who are infected through heterosexual or homosexual activity. Despite the devastating consequences of some STDs, many young adults engage in risky sexual practices, such as not using condoms, and they are especially likely to do so when using alcohol or other drugs. Ways to avoid STDs include condom use or abstinence.

- **Learn to relax** Daily hassles and stress can cause many health problems, including conditions, such as insomnia, that can interfere with your ability to function. Relaxation exercises can help soothe the body and mind. Seek help from trained counselors who can teach you these methods, such as using biofeedback to measure your physiological activity so you can learn to control it. You might also try a relaxing activity, such as yoga.

- **Learn to cope** Negative events are a part of life. Learn strategies for assessing them realistically and seeing what might be positive about them as well as accepting the difficulties they pose. You can learn strategies for dealing with stressors—seeking advice or assistance, attempting new solutions, distracting yourself with more pleasant thoughts or activities, reinterpreting situations humorously, and so on. Find out which strategies work best for you. The important thing is not to allow stress to consume your life. Exercise helps reduce stress and is an excellent daily strategy for keeping it in check.

- **Build a strong support network** Friends and family can help you deal with much of life's stress, from daily frustrations to serious catastrophes. Avoid people who encourage you to act in unhealthy ways or are threatened by your efforts to be healthy. Instead, find people who share your values, who understand what you want from life, who can listen and provide advice, assistance, or simply encouragement. Trusting others is a necessary part of social support, and it is associated with positive health outcomes.

- **Write about troubling events in your life** Write about difficult memories or challenges, or talk about them into a recorder if you prefer. There is good evidence that writing about difficult events can reduce depression and improve overall health.

- **Consider your spiritual life** If you have spiritual beliefs, try incorporating them into your daily living. Benefits can accrue from living a meaningful life and from experiencing the support provided by faith communities.

- **Try some of the happiness exercises** The exercises suggested in Figure 10.17 to enhance happiness include low-risk activities such as expressing gratitude and imagining your "best possible self." By focusing on positive events—and more positive explanations of troubling ones—you may become a happier person.

CONCLUSION

What country in the world has the longest life expectancy? The answer may surprise you. The tiny country of Andorra, in the Pyrenees Mountains between France and Spain, has an average life expectancy of 83.5 years, followed by Japan (80.7 years), San Marino (81.1 years), and Singapore (80.1 years; Associated Press, 2007). A baby born in the United States will live an average of 77.9 years. The shortest life expectancies are in African countries ravished by AIDS, famine, and civil strife: Swaziland has the shortest life expectancy at 34.1 years, followed by Zambia (37.2 years), Zimbabwe (37.8 years), and Angola (38.3 years). The reasons for variations in life expectancy are seemingly simple, but making changes so that everyone can live a long and healthy life has proved to be immensely difficult.

A major reason for some of the disparity among countries with more resources is different health care systems and varying access to high-quality, preventive health care. In addition, increasing numbers of people in the United States and other industrialized countries are obese and fail to get enough exercise—both factors that reduce life expectancies. Americans now work more hours every year than people in any other country of the world, having surpassed the Japanese almost a decade ago in the hours worked. Work hours are increasing in many other industrialized countries as well, so people have more stress and less time for exercise and interpersonal relationships—all of which will take a toll on their health. We know how to live healthier lives, yet too many of us eat foods high in fats, fail to exercise, smoke cigarettes, engage in risky behaviors, and so on. How can people be motivated to change their habits?

Convincing people to live healthier lives will require a large-scale effort on multiple levels. Families need to make a commitment to eating well and engaging in physical activities at all age levels. Schools need to provide better health education and healthy school lunches. Neighborhoods should be safe so people can walk around and play in parks and playgrounds. We need to promote families and other social relationships and provide communities that care. We need to create a caring society committed to tackling problems such as loneliness and social isolation. Everyone needs access to high-quality health care. With a system-wide response, we can all live healthier lives.

Health psychologists apply the research methods and theories of psychology to health, with the goal of enhancing well-being. Researchers in this field recognize that our behaviors contribute to the leading causes of death, an understanding that means we can be active participants in creating and maintaining better health. The biopsychosocial model integrates findings from the biological sciences, psychology, and sociology to explain the simultaneous influences from these three perspectives on health. In thinking about ways to promote health and well-being, we need to adopt a multidisciplinary perspective and attack the problems of ill health at the individual, societal, and biological levels.

■ CHAPTER SUMMARY

Can Psychosocial Factors Affect Health?

- **The Biopsychosocial Model of Health Incorporates Multiple Perspectives for Understanding and Improving Health:** The biopsychosocial model describes the reciprocal and multiple influences of biological predispositions, individual thoughts and actions, and societal variables on health. According to this model, people are active participants in shaping health outcomes.

- **Behavior Contributes to the Leading Causes of Death:** The leading causes of death are all behavioral, especially among teenagers and young adults, who are most likely to die from accidents, homicide, and suicide. Many lifestyle variables, such as eating unhealthy foods, being obese, and leading a sedentary life, contribute to heart disease, cancer, respiratory disease, and other disease states that reduce the quality and length of life. People with certain personality types, such as those with hostile personalities, are at an increased risk for heart disease and earlier death.

- **Placebos Can Be Powerful Medicine:** Placebos can have powerful effects on health and well-being, but a placebo works only if the person taking it believes in its ability to reduce pain or disease. The same brain processes involved in responses to chemically active (nonplacebo) drugs are involved when patients respond to placebos.

How Do People Cope with Stress?

- **Stress Has Physiological Components:** Stressful events cause a cascade of physiological events, most importantly the release of hormones from the hypothalamus, the pituitary gland, and the adrenal glands. Stress-related hormones circulate through the blood stream, affecting organs throughout the body.

- **There Are Sex Differences in Responses to Stressors:** Women and men respond somewhat differently to stress. Women will more likely tend and befriend, whereas men will more likely have a fight-or-flight response. Consistent with an evolutionary perspective on psychology, these different styles may be related to sex-differentiated roles in hunter-gatherer societies and to higher estrogen concentrations in women during childbearing years.

- **The General Adaptation Syndrome Is a Bodily Response to Stress:** Selye outlined the general adaptation syndrome, the steps by which the body responds to stress. The initial response, alarm, is followed by resistance; if the stressor continues, the final response is exhaustion.

- **Stress Affects Health:** A small amount of stress may be healthy, but excessive stress negatively affects health by placing a heavy allostatic load on the physical system, impairing memory and cognition. When we are constantly stressed, our bodies do not have enough time to return to homeostasis, the resting state, to recover from stress reactions.

- **Coping Is a Process:** Coping means adjusting to stress. We have emotion-focused and problem-focused coping strategies. The latter are usually more constructive in the long run because they allow us to find ways to change a stressful situation.

What Behaviors Affect Mental and Physical Health?

- **Obesity Results from a Genetic Predisposition and Overeating:** In industrialized countries around the world, an increasing number of people are obese. Obesity results from a combination of a genetic predisposition and overeating. Restrictive diets rarely help obese people lose weight.

- **Smoking Is a Leading Cause of Death:** Smoking contributes to all the major diseases that kill people, including heart disease and many cancers. People usually start smoking as children or adolescents and continue because of the attractive traits sometimes associated with people who smoke, such as defying authority.

- **Exercise Has Physical, Emotional, and Cognitive Benefits:** Exercise has been shown to reduce depression, improve memory, and speed healing, in addition to its positive effects on muscles and the respiratory system. Exercise can reduce cognitive decline in older adults. Despite these positive effects, too many people fail to exercise.

- **There Are Ethnic Differences in Health Behaviors:** Ethnic and racial differences in health behaviors can explain some of the disparities in health outcomes. As groups become more acculturated to the mainstream culture, they tend to adopt the health behaviors of that culture, positive and negative. Health interventions intended to bring about changes need to consider the behaviors of different groups.

Can a Positive Attitude Keep Us Healthy?

- **Being Positive Has Health Benefits:** A range of evidence shows that there are health benefits to having a positive, optimistic outlook.

- **Social Support and Social Integration Are Associated with Good Health:** Social support is critical to good health because when others care about us, they provide material and psychological support. They can help us reinterpret events more positively. Socially integrated individuals have meaningful relations with others.

- **Trust and Health Are Related across Cultures:** Oxytocin, sometimes called the trust hormone, is secreted during trusting encounters; it is involved in infant/parent attachment and love relationships.

- **Spirituality Contributes to Well-Being:** Being spiritual can give meaning to people's lives; members of religious communities also provide physical assistance to one another and support healthy behaviors.

■ KEY TERMS

allostatic load theory of illness, p. 441
anorexia nervosa, p. 449
biopsychosocial model, p. 429
body mass index (BMI), p. 445
buffering hypothesis, p. 458

bulimia nervosa, p. 450
coping response, p. 434
emotion-focused coping, p. 442
fight-or-flight response, p. 436
general adaptation syndrome, p. 438
health psychology, p. 428

hypothalamic-pituitary-adrenal (HPA) axis, p. 435
immune system, p. 437
lymphocytes, p. 437
oxytocin, p. 437
placebo effect, p. 431
primary appraisal, p. 442

problem-focused coping, p. 442
secondary appraisal, p. 442
social integration, p. 458
stress, p. 434
stressor, p. 434
tend-and-befriend response, p. 436

Type A behavior pattern, p. 440
Type B behavior pattern, p. 440
well-being, p. 428

1. Which of the following comments most accurately represents health psychologists' current understanding of illness?
   a. "Illness is totally under our own control. We can stay healthy simply by making healthy decisions."
   b. "Illness is a matter of luck. If our bodies are destined to become ill, we're out of luck."
   c. "I feel sorry for people with family histories of illnesses such as heart disease, breast cancer, and diabetes. Their genetic predispositions guarantee they'll develop these same illnesses."
   d. "Genetic predispositions to some illnesses exist. But living healthily can help reduce the chances we'll develop an illness."

2. The correct answer to the previous question is consistent with the _____ of health and illness.
   a. biomedical model
   b. biopsychosocial model
   c. moral model
   d. self-efficacy model

3. Latasha is normally an engaged and satisfied employee. For a few months, she becomes very dissatisfied, grumpy, and uninterested in her job. Shortly after participating in a weekend-long seminar about the secrets of success, Latasha begins enjoying her work again. Which of the following attributions for her improved satisfaction at work best reflects the concept of regression to the mean?
   a. "Well, I figured I couldn't stay in that funk forever. Things eventually had to start looking up again."
   b. "That seminar was amazing! Things are really starting to go my way now that I know the secret to success."
   c. "I'm so glad my boss moved to another department. Now that she's gone, things are looking up."
   d. "Everything started going better once I changed my negative attitude."

4. Which of the following individuals is most at risk for developing heart disease, assuming equal levels of physiological risk factors such as blood pressure and cholesterol level?
   a. People describe Sonja as driven. She desires to be the top in her field and packs her calendar with important meetings and educational opportunities to help her meet this goal.
   b. People describe Patti as a complainer. She always finds something to gripe about, whether it is poor service at a restaurant, a driver's failure to use turn signals, or a loud talker on a cell phone.
   c. People describe Kenji as laid back. He always has time for a cup of coffee with friends or to surf the Web.
   d. People describe Oksana as scattered. She is regularly late for class and forgets to turn in assignments. Although apologetic for her tardiness, she does not seem distressed by her behavior.

5. Individuals who are hardy _____. Choose all that apply.

   a. are committed to daily activities
   b. are optimistic
   c. have access to financial resources
   d. have many close friends
   e. see challenges as opportunities for growth
   f. see themselves as able to control their own lives

6. Which of the following statements are true?
   a. Our bodies have natural defenses against weight loss that limit dieting's effectiveness.
   b. Body weight seems to be determined largely by a set-point.
   c. Dieters who lose and regain weight repeatedly tend to become heavier over time.
   d. Exercise is an essential element of any weight control program.

7. Label each of the following statements as applying to anorexia nervosa (AN) and/or bulimia nervosa (BN).
   a. This disorder can result in death if not treated.
   b. A person with this disorder exhibits eating that is out of control and excessive.
   c. The person will be at least 15 percent to 25 percent underweight.
   d. The person refuses to eat.
   e. The person will tend to be average weight or slightly overweight.
   f. This disorder results in a loss of bone density.
   g. This disorder typically develops in early adolescence.
   h. This disorder typically develops in late adolescence.
   i. Typically other people do not realize the person is suffering from this disorder.
   j. The person worries excessively about body weight issues.

8. Imagine your grandparent is preparing to move to a retirement community. Which of the following might you say if you wanted to help her or him promote physical and mental health? Choose all that apply.
   a. "Keep in mind there are a lot of shady characters out there looking to take advantage of people. Be suspicious of new people until you have a reason to trust them."
   b. "Know that I care about you and am here for you if there's anything I can do to help with the transition to your new home."
   c. "Make a point of meeting a lot of other residents."
   d. "Make sure to stay in touch with your close friends."
   e. "Your cable service offers over 100 channels; you won't run out of interesting programs to watch!"

9. Which of the following statements are true regarding oxytocin?
   a. Oxytocin is critical in the fight-or-flight response to stress.
   b. Oxytocin is released when people feel empathy.
   c. Oxytocin is secreted when males engage in aggressive behaviors.
   d. Participants dosed with oxytocin behave more trustingly than control participants do.
   e. Women release oxytocin when they breast-feed infants.

■ PSYCHOLOGY AND SOCIETY

1. Think about a stressor you likely will face in the near future (e.g., starting a new job, moving to a new city, becoming geographically separated from friends or family). Write a journal entry describing concrete strategies you can engage in to cope with the stressor. Be specific, and discuss the extent to which each coping strategy is considered adaptive or maladaptive. If you have a tendency to engage in maladaptive coping strategies (e.g., overeating, procrastination), remind yourself to be careful about these behaviors.

2. You notice a troubling trend in a magazine to which you subscribe: Each month, the magazine touts a new diet "guaranteed" to help people lose weight. Compose a letter to the magazine's editor expressing concern about the editorial team's decision to promote these diets. Use scientific evidence to back up any claims you make about the likely effectiveness of these diets and the physical and psychological effects people attempting to follow these diets might experience.

The answer key for all the Measuring Up exercises and the Practice Tests can be found at the back of the book.

Find more review materials online at www.wwnorton.com/psychologicalscience.

Test Preparation ■ **467**

Human Development

IN 1970, A MOTHER AND HER YOUNG DAUGHTER walked into a welfare office in Los Angeles. The mother was seeking help after escaping an abusive and mentally ill husband, and the girl, later known as "Genie," appeared to be suffering from autism (FIGURE 11.1). When a social worker saw Genie, who was 4 feet 6 inches and 59 pounds, she alerted her supervisor. Although Genie looked much younger, she turned out to be 13 years old. Having suffered severe neglect and abuse, she could not hop, skip, climb, or do anything requiring the full extension of her limbs (Curtiss, 1977; Rymer, 1993). After being admitted to a hospital, she was taken from her parents and placed in foster care.

Genie's early life had been a nightmare. For more than 10 years, her father had locked her in a tiny, dark bedroom. Tied to a chair during the day and caged in a crib at night, she had been poorly fed and beaten for making any noise. She had no one to talk to and nothing to listen to or even look at in her barren room. She was raised with essentially no

---

What Shapes a Child?
- Development Starts in the Womb
- Brain Development Promotes Learning
- Attachment Promotes Survival
- Critical Thinking Skill: Understanding That "Some" Does Not Mean "All"

How Do Children Learn about Their Worlds?
- Perception Introduces the World
- Memory Improves over Childhood
- Piaget Emphasized Stages of Development

- Infants Have Early Knowledge about the World
- Humans Learn from Interacting with Others
- Language Develops in an Orderly Fashion

How Do Children and Adolescents Develop Their Identities?
- Social Systems Influence Development
- Friends Influence Identity and Behavior
- Parental Style Can Affect Children's Well-Being
- Divorce Is Difficult for Children

- Critical Thinking Skill: Recognizing and Avoiding Either/Or Thinking
- Gender Identity Is Determined by Biology and Cultural Norms
- People Define Themselves in Terms of Race and Ethnicity

What Brings Meaning to Adulthood?
- Adults Are Affected by Life Transitions
- Aging Can Be Successful
- Cognition Changes during Aging

FIGURE 11.1 Genie This photo shows Genie in 1971.

developmental psychology The study of changes in physiology, cognition, and social behavior over the life span.

normal human contact and no stimulation from the external world. When she was rescued, Genie had a strange gait, almost like a rabbit's, and held her hands out in front of her like a dog sitting up and begging. She understood just a few words and could form only brief phrases, such as *Stop it* and *No more*. Genie also showed few signs of emotion or interest in connecting with those around her.

For the next four years, scientists from Children's Hospital in Los Angeles cared for Genie as they studied the consequences of her social isolation. For decades, psychological scientists had struggled to understand the extent to which development was affected by nature and by nurture. How much of who we are as humans is hardwired in our genes, and how much is the result of early experience? What is human nature when it is stripped of society and culture? No experiment could be conducted ethically to answer these questions, but would Genie provide insight into what makes us human? Would she be able to learn? Would she develop normal social skills that could allow her to become a full member of society? Would a warm, nurturing environment help her recover from her tragic past? If the ability to acquire language is inborn, would she quickly learn to speak and be able to describe what had happened to her?

In the first few years that Genie was cared for by the scientists, she made some progress in forming social relationships and acquiring minimal language. But she was able to develop only the most rudimentary language skills. She learned many words, but she could not put them together properly in sentences. Sadly, when Genie turned 18, her mother regained custody of her and immediately cut off all contact with the scientific community. Genie lived with her mother for only a short time before she was removed and sent to various foster homes. In at least one home, she was again abused. She now lives in a small group home for adults who cannot look after themselves. The role her social and physical abuse played in her enduring difficulties in interacting with others and acquiring language will never be known. Yet her case provides some tantalizing demonstrations of experience's role in shaping both brain development and psychological capacities.

This chapter examines the ways biological and social forces combine to shape the path of human development. **Developmental psychology** is concerned with changes, over the life span, in physiology, in cognition, and in social behavior. For instance, to study how humans develop cognitive skills, scientists have focused on age-related changes in psychological capacities such as perception, language, and thinking. The mind develops adaptively, as new, useful skills appear at appropriate times, even in the absence of specific training. Infants also develop socially—innately forming bonds with others—an adaptive trait that provides protection and facilitates survival. As children grow, they learn how to communicate with others, how to behave appropriately in various situations, and how to establish and maintain relationships. Socialization also affects human characteristics such as morality, gender, and identity. In exploring these aspects of development, the chapter also examines some of the most fundamental questions about humanity: How do we become members of society? How do we develop into who we are and come to value what we value? How do genes interact with early experiences to produce unique individuals? How do we grow and adapt within our own cultures? How do we change across the life span? These processes shape us into who we become.

LEARNING OBJECTIVES

Describe how the prenatal environment can affect development.

List and describe the types of attachment infants have to their caregivers.

What Shapes a Child?

For the most part, human development follows a predictable progression. Physically, at about the same periods in the life span, each human grows and matures. During the prenatal period, the body develops in a fixed sequence. Depending on its genetic instructions, the developing body turns into a male or female infant. No newborn talks immediately, nor does any baby walk before it can sit up. Virtually all humans make eye contact quickly after they are born; display a first social smile at around six weeks; and learn to roll over, to sit up, to crawl, to stand, to walk, and to talk, in that order (occasionally a step may be skipped or reversed), within a predictable range of ages (**FIGURE 11.2**). This pattern's consistency suggests that our genes set the pace and order of development.

Environment also influences what happens throughout development. For example, children often achieve developmental milestones at different paces, depending on the cultures in which they are raised. For instance, healthy children in Uganda tend to walk by 10 months, whereas children in France often do not walk before 15 months (Berger, 2004). These differences are due in part to different patterns of infant care across cultures, such as whether infants are carried around during the day, whether infants sleep with their parents, or even whether infants sleep on their backs or their stomachs. In recent years, parents in North America have been advised that placing their infants on their backs to sleep minimizes the risk of suffocation. Because it is relatively difficult for infants to turn over, those who sleep on their backs crawl much later than those who sleep on their stomachs. In some other countries, infants are seldom left on the floor to crawl because of hygiene issues. These infants learn to crawl at later ages than infants who are regularly placed on the floor. Parental practices such as these influence how motor skills develop. As discussed in Chapter 3, environment determines which of a person's genes are expressed and how they are expressed: We are the products of both nature and nurture, because genes and experience work together to make us who we are.

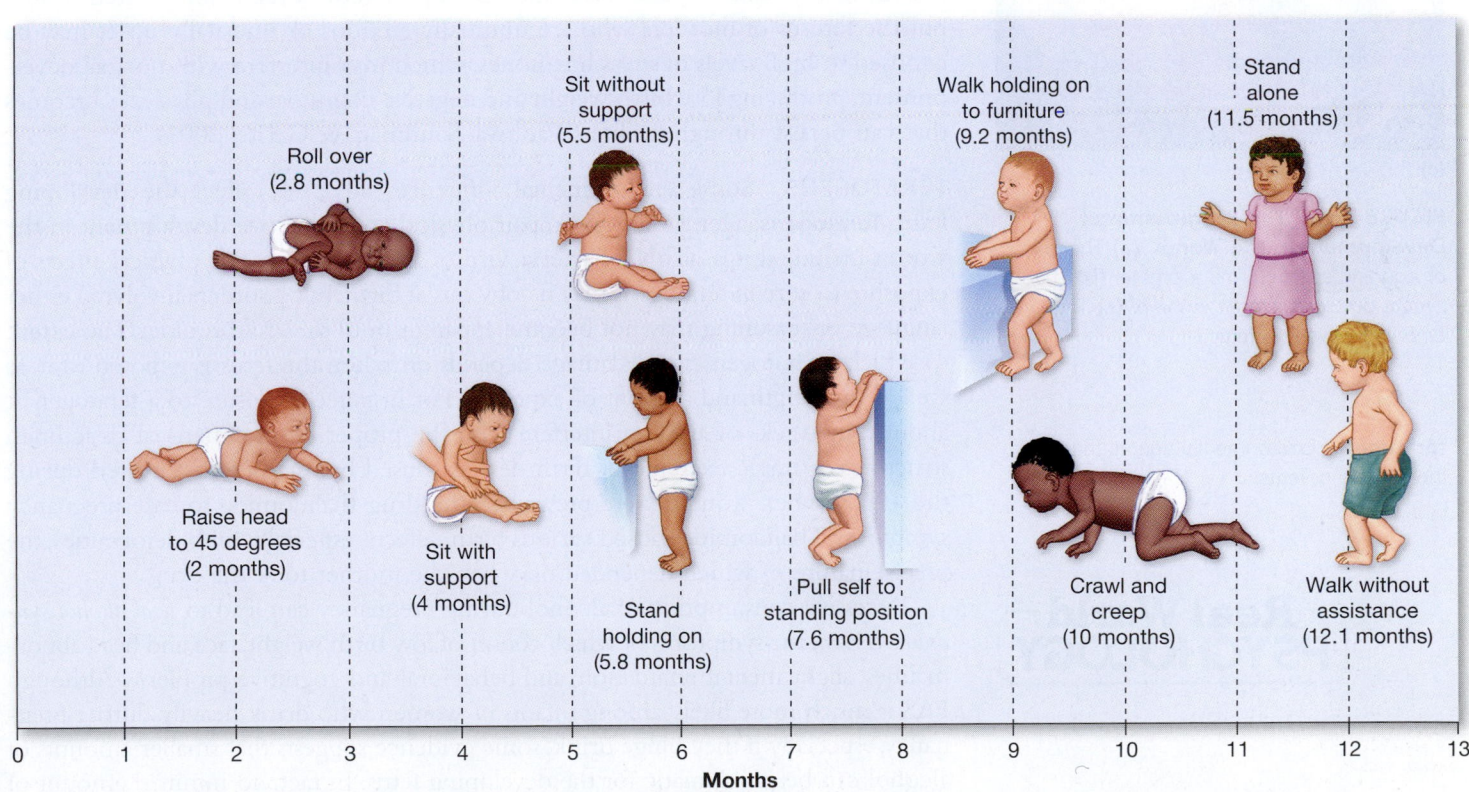

FIGURE 11.2 The Progression of Human Physical Development A baby learns to walk without formal teaching. Learning to walk progresses along a fixed, time-ordered sequence characteristic of all humans.

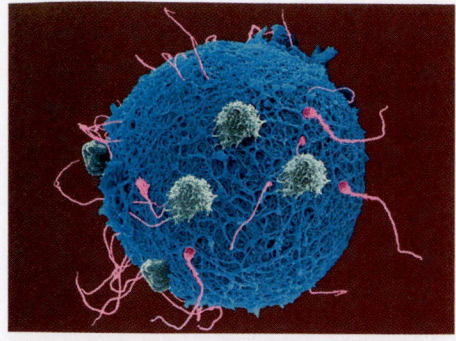
(a)

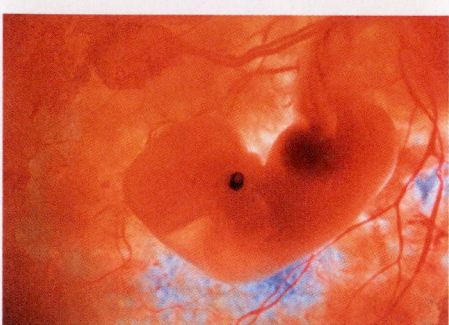
(b)

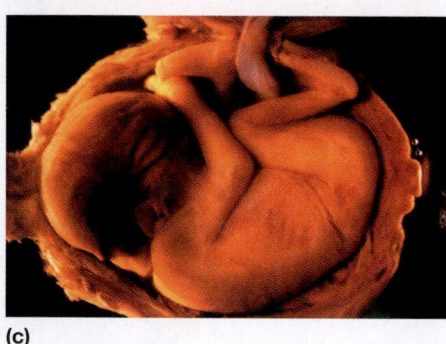
(c)

FIGURE 11.3 The Progression of Development in the Womb **(a)** The union of egg and sperm forms a zygote. **(b)** The zygote develops into an embryo. **(c)** The embryo becomes a fetus.

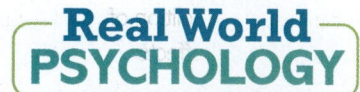

teratogens Environmental agents that harm the embryo or fetus.

Development Starts in the Womb

From conception through birth approximately nine months later, remarkable developments occur (**FIGURE 11.3**). The process begins at the moment of conception, when the sperm from the male unites with the egg from the female to create the *zygote*, the first cell of a new life. From about two weeks to two months, the developing human is known as an *embryo*. During this stage, the internal organs, such as the heart, lungs, liver, kidneys, sex organs, and nervous system, begin to form. After two months, the growing human is called a *fetus* and at this time undergoes a great deal of physical growth as the whole body takes its infant form. The final trimester, or three-month period, puts the finishing touches on the fetus; at this point, a healthy fetus is capable of surviving outside the womb.

PHYSICAL DEVELOPMENT   Genes in combination with the environment in the womb govern much of the human nervous system's prenatal development. Most of the brain's nerve cells develop in a specific sequence in the first seven months of gestation (Rakic, 2000). The basic brain areas begin to form by week 4. The cells that will form the cortex are visible by week 7; those of the thalamus and hypothalamus, by week 10; and those of the left and right hemispheres, by week 12. By the seventh month, the fetus has a working nervous system. By birth, the brain is complex: It has cortical layers, connections among its neurons, and myelination. Yet brain development does not stop at birth—the brain continues to develop throughout childhood and adulthood and into old age.

Hormones that circulate in the womb influence the developing fetus. For instance, if the mother's thyroid does not produce sufficient amounts of hormones, the fetus is at risk for lower IQ and diminished intellectual development. The mother's emotional state can also affect the developing fetus. Pregnancy is often trying, but the fetuses of mothers who are unusually anxious or unusually upset may be exposed to high levels of stress hormones, which may interfere with normal development, producing low birth weight and negative cognitive and physical outcomes that can persist throughout life (Wadhwa, Sandman, & Garite, 2001).

TERATOGENS   Some environmental influences adversely affect the developing fetus. **Teratogens,** agents that can impair physical and cognitive development in the womb, include drugs, alcohol, bacteria, viruses, and chemicals. The physical effects of exposure to certain teratogens may be obvious at birth, but disorders involving either language or reasoning may not become apparent until the child is older. The extent to which a teratogen causes damage depends on when the fetus is exposed to it, as well as the length and amount of exposure. For instance, exposure to a teratogen at about four weeks of age can interfere with the proper development of basic brain structures. A tragic example of birth defects caused by teratogens occurred during the 1950s, when women were prescribed the drug thalidomide to ease pregnancy symptoms. Thalidomide caused various birth defects, especially limb deformities, the precise nature of which depended on when the mother took the drug.

Excessive consumption of alcohol during pregnancy can lead to *fetal alcohol syndrome (FAS),* the symptoms of which consist of low birth weight, face and head abnormalities, slight mental retardation, and behavioral and cognitive problems. Although FAS is much more likely among infants of women who drink heavily during pregnancy, especially if they binge drink, some evidence suggests that smaller amounts of alcohol can be problematic for the developing fetus. In fact, no minimal amount of alcohol has been determined to be safe for pregnant women and their developing babies. For this reason, many health workers recommend that women abstain from drinking alcohol when they are pregnant or trying to become pregnant.

ONEthics Alcohol and Drug Use during Pregnancy

One cause of mental retardation in the Western world is prenatal alcohol exposure, which can result in FAS (Centers for Disease Control and Prevention, 2004). Alcohol interferes with normal brain development and can cause permanent brain damage, especially to the neocortex, hippocampus, and cerebellum (**FIGURE 11.4**). The resulting impairments can negatively affect learning, attention, the inhibition and regulation of behavior, memory, causal reasoning, and motor performance (Guerri, 2002). In the United States, the prevalence of FAS is estimated to be between 0.2 and 2.0 cases per 1,000 live births, though the actual numbers could be higher (Centers for Disease Control and Prevention, 2004).

The use of recreational drugs, such as opiates, cocaine, or cannabis, during pregnancy can also affect a child's development. Premature birth and other complications have been associated with the use of all these drugs during pregnancy (Gillogley et al., 1990; Sherwood et al., 1999). Infants of women taking opiates, particularly methadone, have two to three times greater risk for unexplained sudden death in infancy (Davidson Ward et al., 1990), and cocaine use has also been linked to sudden infant death (Kandall & Gaines, 1991; Hulse, Milne, English, & Holman, 1998). Among infants exposed to opiates in utero, 55 percent to 94 percent show symptoms of newborn withdrawal (American Academy of Pediatrics, 1998), including irritability, high-pitched crying, tremors, vomiting, diarrhea, and rapid breathing. However, some heavy drug users have normal infants, while some moderate users have infants with serious effects, so we cannot say that a baby born to a drug user will necessarily be impaired.

For any case in which prenatal drug or alcohol use puts an infant at high risk of injury, death, or lifelong disability, Norman Fost (1989), a medical ethics professor, poses three questions:

- Does a woman have a duty to abstain from using drugs that are likely to harm the fetus?
- Does the state have an obligation to protect the fetus/newborn from harm?
- Should there be legal measures to reduce the incidence of such harm or to prevent it from occurring?

The central conflict is between, on the one hand, the personal rights and autonomy of the woman and, on the other, the effects of her behavior on both the infant and society. According to the bioethics professor Ruth Macklin (1990), most people would agree that it is better for a baby to be healthy than not healthy and therefore pregnant women are morally obligated

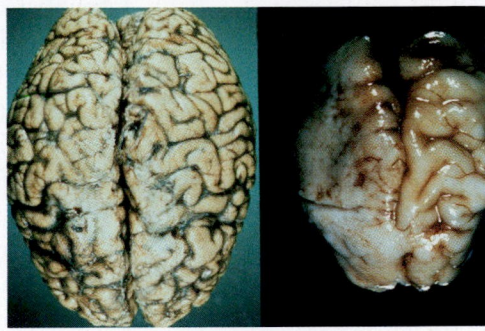

FIGURE 11.4 Fetal Alchohol Syndrome To see the effects of interrupted brain development, compare **(left)** the brain of a normal six-week-old baby with **(right)** the brain of a baby of the same age with FAS.

to do all they can to produce healthy infants. However, many pregnant women are not willing and able to comply.

The ethics committee of the American College of Obstetricians and Gynecologists (2004) has concluded, on the side of patient autonomy, that forcing therapy on pregnant women is almost never justified. For women who abuse drugs, the committee urges screening by physicians, counseling, and treatment. The American Academy of Pediatrics bioethics committee (1988) is more willing to challenge women's decisions and resort to the courts under certain circumstances: (1) The fetus will suffer irrevocable harm without the treatment, (2) the treatment is clearly indicated and likely to be effective, and (3) the risk to the woman is low.

Many psychologists, physicians, and ethicists worry that legally coercive measures will drive pregnant women away from the health care system when they need it most and will result in more harm to both the woman and the fetus. Fost (1989) argues that although this consideration is important, it is difficult to weigh the effects of women's not seeking prenatal health care against the known risks of drug and alcohol use during pregnancy. He makes an analogy to child abuse laws, which may similarly deter some parents from seeking medical care for their children; however, few people would advocate the abolition of child abuse laws because of these potentially harmful effects.

What do you think? Does an unborn infant's right to a healthy life outweigh a pregnant woman's right to personal autonomy? Should pregnant drug users be placed in facilities where they cannot take drugs until their babies are born, and if so, should taxpayers pay for these women's care? What might be some alternative options?

Brain Development Promotes Learning

Newborns normally come into the world able to see, smell, hear, taste, and respond to touch. Although these skills are not fully developed at birth, the newborn is able to process a considerable range of sensory stimuli. For instance, two-hour-old infants prefer sweet tastes to all other tastes (Rosenstein & Oster, 1988). Young infants also have a reasonably acute sense of smell, at least for smells associated with feeding. In a number of studies, infants turned their heads toward a pad containing their own mother's milk but not toward pads containing milk from other breast-feeding mothers (e.g., Winberg & Porter, 1998). The sense of hearing is also quite good at birth: Infants are startled by loud sounds and often will turn their bodies toward the source of the sounds. Newborns' sense of hearing is much better than their sense of vision, however; their range of visual acuity is 8–12 inches, about the distance, during breastfeeding, between an infant's face and its mother's face. This limited visual range may be adaptive, since it encourages the infant to focus on what is most important, the mother's breast and face, and promotes the beginnings of the child's social interaction. As discussed further in the next section, newborns' perceptual skills increase tremendously over the first few months of life.

Although newborn infants cannot survive on their own, they are not completely helpless. Newborns have various basic reflexes that aid survival. Perhaps you have observed the *grasping reflex* when a baby held your finger. Some believe this reflex is a survival mechanism that has persisted from our primate ancestors; after all, young apes grasp their mothers, an adaptive reflex because the offspring need to be carried from place to place. Also innate is the *rooting reflex,* the turning and sucking that infants automatically engage in when a nipple or similar object touches an area near their mouths. These reflexes pave the way for learning more-complicated behavior patterns such as feeding oneself or walking. Thus at birth the brain is sufficiently developed to support basic reflexes, but further brain development appears necessary for cognitive development to occur.

MYELINATION AND NEURONAL CONNECTIONS   Early brain growth has two important aspects: Specific areas within the brain mature and become functional, and regions of the brain learn to communicate with one another through synaptic connections. One important way that brain circuits mature is through myelination, which begins on the spinal cord during the first trimester of pregnancy and on the brain's neurons during the second trimester. As discussed in Chapter 3, myelination is the brain's way of insulating its "wires": Nerve fibers are wrapped with a fatty sheath, much like the plastic coating around electrical wire, to increase the speed with which they are able to transmit signals. Myelination occurs in different brain regions at different stages of development (**FIGURE 11.5**).

The myelinated axons form synapses with other neurons. Far more of these connections develop than the infant brain will ever use. Then something remarkable happens: The brain adopts a very strict "use it or lose it" policy. The frequently used connections are preserved; the unused ones decay and disappear. This process, **synaptic pruning,** occurs in different areas of the brain at different times. As shown in **FIGURE 11.6**, synaptic density is highest in the auditory cortex around age three; in the visual cortex, around ages one and two; and in the prefrontal cortex, which is critical for reasoning, around age six. After adolescence, the density of synapses remains approximately constant in these three brain areas (Thomas & Johnson, 2008). Once connections are established, the brain sets about making them more permanent—for example, by increasing myelination. Some developmental psychologists believe infants do not develop specific cognitive skills until certain brain connections are made. This idea, that the progression of learning is tied closely to brain

synaptic pruning A process whereby the synaptic connections in the brain that are frequently used are preserved, and those that are not are lost.

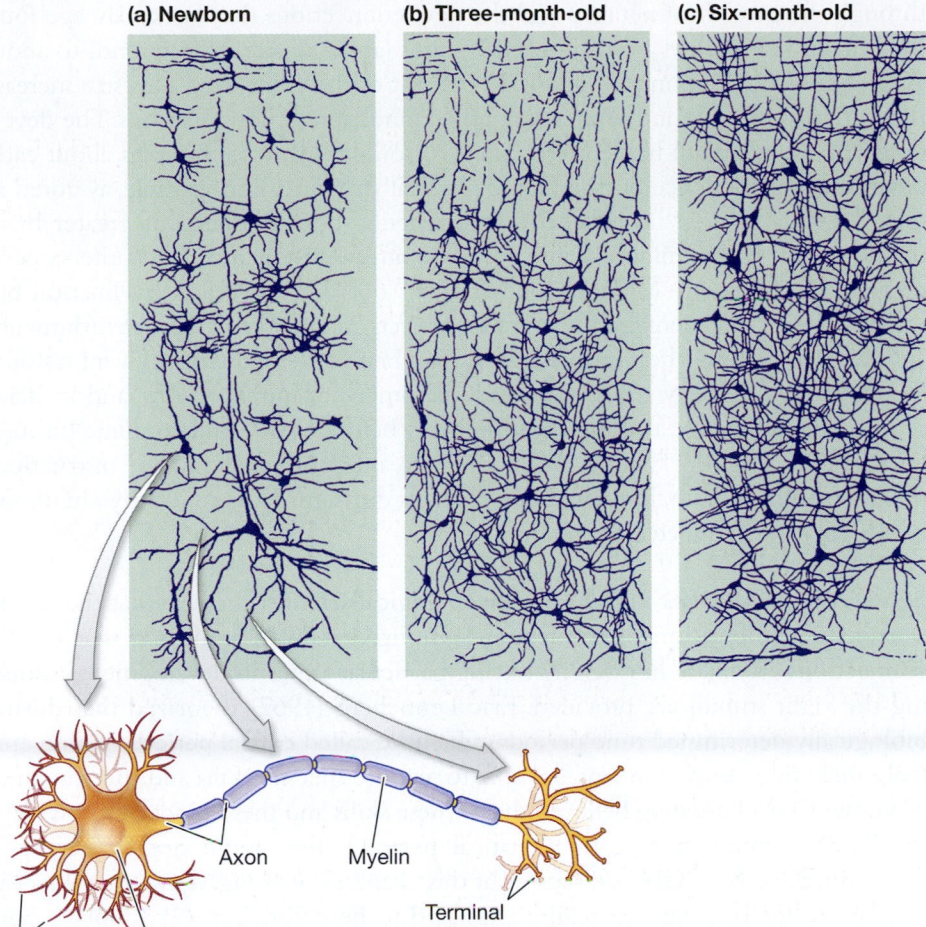

(a) Newborn   **(b) Three-month-old**   **(c) Six-month-old**

Dendrites   Cell body   Axon   Myelin   Terminal buttons

FIGURE 11.5 Myelination Neurons in the visual cortex develop more and more myelination as the infant's brain ages.

development, presents a new and exciting approach for research energized by the biological revolution in psychological science.

The brain grows as determined by genetic instruction, but the organ is also highly "plastic," meaning hardwired to adapt to different environments. Though most neurons are already formed at birth, the brain's physical development continues

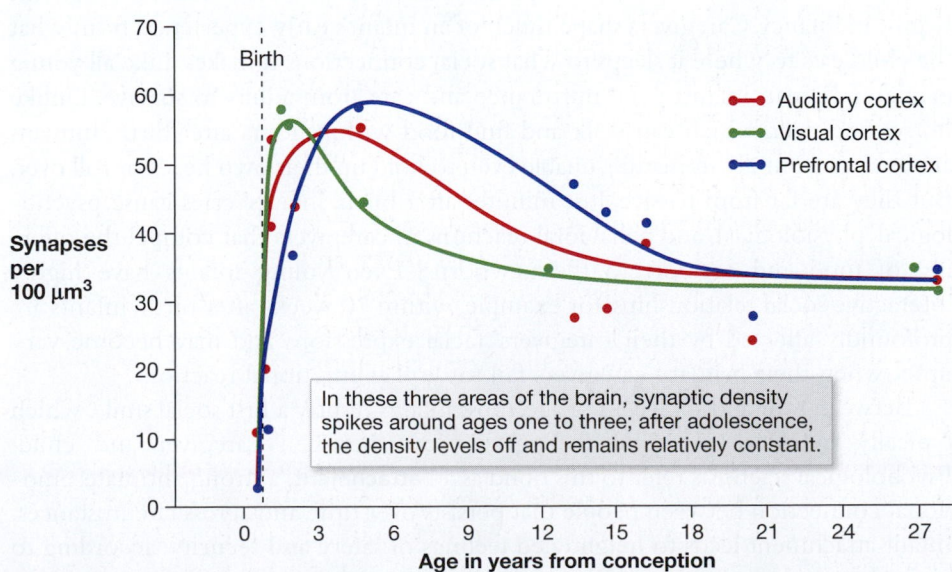

Birth

- ●— Auditory cortex
- ●— Visual cortex
- ●— Prefrontal cortex

Synapses per 100 μm³

In these three areas of the brain, synaptic density spikes around ages one to three; after adolescence, the density levels off and remains relatively constant.

Age in years from conception

FIGURE 11.6 Synaptic Density through Early Adulthood The highest levels of density can be thought of as the times when the brain is most plastic—most able to change.

through the growth of neurons and the new connections they make. By age four, the human brain grows from about 350 grams (approximately .75 pound) to about 1,250 grams (2.75 pounds or about 80 percent of the adult size). This size increase is due to myelination and to new synaptic connections among neurons. The developing brain's plasticity has led researchers to some remarkable findings about early environment's influence on the brain's physical structure. For example, as noted in Chapter 3, rats raised in enriched environments show evidence of greater brain development. Early childhood nutrition also affects myelination and other aspects of brain development. Malnourished children not only have less myelination but might also lack the energy to interact with objects and people in their environments, and this lack of stimulation further undermines brain development. As recent research has confirmed, poverty is bad for the development of human brains, and its deleterious effects begin at a young age—probably before birth—and continue through life (Farah et al., 2006; Farah et al., 2008). Thus, although genes provide instructions for the maturing brain, how the brain changes during infancy and early childhood is also very much affected by environment.

SENSITIVE LEARNING PERIODS Psychological scientists believe that the key to learning is the creation of connections among certain neurons and that certain connections are made most easily during particular times in development, assuming the right stimuli are provided. Eric Lenneberg (1967) theorized that during biologically determined time periods, which he called **critical periods,** young animals, including young humans, are able to acquire specific skills and specific kinds of knowledge. Lenneberg believed that if these skills and these kinds of knowledge were not acquired during their critical periods, they could not be acquired. However, the case of Genie, discussed at this chapter's opening, shows that the critical period for language (generally estimated to be before age 12) is not so rigid as Lenneberg thought. Genie was unable to acquire full language skills, perhaps because she was not exposed to language early in life, but she learned some aspects of language at a later age. The specific points in development at which some skills or kinds of knowledge are learned most easily are now called **sensitive periods.**

Attachment Promotes Survival

Children are shaped not only by biological development but also by their early interactions with other people—especially their caregivers. Social development begins in infancy. Caregivers shape much of an infant's early experience, from what the child eats to where it sleeps to what social connections it makes. Like all young primates, human infants need nurturance and care from adults to survive. Unlike horses and deer, which can walk and find food within hours after birth, humans are born profoundly immature, unable even to hold up their own heads or roll over. But they are far from passive. Just minutes after birth, infants' cries cause psychological, physiological, and behavioral reactions in caregivers that compel the offering of food and comfort to the newborns. Even young infants have highly interactive social relationships; for example, within 10 weeks after birth, infants are profoundly affected by their caregivers' facial expressions and may become very upset when their primary caregivers fail to display emotional reactions.

Between four and six weeks of age, most infants display a first social smile, which typically enhances powerful feelings of love between caregiver and child. Psychological scientists refer to this bond as an **attachment,** a strong, intimate, emotional connection between people that persists over time and across circumstances. Infant attachment leads to heightened feelings of safety and security; according to

critical periods Biologically determined time periods for the development of specific skills.

sensitive periods Biologically determined time periods when specific skills develop most easily.

attachment A strong emotional connection that persists over time and across circumstances.

the psychiatrist John Bowlby, who popularized its importance, it also motivates infants and caregivers to stay in close contact. Bowlby argued that infants have an innate repertoire of attachment behaviors that motivate adult attention. For instance, they prefer to remain close to caregivers, act distressed when caregivers leave and rejoice when they return, and put out their arms to be lifted. Thus attachment is adaptive. Infants who exhibit attachment behaviors have a higher chance of survival through adult protection and consequently are more likely to pass along their genes to future generations.

Adults generally seem predisposed to responding to infants, as in picking up and rocking a crying child. They also tend to respond to infants in ways that infants can understand, as in making exaggerated facial expressions and speaking in a higher-pitched voice than normal. The next time you observe an adult talking to a baby, notice how even the gruffest men with deep voices change their voices to a higher pitch. Babies attend to high-pitched voices; in virtually every culture studied, men, women, and even children intuitively raise their voices' pitch when talking to babies, and babies respond by maintaining eye contact with the adults (Fernald, 1989; Vallabha, McClelland, Pons, Werker, & Amano, 2007). Bowlby argues that these behaviors motivate infants and caregivers to stay in proximity.

ATTACHMENT IN OTHER SPECIES Attachment is important for survival not only in humans but also in many other species. For instance, infant birds communicate hunger through crying, thereby prompting caregivers to find food for them. Some bird species seem to have a critical period in which infants become strongly attached to a nearby adult, even one from another species. This pattern, first noticed in the nineteenth century, occurs for birds such as chickens, geese, and ducks. Because these birds can walk immediately after hatching, they are at risk of straying from their mothers. Therefore, within about 18 hours after hatching, these birds will attach themselves to an adult (usually to their mothers) and then follow the object of their attachment. The ethologist Konrad Lorenz called such behavior *imprinting* and noted that goslings that became imprinted on him did not go back to their biological mothers when later given access to them (**FIGURE 11.7**). However, such birds preferentially imprint on a female of their species if one is available.

During the late 1950s, the psychologist Harry Harlow described one of the most striking examples of nonhuman attachment. At that time, psychologists generally believed infants needed mothers primarily as food sources. For Freudians, the mother was the source of libidinal (life or emotional or sexual) pleasures (see Chapter 13, "Personality"). For behaviorists, the mother was valued as the result of secondary reinforcement, given her role as the provider of food (see Chapter 6, "Learning"). But explanations of attachment that were based on Freudian thinking or learning theory struck Harlow as unsatisfactory, because he recognized that infants needed comfort and security in addition to food.

In a now-famous series of experiments, Harlow placed infant rhesus monkeys in a cage with two different "mothers." One surrogate mother was made of bare wire and could give milk through an attached bottle. The second surrogate mother was made of soft terrycloth and had a monkeylike head (rudimentary features—eyes, nose, mouth, and ears—attached to a flat circle) but could not give milk. Which of these two substitute mothers do you think the infant monkeys preferred—the wire one that provided milk or the soft and cuddly one that looked more like a monkey?

The monkeys' responses were unmistakable: They clung to the cloth mother most of the day and went to it for comfort in times of threat. The monkeys approached the wire mother only when they were hungry. Harlow tested the monkeys' attachment to these mothers in various ways, such as introducing a strange

FIGURE 11.7 Attachment Here, Konrad Lorenz walks the goslings that had imprinted themselves on him. The little geese followed Lorenz as if he were their mother.

object into the cage. He repeatedly found that the infants were calmer, braver, and overall better adjusted when near the cloth mother. Hence, the mother-as-food theory of mother/child attachment was debunked. Harlow's findings established the importance of contact comfort—of allowing an infant to cling to and hold something soft—in social development (**FIGURE 11.8**).

ATTACHMENT STYLE   Attachment behaviors begin during the first months of life and have been observed in children around the world, although normal attachment may vary somewhat depending on cultural practices (Kappenberg & Halpern, 2006). If Bowlby was correct in hypothesizing that attachment encourages proximity between infant and caregiver, then we might expect attachment responses to increase when children naturally start moving away from caregivers. And indeed, just when infants start to crawl, at around 8 to 12 months, they typically display *separation anxiety,* in which they become very distressed when they cannot see or are separated from their attachment figures. This pattern occurs in all human cultures.

To study attachment, the developmental psychologist Mary Ainsworth created the *strange-situation test.* The test involves observing, through a one-way mirror, the child, the caregiver, and a friendly but unfamiliar adult in a series of eight semi-structured episodes in a laboratory playroom. The crux of the procedure is a standard sequence of separations and reunions between the child and each adult. Over the course of the eight episodes, the child experiences increasing distress and a

FIGURE 11.8 **Scientific Method: Harlow's Monkeys and Their "Mothers"**

Hypothesis: Infant monkeys will form an attachment to a surrogate mother that provides warmth and comfort.

Research Method: Infant rhesus monkeys were put in a cage with two different "mothers":

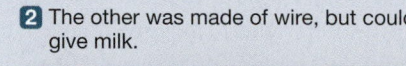

1 One mother was made of cloth and looked like a monkey, but could not give milk.

2 The other was made of wire, but could give milk.

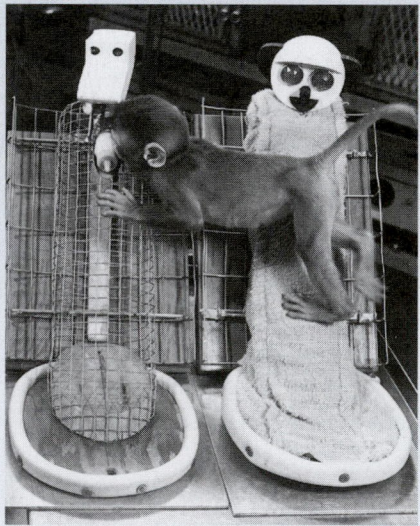

Results: The monkeys clung to the cloth mother and went to it for comfort in times of threat. The monkeys approached the wire mother only when they were hungry.

Conclusion: Infant monkeys will prefer and form an attachment to a surrogate mother that provides warmth and comfort over a wire surrogate mother that provides milk.

greater need for caregiver proximity. The extent to which the child copes with distress and the strategies he or she uses to do so indicate the quality of the child's attachment to the caregiver. Activity level and actions such as crying, playing, and paying attention to the mother and stranger are recorded. Using the strange-situation test, Ainsworth originally identified three types of child attachment: *secure, avoidant, and anxious/ambivalent*.

Secure attachment applies to the majority of children (approximately 65 percent). A secure child is happy to play alone and is friendly to the stranger while the attachment figure is present. When the attachment figure leaves, the child is distressed, whines or cries, and shows signs of looking for the attachment figure. When the attachment figure returns, the child is happy and quickly comforted, and often wants to be held or hugged. The child then returns to playing (**FIGURE 11.9**).

secure attachment Attachment style for a majority of infants, who are readily comforted when their caregiver returns after a brief separation.

FIGURE 11.9 The Strange Situation Test

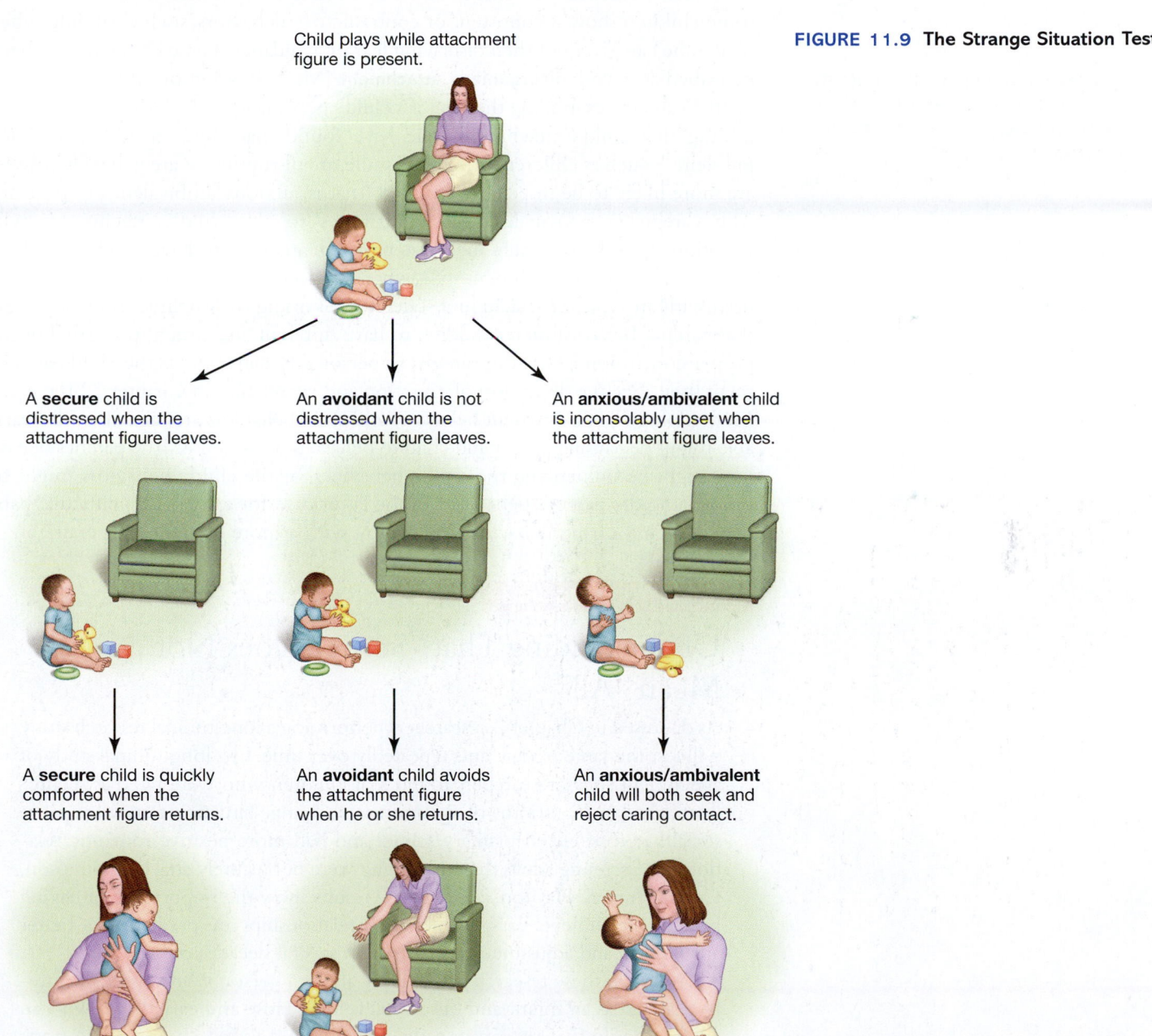

Child plays while attachment figure is present.

A **secure** child is distressed when the attachment figure leaves.

An **avoidant** child is not distressed when the attachment figure leaves.

An **anxious/ambivalent** child is inconsolably upset when the attachment figure leaves.

A **secure** child is quickly comforted when the attachment figure returns.

An **avoidant** child avoids the attachment figure when he or she returns.

An **anxious/ambivalent** child will both seek and reject caring contact.

avoidant attachment Attachment style in which infants ignore their caregiver when he or she returns after a brief separation.

anxious-ambivalent attachment Attachment style in which infants become extremely upset when their caregiver leaves but reject the caregiver when he or she returns.

disorganized attachment Attachment style in which infants give mixed responses when their caregiver leaves and then returns from a short absence.

Avoidant attachment applies to approximately 20 percent to 25 percent of children. The avoidant child does not appear distressed or upset by the attachment figure's departure. If upset, the children may be comforted by the stranger. When the attachment figure returns, the child does not want a reunion, but rather ignores or snubs the attachment figure. If the child approaches the attachment figure, he or she often does so tentatively.

Anxious/ambivalent attachment applies to approximately 10 percent to 15 percent of a given sample. A child with an anxious-ambivalent style is anxious throughout the test. The child clings to the attachment figure after they enter the room; when the attachment figure leaves, the child becomes inconsolably upset. When the attachment figure returns, the child will seek and reject caring contact; for instance, the child may want to be held but then fight to be released. The child may cling to the attachment figure even while trying to hit him or her.

Other researchers have identified variants of these attachment styles. For instance, some children show inconsistent or contradictory behaviors, such as smiling when seeing the caregiver but then displaying fear or avoidance. These children have been described as having **disorganized attachment** (Main & Solomon, 1986).

Researchers examining the role of a child's personality or temperament in determining that child's attachment style have found that children with behavioral problems—such as children who rarely smile, are disruptive, or are generally fussy—are more likely to be insecurely attached (that is, anxious/ambivalent or avoidant). The caregiver's personality also contributes to the child's attachment style. Emotionally or behaviorally inconsistent caregivers tend to have children with an anxious/ambivalent attachment style, whereas rejecting caregivers tend to have children with an avoidant attachment style. It is tempting to conclude from these data that parents' behavior *causes* children to have different attachment patterns, but the proper conclusion is that the caregiver's personality *contributes to* the child's attachment style. (See the discussion of causation and correlation in Chapter 2, "Research Methodology.") When parent behaviors and child behaviors are related, a third variable might be causing parent and child to behave in related ways, the parent's behaviors might be influencing the child's behaviors, or the child's behaviors might be influencing the parent's behaviors. In the latter case, for example, a "difficult" baby may elicit less caring behavior than a baby with a more content temperament.

CRITICAL THINKING SKILL

Understanding That "Some" Does Not Mean "All"

As discussed in Chapter 2, researchers performing a longitudinal research study will test the same participants repeatedly over time. In a longitudinal study of attachment styles, researchers found that children who were rated as securely attached at 12 months of age (using the strange-situation test) were more socially competent in primary school and had more positive romantic relationships as young adults than those who were not securely attached (Simpson, Collins, Tran, & Haydon, 2007). These results show the importance of having positive attachments early in life: Such relationships are predictive of better attachment and adjustment over the next several decades of life.

What do these research findings say about a person who was not securely attached as an infant and did not develop a close and early bond with an adult? Should that person just give up now and forget about having positive romantic relationships? Of course not. Having a secure attachment in infancy makes it *more likely* that an adult will have healthy romantic attachments. But that attachment does not guarantee the result, nor does the lack of attachment to a caregiver in infancy mean that a person will not have strong romantic relationships later in life.

In trying to apply these results to our own lives, however, we might misinterpret the take-home message as something like "If I was securely attached to my caregiver in infancy, I will have better romantic relationships as a young adult." That is, in thinking about such findings, we tend to change relative probabilities (e.g., "If securely attached as an infant, a person is *more likely* to have healthy romantic relationships later in life") to absolute statements (e.g., "If securely attached as an infant, a person *will* have healthy romantic relationships later in life" or the converse, "If *not* securely attached as an infant, a person *will not* have healthy romantic relationships later in life," which is equally wrong). The problem arises when we convert terms such as *some* and *more* into *all*. By focusing on the properly limited meanings of a study's terms, we can draw correct conclusions from that study's results.

"They got extinct because they didn't listen to their mommies."

CHEMISTRY OF ATTACHMENT   In many studies, scientists working at the biological level of analysis have discovered that the hormone oxytocin is related to social behaviors, including infant/caregiver attachment (Carter, 2003; Feldman, Weller, Zagoory-Sharon, & Levine, 2007). Oxytocin plays a role in maternal tendencies, feelings of social acceptance and bonding, and sexual gratification. In the mother and the infant, oxytocin promotes behaviors that ensure the survival of the young. For instance, infant sucking triggers the release of oxytocin in the mother, and this release stimulates biological processes in the mother that move milk into the milk ducts so the infant can nurse. In a study of mothers and their newborn infants, oxytocin was associated with several measures of attachment, such that higher levels of this hormone were predictive of better maternal attachment.

SUMMING UP

What Shapes a Child?

The human genome consists of instructions for building a functioning human being, but from the earliest moment of human development, environmental factors influence how each individual is formed. Throughout the prenatal period, various environmental agents, from the mother's hormones to substances she consumes, can alter the formation of the fetus and its cognitive capacities. Once the child is born, learning is constrained by the development of both brain and body. Except in cases of abuse or some serious illnesses, children crawl and walk when their bodies develop the appropriate musculature and when their brains mature sufficiently to coordinate motor actions. Almost from the moment of birth, humans are social creatures, forming bonds of attachment with caregivers. The quality of these attachments, as well as the children's attitudes, values, and beliefs, are shaped by interactions with their caregivers. Parents and other caregivers influence many aspects of children's lives.

How Do Children Learn about Their Worlds?

In the first few years of life, children normally acquire many skills and absorb many kinds of knowledge. However, they most likely retain very few memories of learning to walk, talk, read, reason, and do countless other things. In studying the early years of human development, psychological scientists seek to understand if children learn through their interactions with the environment, if they are born with innate cognitive abilities, or both. Throughout psychology's history, scientists have vigorously debated the contributions of nature and nurture to development. Nearly everyone now agrees that both are important, and current research focuses on how genes and experience interact to make us who we are.

Perception Introduces the World

To learn, children need to obtain information from the world. They do so principally through their senses. As noted above, newborns have all their senses at birth, although some of their senses are poorly developed. The development of their sensory capacities allows infants to observe and evaluate the objects and events around them. The infants then use the information gained from perception to try to make sense of how the world works.

INFANT-RESEARCH TECHNIQUES How can we tell what a baby knows about the world? Psychological scientists have devised clever experiments for gauging what infants perceive about the objects and events in the infants' environments. Based on the observation that infants tend to look longer at stimuli that interest them, one type of experiment uses the *preferential-looking technique:* Researchers show an infant two things. If the infant looks longer at one of the things, the researchers know the infant can distinguish between the two and finds one more interesting.

Other experiments are based on the *orienting reflex,* humans' tendency to pay more attention to new stimuli than to stimuli to which they have become habituated, or grown accustomed (Fantz, 1966). Even from birth, an infant will look away more quickly from something familiar than from something unfamiliar or puzzling. By using their knowledge of habituation, researchers can create a response preference in an infant for one stimulus over another. For example, they might show the infant a picture or an object until the infant is familiar enough with it that the infant adapts to the stimulus or becomes bored—the amount of time the infant looks at the stimulus declines. At that point, the researchers can measure whether the infant reacts to a change in the stimulus: If shown a new picture or new object, will the infant look longer at it? If so, the infant is noticing a difference between the old and new stimuli. If the infant looks at the new stimulus the same amount of time she looks at the old stimulus, the researchers assume the infant does not distinguish between the two. Such tests are used to gauge everything from infants' perceptual abilities—how and when they can perceive color, depth, and movement, for instance—to their understanding of words, faces, numbers, and laws of physics. So what do we know about infants' early perceptual abilities? What can they learn about their worlds?

VISION   The ability to distinguish differences among shapes, patterns, and colors develops early in infancy. Developmental psychologists use the preferential-looking technique to determine how well an infant can see—that is, the infant's *visual acuity.* Infants respond more to objects with high-contrast patterns, for example, than to other stimuli. In the early 1960s, Robert Fantz and other developmental psychologists showed infants patterns of black-and-white stripes as well as patches of gray and observed the infants' reactions (**FIGURE 11.10**). In these studies, the mother or another caregiver was asked to hold the infant in front of a display of the two images. The experimenter, not knowing which image was on which side, would observe through a peephole to see where the infant preferred to look (**FIGURE 11.11**). This research revealed that infants look at stripes with high contrast more readily than at gray images. The smaller the stripes get—that is, the less contrast between the images—the more difficult it becomes for infants to distinguish them from the gray patches. When infants look at both images equally, researchers assume the infants cannot tell the difference between the two.

Research has indicated that though infants' visual acuity for distant objects is poor when they are first born, it increases rapidly over the first six months (Teller, Morse, Borton, & Regal, 1974). Adult levels of acuity are not reached until about one year. The increase in visual acuity is probably due to the development of the infant's visual cortex as well as the development of cones in the retina (as noted in Chapter 5, the cones are important for perceiving detail).

To assess when depth perception emerges in infancy, the perceptual psychologist Robert Fox and his colleagues (1980) showed infants *stereograms,* in which one view of an image is shown to one eye and another view to the other; this information is then converted into depth perception. If infants cannot use this *disparity information* to perceive depth, they will see only a random collection of dots. To determine whether infants can see stereograms, Fox devised an experiment in which a baby wearing special viewing glasses looks at a screen while

FIGURE 11.10 Vision in Infancy Robert Fantz was the first to determine that infants prefer patterns with high contrast. A more thorough understanding of infants' visual abilities has led parents to buy mobiles and toys that use some of Fantz's testing patterns.

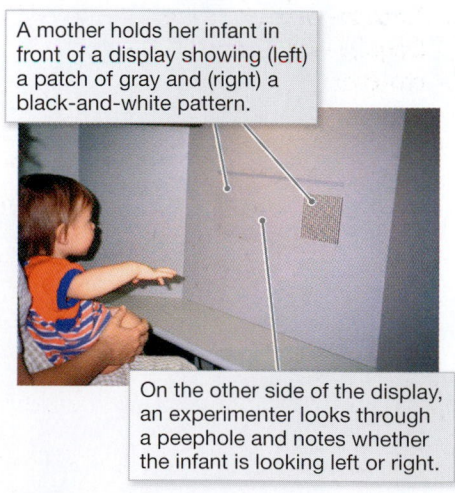

A mother holds her infant in front of a display showing (left) a patch of gray and (right) a black-and-white pattern.

On the other side of the display, an experimenter looks through a peephole and notes whether the infant is looking left or right.

FIGURE 11.11 Testing Visual Acuity in Infants This infant's visual acuity is being tested with the preferential-looking procedure.

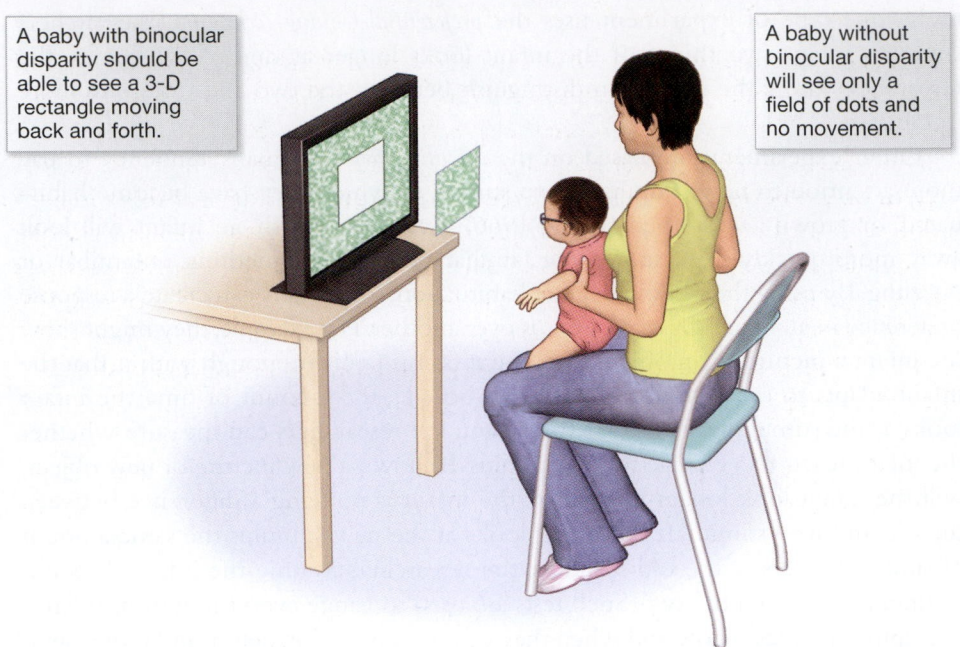

A baby with binocular disparity should be able to see a 3-D rectangle moving back and forth.

A baby without binocular disparity will see only a field of dots and no movement.

FIGURE 11.12 Fox's Experiment to Test Binocular Disparity This test determines whether the baby can use binocular disparity as a cue to depth.

seated on the parent's lap (**FIGURE 11.12**). Fox's results indicate that the ability to perceive depth develops between three and a half and six months of age.

AUDITORY PERCEPTION When infants are presented with rattle sounds in their right or left ears, they turn in the direction of the sounds; this movement indicates both that they have perceived the sound and that they know where it is coming from. Detailed analysis of the tone levels that infants can hear indicates that by six months babies have nearly adult levels of auditory function (DeCasper & Spence, 1986). Infants also seem to have some memory for sounds. Using habituation techniques, researchers have determined that infants can recognize sounds they have heard before. By measuring an infant's rate of sucking on a rubber nipple, researchers can determine if the infant is aroused in response to a specific sound. Anthony DeCasper and William Fifer (1980) used operant conditioning (discussed in Chapter 6, "Learning") to determine what sounds two-day-old infants can remember. In their study, each infant wore earphones and was given a nipple linked to recordings of his or her mother's voice and a stranger's voice. If the infant paused for a longer time between sucking bursts, the mother's voice played. If the infant paused for a shorter time, the stranger's voice played. Even at this young age, the newborns learned to alter their sucking patterns to hear their mother's voices more often. Using a biological level of analysis, researchers sought to determine whether the brain regions activated when someone hears speech are similar for infants and adults. In adults, different brain regions respond to speech and to non-speech (Vouloumanos, Kiehl, Werker, & Liddle, 2001). Would infants' brains show the same distinction? Researchers compared adults' and infants' brain responses to speech and to nonspeech, using *event-related potentials* (EEG measures) that pick up neural activity from the scalp (Dehaene-Lambertz & Gliga, 2004). As they expected, three-month-old infants showed neural responses similar to those obtained from adults. This finding suggests that, from the first three months of life through adulthood, there is a continuity in how the brain processes speech.

Memory Improves over Childhood

The development of memory also helps children learn about the world around them, as they use new information to build on what they already know. In two experiments, Carolyn Rovee-Collier (1999) revealed that from a very young age infants possess some types of memory, though that memory is quite rudimentary. In one experiment, a mobile hanging over a crib was attached to an infant's ankle with a ribbon. The infant learned that he or she could move the mobile by kicking. The rate at which the infant kicked when the mobile was not attached served as the baseline. When the infant was tested later, the ribbon was attached to the ankle but not to the mobile, so the kicks no longer moved the mobile. If the baby recognized the mobile, presumably it would kick faster than the baseline rate to try to make the mobile move. Infants ranging in age from 2 months to 18 months were trained for two days on the mobile and then tested after different lengths of time. The findings indicated that older infants remembered longer. By 18 months, they could remember the event for several weeks (**FIGURE 11.13**).

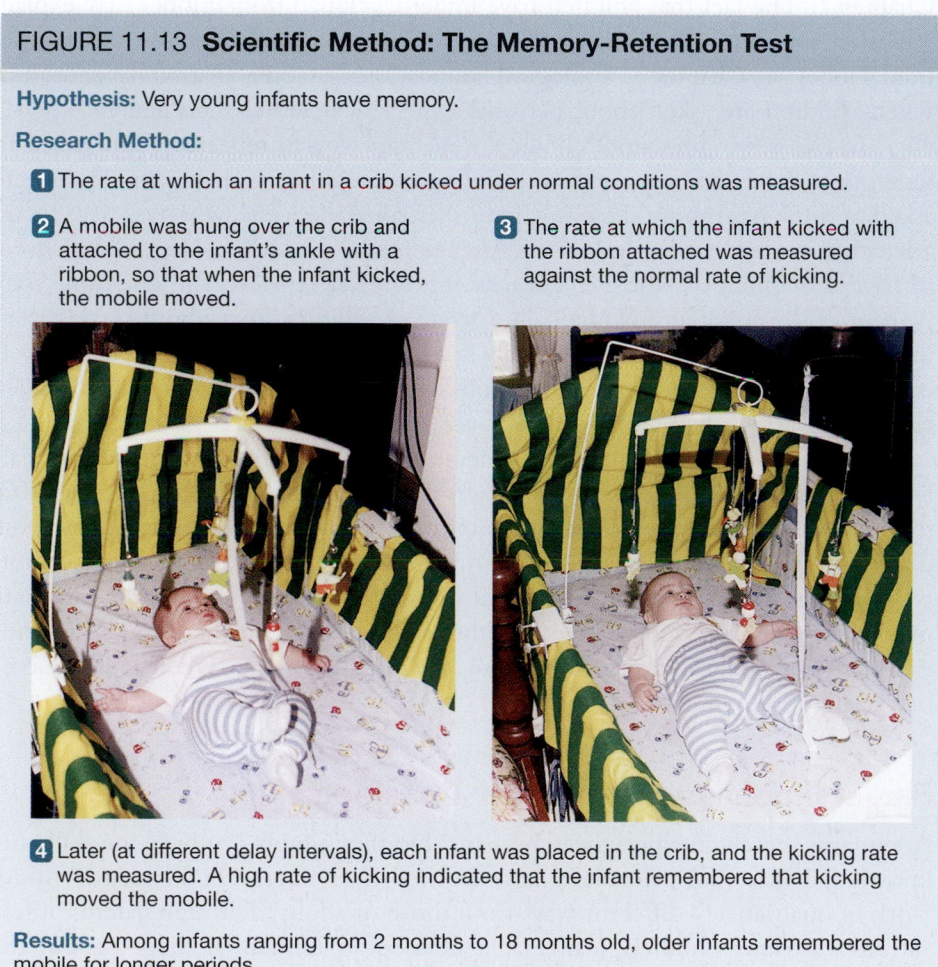

FIGURE 11.13 **Scientific Method: The Memory-Retention Test**

Hypothesis: Very young infants have memory.

Research Method:

1 The rate at which an infant in a crib kicked under normal conditions was measured.

2 A mobile was hung over the crib and attached to the infant's ankle with a ribbon, so that when the infant kicked, the mobile moved.

3 The rate at which the infant kicked with the ribbon attached was measured against the normal rate of kicking.

4 Later (at different delay intervals), each infant was placed in the crib, and the kicking rate was measured. A high rate of kicking indicated that the infant remembered that kicking moved the mobile.

Results: Among infants ranging from 2 months to 18 months old, older infants remembered the mobile for longer periods.

Conclusion: Very young infants have memory, but it is quite rudimentary.

INFANTILE AMNESIA   What is your earliest memory? Most adults remember few events that occurred before they were three or four years old. Freud referred to this inability to remember events from early childhood as **infantile amnesia.** Psychologists have offered various explanations for this phenomenon (Eacott, 1999). Some believe children begin to retain memories after developing the ability to create autobiographical memory based on personal experience—for instance, recalling that "a cat scratched me" rather than "cats scratch." Other psychologists suggest that childhood memory develops with language acquisition because the ability to use words and concepts aids in memory retention.

INACCURATE MEMORY   Young children often have source amnesia (difficulty knowing where they learned something; discussed in Chapter 7, "Attention and Memory"). For example, even when tested immediately after being presented with information, three-year-old children forget the source of the information faster than do five-year-old children (Gopnik & Graf, 1988). Evidence from investigations of source amnesia suggests that many of people's earliest memories come from looking at pictures in family albums, watching home movies, or hearing stories from their parents—not from actual memories of the events.

Children are also known to confabulate (make things up; also discussed in Chapter 7). The fact that children have underdeveloped frontal lobes may explain why they are more likely than adults to engage in this behavior (on the roles of frontal lobes, see Chapter 3, "Biological Foundations"). Confabulation happens most when children are asked about personal experiences rather than general knowledge. In one study, preschool children were interviewed repeatedly and asked to remember if they had ever gotten their fingers caught in a mousetrap. They were asked to think hard about the event and to visualize the scene, who was with them, what they were wearing, and so on. After ten weeks in which the children were to have thought about the event, a new interviewer repeated the question. Sixty percent of the children provided false narratives, telling a story about getting their fingers caught and behaving as if it really had happened. Many of the children developed very elaborate stories with numerous details about why their fingers had been caught and how it had felt (Bruck & Ceci, 1993).

Siblings sometimes argue about a memory, each claiming the same event really happened to them. A team of researchers (Ikier, Tekcan, Gülgöz, & Küntay, 2003) studied such disputed memories and undisputed memories and found many more disputed memories among identical twins than among fraternal twins and nontwin siblings, probably because identical twins are the same sex and tend to share many more life experiences than do other siblings. Most of the disputed memories were for events that occurred during the preschool years, when source memory is still developing.

Piaget Emphasized Stages of Development

Are infants merely inexperienced humans? Do they simply not have the skills and knowledge that adults normally have learned over time? Or do infants' minds work in qualitatively different ways from those of adults? Through careful observations of young children, Jean Piaget devised an influential theory about the development of thinking (**FIGURE 11.14**; for more on Piaget, see Chapter 1, "Introduction"). One crucial aspect of Piaget's research is that he paid as much attention to how children made errors as to how they succeeded on tasks. These mistakes, illogical by adult standards, provided insights into how young minds

FIGURE 11.14 Jean Piaget Piaget introduced the idea that cognitive development occurs in stages.

make sense of the world. By systematically analyzing children's thinking, Piaget developed the theory that children go through four *stages of development—sensorimotor, preoperational, concrete operational,* and *formal operational*—that reflect different ways of thinking about the world (**FIGURE 11.15**). From this perspective, it is not that infants know less than adults but rather that their view of how the world works is based on an entirely different set of assumptions than those held by adults. As discussed below, other researchers have challenged the idea of stages of development.

Piaget proposed that during each stage of development children form new *schemas*. As defined and discussed in Chapter 7, schemas are ways of thinking, conceptual models of how the world works. Piaget believed that each stage builds on the previous one through two learning processes: **Assimilation** is the process through which a new experience is incorporated in an existing schema; **accommodation** (a different term than the one presented in Chapter 5) is the process through which a schema is adapted or expanded to include the new experience.

assimilation The process by which a new experience is placed into an existing schema.

accommodation The process by which a schema is changed to incorporate a new experience that does not easily fit into an existing schema.

FIGURE 11.15 Piaget's Stages of Cognitive Development

Stage	Characterization
1 Sensorimotor (birth–2 years)	• Differentiates self from objects • Recognizes self as agent of action and begins to act intentionally; for example, pulls a string to set a mobile in motion or shakes a rattle to make a noise • Achieves object permanence: realizes that things continue to exist even when no longer present to the senses 
2 Preoperational (2–7 years)	• Learns to use language and to represent objects by images and words • Thinking is still egocentric: has difficulty taking the viewpoint of others • Classifies objects by a single feature; for example, groups together all the red blocks regardless of shape or all the square blocks regardless of color 
3 Concrete operational (7–12 years)	• Can think logically about objects and events • Achieves conservation of number (age 7), mass (age 7), and weight (age 9) • Classifies objects by several features and can order them in a series along a single dimension, such as size 
4 Formal operational (12 years and up)	• Can think logically about abstract propositions and test hypotheses systematically • Becomes concerned with the hypothetical, the future, and ideological problems 

SENSORIMOTOR STAGE (BIRTH TO TWO YEARS) According to Piaget, from birth until about age two children are in the **sensorimotor stage,** acquiring information only through their senses. Thus infants understand objects only when they reflexively react to those objects' sensory input—such as when they suck on a nipple, grasp a finger, or recognize a face. As they begin to control their movements, they develop their first schemas: conceptual models consisting of mental representations of the kinds of actions that can be performed on certain kinds of objects. For instance, the sucking reflex begins as a reaction to the sensory input from the nipple: Infants simply respond reflexively by sucking. Soon they realize they can suck other things, such as a bottle, a finger, a toy, a blanket. Piaget described sucking other objects as an example of assimilation to the schema of sucking. But sucking a toy or a blanket does not result in the same experience as the reflexive sucking of a nipple. The difference between these experiences leads to accommodation with respect to the sucking schema—children must adjust their understanding of sucking.

Piaget believed that all the sensorimotor schemas eventually merge into an exploratory schema. In other words, infants learn they can act on objects—manipulate them to understand them—rather than simply react to them. If you have spent time watching an infant learn about the world, you may have noticed that every new object goes into the infant's mouth. Caregivers may worry about the cleanliness of this way of learning about the world, but the behavior is typical for infants in the sensorimotor stage of development.

According to Piaget, one cognitive concept related to this stage is **object permanence,** the understanding that an object continues to exist even when it is hidden from view. Piaget noted that not until nine months of age will most infants search for objects they have seen being hidden. Even at nine months, when infants will begin to snatch a blanket away to find a hidden toy, their search skills have limits. For instance, suppose during several trials an eight-month-old child watches an experimenter hide a toy under a blanket and the child then finds the toy. If the experimenter then hides the toy under a different blanket, in full view of the child, the child will still look for the toy in the first hiding place. Full comprehension of object permanence was, for Piaget, one key accomplishment of the sensorimotor period.

PREOPERATIONAL STAGE (TWO TO SEVEN YEARS) In the **preoperational stage,** according to Piaget, children can think about objects not in their immediate view and have developed various conceptual models of how the world works. During this stage, they begin to think symbolically—for example, taking a stick and pretending it is a gun. Piaget believed that what they cannot do yet is think "operationally"—they cannot imagine the logical outcome of performing certain actions on objects. They base their reasoning not on logic but on immediate appearance. For instance, children at this stage have no understanding of the law of conservation of quantity: that even if a substance's appearance changes, its quantity may remain unchanged. For instance, if you pour a short, fat glass of water into a tall, thin glass, you know the amount of water has not changed. However, if you ask children in the preoperational stage which glass contains more, they will pick the tall, thin glass because the water is at a higher level. The children will make this error even when they have seen someone pour the same amount of water into each glass—and even when they do it themselves (**FIGURE 11.16**).

CONCRETE OPERATIONAL STAGE (7 TO 12 YEARS) At about seven years of age, children enter the **concrete operational stage,** where they remain until adolescence. Piaget believed that humans do not develop logic until they begin to think about and understand operations. In other words, they then can figure out

1 A six-year-old understands that two identical short glasses of water contain the same amount of water.

2 She pours the water from one of the short glasses into a tall glass.

3 When asked which glass has more water, she points to the taller glass, even though she poured the water from the equivalent shorter glass.

FIGURE 11.16 The Preoperational Stage and the Law of Conservation In the preoperational stage, children cannot yet understand the concept of conservation.

the world by thinking about how events are related. A classic *operation* is an action that can be undone: A light can be turned on and off; a stick can be moved across the table and then moved back. According to Piaget, the ability to understand that an action is reversible enables children to begin to understand concepts such as conservation of quantity. Although this development is the beginning of logical thinking, Piaget believed that children at this stage reason only about concrete things—objects they can act on in the world. They do not yet have the ability to reason abstractly, or hypothetically, about what might be possible.

FORMAL OPERATIONAL STAGE (12 YEARS TO ADULTHOOD) The **formal operational stage** is Piaget's final stage of cognitive development. Formal operations involve abstract thinking, characterized by the ability to form a hypothesis about something and test it through deductive logic. For instance, at this stage teens can systematically begin to test a theory or solve a problem. Piaget described giving students four flasks of colorless liquid and one flask of colored liquid, then telling them that by combining two of the colorless liquids, they could obtain the colored liquid. Adolescents, by systematically trying different combinations, can obtain the correct result. Younger children, who just randomly combine liquids, cannot. One example of psychological science in action is the influence on education of Piaget's research: In the United States, for example, subjects that require abstract reasoning, such as algebra or the scientific method, usually are not taught until around eighth grade, when most of the children are 12 years old.

CHALLENGES TO PIAGET'S THEORY Piaget revolutionized the understanding of cognitive development and was right about many things. However, many subsequent studies have challenged his views. For example, some critics dispute the idea that every person goes through the stages of development in the same order. Piaget also believed that as children progress through each stage, they all use the same kind of logic to solve problems. His framework thus leaves little room for differing cognitive strategies or skills among individuals—or among cultures. Some evidence supports his view, but many children seem to move back and forth between stages. Some developmental psychologists have revised many of Piaget's theories while preserving his basic ideas. These theorists believe that different areas in the brain are responsible for different skills, and that the development of different skills therefore does not have to follow strict stages (Bidell & Fischer, 1995; Case, 1992; Fischer, 1980).

Infants Have Early Knowledge about the World

Piaget suggested that children are not capable of understanding much of the world around them until they go through the various stages of cognitive development. However, recent research indicates that children understand much more and at much earlier ages than was previously believed. Tests using the preferential-looking technique have revealed that infants as young as three months of age can remember an object even when it is no longer in plain sight, a finding that seems to contradict Piaget's ideas about object permanence. Similarly, infants' reactions to novel stimuli indicate that they have cognitive skills quite early in life. For example, if three-month-old infants watch events that do not make rational sense, they will stare at the impossible or unexpected results longer than they would stare at the results of events that make sense.

Suppose you show an infant an apple, lower a screen in front of the apple, and then raise the screen to show the apple. Then you perform the same actions, but

sensorimotor stage The first stage in Piaget's theory of cognitive development, during which infants acquire information about the world through their senses and respond reflexively.

object permanence The understanding that an object continues to exist even when it cannot be seen.

preoperational stage The second stage in Piaget's theory of cognitive development, during which children think symbolically about objects, but reason is based on appearance rather than logic.

concrete operational stage The third stage in Piaget's theory of cognitive development, during which children begin to think about and understand operations in ways that are reversible.

formal operational stage The final stage in Piaget's theory of cognitive development; it involves the ability to think abstractly and to formulate and test hypotheses through deductive logic.

this time raise the screen to show a carrot—a surprising, impossible event. If the infant looks longer at the carrot than it had looked at the apple, you would deduce that the infant expected to see the apple (Baillargeon, 1995). By responding differently to such an impossible event than to possible ones, infants demonstrate some understanding that an object continues to exist when it is out of sight, even though they might not reach for a hidden object in Piaget's object permanence test. Piaget's task probably required too much of infants, perhaps by making them reach for the object. Baillargeon's apple/carrot test revealed that object permanence occurs earlier than Piaget believed.

UNDERSTANDING THE LAWS OF NATURE: PHYSICS The developmental psychologist Elizabeth Spelke and her colleagues have conducted numerous studies indicating that infants have a primitive understanding of some of the basic laws of physics. Consider one such example. Humans are born with the ability to perceive movement: A newborn will follow a moving stimulus with his or her eyes and head and prefer to look at a moving stimulus over a stationary one. Experiments indicate that as infants get older, they use movement information to determine if an object is continuous—that is, if it is all one object, even if the infant cannot see the entire thing because it is partially hidden (Kellman, Spelke, & Short, 1986). In one experiment, the researchers showed four-month-old infants a rod moving back and forth behind a block. Once habituated, the infants were shown two scenes: one in which the block was removed and there was a single rod, and another in which the block was removed and there were two small rods. The infants looked longer at the two small rods (**FIGURE 11.17**). This response indicated that they expected the rod moving behind the block to be one continuous object rather than two small ones. Understanding the relation between the movement and the physical properties of the rod requires various cognitive skills. It requires the ability to see the rod as an object separate from the block and to surmise that since the two ends are moving together, they must be part of the same whole rod, even though part of rod is hidden. If the experiment is conducted with a stationary rod, however, the infants do not look longer at the two small rods. Therefore, infants appear to use movement to infer that objects moving together are continuous, whereas for infants two stationary objects may or may not be continuous.

In a series of studies using impossible events, Renee Baillargeon and her colleagues (Baillargeon, 2008; Wang & Baillargeon, 2008) found that at a very young age children begin to understand what is necessary to support an object in space. The experimenters determined that, by three months of age, infants expect a box on a platform to remain stable if a person holding the box releases it, whereas those infants expect a box with nothing under it to fall if a person holding the box releases it (**FIGURE 11.18**). Thus children seem to have an intuitive sense of the laws that govern the physical world.

UNDERSTANDING THE LAWS OF NATURE: MATHEMATICS How much do you think infants and toddlers know about counting and other mathematical operations? Piaget believed that young children do not understand numbers and therefore must learn counting and other number-related skills through memorization. His experiments consisted of, for example, showing four-to-five-year-old children two rows of marbles. Both rows had the same number of marbles, but in one row the marbles were spread out. The children usually said the longer row had more marbles (**FIGURE 11.19**), and Piaget concluded that children's understanding of quantity—of the concepts *more than* and *less than*—had to do not with number but with length.

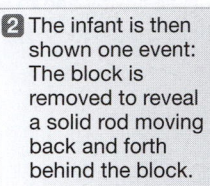

1. A four-month-old is shown a rod that moves back and forth behind an occluding block. The infant becomes habituated to this stimulus.

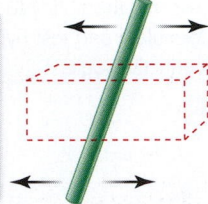

2. The infant is then shown one event: The block is removed to reveal a solid rod moving back and forth behind the block.

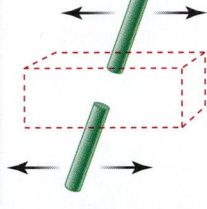

3. Finally, the infant is shown a second event: The block is removed to reveal two separate rods moving back and forth behind the block.

The infant spends much more time looking at the second event (two moving rods) than at the first (one moving rod).

FIGURE 11.17 The Perceptual Effect of Occlusions in Early Infancy Understanding the relation between movement and physical properties requires cognitive skills. Infants appear to use movement to infer that objects moving together are continuous.

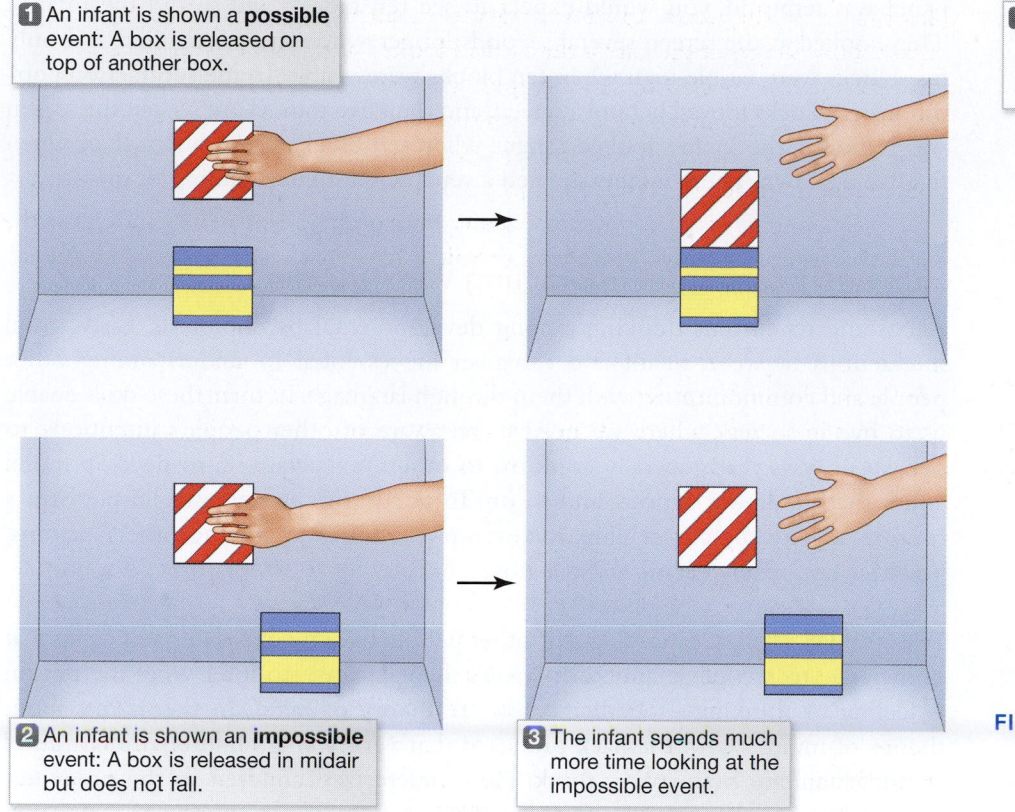

1 An infant is shown a **possible** event: A box is released on top of another box.

2 An infant is shown an **impossible** event: A box is released in midair but does not fall.

3 The infant spends much more time looking at the impossible event.

FIGURE 11.18 Understanding the Laws of Nature Infants seem to intuitively sense that a box placed in midair must fall.

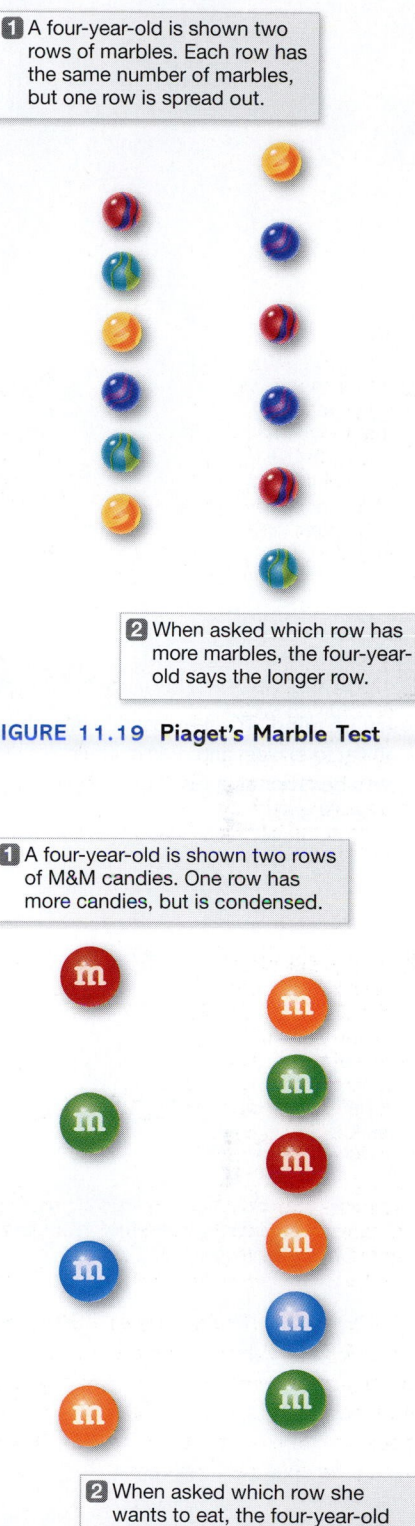

1 A four-year-old is shown two rows of marbles. Each row has the same number of marbles, but one row is spread out.

2 When asked which row has more marbles, the four-year-old says the longer row.

FIGURE 11.19 Piaget's Marble Test

1 A four-year-old is shown two rows of M&M candies. One row has more candies, but is condensed.

2 When asked which row she wants to eat, the four-year-old picks the row with more candies even though it is shorter.

FIGURE 11.20 The M&M Version of Piaget's Marble Test Children who might not have succeeded on Piaget's marble test were able to choose the row that contained more items when those items were M&Ms and the test question was *Which row would you like to eat?*

Challenging Piaget's view, Jacques Mehler and Tom Bever (1967) argued that children younger than three years of age can understand *more than* and *less than*. To demonstrate their point, they cleverly repeated Piaget's experiment using M&Ms candy. They showed the children two rows of four M&Ms each and asked if the rows were the same. When the children said yes, the researchers then transformed the rows. For instance, they would add two candies to the second row, but compress that row so it was shorter than the row with fewer candies. Then they would tell the children to pick the row they wanted to eat. More than 80 percent picked the row with more M&Ms, even though it was the visually shorter row (**FIGURE 11.20**). This research indicated that when children are properly motivated, they understand and can demonstrate their knowledge of *more than* and *less than*. Despite Piaget's enormous contributions to the understanding of cognitive development, the growing evidence that even infants have innate knowledge challenges his theory of distinct stages of cognitive development. For example, subsequent scientific findings indicate that Piaget underestimated young children's mental capacities.

As researchers have developed better methods for studying what infants know and can do, they have learned that very young infants have some amazing numerical abilities. For example, at what age would you guess that children have a basic idea of addition and subtraction? Researchers explored this question with a sample of nine-month-olds (McCrink & Wynn, 2004). They used the habituation paradigm to see if the infants were surprised (looked longer) when they were presented with wrong answers to addition and subtraction problems. Normal nine-month-olds watched a computer monitor where, in the addition condition, five blocks were covered by a panel and then five more blocks moved behind the panel. When the panel was removed, you would expect to see ten blocks, and so did the infants: They looked at the screen several seconds longer when the panel lifted and only five blocks were visible than when ten blocks were visible. In the subtraction condition, ten blocks moved behind a screen, and then five moved out. When the screen was removed, the infants looked longer when ten blocks were shown than when five were shown. These infants showed a remarkable understanding of quantity.

Humans Learn from Interacting with Others

According to current thinking among developmental psychologists, early social interactions between infant and caregiver are essential to understanding other people and communicating with them through language. In turn, these skills enable us to live in society, where we need to be aware of other people's intentions, to behave in ways that generally conform to others' expectations, to develop moral codes that guide our actions, and so on. To safely (that is, defensively) perform a routine activity such as driving, for example, requires predicting others' actions, however potentially erratic those actions.

theory of mind The term used to describe the ability to explain and predict other people's behavior as a result of recognizing their mental state.

THEORY OF MIND   Knowing that other people have mental states and using that knowledge to recognize another person's mental state—to infer what the person is feeling or thinking—together constitute **theory of mind.** In theorizing about theory of mind, David Premack proposed that very young children are not good at understanding how others think. He characterized children in the preoperational stage as egocentric: They cannot see another person's point of view, only their own. For instance, children at this stage might stand in front of a television and, because they can see the picture just fine, not understand they are blocking the screen for others. Evidence from the past two decades, however, has shown that young children are less egocentric than Piaget believed. Beginning in infancy, young children come to understand that other people perform actions for reasons—that the actions are intentional (Gergely & Csibra, 2003; Somerville & Woodward, 2005). The recognition of actions' intentionality reflects a growing capacity for theory of mind and allows people to understand, predict, and attempt to influence others' behavior (Baldwin & Baird, 2001).

In one study, an adult began handing a toy to an infant. On some trials, the adult became unwilling to hand over the toy (e.g., teasing the infant with the toy or playing with it himself or herself). On other trials, the adult became unable to hand it over (e.g., "accidentally" dropping it or being distracted by a ringing telephone). Infants older than nine months showed greater signs of impatience (such as reaching for the toy) when the adult was unwilling than when the adult was unable (Behne, Carpenter, Call, & Tomasello, 2005). In a study that suggests the ability to understand intentions is developed by 13 months of age, infants watched animations of a caterpillar, which searched behind a screen for food. On some trials, the caterpillar had information as to whether a particular food was behind the screen; on other trials, the caterpillar did not have this information. To determine whether the infants expected the caterpillar to find the food, the researchers measured the amounts of time the infants looked at the screen. The infants' expectations appeared to depend on what they believed the caterpillar knew (Surian, Caldi, & Sperber, 2007). In another study, 15-month-old children imitated the actions of an adult trying to pull apart the halves of a dumbbell. On some trials, the children watched the adult's hand slip off the dumbbell before he or she successfully separated it. However, the children imitated the goal of separating the dumbbell rather than the adult's actual movements, such as having the hand slip off (Meltzoff, 1995).

Ann

Sally

Basket   Box

Sally puts her marble in the basket.

Sally goes away.

Ann moves the marble.

"Where will Sally look for her marble?"

FIGURE 11.21 A Classic Test for a Child's Theory of Mind When a child acquires theory of mind, he or she is able to understand that different individuals have both different perspectives and knowledge based on their individual experiences.

These studies and others (e.g., Onishi & Baillargeon, 2006) provide strong evidence that in the first year of life children begin to read intentions and that by the end of the second year, perhaps even by 13 to 15 months of age, they become very good at reading them (Baillargeon, Li, Ng, & Yuan, 2009).

In this light, consider the *false-belief test,* which measures children's ability to predict actions. To complete the test successfully, children must understand that people can act on the basis of false information. In a classic example, the child watches Sally place a marble in a basket and leave the room; the child then sees Ann come in, remove the marble from the basket, and place it in a box. The child is then asked to guess where Sally will look for the marble when she comes back in the room (**FIGURE 11.21**). To answer correctly, the child must develop a theory: Sally put the marble in the basket; Sally does not know Ann moved the marble, so Sally will look in the basket. Children normally are able to solve this problem by age four or five, most likely because by that age they have both sufficient language skills and the ability to coordinate deliberate actions with beliefs.

Children's success at the false-belief test and children's full development of theory of mind appear to coincide with the maturation of the brain's frontal lobes. If the capacity for theory of mind is thus linked to brain development, children in different cultures ought to solve the false-belief test at about the same age. Indeed, a recent study found that children from Canada, India, Peru, Samoa, and Thailand reached the false-belief milestone at around age five (Callaghan et al., 2005). When developmental findings are similar across multiple cultures, the results are considered *culturally universal,* influenced more heavily by biological maturation than by cultural practices (**FIGURE 11.22**).

The frontal lobes' importance for theory of mind is also supported by research with adults. In brain imaging studies, prefrontal brain regions become active when

(a)

(b)

FIGURE 11.22 Culturally Universal Development Around the world—for example, in **(a)** Africa and **(b)** Asia—children display universal aspects of human development.

people are asked to think about others' mental states. People with damage to this region have difficulty attributing mental states to characters in stories (Stone, Baron-Cohen, & Knight, 1998).

Like the abilities to understand math and physics, theory of mind might develop independently of other brain functions. While children with the developmental disorder autism (discussed in Chapter 14, "Disorders of the Mind and Body") cannot solve the false-belief problem, children with Down syndrome can solve it. This finding suggests that theory of mind is not governed by reasoning and general intelligence, since children with Down syndrome are impaired in those areas.

MORAL REASONING AND MORAL EMOTIONS Moral development concerns the way people learn to decide between behaviors with competing social outcomes. In other words, it involves the choices people make that affect others, such as whether to take actions that may harm others or that may break implicit or explicit social contracts. Ideally, morality develops during childhood and into adulthood. Theorists typically have divided it into *moral reasoning,* which depends on cognitive processes, and *moral emotions.* Of course, cognition and emotions are intertwined: Research has shown that if people lack adequate cognitive abilities, their moral emotions may not translate into moral behaviors; similarly, moral reasoning is enhanced by moral emotions.

Psychologists who study the cognitive processes of moral behavior have focused largely on Lawrence Kohlberg's stage theory. Kohlberg (1984) tested moral-reasoning skills by asking people to respond to hypothetical situations in which a main character was faced with a moral dilemma, such as having to steal a drug to save his dying wife. Kohlberg was most concerned with the reasons children and adults provided for their answers. He devised a theory of moral judgment that involved three levels of moral reasoning. At the **preconventional** level, children classify answers in terms of self-interest or pleasurable outcomes. For example, a child at this level may say, "He should steal the drug if he really likes his wife." At the **conventional** level, responses conform to rules of law and order or focus on others' disapproval, as in "He shouldn't take the drug because it is wrong to steal, so everyone will think he is a bad person." At the highest, **postconventional** level, responses center around complex reasoning about abstract principles and values, such as "Sometimes people have to break the law if the law is unjust." Moral reasoning theories have been faulted for emphasizing the cognitive aspects of morality. Some theorists contend that moral reasoning, as such, fails to predict moral behavior; they believe instead that moral actions, such as helping others in need, are influenced more by emotions than by cognitive processes.

Research on moral behavior's emotional components has focused largely on *empathy* and *sympathy,* called moral emotions because they are related to moral behaviors. Empathy arises from understanding another's emotional state and feeling what the other person is feeling or would be expected to feel in the given situation. In contrast, sympathy arises from feelings of concern, pity, or sorrow for another (Eisenberg, 2000). In other words, empathy involves feeling *with* the other person, whereas sympathy involves feeling *for* the other person. Along with embarrassment, the moral emotions are considered self-conscious emotions, because they require comprehension of oneself as a causal agent and an evaluation of one's own responses. Moral emotions form early in life but emerge later than primary emotions (such as happiness or anger), so they are also called *secondary emotions.*

Recent research has shown that parents' behaviors influence their children's level of both moral emotions and prosocial behavior. Parents of sympathetic children

preconventional Earliest level of moral development, in which self-interest determines what is moral.

conventional Middle stage of moral development, in which rules and the approval of others determines what is moral.

postconventional Highest stage of moral development, in which decisions about morality depend on abstract principles.

tend to have certain characteristics: They are high in sympathy, they allow their children to express negative emotions in ways that do not harm others, they do not express hostility in the home, they help their children cope with negative emotions, and they promote an understanding of and focus on others (**FIGURE 11.23**). In contrast, parents of children high in shame tend to show frequent anger, to be lax in discipline, and not to respond positively to the children's appropriate behavior (Ferguson & Stegge, 1995). Thus not all children progress through the stages of moral development at the same rate or in the same order. Research has shown the value of inductive reasoning (coming to a general conclusion from specific instances; discussed in Chapter 8, "Thinking and Intelligence") with children about their behavior. Parents' displays of inductive reasoning—as in "You made Chris cry. It's not nice to hit"—promote their childrens' sympathetic attitudes, appropriate feelings of guilt, and awareness of others' feelings.

PHYSIOLOGICAL BASIS OF MORALITY Some evidence from the biological level of analysis indicates that moral emotions are based in physiological mechanisms that help people make decisions. Antonio Damasio's *somatic-marker hypothesis* states that people have a visceral response (they seem to feel it in the gut or stomach) to real or imagined outcomes and that this response aids decision making. Damasio has found that patients with damage to the prefrontal cortex fail to become emotionally involved in decision making because their somatic markers are not engaged (see Chapter 9, "Motivation and Emotion"). Damasio and his colleagues (Anderson, Bechara, Damasio, Tranel, & Damasio, 1999) studied two people who had experienced prefrontal damage during infancy. Both individuals showed severe deficiencies in moral and social reasoning. When given Kohlberg's moral-dilemma task, both patients scored at the preconventional level. These patients also neglected social and emotional factors in their life decisions. Both failed to express empathy, remorse, or guilt for wrongdoing, and neither had particularly good parenting skills. One engaged in petty thievery, was verbally and physically threatening (once to the point of physical assault), and frequently lied for no apparent reason. Thus the frontal lobes appear to support the capacity for morality. However, children develop a sense of morality through socialization, especially from their parents.

FIGURE 11.23 Parental Behavior Affects Children's Behavior Parents who are high in sympathy and allow their children to express negative emotions without shame or hostility tend to have sympathetic children.

Language Develops in an Orderly Fashion

Communication through language allows humans to learn much more than other animals can. Language enables us to live in complex societies, because through it we learn the history, rules, and values of our culture or cultures. Through language we are able to communicate across cultures, sharing, for example, the new inventions and technologies that have shaped modern civilization. How does this remarkable ability, communication through language, develop?

As the brain develops, so does the ability to speak and form sentences. As children develop social skills, they also improve their language skills. There is some variation in the rate at which language develops, but overall the stages of language development are remarkably uniform across individuals. According to Michael Tomasello (1999), the early social interactions between infant and caregiver are essential to understanding other people and being able to communicate with them through language. Research has demonstrated that infants and caregivers attend to objects in their environment together; this joint attention facilitates learning to speak (Baldwin, 1991). However, the ability to speak can be disrupted by social isolation and lack of exposure to language, as in Genie's case (discussed at this chapter's opening).

FROM ZERO TO 60,000 Language is a system of using sounds and symbols according to grammatical rules to communicate. It can be viewed as a hierarchical structure (**FIGURE 11.24**), in which sentences can be broken down into smaller units, or *phrases,* which can be broken down further into words, each of which consists of *morphemes* (the smallest units that have meaning, including suffixes and prefixes), which consist of *phonemes* (basic sounds). The system of rules that govern how words are combined into phrases and how phrases are combined to make sentences is a language's *syntax.*

Research on the early language capacities of infants has shown that newborns are already well on their way to language learning (Kuhl, 2004: Werker, Gilbert, Humphrey, & Tees, 1981). Patricia Kuhl and her colleagues (2006; Kuhl et al., 2006; Kuhl, Tsao, & Liu, 2003) found that up to six months of age, a baby can discriminate all the speech sounds that occur in all natural languages, even if the sounds do not occur in the language spoken in the baby's home. To study how an infant learns the speech sounds of his or her own language, the researchers used a habituation technique: An experimenter distracted the baby with a toy on one side, and speech sounds were emitted from a box on the other side—for example, *ba, ba, ba.* Then a new speech sound was introduced—for example, *la, la, la.* If the baby turned toward the new sound, the researchers determined that the baby could tell the difference between *la* and *ba.*

In one study, the researchers compared babies from Japanese-language homes to those from English-language homes (Kuhl et al., 2006). In Japanese, the /r/ and /l/ sounds are grouped into a single phonemic category, but these are separate speech sounds in English, where, for example, *rake* and *lake* mean different things. When infants were six months to eight months old, American and Japanese infants were about 65 percent correct in their ability to discriminate between the /r/ and /l/ phonemes, but by the time they were ten months to twelve months old, the American infants were better able to discriminate these speech sounds and the Japanese infants were less able to do so.

In an extension of this research, Kuhl and colleagues studied whether American babies who were exposed to a foreign language would learn to discriminate the speech sounds in that language (Kuhl, Tsao, & Liu, 2003). In the four-week study, native speakers of Mandarin, in 12 sessions lasting approximately 25 minutes each, spoke only in Mandarin to nine-month-old American infants. The researchers then tested these infants on their ability to discriminate speech sounds found in Mandarin but not in English. As the first graph in **FIGURE 11.25** shows, the infants who interacted with the Mandarin speakers were much better at discriminating Mandarin speech sounds than

FIGURE 11.24 The Units of Language

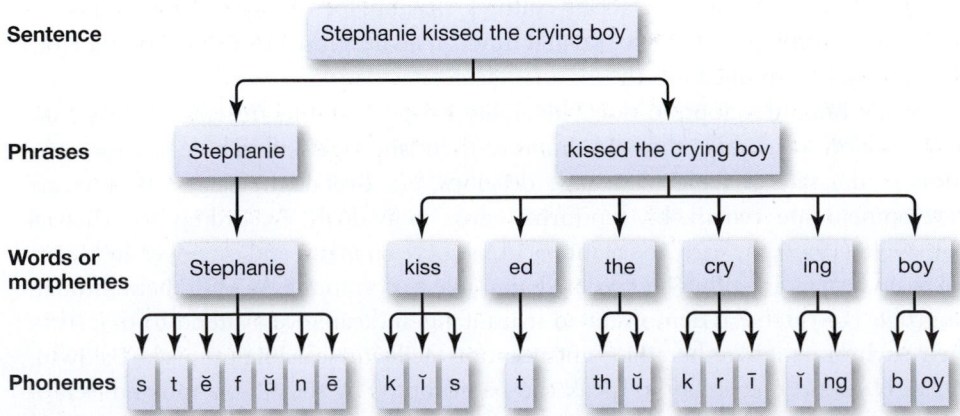

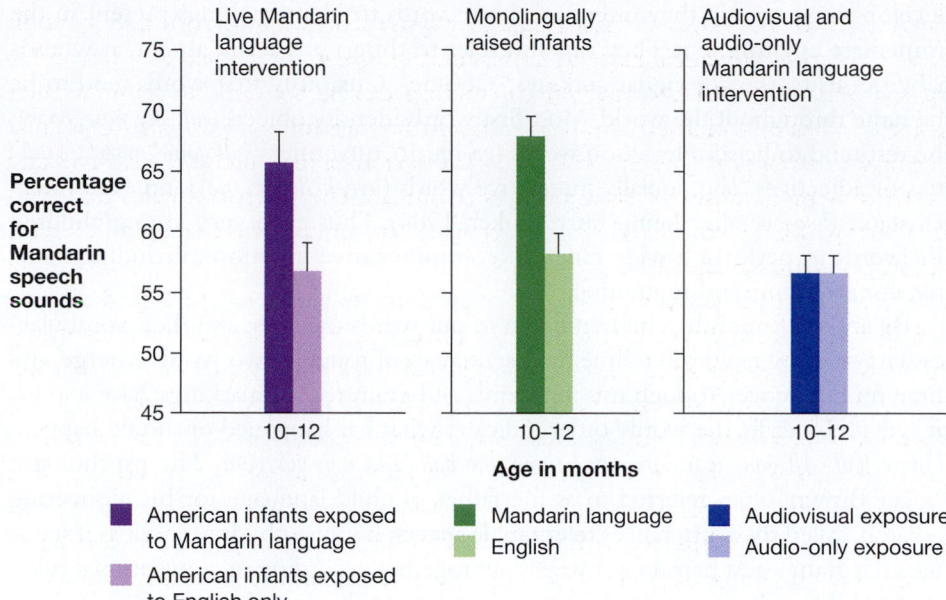

FIGURE 11.25 Mandarin Chinese Phonetic Discrimination
American infants exposed to live Mandarin speakers correctly identified the same percentage of Mandarin speech sounds as infants raised hearing only Chinese. By contrast, infants who saw videos of the Mandarin speakers or heard their audiotapes performed at the same level as infants who heard only English. Live interaction is critical for learning speech sounds.

were infants who did not. In fact, as the second graph shows, the American infants who interacted with the Mandarin speakers were almost as good at discriminating speech sounds in Mandarin as were infants raised hearing only Chinese.

The researchers further wondered whether infants who watched videos of the Mandarin speakers or listened to audiotapes of them speaking would also learn Mandarin speech sounds. As the third graph shows, neither watching the videos nor hearing the tapes enhanced the infants' ability to discriminate Mandarin speech sounds. The learning setting had to include a live interaction to work, a finding that reinforces the importance of social interactions in language learning.

From hearing differences between sounds immediately after birth and continuing to learn the sounds of their own languages, babies go on to develop the ability to speak. Humans appear to go from babbling as babies to employing a full vocabulary of about 60,000 words as adults without working very hard at it, and speech production follows a distinct path. During the first months of life, newborns' actions—crying, fussing, eating, and breathing—generate all their sounds, which are cries, gurgles, or grunts. Cooing and laughing appear at three to five months. From five to seven months, babies begin babbling, using consonants and vowels. From seven to eight months, they babble in syllables (*ba-ba-ba, dee-dee-dee*). By the first year, the syllables are mixed (*ba-dee, dah-dee*), and those babbles begin to take on the sounds and rhythms of the infant's native language. Babbling may be an infant's way of testing the system—checking what the basic parts are and how they are put together.

Language's onset is marked by the first words a baby utters and appears to understand. Babies tend to utter their first words around age one. Babies most often first utter two types of words. One type, *performatives,* consists of wordlike sounds that are learned in a context and that a baby may not be using to represent a meaning. For instance, a baby says "Hello" or something that sounds like it when holding a phone. Does the baby know that *hello* is a greeting used to talk to someone on the other end of the line? Or is the baby simply imitating what it sees people do when they pick up the phone? Chances are it is the latter if the baby does not say "hello" in other appropriate settings. *True words,* in contrast, are clearly meant to represent concepts. For instance, *cat* names the family pet; *book,* a bedtime story. When babies develop single words, they often use those words to identify things present in the immediate environment. They can also refer to things physically absent, as when a baby points to the cookie jar and says "Cookie." Curiously, first words tend to be the same throughout the world. Most first words identify objects (*cat, sky, nose, book*); the rest tend to be simple action words (*go, up, sit*), quantifiers (*all gone! more!*), qualities or adjectives (*hot*), socially interactive words (*bye, hello, yes, no*), and even internal states (*boo-boo* after being hurt; Pinker, 1984). Thus even very young children use words to perform a wide range of communicative functions, including naming, commenting, and requesting.

By about 18 months, children begin to put words together, and their vocabularies start to grow rapidly. Rudimentary sentences of roughly two words emerge, and these minisentences, though missing words and grammatical markings, have a logic, or syntax. Typically, the words' order indicates what has happened or should happen: *Throw ball. All gone* translates as *I threw the ball, and now it's gone.* The psychologist Roger Brown, often referred to as the father of child language for his pioneering research, called these utterances **telegraphic speech** because children speak as if sending a telegram—just bare-bones words put together according to conventional rules.

As children begin to use language in more sophisticated ways, one relatively rare but telling error they make is to overapply new grammar rules they learn. Children may start to make mistakes at ages three to five with words they used correctly at age two or three. For example, when they learn that adding -*ed* makes a verb past tense, they then add -*ed* to every verb, including irregular verbs that do not follow that rule, saying "runned" or "holded" even though they may have said "ran" or "held" at an earlier age. Similarly, they may overapply the rule to add -*s* to form a plural, saying "mouses" and "mans," even if they said "mice" and "men" at a younger age.

Although such overgeneralizations are rare (Marcus, 1996; Marcus et al., 1992), they reflect an important aspect of language acquisition. Children are not simply repeating what they have heard others say, because they most likely have not heard anyone say "runned." Instead, these errors occur because children are able to use language in a generative way. They therefore make more errors with words used less frequently (such as *drank* and *knew*) because they have heard the irregular form less often. Adults tend to do the same thing, but they will more likely make errors on the past tenses of words they do not use often, such as *trod, strove,* or *slew* (saying "treaded," "strived," or "slayed"; Pinker, 1994).

ACQUIRING LANGUAGE WITH THE HANDS If the perception and production of sound are the key neurological determinants of early language acquisition, then babies exposed to signed languages should acquire these languages in fundamentally different ways than babies acquire spoken language. If, however, what makes human language special is its highly systematic patterns and the human brain's sensitivity to them, then babies should acquire signed language and spoken language in highly similar ways. To test this hypothesis, Laura Ann Petitto and her students videotaped deaf babies of deaf parents in households using two entirely different signed languages: American Sign Language (ASL) and the signed language of Quebec, langue des signes quebecoise (LSQ). They found that deaf babies exposed to signed languages from birth acquire these languages on an identical maturational timetable as hearing babies acquire spoken languages (Petitto, 2000; **FIGURE 11.26**). In demonstrating that speech does not drive all human language acquisition, this research shows that humans must possess a biologically endowed sensitivity to aspects of language patterns—a sensitivity that launches a baby into the course of acquiring language.

telegraphic speech The tendency for children to speak using rudimentary sentences that are missing words and grammatical markings but follow a logical syntax.

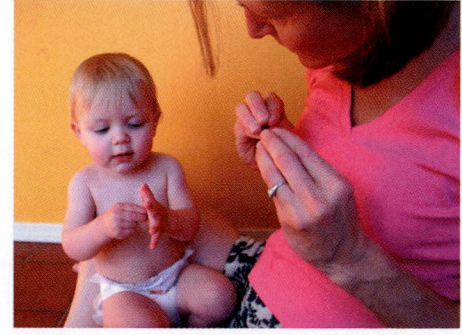

FIGURE 11.26 Acquiring Signed Language Deaf infants have been shown to acquire signed languages at the same rates that hearing infants acquire spoken languages.

UNIVERSAL GRAMMAR Much linguistic and psycholinguistic research is aimed at understanding the detailed steps by which language is assembled, produced, and understood. The linguist Noam Chomsky transformed the field when he argued that language must be governed by *universal grammar,* or innate knowledge of a set of universal and specifically linguistic elements and relations that form the heart of all human languages.

Until Chomsky came on the scene in the late 1950s, linguists had focused on analyzing language and identifying basic components of grammar. All languages include similar elements, such as nouns and verbs, but how those elements are arranged varies considerably across languages. In his early work, Chomsky argued that the way people combine these elements to form sentences and convey meaning is only a language's surface structure, the sound and order of words. He introduced the concept of *deep structure:* the implicit meanings of sentences. For instance, *The fat cat chased the rat* implies that there is a cat, it is fat, and it chased the rat. *The rat was chased by the fat cat* implies the same ideas even though on the surface it is a different sentence. Chomsky believed we automatically and unconsciously transform surface structure to deep structure, the meaning being conveyed. Research has shown that we remember a sentence's underlying meaning, not its surface structure. According to Chomsky, humans are born with a *language acquisition device,* which contains universal grammar, but exposure to a native language narrows down which grammatical rules a person learns. Of course, environment greatly influences a child's acquisition of language; indeed, the fact that you speak English rather than (or in addition to) Swahili is determined entirely by your environment.

The psychologist Lev Vygotsky developed the first major theory that emphasized the role of social and cultural context in the development of both cognition and language. According to Vygotsky, humans are unique because they use symbols and psychological tools, such as speech, writing, maps, art, and so on, through which they create culture. Culture, in turn, dictates what people need to learn and the sorts of skills they need to develop. For example, some cultures value science and rational thinking, whereas others emphasize supernatural and mystical forces. These cultural values shape how people think about and relate to the world around them. Vygotsky distinguished between elementary mental functions, such as innate sensory experiences, and higher mental functions, such as language, perception, abstraction, and memory. As children develop, their elementary capacities are gradually transformed, primarily through culture's influence.

Central to Vygotsky's theories is the idea that social and cultural context influences language development, which in turn influences cognitive development. Children start by directing their speech toward specific communications with others, such as asking for food or for toys. As children develop, they begin directing speech toward themselves, as when they give themselves directions or talk to themselves while playing. Eventually, children internalize their words into inner speech: verbal thoughts that direct both behavior and cognition. From this perspective, your thoughts are based on the language you have acquired through your society and through your culture, and this ongoing inner speech reflects higher-order cognitive processes.

Interaction across cultures also shapes language. The term *creole* describes a language that evolves over time from the mixing of existing languages (**FIGURE 11.27**). A creole language may develop, for example, when a culture colonizes a place, as when the French established themselves in southern Louisiana and acquired slaves who were not native French speakers. The creole develops out of rudimentary communications, as populations that speak several languages attempt to understand each other, often mixing words from the colonists' and natives' languages into a *pidgin,* an informal creole that lacks consistent grammatical rules. The linguist Derek

FIGURE 11.27 Creole Languages Creole languages evolve from a mixing of languages. In Suriname, where this boy is reading a classroom blackboard, over 10 languages are spoken. The official language, Dutch, comes from the nation's colonial background; the other tongues include variants of Chinese, Hindi, Javanese, and half a dozen original Creoles, among them Sranan Tongo (literally, "Suriname tongue").

Bickerton (1998) has found that the colonists' children impose rules on their parents' pidgin, developing it into a creole. Bickerton argues that this is evidence for built-in, universal grammar: The brain changes a nonconforming language by applying the same basic rules to it. Bickerton also has found that creoles formed in different parts of the world, with different combinations of languages, are more similar to each other in grammatical structure than to long-lived languages.

LEARNING TO READ   Reading, like speaking, is nearly effortless for most adults. When we look at letters, we see words and automatically derive meaning from them. But learning to read is challenging for many children, who struggle to figure out which symbols are letters, which letters clump together to make words, and which words go together to make meaningful sentences. So what is the best way to teach children to read?

There are two major schools of thought regarding how to teach reading. Traditional methods use *phonics,* which teaches an association between letters and their phonemes, or sounds. Children learn to spell out words by how they sound. Because of the complexity of the English language, in which the sounds of letters can vary across words, some educators have advocated *whole-language* approaches, which emphasize words' meanings and how words are connected in sentences. The whole-language approach has dominated in most American schools for the past two decades, perhaps in part because the philosophy that guides its instruction emphasizes student interest and enjoyment of reading. But does it do a better job than phonics in helping children learn to read?

In different forms, the phonics method has been popular for over 200 years. In phonics, children learn to make the appropriate sounds for the letters of the English alphabet. They learn a small number of simple words that teach the sounds of letters for most words of the English language. Because of English's irregularities, children first learn the general rules and then learn to recognize exceptions to those general rules. This approach emphasizes memorizing the mappings between letters and their sounds rather than building vocabulary or processing words' meanings.

The general idea behind whole-language instruction is that children should learn to read the way they learn to talk. We do not process speech by breaking down the stream into phonemes; instead, we understand speech as a series of connected words that have meaning in the context of an entire sentence. Thus, according to whole-language proponents, breaking down words into sounds is unnatural, frustrating, and boring. Instead, students should learn to read naturally and unconsciously, by learning individual words and then stringing them together.

Psychological science has made tremendous contributions to understanding not only how children learn to read but also which educational practices work best for most children. A group of psychologists who are experts in reading reviewed the vast literature on how children learn to read and published a comprehensive report for educators' benefit. From this research, they found that classroom and laboratory research over the past three decades has consistently found evidence that phonics instruction is superior to whole-language methods in creating proficient readers (Rayner, Foorman, Perfetti, Pesetsky, & Seidenberg, 2001). This result applies especially to children at risk of becoming poor readers, such as those whose parents do not read to them on a regular basis. The benefits of the whole-language approach are that it motivates students by making reading fun and encourages students to be creative and thoughtful. However, basic reading skills are best provided through phonics—and reading is not fun when children struggle to identify words.

The debate over phonics and whole-language approaches is an excellent example of how scientific research can contribute to important societal issues. The

Real World PSYCHOLOGY

whole-language movement was a progressive philosophy that tried to foster a love of learning. Yet the science of reading is clear—phonics works best (**FIGURE 11.28**). By sharing their research with those who set education policy, psychological scientists are helping children be better readers.

ANIMAL COMMUNICATION Nonhuman animals have ways of communicating with each other, but no other animal uses language the way humans do. Scientists have tried for years to teach language to chimpanzees, one of our nearest living relatives. Chimps lack the vocal ability to speak aloud, so studies have used sign language or visual cues to determine whether they understand words or concepts such as causation. Although chimpanzees can learn some words and have some sense of causation, other research challenges the idea that this learning means they have innate language abilities. Consider the work of the psychologists Herbert Terrace, Laura Ann Petitto, and Tom Bever, who set out to test Noam Chomsky's assertion that language was a uniquely human trait by attempting to teach American Sign Language to a chimpanzee, whom they named Neam Chimpsky (nicknamed Nim; **FIGURE 11.29**). But after years of teaching Nim, the team admitted that Chomsky might be right.

Nim, like all other language-trained chimps, consistently failed to master key components of human language syntax. While Nim was quite adept at communicating with a small set of basic signs ("eat," "play," "more"), he never acquired the ability to generate creative, rule-governed sentences; he was like a broken record, talking about the same thing over and over again in the same old way. Crucially, unlike even the young child who names, comments, requests, and more with his or her first words, Nim and all the ASL-trained chimps used the language almost exclusively to make requests. In the end, the chimps could use bits and pieces of language only to obtain outcomes—to get things (food, more food) from their caretakers—rather than to express meanings, thoughts, and ideas by generating language (Petitto & Seidenberg, 1979).

FIGURE 11.28 Phonics versus Whole-Language Approaches Although the whole-language method of teaching children to read has been popular for over 20 years, researchers have found that phonics— popular for over 200 years—is a more effective way to create proficient readers. Here, as part of phonics instruction, children associate vowel sounds with representative words.

FIGURE 11.29 Laura Ann Petitto with Nim Chimpsky

SUMMING UP

How Do Children Learn about Their Worlds?

Children acquire information through perception. Research, drawing on the fact that young infants look longer at novel stimuli than at familiar stimuli, indicates that infants are capable of learning at very young ages. Piaget emphasized that most young children's cognitive development occurs in consistent stages, each of which builds on previous stages. Though his theory was influential, recent evidence suggests that infants understand much more about objects' physical properties than Piaget believed and that he underestimated infants' innate and early knowledge. For instance, infants can use laws of physics and even demonstrate a basic understanding of addition and subtraction. An important part of learning occurs through social interaction, as young children develop the ability for theory of mind, a capacity that allows people to live in human society. A developing memory system helps children build a store of useful knowledge. The human capacity for language is innate, as there appear to be built-in methods of acquiring words and forming them into sentences. Although language development occurs in an orderly fashion, the specific language a child develops is influenced by environmental and cultural factors. These processes develop together to enable young children to learn and survive as they become members of society.

1. Match each of Piaget's stages of cognitive development with its description. The stages are concrete operational, formal operational, preoperational, and sensorimotor.

   _____ **a.** Children can think about objects they cannot see and can play symbolically.

   _____ **b.** Children can think abstractly and form hypotheses.

   _____ **c.** Object permanence develops along with first schemas.

   _____ **d.** Children show evidence of logical thinking, but still cannot think about abstract concepts.

2. Indicate whether each of the following statements about language learning is true or false.
   a. The ability to differentiate between common phonemes (speech sounds) develops around the time children begin kindergarten.
   b. The average adult knows approximately 250,000 words.
   c. Telegraphic speech is the use of a few words to convey meaning.
   d. Deaf children acquire sign language much more slowly than hearing children acquire spoken language.
   e. An infant younger than six months of age can discriminate speech sounds from only the language to which he or she is regularly exposed.

How Do Children and Adolescents Develop Their Identities?

LEARNING OBJECTIVES

Provide examples of the pervasive effects of gender roles.

Describe the research findings about the effects of divorce on children.

Explain the determinants of gender identity.

social development The maturation of skills or abilities that enable people to live in a world with other people.

As a child develops and learns more about the world, the child begins creating a sense of identity—of who he or she is. Identity formation is an important part of **social development,** the maturation of the skills and abilities that enable people to interact with others. Many factors, including gender, shape the sense of personal identity, which is further influenced by the culture in which a child is raised as well as that culture's beliefs about characteristics such as race and age.

As a child grows older and enters adolescence, the child seeks to understand how he or she fits into the world and to imagine what kind of person he or she will become later in life. Establishing a personal identity means breaking away from childhood beliefs by questioning and challenging parental and societal ideas (Erikson, 1968). Three major changes are believed to cause adolescents to question who they are: (1) changing physical appearance, which leads to changes in self-image; (2) more-sophisticated cognitive abilities, which prompt increased introspection; and (3) heightened pressure to prepare for the future—in particular, to make career choices. Teenagers explore alternative belief systems and wonder what they would be like if they were raised in other cultures, by other parents, or in other historical times. In general, adolescence is a period of struggling to answer essential questions such as *Who am I?* and *Where am I going?* The way an individual answers these questions depends on numerous factors in his or her environment.

Social Systems Influence Development

Urie Bronfenbrenner (1995) proposed the *biocultural systems theory,* which emphasizes the way biology and cultural systems interact to affect development. According to Bronfenbrenner, we can understand development best by considering the context in which it occurs. He theorized that four levels of systems affect the developing person. The *microsystem* is at the center and has the most immediate effects on a child. The microsystem includes, for example, the family and the cultural factors in each child's classroom, which exert direct effects on the developing child (rather than schooling as a whole). An external system, the *exosystem,* includes less direct influences—such as a parents' workplaces or the church the family attends—which create expectations about both behaviors and belief systems and indirectly regulate how much time and energy parents spend with their children. The *macrosystem* is the larger sociocultural context in which the child is reared (for example, being raised in an Asian culture or a South African culture). The *chronosystem* consists of the norms and rules in effect at the historical time when the child is reared. Bronfenbrenner's "system of systems" led to interdisciplinary work in child development because it hypothesized that social and historical contexts are essential to understanding how people develop. Bronfenbrenner cofounded Head Start, a massive federal program in the United States, designed to help children in low-income families develop the skills and abilities fostered by middle-class families (**FIGURE 11.30**). His emphasis on larger social systems translated psychological research into public policy and created a role for government in fostering positive development. Bronfenbrenner's theory emphasizes cultural effects on the way people develop their senses of identity.

FIGURE 11.30 Head Start A Head Start class in Billings, Montana, demonstrates a traditional Crow Indian dance.

Friends Influence Identity and Behavior

Developmental psychologists increasingly recognize peers' importance in shaping identity. Children, regardless of their cultures, tend to spend much of their time interacting with other children, usually playing in various ways. In helping children learn, and practice, skills that will be valuable in adulthood, play is the work of childhood and deserves the same respect we give to the demands of adult life. In developmental terms, attention to peers begins at the end of the first year of life, when infants begin to imitate other children, smile, and make vocalizations and other social signals to their peers (Brownell & Brown, 1992). Children of all ages learn how to behave from their friends, in part because for behaving appropriately they receive social rewards and for behaving inappropriately they receive social punishments. For example, children's math grades are correlated with the average math and verbal skills of the children in their peer group (Kurdek & Sinclair, 2000). Children and their peer group have similar academic motivation, but we cannot know if they select friends who are similar to them or they become similar to their friends (Crosnoe, Cavanagh, & Elder, 2003). Early friends are both playmates and teachers.

How children and adolescents compare their strengths and weaknesses with those of their peers also influences the development of identity. As part of the search for identity, teenagers form friendships with others whose values and worldviews are similar to their own. Despite wide differences in the experiences of teenagers around the world, adolescent peer groups tend to be described by a fairly small set of stereotypic names: jocks, brains, loners, druggies, nerds, and other not-so-flattering designations.

PARENTS VERSUS PEERS The impact of parents versus peers on young people has become a controversial topic in developmental psychology. People often describe individuals as "coming from a good home" or as having "fallen in with the wrong crowd"; these clichés reflect the importance placed on both parents and peers in influencing an individual. Judith Rich Harris (1995) has suggested that beyond choosing where to live and what schools to send their children to, parents contribute surprisingly little to children's social development. In fact, after reviewing numerous psychological studies, Harris concluded that parents have "no important long-term effects on the development of their child's personality" (p. 458). As mentioned in Chapter 3 and discussed in greater detail in Chapter 13, once you control for shared genes, siblings raised in the same house are no more alike than strangers plucked off the street. Likewise, twin studies indicate that growing up with the same parents has only a small influence on personality.

Harris has posited that a child's peers are the most important influence when it comes to socialization. Harris's work is based largely on her *group socialization theory*, which posits that children learn two sets of behaviors, one set for inside the home and one set for outside. The behaviors and responses children learn inside the home, typically those taught by their parents early in life, are not useful in outside social contexts. According to Harris, only those behaviors learned outside the home have long-term effects on personality and on adult behavioral outcomes. Although Harris's theoretical stance has received a great deal of criticism, it has stimulated a fresh look at children's social lives and peers' important influence on children.

In contrast to Harris's theory, much research has confirmed that parents have substantial influence throughout an individual's life. Significantly, researchers have emphasized that neither the peer group nor the family can be assigned the primary role in a child's social development. Instead, the two contexts play complementary roles. B. Bradford Brown and his colleagues (1993) have argued that parents' influence can be direct or indirect. Parents not only contribute to specific individual behaviors but also affect social development indirectly by influencing the choices the child makes about what kind of crowd to join. In observations of 695 young people from childhood through adolescence, Robert and Beverly Cairns (1994) found that parents and teachers played a major role in realigning social groups so they were consistent with family norms. Thus parents and peers seem to be important in children's development.

Parental Style Can Affect Children's Well-Being

Exactly how important are caregivers in shaping the developing child? Do parents affect their children's well-being? Most parents believe their actions profoundly affect how their children turn out and want their children to turn out well, so for their children's sake they sacrifice time, effort, and money. Although some scholars, such as Harris, believe parents' importance has been overemphasized, parenting clearly matters at the extremes, when children are celebrated or when they are abused. Genie, the girl discussed at this chapter's opening, would have turned out quite differently had her parents not abused her. But the evidence suggests that even beyond such extremes caregivers influence children's social development.

Important support for the significance of child/parent interaction comes from the New York Longitudinal Study, begun in 1956 by Stella Chess and Alexander Thomas. The study ran for six years, assessing 141 children from 85 middle- to upper-middle-class families. Chess and Thomas (1984) focused on what they considered the crucial ingredient in child/parent interaction: each child's biologically based temperament, as a combination of typical mood, activity level, and emotional reactivity. For example, general fussiness is not necessarily a signal of a child's temperament type; instead, the frequency of the fussiness as well as the intensity of the fussiness and how easily it can be controlled are better indicators. (The concept of temperament is explored more fully in Chapter 13, "Personality.")

Chess and Thomas found that the fit between the child's temperament and the parents' behaviors is most important in determining social development. For instance, most parents find it frustrating to raise a difficult child, who will tend to have negative moods and a hard time adapting to new situations. Parents who openly demonstrate their frustration with their child's behavior or insist on exposing the child to conflict often unwittingly encourage negative behaviors. For example, if the child is extremely uneasy about entering a new setting, pushing the child can lead to behavioral problems. If the child is very distractible, forcing him or her to concentrate for long periods may lead to emotional upset. In the study, parents who responded to a difficult child calmly, firmly, patiently, and consistently tended to have the most positive outcomes. These parents tended not to engage in self-blame for their child's negative behaviors, and they managed to cope with their own frustration with and disappointment in their child. Chess and Thomas also noted that overprotectiveness can encourage a child's anxiety in response to a new situation, thereby escalating the child's distress. Ultimately, then, the best style of parenting is dynamic and flexible, takes into account the parents' personalities, the child's temperament, and the particular situation.

Other research has shown that parents have multiple influences on their children's attitudes, values, and religious beliefs. Children learn about the world in part from the attitudes expressed by their parents, such as prejudices regarding certain groups of people. Especially nurturing parents tend to raise children who experience more-social emotions, such as appropriate guilt, perhaps because the parents encourage an empathetic attitude toward others. Parents also help determine the neighborhoods in which their children live, the schools they attend, and the extracurricular activities that provide exercise and stimulation—all of which will likely influence the child subtly and not so subtly. Thus, for example, parents who avoid or limit television, regularly go on family hikes, and participate in various sports may have children who are more physically fit than those who plunk their children down in front of the television for hours per day. Of course, nature might contribute to these differences as well: Athletic people might possess genes that promote fitness and pass them along to their children, who might respond positively to being active because they have a genetic predisposition to liking exercise and benefiting from it. As shown throughout this book, biological and environmental influences interact to produce behavior.

Divorce Is Difficult for Children

The rise in divorce rates since the 1960s has prompted concern about divorce's effects on children. In the United States, nearly half of all marriages end in divorce, and each year nearly one million children experience their parents' divorce (Bramlett & Mosher, 2002). The overall picture that emerges from research suggests that divorce is associated with numerous problems for children (**FIGURE 11.31**). Although some children—especially intelligent, socially mature, and responsible ones—cope very well with their parents' divorces, the experience can be quite difficult for many others (Hetherington, Bridges, & Insabella, 1998). Compared with children whose parents stay together, those whose parents divorce tend to do less well in school, have more conduct disorders and psychological problems, and have poor social relations and low self-esteem (Amato, 2001). Children of divorce are also more likely to get divorced as adults, a phenomenon suggesting either that divorce's negative effects continue after childhood or that parents pass on genes to their children predisposing the children to divorce (e.g., by producing particular temperaments). Either way, why is divorce associated with so many negative outcomes?

Divorce may damage a child's relationship with one or both parents, as when the parent with custody moves far away from or restricts contact with the non-custodial parent. The child then loses a potentially important source of both emotional support and guidance. But children who live in households filled with conflict might have psychological problems whether or not their parents stay together.

FIGURE 11.31 Divorce Divorce can be associated with numerous problems for children when it creates conflict and depression in the household. The parents in this divorced family take turns staying in the family house with their children.

Perhaps people who get divorced differ in important ways from those who stay married—they may be more irritable or depressed or may have difficulty coping with conflict, and these personal factors may interfere with their ability to be effective parents. Maybe all these things contribute to negative outcomes for the children of divorce. So what does research show about why divorce is harmful to children?

The past 30 years have seen a significant decline in two-parent families. Approximately one-third of all children born in the United States in 2002 had unwed mothers (Munson & Sutton, 2004). Although children with two parents fare best, children who lose a parent through death have fewer problems than children of divorce (Amato & Keith, 1991). Children raised by single mothers, though, share many of the problems of children of divorce (Clarke-Stewart, Vandell, McCartney, Owen, & Booth, 2000). The overall evidence indicates that the absence of a biological father is associated with a number of negative outcomes (Dunn, 2004). One study found that girls raised without fathers were much more likely to initiate early sexual activity and were much more likely to become pregnant at a young age (Ellis et al., 2003). However, having a stepfather does not resolve these problems—if anything, living with a stepparent may be associated with an increase in psychological problems (Amato & Keith, 1991). Thus two parents are not always better than one.

Why might children of divorce and children raised by single parents be at a disadvantage compared with children from two-parent homes? An alarming number of single mothers live in poverty, and many rely on assistance to provide for their children's basic needs. For mothers and their children, divorce is often associated with a significant decline in financial resources, and such economic decline predicts at least some of divorce's negative outcomes on children. In the United States, within two years of getting divorced, women's family income declines by an average of almost 25 percent (Kunz Center, 2005). Mothers threatened with poverty need to devote considerable time and energy to obtaining money, and their efforts may leave them feeling so overburdened, stressed, and hassled that they have little time or energy for parenting. When the father stays involved in the family economically and emotionally, divorce's effect is reduced considerably (Pett, Wampold, Turner, & Vaughan-Cole, 1999).

Do divorce's economic consequences make it better to stay married for the sake of the children? Just because people do not get divorced does not mean they are happily married. Frequent arguments, fighting, and even physical abuse characterize some long-term marriages. The available evidence suggests that living in a high-conflict family is associated with even greater negative outcomes than is parental divorce (Amato & Keith, 1991). If it is not divorce but living in conflict that causes problems, then children should show the negative outcomes associated with divorce well before the parents separate. Indeed, longitudinal studies offer evidence of greater behavioral and emotional problems among children whose parents later divorce compared with those whose parents stay together (Clarke-Stewart et al., 2000).

In thinking about divorce, keep in mind that data are always about group averages; even if, on average, divorce negatively affects children, many children of divorce do just fine. If your parents have divorced, you are not doomed to being divorced yourself. (Recall the critical skill, discussed above, of not confusing *some* with *all;* this skill might seem simple, but in specific contexts people can be misled by automatically applying group results to themselves or to any single person.) Since some of divorce's negative effects on children are known to result from the reduced income following divorce, feelings of abandonment and turmoil, and the parental hostility surrounding divorce, parents and others can take many actions to reduce these negative effects. Both mothers and fathers need to remain actively involved in their children's lives; parents need to learn how to reduce the turmoil that accompanies divorce by working out arrangements in the children's best interests. On a societal level, newly divorced parents may need financial aid, and/or job training, to avoid poverty. Although divorce is never easy, parents must work together to minimize its impact on their children.

Recognizing and Avoiding Either/Or Thinking

The Caston brothers share unfortunate bonds (**FIGURE 11.32**). As boys, all three suffered neglect and abuse. Now grown, they are in prison for separate murders. Not all neglected and abused children become hardened criminals, and not all hardened criminals were neglected and abused. However, 48 percent of state prisoners report that at least one family member has spent time in prison (Johnson, 2008). How can we understand the forces that cause members of the same family to murder or commit other crimes? Is it nature or nurture that leads people into crime? This question often arises when complex psychological phenomena are discussed.

The nature/nurture question is one example of either/or thinking. Two choices are offered with the implication that one is correct, one is incorrect, and there are no other options. Either/or thinking, also called black-and-white thinking, is the tendency to see issues as falling into one of two categories, whereas complex topics almost always involve shades of gray. Either/or thinking is sometimes difficult to recognize in context. For example, a 2007 survey from a member of the U.S. Congress asked constituents if they were in favor of amnesty for aliens who were in the United States illegally or whether illegal aliens should be deported as quickly as possible. When presented with two choices, most people select the alternative that seems better and do not consider other possibilities. Every time you are presented with an either/or choice, stop to consider other possibilities to avoid being misled into automatically accepting the idea that there are only two possible options (**FIGURE 11.33**). Most complex problems have many possible solutions.

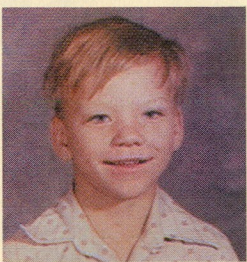
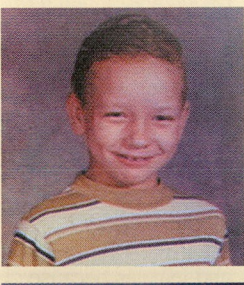
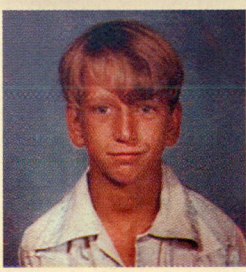

FIGURE 11.32 Caston Brothers
All three Caston brothers (top to bottom: Jesse, Frank, and Sonny) would grow up to be convicted of separate murders.

FIGURE 11.33

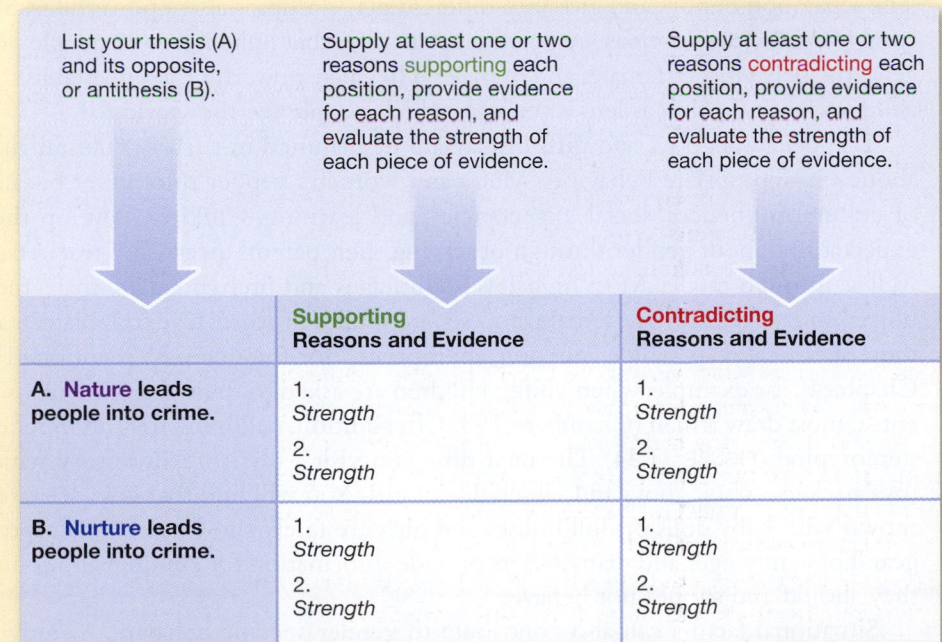

List your thesis (A) and its opposite, or antithesis (B).	Supply at least one or two reasons supporting each position, provide evidence for each reason, and evaluate the strength of each piece of evidence.	Supply at least one or two reasons contradicting each position, provide evidence for each reason, and evaluate the strength of each piece of evidence.
	Supporting Reasons and Evidence	**Contradicting** Reasons and Evidence
A. Nature leads people into crime.	1. *Strength* 2. *Strength*	1. *Strength* 2. *Strength*
B. Nurture leads people into crime.	1. *Strength* 2. *Strength*	1. *Strength* 2. *Strength*

"Do you know its sexual identity?"

gender identity Personal beliefs about whether one is male or female.

gender roles The characteristics associated with males and females because of cultural influence or learning.

gender schemas Cognitive structures that influence how people perceive the behaviors of females and males.

FIGURE 11.34 Try for Yourself: The Development of Gender Roles

Which of these toys are intended for boys and which are intended for girls?

Gender Identity Is Determined by Biology and Cultural Norms

How would you define yourself? Which characteristics would you mention? Most people believe that gender—being female or male—is a major component of who they are. Now try to imagine yourself as the same person but a member of the opposite sex. For many of us this is hard to do. But how different are women and men? Certain physical differences are obvious, but how do women and men differ psychologically? According to evolutionary theory, sex differences ought to reflect different adaptive problems men and women have faced, and this notion is generally supported by research. However, since men and women have faced similar adaptive problems, they are similar on most dimensions.

Many differences between males and females have as much to do with socialization as with genetics. Some psychological scientists use the term *sex* to refer to biological differences and the term *gender* for differences between males and females that result from socialization. However, this distinction is not always easy to make, because the biological and psychosocial aspects of being female or male are usually so entwined that we cannot separate them. Each person is treated in certain ways based on his or her biological sex, and each person's behaviors reflect both biological components and social expectations. For example, as discussed in Chapter 3, researchers have identified some differences between the brains of men and of women, but they have not yet determined whether these differences are the result of genetics, of the way girls and boys are treated during development, or, more likely, a combination of both. Nor do we know how or if sex-related brain differences translate into thoughts and actions.

Whether you think of yourself as female or male is your **gender identity,** which shapes how you behave. Children as young as one or two years old can tell you whether they are boys or girls. Once boys and girls discover that they are boys or girls, they seek out activities that are culturally appropriate for their sex. **Gender roles** are culturally defined norms that differentiate behaviors, and attitudes, according to maleness and femaleness. In North American culture, for example, most parents and teachers discourage girls from playing too roughly and boys from crying. The separation of boys and girls into different play groups is also a powerful socializing force. **Gender schemas** are cognitive structures that influence how people perceive the behaviors of females and of males. They play powerful roles in establishing gender identity, acting as lenses through which people see the world.

The behaviors boys and girls display are determined in part by cultural rules about sex-appropriate behaviors. Men's and women's gender roles differ because of cultural influences, social expectancies, and learning. Children develop their expectations about gender through observing their parents, peers, and teachers, as well as through media. Most high-level politicians and firefighters are male, most nurses and secretaries are female, and so on. Children learn to extrapolate from these statistical facts which jobs are "appropriate" for the sexes. As mentioned in Chapter 8, for example, when young children are asked to draw a picture of a scientist, most draw a man (Chambers, 1983). In addition, children's toys often reflect stereotyping (**FIGURE 11.34**). The next time you visit a toy store, inventory which toys' packages depict boys and which depict girls. You will find that boys are rarely shown with baby dolls or doll houses and girls are rarely shown in contact sports gear. These messages and many others provide information for children about how they should and should not behave.

Situational factors can also contribute to gender-specific behavior. A study of young women talking to their boyfriends or their casual male friends on the telephone illustrates how situation can alter gender-related responses. When the women talked to their boyfriends, their voices changed to a higher pitch and became softer and more relaxed than when they talked to their male friends. The way they spoke to their boyfriends was also more babyish, feminine, and absentminded, as rated by objective judges. When asked, the women said they knew they had spoken in two different ways and that they did so to communicate affection for their boyfriends (Montepare & Vega, 1988).

BIOLOGICAL BASES OF SEXUAL IDENTITY On April 27, 1966, Janet and Ron Reimer brought their seven-month-old twins, Bruce and Brian, to St. Boniface Hospital in Winnipeg, Canada, for routine circumcision. Bruce was operated on first, and his penis was badly damaged in a very rare accident during this common and minor procedure. Its condition deteriorated over the next several days, and within the week it had shriveled up and disappeared. (After what happened to Bruce, no attempt was made to circumcise Brian.) The accident and the events that followed changed not only the lives of the Reimer family but also psychologists' beliefs about the concept of gender.

As recounted in John Colapinto's book *As Nature Made Him: The Boy Who Was Raised as a Girl* (2000), Janet and Ron investigated whether Bruce should undergo sexual reassignment and be raised as a girl. Previous sexual reassignment cases had involved hermaphrodite children, who were born with ambiguous genitalia; the process had never been attempted on a child born with normal genitalia. The Reimers contacted the world-renowned (and controversial) sexologist John Money at Johns Hopkins University, and Money convinced them that sexual reassignment was the best course of action for Bruce's psychological well-being. Bruce was castrated (his testes were removed) when he was 22 months old, renamed Brenda, and raised as a girl (**FIGURE 11.35**). Throughout the 1970s and 1980s, media accounts and psychology textbooks recounted the story as demonstrating that Brenda was happy and well-adjusted and that gender was the result of socialization rather than biology. Unfortunately, Colapinto's recent analysis indicates that Brenda's sexual reassignment was a failure from the start.

Brenda's life can be described as tumultuous at best, hellish at worst. Although her parents let her hair grow long, dressed her in feminine colors and clothing styles, and encouraged her to play with other girls, by all accounts Brenda was not comfortable or happy being a girl. She was teased incessantly for her roughness and aggressiveness. Brenda grew even more uncomfortable after receiving hormones at age 11 to initiate the development of secondary sexual characteristics. The development of her breasts resulted in intense embarrassment and horror for Brenda that did not fade with time.

As the years passed, Janet and Ron were finally forced to consider that Brenda was not—nor would ever truly be—a girl. After 15 years of family and peer problems and intense psychological troubles, Brenda was told the truth about what had happened. A flood of emotions welled up within her, but the most overwhelming feeling was relief. As Brenda later recalled, "I was relieved. Suddenly it all made sense why I felt the way I did. I wasn't some sort of weirdo. I wasn't crazy."

Brenda immediately decided to return to being male. She stopped hormone therapy. She changed her name to David, which she chose because of the biblical story of David and Goliath. New surgical techniques allowed physicians to provide David with a functional artificial penis that could be used for sexual intercourse. At age 23, he met and married a woman with three children, and for many years he lived an apparently happy family life (**FIGURE 11.36**). After a while, however, his marriage failed, and a series of financial setbacks along with the death of his twin brother led him to become despondent. David killed himself in May 2004 at age 38. Most psychologists believe the stress of being a boy raised as a girl contributed to identity problems that

FIGURE 11.35 Brian and Bruce Reimer This photo shows Brian and Bruce (Brenda) Reimer as children. Only his short haircut distinguishes Brian as the boy. The fact that they were identical twins made the situation ideal for studying the effects of culture on gender identity.

FIGURE 11.36 David (Bruce) Reimer This photo shows David (Bruce) living as a man.

troubled him throughout his adult life. The lesson from David's life is that gender identity is not shaped solely by whether a person is treated as a boy or as a girl; biology has a strong effect on whether people identify as female or male. In hindsight, it seems clear that simply changing the sexuality of a child's genitals will not turn that person from a boy into a girl or vice versa, but the general ideas of the 1960s favored environmental explanations for most differences between men and women.

People Define Themselves in Terms of Race and Ethnicity

How individuals develop a sense of their own and others' racial and ethnic identities is an important component of social development. Researchers have studied how children learn the racial and ethnic categories prevalent in their community, identify their own race and ethnic group, and form stable attitudes toward their own and others' groups (Spencer & Markstrom-Adams, 1990).

Several studies have demonstrated that by three months of age, infants can discern racial differences in the faces of strangers (Bar-Haim, Ziv, Lamy, & Hodes, 2006). The researchers recorded how long young infants—Caucasian ones and ones of African (black) descent—looked at African faces and Causcasian faces. Infants generally looked longer at faces from their own race, a finding the researchers interpreted as a preference for the infants' own race. The only infants who did not show this pattern were children of African (black) descent who were living in a predominantly Caucasian culture. These children did not seem to prefer faces of either race. The researchers theorized that this cross-race finding was caused by high levels of interracial contact during the first three months of life (**FIGURE 11.37**).

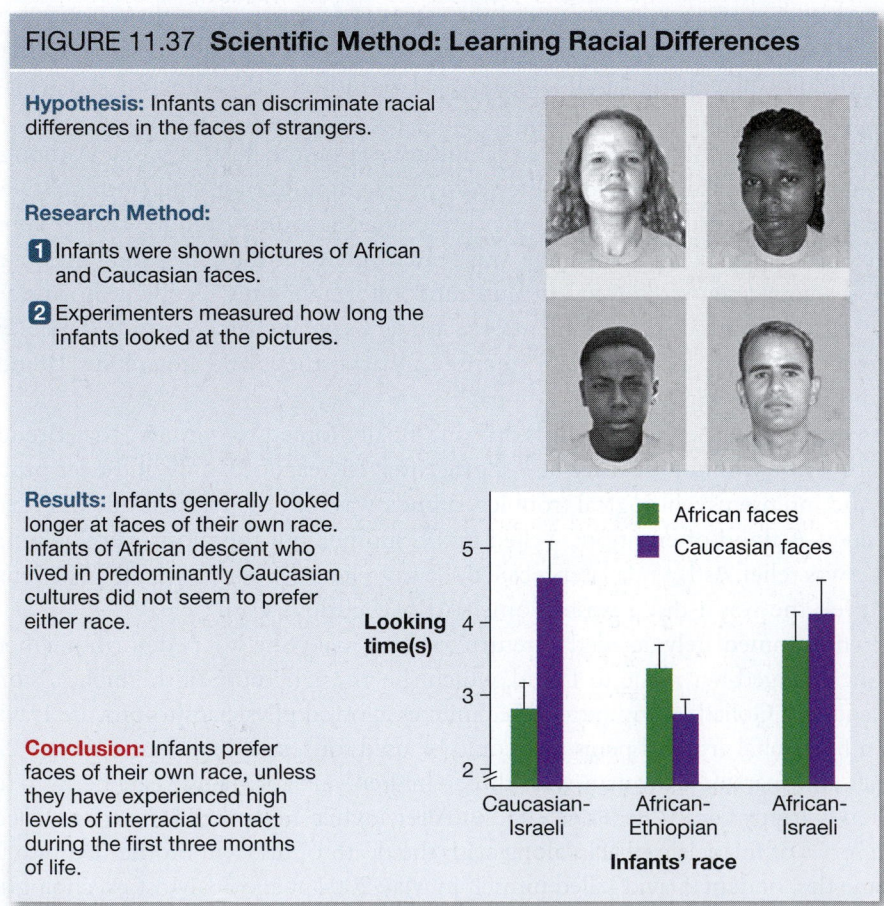

FIGURE 11.37 Scientific Method: Learning Racial Differences

Hypothesis: Infants can discriminate racial differences in the faces of strangers.

Research Method:

1 Infants were shown pictures of African and Caucasian faces.

2 Experimenters measured how long the infants looked at the pictures.

Results: Infants generally looked longer at faces of their own race. Infants of African descent who lived in predominantly Caucasian cultures did not seem to prefer either race.

Conclusion: Infants prefer faces of their own race, unless they have experienced high levels of interracial contact during the first three months of life.

The process of identity formation in a country such as the United States, where people of so many races and ethnicities live together, is particularly complicated. Because of prejudice and discrimination and the accompanying barriers to economic opportunities, children of ethnic minorities often face challenges with regard to the development of their ethnic identities. Children entering middle childhood have acquired an awareness of their ethnic identities to the extent that they know the labels and attributes that the dominant culture applies to their ethnic groups. Many researchers believe that during middle childhood and adolescence, children in ethnic minority groups often engage in additional processes aimed at ethnic identity formation (Phinney, 1990). The factors that influence these processes vary widely among individuals and groups.

The increase in interracial relationships in the United States and many other countries means that a growing proportion of the population is racially mixed, and people increasingly identify themselves as biracial and multiracial to reflect their full racial and ethnic heritages. The golfer Tiger Woods, for example, refers to his multiracial identity as "Cablinasian," a term he invented to reflect his mother's being Thai and his father's being a mix of African American, Caucasian, and Native American. More and more people respond to questions of racial and ethnic identity by refusing to be pigeonholed into one category.

 SUMMING UP

How Do Children and Adolescents Develop Their Identities?

How people define themselves is influenced by cultural beliefs about factors such as race, sex, and age. Even young children classify themselves on the basis of biological sex, but how they come to understand the meaning of being a boy or a girl is largely determined through their socialization into gender roles, in which children adopt behaviors viewed as appropriate for their sex. Adolescents struggle for identity by questioning social values and personal goals, as they try to figure out who they are and what they want to become. Moral development helps people define what they value and what is important to them. Race and ethnicity shape our beliefs and attitudes regarding how we fit into the cultures in which we are raised.

MEASURING UP

1. Choose the statement that is true about divorce.
   a. Children of divorce probably should not get married because they are likely to get divorced.
   b. No data show negative effects of divorce on children.
   c. Parents should always stay together for the sake of their children.
   d. Reduced income and, often, poverty follow divorce and may be responsible for some of the negative effects of divorce on children.

2. The case study of Bruce/Brenda Reimer shows that _____.
   a. gender identity has a strong biological component
   b. gender identity depends almost completely on the way a child is raised
   c. it is fairly easy to teach children they are girls when biologically they are boys or to teach them they are boys when biologically they are girls
   d. changing a child's name after the child has learned her or his name can cause problems with gender identity

LEARNING OBJECTIVES
Describe Erikson's life challenges that mark adult development.

List and describe the cognitive changes that occur as we age.

What Brings Meaning to Adulthood?

For many years, developmental psychologists focused on childhood and adolescence, as if most important aspects of development occurred by age twenty. In recent decades, researchers working in a wide range of fields have demonstrated that important changes in physiology, in cognition, and in social behavior continue throughout adulthood into old age. Therefore, many contemporary psychological scientists consider development from a life-span perspective, trying to understand how mental activity and social relations change over the entire course of life. Such research shows that we should not equate growing old with despair. In fact, many positive things happen as we grow older. Although aging is associated with significant cognitive and physical decline, it is an important part of life and can be very meaningful. And as medical advances allow people to live longer, understanding old age becomes especially important.

One of the first researchers to take this approach was Erik Erikson, who proposed a theory of development emphasizing age-related psychological processes and their effects on social functioning across the life span. Erikson thought of identity development as composed of eight stages, which ranged from an infant's first year to old age (TABLE 11.1). He further conceptualized each stage as having a developmental "crisis," or development challenge to be confronted. Each challenge provides an opportunity for psychological progress, but if progress is not made, further psychosocial development is impaired. This section focuses on the three of Erikson's stages that take place during adulthood.

Erikson's sixth stage, *intimacy versus isolation,* involves the challenge of forming and maintaining committed friendships and romantic relationships. Essentially, it involves finding someone with whom to share your life. The seventh stage, *generativity versus stagnation,* takes place during middle life. This stage involves producing or giving back to society, and it usually includes parenthood or engaging in activities, such as volunteering, that bring additional meaning to life. Erikson's last

Table 11.1 Erikson's Stages of Identity

STAGE	AGE	IDENTITY CHALLENGE	SUCCESSFUL RESOLUTION OF CHALLENGE
Infancy	0–2	Trust versus mistrust	Children learn that the world is safe and that people are loving and reliable.
Toddler	2–3	Autonomy versus shame and doubt	Encouraged to explore the environment, children gain feelings of independence and positive self-esteem.
Preschool	4–6	Initiative versus guilt	Children develop a sense of purpose by taking on responsibilities, but also develop the capacity to feel guilty for misdeeds.
Childhood	7–12	Industry versus inferiority	By working successfully with others, children learn to feel competent.
Adolescence	13–19	Ego identity versus role confusion	By exploring different social roles, adolescents develop a sense of identity.
Young adulthood	20s	Intimacy versus isolation	Young adults gain the ability to commit to long-term relationships.
Middle adulthood	30s to 50s	Generativity versus stagnation	Adults gain a sense that they are contributing to the future and caring for future generations.
Old age	60s and beyond	Integrity versus despair	Older adults feel a sense of satisfaction that they have lived a good life and developed wisdom.

stage, *integrity versus despair*, takes place in old age. Integrity refers to a sense of honesty about oneself. In this stage, older adults reflect on their lives and respond either positively to having had a worthwhile life or with regret and sadness at what has passed. Having a good life could be defined as having intimate relations, giving back to society, and viewing one's life with a sense of integrity. Erikson's theory highlights the way people care about different things as they grow older. The following sections examine the physical, cognitive, and social changes that occur during adulthood and how they affect people's quality of life.

Adults Are Affected by Life Transitions

For many young people, college is a magical time of life: meeting new friends, learning new ideas, having a good time—all as adolescence emerges into adulthood. People in their twenties and thirties undergo significant changes as they pursue career goals and make long-term commitments in relationships, as in getting married and raising children. All this corresponds to Erikson's idea that we face challenges as we mature through adulthood. In essence, the major challenges of adulthood reflect the need to find meaning in our lives. If life involved only getting up in the morning, working, eating, and sleeping, what would be the point? Most people seek more than that from life. They want jobs that fulfill them, and they want family members to share their lives.

CAREER   Children commonly are asked what they want to be when they grow up. Although some college students are committed to achieving specific career goals, many others struggle to find careers they hope will be satisfying. Most people work approximately 100,000 hours in their lives, so a career plays an important role in their overall happiness. A "good job" not only provides material rewards but also brings a sense of accomplishment and purpose. The right career helps you feel that you contribute to society and that other people recognize you for doing so. It brings meaning to your life and helps you grow as a person and become better able to fulfill your life's goals. So how do you find the right job?

Selecting a career path is rarely easy. Sometimes, people who have been toiling in corporate or professional jobs have midlife crises in which they realize that their jobs fail to bring them any meaningful satisfaction. Such situations may result when people focus on making money rather than on finding the right job that will allow them to be the type of person, spouse, parent, or community member they want to be. Career counselors often advise people to follow their passions rather than the wishes of parents or family members. You do not necessarily need a specific plan, but you must be honest with yourself: Assess your strengths and weaknesses and try to develop a general idea of the kind of career you can pursue effectively and are likely to find fulfilling. From Erikson's perspective, the desire for generativity inspires us to want to give something of ourselves to society. The right career allows us to pursue our interests and gain a sense of accomplishment while balancing family and other life goals.

MARRIAGE   In adulthood, people devote a great deal of effort to achieving and maintaining satisfying relationships. Indeed, the vast majority of people around the world marry at some point in their lives or form some type of permanent bond with a relationship partner, although people today marry later in life and the percentage who marry is declining slowly in most industrialized countries. The search for the right partner is an important feature in contemporary Western cultures, while in many Eastern cultures parents (and other elders) decide whom their sons and daughters will marry. It is hard for many Westerners to imagine, but arranged marriages tend to be stable, and in general the people who marry this way report being quite satisfied.

As discussed in Chapter 10, marriage has many health advantages. Numerous theories account for married people's longevity, most of them focusing on the ways marital partners can support each other, such as helping each other deal with stress or assisting each other in meeting life's demands. Married people may also influence their partners' healthful behavior by encouraging them to eat properly, to get exercise, and so on. In an international study of marriage and subjective well-being, involving more than 59,000 people from 42 countries, researchers found that marriage's effect on well-being was fairly similar in all the countries studied despite their diversity (Diener, Gohm, Suh, & Oishi, 2000). Not only were there cross-cultural similarities in response to marriage, but men and women derived approximately equal benefits from marriage (**FIGURE 11.38**). One small difference among countries was the finding that the benefits of being married compared with being divorced were slightly higher in collectivist countries, which emphasize the common good and group values rather than individual achievement. (Countries considered collectivist in the study included China, South Korea, Nigeria, Turkey, and Brazil. Individualist countries included the United States, Great Britain, the Netherlands, Canada, and Switzerland.)

According to national surveys, at any given time the vast majority of married people report satisfaction with their marriages. Those reporting the most satisfaction have sufficient economic resources, share decision making, and together hold the view that marriage should be a lifelong commitment (Amato, Johnson, Booth, & Rogers, 2003). Yet, as mentioned above, in contemporary American society

FIGURE 11.38 Marriage across Cultures
Notice the similarities and differences at the marriages of **(a)** a Sami couple in Norway, **(b)** an Amhara couple in Ethiopia, and **(c)** a Hani couple in China.

(a)

(b)

(c)

approximately half of all marriages end in divorce. (A slight decline in the divorce rate over the last few years may be attributable to factors such as the increasing number of adults who are not marrying and the later ages at which people are marrying.)

HAVING CHILDREN   According to Erikson, one major way that people satisfy the challenge of generativity is through having children. The arrival of a first child is a profound event for most couples, changing their lives in almost every respect. Responding to an infant's cries and trying to figure out why the child is distressed often cause anxiety and frustration for first-time parents. But new parents also experience great joys—seeing a baby's first social smile, watching the first few tentative steps, and hearing a child say "Mommy" or "Daddy" provide powerful reinforcement for parents. Parents often become immersed in their children's lives, making sure the children have playmates, exposing them to new experiences, and trying to make them happy and healthy. Being a parent is central to many adults' self-definitions.

Many people are eager to have children, but research shows that children can strain marriages, especially when time and money are tight. A consistent finding is that couples with children, especially with adolescent children, report less marital satisfaction than those who are childless (Belsky, 1990). Although satisfaction might be lower, the marriages of those with children appear to be more stable. For many people, having children is not about happiness but about redefining their lives to reflect the value they place on family. They look forward to coaching their kids in sports, encouraging them in school, and watching them grow up, have careers, get married, and provide grandchildren. For many people, along with career and marriage, give life meaning.

Aging Can Be Successful

In Western societies, people are living much longer, and the number of people over age 85 is growing dramatically. Indeed, it is becoming commonplace for people to live beyond 100. By 2030, more than 1 in 5 Americans will be over age 65, and these older people will be ethnically diverse, well educated, and physically fit. With this "graying" of the population in Western societies, much greater research attention has been paid to the lives of people over age 60.

The elderly contribute much to modern society. For instance, nearly 40 percent of U.S. federal judges are over 65, and they handle about 20 percent of the caseload (Markon, 2001). Many older adults work productively well past their seventies. Our view of the elderly is likely to change a great deal as the baby boom generation ages. Consider music stars—such as Bruce Springsteen, Tina Turner, and the Rolling Stones—who remain popular and vibrant well into their fifties, sixties, and beyond, certainly in defiance of common stereotypes of old people (**FIGURE 11.39**).

However, the body and mind inevitably start deteriorating slowly at about age 50. Trivial physical changes include the graying and whitening of hair and the wrinkling of skin. Some of the most serious changes affect the brain, whose frontal lobes shrink proportionally more than other brain regions. Although scientists once believed that cognitive problems such as confusion and memory loss were an inevitable, normal part of aging, they now recognize that most older adults remain alert as they grow older, although they do everything a bit more slowly. Older adults who experience a dramatic loss in mental ability often suffer from *dementia,* a brain condition in which thinking, memory, and behavior deteriorate progressively.

FIGURE 11.39 Changing Views of the Elderly The Rolling Stones, now in their 60s, have been making music for over 40 years. If they continue to rock as senior citizens, will we have to revise our sense of "the elderly"?

Dementia has many causes, including excessive alcohol intake and HIV, but for older adults the major causes are Alzheimer's disease and small strokes that affect the brain's blood supply. After age 70, the risk of dementia increases with each year of life. Approximately 3 percent to 5 percent of people will develop Alzheimer's disease by age 70 to 75, and then the proportion of people with the disease doubles every five years. The cause of Alzheimer's is not currently known, but evidence suggests that genes contribute to its development. One gene involved in cholesterol functioning has been shown to be predictive of Alzheimer's, although how this gene is related to the disease is not currently known (Corder et al., 1993). The initial symptoms of Alzheimer's disease are typically minor memory impairments, but the disease eventually progresses to more serious difficulties, such as forgetting daily routines. Eventually, the person loses all mental capacities, including memory and language (**FIGURE 11.40**).

Despite the physical, social, and emotional challenges of aging, most older adults are surprisingly healthy and happy. Indeed, some individuals thrive in old age, especially those with adequate financial resources and good health (Crosnoe & Elder, 2002). Most older adults consider themselves in good health. Moreover, older adults report being just as satisfied with life, if not more so, than younger adults (Mroczek & Kolarz, 1998). Indeed, except for dementia, older adults have fewer mental health problems, including depression, than younger adults.

According to the psychologist Laura Carstensen's *socioemotional selectivity theory*, as people grow older they perceive time to be limited and therefore adjust their priorities to emphasize emotionally meaningful events, experiences, and goals (Carstensen, 1995; Fung & Carstensen, 2004). For instance, they may choose to spend more time with a smaller group of close friends and avoid new people. They may spend an increasing amount of time reflecting on their lives and sharing memories with family members and friends. As they reminisce about their lives, older adults report more positive than negative emotions (Pasupathi & Carstensen, 2003). In essence, older adults want to savor their final years by putting their time and effort into meaningful and rewarding experiences.

According to Erikson, older adults find meaning by looking back and evaluating what they have done with their lives. To the extent that they consider their time well spent, older adults are satisfied and can live their final years gracefully. The crisis at this stage can be triggered by events that highlight the mortal nature of human life, such as the death of a spouse or close friend, or by changing social and occu-

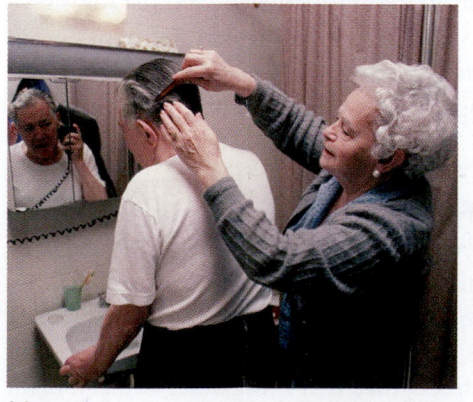

(a)

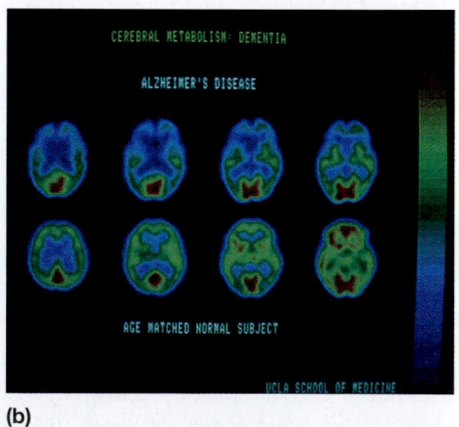

(b)

FIGURE 11.40 Alzheimer's Disease (a) A wife helps her husband, who is an Alzheimer's patient. **(b)** These PET scans compare the brain of an Alzheimer's patient with a healthy brain.

pational roles, such as retirement. Resolving such challenges allows people to come to terms with the reality of death. Although people of all ages are concerned with the meaning of life, it often becomes a preoccupation for the elderly.

Cognition Changes during Aging

Cognitive abilities eventually decline with age, but it is difficult to pinpoint exactly what causes the decline. One of the most consistent and identifiable changes is a slowing of mental processing speed. Experiments that test the time it takes to process a sensory input and react with a motor response show an increase in response time as early as an individual's mid-twenties (Era, Jokela, & Heikkinen, 1986). This increase becomes more rapid as the individual ages. Some sensory-perceptual changes occur with age and may account for some of the observed decline. For instance, as we age, our sensitivity to visual contrast decreases, so activities such as climbing stairs or driving at night may become more difficult and more dangerous. Sensitivity to sound also decreases with age, especially the ability to tune out background noise. This change may make older people seem confused or forgetful when they simply are not able to hear adequately. Aging also affects memory and intelligence, as discussed below.

MEMORY   Older people have difficulty with memory tasks that require the ability to juggle multiple pieces of information at the same time. Tasks in which attention is divided, such as driving while listening to the radio, also prove difficult. Some scientists believe these deficits reflect a decreased ability to store multiple pieces of information in working memory simultaneously (Salthouse, 1992). Consistent evidence indicates that the frontal lobes, which play an important role in working memory (see Chapter 7, "Attention and Memory"), typically shrink as people grow older, and many other cognitive skills that rely on the frontal lobes show impairment with advancing age.

Generally speaking, long-term memory is less affected by aging than is short-term or working memory, although certain aspects of long-term memory appear to suffer in advanced age. Older people often need more time to learn new information, but once they learn it, they use it as efficiently as younger people. The elderly also are better at recognition than at retrieval tasks. For example, they have no trouble recognizing words that have been shown to them if they are asked, "Did you see the word *cat*?" But if they are asked what word they saw, or whether they saw an animal name, they do not do as well. Consistent with the socioemotional selection theory is the finding that older people show better memory for positive than for negative information (Kennedy, Mather, & Carstensen, 2004), perhaps because they selectively ignore negative events (Mather & Carstensen, 2003).

Why do older adults show poor memory? Do they use less efficient strategies for encoding information to be remembered? In an intriguing study, Jessica Logan and colleagues (2002) examined the memory processes of adults in their twenties and adults in their seventies and eighties. As expected, the older adults performed worse than the young adults. They showed less activation in left hemisphere brain areas known to support memory and greater activation in right hemisphere areas that do not aid memory. In a second study, the researchers sought to determine whether the memory deficit could be reduced if they gave the older subjects a strategy to improve memorization. As discussed in Chapter 7, the more deeply an item is encoded, the better it is remembered. Accordingly, the researchers asked older participants to classify words as concrete or abstract, a strategy that leads to deeper

encoding. Undertaking this classification produced better memory and greater activation of the left frontal regions. These findings suggest that one reason for the decline in memory observed with aging is that older adults tend not to use strategies that facilitate memory, which raises the possibility that cognitive training might be useful for postponing age-related memory deficits.

INTELLIGENCE Research has indicated consistently that intelligence, as measured on standard psychometric tests, declines with advanced age. As we age, do we really lose IQ points? Or do older people just have a shorter attention span or lack the motivation to complete such tests? As discussed in Chapter 8, some researchers have distinguished between fluid intelligence and crystallized intelligence (Horn & Hofer, 1992). Many standardized tests measure fluid intelligence, the ability to process new general information that requires no specific prior knowledge (as in recognizing an analogy or arranging blocks to match a picture). Associated with speed of mental processing, fluid intelligence tends to peak in early adulthood and decline steadily as we age. Crystallized intelligence refers to more-specific knowledge, which must be learned or memorized, such as vocabulary, or knowledge of specialized information or reasoning strategies. This type of intelligence usually increases throughout life and breaks down only when declines in other cognitive abilities prevent new information from being processed.

The Seattle Longitudinal Study addressed the question of aging's effects on intelligence, tracking adults age 25 to 81 over seven years and administering tests of cognitive abilities such as verbal and mathematical skills (Schaie, 1990). The study found that intellectual decline does not occur until people are in their sixties or seventies. Further, people who were healthy and remained mentally active demonstrated less decline. Although memory and the speed of processing may decline, the continued ability to learn new information may mitigate those losses in terms of daily functioning. There has been a great deal of excitement lately about the possibility that active social engagement may help older adults maintain their cognitive abilities. For instance, older adults who have more extensive social contacts and remain active through leisure pursuits may be less susceptible to dementia and Alzheimer's disease (Fratiglioni, Paillard-Borg, & Winblad, 2004). Because life expectancies are much longer today than ever before, much more research is likely to be devoted to understanding how people can maintain their cognitive capacities to get the most out of their final years.

SUMMING UP

What Brings Meaning to Adulthood?

Researchers increasingly have been studying humans across the entire life span, from conception to old age. Adulthood requires people to meet certain challenges, such as establishing a career, getting married, and raising a family. An overriding theme that emerges from studying life transitions is that people seek meaning in their lives and that they do so increasingly as they age. Although older adults are often characterized as feeble and senile, they are for the most part healthy, alert, and vital. Indeed, one of the biggest surprises in recent research is the finding that older people are often more satisfied with their lives than are younger adults. Despite declines in memory and speed of mental processing, humans generally maintain their intelligence into very old age, especially if they engage in social and mental activities that help keep their mental skills in shape.

1. Erikson proposed that certain challenges typify the passage through adulthood to old age. Which of the following statements represents these challenges?
   a. As adults, we have the challenge of making a living and caring for our children and other family members.
   b. Across all societies, people have to face the challenge created by a limited life span.
   c. In adulthood, people face the challenge of creating and maintaining close relationships, giving back to society, and responding well to the lives they have lived.
   d. Adults face spiritual challenges that can cause midlife crises and depression.

2. Indicate whether the following statements describe cognitive aging. Either mark the statement "CA" or leave it blank.
   _____ a. Measures of fluid intelligence decline.
   _____ b. Measures of crystallized intelligence decline.
   _____ c. Working (short-term) memory declines.
   _____ d. Declines in long-term memory are usually the earliest signs of cognitive aging.
   _____ e. The frontal lobes of the brain shrink throughout adulthood.
   _____ f. Speed of learning remains mostly unchanged until very old age.

CONCLUSION

Throughout the journey of human development, the interacting forces of nature and nurture shape us into unique persons. At birth, we are capable of advanced cognitive feats, but our mental processes mature as we do. As the brain develops, especially as the frontal lobes become organized, we become social creatures capable of communicating through language, but we also begin to define ourselves as individuals with specific values, morals, beliefs, hopes, and dreams.

■ CHAPTER SUMMARY

What Shapes a Child?

- **Development Starts in the Womb:** Many factors in the prenatal environment, such as nutrition and hormones, can affect development. Exposure to teratogens (e.g., drugs, alcohol, viruses) can result in death, deformity, or mental disorders.

- **Brain Development Promotes Learning:** Brain development involves both maturation and experience. The brain's plasticity allows changes in the development of connections and in the synaptic pruning of unused neural connections. The timing of experiences necessary for brain development is particularly important in the early years.

- **Attachment Promotes Survival:** The emotional bond that develops between a child and a caregiver increases the child's chances of survival. Attachment styles are generally categorized as secure, avoidant, anxious/ambivalent, and disorganized. At the biological level, the hormone oxytocin facilitates attachment.

How Do Children Learn about Their Worlds?

- **Perception Introduces the World:** Experiments using habituation and the preferential-looking technique have revealed infants' considerable perceptual ability. Vision and hearing develop rapidly as neural circuitry develops.

- **Memory Improves over Childhood:** Infantile memory is limited by a lack of both language ability and autobiographical reference. Source amnesia is common in children. Confabulation, common in young children, may result from underdevelopment of the frontal lobes.

- **Piaget Emphasized Stages of Development:** Jean Piaget proposed that through interaction with the environment, children develop mental schemas and proceed through stages of cognitive development. In the sensorimotor stage, children experience the world through their senses and develop object permanence. In the preoperational stage, children's thinking is dominated by the appearance of objects rather than by logic. In the concrete operational stage, children learn the logic of concrete objects. In the formal operational stage, children become capable of abstract, complex thinking.

- **Infants Have Early Knowledge about the World:** Experiments using the habituation paradigm have revealed that infants innately understand some basic laws of physics and of mathematics.

- **Humans Learn from Interacting with Others:** Being able to infer another's mental state is known as theory of mind. Through socialization, children move from egocentric thinking to being able to take another's perspective.

- **Language Develops in an Orderly Fashion:** Infants can discriminate phonemes. Language proceeds from sounds to words to telegraphic speech to sentences. According to Noam Chomsky, all human languages are governed by universal grammar, an innate set of relations between linguistic elements. According to Lev Vygotsky, social interaction is the force that develops language. For language to develop, a child must be exposed to it during the sensitive period.

How Do Children and Adolescents Develop Their Identities?

- **Social Systems Influence Development:** Urie Bronfenbrenner's biocultural theory of development recognizes four levels of context that affect development: The microsystem includes family and classroom; the exosystem includes less direct forces, such as parents' workplace norms; the macrosystem broadens to cultural aspects such as ethnicity; and the chronosystem consists of sociohistorical context.

- **Friends Influence Identity and Behavior:** Social comparisons help shape children's development.

- **Parental Style Can Affect Children's Well-Being:** Although some psychologists believe that parents play a minimal role in their children's development, data show that parents influence many areas of their children's lives, including religiosity and how children experience emotions.

- **Divorce Is Difficult for Childen:** Many children suffer adverse consequences when their parents divorce, but some children manage this life-changing event well. The reduced income following divorce likely contributes to the negative outcomes.

- **Gender Identity Is Determined by Biology and Cultural Norms:** Shaped by biology and culture, gender identity develops in children and shapes their behaviors (i.e., gender roles). Gender schemas are the cognitive constructs of gender.

- **People Define Themselves in Terms of Race and Ethnicity:** By three months of age, infants show a preference for faces of their own race, except for infants reared around large majorities of people from different races. By age four, children begin to categorize themselves and others with regard to race and ethnicity. Ethnic identity is complicated by social prejudice.

What Brings Meaning to Adulthood?

- **Adults Are Affected by Life Transitions:** Erikson believed that people develop throughout the life span and theorized that each stage of life presents important social issues to be resolved. For adults, development focuses on generativity with regard to career and family. Marriage is a central issue, though in Western societies about half of contemporary marriages fail.

- **Aging Can Be Successful:** As the population in many Western societies ages, more research is being done on aging, which inevitably brings physical and mental changes. Dementia has various causes, including Alzheimer's disease. Most older adults are healthy, remain productive, and become selective about their relationships and activities.

- **Cognition Changes during Aging:** Short-term memory, including complex memory and divided attention, is affected by aging. Crystallized intelligence increases; fluid intelligence declines in old age as processing speed declines. Being mentally active and socially engaged preserves cognitive functioning.

■ KEY TERMS

accommodation, p. 487
anxious–ambivalent attachment, p. 480
assimilation, p. 487
attachment, p. 476
avoidant attachment, p. 480

concrete operational stage, p. 489
conventional, p. 494
critical periods, p. 476
developmental psychology, p. 470
disorganized attachment, p. 480

formal operational stage, p. 489
gender identity, p. 508
gender roles, p. 508
gender schemas, p. 508
infantile amnesia, p. 486
object permanence, p. 488
postconventional, p. 494

preconventional, p. 494
preoperational stage, p. 488
secure attachment, p. 479
sensitive periods, p. 476
sensorimotor stage, p. 488

social development, p. 502
synaptic pruning, p. 474
telegraphic speech, p. 498
teratogens, p. 472
theory of mind, p. 492

■ PRACTICE TEST

1. A one-week-old infant normally can _____.
   a. differentiate between sweet and nonsweet tastes
   b. display social smiles
   c. grasp a caregiver's finger
   d. make eye contact
   e. orient toward loud sounds
   f. recognize his or her name
   g. roll over from stomach to back
   h. see a caregiver across the room
   i. turn his or her head toward the smell of the mother's breast milk
   j. turn toward a nipple near his or her mouth

2. Which of the following statements best summarizes the key finding from Harry Harlow's study of infant rhesus monkeys?
   a. Contact with "mothers" who provided food promoted normal cognitive development.
   b. Contact with "mothers" who provided food promoted normal social development.
   c. Contact with comforting "mothers" promoted normal cognitive development.
   d. Contact with comforting "mothers" promoted normal social development.

3. A nine-month-old child watches as three cubes are covered by a panel, then as three more cubes appear to move behind the panel. Once the panel is lifted, only three cubes appear. Which of the following statements describes the infant's likely reaction?
   a. The infant quickly will lose interest in the screen.
   b. The infant will try to grab the three remaining cubes.
   c. The infant will stare at the researcher's face.
   d. The infant will stare at the three remaining cubes for a relatively long time.

4. Imagine reading a young child a story. In the story, Schuyler calls Emma a mean name. Emma retaliates by biting Schuyler. You ask the child what she thinks about the fact that Emma bit Schuyler. Three possible responses appear below. Label each as typical of one of the levels of moral reasoning described by Kohlberg: preconventional, conventional, or postconventional.
   a. "Emma is mad."
   b. "It is not okay to hurt people just because they hurt you."
   c. "It is wrong to bite people. Emma is going to get a time out."

5. Indicate whether each of the following phenomena is associated with the scholarship of Chomsky or with that of Vygotsky.
   a. culture dictating what people need to learn
   b. culture being created through symbols
   c. deep structure

   d. language acquisition device
   e. language development influencing cognitive development
   f. social context influencing language development
   g. surface structure
   h. universal grammar

6. Which of the following conclusions about the relationship between parenting style and child well-being is supported by empirical research? Optimal social development occurs when _____.
   a. parents accompany a child in the exploration of novel environments and novel situations
   b. parents attempt to grant a child's every wish
   c. parents determine the child's needs without input from the child
   d. the parenting style fits the child's temperament

7. Which of the following comments violate the critical thinking skills addressed in this chapter: understanding that some does not mean all and avoiding either/or thinking? Choose all that apply.
   a. "Alcoholism runs in my family, but that doesn't mean I'll necessarily become a problem drinker."
   b. "I can't believe I drank a beer before I knew I was pregnant! My baby is going to suffer from fetal alcohol syndrome."
   c. "I don't care who my kid's friends are. I've raised him to be a good boy, and they can't change who he is."
   d. "My teen has a pretty hyper disposition, but all that caffeine he drinks isn't helping the situation."

8. Igor is 83 years old. Which of his behaviors and cognitions are consistent with the socioemotional selectively theory?
   a. Anticipating he will die within the next few years, he sells his house and invests his money in a start-up company.
   b. He gets together with his friends and family to reminisce about the good old days.
   c. He spends his days sitting on the porch feeling sorry for himself.
   d. He travels for a few months in Bolivia, a country he has always wanted to learn more about.
   e. He volunteers his time mentoring boys in a residential home for troubled youth.

9. Which of the following characteristics describe most older adults? Select all that apply.
   a. happy
   b. mentally healthy
   c. feeling more positive emotions than negative ones
   d. greedy
   e. physically well
   f. senile

■ PSYCHOLOGY AND SOCIETY

1. Think back to an early memory. Write a description of the memory and share it with people who might remember the same event. How are their memories of the event similar to and different from your recollection? Then apply concepts from this chapter—such as infantile amnesia, source amnesia, confabulation, and disputed memories—to analyze why the similarities and differences exist.

2. Visit a toy store and compare toys marketed to girls with those marketed to boys. How are the toys packaged? What images appear on the packages? What words are used to describe the toys? How would children play with the toys (e.g., quiet play versus loud play; solo play versus group play)? Write an essay reflecting on the messages these toys and their packaging communicate to kids about gender.

The answer key for all the Measuring Up exercises and the Practice Tests can be found at the back of the book.

Social Psychology

ACCORDING TO THE GENEVA CONVENTIONS, prisoners of war should be treated with respect and dignity. Even amid the horrors of war, we expect the military to behave in a civilized and professional manner. This is why the events at Abu Ghraib prison, in Iraq, were so shocking. American soldiers brutalized and humiliated Iraqi detainees, threatening them with dogs, beating them with broom handles and chairs, and forcing them to lie on top of each other naked and simulate oral sex and masturbation. When photographs of these actions appeared on the Internet, outrage and condemnation of the deplorable conduct were immediate. Responding quickly to this fury, U.S. government officials stressed that these were isolated incidents carried out by a small group of wayward soldiers. The idea that only a few troubled individuals were responsible for torturing and humiliating Iraqi prisoners is bizarrely comforting. Somehow we are relieved to know that their deviant behavior does not reflect on ordinary people. Surely most of us would not inflict such humiliation and pain on prisoners, many of whom were just teenagers and young men rounded up for questioning. Or would we?

Would you beat up or humiliate someone simply because you were ordered to do so or were in a situation where others were doing so? Or would you defy authority and resist peer pressure? How do we explain the guards' actions at Abu Ghraib, whether or not the guards were ordered to perform them? The case of Abu Ghraib challenges many commonsense notions about human nature and forces us to consider questions about humanity's dark side. People beat, rape, torture, and murder others. Is something wrong with these people?

According to social psychologists, nothing typically is wrong with people such as the guards at Abu Ghraib. Rather, they are probably normal people caught up in overwhelming situations that shape their actions. Social psychologists point out a number of situational factors that likely influenced the guards' behavior at Abu Ghraib, such as an unclear chain of command and a diffusion of responsibility. Moreover, social psychologists know that people typically are obedient to authority, especially in times of war. Also, the working conditions promoted aggression: One of the Abu Ghraib units had expected to be in Iraq a short time, working in traffic control; instead, they found themselves in an overcrowded prison (with a notorious reputation, before the war, for having been a torture chamber under Saddam Hussein's regime) where they worked long hours, six or seven days a week, in extremely hot temperatures while under frequent mortar attack. Finally, during wartime, people are especially likely to view the world as consisting of "us" and "them." Members of the enemy group are viewed as being all the same, often as evil and inferior, and are treated in a dehumanized fashion. All these factors contributed to the mistreatment of prisoners at Abu Ghraib.

In a classic study that illuminates the forces at work in situations like Abu Ghraib, the psychologists Philip Zimbardo and Chris Haney had male Stanford undergraduates play the roles of prisoners and guards in a mock prison (Haney, Banks, & Zimbardo, 1973). The students, who had all been screened and found to be psychologically stable, were randomly assigned to their roles. What happened was unexpected and shocking. Within days, the guards became brutal and sadistic. They constantly harassed the prisoners, forcing them to engage in meaningless and tedious tasks and exercises. Although the study was scheduled to last two weeks, it became necessary to stop it after only six days. The Stanford prison study demonstrated the speed at which apparently normal college students could be transformed into the social roles they were playing. Similarly, the guards at Abu Ghraib believed it was their job to "soften up" the prisoners for interrogation, and their actions were strikingly similar to those of the Stanford participants (FIGURE 12.1).

When people act brutally and sadistically, we assume they are brutal and sadistic. We neglect to consider the situation in which they have acted brutally and sadistically and to assess how much power it had in shaping their behavior. This is not to suggest that individual traits are unimportant or that people are not responsible for their behavior; however, many behaviors become more understandable within particular contexts.

Humans are social animals who live in a highly complex world. At any moment, hundreds of millions of people are talking with friends, forming impressions of strangers, arguing with family members, even falling in love with potential mates. Our regular interactions with others—even imagined others—shape who we are and how we understand the world. Social psychology is concerned with how people influence other people's thoughts, feelings, and actions. Because almost every human activity

(a)

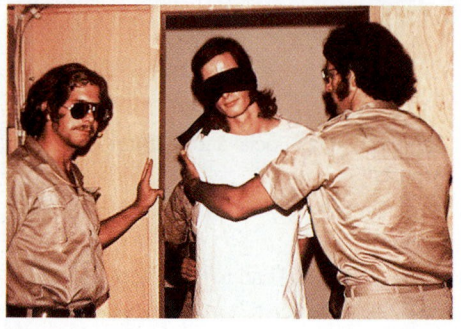

(b)

FIGURE 12.1 When Good People Go Bad (a) Were soldier-guards at Abu Ghraib who harassed, threatened, and tortured prisoners just a few "bad apples," or were they normal people reacting to an extreme situation? **(b)** In the Stanford prison study, student-guards took on their roles with such vigor that the study was ended early because of concerns for the well-being of the "guards" and the "prisoners."

has a social dimension, research in social psychology covers expansive and varied territory: how we perceive ourselves and others, how we function in groups, why we hurt or help people, why we fall in love, why we stigmatize and discriminate against certain people. In this chapter, you will learn the basic principles of how people interact with each other. You will see that research in social psychology provides insights into situations such as Abu Ghraib, revealing to us not that humans are inherently flawed or evil but rather that social context is powerful.

How Do Attitudes Guide Behavior?

How do you feel about the Abu Ghraib prisoner abuse scandal? You quite likely had feelings, opinions, and beliefs about it before you started reading this chapter, just as you have feelings, opinions, and beliefs about yourself, your friends, your favorite television program, and so on. These feelings, opinions, and beliefs are called attitudes. The concept of **attitudes**—our evaluations of objects, of events, or of ideas—is central to social psychology. Attitudes are shaped by social context and play an important role in how we evaluate and interact with other people. We have attitudes about all sorts of things, from trivial and mundane matters such as which deodorant works best to grand issues such as politics, morals, and religion—that is, the core beliefs and values that define who we are as human beings. Some of these attitudes we are aware of, whereas others we do not even know we hold. Some attitudes are complex and involve multiple components. You might enjoy eating ice cream but believe it is bad for your health. You might be disgusted with the Abu Ghraib prisoner abuse but have pity for the U.S. soldiers caught up in the horrific situation. This section considers how attitudes affect our daily lives.

LEARNING OBJECTIVES
Identify the processes by which attitudes are formed and changed.

Recognize situations in which people will most likely behave in ways consistent with their attitudes.

attitudes The evaluation of objects, events, or ideas.

We Form Attitudes through Experience and Socialization

Direct experience of or exposure to things provides information that shapes attitudes. As we encounter new objects, we explore them and learn about them. In general, people develop negative attitudes about new objects more quickly than they develop positive attitudes (Fazio, Eisner, & Shook, 2004).

We talk about acquiring a taste for foods that we did not like originally, such as coffee or sushi, but how do we come to like something that we could not stand the first time we were exposed to it? Typically, the more a person is exposed to something, the more he or she tends to like it. In a classic set of studies, Robert Zajonc (1968, 2001) exposed people to unfamiliar items a few times or many times. Greater exposure to the item, and therefore greater familiarity with it, caused people to have more positive attitudes about the item; this process is known as the *mere exposure effect*. For example, when people are presented with normal and reversed photographs of themselves, they tend to prefer the reversed images, which correspond to what they see when they look in the mirror (**FIGURE 12.2**). Their friends and family members prefer the true photographs, which correspond to how they view the people.

Attitudes can be conditioned (on conditioning, see Chapter 6, "Learning"). Advertisers often use classical conditioning: When we see an attractive celebrity paired with a product, we develop more-positive attitudes about the product. After conditioning, a formerly neutral stimulus, such as a deodorant, triggers the same attitude response as the paired object, such as Brad Pitt (if Brad Pitt were to endorse a deodorant). Operant conditioning also shapes attitudes: If you are rewarded with good grades each time you study, you will develop a more positive attitude toward studying.

FIGURE 12.2 The Mere Exposure Effect If he is like most people, U.S. president Barack Obama will prefer **(right)** his mirror image, with which he is more familiar, to **(left)** his photographic image.

Attitudes are also shaped through socialization. Caregivers, media, teachers, religious leaders, and politicians guide our attitudes about many things, including what kinds of music we should like, how we should feel about people who behave in certain ways, and how we should treat the environment. Society socializes many of our basic attitudes, including which things are edible. For instance, many Hindus do not eat beef, whereas many Jews do not eat pork. Would you eat a worm? Most Westerners would find it disgusting. But in some cultures worms are a delicacy.

Behaviors Are Consistent with Strong Attitudes

To the extent that attitudes are adaptive, they should guide behavior. In general, the stronger and more personally relevant the attitude, the more likely it will predict behavior, be consistent over time, and be resistant to change. For instance, someone who grew up in a strongly Democratic household, especially one where derogatory comments about Republicans were expressed frequently, will more likely register as a Democrat and vote Democratic than someone who grew up in a more politically neutral environment. Moreover, the more specific the attitude, the more predictive it is. For instance, your attitudes toward recycling are more predictive of whether you take your soda cans to a recycling bin than are your general environmental beliefs. Attitudes formed through direct experience also tend to predict behavior better. No matter what kind of parent you think you will be, for example, once you have seen one child through toddlerhood, you will have formed very strong attitudes about child-rearing techniques, and these attitudes will predict how you approach the early months and years of your second child.

The ease with which memories related to an attitude are retrieved—*attitude accessibility*—predicts behavior consistent with the attitude. Russell Fazio (1995) has shown that easily activated attitudes are more stable, predictive of behavior, and resistant to change. Thus the more quickly you recall that you like your psychology course, the more likely you will attend lectures and read the textbook.

Attitudes can be *explicit* or *implicit*. **Explicit attitudes** are those you know about and can report to other people. If you say you like bowling, you are stating your explicit attitude toward it. Anthony Greenwald and Mahzarin Banaji (1995) have noted that our many **implicit attitudes** influence our feelings and behaviors at an unconscious level. We access implicit attitudes from memory quickly, with little conscious effort or control. Just as implicit memory (see Chapter 7, "Attention and Memory") allows us to perform actions, such as riding a bicycle, without thinking through all the required steps, so implicit attitudes shape behavior without our awareness. For instance, you might purchase a product endorsed by a celebrity even though you have no conscious memory of having seen the celebrity use the product. (Maybe Brad Pitt *has* endorsed a deodorant?) Some evidence suggests that implicit attitudes involve brain regions associated with implicit memory in general (Lieberman, 2000). Also as with implicit memory, researchers assess implicit attitudes through indirect means, such as through behaviors rather than through self-reports.

One method researchers use to assess implicit attitudes is the Implicit Association Test (IAT; Greenwald, McGhee, & Schwartz, 1998), a reaction time test that can identify implicit attitudes. The IAT measures how quickly we associate concepts or objects with positive or negative words (**FIGURE 12.3**). Responding more quickly to the association of *female = bad* than *female = good* indicates your implicit attitude about females. Implicit attitudes are also revealed in people's behaviors. Under particular circumstances, for example, even people who claim to harbor no racist beliefs might respond differently to people of other races than to people of

explicit attitudes Attitudes that people can report.

implicit attitudes Attitudes that influence our feelings and behavior at an unconscious level.

FIGURE 12.3 Try for Yourself: Implicit Association Test

At the Web site Project Implicit® (https://implicit.harvard.edu/implicit), you can try your hand at various association tests on topics such as age, race, and gender.

After answering questions or responding to certain words and images, you will receive your results and information about the preferences of others.

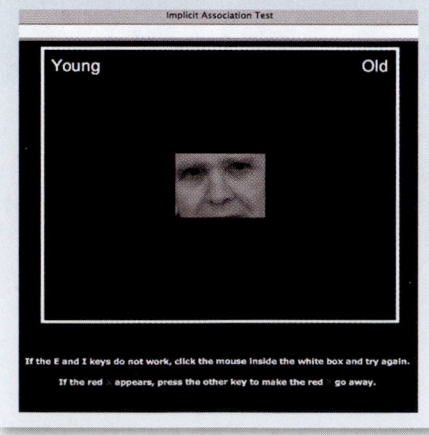

their own race (say, if a person of one race is in a situation where the majority of people are of a different race). Indeed, a recent meta-analysis of more than 100 studies found that, in socially sensitive situations in which people might not want to admit their real attitudes, the IAT is a better predictor of behavior than are explicit self-reports (Greenwald, Poehlnan, Uhlmann, & Banaji, in press). And as discussed below, implicit attitudes are important for understanding racial stereotypes.

Discrepancies Lead to Dissonance

Most people expect attitudes to guide behavior. We expect people to vote for candidates they like and to avoid eating foods they do not like. In 1957, Leon Festinger, studying how people resolved situations in which they held conflicting attitudes, proposed an elegant theory that was to become one of the most important catalysts of research in experimental social psychology (**FIGURE 12.4**). He proposed that **cognitive dissonance** occurs when there is a contradiction between two attitudes or between an attitude and a behavior. For example, people experience cognitive dissonance when they smoke even though they know that smoking might kill them. A basic assumption of dissonance theory is that dissonance causes anxiety and tension and therefore motivates people to reduce the dissonance and relieve displeasure. Generally, people reduce dissonance by changing their attitudes or behaviors; they sometimes also rationalize or trivialize the discrepancies.

Dissonance theory provides important insights into many perplexing behaviors. Consider the American soldiers who served as prison guards at Abu Ghraib. Their treatment of prisoners likely was dissonant from their views on how people generally should be treated. In such poorly run, overcrowded wartime prisons, guards commonly develop extremely negative attitudes about their prisoners, even viewing them as subhuman. Although this might resolve dissonance for the guards, it encourages mistreatment of the prisoners. The following sections examine how dissonance affects attitudes and behavior.

POSTDECISIONAL DISSONANCE According to cognitive dissonance theory, holding positive attitudes about two options but having to choose one of them causes dissonance. For example, a person might have trouble deciding which college to attend. The person might narrow the choice to two or three alternatives and then have to choose. *Postdecisional dissonance* then motivates the person to focus on one school's—the chosen school's—positive aspects and the other schools' negative aspects. Similarly, a person leaning toward buying a truck rather than a car might suddenly think of many reasons for owning a truck rather than a car, whereas a person buying a car might do just the opposite. This effect occurs automatically, with minimal cognitive processing, and apparently without awareness. Indeed, even patients with long-term memory loss may show postdecisional effects for past choices, even if the patients do not consciously recall the outcomes of those choices (Lieberman, Ochsner, Gilbert, & Schacter, 2001).

ATTITUDE CHANGE In one of the original dissonance studies (Festinger & Carlsmith, 1959), each participant performed an extremely boring task for an hour. The experimenter then paid the participant $1 or $20 to lie and tell the next participant that the task was really interesting, educational, and worthwhile. Nearly all the participants subsequently provided the false information. Later, under the guise of a different survey, the same participants were asked how worthwhile and enjoyable the task had actually been. You might think that those paid $20 remembered the task as more enjoyable, but just the opposite happened.

FIGURE 12.4 Leon Festinger Festinger developed the influential theory of cognitive dissonance.

cognitive dissonance An uncomfortable mental state due to conflicts between attitudes or between attitudes and behavior.

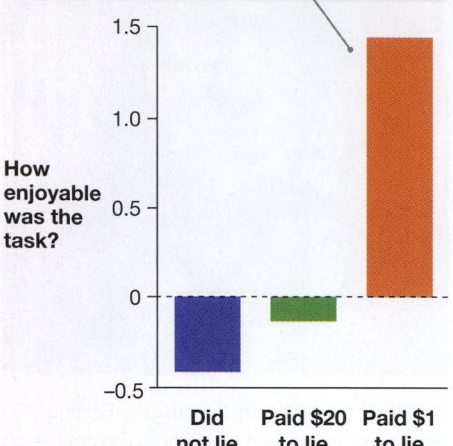

Participants who were paid only $1 to mislead a fellow participant experienced cognitive dissonance, which led them to alter their attitudes about how pleasurable the task had been.

How enjoyable was the task?

1.5

1.0

0.5

0

−0.5

Did not lie — Paid $20 to lie — Paid $1 to lie

FIGURE 12.5 Cognitive Dissonances In Festinger's dissonance studies, participants performed an extremely boring task and then reported to other participants how enjoyable it was. Some participants were paid $20 to lie, and some were paid $1.

FIGURE 12.6 Justifying Effort In early 2008, the University of Maryland removed the Delta Sigma chapter of the Delta Tau Delta fraternity from the College Park campus. Photos such as this one revealed that the fraternity's hazing included abusive alcohol consumption and mental, emotional, and physical duress. Might the pledges have justified their mistreatment by feeling intensely committed to the group?

persuasion The active and conscious effort to change attitudes through the transmission of a message.

Participants who had been paid $1 rated the task much more favorably than those who had been paid $20. According to the researchers, this effect occurred because those paid $1 had insufficient monetary justification for lying. Therefore, to justify why they went along with the lie, they changed their attitudes about performing the dull experimental task. Those paid $20 had plenty of justification for lying, since $20 was a large amount of money in 1959 (roughly equivalent to $140 today), so they did not experience dissonance and did not have to change their attitudes about the task (**FIGURE 12.5**). As this research shows, one way to get people to change their attitudes is to change their behaviors first, using as few incentives as possible. As discussed in Chapter 9, for example, giving children rewards for drawing creatively with colored pens undermines how much they subsequently use the pens.

JUSTIFYING EFFORT If people's attitudes can be changed so easily by changes in their behavior, what effect might extreme group-related behaviors, such as initiation rites, have on members' attitudes about the groups? On college campuses, administrators impose rules and penalties to discourage hazing, yet fraternities and sororities have continued to do it. They do not simply select new members and let them in without initiation because requiring people to undergo embarrassing or difficult rites of passage makes membership in the group seem much more valuable and makes the group more cohesive. To test these ideas, Eliot Aronson and Judson Mills (1959) required women to undergo a test to see if they qualified to take part in a research study. One group of women had to read a list of obscene words and sexually explicit passages in front of the male experimenter, whereas a control group read a list of milder words (such as *prostitute*). Both groups then listened to a boring and technical presentation about mating rituals in lower animals. Women who read the embarrassing words reported that the presentation was much more interesting, stimulating, and important than did the women who read the milder words.

As this research shows, when people put themselves through pain, embarrassment, or discomfort to join a group, they experience a great deal of dissonance. After all, they typically would not choose to be in pain, embarrassed, or uncomfortable. Yet they made such a choice. They resolve the dissonance by inflating the importance of the group and their commitment to it. This justification of effort helps explain why people are willing to subject themselves to humiliating experiences such as hazing (**FIGURE 12.6**). More tragically, it may help explain why people who give up connections to families and friends to join cults or to follow enigmatic leaders are willing to die rather than leave the groups. If they have sacrificed so much to join a group, people believe, the group must be extraordinarily important.

Attitudes Can Be Changed through Persuasion

A number of forces other than dissonance can conspire to change attitudes. We are bombarded by television advertisements; lectures from parents, teachers, and physicians; public service announcements; politicians appealing for our votes; and so on. **Persuasion** is the active and conscious effort to change attitudes through the transmission of a message. The earliest scientific work on persuasion was conducted by Carl Hovland and his colleagues (1953), who emphasized that persuasion is most likely to occur when people pay attention to a message, understand it, and find it convincing; in addition, the message must be memorable, so its impact lasts over time.

Researchers have noted that persuasion leads to attitude change in two fundamental ways (**FIGURE 12.7**). According to Richard Petty and John Cacioppo's

elaboration likelihood model (1986), persuasion works via two routes: The *central route*—in which people pay attention to arguments, consider all the information, and use rational cognitive processes—leads to strong attitudes that last over time and are resistant to change. The *peripheral route*—in which people minimally process the message—leads to more-impulsive action, as when a person decides to purchase a product because a celebrity has endorsed it.

The cues that influence a message's persuasiveness include the *source* (who delivers the message), the *content* (what the message says), and the *receiver* (who processes the message). Sources who are both attractive and credible are the most persuasive. Thus television ads for medicines and medical services often feature very attractive people playing the roles of physicians. The message is effective because of peripheral processing. Even better, of course, is when a drug company ad uses a spokesperson who is both attractive *and* an actual doctor. Credibility and persuasiveness may also be heightened when the receiver perceives the source as similar to himself or herself.

Of course, the arguments in the message are also important for persuasion. Strong arguments that appeal to our emotions are the most persuasive. Advertisers also use the mere exposure effect, repeating the message over and over in the hope that multiple exposures will lead to increased persuasiveness. For this reason, politicians often make the same statements over and over during campaigns. Those who want to persuade (including, of course, politicians) also have to decide whether to deliver one-sided arguments or to consider both sides of particular issues. One-sided arguments work best when the audience is on the speaker's side or is gullible. With a more skeptical crowd, speakers who acknowledge both sides but argue that one is superior tend to be more persuasive than those who completely ignore the opposing view.

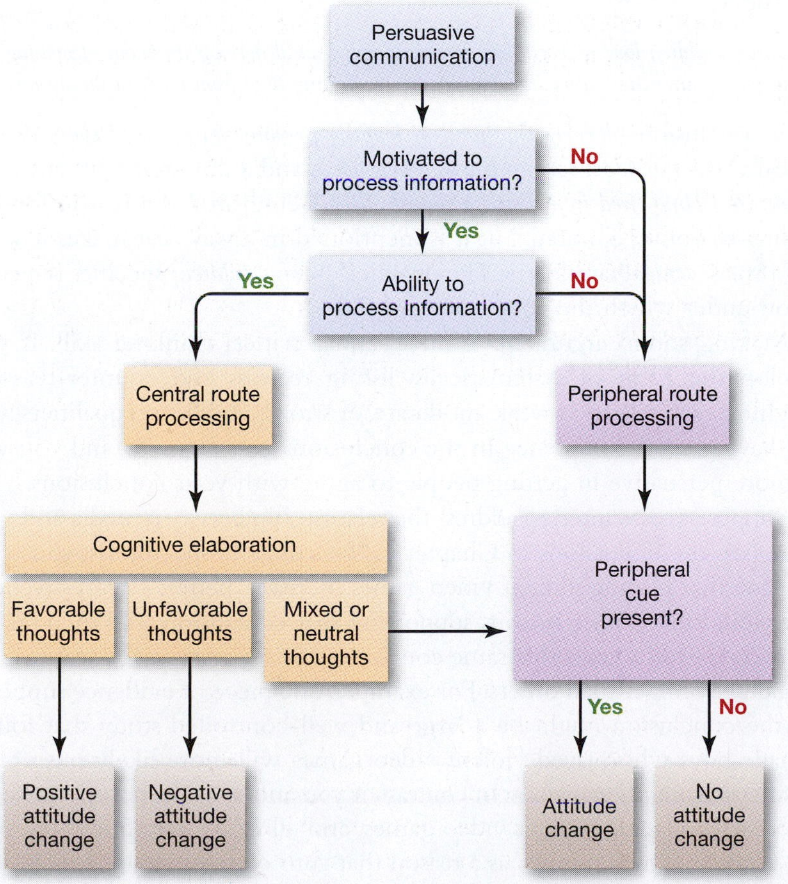

elaboration likelihood model A theory of how persuasive messages lead to attitude changes.

FIGURE 12.7 The Elaboration Likelihood Model When people are motivated to consider information carefully, they process it via the central route, and their attitude changes reflect cognitive elaboration **(left)**. When they are not motivated, they process information via the peripheral route, and their attitude changes reflect the presence or absence of shallow peripheral cues **(right)**.

Making Sound Arguments

In everyday language, the word *argument* refers to a dispute between people. In terms of *rhetoric*—the art of speaking or writing as a means of communication or persuasion—it has a somewhat different and more precise meaning: An argument consists of one or more statements, called reasons or premises, used to support a conclusion (i.e., to persuade the reader or listener that the conclusion is true or probably true). Such arguments appear in much of the information we consume, from blog entries to this textbook. An argument may include a qualifier, a constraint or restriction on the conditions under which the conclusion is supported. It may also include a counterargument, or reasons that run counter to the conclusion: A person strengthens his or her argument by acknowledging alternative opinions, showing that various points of view have been taken into account in reaching the argument's conclusion.

Because an argument must have a conclusion and reasons—though not necessarily in that order—a statement such as

Psychology is my favorite subject.

is not an argument; it is just a simple statement about a preference. However,

Get plenty of exercise because it helps relieve stress.

is a simple argument, with one conclusion (*Get plenty of exercise*) and one reason that supports the conclusion (*because it helps relieve stress*). The argument

Young children love to learn from books, so you should develop the habit of reading to your young child every day, even if you are feeling tired from work or family life.

has a conclusion (*develop the habit of reading to your young child every day*), a reason (*Young children love to learn from books*), and a counterargument (*even if you are feeling tired from work or family life*). Being tired is a reason for not reading to young children, but it is mentioned in a way that makes it seem like a weak counterargument. The qualifier (*Young children*) specifies the condition under which the conclusion is valid.

Making sound arguments is an essential critical thinking skill. If you develop the habit of systematically listing reasons and counter-reasons; weighing each reason as weak, moderate, or strong; and listing qualifiers, you will have greater confidence in the conclusions you come to, and you will be more persuasive in getting people to agree with your conclusions.

Suppose you wanted to address the relationship between media and violence (see the discussions in Chapter 6, "Learning"). Specifically, you want to argue that playing violent video games increases people's aggressiveness. You would first gather reasons supporting that conclusion, and then gather counter-reasons against that same conclusion. Some reasons, for and against, would be stronger than others. For example, one piece of evidence supporting the conclusion might be a large and well-controlled study that found teenage boys who played violent video games will more likely push people after playing these games. In contrast, if you and your friends spend hours every week playing violent video games, and all of you are not aggressive, you could list this "finding" as a reason that runs counter to the conclusion.

The results from the study would provide strong support for the conclusion, however, while your personal experience would be weak (because anecdotal) evidence against the conclusion. (On the weakness of anecdotal evidence, see the discussion of ESP in Chapter 5, "Sensation and Perception.")

When making your own arguments or analyzing arguments presented to you, you must consider the strengths of both the reasons supporting the conclusion and those running counter to the conclusion. You need to combine this information to determine if the overall support for the conclusion is strong, medium, weak, or nonexistent. To assess the argument's overall strength, you also need to take into account everything you know about good research and about critical thinking. Assessing arguments in this way is not about making everyone think the same; rather, it is about focusing on important information and becoming a better thinker (**FIGURE 12.8**).

FIGURE 12.8 Think Critically: **Argument Template**

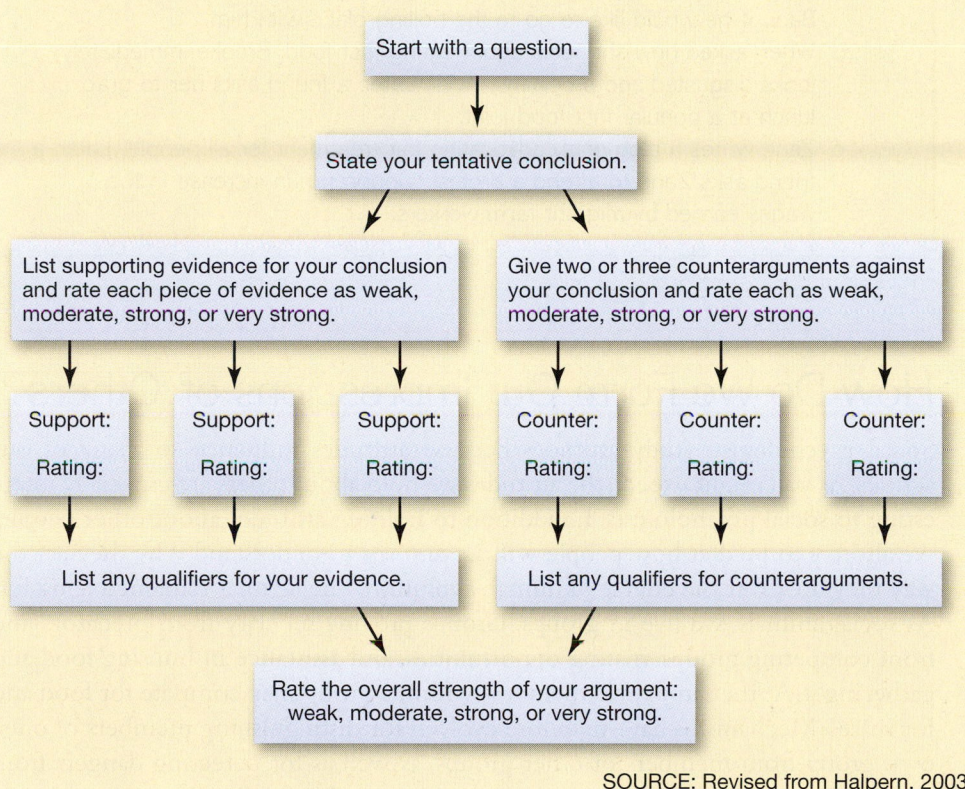

SOURCE: Revised from Halpern, 2003.

⊳ SUMMING UP

How Do Attitudes Guide Behavior?

Attitudes are evaluations of objects, of events, or of ideas. They are formed through socialization and direct experience and best predict behavior when they are strong and easily accessible. Discrepancies between attitudes, or between attitudes and behavior, lead to cognitive dissonance. Dissonance theory can be used to explain a wide range of human behavior. Attitudes can be changed through persuasion centrally, when people think carefully about the issues, or peripherally, when they receive the message to a much smaller extent.

1. Identify the attitude formation(s) or change process(es) described in each of the following examples. Choose from cognitive dissonance, conditioning, mere exposure effect, persuasion, and socialization.
   a. Akira returns home from her first day of kindergarten. She tells her parents, "I don't like my teacher." A few weeks later, her parents hear Akira talking about how much she likes her teacher.
   b. Arnie always wears his seat belt, because his parents taught him to when he was a child.
   c. Given the choice between a Coke or a Pepsi, Manish chooses a Coke. Later that night, he watches his favorite TV show and realizes that Coca-Cola is one of its sponsors.
   d. Sam proclaims her love of coffee to her date. Later, the couple goes to a café. Although Sam is really craving an Italian soda, she orders a coffee.

2. For each of the following scenarios, indicate whether the attitude is likely to predict the subsequent behavior. In a few words, explain why or why not.
   a. Badu somewhat agrees that it is important to vote. Later, a friend asks Badu if he would like to go to the polling place with him.
   b. When asked how she feels about eating fast food, Brooke immediately looks disgusted and proclaims, "Ick!" Later, a friend asks her to grab lunch at a popular fast food joint.
   c. Zane writes a blog entry advocating fair treatment for all people. Later, a friend asks Zane to attend a protest supporting an increase in the wages earned by migrant farm workers.

How Do We Form Our Impressions of Others?

Social psychologists study attitudes because attitudes influence so many of our actions. As you might expect, the attitudes we hold about others are especially interesting to social psychologists. In addition to holding attitudes about other people, we also try to predict how people will act and try to understand why they act the way they do. Over the course of human evolution, one fact has remained constant: As social animals, we live in groups. Groups provide security from predators and from competing groups, mating opportunities, and assistance in hunting food and gathering it. At the same time, members within a group may compete for food and for mates. Mechanisms have therefore evolved for distinguishing members of one's own group from members of other groups, as well as for detecting dangers from within the group, such as deception, coercion, and infidelity. We constantly are required to make social judgments, assessing whether people are friends or foes, potential mates or potential challengers, honest or dishonest, trustworthy or unreliable, and so on. We also automatically classify people into social categories, and doing so can have major implications for how we treat them.

Nonverbal Actions and Expressions Affect Our Impressions

Real World PSYCHOLOGY

Over the years, social psychology has confirmed the importance of first impressions on long-term evaluations of people. Suppose someone is walking toward you. You make a number of quick judgments, such as whether you know the person, whether the person poses danger, and whether you want to know the person better. How you initially feel about that person will be determined mostly by nonverbal behaviors. Facial expressions, gestures, walking style, and fidgeting are all examples of **nonverbal behavior,** sometimes referred to as *body language* (**FIGURE 12.9**). Many factors influence impression formation, ranging from the observer's expectations and attitudes to what the observed person says, as well as his or her nonverbal gestures and physical appearance.

nonverbal behavior The facial expressions, gestures, mannerisms, and movements by which one communicates with others.

FACIAL EXPRESSIONS

The first thing we notice about another person is usually the face. When human babies are less than an hour old, they prefer to look at and will track a picture of a human face rather than a blank outline of a head (Morton & Johnson, 1991). The face communicates a great deal, such as emotional state, interest, and distrust. People use their eyes, for example, to indicate anger, to flirt, to catch the attention of a passing waiter, and so on. Eye contact is important in social situations, though how we perceive it depends on our culture. People from Western cultures tend to seek eye contact when they speak to someone. If the other person does not meet their eyes, they might assume, perhaps incorrectly, that the person is embarrassed, ashamed, or lying, whereas they tend to view a person who looks them in the eyes as truthful and friendly. For this reason, people wearing sunglasses are often described as cold and aloof, and police officers sometimes wear sunglasses partly to seem intimidating. In other groups, such as certain Native American tribes, making direct eye contact, especially with the elderly, is considered disrespectful.

FIGURE 12.9 Nonverbal Behavior People's body language affects our impressions of the people and their situations. For example, observers of this couple might assume they are having a conflict.

BODY LANGUAGE

How much can be learned from nonverbal behavior? Nalini Ambady and Robert Rosenthal have found that people can make accurate judgments based on only a few seconds of observation, what they refer to as *thin slices of behavior.* For instance, videotapes of judges giving instructions to juries reveal that judges' nonverbal actions can predict whether juries find defendants guilty or not guilty. Judges, perhaps unconsciously, may indicate their beliefs about guilt or innocence through facial expressions, tone of voice, and physical gestures. In one study, participants viewed soundless 30-second film clips of college teachers lecturing. Based solely on nonverbal behaviors, the participants' ratings corresponded very highly to the ratings given by the instructor's students (Ambady & Rosenthal, 1993).

One important nonverbal cue is how people walk, known as *gait.* Gait provides information about affective state. People with a bounce in their step, who walk along swinging their arms, are seen as happy. By contrast, people who scurry along, taking short steps while stooped over, are perceived as hostile, while those taking long strides with heavy steps are perceived to be angry. In an intriguing study, researchers found that participants accurately judged sexual orientation at a better-than-chance rate after watching a 10-second silent video or a dynamic figural outline of someone walking or gesturing (Ambady, Hallahan, & Conner, 1999; **FIGURE 12.10**). What aspects of behavior gave cues to sexual orientation? According to recent research, the extent to which body shape and body motion differed from those of the typical male or female was the primary cue used by perceivers (Johnson, Gill, Reichman, & Tassinary, 2007). Such thin slices of behavior are powerful cues for impression formation.

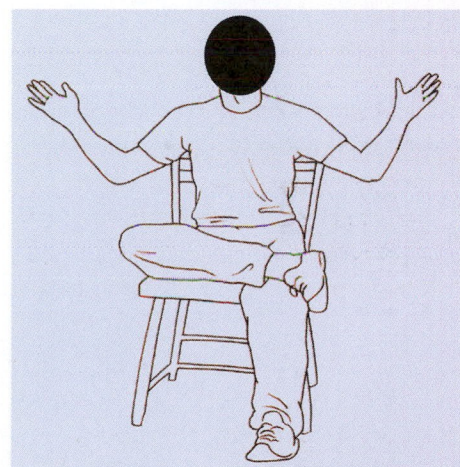

FIGURE 12.10 Nonverbal Cues from Body Shape After watching a 10-second clip of a figural outline such as this one, participants correctly guessed the figure's sexual orientation at a better-than-chance rate.

We Make Attributions about Others

We constantly try to explain other people's motives, traits, and preferences. Why did she say that? Why is he crying? Why does she study so hard? and so on. **Attributions** are people's causal explanations for events or actions, including other

attributions People's causal explanations for why events or actions occur.

people's behavior. People are motivated to draw inferences in part by a basic need for both order and predictability. The world can be a dangerous place in which many unexpected things happen. People prefer to think that things happen for reasons, and that therefore they can anticipate future events. For instance, you might expect that if you study for an exam you will do well on it. Indeed, when a violent act, such as a rape or murder, appears to be senseless, people often make attributions about the victim, such as "she deserved it" or "he provoked it." Such attributions are part of what is referred to as the *just world hypothesis.* From this perspective, victims must have done something to justify what happened to them. People might apply the just world hypothesis, for example, by saying that the Iraqi detainees at the Abu Ghraib prison probably did something that led them to be arrested and therefore were in a sense responsible for and deserving of the abuse they received. It is simply easier to believe that the prisoners, not the guards, must be guilty of criminal actions. Such attributions make the mistreatment seem more understandable and more justified and make the world seem safer and saner.

ATTRIBUTIONAL DIMENSIONS   In any situation, there are dozens of plausible explanations for specific outcomes. Doing well on a test, for example, could be due to brilliance, luck, intensive studying, the test's being unexpectedly easy, or a combination of factors. Fritz Heider, the originator of attribution theory, drew the essential distinction between *personal* and *situational attributions.* **Personal attributions,** also known as *internal* or *dispositional attributions,* are explanations that refer to things within people, such as abilities, traits, moods, or efforts. By contrast, **situational attributions,** also known as *external attributions,* refer to outside events, such as the weather, accidents, or people's actions. Bernard Weiner (1974) noted that attributions can vary on other dimensions, such as whether they are stable over time versus unstable, or controllable versus uncontrollable. For instance, weather is situational, unstable, and uncontrollable. Good study habits are personal, stable, and controllable. Weiner's theory has been used to explain psychological states such as depression. As discussed in Chapters 13 and 14, depressed people attribute their failures to their own incompetence, which they believe is permanent. By contrast, those who are not depressed often self-servingly attribute their failures to situational, unstable, or uncontrollable attributes. Essentially, nondepressed people tend to attribute their failures to temporary aspects of situations, as in blaming failing a test on not getting enough sleep or on the professor's creating a bad exam. By contrast, they attribute success to personal, permanent factors, as in doing well on an exam because they are smart.

ATTRIBUTIONAL BIAS   So is it the person? Or is it the situation? When explaining other people's behavior, we tend to overemphasize the importance of personality traits and underestimate the importance of situation. This tendency is so pervasive that it has been called the **fundamental attribution error.** Theorists such as Fritz Heider and Harold Kelley have described people as intuitive scientists who try to draw inferences about others and make attributions about events. Unlike objective scientists, however, people tend to be systematically biased in their social-information processing. They make self-serving attributions consistent with their preexisting beliefs, and they generally fail to take into account that other people are influenced by social circumstances (**FIGURE 12.11**). Edward Jones originated the idea of fundamental attribution error during the 1960s (though he called it the *correspondence bias,* emphasizing that people expect others' behaviors to correspond with their own beliefs and personalities). In contrast, according to Jones, when people make attributions about themselves, they tend to focus on situations rather than on their personal dispositions, an error that, in conjunction with the

personal attributions   Explanations that refer to internal characteristics, such as abilities, traits, moods, and effort.

situational attributions   Explanations that refer to external events, such as the weather, luck, accidents, or the actions of other people.

fundamental attribution error   The tendency to overemphasize personal factors and underestimate situational factors in explaining behavior.

fundamental attribution error, leads to the *actor/observer discrepancy.* For instance, people tend to attribute their own lateness to external factors, such as traffic or competing demands, but they tend to attribute other people's lateness to personal characteristics, such as laziness or lack of organization.

A meta-analysis of 173 studies found that the actor/observer effect is observed most commonly for negative events (Malle, Knobe, & Nelson, 2007). Indeed, we tend to attribute positive events to our dispositions and negative events to outside forces. (For a further examination of this tendency, the *self-serving bias,* see Chapter 13, "Personality.")

Is the fundamental attribution error really fundamental? Might there also be cultural differences in the attributional styles that typify people from Eastern and Western societies? Indeed, as discussed in Chapter 1, people in Eastern cultures tend to be more holistic in how they perceive the world, seeing the forest rather than individual trees. The variation within all cultures is important, of course, but on average the evidence indicates that people from Eastern cultures use much more information when making attributions than do people in Western cultures, and they are more likely to believe that human behavior is the outcome of both personal and situational factors (Choi, Dalal, Kim-Prieto, & Park, 2003; Miyamoto & Kitayama, 2002). Easterners may not be susceptible to some of the same attributional biases as Westerners, but they are more likely to take situational forces into account, whereas people in the West place overriding emphasis on personal factors. Thus the basic predictions derived from the fundamental attribution error are found across cultures, though there is a difference in the extent to which people in different cultures attribute others' behaviors to personality traits rather than to the situations.

FIGURE 12.11 Fundamental Attribution Error As casual observers, we might wonder why these women in Mumbai, India, are fighting to board the train. Are they late for work? Is it the last train? But if we could see what is happening beyond the picture, we might see that the larger situation—the context in the station, in Mumbai, and so on—reveals other reasons for the women's urgency.

Identifying and Avoiding the Actor/Observer Discrepancy

An important part of critical thinking is understanding the way we assign causes to our own and others' behaviors. According to the actor/observer discrepancy, people strongly tend to believe that individual attributes underlie other peoples' actions ("She failed the quiz because she is stupid") but to see their own actions as caused by circumstances ("I failed the quiz because I was tired"). With a little attention, you will begin to see people around you making such attributions. During a political campaign, listen to the way the various candidates explain their own behaviors and those of their opponents. This bias is especially noticeable when a candidate says or does something controversial. For example, a candidate who has changed his or her position on an important policy issue likely will claim to have done so for situational reasons, perhaps because of a lack of access to certain information when making the initial statement. However, if that candidate's opponent has changed position on another issue, the first candidate likely will attribute this change of stance to a lack of firm convictions or another personality flaw on the opponent's part.

It is easier to recognize the actor/observer discrepancy in others' thinking than in your own, but once you are aware of this bias, it becomes easier to avoid it. Consider the following scenario: If you have a quick encounter with someone who seems rude or inattentive, do you immediately think,

"Wow, what a nasty person"? Now turn the situation around: Suppose a troubling family problem has made you late for class. As you rush across campus, someone stops you and asks a question. How likely is it that you will think, "Can't this person see I'm busy?" and be somewhat rude and inattentive? Yet you might feel justified in behaving this way because of your immediate situation. By learning to recognize the actor/observer discrepancy in your own thinking, you will be able to judge others' behavior more fairly and to take more responsibility for your own.

Stereotypes Are Based on Automatic Categorization

What are Italians like—do they all have fiery tempers? Do all Canadians like hockey? Can white men jump? We hold attitudes and beliefs about groups because they allow us to answer these sorts of questions quickly. Such attitudes and beliefs are **stereotypes,** cognitive schemas that help us organize information about people on the basis of their membership in certain groups. Stereotypes are mental shortcuts that allow for easy, fast processing of social information. As discussed in Chapter 8, heuristic processing allows us to make quick decisions. Stereotyping occurs automatically and, in most cases, outside of our awareness. In and of themselves, stereotypes are neutral and simply reflect efficient cognitive processes. Indeed, some stereotypes are based in truth: Men tend to be more violent than women, and women tend to be more nurturing than men. However, these are true on average; not all men are violent, nor are all women nurturing.

People construct and use categories to streamline their impression formation and to deal with the limitations inherent in mental processing. That is, because of limited mental resources, people cannot scrutinize every person they encounter. Rather than consider each person as unique and unpredictable, they categorize people as belonging to particular groups about which they hold knowledge in long-term memory. For example, they might automatically categorize people on the basis of their clothing or hairstyles. Once they have categorized those people, they will have beliefs about them based on their stereotypes about the particular categories. That is, stereotypes affect impression formation (Kunda & Spencer, 2003). For example, people are more likely to falsely remember a male name than a female name as that of a famous person (the false fame effect, discussed in Chapter 7), apparently because of the stereotype that men are more likely than women to be famous (Banaji & Greenwald, 1995).

Once people form stereotypes, they maintain them by a number of processes. As schematic structures, stereotypes guide attention toward information that confirms the stereotypes and away from disconfirming evidence. People's memories are also biased to match stereotypes. These biases lead to illusory correlations in which people believe relationships exist when they do not. A professor who notices one black student performing poorly but fails to notice other black students doing well is confirming a false belief relating race to performance. Similarly, the same behavior might be perceived in different ways so it is consistent with a stereotype. Thus a white man's success may be attributed to hard work and determination, whereas a black man's success may be attributed to outside factors, such as luck or affirmative action. A lawyer described as aggressive

stereotypes Cognitive schemas that allow for easy, fast processing of information about people based on their membership in certain groups.

and a construction worker described as aggressive conjure up different images. Moreover, when people encounter someone who does not fit a stereotype, they put that person in a special category rather than alter the stereotype, a process known as *subtyping*. Thus a racist who believes blacks are lazy may categorize a superstar such as Michael Jordan as an exception to the rule rather than as evidence for the stereotype's invalidity. Forming a subtype that includes successful blacks allows the racist to maintain the stereotype that most blacks are unsuccessful.

SELF-FULFILLING EFFECTS   How does being treated as members of stereotyped groups affect people? Initially untrue stereotypes can become true through **self-fulfilling prophecy,** in which people come to behave in ways that confirm their own or others' expectations. In the 1960s, the psychologist Robert Rosenthal and a school principal, Lenore Jacobsen, conducted one of the most impressive early examinations of this process. In this study, elementary-school students took a test that supposedly identified some of them, called *bloomers,* as being especially likely to show large increases in IQ during the school year. Teachers were given a list of the bloomers in their classes. At the end of the year, standardized testing revealed that the bloomers showed large increases in IQ. As you might have guessed, the bloomers had been chosen at random rather than through the test, and therefore their increases in IQ seemed to have resulted from the extra attention and encouragement provided by the teachers. Thus teacher expectations turned into reality. Of course, negative stereotypes can become self-fulfilling as well. Teachers who expect certain students to fail might, however unconsciously, subtly undermine those students' self-confidence or motivation. For instance, offering unwanted help, even with the best intentions, can send the message that the teacher does not believe the students have what it takes to succeed.

In another study, each man believed he was speaking with either an attractive woman or an unattractive woman on the phone about a potential date (Snyder, Tanke, & Berscheid, 1977). The men who thought the women they talked with were attractive, based on a photo, rated the women as more sociable, poised, and humorous than did men who thought they were talking with unattractive women. Perhaps this finding is not surprising. In addition, however, other participants, who did not know which women were believed to be attractive, listened to only the women's sides of the conversations; those participants also rated the women believed to be attractive in more positive terms. That is, women interacting with men who believed they were attractive behaved more pleasantly than those interacting with men who believed they were unattractive. The men's behavior helped confirm their stereotypes. This study is another example of the ways our thoughts and behaviors are influenced by events about which we are not consciously aware.

Yet another example of how expectations can affect performance is stereotype threat. As discussed in Chapter 8, stereotype threat applies to any group for which there is a negative stereotype. For instance, when women are asked to indicate if they are male or female and then tested on their math ability, they tend to perform more poorly than when they are not initially reminded of their sex (Shih, Pittinsky, & Ambady, 1999). Stereotype threat may partly explain the underlying disparity between the numbers of men and women in science careers. Stereotype threat is among the most studied topics in social psychology over the past decade, as researchers have sought to understand what causes it and how to prevent it. A recent review of the literature identified three interrelated mechanisms as responsible for producing decreased performances following threat: (1) physiological stress affecting prefrontal functioning; (2) a tendency for people to think about their performances, which can distract them from the tasks; and (3) attempts to suppress

self-fulfilling prophecy   People's tendency to behave in ways that confirm their own or others' expectations.

negative thoughts and emotions, which require a great deal of effort (Schmader, Johns, & Forbes, 2008). A recent brain imaging study found that women exposed to a math stereotype threat showed reduced activity in brain regions associated with math performance and increased activation in brain regions involved in social and emotional processing, supporting the idea that stereotype threat undermines cognitive processes by raising performance anxiety (Krendl, Richeson, Kelley, & Heatherton, 2008). In each of these examples, people's beliefs about how others viewed them altered their behaviors in ways that confirmed the stereotypes, even though they had no conscious knowledge of these influences.

Stereotypes Can Lead to Prejudice

prejudice The usually negative affective or attitudinal responses associated with stereotypes.

discrimination The inappropriate and unjustified treatment of people based solely on their group membership.

Stereotypes may be neutral categories, but negative stereotypes of groups lead to prejudice and discrimination. **Prejudice** consists of the affective or attitudinal responses associated with stereotypes, and it usually involves negative judgments about people based on their group membership. **Discrimination** is the unjustified and inappropriate treatment of people as a result of prejudice. Prejudice and discrimination are responsible for much of the conflict and warfare around the world. Within nearly all cultures, some groups of people are treated negatively because of prejudice. Social psychologists have spent the last half century studying the causes and consequences of prejudice as well as trying to find ways to reduce its destructive effects.

Why do stereotypes so often lead to prejudice and discrimination? Various researchers have theorized that only certain types of people are prejudiced, that people treat others as scapegoats to relieve the tensions of daily living, and that people discriminate against others to protect their own self-esteem. One explanation, consistent with the theme that the mind is adaptive, is that evolution has led to two processes that produce prejudice and discrimination: We tend to favor our own groups over other groups, and we tend to stigmatize those who pose threats to our groups.

FIGURE 12.12 Ingroup/Outgroup Bias People tend to identify strongly with the groups to which they belong. Here, Croatian and Turkish soccer fans clash before the Euro 2008 quarter-final soccer match between their two countries.

INGROUP/OUTGROUP BIAS We are powerfully connected to the groups to which we belong. We cheer them on, fight for them, and sometimes are even willing to die for them. Those groups to which we belong are *ingroups;* those to which we do not belong are *outgroups* (**FIGURE 12.12**). As discussed in Chapter 6, when people participate in conditioning experiments in which aversive stimuli are paired with members of their own racial group or members of a different racial group, they more easily associate the negative stimuli with outgroup members (Olsson, Ebert, Banaji, & Phelps, 2005). This finding suggests that people are predisposed to be wary of others who do not belong to their own groups, since presumably outgroup members have been more dangerous over the course of human evolution. However, people low in racial bias, on both implicit and explicit measures, are less likely to acquire negative associations to neutral stimuli in a classical conditioning paradigm (Livingston & Drwecki, 2007). That is, some people quickly learn that some neutral unfamiliar pictures are repeatedly paired with negative images whereas others resist making those associations. Livingston and Drwecki found that the latter group is less likely to show race bias, and Caucasian people in this group are more likely to be recognized by their African American friends as not prejudiced.

The separation of people into ingroup and outgroup members appears to occur early in development. As noted in Chapter 5, people are better able to remember faces of people of their own race than those of people of other races. Researchers have found that three-month-old Caucasian infants in the United Kingdom recognize faces from their own group as well as they recognize faces from other groups

(African, Middle Eastern, and Chinese). However, by six months of age the infants recognize only Caucasian and Chinese faces, and by nine months they recognize only Caucasian faces (Kelly et al., 2007). When researchers examined implicit race attitudes of Caucasian children using the IAT, they found that six-year-olds showed as much implicit racial bias as 10-year-olds and adults, although by age 10 children reported more egalitarian explicit attitudes (Baron & Banaji, 2006).

Once people categorize others as ingroup or outgroup members, they treat them accordingly. For instance, due to the *outgroup homogeneity effect,* people tend to view outgroup members as less varied than ingroup members. UCLA students may think Berkeley students are all alike, but when they think about UCLA students they cannot help but notice the wide diversity of different student types. Of course, for Berkeley students, the reverse is true about UCLA students and themselves. Similarly, most people recognize that residents of their home countries differ in substantial ways; but Westerners, for example, tend to view Arabs as being very similar to one another, sharing similar values and even attitudes about the West, while Arabs tend to hold the same sort of views about Westerners.

The consequence of categorizing people as ingroup or outgroup members is **ingroup favoritism,** in which people will more likely distribute resources to ingroup members than to outgroup members. In addition, people are more willing to do favors for ingroup members or to forgive their mistakes or errors. The power of group membership is so strong that people exhibit ingroup favoritism even if the groups are determined by arbitrary processes. Henri Tajfel and John Turner (1979) randomly assigned volunteers to two groups, using meaningless criteria such as flipping a coin. Participants were then given a task in which they divided up money. Not surprisingly, they gave more money to their ingroup members, but they also tried to prevent the outgroup members from getting any money, even when they were told that the basis of group membership was arbitrary and that giving money to the outgroup would not affect how much money their own group obtained.

Why do people value members of their own groups? We can speculate that over the course of human evolution, personal survival has depended on group survival. Especially when there is competition for scarce resources, those who work together to keep resources within their group and deny resources to outgroup members have a selective advantage over those willing to share with the outgroup. At the psychological level, our group memberships are an important part of our social identity and contribute to our overall sense of self-esteem. In addition, women show a much greater automatic ingroup bias toward other women than men do toward other men (Rudman & Goodwin, 2004). Although men generally favor their ingroups, they fail to do so when the category is sex. Rudman and Goodwin speculate that men and women depend on women for nurturing and that both are threatened by male violence. Moreover, although women can freely express their affection for their female friends, males appear to be less comfortable doing so, perhaps because it might threaten their sexual identities.

STEREOTYPES AND PERCEPTION   How can social psychology help us understand a tragedy such as the killing of Amadou Diallo by New York City police officers, described in the opening of Chapter 1? In crossing levels of analysis, we find that implicit social attitudes can influence basic perceptual processes. In two experiments that demonstrated this, Payne (2001) showed pictures of various objects to white participants and asked them to classify the objects as guns or tools as quickly as possible. Immediately before seeing a picture, the participants briefly were shown a picture of a white face or a black one. Priming by a black face led participants to identify guns more quickly and to mistake tools for guns

ingroup favoritism   The tendency for people to evaluate favorably and privilege members of the ingroup more than members of the outgroup.

(**FIGURE 12.13**). A more recent study, in which over 90% of the participants were white, found that the reverse is also true: Priming people with pictures of weapons (e.g., guns and knives) leads them to pay greater attention to black faces than to white faces (Eberhardt, Goff, Purdie, & Davies, 2004). Such findings suggest that implicit bias may have been involved in the Diallo shooting. The officers were looking for individuals who fit a specific racial profile. When forced to make a split-second decision, they mistook Diallo's wallet for a weapon.

In a virtual reality simulation of the Diallo shooting, Greenwald, Oakes, and Hoffman (2003) required each participant, in the role of a police officer, to respond to a criminal holding a gun (by clicking a computer mouse to shoot him), to a fellow police officer holding a gun (by pressing the space bar), or to a civilian holding a neutral object (by doing nothing). In some trials, the criminal holding a gun was a white male and the police officer holding a gun was a black male. In the other trials, these racial matches were reversed. Whatever their roles in the study, blacks were more likely to be incorrectly shot, in part because the objects they held were more likely to be identified as weapons. Fortunately, recent evidence suggests that computerized training, in which race is unrelated to the presence of a weapon, can eliminate this racial bias in shooting behavior among police officers (Plant & Peruche, 2005). Indeed, research comparing police officers and community members on simulated decisions to shoot or not shoot blacks and whites found that police officers were much less likely to shoot unarmed people and were equally likely to shoot blacks and whites (Correll et al., 2007). Community members were more likely to shoot unarmed black targets, suggesting that the extensive training received by police officers helps them avoid race bias in deciding whether to shoot.

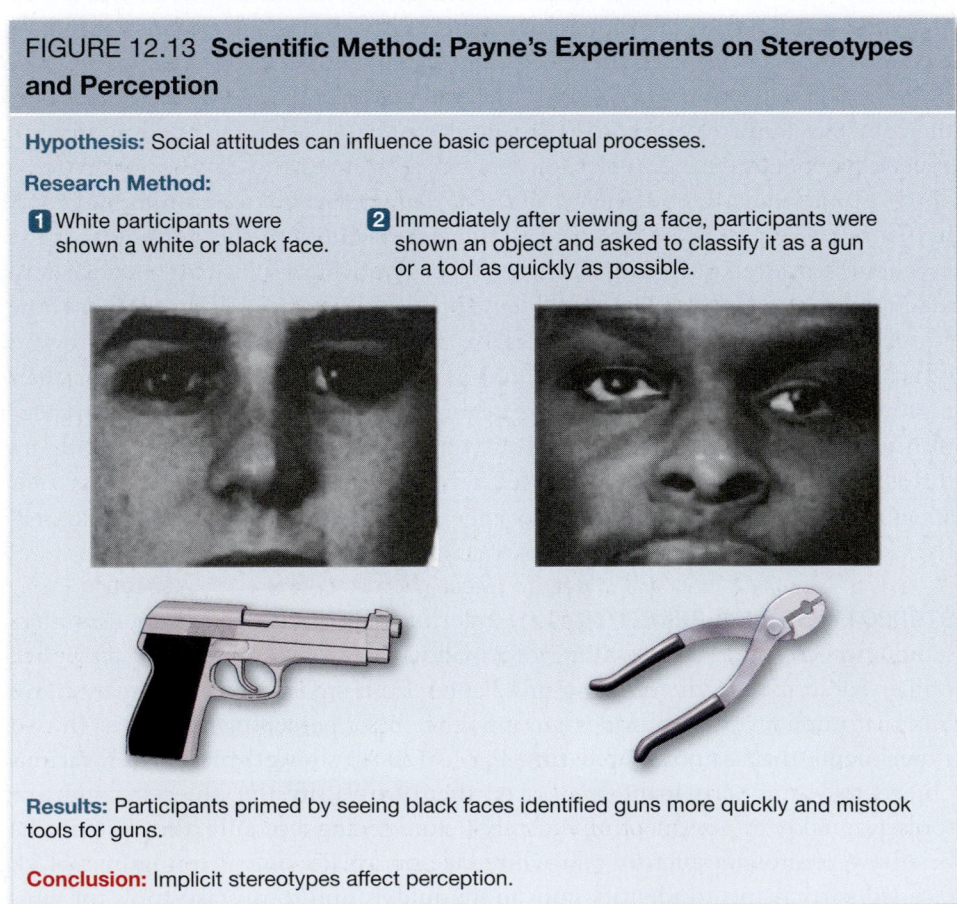

FIGURE 12.13 **Scientific Method: Payne's Experiments on Stereotypes and Perception**

Hypothesis: Social attitudes can influence basic perceptual processes.

Research Method:

1 White participants were shown a white or black face.

2 Immediately after viewing a face, participants were shown an object and asked to classify it as a gun or a tool as quickly as possible.

Results: Participants primed by seeing black faces identified guns more quickly and mistook tools for guns.

Conclusion: Implicit stereotypes affect perception.

ON Ethics   Psychological Testing for Prejudice

Knowing if a person has racist views or how well a person can control his or her responses in situations where negative stereotypes may come into play would seem to be helpful in many situations, from hiring police officers and teachers to selecting jury panels. But if racist views could be determined by psychological testing and fMRI brain scanning (on such techniques, see Chapter 2, "Research Methodology"), would it be ethical to do so? If a couple of tests and a brain scan could eliminate all racial problems within the police force, would such testing be justified (**FIGURE 12.14**)? Similarly, is it ethical to require potential jurors to have their thoughts "read" by a machine and put on public record? What if it meant that every defendant would more likely have a fair trial? In other words, do we have a right to keep our thoughts private, or does the right to a fair trial supercede the individual juror's rights?

Quickly categorizing all sensory input is what our brains do, and luckily for us they are pretty good at it. We instantly know if an object is animate or inanimate, a plant or an animal, a cat or a lion. We are also good at distinguishing males from females and children from adults. We might be able to tell a gang member from a police officer patrolling the streets, but if the police officer and the gang member traded clothing, we might no longer be able to put each in his or her group.

It appears that a process in the brain also makes it likely that people will categorize others on the basis of race. As noted in Chapter 1, fMRI studies done by Elizabeth Phelps and Mahzarin Banaji revealed that the amygdalas of some white men are activated by the sight of an unknown black man's face. This response is triggered by an automatic, unconscious assessment of potential threat signified by sensory, social, and emotional stimuli. Yet responding this way is not the same thing as being racist, nor does it always happen. The ability to categorize is probably necessary for racism but does not necessarily lead to it; many people override this automatic activation and act in a nondiscriminatory fashion.

Robert Kurzban and his colleagues (2001) examined claims that people encode the race of each individual they encounter. From an evolutionary psychologist's perspective, these claims make no sense. Our hunter-gatherer ancestors rarely, if ever, traveled far enough to come in contact with people of a different race, so there would have been no selection pressure for an adaptation that automatically encoded race. Race must therefore be encoded as a side effect of some other function, perhaps as a by-product of computational mechanisms that evolved for tracking coalitions and alliances (Cosmides, Tooby,

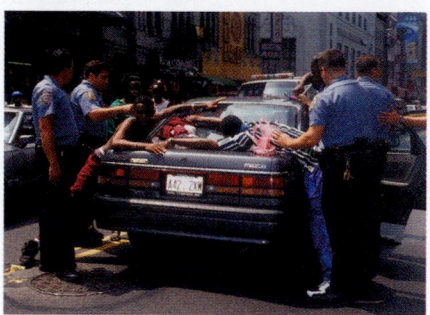

FIGURE 12.14
Testing for Prejudice Critics charge that prejudice often influences random searches. Might testing eliminate potentially prejudiced officers from the force?

& Kurzban, 2003). In a four-minute experiment, Kurzban found that when categorization cues stronger than race were present (he used shirt color to indicate coalitional alliances), the categorization based on race was diminished or eliminated. For example, when you watch a football game between the Broncos and the Cowboys, you see Broncos and Cowboys, not white players and black ones. You are categorizing by coalitional alliance, not by race.

Mary Wheeler and Susan Fiske (2005) investigated whether social goals such as social categorization (e.g., guessing the age of the black or white person in a photo), social individuation (e.g., guessing a person's vegetable preference), and simple visual inspection (e.g., detecting a dot on the face) would affect the amygdala response and cognitive responses to racial outgroups. One study recorded brain activity in the amygdala using fMRI, and another measured cognitive activation of stereotypes by word priming. They found that neither response to racial outgroups was inevitable; instead, both responses depended on perceivers' current social-cognitive goals. Changing the social context in which a target person is viewed affects the outgroup perception, measurable in both the brain and reaction time behavior.

Even if someday we are able to link specific brain activity to racist thoughts, it will not mean that racist thoughts necessarily lead to racist acts. Since categorizing people need not entail mistreating them, should the products of automatic processing be revealed and used to judge people? Is the use of psychological testing and of brain scans for racist thoughts justified if it prevents even one race-based death, such as Amadou Diallo's (see Chapter 1), or prevents a jury from unjustly convicting even one innocent person because of race bias? Might it be worthwhile to use such tests to identify which police officers may need special sensitivity training or which jurors should not be chosen for a case in which race might be a factor?

INHIBITING STEREOTYPES   Most people do not consider themselves prejudiced, and many are motivated to avoid stereotyping others. Yet according to many social cognition researchers, categorization and stereotyping occur automatically, without people's awareness or intent (Bargh & Ferguson, 2000). Patricia Devine (1989) has made the important point that people can override the stereotypes they hold and act in nondiscriminatory ways. For instance, most people in North America know the negative stereotypes associated with African Americans, and when a nonblack person encounters a black person, the information in the stereotypes becomes cognitively available. According to Devine, people low in prejudice override this automatic activation and act in a nondiscriminatory fashion. While some automatic stereotypes alter how we perceive and understand the behavior of those we stereotype, simply categorizing people need not lead to mistreating them.

Indeed, numerous studies have shown that we can consciously alter our automatic stereotyping (Blair, 2002). For instance, Dasgupta and Greenwald (2001) found that presenting positive examples of admired black individuals (e.g., Denzel Washington) produced more favorable attitudes toward African Americans on the IAT. In another study, training people to respond counter-stereotypically, as in having them press a "no" key when they saw an elderly person paired with a stereotype of the elderly, led to reduced automatic stereotyping in subsequent tasks (Kawakami, Dovidio, Moll, Hermsen, & Russin, 2000). Telling people their tests scores indicate that they hold negative stereotypes can motivate people to correct their attitudes, and the worse they feel about holding those attitudes, the harder they try not to be biased (Monteith, 1993).

Inhibiting stereotyped thinking in everyday life is difficult and requires self-regulation (Monteith, Ashburn-Nardo, Voils, & Czopp, 2002), in part because of the brain activity involved. As discussed throughout this book, the frontal lobes are important for controlling both thoughts and behavior. In one brain imaging study, briefly showing white participants pictures of black faces produced amygdala activity. The amygdala is involved in detecting threat; in this context, the amygdala activity may indicate that the participants' immediate responses to black faces were negative. However, if the faces were presented longer, the frontal lobes became active and the amygdala response decreased; thus the frontal lobes appear to have overridden this immediate reaction. This reaction happened more for those whose IAT scores indicated negative stereotypes about blacks (Cunningham et al., 2004). In another study, when white participants observed black faces their frontal lobe activity was associated with poor performance on a subsequent task of mental function, a finding that implies controlling stereotypes is mentally taxing (Richeson et al., 2003). The general pattern indicates that those with high levels of motivation to avoid appearing racist have an anxious arousal response when interacting with African Americans, a response that subsequently can interfere with cognition (Richeson & Trawalter, 2008).

Cooperation Can Reduce Prejudice

Can social psychologists use what they have learned in the laboratory to help reduce prejudice and to encourage peace? Since the 1950s, numerous such attempts have been made to alleviate the hostility and violence between factions, but it is extraordinarily difficult to change cultural and religious beliefs, and attitudes toward ethnic groups are embedded deeply in both. Around the world, groups clash over disputes that predate the births of most of the combatants, and sometimes people cannot even remember the original sources of particular conflicts. Yet as the global response to the deadly tsunami of late 2004 indicates, people can work together and, in doing so, overcome intergroup hostilities if they have a greater purpose, such as dealing with a natural catastrophe that killed hundreds of thousands and left millions homeless.

Social psychology may be able to suggest strategies for promoting intergroup harmony and producing greater tolerance for outgroups. The first study to suggest so was conducted by the psychologist Muzafer Sherif and his colleagues in the late 1950s. Sherif arranged for 22 well-adjusted and intelligent white fifth-grade boys from Oklahoma City to attend a summer camp. None of the boys knew each other before that summer. Before arriving at camp, the boys were divided into two groups that were essentially the same. During the first week, the boys lived in separate camps, each unaware that a similar group of boys was across the lake.

The next week, over a four-day period, the groups competed in a number of athletic competitions, such as tug-of-war, football, and softball. The stakes were high: The winning team would get a trophy, individual medals, and appealing prizes; the losers would receive nothing. The groups named themselves the Rattlers and the Eagles. Group pride was extremely strong, and animosity between the groups quickly escalated. The Eagles burned the Rattlers' flag, and the Rattlers retaliated by trashing the Eagles' cabin. Eventually, confrontations and physical fights had to be broken up by the experimenters. All the typical signs of prejudice emerged, including the outgroup homogeneity effect and ingroup favoritism.

Phase 1 of the study was complete. Sherif had shown how easy it was to get people to hate each other—simply divide them into groups and have the groups compete, and prejudice and mistreatment would result. Phase 2 of the study then explored whether the hostility could be undone.

Sherif first tried what made sense at the time, simply having the groups come into contact with one another. This approach failed miserably. The hostilities were too strong, and skirmishes continued. Sherif reasoned that if competition led to hostility, then cooperation should reduce hostility. The experimenters created situations in which members of both groups had to cooperate to achieve necessary goals. For instance, the experimenters rigged a truck to break down. Getting the truck moving required all the boys to pull together—in an ironic twist—on the same rope used earlier in the tug-of-war. When they succeeded, a great cheer arose from the boys, with plenty of backslapping all around. After a series of tasks that required cooperation, the walls between the two sides broke down, and the boys became friends across the groups. Among strangers, competition and isolation created enemies. Among enemies, cooperation created friends (**FIGURE 12.15**).

FIGURE 12.15 **Scientific Method: Sherif's Study of Competition and Cooperation**

Hypothesis: Just as competition between groups promotes prejudice and hostility, so cooperation between groups can promote harmony.

Research Method:

1 In Phase 1 of the experiment, boys from two summer camps were pitted against each other in athletic competitions:

2 In Phase 2, the boys from the two camps were required to work together as one group to achieve common goals.

Results: Competition created tension and hostility, but after a series of cooperative efforts, the boys began to make friends across groups.

Conclusion: Shared goals requiring cooperation across group lines can reduce hostility between groups.

Research over the past four decades has indicated that only certain types of contact between hostile groups will likely reduce prejudice and discrimination. Shared *superordinate* goals—those that require people to cooperate—reduce hostility between groups. People who work together to achieve a common goal often break down subgroup distinctions as they become one larger group (Dovidio et al., 2004). For example, athletes on multiethnic teams often develop positive attitudes toward other ethnicities.

JIGSAW CLASSROOM   The programs that most successfully bring groups together involve person-to-person interaction. A good example is Eliot Aronson's jigsaw classroom, which he developed with his students in the 1970s. In this program, students work together in mixed-race or mixed-sex groups in which each member of the group is an expert on one aspect of the assignment. For instance, when studying Mexico, one group member might study its geography, another its history, and so on. The various geography experts from each group get together and master the material. They then return to their own groups and teach the material to their team members. Thus cooperation is twofold: Each group member cooperates not only with members of other groups but also within the group. More than 800 studies of the jigsaw classroom have demonstrated that it leads to more-positive attitudes toward other ethnicities and that students learn the material better and perform at higher levels. According to Aronson, children in jigsaw classrooms grow to like each other more and develop higher self-esteem than do children in traditional classrooms. The lesson is clear: Communal work toward superordinate goals can reduce prejudice.

 SUMMING UP

How Do We Form Our Impressions of Others?

Human social interaction requires people to form impressions of others. People are highly sensitive to nonverbal information and can develop accurate impressions of others on the basis of very thin slices of behavior. People also are motivated to figure out what causes other people to behave the way they do. People often make biased attributions about others. They tend to attribute other people's behavior to dispositions rather than to situations, and they use heuristic processing, which biases social judgment. Stereotypes result from the normal cognitive process of categorization. However, negative stereotypes and prejudice lead to discrimination. Humans tend to discriminate against those who are threatening, such as outgroup members.

 MEASURING UP

1. Label each of the following statements as an example of stereotyping, prejudice, or discrimination.
   a. "People from New York are loud and obnoxious."
   b. "What can I say, I just don't like people from New York."
   c. Walter tells a joke that makes fun of people from New York.

2. Max was arrested for driving while under the influence of alcohol. Label each of the following statements as an example of personal attribution, situational attribution, or fundamental attribution error.
   a. Max says, "Nobody would give me a ride home. I couldn't sleep at the bar, so I had to get home. I had no other option."
   b. Max's friend says, "Max should know better, but he is a selfish and irresponsible jerk."
   c. Max says, "That was really stupid of me. Maybe I have a drinking problem."

How Do Others Influence Us?

We humans have an overriding motivation to fit in with the group. One way we try to fit in is by presenting ourselves positively, as in being on our best behavior and in trying not to offend others. But we also conform to group norms, obey authorities' commands, and are easily influenced by others in our social groups. The desire to fit in with the group and avoid being ostracized is so great that under some circumstances we willingly engage in behaviors we otherwise would condemn. As noted throughout this chapter, the power of the social situation is much greater than most people believe—and this truth is perhaps the single most important lesson from social psychology. The importance of social influences was summed up by Philip Zimbardo, who commented that it is difficult to remain a cucumber while those around you become pickles.

<aside>
LEARNING OBJECTIVES

Differentiate among conformity, compliance, and obedience.

Apply principles of social influence to common educational situations.
</aside>

Groups Influence Individual Behavior

The first social psychology experiment was conducted in 1897, by Norman Triplett, who showed that bicyclists pedal faster when riding with other people than when riding alone. They do so because of **social facilitation,** in which the presence of others enhances performance. Social facilitation also occurs in other animals, including horses, dogs, rats, birds, fish, and even cockroaches. Robert Zajonc (1965) proposed a model of social facilitation that involves three basic steps (**FIGURE 12.16**). According to Zajonc, all animals are genetically predisposed to become aroused by the presence of others of their own species, since others are associated with most of life's rewards and punishments. Zajonc then invoked Clark Hull's well-known learning principle that arousal leads animals to emit a dominant response, that is, the response most likely to be performed. In front of food, for example, the dominant response is to eat. Zajonc's model expands on Triplett's, predicting that social facilitation can enhance or impair performance. The presence of others improves the performance of a simple task for which the dominant response is well learned, such as the adding of single digits, but it interferes with the performance of a complex task that requires greater thought, such as differential calculus. If employees are performing simple tasks such as database entry, they might work best in a fairly open environment, either around a common table or in cubicles, where each person is aware of the rate at which others are performing. If employees are performing more complicated tasks, such as editing manuscripts, they might work best in private offices, since concentration is paramount and an awareness of how others are performing is irrelevant to the complex work at hand.

SOCIAL LOAFING   In some cases, people work less hard when in a group than when working alone. This **social loafing** occurs when people's efforts are pooled so that no one individual feels personally responsible for the group's output. In a classic study, six blindfolded people wearing headphones were told to shout as loudly as they could. Some were told they were shouting alone; others were told that they were shouting with other people. Participants did not shout as loudly when they believed that others were shouting as well (Latané, Williams, & Harkins, 1979). However, making it clear that individual efforts can be monitored eliminates social loafing. Thus if a group is working on a project, each person must feel personally responsible for some component of the project for everyone to exert maximum effort.

DEINDIVIDUATION   People sometimes lose their individuality when they become part of a group. **Deindividuation** occurs when people are not self-aware and therefore are not paying attention to their personal standards. Recall that self-awareness

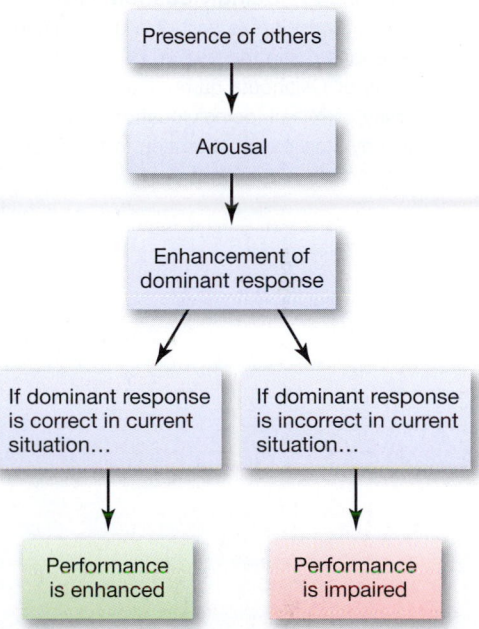

FIGURE 12.16 Social Facilitation The mere presence of other people leads to increased arousal, which in turn favors the dominant response. If this is the correct response, performance is enhanced, but if it is the incorrect response, performance suffers.

social loafing   The tendency for people to work less hard in a group than when working alone.

deindividuation   A phenomenon of low self-awareness, in which people lose their individuality and fail to attend to personal standards.

typically causes people to act in accordance with the values and beliefs they hold. When self-awareness disappears, so do restraints. Deindividuated people often do things they would not do if they were alone or self-aware. A good example is crowd behavior. Most of us like to think we would try to help a person who was threatening suicide. But people in crowds often not only fail to intercede but also sometimes egg the person on, yelling "Jump!, Jump!" to someone teetering on a ledge.

People are especially likely to become deindividuated when they are aroused and anonymous and when responsibility is diffused. Rioting by fans, looting following disasters, and other mob behaviors are the products of deindividuation. Recall the Stanford prison study, mentioned at the beginning of this chapter. The study had to be stopped after just six days because the students became so immersed in their roles that many guards acted brutally and many prisoners became listless and apathetic. The situation was powerful enough to radically alter people's behavior through a process of deindividuation. Most militaries around the world require each of their members to have a standard haircut and an identical uniform because people who look similar are more likely to conform and respond to orders—including orders to commit acts of violence against an enemy. Not all deindividuated behavior is so serious, of course. Gamblers in crowded casinos, fans doing the wave, and people dancing the funky chicken while inebriated at weddings are most likely in deindividuated states, and accordingly they act in ways they would not if they were self-aware (**FIGURE 12.17**).

GROUP DECISION MAKING It has been said that a group's intelligence can be determined by averaging its members' IQs and then dividing that average by the number of people in the group. In other words, groups are known for making bad decisions. Social psychologists have shown that being in a group influences decision making in curious ways. For instance, in the 1960s the psychologist James Stoner found that groups often made riskier decisions than individuals did. This phenomenon, the *risky-shift effect,* accounts for why children in a group may try something dangerous that none of them would have tried alone. Subsequent research has demonstrated that groups are sometimes riskier than individuals and sometimes more cautious, as groups tend to enhance the initial attitudes of members who already agree. This process is known as *group polarization.* For example, discussion tends to make people on juries believe more strongly in their initial opinions about defendants' guilt or innocence. When groups make risky decisions, they usually do so because the individuals initially favor a risky course of action and, through mutual persuasion, come to agreement.

Sometimes group members are particularly concerned with maintaining the group's cohesiveness, so for the sake of cordiality the group will make a bad decision. In 1972, the social psychologist Irving Janis coined the term *groupthink* to describe this extreme form of group polarization. Contemporary examples of groupthink include the decision to launch the space shuttle *Challenger* despite the clear evidence of a problem with a part; choices made by President Bill Clinton and his advisers following the allegations of his affair with Monica Lewinsky, a sequence of events that ultimately led to his impeachment; and the second Bush administration's decision to go to war with Iraq over weapons of mass destruction that did not exist, as later investigations showed (see "Critical Thinking Skill: Recognizing and Correcting for Belief Persistence ...," in Chapter 9). Groupthink typically occurs when a group is under intense pressure, is facing external threats, and is biased in a particular direction. The group does not carefully process all the information available to it, dissension is discouraged, and group members assure each other they are doing the right thing. To prevent groupthink, leaders must refrain from expressing their opin-

FIGURE 12.17 Deindividuation When people are swept up as part of a group, such as these fans doing the "wave" during a University of Oklahoma game against the University of Miami, deindividuation can happen if they stop paying attention to their personal standards.

FIGURE 12.18 Try for Yourself: Working Effectively in Groups

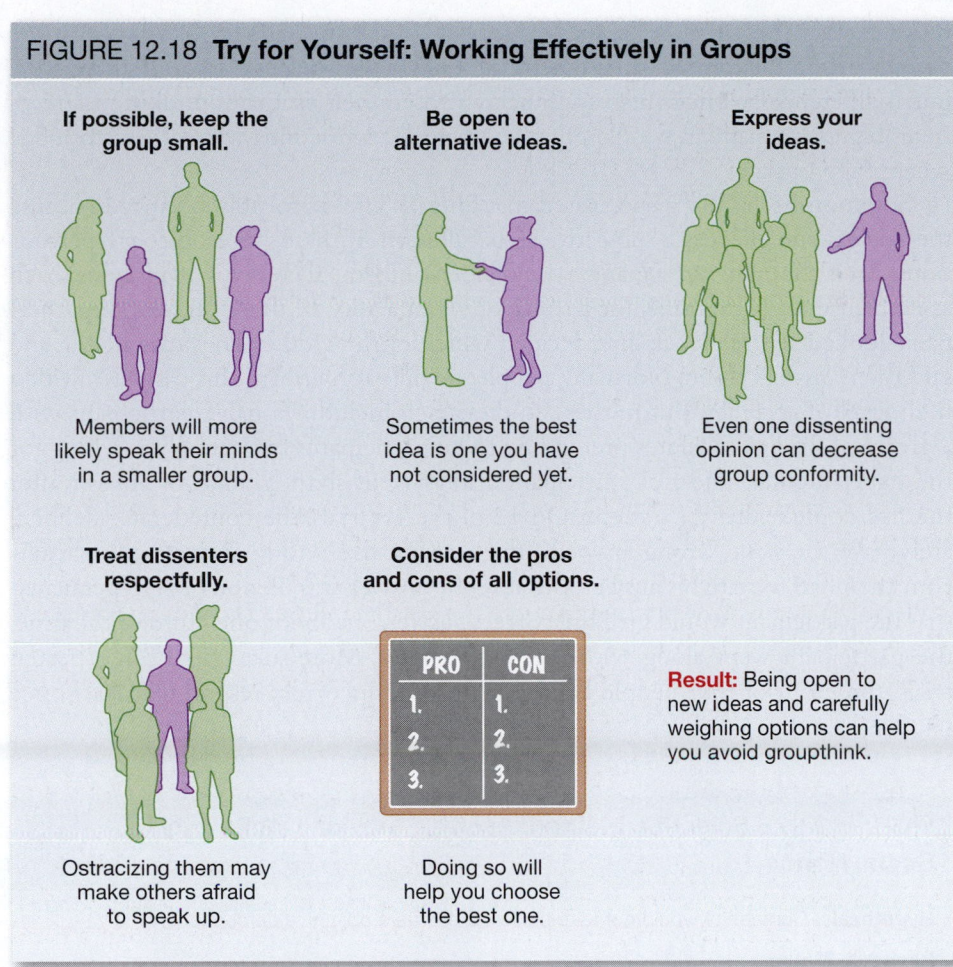

If possible, keep the group small.

Members will more likely speak their minds in a smaller group.

Be open to alternative ideas.

Sometimes the best idea is one you have not considered yet.

Express your ideas.

Even one dissenting opinion can decrease group conformity.

Treat dissenters respectfully.

Ostracizing them may make others afraid to speak up.

Consider the pros and cons of all options.

PRO	CON
1.	1.
2.	2.
3.	3.

Doing so will help you choose the best one.

Result: Being open to new ideas and carefully weighing options can help you avoid groupthink.

---

ions too strongly at the beginning of discussions. The group should be encouraged to consider alternative ideas, either by having someone play devil's advocate or by purposefully examining outside opinions. Carefully going through alternatives and weighing the pros and cons of each can help people avoid groupthink (**FIGURE 12.18**).

We Conform to Social Norms

Society needs rules. Imagine, for example, the problems you would cause if you woke up one morning and decided that from then on you would drive on the wrong side of the road. **Social norms**—expected standards of conduct—influence behavior in multiple ways, such as indicating which behavior is appropriate in a given situation. Standing in line is a social norm, and people who violate that norm by cutting in line are often reprimanded and directed to the back of the line. **Conformity,** the altering of one's behaviors or opinions to match those of others or to match social norms, is also a powerful form of social influence.

How much do people conform? Muzafer Sherif was one of the first researchers to demonstrate the power of norms and conformity in social judgment. His studies, conducted in the 1930s, relied on a perceptual phenomenon known as the *autokinetic effect,* in which a stationary point of light appears to move when viewed in a totally dark environment. This effect occurs because people have no frame of reference and therefore cannot correct for small eye movements. Sherif asked participants who were alone in a room to estimate how far the light moved. Individual differences were considerable; some saw the light move only an inch or two, whereas others saw it

social norms Expected standards of conduct, which influence behavior.

conformity The altering of one's opinions or behaviors to match those of others or to match social norms.

move eight inches or more. In the second part of the study, Sherif put two or more participants in the room and had them call out their estimates. Although there were initial differences, participants very quickly revised their estimates until they agreed. In ambiguous situations, people often compare their reactions with others' to judge what is appropriate.

Solomon Asch (1955) speculated that Sherif's effect probably occurred because the autokinetic effect is a subjective visual illusion. If there were objective perceptions, Asch thought, participants would not conform. To test his hypothesis, Asch assembled male participants for a study of visual acuity. In the 18 trials, the participants looked at a reference line, decided which of three other lines matched it, and said their answers aloud. Normally, people are able to perform this easy task with a high level of accuracy. But in these studies, Asch included a naive participant with a group of five confederates pretending to be participants but actually working for the experimenter. The real participant always went sixth, giving his answer after the five confederates gave theirs. On 12 of the 18 trials, the confederates deliberately gave the same wrong answer. After hearing five wrong answers, the participant then had to state his answer. Because the answer was obvious, Asch speculated that the participant would give the correct answer, but about one-third of the time, the participant went along with the confederates. More surprisingly, in repeated trials, three out of four people conformed to the incorrect response at least once (**FIGURE 12.19**).

FIGURE 12.19 Scientific Method: Asch's Study on Conformity to Social Norms

Hypothesis: Conformity would not take place if there were objective perceptions.

Research Method:

1 A participant joined a group of five other participants—who were confederates, secretly in league with the researcher. Each participant was asked to look at a reference line **(left)** and then say out loud which of three comparison lines matched it **(right)**.

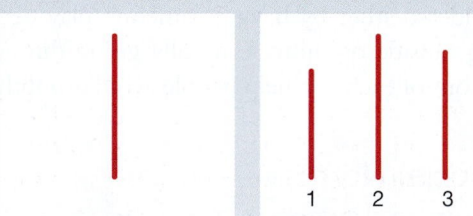

Reference line   Comparison lines

2 The five confederates deliberately gave the wrong answer in 12 out of 18 trials (the real participant is in the middle of the photos below, with glasses).

The real participant hears the answer given by the confederates.

He has a hard time believing their wrong answers.

But he starts to doubt his own eyes.

Results: When confederates gave false answers first, three-quarters of the real participants conformed by giving the wrong answer at least once.

Conclusion: People tend to conform to social norms, even when those norms are obviously wrong.

Research consistently has demonstrated that people tend to conform to social norms. This effect can be seen outside the laboratory as well: Adolescents conform to peer pressure to smoke; jury members go along with the group rather than state their own opinions; people stand in line to buy tickets. But when do people reject social norms? In a series of follow-up studies, Asch and others identified factors that decrease the chances of conformity. One factor is group size. If there are only one or two confederates, a naive participant usually does not conform; as soon as the confederates number three or more, the participant conforms. However, conformity seems to level off at a certain point. Subsequent research has found that even groups as large as 16 do not lead to greater conformity than groups of 7.

Asch found that lack of unanimity is another factor that diminishes conformity. If even one confederate gives the correct answer, conformity to the group norm decreases a great deal. Any dissent from majority opinion can diminish the influence of social norms. But dissenters are typically not treated well by groups. In 1951, Stanley Schachter conducted a study in which a group of students debated the fate of a juvenile delinquent, Johnny Rocco. A confederate deviated from the group judgment of how Johnny should be treated. When it became clear that the confederate would not be persuaded by group sentiment, the group began to ostracize him. When group members subsequently were given the opportunity to reduce group size, they consistently rejected the "deviant" confederate. The bottom line is that groups enforce conformity, and those who fail to go along are rejected. The need to belong, and the anxiety associated with the fear of social exclusion, gives a group powerful influence over its members. Indeed, a brain imaging study that used a conformity test similar to Asch's found activation of the amygdala, perhaps a fear response, in participants whose answers did not conform to the group's incorrect answer (Berns et al., 2005).

Universities across North America have tried to harness the power of social norms to reduce binge drinking on campus. They have used social norms marketing in attempts to correct faulty misperceptions regarding peer drinking; proponents might put up posters saying, for example, "Most students have fewer than four drinks when they party." Unfortunately, social norms marketing may inadvertently increase drinking among light drinkers, whose behavior is also susceptible to social norms (Russell, Clapp, & Dejong, 2005); students who usually have only one drink at a time might interpret the posters as suggesting that the norm is to have two or three drinks, and they might adjust their behavior accordingly. One team of researchers demonstrated that simply providing descriptive norms (i.e., the frequency of behavior) can cause this sort of backfire effect. They found that adding a message that the behavior is undesirable might help prevent social norms marketing from increasing the behavior it is meant to reduce (Schultz, Nolan, Cialdini, Goldstein, & Griskevicius, 2007).

We Are Compliant

Often people influence the behavior of others simply by asking them to do things. If the others do the requested things, they are exhibiting **compliance.** A number of factors increase compliance. For instance, Joseph Forgas (1998) has demonstrated that people in good moods are especially likely to comply. This tendency may be the basis for "buttering up" others when we want things from them. According to Robert Cialdini (2008), people often comply with requests because, failing to pay attention, they respond without fully considering their options; they are following a standard mental shortcut to avoid conflict. For instance, if you give people a reason for a request, they will much more likely comply, even if the reason makes little sense.

compliance The tendency to agree to do things requested by others.

People can use a number of powerful strategies to influence others to comply. For instance, because of the *foot-in-the-door effect,* people will more likely comply with a large and undesirable request if earlier they have agreed to a small request. Jonathan Freedman and Scott Fraser (1966) asked homeowners to allow a large, unattractive "DRIVE CAREFULLY" sign to be placed on their front lawns. As you might imagine, fewer than one in five people agreed to do so. However, another group of homeowners first was asked to sign a petition supporting legislation that would reduce traffic accidents. A few weeks later, these same people were approached about having the large sign placed on their lawns, and more than half agreed. Once people commit to a course of action, they behave in ways consistent with that course.

The opposite influence technique is the *door in the face,* thanks to which people will more likely agree to a small request after they have refused a large request, because the second request seems modest in comparison and they want to seem reasonable. Salespeople often use this technique. Another favorite among salespeople is the *low-balling strategy,* which begins when a salesperson offers a product—for example, a car—for a very low price. Once the customer agrees, the salesperson may claim that the manager did not approve the price or that there will be additional charges. Whatever the reason, a person who has agreed to buy a product will often agree to pay the increased cost.

We Are Obedient to Authority

One of the most famous and most disturbing psychology experiments was conducted in the early 1960s by Stanley Milgram, who wanted to understand why apparently normal German citizens willingly obeyed orders to injure or kill innocent people during World War II (**FIGURE 12.20**). Milgram was interested in the determinants of *obedience*—that is, the factors that influence people to follow orders given by an authority. Try to imagine yourself as a participant in Milgram's experiment. You have agreed to take part in a study of learning. On arriving at the laboratory, you meet your fellow participant, a 60-year-old grandfatherly type. The experimenter describes the study as consisting of a teacher administering electric shocks to a learner engaged in a simple memory task involving word pairs. Your role as the teacher is determined by an apparently random drawing of your name from a hat. On hearing that he may receive electric shocks, the learner reveals that he has a heart condition and expresses minor reservations. The experimenter says that although the shocks will be painful, they will not cause permanent tissue damage. You help the experimenter take the learner to a small room and hook him up to the electric shock machine. You then proceed to a nearby room and sit at a table in front of a large shock generator with switches from 15 to 450 volts. Each voltage level carries a label, ranging from "slight" to "danger—severe shock" to, finally, an ominous "XXX."

You perform your task, giving the learner a shock each time he makes a mistake and increasing the voltage with each subsequent error. When you reach 75 volts, over the intercom you hear the man yelp in pain. At 150 volts, he screams, bangs on the wall, and demands that the experiment be stopped. The

FIGURE 12.20 Stanley Milgram Milgram, pictured here with his infamous shock generator, demonstrated that average people will obey even hideous orders given by an authority figure.

man is clearly in agony as—at the experimenter's command—you apply additional, stronger shocks. Each time you say you are quitting and try to stop the experiment, the experimenter replies, "The experiment requires that you continue," "It is essential that you go on," "There is no other choice; you must go on!" So you do. At 300 volts, the learner refuses to answer any more questions. After 330 volts, the learner is silent. All along you have wanted to leave, and you severely regret participating in the study. You might have killed the man, for all you know.

Does this scenario sound crazy to you? If you really were the teacher, at what level would you stop administering the shocks? Would you quit as soon as the learner started to complain? Would you go up to 450 volts? The various people Milgram asked predicted that most participants would go no higher than 135 volts and that fewer than one in a thousand people would administer the highest level of shock. But that is not what happened. What did happen changed how people viewed the power of authority.

Milgram found that although almost all the participants tried to quit, nearly two-thirds completely obeyed all the experimenter's directives (**FIGURE 12.21**), despite believing they were administering 450 volts to an older man with a heart condition (actually a confederate). These findings have been replicated by Milgram and others around the world. The conclusion of these studies is that ordinary people can be coerced into obedience by insistent authorities, even when what they are coerced into goes against the way they usually would behave. At the same time, these results do not mean all people are equally obedient. Indeed, some aspects of personality seem related to being obedient, such as the extent to which people are concerned about how others view them (Blass, 1991). As discussed in the next chapter, both situation and personality influence behavior.

Surprised by the results of his study, Milgram next set out to study how to reduce obedience. He found that some situations produced less compliance. For instance, if the teacher could see or had to touch the learner, obedience decreased. When the experimenter gave the orders over the telephone and thus was more removed from the situation, obedience dropped dramatically.

Throughout these studies, Milgram was highly concerned with his participants' mental states. In systematic debriefings, he carefully revealed the true nature of the experiments to the participants, and he made sure that the teachers met the confederate learners and that the teachers could see that the learners were not hurt in any way. Milgram also followed his participants over time to ensure that they experienced no long-term negative effects. Actually, many people were glad they had participated, feeling that they had learned something about themselves and about human nature. Most of us assume that only sadistic miscreants would willingly inflict injury on others when ordered to do so. Milgram's research, and studies that followed up on it, demonstrated that ordinary people may do horrible things when ordered to do so by an authority (**FIGURE 12.22**). Although some people speculate that these results would not be true today, a recent replication found that 70 percent of the participants were obedient up to the maximum voltage in the experiment (Burger, 2009).

All the background data available on the prison guards at Abu Ghraib (see the discussion at the opening of this chapter), for example, suggest they were ordinary people. Investigators do not know exactly what the guards were ordered to do, but a number of social factors, from deindividuation to social facilitation to inappropriate norms and conformity, contributed to the situation and likely played prominent roles in the mistreatment of Abu Ghraib prisoners. As noted earlier, all of us need to be aware of situational influences when we evaluate our own behavior and that of others, particularly when our core beliefs and values are at risk.

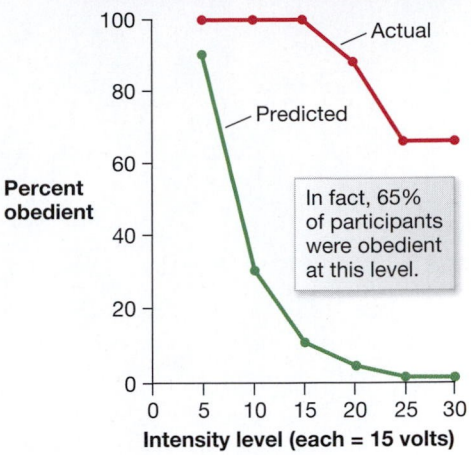

The overall prediction was that fewer than one-tenth of a percent of participants in the Milgram experiments would obey completely and provide the maximum level of shock.

In fact, 65% of participants were obedient at this level.

FIGURE 12.21 Predicting the Results Psychiatrists, college sophomores, middle-class adults, and both graduate students and professors in the behavioral sciences offered predictions about the results of Milgram's experiments. Their predictions were incorrect.

FIGURE 12.22 Scientific Method: Milgram's Shock Experiments on Obedience

Hypothesis: People are obedient to authority figures.

Research Method:

1 In one condition, each participant was instructed to "shock," from another room, a participant (learner) who was secretly in league with the experimenter.

2 In another condition, each participant was instructed to touch and "shock" a learner sitting next to the participant. In both conditions, the experimenter would instruct the participant to give the learner increasingly severe shocks.

3 After the experiment, each participant was introduced to the confederate learner and could see that the learner had not been harmed.

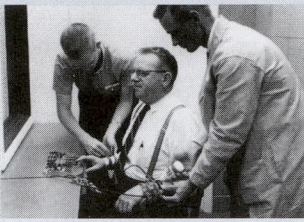  

Results: In the first condition, almost all the participants tried to quit, but nearly two-thirds obeyed the experimenter's directives. In the "touch" condition, fewer than one-third of the participants obeyed the experimenter's orders.

Conclusion: Most people will obey even hideous orders given by insistent authority figures, but this willingness is lessened when people are made more personally responsible.

SUMMING UP

How Do Others Influence Us?

For the most part, people follow group norms, are influenced by others' opinions, and are obedient to authority. Most people underestimate the power of these effects or do not believe that they themselves are affected by social influence. Yet the evidence is overwhelming that in many situations people will engage in behaviors quite inconsistent with their own standards. Sometimes, for example, people in a state of deindividuation lose awareness of the values and beliefs they hold. Those who are aware of the power of social influence often use specific strategies to manipulate others' behavior, such as by using foot-in-the-door, door-in-the-face, and low-balling techniques. The more each of us is aware of our own values and beliefs, the more capable we are of upholding our own standards.

MEASURING UP

1. Label each of the following scenarios as an example of conformity, compliance, or obedience.
   a. Bettina decides to join Facebook because all her friends have already created profiles.
   b. Elisa says to her son, "Wash the dishes before you go outside to play." He does so.
   c. Randall goes into an office supply store to make photocopies. There are long lines at each copier. As a woman steps up to one of the machines to take her turn, he approaches her and asks, "Do you mind if I go next? I need to make a copy." She says yes.

2. Match each of the following social influence constructs with the correct definition: deindividuation, group polarization, social facilitation, and social loafing.
   a. A lack of self-awareness has a disinhibiting effect, allowing people to act in ways that are inconsistent with the beliefs and values they hold.
   b. People make less individual effort when their efforts are pooled than when they work alone.
   c. Over the course of group discussion, individuals become increasingly committed to attitudes they held before the group discussion.
   d. The presence of others enhances performance of simple tasks that are well learned.

When Do We Harm or Help Others?

Although obedience can lead people to commit horrible acts, the need to belong to a group also can lead us to acts of altruism and of generosity. Events of the last few years have revealed the human capacities for harming and helping others. We have seen terrorists killing civilians in Mumbai, guards abusing prisoners at Abu Ghraib, and tribal warfare in the Darfur region of Sudan. Yet people also can be kind, compassionate, and giving, as evidenced by the outpouring of support to the victims of the 2004 tsunami (noted earlier in this chapter). Similarly, members of the group Doctors Without Borders travel to dangerous regions around the globe to care for those in need. This tension between our aggressive and altruistic sides is at the core of who we are as a species. Psychological scientists working at all levels of analysis have provided much insight into the roles that nature and nurture play in these fundamental human behaviors.

Aggression Can Be Adaptive

Aggression can be expressed through countless behaviors, all involving the intention to harm someone else. Among nonhuman animals, it often occurs in the context of fighting over a mate or defending territory from intruders, though in the latter case just the threat of aggressive action may be sufficient to dissuade. Among humans, physical aggression is common among young children but relatively rare in adults; adults' aggressive acts more often involve words, or other symbols, meant to threaten, intimidate, or emotionally harm others. Aggression can be considered across the levels of analysis, from basic biology to cultural context.

aggression Any behavior or action that involves the intention to harm someone else.

BIOLOGICAL FACTORS At the biological level of analysis—largely involving research with nonhuman animals—we see that stimulating certain brain regions or altering neurochemicals can lead to substantial changes in behavior. Stimulating or damaging the septum, amygdala, or hypothalamus regions in the brain (see Figure 3.28) leads to corresponding changes in the level of aggression displayed. For example, stimulating a cat's amygdala with an electric probe causes the animal to attack, whereas damaging the amygdala leads to passive behavior. In 1937, researchers Heinrich Kluver and Paul Bucy produced a striking behavioral change by removing the amygdalas of normally very aggressive rhesus monkeys. Following the surgery, the monkeys were tame, friendly, and easy to handle. They began to approach and explore normally feared objects, such as snakes. They also showed unusual oral behavior, putting anything within reach into their mouths, including snakes, matches, nails, dirt, and feces. The behavior associated with damage to this region is now referred to as *Kluver-Bucy syndrome*.

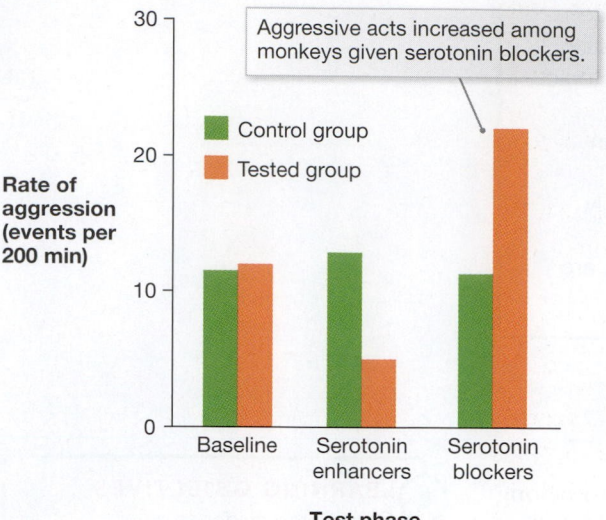

Aggressive acts increased among monkeys given serotonin blockers.

Control group
Tested group

Rate of aggression (events per 200 min)

30

20

10

0

Baseline   Serotonin   Serotonin
            enhancers   blockers

Test phase

FIGURE 12.23 Serotonin and Aggression Male vervet monkeys were given either serotonin enhancers or serotonin blockers. The results suggest serotonin is important in the control of aggressive behavior.

FIGURE 12.24 Frustration-Aggression Hypothesis Frustration generally leads to aggression. For example, road rage is most likely to occur where traffic is heavy and drivers feel frustrated.

In terms of neurochemistry, several lines of evidence suggest that serotonin is especially important in the control of aggressive behavior (Caramaschi, de Boer, & Koolhaus, 2007). In a study using monkeys, drugs that enhance the activity of serotonin lowered aggression, whereas those that interfere with serotonin increased aggression (Raleigh, McGuire, Brammer, Pollack, & Yuwiler, 1991; **FIGURE 12.23**). In humans, low levels of serotonin have been associated with aggression in adults and hostility and disruptive behavior in children (Kruesi et al., 1992). In a large sample of men from New Zealand, low serotonin levels were associated with violence but not with criminal acts in general (Moffitt et al., 1998). Additionally, postmortem examinations of suicide victims have revealed extremely low serotonin levels. Although suicide may seem very different from aggression, many psychologists believe suicide and violence toward others are manifestations of the same aggressive tendencies. Indeed, low serotonin levels were found among those who had killed themselves violently (such as by shooting themselves) but not among those who had done so nonviolently (such as by taking drug overdoses; Asberg, Shalling, Traskman-Bendz, & Wagner, 1987).

Decreased serotonin levels may interfere with good decision making in the face of danger or of social threat. For instance, monkeys with the lowest serotonin levels are the least socially skilled (Higley et al., 1996). This lack of social competence often leads the other monkeys to attack and kill them. Monkeys with low serotonin also likely will pick fights with much larger monkeys. Do these findings have implications for humans? Possibly. In one study, participants given a drug that enhances serotonin activity were found to be less hostile and more cooperative over time, compared with the control group (Knutson et al., 1998).

INDIVIDUAL FACTORS In the 1930s, John Dollard and his colleagues proposed the first major psychological model of aggression. According to their **frustration-aggression hypothesis,** the extent to which people feel frustrated predicts the likelihood that they will be aggressive. The more people's goals are blocked, the greater their frustration and therefore the greater their aggression. Slow traffic is frustrating, for example, and if it impedes you from getting somewhere you really want or need to go, you may feel especially frustrated. If another driver then cuts in front of you, you may feel especially angry and perhaps make an aggressive hand gesture, shout, or otherwise express yourself (**FIGURE 12.24**).

According to Leonard Berkowitz's *cognitive-neoassociationistic model* (1990), frustration leads to aggression by eliciting negative emotions. Similarly, any situation that induces negative emotions, such as being insulted, afraid, overly hot, or in pain, can trigger physical aggression even if it does not induce frustration. Berkowitz proposed that negative emotion leads to aggression because it primes cognitive knowledge associated with aggression; in other words, negative events activate thoughts related to escaping or fighting, and those thoughts prepare a person to act aggressively. Whether someone behaves aggressively depends on the situational context. If the situation also cues violence—for example, if the person has recently watched a violent movie or been in the presence of weapons—the person more likely will act aggressively.

Aggression Has Social and Cultural Aspects

An evolutionary approach to aggression would call for similar patterns of aggressive behavior to exist in all human societies. After all, if aggression provided a selective advantage for human ancestors, it should have done so for all humans. But the data show that violence varies dramatically across cultures and even within cultures at different times. For example, over the course of 300 years, Sweden went from being one of the most violent nations on Earth to being one of the most peaceable, a change that did not correspond with a change in the gene pool. Moreover, murder rates are far higher in some countries than in others (**FIGURE 12.25**). Analysis of crime statistics in the United States reveals that physical violence is much more prevalent in the South than in the North. Aggression may be part of human nature, but culture influences people's tendencies to commit acts of physical violence.

Some cultures may be violent because they subscribe to a *culture of honor,* a belief system in which men are primed to protect their reputations through physical aggression. Men in the southern United States, for example, traditionally were (and perhaps still are) raised to be ready to fight for their honor and to respond aggressively to personal threats. To determine whether southern males are more likely to be aggressive than northern males, researchers conducted a series of studies at the University of Michigan (Cohen, Nisbett, Bowdle, & Schwarz, 1996). In each study, a male participant walking down a narrow hallway had to pass a male confederate who was blocking the hallway at a filing cabinet. As the participant tried to edge past the confederate, the confederate responded angrily and insulted the participant. Compared with participants raised in the North, those raised in the South became more upset and were more likely to feel personally challenged, more

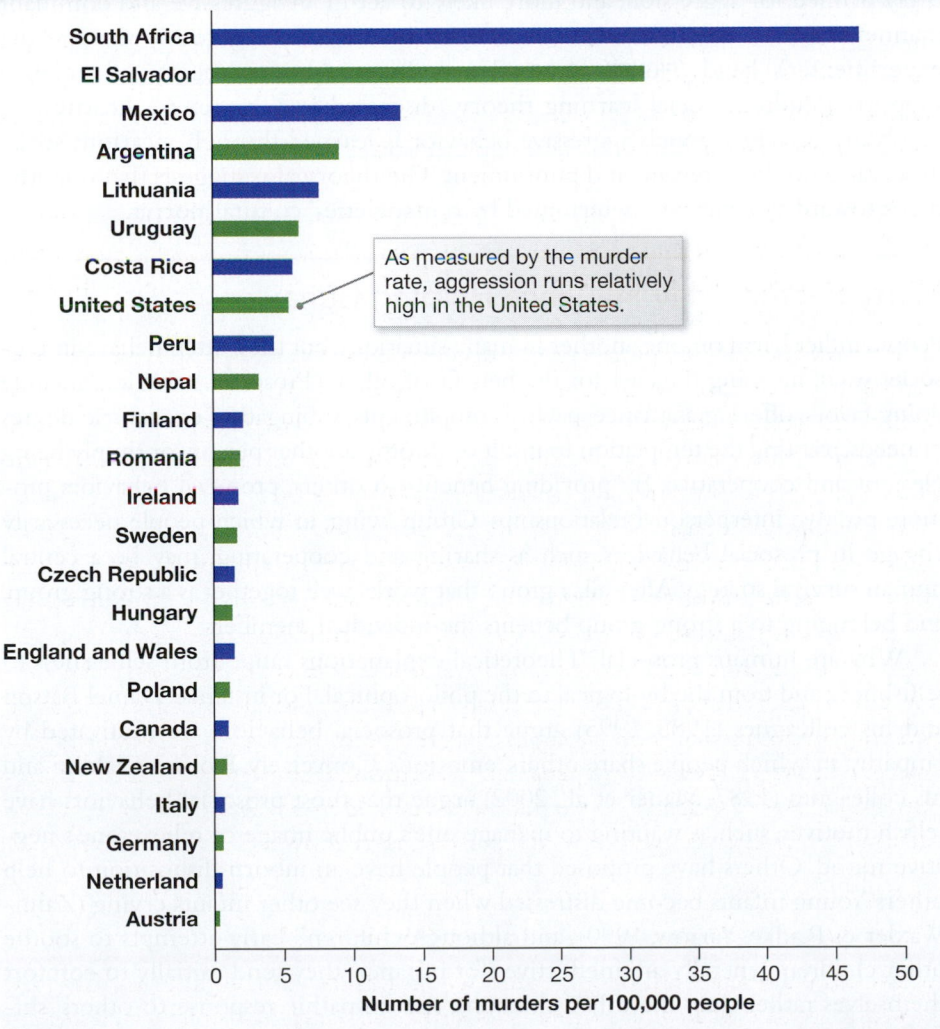

FIGURE 12.25 Aggression Varies across Cultures

As measured by the murder rate, aggression runs relatively high in the United States.

Number of murders per 100,000 people

SOURCE: United Nations, 2002.

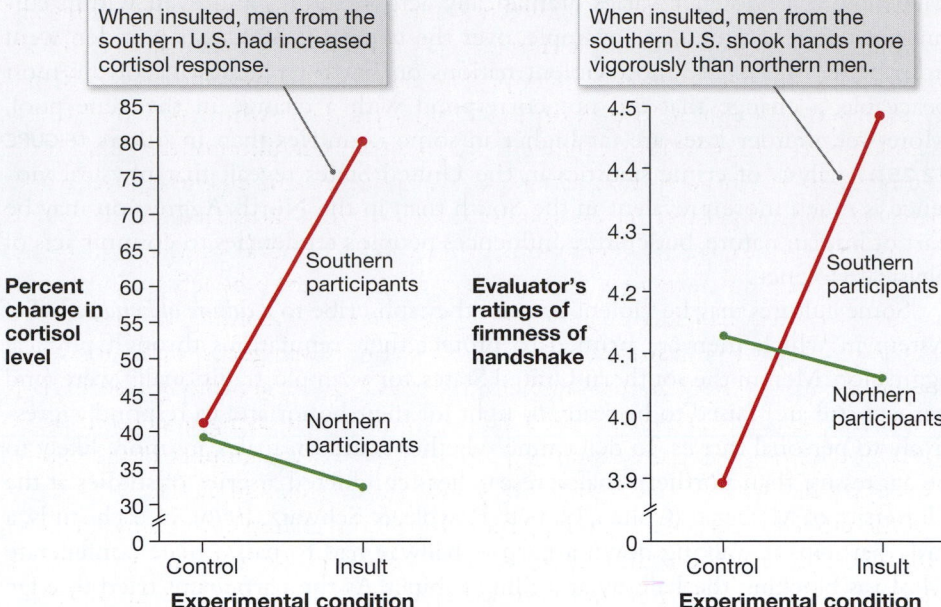

FIGURE 12.26 Aggressive Responses to Insults

physiologically aroused (measured by cortisol and testosterone increases), more cognitively primed for aggression, and more likely to act in an aggressive and dominant manner for the rest of the experiment—for instance, by vigorously shaking the experimenter's hand (**FIGURE 12.26**). The culture-of-honor theory of violence supports Bandura's social learning theory (discussed in Chapter 6, "Learning"), according to which much aggressive behavior is learned through vicarious social observation of both reward and punishment. The theory also suggests that our attitudes toward violence are determined by our societies' cultural norms.

Many Factors May Influence Helping Behavior

prosocial Tending to benefit others.

People inflict harm on one another in many situations, but they often behave in **prosocial** ways, meaning they act for the benefit of others. Prosocial behaviors include doing favors, offering assistance, paying compliments, subjugating egocentric desires or needs, resisting the temptation to insult or throttle another person, or simply being pleasant and cooperative. By providing benefits to others, prosocial behaviors promote positive interpersonal relationships. Group living, in which people necessarily engage in prosocial behaviors such as sharing and cooperating, may be a central human survival strategy. After all, a group that works well together is a strong group, and belonging to a strong group benefits the individual members.

Why are humans prosocial? Theoretical explanations range from selflessness to selfishness, and from the biological to the philosophical. For instance, Daniel Batson and his colleagues (1988; 1995) argue that prosocial behaviors are motivated by empathy, in which people share others' emotions. Conversely, Robert Cialdini and his colleagues (1987; Maner et al., 2002) argue that most prosocial behaviors have selfish motives, such as wanting to manage one's public image or relieve one's negative mood. Others have proposed that people have an inborn disposition to help others. Young infants become distressed when they see other infants crying (Zahn-Waxler & Radke-Yarrow, 1990), and although children's early attempts to soothe other children generally are ineffective (for instance, they tend initially to comfort themselves rather than the other children), this empathic response to others' suffering suggests that prosocial behavior is hardwired.

Altruism is the providing of help when it is needed, without any apparent reward for doing so. The fact that people help others, and even risk personal safety to do so, may seem contrary to evolutionary principles; after all, those who protect themselves first would appear to have an advantage over those who risk their lives to help others. During the 1960s, the geneticist William Hamilton offered an answer to this riddle; he proposed that natural selection occurs at the genetic level rather than at the individual level. As discussed in Chapter 1, the "fittest" animals pass along the most genes to future generations, through the survival of their offspring. Hamilton's concept of *inclusive fitness* describes the adaptive benefits of transmitting genes rather than focusing on individual survival. According to this model, people are altruistic toward those with whom they share genes, a phenomenon known as *kin selection*. A good example of kin selection occurs among insects, such as ants and bees, whose workers feed and protect the egg-laying queen but never reproduce. By protecting the group's eggs, they maximize the number of their common genes that will survive into future generations (Dugatkin, 2004).

Of course, sometimes animals help nonrelatives: For example, dolphins and lions will look after orphans within their own species. Similarly, a person who jumps into a lake to save a drowning stranger is probably not acting for the sake of genetic transmission. Robert Trivers (1971) proposed the idea of *reciprocal helping* to explain altruism toward nonrelatives. According to Trivers, one animal helps another because the other may return the favor in the future. Consider grooming, in which primates take turns cleaning each other's fur: "You scratch my back, and I'll scratch yours." For reciprocal helping to be adaptive, benefits must outweigh costs, and indeed people will less likely help when the costs of doing so are high. Reciprocal helping will also much more likely occur among animals, such as humans, that live in social groups because their species survival depends on cooperation. Thus, as discussed above, people will more likely help members of their ingroups than those of outgroups. From an evolutionary perspective, then, altruism confers benefits, either by increasing the transmission of genes or by increasing the likelihood that others in the social group will reciprocate when needed.

Some Situations Lead to Bystander Apathy

In 1964, a young woman named Kitty Genovese was walking home from work in a relatively safe area of New York City. An assailant savagely attacked her for half an hour, eventually killing her. At the time, a newspaper reported that none of the 38 witnesses to the crime tried to help or called the police (**FIGURE 12.27**). As you might imagine, most people who followed the story were outraged that 38 people could sit by and watch a brutal murder. That story appears to have been wrong, however, as none of the few witnesses was in a position to observe what was happening to Genovese (Manning, Levine, & Collins, 2007).

Yet the idea of 38 silent witnesses prompted researchers to undertake important research on how people react in emergencies. Shortly after the Genovese murder, social psychologists Bibb Latané and John Darley examined situations that produce the **bystander intervention effect,** or the failure to offer help to someone observed to be in need. Although common sense might suggest that the more people there are available to help, the more likely it is that a victim will be helped, Latané and Darley made the paradoxical claim that a person will less likely help if other bystanders are around.

To test their theory, Latané and Darley conducted studies in which people were placed in situations that indicated they should seek help. In one of the first situations (Latané & Darley, 1968), male college students filling out questionnaires in a

altruism The providing of help when it is needed, without any apparent reward for doing so.

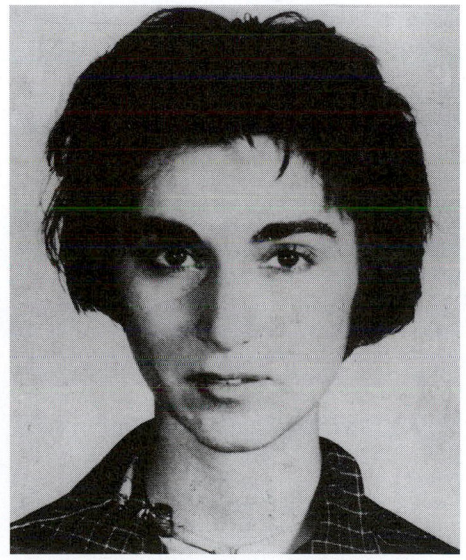

FIGURE 12.27 Kitty Genovese When Genovese was murdered, was she also the victim of bystander apathy?

bystander intervention effect The failure to offer help by those who observe someone in need.

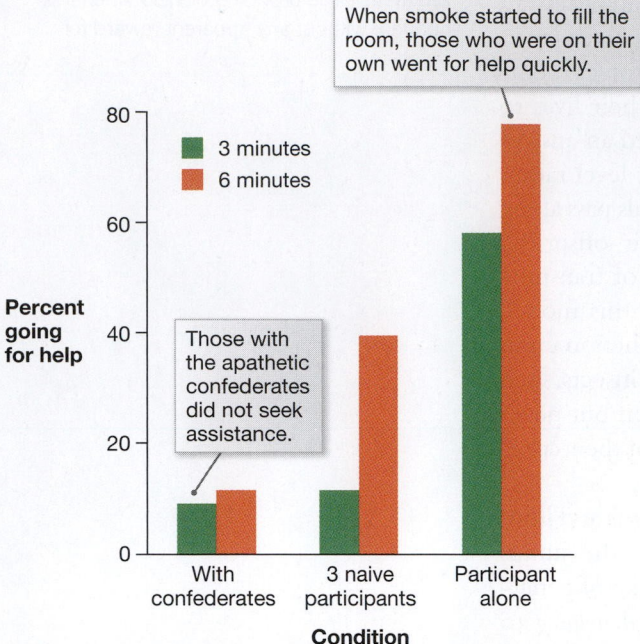

When smoke started to fill the room, those who were on their own went for help quickly.

Those with the apathetic confederates did not seek assistance.

Percent going for help

- 3 minutes
- 6 minutes

Condition

With confederates | 3 naive participants | Participant alone

FIGURE 12.28 The Bystander Intervention Effect Participants waited with two apathetic confederates, with two other naive participants, or alone. This chart records their reactions to smoke filling the room.

room were exposed to pungent smoke puffing in through the heating vents. Some participants were alone, some were with two other naive participants, and some were with two confederates, who noticed the smoke, shrugged, and continued filling out their questionnaires. When participants were on their own, most went for help. However, when three naive participants were together, few initially went for help. With the two calm confederates, only 10 percent of participants went for help in the first six minutes (**FIGURE 12.28**). The other 90 percent "coughed, rubbed their eyes, and opened the window—but they did not report the smoke" (p. 218). Similar results were obtained in subsequent studies, in which people were confronted with mock crimes, apparent heart attack victims in subway cars, and people passed out in public places. The bystander intervention effect, also called *bystander apathy,* has been shown to occur in a wide variety of contexts. Even divinity students, while rushing to give a lecture on the Good Samaritan, failed to help a person in apparent need of medical attention (Darley & Batson, 1973).

Years of research have indicated four major reasons for the bystander intervention effect. First, a diffusion of responsibility occurs, such that people expect other bystanders to help. Thus the greater the number of people who witness someone in need of help, the less likely it is that any of them will step forward. Second, people fear making social blunders in ambiguous situations. All the laboratory situations had some degree of ambiguity, and people may have worried that they would look foolish if they sought help that was not needed. Evidence indicates that people feel less constrained from seeking help as the need for help becomes clearer. In the Genovese murder case, the few witnesses found the situation unclear and therefore might have been reluctant to call the police. Third, people will less likely help when they are anonymous and can remain so. Therefore, if you need help, it is often wise to point to a specific person and request his or her help by saying something like, "You, in the red shirt, call an ambulance!" Fourth, people weigh how much harm to themselves they risk by helping against what benefits they may have to forgo if they help. Imagine you are walking to a potentially dull class on a beautiful day, and in front of you someone falls down, twists an ankle, and needs transportation to the nearest clinic. You probably would be willing to help. Now imagine you are running to a final exam that counts for 90 percent of your grade. In this case, you probably would be much less likely to offer assistance.

 SUMMING UP

When Do We Harm or Help Others?

Humans in all cultures engage in aggressive acts. Frustration can lead to aggression, as can other factors that induce negative affect. This effect may occur because negative emotion primes aggressive thoughts. Beliefs and cultural norms can alter the expression of aggressive behavior. People often are willing to offer help to others, especially if the person needing help is a relative. However, people will less likely offer help when there are personal risks involved and when responsibility is diffused.

1. Indicate whether each of the following statements supports a biological, individual-differences, or sociocultural explanation for aggression.
   a. Drugs that enhance serotonin activity decrease aggressive behaviors.
   b. If some people recently watched a violent movie, they will more likely act aggressively.
   c. Levels and types of violence vary across cultures.
   d. Levels and types of violence vary within cultures across time.
   e. Physical violence is more prevalent in the southern United States than in the northern United States.
   f. Postmortem examinations of people who committed suicide reveal extremely low serotonin levels.
   g. Removing the amygdala in a rhesus monkey tames this normally aggressive creature.
   h. Stimulating a cat's amygdala with an electric shock causes the animal to attack.
   i. The more an individual's goals are blocked, the greater his or her frustration and aggression.

2. For each of the following scenarios, indicate whether the individuals are likely to evidence bystander apathy. Briefly explain why or why not.
   a. A college student is in an academic building late one Friday afternoon, when almost everyone has gone home for the weekend. She sees one of her professors lying in the hallway; his breathing is shallow, and he is grasping his chest.
   b. A driver hurrying to a meeting sees a man hovering over a woman sitting on a park bench. The man is shaking his fist violently, and the woman is looking up at him with terror in her eyes.
   c. College students are walking across campus after a night on the town. They come across a person who appears to be homeless, curled up on the sidewalk. His eyes and mouth are open, but he does not seem alert.

What Determines the Quality of Relationships?

You might expect that studying relationships—how people select their friends and romantic partners—would be a high priority for psychological scientists. But until the last decade or so, the topic was given little attention, perhaps because of the difficulty of developing rigorous experiments to test complex and fuzzy concepts such as love, a mysterious state that some think is more appropriate for consideration by poets than by scientists. However, researchers have made considerable progress in identifying the factors that lead us to form friendships and other close relationships (Berscheid & Regan, 2005). Many of these findings consider the adaptiveness of forming lasting affiliative bonds with others. As discussed in Chapter 9, humans have a strong need for social contact, and various factors influence how people select mates. The following section considers the factors that determine the quality of human relationships: how friendships develop, why people fall in love, and why love relationships sometimes fail. As you will see, many of the same principles are involved in choosing our friends and choosing our lovers.

◀ **LEARNING OBJECTIVES**
Describe passionate and companionate love.

Distinguish between relationships that are likely to last and relationships that are not.

Situational and Personal Factors Influence Friendships

Psychological scientists have discovered a number of factors that promote friendships. In 1950, Leon Festinger, Stanley Schachter, and Kurt Back examined friends in a college dorm. Because room assignments were random, the researchers were able to examine the effects of proximity, or how often people come into contact, on friendship. They found that the more often students came into contact, the more likely they would become friends. Indeed, friendships often form among people who belong to the same groups, clubs, and so on.

Proximity might have its effects because of familiarity: People like familiar things more than unfamiliar ones. In fact, humans generally fear anything novel, a phenomenon known as *neophobia*. As discussed earlier, repeatedly being exposed to something leads to increased liking—the mere exposure effect. This effect has been demonstrated in hundreds of studies using various objects, including faces, geometric shapes, Chinese characters, and nonsense words (Zajonc, 2001). However, familiarity can breed contempt rather than liking, as when the more we get to know someone, the more aware we become of how different that person is from us (Norton, Frost, & Ariely, 2007).

BIRDS OF A FEATHER   Another factor that increases liking is similarity. Birds of a feather really do flock together. People similar in attitudes, values, interests, backgrounds, and personalities tend to like each other. In high school, people tend to be friends with those of the same sex, race, age, and year in school. College roommates who are most similar at the beginning of the school year are most likely to become good friends. The most successful romantic couples also tend to be the most physically similar, a phenomenon called the *matching principle* (Bentler & Newcomb, 1978; Caspi & Herbener, 1990). Of course, people can and do become friends with, become romantic partners with, and marry people of other races, people who are much older or younger, and so on, but such friendships and relationships tend to be based on other important similarities—values, education, socioeconomic status, and so on.

PERSONAL CHARACTERISTICS   People tend especially to like those who have admirable personality characteristics and who are physically attractive, both as friends and as lovers. In a now-classic study conducted in the 1960s, Norman Anderson asked college students to rate 555 trait descriptions by how much they would like others who possessed those traits. As you might guess from the earlier discussion of who is rejected from social groups, people dislike cheaters and others who drain group resources. Indeed, as shown in **TABLE 12.1**, the least likable characteristics are dishonesty, insincerity, and lack of personal warmth. Conversely, people especially like those who are kind, dependable, and trustworthy. Generally, people like those who have personal characteristics valuable to the group. For example, people like those whom they perceive to be competent much more than those they perceive to be incompetent or unreliable, perhaps because competent people make valuable group members. However, people who seem overly competent or too perfect make others feel uncomfortable or inadequate, and small mistakes can make a person seem more human and therefore more likable. In one study, a highly competent person who spilled a cup of coffee on himself was rated more highly than an equally competent person who did not perform this clumsy act (Helmreich, Aronson, & LeFan, 1970).

PHYSICAL ATTRACTIVENESS   What determines physical attractiveness? Although some standards of beauty, such as preferences for particular body types,

Table 12.1 The Ten Most Positive and Most Negative Personal Characteristics

MOST POSITIVE	MOST NEGATIVE
Sincere	Unkind
Honest	Untrustworthy
Understanding	Malicious
Loyal	Obnoxious
Truthful	Untruthful
Trustworthy	Dishonest
Intelligent	Cruel
Dependable	Mean
Thoughtful	Phony
Considerate	Liar

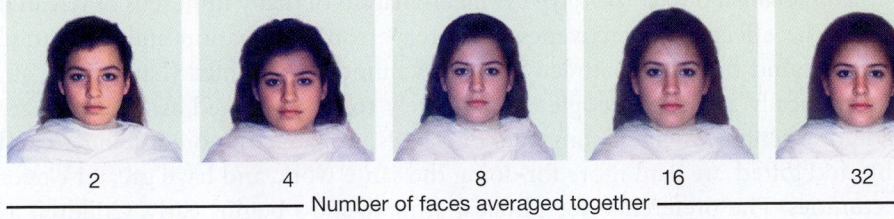

2 4 8 16 32

Number of faces averaged together

appear to change over time and across cultures, how people rate attractiveness is generally consistent across all cultures (Cunningham, Roberts, Barbee, Druen, & Wu, 1995). In a cleverly designed study of what people find attractive, Langlois and Roggman (1990) used a computer program to combine (or "average") various faces without regard to individual attractiveness. They found that as more faces were combined, participants rated the "averaged" faces as more attractive (**FIGURE 12.29**). People may view averaged faces as attractive because of the mere exposure effect, in that such faces may be more familiar than unusual faces (**FIGURE 12.30**). However, other researchers contend that although averaged faces might be attractive, averaged attractive faces are rated more favorably than averaged unattractive faces (Perrett, May, & Yoshikawa, 1994).

Most people find symmetrical faces more attractive than asymmetrical ones. This preference may be adaptive, in that a lack of symmetry could indicate poor health or a genetic defect. There are no racial differences in the extent to which faces are symmetrical, but biracial people tend to have more symmetrical facial features and correspondingly are rated as more attractive than those who are uniracial (Phelan, 2002). It does not seem to matter which two races comprise the genetic makeup. (We do not yet have data on the attractiveness of multiracial people.)

Attractiveness can bring important social benefits: Most people are drawn to those they find physically attractive. Attractive people are typically judged to be happier, more intelligent, more sociable, more successful, and less socially deviant. Taken together, these findings point to what Karen Dion and her colleagues (1972) dubbed

---

FIGURE 12.30 **Try for Yourself: Which Average Is More Attractive?**

Which face do you find most attractive?

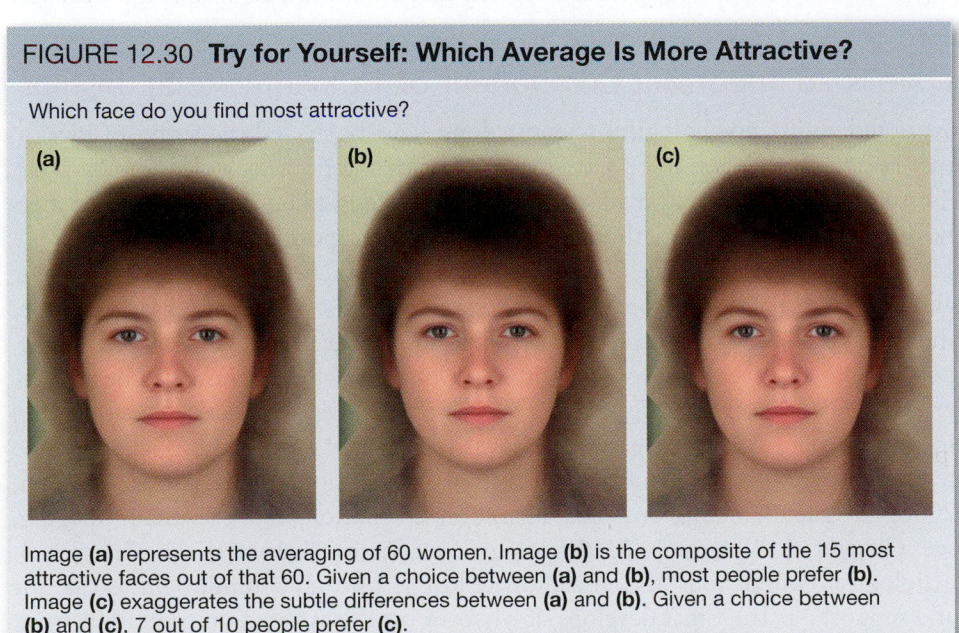

(a) (b) (c)

Image **(a)** represents the averaging of 60 women. Image **(b)** is the composite of the 15 most attractive faces out of that 60. Given a choice between **(a)** and **(b)**, most people prefer **(b)**. Image **(c)** exaggerates the subtle differences between **(a)** and **(b)**. Given a choice between **(b)** and **(c)**, 7 out of 10 people prefer **(c)**.

Explanation: Female faces that have stereotypically feminine features, such as larger eyes, a smaller nose, plumper lips, and a smaller chin, tend to be rated most attractive.

the *"what is beautiful is good" stereotype.* A meta-analysis of many hundreds of research studies of the effects of attractiveness on interpersonal evaluation and behavioral outcomes found that being attractive confers numerous benefits (Langlois et al., 2000). Physically attractive people are less likely to be perceived as criminals, are given lighter sentences when convicted of crimes, are rated as more intelligent and capable and gifted, are paid more for doing the same work, and have greater career opportunities. The preference for physical attractiveness begins early. Children as young as six months prefer to look at attractive faces, and young children prefer attractive over unattractive playmates (Rubenstein, Kalakanis, & Langlois, 1999). Even mothers treat attractive children differently from unattractive children. In one study, researchers observed more than 100 mothers feeding and playing with their just-born babies (while still in the hospital) and then again three months later (Langlois, Ritter, Casey, & Sawin, 1995). Mothers of attractive infants were much more affectionate and playful than mothers of unattractive children, who attended to other people more than to their infants. Mothers of attractive infants also expressed slightly more positive attitudes about those infants.

Given such preferential treatment, do physically attractive people actually possess characteristics consistent with the "what is beautiful is good" stereotype? The evidence on this issue is mixed. Attractive people tend to be more popular, more socially skilled, and healthier, but they are not necessarily smarter or happier. Among studies of college students, the correlation between objective ratings of attractiveness and other characteristics appears small. In one study that examined physical attractiveness, objectively rated by multiple judges, the researchers did not find any relation between appearance and grades, number of personal relationships, financial resources, or just about anything (Diener, Wolsic, & Fujita, 1995). In addition, attractive people are similar to less attractive people in intelligence, life satisfaction, and self-esteem. Why does having all the benefits of attractiveness not lead to greater happiness? Possibly, attractive people learn to distrust attention from others, and especially from the opposite sex, because they assume people like them simply for their looks. Believing that good things happen to them primarily because they are good looking may leave people feeling insecure, given that looks can fade or change with age.

Love Is an Important Component of Romantic Relationships

As noted above, psychological scientists long have neglected the study of love, in part because love seems to be a mysterious state that defies sensible comprehension. Thanks to the pioneering work of Elaine Hatfield and Ellen Berscheid, researchers now can use scientific methods to examine this important interpersonal bond. Hatfield and Berscheid have drawn an important distinction between *passionate love* and *companionate love.* Passionate love is a state of intense longing and sexual desire, the kind of love often portrayed stereotypically in the movies. In passionate love, people fall head over heels for each other, feel an overwhelming urge to be together, and are continually sexually aroused in each other's presence (**FIGURE 12.31A**). Brain imaging studies show that passionate love is associated with activity in dopamine reward systems, the same ones involved in drug addiction (Fisher, Aron, & Brown, 2006; Ortigue, Bianchi-Demicheli, Hamilton, & Grafton, 2007; on brain imaging, see Chapter 2, "Research Methodology"; on brain chemistry, see Chapter 3, "Biological Foundations"). Companionate love is a strong commitment to care for and support a partner that develops slowly over time. It is based on friendship, trust, respect, and intimacy (**FIGURE 12.31B**). Although people experience passionate love early in relationships, in most enduring relationships it evolves into a more companionate love, in which intimacy and commitment dominate (Sternberg, 1986).

(a)

(b)

FIGURE 12.31 Passionate versus Companionate Love **(a)** The arts tend to focus on passionate love, as in this scene from the 1996 movie version of William Shakespeare's *Romeo and Juliet,* starring Claire Danes and Leonardo DiCaprio. **(b)** Romances such as *Sleepless in Seattle* (1993), however, focus on older, more mature partners. Although Sam (Tom Hanks) and Annie (Meg Ryan) spend very little time together on screen, this final scene suggests that companionate love will develop between them. Their status as a family-to-be is represented here by Sam's son, Jonah (Ross Malinger).

One theory of love is based on attachment theory. As discussed in Chapter 11, infants can form different levels of attachment with their parents. According to Cindy Hazan and Phillip Shaver (1987), adult relationships, especially romantic relationships, also vary in their attachment styles. The types of attachment styles people have as adults are assumed to relate to how their parents treated them as children (Fraley & Shaver, 2000). Those who believe their parents were warm, supportive, and responsive report having secure attachments in their relationships. They find it easy to get close to others and do not fear being abandoned. Just under 60 percent of adults report having this attachment style (Mickelson, Kessler, & Shaver, 1997). Those who believe their parents were cold and distant, about 25 percent of the population, report having avoidant attachments. They find it hard to trust or depend on others, and they are wary of those who try to become close to them. Relationship partners make them uncomfortable. Those whose parents treated them inconsistently—sometimes warm and sometimes not—have anxious/ambivalent attachments. This 11 percent of the population is best described as clingy. They worry that people do not really love them and are bound to leave them. However, these findings are based partly on people's recollections of how their parents treated them, and it is possible that their memories are distorted.

Most people enter into romantic relationships of one form or another. As discussed in Chapter 10, people in long-term, committed relationships tend to live longer, healthier lives. But love, which is so important to so many people, can be elusive. Many people struggle to find their "one true love," as they date and reject potential partners who fall short of their ideals. As mentioned in Chapter 11, people now tend to marry much later than they did in the past. Even people in loving, committed relationships encounter challenges to their relationships. What can social psychology tell us about the factors that make relationships successful?

Making Love Last Is Difficult

Many contemporary Western marriages fail. In North America, approximately half of marriages end in divorce or separation, often within the first few years. In addition, many couples who do not get divorced live together unhappily, in a constant state of tension or as strangers sharing a home. The social psychologist Rowland Miller notes that "married people are meaner to each other than they are to total strangers" (1997, p. 12). People often take their relationship partners for granted, openly criticize them, and take out their frustrations on them by being cruel or cold. Perhaps unsurprisingly, then, relatively few marriages meet the blissful ideals that newlyweds expect.

As noted above, passion typically fades over time. The long-term pattern of sexual activity within relationships shows a rise and then a decline. Typically, for a period of months or even years, the two people experience frequent, intense desire for one another and have sex as often as they can arrange it. Past that peak, however, their interest in sex with each other wanes. Frequency of sex declines by about half from the first year of marriage to the second, for example, and it continues to decline, although more gradually, thereafter. Not only does frequency of sex decline, but people typically experience less passion for their partners over time. Unless people develop other forms of satisfaction in their romantic relationships, such as friendship, social support, and intimacy, the loss of passion leads to dissatisfaction and often to the eventual dissolution of the relationship (Berscheid & Regan, 2005).

JEALOUSY AND POSSESSIVENESS   Even when people lose some of their sexual desire for one another, they generally do not want their mates to have sex with other people. Some degree of sexual possessiveness and jealousy is found in all cultures, although with variation as to what makes people jealous and how they express the feeling. Although people may disapprove of sexual infidelity, many eventually engage in it. Even so, infidelity is far less frequent than many people think. The best estimates are that one out of four husbands and one out of nine wives have extramarital sex. Earlier estimates suggesting that half of married men and almost as many women were unfaithful may have reflected the more permissive patterns of the then ongoing "sexual revolution" of the 1960s and 1970s, and people may well be more faithful now than they were a couple of decades ago.

DEALING WITH CONFLICT   Even in the best relationships, some conflict is inevitable, and couples continually need to resolve strife. Confronting and discussing important issues is clearly an important aspect of any relationship. The way a couple deals with conflict often determines whether the relationship will last. John Gottman (1994) describes four interpersonal styles that typically lead couples to discord and dissolution, and he calls these patterns of interacting the "Four Horsemen of the Apocalypse" to reflect their threats to relationships. These maladaptive strategies are *being overly critical, holding the partner in contempt, being defensive,* and *mentally withdrawing from the relationship.* For example, when one partner voices a complaint, the other responds with his or her own complaint(s) and often raises the stakes by recalling all of the other person's failings. People use sarcasm and sometimes insult or demean their partners. Inevitably, any disagreement, no matter how small, escalates into a major fight over the core problems, which often center around a lack of money or of sex or of both. More-satisfied couples tend to express concern for each other even while disagreeing, try to see each other's point of view, and manage to stay relatively calm. Delivering criticism lightheartedly and playfully is also a strategy for relationship satisfaction (Keltner, Young, Heerey, Oemig, & Monarch, 1998). In addition, optimistic people are more likely to use cooperative problem solving; as a result, optimism is linked to having satisfying and happy romantic relationships (Assad, Donnellan, & Conger, 2007; Srivastava, McGonigal, Richards, Butler, & Gross, 2006).

ATTRIBUTIONAL STYLE AND ACCOMMODATION   Unhappy couples also differ from happy couples in *attributional style,* or how one partner explains the other's behavior (Bradbury & Fincham, 1990). Essentially, happy couples attribute good outcomes to one another and bad outcomes to situations, whereas distressed couples do the opposite. Happy couples make partner-enhancing attributions in which they overlook bad behavior or respond constructively, a process called *accommoda-*

tion (Rusbult & Van Lange, 1996). In contrast, unhappy couples make distress-maintaining attributions, in which they view one another in the most negative ways possible. In unhappy couples, if one partner comes home with flowers, for example, the other partner wonders what ill deed the first partner committed rather than reflecting on that partner's generosity and sweetness.

Over the past two decades, a number of psychological scientists have conducted research on healthy and unhealthy relationships. Among the foremost of these researchers is John Gottman, who has studied thousands of married couples to understand what predicts marital outcomes (Gottman, 1998). In his 1994 book, *Why Marriages Succeed or Fail and How You Can Make Yours Last,* Gottman outlines numerous differences between couples who are happy and those who are not. He also dispels some common myths about couples—for instance, that couples who have the most sex are the happiest. Actually, couples who *agree* on the frequency of sex are happiest. No matter the frequency, if one person thinks it is too often and the other thinks it is not often enough, that spells conflict. Furthermore, many people believe that conflict is a sign of a troubled relationship and that couples who never fight must be the happiest, but these ideas are not true either. According to research by Gottman and others, fighting, especially when it allows grievances to be aired, is one of the healthiest things a couple can do for their relationship. Conflict is inevitable in any serious relationship, but resolving conflict positively is the key to happiness as a couple.

Gottman asserts that the most successful type of couple is what he calls a *validating* couple, in which partners may disagree—may respond to particular situations by having different opinions and feeling different emotions—but each partner considers the other partner's opinions and emotions valid. People in such relationships make statements like "I know that it makes you angry when I hang the toilet paper the wrong way, but it was never a big deal to me which way it should hang." Validating couples try to compromise and to demonstrate mutual respect. Quite simply, they do the hard work of working things out.

Based on his research, Gottman believes that as long as there are about five positive interactions for every negative one in a relationship, chances are good that the relationship will be stable. Couples headed for breakup fall below this level, and if there are as many negatives as positives in a relationship, the prognosis is pretty bleak. Therefore, the task for any couple is to seek opportunities for positive feelings within the relationship. According to Gottman and others, the same principles apply to all long-term, committed relationships, heterosexual or homosexual:

- Show interest in your partner. Listen to him or her describe the events of the day. Pay attention while he or she is speaking and maintain eye contact. Try to be empathetic; show that you really understand and can feel what your partner is feeling. Such empathy and understanding cannot be faked, but saying, for example, "That must have been really annoying" conveys that you understand your partner's feelings.

- Be affectionate. You can show love in very quiet ways, such as simply touching the person once in a while. Reminisce about happy times together. Appreciate the benefits of the relationship. A couple who talk about the joys of their relationship, including comparing their partnership favorably to those of other people, tend to be happier with their relationship.

- Show you care. Many people take their partners for granted. Try to do spontaneous things such as buying flowers or calling your partner at an

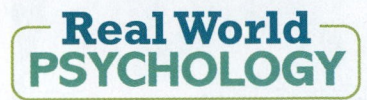

Real World PSYCHOLOGY

(a)

(b)

FIGURE 12.32 Principles for a Committed Relationship Positive interactions help keep a relationship stable. **(a)** A thoughtful gesture is one way to show your partner you care. **(b)** Doing activities you both enjoy is one way to spend quality time together.

unexpected time just to see how he or she is doing (**FIGURE 12.32A**). Such actions let your partner know you think about him or her, even when you are not together. When we are dating people, we flirt with them, give them compliments, and display our best manners. Being in a committed relationship does not mean you do not have to do any of these things. Be nice to your partner and try to make him or her feel that you value your mutual companionship. Praise your partner whenever possible. In turn, he or she will feel free to act in kind, which will help you feel good about yourself.

- Spend quality time together. It is easy for a couple to drift apart and develop separate lives. Find time to explore joint interests, such as hobbies or other activities (**FIGURE 12.32B**). Partners should pursue independent interests, but having some activities and goals in common helps bring a couple closer. Having fun together is an important part of any relationship. Share private jokes, engage in playful teasing, be witty. Enjoy each other.

- Maintain loyalty and fidelity. Outside relationships can be threatening to an intimate partnership. Believing your partner is emotionally or physically involved with another person can pose harm to even the healthiest relationship, as can being distrustful or jealous for no reason. At their core, relationship partners have to trust one another. Anything that threatens that basic sense of trust will harm the relationship.

- Learn how to handle conflict. Do not avoid it and pretend you have no serious issues. Rather, calm down, try to control your anger, and avoid name-calling, sarcasm, or excessive criticism. Validate your partner's feelings and beliefs even as you express your own feelings and beliefs. Look for areas of compromise.

Although much of this advice seems like common sense, many couples lose sight of how to express their love and commitment. Partners can get so caught up in everything else in their lives, from work to raising children, that it becomes easier to focus on what is wrong in a relationship than on what is right. When that happens, the relationship has taken a wrong turn. To make a relationship stronger, partners must put considerable effort into recognizing and celebrating all that is good about the relationship. Those affirming experiences make relationships succeed.

 SUMMING UP

What Determines the Quality of Relationships?

People form friendships based on proximity, familiarity, similarity, and personal characteristics, such as personality traits and attractiveness. Love is an important component of romantic relationships. Relationships based solely on sexual passion may fail when that passion starts to wane, as it often does over time. How a couple deals with conflict is an important determinant of whether the relationship will endure. Happy couples tend to make positive attributions for the partners' behaviors, whereas unhappy couples tend to make negative attributions.

MEASURING UP

1. Label each of the following characteristics as an attribute of passionate love or companionate love.
   a. a longing to be together
   b. associated with dopamine reward systems

c. based on friendship
d. develops slowly over time
e. emotionally volatile
f. strong commitment to care for and support partner
g. typified by sexual desire
h. typified by trust and respect

2. For each of the following situations, select the comment that, according to empirical findings, indicates a lasting relationship.

Situation 1: Chris finds a receipt in Sam's pocket for a $200 pair of pants. Because they are on a tight budget, this expense angers Chris. Chris confronts Sam about the expense.
a. Sam replies, "It seems only fair that I get to treat myself when you have your $70-a-month gym membership."
b. Sam replies, "I understand why you're upset. I really do need a new pair of pants, but I don't need a $200 pair of pants, so I'll return these tomorrow and get a less expensive pair."

Situation 2: Jordan and Jane receive a letter from the Internal Revenue Service saying they owe $3,000 in back taxes because of an error in the documents their accountant filed a few years ago.
a. Jordan notes, "The accountant made this error, and now we have to come up with the money to pay for it! Well, good thing we've been saving."
b. Jordan notes, "Didn't you say you reviewed those documents? Next time, you have to be more careful."

CONCLUSION

Even as we feel in control of our own behavior and believe we can make sense of others' actions, we often fail to take into account how powerfully social situations can influence behavior, attitudes, and beliefs. Moreover, much of how we think about ourselves and others occurs automatically and is based on minimal information. These judgments are often biased in ways that make us feel good about ourselves, frequently at others' expense. Research crossing levels of analysis has shown that stereotypes alter the way people perceive and process information about others. Brain activity often indicates that people do not report, or perhaps even know about, attitudes they hold, such as negative ones about ethnic minorities. Using only some of their mental resources, human minds automatically categorize others, with the outcome that people fail to treat others individually and with respect. People easily develop ingroups and outgroups; a group can consist of as few as three people. Yet social psychologists have discovered that cooperative learning systems can benefit the self and society. The challenge now is to adapt these systems to larger groups in society and to motivate these groups to use them.

Much of the strength of the social situation comes from the human need to belong. People favor their groups, go along with their leaders, and are motivated to avoid conflict to maintain group harmony. However, pressure to conform to the group leaves people susceptible to social influence and causes them to act in ways that conflict with their personal standards. Understanding the power of social situations allows us to at least partially understand humans' inhumane acts and to more fully understand humans' everyday behavior.

■ CHAPTER SUMMARY

How Do Attitudes Guide Behavior?

- **We Form Attitudes through Experience and Socialization:** Attitudes are influenced by familiarity (the mere exposure effect) and can be shaped by conditioning and through socialization.

- **Behaviors Are Consistent with Strong Attitudes:** Implicit attitudes (those that are automatic and easily activated from memory) can influence behavior and may differ from explicit attitudes (those we profess).

- **Discrepancies Lead to Dissonance:** A mismatch between attitudes or between an attitude and a behavior causes cognitive dissonance, which is usually resolved by a change in attitude. A behavioral change is possible but more difficult to accomplish. To justify behavior that does not reflect attitudes, people often inflate positive aspects of the experience.

- **Attitudes Can Be Changed through Persuasion:** Persuasion often works by focusing on either the message (the central route) or the feelings the message generates (the peripheral route).

How Do We Form Our Impressions of Others?

- **Nonverbal Actions and Expressions Affect Our Impressions:** Nonverbal behavior (body language) is interpreted quickly and provides valuable information.

- **We Make Attributions about Others:** We use personal dispositions and situational factors to explain others' behavior. Fundamental attribution error occurs when personal attributions are favored over situational attributions in explaining others' behavior.

- **Stereotypes Are Based on Automatic Categorization:** Stereotypes are cognitive schemas that allow for fast, easy processing of social information; they can lead to bias and illusory correlations. Self-fulfilling prophecies occur when people behave in ways that confirm the biases of stereotypes.

- **Stereotypes Can Lead to Prejudice:** Prejudice occurs when the attitude associated with a stereotype is negative. Having a negative bias can lead to discriminatory action. We show a preference for members of our ingroup versus those in outgroups.

- **Cooperation Can Reduce Prejudice:** Sharing superordinate goals that require cooperation leads to reduced prejudice and discrimination.

How Do Others Influence Us?

- **Groups Influence Individual Behavior:** The presence of others can improve performance (social facilitation) or create laziness (social loafing). Loss of personal identity and of self-awareness (deindividuation) can occur in groups. Group decisions can be extreme.

- **We Conform to Social Norms:** Socially determined influences on behavior occur through awareness of social norms. Lack of unanimity diminishes conformity.

- **We Are Compliant:** Various factors influence the likelihood of compliance, among them what mood we are in and whether we have previously agreed to a lesser request (foot-in-the-door effect).

- **We Are Obedient to Authority:** People readily behave in ways directed by authorities, even to the extent of harming others.

When Do We Harm or Help Others?

- **Aggression Can Be Adaptive:** Brain structures, neurochemistry, and hormones influence aggression. Biologically based responses can be adaptive. Frustration can lead to aggression.

- **Aggression Has Social and Cultural Aspects:** Aggression is not entirely adaptive and is influenced by our social and cultural experiences.

- **Many Factors May Influence Helping Behavior:** Prosocial behaviors maintain social relations. Altruism toward kin may favor inclusive fitness. Reciprocal helping is more likely in social groups in which survival depends on cooperation.

- **Some Situations Lead to Bystander Apathy:** The presence of others in an emergency may diffuse responsibility and lead to individual inaction.

What Determines the Quality of Relationships?

- **Situational and Personal Factors Influence Friendships:** People affiliate with others who are similar to themselves and who possess valued characteristics, such as attractiveness.

- **Love Is an Important Component of Romantic Relationships:** In successful romantic relationships, passionate love tends to evolve into companionate love.

- **Making Love Last Is Difficult:** As passion fades, couples must develop other areas of satisfaction. Jealousy arises out of fears of infidelity. How a couple deals with conflict influences the stability of the relationship. Generally, in a happy couple the partners have positive views of each other and their relationship.

■ KEY TERMS

aggression, p. 553
altruism, p. 557
attitudes, p. 525
attributions, p. 533
bystander intervention effect, p. 557
cognitive dissonance, p. 527

compliance, p. 549
conformity, p. 547
deindividuation, p. 545
discrimination, p. 538
elaboration likelihood model, p. 529
explicit attitudes, p. 526

frustration-aggression hypothesis, p. 554
fundamental attribution error, p. 534
implicit attitudes, p. 526
ingroup favoritism, p. 539

nonverbal behavior, p. 533
personal attributions, p. 534
persuasion, p. 528
prejudice, p. 538
prosocial, p. 556

self-fulfilling prophecy, p. 537
situational attributions, p. 534
social facilitation, p. 545
social loafing, p. 545
social norms, p. 547
stereotypes, p. 536

■ PRACTICE TEST

1. Which of the following scenarios illustrates postdecisional dissonance?
   a. Josh has always wanted to attend College A. During his senior year of high school, he applies to College A and College B. Although he receives acceptance letters from both institutions, he decides to attend College A. When asked to explain why he wants to attend College A, he says, "I like that I can live on campus. There's a great community vibe here. Plus I can major in international business. None of these things are true of the other school."

The answer key for all the Measuring Up exercises and the Practice Tests can be found at the back of the book.

b. Adrianna wants to go on a community service trip during her spring break. After struggling for weeks to decide between two options, she opts to build houses in rural Mexico instead of doing hurricane cleanup in Louisiana. When asked to explain why she made this decision, she says, "The Mexico trip will give me a chance to travel outside the United States, which I've always wanted to do. Plus, the Louisiana trip sounded pretty stale."

2. Which of the following scenarios illustrates justification of effort?
   a. David's boss regularly asks him to do a lot of extra tasks around the office, but David's pay does not reflect the extra effort he puts into emptying the recycling bin, washing out coffee mugs, or refilling the printer paper. When asked why he does all these extra tasks, David replies, "I'm happy to do whatever it takes to make our office as welcoming and efficient as possible."
   b. Sasha elects to attend an intensive, summer-long math program. When asked why she gave up her summer vacation for this program, Sasha says, "I'll be able to get college credit for the courses I took there, plus I got a scholarship that paid for my tuition, room, and board. It was a deal I couldn't refuse."

3. Some of the following statements illustrate cognitive or behavioral outcomes of stereotyping. As appropriate, label those statements as examples of illusory correlation, ingroup favoritism, outgroup homogeneity, and self-fulfilling prophecy. Not all response options will be used.
   a. A first-year college student states, "Students at our college are so unique! Each person has his or her own passions and aptitudes."
   b. A professor mistakenly comments to a colleague, " The athletes in my class always seem to ask for extensions on their homework; none of my other students ever ask for extensions."
   c. A senior College A tells her friend, "Whatever you do, don't go to parties at College B. They all drink way too much, and the guys can't keep their hands off the women at their parties."

4. Dorm A and Dorm B have a long-standing rivalry. Recently, the rivalry has intensified, resulting in destructive acts to property and harrassment of outgroup members. A couple students from each dorm encourage the students to get together to brainstorm possible strategies for easing the tension. According to the ideas presented in this chapter, which suggestion would be most effective?
   a. "Let's hold a series of dorm dinners. Dorm A can invite people from Dorm B over one week, and Dorm B can invite people from Dorm A over the following week."
   b. "Since people in Dorm A are such strong math students, we could have Dorm A offer math tutoring to students from Dorm B."
   c. "The administration should hold a meeting with the dorm presidents to let them know that funding for dorm activities will be cut unless the interdorm tension subsides."
   d. "We can hold an all-campus competition, where teams of dorms would compete for prizes. Dorm A and Dorm B could be on one team; Dorm C and Dorm D could be on the other team."

5. Which of the following examples of social norms marketing would most likely be most effective?
   a. 80 percent of the residents in your neighborhood recycle.
   b. 80 percent of the residents in your neighborhood recycle. Keep up the great work!
   c. Recycle!
   d. Recycle! It's the right thing to do!

6. Some of the following scenarios illustrate compliance strategies discussed in this chapter. As appropriate, label each scenario as an example of door in the face, foot in the door, or low-balling. Not all response options will be used, and not every example will have an appropriate label.
   a. After a grueling series of abdominal crunches, a fitness instructor tells her class, "C'mon, just eight more!" Then, after the eight crunches, she says, "OK, now crunch up and hold for eight counts!"
   b. A professor tells her students, "As you know, we're going on a class field trip this Saturday. I'd like us to all meet up at 8:00 A.M. Will that time work for everyone?" Then, upon encountering much resistance from the class, she says, "Okay, okay. Instead of 8:00, let's meet at 9:00."
   c. You see an informercial for a collection of fancy knives. A countdown timer appears in the corner of the screen, reminding you the deal will be available for only three more minutes.

7. Which of the following examples most accurately describes the relationship between relationship length and frequency of sex?
   a. After an initial period of frequent sex, there is a negative correlation between relationship length and frequency of sex.
   b. There is a near-zero correlation between relationship length and frequency of sex.
   c. There is a negative correlation between relationship length and frequency of sex.
   d. There is a positive correlation between relationship length and frequency of sex.

8. Match each definition below with the appropriate term: altruism, inclusive fitness, kin selection, reciprocal helping.
   a. a process in which individuals behave helpfully toward those with whom they share genes
   b. providing help without any apparent reward for doing so
   c. the tendency for one animal to help another because the other can return the favor in the future
   d. the adaptive benefits of transmitting genes rather than focusing on individual survival

9. Which statement below about Shelly, who is very attractive, is most consistent with the "what is beautiful is good" stereotype?
   a. "Shelly is a total ditz!"
   b. "Shelly is easily the happiest person I know!"
   c. "Shelly sure knows how to manipulate other people with her looks!"
   d. "Shelly's parents are really attractive, too."

■ PSYCHOLOGY AND SOCIETY

1. Seek out examples of public service announcements. You can find them on television, in print, or on the Internet (for example, check out adcouncil.org). Analyze the ads using ideas from the elaboration likelihood model. Make clear whether the ads use the central or peripheral routes to persuasion, identify cues (source, content, receiver) likely to influence the persuasiveness of the message, and note whether the ads use a social norms marketing approach.

2. Our social worlds are full of norms: how to act, how to dress, when to eat, what to say, how to say it, and so on. For one 24-hour period, write down as many social norms as you can identify. You might find it helpful to ask, "How would others react if I _____?" In the blank, fill in any nonstandard behavior. Would people laugh at you or give you a dirty look? If so, you probably would be violating a norm. After logging the observed norms, write a brief essay reflecting on what you learned as a result of engaging in this activity.

Personality

TOM HANKS HAS BEEN WELL KNOWN AS AN ACTOR since he costarred in the television show *Bosom Buddies* in the early 1980s; he later won Academy Awards for his performances in *Philadelphia* and *Forrest Gump,* as well as several Golden Globe Awards. He tends to play likable characters and has won a strong popular following. Given everything that you know about Hanks, what kind of person do you think he is (FIGURE 13.1)? What do you suppose makes people find him so appealing on-screen?

Would it surprise you to learn that Tom Hanks was painfully shy when he was growing up? He attributes this shyness to the frequent changes he experienced: By age 10, Hanks had had one mother and two stepmothers, had attended five schools, and had lived in ten houses, all of which made it difficult for him to form lasting friendships. Lacking the social

How Have Psychologists Studied Personality?

- Psychodynamic Theories Emphasize Unconscious and Dynamic Processes
- Humanistic Approaches Emphasize Integrated Personal Experience
- Type and Trait Approaches Describe Behavioral Dispositions
- Personality Reflects Learning and Cognition

How Is Personality Assessed, and What Does It Predict?

- Personality Refers to Both Unique and Common Characteristics
- Researchers Use Objective and Projective Methods to Assess Personality
- Observers Show Accuracy in Trait Judgments
- People Sometimes Are Inconsistent
- Behavior Is Influenced by the Interaction of Personality and Situations
- There Are Cultural and Gender Differences in Personality

What Are the Biological Bases of Personality?

- Animals Have Personalities
- Personality Is Rooted in Genetics
- Temperaments Are Evident in Infancy
- Personality Is Linked to Specific Neurophysiological Mechanisms
- Personality Is Adaptive

- Critical Thinking Skill: Avoiding Single-Cause Explanations
- Personality Traits Are Stable over Time

How Do We Know Our Own Personalities?

- Our Self-Concepts Consist of Self-Knowledge
- Perceived Social Regard Influences Self-Esteem
- Critical Thinking Skill: Resisting Appeals to Snobbery
- We Use Mental Strategies to Maintain Our Views of Self
- There Are Cultural Differences in the Self

(a)

(b)

FIGURE 13.1 Two Sides of Tom Hanks **(a)** Is Hanks an outgoing performer, as seen here in *Charlie Wilson's War* (2007) or **(b)** a reserved individual, as seen here on the set of *Angels & Demons* in 2008? Or is he both?

skills to make friends, Hanks found he could get attention by being the class clown. He would take on different personas and make people laugh, unknowingly training himself to become an actor. In fact, he had a natural skill for changing his personality to suit any situation. In 1997 he told the *Guardian* newspaper that he had learned to adjust his behavior to whatever was expected: "If I was supposed to be repressed, I could repress myself; if I was supposed to be outgoing, I could be outgoing; if I was supposed to be raucous, I could be raucous. I think I still do that sometimes, I'm still good at it."

So who is the real Tom Hanks? Does knowing that he moved around a lot as a child help us understand his unique nature? Does knowing that he was shy as a child tell us anything about what he is like as an adult? If Hanks is still shy, how can he stand in front of thousands of people to give an acceptance speech at the Academy Awards ceremony? Did becoming involved in acting as a teenager allow Hanks to overcome his shyness? Or did he just decide not to be shy? Psychologists consider these sorts of questions as they seek to understand what makes each person—a movie star, a college student, or any person—unique.

Understanding personality may be one of the oldest quests in psychology. Since antiquity, a vast array of theories has been proposed to explain basic differences among individuals. **Personality** consists of the characteristic thoughts, emotional responses, and behaviors that are relatively stable in an individual over time and across circumstances. (The word *personality* comes from the Latin *persona,* meaning "mask"; in ancient Greek and Roman theater, actors would speak through masks, each representing a separate personality.) People constantly try to figure out other people—to understand why they behave in certain ways and to predict their behavior. In fact, many students take psychology courses partly because they want to know what makes other people tick.

One challenge of figuring out people is that they may act differently depending on the situation. How much can a person's behavior tell us about his or her personality? What else do we need to know to understand someone? If each person is unique, what determines this uniqueness? For instance, what factors during childhood affect personality? Also, to what extent does a person's personality change throughout that person's life?

personality The characteristic thoughts, emotional responses, and behaviors that are relatively stable in an individual over time and across circumstances.

Personality psychologists study the processes that influence personality, and their research explores the influence of culture, learning, biological and cognitive factors. Some personality psychologists are most interested in understanding *whole persons*—that is, what makes each person unique. Another approach is to study individual traits—that is, how people differ on one or a few dimensions. People obviously differ in many ways: Some are hostile, some are nurturing, some are withdrawn. Each characteristic is a **personality trait**, a dispositional tendency to act in a certain way over time and across circumstances. What sort of person are you? More to the point, why are you who you are?

personality trait A characteristic; a dispositional tendency to act in a certain way over time and across circumstances.

How Have Psychologists Studied Personality?

Dan McAdams, a leading personality researcher, has asked, "What must we know to know a person well?" Different psychological scientists try to answer this question in different ways, often depending on their theoretical approaches. Some personality psychologists emphasize biological and genetic factors. Others emphasize culture, patterns of reinforcement, or mental and unconscious processes. To understand people well is to understand everything about them—their biological make-ups, their childhood experiences, their cultural backgrounds, the way they think. All these factors shape people in unique ways. Therefore, personality psychologists approach the study of personality on many levels.

Gordon Allport gave a classic scientific definition of personality: "the dynamic organization within the individual of those psychophysical systems that determine his characteristic behavior and thought" (1961, p. 28; **FIGURE 13.2**). This definition includes many of the concepts most important to a contemporary understanding of personality. The notion of *organization* indicates that personality is not just a list of traits but a coherent whole. Moreover, this organized whole is *dynamic* in that it is goal seeking, sensitive to context, and adaptive to environment. By emphasizing *psychophysical systems*, Allport highlights the psychological nature of personality while recognizing that personality arises from basic biological processes. In addition, his definition stresses that personality causes people to have *characteristic* behaviors and thoughts (and feelings). In other words, they do and think and feel things relatively consistently over time.

LEARNING OBJECTIVE
List the major theorists and concepts associated with four general approaches to the study of personality.

FIGURE 13.2 Gordon Allport In 1937, Allport published the first major textbook of personality psychology, which defined the field. He also championed the study of individuals and established traits as a central concept in personality research.

Psychodynamic Theories Emphasize Unconscious and Dynamic Processes

As discussed in Chapter 1, Sigmund Freud was a physician whose theories dominated psychological thinking for many decades. Focusing on the individual level of analysis, Freud developed many ideas about personality by observing patients he was treating for psychological disturbances, such as paralysis without any apparent physical cause. The central premise of Freud's **psychodynamic theory** of personality is that unconscious forces influence behavior. Freud referred to these psychic forces as *instincts* (although he used the term in a way slightly different from its contemporary use), defining them as mental representations arising out of biological or physical need. For instance, he proposed that people satisfy the *life instinct* by following the *pleasure principle,* which directs people to seek pleasure and to avoid pain. The energy that drives the pleasure principle is the *libido.* Although today the term has a sexual connotation, Freud used it to refer more generally to the energy that promotes pleasure seeking. The life instinct can be viewed as the desire to satisfy libidinal urges for pleasure. Multiple forces can be in conflict, and Freud viewed such conflict as the essential cause of mental illness.

psychodynamic theory Freudian theory that unconscious forces, such as wishes and motives, influence behavior.

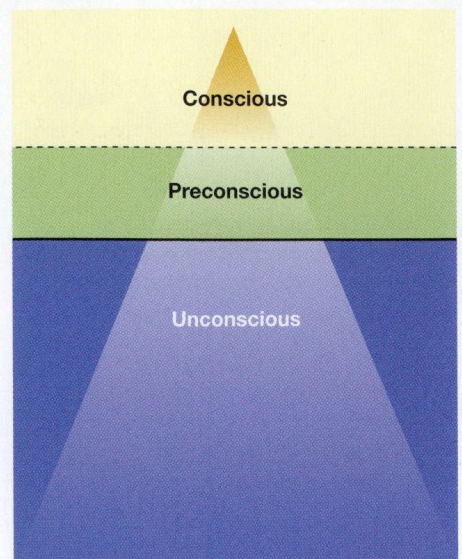

FIGURE 13.3 Levels of Consciousness
Sigmund Freud theorized that mental activity occurred in these three zones. He believed that much of human behavior was influenced by unconscious processes.

psychosexual stage According to Freud, the developmental stages that correspond to the pursuit of satisfaction of libidinal urges.

A TOPOGRAPHICAL MODEL OF MIND Freud believed that most of the conflict between psychological forces occurs below the level of conscious awareness. In his *topographical model,* he proposed that the structure of the mind, or its topography, is divided into three zones of mental awareness (**FIGURE 13.3**). At the *conscious* level, people are aware of their thoughts. The *preconscious* level consists of content that is not currently in awareness but that could be brought to awareness; it is roughly analogous to long-term memory. The *unconscious* level contains material that the mind cannot easily retrieve. According to Freud, the unconscious mind contains wishes, desires, and motives, and they are associated with conflict, anxiety, or pain; to protect the person from distress, they are not accessible. Sometimes, however, this information leaks into consciousness, such as occurs during a *Freudian slip,* in which a person accidentally reveals a hidden motive (e.g., introducing herself or himself to someone attractive by saying, "Excuse me, I don't think we've been properly seduced").

DEVELOPMENT OF SEXUAL INSTINCTS An important component of Freudian thinking is the idea that early childhood experiences have a major impact on the development of personality. Freud believed that children go through developmental stages corresponding to their pursuit of satisfaction of libidinal urges. At each **psychosexual stage,** libido is focused on one of the *erogenous zones:* the mouth, the anus, or the genitals. The *oral stage* lasts from birth to approximately 18 months, during which time pleasure is sought through the mouth; hungry infants experience relief when they breastfeed and thus associate pleasure with sucking. When children are two to three years old, toilet training leads them to focus on the anus; learning to control the bowels is the focus of the *anal phase.* From age three to five, children enter the *phallic stage* and direct their libidinal energies toward the genitals. Children often discover the pleasure of rubbing their genitals during this time, although they have no sexual intent per se.

One of the most controversial Freudian theories (there are few data to support it) applies to children in the phallic stage. According to Freud, children desire an exclusive relationship with the opposite-sex parent. Because the same-sex parent is thus considered a rival, children develop hostility toward that parent; in boys, this is known as the *Oedipus complex* (after the Greek character Oedipus, who unknowingly killed his father and married his mother). Freud believed that children develop unconscious wishes to kill the one parent in order to claim the other and that they resolve this conflict through identification with the same-sex parent, taking on many of that parent's values and beliefs. This theory was mostly applicable to boys. Freud's theory for girls was more complex and even less convincing.

Following the phallic stage, according to Freud, children enter a brief *latency stage,* in which libidinal urges are suppressed or channeled into doing schoolwork or building friendships. Finally, in the *genital stage,* adolescents and adults attain mature attitudes about sexuality and adulthood. Libidinal urges are centered on the capacity to reproduce and contribute to society.

According to Freud, progression through these psychosexual stages profoundly affects personality. For example, some people become *fixated* at a stage during which they receive excessive parental restriction or indulgence. Those fixated at the oral stage develop *oral personalities;* they continue to seek pleasure through the mouth, such as by smoking, and are excessively needy. Those fixated at the anal phase may have *anal-retentive personalities,* being stubborn and highly regulating. Anal fixation may arise from overly strict toilet training or excessively rule-based child rearing.

STRUCTURAL MODEL OF PERSONALITY Freud proposed an integrated model of how the mind is organized, consisting of three theoretical structures that vary in degree of consciousness. At the most basic level and completely submerged in the unconscious is the **id,** which operates according to the pleasure principle, acting on impulses and desires. The innate forces driving the id are sex and aggression. Acting as a brake on the id is the **superego,** the internalization of parental and societal standards of conduct. Developed during the phallic phase, the superego is a rigid structure of morality, or conscience. Mediating between the superego and the id is the **ego,** which tries to satisfy the wishes of the id while being responsive to the dictates of the superego. The ego operates according to the *reality principle,* which involves rational thought and problem solving.

Conflicts between the id and the superego lead to anxiety, which the ego copes with through various **defense mechanisms,** unconscious mental strategies that the mind uses to protect itself from distress. For instance, people often *rationalize* their behavior by blaming situational factors over which they have little control, as when you tell your parents you did not call them because you were too busy studying for an exam. Finding good excuses keeps people from feeling bad and can also prevent others from getting mad at them. Much of the theoretical work on defense mechanisms can be credited to Freud's daughter, Anna Freud (1936; **FIGURE 13.4**). (Several common defense mechanisms are listed in **TABLE 12.1.**) Research in psychology over the past 40 years has provided considerable support for the existence of many of these defense mechanisms (Baumeister, Dale, & Sommers, 1998), although contemporary researchers believe these mechanisms protect self-esteem rather than relieve unconscious conflict over libidinal desires. For instance, *reaction formation* occurs when a person wards off an uncomfortable thought about the self by embracing the opposite thought. In one study of reaction formation in men, participants who had earlier expressed the most negative views of homosexuality showed greater physiological arousal when viewing video depictions of homosexual sex than did men who were more accepting of homosexuality (Adams, Wright, & Lohr, 1996). These findings suggest homophobia might result from repression of homosexual impulses, leading to reaction formation.

PSYCHODYNAMIC THEORY SINCE FREUD Although Freud is the thinker most closely identified with psychodynamic theory, a number of scholars, while rejecting certain aspects of Freudian thinking, embraced the notion of unconscious conflict. These *neo-Freudians* include Carl Jung, Alfred Adler, and Karen Horney, all of whom modified Freud's ideas in their own psychodynamic theories. For instance, Adler and Horney strongly criticized Freud's view of women, finding many of his theories misogynist. The phallic stage of development, for example, is named for the male sex organ, yet Freud used this label for female and male development. Many neo-Freudians rejected Freud's emphasis on sexual forces and instead focused on social interactions, especially children's emotional attachments to their parents. This focus is embodied in *object relations theory,* in which the object of attachment is another person, such as a parent or spouse. In addition, some neo-Freudians, including Horney and Erik Erikson, emphasized the influence of culture, which Freud saw monolithically as "civilization."

Psychological scientists largely have abandoned psychodynamic theories because Freud's central premises cannot be examined through accepted scientific methods. However, Freud has to be understood in the context of his time and the methods he had at his disposal. He was an astute observer of behavior and a creative theorist. His observations and ideas continue to affect personality psychology and have framed much of the research in personality over the last century (Westen, 1998; Hines, 2003).

id In psychodynamic theory, the component of personality that is completely submerged in the unconscious and operates according to the pleasure principle.

superego In psychodynamic theory, the internalization of societal and parental standards of conduct.

ego In psychodynamic theory, the component of personality that tries to satisfy the wishes of the id while being responsive to the dictates of the superego.

defense mechanisms Unconscious mental strategies the mind uses to protect itself from conflict and distress.

FIGURE 13.4 Anna Freud Anna Freud studied defense mechanisms and contributed to the understanding of children's development.

Humanistic Approaches Emphasize Integrated Personal Experience

By the early 1950s, most psychological theories of personality were heavily deterministic; that is, personality and behavioral characteristics were considered to arise from forces beyond a person's control. Whereas Freud believed that personality is determined by unconscious conflicts, behaviorists such as B. F. Skinner (see Chapter 6, "Learning") argued that patterns of reinforcement determine response tendencies, which are the basis of personality. Against this backdrop emerged a view of personality that emphasizes the uniqueness of the human condition. **Humanistic approaches** emphasize personal experience and belief systems and propose that humans seek to fulfill their potential for personal growth through greater self-understanding; this process is referred to as *self-actualization.* Humanism focuses on subjective human experience, or *phenomenology,* and views each person as inherently good. Abraham Maslow's theory of motivation (see Chapter 9, "Motivation and Emotion") is an example: Maslow believed that the desire to become self-actualized is the ultimate and most important human motive.

The most prominent humanistic psychologist was Carl Rogers, whose *person-centered approach* to personality emphasizes people's personal understandings, or phenomenology (**FIGURE 13.5**). In the therapeutic technique Rogers advocated, the therapist would create a supportive and accepting environment and would deal with clients' problems and concerns as clients understood them. Rogers's theory highlights the importance of how parents show affection for their children and how parental treatment affects personality development. Rogers speculated that most parents provide love and support that is conditional: The parents love their children as long as the children do what the parents want them to do. Parents who disapprove of their children's behavior may withhold their love; as a result, children quickly abandon their true feelings, dreams, and desires and accept only those parts of themselves that elicit parental love and support. Thus people lose touch with their true selves in their pursuit of positive regard from others. To counteract this effect, Rogers encouraged parents to raise their children with *unconditional positive regard,* in which the children are accepted, loved, and prized no matter how they behave. Parents may express disapproval of bad behavior, but in a context that ensures the children feel loved. According to Rogers, a child raised with unconditional positive regard will develop a healthy sense of self-esteem and will become a *fully functioning person.*

Humanistic psychology has not been overly concerned with the scientific study of personality, emphasizing instead subjective personal experience. Recently, as discussed in Chapter 10, psychologists have begun to use the methods of science to study humanity's positive aspects. The *positive psychology movement* was launched by the clinical psychologist Martin Seligman (Seligman & Csikszentmihalyi, 2000). Seligman and others have encouraged the scientific study of qualities such as faith, values, creativity, courage, and hope. For instance, Ed Diener (2000) has conducted extensive research on *subjective well-being,* a general term for the degree of happiness and satisfaction people feel (**FIGURE 13.6**). He has found that well-being varies across cultures, such that the wealthiest countries often have the highest levels of satisfaction (a finding that fits well with Maslow's proposal that people need to satisfy basic needs such as food, shelter, and safety before they can address self-esteem needs). More recently, Michele Tugade and Barbara Frederickson (2004) have found that people who are resilient, who can bounce back from negative events, experience positive emotions even when under stress. According to the *broaden-and-build theory,* positive emotions prompt people to consider novel solutions to their

humanistic approaches Approaches to studying personality that emphasize personal experience and belief systems; they propose that people seek personal growth to fulfill their human potential.

FIGURE 13.5 Carl Rogers Rogers emphasized people's subjective understandings of their whole lives.

FIGURE 13.6 Try for Yourself: Measuring Subjective Well-Being

Satisfaction with Life Scale

Using the 1–7 scale below, indicate your agreement with each item by placing the appropriate number on the line preceding that item. Be open and honest in your responding. Then add the five numbers to determine your overall life satisfaction.

7 = strongly agree   3 = slightly disagree
6 = agree   2 = disagree
5 = slightly agree   1 = strongly disagree
4 = neither agree nor disagree

____ In most ways, my life is close to my ideal.
____ The conditions of my life are excellent.
____ I am satisfied with my life.
____ So far, I have gotten the important things I want in life.
____ If I could live my life over, I would change almost nothing.

35–31 extremely satisfied   15–19 slightly dissatisfied
26–30 satisfied   10–14 dissatisfied
21–25 slightly satisfied   5–9 extremely dissatisfied
20   neutral

Result: The Satisfaction with Life Scale has been found to reliably and validly assess a person's general satisfaction in life.

SOURCE: Pavot and Diener, 1993.

problems, and thus resilient people tend to draw on their positive emotions in dealing with setbacks or negative life experiences (Frederickson, 2001).

Type and Trait Approaches Describe Behavioral Dispositions

Psychodynamic and humanistic approaches seek to explain the mental processes that shape personality. The same underlying processes likely occur in everyone, but individuals differ because they experience different conflicts, are treated differently by their parents, and so on. Other approaches to personality focus more on description than explanation. For example, in describing a friend you probably would not delve into unconscious conflicts; rather, you would describe the person as a certain type, such as an *introvert* or an *extravert*. **Personality types** are discrete categories of people; we fill in gaps in our knowledge about individuals with our beliefs about the behaviors and dispositions associated with these types. Our tendency to assume that certain personality characteristics go together, and therefore to make predictions about people based on minimal evidence, is called *implicit personality theory*. For example, we might think that introverts dislike parties, like books, and are sensitive.

personality types Discrete categories based on global personality characteristics.

Many personality psychologists are concerned with *traits* in addition to types (remember that traits are behavioral dispositions that endure over time and across situations). Traits exist on a continuum—most people fall toward the middle and relatively few at the extremes. Thus, for example, people range from being very introverted to very extraverted, but most are somewhere in the middle. The **trait approach** to personality provides a method for assessing the extent to which individuals differ in personality dispositions, such as sociability, cheerfulness, and aggressiveness (Funder, 2001).

trait approach An approach to studying personality that focuses on the extent to which individuals differ in personality dispositions.

How many traits are there? Early in his career, Gordon Allport, along with his colleague Henry Odbert, counted the dictionary words that could be used as personality traits. They found nearly 18,000. During the 1950s, the researcher Raymond

Cattell set out to ascertain the basic elements of personality, believing that statistical procedures would enable him to take the scientific study of personality to a higher level and perhaps to uncover the basic structure of personality. Cattell's participants filled out personality questionnaires containing a number of trait items, which he had reduced from the larger set produced by Allport and Odbert. Cattell then performed *factor analysis,* grouping items according to their similarities. For instance, all the terms that referred to friendliness (*nice, pleasant, cooperative,* and so on) were grouped together. Through this procedure, Cattell (1965) identified 16 basic dimensions of personality, such as those relating to intelligence, sensitivity, dominance, and self-reliance. Many were given rather unusual names to avoid confusion with everyday language; most personality psychologists no longer use these terms.

EYSENCK'S HIERARCHICAL MODEL Further reducing the number of basic traits was the psychologist Hans Eysenck, who in the 1960s proposed a hierarchical model of personality (**FIGURE 13.7**), the basic structure begins at the *specific response level,* which consists of observed behaviors. For instance, a person might buy an item because it is on sale and then repeat the behavior on different occasions; these behaviors are at the *habitual response level* (i.e., some people cannot pass up sale items, whether they need them or not). If a person is observed to behave the same way on many occasions, the person is characterized as possessing a *trait*. Traits such as impulsiveness and sociability can be viewed as components of *superordinate traits,* of which Eysenck proposed three: introversion/extraversion, emotional stability, and psychoticism.

Introversion/extraversion, coined by the psychoanalyst Carl Jung, refers to the extent to which people are shy, reserved, and quiet versus sociable, outgoing, and bold. As discussed later in this chapter, Eysenck believed that this dimension reflects differences in biological functioning. *Emotional stability* refers to the extent to which people's moods and emotions change; those low in emotional stability, *neurotic* people, experience frequent and dramatic mood swings, especially toward negative emotions, compared with people who are more stable. Highly neurotic people report often feeling anxious, moody, and depressed, and they generally hold very low opinions of themselves. *Psychoticism* is a mix of aggression, impulse control, and empathy; those high in psychoticism are more aggressive, impulsive, and self-centered than those low in psychoticism. The term *psychoticism* implies a level of psychopathology that Eysenck did not intend. More-recent conceptions of this superordinate trait call it *constraint:* People range from restrained to disinhibited (Watson & Clark, 1997).

FIGURE 13.7 Eysenck's Hierarchical Model of Personality Extraversion is a superordinate trait made up of sociability, dominance, assertiveness, activity, and liveliness. Each of these subordinate traits is made up of habitual and specific responses.

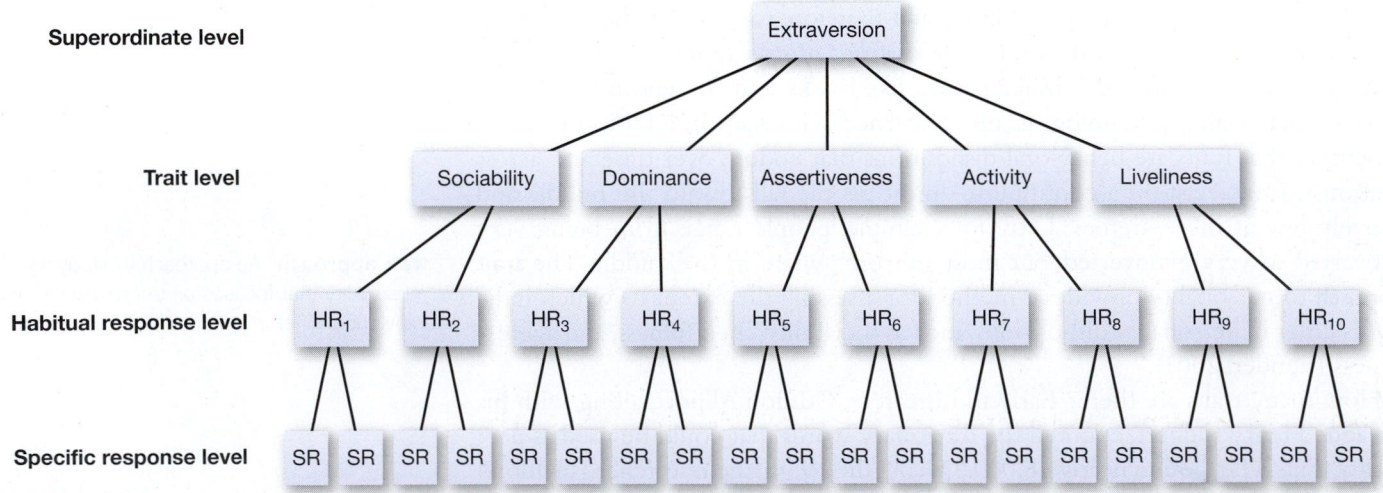

THE BIG FIVE In the last 20 years or so, many personality psychologists have embraced the **five-factor theory,** which is similar to Eysenck's model and identifies five basic personality traits (McCrae & Costa, 1999). The so-called *Big Five* are *openness to experience, conscientiousness, extraversion, agreeableness,* and *neuroticism* (**FIGURE 13.8**). Each factor is a higher-order trait comprising interrelated lower-order traits. For instance, conscientiousness is determined by how careful and organized one is, while agreeableness reflects the extent to which one is trusting and helpful. Those high in openness to experience are imaginative and independent; those low in this basic trait are down-to-earth and conformist.

Considerable evidence supports the five-factor theory (John, 1990). The Big Five emerge across cultures, among adults and children, even when vastly different questionnaires assess the factors, and the same five factors appear whether people rate themselves or are rated by others. Some cross-cultural differences emerge, however. For example, personality studies conducted in China have shown that interpersonal relatedness, or harmony, is an important personality trait there but not in Western cultures (Cheung et al., 2001; Cheung, Cheung, & Leung, 2008)—possibly because many Chinese live in densely populated areas, so getting along with others is more essential than in societies where people live farther apart.

Some researchers have questioned whether the five-factor theory really clarifies personality, since the factor terms are descriptive rather than explanatory, and reducing all of human personality to five dimensions ignores individual subtleties. However, the theory is valuable as an organizational structure for the vast number of traits that describe personality; by providing a common descriptive framework, it integrates and invigorates the trait approach (John & Srivastava, 1999). Moreover, the factors uniquely predict certain outcomes. For instance, conscientiousness predicts grades in college but not scores on standardized tests, whereas openness to experience predicts scores on standardized tests but not grades (Noftle & Robins, 2007). These effects may occur because highly conscientious people tend to work very hard, a characteristic that matters for grades, whereas people who are high in openness tend to use words very well, a characteristic that matters for achievement tests. Thus factors exist at more than a descriptive level. Working across levels of analysis provides new ways to understand the basic traits (Clark & Watson, 1999).

five-factor theory The idea that personality can be described using five factors: openness to experience, conscientiousness, extraversion, agreeableness, and neuroticism.

OPENNESS TO EXPERIENCE
Imaginative vs. down to earth
Likes variety vs. likes routine
Independent vs. conforming

CONSCIENTIOUSNESS
Organized vs. disorganized
Careful vs. careless
Self-disciplined vs. weak-willed

Personality

NEUROTICISM
Worried vs. calm
Insecure vs. secure
Self-pitying vs. self-satisfied

EXTRAVERSION
Social vs. retiring
Fun-loving vs. sober
Affectionate vs. reserved

AGREEABLENESS
Softhearted vs. ruthless
Trusting vs. suspicious
Helpful vs. uncooperative

FIGURE 13.8 The Big Five Personality Factors The acronym OCEAN is a good way to remember these terms.

Personality Reflects Learning and Cognition

In contrast to psychologists who saw personality as the result of internal processes, behaviorists such as B. F. Skinner viewed personality mainly as learned responses to patterns of reinforcement. However, growing dissatisfaction with strict models of learning theory led researchers to incorporate cognition into the understanding of personality. For instance, the early cognitive theorist George Kelly (1955) emphasized the importance of people's understandings, or *personal constructs,* of their circumstances. These constructs are personal theories of how the world works. Kelly thought that people viewed the world as if they were scientists, constantly testing out their theories by observing ongoing events and then revising those theories

FIGURE 13.9 Expectancies and Value
The expectation of positive reinforcement from doing well on a test may be enough to keep this student studying in his dorm room rather than going out to a party.

based on what they observe. According to Kelly, personal constructs develop through people's experiences and represent their interpretations and explanations for events in their social worlds. Julian Rotter (1954) built further on the cognitive approach by introducing the idea that behavior is a function of people's *expectancies* for reinforcement, as well as the *values* they ascribe to particular reinforcers. Thus a person deciding whether to study for an exam or go to a party will weigh the likelihood that studying will lead to a good grade, as well as how much that grade matters, against the likelihood that the party will be fun and the extent to which he or she values having fun (**FIGURE 13.9**). Rotter proposed that people differ in their beliefs that their efforts will lead to positive outcomes. People with an *internal locus of control* believe they bring about their own rewards, whereas those with an *external locus of control* believe that rewards—and therefore their personal fates—result from forces beyond their control. These generalized beliefs affect individuals' psychological adjustment.

The incorporation of cognition into learning theories led to the development of *cognitive-social theories* of personality, which emphasize how personal beliefs, expectancies, and interpretations of social situations shape behavior and personality. For instance, Albert Bandura (1977) argued that humans possess mental capacities, such as beliefs, thoughts, and expectations, that interact with environment to influence behavior. For Bandura, as discussed in Chapter 9, the extent to which people believe they can achieve specific outcomes, called *self-efficacy,* is an important determinant of behavior. Moreover, as discussed in Chapter 6, Bandura proposed that people develop expectancies in part through *observational learning,* such as by noticing whether others are rewarded, or punished, for acting in certain ways.

One of the most influential cognitive-social theorists has been Walter Mischel, who approached the study of personality at the social level of analysis. Mischel sparked controversy by proposing that personality traits often fail to predict behavior across different circumstances. According to his *cognitive-affective personality system (CAPS;* Mischel & Shoda, 1995), people's responses are influenced by how they perceive a given situation, their affective (emotional) response to the situation, their skills in dealing with challenges, and their anticipation of the outcomes of their behavior (**FIGURE 13.10**).

Imagine, for instance, a person who walks into a party expecting to make a good impression, having done so many times in the past. This person will act very differently from someone whose past experiences of awkwardness, discomfort, and shyness lead to the expectation of rejection. Consider also the personality style *defensive pessimism,* studied by Julie Norem and Nancy Cantor. Defensive pessimists expect to fail and therefore enter test situations with dread. By contrast, optimists enter test situations with high expectations. Yet pessimists and optimists tend to perform similarly on exams (Norem, 1989). These two personality styles reflect different motivational strategies: Pessimists expect the worst so they can be relieved when they succeed, whereas optimists focus on positive outcomes.

FIGURE 13.10 CAPS Model Mischel and Shoda believed personality traits alone could not predict behavior.

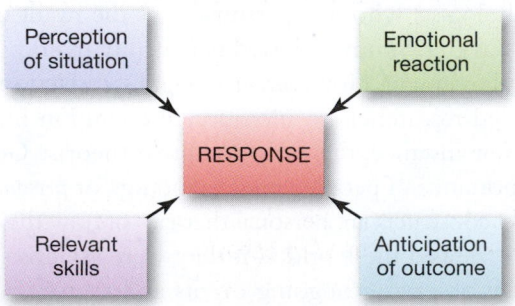

The CAPS model and other cognitive–social theories of personality also emphasize *self-regulatory capacities*, in which people set personal goals, evaluate their progress, and adjust their behavior accordingly. Indeed, many personality psychologists believe that motives and strivings, such as those for achievement, power, or intimacy, are an essential aspect of personality (Snyder & Cantor, 1998). Personality, then, represents behavior that emerges from people's interpretations of their social worlds and from their beliefs about how they will affect and be affected by their social situations.

 ## SUMMING UP

How Have Psychologists Studied Personality?

According to the psychodynamic approach, unconscious motives and conflicts that are experienced throughout life, but especially in childhood, shape personality. Humanists believe each person is unique and capable of fulfilling great potential. Trait theorists describe behavior on the basis of dispositions. Cognitive-social theorists focus on how beliefs and cognitive interpretations affect people's perceptions of their social environments. These varied approaches share a goal of trying to understand the ways in which people are similar to and different from one another.

MEASURING UP

1. Indicate which theorists are associated with each of the following four approaches to studying personality: psychodynamic, humanistic, type and trait, and learning and cognition.

   a. Abraham Maslow   h. Gordon Allport
   b. Albert Bandura   i. Hans Eysenck
   c. Anna Freud   j. Karen Horney
   d. Carl Jung   k. Martin Seligman
   e. Carl Rogers   l. Raymond Cattell
   f. Erik Erikson   m. Sigmund Freud
   g. George Kelly   n. Walter Mischel

2. Indicate which concepts are associated with each of the four approaches to studying personality (see question 1).

   a. defense mechanisms
   b. id, ego, superego
   c. describing how individuals differ from one another
   d. locus of control
   e. people seeking to fulfill their potential for personal growth through greater self-understanding
   f. personal beliefs, expectations, and interpretations of social situations shaping personality
   g. personality traits
   h. personality types
   i. self-efficacy
   j. sexual instincts
   k. the Big Five
   l. unconditional positive regard
   m. unconscious forces influencing behavior

How Is Personality Assessed, and What Does It Predict?

Personality researchers have yet to agree on the best method for assessing aspects of personality. As mentioned, personality encompasses thoughts, feelings, and behaviors, all of which need to be considered. Psychological scientists measure personality by having people report on themselves, by asking people's friends or relatives to describe them, or by watching how people behave. Each method has strengths and limitations. The following section considers how psychological scientists assess personality and how the different methods influence our understanding of individuals.

Personality Refers to Both Unique and Common Characteristics

idiographic approaches Person-centered approaches to studying personality that focus on individual lives and how various characteristics are integrated into unique persons.

nomothetic approaches Approaches to studying personality that focus on how people vary across common traits.

Allport divided the study of personality into two approaches: **Idiographic approaches** are *person-centered* in that they focus on individual lives and how various characteristics are integrated into unique persons. **Nomothetic approaches,** in contrast, focus on characteristics common among all people but on which individuals vary. In other words, idiographic approaches use a different metric for each person, whereas nomothetic approaches use the same metric to compare all people.

Idiographic approaches assume all individuals are unique. If your classmates were to identify 10 personality traits that described them, although there would be some overlap each person would probably list some different traits. After all, people like to be distinctive, so they tend to choose traits that are particularly descriptive of themselves compared with other people. These *central traits* are especially important for how individuals define themselves. In contrast, people consider *secondary traits* less personally descriptive or not applicable. In general, central traits are more predictive of behavior than are secondary traits.

Researchers who use idiographic approaches often examine case studies of individuals through interviews or biographical information. For example, many scholars, including Henry Murray, who pioneered the approach, have tried to account for Adolf Hitler's behavior in Nazi Germany by studying his early childhood experiences, his physical stature, and his personal motivations (**FIGURE 13.11**). This type of study emphasizes the idea that personality unfolds over the life course as people react to their particular circumstances.

Another idiographic approach considers a human life as a narrative (McAdams, 1999, 2001). According to Dan McAdams, to give life meaning and make sense of the world, each person weaves a *life story* that integrates self-knowledge into a coherent whole. The life story is a reconstructive and imaginative process in which the person links his or her motives, goals, and beliefs with events, people, and circumstances. In so doing, the individual creates *personal myths* that bind together past events and future possibilities. To study personality, then, narrative psychologists pay attention to the stories people tell about their lives.

Nomothetic approaches focus on common traits (e.g., agreeable/disagreeable) rather than individual uniqueness. Researchers in this tradition compare people by using common trait measures, such as questionnaires or other similar methods. For example, they might give participants a list of 100 personality traits and have them rate themselves on each, using a scale from 1 to 10. From the nomothetic perspective, individuals are unique because of their unique combinations of common traits.

FIGURE 13.11 Adolf Hitler In his personality analysis of Hitler, Henry Murray (1943) stated the German leader was impotent in heterosexual relations and had engaged in a homosexual relationship. Murray's collaborative report predicted Hitler's suicide.

Researchers Use Objective and Projective Methods to Assess Personality

Researchers use numerous methods to assess personality, ranging from self-reports to clinical interviews to observer reports. In addition, the way researchers choose to measure personality depends to a great extent on their theoretical orientations. For instance, trait researchers use personality descriptions, whereas humanistic psychologists use more holistic approaches. At the broadest level, assessment procedures can be grouped into projective and objective measures.

PROJECTIVE MEASURES According to psychodynamic theory, personality is influenced by unconscious conflicts. **Projective measures** explore the unconscious by having people describe or tell stories about ambiguous stimulus items. The general idea is that people will project their mental contents onto the ambiguous items, thereby revealing hidden aspects of personality such as motives, wishes, and unconscious conflicts. Many such procedures are used to assess psychopathology. One of the best-known projective measures is the *Rorschach inkblot test,* in which people look at an apparently meaningless inkblot and describe what it looks like to them. How a person describes the inkblot is supposed to reveal unconscious conflicts and other problems. However, the Rorschach does a poor job of diagnosing specific psychological disorders, and it finds many normal adults and children to be psychologically disturbed (Wood, Garb, Lilienfeld, & Nezworski, 2002).

One classic projective measure used by personality psychologists is the *Thematic Apperception Test (TAT),* developed by Henry Murray and Christiana Morgan to study achievement motivation. A person is shown an ambiguous picture and is asked to tell a story about it (**FIGURE 13.12**). Scoring of the story is based on the motivational schemes that emerge, which are assumed to reflect the storyteller's personal motives. Although many projective measures have been criticized for being too subjective and poorly validated, the TAT has been useful for measuring motivational traits, especially those related to achievement, power, and affiliation, and therefore it continues to be used in contemporary research (McClelland, Koestner, & Weinberger, 1989). Indeed, evidence shows that the TAT, if used properly, reliably predicts how interpersonally dependent people are—for example, how much they seek approval and support from others (Bornstein, 1999).

projective measures Personality tests that examine unconscious processes by having people interpret ambiguous stimuli.

FIGURE 13.12 Thematic Apperception Test Pictures of this type are used in the TAT.

OBJECTIVE MEASURES **Objective measures** of personality make no pretense of uncovering hidden conflicts or secret information. They measure only what the raters believe or observe. Personality researchers use them to compare people's responses and assess the extent to which the answers predict behavior. Objective measures are straightforward assessments, usually involving self-report questionnaires or observer ratings. A questionnaire might target a specific trait, such as how much excitement a person seeks out of life, but more often objective measures are large personality inventories, such as the *NEO Personality Inventory,* which consists of 240 items designed to assess the Big Five personality factors (Costa & McCrae, 1992). Although they are called objective, the tests require people to make subjective judgments. Self-reports can be affected by desires to avoid looking bad and by biases in self-perception.

It can be difficult to compare self-reported objective measures directly, because individual respondents do not have objective standards against which to rate themselves. For example, two individuals reporting a 5 on a 7-point shyness scale may not be equally shy because the term can mean different things to different people.

objective measures Relatively direct assessments of personality, usually based on information gathered through self-report questionnaires or observer ratings.

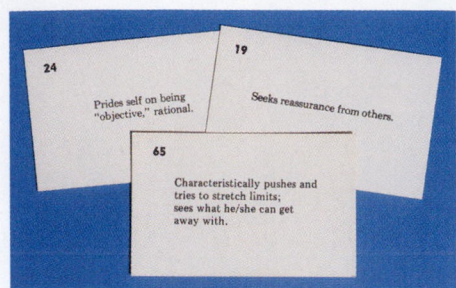

FIGURE 13.13 California Q-Sort These are three of the cards participants sort when taking the Q-Sort assessment.

situationism The theory that behavior is determined more by situations than by personality traits.

One technique that assesses traits is the *California Q-Sort,* in which people sort 100 statements printed on cards into nine piles according to how accurately the statements describe them. The piles represent categories ranging from "not at all descriptive" to "extremely descriptive" (**FIGURE 13.13**). A participant may place only so many cards in each pile, with fewer cards being allowed for the extreme ends of the scale. Because most of the cards must be piled in the moderately descriptive categories, the Q-Sort has a built-in procedure for identifying central dispositions. The Q-Sort, like most objective measures, can also be used by observers, such as parents, teachers, therapists, and friends.

Observers Show Accuracy in Trait Judgments

Do other people know you pretty well? Imagine that you often feel shy in new situations, as many people do. Would others know that shyness is part of your personality? Some shy people force themselves to be outgoing to mask their feelings, so their friends might have no idea that they feel shy. Others react to the fear of social situations by remaining quiet and aloof, so observers might believe them to be cold, arrogant, and unfriendly. Indeed, we are all judged by others throughout our lives, but how accurate are those judgments? And how well do observers' personality judgments predict others' behavior?

An important study by David Funder (1995) found a surprising degree of accuracy for trait judgments under certain circumstances. For instance, a person's close acquaintances may predict the person's behavior more accurately than the person does. In one study, for example, friends predicted assertiveness and other behaviors better than did the person's own ratings (Kolar, Funder, & Colvin, 1996; Vazire & Mehl, 2008). This effect may occur because our friends observe how we behave in situations, whereas we may be preoccupied with evaluating other people and therefore fail to notice how we actually behave. Another possibility is that our subjective perceptions may diverge from our objective behaviors. In either case, the study implies that there is a disconnect between how people view themselves and how they behave. Not surprisingly, evidence indicates that people come to know others better over time, as they witness others' behavior across different circumstances; thus we are more accurate in predicting a close friend's behavior than that of a mere acquaintance (Biesanz, West, & Millevoi, 2007).

People Sometimes Are Inconsistent

Imagine again that you are shy. Are you shy in all situations? Probably not. Shy people tend to be most uncomfortable in new situations in which they are being evaluated; they usually are not shy around family and close friends. In 1968, Walter Mischel dropped a bombshell on the field of personality by proposing that behaviors are determined more by situations than by personality traits, a theory referred to as **situationism.** For evidence, he referred to studies in which people who were dishonest in one situation were completely honest in another. For instance, a student who is not totally honest with a professor in explaining why a paper is late probably is no more likely to steal or to cheat on taxes than is a student who admits to oversleeping. Mischel's critique of personality traits caused considerable rifts between social psychologists, who emphasize situational forces, and personality psychologists, who focus on individual dispositions. After all, the most basic definition of personality holds that it is relatively stable across situations and circumstances. If Mischel was correct and there was relatively little stability, the whole concept of personality seemed empty.

As you might expect, there was a vigorous response to Mischel's critique. The argument made by personality researchers in the *person/situation debate* is that the extent to which a trait predicts behavior depends on the *centrality* of the trait, the *aggregation* of behaviors over time, and the *type* of trait being evaluated. People tend to be more consistent in their central traits than in their secondary traits, since the former are most relevant to them. In addition, if behaviors are averaged across many situations, personality traits are more predictive of behavior. Shy people may not be shy all the time, but on average they are shy more than those who are not shy. Moreover, people who report being shy in college continue to report being shy many years later, so the trait of shyness seems to be stable. Some traits, such as honesty, will also more likely be consistent across situations, whereas others, such as shyness, might vary depending on the situation. Finally, some people may be more consistent than others. Consider the trait of *self-monitoring,* which involves being sensitive to cues of situational appropriateness. Those high in self-monitoring alter their behavior to match the situation, so they exhibit low levels of consistency. By contrast, those low in self-monitoring are less able to alter their self-presentations to match situational demands, so they tend to be much more consistent across situations.

Behavior Is Influenced by the Interaction of Personality and Situations

Considerable evidence indicates that personality traits are predictive of behavior. For instance, people high in neuroticism tend to be more depressed and have more illnesses, are more likely to have midlife crises, and so on. Indeed, being highly neurotic is the best personality predictor of marital dissatisfaction and divorce (Karney & Bradbury, 1995). Likewise, those high in sensation seeking are more likely to smoke, use drugs, have sex, be impulsive, watch erotic movies, begin conversations, and engage in physically risky activities such as mountain climbing. Researchers have found strong evidence that personality dispositions are meaningful constructs that predict behavior over time and across circumstances. Yet people are also highly sensitive to social context, and most conform to situational norms. Few people would break the law in front of a police officer or drive on the wrong side of the road just because they felt like it; the situation dictates behavior irrespective of personality.

Situational influences can be subtle. Consider your own behavior. You may reveal different aspects of your personality during your interactions with different people. Your goals for social interaction change, as do the potential consequences of your actions. For example, your family may be more tolerant of your bad moods than your friends are. Thus you may feel freer to express your bad moods around your family.

Situations differ in the extent to which they constrain the expression of personality (Kenrick & Funder, 1991). Consider two people, one highly extraverted, aggressive, and boisterous, and the other shy, thoughtful, and restrained. At a funeral, it might be hard to tell them apart based on their behavior, but at a party the differences would be obvious. Personality psychologists differentiate between *strong situations* (e.g., elevators, religious services, job interviews) and *weak situations* (e.g., parks, bars, one's house); the former mask differences in personality because of the power of the social environment (**FIGURE 13.14**). Most trait theorists are

(a)

(b)

FIGURE 13.14 Strong and Weak Situations (a) A strong situation, such as a funeral, tends to discourage displays of personality. (b) A weak situation, such as hanging out with friends, tends to let people behave more freely.

interactionists Theorists who believe that behavior is determined jointly by underlying dispositions and situations.

interactionists, believing that behavior is determined jointly by situations and underlying dispositions.

People also affect their social environments, however. First, people choose their situations. Introverts tend to avoid parties or other situations in which they might feel anxious, whereas extraverts seek out social opportunities. Once people are in situations, their behavior affects those around them. Some extraverts may draw people out and encourage them to have fun, whereas others might act aggressively and turn people off. Some introverts might create an intimate atmosphere that encourages people to open up and reveal personal concerns, whereas others might make people uncomfortable and anxious. A reciprocal interaction occurs between the person and the social environment so that they simultaneously influence each other. The important point is that personality reflects both underlying dispositions and the activation of goals and of emotional responses in given situations.

There Are Cultural and Gender Differences in Personality

How similar are people around the world? Certainly there are stereotypes about people from different countries, as well as about men and women. But is there any truth to these stereotypes? Does scientific evidence document differences in personality among cultures or between women and men?

Studying cultural differences in personality presents many challenges. As noted in Chapter 2, cross-cultural research can be difficult when language is a central component of what is being studied. Recall from Chapter 1 that people from Eastern cultures tend to think in terms of relations with other people, whereas those from Western cultures tend to think in terms of independence (how this affects the sense of self is discussed later in this chapter). People from various cultures might therefore interpret any question about personality traits from different perspectives, such as what it means for their family or group (Eastern) versus what it means for them alone (Western). Comparing across cultures also requires the use of standardized questionnaires that are reliably translated so that the questions clearly refer to the same personality trait in all cultures and all respondents interpret the questions in the same way. Another problem involves sampling: Often researchers use samples of convenience, such as college students taking the researchers' classes, but in different countries different types of people may go to college or university. Thus apparent cultural differences result from examining different types of people in the different cultures.

Recognizing these issues, one research team conducted a careful investigation of personality differences across 56 nations (Schmitt et al., 2007). They found support for the Big Five personality traits across all the countries, in turn supporting the argument that those traits are universal for humans. However, the investigators found modest differences in Big Five traits across the 56 nations; people from East Asia (e.g., Japan, China, Korea) rated themselves comparatively lower than other respondents on extraversion, agreeableness, and conscientiousness, and comparatively higher on neuroticism (**FIGURE 13.15**). By contrast, respondents from countries in Africa rated themselves as more agreeable and conscientious and less neurotic than did people from most other countries. However, these ratings might have reflected differences in cultural norms for saying good and bad things about oneself, and people from East Asian countries might be the most modest.

Clear from research, however, is that self-reports often do not match cultural stereotypes about the respondents. One team of researchers examined beliefs about personality characteristics typical of people from 49 cultures and then compared those ratings to self-reports and observer reports of people from those cultures

(Terracciano et al., 2005). There was little correspondence. For instance, Canadians were widely believed to be relatively low in neuroticism and high in agreeableness, yet self-reports by Canadians did not support this pattern; they reported themselves to be just as neurotic and disagreeable as people from other cultures. Steven Heine and his colleagues (2008) have argued that national reputations may be accurate and that self-reports might be biased by individuals' comparisons of themselves to their national reputations. Imagine that everyone in Country X works extremely hard and is always on time; therefore, these people are high in conscientiousness compared with those in Country Y, who work only when the urge strikes them. An individual in Country X may be just as conscientious as a person in Country Y, but compared to his or her fellow citizens the person in Country X may feel average, whereas the person in Country Y would feel far above average. Thus people can view the same behavior differently depending on how they compare themselves to others. In other words, maybe Canadians really are especially agreeable, and it is simply hard to notice one person's agreeableness around all those other agreeable Canadians.

What about gender? Are the stereotypes about men and women accurate? Women and men are much more similar than different in terms of personality, but the differences between them largely support the stereotypes. That is, across various studies, women typically report and are rated as being more empathetic and agreeable than men, but also as being somewhat more neurotic and concerned about feelings. By contrast, men tend to report and are rated as being more assertive (Costa, Terracciano, & McCrae, 2001; Feingold, 1994; Maccoby & Jacklin, 1974).

Of particular interest is how gender differences emerge across cultures. You might guess that the more egalitarian and developed a society, the more similarity between the sexes would be observed. After all, if we treat boys and girls equally, we might expect them to turn out to be more similar than they would if we treat them differently. Thus it is puzzling to discover that gender differences in personality are largest in societies in North America and Europe, which provide more equal opportunities and treatment than many other societies, and smallest in Asian and African communities (Costa et al., 2001; Guimond et al., 2007; Schmitt, Realo, Voracek, & Allik, 2008). One theory to explain this pattern is that prosperous, developed societies that emphasize women's rights to education and to work allow for greater personal expression of individuality (Schmitt et al., 2008). Still, why might differences between females and males emerge when people can express themselves freely? According to the social psychologist Serge Guimond (2008), people in individualistic cultures, such as within Western Europe and North America, tend to compare themselves against other groups. Thus women in such cultures describe themselves in ways that differentiate them from men, thereby creating gender differences in personality. From this perspective, the apparent cultural differences in the gender gap result from cultural differences in how people compare themselves rather than from any genuine cultural differences. However, as you will see later in this chapter, some evidence suggests that certain sex differences in characteristics related to personality emerge during early childhood.

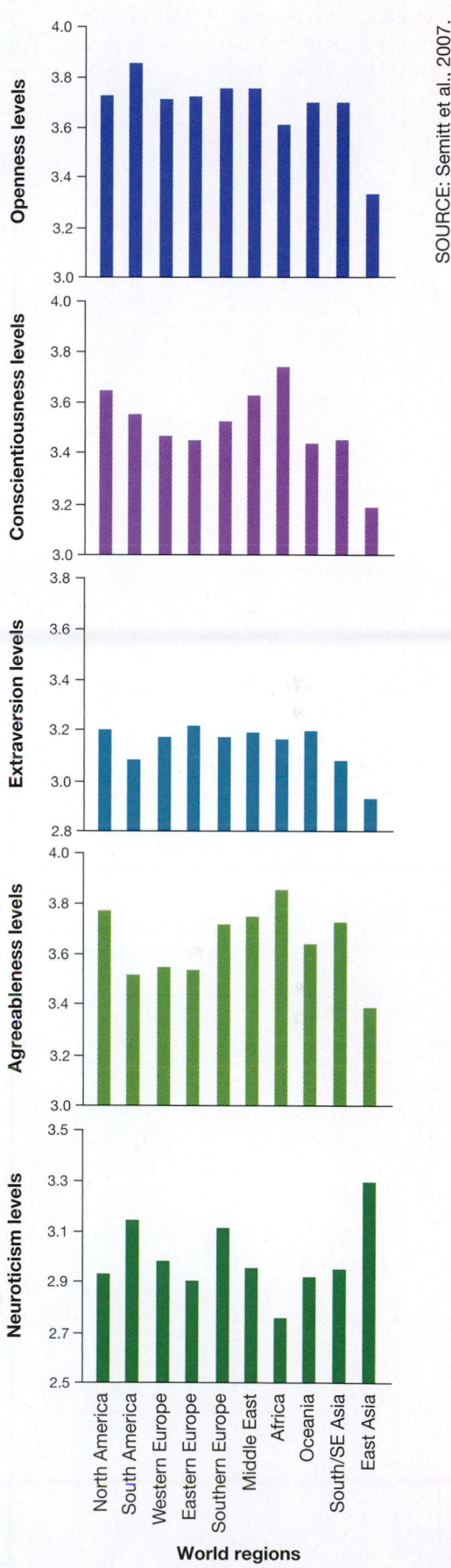

SOURCE: Semitt et al., 2007.

FIGURE 13.15 Cross-Cultural Research on Personality Traits A team of more than 120 scientists investigated the Big Five personality traits around the world, from Argentina to Zimbabwe.

► SUMMING UP

How Is Personality Assessed, and What Does It Predict?

Personality is assessed through projective or objective measures, depending on the researcher's goals. Sometimes personality psychologists examine individuals—for example, by studying personal myths. Sometimes they examine many people by using a common measure to assess whether individual differences predict behavior. People are relatively good at assessing others' personality traits, and some evidence suggests that observers might be better at predicting others' behavior than people are at predicting their own. Observers may be more sensitive to environmental cues that shape behavior. Indeed, traits interact with environments, such that situations sometimes constrain behavior, and personality sometimes influences situations. The structure of personality is stable across cultures, although self-reports concerning some traits differ across cultures. These differences may be attributed to biases in self-report. Reliable gender differences in personality are somewhat consistent with common sex stereotypes. Gender differences more likely emerge in prosperous and developed societies.

► MEASURING UP

1. Match the strengths and limitations listed below to the following assessment methods: California Q-Sort, NEO Personality Inventory, Rorschach inkblot test, Thematic Apperception Test. (Each method may be associated with multiple strengths and multiple limitations.)

   Strengths:
   a. Can be completed by an individual or by observers who evaluate that individual.
   b. Can reveal hidden aspects of personality.
   c. Effectively measures motivational states.
   d. Offers a built-in procedure for identifying traits perceived to be most central to the rater.

   Limitations:
   e. Can be biased by the rater's desire to avoid looking bad.
   f. Does a poor job of diagnosing psychological disorders.
   g. Many normal individuals who take this test are misdiagnosed as being psychologically disturbed.

2. For each scenario, indicate which person is most likely to engage in the behavior described, and explain why in a sentence.

   Scenario 1: The two people described below each have a birthday party. After the party, who is more likely to follow through on his plan to send thank-you cards to the guests? Why?
   a. Chad describes himself as highly conscientious; moreover, he says his conscientiousness is vital to who he is.
   b. Malik takes the NEO Personality Inventory. He is a little surprised by the results, which indicate he is highly conscientious.

   Scenario 2: The two people described below are each engaged in conversations with total strangers. Which person is most likely to give an honest answer when asked, "How are you doing?" Why?
   a. Hayley is in an office conference room, talking with the boss's administrative assistant while waiting for the boss to arrive for Hayley's interview.
   b. Roxanne is at a bar talking to the bartender while sipping her drink.

Being positive seems to have many survival advantages. Happy people reap benefits including more friends, more social support, higher incomes, a better chance of staying married, greater creativity, and greater productivity. Happy people have greater self-control, better self-regulatory and coping abilities, stronger immune systems, and longer lives. They are more cooperative, social, charitable, and "other-centered" (Lyubomirsky, Sheldon, & Schkade, 2005). It also appears that a majority of people are generally happy. In one survey, the self-rated level of subjective well-being was above neutral in 86 percent of 43 nations (Diener & Diener, 1996). In the United States, in all socioeconomic groups, whites and African Americans score well above the neutral point (Andrew, 1991).

To a great extent, happiness seems to be something a person wins in the lottery at birth. Research on twins has shown that 50 percent to 80 percent of the variance in average levels of happiness can be accounted for by genes rather than by life experience (Lykken & Tellegen, 1996). Every individual has a characteristic and highly heritable range of happiness; at what point in that range he or she operates is determined by external factors that fall into two groups: conditions and voluntary activities. Conditions include wealth, marital status, where the person lives, age, sex, race, and physical abilities. Voluntary activities are things the person chooses to do, such as learning a new skill or language, meditating, traveling, engaging in hobbies, exercising, and socializing.

Might taking drugs be a way to increase happiness? In many individuals diagnosed with disorders such as depression, selective serotonin reuptake inhibiters (SSRIs) such as Prozac, Paxil, Zoloft, Lexapro, or Celexa brighten or stabilize moods, presumably as a result of the increased availability of serotonin in certain crucial places in the brain (**FIGURE 13.16**). Serotonin, a neurotransmitter, is released from one neuron to activate another. (On neurotransmitters, neurons, and brain chemistry generally, see Chapter 3, "Biological Foundations.") The brain recycles serotonin after each release by means of a reuptake system. SSRIs inhibit the serotonin reuptake system, thereby increasing the concentration of serotonin. Although scientists do not know how serotonin functions, how inhibiting serotonin reuptake alters the mental state, or even whether serotonin deficiency causes depression in the first place, millions of Americans take SSRIs. Many of these people suffer from severe depression, but some doctors prescribe mood-brighteners for people whose moods are not extreme and whose neurochemistry may be normal.

For more information talk to your doctor

FIGURE 13.16 **Mood-Enhancing Drugs** Advertisements for mood-enhancing drugs, such as this one for the antidepressant Paxil, depict them as a sure-fire way to produce happiness.

Prescribing mood enhancers for individuals who have no mental disorders raises ethical issues. First, safety is a primary concern for healthy people using these drugs long-term, since little is known about the physical effects of long-term use. There may also be social effects, whereby having an easy way to achieve well-being might lead to a redefinition and narrowing of the range of normal emotions, moods, and temperaments. More and more people might feel pressured to take SSRIs because their chemically enhanced peers have set a new standard for cheerfulness. In a more extreme scenario, such treatments could be misused for social control.

Third, mood enhancement raises issues of personal identity and truth. If SSRIs change a user's personality, do the drugs alter who the person actually is? If Katie is taking an SSRI, are Katie on meds and Katie off meds two different people? If Keith falls in love with Katie, has Keith fallen in love with Katie or with Katie on medication?

Fourth, SSRIs give an overall sense of well-being but do not promote well-being itself, so people taking them may lack the motivating force of discontent to make beneficial changes. Thus they may become emotionally estranged from reality and fail to respond to experiences properly. Would popping a mood-brightening drug be such an easy fix that people would engage less in mood-enhancing activities that may also benefit society, and would this shift eventually change society for the worse?

What Are the Biological Bases of Personality?

Where does personality come from? Freud emphasized early childhood experiences in his theory of psychosexual stages, and Rogers believed that unconditional positive regard leads to positive mental health. Most people assume that how a child is treated—by parents, guardians, and so on—will substantially affect that child's personality and subsequent development. As discussed above, both gender and culture influence personality. So what role does biology play? Is each person born with certain predispositions? How do the workings of body and of brain affect the development of personality?

Over the past few decades, evidence has emerged that biological factors—such as genes, brain structures, and neurochemistry—play an important role in determining personality. This is not to say that these factors are insensitive to experience. As discussed in Chapter 3, every cell in the body contains the genome, or master recipe, that provides detailed instructions for physical processes. Gene expression—whether the gene is turned off or on—underlies all psychological activity. Ultimately, genes have their effects only if they are expressed, and environment determines when or if this happens. In terms of personality, genetic makeup may predispose certain traits or characteristics, but whether these genes are expressed depends on the unique circumstances that each child faces during development. For instance, as noted in Chapter 3, children with a certain gene variation were found to be more likely to become violent criminals as adults if they were abused during childhood. An important theme throughout this book is that nature and nurture work together to produce individuals; this theme holds particularly true for personality.

Animals Have Personalities

Real World PSYCHOLOGY

If you have ever owned a pet, you probably felt that your pet had a distinct personality. For most of the history of psychological science, your intuition would have been regarded skeptically, the assumption being that you were projecting your own sense of personality onto your pet. However, the principles of evolution suggest a continuity across species in that humans and other animals evolved as they solved occasionally similar adaptive challenges; this view raises the possibility that animals might display consistent individual differences in behaviors, across circumstances, that reflect underlying biological bases of personality (Gosling, 2001). But how do psychological scientists determine animals' personalities?

Sam Gosling, studying the behavior of a group of 34 spotted hyenas, created a personality scale consisting of 44 traits applicable to both humans and hyenas (Gosling, 1998). Four observers who knew hyenas well used the scale independently to rate the animals. Agreement among raters was as high as is typically found in personality studies of humans, suggesting that the raters could assess the hyenas reliably. Using factor analysis, Gosling found that the traits clustered into five factors, albeit not exactly the same five factors found for humans. Although there were rough similarities between humans and hyenas in traits related to agreeableness, neuroticism, and openness to experience, hyenas showed no evidence of a conscientiousness factor, and extraversion seemed to exist mainly in the form of assertiveness—a finding that makes sense given that hyenas form dominance hierarchies (**FIGURE 13.17**).

Gosling and Oliver John (1999) summarized the findings of 19 studies that assessed multiple personality traits in modestly large samples of nonhuman animals, including household pets, monkeys and other primates, pigs, donkeys, and aquatic animals. They found evidence that traits similar to extraversion, neuroticism, and

FIGURE 13.17 Scientific Method: Gosling's Study of Personality in Animals

Hypothesis: Nonhuman animals can be described in terms of basic personality traits.

1 The researchers defined 44 traits and asked four observers to rate 34 spotted hyenas on each trait.

2 Through factor analysis, the 44 traits were clustered into five principal dimensions:

ASSERTIVENESS   CURIOSITY

EXCITABILITY   HUMAN-DIRECTED AGREEABLENESS

SOCIABILITY

Results: The four judges' ratings showed as much agreement as in most personality studies of humans, and the five personality dimensions could not be accounted for by other factors, such as sex or age.

Conclusion: The finding that hyenas can reliably be described in terms of personality traits lends support for further personality research on nonhuman animals.

agreeableness could be seen in most species. Extraversion reflected different levels of energy, approachability, and sociability. Neuroticism indicated differences in emotional reactivity, fearfulness, and excitability, whereas agreeableness reflected differences in aggression, hostility, and affinity for mates. For openness to experience, animals in about half the species displayed individual differences in both curiosity and play, and Gosling and John speculated that animals' openness might be similar to behaviors observed in young children. Conscientiousness, a core human trait, was found only among chimpanzees, some of whom showed more unpredictability and disorganized behavior than others. The finding that only chimpanzees showed any signs of conscientiousness may not be surprising, since they are humans' closest relatives. Indeed, a recent study of personality in orangutans also failed to find evidence of conscientiousness, but it found evidence for the other four of the Big Five traits (Weiss, King, & Perkins, 2006).

Do these judgments of personality in animals reflect true variations, or are they just stereotypes of certain species or breeds (**FIGURE 13.18**)? To test whether differences in personality traits among animals exist and can be measured, Gosling and his colleagues (2003) examined personality judgments for domestic dogs and compared those to judgments made for humans. The researchers selected three measures of accuracy: (1) the extent to which ratings by the same judges were consistent for similar behaviors over time, (2) whether there was agreement among independent judges viewing the same behavior, and (3) the extent to which the behavior corresponded to the definition of the trait, as when a dog was rated as aggressive

(a)

(b)

FIGURE 13.18 Do Dogs Have Personalities? Which is friendlier, **(a)** a golden retriever or **(b)** a rottweiler? How might you test your hypothesis?

for baring its teeth angrily. Using these measures of accuracy, Gosling asked each dog owner to rate his or her animal and also to provide the name of a friend who knew the dog well enough to rate it. Independent judges also assessed the behavior of the dog while it played in a park and performed a wide array of tasks. The dogs were assessed on four personality factors that corresponded roughly to openness to experience, extraversion, agreeableness, and neuroticism. The findings generally indicated that the ratings of the dogs were consistent over time, that the judges agreed, and that the trait behaviors displayed by the dogs corresponded to ratings of those traits made by independent judges. To rule out the possibility that breed stereotypes based solely on appearance influenced the ratings, another group of judges rated only pictures of the dogs. The personality ratings remained accurate even after statistical controlling for the ratings made of the pictures. This study suggests that dogs' personalities can be rated with impressive accuracy. That animals show clear evidence of basic personality traits suggests that these traits are biologically based and passed along through genes.

Personality Is Rooted in Genetics

Overwhelming evidence indicates that nearly all personality traits have a genetic component (Plomin & Caspi, 1999). One of the earliest studies to document the heritability of personality was conducted by James Loehlin and Robert Nichols (1976), who examined similarities in personality between more than 800 pairs of twins. Across a wide variety of traits, identical twins proved much more similar than fraternal twins. As discussed in Chapter 3, this pattern reflects the actions of genes, since identical twins share nearly the same genes whereas fraternal twins do not. Numerous twin studies subsequently have found that genetic influence accounts for approximately half the variance (40 percent to 60 percent) between individuals in personality traits, including the Big Five (**FIGURE 13.19**), and the genetic basis of these five traits has been shown to be the same across cultures (Yamagata et al., 2006). These patterns persist whether the twins rate themselves or whether friends, family, or trained observers rate them.

Of course, identical twins might receive more similar treatment than other siblings, and that treatment might explain the similarities in personality. The best evidence refuting this idea was obtained by Thomas Bouchard and his colleagues (1990). Their studies of twins raised apart (as described in Chapter 3, "Biological Foundations") revealed that these twins are often as similar as, or even more similar than, twins raised together. One possibile explanation for this finding is that parents strive to bring out individual strengths in each twin so that each feels unique and special. Thus parenting style may foster differences rather than similarities. If this explanation is correct, we might expect stronger correlations between personality traits for older twins than for younger twins, since the effects of parenting would diminish over time. And indeed, identical twins become more alike as they grow older. By contrast, siblings and fraternal twins do not.

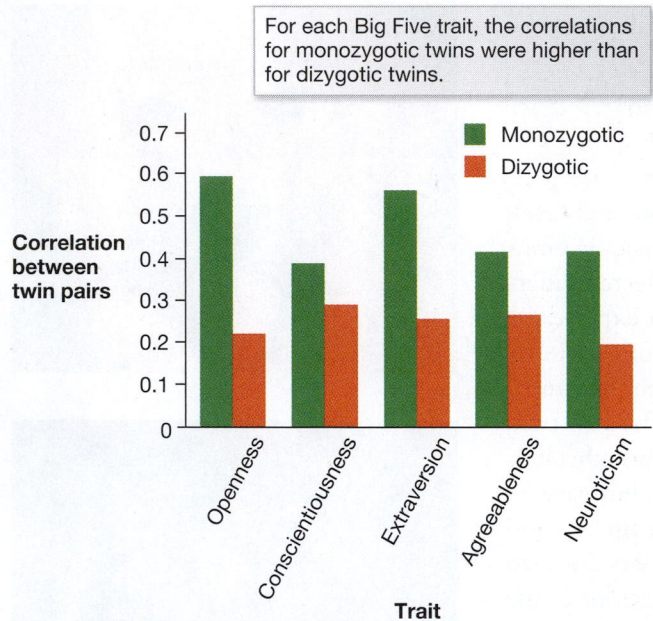

FIGURE 13.19 Correlations in Twins
Researchers examined correlations between 123 pairs of identical twins (monozygotic) and 127 pairs of fraternal twins (dizygotic) in Vancouver, Canada.

ADOPTION STUDIES Further evidence for the genetic basis of personality comes from adoption studies, although such studies usually yield lower estimates of gene influence than do twin studies. Siblings who are adopted (and not biologically related) and raised in the same household are no more alike in personality than any two strangers randomly plucked off the street (Plomin & Caspi, 1999). Moreover, the personalities of adopted children bear no significant relationship to those of the adoptive parents. These findings suggest that parenting style may have relatively little impact on personality. In fact, current evidence suggests that parenting style has much less impact than has long been assumed. For instance, although studies typically find only small correlations in personality between biological siblings or between children and their biological parents, these correlations are still larger than for adopted children, suggesting that the similarities have a genetic component. Why are children raised together in the same household (who are not identical twins) so different? One explanation is that the lives of siblings diverge as they establish friendships outside the home, and even though they are raised in the same home, their environments differ as a function of age and the fact that they have younger or older sisters or brothers. Siblings' personalities slowly grow apart as their initial differences become magnified through their interactions with the world.

Although the small correlations in personality among siblings might imply that parenting style has little effect, this does not mean that parents are unimportant (see Chapter 11, "Human Development"). David Lykken (2000), a leading behavioral genetics researcher, has argued that children raised with inadequate parenting are not socialized properly and therefore will much more likely become delinquent or display antisocial behavior. Thus a minimum level of parenting is crucial, but the particular style of parenting may not have a major impact on personality.

"I could cry when I think of the years I wasted accumulating money, only to learn that my cheerful disposition is genetic."

ARE THERE SPECIFIC GENES FOR PERSONALITY? Research has revealed genetic components for particular behaviors such as viewing television or getting divorced, and even for specific attitudes such as feelings about capital punishment or appreciation of jazz (Tesser, 1993). These findings do not mean, of course, that genes lurking in people's DNA determine the amount or types of television people watch. Rather, genes predispose certain personality traits associated with behavioral tendencies. In most cases, researchers note the influence of multiple genes that interact independently with the individual's environment to produce general dispositions, such as a preference for indoor activities over outdoor pursuits.

However, growing evidence indicates that genes can be linked with some specificity to personality traits. For instance, a gene that regulates one particular dopamine receptor has been associated with novelty seeking (Cloninger, Adolfsson, & Svrakic, 1996; Ekelund, Lichtermann, Jaervelin, & Peltonen, 1999). The theory is that people with one form of this gene are deficient in dopamine and seek out novel experiences to increase the release of dopamine. Research on neuroticism and agreeableness implicates a gene that regulates serotonin, although the effect is not large (Jang et al., 2001). These genes and perhaps thousands of others contribute to specific traits that combine to influence a person's overall personality and sense of psychological well-being (Weiss, Bates, & Luciano, 2008). For instance, some pairs of genes seem to work in opposite ways, such as making people more or less neurotic, and therefore they may cancel each other out (Savitz & Ramesar, 2004).

David Lykken and his colleagues (1992) note that it may be the chance aggregation of genes that produces unique individuals. They provide the analogy of a poker hand, in which the mother has dealt the ten and king of hearts and the father has dealt the jack, queen, and ace of hearts. Although neither parent alone has dealt a meaningful hand, together they have passed on a royal flush. Of course,

"Oh, he's cute, all right, but he's got the temperament of a car alarm."

temperaments Biologically based tendencies to feel or act in certain ways.

some people receive winning hands and others receive difficult hands to play. The point is that each person's personality reflects the genetic hand dealt jointly by both of that person's parents. Moreover, each person experiences different circumstances that may cause the selective expression of certain genes. Given the complexity of most personalities, the complexity of their underlying physiology is hardly surprising. As psychological scientists gain a greater understanding of the human genome in general, they likely will continue to identify how specific genes interact with environments to produce various aspects of personality.

Temperaments Are Evident in Infancy

Genes work by affecting biological processes. Therefore, to the extent that genes influence personality, there ought to be corresponding biological differences in personality, called **temperaments.** Temperaments, which are considered broader than traits, are general tendencies to feel or act in certain ways. Most of the research on temperaments focuses on infants, because personality differences very early in life likely indicate the actions of biological mechanisms. Although later life experiences may alter personality traits, temperaments represent the innate biological structures of personality.

Arnold Buss and Robert Plomin (1984) have argued that three personality characteristics can be considered temperaments. *Activity level* is the overall amount of energy and of behavior a person exhibits. For example, some children race around the house, others are less vigorous, and still others are slow-paced. *Emotionality* describes the intensity of emotional reactions. For example, children who cry often or easily become frightened, as well as adults who quickly anger, are likely high in emotionality. Finally, *sociability* refers to the general tendency to affiliate with others. People high in sociability prefer to be with others rather than to be alone. According to Buss and Plomin, these three temperamental styles are the main personality factors influenced by genes. Indeed, evidence from twin studies, adoption studies, and family studies indicates a powerful effect of heredity on these core temperaments.

LONG-TERM IMPLICATIONS OF TEMPERAMENTS To what extent do infant temperaments predict adult personality? Recent research has documented compelling evidence that early childhood temperaments significantly influence behavior and personality structure throughout a person's development (Caspi, 2000). In one study (also discussed in Chapter 3, "Biological Foundations"), researchers investigated the health, development, and personalities of more than 1,000 people born during a one-year period (Silva & Stanton, 1996). These individuals were examined approximately every two years. At three years of age, children were classified into temperamental types based on examiners' ratings. The classification at age three predicted personality structure and a variety of behaviors in early adulthood (**FIGURE 13.20**). For instance, inhibited children were much more likely to become depressed. These findings suggest that early childhood temperaments may be good predictors of later behaviors.

GENDER AND TEMPERAMENTS As discussed earlier, reliable differences exist between males and females in terms of personality traits, at least within Western cultures. How early do these differences emerge? Do temperament differences exist between girls and boys? A recent meta-analysis found robust gender differences in temperament in early childhood (Else-Quest, Hyde, Goldsmith, & Van

Hulle, 2006). Girls demonstrated a stronger ability to control their attention and to resist their impulses, whereas boys were more physically active and experienced more high-intensity pleasure, such as in rough-and-tumble play. However, there were no temperamental differences in negative emotions, such as being angry or neurotic, during childhood.

SHYNESS AND INHIBITION This chapter frequently uses the example of shyness, or feelings of discomfort and of inhibition during interpersonal situations (Henderson & Zimbardo, 1998). The extent to which people are shy has been linked to early differences in temperament. Research has shown that children as young as six weeks of age can be identified as likely to be shy (Kagan & Snidman, 1991). Approximately 15 percent to 20 percent of newborns react to new situations or strange objects by becoming startled and distressed, crying, and vigorously moving their arms and legs. Kagan refers to these children as *inhibited*, a characteristic he views as biologically determined. Showing signs of inhibition at two months of age predicts later parental reports that the children are shy at four years of age, and such children are likely to be shy well into their teenage years. Indeed, measures of brainstem reactivity, indicating the ease with which a person is aroused, at ages 10 to 12 correspond to ratings made of these children at four months of age (Woodward et al., 2001), such that inhibited children show greater reactivity. Similar genetic findings for inhibited behavior have been found in species including dogs and monkeys. The biological evidence suggests that the amygdala—the brain region involved in emotional responses, especially fear—is involved in shyness. For instance, in one study, socially phobic (i.e., extremely shy) participants had much greater amygdala activation when shown unfamiliar faces than did control participants (Birbaumer et al., 1998).

Although shyness has a biological component, it has a social component as well: Approximately one-quarter of behaviorally inhibited children are not shy later in childhood. This development typically occurs when parents create supportive and calm environments in which children can deal with stress and novelty at their own paces. But these parents do not completely shelter their children from stress, so the children gradually learn to deal with their negative feelings in novel situations. Moreover, shyness varies across cultures: For example, it is quite common in Japan and less common in Israel. Such social and cultural factors highlight the interplay between nature and nurture.

Personality Is Linked to Specific Neurophysiological Mechanisms

Genes act to produce temperaments, which affect how children respond to and shape their environments, which in turn interact with temperament to shape personality. But how do these genetic predispositions produce personality? That is, what neurophysiological mechanisms are linked to personality? Some theories focus on the biological processes that produce the thoughts, emotions, and behaviors that make up personality. From this perspective, personality differences may reflect differences in the relative activation of different biological systems (Canli, 2006). Most research on the neurobiological underpinnings of personality has explored the dimension of extraversion/introversion.

AROUSAL AND EXTRAVERSION/INTROVERSION The intellectual founder of the modern biological approach to personality was Hans Eysenck, who believed that differences in cortical arousal produce the behavioral differences between

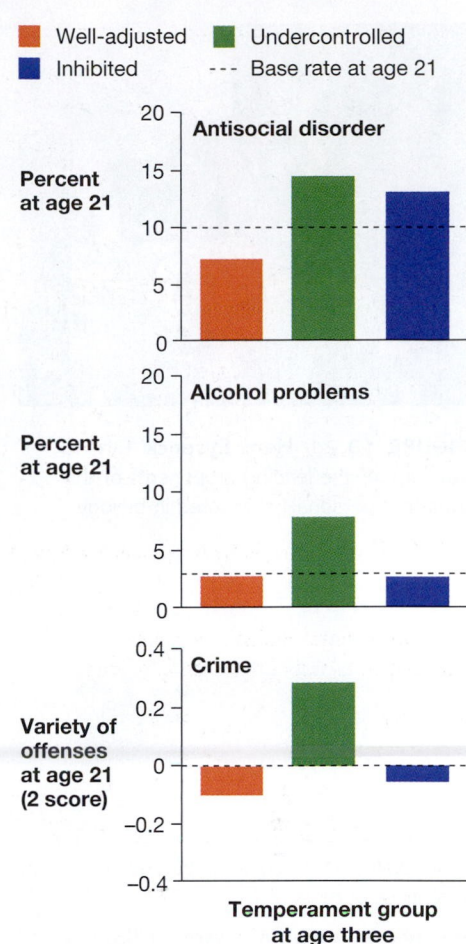

FIGURE 13.20 Predicting Behavior
Researchers investigated the personality development of more than 1,000 people, 97 percent of whom remained in the study through their 21st birthdays. Those judged undercontrolled at age three were later more likely to have alcohol problems, to be criminals or unemployed, to attempt suicide, to be antisocial and anxious, and to have less social support than those judged either well adjusted or inhibited.

FIGURE 13.21 Hans Eysenck Eysenck was one of the leading proponents of the idea that personality is rooted in biology.

behavioral approach system (BAS) The brain system involved in the pursuit of incentives or rewards.

behavioral inhibition system (BIS) The brain system that is sensitive to punishment and therefore inhibits behavior that might lead to danger or pain.

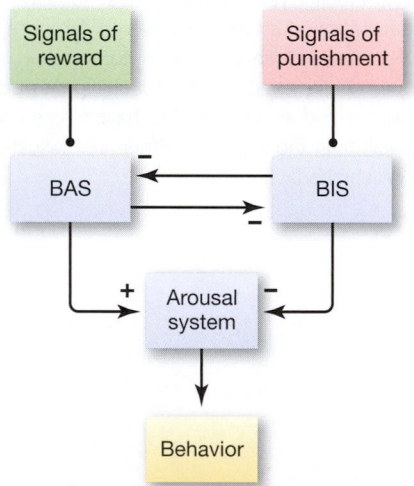

FIGURE 13.22 Behavioral Approach System and Behavioral Inhibition System Signals of potential reward are processed by the BAS. Signals of potential punishment are processed by the BIS. Based on the information each receives, the BAS activates behavior and the BIS inhibits behavior.

extraverts and introverts (**FIGURE 13.21**). Cortical arousal, or alertness, is regulated by the *ascending reticular activating system (ARAS),* and Eysenck proposed that this system differs between extraverts and introverts. He noted that extraverts seem constantly to seek additional arousal—for example, by attending parties or meeting new people. By contrast, introverts seem to avoid arousal by preferring solitary, quiet activities such as reading. According to earlier psychological theories, each person prefers to operate, and operates best, at some *optimal level of arousal* (see Chapter 9, "Motivation and Emotion"). Eysenck proposed that the resting levels of the ARAS are higher for introverts than for extraverts. Extraverts typically are below their optimal levels, such that they are chronically underaroused. To operate efficiently, they have to find arousal, so they impulsively seek out new situations and new emotional experiences. Introverts, whose arousal is above their optimal levels, do not want any additional arousal. They prefer quiet solitude with few stimuli. If you are an introvert, a noisy environment will distract you; if you are an extravert, quiet places will bore you. Consistent with Eysenck's theory, research has demonstrated that extraverts perform better in noisy settings (Geen, 1984).

If introverts are chronically more aroused than extraverts, they ought to be more sensitive to stimuli at all levels of intensity. Generally, introverts do appear more sensitive—to pain, for example, and to sourness (they salivate more when lemon juice is placed on their tongues than extraverts do). However, evidence for baseline differences in arousal has been more difficult to produce. Thus what differentiates introverts from extraverts appears to be their level of *arousability,* or reactivity to stimuli, such that introverts are more arousable.

Marvin Zuckerman (1994) describes the arousal-based trait of *sensation seeking* as similar to extraversion but with an impulsive element that more closely matches psychoticism, one of Eysenck's superordinate traits. According to Zuckerman, sensation seekers have a neurochemical deficiency that motivates them to seek arousal through adventures and new experiences. Moreover, sensation seekers tend to be easily bored and to escape boredom through the use of drugs and/or alcohol.

NEUROPHYSIOLOGY OF EXTRAVERSION/INTROVERSION A number of theorists have offered refinements to Eysenck's initial work that reflect more recent understandings of how the brain functions. The various theories have some common features, including a basic differentiation between approach learning and avoidance learning. Jeffrey Gray (1987) incorporated this distinction in his approach/inhibition model of the relation between learning and personality. Gray proposed that personality is rooted in motivational functions that have evolved to help organisms respond efficiently to reinforcement and punishment. In Gray's model, the **behavioral approach system (BAS)** consists of the brain structures that lead organisms to approach stimuli in pursuit of rewards. This is the *"go" system.* The *"stop" system,* known as the **behavioral inhibition system (BIS),** is sensitive to punishment and therefore inhibits behavior that might lead to danger or pain (**FIGURE 13.22**). According to Gray, extraverts have a stronger BAS than BIS, so they are more influenced by rewards than by punishments. Indeed, extraverts tend to act impulsively in the face of strong rewards, even following punishment (Patterson & Newman, 1993). By contrast, introverts have a more active BIS. Their chronic anxiety often leads them to avoid social situations in which they anticipate possible negative outcomes.

The BIS is associated with activity in the frontal lobes, which help inhibit inappropriate social behavior. Those with injury to the frontal lobes, especially the prefrontal cortex, exhibit social incompetence, disinhibition, impaired social judgment, and a lack of sensitivity to social cues. (For an image of these brain regions, see

Figure 3.28.) One imaging study found that introversion was associated with greater activation of the frontal lobes (Johnson et al., 1999), a finding that supports Gray's model of BIS. The amygdala is another brain region involved in both social sensitivity and the processing of cues related to possible punishment. As mentioned previously, some researchers believe personality traits such as fearfulness, anxiousness, and shyness are associated with excessive activation of the amygdala (Zuckerman, 1995). People who are usually anxious show a heightened amygdala response when observing pictures of neutral facial expressions, perhaps because such people are especially sensitive to signs of social rejection, so the neutral faces may trigger evaluation concerns (Somerville, Kim, Johnstone, Alexander, & Whalen, 2004).

We still have much to learn about the biological bases of personality. Only with recent advances in technology have researchers started to explore personality's genetic and neurophysiological correlates. For example, in one study of people who possess a particular form of a serotonin gene associated with greater fearfulness and negativity, participants showed greater amygdala activity when looking at pictures of human faces with emotional expressions than did participants with the other form of the gene (Hariri et al., 2002). Using brain imaging and gene data together may become a powerful new way to assess the biological basis of personality. We can anticipate many exciting new discoveries relevant to personality and temperament as a result of the biological revolution in psychological science (Canli, 2004).

Personality Is Adaptive

As natural selection has shaped the human genome over the course of evolution, adaptive characteristics likely spread through the gene pool and occurred in increasing numbers from generation to generation. Thus we might expect that personality traits useful for survival and reproduction were favored. It is easy to imagine how being competitive might lead an individual to obtain great rewards or to enjoy increased value in his or her social group. But traits also provide important information about desirable and undesirable qualities in mates, such as whether a person is conscientious, agreeable, neurotic, and so on. David Buss (1999) has argued that the Big Five personality traits emerged as foundational because each one provides important information regarding mate selection.

But if traits are adaptive, why do individuals differ so greatly? Natural selection ought to have made people more similar rather than more different. One possible explanation is that individual differences reflect characteristics, perhaps resulting from random processes, that were of trivial importance over the course of evolution (Tooby & Cosmides, 1990). However, Buss and Greiling (1999) have proposed that individual differences may reflect the inheritance of alternative strategies that become activated according to situational contexts. For example, consider a situation in which most people are honest and cooperative and therefore trust others to be honest and cooperative as well. A dishonest person in such a system could do well by exploiting others' basic trust. Of course, if too many people acted dishonestly, the system would change or collapse. The important point is that evolution has allowed for multiple strategies that are differentially adaptive depending on environmental demands.

Another possible explanation for individual differences is that human groups whose members possess diverse skills have a selective advantage over other human groups (Caporael, 2001). Members of successful groups are all more likely to survive and reproduce. Consider the trait of novelty seeking. Having group members who seek out and explore new territory might lead to the discovery of new resources, such as an abundant food supply. At the same time, novelty seekers expose themselves to greater risks, and the group would suffer if all its members followed this strategy. Therefore, it is to the group's advantage to have cautious members as well; these individuals may enhance the group in other ways, perhaps by being more considerate or providing social support.

Avoiding Single-Cause Explanations

Imagine you are talking to two people who are brother and sister. The brother explains that he is a terrible spendthrift because he grew up very poor, whereas his sister explains that she is thrifty, to the point of being cheap, because she grew up very poor. In other words, they provide the same explanation for opposite behaviors. Although most of us understand that differences among people result from multiple causal factors, we often act as though single explanations are correct (Nisbett and Ross, 1980).

Most people prefer single explanations that confirm their preexisting biases. (See the discussion of confirmation bias in Chapter 8, "Thinking and Intelligence," and see the discussion of belief persistence in Chapter 9, "Motivation and Emotion.") For example, people who have never received welfare (assistance from the government for basic necessities) are likely to describe welfare recipients as lazy. People on welfare, in contrast, might explain that they need the help because they have been unlucky or because a weak economy does not provide enough job opportunities. (Notice that these single explanations also reflect the actor/observer discrepancy bias, discussed in Chapter 12, "Social Psychology"; it is the tendency to explain other people's behavior as caused by their own actions and to view one's own behavior as caused by external events.)

In the debate over why men or women constitute the majority in different occupations (e.g., women in nursing and clerical jobs, men in the building trades and architecture), most people argue from the standpoint of either nature or nurture, even though they admit that both must be important. Similarly, individuals usually are on welfare for multiple reasons, such as insufficient education, poverty in childhood, limited access to good jobs, poor health, and so on. Whenever you hear people claiming single causes for complex phenomena, or when you find yourself starting to do so, remember to consider multiple causes instead (**FIGURE 13.23**).

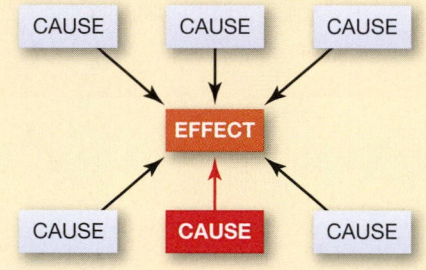

FIGURE 13.23 Think Critically: Cause(s) and Effect Be sure to consider multiple causes of a phenomenon, not just the one that jumps out at you.

Personality Traits Are Stable over Time

The Jesuit maxim *Give me a child until he is seven, and I will show you the man* is the thesis of Michael Apted's *Up* series of documentary films, which follows the development of a group of British schoolchildren through interviews at ages 7, 14, 21, 28, 35, and 42. A striking aspect of these films is the apparent stability of personality over time. The child interested in the stars and science becomes a professor of physics; the boy who finds his childhood troubling and confusing develops an apparent schizo-affective personality; the reserved, well-mannered, upper-class girl at age 7 grows into the reserved, well-mannered woman in her pastoral retreat at age 35. Are people really so stable? Childhood temperaments may predict behavioral outcomes in early adulthood, but what about change during adulthood?

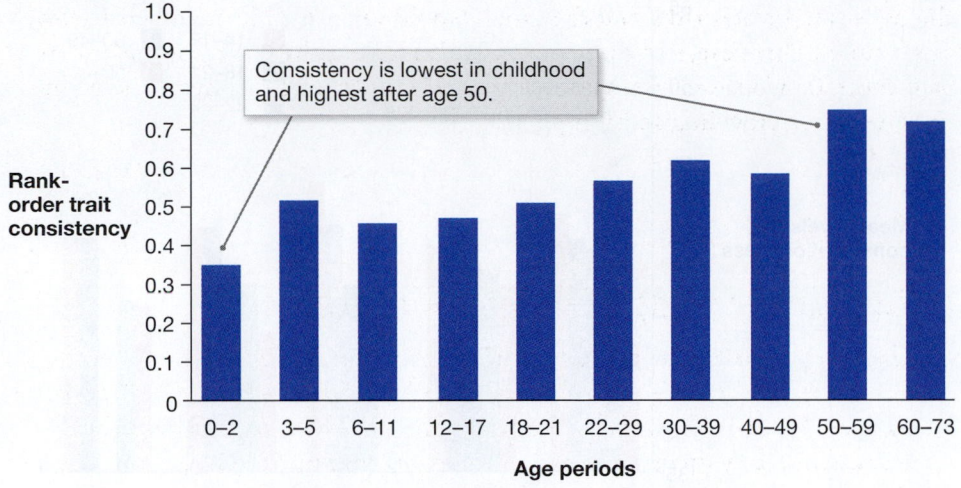

FIGURE 13.24 The Stability of Personality This graph shows the levels of consistency, at different ages, of the study participants' personalities.

Indeed, the foundation of clinical psychology is the belief that people can and do change important aspects of their lives. They exert considerable energy trying to change—they attend self-help groups, read self-help books, pay for therapy sessions, and struggle to make changes in their lives. But how much can people really change?

How we define the essential features of personality has tremendous implications for whether it is fixed or changeable. Continuity over time and across situations is inherent in the definition of *trait,* and most research finds personality traits to be remarkably stable over the adult life span (Heatherton & Weinberger, 1994). For instance, over many years the relative rankings of individuals on each of the Big Five personality traits remain stable (McCrae & Costa, 1990). A meta-analysis of 150 studies consisting of nearly 50,000 participants, who had been followed for at least one year, found strong evidence for stability in personality (Roberts & Friend-DelVecchio, 2000). The rank orderings of individuals on any personality trait were quite stable over long periods across all age ranges. However, stability was lowest for young children and highest for those over age 50 (**FIGURE 13.24**). This finding suggests that personality changes somewhat in childhood but becomes more stable by middle age. Such findings support the contention of the psychologist William James, who stated in 1890, "For most of us, by age 30, the character has set like plaster and will never soften again" (p. 12b). According to the meta-analysis, James was right that personality becomes set, but it appears to happen a little later than age 30.

AGE-RELATED CHANGE Stability in rank ordering means that individuals stay the same as compared with others. However, might all people change in personality as they grow older, while retaining their relative rankings? For instance, do people always become wiser and more cautious as they get older? In general, people become less neurotic, less extraverted, and less open to new experiences. They also tend to become more agreeable and more conscientious (Srivastava, John, Gosling, & Potter, 2003). These effects are not large, but they are consistent (Roberts, Walton, & Viechtbauer, 2006). Moreover, the pattern holds in different cultures (McCrae et al., 2000; **FIGURE 13.25**); this finding suggests that age-related changes in personality occur independently of environmental influences and therefore that personality change itself may be based in human physiology. Indeed, evidence shows that personality change has a genetic component, such that the extent of change is more similar in monozygotic twins than in dizygotic twins (McGue, Bacon, & Lykken, 1993).

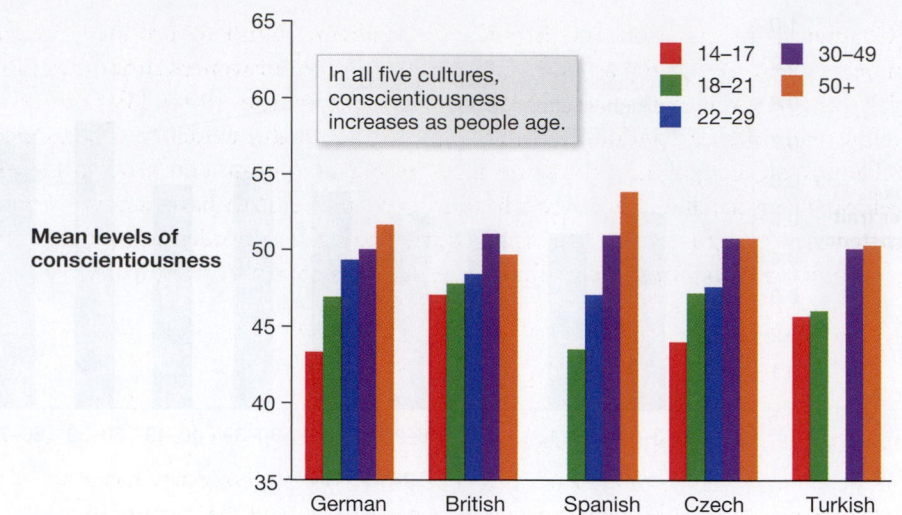

FIGURE 13.25 **Mean Levels of Conscientiousness at Different Ages in Five Cultures**

CHARACTERISTIC ADAPTATIONS In their research on potential change in personality, Robert McCrae and Paul Costa (1999) emphasize an important distinction between basic tendencies of personality and characteristic adaptations (**FIGURE 13.26**). *Basic tendencies* are dispositional traits determined largely by biological processes; as such, they are very stable. *Characteristic adaptations* are adjustments to situational demands; such adaptations tend to be somewhat consistent because they are based on skills, habits, roles, and so on. But changes in behavior produced by characteristic adaptations do not indicate changes in basic tendencies. Consider a highly extraverted woman: In her youth, she may go to parties frequently, be a thrill seeker, and have multiple sexual partners. In her old age, she will less likely do these things, but she may have many friends and enjoy traveling. Although the exact behaviors differ, they reflect the core trait of extraversion.

Overall, then, personality appears to be relatively stable, especially among adults, because of numerous factors. If personality is determined partly by biological mechanisms, some of its changes will be tied to changes in biological makeup. Indeed, damage to certain brain regions is associated with dramatic changes in personality. For example, damage to the frontal lobes (such as in the railroad worker Phineas Gage, described in Chapter 4, "The Mind and Consciousness," or Elliot, described

FIGURE 13.26 McCrae and Costa's Model of Personality Basic tendencies are biologically based, but characteristic adaptations are influenced by situations. The lines with arrows indicate some of the ways in which the different components interact. The important point is that basic tendencies do not change across situations, but observable behavior (objective biography) does because it is influenced by personal goals and motives as well as by situations.

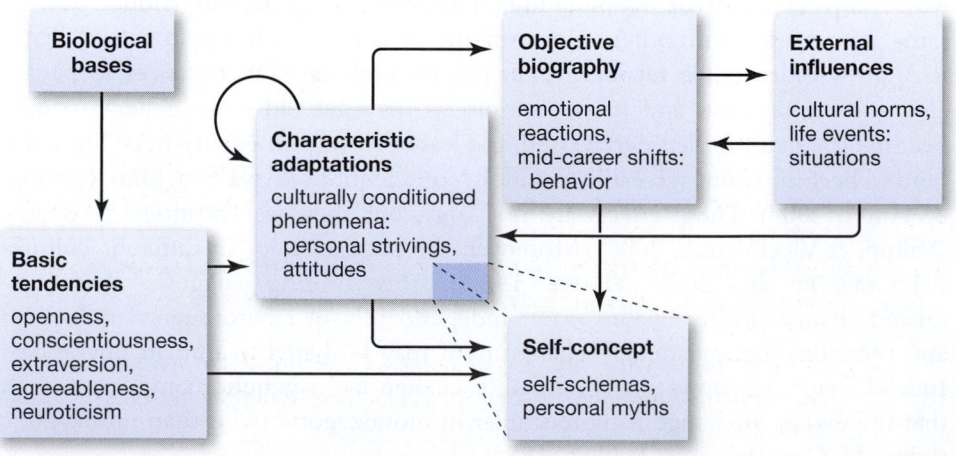

in Chapter 9, "Motivation and Emotion") has been found to produce various changes in personality, such as increased extraversion, impulsiveness, moodiness, and socially inappropriate behavior (Stuss, Gow, & Hetherington, 1992). That the brain develops well into early adulthood may explain the greater evidence of personality change before age 30. At the same time, people's environments tend to be relatively stable, especially after early adulthood. People tend to have successive jobs with the same status level and to marry those similar in attitudes and personality. The stability of situations likely contributes to the stability of personality.

SUMMING UP

What Are the Biological Bases of Personality?

Evidence from behavioral genetics has demonstrated that personality has a substantial genetic component accounting for approximately half the variance in most traits. Temperaments, biology-based personality tendencies, are evident in early childhood and have long-term implications for adult behavior. Temperamental styles reflect underlying differences in biological processes, especially those related to neurophysiology. Such differences may reflect adaptive advantages over the course of human evolution. Given that personality is rooted partly in biology, it is not surprising that most people's personalities remain relatively stable over time, especially in adulthood.

MEASURING UP

1. Which of the following statements are true regarding the relationships among environment, genes, personality traits, and temperament? Select all that apply.
   a. Environment interacts with personality traits to shape temperament.
   b. Environment interacts with temperament to shape personality traits.
   c. Genes act to produce temperament.
   d. Temperament affects how each child responds to and shapes his or her environment.
   e. The influence of genes on temperament and on personality traits changes over the life span.

2. Which of the following findings support biological bases of personality?
   a. Children as young as six weeks of age can be classified as evidencing specific temperaments (Kagan & Snidman, 1991).
   b. Factor analysis reveals five basic personality traits (McCrae & Costa, 1999).
   c. Introversion is associated with greater activation of the frontal lobes (Johnson et al., 1999).
   d. Personality traits can predict academic outcomes, including scores on standardized tests and grades in college (Noftle & Robins, 2007).
   e. Changes in personality as people age occur the same across all cultures (McCrae et al., 2000).
   f. Siblings who are adopted (and not biologically related) and raised in the same household are no more alike in personality than random strangers (Plomin & Caspi, 1999).
   g. Twin studies suggest that 40 percent to 60 percent of the variance between individuals in personality traits can be accounted for by genetics.

How Do We Know Our Own Personalities?

In the previous sections, the subject was people's personalities generally, and the central question was *What must we know to know a person well?* In considering our own personalities, we can rephrase that question as *What must we know to know ourselves well?* The following section examines how we process information about ourselves and how that processing shapes our personalities.

Although we all have a notion of something we refer to as the "self," the self is difficult to define. At a general level, it involves each person's mental representation of personal experience and includes his or her thought processes, physical body, and conscious awareness of being separate from others and unique. This sense of self is a unitary experience, continuous over time and space. When you wake up in the morning, for example, you do not have to figure out who you are (even if you sometimes have to figure out where you are, such as when you are on vacation).

Our Self-Concepts Consist of Self-Knowledge

Write down 20 answers to the question *Who am I?* The information in your answers is part of your *self-concept,* which is everything you know about yourself (**FIGURE 13.27**). For example, answers commonly given by college students include gender, age, student status, interpersonal style (e.g., shy, friendly), interpersonal characteristics (e.g., moody, optimistic), and body image. But how would thinking of yourself as shy or optimistic or overweight affect how you feel and function from day to day? Many psychologists view the self-concept as a cognitive knowledge structure that guides your attention to information relevant to you and that helps you adjust to your environment. If you think of yourself as shy, you might avoid a raucous party; if you believe yourself to be optimistic, you might easily bounce back from a poor grade in organic chemistry; and so on.

SELF-AWARENESS William James and the sociologist George Herbert Mead were among the first modern thinkers to consider the nature of the self, and both differentiated between the self as the knower ("I") and the self as the object that is known ("me")—now called the *objectified self.* As the knower, the self is the subject doing the thinking, feeling, and acting. It is involved in executive functions such as choosing, planning, and exerting control. The objectified self is the knowledge the subject holds about itself, such as its best and worst qualities. The sense of self as the object of attention is the psychological state known as *self-awareness—* when the "I" thinks about the "me."

What are the consequences of being self-aware? In 1972, the psychologists Shelley Duval and Robert Wicklund introduced the theory of objective self-awareness, which proposes that self-awareness leads people to act in accordance with the values and beliefs they hold. For instance, one study showed that college students are less likely to cheat, when given the opportunity, if they are sitting in front of mirrors (Diener & Wellborn, 1976). Perhaps seeing their own faces reminds them that they do not value cheating. As discussed in Chapter 9, discrepancies between personal standards (e.g., not cheating) and goals (e.g., passing the test) can motivate behaviors (e.g., studying) that reduce the discrepancy. According to the psychologist Tory Higgins's *self-discrepancy theory* (1987), this awareness of differences between personal standards and goals leads to strong emotions. For instance, being aware of a discrepancy between seeing yourself as lazy and preferring to see yourself as hardworking can lead you to feel disappointed, frustrated, and depressed; being aware

FIGURE 13.27 Sense of Self Each of us has a self-concept.

of a discrepancy between seeing yourself as lazy and wanting others to see you as hardworking can lead you to feel anxious and guilty. So if you fail an important class because you did not study enough, you might feel depressed; but if you think about how your parents will feel when you fail an important class because you did not study enough, you might feel anxious.

From studies of patients with brain injuries, we know that self-awareness is highly dependent on normal development of the frontal lobes. People with damage to the frontal lobes tend to be only minimally self-reflective and seldom report daydreaming or other types of introspection. They also often show a lack of interest in or knowledge about their disorders. Such individuals are not completely unaware of themselves, but they do not find information about the self personally significant. The neuropsychologist Donald Stuss (1991) reported on a highly intelligent patient who had a tumor removed from his frontal lobes. Subsequently, the patient had difficulty at work and became extremely unproductive, even though his intelligence and knowledge about the world were intact. As noted in Chapter 3, people with damage to the frontal lobes often have social and motivational impairments, which may interfere with job performance. Despite 18 months of therapy, the patient continued to do poorly on the job, but he could not recognize that he had a problem. When asked to role-play the situation as if he were the boss, he quickly recognized the problem and made appropriate recommendations—that the worker (himself) be put on a disability pension. However, when asked to evaluate himself from his own subjective perspective, he disagreed with the recommendation he had just made. Dramatic examples such as this one show the types of distortion that frontal-lobe patients may experience in processing information about the self.

SELF-SCHEMA Have you ever been at a loud, crowded party where you could barely hear yourself speak, but when someone across the room mentioned your name, you heard it clearly above the noise? As discussed in Chapter 7, the *cocktail party phenomenon* occurs because information about the self is processed deeply, thoroughly, and automatically. According to Hazel Markus (1977), the self-schema is the cognitive aspect of the self-concept, consisting of an integrated set of memories, beliefs, and generalizations about the self. The self-schema can be viewed as a network of interconnected knowledge about the self (**FIGURE 13.28**). It helps us perceive, organize, interpret, and use information about the self; it also helps filter information so that each of us will likely notice things that are self-relevant, such as our own names. Examples of our behavior, and aspects of our personalities, that are important to us become prominent in our self-schemas. For instance, being a good athlete or a good student may be a major component of your self-schema, whereas having few cavities probably is not. Thus when asked if you are ambitious, you can answer without sorting through occasions in which you did or did not act ambitiously. Your self-schema summarizes the relevant past information.

Self-schemas may lead to enhanced memory for information processed in a self-referential manner. Tim Rogers and his colleagues (1977) showed that trait adjectives processed with reference to the self (e.g., "Does the word *honest* describe you?") were better recalled than comparable items processed only for their general meanings (e.g. "Does the word *honest* mean the same as *trustworthy*?"). Researchers more recently have examined the neural dimensions of self-referential processing (Gillihan & Farah, 2005). A typical finding is activation of the middle of the frontal lobes when people process information about

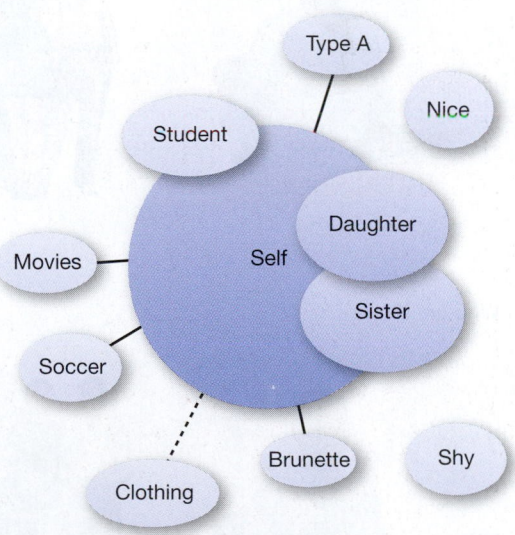

FIGURE 13.28 Self-Schema The self-schema consists of interrelated knowledge about the self.

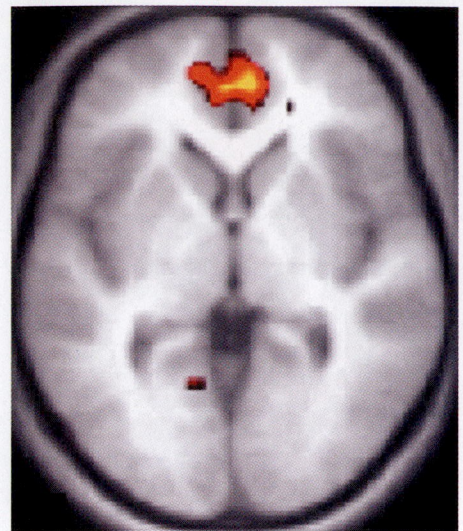

FIGURE 13.29 Frontal Lobe Activity On this brain scan from the study by Kelley et al., the red, orange, and yellow area indicates the activation.

FIGURE 13.30 Working Self-Concept When considering themselves or their personalities, people are especially likely to mention characteristics that distinguish them from other people.

themselves (Kelley et al., 2002; **FIGURE 13.29**). This brain region is more active when we answer questions about ourselves (e.g., "Are you honest?") than when we answer questions about other people (e.g., "Is Madonna honest?"). The greater the activation of this area during self-referencing, the more likely we will remember the item later during a surprise memory task (Macrae, Moran, Heatherton, Banfield, & Kelley, 2004). Along with the self-awareness deficit shown in neurological patient studies, this finding further supports the idea that the frontal lobes are important for processing information about the self.

WORKING SELF-CONCEPT The immediate experience of self, the *working self-concept,* is limited to the amount of personal information that can be processed cognitively at any given time. Because the working self-concept includes only part of the vast array of self-knowledge, the sense of self varies from situation to situation. For instance, at a party you might think of yourself as fun-loving rather than as intelligent, even though both traits are aspects of your self-concept. Thus your self-descriptions vary as a function of which memories you retrieve, which situation you are in, which people you are with, and your role in that situation.

When people consider who they are or think about different features of their personalities, they often emphasize characteristics that make them distinct from others. For instance, think back to your 20 responses to the question *Who am I?* Which answers stressed your similarity to other people or membership in a group? Which ones stressed your differences from other people, or at least from the people immediately around you? Respondents are especially likely to mention features such as ethnicity, gender, or age if the respondents differ from other people around them at the moment (**FIGURE 13.30**). Thus Canadians would more likely note their nationality if they were in Boston, for example, than if they were in Toronto. Because the working self-concept guides behavior, this tendency implies that Canadians also would more likely feel and act like "Canadians" when in Boston than when in Toronto. Most people have optimal levels of distinctiveness, however, since generally they want to avoid standing out too much; teenagers especially want to stand out and fit in at the same time.

Perceived Social Regard Influences Self-Esteem

North American culture has been obsessed with self-esteem since at least the 1980s. At a basic level, *self-esteem* is the evaluative aspect of the self-concept, indicating people's emotional response as they contemplate various characteristics about themselves (e.g., worthy or unworthy, good or bad). Although self-esteem is related to self-concept, people can objectively believe positive things about themselves without liking themselves very much. Conversely, people can like themselves very much, and therefore have high self-esteem, even when objective indicators do not support such positive self-views.

Many theories assume that people's self-esteem is based on how they believe others perceive them. According to this view, known as *reflected appraisal,* people internalize the values and beliefs expressed by important people in their lives, adopting those attitudes (and related behaviors) as their own.

Consequently, people come to respond to themselves in manners consistent with how others respond to them. From this perspective, when important figures reject, ignore, demean, or devalue a person, the person likely will experience low self-esteem.

This social view of self-esteem, as espoused by psychologists such as Carl Rogers, has led some theorists to promote parents' unconditional acceptance of their children. Later theorists have noted, however, that unconditional acceptance must occur in the context of relatively strict parenting, in which parents define limits clearly and enforce them by providing positive reinforcement for behaviors within, and punishment for behaviors outside, those limits (Coopersmith, 1967). In other words, children will be accepted and loved no matter what they do, but their inappropriate behaviors will be corrected through punishment.

SOCIOMETER THEORY In a novel and important account of self-esteem, Mark Leary and his colleagues (1995) have proposed that self-esteem monitors the likelihood of social exclusion. This theory assumes that, as discussed in Chapter 12, humans have a fundamental, adaptive need to belong. For most of human evolution, those who belonged to social groups have been more likely to survive and reproduce than those who were excluded and left to survive on their own. When people behave in ways that increase the likelihood that they will be rejected, they experience a reduction in self-esteem. Thus self-esteem is a **sociometer,** an internal monitor of social acceptance or rejection (**FIGURE 13.31**). Those with high self-esteem have sociometers indicating a low probability of rejection; such individuals do not worry about how they are perceived by others. By contrast, those with low self-esteem have sociometers indicating the imminent possibility of rejection; therefore they are highly motivated to manage their public image. An abundance of evidence supports the sociometer theory, including the consistent finding that low self-esteem correlates highly with social anxiety (Leary, 2004; Leary & MacDonald, 2003).

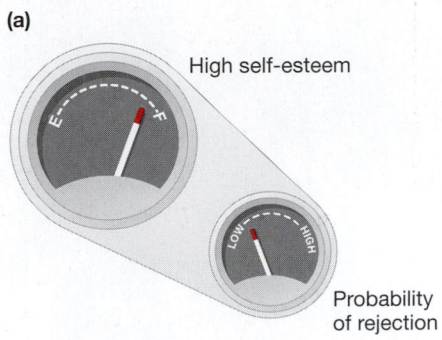

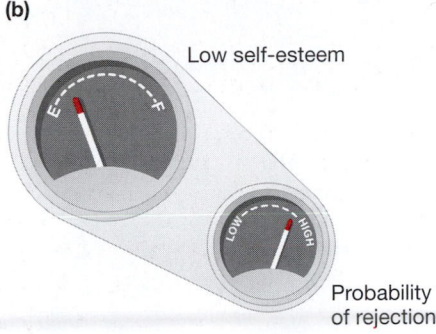

FIGURE 13.31 Sociometers According to sociometer theory, self-esteem is the gauge that measures the extent to which a person believes he or she is being **(a)** included in or **(b)** excluded from a social group.

sociometer An internal monitor of social acceptance or rejection.

Resisting Appeals to Snobbery

Choosy mothers choose Jif.
Inquiring minds want to know.
L'Oreal: Because you're worth it.
When you care enough to send the very best.

Appeals to snobbery, such as these advertising slogans, effectively play on people's desire to perceive themselves (and be perceived by others) as superior—more sophisticated, intelligent, stylish, wealthy, or educated. Such advertisements might suggest that you, as the consumer, are among the select few who can appreciate the product (**FIGURE 13.32**). The messages are not always verbal. An appeal to snobbery might be conveyed through images—by portraying well-dressed, attractive people in luxurious homes, for example. On television, the radio, and the Internet, sounds such as background music or actors' accents can provide subtle cues suggesting wealth, high social class, and advanced education.

FIGURE 13.32 Appeals to Snobbery This advertisement, for a residential development in Dubai, presents housing as not just a place to live but also a lifestyle.

Not all appeals to snobbery have an economic objective, however. Political advertisements often convey subtle messages about the type of people who support a certain political candidate or party—intelligent and hardworking people, who will not be fooled by the opposing candidate's rhetoric. The message is that if you belong to (or want to belong to) this group of people, you will support the candidate.

With practice, you will recognize when a persuasive message is trying to play on your desire to be better than others. The next time you watch television or leaf through a magazine, look for advertisements that make appeals based on consumers' snobbery. How do the advertisers convey their messages? What desired traits do they associate with their product? Most important, if you buy this product, will it make you feel smarter, trendier, or classier than everyone else, or will you be falling prey to clever advertising?

SELF-ESTEEM AND DEATH ANXIETY One provocative theory proposes that self-esteem provides meaning for individuals by staving off anxiety over their mortality (Greenberg, 2008). According to *terror management theory,* self-esteem protects people from the horror associated with knowing they eventually will die (Greenberg, Solomon, & Pyszczynski, 1997; Pyszczynski, Greenberg, Solomon, Arndt, & Schimel, 2004). People counter mortality fears by creating a sense of symbolic immortality through contributing to their culture and upholding its values. From this cultural perspective, self-esteem develops from a person's belief that he or she is living up to criteria valued within the culture. Accordingly, exaggerations of personal importance reflect attempts to buffer anxiety about inevitable death. Research has demonstrated that reminding people of their mortality leads them to act in ways that enhance their self-esteem (Goldenberg, McCoy, Pyszczynski, Greenberg, & Solomon, 2000).

SELF-ESTEEM AND LIFE OUTCOMES With such emphasis placed on self-esteem within Western culture, you might expect that having high self-esteem is the key to life success. However, the evidence from psychological science indicates that self-esteem may be less important than is commonly believed. After reviewing several hundred studies, Roy Baumeister and his colleagues (2003, 2005) found that although people with high self-esteem report being much happier, self-esteem is weakly related to objective life outcomes. People with high self-esteem who consider themselves smarter, more attractive, and better liked do not necessarily have higher IQs and are not necessarily thought of more highly by others. Many people with high self-esteem are successful in their careers, but so are many people with low self-esteem. Moreover, to the extent a small relationship exists between self-esteem and life outcomes, perhaps success causes high self-esteem; people might have higher self-esteem because they have done well in school or in their careers. Correlation does not prove causation.

In fact, there may even be some downsides to having very high self-esteem. Violent criminals commonly have very high self-esteem; indeed, some people become violent when they feel that others are not treating them with an appropriate level of respect (Baumeister, Smart, & Boden, 1996). School bullies also often have high self-esteem (Baumeister et al., 2003). When people with high self-esteem believe their abilities have been challenged, they may act in ways (e.g., antagonistic or boastful) that cause people to dislike them (Heatherton & Vohs, 2000; Vohs & Heatherton,

2004). Thus although having high self-esteem seems to make people happier, it does not necessarily lead to successful social relationships or life success.

A personality trait associated with inflated self-esteem is *narcissism,* in which self-centered people view themselves in grandiose terms, feel entitled to special treatment, and are manipulative (Bosson et al., 2008). (The term comes from Greek mythology, in which Narcissus rejected the love of others and fell in love with his own reflection in a pond.) Narcissists' greatest love is for the self, and they tend to have poor relations with others (Campbell et al., 2005). They become angry when challenged (Rhodewalt & Morf, 1998), become abusive to those who do not share their lofty opinions of themselves (Bushman & Baumeister, 1998; Twenge & Campbell, 2003), and are manipulative, selfish, and unfaithful in their relationships (Campbell, Foster, & Finkel, 2002). You might be interested to note that a meta-analysis found increasing narcissism among American college students between 1979 and 2006 (Twenge et al., 2008). According to the researchers, contributing factors might include programs aimed at increasing self-esteem among young schoolchildren (such as having them sing songs about how they are special), grade inflation that makes students feel more capable than they might really be, and a rise in the use of self-promotion Web sites such as Facebook and MySpace. However, a different team of researchers was unable to replicate this finding, and there is controversy regarding what the pattern observed by Twenge et al. means (Trzesniewski, Donnellan, & Roberts, 2008).

We Use Mental Strategies to Maintain Our Views of Self

Most people show favoritism to anything associated with themselves. For example, people consistently prefer their belongings to things they do not own (Beggan, 1992), and they even prefer the letters of their own names, especially their initials, to other letters (Koole, Dijksterhuis, & van Knippenberg, 2001; **FIGURE 13.33**). Sometimes these positive views of the self seem inflated. For instance, 90 percent of adults claim they are better-than-average drivers, even if they have been hospitalized for injuries caused by car accidents (Guerin, 1994; Svenson, 1981). Similarly,

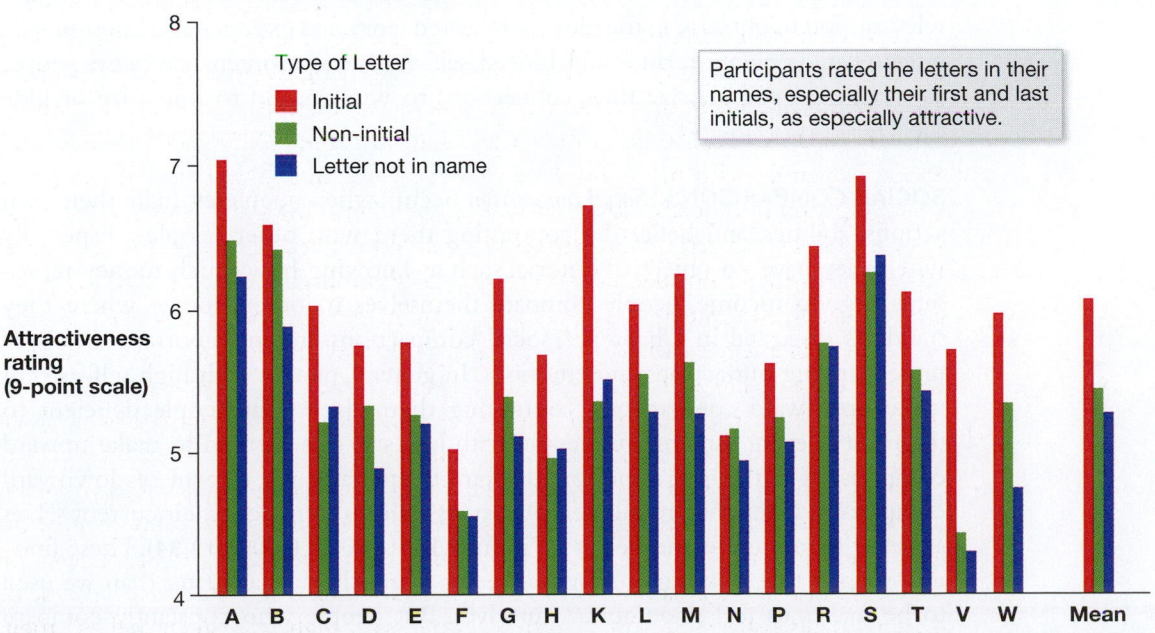

FIGURE 13.33 Favoritism This graph shows the study participants' ratings of the letters of the alphabet.

in a College Entrance Examination Board survey of more than 800,000 college-bound seniors, none rated themselves as below average, and a whopping 25 percent rated themselves in the top 1 percent (Gilovich, 1991). Most people describe themselves as above average in nearly every way, a phenomenon referred to as the *better-than-average effect* (Alicke, Klotz, Breitenbecher, Yurak, & Vredenburg, 1995). People with high self-esteem are especially likely to do so.

According to Shelley Taylor and Jonathan Brown (1988), most people have positive illusions—overly favorable and unrealistic beliefs—in at least three domains. First, they continually experience the better-than-average effect. Second, they unrealistically perceive their personal control over events. For example, some fans believe they help their favorite sports teams win if they attend games or wear their lucky jerseys. Third, most people are unrealistically optimistic about their personal futures, believing they probably will be successful, marry happily, and live long lives. Although positive illusions can be adaptive when they promote optimism in meeting life's challenges, they can lead to trouble when people overestimate their skills and underestimate their vulnerabilities.

Life is filled with failure, rejection, and disappointment, yet most people feel pretty good about themselves. How do people maintain such positive views? Psychologists have cataloged (though not necessarily endorsed) a number of unconscious strategies that help people maintain a positive sense of self. Among the most common are *self-evaluative maintenance, social comparisons,* and *self-serving biases.*

SELF-EVALUATIVE MAINTENANCE Abraham Tesser (1988) notes that self-esteem can be affected not only by how people perform but also by how relevant their performances are to their self-concepts and how their performances compare with those of significant people around them. According to the theory of *self-evaluative maintenance,* people can feel threatened when someone close to them outperforms them on a task that is personally relevant. If you had a twin brother who shared your aspiration to be a world-class chef, his brilliant success at cooking would have important implications for how you felt about yourself. To maintain your sense of self-esteem, Tesser argues, you would either distance yourself from the relationship or select a different aspiration. Of course, if your twin brother excels at something you do not find relevant, you might bask in the glow of reflected glory and experience a boost in self-esteem based on your relationship. Indeed, self-evaluative maintenance causes people to exaggerate or publicize their connections to winners and to minimize or hide their relations to losers.

SOCIAL COMPARISONS *Social comparison* occurs when people evaluate their own actions, abilities, and beliefs by contrasting them with other people's. Especially when they have no objective criteria, such as knowing how much money represents a good income, people compare themselves to others to see where they stand. As discussed in Chapter 9, social comparisons are an important means of understanding our actions and emotions. In general, people with high self-esteem make downward comparisons, contrasting themselves with people deficient to them on relevant dimensions. People with low self-esteem tend to make upward comparisons with those superior to them. People also use a form of downward comparison when they recall their own pasts—they often view their current selves as better than their former selves (Wilson & Ross, 2001; **FIGURE 13.34**). These findings suggest that viewing ourselves as better than others or as better than we used to be makes us feel good about ourselves. But people who constantly compare themselves with others who do better may confirm their negative self-feelings.

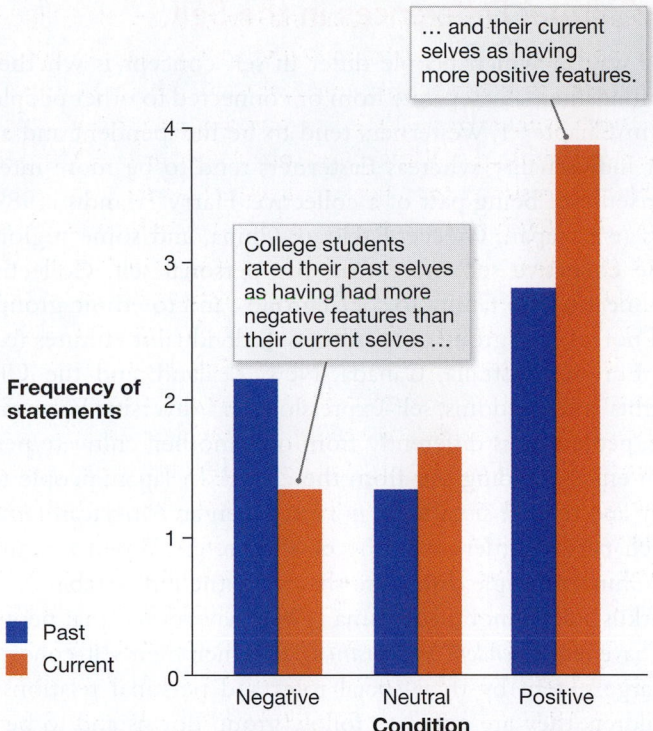

... and their current selves as having more positive features.

College students rated their past selves as having had more negative features than their current selves ...

Frequency of statements

- Past
- Current

Negative   Neutral   Positive
Condition

FIGURE 13.34 Making Comparisons This graph shows the results of Wilson and Ross's 2001 study.

SELF-SERVING BIASES People with high self-esteem tend to take credit for success but blame failure on outside factors, a tendency referred to as a **self-serving bias.** For instance, students who do extremely well on exams often explain their performance by referring to their skills or hard work. Those who do poorly might describe the test as an arbitrary examination of trivial details. People with high self-esteem also assume that criticism is motivated by envy or prejudice. Indeed, members of groups prone to discrimination (e.g., the disabled; ethnic minorities) tend to have high self-esteem. One theory, proposed by Jennifer Crocker and Brenda Major (1989), suggests that members of these groups maintain positive self-esteem by taking credit for success and blaming negative feedback on prejudice. Thus if they succeed, the success is due to personal strengths and occurs despite the odds. If they fail, the failure is due to external factors and unfair obstacles.

Over the last thirty years, psychologists have documented many ways that people show bias in thinking about themselves compared with how they think about others (Campbell & Sedikides, 1999). In thinking about our failures, for example, we compare ourselves with others who did worse, we diminish the importance of the challenge, we think about the things we are really good at, and we bask in the reflected glory of both family and friends. The overall picture suggests we are extremely well equipped to protect our positive beliefs about ourselves. Some researchers have even argued that self-serving biases reflect healthy psychological functioning (Mezulis, Abramson, Hyde, & Hankin, 2004; Taylor & Brown, 1988). However, recall the earlier discussion of narcissism, which reflects more of a disorder of personality than healthy functioning.

self-serving bias The tendency for people to take personal credit for success but blame failure on external factors.

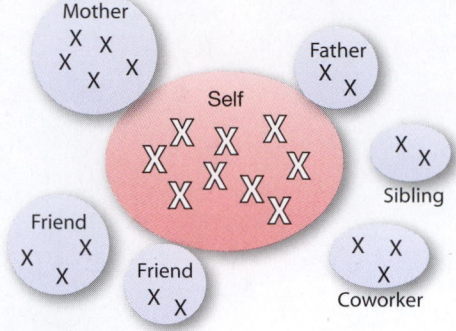

(a) Individualist

Mother
Self
Father
Sibling
Friend
Friend
Coworker

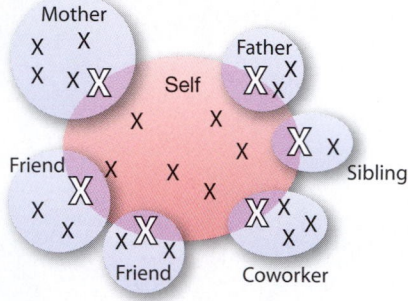

(b) Collectivist

Mother
Father
Self
Friend
Sibling
Friend
Coworker

FIGURE 13.35 Self-Construals
Self-construals differ in **(a)** individualist and **(b)** collectivist cultures.

There Are Cultural Differences in the Self

An important way in which people differ in self-concept is whether they view themselves as fundamentally separate from or connected to other people. For example, as noted in Chapter 1, Westerners tend to be independent and autonomous, stressing their individuality, whereas Easterners tend to be more interdependent, stressing their sense of being part of a collective. Harry Triandis (1989) notes that some cultures (e.g., Japan, Greece, Pakistan, China, and some regions of Africa) emphasize the collective self more than the personal self. Collectivist cultures emphasize connections to family, to social groups, and to ethnic groups; conformity to societal norms; and group cohesiveness. Individualist cultures (e.g., northern and western Europe, Australia, Canada, New Zealand, and the United States) emphasize rights and freedoms, self-expression, and diversity. For example, in the United States, people dress differently from one another, cultivate personal interests, and often enjoy standing out from the crowd. In Japan, people tend to dress more similarly and respect situational norms. When an American family goes to a restaurant, each person orders what he or she prefers. When a family goes to a restaurant in China, multiple dishes are shared by the entire table.

Hazel Markus and Shinobu Kitayama (1991) have noted that people in collectivist cultures have *interdependent self-construals,* in which their self-concepts are determined to a large extent by their social roles and personal relationships (**FIGURE 13.35**). As children, they are raised to follow group norms and to be obedient to parents, teachers, and other people in authority. They are expected to find their proper place in society and not to challenge or complain about their status. By contrast, people in individualist cultures have *independent self-construals.* Parents and teachers encourage children to be self-reliant and to pursue personal success, even at the expense of interpersonal relationships. Thus children's senses of self are based on their feelings of being distinct from others. Note, however, that within these broad patterns—in individualist and collectivist cultures—there is variability in terms of independent/interdependent self-construals.

CULTURE AND SELF-SERVING BIAS Psychologists generally have viewed the self-enhancing bias as a universal human trait—like eating, it is part of human nature (Sedikides & Gregg, 2008). Although depressed people might fail to show the effect, the assumption is that most healthy, functioning individuals show robust self-enhancement. Some researchers, however, have questioned whether the self-serving bias is truly universal across cultures. Steven Heine and his colleagues (1999) have argued that the self-serving bias may be more common in Western cultures, in which individuality is emphasized, than in Eastern cultures, in which the collective self is emphasized (**FIGURE 13.36**). That is, believing that you are an especially talented individual presupposes you are better than others. Such an attitude is not acceptable in Eastern cultures, in which the group, rather than the individual, is special.

What does the evidence indicate about whether the self-serving bias is universal? Consider a study by Endo and Meijer (2004), who asked American and Japanese students to list as many of the students' own successes and failures as they could. The Americans showed a bias for listing successes, whereas the Japanese students listed failures and successes equally. In addition, the Americans used outside forces to explain failure, but the Japanese students used them to explain success. Indeed, Markus and Kitayama (1991) have argued that self-criticism rather than self-promotion is the most common social norm in Asian cultures. The overall evidence supports the view that people in individualistic cultures are more concerned with self-enhancement than those in collectivist, particularly Asian, cultures (Heine, 2003). For example, in a meta-analysis involving more than 500 studies, people in Western cultures showed a much larger self-serving bias than those in Eastern cultures (Mezulis et al., 2004). Although some Eastern cultures, especially China and Korea, show a modest self-serving bias, it typically is much smaller than in most Western cultures.

Might these differences reflect cultural rules about publicly admitting positive self-views? Perhaps people in the East are just more modest in public even though they engage in strategic self-enhancement. However, in studies using anonymous reporting, where presumably there is less call for modesty, Easterners continue to show a low level of self-serving bias (Heine, 2003). At the same time, indirect evidence indicates that people from China and Japan show a positivity bias (a tendency to see themselves as better than others) equivalent to Americans' (Yamaguchi et al., 2007). The researchers used an implicit measure of self-esteem that does not rely on self-reports but on how easily participants associate positive things with themselves versus with others. (As discussed in Chapter 12, implicit attitude assessment is useful for situations in which people are hesitant to make explicit reports.) This finding suggests that although Easterners value themselves just as much as Westerners, they are hesitant to admit it.

Critics also have argued that researchers have a Western bias in the domains they study and therefore have failed to assess Eastern research participants in crucial domains. Some findings indicate that those from Asian cultures self-enhance in domains particularly important to them (Brown & Kobayashi, 2002). The assumption is that if a culture values industriousness, people will describe themselves as especially hardworking; but if the culture values kindness, people will emphasize how nice they are. People in Eastern cultures may emphasize what good group members they are as a method of self-enhancement (Sedikides, Gaertner, & Toguchi, 2003). According to this perspective, self-enhancement is universal but the traits people focus on to achieve it vary across cultures. Thus when the culture emphasizes personal achievement, people self-enhance as individuals; when the culture emphasizes group achievement, people self-enhance as group members.

(a)

(b)

FIGURE 13.36 Individualist versus Collectivist Cultures (a) Western cultures tend to highlight individual success, whereas **(b)** Eastern cultures tend to value those who fall in line with the masses.

The question of whether self-serving bias is universal has led to lively debate among psychologists, in part because it relates to important questions about how culture shapes the sense of self (Heine, 2005; Sedikides et al., 2003). How much do *you* believe people really differ around the world? Is it more important to be respected by others or to feel good about yourself no matter what others think? Might people in Eastern cultures feel better about themselves when they demonstrate that they are modest and self-effacing, whereas Westerners feel better when they can show they are successful? What function does self-enhancement serve in different cultures?

 ### SUMMING UP

How Do We Know Our Own Personalities?

Everything we know about ourselves constitutes our self-concepts. Often people are especially aware of their objective selves, a tendency that leads them to behave according to their personal standards and beliefs. Information about the self is processed efficiently and quickly through a self-schema, although how people describe themselves may vary depending on the situation. Researchers have found cultural differences in how the self is construed: Collectivist cultures emphasize the interdependent self, and individualistic cultures emphasize the independent self. Self-esteem is the evaluative aspect of the self-concept. Most people have moderate to high levels of self-esteem, viewing themselves as better than average on a number of dimensions. These and other strategies help people maintain positive self-esteem.

 ### MEASURING UP

1. Imagine that while browsing the shelves of a local bookstore, you discover a series of books about self-esteem. Which of the following three theoretical perspectives is most likely addressed in each book: self-evaluation maintenance theory, sociometer theory, or terror management theory?
   a. *Protecting Your Self-Esteem When Your Best Friend Is Better at Everything*
   b. *Anxious about Your Inevitable Death? Self-Esteem Can Help*
   c. *Feeling Bad about Feeling Left Out: What Your Self-Esteem Is Trying to Tell You*

2. Sort the following list of attributes into two groups: those more often evidenced in collectivist cultures and those more often evidenced in individualist cultures.
   a. emphasis on the collective self
   b. emphasis on the personal self
   c. encouragement to pursue personal success, even at the expense of interpersonal relationships
   d. fundamental separation of people
   e. inherent connection between people
   f. less variation in how people dress
   g. particular concern with self-enhancement
   h. emphasis on obedience to authority
   i. emphasis on self-reliance
   j. self-concepts determined largely by social roles and by personal relationships
   k. self-criticism more normative than self-promotion
   l. greater tendency to respect situational norms

CONCLUSION

The study of personality is complex because each person is unique. By examining conscious and unconscious cognitive processes, behavioral dispositions, and people's life narratives, researchers have come to understand some principles underlying personality. We now know that the basic blueprint for personality is genetically determined and is manifest through biologically based temperaments. Yet these temperaments do not predetermine personality; interactions between people and their social worlds create unique individuals. Clearly, personality is coherent and stable. Although people change jobs, relationships, and living circumstances, the core of each person's personality stays the same throughout life.

Most of us see ourselves in a positive light, and we are quite capable of dismissing challenges to our positive self-views. Learning about aspects of personality and people's biases in how they think about themselves gives us better insight into ourselves and others.

■ CHAPTER SUMMARY

How Have Psychologists Studied Personality?

- **Psychodynamic Theories Emphasize Unconscious and Dynamic Processes:** Freud believed that personality resulted partly from unconscious conflicts. The personality results from the ego's use of defense mechanisms to reduce the anxiety of the oppositional demands of the id and the superego. Stages of psychosexual development occur from birth to adolescence. Neo-Freudians have focused on relationships, especially children's emotional attachments to their parents.

- **Humanistic Approaches Emphasize Integrated Personal Experience:** Humanists view personality as the result of experiences and beliefs. Humans strive to realize their full potential and may be hampered in doing so if they do not receive unconditional positive regard from their parents and/or guardians. The positive psychology movement researches subjective well-being.

- **Type and Trait Approaches Describe Behavioral Dispositions:** Personality type theories focus more on description than on explanation. Trait theorists assume that personality is a collection of traits that vary and that exist in a hierarchy of importance. In Eysenck's model of personality, lesser traits are organized under larger biologically based traits (extraversion, emotional stability, psychoticism). The Big Five theory considers personality to be composed of openness to new experience, conscientiousness, extraversion, agreeableness, and neuroticism.

- **Personality Reflects Learning and Cognition:** Through interaction with their environment, people learn patterns of responding that are guided by both expectancies and values. Self-efficacy, the extent to which people believe they can achieve specific outcomes, is an important determinant of behavior. The cognitive-affective personality system (CAPS) emphasizes self-regulation.

How Is Personality Assessed, and What Does It Predict?

- **Personality Refers to Both Unique and Common Characteristics:** Idiographic approaches are person-centered; they evaluate personality by assessing the unique pattern of an individual's characteristics. Nomothetic approaches focus on characteristics common among all people but on which individuals vary (i.e., traits).

- **Researchers Use Objective and Projective Methods to Assess Personality:** Projective measures subjectively evaluate the unconscious issues a person projects onto ambiguous stimuli. Objective measures are straightforward assessments, usually involving self-report questionnaires or observer ratings.

- **Observers Show Accuracy in Trait Judgments:** Close acquaintances may better predict a person's behavior than the person can.

- **People Sometimes Are Inconsistent:** Mischel proposed that situations are more important than traits in predicting behavior.

- **Behavior Is Influenced by the Interaction of Personality and Situations:** Situations vary in the extent to which they both influence behavior and interact with personality to determine behavior.

- **There Are Cultural and Gender Differences in Personality:** Cross-cultural research presents problems because of translation issues, cultural norms for self-reporting, and individuals' judgments of themselves relative to other people from their own cultures. Some research suggests that the Big Five personality factors are universal for humans.

What Are the Biological Bases of Personality?

- **Animals Have Personalities:** Research on a wide variety of animal species has shown that animals have distinct personality traits that correspond roughly to the Big Five in humans.

- **Personality Is Rooted in Genetics:** Twin and adoption studies have found that 40 percent to 60 percent of personality variation is due to genetics. Personality characteristics are influenced by multiple genes, and their expression is the result of interaction with environments.

- **Temperaments Are Evident in Infancy:** Temperaments, the general tendencies of how people behave, are biologically mediated and observable in infants.

- **Personality Is Linked to Specific Neurophysiological Mechanisms:** Cortical arousal is regulated by the ascending reticular activating system and results in characteristics of introversion/extraversion. The behavioral approach system and the behavioral inhibition system affect variations in arousal and the behavioral responses.

- **Personality Is Adaptive:** Variations in individuals' personality and skills benefit a group and provide an advantage for group survival.

- **Personality Traits Are Stable over Time:** Trait consistency is lowest for young children and highest for those over age 50. Biological and environmental factors are more stable in adulthood. Characteristic adaptations change across time and circumstances.

How Do We Know Our Own Personalities?

- **Our Self-Concepts Consist of Self-Knowledge:** Self-schemas are the cognitive aspects of self-knowledge, and the working self-concept is the immediate experience of self at any given time.

- **Perceived Social Regard Influences Self-Esteem:** Self-esteem is influenced by people's beliefs about how other people view them. According to sociometer theory, the need to belong influences social anxiety relative to self-esteem. Self-esteem may also be influenced by death anxiety.

- **We Use Mental Strategies to Maintain Our Views of Self:** Positive illusions of self are common. Self-esteem is influenced by comparisons to others. A self-serving bias helps maintain positive self-esteem and may be culturally influenced.

- **There Are Cultural Differences in the Self:** People from collectivist cultures (e.g., regions of Asia and Africa) tend to have interdependent self-concepts; people from individualist cultures (e.g., the United States, Canada, Europe) tend to have independent self-concepts.

■ KEY TERMS

behavioral approach system (BAS), p. 596

behavioral inhibition system (BIS), p. 596

defense mechanisms, p. 575

ego, p. 575

five-factor theory, p. 579

humanistic approaches, p. 576

id, p. 575

idiographic approaches, p. 582

interactionists, p. 586

nomothetic approaches, p. 582

objective measures, p. 583

personality, p. 572

personality trait, p. 573

personality types, p. 577

projective measures, p. 583

psychodynamic theory, p. 573

psychosexual stage, p. 574

self-serving bias, p. 609

situationism, p. 584

sociometer, p. 605

superego, p. 575

temperaments, p. 594

trait approach, p. 577

1. Your psychology instructor asks the students in your class to form groups of five and then take turns answering the question *What do we need to know about you to truly know you?* The people in your group give the following answers; label each as representative of psychodynamic, humanistic, type and trait perspectives, or learning and cognition perspectives.
   a. "To know me, you would have to ask me questions about myself. I took a survey once that said I am an extremely intuitive introvert."
   b. "To know me, you would have to know that I can't control anything in my world. External forces determine my outcomes."
   c. "To know me, you would have to figure out a way to peer into my unconscious. There's so much I can't even know about myself; I'm not sure you could ever really know me."
   d. "To know me, you would have to know about my hopes and aspirations. I seek to become the best person I can be."

2. June asks people to watch a five-minute recording of a play in which two characters find themselves in a dangerous situation. Then she asks her research participants to write an ending to the story, which she codes to reveal features of each participant's personality. This proposed measure of personality can best be described as _____ and _____.
   a. idiographic; projective
   b. nomothetic; projective
   c. idiographic; objective
   d. nomothetic; objective

3. Which of the following statements might explain why our close acquaintances sometimes are better able to predict our behaviors than we are? Select all that apply.
   a. Our ego defense mechanisms prevent us from knowing our true personalities and thus undermine our abilities to accurately predict our own behaviors.
   b. Predictions of our own behaviors may be biased in favor of our subjective perceptions (how we *think* we act) rather than our objective behaviors (how we *do* act).
   c. We tend to pay more attention to others than to ourselves and thus fail to notice our own behavior; others notice how we behave and are better able to predict our future behaviors.

4. Which of the following are associated with the behavioral approach system (BAS), and which are associated with the behavioral inhibition system (BIS)?
   a. "go" system
   b. avoiding punishments
   c. frontal lobe and amygdala activity
   d. pursuit of rewards
   e. "stop" system

5. Which of the following statements best describes the distinctions among traits, temperaments, and characteristic adaptations?
   a. Temperaments, which are broader than traits, influence personality throughout development. Situational demands can lead to characteristic adaptations, which, although they do not reflect changes in the underlying dispositions, can reflect changes in how these dispositions are expressed.
   b. Temperaments, which are broader than traits, influence personality throughout development. After childhood, situational demands lead to characteristic adaptations, which reflect changes in underlying dispositions.
   c. Temperaments, which are narrower than traits, influence personality only during childhood. After childhood, situational demands lead to characteristic adaptations, which reflect changes in underlying dispositions.
   d. Temperaments, which are narrower than traits, influence personality only during childhood. Situational demands can lead to characteristic adaptations, which, although they do not reflect changes in the underlying dispositions, can reflect changes in how these dispositions are expressed.

6. By extrapolating from research on self-schemas, indicate which of the following memorization techniques should be most effective in memorizing a list of nouns.
   a. Imagine a friend or acquaintance doing something with each noun (e.g., "My friend bends over to tie his *shoe*").
   b. Imagine yourself doing something with each noun (e.g., "I wiggle my toes inside my *shoe*").
   c. Repeat the word three times (e.g., *shoe, shoe, shoe*).
   d. Think of a word that rhymes with the noun (e.g., *shoe* rhymes with *who*).

7. A professional athlete makes the following statements during an interview with a sports reporter. Which statements are most likely to be positive illusions?
   a. "I had a better-than-average game today."
   b. "I'm sure that wearing my lucky socks helped."
   c. "But it also helped that I've been taking care of my injury—lots of ice and physical therapy."
   d. "I'm done with injuries. From here on out, I'll have a clean bill of health."

8. Braunwin prides herself on her musical ability. Which of the following successes would most likely lead Braunwin to feel bad about herself? Which would most likely lead her to feel good? Why?
   a. A student at Braunwin's college is selected to play on the national volleyball team.
   b. A student at Braunwin's college receives a competitive scholarship to study music.
   c. Braunwin's best friend is asked to play a solo during the band concert.
   d. Braunwin's sister receives a prestigious athletic scholarship.

■ PSYCHOLOGY AND SOCIETY

1. In 1953, the psychologist Henry A. Murray and the anthropologist Clyde Kluckhon claimed that every person is like all other people, like some other people, and like no other person. Based on your understanding of the ideas from this chapter, describe the ways in which each individual is like all other people, like some other people, and like no other person.

2. Imagine your friend John is emotionally volatile and easily upset, and he often reports feeling anxious and depressed. He could be said to be high in neuroticism, one of the Big Five personality traits. Describe at least two ways in which John's personality might influence his social environment and at least two ways in which his social environment might influence the expression of his personality.

The answer key for all the Measuring Up exercises and the Practice Tests can be found at the back of the book.

Disorders of the Mind and Body

GERTRUDE AND HENRY MET IN THE 1930s. She found him annoying but eventually agreed to marry him after he threatened suicide. Gertrude became pregnant after three years of marriage, and in the fifth month of the pregnancy Gertrude's doctor predicted that she would have twins. In fact, she had quadruplets: Nora, Iris, Myra, and Hester (FIGURE 14.1). (Their names have been changed to protect their privacy.) Henry was frequently unemployed, so the couple could not afford to support four babies. A local newspaper raised money, and a house was donated to the family. A steady stream of visitors wanted to see the babies, and Henry began charging admission. After a while, however, he became worried about his family's safety, so he barred all visitors. At one point, he mistook his wife for an intruder and fired a pistol at her.

How Are Mental Disorders Conceptualized and Classified?

- Mental Disorders Are Classified into Categories
- Mental Disorders Must Be Assessed
- Critical Thinking Skill: Recognizing When Categories Represent Continuous Dimensions
- Dissociative Identity Disorder Is a Controversial Diagnosis
- Mental Disorders Have Many Causes

Can Anxiety Be the Root of Seemingly Different Disorders?

- There Are Different Types of Anxiety Disorders

- Anxiety Disorders Have Cognitive, Situational, and Biological Components

Are Mood Disorders Extreme Manifestations of Normal Moods?

- There Are Different Types of Mood Disorders
- Mood Disorders Have Cognitive, Situational, and Biological Components

What Is Schizophrenia?

- Schizophrenia Has Positive and Negative Symptoms
- Schizophrenia Is Primarily a Brain Disorder
- Environmental Factors Influence Schizophrenia

Are Personality Disorders Truly Mental Disorders?

- Personality Disorders Are Maladaptive Ways of Relating to the World
- Borderline Personality Disorder Is Associated with Poor Self-Control
- Antisocial Personality Disorder Is Associated with a Lack of Empathy

Should Childhood Disorders Be Considered a Unique Category?

- Autism Is a Lack of Awareness of Others
- Critical Thinking Skill: Recognizing and Resisting Hindsight Bias
- Attention-Deficit/Hyperactivity Disorder Is a Disruptive Impulse Control Disorder

617

FIGURE 14.1 The Genain Quadruplets as Adults

Henry and Gertrude believed that the girls represented one person split into four. They consistently preferred the two larger babies, Nora and Myra, over the other two, and Gertrude took a particular dislike to Hester, especially after she caught her masturbating. Gertrude continued to worry excessively about masturbation, and after she caught Hester and Iris engaging in mutual masturbation, she had a doctor remove their clitorises. As the girls got older, Henry insisted on watching them dress and undress and even watched them change their sanitary pads. In high school, Hester became irritable and depressed; her behavior was at times destructive and bizarre. She "admitted" to engaging in a series of sexual activities dating back to elementary school. Instead of fully exploring the causes for this behavior, her parents concluded that masturbation had made her mentally retarded. She was heavily sedated and kept at home. Although the other girls graduated from high school and even held jobs for a while, they all had psychotic episodes resulting in hospitalization. All four women eventually were diagnosed with schizophrenia. The National Institute of Mental Health (NIMH) offered free care in return for the opportunity to study them. To preserve their anonymity, the NIMH assigned the Genain quadruplets first names beginning with the initials of NIMH (information from Rosenthal, 1963).

Although today the Genains are recognized as having mental disorders and receive appropriate treatment, throughout history the mentally disordered have not always been viewed humanely. In the Middle Ages, the Genain quadruplets might have been regarded as possessed by demons and been persecuted. In the 1700s, they likely would have languished in understaffed, overcrowded mental institutions, where there would have been little attempt to understand their disorders and even less of an attempt to treat them. In the 1800s, the focus would have been on environmental factors contributing to their disorder, such as physical abuse and their father's bizarre and inappropriate behavior. Although their early experiences undoubtedly contributed to the development of their mental disorders, we now understand that biology plays a critical role in schizophrenia. Indeed, an important lesson in this chapter is that environment and biology interact to produce mental disorders. As noted throughout the book, it is meaningless to state that a condition is caused by either biology or environment; both affect all mental disorders to some extent. Advances in research have demonstrated that most mental disorders are ultimately disorders of both mind and body, attributable to both psychological and biological factors.

Over the course of history, people have struggled with how best to understand **psychopathology**—literally, sickness or disorder of the mind. Throughout recorded history, from the writings of Aristotle to those of Freud, accounts exist of people suffering from various forms of psychopathology. Mental disorders are common around the globe, in all countries and all societies. Indeed, about one in four Americans over age 18 has a diagnosable mental disorder in a given year (Kessler et al., 2005a), and about 1 in 5 adults receives treatment over any two-year period (Kessler et al., 2005b). Indeed, nearly 1 in 2 people will have some form of mental disorder at some point in their lives, the most common being mood disorders (such as depression), impulse control disorders (such as hyperactivity and problems paying attention), anxiety disorders, and substance abuse disorders (Kessler & Wang, 2008). Of course, mental disorders range in severity; only about 7 percent of the U.S. population is severely affected. This group also tends to suffer from multiple mental disorders, such that at a given time someone might be anxious and depressed and also abuse drugs or alcohol. There are also enormous gender differences in psychopathology; some

psychopathology A disorder of the mind.

disorders are much more likely in women (such as depression and anxiety disorders), and some are much more likely in men (such as antisocial personality disorder and autism). These gender differences likely reflect biology and culture, as the sexes may differ in their predispositions to mental disorders and in how cultural values influence the degree to which different disorders are diagnosed for women and for men.

Given that mental disorders are common and vary in severity, most people have symptoms of mental disorders at some point in their lives. Who among us has not felt exceedingly sad on occasion or has not felt anxious when contemplating some difficult challenge? As noted in Chapter 9, emotions are a central aspect of being human. Drawing the line between a natural emotional experience and a mental disorder can be challenging, because different people respond to events differently and personal suffering is hard to determine objectively. Mental problems that disrupt a person's life and cause significant distress over a long period are considered a disorder rather than the normal ups and downs of everyday life. This means that you may have experienced some of the symptoms of many of the mental disorders discussed below. As you read, however, resist the urge to make diagnoses, even if particular symptoms seem to describe you, or anyone you know, perfectly. Just like medical students who worry they have every disease they learn about, you need to guard against overanalyzing yourself and others. At the same time, what you learn in this chapter and the next (on treating disorders) may help you understand the mental health problems you or people you care about might experience at some point.

How Are Mental Disorders Conceptualized and Classified?

How do you know if a person has a mental disorder? It can be challenging to decide if a given behavior is caused by psychopathology, because behavior—especially unusual behavior—always must be reviewed according to the situation. A woman running through the streets screaming, sobbing, and grabbing and hugging people might have some form of mental disorder—or she might be celebrating because she just won the lottery. Many behaviors considered normal in one setting may be considered deviant in other settings. For example, some tribes in Africa spread feces in their hair as part of rituals; some Native American and East Asian cultures consider it a great honor to hear the voices of spirits. In urban America, the former would be seen as deviant behavior, and the latter as evidence of auditory hallucinations. However, it is important to consider certain criteria in determining whether behavior represents psychopathology: (1) Does the behavior deviate from cultural norms? (2) Is the behavior maladaptive? (3) Is the behavior causing the individual personal distress?

Because it is hard to draw the line between normal and abnormal, psychopathology increasingly is defined as thoughts, and behaviors, that are maladaptive rather than deviant. Excessive hand-washing can be deviant but adaptive—after all, it is the best way of avoiding contagious disease. The same behavior, however, can be maladaptive when people cannot stop until they have washed their hands raw. Indeed, the diagnostic criteria for all the major disorder categories stipulate that the symptoms of the disorder must interfere with at least one aspect of the person's life, such as work, social relations, or self-care. This component is critical in determining whether a given behavior or set of behaviors represents a mental disorder or is simply unusual.

LEARNING OBJECTIVES

Differentiate among common methods for assessing mental disorders.

Describe different theoretical models that seek to explain the etiology of mental disorders.

Mental Disorders Are Classified into Categories

Despite the problems in conceptualizing mental disorders, there are clear advantages to categorizing them. To investigate the **etiology** (factors that contribute to the development) and possible treatments of mental disorders, psychologists need to group these disorders into meaningful categories. Researchers and clinicians have struggled for many years with how best to categorize mental disorders. In the late 1800s, for example, the psychiatrist Emil Kraepelin recognized that not all patients with mental disorders suffer from the same disorder, and he identified mental disorders on the basis of groups of symptoms that occur together (**FIGURE 14.2**).

The idea of categorizing mental disorders systematically was not officially adopted until the first edition of the *Diagnostic and Statistical Manual of Mental Disorders (DSM)* was published, in 1952. Although it has undergone several revisions, the *DSM* remains the standard in psychology and psychiatry. Earlier versions focused on the presumed causes of mental disorders, but beginning with the *DSM-III,* in 1980, there was a return to classifying psychopathology based on observable symptoms. In the current edition, the fourth, disorders are described in terms of such symptoms, and a patient must meet specific criteria to receive a particular diagnosis. In addition, a patient does not receive a single label but rather is classified through a **multiaxial system** (detailed in **TABLE 14.1**), which is based on the growing realization that various factors affect mental health. Diagnoses include evaluations on five dimensions, or axes: (1) clinical disorders, (2) mental retardation or personality disorders, (3) medical conditions, (4) psychosocial problems, and (5) global or overall assessment of how well the person is functioning. Diagnosing a patient on all five axes provides a more complete picture of the person than simply assigning a clinical category.

Mental Disorders Must Be Assessed

Physical disorders often can be detected by medical tests, such as blood tests or biopsies, but determining whether a person has a mental disorder is not as straightforward. Clinical psychologists often work like detectives, tracking down information

etiology Factors that contribute to the development of a disorder.

FIGURE 14.2 Emil Kraepelin Kraepelin was one of the first researchers to propose a classification system for mental disorders.

multiaxial system The system used in the *DSM* that provides assessment along five axes describing important mental health factors.

Table 14.1 *DSM-IV* Multiaxial Classification System	
Axis I	Clinical disorders and other conditions that may be a focus of clinical attention (e.g., schizophrenia, mood disorders, anxiety disorders, sexual and gender disorders, sleep disorders, eating disorders).
Axis II	Mental retardation and personality disorders (e.g., antisocial personality disorder, paranoid personality disorder, borderline personality disorder).
Axis III	General medical conditions that may be relevant to mental disorders (e.g., cancer, epilepsy, obesity, Parkinson's disease, Alzheimer's disease).
Axis IV	Psychosocial and environmental problems that might affect the diagnosis, treatment, and prognosis of mental disorders (e.g., unemployment, divorce, legal problems, homelessness, poverty, parental overprotection).
Axis V	Global assessment of functioning (social, psychological, and occupational). Rated on a scale from 1 to 100, with 1 representing danger of hurting self or others and 100 meaning superior functioning in a wide range of areas.

SOURCE: *Diagnostic and Statistical Manual of the American Psychiatric Association*, 1994.

from sources including self-reports, observations, and interviews. The process of examining a person's mental functions and psychological health is known as **assessment.** The first goal of assessment is to make a *diagnosis* so that appropriate treatment can be provided. Because the course and probable outcome, or *prognosis,* of different mental disorders can vary, the correct diagnosis helps the patient and family understand what the future might bring. Assessment does not stop with diagnosis, however, as ongoing assessment helps mental health workers understand whether specific situations might cause a worsening of the disorder, whether progress is being made in treatment, and any other factors that might help in understanding unique aspects of a given case (**FIGURE 14.3**).

The method of initial assessment sometimes depends on how a person comes into contact with mental health workers. People often come to emergency rooms showing confusion, memory problems, or other mental impairments. A patient in this condition may be given a *mental status exam* to provide a snapshot of his or her psychological functioning. The exam involves behavioral observations that evaluate the person for characteristics such as personal grooming, ability to make eye contact, tremors or twitches, mood, speech, thought content, and memory. This evaluation can offer insights into whether a person has a mental disorder. For example, a patient who arrives in a disheveled state and wearing excess layers of clothing more likely suffers from schizophrenia than from an anxiety disorder. The mental status exam is also useful for determining whether the mental impairments are due to a psychological condition or a physical condition, such as stroke or head injury.

Most symptoms of psychological problems develop over fairly long periods, and a person seeking help for such problems frequently is encouraged to see a mental health professional by family members or by a physician. A psychologist's first step in an assessment is to ask the person about current symptoms and about recent experiences that might be causing distress—for example, if the person is feeling depressed, the psychologist will likely ask whether he or she recently has experienced some sort of loss. In this *clinical interview,* the interviewer's skills determine the quantity and value of information obtained. A good interviewer expresses empathy, builds rapport quickly, is nonjudgmental and trusting, and supports the client's efforts to find out what is wrong and how it might be addressed.

STRUCTURED VERSUS UNSTRUCTURED INTERVIEWS Since the beginning of modern psychology, most interviews have been *unstructured,* such that the topics of discussion vary as the interviewer probes different aspects of the person's problems. The interview is guided by the clinician's past experiences as well as by his or her observations of the client and the type of problems that are most likely. Unstructured interviews are highly flexible—indeed, no two unstructured interviews will likely elicit identical information from the same patient. They also are overly dependent on the interviewer's skills. In *structured interviews,* standardized questions are asked in the same order each time. The patient's answers are coded according to a predetermined formula; the diagnosis is based on the specific patterns of responding. The most commonly used structured interview is the *Structured Clinical Interview for DSM (SCID),* through which diagnoses are made according to *DSM* criteria (Spitzer, Williams, Gibbon, & First, 1992). The SCID begins with general questions such as *What kind of work do you do?* and proceeds to questions about the client's symptoms, such as about their frequency and severity. The SCID is also valuable for research and treatment, because the results obtained from one group of patients will likely apply to other patients diagnosed with the same disorder

assessment In psychology, examination of a person's mental state to diagnose possible psychological disorders.

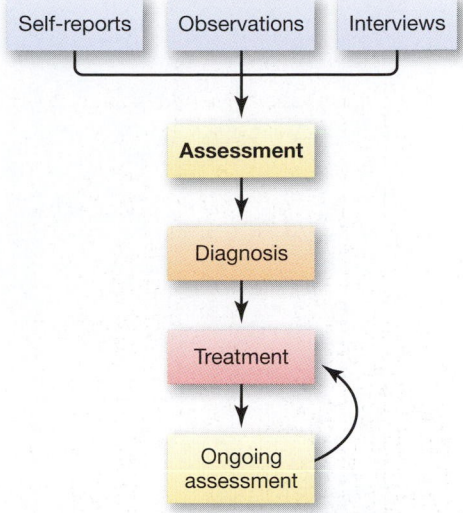

FIGURE 14.3 Assessing a Patient
Clinical psychologists examine a person's mental functions and psychological health to diagnose a mental disorder.

TYPES OF TESTING A psychological assessor often can gain valuable information simply by observing the client's *behavior*. For instance, a client who avoids eye contact during an examination might suffer from social anxiety; a client whose eyes dart around nervously may feel paranoid. Behavioral assessments often are useful with children—for instance, observing their interactions with others or seeing whether they can sit still in a classroom.

Another source of information regarding psychopathology is *psychological testing*. Chapter 13 provides examples of these types of tests for assessing personality. Of the thousands of psychological tests available to clinicians, some are for specific mental disorders, such as the widely used Beck Depression Inventory (Beck, Steer, & Brown, 1996; Beck, Ward, Mendelson, Mock, & Erbaugh, 1961). Other measures assess both a broad range of mental disorders and general mental health. The most widely used questionnaire for psychological assessment is the *Minnesota Multiphasic Personality Inventory (MMPI)*. Developed during the 1930s, the MMPI was updated in the 1990s for language changes. The latest version consists of 567 true/false items that assess emotions, thoughts, and behaviors. The MMPI has ten clinical scales (e.g., paranoia, depression, mania, hysteria) that generate a profile indicating whether the client may have a particular mental disorder.

As discussed in Chapter 2, a common problem with all self-report assessments, such as the MMPI, is that to make a favorable impression respondents sometimes distort the truth or lie outright. To avoid detection of a mental disorder, a test-taker might be evasive or defensive. To look especially troubled, another test-taker might untruthfully lean toward negative items. To counter such response biases, the MMPI includes validity scales, which measure the probability that respondents are being less than truthful. For instance, a person might try to present himself or herself too positively by agreeing with a large number of items such as "I always make my bed" and "I never tell lies"; a high score on this category would indicate an attempt to present a perfectly positive image. Even if the test-taker is not responding in this way consciously, the scoring of answers on the other items must take into account the positivity bias in responses. Other validity scales examine whether the test-taker answers similar questions in the same manner each time and whether he or she responds "true" to items that are extremely rare or to an especially large number of negative items (known as *faking bad*).

Although tests such as the MMPI are used widely in psychological assessment, they are seldom the sole source of information. Indeed, most clinicians do not diagnose until they have consistent results from psychological tests and structured interviews. In addition, although in North America the MMPI generally has been a reliable and valid assessment tool, it has been criticized as inappropriate for use in other countries or among groups such as the poor, the elderly, and racial minorities. The problem here is that scores considered "normal" on the MMPI are based on studies in which such people were inadequately represented.

Another assessment method is *neuropsychological testing*. In this method, the client performs actions such as copying a picture; drawing a design from memory; sorting cards that show various stimuli into categories based on size, shape, or color; placing blocks into slots on a board while blindfolded; and tapping fingers rapidly (**FIGURE 14.4**). Each task requires an ability such as planning, coordinating, or remembering. By highlighting actions that the client performs poorly, the assessment might indicate problems with a particular brain region. For instance, people who have difficulty switching from one rule to another for categorizing objects, such as sorting by shape rather than by color, may have impairments in the frontal lobes. Subsequent assessment with MRI or PET might indicate brain damage caused by a tumor or by an injury (on these techniques, see Chapter 2, "Research Methodology").

FIGURE 14.4 Neuropsychological Testing The assessment depicted here uses a neuropsychological test to examine mental function. In this timed test, a researcher watches a client fit wooden blocks into a corresponding template to test for signs of Alzheimer's disease.

EVIDENCE-BASED ASSESSMENT One key theme of this book is that scientific research informs the understanding of mind, brain, and behavior, and assessment procedures are no exception. *Evidence-based assessment* is an approach to clinical evaluation in which research guides the evaluation of mental disorders, the selection of appropriate psychological tests and neuropsychological methods, and the use of critical thinking in making a diagnosis (Hunsley & Mash, 2007; Joiner, Walker, Pettit, Perez, & Cukrowicz, 2005). For instance, scientific research indicates that many mental disorders occur together, a state known as *comorbidity* (**FIGURE 14.5**). For example, people who are depressed often have substance abuse disorders, so an evidence-based assessment approach would indicate that people found to be depressed should also be assessed for comorbid conditions such as substance abuse.

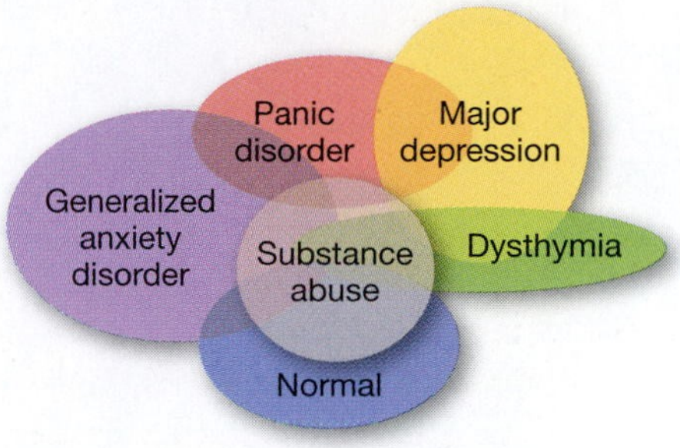

FIGURE 14.5 Comorbidity As this diagram illustrates, mental disorders commonly overlap.

CRITICAL THINKING SKILL

Recognizing When Categories Represent Continuous Dimensions

Can a woman be "a little bit" pregnant? Most people would agree that pregnancy is an all-or-none state and that a woman who is a few days pregnant is every bit as pregnant as a woman in her ninth month.

Many other categories are not so cut and dried. Is a person honest or dishonest? Smart or unintelligent? Good looking or ugly? Like these, most categories represent points along a continuum. Most dimensions in life (e.g., hot/cold, day/night) do not represent absolute differences. The same is true for mental health versus mental disorders: A diagnosis of a mental disorder indicates membership in a category, but the underlying dimension is continuous.

Suppose your neighbor has been diagnosed with an anxiety disorder. This means that a mental health practitioner such as a clinical psychologist has decided that your neighbor's symptoms of anxiety are beyond what is considered normal. This label, or diagnosis, carries the understanding that to alleviate the symptoms your neighbor needs counseling or medication. The label lumps your neighbor with all people who share the diagnosis, though the severity of the disorder can range from just slightly more anxious than normal to extremely anxious in a way that interferes with daily living. You do not know from the diagnosis exactly where your neighbor falls along the continuum (**FIGURE 14.6**).

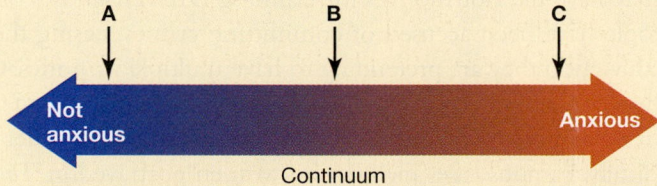

FIGURE 14.6 Think Critically: Recognizing When Categories Represent Continuous Dimensions It may seem obvious that a person at point A is not anxious and a person at point C is anxious, but how should a person at point B be classified?

Dissociative Identity Disorder Is a Controversial Diagnosis

Sometimes the available evidence raises doubts about the validity of certain diagnoses. Consider multiple personalities. In 1978, Billy Milligan was found innocent of robbery and rape charges on the grounds that he had been diagnosed with multiple personality disorder. Milligan clearly committed the robberies and rapes, but his lawyers successfully argued that he had multiple personalities and that different ones committed the crimes; therefore, Billy could not be held responsible. In his book *The Minds of Billy Milligan* (1981), Daniel Keyes describes the 24 separate personalities sharing the body of 26-year-old Billy Milligan. One is Arthur, who at age 22 speaks with a British accent and is self-taught in physics and biology. He reads and writes fluent Arabic. Eight-year-old David is the keeper of the pain; anytime something physically painful happens, David experiences it. Christene is a three-year-old dyslexic girl who likes to draw flowers and butterflies. Regan is 23 and Yugoslavian; speaks with a marked Slavic accent; and reads, writes, and speaks Serbo-Croatian. He is the protector of the "family" and acknowledges robbing his victims, but he denies raping them. Adalana, a 19-year-old lesbian who writes poetry, cooks, and keeps house for the others, later admitted to committing the rapes. After his acquittal, Milligan spent close to a decade in various mental hospitals. In 1988, psychiatrists declared that Milligan's 24 personalities had merged into one and that he was no longer a danger to society. Milligan was released and reportedly has lived quietly since then. Many people respond to reports such as this with astonishment and incredulity, believing that people such as Milligan must be faking. To judge the facts, we need to examine what is known about his condition and how it is diagnosed.

dissociative identity disorder (DID) The occurrence of two or more distinct identities in the same individual.

Dissociative identity disorder (DID), formerly called *multiple personality disorder,* involves the occurrence of two or more distinct identities in the same individual. DID is an example of the *DSM* category of *dissociative disorders,* which involve disruptions of identity, of memory, and of conscious awareness. Most people diagnosed with DID are women who report being severely abused as children. According to the most common theory of DID, children cope with abuse by pretending it is happening to someone else and entering a trancelike state in which they dissociate their mental states from their physical bodies. Over time, this dissociated state takes on its own identity. Different identities develop to deal with different traumas. Often the identities have periods of amnesia, and sometimes only one identity is aware of the others. Indeed, diagnosis often occurs only when a person has difficulty accounting for large chunks of his or her day. The separate identities usually differ substantially, such as in gender, sexual orientation, age, language spoken, interests, physiological profiles, and patterns of brain activation (Reinders et al., 2003). Even their handwritings can differ (**FIGURE 14.7**).

Despite this evidence, many researchers remain skeptical about whether DID is a genuine mental disorder or whether it exists at all (Kihlstrom, 2005). Moreover, some people may have ulterior motives for claiming DID. Diagnoses of DID often occur after people have been accused of committing crimes, raising the possibility that to avoid conviction they are pretending to have multiple identities. Other skeptics point to the sharp rise in reported cases as evidence that the disorder might not be real or that it is diagnosed far too often. Before the 1980s, this disorder was reported only sporadically. Famous cases include the women portrayed in *The Three Faces of Eve* (Thigpen & Cleckley, 1954) and *Sybil* (Schreiber, 1974). In the 1990s, the number of cases skyrocketed into the tens of thousands. Moreover, those displaying the disorder went from having two or three identities to having several dozen or even hundreds. What can explain these changes? Some of these patients may have developed DID after seeing therapists who believed strongly in the disorder. Indeed, in most cases those diagnosed as having DID were unaware of their other identities until after many therapy sessions. The 1980s and 1990s saw a surge of therapists who believed that childhood trauma frequently was repressed and that it needed to be uncovered during treatment. These therapists tended to use hypnosis, and they might have suggested DID symptoms to the patients they were assessing.

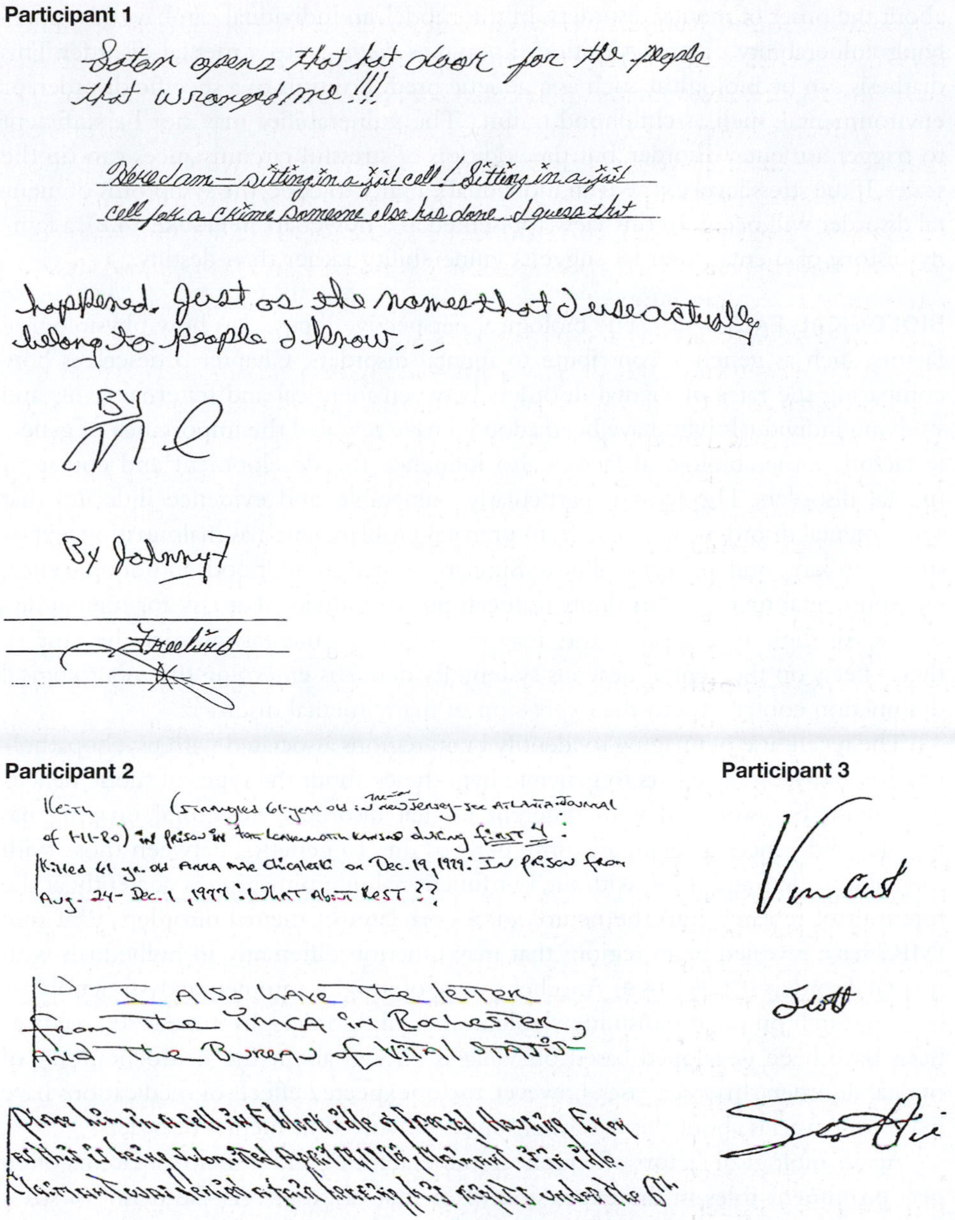

Participant 1

Satan opens that hot door for the people that wronged me!!!

Here I am — sitting in a jail cell! Sitting in a jail cell for a crime someone else has done. I guess that

happened just as the names that I use actually belong to people I know...

By

By Johnny7

Participant 2

Keith (strangled 61-yr old in New Jersey—see Atlanta Journal of 1-11-80) In prison in Leavenworth Kansas during Test 4 : Killed 61 yr. old Anna mae Chicalek on Dec. 19, 1979: In prison from Aug. 24- Dec. 1, 1979 : What about Rest 3 ?

I Also have the letter from the YMCA in Rochester, and the Bureau of Vital Statis

Participant 3

Von Cart

Scott

FIGURE 14.7 Handwriting Samples of Three People Diagnosed with Dissociative Identity Disorder When researchers studied 12 murderers diagnosed with DID, writing samples from 10 of the participants revealed markedly different handwriting in each of their identities. Here, handwriting samples from three of the participants show different identities expressing themselves.

Despite this counterevidence, independent reports have verified that at least some patients with DID were abused, and physical or sexual abuse can cause psychological problems, including distortions of consciousness. But how can we know whether a diagnosis of DID is valid? As mentioned above, most often there is no objective, definitive test for diagnosing mental disorders. Ultimately, it is difficult to tell if a person is faking, whether he or she has come to believe what a therapist said, or whether he or she has a genuine mental disorder.

Mental Disorders Have Many Causes

Although there is not complete agreement for the causes of most mental disorders, including dissociative identity disorder, some factors are thought to play important developmental roles. As discussed throughout this book, both nature and nurture matter, and it is futile to try to identify biology or environment as solely responsible for a given disorder. The **diathesis-stress model** provides one way of thinking

diathesis-stress model A diagnostic model that proposes that a disorder may develop when an underlying vulnerability is coupled with a precipitating event.

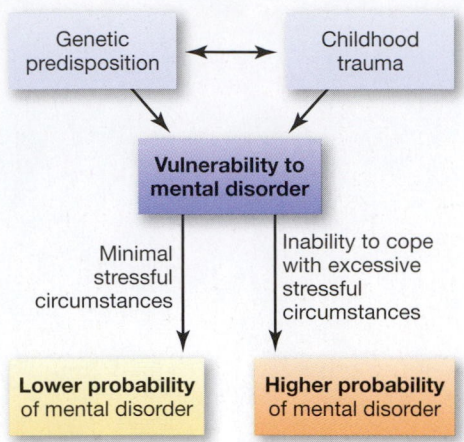

FIGURE 14.8 **Diathesis-Stress Model** In this model, nature and nurture work together: A person can be vulnerable to a mental disorder because of an inherited predisposition, an environmental influence, or both. Stress then may act upon the person's vulnerability.

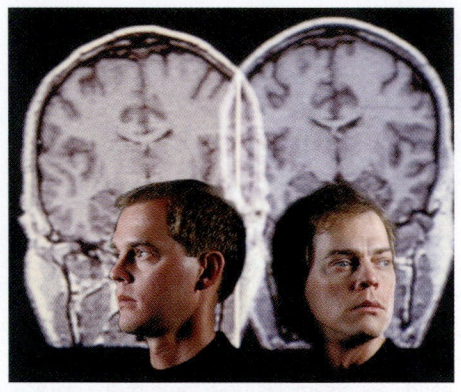

FIGURE 14.9 **Biological Factors in Mental Disorders** Although these men are twins, the one on the right has schizophrenia and the one on the left does not. Note the larger ventricles in the schizophrenic twin's MRI (these fluid-filled cavities appear dark in the image). This same pattern has emerged in the study of other twin pairs in which one has schizophrenia and the other does not.

family systems model A diagnostic model that considers symptoms within an individual as indicating problems within the family.

about the onset of mental disorders. In this model, an individual can have an underlying vulnerability or predisposition (known as *diathesis*) to a mental disorder. This diathesis can be biological, such as a genetic predisposition to a specific disorder, or environmental, such as childhood trauma. The vulnerability may not be sufficient to trigger a mental disorder, but the addition of stressful circumstances can tip the scales. If the stress level exceeds an individual's ability to cope, the symptoms of mental disorder will occur. In this view (presented as a flowchart in **FIGURE 14.8**), a family history of mental disorder suggests vulnerability rather than destiny.

BIOLOGICAL FACTORS The biological perspective focuses on how physiological factors, such as genetics, contribute to mental disorders. Chapter 3 describes how comparing the rates of mental disorders between identical and fraternal twins and studying individuals who have been adopted have revealed the importance of genetic factors. Other biological factors also influence the development and course of mental disorders. The fetus is particularly vulnerable, and evidence indicates that some mental disorders may arise from prenatal problems such as malnutrition, exposure to toxins, and maternal illness. Similarly, during childhood and adolescence, environmental toxins and malnutrition can put an individual at risk for mental disorders. All these biological factors may contribute to mental disorders because of their effects on the central nervous system. Evidence is emerging that neurological dysfunction contributes to the expression of many mental disorders.

The recent use of imaging to identify brain regions associated with psychopathology has allowed researchers to generate hypotheses about the types of subtle deficits that might be associated with different mental disorders. Structural imaging has revealed differences in brain anatomy, perhaps due to genetics, between those with mental disorders and those without, but functional neuroimaging is currently at the forefront of research into the neurological correlates of mental disorders. PET and fMRI have revealed brain regions that may function differently in individuals with mental disorders (**FIGURE 14.9**). Another source of insights into neural dysfunction has been research on neurotransmitters' role in mental disorders. In some cases, medications have been developed based on what is known about the neurochemistry of mental disorders. In other cases, however, the unexpected effects of medications have led to discoveries about the neurotransmitters involved in mental disorders.

Again, biological factors often reflect vulnerabilities, and situational factors often play prominent roles in the expression of mental disorders. As the diathesis–stress model reminds us, single explanations (nature or nurture) are seldom sufficient for understanding mental disorders.

PSYCHOLOGICAL FACTORS The first edition of the *DSM* was influenced heavily by Freudian psychoanalytic theory. Freud believed that mental disorders were mostly due to unconscious conflicts, often sexual in nature, that dated back to childhood. Consistent with this perspective, many disorders in the first edition of the *DSM* were described as reactions to environmental conditions or as involving various defense mechanisms. Although Freud made important historical contributions in shaping psychology, most of his theories—particularly his theories on the causes of mental health disorders—have not stood the test of time. However, psychological factors clearly play an important role in the expression and treatment of mental disorders. At the social level of analysis, thoughts and emotions are shaped by environment and can profoundly influence behavior, including disordered behavior. Not only traumatic events but also less extreme circumstances, such as constantly being belittled by a parent, can have long-lasting effects. The **family systems model** proposes that an individual's behavior must be considered within a social context, particularly within

(a)

(b)

FIGURE 14.10 Sociocultural Model According to the sociocultural model, psychopathology results from the interaction between individuals and their cultures. These images exemplify such interactions. **(a)** This billboard, denouncing the use of anorexic fashion models, appeared in Milan during Italian fashion week. **(b)** This homeless schizophrenic man lives on the streets in Notting Hill, a fashionable area of London.

the family. Problems that arise within an individual are manifestations of problems within the family (as was the case for the Genain quadruplets, described at the beginning of the chapter). Developing a profile of an individual's family interactions can be important not only for understanding possible factors contributing to the disorder but also for determining whether the family is likely to be helpful or detrimental to the client's progress in therapy.

Similarly, the **sociocultural model** views psychopathology as the result of the interaction between individuals and their cultures. Disorders such as schizophrenia appear more common among the lower socioeconomic classes, whereas disorders such as anorexia nervosa appear more common among the middle and upper classes (**FIGURE 14.10**). From the sociocultural perspective, these differences in occurrence are due to differences in lifestyles, in expectations, and in opportunities among classes. There may be cultural biases in people's willingness to ascribe disorders to different social classes, however. Eccentric behavior among the wealthy elite might be tolerated or viewed as amusing, whereas the same behaviors observed among those living in poverty might be taken as evidence of mental disorders. Moreover, people who develop schizophrenia may have trouble finding work and so experience financial problems because of their disorder.

sociocultural model A diagnostic model that views psychopathology as the result of the interaction between individuals and their cultures.

COGNITIVE-BEHAVIORAL FACTORS At the level of the individual, the central principle of the **cognitive-behavioral approach** is that abnormal behavior is learned. As discussed in Chapter 6, through classical conditioning an unconditioned stimulus produces an unconditioned response. For example, a loud noise produces a startled response. A neutral stimulus paired with this unconditioned stimulus can eventually by itself produce a similar response. As was the case with Little Albert, if a child is playing with a fluffy white rat and is frightened by a loud noise, the white rat alone can later cause fear in the child. In fact, this process is

cognitive-behavioral approach A diagnostic model that views psychopathology as the result of learned, maladaptive cognitions.

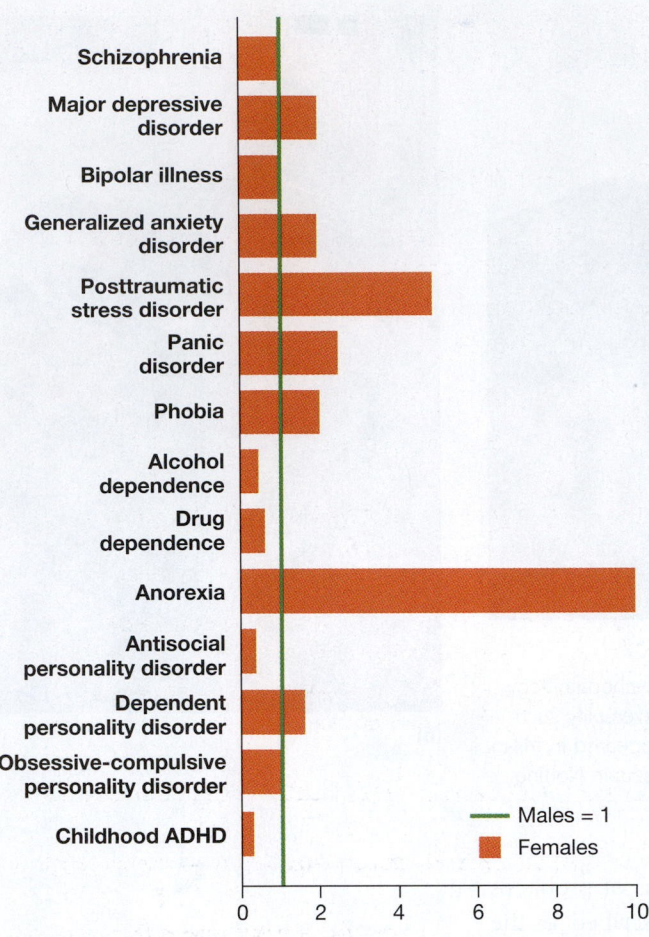

SOURCE: NIAAA;NIMH; R. Kessler/Harvard University.

FIGURE 14.11 Sex Differences in Mental Disorders In this graph, males are set as the baseline of 1 for comparison purposes.

FIGURE 14.12 Externalizing and Internalizing Model of Mental Disorders Internalizing is more prevalent in females, and externalizing is more prevalent in males.

how John B. Watson, the founder of behaviorism, demonstrated that many fears are learned rather than innate.

Proponents of strict behaviorism argue that mental disorders result from classical and operant conditioning. Strict behaviorists originally defined behavior as overt and observable actions, but later this view was challenged. According to the revised cognitive-behavioral perspective, thoughts and beliefs are types of behavior and can be studied empirically. The premise of this approach is that thoughts can become distorted and produce maladaptive behaviors and maladaptive emotions. In contrast to the psychoanalytical perspective, cognitive-behavioral psychologists believe that thought processes are available to the conscious mind; individuals are aware of, or easily can be made aware of, the thought processes that give rise to maladaptive emotions and behaviors.

SEX DIFFERENCES IN MENTAL DISORDERS Some mental disorders are more common for males and others for females. The reasons for these differences are both environmental and biological. As **FIGURE 14.11** shows, dependence on alcohol and/or drugs, antisocial personality disorders, and childhood attention-deficit/hyperactivity disorder are twice as likely to occur in males as in females. In contrast, anorexia is 10 times more likely to occur in females, posttraumatic stress disorder is four times more likely in females, and panic disorders are almost twice as likely in females. Some disorders, such as schizophrenia and bipolar disorder, are equally likely in the sexes. One way of categorizing mental disorders is to divide them into two major groups: *internalizing disorders,* those characterized by negative emotions such as distress and fear, and *externalizing disorders,* those characterized by disinhibition, such as alcoholism, conduct disorders, and antisocial behavior. (A schematic diagram of this model of mental disorders appears in **FIGURE 14.12.**) In general, the disorders associated with internalizing are more prevalent in females, and those associated with externalizing are more prevalent in males (Krueger & Markon, 2006).

CULTURE AND MENTAL DISORDERS Increasingly, psychologists and other mental health professionals are recognizing the importance of culture on many aspects of our lives. Most mental disorders show universal and culture-specific symptoms; that is, they may be very similar around the world but still reflect cultural differences.

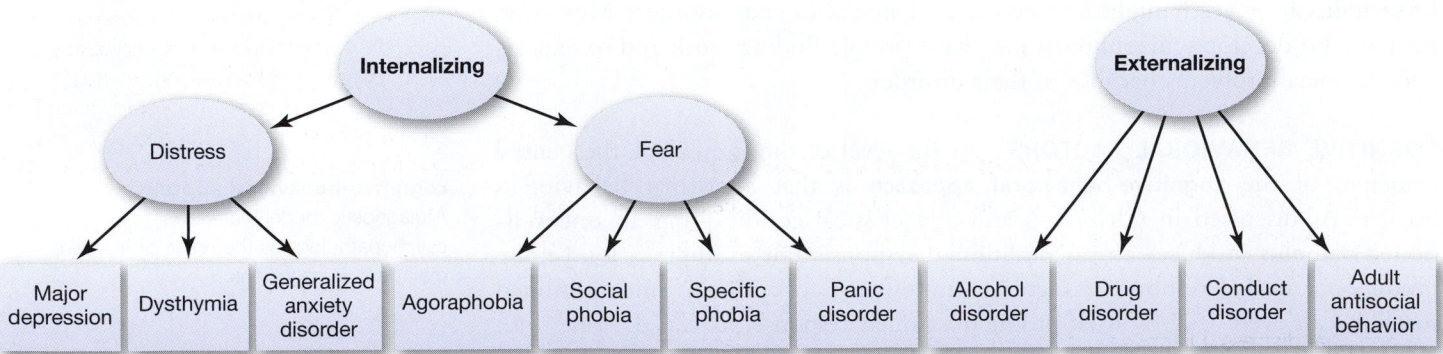

SOURCE: Krueger & Markon, 2006.

Table 14.2 Culture-Bound Syndromes

Name	Definition and Location
Amok	A sudden outburst of explosive and assaultive violence preceded by period of social withdrawal and apathy (Southeast Asia, Philippines).
Ataque de nervios	Uncontrollable shouting and/or crying. Verbal and physical aggression. Heat in chest rising to head. Feeling of losing control. Occasional amnesia for experience (Caribbean Latinos and South American Latinos).
Hwa-byung	Acute panic, fear of death, fatigue, anorexia, dyspnea, palpitations, lump in upper stomach (Korea).
Latah	Startle reaction followed by echolalia and echopraxia, and sometimes coprolalia and altered consciousness (Malaysia and Indonesia).
Kuro (shook yong)	Intense fear following perception that one's genitalia (men/women) or breasts (women) are withdrawing into one's body. Shame may also be present if perception is associated in time with immoral sexual activity (Chinese populations in Hong Kong and Southeast Asia).
Phii pob	Belief that one is possessed by a spirit. Numbness of limbs, shouting, weeping, confused speech, shyness (Thailand).
Pissu	Burning sensations in stomach, coldness in body, hallucinations, dissociation (Ceylon).
Suchi-bai	Excessive concerns for cleanliness; changes street clothes, washes money, hops while walking to avoid dirt, washes furniture, remains immersed in holy river (Bengal, India—especially Hindu widows).
Susto (espanto)	Strong sense of fear that one has lost one's soul. Accompanied by anorexia, weight loss, skin pallor, fatigue, lethargy, extensive thirst, untidiness, tachycardia, and withdrawal (Latinos in South and Central America, Mexico; Latino migrants to North America).
Taijin kyofusho	Intense fear of interpersonal relations. Belief that parts of the body give off offensive odors or displease others (Japan).
Tawatl ye sni	Total discouragement. Preoccupation with death, ghosts, spirits. Excessive drinking, suicide thoughts and attempts (Sioux Indians).
Uquamairineq	Hypnotic states, disturbed sleep, sleep paralysis, dissociative episodes, and occasional hallucinations (Native Alaskans: Inuit, Yuit).

Disorders with a strong biological component are more similar across cultures, whereas those heavily influenced by learning and by context will more likely differ across cultures. For example, depression is a major mental health problem around the world, but the manifestations of depression differ by culture.

Since the 1994 edition, the *DSM* has included a section on *culture-bound syndromes,* disorders mainly found in specific cultures or regions. (**TABLE 14.2** lists examples of culture-bound disorders; **FIGURE 14.13** depicts one example.) Clinicians and researchers need to be sensitive to cultural issues to avoid making mistakes in their diagnoses and treatments (Marsalla & Yamada, 2007). Cultural factors can be critical in determining how a disorder is expressed and how an individual will respond to different types of therapies.

FIGURE 14.13 Suchi-Bai Disorder
Suchi-bai disorder involves an excessive concern for cleanliness and is particularly common among Hindu widows. In India, widows—such as this one, washing herself in an ashram—often are discriminated against and blamed for the deaths of their husbands.

SUMMING UP

How Are Mental Disorders Conceptualized and Classified?

Because psychopathology takes many forms, mental disorders are difficult to define and categorize. Although the behavioral manifestations vary widely, people diagnosed with these disorders have three things in common: Their behavior is maladaptive, it interferes with some important aspect of their lives, and it causes personal distress. Diagnoses of specific mental disorders are based on the checklist system of the *DSM*. Clinical assessments typically consisting of interviews and psychological tests are used to examine a person's mental functions and psychological health, and there is growing emphasis on evidence-based assessments. Some diagnoses, such as DID, are controversial because evidence for the existence of these particular mental disorders is questionable. The specific causes of most mental disorders are unknown and may be complex interactions of psychological, biological, and cognitive-behavioral factors. In general, females will more likely suffer from internalizing disorders such as distress and fear, and males will more likely suffer from externalizing disorders such as alcoholism and antisocial behavior. Disorders largely biological in origin are more similar throughout the world, and disorders that may be learned in a context vary more across cultures. Culture-bound disorders are found mainly in certain regions or cultures.

▶ MEASURING UP

1. Indicate whether each of the following scenarios is best described as a mental status exam, a structured interview, an unstructured interview, a behavioral test, a psychological test, or a neuropsychological test.
   a. A child psychologist asks a young client to study a series of words and then to list the words immediately afterward; memory for the words is assessed again later in the session.
   b. A social worker at a homeless shelter conducts systematic behavioral observations of new clients as they register for services.
   c. The staff member in charge of assessing the mental health status of recently incarcerated persons asks the same series of questions of each new inmate.

2. While at a conference on mental disorders, you attend a symposium titled *Understanding the Origins of Mental Health*. Excerpts from three of the presentations appear below. Match each excerpt to one of the etiological models discussed in this chapter: diathesis-stress model, biological model, family systems model, sociocultural model, and cognitive-behavioral approach. Not all the models will have matches.
   a. "By understanding the mechanisms by which neurotransmitters affect behavior and cognition and emotion, we gain insight into the underlying causes of mental illness."
   b. "Children are not raised in vacuums; they are raised in families. Therefore, to understand the origins of mental illness, we must understand the dynamics of the client's family."
   c. "Some individuals are predisposed—whether as a function of their biology or of their past experiences—to develop psychological disorders. Stressful circumstances amplify these predispositions, making the individual more likely to evidence symptoms of psychopathology."

LEARNING OBJECTIVES

Identify common symptoms experienced by people with anxiety disorders.

Provide evidence supporting the cognitive, situational, and biological underpinnings of anxiety disorders.

Can Anxiety Be the Root of Seemingly Different Disorders?

What does the fear of spiders have in common with the need to repeatedly check that the stove is turned off? They are both manifestations of anxiety disorders. Anxiety itself is normal and even useful. It can prepare us for upcoming events and motivate us to learn new ways of coping with life's challenges. Being anxious about tests reminds us to keep up with our homework and study. Likewise, being slightly anxious when meeting new people helps us avoid doing bizarre things and making bad impressions. For some people, however, anxiety can become debilitating and can interfere with every aspect of life. *Anxiety disorders* are characterized by excessive anxiety in the absence of true danger. It is normal to be anxious in stressful or threatening situations. It is abnormal to feel strong chronic anxiety without cause.

There Are Different Types of Anxiety Disorders

More than 1 in 4 people will have some type of anxiety disorder during their lifetimes (Kessler & Wang, 2008). Those suffering from anxiety disorders feel tense, anxious, and apprehensive. They are often depressed and irritable because they cannot see any solution to their anxiety. Constant worry can make falling asleep and staying asleep difficult, and attention span and concentration can be impaired. Because of the arousal of the autonomic nervous system, chronic anxiety also causes bodily symptoms such as sweating, dry mouth, rapid pulse, shallow breathing, increased blood pressure, and increased muscular tension. Chronic arousal can also result in hypertension, headaches, and intestinal problems and can even cause illness or tissue damage. Because of their high levels of autonomic arousal, those who suffer from anxiety disorders also exhibit restless and pointless motor behaviors. Exaggerated startle response is typical, and behaviors such as toe tapping and excessive fidgeting are common. Problem solving and judgment may suffer as well. Recent research has shown that chronic stress can produce atrophy in the hippocampus, a brain structure involved in learning and memory (McEwen, 2000). The fact that chronic stress can damage the body and brain indicates the importance of identifying and effectively treating disorders that involve chronic anxiety. Different anxiety disorders share some emotional, cognitive, somatic, and motor symptoms, even though the behavioral manifestations of these disorders are quite different (Barlow, 2002).

PHOBIC DISORDER As discussed in Chapter 6, a *phobia* is a fear of a specific object or situation. Fear can be adaptive, as it can lead us to avoid potential dangers, such as poisonous snakes and rickety bridges. In phobias, however, the fear is exaggerated and out of proportion to the actual danger. Phobias are classified based on the object of the fear. *Specific phobias,* which affect about 1 in 8 people, involve particular objects and situations, such as snakes (ophidiophobia), enclosed spaces (claustrophobia), and heights (acrophobia). (**TABLE 14.3** lists some unusual

---

Table 14.3 Some Unusual Specific Phobias

- **Arachibutyrophobia:** fear of peanut butter sticking to the roof of one's mouth
- **Automatonophobia:** fear of ventriloquists' dummies
- **Barophobia:** fear of gravity
- **Dextrophobia:** fear of objects at the right side of the body
- **Geliophobia:** fear of laughter
- **Gnomophobia:** fear of garden gnomes
- **Hippopotomonstrosesquippedaliophobia:** fear of long words
- **Ochophobia:** fear of being in a moving automobile
- **Panophobia:** fear of everything
- **Pentheraphobia:** fear of mothers-in-law
- **Triskaidekaphobia:** fear of the number 13

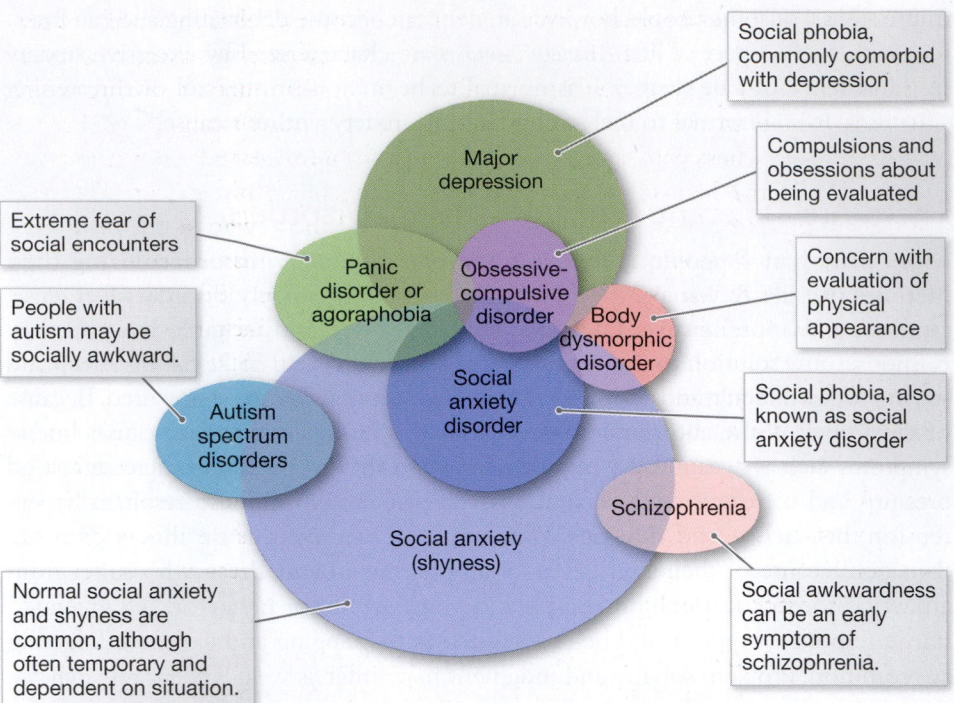

FIGURE 14.14 Social Phobias Social phobia is comorbid with many other psychological disorders, all of which need to be considered to make a correct diagnosis.

Labels in figure:
- Social phobia, commonly comorbid with depression
- Compulsions and obsessions about being evaluated
- Concern with evaluation of physical appearance
- Social phobia, also known as social anxiety disorder
- Social awkwardness can be an early symptom of schizophrenia.
- Extreme fear of social encounters
- People with autism may be socially awkward.
- Normal social anxiety and shyness are common, although often temporary and dependent on situation.
- Major depression
- Panic disorder or agoraphobia
- Obsessive-compulsive disorder
- Body dysmorphic disorder
- Social anxiety disorder
- Autism spectrum disorders
- Social anxiety (shyness)
- Schizophrenia

specific phobias.) A common phobia is fear of flying. Even though the odds of dying in a plane crash, compared with a car crash, are extraordinarily small, some people find flying terrifying. For those who need to travel frequently for their jobs, a fear of flying can cause significant impairment in daily living.

Social phobia, a specific phobia that is sometimes called *social anxiety disorder,* is a fear of being negatively evaluated by others. It includes being afraid of public speaking, speaking up in class, meeting new people, and eating in front of others. About 1 in 8 people will experience social phobia at some point in their lifetimes, and around 7 percent are experiencing social phobia at any given time (Ruscio et al., 2008). It is one of the earliest forms of mental disorder to develop, often beginning around age 13; and the more social fears a person has, the more likely he or she is to develop other disorders, particularly depression and substance abuse problems. Indeed, assessment must consider the overlap between social phobia and related disorders to make an informed diagnosis (Stein & Stein, 2008; **FIGURE 14.14**).

GENERALIZED ANXIETY DISORDER   Whereas the anxiety in phobic disorders has a specific focus, the anxiety in **generalized anxiety disorder (GAD)** is diffuse and always present. People with this disorder are constantly anxious and worry incessantly about even minor matters (Sanderson & Barlow, 1990). They even worry about being worried! Because the anxiety is not focused, it can occur in response to almost anything, so the sufferer is constantly on the alert for problems. This hypervigilance results in distractibility, fatigue, irritability, and sleep problems, as well as headaches, restlessness, light-headedness, and muscle pain. Just under 6 percent of the population is affected by this disorder at some point in their lives, though women are more often diagnosed than men (Kessler et al., 1994; Kessler & Wang, 2008).

PANIC DISORDER   Panic disorder affects an estimated 3 percent of the population in a given year, and women are twice as likely to be diagnosed as men (Kessler

generalized anxiety disorder (GAD)
A diffuse state of constant anxiety not associated with any specific object or event.

& Wang, 2008). **Panic disorder** involves sudden and overwhelming attacks of terror that seemingly come out of nowhere or are cued by external stimuli or internal thought processes. Panic attacks typically last for several minutes, during which the victim begins to sweat and tremble; feels his or her heart racing, feels short of breath, and feels chest pain; and may feel dizzy and light-headed, with numbness and tingling in the hands and feet. People experiencing panic attacks often feel that they are going crazy or that they are dying, and those who suffer from persistent panic attacks attempt suicide much more frequently than those in the general population (Fawcett, 1992; Korn et al., 1992; Noyes, 1991). People who experience panic attacks during adolescence are especially likely to develop other anxiety disorders, such as posttraumatic stress disorder (PTSD) and generalized anxiety disorder, in adulthood (Goodwin et al., 2004).

A related disorder is **agoraphobia,** a fear of being in situations in which escape is difficult or impossible (e.g., being in a crowded shopping mall) to the extent that being in such situations causes panic attacks. People who suffer from agoraphobia avoid going into open spaces or to places where there might be crowds. In extreme cases, sufferers may feel unable to leave their homes, in part because they fear having a panic attack in public:

> Ms. Watson began to dread going out of the house alone. She feared that while out she would have an attack and would be stranded and helpless. She stopped riding the subway to work out of fear she might be trapped in a car between stops when an attack struck, preferring instead to walk the 20 blocks between her home and work. She also severely curtailed her social and recreational activities—previously frequent and enjoyed—because an attack might occur, necessitating an abrupt and embarrassing flight from the scene. (Spitzer, Skodol, Gibbon, & Williams, 1983)

This description demonstrates the clear links between panic attacks and agoraphobia. Indeed, agoraphobia without panic is quite rare (Kessler & Wang, 2008).

OBSESSIVE-COMPULSIVE DISORDER   Affecting 1 percent to 2 percent of the population, **obsessive-compulsive disorder (OCD)** involves frequent intrusive thoughts and compulsive actions (Kessler & Wang, 2008). It is more common in women than men and generally begins in early adulthood (Robins & Regier, 1991; Weissman et al., 1994). *Obsessions* are recurrent, intrusive, and unwanted thoughts or ideas or mental images; they often include fear of contamination, of accidents, or of one's own aggression (**FIGURE 14.15**). *Compulsions* are particular acts that the OCD patient feels driven to perform over and over again. The most common compulsive behaviors are cleaning, checking, and counting. For instance, a person might continually check to make sure a door is locked, because of an obsession that his or her home might be invaded, or a person might engage in superstitious counting to protect against accidents, such as counting the number of telephone poles while driving. Those with OCD anticipate catastrophe and loss of control. However, as opposed to those who suffer from other anxiety disorders, who fear what might happen to them, those with OCD fear what they might do or might have done, and checking is the only way to calm the anxiety:

> While in reality no one is on the road, I'm intruded with the heinous thought that I *might* have hit someone . . . a human being! God knows where such a fantasy comes from. . . . I try to make reality chase away this fantasy. I reason, "Well, if I hit someone while driving, I would have *felt* it." This brief trip into reality helps the pain dissipate . . . but only for a second. . . . I start ruminating, "Maybe I did hit someone and didn't realize it. . . . Oh my God! I might have killed somebody! I have to go back and check." (Rapoport, 1990, pp. 22–27)

panic disorder An anxiety disorder characterized by sudden, overwhelming attacks of terror.

agoraphobia An anxiety disorder marked by fear of being in situations in which escape may be difficult or impossible.

obsessive-compulsive disorder (OCD) An anxiety disorder characterized by frequent intrusive thoughts and compulsive actions.

FIGURE 14.15 Howie Mandel The comedian Howie Mandel is a diagnosed sufferer of obsessive-compulsive disorder. Like many people with OCD, Mandel suffers from mysophobia, or the fear of germs. He has admitted that his trademark shaved head helps him with this problem, as it makes him feel cleaner. Mandel even built a second, sterile house, to which he can retreat if he feels he might be contaminated by anyone around him.

Anxiety Disorders Have Cognitive, Situational, and Biological Components

Although the behavioral manifestations of anxiety disorders can be quite different, they share some causal factors (Barlow, 2002). *Cognitive factors* make up one group. For example, when presented with ambiguous or neutral situations, anxious individuals tend to perceive them as threatening, whereas nonanxious individuals assume they are nonthreatening (Eysenck, Mogg, May, Richards, & Matthews, 1991; for an example, see **FIGURE 14.16**). Anxious individuals also focus excessive attention on perceived threats (Rinck, Reinecke, Ellwart, Heuer, & Becker, 2005). They thus recall threatening events more easily than nonthreatening events, exaggerating their perceived magnitude and frequency.

In addition to cognitive components, *situational factors* play a role in the development of anxiety disorders. As discussed in Chapter 6, monkeys develop a fear of snakes if they observe other monkeys responding to snakes fearfully. Similarly, a person could develop a fear of flying by observing another person's fearful reaction to the closing of cabin doors. Such a fear might then generalize to other enclosed spaces, resulting in claustrophobia. *Biological factors* also seem important in the development of anxiety disorders; recent investigations have resulted in a number of exciting findings. For instance, as noted in Chapter 13, children who have an inhibited temperamental style are usually shy and tend to avoid unfamiliar people and novel objects. These inhibited children will more likely have anxiety disorders later in life (Fox, Henderson, Marshall, Nichols, & Ghera, 2005) and are especially at risk for developing social phobia (Biederman et al., 2001). In one study, adults who had been categorized as inhibited before age two received brain scans while viewing pictures of familiar faces and of novel faces. Compared with adults who had been categorized as uninhibited before age two, the inhibited group showed greater activation of the amygdala, a brain region involved when people are threatened, while viewing the novel faces (Schwartz, Wright, Shin, Kagan, & Rauch, 2003). This finding suggests that some aspects of childhood temperament are preserved in the adult brain (**FIGURE 14.17**). To understand these factors more fully, we need to examine the causes of obsessive-compulsive disorder.

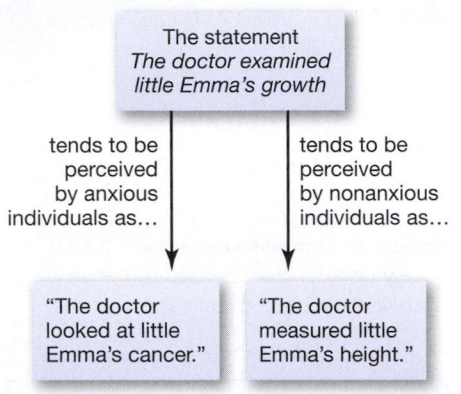

FIGURE 14.16 Anxiety Disorders Anxious individuals tend to perceive ambiguous situations as threatening.

FIGURE 14.17 Scientific Method: Inhibition and Social Anxiety

Hypothesis: People who had an inhibited temperamental style as children will more likely have anxiety disorders later in life.

Research Method:

1 Adults who were categorized as inhibited during their second year of life, and adults who were categorized as uninhibited before age two, received brain scans while viewing pictures of familiar faces and of novel faces.

2 Two areas of the brain were more activated by novel faces—the amygdala (marked "Amy") and the occipitotemporal cortex (marked "OTC"), a brain region active when people see faces.

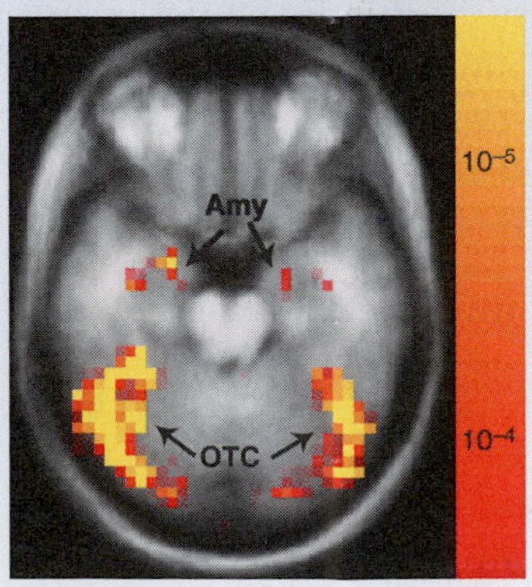

Results: When shown the novel faces, the inhibited group showed greater activation of the amygdala, a brain region involved when people are threatened.

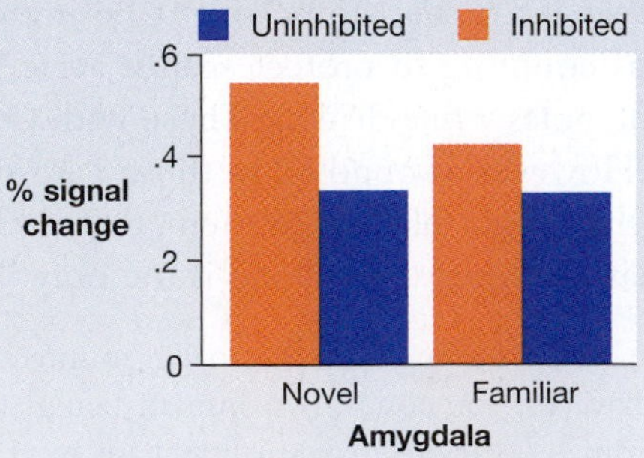

Conclusion: Biological factors seem to play an important role in the development of anxiety disorders.

A paradoxical aspect of OCD is that people are aware that their obsessions and compulsions are irrational, yet they are unable to stop them. One explanation is that the disorder results from conditioning. Anxiety is somehow paired to a specific event, probably through classical conditioning, and the person engages in behavior that reduces anxiety and therefore is reinforced through operant conditioning. This reduction of anxiety is reinforcing and increases the person's chance of engaging in that behavior again. For example, say you are forced to shake hands with someone who has a bad cold, and you have just seen him wiping his nose with his right hand. Shaking that hand might cause you to be anxious or uncomfortable because you do not want to get sick yourself. As soon as the pleasantries are over, you run to the bathroom and wash your hands. You feel relieved. You have just paired hand washing with a reduction in anxiety, thus increasing the chances of hand washing in the future. (This example is rendered as a flowchart in **FIGURE 14.18**.)

There is good evidence that the etiology of OCD is in part genetic (Crowe, 2000). Indeed, various behavioral genetics methods, such as twin studies, have shown that OCD runs in families. Although the specific mechanism has not been identified, evidence points to genes that control the neurotransmitter glutamate, which (as noted in Chapter 3) is the major excitatory transmitter in the brain, causing increased neural firing (Pauls, 2008).

Brain imaging has provided some evidence regarding which brain systems are involved in OCD. The caudate, a brain structure involved in suppressing impulses, is smaller and has structural abnormalities in people with OCD (Baxter, 2000). Moreover, PET studies show abnormal activity in the thalamus and caudate of those with OCD compared to those of controls (Saxena, Maulik, Sharan, Levav, & Saraceno, 2004; **FIGURE 14.19**). In addition, patients with diseases in this area of the brain often have symptoms of OCD. Because this region is involved in impulse suppression, dysfunction in this region may result in the leak of impulses into consciousness. The prefrontal cortex, which is involved in conscious control of behavior, then becomes overactive in an effort to compensate (Whiteside, Port, & Abramowitz, 2004; Yucel et al., 2007). As discussed in Chapter 15, deep brain electrical stimulation of the caudate has been successful in alleviating the symptoms of OCD, providing additional evidence that this brain structure is involved in OCD (Aouizerate et al., 2004).

Growing evidence also indicates that OCD sometimes can be triggered by environmental factors. In particular, a streptococcal infection apparently can cause a severe form of OCD in some young children. Originally identified in 1998 by Susan Swedo and her colleagues at the National Institute of Mental Health, this syndrome strikes virtually overnight, as children suddenly display odd symptoms of OCD such as engaging in repetitive behaviors, developing irrational fears and obsessions, and having facial tics. Researchers have speculated that an autoimmune response damages the caudate, thereby producing the symptoms of OCD (Snider & Swedo, 2004). Treatments that enhance the immune system have been found to diminish the symptoms of OCD in children with this syndrome. Why some children are susceptible to this autoimmune response is unknown.

Most likely, biological and cognitive-behavioral factors interact to produce the symptoms of OCD. A dysfunctional caudate allows impulses to enter consciousness, and these impulses may give rise to the obsessions of OCD. The prefrontal cortex becomes overactive in an attempt to compensate, thereby establishing associations between obsessions and behaviors that reduce the anxiety arising from the obsessions. These behaviors thus become compulsions through conditioning.

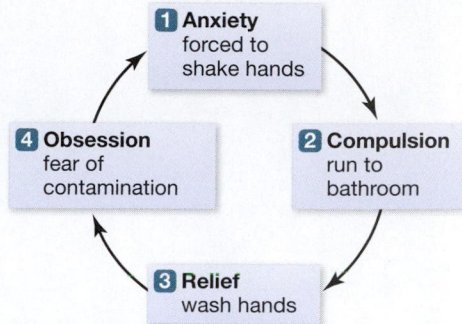

FIGURE 14.18 OCD Cycle Classical conditioning (here, step 1) and operant conditioning (steps 2–3) may contribute to a person's developing OCD (step 4).

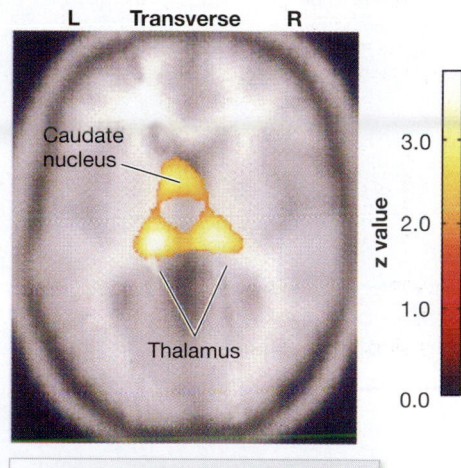

This PET scan shows abnormal activity in the thalamus and caudate brain regions of an OCD patient.

FIGURE 14.19 OCD Brain Scan

"Is the Itsy Bitsy Spider obsessive-compulsive?"

Are Mood Disorders Extreme Manifestations of Normal Moods?

Our moods color every aspect of our lives. When we are happy, the world seems like a wonderful place, and we are filled with boundless energy. When we are sad, we view the world in a decidedly less rosy light, feeling hopeless and isolated. Few of us, however, experience these symptoms day after day until they disrupt our ability to work, learn, and play. In addition, although it is easy to imagine how periods of sadness can interfere with daily life, periods of excessive elation can be equally devastating.

There Are Different Types of Mood Disorders

Mood disorders reflect extreme emotions: Depressive disorders feature persistent and pervasive feelings of sadness, and bipolar disorders involve radical fluctuations in

Real World PSYCHOLOGY

mood. Although some of their characteristics overlap, the two categories represent fundamentally different disorders.

DEPRESSIVE DISORDERS Depressive disorders can be major or less severe. To be diagnosed with **major depression,** a person must have one of two symptoms: depressed (often irritable) mood or loss of interest in pleasurable activities. In addition, the person must have other symptoms such as appetite and weight changes, sleep disturbances, loss of energy, difficulty concentrating, feelings of self-reproach or guilt, and frequent thoughts of death and suicide. The following excerpt is from a case study of a 56-year-old woman diagnosed with depression:

> She described herself as overwhelmed with feelings of guilt, worthlessness, and hopelessness. She twisted her hands almost continuously and played nervously with her hair. She stated that her family would be better off without her and that she had considered taking her life by hanging herself. She felt that after death she would go to hell, where she would experience eternal torment, but that this would be a just punishment. (Andreasen, 1984, p. 39)

Although feelings of depression are relatively common, only long-lasting episodes that impair a person's life are diagnosed as mood disorders. Major depression affects about 6 percent to 7 percent of people in a given 12-month period, whereas approximately 16 percent of people will experience major depression at some point in their lives (Kessler & Wang, 2008). Although major depression varies in severity, those who receive a diagnosis are highly impaired by the condition, and it tends to persist over time for them, often lasting for many years (Kessler, Merikangas, & Wang, 2007). Women are nearly twice as likely to be diagnosed with major depression as men are (Kessler et al., 2003).

Unlike major depression, **dysthymia** is of mild to moderate severity. Those diagnosed with dysthymia, approximately 2 percent to 3 percent of the population, must have a depressed mood most of the day, more days than not, for at least two years. However, the depression is not severe enough to merit a diagnosis of major depression. Periods of dysthymia last from 2 to 20 or more years, although the typical duration is about 5 to 10 years. Because the depressed mood is so long-lasting, some psychological scientists consider it a personality disorder rather than a mood disorder. The distinction among a depressive personality, dysthymic disorder, and major depression is unclear. In fact, they may be points along a continuum rather than distinct disorders. In support of this view, researchers have found that dysthymia often precedes major depression (Lewinsohn, Allen, Seeley, & Gotlib, 1999; Lewinsohn, Rodhe, Seeley, & Hops, 1991).

Depression is so prevalent that it is sometimes called the common cold of mental disorders. In its most severe form, depression is the leading cause of disability in the United States and worldwide (Worley, 2006). The stigma associated with this disorder has especially dire consequences in developing countries, where people do not take advantage of the treatment options because they do not want to admit to being depressed. Depression is the leading risk factor for suicide, which claims approximately a million lives annually around the world and is among the top three causes of death for people between 15 and 35 years of age (Insel & Charney, 2003). One way to combat the stigma of mental disorders is to focus attention on their high incidence and to educate more people about effective treatments (see Chapter 15, "Treating Disorders of the Mind and Body").

Although many people suffer from depression, twice as many women as men suffer from it across multiple countries and contexts (Ustun, Ayuso-Mateos, Chatterji, Mathers, & Murray, 2004). In fact, suicide is the leading cause of death

major depression A disorder characterized by severe negative moods or a lack of interest in normally pleasurable activities.

dysthymia A form of depression that is not severe enough to be diagnosed as major depression.

FIGURE 14.20 Depression An elderly woman sells produce on the street in Temuco, Chile.

bipolar disorder A mood disorder characterized by alternating periods of depression and mania.

FIGURE 14.21 Kay Redfield Jamison Jamison was able to overcome her crippling bipolar disorder to succeed as a teacher, researcher, and author.

among young women in India and China (Khan, 2005), and the highest rates of depression are found in women in developing countries, with especially high rates reported for women in rural Pakistan (Mumford, Saeed, Ahmad, Latif, & Mubbashar, 1997).

Why are the rates of depression so much higher for women than men? Some researchers have suggested that women's multiple roles in most societies as wage earners and family caregivers cause stress that results in increased incidence of depression, but other researchers have pointed out the health benefits of having multiple roles, such as being a wife, mother, and employee (Barnett & Hyde, 2001). Thus it is not multiple roles per se but more likely overwork and lack of support that contribute to the high rate of depression in women. Research in India, Brazil, and Chile shows that low income, lack of education, and difficult family relationships contribute to mental disorders in women (Blue & Harpham, 1996; **FIGURE 14.20**).

Furthermore, men present symptoms in a way that is more in line with the male gender role. For example, when men are distressed they will more likely abuse alcohol and other drugs and engage in violent and risky behaviors, including unsafe sexual practices, because having a disorder can make men feel as though they are admitting to weakness (Doyal, 2001). One theory is that women respond to stressful events by "internalizing" their feelings, which leads to depression and anxiety, whereas men "externalize" with alcohol, drugs, and violence (Holden, 2005).

BIPOLAR DISORDERS   Although we all experience variations in moods, normal fluctuations from sadness to exuberance seem minuscule compared to the extremes experienced by those with **bipolar disorder.** This disorder previously was known as manic depression, because those who are diagnosed with the disorder have periods of major depression but also experience episodes of mania. *Manic episodes* are characterized by elevated mood, increased activity, diminished need for sleep, grandiose ideas, racing thoughts, and extreme distractibility. During episodes of mania, heightened levels of activity and euphoria often result in excessive involvement in pleasurable but foolish activities—such as sexual indiscretions, buying sprees, and risky business ventures—that the individual comes to regret once the mania has subsided.

Whereas some sufferers of bipolar disorder experience true manic episodes, others may experience less extreme mood elevations. These *hypomanic episodes* are often characterized by heightened creativity and productivity and can be extremely pleasurable and rewarding; they are not too disruptive in people's lives. Bipolar disorder is much less common than depression; the lifetime prevalence for any type is estimated at around 4 percent (Kessler & Wang, 2008). In addition, whereas depression is more common in women, the prevalence of bipolar disorder is equal in women and men. Bipolar disorder most commonly emerges during late adolescence or early adulthood.

The psychology professor Kay Redfield Jamison acknowledged her own struggles with manic depression in her award-winning memoir, *An Unquiet Mind* (1995; **FIGURE 14.21**). Her work has helped shape the study of the disorder, and her 1990 textbook on manic-depressive disorder, coauthored with Frederick Goodwin, is considered the standard for the field. In *An Unquiet Mind,* Jamison details how as a child she was intensely emotional and occasionally obsessive. When she was 17, she had her first serious bout of what she describes as psychotic, profoundly suicidal depression. Jamison experienced deepening swings from nearly psychotic exuberance to paralyzing depression throughout her undergraduate years. In 1975, after obtaining her Ph.D. in clinical psychology, she joined the UCLA Department of Psychiatry, where she directed the Affective Disorders Clinic. Within months after she began this job, her condition deteriorated dramatically. She began hallucinating and feared that she was losing her mind. This state so terrified her that she sought out a psychiatrist, who quickly diagnosed her as having manic-depressive disorder and prescribed a drug called lithium. (For more about lithium and other treatments for bipolar disorder, see Chapter 15, "Treating Disorders of the Mind and Body.")

One of the unfortunate side effects of lithium is that it blunts positive feelings. Those with bipolar disorder experience profoundly enjoyable highs during their manic phases. Even though patients with bipolar disorder know that lithium helps them, they resent the drug and often refuse to take it. Although lithium has helped Jamison, she also credits the psychological support of her psychiatrist, as well as the support of her family and friends. Jamison has made the point that lithium can rob people of creative energy. In her book *Touched with Fire* (1993), she asks whether lithium would have dampened the genius of those major artists and writers who may have had mood disorders, such as Michelangelo, Vincent van Gogh, Georgia O'Keeffe, Emily Dickinson, and Ernest Hemingway. Jamison demonstrates the strong association between manic depression and artistic genius, and she raises the disturbing question of whether eradicating the disorder would rob society of much great art. Jamison embodies this irony: Her early career benefited from the energy and creativity of her manic phases even as her personal life was threatened by devastating depression.

Mood Disorders Have Cognitive, Situational, and Biological Components

Mood disorders can be devastating. The sadness, hopelessness, and inability to concentrate that characterize major depression can result in the loss of jobs, of friends, and of family relationships. Because of this disorder's profound effects, particularly the danger of suicide, much research has focused on understanding the causes of major depression and treating it. People with bipolar disorder are also at risk for suicide. In addition, errors in judgment during manic episodes can have devastating effects.

Studies of twins, of families, and of adoptions support the notion that depression has a genetic component. Although there is some variability among studies, *concordance rates* (i.e., the percentage of twins who share the same disorder) between identical twins are generally around four times higher than rates between fraternal twins (Gershon, Berrettini, & Goldin, 1989). Thus the genetic contribution to depression is somewhat weaker than the genetic contribution to schizophrenia or to bipolar disorder (Belmaker & Agam, 2008).

Twin studies reveal that the concordance for bipolar disorder in identical twins is more than 70 percent, versus only 20 percent in fraternal, or dizygotic, twins (Nurnberger, Goldin, & Gershon, 1994). In the 1980s, a genetic research study was carried out on the Amish, an ideal population because they keep good genealogical records and few outsiders marry into the community. In addition, substance abuse is virtually nonexistent among Amish adults, so mental disorders are easier to detect. The research results revealed that bipolar disorder ran in a limited number of families and that all of those afflicted had a similar genetic defect (Egeland et al., 1987). However, genetic research suggests that the hereditary nature of bipolar disorder is complex and not linked to just one gene. Current research focuses on identifying genes that may be involved. In addition, it appears that in families with bipolar disorder, successive generations have more severe disorders and earlier age of onset (McInnis et al., 1993; Petronis & Kennedy, 1995). Research on this pattern of transmission may help reveal the genetics of the disorder, but the specific nature of the heritability of bipolar disorder remains to be discovered.

The existence of a genetic component implies that biological factors are involved in depression, and much evidence suggests that major depression involves a deficiency of one or more monoamines. (As discussed in Chapter 3, monoamines are neurotransmitters that regulate emotion and arousal and motivate behavior.) For instance, psychological scientists know that medications that increase the availability of norepinephrine, a monoamine, alleviate depression, whereas those that decrease levels of this neurotransmitter can cause depression. Medications such as Prozac—a *selective serotonin reuptake inhibitor (SSRI)*—selectively increase another monoamine, serotonin, and there is increased interest in understanding the role of this neurotransmitter in mood disorders (Barton et al., 2008; SSRIs and other medications are discussed in Chapter 15). Studies of brain function have suggested that certain neural structures may be involved in mood disorders. Damage to the left prefrontal cortex can lead to depression, but damage to the right hemisphere does not. The brain waves of depressed people show low activity in these same regions in the left hemisphere. Interestingly, this pattern persists in patients who have been depressed but are currently in remission; it therefore may be a kind of biological marker of predisposition to depression.

Biological rhythms also have been implicated in depression. Depressed patients enter REM sleep more quickly and have more of it. In fact, one symptom of depression is excessive sleeping and tiredness. In addition, many people show a cyclical pattern of depression depending on the season. This disorder, known as *seasonal affective disorder (SAD),* results in periods of depression corresponding to the shorter days of winter in northern latitudes.

Although biological factors may play a role in depression, situational factors are also important. A number of studies have implicated life stressors in many cases of depression (Hammen, 2005). Particularly relevant for depression is interpersonal loss, such as the death of a loved one or a divorce (Paykel, 2003). In one classic study, depression was especially likely in the face of multiple negative events (Brown & Harris, 1978). Another study found that depressed patients had more negative life events during the year before the onset of their depression (Dohrenwend, Shrout, Link, Skodol, & Martin, 1986). How an individual reacts to stress, however, can be influenced by interpersonal relationships, which play an extremely important role in depression (Joiner, Coyne, & Blalock, 1999). Regardless of any other factors, relationships contribute to the development of depression, alter people's experiences when depressed, and ultimately may be damaged by the constant needs of the depressed person. Many people report negative reactions to depressed people, perhaps because of their frequent complaining. Over time, people may avoid interactions with those who are depressed, thus initiating a downward spiral by making the depressed people even more depressed (Dykman, Horowitz, Abramson, & Usher, 1991). By contrast, a person who has a close friend or group of friends is less likely to become depressed when faced with stress. This protective factor is not related to the number of friends but to the quality of the friendships: One good friend is more protective than a large number of casual acquaintances.

Cognitive processes also play a role in depression. The psychologist Aaron Beck has proposed that depressed people think negatively about themselves, their situation, and the future, subjects he groups as the *cognitive triad* (Beck, 1967, 1976; Beck, Brown, Seer, Eidelson, & Riskind, 1987; Beck, Rush, Shaw, & Emery, 1979; **FIGURE 14.22**). Depressed people blame misfortunes on personal defects while seeing positive occurrences as the result of luck. Nondepressed people do the opposite. Beck also notes that depressed people make *errors in logic,* such as overgeneralizing based on single events, magnifying the seriousness of bad events, and taking responsibility for bad events that actually have little to do with them.

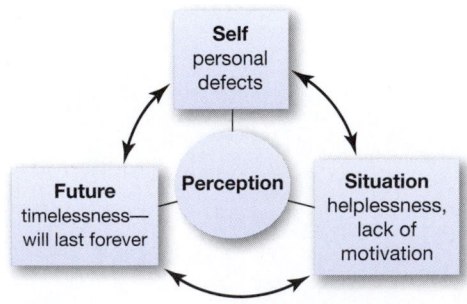

FIGURE 14.22 Cognitive Triad According to Beck, depressed people perceive themselves, situations, and the future negatively.

A second cognitive model of depression is the **learned helplessness model** (Seligman, 1974, 1975), in which people see themselves as unable to have any effect on events in their lives. Martin Seligman's model is based on years of research demonstrating that animals placed in aversive situations they could not escape eventually became passive and unresponsive, lacking the motivation to try new methods of escape when given the opportunity. People suffering from learned helplessness come to expect that bad things will happen to them and believe they are powerless to avoid negative events. The attributions, or explanations, they make for negative events refer to personal factors that are stable and global, rather than to situational factors that are temporary and specific. This attributional pattern leads people to feel hopeless about making positive changes in their lives (Abramson, Metalsky, & Alloy, 1989). The accumulation of evidence suggests that dysfunctional cognitive patterns are a cause rather than a consequence of depression.

learned helplessness model A cognitive model of depression in which people feel unable to control events around them.

> ## SUMMING UP
>
> ### Are Mood Disorders Extreme Manifestations of Normal Moods?
>
> Although everyone experiences both extreme moods and fluctuations in mood, mood disorders are qualitatively different from normal variations in emotion. Mood disorders disrupt a person's ability to function for significant lengths of time, and they are accompanied by a number of psychological and physiological elements. Depressive and bipolar disorders are included in the same *DSM* category and share some behavioral characteristics, but they are distinctly different disorders. Depressive disorders seem to result from various psychological, cognitive, and biological factors, whereas bipolar disorders seem to arise from predominantly biological factors.
>
> ## MEASURING UP
>
> 1. Indicate whether each of the symptoms and causes listed below is associated with major depression, bipolar disorder, or both.
>   a. appetite changes
>   b. disorder caused partly by dysfunctional cognitive patterns
>   c. disorder caused partly by life stressors
>   d. excessive involvement in pleasurable activities
>   e. extreme distractibility
>   f. heightened creativity and heightened productivity
>   g. hereditary component
>   h. loss of interest in pleasurable activities
>   i. racing thoughts
>   j. risk factor for suicide
>   k. sleep disturbances
>   l. typified by extreme emotion
> 2. Which of the following statements represent dysfunctional cognitive patterns believed to cause depression? If a statement is an example of dysfunctional cognition, briefly describe why.
>   a. "I didn't make the soccer team. I fail at everything."
>   b. "I didn't get a raise because I was late to work a number of times over the past quarter."
>   c. "There's nothing I can do about the fact that my boss is so mean to me."
>   d. "This assignment is really hard. I need to go to my instructor's office hours."

What Is Schizophrenia?

LEARNING OBJECTIVES

Distinguish between positive and negative symptoms of schizophrenia.

Identify biological and environmental factors believed to lead to schizophrenia.

schizophrenia A mental disorder characterized by alterations in perceptions, emotions, thoughts, or consciousness.

FIGURE 14.23 Schizophrenia In the 2001 film *A Beautiful Mind,* Russell Crowe plays real-life Princeton mathematics professor and Nobel laureate John Forbes Nash. Nash has suffered from schizophrenia.

positive symptoms Symptoms of schizophrenia, such as delusions and hallucinations, that are excesses in behavior.

negative symptoms Symptoms of schizophrenia marked by deficits in functioning such as apathy, lack of emotion, and slowed speech and movement.

Schizophrenia, which literally means "splitting of the mind," refers to a split between thought and emotion (**FIGURE 14.23**). In popular culture, schizophrenia is often confused with dissociative identity disorder, or split personality, but the two disorders have little in common. Schizophrenia is a *psychotic disorder,* meaning it is characterized by alterations in thoughts, in perceptions, or in consciousness. Current estimates are that between 0.5 percent and 1.0 percent of the population has schizophrenia (Tandon, Keshavan, & Nasrallah, 2008). A recent meta-analysis of 188 studies from 46 countries found similar rates for men and women, roughly 4 to 7 per 1,000 people (Saha, Chant, Welham, & McGrath, 2006). These researchers also found that the rate of schizophrenia was slightly lower in developing nations. Interestingly, the prognosis is better in developing than in developed cultures (Kulhara & Chakrabarti, 2001), perhaps because there is more tolerance for symptoms or greater sympathy for unusual or different people in developing countries. Not all cases of schizophrenia are identical; the disorder has distinct subtypes. Clinicians and researchers rely on lists of symptoms to diagnose these various subtypes of schizophrenia (**TABLE 14.4**).

Schizophrenia Has Positive and Negative Symptoms

For the victim and for the family, schizophrenia is arguably the most devastating mental disorder. It is characterized by a combination of abnormalities—motor, cognitive, behavioral, and perceptual—that result in impaired social, personal, and/or vocational functioning. Some researchers have grouped these characteristics into two categories: **Positive symptoms** are excesses (they are not positive in the sense of being good or desirable), whereas **negative symptoms** are deficits in functioning.

Table 14.4 *DSM-IV* Subtypes of Schizophrenia	
SUBTYPE	**CHARACTERISTICS**
Paranoid type	Preoccupation with delusions or auditory hallucinations. Little or no disorganized speech, disorganized or catatonic behavior, or inappropriate or flat affect.
Disorganized type	All the following—disorganized speech, disorganized behavior, and inappropriate or flat affect—are prominent in behavior, but catatonic-type criteria are not met. Delusions or hallucinations may be present, but only in fragmentary or noncoherent form.
Catatonic type	At least two of the following: extreme motor immobility, purposeless excessive motor activity, extreme negativism (motionless resistance to all instructions) or mutism (refusing to speak), peculiar or bizarre voluntary movement, echolalia.
Undifferentiated type	Does not fit any of the subtypes above, but meets the symptom criteria for schizophrenia.
Residual type	Has experienced at least one episode of schizophrenia, but currently does not have prominent positive symptoms (delusions, hallucinations, disorganized speech or behavior). However, continues to show negative symptoms and a milder variation of positive symptoms (odd beliefs, eccentric behavior).

SOURCE: *Diagnostic and Statistical Manual of the American Psychiatric Association,* 1994.

Table 14.5 Delusions and Associated Beliefs

Persecution	Belief that others are persecuting, spying on, or trying to harm them.
Reference	Belief that objects, events, or other people have particular significance to them.
Grandeur	Belief that they have great power, knowledge, or talent.
Identity	Belief that they are someone else, such as Jesus Christ or the president of the United States.
Guilt	Belief that they have committed a terrible sin.
Control	Belief that their thoughts and behaviors are being controlled by external forces.

POSITIVE SYMPTOMS OF SCHIZOPHRENIA   Delusions and hallucinations are the positive (i.e., excessive) symptoms most commonly associated with schizophrenia. **Delusions** are false beliefs based on incorrect inferences about reality (common types of delusions are listed in **TABLE 14.5**). Delusional people persist in their beliefs despite evidence that contradicts those beliefs. An example of a *paranoid delusion* arose in response to the Domino's Pizza advertising campaign "Avoid the Noid." The Noid was depicted as an elflike creature who turned pizzas cold. In 1989, Kenneth Noid, a 22-year-old man from Georgia, concluded that this ad campaign was directed at him, and in retaliation he took two Domino's employees hostage. The hostages escaped, and Noid surrendered to the police.

Although delusions are characteristic of schizophrenia regardless of the culture, the type of delusion can be influenced by cultural factors (Tateyama et al., 1993). When the delusions of German and Japanese schizophrenia patients were compared, the two groups had similar rates of *delusions of grandeur,* believing themselves much more powerful and important than they really were. However, the two groups differed significantly for other types of delusions. The German patients had delusions involving guilt and sin, particularly as these concepts related to religion. They also suffered from *delusions of persecution,* whereas the Japanese patients had *delusions of harassment,* such as the belief that they were being slandered by others. The types of delusions that schizophrenic people have can also be affected by current events:

> In summer, 1994, mass media in the U.S. reported that North Korea was developing nuclear weapons. At that time, in New York, a middle-age woman with schizophrenia told me that she feared a Korean invasion. In fall, 1995, during a psychiatric interview a young woman with psychotic disorder told me that she had secret connections with the United Nations, the Pope, and O. J. Simpson, and they were helping her. The celebration of the 50th Anniversary of the United Nations, the visit of the Pope to the U.S., and the O. J. Simpson criminal trial were the highly publicized events in the United States at that time. (Sher, 2000, p. 507)

Hallucinations are frequently auditory, although they can also be visual, olfactory, or somatosensory:

> I was afraid to go outside and when I looked out of the window, it seemed that everyone outside was yelling, "kill her, kill her.". . .Things continued to get worse. I imagined that I had a foul body odor and I sometimes took up to six showers a day. I recall going to the grocery store one day, and I imagined that the people in the store were saying "Get saved, Jesus is the answer." (O'Neal, 1984, pp. 109–110)

Auditory hallucinations are often voices that are accusatory, telling the person he or she is evil or inept, or that command the person to do dangerous things. Sometimes

delusions False personal beliefs based on incorrect inferences about reality.

hallucinations False sensory perceptions that are experienced without an external source.

the person hears a cacophony of sounds with voices intermingled. Although the cause of hallucinations remains unclear, neuroimaging studies suggest hallucinations are associated with activation in cortical areas that process external sensory stimuli. For example, auditory hallucinations accompany increased activation in brain areas activated in normal subjects when they engage in inner speech (Stein & Richardson, 1999). This finding has led to speculation that auditory hallucinations might be caused by a difficulty in distinguishing normal inner speech (i.e., the type we all engage in) from external sounds. Schizophrenics need to learn to ignore the voices in their heads, but doing so is extremely difficult and sometimes impossible.

Loosening of associations, another characteristic associated with schizophrenia, occurs when an individual shifts between seemingly unrelated topics as he or she speaks, making it difficult or impossible for a listener to follow the speaker's train of thought:

> They're destroying too many cattle and oil just to make soap. If we need soap when you can jump into a pool of water, and then when you go to buy your gasoline, my folks always thought they could get pop, but the best thing to get is motor oil, and money. May as well go there and trade in some pop caps and, uh, tires, and tractors to car garages, so they can pull cars away from wrecks, is what I believed in. (Andreasen, 1984, p. 115)

More-extreme cases involve *clang associations*—the stringing together of words that rhyme but have no other apparent link. Such strange speaking patterns make it very difficult for people with schizophrenia to communicate (Docherty, 2005).

Another common symptom of schizophrenia is **disorganized behavior,** such as wearing multiple layers of clothes even on hot summer days. Those with schizophrenia may walk along muttering to themselves, alternating between anger and laughter, or they might pace, wringing their hands as if extremely worried. Those who have *catatonic schizophrenia* might mindlessly repeat words they hear, a behavior called *echolalia;* or they might remain immobilized in one position for hours, with a rigid, masklike facial expression and eyes staring into the distance. Catatonic behavior may be an extreme fear response—akin to how animals respond to sudden dangers—in which the person is literally "scared stiff" (Moskowitz, 2004).

NEGATIVE SYMPTOMS OF SCHIZOPHRENIA A number of behavioral deficits associated with schizophrenia result in patients' becoming isolated and withdrawn. People with schizophrenia often avoid eye contact and seem apathetic; they do not express emotion even when discussing emotional subjects; and they use slowed speech, reduced speech output, and a monotonous tone of voice. Their speech may be characterized by long pauses before answering, failure to respond to a question, or inability to complete an utterance after initiating it. There is often a similar reduction in overt behavior: Patients' movements may be slowed and their overall amount of movement reduced, with little initiation of behavior and no interest in social participation. These symptoms, though less dramatic than delusions and hallucinations, can be equally serious. Negative symptoms are more common in men than women (Raesaenen, Pakaslahti, Syvaelahti, Jones, & Isohanni, 2000) and are associated with a poorer prognosis.

Although the positive symptoms of schizophrenia can be dramatically reduced or eliminated with antipsychotic medications, the negative symptoms often persist. The fact that negative symptoms are more resistant to medications has led researchers to speculate that positive and negative symptoms have different organic causes. Since positive symptoms respond to a class of medications (known as *antipsychotics*) that act on neurotransmitter systems, these symptoms are thought to result from neurotransmitter dysfunction. In contrast, negative symptoms may be

loosening of associations A speech pattern among schizophrenic patients in which their thoughts are disorganized or meaningless.

disorganized behavior Acting in strange or unusual ways, including strange movement of limbs, bizarre speech, and inappropriate self-care, such as failing to dress properly or bathe.

associated with abnormal brain anatomy, since structural brain deficits are not affected by changes in neurochemistry. Some researchers believe that schizophrenia with negative symptoms is a separate disorder from schizophrenia with positive symptoms (Messias et al., 2004).

Schizophrenia Is Primarily a Brain Disorder

Although schizophrenia runs in families, the etiology of the disorder is complex and not well understood. Early theories attributed this disorder to the patients' mothers, who were described as simultaneously accepting and rejecting their children. According to these theories, the mothers' contradictory behavior caused their children to develop schizophrenia. However, genetics plays a role in the development of schizophrenia (**FIGURE 14.24**). If one twin develops schizophrenia, the likelihood of the other's also succumbing is almost 50 percent if the twins are identical but only 14 percent if the twins are fraternal. If one parent has schizophrenia, the risk of a child's developing the disease is 13 percent. If, however, both parents have schizophrenia, the risk jumps to almost 50 percent (Gottesman, 1991). Yet the genetic component of schizophrenia represents a predisposition rather than destiny. If schizophrenia were caused solely by genetics, concordance in identical twins would approach 100 percent. Although this percentage was true for the Genains, the identical quadruplets introduced at the beginning of this chapter, there are marked differences in the severity of the disorder among the four sisters (Mirsky et al., 2000). Because the Genains are nearly identical genetically, the differences in severity of the disorder cannot be accounted for by genetics.

Recent research indicates that those with schizophrenia have rare mutations of their DNA about three to four times more often than do healthy individuals, especially in genes related to brain development and to neurological function (Walsh et al., 2008). These mutations may result in abnormal brain development, which might lead to schizophrenia. No single gene causes schizophrenia, but rather multiple genes likely contribute in subtle ways to the expression of the disorder. Indeed, each of at least two dozen candidate genes might modestly influence the development of schizophrenia (Gottesman & Hanson, 2005). Indeed, researchers recently have theorized that competition between the mother's and father's genes may predispose many forms of mental illness, including schizophrenia (Badcock & Crespi, 2008). That is, the mother's egg and the father's sperm may affect which genes are expressed. Mental disorders may result when this struggle leads to an unbalanced autome.

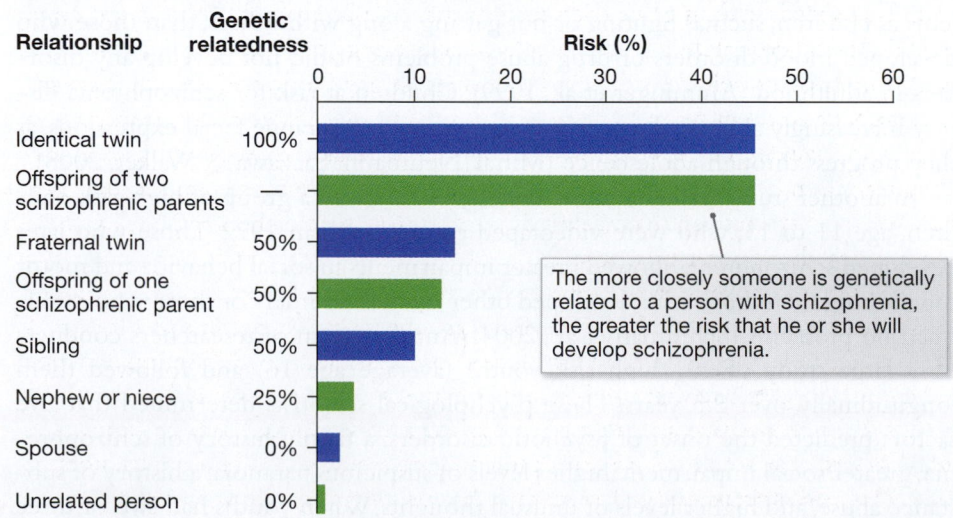

FIGURE 14.24 Genetics and Schizophrenia

Schizophrenia is primarily a brain disorder (Walker, Kestler, Bollini, & Hochman, 2004). The advent of techniques that image both the structure and the function of the brain have documented consistent abnormalities among those with schizophrenia. (On imaging techniques, see Chapter 2, "Research Methodology." On the structure and function of the brain, see Chapter 3, "Biological Foundations.") As seen in structural brain imaging studies, the ventricles are enlarged in schizophrenics, meaning that actual brain tissue is reduced (see Figure 14.9). Moreover, greater reductions in brain tissue are associated with more negative outcomes (Mitelman, Shihabuddin, Brickman, Hazlett, & Buchsbaum, 2005), and longitudinal studies show continued reductions over time (Ho et al., 2003). This reduction of tissue occurs in many regions of the brain, especially the frontal lobes and medial temporal lobes. Moreover, in functional brain imaging studies, typical results indicate reduced activity in frontal and temporal regions (Barch, Sheline, Csernansky, & Snyder, 2003).

Given that abnormalities occur throughout many brain regions in schizophrenics, some researchers have speculated that schizophrenia is more likely a problem of connection between brain regions than the result of diminished or changed functions of any particular brain region (Walker et al., 2004). One possibility is that schizophrenia results from abnormality in neurotransmitters. Since the 1950s, scientists have believed that dopamine may play an important role; drugs that block dopamine activity decrease symptoms, whereas drugs that increase the activity of dopamine neurons increase symptoms. However, evidence from the past two decades has implicated a number of other neurotransmitter systems. More recently, researchers have suggested that schizophrenia might involve abnormalities in the glial cells that make up the myelin sheath (Davis et al., 2003; Moises & Gottesman, 2004). Such abnormalities would impair neurotransmission throughout the brain.

If schizophrenia is a brain disorder, when do these brain abnormalities emerge? Because schizophrenia is most often diagnosed when people are in their twenties or thirties, it is hard to assess whether brain impairments occur earlier in life. New evidence suggests that some neurological signs of schizophrenia can be observed long before the disorder is diagnosed. Elaine Walker and her colleagues have analyzed home movies taken by parents whose children later developed schizophrenia. Compared with their siblings, those who developed the disorder displayed unusual social behaviors, more severe negative emotions, and motor disturbances, all of which often went unnoticed during the schizophrenic's childhood (Walker et al., 2004). One study followed a group of children at risk for developing psychopathology because their parents suffered from a mental disorder. Adults who developed schizophrenia were much more likely to have displayed behavioral problems as children, such as fighting or not getting along with others, than those who developed mood disorders or drug abuse problems or did not develop any disorders in adulthood (Amminger et al., 1999). Children at risk for schizophrenia display increasingly abnormal motor movements, such as strange facial expressions, as they progress through adolescence (Mittal, Neumann, Saczawa, & Walker, 2008).

In another study, Walker and her colleagues followed a group of high-risk children, age 11 to 13, who were videotaped eating lunch in 1972. Those who later developed schizophrenia showed greater impairments in social behavior and motor functioning than those who developed other mental disorders or those who developed no problems (Schiffman et al., 2004). Another team of researchers conducted a large study of 291 high-risk youths (average age 16) and followed them longitudinally over 2.5 years. These psychological scientists determined that five factors predicted the onset of psychotic disorders: a family history of schizophrenia, greater social impairment, higher levels of suspicion/paranoia, a history of substance abuse, and higher levels of unusual thoughts. When youths had two or three of the first three factors, nearly 80 percent of them developed full-blown psychosis (Cannon et al., 2008). These studies suggest that schizophrenia develops over the life course but that obvious symptoms often emerge by late adolescence, and that hints of future problems may be evident even among young children.

Environmental Factors Influence Schizophrenia

Since genetics does not account fully for the onset and severity of schizophrenia, other factors must also be at work. In those at risk for schizophrenia, environmental stress seems to contribute to its development (Walker et al., 2004). A study of adopted children whose biological mothers were diagnosed with schizophrenia found that if the adoptive families were psychologically healthy, none of the children became psychotic, but if the adoptive families were severely disturbed, 11 percent of the children became psychotic and 41 percent had severe psychological disorders (Tienari et al., 1990, 1994).

Some researchers have theorized that the increased stress of urban environments can trigger the onset of the disorder, since being born or raised in an urban area approximately doubles the risk of developing schizophrenia later in life (Torrey, 1999). Others have speculated that some kind of *schizovirus* exists and that living in the close quarters of a big city increases the likelihood of the virus spreading. In support of the virus hypothesis, some researchers have reported finding antibodies in the blood of schizophrenics that are not found in those without the disorder (Waltrip et al., 1997). Moreover, those diagnosed with schizophrenia are more likely to have been born during late winter and early spring (Mednick, Huttunen, & Machon, 1994; Torrey, Torrey, & Peterson, 1977). Mothers of children born in late winter and early spring were in their second trimester of pregnancy during flu season; retrospective studies suggest that the mothers of those with schizophrenia are more likely than other mothers to have contracted influenza during this critical period. During the second trimester, a great deal of fetal brain development occurs, so at that time trauma or pathogens can interfere with the organization of brain regions.

SUMMING UP

What Is Schizophrenia?

Schizophrenia consists of negative and positive symptoms, and it is largely a biological disorder. Twin and adoption studies have highlighted the critical role of genetics in the development of schizophrenia, and recent advances in genetic analysis have yielded more insights into the complexities of this disorder. In addition, research suggests the presence of chemical and anatomical abnormalities in the brains of those afflicted with schizophrenia. Despite all this evidence, however, the specific ways in which genetics, neurochemistry, and brain anatomy contribute to this disorder remain unclear. Also, most researchers agree that environmental factors play a role, but little is known about how environment interacts with biological factors.

MEASURING UP

1. Indicate whether each of the following phenomena is a negative or a positive symptom of schizophrenia.
   a. social withdrawal
   b. flat affect

        c. delusions
        d. hallucinations
        e. slowed motor movement
        f. loosening of associations

    2. Indicate whether each of the following phenomena is a biological or an environmental factor contributing to schizophrenia.
        a. abnormalities in brain function
        b. abnormalities in brain structure
        c. family members' mental health
        d. hereditary predisposition
        e. stress

Are Personality Disorders Truly Mental Disorders?

Personality reflects each person's unique response to environment. Although people change somewhat over time (see Chapter 13, "Personality"), the ways they interact with the world and cope with events are fairly fixed by the end of adolescence. Some people interact with the world in maladaptive and inflexible ways; when this style of interaction is long-lasting and causes problems in work and in social situations, it becomes a *personality disorder*. All of us at some point likely have exhibited certain symptoms of personality disorders. We might be indecisive, self-absorbed, or emotionally unstable. Indeed, personality disorders are relatively common, affecting just under 1 in 10 people (Lenzenweger, Lane, Loranger, & Kessler, 2007); but those with true personality disorders consistently behave in maladaptive ways, show a more extreme level of maladaptive behavior, and experience more personal distress and more problems as a result of their behavior.

Personality Disorders Are Maladaptive Ways of Relating to the World

Whereas the other disorders discussed in this chapter are classified on Axis I of Table 14.1, personality disorders are classified on Axis II, along with mental retardation. Personality disorders and mental retardation are grouped together because they usually last throughout the life span with no expectation of significant change.

The personality disorders generally are divided into three groups, as listed in **TABLE 14.6**. People with the first group of disorders display odd or eccentric behavior. *Paranoid, schizoid,* and *schizotypal* personality disorders are included in this group. Such individuals are often reclusive and suspicious, and they have difficulty forming personal relationships because of their strange behavior and aloofness. The second group—*histrionic, narcissistic, borderline,* and *antisocial* personality disorders—is characterized by dramatic, emotional, and erratic behaviors. Borderline and antisocial personality disorders have been the focus of much research, and they are considered in more detail in the following sections. The third group of personality disorders—*avoidant, dependent,* and *obsessive-compulsive*—involves anxious or fearful behaviors. Although this group shares some characteristics of anxiety disorders, these personality disorders refer more to a general way of interacting with others and of responding to events. For instance, a person with an obsessive-compulsive personality disorder may be excessively neat and orderly, always eating the same food at

Table 14.6 Personality Disorders and Associated Characteristics

Odd or Eccentric Behavior

Paranoid	Tense, guarded, suspicious; holds grudges.
Schizoid	Socially isolated, with restricted emotional expression.
Schizotypal	Peculiarities of thought, appearance, and behavior that are disconcerting to others; emotionally detached and isolated.

Dramatic, Emotional, or Erratic Behavior

Histrionic	Seductive behavior; needs immediate gratification and constant reassurance; rapidly changing moods; shallow emotions.
Narcissistic	Self-absorbed; expects special treatment and adulation; envious of attention to others.
Borderline	Cannot stand to be alone; intense, unstable moods and personal relationships; chronic anger; drug and alcohol abuse.
Antisocial	Manipulative, exploitive; dishonest; disloyal; lacking in guilt; habitually breaks social rules; childhood history of such behavior; often in trouble with the law.

Anxious or Fearful Behavior

Avoidant	Easily hurt and embarrassed; few close friends; sticks to routines to avoid new and possibly stressful experiences.
Dependent	Wants others to make decisions; needs constant advice and reassurance; fears being abandoned.
Obsessive-compulsive	Perfectionistic; overconscientious; indecisive; preoccupied with details; stiff; unable to express affection.

precisely the same time, perhaps reading a newspaper in a particular order each time. This pattern becomes problematic only when it interferes with the person's life, as in making it impossible to travel or to maintain relationships.

Personality disorders remain controversial in modern clinical practice for several reasons. First, personality disorders appear to be extreme versions of normal personality traits, again demonstrating the continuum between what is considered normal versus abnormal. For example, indecisiveness is characteristic of obsessive-compulsive personality disorder, but the *DSM* does not define the degree to which someone must be indecisive to be diagnosed as obsessive-compulsive. Second, there is overlap among the traits listed as characteristic of different personality disorders, so the majority of people diagnosed with one personality disorder also meet the criteria for another (Clark, 2007). This overlap suggests that the categories may not be mutually exclusive and that fewer types of personality disorders may exist than are listed in the *DSM*. Also, some aspects of personality disorders are less stable over time than has been assumed.

Personality disorders may not seem to affect daily life as much as do some of the Axis I disorders (clinical diagnoses) discussed in this chapter, such as schizophrenia or bipolar disorder. However, although people with personality disorders do not hallucinate or experience radical mood swings, their ways of interacting with the world can have serious consequences. The following in-depth consideration of borderline personality disorder and antisocial personality disorder illustrates the devastating effect of these disorders on the individual, family and friends, and society.

Borderline Personality Disorder Is Associated with Poor Self-Control

borderline personality disorder
A personality disorder characterized by identity, affective, and impulse disturbances.

Borderline personality disorder, characterized by disturbances in identity, in affect, and in impulse control, was officially recognized as a diagnosis in 1980. The term *borderline* was initially used because these patients were considered on the border between normal and psychotic (Knight, 1953). The wide variety of clinical features of this disorder reflects its complexity (see **TABLE 14.7**). Approximately 1 percent to 2 percent of adults meet the criteria for borderline personality disorder (Lenzenweger et al., 2007; Swartz, Blazer, George, & Winfield, 1990; Torgerson, Kringlen, & Cramer, 2001); it is more than twice as common in women as in men.

People with borderline personality disorder seem to lack a strong sense of self. They cannot tolerate being alone and have an intense fear of abandonment. Because they desperately need an exclusive and dependent relationship with another person, they can be very manipulative in their attempts to control relationships, as shown in the following example:

> A borderline patient periodically rented a motel room and, with a stockpile of pills nearby, would call her therapist's home with an urgent message. He would respond by engaging in long conversations in which he "talked her down." Even as he told her that she could not count on his always being available, he became more wary of going out evenings without detailed instructions about how he could be reached. One night the patient couldn't reach him due to a bad phone connection. She fatally overdosed from what was probably a miscalculated manipulation. (Gunderson, 1984, p. 93)

In addition to problems with identity, borderline individuals have affective disturbances. Emotional instability is paramount, with sudden episodes—of depression, anxiety, anger, and irritability—that can last from a few hours to a few days. Shifts from one mood to another usually occur with no obvious precipitating cause, as is evident in the therapist Molly Layton's description of her patient Vicki:

> She had chronic and debilitating feelings of emptiness and paralyzing numbness, during which she could only crawl under the covers of her bed and hide. On these days, she was sometimes driven to mutilate her thighs with scissors. Although highly

---

Table 14.7 Clinical Features of Borderline Personality Disorder

A person having at least five of these characteristics might be considered to have borderline personality disorder.

1. Employment of frantic efforts to avoid real or imagined abandonment.

2. Unstable and intense interpersonal relationships.

3. Persistent and markedly disturbed, distorted, or unstable sense of self (e.g., a feeling that one doesn't exist or that one embodies evil).

4. Impulsiveness in such areas as sex, substance use, crime, and reckless driving.

5. Recurrent suicidal thoughts, gestures, or behavior.

6. Emotional instability, with periods of extreme depression, irritability, or anxiety.

7. Chronic feelings of emptiness.

8. Inappropriate intense anger or lack of control of anger (e.g., loss of temper, recurrent physical fights).

9. Transient, stress-related paranoid thoughts or severe dissociative symptoms.

SOURCE: *Diagnostic and Statistical Manual of the American Psychiatric Association*, 1994.

accomplished as a medical student and researcher, who had garnered many grants and fellowships, she would sometimes panic and shut down in the middle of a project, creating unbearable pressures on herself to finish the work. While she longed for intimacy and friendship, she was disablingly shy around men. (Layton, 1995, p. 36)

The third hallmark of borderline personality disorder is impulsivity, which can include sexual promiscuity, physical fighting, and binge eating and purging. As was the case with Vicki, however, self-mutilation is most commonly associated with this disorder. Cutting and burning of the skin are typical, as well as a high risk for suicide. Some evidence indicates that those with borderline personality disorder have diminished capacity in the frontal lobes, which normally help control behavior (Silbersweig et al., 2007).

Evidence from twin studies strongly suggests that borderline personality disorder has a genetic component (Skodol et al., 2002). Rates of mood disorders in the families of borderline patients also tend to be high, and these patients often show sleep abnormalities characteristic of depression. One possible reason that borderline personality disorder and affective disorders such as depression may be linked is that both appear to involve the neurotransmitter serotonin. Evidence has linked low serotonin levels to the impulsive behavior seen in borderline personality disorder (Skodol et al., 2002).

Borderline personality disorder may also have an environmental component, as a strong relationship exists between the disorder and trauma or abuse (Lieb, Zanarini, Schmahl, Linehan, & Bohus, 2004). Some studies have reported that 70 percent to 80 percent of patients with borderline personality disorder have experienced physical or sexual abuse or observed some kind of extreme violence. Other theories implicate early interactions with caretakers. Borderline patients may have had caretakers who did not accept them or were unreliable or unavailable. The constant rejection and criticism made it difficult for the individuals to learn to regulate emotions and understand emotional reactions to events (Linehan, 1987). An alternative theory is that caregivers encouraged dependence and therefore borderline patients did not adequately develop a sense of self. They become extremely sensitive to others' reactions, and if they are rejected, they reject themselves.

Antisocial Personality Disorder Is Associated with a Lack of Empathy

In the 1800s, the term *psychopath* was coined to describe people who seem willing to take advantage of and to hurt others without any evidence of concern or of remorse (Koch, 1891). In his classic 1941 book the *Mask of Sanity,* the psychiatrist Hervey Cleckley described characteristics of psychopathic individuals from his clinical experience, such as that they could be superficially charming and rational; be insincere, unsocial, and incapable of love; lack insight; and be shameless. In 1980, the *DSM* dropped the label *psychopath,* which was seen as pejorative, and adopted **antisocial personality disorder (APD).** This change has led to confusion because the two terms are overlapping but not identical. APD is the catchall diagnosis for individuals who behave in socially undesirable ways, such as breaking the law, being deceitful and irresponsible, and feeling a lack of remorse for their behavior. Those with this disorder tend to be hedonistic, seeking immediate gratification of wants and needs without any thought of others.

Psychopaths display the extreme version of APD. They are pathological in their degree of callousness and are particularly dangerous. For instance, one study of murderers found that those with psychopathic tendencies nearly always killed

antisocial personality disorder
A personality disorder marked by a lack of empathy and remorse.

intentionally—to gain something they wanted, such as money, sex, or drugs—whereas those without psychopathic tendencies were much more likely to commit murder impulsively, when provoked or angry (Woodworth & Porter, 2002). Psychopaths fit the stereotype of cold-blooded killers, such as Jeffrey Dahmer, Dennis Rader (the BTK strangler), and Gary Gilmore (**FIGURE 14.25**), who was executed for the murder he describes here:

> I went in and told the guy to give me the money. I told him to lay on the floor and then I shot him. I then walked out and was carrying the cash drawer with me. I took the money and threw the cash drawer in a bush and I tried to push the gun in the bush, too. But as I was pushing it in the bush, it went off and that's how come I was shot in the arm. It seems like things have always gone bad for me. It seems like I've always done dumb things that just caused trouble for me. I remember when I was a boy I would feel like I had to do things like sit on a railroad track until just before the train came and then I would dash off. Or I would put my finger over the end of a BB gun and pull the trigger to see if a BB was really in it. Sometimes I would stick my finger in water and then put my finger in a light socket to see if it would really shock me. (Spitzer et al., 1983, p. 66–68)

ASSESSMENT AND CONSEQUENCES Antisocial personality disorder is much more common in men than in women (Robins & Regier, 1991), with estimates varying from 1 percent to 4 percent of the population, and with those displaying psychopathic traits being more infrequent (Compton, Conway, Stinson, Colliver, & Grant, 2005; Lenzenwegger et al., 2007). The disorder is most apparent in late adolescence and early adulthood, and it generally improves around age 40 (Hare, McPherson, & Forth, 1988), at least for those without psychopathic traits. According to the diagnostic criteria, APD cannot be diagnosed before age 18, but the person must have displayed antisocial conduct before age 15. This stipulation ensures that only those with a lifetime history of antisocial behaviors can be diagnosed with antisocial personality disorder. They also must meet criteria such as repeatedly performing illegal acts, repeatedly lying or using aliases, and showing reckless disregard for their own safety or others' safety. Because many such individuals are quite bright and highly verbal, they can talk their way out of bad situations. In any event, punishment seems to have very little effect on them (Lykken, 1957, 1995), and they often repeat the problem behaviors a short time later.

Perhaps as much as 50 percent of the prison population meets criteria for antisocial personality disorder (Hare, 1993; Widiger & Corbitt, 1995). Because of the prevalence of the disorder in the prison population, much of the research on antisocial personality disorder has been conducted in this setting. One researcher, however, came up with an ingenious way of finding research participants outside of prison. She put the following advertisement in a counterculture newspaper: "Wanted: charming, aggressive, carefree people who are impulsively irresponsible but are good at handling people and at looking after number one. Send name, address, phone, and short biography proving how interesting you are to . . ." (Widom, 1978, p. 72). Seventy-three people responded, about one-third of whom met the criteria for antisocial personality disorder. These individuals were then interviewed and given a battery of psychological tests. Their characteristics proved very similar to those of prisoners diagnosed with antisocial personality disorder, except that the group that responded to the ad had avoided imprisonment. Indeed, these findings fit Cleckly's view of those with psychopathic traits as often being charming and intelligent. Lacking remorse, willing to lie or cheat, and lacking empathy, some psychopaths manage to be successful professionals and to elude detection for

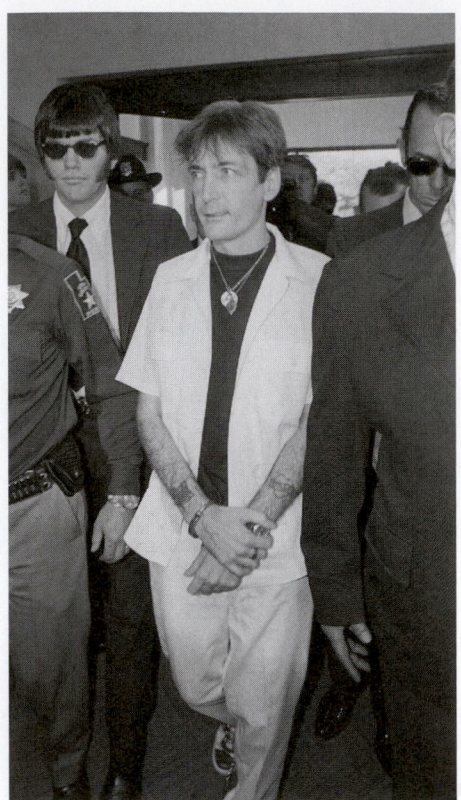

FIGURE 14.25 Gary Gilmore after His Arrest Under the *DSM-IV,* Gilmore would have been given a diagnosis of antisocial personality disorder.

In 1899, a separate justice system for juveniles was founded in the United States, based on the premise that developmental differences existed between youths and adults. More recently, however, rising violent juvenile crime has caused the separation of the two justice systems to erode, such that many states are now trying juveniles in criminal courts and putting them in prison with adults. When a judge decides whether a juvenile will stand trial in an adult court, he or she considers the juvenile's potential for future violence and the possible success of treatment or rehabilitation in the juvenile system. But how can a judge predict which juveniles will be repeat offenders and which can be rehabilitated?

Among adults, one robust predictor of criminal violence is psychopathy (Salekin, Rogers, & Sewell, 1996), and psychopaths are more likely to commit additional violent offenses after release from incarceration (Harris, Rice, & Cormier, 1991; Heilbrun, et al., 1998); the same seems to be true among adolescents. Psychopathy in both childhood (psychopathic tendencies) and adulthood involves both callous-unemotional traits—such as lack of empathy, lack of guilt, and shallow emotions—and overt antisocial behavior (Blair, 2001). Children who show antisocial behavior early on are at great risk for antisocial and criminal behavior in adulthood (Moffitt, 2003). Callous-unemotional traits may be a risk factor that makes children vulnerable for long-term persistent serious antisocial behavior (Frick, 1998) that is often predatory in nature (Hart & Hare, 1997).

One problem for diagnosis is that normal adolescent behavior shares some characteristics with psychopathy—such as impulsivity and sensation seeking, as well as deficits in judgment, in long-range planning, in perspective taking, and in empathy—but the traits that indicate adolescent psychopathy are more serious variants or more extreme ones. A normal adolescent may score high on one or two traits, but those who fall into the psychopathy range score high on several traits at once. The leading measure of adult psychopathy is the *Psychopathy Checklist-Revised (PCL-R)*, developed by Robert Hare (2003), and a version of this test for youths, the *PCL-YV*, has also been developed. While normally developing youths typically score less than 5 on the *PCL-YV*, the average score of a young offender is at least 20 (Forth, Kosson, & Hare, 2003). In fact, the *PCL-YV* has been shown to be good at predicting general and violent recidivism in the short term, and a 10-year retrospective study showed that high scores were associated with an increased likelihood of violent offenses and a shorter time between testing and the first violent offense (Gretton, Hare, & Catchpole, 2004).

Do all children with psychopathic traits turn into adult psychopaths? How stable are these traits over time? A study that examined the link between childhood psychopathy and adult psychopathy found that boys who were high in psychopathy at age 13 tended to remain high at age 24, and no moderating factors the researchers investigated appeared to reduce future psychopathy among those at high risk. However, boys who were low in psychopathy at age 13 were influenced by environmental factors: Those who had grown up in wealthier families, had fewer antisocial peers, and had less physical punishment remained low in psychopathy, while those who had grown up poorer, had antisocial friends, and had more physical punishment became more psychopathic over time (Lynam, Loeber, & Stouthamer-Loeber, 2008). A three-year study of moderately aggressive 9-year-olds also found a relatively stable pattern, except that the children with better social functioning had decreased psychopathic characteristics over time. Apparently, some children have stable psychopathic traits that carry on into adulthood, but others do not, and further research may improve psychologists' ability to distinguish the two types of children.

If we can identify psychopathic adolescents, can they be prevented from committing crimes? One study has shown modest success over a two-year period in an intensive treatment program of repeat offenders, which resulted in relatively slower and lower rates of repeated crimes, although the level was still high (Caldwell, Skeem, Salekin, & Van Rybroek, 2006).

Is it ethical to screen children with conduct disorders for psychopathy, given that they may be receptive to treatment and that certain environmental factors can improve or worsen the disorder? Should children with psychopathic tendencies be watched more closely? If so, by whom? Should their parents receive special counseling and training? Finally, should scores on the *PCL-YV* be used to determine the sentences for adolescents who commit violent crimes, such that those with high scores would be tried through the adult rather than the juvenile criminal justice system?

crimes they may commit. Their psychopathic traits may even provide advantages in some occupations, such as business and politics.

THE CAUSES OF ANTISOCIAL PERSONALITY DISORDER In 1957, David Lykken reported that psychopaths do not become anxious when subjected to aversive stimuli. He and other investigators have continued this line of work, showing that such individuals do not seem to feel fear or anxiety (Lykken, 1995). Electroencephalogram (EEG) examinations have demonstrated that criminals who meet the criteria for antisocial personality disorder have slower alpha-wave activity (Raine, 1989). This finding indicates a lower overall level of arousal and may explain why these people engage in sensation-seeking behavior, as well as why they do not learn from punishment—because of their low arousal, they do not experience punishment as particularly aversive. This pattern of reduced psychophysiological response in the face of punishment also occurs in adolescents at risk for developing psychopathy (Fung et al., 2005). In addition, there is evidence of amygdala abnormalities in those with antisocial tendencies, such as having a smaller amygdala and being less responsive to negative stimuli (Blair, 2003). Deficits in frontal-lobe functioning have also been found and may account for the lack of forethought and the inability to consider the implications of actions characteristic of antisocial personality disorder (Seguin, 2004).

Evidence indicates that genetic and environmental factors are important for antisocial personality disorder, although genetics may be more important for psychopathy. Identical twins have a higher concordance of criminal behavior than do fraternal twins (Lykken, 1995), although the research just cited did not rule out the role of shared environment. A large study of 14,000 adoptions (Mednick, Gabrielli, & Hutchings, 1987) found that adopted male children had a higher rate of crime if their biological fathers had criminal records. In addition, the greater the criminal record of the biological father, the more likely that the adopted son engaged in criminal behavior. Although genes may be at the root of antisocial behaviors and psychopathy, factors such as low socioeconomic status, dysfunctional families, and childhood abuse may also be important. Indeed, malnutrition at age 3 has been found to predict antisocial behavior at age 17 (Liu, Raine, Venables, & Mednick, 2004). An enrichment program for children that included a structured nutrition component was associated with less criminal and antisocial behavior 20 years later (Raine, Mellingen, Liu, Venables, & Mednick, 2003). This finding raises the possibility that malnutrition or other, similar environmental factors might contribute to the development of antisocial personality disorder.

 SUMMING UP

Are Personality Disorders Truly Mental Disorders?

Personality disorders are diagnosed along a different axis from that of the other mental disorders discussed thus far. Personality disorders are not considered clinical disorders, yet they can have devastating effects on the individual, the family, and society. Borderline personality disorder is characterized by disturbances in identity, in affect, and in impulse control. Those with the disorder often have a history of abuse or rejection by caregivers. Those with antisocial personality disorder are hedonistic and sensation seeking, and lack empathy for others. Although the outward symptoms of these disorders are not as severe as those of some clinical disorders, they are highly resistant to change and can cause significant personal and societal problems.

MEASURING UP

The *DSM-IV* groups together seemingly different disorders—such as borderline personality disorder, antisocial personality disorder, and mental retardation. What features of these disorders justify this grouping? Check all that apply.

   a. They last throughout the life span.
   b. They likely will change with appropriate intervention.
   c. There is no expectation of significant change.
   d. These are all clinical disorders.

Should Childhood Disorders Be Considered a Unique Category?

In his classic text on the classification of mental disorders, published in 1883, Emil Kraepelin did not mention childhood disorders. The first edition of the *DSM,* published 70 years later, essentially considered children small versions of adults, and consequently it did not consider childhood disorders separately from adulthood disorders. Currently, in response to the belief that cognitive, emotional, and social abilities should be considered in the context of the individual's developmental state, the *DSM* has a category in Axis I called "disorders usually first diagnosed in infancy, childhood, or adolescence." This category includes a wide range of disorders, from those affecting only circumscribed areas of a child's world, such as reading disorders and stuttering, to those affecting every aspect of a child's life, such as autism, attention–deficit/hyperactivity disorder, and others listed in **TABLE 14.8**.

LEARNING OBJECTIVES

Identify three categories of deficits exhibited by children with autism.

Describe differences in brain structure and brain function among people with and without attention-deficit/hyperactivity disorder.

Table 14.8 Childhood Disorders

DISORDER	DESCRIPTION
Attention-deficit/hyperactivity	A pattern of hyperactive, inattentive, and impulsive behavior that causes social or academic impairment.
Autism	Characterized by unresponsiveness; impaired language, social, and cognitive development; and restricted and repetitive behavior.
Elimination disorders	The repeated passing of feces or urination in inappropriate places by children from whom continence should be expected.
Learning disorders	Marked by substantially low performance in reading, mathematics, or written expression with regard to what is expected for age, amount of education, and intelligence.
Mental retardation	Characterized by below-average intellectual functioning (IQ lower than 70) and limited adaptive functioning that begins before age 18.
Rumination disorder	The repeated regurgitation and rechewing of partially digested food, not related to nausea or gastrointestinal disorder.
Selective mutism	Failure to speak in certain social situations, despite the ability to speak in other situations; interferes with social or academic achievement.
Tourette's disorder	Recurrent motor and vocal tics that cause marked distress or impairment and are not related to a general medical condition.

Despite the variety of disorders in this category, they should all be considered within the context of knowledge about normal childhood development. Some symptoms of childhood mental disorders are extreme manifestations of normal behavior or are actually normal behaviors for children at an earlier developmental stage. Bedwetting, for example, is normal for two-year-olds but not for 10-year-olds. Other behaviors, however, deviate significantly from normal development. Two disorders of childhood, autism and attention-deficit/hyperactivity disorder, are explored here as illustrations.

Autism Is a Lack of Awareness of Others

Autism is characterized by deficits in social interaction, by impaired communication, and by restricted interests (Volkmar, Chawarska, & Klin, 2005). Autism was first described in 1943 by Leo Kanner, who was struck by the profound isolation of some children and coined the term *early infantile autism*. Approximately 3 to 6 children out of 1,000 show signs of autism, and autistic males outnumber autistic females 3 to 1 (Muhle, Trentacoste, & Rapin, 2004). From 1991 to 1997, there was a dramatic increase of 556 percent in the number of children diagnosed with autism (Stokstad, 2001), likely due to a greater awareness of symptoms by parents and physicians and a willingness to apply the diagnosis to a wider spectrum of behaviors (Rutter, 2005). In other words, the notion that autism is epidemic overstates reality. Indeed, the psychological scientist Morton Ann Gernsbacher and her colleagues have identified several serious problems with studies that claim huge increases in cases of autism (Gernsbacher, Dawson, & Goldsmith, 2005). Recognizing how changing criteria may alter diagnosis rates underscores the value of critical thinking in understanding important health issues.

Autism varies in severity, from mild social impairments to severe social and intellectual impairments. *Asperger's syndrome* is high-functioning autism, in which children of normal intelligence have deficits in social interaction, reflecting an underdeveloped theory of mind. As discussed in Chapter 11, theory of mind is both the understanding that other people have mental states and the ability to predict their behavior accordingly. Perhaps the most famous person with Asperger's is Temple Grandin, an accomplished scientist who now designs humane slaughterhouse facilities (Grandin, 1995). Although extremely intelligent, she has great difficulty understanding the subtle social motives and the behaviors of other humans, and she finds it easier to relate to animals. Grandin understands the environment from an animal's point of view, which allows her to design facilities that are calming.

CORE SYMPTOMS OF AUTISM Children with severe autism are seemingly unaware of others. As babies, they do not smile at their caregivers, do not respond to vocalizations, and may actively reject physical contact with others. Autistic children do not establish eye contact and do not use their gazes to gain or direct the attention of those around them. One group of researchers had participants view video footage of autistic children's first birthdays to see if characteristics of autism could be detected before the children were diagnosed (Osterling & Dawson, 1994). By considering only the number of times a child looked at another person's face, the participants correctly classified the children as autistic or normal 77 percent of the time (**FIGURE 14.26**). Thus, as with schizophrenia, early signs of autism may be overlooked, probably because they are within the broad bounds of what is normal at a young age.

Deficits in communication are the second major cluster of behaviors characteristic of autism. Such deficits are evident by 14 months of age among children

autism A developmental disorder involving deficits in social interaction, impaired communication, and restricted interests.

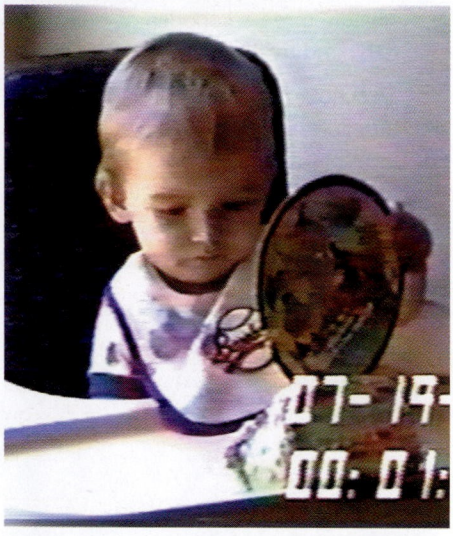

(a)

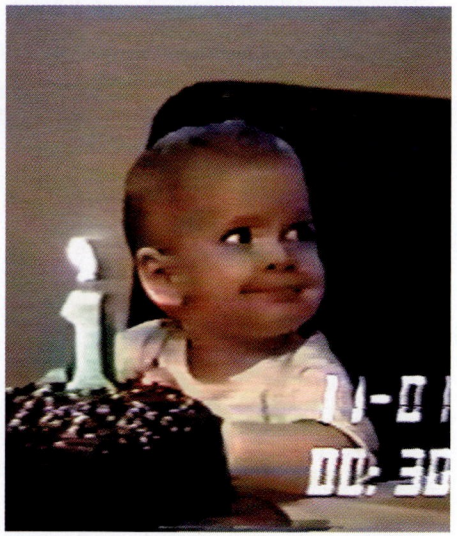

(b)

FIGURE 14.26 Scenes from Videotapes of Children's Birthday Parties (a) This child focused more on objects than on people and was later diagnosed with autism. **(b)** This child developed normally.

who subsequently are diagnosed with autism (Landa, Homan, & Garrett-Mayer, 2007). Autistic children show severe impairments in verbal and nonverbal communication. Even if they vocalize, it is often not with any intent to communicate. Autistics who develop language usually exhibit odd speech patterns, such as echolalia and *pronoun reversal*. Echolalia, mentioned earlier as a symptom of catatonia, involves the repetition of words or phrases, sometimes including an imitation of the intonation and sometimes using a high-pitched monotone. Pronoun reversal, in which autistic children replace "I" with "you," may be related to echolalia, but normal children also reverse pronouns as they learn language. For example, a preschooler might say "pick you up" when he wants to be picked up. Even if autistic children cease being echolalic, their pronoun confusion often persists beyond the years of basic language-learning. Those who develop functional language also often interpret words literally, use language inappropriately, and lack verbal spontaneity.

A third category of deficits includes restricted activities and interests. Although autistic children appear oblivious to people around them, they are acutely aware of their surroundings. Although most children automatically pay attention to the social aspects of a situation, those with autism may focus on seemingly inconsequential details (Klin, Jones, Schultz, & Volkmar, 2003; **FIGURE 14.27**). Any changes in daily routine or in the placement of furniture or of toys are very upsetting and can result in extreme agitation and tantrums. Also, autistic children's play tends to be repetitive and obsessive, with a focus on objects' sensory aspects. They may smell and taste objects, or spin and flick them for visual stimulation. Similarly, their own behavior tends to be repetitive, with strange hand movements, body rocking, and hand flapping. Self-injury is common, and some children must be forcibly restrained to keep them from hurting themselves.

Area focused on by an autistic two-year-old

FIGURE 14.27 Toddler Viewer with Autism A two-year-old with autism focuses on the unimportant details in the scene rather than on the social interaction.

CRITICAL THINKING SKILL

Recognizing and Resisting Hindsight Bias

As the saying goes, hindsight is 20/20, because we can see clearly how events occurred after they happen. Indeed, after an event occurs, we frequently have an inflated idea of the extent to which we "saw it coming." This tendency is *hindsight bias,* also called the "I knew it all along" bias (Christensen-Szalanski & Wilham, 1991; Fischhoff, 1975). Once we know something is true, we feel we knew it all along—or that someone else should have.

Hindsight bias operates in all sorts of contexts. For example, if you break up with your girlfriend or boyfriend, your close friends may tell you they saw it coming. If you learn that a neighbor's child has been diagnosed as autistic, you might look back at the child's infant behaviors and conclude that the problem should have been recognized much earlier.

Hindsight bias can operate on a larger scale as well. In newspaper commentaries after a disaster, such as a bridge collapse or a landslide after a heavy rain, experts and laypeople alike point out that they knew this would happen—and, by extension, that the government authorities were negligent because they did not act before the disaster to prevent it. Whenever

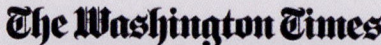

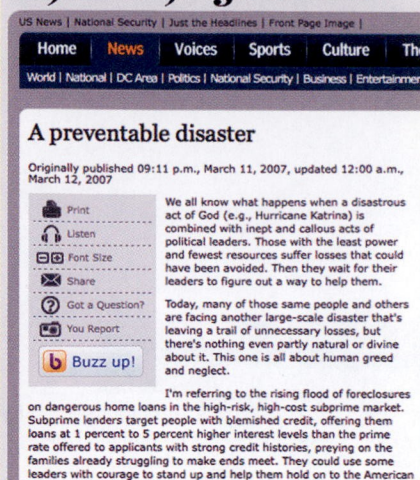

A preventable disaster

Originally published 09:11 p.m., March 11, 2007, updated 12:00 a.m., March 12, 2007

We all know what happens when a disastrous act of God (e.g., Hurricane Katrina) is combined with inept and callous acts of political leaders. Those with the least power and fewest resources suffer losses that could have been avoided. Then they wait for their leaders to figure out a way to help them.

Today, many of those same people and others are facing another large-scale disaster that's leaving a trail of unnecessary losses, but there's nothing even partly natural or divine about it. This one is all about human greed and neglect.

I'm referring to the rising flood of foreclosures on dangerous home loans in the high-risk, high-cost subprime market. Subprime lenders target people with blemished credit, offering them loans at 1 percent to 5 percent higher interest levels than the prime rate offered to applicants with strong credit histories, preying on the families already struggling to make ends meet. They could use some leaders with courage to stand up and help them hold on to the American dream of homeownership.

FIGURE 14.28 Think Critically: Recognizing and Resisting Hindsight Bias When we already know the outcome of an event, it is important to recognize the limits of what was known or could have been known before the event.

you hear people discussing the causes of an event after it happened and how obvious the conclusion should have been, remember to recognize the limits of what was known or could have been known before the event occurred. You will judge your own behaviors more accurately and those of others more charitably if you take this perspective after events occur (**FIGURE 14.28**).

AUTISM IS PRIMARILY A BIOLOGICAL DISORDER   Kanner, one of the first scientists to study autism, believed it was an innate disorder exacerbated by cold and unresponsive mothers, whom he called "ice box mothers" or "refrigerator mothers." He described the parents of autistic children as insensitive, meticulous, introverted, and highly intellectual. This view is given little credence today, as it is now well established that autism is the result of undetermined biological factors. Genetic studies of autism have been hampered by the rarity of the disorder and by the fact that autistic persons rarely marry and almost never have children. Despite the limited genetic research, there are indications that the disorder has a strong hereditary component (Muhle et al., 2004). If one child in a family is autistic, the probability of a second also being diagnosed is anywhere from 2 percent to 9 percent (Jorde et al., 1990; Szatzmari et al., 1993). Although this probability is relatively low, it is significantly higher than the estimated 0.4 percent prevalence of the disorder in the population at large. If two siblings are autistic, the chance of a third sharing the same diagnosis jumps to 35 percent. A number of studies have found concordance rates in twins to be 70 percent to 90 percent for identical twins and 10 percent for fraternal twins (Bailey et al., 1995; Steffenburg et al., 1989).

Research into the causes of autism points to prenatal and/or neonatal events that may result in brain dysfunction. The brains of children with autism grow unusually large during the first two years of life, and then growth slows until age five (Courchesne et al., 2007; Courchesne, Redcay, & Kennedy, 2004). Their brains also do not develop normally during adolescence (Amaral, Schumann, & Nordahl, 2008). Researchers are investigating genetic and nongenetic factors that might explain this overgrowth/undergrowth pattern. That some mothers of autistic children have bled significantly during the second trimester of pregnancy suggests trauma during the critical period for brain development. Autistic children also have a higher rate of neonatal complications such as apnea (periods when breathing stops or is reduced), seizures, and delay in breathing. Moreover, autistic children are more likely to have minor physical anomalies, such as digestive problems and unusually shaped ears, to be the product of a first pregnancy, and to be born to an older mother (Gilberg, 1980).

Three exciting new developments may help focus future autism research. A deficit in oxytocin, a neuropeptide involved in social behavior, may be related to some of the behavioral manifestations of autism. Mice lacking oxytocin behave normally, except that they cannot recognize other mice or their mother's scent; a single dose of oxytocin cures them (Ferguson et al., 2000). In one study, autistic adults who received injections of oxytocin showed a dramatic improvement in their symptoms (Novotny et al., 2000). Such injections seem particularly useful for reducing repetitive behaviors (e.g., repeating the same phrase), questioning, inappropriate touching, and self-injury (Hollander et al., 2003). A second recent finding suggests that levels of four proteins in the blood are elevated in 97 percent of autistic children and in 92 percent of retarded children, but in none of the healthy controls. These elevated protein levels were found in blood samples taken at birth, and all four proteins are involved in brain development (Nelson et al., 2001). These proteins may be involved in the pattern of overgrowth and undergrowth of the brain for those with autism. However, whether these proteins are influenced by genetic or environmental factors and what role they play in the development of autism are matters for future research.

In recent research, investigators found abnormal antibodies in the blood of the mothers of 11 percent of children with autism but not in a large sample of mothers with healthy children or mothers of children with other developmental disorders (Braunschweig et al., 2008). Following up on this study, the psychological scientist David Amaral and his colleagues injected four pregnant rhesus monkeys with the antibody from the mothers of autistic children. All the offspring of these monkeys demonstrated unusual behaviors characteristic of autism, such as repetitive movements and hyperactive limb movements (Martin et al., 2008). None of the offspring of monkeys injected with normal antibodies from mothers of healthy children showed this unusual behavior.

Attention-Deficit/Hyperactivity Disorder Is a Disruptive Impulse Control Disorder

> A hyperactive child's mother might report that he has difficulty remembering not to trail his dirty hand along the clean wall as he runs from the front door to the kitchen. His peers may find that he spontaneously changes the rules while playing Monopoly or soccer. His teacher notes that he asks what he is supposed to do immediately after detailed instructions were presented to the entire class. He may make warbling noises or other strange sounds that inadvertently disturb anyone nearby. He may seem to have more than his share of accidents—knocking over the tower his classmates are erecting, spilling his cranberry juice on the linen tablecloth, or tripping over the television cord while retrieving the family cat—and thereby disconnecting the set in the middle of the Super Bowl game. (Whalen, 1989)

Although these symptoms can seem humorous in the retelling, the reality is a different story. Children with **attention-deficit/hyperactivity disorder (ADHD)** are restless, inattentive, and impulsive. They need to have directions repeated and rules explained over and over. Although these children are often friendly and talkative, they can have trouble making and keeping friends because they miss subtle social cues and make unintentional social mistakes. Many of these symptoms are exaggerations of typical toddler behavior; thus the line between normal and abnormal behavior is hard to draw, and as many as 50 percent of mothers of four-year-old boys believe their sons are hyperactive (Varley, 1984).

THE ETIOLOGY OF ADHD Although estimates vary widely, the best available evidence for children in the United States is that 11 percent of boys and 4 percent of girls have ADHD (Bloom & Cohen, 2007). The causes of the disorder are unknown; one of the difficulties in pinpointing the etiology is that ADHD is most likely a heterogeneous disorder. In other words, the behavioral profiles of children with ADHD vary, so the causes of the disorder most likely vary as well. Children with ADHD may be more likely than other children to come from disturbed families. Factors such as poor parenting and social disadvantage may contribute to the onset of symptoms, as is true for all mental disorders.

ADHD clearly has a genetic component: Concordance is estimated at 55 percent in identical twins and 32 percent in fraternal twins (Goodman & Stevenson, 1989; Sherman, McGue, & Iacono, 1997). In an imaging study, Zametkin and his colleagues (1990) found that adults who had been diagnosed with ADHD in childhood had reduced metabolism in brain regions involved in self-regulation of

attention-deficit/hyperactivity disorder (ADHD) A disorder characterized by restless, inattentive, and impulsive behaviors.

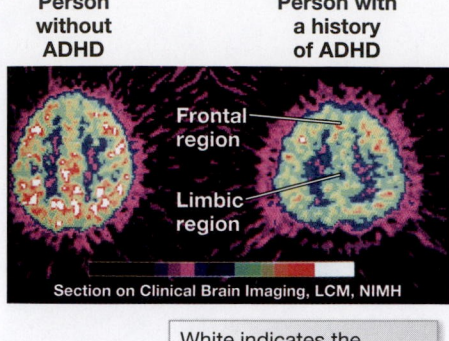

Person without ADHD **Person with a history of ADHD**

Frontal region

Limbic region

Section on Clinical Brain Imaging, LCM, NIMH

White indicates the highest level of activation.

FIGURE 14.29 ADHD and the Brain The brain image of a person with a history of ADHD shows lesser overall activation (at the red and white levels), especially in the frontal and limbic regions.

FIGURE 14.30 Living with ADHD Paula Luper, of North Carolina, was diagnosed with ADHD in elementary school. Here, as a senior in high school, she is taking a quiz in the teachers lounge to avoid distraction.

motor functions and of attentional systems (**FIGURE 14.29**). These researchers postulated that the connection between the frontal lobes and the limbic system is impaired in ADHD patients. The symptoms of ADHD are similar to those seen in patients with frontal-lobe damage: problems with planning, sustaining concentration, using feedback, and thinking flexibly. Other imaging studies have found prefrontal abnormalities when adolescents with ADHD perform tasks that require inhibiting motor responses. Greater impairments in performance on the tasks are associated with abnormal activation of these prefrontal regions (Schulz et al., 2004). Current research continues to focus on the frontal lobes (Barkely, 1997; Neidemeyer & Naidu, 1997) but also implicates subcortical structures. In particular, researchers have demonstrated differences in the basal ganglia in the brains of some ADHD patients (Aylward, Reiss, Reader, & Singer, 1996; Castellanos, Giedd, Eckberg, & Marsh, 1998; Fillipek et al., 1997). Because this region is involved in regulating motor behavior and impulse control, dysfunction in these structures could contribute to the hyperactivity characteristic of ADHD (**FIGURE 14.30**).

ADHD ACROSS THE LIFE SPAN Children generally are not given diagnoses of ADHD until they enter structured settings in which they must conform to rules, get along with peers, and sit in seats for long periods. In the past, these things happened when children entered school, between ages five and seven. Now, with the increasing prevalence of structured day-care settings, the demands on children to conform are occurring much earlier. Although it is reasonable to expect a six-year-old to sit quietly and share crayons, it is probably unrealistic to expect the same of a three-year-old. Many preschoolers considered inattentive and overactive by their parents and teachers are simply going through a normal developmental stage that will not become the persistent pattern of ADHD. Certain characteristics distinguish children who go on to develop ADHD from those who do not. For example, infants who are later diagnosed with ADHD have difficulty establishing regular patterns for eating and sleeping (Ross & Ross, 1982). Toddlers exhibit excessive activity and temperamental behavior quite early in life (Hartsough & Lambert, 1985). They are very curious and engage in vigorous play, and consequently they are quite accident prone. Older children generally do not demonstrate excess motor activity but are instead restless and fidgety (Pelham & Bender, 1982).

It previously was thought that children outgrow ADHD by the time they enter adulthood. Recent longitudinal studies, however, dispute this notion (McGough & Barkley, 2004). Between 30 percent and 80 percent of those with ADHD in childhood continue to show symptoms of the disorder in adulthood (Weiss & Hechtman, 1993). Adults with ADHD symptoms, about 4 percent of the population (Kessler et al., 2006), may struggle academically and vocationally. They generally reach a lower-than-expected socioeconomic level and change jobs more frequently than other adults (Bellak & Black, 1992; Mannuzza et al., 1991). The impact of ADHD on society is apparently greater than previously believed. However, some ADHD patients learn to adapt and are successful in their personal and vocational lives.

>
>
> ## SUMMING UP
>
> ### Should Childhood Disorders Be Considered a Unique Category?
>
> Until recently, children were considered small versions of adults, and mental disorders in children were classified according to adult categories. Currently, disorders in children are considered in the context of normal development. In some cases, mental disorders identified in childhood have lasting impacts on the individual, and

the problems apparent early in life continue throughout maturation. This outcome is clearly the case for autism, in which the social and cognitive characteristics of the disorder deviate significantly from normal childhood development and continue to have a major impact throughout the life span. The impact of childhood ADHD on adult functioning is less certain.

MEASURING UP

1. Children with autism exhibit deficits in which of the following categories?
   a. awareness of other people
   b. communication
   c. craving for frequent changes in environment
   d. impulsivity
   e. restricted activities and interests

2. Compared with people without ADHD, people with ADHD show _____ activation in the _____ of the brain.
   a. less; frontal lobes and limbic regions
   b. less; temporal lobes and Broca's area
   c. more; frontal lobes and limbic regions
   d. more; temporal lobes and Broca's area

CONCLUSION

This book emphasizes the adaptive nature of the human mind, in that the mind solves problems of survival and performs complex functions such as perceiving and remembering. But sometimes the mind fails to work properly, producing maladaptive thoughts, emotions, and behaviors. For instance, people can become too afraid to leave their houses, too depressed to get out of their beds, or so manic that they take dangerous risks. Others hear voices or believe family members are trying to poison them. Sometimes people are incapable of interacting with others.

This chapter has explored the nature and causes of psychopathology. From Freud's time, most mental disorders were viewed as arising from mistreatment by mothers; for instance, autism was (falsely) believed to be the result of cold, uncaring mothers. We now know that biology plays an important role. Indeed, the biological revolution has provided compelling evidence that many mental disorders involve genetic predispositions, abnormalities in neurotransmitter systems, or brains that do not function normally. At the same time, psychological and social factors are implicated in the development and course of most mental disorders. An obvious example is the distorted thought patterns that afflict those with major depression and other mood disorders.

Various environmental factors also contribute to psychopathology. Parental maltreatment can damage children, as was the case with the Genain quadruplets and with those who display multiple identities, but these effects work in conjunction with biological propensities. Prenatal and early childhood factors, such as malnutrition, exposure to toxins and to viruses, and poverty, seem to increase the risk of psychopathology. In addition, the experience of loss or trauma can produce mood disorders among otherwise mentally healthy adults. To understand psychopathology thoroughly, we need to recognize the effects of social, psychological, and biological factors in those who are susceptible. Crossing levels of analysis to understand the causes of mental disorders is especially useful for determining the best ways to treat them, which are discussed in Chapter 15.

■ CHAPTER SUMMARY

How Are Mental Disorders Conceptualized and Classified?

- **Mental Disorders Are Classified into Categories:** The *Diagnostic and Statistical Manual of Mental Disorders* is a multiaxial system for diagnosing groups of symptoms in the contexts of related factors.

- **Mental Disorders Must Be Assessed:** Assessment is the process of examining a person's mental functions and psychological health to make a diagnosis. Assessment is accomplished through interviews, behavioral evaluations, and psychological testing.

- **Dissociative Identity Disorder Is a Controversial Diagnosis:** Also called multiple personality disorder, dissociative identity disorder involves two or more distinct identities within one person. It is a controversial diagnosis because people may fake its symptoms.

- **Mental Disorders Have Many Causes:** Disorders may arise from psychological factors, such as family dynamics or sociocultural context. They may be the result of learned, maladaptive cognitions. Biological factors also underlie mental illness. The diathesis-stress model looks at mental disorders as an interaction among multiple factors. In this model, stressful circumstances may trigger a disorder in an individual with underlying vulnerabilities.

Can Anxiety Be the Root of Seemingly Different Disorders?

- **There Are Different Types of Anxiety Disorders:** Phobias are exaggerated fears of specific stimuli. Generalized anxiety disorder is diffuse and omnipresent. Panic attacks cause sudden overwhelming terror and may lead to agoraphobia. Obsessive-compulsive disorders involve anxiety-related thoughts and behaviors.

- **Anxiety Disorders Have Cognitive, Situational, and Biological Components:** The etiology of OCD involves genetics as well as brain dysfunction. The irrational thoughts that accompany panic attacks may lead to agoraphobia through cognitive-behavioral connections.

Are Mood Disorders Extreme Manifestations of Normal Moods?

- **There Are Different Types of Mood Disorders:** Depressive disorders may be major or bipolar and are more severe than dysthymia.

- **Mood Disorders Have Cognitive, Situational, and Biological Components:** The biological factors of depression include genetics, frontal-lobe functioning, and serotonin modulation, as well as biological rhythms. Negative thinking and poor interpersonal relations also contribute to depression.

What Is Schizophrenia?

- **Schizophrenia Has Positive and Negative Symptoms:** Positive symptoms include excesses, such as delusions and hallucinations. Negative symptoms are deficits in functioning, such as social withdrawal and reduced bodily movement.

- **Schizophrenia Is Primarily a Brain Disorder:** The brains of schizophrenics have larger ventricles and less brain mass, with reduced frontal- and temporal-lobe activation. A variety of neurochemical and neural structural abnormalities exist as well.

- **Environmental Factors Influence Schizophrenia:** Urban environments may trigger the onset of schizophrenia. Trauma or pathogens encountered by pregnant women may increase the likelihood of the disorder in their children.

Are Personality Disorders Truly Mental Disorders?

- **Personality Disorders Are Maladaptive Ways of Relating to the World:** Odd behaviors, extreme emotions, and fearful behaviors are characteristic of personality disorders. Whether some of these extremes are true psychopathologies is controversial.

- **Borderline Personality Disorder Is Associated with Poor Self-Control:** Borderline personality disorder involves disturbances in identity, in affect, and in impulse control. A strong relationship exists between the disorder and both trauma and abuse.

- **Antisocial Personality Disorder Is Associated with a Lack of Empathy:** Antisocial personality disorder is marked by a lack of both empathy and remorse and by a tendency to be manipulative. Both genetics and environment seem to be contributing factors.

Should Childhood Disorders Be Considered a Unique Category?

- **Autism Is a Lack of Awareness of Others:** Autism, a biological disorder, emerges in infancy and is marked by avoidance of eye contact and impairment in verbal and nonverbal communication. Asperger's syndrome is a high-functioning variation of autism. The biological factors involved in autism may include abnormalities in oxytocin, in brain growth, and in blood proteins.

- **Attention-Deficit/Hyperactivity Disorder Is a Disruptive Impulse Control Disorder:** Children with ADHD are restless, inattentive, and impulsive. Its causes may include environmental factors such as poor parenting and social disadvantages; genetic factors; and brain abnormalities, particularly with regard to activation of the frontal lobes and subcortical basal ganglia. ADHD continues into adulthood, presenting challenges to academic work and to career pursuits.

■ KEY TERMS

agoraphobia, p. 633

antisocial personality disorder, p. 651

assessment, p. 621

attention-deficit/hyperactivity disorder (ADHD), p. 659

autism, p. 656

bipolar disorder, p. 638

borderline personality disorder, p. 650

cognitive-behavioral approach, p. 627

delusions, p. 643

diathesis-stress model, p. 625

disorganized behavior, p. 644

dissociative identity disorder (DID), p. 624

dysthymia, p. 637

etiology, p. 620

family systems model, p. 626

generalized anxiety disorder (GAD), p. 632

hallucinations, p. 643

learned helplessness model, p. 641

loosening of associations, p. 644

major depression, p. 637

multiaxial system, p. 620

negative symptoms, p. 642

obsessive-compulsive disorder (OCD), p. 633

panic disorder, p. 633

positive symptoms, p. 642

psychopathology, p. 618

schizophrenia, p. 642

sociocultural model, p. 627

■ PRACTICE TEST

1. Which of the following questions would a clinician ask to determine whether a behavior represents psychopathology? Select all that apply.
   a. Does the behavior deviate from cultural norms?
   b. Is the behavior causing the individual personal distress?
   c. Is the behavior maladaptive?
   d. Is the behavior unusual?
   e. Is the behavior upsetting to members of the client's social network?

2. Two students visit the campus health center. Student A describes feeling constantly fearful and anxious. Student B describes feeling persistently agitated and often exhibiting violent outbursts. Student A's symptom's are consistent with an _____ disorder, which are more common in _____; student B's symptom's are consistent with an _____ disorder, which are more common in _____. Choose from the following pairs of words to fill in the blanks.
   a. externalizing, females; internalizing, males
   b. externalizing, males; internalizing, females
   c. internalizing, females; externalizing, males
   d. internalizing, males; externalizing, females

3. Indicate whether each of the following constellations of symptoms is best described as phobic disorder, generalized anxiety disorder, panic disorder, or obsessive-compulsive disorder.
   a. Harlow is hypervigilant, constantly on the lookout for problems. For example, he tried calling his parents, but the line was busy. He tried again an hour later, but the line was still busy. Harlow jumped to the conclusion that his father must have been home alone, had a heart attack, and tried to dial 911. Although Harlow recognizes that his intense worry over a busy phone line is irrational, he cannot shake the worry.
   b. While hiking a looped path, Susan comes across a snake sunning itself. She considers turning around, but decides not to out of fear she will find another snake and will end up being trapped between two snakes.

4. Indicate whether each of the following constellations of symptoms is best described as major depression, dysthymia, or bipolar disorder.
   a. Claudia has felt a sense of sadness for the past couple years. She seems to function well enough in her daily life, but she always feels glum.
   b. Lorenzo's mother died about a year ago. Since then, he has not found any satisfaction in his hobbies, spends most nights lying awake in bed, and has lost nearly 10 pounds.

5. Match each of the following statements with the correct label for that symptom of schizophrenia: delusion of grandeur, delusion of persecution, flat affect, hallucination, loosening of associations, social withdrawal. Not all labels will be used.
   a. "I sat on the rock dock clock clock clock."
   b. "People from the Central Intelligence Agency are following me; they are out to get me. You and I will need to talk in the elevator so they can't listen in on our conversation."
   c. "The bugs keep crawling on my skin; I wipe them off, but they keep coming."

6. Which of the following statements describe key objections to categorizing personality disorders as true mental disorders? Check all that apply.
   a. If environmental factors contribute to the expression of personality disorders, it makes more sense to label the environment as disordered rather than the person.
   b. Overlap in the characteristics of different disorders suggests that the categories may not be conceptually clear cut.
   c. Some features of personality disorders are not as stable as researchers once thought.
   d. The features of personality disorders are merely extreme versions of normal personality traits.

7. Royce takes swimming lessons at the community pool. He often arrives without all the things he needs for practice, such as his towel, a change of clothes, and goggles. As the teacher instructs the class, Royce often blows bubbles at the water's surface. And although he listens to what the teacher tells him about how to modify his swim strokes, he has difficulty using the suggestions. Based on this description, which of the following disorders does Royce most likely have?
   a. agoraphobia
   b. attention-deficit/hyperactivity disorder
   c. autism
   d. obsessive-compulsive disorder

8. Are females or males more likely to be diagnosed with each of the following disorders?
   a. antisocial personality disorder
   b. attention-deficit/hyperactivity disorder
   c. autism
   d. borderline personality disorder
   e. depression
   f. generalized anxiety disorder
   g. obsessive-compulsive disorder
   h. panic disorder

■ PSYCHOLOGY AND SOCIETY

1. Of the disorders discussed in this chapter, which one do you think would be most difficult to live with, and why? Which one would be most difficult from a family member's perspective? Why?

2. After reading this chapter, (1) identify three things you learned that you find particularly interesting, and explain why; (2) identify your previous misconceptions about mental illness; and (3) describe how a more complete understanding of mental illness will inform your beliefs about and actions toward people with mental illnesses.

The answer key for all the Measuring Up exercises and the Practice Tests can be found at the back of the book.

 Find more review materials online at www.wwnorton.com/psychologicalscience.

Treating Disorders of the Mind and Body

DENNIS WAS A 31-YEAR-OLD INSURANCE SALESMAN. One day, while shopping in a mall with his fiancée, Dennis suddenly felt very sick. His hands began to shake, his vision became blurred, and he felt a great deal of pressure in his chest. He began to gasp and felt weak all over. All of this was accompanied by a feeling of overwhelming terror. Without stopping to tell his fiancée what was happening, he ran from the store and sought refuge in the car. He opened the windows and lay down, and he started to feel better in about 10 minutes. Later, Dennis explained to his fiancée what had happened and revealed that he had experienced this sort of attack before. Because of this, he would often avoid places like shopping malls. At the urging of his fiancée, Dennis agreed to see a psychologist. During his first several treatment sessions, Dennis downplayed his problems, clearly concerned that others might think him crazy. He was also reluctant to rely on medications because of the stigma

---

How Are Mental Disorders Treated?

- Psychotherapy Is Based on Psychological Principles
- Culture Can Affect the Therapeutic Process
- Medication Is Effective for Certain Disorders
- Alternative Biological Treatments Are Used in Extreme Cases
- Pseudotherapies Can Be Dangerous

What Are the Most Effective Treatments?

- Treatments That Focus on Behavior and on Cognition Are Superior for Anxiety Disorders

- Many Effective Treatments Are Available for Depression
- Lithium Is Most Effective for Bipolar Disorder
- Pharmacological Treatments Are Superior for Schizophrenia
- There Are Important Considerations in Selecting a Psychotherapist
- Critical Thinking Skill: Avoiding the Sunk Costs Fallacy

Can Personality Disorders Be Treated?

- Dialectical Behavior Therapy Is Most Successful for Borderline Personality Disorder

- Antisocial Personality Disorder Is Difficult to Treat

How Should Childhood and Adolescent Disorders Be Treated?

- The Use of Medication to Treat Adolescent Depression Is Controversial
- Children with ADHD Can Benefit from Various Approaches
- Critical Thinking Skill: Evaluating Alternatives in Decision Making
- Autistic Children Benefit from a Structured Treatment Approach

attached. He had read about cognitive-behavioral therapy and was interested in trying this approach to address his problem.

The therapist explained that Dennis was experiencing panic attacks combined with agoraphobia. The therapist believed Dennis's problems were the result of vulnerability to stress combined with thoughts and behaviors that exacerbated anxiety. The first step in treatment was therefore relaxation training, to give Dennis a strategy to use when he became anxious and tense. The next step was to modify his maladaptive thought patterns. Dennis kept a diary for several weeks to identify situations in which his distorted thoughts might be producing anxiety, such as meeting with prospective clients. Before meeting with a client, Dennis would become extremely anxious because he felt it would be catastrophic if he was unable to make the sale. With his therapist's help, Dennis came to recognize that being turned down by a client was difficult but manageable and that it was unlikely to have long-term impact on his career. The final phase of treatment was to address Dennis's avoidance of situations that he associated with panic attacks (FIGURE 15.1). Dennis and his therapist constructed a hierarchy of increasingly stressful situations. The first was an easy situation, involving a short visit to a department store on a not-too-crowded weekday morning. Dennis's fiancée accompanied him so that he would feel less vulnerable. After completing this task, he moved on to increasingly difficult situations, using relaxation techniques as necessary to control his anxiety. After six months, therapy was discontinued. Dennis's anxiety levels were significantly reduced, and he was able to make himself relax when he did become tense. In addition, he had not experienced a panic attack during that period and was no longer avoiding situations he previously had found stressful (Oltmans, Neale, & Davison, 1999).

Chapter 14 discussed various mental disorders, including ones like Dennis's. At this time, there are no instant cures for mental disorders. They need to be managed over time through treatment that helps alleviate symptoms so people can function in their daily lives. Scientific research has produced tremendous advances in ways of treating many mental disorders. The choice of treatment depends on both the type of disorder and the needs of the individual suffering from the disorder. As you will learn throughout this chapter, some treatments are more effective than others for certain disorders. Dennis's case illustrates the effectiveness of cognitive-behavioral therapy, a form of psychotherapy that is extremely effective and long-lasting for many mental disorders. Other mental disorders, such as schizophrenia and bipolar disorder, respond best to medications and show little improvement with psychotherapy alone. This chapter explores the basic principles of therapy and describes the various treatment approaches to specific mental disorders.

FIGURE 15.1 Panic Attacks The stress of being in a crowd can bring on a panic attack in someone who has an anxiety disorder.

How Are Mental Disorders Treated?

LEARNING OBJECTIVES

Recognize different styles of psychotherapy.

Describe the uses, mechanisms, and side effects of common psychotropic medications.

psychotherapy The generic name given to formal psychological treatment.

biological therapies Treatment based on medical approaches to illness and to disease.

Research shows that most mental disorders can be treated in more than one way, although often a particular method is most successful for a specific disorder. Psychologists use two basic categories of techniques to treat mental disorders: psychological and biological. The generic name given to formal psychological treatment is **psychotherapy,** but the particular techniques used may depend on the practitioner's training. All forms of psychotherapy involve interactions between practitioner and client aimed at helping the client understand his or her symptoms and problems and providing solutions for them. **Biological therapies** reflect medical approaches to illness and to disease. They are based on the notion that mental disorders result from abnormalities in neural and bodily processes—imbalances in specific neurotransmitters, for example, or malfunctions in certain brain regions.

Treatments range from drugs to electrical stimulation of brain regions to surgical interventions. In particular, *psychopharmacology,* the use of medications that affect brain or body functions, has proved to be effective, at least on a short-term basis. However, one limitation of biological therapies is that long-term success may require the person to continue treatment, sometimes indefinitely. Moreover, sometimes nonbiological treatments are more effective. For many disorders, the recent focus has been on combining biological therapies with other approaches to optimize treatment for each patient.

As outlined in Chapter 14, a number of theories have been proposed to account for psychopathology. These approaches propose treatment strategies based on assumptions about the causes of mental disorders. However, gaining a better understanding of the etiology (i.e., the cause) of a mental disorder does not always provide further insights into how best to treat it. For example, autism clearly is caused by biological factors, but this knowledge has not led to any significant advances in therapies for the disorder. In fact, the best available treatment, as you will discover later in this chapter, is based on behavioral, not biological, principles. Likewise, in a situation where the patient's loss of a parent has led to clinical depression, drugs might be useful for treatment, even though the depression was caused by the situation, not by biological factors.

Psychotherapy Is Based on Psychological Principles

Psychotherapy, regardless of the treatment provider's theoretical perspective, generally is aimed at changing patterns of thought or of behavior. However, the ways in which such changes are effected can differ dramatically—it has been estimated that there are more than 400 approaches to treatment (Kazdin, 1994). The following discussion highlights the major components of the most common approaches and describes how therapists use these methods to treat specific mental disorders. Today, many practitioners use a mix of techniques based on what they believe is best for each client's particular condition. One factor known to affect the outcome of therapy is the relationship between the therapist and the client, in part because a good relationship can foster an expectation of receiving help (Miller, 2000; Talley, Strupp, & Morey, 1990). Most people in the mental health field use the curative power of client expectation to help their patients achieve success in therapy. This approach is not limited to mental disorders, however—a good relationship with a service provider is important for any aspect of physical or mental health.

insight A goal of some types of therapy; a patient's understanding of his or her own psychological processes.

PSYCHODYNAMIC THERAPY FOCUSES ON INSIGHT Among the first people to develop psychological treatments for mental disorders was Sigmund Freud, who believed that such disorders were caused by prior experiences, particularly early traumatic experiences. Along with Josef Breuer, he pioneered the method of psychoanalysis. In early forms of psychoanalysis, the client would lie on a couch while the therapist sat out of view, to reduce the client's inhibitions and allow freer access to unconscious thought processes (**FIGURE 15.2**). Treatment involved uncovering unconscious feelings and drives that, Freud believed, gave rise to maladaptive thoughts and behaviors. Techniques included *free association,* in which the client would say whatever came to mind, and *dream analysis,* in which the therapist would interpret the hidden meaning of the client's dreams. The general goal of psychoanalysis is to increase clients' awareness of these unconscious processes and how they affect daily functioning. With this **insight,** or personal understanding of their own psychological processes (a different use of the term from the one in Chapter 8, where it refers to the sudden solution of a problem), clients are freed

FIGURE 15.2 Psychoanalysis As part of the treatment process, Freud sat behind his desk while his clients lay on the couch facing away from him.

from these unconscious influences, and symptoms disappear. Some of Freud's ideas have since been reformulated; these later adaptations collectively are known as *psychodynamic therapy.* Psychologists who use this approach help people understand why they are distressed by examining their needs, defenses, and motives. Although most proponents of the psychodynamic perspective today have replaced the couch with a chair, they continue to embrace Freud's "talking therapy," though in a more conversational format.

During the past few decades, the use of psychodynamic therapy has become increasingly controversial. Traditional psychodynamic therapy is expensive and time consuming, sometimes continuing for many years. Some psychological scientists question whether psychodynamic treatments are effective for treating serious forms of psychopathology. Some evidence indicates that psychodynamic theory has promise for certain disorders, such as borderline personality disorder (Gibbons, Crits-Chistoph, & Hearon, 2008), but evidence for its effectiveness in treating most mental disorders is weak or absent. A new approach to psychodynamic therapy consists of offering fewer sessions and focusing more on current relationships than on early childhood experiences. Proponents argue that this short-term psychodynamic therapy can be useful for treating psychological disorders including depression, eating disorders, and substance abuse (Leichsenring, Rabung, & Leibing, 2004), although the dropout rates in these studies are extremely high (Winfried & Hofmann, 2008) and it is not clear whether the psychodynamic aspects are superior to other brief forms of therapy, such as simply talking to a caring therapist.

client-centered therapy An empathic approach to therapy; it encourages personal growth through greater self-understanding.

HUMANISTIC THERAPIES FOCUS ON THE WHOLE PERSON As noted in Chapter 13, the humanistic approach to personality emphasizes personal experience and belief systems and the phenomenology of individuals. The goal of humanistic therapy is to treat the person as a whole, not as a collection of behaviors or a repository of repressed thoughts. One of the best-known humanistic therapies is **client-centered therapy,** developed by the psychologist Carl Rogers, which encourages people to fulfill their individual potentials for personal growth through greater self-understanding. A key ingredient of client-centered therapy is to create a safe and comforting setting for clients to access their true feelings. Therapists strive to be empathic, to take the client's perspective, and to accept the client through unconditional positive regard. Instead of directing the client's behavior or passing judgment on the client's actions or thoughts, the therapist helps the client focus on his or her subjective experience, often by using *reflective listening,* in which the therapist repeats the client's concerns to help the person clarify his or her feelings. One current treatment for problem drinkers, known as *motivational interviewing,* uses a client-centered approach over a very short period (such as one or two interviews). Motivational interviewing has proven a valuable treatment for drug and alcohol abuse, as well as for increasing both healthy eating habits and exercise (Burke, Arkowitz, & Menchola, 2003). William Miller (2000) attributes the outstanding success of this brief form of empathic therapy to the warmth expressed by the therapist toward the client. Although relatively few practitioners follow the tenets of humanistic theory strictly, many techniques advocated by Rogers are used currently to establish a good therapeutic relationship between practitioner and client.

COGNITIVE-BEHAVIORAL THERAPY TARGETS THOUGHTS AND BEHAVIORS

Many of the most successful therapies involve trying to change people's behavior and cognition directly. Whereas insight-based therapies consider maladaptive behavior the result of an underlying problem, behavioral and cognitive therapies treat the thoughts and behaviors as the problem and directly target them in therapy. For behavioral therapy, the premise is that behavior is learned and therefore can be unlearned using the principles of classical and operant conditioning (see Chapter 6, "Learning"). Behavior modification, based on operant conditioning, rewards desired behaviors and ignores or punishes unwanted behaviors; however, for desired behavior to be rewarded, the client first must exhibit the behavior. *Social-skills training* is an effective way to elicit desired behavior. When a client has particular interpersonal difficulties, such as with initiating a conversation, he or she learns appropriate ways to act in specific social situations. The first step is often *modeling,* in which the therapist acts out an appropriate behavior. The client is encouraged to imitate this behavior, rehearse it in therapy, and later apply the learned behavior to real-world situations.

Cognitive therapy is based on the theory that distorted thoughts can produce maladaptive behaviors and emotions. Treatment strategies that modify these thought patterns should eliminate the maladaptive behaviors and emotions. A number of approaches to cognitive therapy have been proposed. Aaron T. Beck has advocated **cognitive restructuring,** in which clinicians help their clients recognize maladaptive thought patterns and replace them with ways of viewing the world that are more in tune with reality (**FIGURE 15.3** and **15.4**). Albert Ellis, another major thinker in this area, has introduced *rational-emotive therapy,* in which therapists act as teachers who explain and demonstrate more-adaptive ways of thinking and behaving. In both types of therapies, maladaptive behavior is assumed to result from individual belief systems and ways of thinking rather than from objective conditions. An approach that integrates insight therapy with cognitive therapy is *interpersonal therapy* (Markowitz & Weissman, 1995), which focuses on relationships the client attempts to avoid. Because interpersonal functioning is seen as critical to psychological adjustment, treatment focuses on helping clients express their emotions and explore interpersonal experiences (Blagys & Hilsenroth, 2000).

Perhaps the most widely used version of psychotherapy is **cognitive-behavioral therapy (CBT),** which incorporates techniques from both behavioral therapy and cognitive therapy. CBT tries to correct faulty cognitions and to train the client to engage in new behaviors. For instance, a person with social phobia, who fears negative evaluation, might be taught social skills. At the same time, the therapist helps the client understand how the client's appraisals of other peoples' reactions to him or her might be inaccurate. CBT is one of the most effective forms of psychotherapy for many types of mental disorders, especially anxiety disorders and mood disorders (Deacon & Abromowitz, 2004; Hollon, Thase, & Markowitz, 2002).

Many cognitive-behavioral therapies for phobia include **exposure,** in which the client is exposed repeatedly to the anxiety-producing stimulus or situation. The theory, based on classical conditioning, is that when individuals avoid feared stimuli or situations, they experience reductions in anxiety that reinforce avoidance behavior. Repeated exposure to a feared stimulus increases the client's anxiety, but if the client is not permitted to avoid the stimulus, the avoidance response

FIGURE 15.3 Aaron T. Beck Beck is one of the pioneers of cognitive therapy for mental disorders, especially depression.

cognitive therapy Treatment based on the idea that distorted thoughts produce maladaptive behaviors and emotions.

cognitive restructuring A therapy that strives to help patients recognize maladaptive thought patterns and replace them with ways of viewing the world that are more in tune with reality.

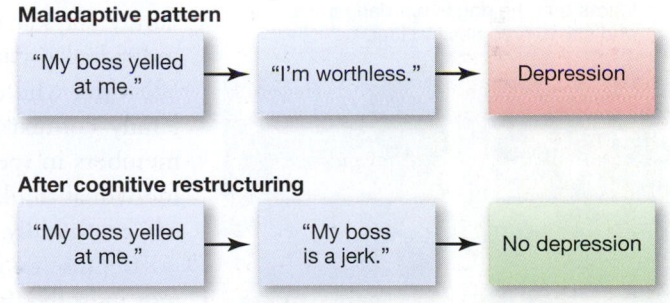

FIGURE 15.4 Cognitive Restructuring Cognitive restructuring involves replacing maladaptive thought patterns with more realistic, positive ones.

cognitive-behavioral therapy (CBT) A therapy that incorporates techniques from behavioral therapy and cognitive therapy to correct faulty thinking and change maladaptive behaviors.

exposure A behavioral therapy technique that involves repeated exposure to an anxiety-producing stimulus or situation.

1 The little girl in the white shirt (on the right) has a phobia about dogs.

2 She is encouraged to approach a dog that scares her.

3 From this mild form of exposure she learns that the dog is not dangerous, and she overcomes her fear.

FIGURE 15.5 Exposure Exposure is a common feature of many cognitive-behavioral therapies for phobia.

expressed emotion A pattern of interactions that includes emotional over-involvement, critical comments, and hostility directed toward a patient by family members.

is eventually extinguished. (**FIGURE 15.5** shows a girl gradually overcoming her fear of dogs by slowly increasing her level of exposure to a dog.) This treatment is reliable for many phobias and can be tried at home for mild cases, as long as the person with the phobia can control how quickly and how close he or she comes to the feared object.

GROUP THERAPY BUILDS SOCIAL SUPPORT Group therapy rose in popularity after World War II, when there were more people needing therapy than there were therapists available to treat them. Subsequently, therapists realized that in some instances group therapy offers advantages over individual therapy. The most obvious benefit is cost, since group therapy is often significantly less expensive than individual treatment. In addition, the group setting provides an opportunity for members to improve their social skills and learn from one another's experiences. Group therapies vary widely in the types of clients enrolled in the group, the duration of treatment, the theoretical perspective of the therapist running the group, and the group size—although some practitioners believe eight clients is the ideal number. Many groups are organized around a particular type of problem (e.g., sexual abuse) or around a particular type of client (e.g., adolescents). Often, groups continue over long periods, with some members leaving and others joining the group at various intervals. Depending on the approach favored by the therapist, the group may be highly structured, or it may be a more loosely organized forum for discussion. Behavioral and cognitive-behavioral groups usually are highly structured, with specific goals and techniques designed to modify the thought and behavior patterns of group members. This type of group has been effective for disorders such as bulimia and obsessive-compulsive disorder. In contrast, less structured groups usually focus on increasing insight and providing social support. In fact, the social support that group members can provide each other is one of the most beneficial aspects of this type of therapy, and it often is used to augment individual psychotherapy.

FAMILY THERAPY FOCUSES ON THE FAMILY CONTEXT Although the therapy a client receives is an important element in treating a mental disorder, the client's family plays an almost equally important role. According to a *systems approach*, an individual is part of a larger context, and any change in individual behavior will affect the whole system. This effect is often clearest at the family level. Within the family context, each person plays a particular role and interacts with the other members in specific ways (**FIGURE 15.6**). Over the course of therapy, the way the individual thinks, behaves, and interacts with others may change, and this change can profoundly affect the family dynamics.

Because family attitudes are often critical to long-term prognoses, some therapists insist that family members be involved in therapy. Indeed, evidence suggests that helping families provide appropriate social support leads to better therapy outcomes and reduces relapses. The key is the type of family involvement. For instance, studies have documented the importance of attitudes expressed by family members toward schizophrenics. Negative **expressed emotion** includes making critical comments about the client, being hostile toward the client, and being emotionally overinvolved (e.g., being overprotective or crying excessively). Families' levels of negative expressed emotion correspond to the relapse rate for patients with schizophrenia (Hooley & Gotlib, 2000), and relapse rates are highest if the client has a great deal of contact with the family. Jill Hooley (2007) notes that expressed emotion predicts relapse in countries ranging from Australia to Denmark to China to Iran, although the patterns of expressed emotion that affect relapse differ across those countries and cultures, in part because behaviors such as emotional overinvolvement are more acceptable in some cultures. In turn, culture affects the relationship between expressed emotion and relapse; schizophrenia relapse is more common in hostile families in India than in Japan, whereas relapse is more common in emotionally overinvolved families in Japan than in India.

FIGURE 15.6 Family Therapy Family members' actions, reactions, and interactions can become important topics during therapy.

CONFESSION IS GOOD FOR THE SPIRIT Irrespective of type of therapist or type of treatment, might simply talking to someone about personal problems make a person feel better? The ancient Greek philosopher Aristotle coined the term *catharsis* to describe the way certain messages evoke powerful emotional reactions and subsequent relief. Freud later incorporated this idea into his psychoanalytic approach to the treatment of mental disorders. He believed that uncovering unconscious material and talking about it would bring about catharsis and subsequent relief from symptoms. Although other approaches do not rely on this process explicitly, the opportunity to talk about one's problems to someone who will listen plays a role in all therapeutic relationships. Indeed, just the act of telling someone about your problems can have healing power. As discussed in Chapter 10, James Pennebaker has explored this theory extensively. He finds that when people reveal intimate and highly emotional material, they go into an almost trancelike state. The pitch of their voices goes down, their rate of speech speeds up, and they lose track of both time and place. Subsequent research has revealed that talking or writing about emotionally charged events reduces blood pressure, muscle tension, and skin conduction during the disclosure and immediately thereafter (Pennebaker, 1990, 1995). Even writing about emotional topics via e-mail produces positive health outcomes (Sheese, Brown, & Graziano, 2004). In addition to these short-term benefits, evidence indicates that writing about emotional events improves immune function, even in people with HIV (Petrie, Fontanilla, Thomas, Booth, & Pennebaker, 2004). Other research has shown that such "confessional" therapies can lead to better performance in work and school and can improve memory and cognition. In addition, talking about troubling events may help individuals reinterpret the events in less threatening ways, and such reinterpretation is a central component of many cognitive therapies.

Culture Can Affect the Therapeutic Process

Societal definitions of both mental health and mental disorders are central to the treatments used in psychotherapy. As discussed above, for example, people with schizophrenia relapse more often if they come from emotionally overinvolved Japanese families than if they come from emotionally overinvolved Indian families. Culture has multiple influences on the way mental disorders are expressed, which people with mental disorders are likely to recover, and people's willingness to seek help. Depression, anxiety, alcoholism, and other mental disorders can be debilitating for anyone, but when a stigma is associated with any of these disorders, the problems are exacerbated because people will often then suffer in silence, failing to get the psychotherapy that can help them. Psychotherapy is accepted to different extents in different countries. Some countries, such as China, have relatively few psychotherapists, but many of those countries are seeing a growing demand, as the last two decades or so of economic expansion have brought increasingly stressful lifestyles and an awareness of the mental health problems that come with them.

Real World PSYCHOLOGY

FIGURE 15.7 Cultural Effects on Therapy A psychologist counsels a young victim of the massive earthquake in the Sichuan province in China, 2008.

In 2008, the massive earthquake in China's Sichuan province demonstrated a new acceptance of psychotherapy in that region. At first, mental health workers rushed in to assist the survivors. But it is critical to understand cultural beliefs about psychotherapy to deliver it effectively, and few of the displaced and grieving Chinese showed up for mental health services offered under the banner "Earthquake Psychological Health Station." Because of traditional cultural beliefs, many Chinese distrust emotional expression and avoid seeking help for depression, anger, or grief (Magnier, 2008). Despite such cultural stigmas against getting help for mental disorders, the Chinese government then sent large numbers of psychotherapists into the region to provide culturally sensitive assistance for coping with the earthquake's aftermath (**FIGURE 15.7**). (You will learn later in this chapter that simply encouraging venting following disasters can backfire and cause a worsening of emotional problems.)

The Indian government is recognizing that mental disorders, such as depression, can be as debilitating as malaria and other physical diseases and that the economic consequences of mental disorders are enormous. In one program in India, a corps of health counselors is being trained to screen for mental disorders whenever someone enters a medical office. Because of the stigma of mental disorders, terms such as *mental illness, depression,* and *anxiety* are avoided; instead, terms such as *tension* and *strain* are used to communicate mental health problems (Kohn, 2008).

Culture also plays a critical role in determining the availability, use, and effectiveness of different types of psychotherapy for various cultural and ethnic groups living within any country. Psychotherapy and definitions of mental health are based on the dominant cultural paradigm. Beverly Greene (2007) describes the problem this way: "Women, people of color, people with disabilities, members of sexual minority groups, and people who are poor have all been unfairly stigmatized and have suffered to a greater or lesser extent because of the way psychology has defined what is normal" (p. 47). She urges psychotherapists not to gloss over or deny differences in the life experiences of people from different racial, ethnic, and cultural backgrounds in the United States, such as how they are affected by discrimination. Anderson Franklin (2007) makes a similar point in terms of African American men. Early in psychotherapy, most clients and therapists avoid the complex issues at the intersection of race and gender, acting as though the mental disorders of African American men are no different from those of white American men. But Franklin cautions that African American men's experiences differ in multiple ways that have a cumulative effect on mental disorders, and these differences must be addressed early in therapy.

Another study explored the way Muslim Americans' religious beliefs can influence the outcomes of psychotherapy. Religious minorities in any society need to find healthy ways to reaffirm their faith and deal with discrimination. Psychotherapy can be helpful in this regard if therapists have a fundamental understanding of their clients' culture and can modify their own style and type of therapy to be more culturally appropriate (Ali, Liu, & Humedian, 2004).

Medication Is Effective for Certain Disorders

Drugs have proved effective for treating some mental disorders. Those that affect mental processes are called **psychotropic medications.** They act by changing brain neurochemistry—for example, by inhibiting action potentials or by altering

psychotropic medications Drugs that affect mental processes.

synaptic transmission to increase or decrease the action of particular neurotransmitters (see Chapter 3, "Biological Foundations").

The success of medication in the treatment of mental disorders is largely responsible for the era of deinstitutionalization, in which scores of patients were discharged from mental hospitals and treated with drugs as outpatients. In California during the 1980s, the number of hospital beds for mentally ill patients decreased from 40,000 to 5,000. The smaller number of inpatients meant that institutions could provide better treatment for those still under their care.

Although numerous drugs are available, most psychotropic medications fall into three categories: anti-anxiety drugs, antidepressants, and antipsychotics. **Anti-anxiety drugs,** commonly called *tranquilizers,* are used for the short-term treatment of anxiety. Benzodiazepines (such as Xanax and Ativan) increase the activity of GABA, an inhibitory neurotransmitter. Although these drugs reduce anxiety and promote relaxation, they also induce drowsiness and are highly addictive; they should therefore be used sparingly.

anti-anxiety drugs A class of psychotropic medications used for the treatment of anxiety.

A second class of psychotropic medications is the **antidepressants,** which are used to treat depression. Monoamine oxidase (MAO) inhibitors were the first antidepressants to be discovered. *Monoamine oxidase* is an enzyme that converts serotonin into another chemical form. *MAO inhibitors* therefore result in more serotonin being available in the brain synapses. These drugs also raise levels of norepinephrine and dopamine. A second category of antidepressant medications is the *tricyclic antidepressants,* named after their core molecular structure of three rings. These drugs inhibit the reuptake of certain neurotransmitters, resulting in more of each neurotransmitter being available in the synapse. More recently, *selective serotonin reuptake inhibitors (SSRIs)* have been introduced; the best-known is Prozac. These drugs inhibit the reuptake of serotonin, but they also act on other neurotransmitters to a significantly lesser extent. (**FIGURE 15.8** depicts the way SSRIs work.) Some critics have charged that SSRIs are too often used to treat people who are sad and have low self-esteem but who are not clinically depressed. Such widespread

antidepressants A class of psychotropic medications used to treat depression.

FIGURE 15.8 Selective Serotonin Reuptake Inhibitors SSRIs, such as Prozac, work by blocking reuptake into the presynaptic neuron, thereby allowing serotonin to remain in the synapse, where its effects on postsynaptic receptors are prolonged.

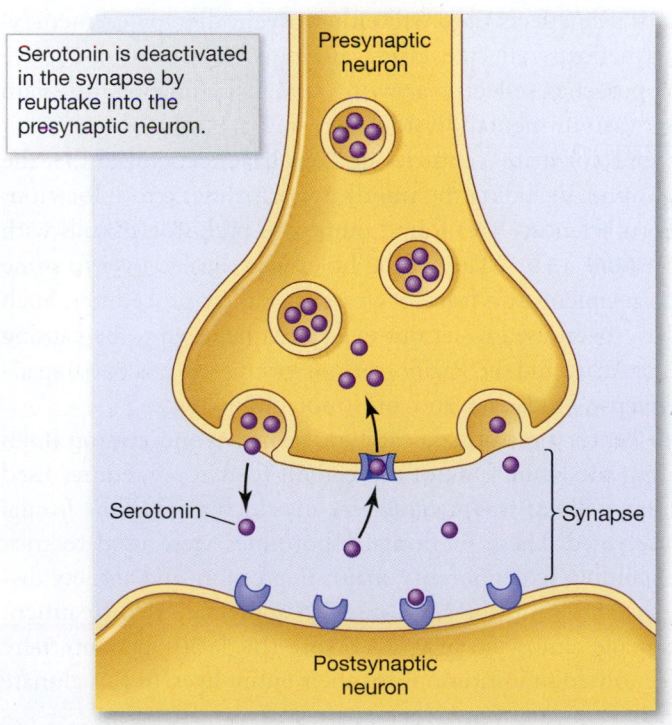

Serotonin is deactivated in the synapse by reuptake into the presynaptic neuron.

Presynaptic neuron

Serotonin

Synapse

Postsynaptic neuron

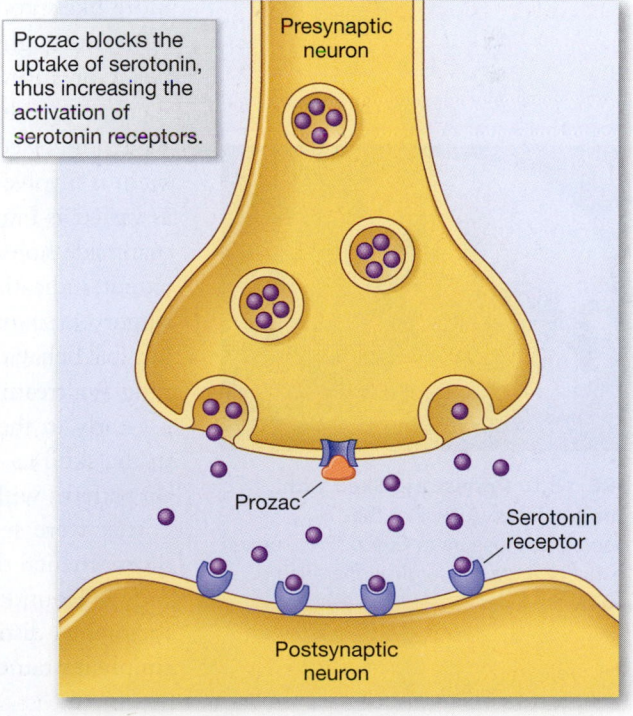

Prozac blocks the uptake of serotonin, thus increasing the activation of serotonin receptors.

Presynaptic neuron

Prozac

Serotonin receptor

Postsynaptic neuron

antipsychotics A class of drugs used to treat schizophrenia and other disorders that involve psychosis.

prescribing of SSRIs is a problem because, like all drugs, SSRIs have side effects, one of which is sexual dysfunction. At the same time, SSRIs have been valuable for a variety of disorders, not just for depression. Indeed, they are often used to treat anxiety disorders.

Antipsychotics, also known as *neuroleptics,* are used to treat schizophrenia and other disorders that involve psychosis. These drugs reduce symptoms such as delusions and hallucinations. Traditional antipsychotics bind to dopamine receptors, thus blocking the effects of dopamine. Antipsychotics are not always effective, however, and they have significant side effects that can be irreversible—such as *tardive dyskinesia,* the involuntary twitching of muscles, especially in the neck and face. Moreover, these drugs are not useful for treating the negative symptoms of schizophrenia, such as apathy and social withdrawal (see Chapter 14, "Disorders of the Mind and Body"). Clozapine, one of the newer antipsychotics, is significantly different in that it acts not only on dopamine receptors but also on serotonin, norepinephrine, acetylcholine, and histamine. Many patients who do not respond to the other antipsychotics improve on clozapine. Newer drugs, such as Risperdal and Zyprexa, are used widely because they are safer than clozapine. However, as discussed below, they can cause serious problems with white blood cells, and they may not be as effective as clozapine.

Other drugs used to treat mental disorders do not fall into traditional categories. *Lithium* is the most effective treatment for bipolar disorder, although the neural mechanisms of how it works are unknown. Drugs that prevent seizures, called *anticonvulsants,* can also regulate moods in bipolar disorder.

Alternative Biological Treatments Are Used in Extreme Cases

Not all people are treated successfully with psychotherapy or medication. To alleviate their disorders, these individuals may attempt alternative biological methods, including brain surgery, the use of magnetic fields, or electrical stimulation, all to alter brain function. These treatments often are used as last resorts because they are more likely to have serious side effects than will either psychotherapy or medication. Although many early efforts reflected crude attempts to control disruptive behavior, more recent approaches reflect a growing understanding of the brain mechanisms that underlie various mental disorders.

As discussed in Chapter 1, for many centuries humans have recognized that the brain is involved with the mind, including the mind's abnormalities. From locations as varied as France and Peru, scientists have found numerous prehistoric skulls with manmade holes in them (**FIGURE 15.9**). Many of the holes were healed over to some extent, indicating that the recipients survived for years after their procedures. Such surgery, *trepanning,* may have been used to let out evil spirits believed to be causing unusual behavior. In parts of Africa and the Pacific, various groups still practice trepanning as a treatment for epilepsy, headaches, and, most notably, insanity.

Early in the twentieth century, medical researchers went beyond cutting holes in the skull to manipulating the brain. One of the earliest formal procedures used on patients with severe mental illness was *psychosurgery,* in which areas of the frontal cortex were selectively damaged. These prefrontal lobotomies were used to treat severe mental disorders including schizophrenia, major depression, and anxiety disorders. To understand such drastic measures, we need to appreciate that treatment for mental disorders had made almost no progress before the 1950s; patients were simply restrained and warehoused in institutions for their entire lives. In this climate

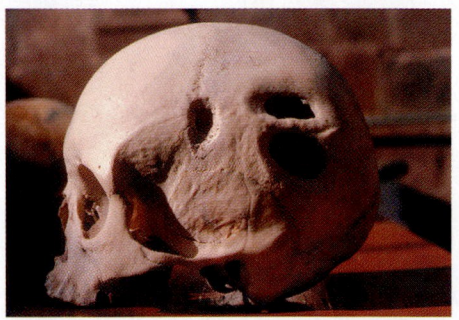

FIGURE 15.9 Prehistoric Skull with Manmade Holes A skull at the Archaeological Museum in Cusco, Peru, bears the marks of a cranial surgical operation performed by the Incas.

of medical desperation, various risky procedures were explored. Although some brain surgeries were performed as early as the 1880s, Egas Moniz generally is credited with bringing the practice to the attention of the medical world in the 1930s. His surgical procedure, later known as prefrontal lobotomy, involved severing nerve-fiber pathways in the prefrontal cortex. Patients who received lobotomies were often listless and had flat affect (on a similar state, see the discussion of Elliot in Chapter 9, "Motivation and Emotion"). Moreover, the procedure often impaired many important mental functions, such as abstract thought, planning, motivation, and social interaction. With the development of effective pharmacological treatments in the 1950s, the use of lobotomy was discontinued. Nowadays some brain surgery is used for mental disorders, but it involves small regions of the brain and typically is performed only as a last resort.

ELECTROCONVULSIVE THERAPY **Electroconvulsive therapy (ECT)** was developed in Europe in the 1930s and tried on the first human in 1938. ECT involves placing electrodes on a patient's head and administering an electrical current strong enough to produce a seizure (**FIGURE 15.10**). The procedure was common in the 1950s and 1960s to treat mental disorders including schizophrenia and depression. The general public views ECT in a predominately negative manner. Ken Kesey's 1962 novel *One Flew over the Cuckoo's Nest,* as well as the award-winning 1975 film version, did a great deal to expose the abuses in mental health care and graphically depicted ECT as well as the tragic effects of lobotomy. Although care for the mentally ill is still far from perfect, many reforms have been implemented. ECT now generally occurs under anesthesia with powerful muscle relaxants to eliminate motor convulsions and confine the seizure to the brain. As you will learn, ECT is particularly effective for some cases of severe depression, although there are some risks to its use.

TRANSCRANIAL MAGNETIC STIMULATION During *transcranial magnetic stimulation (TMS),* as discussed in Chapter 2, a powerful electrical current produces a magnetic field (about 40,000 times Earth's magnetic field) that, when rapidly switched on and off, induces an electrical current in the brain region directly below the coil, thereby interrupting neural function in that region (**FIGURE 15.11**). In *single-pulse TMS,* the disruption of brain activity occurs only during the brief period of stimulation. For instance, a pulse given over a motor region might interfere with a person's ability to reach smoothly toward a target object, whereas a pulse given over the speech region may disrupt speaking momentarily. If multiple pulses of TMS occur over extended time (known as *repeated TMS*), the disruption can last beyond the period of direct stimulation. Recently, researchers have begun investigating the therapeutic potential of TMS in treating mental disorders; as noted later in this chapter, it may be especially useful for depression (Loo & Mitchell, 2005).

electroconvulsive therapy (ECT) A procedure used to treat depression; it involves administering a strong electrical current to the patient's brain.

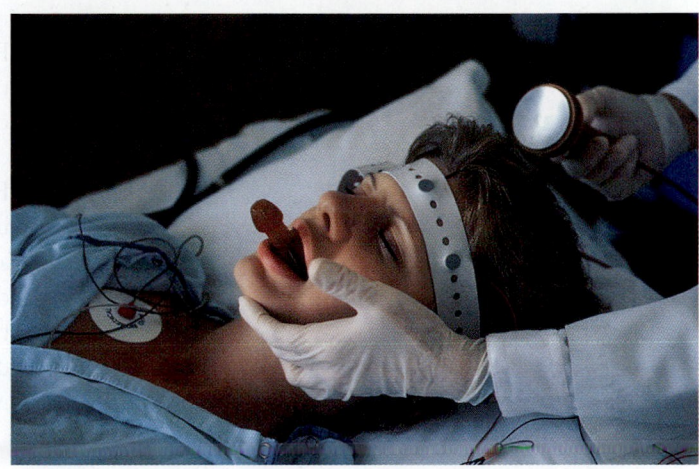

FIGURE 15.10 **Electroconvulsive Therapy** A woman being prepared for electroconvulsive therapy has a soft object placed between her teeth, to prevent her from swallowing her tongue.

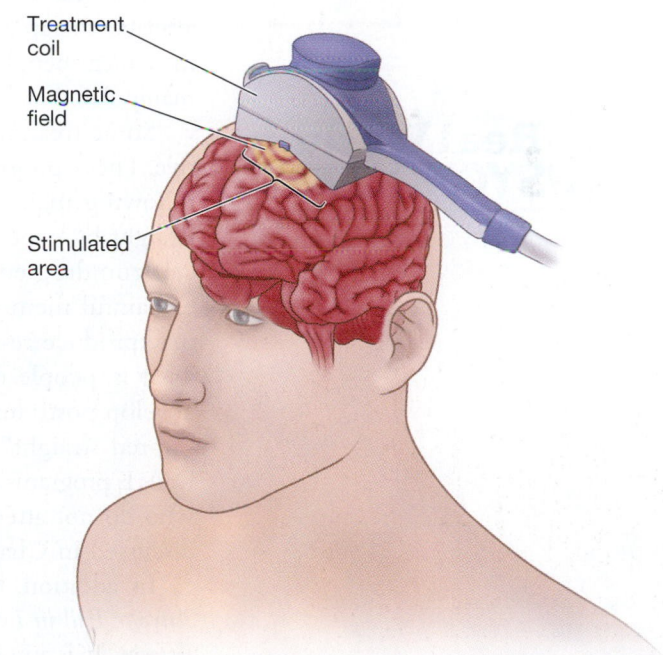

Treatment coil

Magnetic field

Stimulated area

FIGURE 15.11 **Transcranial Magnetic Stimulation** In TMS, current flows through a wire coil placed over the scalp area to be stimulated.

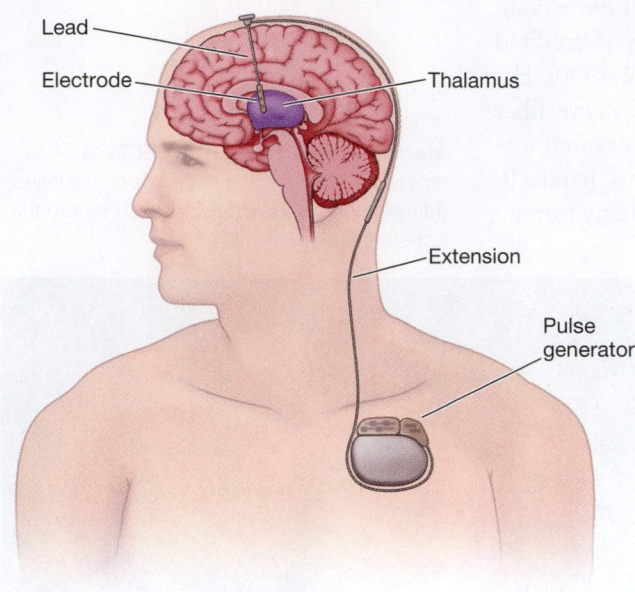

FIGURE 15.12 **Deep Brain Stimulation** In DBS, an electrical generator placed just under the skin below the collarbone sends out continuous stimulation to the implanted electrodes.

DEEP BRAIN STIMULATION One of the most dramatic new techniques for treating severe mental disorder involves surgically implanting electrodes deep within the brain and then using mild electricity to stimulate the brain at an optimal frequency and intensity, much the way a pacemaker stimulates the heart (**FIGURE 15.12**). *Deep brain stimulation (DBS)* was first widely used to treat the symptoms of Parkinson's disease, which (as discussed in Chapter 3) is a disorder of the dopamine system that causes problems with movement. Electrodes implanted into motor regions of the brains of Parkinson's patients reverse many of the movement problems associated with the disease (DeLong & Wichmann, 2008). The success of DBS for Parkinson's is so great that it is now the treatment of choice for many patients, in part because the drugs used to treat Parkinson's often cause undesirable side effects, such as increased involuntary movements. By contrast, DBS has few side effects and a low complication rate, as is typical of any minor surgical procedure. Given DBS's tremendous success in treating Parkinson's, it is being tested for treating other disorders, including mental disorders. As you will learn, DBS might be especially valuable for treating severe OCD and depression.

Pseudotherapies Can Be Dangerous

Chapter 1 talked about pseudoscience, or flawed science. Just as people need to recognize and avoid pseudoscience, they also need to recognize and avoid pseudotherapies—therapies with no scientific basis to suggest they are effective. As the next section will discuss, most psychologists recommend treatments that careful empirical research has proved to be effective (Kazdin, 2008). Unfortunately, many available therapies have no scientific basis—such as those (not discussed in this book) in which people reenact their own births, scream, or have their body parts manipulated.

Some treatments widely believed to be effective are actually counterproductive. These programs include encouraging people to describe their experiences following major trauma such as an earthquake, scaring adolescents into going straight by exposing them to prisoners or tough treatments, having police officers run drug education programs such as DARE, and using hypnosis to recover painful memories. These methods not only lack adequate evidence but also may produce results opposite to those intended (Hines, 2003; Lilienfeld, 2007). That is, people debriefed following natural disasters are slightly more likely to develop posttraumatic stress disorder than those who are not debriefed, teens in "scared straight" programs show an increase in conduct problems, children in DARE programs are more likely to drink alcohol and smoke cigarettes than children who do not attend such programs, and hypnosis can produce false memories (as discussed in Chapter 7).

In addition, many self-help books make questionable claims, such as *Make Anyone Fall in Love with You in 5 Minutes* or *Three Easy Steps for Having High Self-Esteem*. It is important to recognize the difference between evidence-based psychotherapies and "alternative" or "fringe" pseudotherapies because the latter can prevent people from getting effective treatment and may even be dangerous. In one tragic case, a 10-year-old girl died from suffocation after being wrapped in a blanket for 70 minutes during a supposed therapy session to simulate her own birth, an unproven and unscientific method being used to correct the child's unruly behavior (Lowe, 2001). The people conducting the session were unlicensed, which means they had not passed the state tests that certify knowledge about psychotherapy.

 SUMMING UP

How Are Mental Disorders Treated?

There are many ways to treat mental disorders. Psychotherapy uses psychological methods based on the practitioner's theoretical orientation. Some therapies help people gain insight into the ways they think, behave, and interact. Other methods are more concerned with action than with insight and try to correct faulty or biased thinking or to teach new behaviors. An individual's cultural background can be an important determinant of whether he or she will seek therapy and what type of therapy will most likely be effective. Psychopharmacology is based on the idea that maladaptive behavior results from neurological dysfunction, and psychotropic medications therefore are aimed at correcting imbalances of neurotransmitters in the brain. When traditional treatments fail, alternative methods such as ECT, TMS, and DBS sometimes are used. Pseudotherapies are ineffective and sometimes dangerous.

 MEASURING UP

1. Identify the psychotherapeutic orientation each of the following scenarios typifies. Response options include client-centered therapy, cognitive-behavioral therapy, group therapy, and psychodynamic therapy.
    a. Allen seeks therapy to help him cope with social anxiety and panic attacks. During a review of Allen's thought records from the previous week, Allen's therapist says, "Allen, I see you had one panic attack last week during one of your attempts to socialize. On a scale of 0 to 10 in severity, you rated the panic attack as an 8. Tell me about the thoughts you had just before and during the attack. This will help us understand what triggered your panic attack."
    b. During a therapy session, Carlos's therapist says, "Carlos, you've described feeling angry toward your wife when she asks how you're dealing with your father's death. I sensed frustration and anger toward me when I asked you about his death just a moment ago. Usually anger covers more uncomfortable feelings, like hurt, pain, and anguish. If you put your anger aside for a moment, what emotion comes to the surface?"
    c. Following Parin's expression of despair that his girlfriend broke up with him, his therapist responds empathically by saying, "Parin, you feel devastated knowing your love for her was not enough to keep the two of you together. I am sorry you are experiencing so much pain."

2. Identify the disorder most commonly treated with each medication. Response options are anxiety, depression, and schizophrenia.
    a. antipsychotics
    b. selective serotonin reuptake inhibitors
    c. tranquilizers

What Are the Most Effective Treatments?

Research over the past three decades has shown that certain types of treatments are particularly effective for specific types of mental disorders (Barlow, 2004). Because outcomes are influenced by the interaction of client and therapist, it is difficult to make comparisons across disorders and therapists. Nonetheless, some treatments have empirical support for use with specific disorders and others do not. Moreover, the scientific study of treatment indicates that although some mental disorders are quite easily treated, others are not. For instance, highly effective treatments exist for anxiety disorders, mood disorders, and sexual dysfunction, but few treatments for alcoholism are superior to the natural course of recovery that many people undergo without psychological treatment (Seligman, Walker, & Rosenhan, 2001). People who experience depression following the death of a loved one usually feel better with the passage of time. That is, people often resolve personal problems on their own without psychological treatment. Because people tend to enter therapy when they experience crises, they often show improvements no matter what therapy they receive.

As in all other areas of psychological science, the only way to know whether a treatment is valid is to conduct empirical research that compares the treatment to a control condition, such as receiving helpful information or having supportive listeners (Kazdin, 2008). David Barlow, a leading researcher in anxiety disorders, points out that findings from medical studies often lead to dramatic changes in treatment practice (Barlow, 2004). He provides the example of the sharp downturn in the use of hormone replacement therapy in postmenopausal women following evidence that this treatment causes cardiovascular and neurological problems. Similarly, within a year after evidence emerged that arthroscopic knee surgery did not produce better outcomes than sham surgery (in which there was no actual procedure), use of the knee surgery declined dramatically. Such developments reflect the increasing importance of *evidence-based treatments* in medicine. Barlow argues that psychological disorders should always be treated in ways that scientific research has shown to be effective; he prefers the term *psychological treatments* to distinguish evidence-based treatment from the more generic term *psychotherapy,* which refers to any form of talk therapy.

Although there is some debate regarding the most appropriate methods and criteria used to assess clinical research (e.g., Benjamin, 2005; Westen, Novotny, & Thompson-Brenner, 2004), according to Barlow three features characterize psychological treatments. First, they vary according to the particular mental disorder and the client's specific psychological symptoms. Just as treatment for asthma differs from that for psoriasis, treatments for panic disorder will likely differ from those for bulimia nervosa. Second, the techniques used in these treatments have been developed in the laboratory by psychological scientists, especially behavioral, cognitive, and social psychologists. Third, no overall grand theory guides treatment; rather, treatment is based on evidence of its effectiveness. The following section examines the evidence to find out the treatment of choice for some of the most common mental disorders.

Treatments That Focus on Behavior and on Cognition Are Superior for Anxiety Disorders

Over the years, treatment approaches to anxiety disorders have had mixed success. In the era when Freudian psychoanalytic theory governed the classification of mental disorders, anxiety disorders were thought to result from repressed sexual and aggressive impulses; this underlying cause, rather than specific symptoms, was of interest to the therapist. Ultimately, psychoanalytic theory did not prove useful for treating anxiety disorders. The accumulated evidence suggests that cognitive-behavioral therapy works best to treat most adult anxiety disorders (Hofmann & Smits, 2008). Anxiety-reducing drugs are also beneficial in some cases, although there are risks of side effects and, after drug treatment is terminated, the risk of relapse. For instance, tranquilizers work in the short term for generalized anxiety disorder, but they do little to alleviate the source of anxiety and are addictive; therefore, they are not used much today. Antidepressant drugs that block the reuptake of both serotonin and norepinephrine, such as Effexor and Cymbalta, have been effective for treating generalized anxiety disorder (Hartford et al., 2007; Nicolini et al., 2008), but as with all drugs, the effects may be limited to the period during which the drug is taken. By contrast, the effects of cognitive-behavioral therapy persist long after treatment (Hollon, Stewart, & Strunk, 2006).

SPECIFIC PHOBIAS Specific phobias are characterized by the fear and avoidance of particular stimuli, such as heights, blood, and spiders. Learning theory suggests these fears are acquired either through experiencing a trauma or by observing similar fear in others. As discussed in Chapter 14, however, most phobias apparently develop in the absence of any particular precipitating event. Although learning theory cannot completely explain the development of phobias, behavioral techniques are the treatment of choice. In one of the classic methods used to treat phobias, systematic desensitization therapy, the client first makes a *fear hierarchy,* a list of situations in which fear is aroused, in ascending order. The example in **TABLE 15.1** is from a client's therapy to conquer a fear of heights in order to go mountain climbing. The next step is relaxation training, in which the client learns to alternate muscular tension with muscular relaxation and to use relaxation techniques. Exposure therapy is often the next step. While the client is relaxed, he or she is asked to imagine or enact scenarios that become progressively more upsetting. New scenarios are not presented until the client is able to maintain relaxation at the previous levels. The theory behind this technique is that the relaxation response competes with and eventually replaces the fear response. Evidence indicates that it is exposure to the feared object rather than the relaxation that extinguishes the phobic response. Thus many contemporary practitioners leave out the relaxation component. One way to expose people without putting them in danger is to use *virtual environments,* sometimes called *virtual reality.* Computers can simulate the environments and the feared objects, such as by having a person *virtually* stand on the edge of a very tall building or fly in an aircraft (**FIGURE 15.13**). Substantial evidence indicates that exposure to these virtual environments can reduce fear responses (Rothbaum et al., 1999).

Table 15.1 Anxiety Hierarchy

Degree of fear	Situation
5	I'm standing on the balcony of the top floor of an apartment tower.
10	I'm standing on a stepladder in the kitchen to change a lightbulb.
15	I'm walking on a ridge. The edge is hidden by shrubs and treetops.
20	I'm sitting on the slope of a mountain, looking out over the horizon.
25	I'm crossing a bridge 6 feet above a creek. The bridge consists of an 18-inch-wide board with a handrail on one side.
30	I'm riding a ski lift 8 feet above the ground.
35	I'm crossing a shallow, wide creek on an 18-inch-wide board, 3 feet above water level.
40	I'm climbing a ladder outside the house to reach a second-story window.
45	I'm pulling myself up a 30-degree wet, slippery slope on a steel cable.
50	I'm scrambling up a rock, 8 feet high.
55	I'm walking 10 feet on a resilient, 18-inch-wide board, which spans an 8-foot-deep gulch.
60	I'm walking on a wide plateau, 2 feet from the edge of a cliff.
65	I'm skiing an intermediate hill. The snow is packed.
70	I'm walking over a railway trestle.
75	I'm walking on the side of an embankment. The patch slopes to the outside.
80	I'm riding a chair lift 15 feet above the ground.
85	I'm walking up a long, steep slope.
90	I'm walking up (or down) a 15-degree slope on a 3-foot-wide trail. On one side of the trail the terrain drops down sharply; on the other side is a steep upward slope.
95	I'm walking on a 3-foot-wide ridge. The trail slopes on one side are more than 25 degrees steep.
100	I'm walking on a 2-foot-wide ridge. The trail slopes on either side are more than 25 degrees.

FIGURE 15.13 **Using Virtual Environments to Conquer Fear** Computer-generated images can simulate feared environments, such as heights, flying, or social interactions. Clients can conquer these virtual environments before taking on the feared situations in real life.

Used along with the behavioral methods, some cognitive strategies have also proved useful for the treatment of phobia. If the client is not aware that the particular fear is irrational, therapy will likely begin by increasing his or her awareness of the thought processes that maintain the fear of the stimulus. Brain imaging data indicate that successful treatment with cognitive-behavioral therapy alters the way the brain processes the fear stimulus. In one study, research participants suffering from severe spider phobia received brain scans while looking at pictures of spiders (Paquette et al., 2003). Those whose treatment had been successful showed decreased activation in a frontal brain region involved in emotion regulation. These findings suggest that psychotherapy effectively "rewires" the brain and, therefore, that both psychotherapy and medication affect the underlying biology of mental disorders.

Pharmacological treatments for phobias include tranquilizers, which can help people handle immediate fear; but as soon as the drugs wear off, the fears return. Recent studies have suggested that SSRIs might be useful for social phobia. Indeed, in the most comprehensive study conducted to date, researchers found that both Prozac and cognitive-behavioral therapy were effective in treating social phobia (Davidson et al., 2004). After fourteen weeks, symptoms exhibited by participants in the study did not differ. However, those taking Prozac had more physical complaints, such as a lack of sexual interest. Evidence indicates that cognitive-behavioral therapies are the treatments of choice for phobia.

PANIC DISORDER Although many of us at some point experience symptoms of a panic attack, we react to these symptoms in different ways. Some shrug off the symptoms, while others interpret heart palpitations as the beginnings of a heart attack or hyperventilation as a sign of suffocation. Panic disorder has multiple components, each of which may require a different treatment approach.

This clinical observation is supported by the finding that imipramine, a tricyclic antidepressant, prevents panic attacks but does not reduce the anticipatory anxiety that occurs when people fear they might have an attack. To break the learned association between the physical symptoms and the feeling of impending doom, cognitive-behavioral therapy can be effective, as this chapter's opening case study illustrated.

The most important psychotherapeutic methods for treating panic disorder are based on cognitive therapy. When people feel anxious, they tend to overestimate the probability of danger, potentially contributing to their rising feelings of panic. Cognitive restructuring addresses ways of reacting to the symptoms of a panic attack. First, clients identify their specific fears, such as having a heart attack or fainting. Clients then estimate how many panic attacks they have had. The therapist helps them assign percentages to specific fears and then compare these numbers with the actual number of times the fears have been realized. For example, a client might estimate that she fears having a heart attack during 90 percent of her panic attacks and fainting during 85 percent of her attacks. The therapist can then point out that the actual rate of occurrence was zero. In fact, people do not faint during panic attacks; the physical symptoms of a panic attack, such as having a racing heart, are the opposite of fainting.

Even if clients recognize the irrationality of their fears, they often still suffer panic attacks. From a cognitive-behavioral perspective, the attacks continue because of a conditioned response to the trigger (e.g., shortness of breath). The goal of therapy is to break the connection between the trigger symptom and the resulting panic. This break can be made by exposure treatment, which induces feelings of panic—perhaps by having the client breathe in and out through a straw to induce hyperventilation or by spinning the client rapidly in a chair. Whatever the method, it is done repeatedly to induce habituation and then extinction. Cognitive-behavioral therapy appears to be as effective as or more effective than medication in the treatment of panic attacks.

David Barlow and his colleagues (2000) have found that in the short term, cognitive-behavioral therapy alone and imipramine alone were more effective than placebo for treating panic disorder and that they did not differ in results. However, six months after treatment had ended, those who received psychotherapy were less likely to relapse than those who had taken medication. Thus cognitive-behavioral therapy is the treatment of choice for panic disorder. For those who have panic disorder with agoraphobia, the combination of CBT and drugs is better than either treatment alone (Starcevic, Linden, Uhlenhuth, Kolar, & Latas, 2004).

OBSESSIVE-COMPULSIVE DISORDER   Obsessive-compulsive disorder (OCD) is a combination of recurrent intrusive thoughts (obsessions) and behaviors that an individual feels compelled to perform over and over (compulsions; **FIGURE 15.14A**). Evidence that OCD is partly genetic and appears to be related to Tourette's syndrome, a neurological disorder characterized by motor and vocal tics, convinced many practitioners that people with OCD would respond to drug treatment. However, traditional antianxiety drugs are completely ineffective for OCD. When SSRIs were introduced to treat depression, they were particularly effective in reducing the obsessive components of some depressions—for example, constant feelings of worthlessness. Therefore, SSRIs were tried with patients suffering from OCD and were found to be effective (Rapoport, 1989, 1991). The drug of choice for OCD is the potent serotonin reuptake inhibitor clomipramine. It is not a true SSRI, since it blocks reuptake of other neurotransmitters as well, but its strong enhancement of the effects of serotonin appears to make it effective for OCD.

Cognitive-behavioral therapy is also effective for OCD and is especially valuable for those who do not benefit from or who do not want to rely on medication. The two most important components of behavioral therapy for OCD are exposure and response prevention. The client is directly exposed to the stimuli that trigger compulsive behavior but is prevented from engaging in the behavior. This treatment derives from the theory that a particular stimulus triggers anxiety and

FIGURE 15.14 Obsessive-Compulsive Disorder (a) Hand washing is one OCD ritual. **(b)** Treatments for OCD can include the drug clomipramine, exposure, and ritual prevention, with varying rates of success.

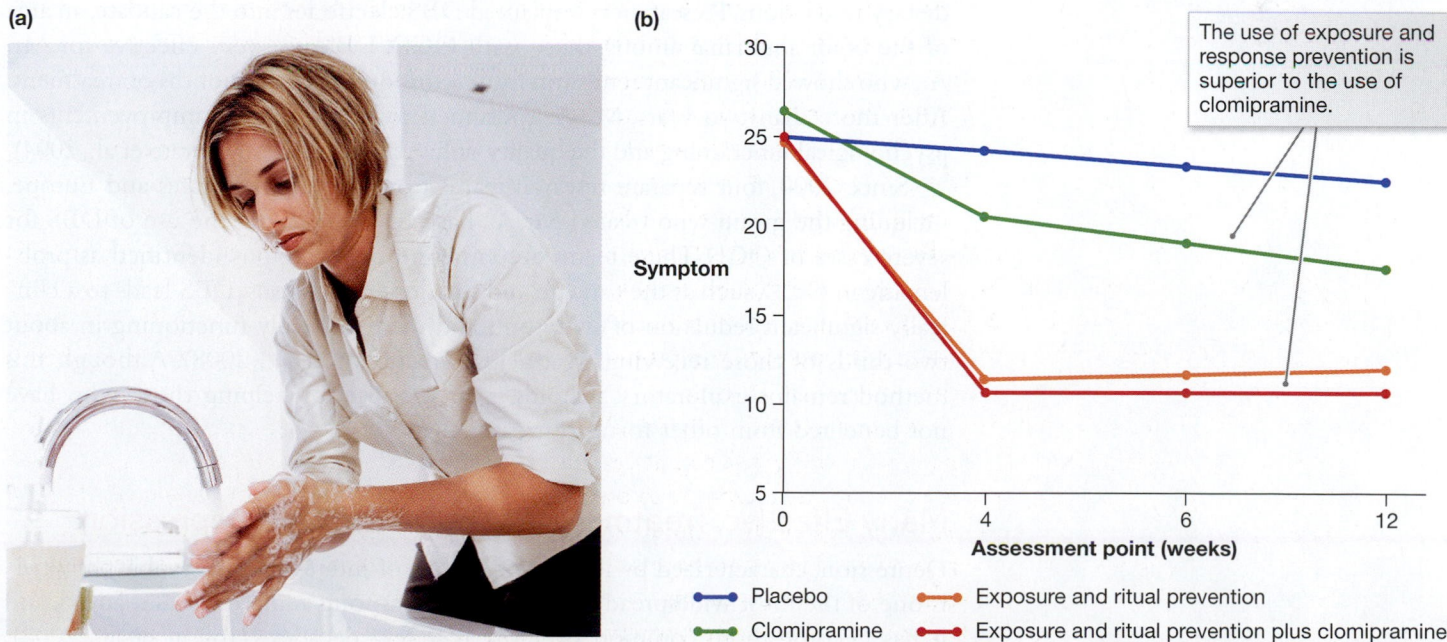

(a)

(b)

The use of exposure and response prevention is superior to the use of clomipramine.

Symptom

Assessment point (weeks)

- Placebo
- Clomipramine
- Exposure and ritual prevention
- Exposure and ritual prevention plus clomipramine

that performing the compulsive behavior reduces the anxiety. For example, a client might compulsively wash his hands after touching a doorknob, using a public telephone, or shaking hands with someone. In exposure and response-prevention therapy, the client would be required to touch a doorknob and then would be instructed not to wash his hands afterward. As with exposure therapy for panic disorder, the goal is to break the conditioned link between a particular stimulus and a compulsive behavior. Some cognitive therapies are also useful for OCD, such as helping the client recognize that most people occasionally experience unwanted thoughts and compulsions and that they are a normal part of human experience.

In the 1990s, researchers imaged the brains of patients with OCD who were being treated either with Prozac or with cognitive-behavioral therapy. Patients in both treatment groups showed the same changes in neural activity (Baxter et al., 1992; Schwartz, Stoessel, Baxter, Martin, & Phelps, 1996). Recall the findings, discussed above, that the treatment for a spider phobia led to changes in brain activity; these studies provide further evidence that psychotherapies in which people reinterpret their fears and change their behaviors can in fact change the way their brains function. How does drug treatment compare with cognitive-behavioral therapy for OCD? In one recent study, the use of exposure and response prevention proved superior to the use of clomipramine, the drug of choice for OCD, although both were better than a placebo (Foa et al., 2005; **FIGURE 15.14B**). Cognitive-behavioral therapy may thus be a more effective way of treating OCD than medication, especially over the long term (Foa et al., 2005). At a minimum, evidence suggests that adding CBT to SSRI treatment improves outcomes (Simpson et al., 2008).

One exciting possibility is that deep brain stimulation (DBS) may be an effective treatment for those with OCD who have not found relief from CBT or medications. Early studies used psychosurgery to remove brain regions thought to contribute to OCD. Although there were promising outcomes and these surgical interventions involved much less damage than earlier methods such as lobotomy, brain surgery is inherently a risky therapy because it is irreversible. However, deep brain stimulation offers new hope. Consider the case of Mr. A., a 56-year-old man suffering from a severely debilitating case of OCD that had lasted for more than four decades. Mr. A. had a number of obsessions about body parts and about gastrointestinal functioning, and his compulsions included repetitive movements and dietary restrictions. Researchers implanted DBS electrodes into the caudate, an area of the brain abnormal among those with OCD. DBS was very effective for Mr. A., who showed significant remission from symptoms after six months of treatment. After more than two years, Mr. A. continued to have stunning improvements in psychological functioning and the quality of his daily living (Aouizerate et al., 2004).

Since 2000, four separate research teams from the United States and Europe, including the group who treated Mr. A., have been exploring the use of DBS for severe cases of OCD. These teams are targeting brain regions identified as problematic in OCD, such as the caudate and surrounding regions. DBS leads to a clinically significant reduction of symptoms and increased daily functioning in about two-thirds of those receiving treatment (Greenberg et al., 2008). Although this method remains exploratory, it holds great promise for helping those who have not benefited from other forms of treatment.

Many Effective Treatments Are Available for Depression

Depression, characterized by low mood or loss of interest in pleasurable activities, is one of the most widespread mental disorders among adolescents and adults, and it has become more common over the past few decades (Hollon et al., 2002).

Fortunately, scientific research has validated a number of effective treatments. There is no "best" way to treat depression; many approaches are available, and ongoing research is determining which type of therapy works best for individuals.

PHARMACOLOGICAL TREATMENT In the 1950s, tuberculosis was a major health problem in the United States, particularly in urban areas. A common treatment was iproniazid, a drug that reduced tubercule bacilli in patients' sputum. It also stimulated patients' appetites, increased their energy levels, and gave them an overall sense of well-being. In 1957, researchers who had noted the drug's effect on mood reported preliminary success in using it to treat depression. In the following year, nearly half a million depressed patients were given iproniazid, an MAO inhibitor. Although they can relieve depression, MAO inhibitors can be toxic because of their effects on various physiological systems. Patients taking these drugs must avoid ingesting any substances containing tyramine, including red wine and aged cheeses, because they can experience severe, sometimes lethal elevations in blood pressure. Interactions with both prescription and over-the-counter medications can also be fatal, so MAO inhibitors are generally reserved for patients who do not respond to other antidepressants.

Tricyclics, another type of antidepressant, were also identified in the 1950s. One of these—imipramine, developed as an antihistamine—was found effective in relieving clinical depression. This drug and others like it act on neurotransmitters as well as on the histamine system. Tricyclics are extremely effective antidepressants. However, as a result of their broad-based action they have a number of unpleasant side effects, such as drowsiness, weight gain, sweating, constipation, heart palpitations, and dry mouth.

The discovery of these early antidepressants was largely serendipitous, but subsequently researchers began to search for antidepressants that did not affect multiple physiological and neurological systems and so would not have such troublesome side effects. In the 1980s, researchers developed Prozac, an SSRI. Because this drug does not affect histamine or acetylcholine, it has none of the side effects associated with the tricyclic antidepressants, although it occasionally causes insomnia, headache, weight loss, and sexual dysfunction. Because they have fewer serious side effects than MAO inhibitors, Prozac and other SSRIs began to be prescribed more frequently. A number of other drug treatments for depression have also been validated, such as bupropion (brand name Wellbutrin), which affects many neurotransmitter systems but has fewer side effects for most people than other drugs. For instance, unlike most antidepressants, bupropion does not cause sexual dysfunction. Interestingly, unlike SSRIs, bupropion is an ineffective treatment for panic disorder and OCD.

Approximately 60 percent to 70 percent of patients who take antidepressants experience relief from their symptoms, compared with about 30 percent who respond to placebos. Such findings indicate that these drugs are quite effective, since placebo effects are a component of all therapeutic outcomes. Indeed, recent evidence indicates that placebo treatment for depression leads to changes in brain activity (Leuchter, Cook, Witte, Morgan, & Abrams, 2002). In this study, 38 percent of participants receiving placebos showed improvement in depressive symptoms and increased activity in the prefrontal cortex, a different pattern of brain activation from that observed for participants receiving antidepressants. Such evidence suggests

"Before Prozac, she loathed company."

that placebo treatments are associated with changes in neurochemistry and alleviate symptoms for some people. Placebos may work by giving people hope that they will feel better, a positive expectancy that may alter brain activity.

Despite attempts to predict individual patients' responses to antidepressants, physicians often must resort to a trial-and-error approach in treating depressed patients. No single drug stands out as being most effective. Some evidence suggests that tricyclics might be beneficial for the most serious forms of depression, especially for hospitalized patients (Anderson, 2000), but SSRIs are generally considered first-line medications because they have the fewest serious side effects (Olfson et al., 2002). Often the decision of which drug to use depends on the patient's overall medical health and the possible side effects of each medication. Once the depressive episode has ended, should patients continue taking medication? Research has shown that those who continue taking medication for at least a year have only a 20 percent relapse rate, whereas those who remain on a placebo have an 80 percent relapse rate (Frank et al., 1990).

COGNITIVE-BEHAVIORAL TREATMENT OF DEPRESSION Despite the success of antidepressant medications, not all patients benefit from these drugs. Moreover, others cannot or will not tolerate the side effects. Fortunately, evidence indicates that cognitive-behavioral therapy is just as effective as biological therapies in treating depression (Hollon et al., 2002). From a cognitive perspective, people who become depressed do so because of automatic, irrational thoughts. According to the cognitive distortion model developed by Aaron Beck, depression is the result of a cognitive triad of negative thoughts about oneself, the situation, and the future (see Figure 14.22). Depressed patients' thought patterns differ from those of people with anxiety disorders. Whereas people with anxiety disorders worry about the future, depressed people think about how they have failed in the past, how poorly they are dealing with the present situation, and how terrible the future will be.

The goal of the cognitive-behavioral treatment of depression is to help the client think more adaptively, a change intended to improve mood and behavior. Although the specific treatment is adapted to the individual client, some general principles apply to this type of therapy. Clients may be asked to recognize and record negative thoughts (**FIGURE 15.15**). Thinking about situations in a negative manner can become automatic, and recognizing these thought patterns can be difficult. Once the patterns are identified and monitored, the clinician can help the client recognize other ways of viewing the same situation that are not so dysfunctional.

Although cognitive-behavioral therapy can be effective on its own, combining it with antidepressant medication is often more effective than either one of these approaches alone (McCullough, 2000). In addition, the response rates and remission rates of the combined-treatment approach are extremely good (Keller et al., 2000; Kocsis et al., 2003). The issue is not drugs versus psychotherapy but rather which treatments provide relief for individual clients. For instance, for clients who are suicidal, in acute distress, or unable to commit to regular attendance with a therapist, drug treatment may be most effective. For many others, especially those who have physical problems such as liver impairment or cardiac problems, psychotherapy may be the treatment of choice because it is long-lasting and does not have the side effects associated with medications (Hollon et al., 2006). As with other mental disorders, treatment of depression with psychotherapy leads to changes in brain activation similar to those observed for drug treatments (Brody et al., 2001). However, one study found that although psychotherapy and drugs involved the same brain regions, activity in those regions was quite different during the two treatments, a finding that suggests they operate through different mechanisms (Goldapple et al., 2004).

FIGURE 15.15 Try for Yourself: Recording Thoughts

Patients in cognitive-behavioral therapy may be asked to keep a record of their automatic thoughts. This example comes from a person suffering from depression.

Date	Event	Emotion	Automatic thoughts
April 4	Boss seemed annoyed.	Sad, anxious, worried	Oh, what have I done now? If I keep making him angry, I'm going to get fired.
April 5	Husband didn't want to make love.	Sad	I'm so fat and ugly.
April 7	Boss yelled at another employee.	Anxious	I'm next.
April 9	Husband said he's taking a long business trip next month.	Sad, defeated	He's probably got a mistress somewhere. My marriage is falling apart.
April 10	Neighbor brought over some cookies.	A little happy, mostly sad	She probably thinks I can't cook. I look like such a mess all the time. And my house was a disaster when she came in!

A log of such events and reactions to those events can help identify patterns in thinking.

Try keeping a log of your own reactions to certain situations, and see if you can identify patterns in your thinking.

ALTERNATIVE TREATMENTS In patients with seasonal affective disorder (SAD), episodes of depression will more likely occur during winter. A milder form of SAD has been called the winter blues. The rate of these disorders increases with latitude (**FIGURE 15.16**). Many of these patients respond favorably to *phototherapy*, which involves exposure to a high-intensity light source for part of each day.

(a)

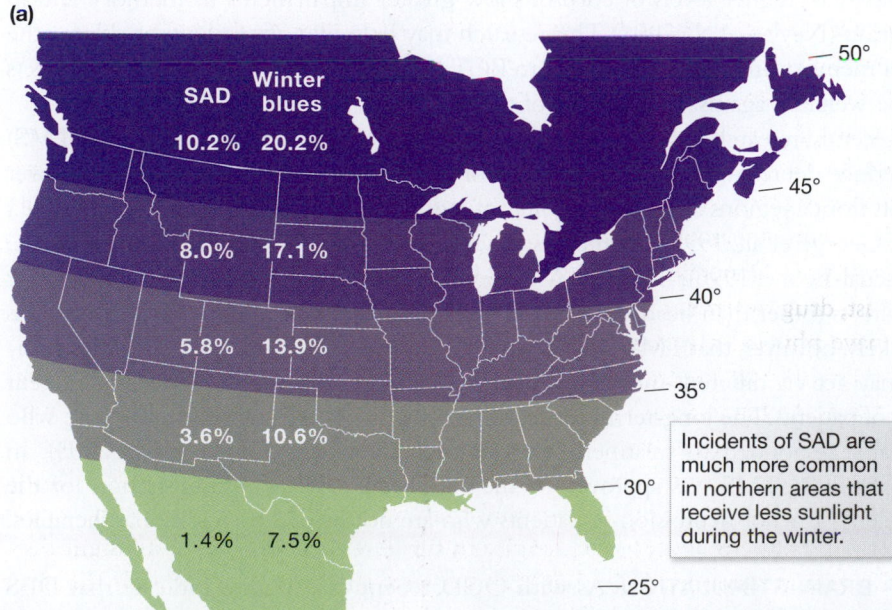

Incidents of SAD are much more common in northern areas that receive less sunlight during the winter.

(b)

FIGURE 15.16 Seasonal Affective Disorder (a) Incidence of SAD varies by latitude. (b) One treatment is phototherapy, where a patient sits in front of strong lighting for several hours each day to reduce symptoms.

For some depressed patients, regular aerobic exercise can reduce depression and prevent recurrence (Pollock, 2004). As described in Chapter 10, aerobic exercise may reduce depression because it releases endorphins, which are chemically related to norepinephrine, a neurotransmitter implicated in depression. Release of endorphins can cause an overall feeling of well-being (a feeling marathoners sometimes experience as "runner's high"). Aerobic exercise may also regularize bodily rhythms, improve self-esteem, and provide social support if people exercise with others. Depressed patients, however, may have difficulty finding the energy and motivation to begin an exercise regime.

In addition to these somewhat benign interventions, electroconvulsive therapy (ECT) has been effective for some people with major depression. Although ECT frequently results in a reduction of depressed mood, the mechanism by which this occurs is unknown (Fink, 2001). ECT may affect neurotransmitters or the neuroendocrine system; it has been shown to increase levels of acetylcholine, and drugs that block the action of acetylcholine reverse its beneficial effects. Regardless of how it works, ECT is a very effective treatment for those who are severely depressed and do not respond to conventional treatments (Hollon et al., 2002).

For a number of reasons, ECT might be preferable to other treatments for depression. Antidepressants can take weeks to be effective, whereas ECT works quickly. For a suicidal patient, waiting several weeks for relief can literally be deadly. In addition, ECT may be the treatment of choice for depression in pregnant women, since no evidence indicates that the seizures harm the developing fetus. Many psychotropic medications, in contrast, can cause birth defects. Most important, ECT has proved effective in patients for whom other treatments have failed.

ECT does, however, have some serious limitations, including a high relapse rate, (often necessitating repeated treatments), and memory impairments (Fink, 2001). In most cases, memory loss is limited to the day of ECT treatment. Some patients, however, experience substantial permanent memory loss (Donahue, 2000). Some centers perform unilateral ECT over only the hemisphere not dominant for language, a treatment that seems to reduce memory disruption (Papadimitrious, Zervas, & Papakostas, 2001). New research suggests the degree of memory and cognitive impairment resulting from ECT may be related to levels of cortisol, a hormone released in response to physical and psychological stress (see Chapter 10, "Health and Well-Being"). Depressed patients with higher levels of cortisol show greater impairments in memory and in cognition (Neylan et al., 2001). This research may help identify patients at risk for the loss of memory and of cognition due to ECT, and these potentially serious side effects can be weighed against the benefits of the treatment.

Recently, research has explored whether transcranial magnetic stimulation (TMS) can reduce depressive symptoms. A series of studies has demonstrated that TMS over the left frontal regions results in a significant reduction in depression (Chistyakov et al., 2004; George et al., 1995; George, Lisanby, & Sackheim, 1999; Pascual-Leone, Catala, & Pascual-Leone, 1996). Because TMS does not involve anesthesia or have any major side effects (other than headache), it can be administered outside hospital settings. It is not likely, however, that TMS will ever completely replace ECT, since the two methods may act via different mechanisms and may therefore be appropriate for different types of patients. The long-term value of TMS is that it is effective even for those who have not responded to treatment with antidepressants (Fitzgerald et al., 2003). In October 2008, TMS was approved by the U.S. Federal Drug Administration for the treatment of major depression in patients who are not helped by traditional therapies.

DEEP BRAIN STIMULATION As with OCD, recent case studies indicate that DBS might be valuable for treating severe depression when all other treatments have failed. Helen Mayberg and her colleagues were the first to try out this novel treatment, in 2003. Mayberg's earlier research had pointed to an area of the prefrontal cortex as abnormal in depression; following the logic of using DBS for Parkinson's, neurosurgeons inserted electrodes into this brain region in six severely depressed patients (Mayberg et al., 2005; McNeely et al., 2008). The results were stunning for four of the patients, some of whom felt relief as soon as the switch was turned on. For them, it was as if a horrible noise had stopped and a weight had been lifted, as if they had emerged into a more beautiful world (Dobbs, 2006; Ressler & Mayberg, 2007; **FIGURE 15.17**). DBS differs from other treatments in that researchers can relatively straightforwardly alter the electrical current, without the patients knowing, to demonstrate that the DBS is responsible for improvements in psychological functioning. Research using DBS to treat severe depression is now under way at a number of sites around the globe.

GENDER ISSUES IN TREATING DEPRESSION As noted in Chapter 14, women are twice as likely to be diagnosed with depression as men are. Some portion of this difference relates to high rates of domestic and other violence against women, reduced economic resources, and inequities at work (American Psychological Association, 2007). Women are also the primary consumers of psychotherapy. The American Psychological Association therefore has published *Guidelines for Psychological Practice with Girls and Women* (2007), which reminds therapists to be aware of gender-specific stressors such as the way work and family interact to place additional burdens on women and the biological realities of reproduction and of menopause. The guidelines also point out that women of color, lesbians, and women with disabilities are often stereotyped in ways that signal disregard for the choices they have made and the challenges they face; all these factors can interfere with the therapeutic process.

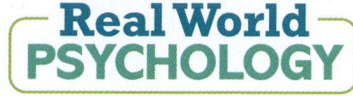

FIGURE 15.17 **Scientific Method: Mayberg's Study of DBS for Depression**

Hypothesis: Deep brain stimulation of an area of the prefrontal cortex may alleviate depression.

Research Method:

1 A pair of small holes were drilled into the skulls of six participants.

2 A pulse generator was attached under the collarbone, connecting to electrodes that passed through the holes in the skull to a specific area of the prefrontal cortex.

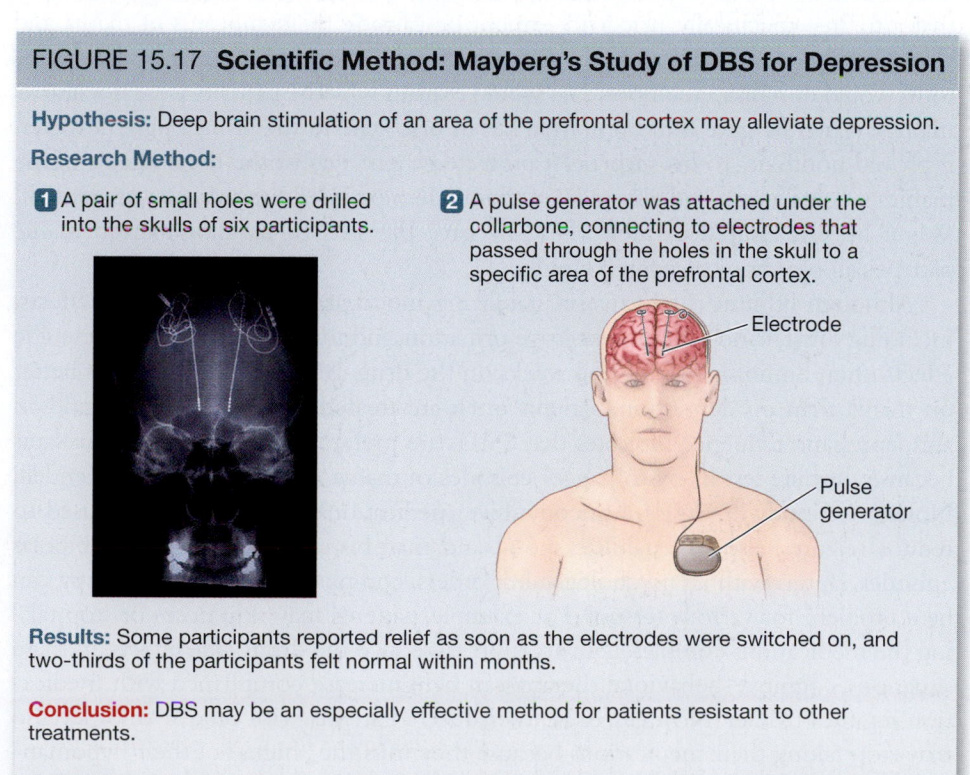

Electrode

Pulse generator

Results: Some participants reported relief as soon as the electrodes were switched on, and two-thirds of the participants felt normal within months.

Conclusion: DBS may be an especially effective method for patients resistant to other treatments.

Problems also exist in the treatment of depression in men. Men's reluctance to admit to depression and even greater reluctance to seek appropriate therapy have been described as "a conspiracy of silence that has long surrounded depression in men" (Brody, 1997). Two prominent men—Mike Wallace, a news correspondent and television news anchor, and William Styron, a Pulitzer Prize–winning author—have talked openly about their battles with depression. Wallace describes it this way: "The sunshine means nothing to you at all. The seasons, friends, good food mean nothing. All you focus on is yourself and how bad you feel." Styron writes, "In severe depression, the entire body and spirit of a person is in a state of shipwreck, of desolate lostness. Nothing animates the body or spirit. It's a total wipeout" (both qtd. in Brody, 1997, paragraphs 2–3). Public statements from such well-respected men may help break the silence surrounding depression in men and increase the number of men who seek psychotherapy. One goal is to help men stop masking their depression with alcohol, isolation, and irritability, any of which may be a symptom of unacknowledged depression.

Lithium Is Most Effective for Bipolar Disorder

Although major depression and bipolar disorder are disorders of mood, they are fundamentally different and require different treatments. Bipolar disorder, in which mood cycles between mania and depression, is one of the few mental disorders for which there is a clear optimal treatment: psychotropic medications, especially lithium (Geddes, Burgess, Hawton, Jamison, & Goodwin, 2004). In one study, only about 20 percent of patients maintained on lithium experienced relapses (Keller & Baker, 1991). The mechanisms by which lithium stabilizes mood are not well understood, but the drug seems to modulate neurotransmitter levels, balancing excitatory and inhibitory activities (Jope, 1999). As with other psychotropic drugs, the discovery of lithium for the treatment of bipolar disorder was serendipitous. In 1949, the researcher John Cade found that the urine of manic patients was toxic to guinea pigs. He believed that a toxin—specifically, uric acid—might be causing the symptoms of mania and that once the uric acid was removed from the body through the urine, the symptoms would diminish (a solution that would explain why the patients were not always manic). When he gave lithium urate, a salt in uric acid, to the guinea pigs, however, it proved nontoxic. To his surprise, it protected them against the toxic effects of the manic patients' urine and also sedated them. He next tried lithium salts on himself. When he was assured of their safety, he gave the salts to ten hospitalized manic patients, all of whom recovered rapidly.

Although lithium is effective in stabilizing mood, it has unpleasant side effects, including thirst, hand tremors, excessive urination, and memory problems. These side effects often diminish after several weeks on the drug. Because lithium works better on mania than on depression, patients often are treated with both lithium and an antidepressant. Evidence indicates that SSRIs are preferable to other antidepressants because they are less likely to trigger episodes of mania (Gijsman, Geddes, Rendell, Nolen, & Goodwin, 2004). Anticonvulsive medications, more commonly used to reduce seizures, also can stabilize mood and may be effective for intense bipolar episodes. But as with all psychological disorders, compliance with drug therapy can be a problem for various reasons. For example, patients may skip doses or stop taking the medications completely in an effort to reduce the drugs' side effects. In these situations, cognitive-behavioral therapy can help increase compliance with medication regimes (Miller, Norman, & Keitner, 1989). Patients with bipolar disorder also may stop taking their medications because they miss the "highs" of their hypomanic and manic phases (Chapter 14 quotes Kay Redfield Jamison's description of the intoxicating pleasure of mania.) Psychological therapy can help patients accept their need for medication and understand the impact their disorder has on them and on those around them.

Pharmacological Treatments Are Superior for Schizophrenia

In the early 1900s, Freud's psychoanalytic theory and treatments based on it were widely touted as the answer to many mental disorders. Even Freud, however, admitted that his techniques were effective only for what he termed "neuroses" and were unlikely to benefit patients with more severe psychotic disorders such as schizophrenia. Because psychotic patients were difficult to handle and even more difficult to treat, they generally were institutionalized in large mental hospitals. By 1934, according to estimates, the physician-to-patient ratio in such institutions in New York State was less than 1 to 200. In this undesirable situation, the staff and administration of mental hospitals were willing to try any inexpensive treatment that had a chance of decreasing the patient population or that at least might make the inmates more manageable. Brain surgery, such as prefrontal lobotomy, was considered a viable option for patients with severe mental disorders. Although Moniz initially reported that the operation was frequently successful (see "Alternative Biological Treatments Are Used in Extreme Cases," above), it soon became evident to him that anxious or depressed patients benefited most from the surgery. Schizophrenic patients did not seem to improve following the operation. Fortunately, as noted earlier, the introduction of psychotropic medications in the 1950s eliminated the use of lobotomy.

PHARMACOLOGICAL TREATMENTS Since the sixteenth century, extracts from dogbane, a toxic herb, had been used to calm highly agitated patients. The critical ingredient was isolated in the 1950s and named *reserpine*. When given to schizophrenic patients, it not only had a sedative effect but also was an effective antipsychotic, reducing the positive symptoms of schizophrenia such as delusions and hallucinations. Shortly afterward, a synthetic version of reserpine was created that had fewer side effects. This drug, *chlorpromazine*, acts as a major tranquilizer. It reduces anxiety, sedates without inducing sleep, and decreases the severity and frequency of the positive symptoms of schizophrenia. Later, another antipsychotic, *haloperidol*, was developed that was chemically different and had less of a sedating effect than chlorpromazine.

Haloperidol and chlorpromazine revolutionized the treatment of schizophrenia and became the most frequently used treatment for this disorder. Schizophrenic patients who had been hospitalized for years were able to walk out of mental institutions and live independently. These antipsychotics are not without drawbacks, however. For example, the medications have little or no impact on the negative symptoms of schizophrenia. In addition, they have significant side effects. Chlorpromazine sedates patients, can cause constipation and weight gain, and causes cardiovascular damage. Although haloperidol does not cause these symptoms, both drugs have significant motor side effects that resemble symptoms of Parkinson's disease: immobility of facial muscles, trembling of extremities, muscle spasms, uncontrollable salivation, and a shuffling walk. Tardive dyskinesia—involuntary movements of the lips, tongue, face, legs, or other parts of the body—is another devastating side effect of these medications and is irreversible once it appears. Despite these side effects, haloperidol and chlorpromazine were the only available options.

The late 1980s saw the introduction of *clozapine*, which is significantly different from previous antipsychotic medications in a number of ways. First, it acts not only on dopamine receptors but also on those for serotonin, norepinephrine,

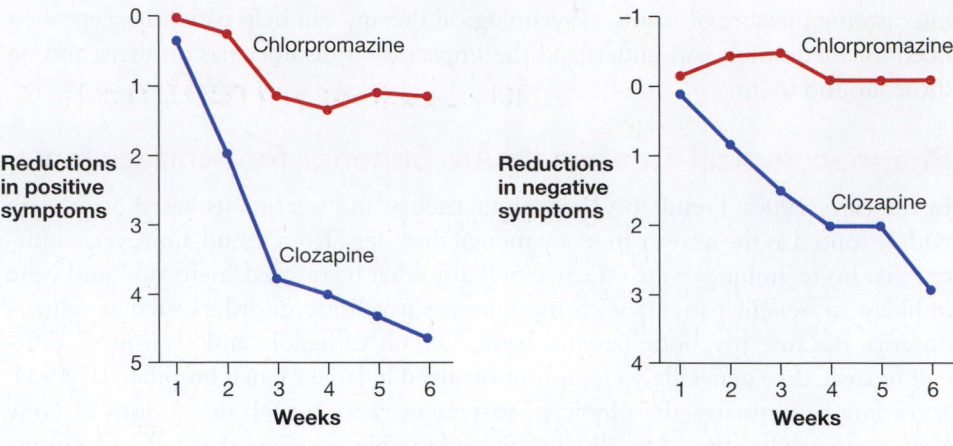

FIGURE 15.18 The Effectiveness of Clozapine

Many patients who had not responded to the previously available neuroleptics found that clozapine reduced the positive and negative symptoms of schizophrenia.

acetylcholine, and histamine. Second, it is beneficial in treating the negative as well as the positive symptoms of schizophrenia (**FIGURE 15.18**). Many patients who had not responded to the previously available neuroleptics improved on clozapine. Third, no signs of Parkinson's symptoms or of tardive dyskinesia appeared in any of the patients taking the drug. Clozapine has fewer side effects than either chlorpromazine or haloperidol, but its side effects are serious: seizures, heart arrhythmias, and substantial weight gain. Of even greater concern is that clozapine can cause a fatal reduction in white blood cells. Although the risk of this problem is low, patients taking the drug must have frequent blood tests. The cost of the blood tests, in addition to the high cost of the medication, has made this drug treatment prohibitively expensive for many patients. More recently, other medications similar to clozapine in structure, pharmacology, and effectiveness have been introduced that do not reduce white blood cell counts. Called *second-generation antipsychotics,* these drugs are now the first line in treatment for schizophrenia (Walker, Kestler, Bollini, & Hochman, 2004). An analysis of 11 studies of a total of 2,769 patients found that these second-generation antipsychotics have about one-fifth the risk of producing tardive dyskinesia as first-generation drugs (Correll, Leucht, & Kane, 2004).

PSYCHOSOCIAL TREATMENTS Medication is essential in the treatment of schizophrenia. Without it, patients may deteriorate, experiencing more frequent and more severe psychotic episodes. When antipsychotic drugs became available, other types of therapies for schizophrenia were virtually dismissed. It became clear over time, however, that although medication effectively reduces delusions and hallucinations, it does not substantially affect patients' social functioning. Thus antipsychotic drugs fall short of being a cure and require combination with other treatment approaches to help people lead productive lives.

Social skills training, for example, is an effective way to address some deficits in schizophrenics (**FIGURE 15.19**). These patients can benefit from intensive training on regulating affect, recognizing social cues, and predicting the effects of their behavior in social situations. With intensive long-term training, schizophrenic patients can generalize the skills learned

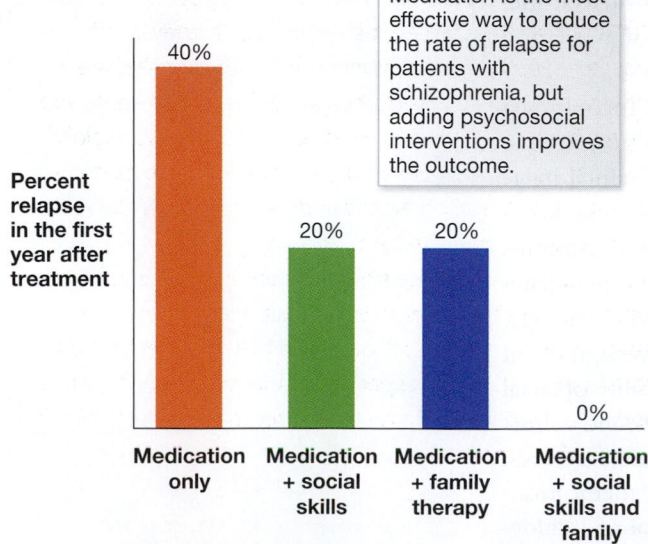

Medication is the most effective way to reduce the rate of relapse for patients with schizophrenia, but adding psychosocial interventions improves the outcome.

FIGURE 15.19 The Effectiveness of Antipsychotic Medications and Social Skills Training

Suppose you are hurrying to class one winter morning, slip on some ice, fall, and sprain your ankle. You may not realize that your ankle is sprained, but you know you are injured. Another student offers to help you to the infirmary, and you gladly accept. However, if you were suffering from *anosognosia,* a condition caused by a brain disease or injury to the parietal lobe, you would not know you were injured. People with this condition may have quite dramatic impairments, such as paralysis and blindness, but are unaware of their problems.

Approximately 50 percent of individuals with schizophrenia, and 40 percent of individuals with bipolar disorder, are unaware of their disorder. However, unlike anosognosia, in which a parietal lobe defect can be seen on a brain scan, there are no objective markers for unawareness of mental disorders. This failure to recognize a disorder is the most common reason that people with these diagnoses do not take their medication, often resulting in worsening of symptoms and increased likelihood of victimization, homelessness, joblessness, incarceration, rehospitalization, and violent acts against others and themselves. In addition, if a person is not treated, the disorder may progress to the point where it is no longer treatable; research has shown, for example, that delaying treatment for schizophrenia causes the disorder to become more severe.

Many family members have been frustrated trying to get help for relatives who are unaware of their own disorders, refuse treatment, and deteriorate. Community members have been frustrated in their inability to help the homeless, who, depending on the state, legally may have the right to refuse treatment. Should people unaware of their own mental disorders be treated even if they do not want to be?

We do not force treatment on people with medical problems, even if their reasoning for rejecting treatment is illogical. Treating mental disorders is even more of an ethical quagmire, mainly because we do not understand many of the disorders completely. As discussed in Chapter 14, the neural underpinnings of depression, bipolar disorder, and schizophrenia are still being studied. Diagnoses are based on behaviors, not on blood tests, and those behaviors may have different origins and be open to various interpretations. In addition, a minority of both psychologists and psychiatrists do not agree that many mental disorders have biological bases; instead, they explain them as emotional reactions to negative life circumstances, stress, or acute trauma. Until research can prove direct causation of mental disorders by biologic processes and can uncover the mechanisms that cause and can treat them, these practitioners believe any involuntary treatments violate an individual's right of self-determination.

Safety is also an ethical issue. Even if a diagnosis is agreed upon, treatments vary in side effects, costs, and effectiveness. When a person is treated involuntarily, who should determine what treatments to use—the family (if there is one), the physician, the community, the government? The optimal treatment as seen by the community or government may be the most cost-effective one, whereas the optimal treatment for the individual may not be. Ethicists also worry that if individuals are threatened with involuntary treatment, they will less likely seek treatment when they need it or may be reluctant to continue it once they have started.

Studies done from the ethical standpoint of fairness and justice suggest a different treatment modality. A sense of fairness and "being heard" can matter almost as much as treatment pressures. Therefore, any treatment must respect the person with the disorder and treat the person fairly. One such treatment that has proved highly effective and has markedly decreased rehospitalizations involves offering patients a contract in which they receive a small amount of money or gift certificates for treatment compliance. This cognitive-behavioral technique, in which positive or healthy behavior is reliably and clearly rewarded, may be perceived as coercion or as exploitation of poor patients. However, the majority of patients do not consider the practice coercive and understand that, unlike involuntary treatment, they can turn it down.

What would you do if your sibling or parent, for example, was experiencing psychotic episodes but was unaware of having a disorder and refused medical evaluation or treatment? Would you consider it ethical to respect your relative's autonomy and do nothing, or would you force him or her to go for treatment?

in therapy to other social environments. Also, when self-care skills are deficient, behavioral interventions can focus on areas such as grooming and bathing, management of medications, and financial planning. Training in specific cognitive skills, such as in modifying thinking patterns and in coping with auditory hallucinations, has been less effective.

Recently, Aaron Beck has proposed that an intensive form of cognitive-behavioral therapy (CBT) is effective for treating schizophrenia (Beck & Rector, 2005). Beck believes that brain dysfunction gives rise to disordered beliefs and behaviors and that schizophrenia may be due partly to limited cognitive resources and an inability to inhibit the intrusion of inappropriate thoughts. From this perspective, delusions and hallucinations reflect biased information processing. In CBT for schizophrenia, much initial effort involves getting the client to trust the therapist as nonjudgmental and understanding of the client's perspective. Over time, the therapy becomes more formal as the therapist helps the client understand how stressful life circumstances contribute to disordered thoughts and how alternative explanations might exist for delusions and hallucinations. Initial studies using CBT for schizophrenia indicate that it is more effective than other psychological treatments in reducing symptoms such as delusions and hallucinations.

PROGNOSIS IN SCHIZOPHRENIA Most patients diagnosed with schizophrenia experience multiple psychotic episodes over the course of the disorder. In some patients, the disorder apparently progresses; each schizophrenic episode lays the groundwork for increasingly severe symptoms in the future. Thus it is in the schizophrenic patient's best interest to treat the disorder early and aggressively.

Although the disorder becomes progressively more severe in some affected individuals, most schizophrenic patients improve over time. One long-term study that followed participants for an average of 32 years showed that between half and two-thirds were recovered or had had considerable improvement in functioning on follow-up (Harding, Zubin, & Strauss, 1987). No one knows why most schizophrenics apparently improve as they grow older. Perhaps they find a treatment regimen most effective for them, or perhaps changes in the brain that occur with aging somehow result in fewer psychotic episodes. Dopamine levels may decrease with age, and this decrease may be related to the improvement in symptoms.

The prognosis for schizophrenic patients depends on factors including age of onset, gender, and culture. Those diagnosed later in life tend to have a more favorable prognosis than those who experience their first symptoms during childhood or adolescence (McGlashan, 1988). Women tend to have better prognoses than men do (Hambrecht, Maurer, Hafner, & Sartorius, 1992), perhaps because schizophrenia in women tends to appear later than in men. Interestingly, culture also plays a role in prognosis. In developing countries, schizophrenia often is not so severe as in developed countries (Jablensky, 1989; Leff, Sartorius, Jablensky, Korten, & Ernberg, 1992), possibly because more extensive family networks in developing countries provide more support for schizophrenic patients.

There Are Important Considerations in Selecting a Psychotherapist

In 1999, the surgeon general of the United States reported that in any given year approximately 1 in 5 Americans has some form of diagnosable mental illness and about 15 percent of Americans seek mental health treatment of some kind. The cost of treating mental disorders in the United States is more than $100 billion each year. A dizzying array of providers offer treatment, ranging from those with limited training (e.g., former addicts who provide peer counseling) to those with advanced degrees in psychopathology and its treatment. In addition to mental health specialists, regular health care providers (e.g., internists, pediatricians), human-service workers (e.g., school counselors), and volunteers (e.g., self-help groups) also assist those with mental problems. No matter who administers the therapy, however, most of the techniques used have emerged from psychological laboratories.

Table 15.2 The Major Types of Specialized Mental Practitioners

Specialty	Degree	Placement
Clinical psychologists	PhD or PsyD	Academic or hospital settings
Psychiatrists	Medical degree (MD)	Hospitals or private practice
Counseling psychologists	PhD	Schools/colleges (counselors)
Psychiatric social workers	Master's in social work (MSW)	Psychiatric hospitals, house calls
Psychiatric nurses	Bachelor's in nursing (BSN)	Hospitals or in-treatment centers
Paraprofessionals	Limited advanced training	Outreach programs, residential treatment centers

As summarized in **TABLE 15.2**, the major types of specialized mental practitioners include the following:

- *Clinical psychologists* typically have a doctoral degree. The graduate training for a PhD takes four to six years, and it emphasizes the design and analysis of research and the use of treatments that have empirical support. Many clinical psychologists work in academic or hospital settings, where they conduct research in addition to providing treatment. A relatively new training program in clinical psychology leads to the PsyD. This program emphasizes clinical skills over research and is meant for those who intend to provide direct mental health services. Clinical psychologists typically are not able to prescribe medications, although efforts are under way to give them such privileges. In New Mexico and Louisiana, clinical psychologists with specialized training in psychoactive drugs can prescribe medications; similar legislation is being proposed elsewhere in the United States.

- *Psychiatrists* have a medical degree (MD) and three to four additional years of specialized training in residency programs. They often work in hospitals or in private practice. Psychiatrists are the only mental health practitioners legally authorized to prescribe drugs in most of the United States.

- *Counseling psychologists* often have a PhD in counseling psychology. They typically deal with problems of adjustment and life stress that do not involve mental illness, such as stress related to scholastic, marital, and occupational problems. Most colleges have staff members who specialize in problems common to students, such as test anxiety, learning disorders, sleep problems, and family issues.

- *Psychiatric social workers* most often have a master's degree in social work (MSW) and specialized training in mental health care. In addition to working with patients in psychiatric hospitals, they may visit people in their homes and address problems arising from the home environments. Their work might include helping clients receive appropriate resources from social and community agencies.

- *Psychiatric nurses* typically have a bachelor's degree in nursing (BSN) and special training in the care of mentally ill patients. They often work in hospitals or in treatment centers that specialize in serious mental illness.

- *Paraprofessionals* have limited advanced training and usually work under supervision. They assist those with mental health problems in the challenges of daily living. For example, they may work in crisis intervention, pastoral counseling, or community outreach programs, or they may supervise clients of residential treatment centers.

Choosing the right therapist is difficult but extremely important for ensuring successful treatment. The right therapist must have the appropriate training and experience for the specific mental disorder, and the person seeking help must believe the therapist is trustworthy and caring. The initial consultation should make the person feel at ease and hopeful that his or her psychological problem can be resolved. If not, the person should seek another therapist. The ability to prescribe medication should play only a minor role in the choice of therapist, since almost all practitioners have arrangements with physicians who can prescribe medications. It is more important to find someone who is both empathic and experienced in the methods known to be effective in treating specific mental disorders.

The Internet provides a growing number of resources for those dealing with life problems on their own. These self-help programs are meant for minor stresses associated with daily living rather than for more serious mental disorders. The Web sites of the American Psychological Association (www.apa.org) and the National Institute of Mental Health (www.nimh.nih.gov) offer additional information about choosing mental health practitioners.

CRITICAL THINKING SKILL

Avoiding the Sunk Costs Fallacy

Suppose you are in therapy with someone who has a good reputation and was highly recommended to you by a good friend or your family physician. You have been meeting with this therapist once a week for the last three months. Despite this sizable commitment of both time and money, you do not feel you are doing any better or that the therapist is committed to helping you lessen your problem. Would you reason that since you have already spent so much time and money working with this therapist you should continue, or would you look for a new therapist?

If you stick with a therapist simply because of what you have invested, you are demonstrating the "sunk costs" fallacy. The time and money spent are gone, and you cannot get them back. Future actions cannot be justified by thinking about prior, or "sunk," costs. This fallacy can occur in various settings, so it is important to learn how to recognize and avoid such thinking. Here are some other examples.

Suppose you have bought expensive tickets for a play. By intermission, you have not enjoyed the play at all. Do you stay because of the time and money you have already spent, or do you leave and spend the next hour doing something you might enjoy more? If you reason that you should stay because of what you have already spent, you are demonstrating the sunk costs fallacy. If you stay for more of the play, you might regret not having done something more fun. Other scenarios may have graver implications. For example, a government might reason that because it has invested many millions (or billions) of dollars in a war, in which thousands of people have died, withdrawing its troops from that war would mean losing the investments in money and in human lives. Nothing can bring back the money and the lives, however, so the decision about what to do next should not rest on how much has been spent or lost thus far. Instead, the decision should rest on what is the best option at this point.

SUMMING UP

What Are the Most Effective Treatments?

Psychotherapy and biological therapy are used to treat mental disorders. When the two are equally effective, psychotherapy is preferred because it has fewer side effects and persists beyond treatment. Cognitive and behavioral therapies, especially exposure and response prevention, are particularly useful for anxiety disorders, although drug treatments are also used for panic disorder and OCD. Among the treatment strategies for mood disorders are exercise, antidepressants, cognitive-behavioral therapy, electroconvulsive therapy, transcranial magnetic stimulation, and deep brain stimulation. Differences in the incidence of depression for men and women have led to specific suggestions for psychotherapy, which include a greater awareness of the way sex role expectations affect the willingness to admit to depression and seek treatment for it, and the biological and social realities of being female or male. Psychopharmacology is the recommended treatment for bipolar disorder and schizophrenia. Various drugs are safe for schizophrenia, but they are most effective when combined with other treatment approaches. Training in social and self-care skills can help patients improve their abilities to interact with others and to take care of themselves. Behavioral interventions can promote improved self-care and increased compliance with medication. In choosing among the many types of psychotherapists, it is most important to find someone the patient can trust and with whom he or she can establish a productive therapeutic relationship.

MEASURING UP

Indicate whether cognitive-behavioral therapy, drug therapy, or a combination of the two is the recommended treatment for each disorder listed.
   a. bipolar disorder
   b. depression
   c. generalized anxiety disorder
   d. obsessive-compulsive disorder
   e. panic disorder
   f. phobias
   g. schizophrenia

Can Personality Disorders Be Treated?

Just as not much is known about the causes of personality disorders such as borderline personality disorder and antisocial personality disorder, little is known about how best to treat them. There is a growing literature of case studies describing treatment approaches for personality disorders, but few large, well-controlled studies have been undertaken. The one thing about personality disorders that most therapists agree on is that they are notoriously difficult to treat. Individuals with personality disorders who are in therapy are usually also being treated for an Axis I disorder—such as OCD or depression—which typically is the problem for which they sought therapy in the first place. People rarely seek therapy for personality disorders because one hallmark of these disorders is that patients see the environment rather than their own behavior as the cause of their problems. This

LEARNING OBJECTIVE
Explain why personality disorders are difficult to treat.

outlook often makes individuals with personality disorders very difficult to engage in therapy.

Dialectical Behavior Therapy Is Most Successful for Borderline Personality Disorder

The impulsivity, emotional disturbances, and identity disturbances characteristic of borderline personality disorder make therapy for those affected very challenging. Traditional psychotherapy approaches have been largely unsuccessful, so therapists have attempted to develop approaches specific to borderline personality disorder.

dialectical behavior therapy (DBT) A form of therapy used to treat borderline personality disorder.

The most successful treatment approach to date for borderline personality disorder was developed by Marsha Linehan in the 1980s. **Dialectical behavior therapy (DBT)** combines elements of the behavioral, cognitive, and psychodynamic approaches (Lieb, Zanarini, Schmahl, Linehan, & Bohus, 2004). All patients are seen in both group and individual sessions, and the responsibilities of the patient and the therapist are made explicit. Therapy proceeds in three stages. In the first stage, the therapist targets the patient's most extreme and dysfunctional behaviors. Often these are self-cutting and suicidal threats or attempts. The focus is on replacing these behaviors with more appropriate ones. The patient learns problem-solving techniques and more effective and acceptable ways of coping with his or her emotions. In the second stage, the therapist helps the patient explore past traumatic experiences that may be at the root of emotional problems. In the third stage, the therapist helps the patient develop self-respect and independent problem-solving. This stage is crucial because borderline patients depend heavily on others for support and validation, and they must be able to generate these attitudes and skills themselves or they likely will revert to their previous behavior patterns.

Because the symptoms experienced by individuals with borderline personality disorder can border on psychosis or mirror depression, researchers previously believed that these patients would develop an Axis I disorder such as schizophrenia or depression. Studies that have followed these individuals over time, however, have demonstrated that instead their symptoms remain relatively unchanged (Plakun, Burkhardt, & Muller, 1985). The only group that shows long-term improvement is borderline patients of a high socioeconomic level who receive intensive treatment; they demonstrate improved interpersonal relationships and often achieve full-time employment (Stone, Stone, & Hurt, 1987). In the remainder of borderline patients, however, interpersonal and occupational problems are the norm. Substance abuse is common, and many patients attempt suicide multiple times.

Therapeutic approaches targeted at borderline personality disorder, such as DBT, may improve the prognosis for these patients. Studies have demonstrated that those undergoing DBT are more likely to remain in treatment and less likely to be suicidal than are patients in other types of therapy (Linehan, Armstrong, Suarez, Allmon, & Heard, 1991; Linehan, Heard, & Armstrong, 1993). SSRIs are often prescribed along with DBT to treat feelings of depression. Although DBT was initially developed as an outpatient therapy, it recently has been adapted for use in an inpatient setting (Swenson, Sanderson, Dulie, & Linehan, 2001). Because borderline patients thrive on attention, inpatient settings not designed for these patients can inadvertently reinforce dysfunctional behaviors, such as self-injury and suicide attempts, that bring them attention. The result is often both a worsening of symptoms and long-term hospitalization (Rosenbluth & Silver, 1992). The DBT program begins with a three-month inpatient stay followed by long-term outpatient therapy. It has been very effective in reducing depression, anxiety, and suicidal discussions and attempts (Bohus et al., 2004; Lynch, Trost, Salsman, & Linehan, 2007).

Antisocial Personality Disorder Is Difficult to Treat

Although treating borderline patients may be very difficult, treating those with antisocial personality disorder often seems impossible. These patients lie without thinking twice about it, care little for others' feelings, and live for the present without consideration of the future. All these factors make development of a therapeutic relationship and motivation for change remote possibilities at best. Antisocial individuals are often more interested in manipulating their therapists than in changing their own behavior. Therapists working with these patients must be constantly on guard.

THERAPEUTIC APPROACHES FOR ANTISOCIAL PERSONALITY DISORDER

Numerous treatment approaches have been tried for antisocial personality disorder (and its extreme variant called *psychopathy*). Because antisocial individuals apparently have diminished cortical arousal, stimulants have been prescribed to normalize arousal levels. Evidence indicates that these drugs are beneficial in the short term but not the long term. Anti-anxiety drugs may lower hostility levels somewhat, and lithium has shown promise in treating the aggressive, impulsive behavior of violent criminals who are psychopathic. Overall, however, psychotropic medications have not been effective in treating this disorder.

Similarly, traditional psychotherapeutic approaches seem of little use in treating antisocial personality disorder. Behavioral and cognitive approaches have had somewhat more success. Behavioral approaches reinforce appropriate behavior and ignore or punish inappropriate behavior in an attempt to replace maladaptive behavior patterns with more socially appropriate ones. This approach seems to work best when the therapist controls reinforcement, the client cannot leave treatment, and the client is part of a group. Individual therapy sessions rarely produce any change in antisocial behavior. Clearly, the behavioral approach cannot be implemented on an outpatient basis, since the client will receive reinforcement for his or her antisocial behavior outside of therapy and can leave treatment at any time. For these reasons, therapy for this disorder is most effective in a residential treatment center or a correctional facility.

More recently, cognitive approaches have been tried for antisocial personality disorder. Aaron Beck and his colleagues (1990) have conceptualized this disorder as a series of faulty cognitions. The antisocial individual believes his or her desire for something justifies any actions he or she takes to attain it. The person believes those actions will not have negative consequences or, if they do, that these consequences are not important. The person also believes he or she is always right and what others think is unimportant. Therapy therefore focuses on making the client aware of these beliefs and challenging their validity. Therapists try to demonstrate that the client can meet his or her goals more easily by following the rules of society than by trying to get around them, as in the following example (Beck et al., 1990):

> Therapist: How well has the "beat-the-system" approach actually worked out for you over time?
>
> Brett: It works great . . . until someone catches on or starts to catch on. Then you have to scrap that plan and come up with a new one.
>
> Therapist: How difficult was it, you know, to cover up one scheme and come up with a new one?
>
> Brett: Sometimes it was really easy. There are some real pigeons out there.
>
> Therapist: Was it always easy?
>
> Brett: Well, no. Sometimes it was a real bitch. . . . Seems like I'm always needing a good plan to beat the system.

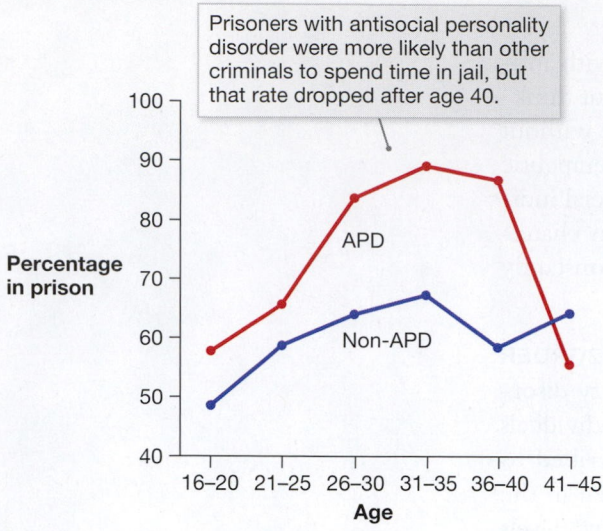

Prisoners with antisocial personality disorder were more likely than other criminals to spend time in jail, but that rate dropped after age 40.

FIGURE 15.20 Antisocial Personality Disorder For this longitudinal study, the percentage of participants in prison during each five-year period is shown.

Therapist: Do you think it's ever easier to go with the system instead of trying to beat it in some way?

Brett: Well, after all that I have been through, I would have to say yes, there have been times that going with the system would have been easier in the long run. . . . But . . . it's such a challenge to beat the system. It feels exciting when I come up with a new plan and think I can make it work.

This dialogue illustrates both the cognitive approach and why these clients are so difficult to work with. Even if they know what they are doing is wrong, they do not care. They live for the thrill of getting away with something.

PROGNOSIS FOR ANTISOCIAL PERSONALITY DISORDER The prognosis that antisocial patients will change their behaviors as a result of therapy is poor, and this is especially true for those with psychopathic traits. Some of the more recently developed cognitive techniques show promise, but no good evidence indicates that they produce long-lasting or even real changes. Fortunately for society, antisocial individuals without psychopathy typically improve after age 40 (**FIGURE 15.20**). The reasons for this improvement are unknown, but it may be due to a reduction in biological drives. Alternative theories suggest these individuals may gain insight into their self-defeating behaviors or may just get worn out and be unable to continue their manipulative ways. The improvement, however, is mainly in the realm of antisocial behavior. The underlying egocentricity, callousness, and manipulativeness can remain unchanged (Harpur & Hare, 1994), especially for those who are psychopathic. In fact, although criminal acts decrease among those with antisocial personality disorder after age 40, more than half of individuals with psychopathic traits continue to be arrested after age 40 (Hare, McPherson, & Forth, 1988). Thus although some aspects of their behavior mellow with age, psychopaths remain rather indifferent to traditional societal norms.

Because of the limited effectiveness of therapy for this disorder, time and effort may be better spent in prevention. *Conduct disorder* is a childhood condition known to be a precursor to antisocial personality disorder. Some of the environmental and developmental risk factors for conduct disorder have been identified, and focusing on these may reduce the likelihood that a child with conduct disorder will grow up to have antisocial personality disorder.

 SUMMING UP

Can Personality Disorders Be Treated?

Personality disorders are characterized by long-standing maladaptive ways of interacting with the world, and they are notoriously difficult to treat. Efforts have been made to develop treatment programs for borderline and antisocial personality disorders because they can have devastating effects on the individual, the family, and society. Dialectical behavior therapy is the most successful method of treating borderline personality disorder. At this point, no treatment approach appears particularly successful for antisocial personality disorder, especially its psychopathic variant.

Why are personality disorders so difficult to treat? Select all that apply.
a. People with personality disorders are difficult to engage in therapy because they do not believe their actions cause their problems.
b. People with personality disorders believe their problems are caused by their environments.
c. People with personality disorders believe they are fundamentally flawed individuals unworthy of help.

How Should Childhood and Adolescent Disorders Be Treated?

It is estimated that in the United States more than 12 percent of children and adolescents suffer from mental disorders (Leckman et al., 1995). Childhood experience and development are critically important to adult mental health. Problems not addressed during childhood will persist into adulthood and will likely be more significant and more difficult to treat. Most theories of human development regard children as more malleable than adults and therefore more amenable to treatment. Thus childhood disorders should be the focus of research into etiology, prevention, and treatment. To illustrate the issues involved in treating childhood disorders, the following section considers treatment approaches for adolescent depression, ADHD, and autism.

LEARNING OBJECTIVE

Explain key arguments in the debate about prescribing medication to children with depression and ADHD.

Understand that sometimes behavioral treatments are best for biological disorders such as autism.

The Use of Medication to Treat Adolescent Depression Is Controversial

Adolescent depression is a serious problem, affecting approximately 1 in 20 American adolescents at any time (Angold & Costello, 2001). Untreated depression is associated with drug abuse, dropping out of school, and suicide. In the United States, approximately 5,000 teenagers kill themselves each year, making it the third leading cause of death for that age group (Arias, MacDorman, Strobino, & Guyer, 2003). For many years, depression in children and adolescents was ignored or viewed as a typical part of growing up. According to a report of the U.S. surgeon general, fewer than 30 percent of children who have mental health problems receive any type of treatment (USDHHS, 1999). Understandably, then, many in the mental health community reacted favorably to the initial use of SSRIs such as Prozac to treat adolescent depression. Studies had found tricyclic antidepressants ineffective and the side effects potentially dangerous for adolescents, but the first studies using SSRIs found them effective and safe (e.g., Emslie et al., 1997).

From the time that SSRIs were introduced as treatments for adolescent depression, some mental health researchers raised concerns that the drugs might cause some adolescents to become suicidal (Jureidini et al., 2004), partly on the basis of findings that SSRIs cause some adults to feel restless, impulsive, and suicidal. Following a report by one drug company of an increase in suicidal thoughts among adolescents taking its product, the U.S. Food and Drug Administration (FDA) asked all drug companies to analyze their records for similar reports. An analysis of reports on more than 4,400 children and adolescents found that about twice as many of those taking SSRIs reported having suicidal thoughts (4 percent) as those taking a placebo (2 percent), but none of the children or adolescents committed suicide.

Given evidence of increased thoughts of suicide, the FDA voted in 2004 to require manufacturers to add to their product labels a warning that antidepressants increase the risk of suicidal thinking and behavior in depressed children and adolescents and that physicians prescribing these drugs need to balance risk with clinical need. Physicians were also advised to watch their patients closely, especially in the first few weeks of treatment. Suddenly many parents were wondering whether SSRIs were safe for their children.

Many issues concerning SSRIs and children need to be evaluated critically. First, are SSRIs effective for young people, and if so, are they more effective than other treatments? Second, do these drugs cause suicidal feelings, or are depressed adolescents likely to feel suicidal whether or not they take medication? Finally, how many adolescents would be suicidal if their depression was left untreated?

The Treatment of Adolescents with Depression Study (TADS, 2004), an ambitious research program supported by the U.S. National Institutes of Health, provides clear evidence that the SSRI Prozac is effective in treating adolescent depression. This study examined 439 patients age 12 to 17 who had been depressed for an average of 40 weeks before the study began. Participants were assigned randomly to a type of treatment and followed for 12 weeks. The results indicated that 61 percent of participants taking Prozac showed improvement in symptoms, compared with 43 percent receiving cognitive-behavioral therapy and 35 percent taking a placebo. The group receiving Prozac and CBT did best (71 percent improved); this finding is consistent with those of other studies, which have shown that combining drugs and psychotherapy often produces the strongest results for treating depression. A more recent, 36-week follow-up of the TADS treatment sample found that although the combined group had the best outcomes (86 percent improvement), improvement with CBT alone (81 percent) was similar to that with Prozac alone (81 percent; March et al., 2007; **FIGURE 15.21**). In terms of suicidality, the results were more mixed. All treatment groups experienced a reduction in thoughts of suicide compared with the baseline. However, participants in the Prozac group were twice as likely to have serious suicidal thoughts or intentions compared with those undergoing other treatments, and of the 7 adolescents who attempted suicide during the study, 6 were taking Prozac. The greater risk of suicidal thoughts or events continued through 36 weeks. Critics of adolescents receiving drugs point out that these findings are consistent with other studies showing a risk from SSRIs (Antonuccio & Burns, 2004).

A few things should be kept in mind in analyzing of the use of SSRIs for adolescent depression. In the TADS study, suicide attempts were quite uncommon (7 of 439 patients). This result is consistent with the FDA finding that about 4 percent of adolescents taking Prozac will become suicidal. Moreover, only a small number of the 5,000 adolescents who kill themselves each year are taking antidepressants of any kind. The question is whether the millions of children who take antidepressants experience more benefits than risks. In addition, the suicide rates have dropped since the use of SSRIs became widespread (**FIGURE 15.22**). The greater the increase in the number of SSRI prescriptions for adolescents within a region, the greater the reduction in teenage suicides (Olfson, Shaffer, Marcus, & Greenberg, 2003). Thus not providing SSRIs to adolescents may raise the suicide rate (Brent, 2004).

According to some researchers, the relative success of psychotherapy for teenage depression makes it a better treatment choice. Indeed, considerable evidence shows that psychotherapy is effective on its own (Mufson et al., 2004) and also enhances drug treatment. Psychological treatments such as interpersonal psychotherapy are successful as well (Hollon et al., 2002). But getting adolescents to comply with psychotherapy can be challenging. Psychotherapy is also time consuming and expensive, and many health insurance companies provide only minimal support (Rifkin

FIGURE 15.21 Scientific Method: The Treatment of Adolescents with Depression Study

Hypothesis: Prozac is the most effective method for treating adolescent depression.

Research Method:

1 Patients aged 12 to 17 were randomly assigned to a type of treatment and followed it for 12 weeks.

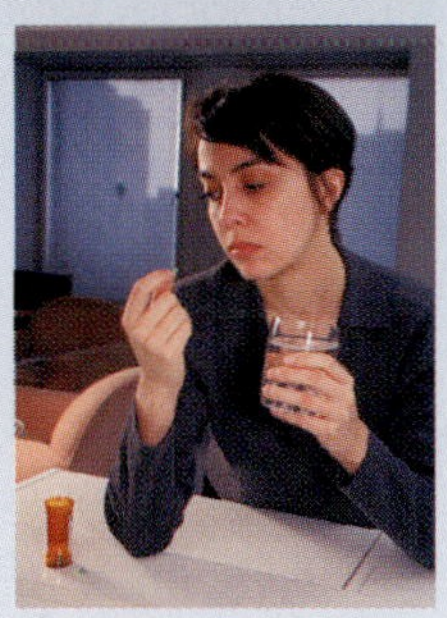

2 Some of the patients were given Prozac, some cognitive-behavioral therapy, some a placebo, and some Prozac and cognitive-behavioral therapy together.

Results: The group receiving Prozac and CBT did best. A follow-up of the TADS treatment sample found that although the combined group continued to have the best outcomes, improvement with CBT alone was similar to that with Prozac alone.

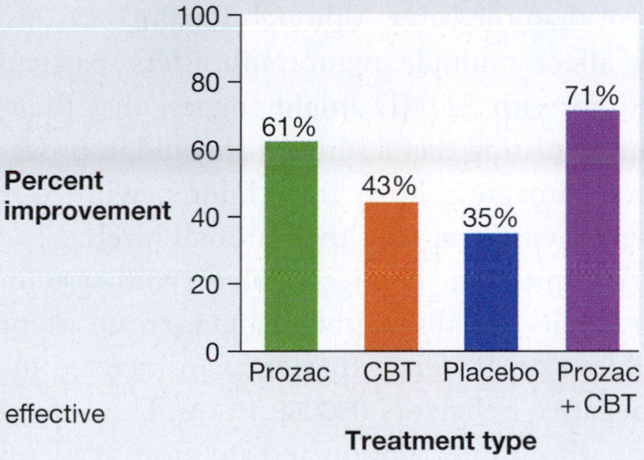

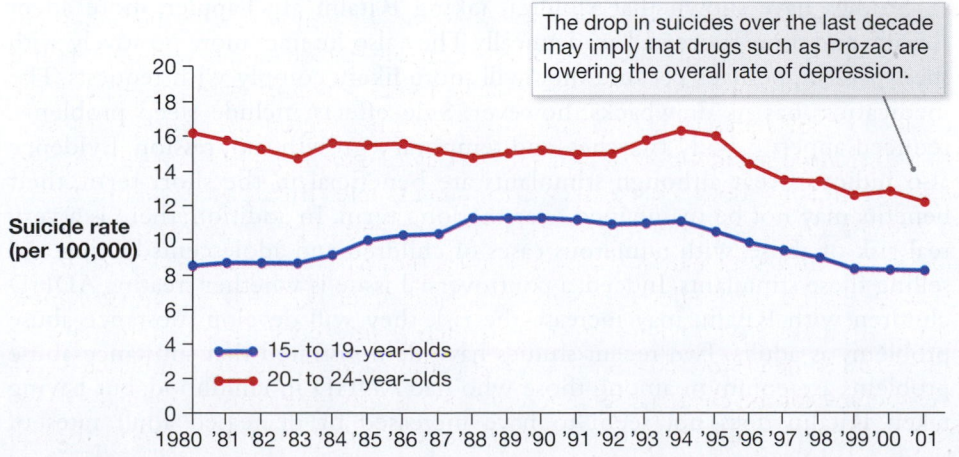

Percent improvement

- Prozac: 61%
- CBT: 43%
- Placebo: 35%
- Prozac + CBT: 71%

Treatment type

Conclusion: Both CBT and Prozac are effective in treating adolescent depression.

& Rifkin, 2004). In addition, it is unrealistic to expect there to be sufficient resources to provide psychotherapy to all adolescents who need it in the near future. By contrast, it is relatively easy for pediatricians and family physicians to prescribe drugs. Unfortunately, the prescribing of such medications by general practitioners can be problematic because these individuals do not have training in treating psychological disorders. Thus although prescribing drugs without CBT might be cost effective (Domino et al., 2008), it may not be in the best interests of depressed children.

FIGURE 15.22 Suicide Rates among People 15 to 24 Years of Age

The drop in suicides over the last decade may imply that drugs such as Prozac are lowering the overall rate of depression.

Suicide rate (per 100,000)

- 15- to 19-year-olds
- 20- to 24-year-olds

1980 '81 '82 '83 '84 '85 '86 '87 '88 '89 '90 '91 '92 '93 '94 '95 '96 '97 '98 '99 '00 '01

Children with ADHD Can Benefit from Various Approaches

There is some dispute about whether attention-deficit/hyperactivity disorder is a mental disorder or simply a troublesome behavior pattern that children eventually outgrow. Some people diagnosed with ADHD as children grow out of it. Many more, however, suffer from the disorder throughout adolescence and adulthood. Longitudinal studies show that 70 percent of individuals diagnosed with ADHD during childhood still meet the criteria for the disorder as adolescents. These individuals are more likely to drop out of school and to reach a lower socioeconomic level than expected. They show continued patterns of inattention, of impulsivity, and of hyperactivity, and they are at increased risk for other psychiatric disorders (Wilens, Faraone, & Biederman, 2004). Because of this somewhat bleak long-term prognosis, effective treatment early in life may be of great importance.

PHARMACOLOGICAL TREATMENT OF ADHD The most common treatment for ADHD is a central-nervous-system stimulant such as *methylphenidate*—most commonly, under the brand name Ritalin. The effects of this drug are similar to those of caffeine and amphetamines, but it is more potent than the former and less potent than the latter. Although Ritalin's actions are not fully understood, the drug may affect multiple neurotransmitters, particularly dopamine. The behavior of children with ADHD might suggest that their brains are overactive, and it may seem surprising that a stimulant would improve their symptoms. In fact, functional brain imaging shows that children with ADHD have underactive brains; their hyperactivity may raise their arousal levels.

At appropriate doses, central-nervous-system stimulants such as Ritalin decrease overactivity and distractibility and increase attention and the ability to concentrate. Children on Ritalin experience an increase in positive behaviors and a decrease in negative behaviors (**FIGURE 15.23**). They are able to work more effectively on a task without interruption and are more academically productive; even their handwriting seems to improve. They also are less disruptive and noisy. This improved behavior likely has contributed to the large number of children who take this medication, since parents often feel pressured by school systems to medicate children who have ongoing behavior problems, and since parents often pressure physicians to prescribe the drug because its effects can make home life much more manageable. One study measured Ritalin's effects on the behavior of children playing baseball (Pelham et al., 1990). Children with ADHD who were taking the medication would assume the ready position in the outfield and could keep track of the game. Children with ADHD who were not taking the drug would often throw or kick their mitts even while the pitch was in progress.

Studies have shown that children taking Ritalin are happier, more adept socially, and more successful academically. They also interact more positively with their parents, perhaps because they will more likely comply with requests. The medication has its drawbacks, however. Side effects include sleep problems, reduced appetite, body twitches, and temporary growth suppression. Evidence also indicates that although stimulants are beneficial in the short term, their benefits may not be maintained over the long term. In addition, there is a very real risk of abuse, with numerous cases of children and adolescents buying and selling these stimulants. Indeed, a controversial issue is whether treating ADHD children with Ritalin may increase the risk they will develop substance abuse problems as adults. Two recent studies have demonstrated that substance abuse problems are common among those who had ADHD in childhood, but having taken Ritalin does not seem to have increased or decreased adult rates of

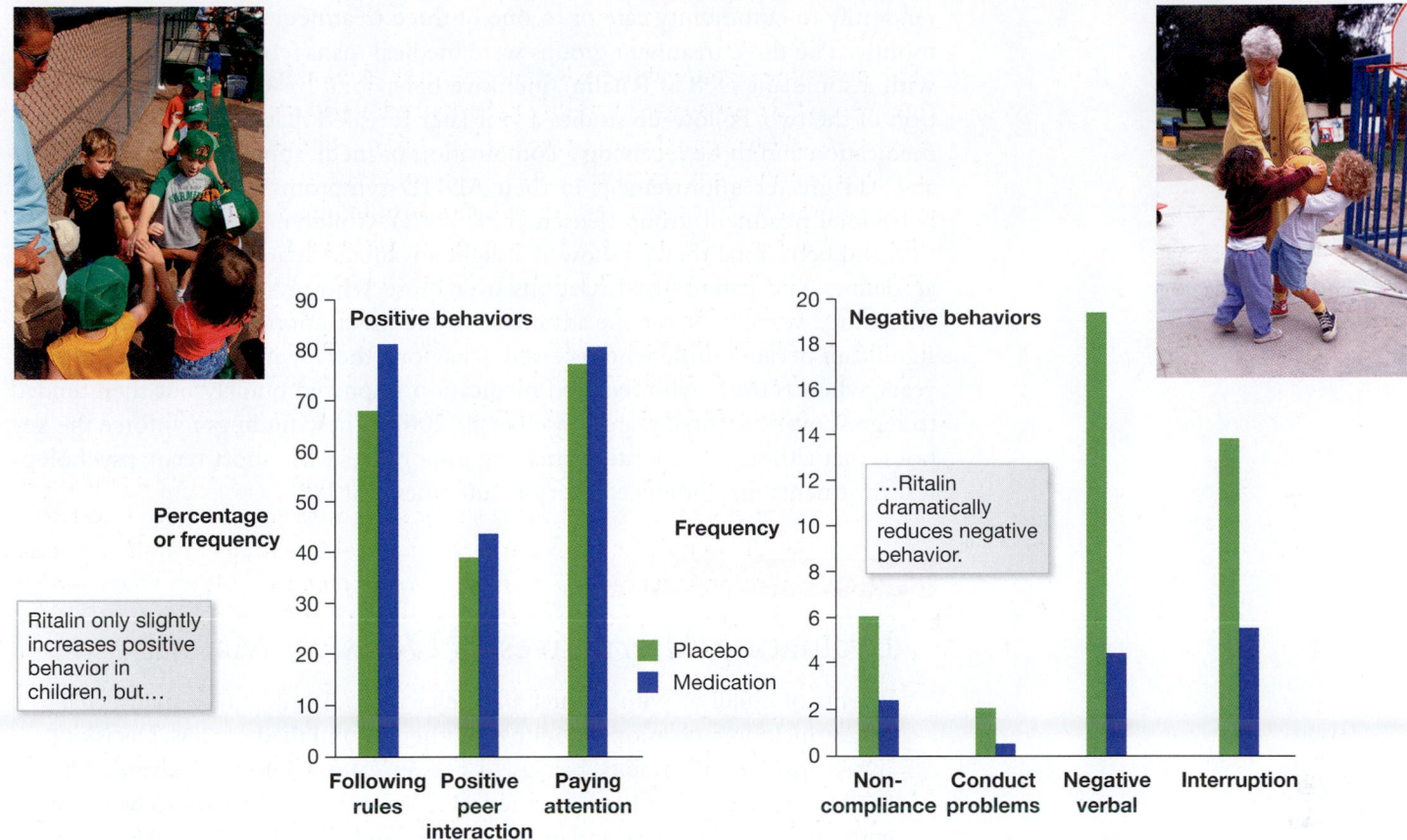

Ritalin only slightly increases positive behavior in children, but…

…Ritalin dramatically reduces negative behavior.

FIGURE 15.23 The Effects of Ritalin

substance abuse (Biederman et al., 2008; Mannuzza et al., 2008). Perhaps most important, some children on medication may see their problems as beyond their control. They may not feel responsible for their behaviors and may not learn coping strategies they will need if they discontinue their medication or if it ceases to be effective. Most therapists believe medication should be supplemented by psychological therapies such as behavior modification, and some even urge that medication be replaced by other treatment approaches when possible. Nonetheless, the data make clear that treatment progresses much better if drugs are part of the overall treatment plan.

BEHAVIORAL TREATMENT OF ADHD Behavioral treatment of ADHD aims to reinforce positive behaviors and ignore or punish problem behaviors. The difficulties with this treatment approach are similar to those discussed in the following section, on autism. Treatment is very intensive and time consuming. In addition, although it is often not difficult to improve behaviors in a structured setting, therapy's effects do not necessarily generalize beyond the clinic or classroom. Many therapists advocate combining behavioral approaches with medication. The medication is used to gain control over the behaviors, and then behavioral modification techniques can be taught and the medication slowly phased out. Others argue that medication should be used only if behavioral techniques do not reduce inappropriate behaviors. This controversy is ongoing, but recent research has shown that medication plus behavioral therapy is more effective than either approach alone.

The National Institute of Mental Health, in collaboration with teams of investigators, began the Multimodal Treatment of Attention-Deficit Hyperactivity Disorder (MTA) in 1992. The study involved 579 children, who were assigned randomly to community care or to one of three treatment groups, each lasting 14 months. The three treatment groups were medical management (usually treatment with a stimulant such as Ritalin), intensive behavioral treatment, and a combination of the two. Follow-up studies a year later revealed that the children receiving medication and those receiving a combination of medication and behavioral therapy had greater improvement in their ADHD symptoms than did those in the behavioral treatment group (Jensen et al., 2001). Children who received medication and behavioral therapy showed a slight advantage in areas such as social skills, academics, and parent-child relations over those who received only medication. After three years, however, the advantage of the medication therapy was no longer significant because those who received behavioral therapy improved over the three years, whereas those who received medication improved quickly but then tended to regress over the three years (Jensen et al., 2007). These findings reinforce the key point that although medications may be important in the short term, psychological treatments may produce superior outcomes that last.

CRITICAL THINKING SKILL

Evaluating Alternatives in Decision Making

Parents of children with mental and behavioral disorders face many challenges, including decisions about psychotherapy and medications. Decisions always involve uncertainty because a person cannot know in advance the consequences of his or her future actions. Decisions usually have to be made with missing information and involve guesses and predictions. Decision making is a recursive, or recycling, process because the nature of the decision may change as more alternatives are generated and evaluated. The decision also requires an action, although it may not be an overt movement—a person could decide which of two opinions to believe, for example—and sometimes the decision may be to do nothing.

Careful decision making is a time-consuming process, but when the decision is important, the time is well spent. The basic processes of decision making are the same whether the decision involves, for example, what to do about a child who has just been diagnosed with ADHD, what career to pursue, or what to have for lunch, though certainly some decisions are more important than others. The first step is to frame the question that needs deciding: *What should I do to help my child who was diagnosed with ADHD to succeed and be happy?* is different from *Should my child take Ritalin?* The first question allows for a broader range of options, which might include alternative schooling or psychotherapy or nothing at all. In general, a broader frame for a decision will yield a larger number of alternatives—the list of possible decisions. If you had a child with ADHD, you might seek the help of different types of professionals in generating a list of alternatives. You would then evaluate each alternative along many dimensions. For example, doing nothing would be an inexpensive alternative, but it probably would not help a child with ADHD lead a happy and successful life. Ritalin would be another alternative. You would continue evaluating alternatives until the best solution emerged. This decision making procedure allows you to compare multiple alternatives. By putting the decision making process on paper, you can consider many complex options simultaneously without being limited by the capacity of your working memory (**FIGURE 15.24**).

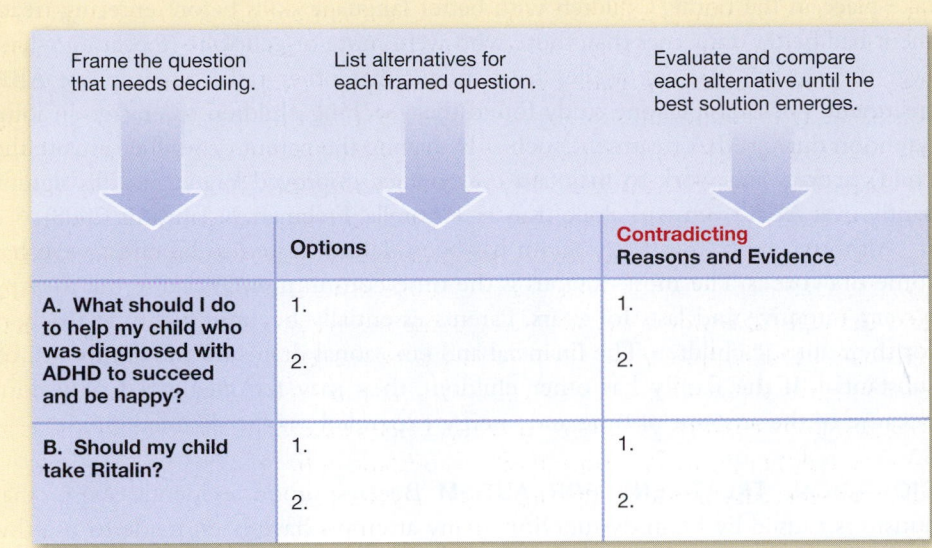

	Options	Contradicting Reasons and Evidence
A. What should I do to help my child who was diagnosed with ADHD to succeed and be happy?	1. 2.	1. 2.
B. Should my child take Ritalin?	1. 2.	1. 2.

FIGURE 15.24 Think Critically: Evaluating Alternatives

Autistic Children Benefit from a Structured Treatment Approach

The treatment of autistic children presents unique challenges to mental health professionals. The core symptoms of autism—impaired communication, restricted interests, and deficits in social interaction—make these children particularly difficult to work with. They often exhibit extreme behaviors as well as public self-stimulation. Although these behaviors must be reduced or eliminated before progress can occur in other areas, doing so is difficult because effective reinforcers are hard to find. Although normal children respond positively to social praise and small prizes, autistic children often are oblivious to these rewards. In some cases, food is the only effective reinforcement in the initial stages of treatment. Another characteristic of autistic children is an overselectivity of attention. This tendency to focus on specific details while ignoring others interferes with generalizing learned behavior to other stimuli and situations. For example, a child who learns to set the table with plates may not know what to do when presented with bowls instead. Generalization of skills must be explicitly taught. For this reason, structured therapies are more effective for these children than unstructured interventions such as play therapy.

applied behavioral analysis (ABA) An intensive treatment for autism, based on operant conditioning.

BEHAVIORAL TREATMENT FOR AUTISM One of the best-known and perhaps most effective treatments for autistic children was developed by Ivar Lovaas and his colleagues. The program, **applied behavioral analysis (ABA),** is based on principles of operant conditioning: Behaviors that are reinforced should increase in frequency, while behaviors that are not reinforced should be extinguished (**FIGURE 15.25**). This very intensive approach requires a minimum of 40 hours of treatment per week. In Lovaas's study, preschool-age children with autism were treated by teachers and by their parents, who received specific training. After more than two years of ABA treatment, the children had gained about 20 IQ points on average and most of them were able to enter a normal kindergarten program (Lovaas, 1987). In contrast, IQ did not change in a comparable control group of children who did not receive any treatment. A group of children who received 10 hours of treatment per week fared no better than the control group. Initiating treatment at a younger age also yielded better results, as did involving the parents and having at least a portion of the therapy

FIGURE 15.25 Applied Behavioral Analysis This form of treatment involves intensive interaction between autistic children and their teachers and parents.

take place in the home. Children with better language skills before entering treatment had better outcomes than those who were mute or echolalic (repeating whatever they heard). Recent studies have shown that other tasks can improve ABA treatment. For example, one study found that teaching children to engage in joint attention during ABA treatment, such as by having the parent or teacher imitate the child's actions and work to maintain eye contact, improved language skills significantly over ABA treatment alone (Kasari, Paparella, Freeman, & Jahromi, 2008).

Although Lovaas's ABA program has been demonstrated to be effective, it has some drawbacks. The most obvious is the time commitment, because the therapy is very intensive and lasts for years. Parents essentially become full-time teachers for their autistic children. The financial and emotional drains on the family can be substantial. If the family has other children, they may feel neglected or jealous because of the amount of time and energy expended on the disabled child.

BIOLOGICAL TREATMENT FOR AUTISM Because good evidence exists that autism is caused by brain dysfunction, many attempts have been made to use this knowledge to treat the disorder. It is easy to find reports of children who have benefited from alternative treatment approaches. These case studies are compelling, but when the treatments are assessed in controlled studies, little or no evidence indicates that most are effective. However, a few biologically based treatment approaches have shown some promise, as discussed in Chapter 14.

One approach involves serotonin. Because SSRIs such as Prozac reduce compulsions in patients diagnosed with obsessive-compulsive disorder, and because autism involves compulsive and repetitive behavior, and because some evidence indicates abnormal serotonin metabolism in autistic children, SSRIs have been tried as a treatment for autism. Indeed, in some autistic children the drug reduces repetitive motor behavior and self-injury and improves social interactions (McDougle, 1997). More-recent research has examined whether the hormone oxytocin, which is important in bonding between mothers and infants, is involved in autism. In one study, high-functioning autistic adults were injected with oxytocin and then performed a social cognition task in which they listened to spoken sentences (e.g., "The boy went to the store") and had to identify the speaker's emotional tone. Those who received oxytocin were better able to tell if the sentence was read in an angry, sad, happy, or indifferent tone than those who received the placebo (Hollander et al., 2007). At this point, the neurobiology of autism is not well understood, and although attempts to use psychopharmacology to treat the disorder have led to some improvements in behavior, much remains to be learned.

PROGNOSIS FOR CHILDREN WITH AUTISM Despite a few reports of remarkable recovery from autism, the long-term prognosis is poor. A follow-up study of men in their early twenties revealed that they continued to show the ritualistic behavior typical of autism. In addition, nearly three-quarters had severe social difficulties and were unable to live and work independently (Howlin, Mawhood, & Rutter, 2000). Several factors affect the prognosis. Although therapists once believed the prognosis was particularly poor for children whose symptoms were apparent before age two (Hoshino et al., 1980), possibly only the most severe cases of autism were diagnosed before public recognition of the disorder increased. Early diagnosis clearly allows for more effective treatments (National Research Council, 2001). Still, severe cases—especially those involving notable cognitive deficiencies—are less likely to improve with treatment. Early language ability is associated with better outcome (Howlin et al., 2000), as is higher IQ. Autistic children have difficulty generalizing from the therapeutic setting to the real world, and this limitation severely restricts their social functioning (Handleman, Gill, & Alessandri, 1988); a higher IQ may mean a better ability to generalize learning and therefore a better overall prognosis.

To understand how autism affects families and how treatment can be beneficial, consider the following case study. John O'Neil, a deputy editor at the *New York Times,* has described what it is like to be the parent of an autistic child (O'Neil, 2004). O'Neil's son James began to show signs of being "different" in early childhood. Although he had been an easy baby, as a toddler he seemed to have difficulty looking his parents in the eye and did not display a strong sense of connection. James indicated little interest in objects, even toys, that were given or shown to him, instead repeating behaviors to the point of harming himself—for example, pulling on and off his cowboy boots until his feet were raw. He responded to loud noises by crying. James's behavior really started to deteriorate when he was two and a half, following the arrival of a baby brother and a move to a new house. His parents assumed he was overwhelmed, but the director of James's new preschool noticed the telltale signs of autism. On her recommendation, a professional assessed James and determined that he had autism. During the first visit to a speech therapist, James's mother learned just how much her son needed treatment: He had forgotten his name.

The discovery of James's autism follows a familiar pattern. Although most diagnoses of autism are made by age three, the disorder can be detected earlier if parents or pediatricians know what to look for. Many children who will develop autism show abnormal social behavior in infancy. Other signs include staring at objects for long periods and not reaching developmental milestones, such as speaking. Sometimes autism appears to strike suddenly in an otherwise normally developing child. The child simply withdraws from social contact, stops babbling, and may become self-abusive. Parents and pediatricians who notice symptoms of autism in such a child may write them off as quirks or feel that the child is just a little slow to develop. Luckily for James, the preschool staff recommended a professional evaluation because of his unusual behavior. As mentioned above, research has shown that the earlier treatment begins, the better the prognosis.

On finding out that treatments for autism existed, the O'Neils were relieved. But then they heard the bad news: Treatment is expensive, difficult, and time consuming—as noted earlier, the recommended amount of treatment is over 40 hours per week. Most versions of treatment are based on Lovaas's ABA therapy, which requires parents and teachers to spend hours helping children with autism learn basic skills, such as saying their names, by using operant conditioning to reward even small behaviors. The same behaviors, repeated over and over, for hours on end: That is the nature of ABA. It teaches each task as a series of simple steps, attempting to actively engage the child's attention in highly structured activities, and it provides regular reinforcement of desired behaviors.

As is the case in many school districts, resources were insufficient for James to receive full treatment in school. His mother, a physician, gave up her full-time position to set up a home-based program for James. He spent up to eight hours every day performing tasks that most children would find extremely boring, such as repeatedly imitating the therapist's placing two blocks next to each other or touching her nose. James's day might begin with physical activities to strengthen coordination and build body awareness, followed by a snack break during which appropriate social behaviors were reinforced and language skills were stressed. Each part of the day was designed to work on James's problem areas. Along the way progress was charted to guide subsequent sessions. At one point, James's language skills clearly had to improve if he was going to be able to attend mainstream school. Encouraged by being given any treat he asked for, James learned to talk.

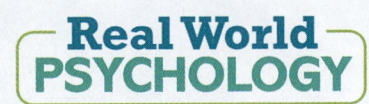

Real World PSYCHOLOGY

FIGURE 15.26 James O'Neil At the time of this photo, James, center, was eight years old. At left is his friend Larry, also eight. At right is James's brother Miles, six.

He started school with the assistance of one of his full-time instructors, who attended class with him. Despite some rocky moments, James has made tremendous progress. He still has problems—in areas such as reading comprehension, math, attention, and social skills—and he does not understand why he has a disorder and why other kids do not. But James has triumphed. Perhaps his biggest accomplishment was making friends with a classmate named Larry (**FIGURE 15.26**). Why, O'Neil speculates, was Larry attracted to James as a friend? Perhaps they shared a love of potty humor, or perhaps they were similarly warm and enthusiastic. One day O'Neil overheard the two friends engaged in silly conversation, telling stupid jokes and gossiping about their "girlfriends." In that moment, O'Neil realized just how many of his dreams for James had been realized.

> ## SUMMING UP
>
> ### How Should Childhood and Adolescent Disorders Be Treated?
>
> Approximately 1 out of 20 adolescents experiences depression. Using drugs such as Prozac with adolescents is controversial: Although these drugs are effective in managing symptoms, they have a slight risk of increasing suicidal behaviors. The use of psychological treatments is most effective over the long run, although the cost is significantly greater and such therapies require more effort by the adolescents. Medications such as Ritalin can be quite effective in treating children with ADHD. However, side effects and ethical concerns are associated with this type of medication. For these reasons, many parents and clinicians have turned to other approaches, such as behavioral therapy. Recent research suggests that the most effective management strategy for ADHD may be a combination of medication and behavioral therapy. In contrast, the most effective treatment for autism currently is structured and intensive behavioral therapy.
>
> ## MEASURING UP
>
> Label each point below as an argument either for or against the practice of prescribing SSRI medications to adolescents with depression.
> a. Depressed adolescents taking SSRIs report having suicidal thoughts twice as often as depressed adolescents not taking SSRIs.
> b. Many depressed adolescents improve when taking SSRIs.
> c. Psychotherapy alone is an effective treatment option.
> d. SSRIs are widely available.
> e. SSRIs offer a relatively inexpensive treatment.
> f. Suicide rates have dropped since the use of SSRIs became widespread.

CONCLUSION

Although great strides have been made in identifying the etiology of mental disorders, this growing knowledge has not always given rise to new treatment approaches. Treatment of mental disorders is aimed at helping the individual think and behave in more adaptive ways, but the approaches vary tremendously. For some disorders, several approaches are equally effective. For other disorders, some approaches are more effective than others. New understanding of the ways in which mental disorders affect neural functioning may lead to the discovery of more effective psychotropic medications. History teaches us, however, that medication is not the magic bullet for mental disorders. Even with the creation of more effective medications, other interventions remain crucial. A pill may help relieve the symptoms of mental disorder, but it cannot help a patient cope with the effects of the disorder, interact with others, or think and behave in more adaptive ways. Psychological, cognitive, and behavioral interventions can address these issues more effectively than medication. Indeed, recent evidence indicates that although drugs may be more effective over the short term, psychological treatments are more effective over the long term. This finding recently was confirmed in studies with children being treated for depression and for ADHD.

The best treatments are those supported by careful empirical research. One of the major themes in this textbook is that our understanding of the human condition has progressed through the administration of the scientific method. This sense of progress is particularly true for the treatment of mental disorders, where pop psychology and pseudotherapies can lead people astray to devote time, money, and energy on ineffective or even dangerous efforts. The careful assessment of treatments for mental health disorders has given therapists a better idea of what works and what does not, freeing them to invest their efforts in identifying needed treatments. The continued application of the scientific method to understanding the treatment of mental disorders is crucial for providing the most effective care.

■ CHAPTER SUMMARY

How Are Mental Disorders Treated?

- **Psychotherapy Is Based on Psychological Principles:** Psychotherapeutic treatments focus on insights. Psychodynamic forms focus on uncovering the unconscious. Humanistic approaches focus on clarifying feelings and motives. Behavioral approaches focus on modifying maladaptive behaviors. Cognitive approaches restructure thinking. Group therapy provides support, and a systems approach is part of family therapy. Common factors across treatments include both the value of confession and expectations that things will get better.

- **Culture Can Affect the Therapeutic Process:** The dominant culture in any country defines mental health and mental disorders; it also determines who needs psychotherapy and what type of therapy should be made available. Psychologists need to have multicultural knowledge if they are to provide competent psychotherapy to people from different backgrounds and with different belief systems.

- **Medication Is Effective for Certain Disorders:** Psychotropic medications change neurochemistry. Anti-anxiety drugs increase GABA activity. Antidepressants affect serotonin availability. Antipsychotics reduce positive symptoms.

- **Alternative Biological Treatments Are Used in Extreme Cases:** When traditional treatments are not successful, alternative treatments are used. These include psychosurgery, electroconvulsive therapy, transcranial magnetic stimulation, and deep brain stimulation.

- **Pseudotherapies Can Be Dangerous:** Increasingly, psychologists are turning to evidence-based practices. Pseudotherapies are treatment approaches that have no credible evidence to support their use. Some pseudotherapies have proved lethal, and all may prevent or delay a patient from seeking help through an evidence-based therapy.

What Are the Most Effective Treatments?

- **Treatments That Focus on Behavior and on Cognition Are Superior for Anxiety Disorders:** Behavioral methods alleviate specific phobias. Cognitive restructuring is effective in treating panic disorders. Obsessive-compulsive disorder (OCD) responds to medications that block serotonin reuptake and to cognitive-behavioral therapy.

- **Many Effective Treatments Are Available for Depression:** Pharmacological treatments include MAO inhibitors, tricyclics, and SSRIs. Cognitive-behavioral treatments are most effective when combined with antidepressants. Alternative therapies include phototherapy for seasonal affective disorder (SAD) and both electroconvulsive therapy and transcranial magnetic stimulation for severe depression.

- **Lithium Is Most Effective for Bipolar Disorder:** The psychotropic medication lithium has been the most effective in stabilizing mood in bipolar patients but has considerable side effects. Psychological therapy can help support compliance with drug treatment.

- **Pharmacological Treatments Are Superior for Schizophrenia:** Antipsychotic medications are most effective for reducing the positive symptoms of schizophrenia. Tardive dyskinesia and other side effects are common with the older antipsychotic drugs. Clozapine acts specifically on dopamine receptors and reduces positive and negative symptoms, with fewer side effects. The prognosis for patients depends on factors including age of onset, gender, and culture.

- **There Are Important Considerations in Selecting a Psychotherapist:** Many types of education and training exist for psychotherapists. In selecting a psychotherapist, it is important to find someone with whom the client can establish a good relationship and who the patient believes is committed to his or her improvement.

Can Personality Disorders Be Treated?

- **Dialectical Behavior Therapy Is Most Successful for Borderline Personality Disorder:** DBT combines elements of behavioral, cognitive, and psychodynamic therapy. Therapy proceeds in three stages. First, the most extreme behaviors are targeted and replaced with more appropriate behaviors. Next, the therapist explores past traumatic events. Finally, the therapist helps the patient develop self-respect and independence.

- **Antisocial Personality Disorder Is Difficult to Treat:** Psychotherapeutic approaches have not proved effective for treating antisocial personality disorder. Behavioral and cognitive approaches have been more effective, primarily in a controlled residential treatment environment. Generally, the prognosis is poor. Focusing on prevention by addressing conduct disorder in childhood may be the best strategy.

How Should Childhood and Adolescent Disorders Be Treated?

- **The Use of Medication to Treat Adolescent Depression Is Controversial:** The use of medication, such as Prozac, is increasing as a treatment for adolescent depression. Such medications may lead to increased suicidality, but the available evidence indicates that medications may have more benefits than costs. Cognitive-behavioral treatment is also beneficial and may be preferred because its effects are long-lasting.

- **Children with ADHD Can Benefit from Various Approaches:** Ritalin, despite its side effects, is an effective pharmacological treatment and works best as part of an overall treatment plan including psychotherapy, particularly behavioral treatment.

- **Autistic Children Benefit from a Structured Treatment Approach:** Behavioral approaches have been effective in improving language and social behavior. The treatment strategy is very time intensive and extends for years. In general, the long-term prognosis is poor.

■ KEY TERMS

anti-anxiety drugs, p. 673

antidepressants, p. 673

antipsychotics, p. 674

applied behavioral analysis (ABA), p. 705

biological therapies, p. 666

client-centered therapy, p. 668

cognitive-behavioral therapy (CBT), p. 669

cognitive restructuring, p. 669

cognitive therapy, p. 669

electroconvulsive therapy (ECT), p. 675

exposure, p. 669

expressed emotion, p. 670

insight, p. 667

psychotherapy, p. 666

psychotropic medications, p. 672

1. Which of the following statements are true regarding how culture can affect the therapeutic process?
   a. Culture can influence people's willingness to seek help.
   b. Culture can influence the expression of mental disorders.
   c. Definitions of mental health are consistent across cultures.
   d. Strategies for assessing mental illness are consistent across cultures.
   e. The extent to which mental illness is stigmatized varies by culture.

2. Which of the following statements are true regarding pseudotherapies?
   a. Because clients engaged in pseudotherapies may believe them to be valid, these clients may not seek effective therapies.
   b. Pseudotherapies lack scientific evidence of their efficacy.
   c. Some pseudotherapies are counterproductive, leading to increased levels of the behaviors they are intended to decrease.
   d. Some pseudotherapies are physically dangerous, exposing clients to bodily harm or even death.
   e. Special certifications are required for therapists wishing to practice pseudotherapies.

3. Barlow advocates distinguishing between psychological treatments and general talk therapy. Which of the following attributes characterize psychological treatments?
   a. Treatments should be based on evidence of their effectiveness.
   b. Treatments should be appropriate for the particular disorders.
   c. Specific techniques for treatment should be developed in the laboratory by psychological scientists.
   d. Treatments should be guided by grand theories.

4. Dialectical behavior therapy takes place in three stages. Place the descriptions of the three stages below in the correct order.
   a. The therapist helps the client explore past traumatic experiences that may be at the root of emotional problems.
   b. The therapist helps the patient develop self-respect and independent problem solving.
   c. The therapist works with the client to replace the most dysfunctional behaviors with more appropriate behaviors.

5. During his early adult years, Joshua was diagnosed with antisocial personality disorder. Joshua is now 40. Over the coming years, his friends and family will likely see a decrease in which of the following behaviors? Select all that apply.
   a. Joshua's lack of remorse for hurting others' feelings.
   b. Joshua's tendency to feel entitled to special treatment.
   c. Joshua's tendency to get into fistfights.

6. Label each point below as an argument either for or against the practice of prescribing Ritalin (methylphenidate) to children with ADHD.
   a. Children taking Ritalin are happier, more socially adept, and more academically successful than those who do not receive treatment.
   b. Children taking Ritalin can experience disordered sleep, reduced appetite, bodily twitches, and temporary growth suppression.
   c. Children taking Ritalin may come to see their ADHD as a problem beyond their control and may not learn coping strategies they will need later if they discontinue their medication or if it ceases to be effective.
   d. Children taking Ritalin show a decrease in negative behaviors and an increase in positive behaviors.
   e. People commonly use Ritalin in nonprescribed ways for reasons other than treating ADHD.
   f. The benefits of Ritalin are not maintained over the long run.

7. Three-year old Marley recently received a diagnosis of autism. Which of the following are true about her likely treatment?
   a. Many individuals will need to be involved in Marley's treatment, including parents, teachers, and mental health practitioners.
   b. Marley's treatment is likely to strain family dynamics and family finances.
   c. Marley's treatment will focus largely on using social praise and small gifts to reinforce desired behavior.
   d. Marley's treatment will need to be highly structured.
   e. Marley's treatment will require a minimum of 20 hours per week and will likely last for two to three months.

8. Imagine you are asked to evaluate the quality of the following two methodologies for an empirical evaluation of a new treatment for ADHD. Label each of the methodologies as strong or weak. If a methodology is strong, briefly explain why. If a methodology is weak, provide a brief recommendation for strengthening it.
   a. Parents will be asked whether they would like their child to receive medication or the new psychotherapy. Each child will be assigned to a condition based on the parents' preference.
   b. The study will include four conditions: a nontreatment control group, a group receiving medication only, a group receiving the new psychotherapy only, and a group receiving both medication and the new psychotherapy.

■ PSYCHOLOGY AND SOCIETY

1. In a 2005 interview, the actor Tom Cruise claimed that "all [antidepressants do] is mask the problem. There's ways with vitamins, and through exercise and various things. . . . Drugs aren't the answer. That these drugs are very dangerous; they're mind-altering drugs." First identify subclaims within the quote and then provide evidence supporting and refuting each subclaim, drawing from Chapters 14 and 15.

2. Imagine your 10-year old cousin has been diagnosed with ADHD. Your aunt and uncle ask if you have any advice on how to select a therapist and how to decide which treatments are most appropriate. Write an e-mail to your relatives advising them on how to select a therapist and the kind of questions they will want to ask themselves and the therapist before choosing among treatment options.

The answer key for all the Measuring Up exercises and the Practice Tests can be found at the back of the book.

GLOSSARY

absentmindedness   The inattentive or shallow encoding of events.

accommodation   The process by which a schema is changed to incorporate a new experience that does not easily fit into an existing schema.

accuracy   The extent to which an experimental measure is free from error.

acetylcholine (ACh)   The neurotransmitter responsible for motor control at the junction between nerves and muscles; also involved in mental processes such as learning, memory, sleeping, and dreaming.

acquisition   The gradual formation of an association between the conditioned and unconditioned stimuli.

action potential   The neural impulse that passes along the axon and subsequently causes the release of chemicals from the terminal buttons.

activation-synthesis hypothesis   A theory of dreaming that proposes that neural stimulation from the pons activates mechanisms that normally interpret visual input.

adaptations   In evolutionary theory, the physical characteristics, skills, or abilities that increase the chances of reproduction or survival and are therefore likely to be passed along to future generations.

additive color mixing   A way to produce a given spectral pattern in which different wavelengths of lights are mixed. The percept is determined by the interaction of these wavelengths with receptors in the eye and is a psychological process.

aggression   Any behavior or action that involves the intention to harm someone else.

agonist   Any drug that enhances the actions of a specific neurotransmitter.

agoraphobia   An anxiety disorder marked by fear of being in situations in which escape may be difficult or impossible.

all-or-none principle   The principle whereby a neuron fires with the same potency each time, although frequency can vary; it either fires or not—it cannot partially fire.

allostatic load theory of illness   When people are continually stressed, they are unable to return to bodily states that characterize normal stress levels.

altruism   The providing of help when it is needed, without any apparent reward for doing so.

amnesia   Deficits in long-term memory that result from disease, brain injury, or psychological trauma.

amygdala   A brain structure that serves a vital role in our learning to associate things with emotional responses and in processing emotional information.

analogical representation   A mental representation that has some of the physical characteristics of an object; it is analogous to the object.

anorexia nervosa   An eating disorder characterized by an excessive fear of becoming fat and thus a refusal to eat.

antagonist   Any drug that inhibits the action of a specific neurotransmitter.

anterograde amnesia   An inability to form new memories.

anti-anxiety drugs   A class of psychotropic medications used for the treatment of anxiety.

antidepressants   A class of psychotropic medications used to treat depression.

antipsychotics   A class of drugs used to treat schizophrenia and other disorders that involve psychosis.

antisocial personality disorder   A personality disorder marked by a lack of empathy and remorse.

anxious-ambivalent attachment   Attachment style in which infants become extremely upset when their caregiver leaves but reject the caregiver when he or she returns.

applied behavioral analysis (ABA)   An intensive treatment for autism, based on operant conditioning.

arousal   Psychological activation, such as increased brain activity, autonomic responses, sweating, or muscle tension.

assessment   In psychology, examination of a person's mental state to diagnose possible psychological disorders.

assimilation   The process by which a new experience is placed into an existing schema.

attachment   A strong emotional connection that persists over time and across circumstances.

attention-deficit/hyperactivity disorder (ADHD)   A disorder characterized by restless, inattentive, and impulsive behaviors.

attitudes   The evaluation of objects, events, or ideas.

attributions   People's causal explanations for why events or actions occur.

audition   The sense of sound perception.

autism   A developmental disorder involving deficits in social interaction, impaired communication, and restricted interests.

autonomic nervous system (ANS)   A major component of the peripheral nervous system; it regulates the body's internal environment by stimulating glands and by maintaining internal organs such as the heart, gall bladder, and stomach.

availability heuristic   Making a decision based on the answer that most easily comes to mind.

avoidant attachment   Attachment style in which infants ignore their caregiver when he or she returns after a brief separation.

axon   A long narrow outgrowth of a neuron by which information is transmitted to other neurons.

basal ganglia   A system of subcortical structures that are important for the initiation of planned movement.

behavior modification   The use of operant-conditioning techniques to eliminate unwanted behaviors and replace them with desirable ones.

behavioral approach system (BAS)   The brain system involved in the pursuit of incentives or rewards.

behavioral inhibition system (BIS)   The brain system that is sensitive to punishment and therefore inhibits behavior that might lead to danger or pain.

behaviorism   A psychological approach that emphasizes the role of environmental forces in producing behavior.

binocular depth cues   Cues of depth perception that arise from the fact that people have two eyes.

binocular disparity (or *retinal disparity*)   A cue of depth perception that is caused by the distance between a person's eyes, which provides each eye with a slightly different image.

biological therapies   Treatment based on medical approaches to illness and to disease.

biopsychosocial model   A model of health that integrates the effects of biological, behavioral, and social factors on health and illness.

bipolar disorder   A mood disorder characterized by alternating periods of depression and mania.

blindsight   A condition in which people who are blind have some spared visual capacities in the absence of any visual awareness.

blocking   The temporary inability to remember something that is known.

body mass index (BMI)   A ratio of body weight to height, used to measure obesity.

borderline personality disorder   A personality disorder characterized by identity, affective, and impulse disturbances.

bottom-up processing   A hierarchical model of pattern recognition in which data are relayed from one processing level to the next, always moving to a higher level of processing.

brain imaging   A range of experimental techniques that make brain structures and brain activity visible.

brainstem   A section of the bottom of the brain, housing the most basic programs of survival, such as breathing, swallowing, vomiting, urination, and orgasm.

Broca's area   The left frontal region of the brain, crucial for the production of language.

buffering hypothesis   The idea that other people can provide direct support in helping individuals cope with stressful events.

bulimia nervosa   An eating disorder characterized by dieting, binge eating, and purging.

bystander intervention effect   The failure to offer help by those who observe someone in need.

case study   A research method that involves the intensive examination of one person.

cell body   In the neuron, where information from thousands of other neurons is collected and processed.

central nervous system (CNS)   The brain and spinal cord.

central tendency   A measure that represents the typical behavior of the group as a whole.

cerebellum   A large, convoluted protuberance at the back of the brainstem, essential for coordinated movement and balance.

cerebral cortex   The outer layer of brain tissue, which forms the convoluted surface of the brain.

change blindness   The common failure to notice large changes in environments.

chromosomes   Structures within the cell body that are made up of genes.

chunking   Organizing information into meaningful units to make it easier to remember.

circadian rhythms   The regulation of biological cycles into regular patterns.

classical conditioning, or Pavlovian conditioning   A type of learned response that occurs when a neutral object comes to elicit a reflexive response when it is associated with a stimulus that already produces that response.

client-centered therapy   An empathic approach to therapy; it encourages personal growth through greater self-understanding.

cognition   Mental activity such as thinking or representing information.

cognitive dissonance   An uncomfortable mental state due to conflicts between attitudes or between attitudes and behavior.

cognitive map   A visual/spatial mental representation of an environment.

cognitive neuroscience   The study of the neural mechanisms that underlie thought, learning, and memory.

cognitive psychology   The study of how people think, learn, and remember.

cognitive restructuring   A therapy that strives to help patients recognize maladaptive thought patterns and replace them with ways of viewing the world that are more in tune with reality.

cognitive therapy   Treatment based on the idea that distorted thoughts produce maladaptive behaviors and emotions.

cognitive-behavioral approach   A diagnostic model that views psychopathology as the result of learned, maladaptive cognitions.

cognitive-behavioral therapy (CBT)   A therapy that incorporates techniques from behavioral therapy and cognitive therapy to correct faulty thinking and change maladaptive behaviors.

compliance   The tendency to agree to do things requested by others.

concept   A mental representation that groups or categorizes objects, events, or relations around common themes.

concrete operational stage   The third stage in Piaget's theory of cognitive development, during which children begin to think about and understand operations in ways that are reversible.

conditioned response (CR)   A response that has been learned.

conditioned stimulus (CS)   A stimulus that elicits a response only after learning has taken place.

cones   Retinal cells that respond to higher levels of illumination and result in color perception.

confabulation   The false recollection of episodic memory.

conformity   The altering of one's opinions or behaviors to match those of others or to match social norms.

confound   Anything that affects a dependent variable and may unintentionally vary between the experimental conditions of a study.

consciousness   The subjective experience of the world and of mental activity.

consolidation   A hypothetical process involving the transfer of contents from immediate memory into long-term memory.

continuous reinforcement   A type of learning in which the desired behavior is reinforced each time it occurs.

control (or comparison) group   The participants in a study that receive no intervention or an intervention different from the one being studied.

conventional   Middle stage of moral development, in which rules and the approval of others determines what is moral.

coping response   Any response an organism makes to avoid, escape from, or minimize an aversive stimulus.

cornea   The clear outer covering of the eye.

correlational study   A research method that examines how variables are naturally related in the real world, without any attempt by the researcher to alter them.

critical periods   Biologically determined time periods for the development of specific skills.

critical thinking   A systematic way of evaluating information to reach reasonable conclusions.

cross-sectional studies   A research method that compares participants in different groups (e.g., young and old) at the same time.

cryptomnesia   A type of misattribution that occurs when a person thinks he or she has come up with a new idea, yet has only retrieved a stored idea and failed to attribute the idea to its proper source.

crystallized intelligence   Knowledge acquired through experience and the ability to use that knowledge.

culturally sensitive research   Studies that take into account the ways culture affects thoughts, feelings, and actions.

culture   The beliefs, values, rules, and customs that exist within a group of people who share a common language and environment and that are transmitted through learning from one generation to the next.

data   Objective observations or measurements.

decision making   Attempting to select the best alternative among several options.

declarative memory   The cognitive information retrieved from explicit memory; knowledge that can be declared.

deductive reasoning   Using a belief or rule to determine if a conclusion is valid (follows logically from the belief or rule).

defense mechanisms   Unconscious mental strategies the mind uses to protect itself from conflict and distress.

defining attribute model   The idea that a concept is characterized by a list of features that are necessary to determine if an object is a member of the category.

deindividuation   A phenomenon of low self-awareness, in which people lose their individuality and fail to attend to personal standards.

delusions   False personal beliefs based on incorrect inferences about reality.

dendrites   Branchlike extensions of the neuron that detect information from other neurons.

dependent variable   In an experiment, the measure that is affected by manipulation of the independent variable.

descriptive statistics   Overall summary of data.

descriptive studies   A research method that involves observing and noting the behavior of people or other animals in order to provide a systematic and objective analysis of behavior.

developmental psychology   The study of changes in physiology, cognition, and social behavior over the life span.

dialectical behavior therapy (DBT)   A form of therapy used to treat borderline personality disorder.

diathesis-stress model   A diagnostic model that proposes that a disorder may develop when an underlying vulnerability is coupled with a precipitating event.

directionality problem   When researchers find a relationship between two variables in a correlational study, they cannot determine which variable may have caused changes in the other variable.

discrimination   The inappropriate and unjustified treatment of people based solely on their group membership.

disorganized attachment   Attachment style in which infants give mixed responses when their caregiver leaves and then returns from a short absence.

disorganized behavior   Acting in strange or unusual ways, including strange movement of limbs, bizarre speech, and inappropriate self-care, such as failing to dress properly or bathe.

display rules   Rules learned through socialization that dictate which emotions are suitable to given situations.

dissociative identity disorder (DID)   The occurrence of two or more distinct identities in the same individual.

dizygotic twins   Twin siblings who result from two separately fertilized eggs (i.e., fraternal twins).

dominant gene   A gene that is expressed in the offspring whenever it is present.

dopamine   A monoamine neurotransmitter involved in reward, motivation, and motor control.

dreams   The product of an altered state of consciousness in which images and fantasies are confused with reality.

drive   Psychological state that motivates an organism to satisfy its needs.

dysthymia   A form of depression that is not severe enough to be diagnosed as major depression.

eardrum (tympanic membrane)   A thin membrane, which sound waves vibrate, that marks the beginning of the middle ear.

ego   In psychodynamic theory, the component of personality that tries to satisfy the wishes of the id while being responsive to the dictates of the superego.

elaboration likelihood model   A theory of how persuasive messages lead to attitude changes.

electroconvulsive therapy (ECT)   A procedure used to treat depression; it involves administering a strong electrical current to the patient's brain.

electroencephalogram (EEG)   A device that measures electrical activity in the brain.

emotion   Feelings that involve subjective evaluation, physiological processes, and cognitive beliefs.

emotional intelligence (EQ)   A form of social intelligence that emphasizes the ability to perceive, understand, manage, and use emotions to guide thoughts and actions.

emotion-focused coping   A type of coping in which people try to prevent having an emotional response to a stressor.

encoding   The processing of information so that it can be stored.

encoding specificity principle   Any stimulus that is encoded along with an experience can later trigger memory for the experience.

endocrine system   A communication system that uses hormones to influence thoughts, behaviors, and actions.

endorphins   A neurotransmitter involved in natural pain reduction and reward.

epinephrine   The neurotransmitter responsible for adrenaline rushes, bursts of energy caused by its release throughout the body.

episodic memory   Memory for one's personal past experiences.

etiology   Factors that contribute to the development of a disorder.

evolutionary theory   In psychological science, a theory that emphasizes the inherited, adaptive value of behavior and mental activity throughout the history of a species.

exemplar model   Information stored about the members of a category is used to determine category membership.

experiment   A study that tests causal hypotheses by measuring and manipulating variables.

experimental (or treatment) group   The participants in a study that receive the intervention.

experimenter expectancy effect   Actual change in the behavior of the people or animals being observed that is due to observer bias.

explicit attitudes   Attitudes that people can report.

explicit memory   The processes involved when people remember specific information.

exposure   A behavioral therapy technique that involves repeated exposure to an anxiety-producing stimulus or situation.

expressed emotion   A pattern of interactions that includes emotional over-involvement, critical comments, and hostility directed toward a patient by family members.

extinction   A process in which the conditioned response is weakened when the conditioned stimulus is repeated without the unconditioned stimulus.

extrinsic motivation   Motivation to perform an activity because of the external goals toward which that activity is directed.

family systems model   A diagnostic model that considers symptoms within an individual as indicating problems within the family.

fight-or-flight response   The physiological preparedness of animals to deal with danger.

five-factor theory   The idea that personality can be described using five factors: openness to experience, conscientiousness, extraversion, agreeableness, and neuroticism.

fixed schedule   A schedule in which reinforcement is consistently provided upon each occurrence.

flashbulb memories   Vivid memories for the circumstances in which one first learned of a surprising, consequential, and emotionally arousing event.

fluid intelligence   Information processing in novel or complex circumstances.

forgetting   The inability to retrieve memory from long-term storage.

formal operational stage   The final stage in Piaget's theory of cognitive development; it involves the ability to think abstractly and to formulate and test hypotheses through deductive logic.

fovea   The center of the retina, where cones are densely packed.

framing   The effect of presentation on how information is perceived.

frontal lobes   The region at the front of the cerebral cortex concerned with planning and movement.

frustration-aggression hypothesis   The extent to which people feel frustrated predicts the likelihood that they will act aggressively.

functional magnetic resonance imaging (fMRI)   An imaging technique used to examine changes in the activity of the working human brain.

functionalism   An approach to psychology concerned with the adaptive purpose, or function, of mind and behavior.

fundamental attribution error   The tendency to overemphasize personal factors and underestimate situational factors in explaining behavior.

GABA   (gamma-aminobutyric acid) The primary inhibitory transmitter in the nervous system.

gender identity   Personal beliefs about whether one is male or female.

gender roles   The characteristics associated with males and females because of cultural influence or learning.

gender schemas   Cognitive structures that influence how people perceive the behaviors of females and males.

gene   The unit of heredity that determines a particular characteristic in an organism.

general adaptation syndrome   A consistent pattern of responses to stress that consists of three stages: alarm, resistance, and exhaustion.

general intelligence (g)   The idea that one general factor underlies all mental abilities.

generalized anxiety disorder (GAD)   A diffuse state of constant anxiety not associated with any specific object or event.

genotype   The genetic constitution determined at the moment of conception.

Gestalt theory   A theory based on the idea that the whole of personal experience is different from simply the sum of its constituent elements.

glutamate   The primary excitatory transmitter in the nervous system.

gonads   The main endocrine glands involved in sexual behavior: in males, the testes; in females, the ovaries.

gustation   The sense of taste.

habituation   A decrease in behavioral response following repeated exposure to nonthreatening stimuli.

hallucinations   False sensory perceptions that are experienced without an external source.

haptic sense   The sense of touch.

health psychology   The field of psychological science concerned with the events that affect physical well-being.

heritability   A statistical estimate of the variation, caused by differences in heredity, in a trait within a population.

heuristics   In problem solving, shortcuts (rules of thumb or informal guidelines) used to reduce the amount of thinking that is needed to move from an initial state to a goal state.

hippocampus   A brain structure important for the formation of certain types of memory.

homeostasis   The tendency for bodily functions to maintain equilibrium.

hormones   Chemical substances, typically released from endocrine glands, that travel through the bloodstream to targeted tissues, which are subsequently influenced by the hormones.

humanistic approaches   Approaches to studying personality that emphasize personal experience and belief systems; they propose that people seek personal growth to fulfill their human potential.

hypnosis   A social interaction during which a person, responding to suggestions, experiences changes in memory, perception, and/or voluntary action.

hypothalamic-pituitary-adrenal (HPA) axis   The biological system responsible for the stress response.

hypothalamus   A small brain structure that is vital for temperature regulation, emotion, sexual behavior, and motivation.

hypothesis   A specific prediction of what should be observed in the world if a theory is correct.

id   In psychodynamic theory, the component of personality that is completely submerged in the unconscious and operates according to the pleasure principle.

idiographic approaches   Person-centered approaches to studying personality that focus on individual lives and how various characteristics are integrated into unique persons.

immune system   The body's mechanism for dealing with invading microorganisms, such as allergens, bacteria, and viruses.

implicit attitudes   Attitudes that influence our feelings and behavior at an unconscious level.

implicit memory   The system underlying unconscious memories.

incentives   External stimuli that motivate behaviors (as opposed to internal drives).

independent variable   In an experiment, the condition that is manipulated by the experimenter to examine its impact on the dependent variable.

inductive reasoning   Using examples or instances to determine if a rule or conclusion is likely to be true.

infantile amnesia   The inability to remember events from early childhood.

inferential statistics   A set of procedures used to make judgments about whether differences actually exist between sets of numbers.

ingroup favoritism   The tendency for people to evaluate favorably and privilege members of the ingroup more than members of the outgroup.

insight   (1) The sudden realization of a solution to a problem. (2) A goal of some types of therapy; a patient's understanding of his or her own psychological processes.

insomnia   A disorder characterized by an inability to sleep.

institutional review boards (IRBs)   Groups of people responsible for reviewing proposed research to ensure that it meets the accepted standards of science and provides for the physical and emotional well-being of research participants.

intelligence   The human ability to use knowledge, solve problems, understand complex ideas, learn quickly, and adapt to environmental challenges.

intelligence quotient (IQ)   The number computed by dividing a child's estimated mental age by the child's chronological age, and then multiplying this number by 100.

interactionists   Theorists who believe that behavior is determined jointly by underlying dispositions and situations.

interneurons   One of the three types of neurons, these neurons communicate only with other neurons, typically within a specific brain region.

interpreter   A left hemisphere process that attempts to make sense of events.

interval schedule   A schedule in which reinforcement is available after a specific unit of time.

intrinsic motivation   Motivation to perform an activity because of the value or pleasure associated with that activity, rather than for an apparent external goal or purpose.

introspection   A systematic examination of subjective mental experiences that requires people to inspect and report on the content of their thoughts.

iris   The colored muscular circle on the surface of the eye; it changes shape to let in more or less light.

kinesthetic sense   Perception of our limbs in space.

latent content   What a dream symbolizes, or the material that is disguised in a dream to protect the dreamer.

latent learning   Learning that takes place in the absence of reinforcement.

lateral inhibition   A visual process in which adjacent photoreceptors tend to inhibit one another.

law of effect   Thorndike's general theory of learning: Any behavior that leads to a "satisfying state of affairs" will more likely occur again, and any behavior that leads to an "annoying state of affairs" will less likely recur.

learned helplessness model   A cognitive model of depression in which people feel unable to control events around them.

learning   An enduring change in behavior, resulting from experience.

longitudinal studies   A research method that measures the same participants multiple times.

long-term memory (LTM)   The relatively permanent storage of information.

long-term potentiation (LTP)   The strengthening of a synaptic connection so that postsynaptic neurons are more easily activated.

loosening of associations   A speech pattern among schizophrenic patients in which their thoughts are disorganized or meaningless.

lymphocytes   Specialized white blood cells known as B cells, T cells, and natural killer cells that make up the immune system.

magnetic resonance imaging (MRI)   A method of brain imaging that produces high-quality images of the brain.

major depression   A disorder characterized by severe negative moods or a lack of interest in normally pleasurable activities.

manifest content   The plot of a dream; the way a dream is remembered.

mean   A measure of central tendency that is the arithmetic average of a set of numbers.

median   A measure of central tendency that is the value in a set of numbers that falls exactly halfway between the lowest and highest values.

meditation   A mental procedure that focuses attention on an external object or on a sense of awareness.

meme   A unit of knowledge transferred within a culture.

memory   The nervous system's capacity to acquire and retain usable skills and knowledge.

memory bias   The changing of memories over time in ways consistent with prior beliefs.

mental age   An assessment of a child's intellectual standing relative to that of his or her peers; determined by a comparison of the child's test score with the average score for children of each chronological age.

mental set   A problem solving strategy that has worked in the past.

meta-analysis   A "study of studies" that combines the findings of multiple studies to arrive at a conclusion.

microsleeps   Brief, unintended sleep episodes, ranging from a few seconds to a minute, caused by chronic sleep deprivation.

mind/body problem   A fundamental psychological issue that considers whether mind and body are separate and distinct or whether the mind is simply the subjective experience of the physical brain.

mirror neurons   Neurons that are activated during observation of others performing an action.

mnemonics   Strategies for improving memory.

modal memory model   The three-stage memory system that involves sensory memory, short-term memory, and long-term memory.

mode   A measure of central tendency that is the most frequent score or value in a set of numbers.

modeling   The imitation of behavior through observational learning.

monocular depth cues Cues of depth perception that are available to each eye alone.

monozygotic twins Twin siblings who result from one zygote splitting in two and therefore share the same genes (i.e., identical twins).

motivation Factors that energize, direct, or sustain behavior.

motor neurons One of the three types of neurons, these efferent neurons direct muscles to contract or relax, thereby producing movement.

multiaxial system The system used in the DSM that provides assessment along five axes describing important mental health factors.

multiple intelligences The idea that people can show different skills in a variety of different domains.

myelin sheath A fatty material, made up of glial cells, that insulates the axon and allows for the rapid movement of electrical impulses along the axon.

narcolepsy A sleep disorder in which people fall asleep during normal waking hours.

natural selection Darwin's theory that those who inherit characteristics that help them adapt to their particular environments have a selective advantage over those who do not.

naturalistic observation A passive descriptive study in which observers do not change or alter ongoing behavior.

nature/nurture debate The arguments concerning whether psychological characteristics are biologically innate or acquired through education, experience, and culture.

need State of biological or social deficiencies.

need hierarchy Maslow's arrangement of needs, in which basic survival needs are lowest priority and personal growth needs are highest priority.

need to belong theory The need for interpersonal attachments is a fundamental motive that has evolved for adaptive purposes.

negative punishment Punishment that occurs with the removal of a stimulus and thus decreases the probability of a behavior's recurring.

negative reinforcement The increase in the probability of a behavior's being repeated through the removal of a stimulus.

negative symptoms Symptoms of schizophrenia marked by deficits in functioning such as apathy, lack of emotion, and slowed speech and movement.

neuron The basic unit of the nervous system; it operates through electrical impulses, which communicate with other neurons through chemical signals. Neurons receive, integrate, and transmit information in the nervous system.

neurotransmitter A chemical substance that carries signals from one neuron to another.

nodes of Ranvier Small gaps of exposed axon, between the segments of myelin sheath, where action potentials are transmitted.

nomothetic approaches Approaches to studying personality that focus on how people vary across common traits.

nonverbal behavior The facial expressions, gestures, mannerisms, and movements by which one communicates with others.

norepinephrine The neurotransmitter involved in states of arousal and awareness.

object permanence The understanding that an object continues to exist even when it cannot be seen.

objective measures Relatively direct assessments of personality, usually based on information gathered through self-report questionnaires or observer ratings.

observational learning Learning that occurs when behaviors are acquired or modified following exposure to others performing the behavior.

observational technique A research method of careful and systematic assessment and coding of overt behavior.

observer bias Systematic errors in observation that occur because of an observer's expectations.

obsessive–compulsive disorder (OCD) An anxiety disorder characterized by frequent intrusive thoughts and compulsive actions.

occipital lobe A region of the cerebral cortex, at the back of the brain, important for vision.

olfaction The sense of smell, which occurs when receptors in the nose respond to chemicals.

olfactory bulb The brain center for smell, located below the frontal lobes.

olfactory epithelium The thin layer of tissue, within the nasal cavity, that is embedded with smell receptors.

operant conditioning, or instrumental conditioning A learning process in which the consequences of an action determine the likelihood that it will be performed in the future.

oxytocin A hormone that is important for mothers in bonding to newborns.

panic disorder An anxiety disorder characterized by sudden, overwhelming attacks of terror.

parallel processing Processing multiple types of information at the same time.

parasympathetic division of ANS A division of the autonomic nervous system; it returns the body to its resting state.

parietal lobe A region of the cerebral cortex, in front of the occipital lobes and behind the frontal lobes, important for the sense of touch and of the spatial layout of an environment.

Parkinson's disease A neurological disorder that seems to be caused by dopamine depletion, marked by muscular rigidity, tremors, and difficulty initiating voluntary action.

partial reinforcement A type of learning in which behavior is reinforced intermittently.

partial-reinforcement extinction effect The greater persistence of behavior under partial reinforcement than under continuous reinforcement.

participant observation A type of descriptive study in which the researcher is actively involved in the situation.

perception The processing, organization, and interpretation of sensory signals; it results in an internal representation of the stimulus.

perceptual constancy People correctly perceive objects as constant in their shape, size, color, and lightness, despite raw sensory data that could mislead perception.

peripheral nervous system (PNS) All nerve cells in the body that are not part of the central nervous system. The PNS includes the somatic and autonomic nervous systems.

personal attributions Explanations that refer to internal characteristics, such as abilities, traits, moods, and effort.

personality The characteristic thoughts, emotional responses, and behaviors that are relatively stable in an individual over time and across circumstances.

personality trait A characteristic; a dispositional tendency to act in a certain way over time and across circumstances.

personality types Discrete categories based on global personality characteristics.

persuasion   The active and conscious effort to change attitudes through the transmission of a message.

phenotype   Observable physical characteristics that result from both genetic and environmental influences.

phobia   An acquired fear that is out of proportion to the real threat of an object or of a situation.

pituitary gland   Located at the base of the hypothalamus; the gland that sends hormonal signals controlling the release of hormones from endocrine glands.

placebo effect   A drug or treatment, unrelated to the particular problem of the person who receives it, may make the recipient feel better because the person believes the drug or treatment is effective.

plasticity   A property of the brain that allows it to change as a result of experience, drugs, or injury.

population   Everyone in the group the experimenter is interested in.

positive punishment   Punishment that occurs with the administration of a stimulus and thus decreases the probability of a behavior's recurring.

positive reinforcement   The increase in the probability of a behavior's being repeated following the administration of a stimulus.

positive symptoms   Symptoms of schizophrenia, such as delusions and hallucinations, that are excesses in behavior.

positron emission tomography (PET)   A method of brain imaging that assesses metabolic activity by using a radioactive substance injected into the bloodstream.

postconventional   Highest stage of moral development, in which decisions about morality depend on abstract principles.

posttraumatic stress disorder (PTSD)   A mental disorder that involves frequent nightmares, intrusive thoughts, and flashbacks related to an earlier trauma.

preconventional   Earliest level of moral development, in which self-interest determines what is moral.

prefrontal cortex   A region of the frontal lobes, especially prominent in humans, important for attention, working memory, decision making, appropriate social behavior, and personality.

prejudice   The usually negative affective or attitudinal responses associated with stereotypes.

preoperational stage   The second stage in Piaget's theory of cognitive development, during which children think symbolically about objects, but reason is based on appearance rather than logic.

primary appraisal   Part of the coping process that involves making decisions about whether a stimulus is stressful, benign, or irrelevant.

primary emotions   Evolutionarily adaptive emotions that humans share across cultures; they are associated with specific biological and physical states.

proactive interference   When prior information inhibits the ability to remember new information.

problem solving   Finding a way around an obstacle to reach a goal.

problem-focused coping   A type of coping in which people take direct steps to confront or minimize a stressor.

procedural memory   A type of implicit memory that involves motor skills and behavioral habits.

projective measures   Personality tests that examine unconscious processes by having people interpret ambiguous stimuli.

prosocial   Tending to benefit others.

prospective memory   Remembering to do something at some time in the future.

prototype model   An approach to object categorization that is based on the premise that within each category, some members are more representative than others.

psychological science   The study of mind, brain, and behavior.

psychoanalysis   A method developed by Sigmund Freud that attempts to bring the contents of the unconscious into conscious awareness so that conflicts can be revealed.

psychodynamic theory   Freudian theory that unconscious forces, such as wishes and motives, influence behavior.

psychopathology   A disorder of the mind.

psychosexual stage   According to Freud, the developmental stages that correspond to the pursuit of satisfaction of libidinal urges.

psychotherapy   The generic name given to formal psychological treatment.

psychotropic medications   Drugs that affect mental processes.

pupil   The small opening in the eye; it lets in light waves.

random assignment   The procedure for placing research participants into the conditions of an experiment in which each participant has an equal chance of being assigned to any level of the independent variable.

ratio schedule   A schedule in which reinforcement is based on the number of times the behavior occurs.

reactivity   When the knowledge that one is being observed alters the behavior being observed.

reasoning   Using information to determine if a conclusion is valid or reasonable.

receptive field   The region of visual space to which neurons in the primary visual cortex are sensitive.

receptors   In neurons, specialized protein molecules, on the postsynaptic membrane, that neurotransmitters bind to after passing across the synaptic cleft.

recessive gene   A gene that is expressed only when it is matched with a similar gene from the other parent.

reconsolidation   Neural processes involved when memories are recalled and then stored again for later retrieval.

reinforcer   A stimulus that follows a response and increases the likelihood that the response will be repeated.

reliability   The extent to which a measure is stable and consistent over time in similar conditions.

REM sleep   The stage of sleep marked by rapid eye movements, dreaming, and paralysis of motor systems.

replication   Repetition of an experiment to confirm the results.

representativeness heuristic   A rule for categorization based on how similar the person or object is to our prototypes for that category.

Rescorla–Wagner model   A cognitive model of classical conditioning; it states that the strength of the CS–US association is determined by the extent to which the unconditioned stimulus is unexpected.

research   Scientific process that involves the systematic and careful collection of data.

response performance   A research method in which researchers quantify perceptual or cognitive processes in response to a specific stimulus.

resting membrane potential   The electrical charge of a neuron when it is not active.

restructuring   A new way of thinking about a problem that aids its solution.

retina The thin inner surface of the back of the eyeball. The retina contains the photoreceptors that transduce light into neural signals.

retrieval The act of recalling or remembering stored information to use it.

retrieval cue Anything that helps a person (or other animal) recall information from memory.

retroactive interference When new information inhibits the ability to remember old information.

retrograde amnesia The condition in which people lose past memories, such as memories for events, facts, people, or even personal information.

reuptake The process whereby a neurotransmitter is taken back into the presynaptic terminal buttons, thereby stopping its activity.

rods Retinal cells that respond to low levels of illumination and result in black-and-white perception.

sample A subset of a population.

scatterplot A graphical depiction of the relationship between two variables.

schema A hypothetical cognitive structure that helps us perceive, organize, process, and use information.

schizophrenia A mental disorder characterized by alterations in perceptions, emotions, thoughts, or consciousness.

scientific method A systematic procedure of observing and measuring phenomena to answer questions about *what* happens, *when* it happens, *what* causes it, and *why*.

secondary appraisal Part of the coping process during which people evaluate their options and choose coping behaviors.

secondary emotions Blends of primary emotions, including states such as remorse, guilt, submission, and anticipation.

secure attachment Attachment style for a majority of infants, who are readily comforted when their caregiver returns after a brief separation.

selection bias When participants in different groups in an experiment differ systematically.

self-actualization A state that is achieved when one's personal dreams and aspirations have been attained.

self-fulfilling prophecy People's tendency to behave in ways that confirm their own or others' expectations.

self-report method A method of data collection in which people are asked to provide information about themselves, such as in questionnaires or surveys.

self-serving bias The tendency for people to take personal credit for success but blame failure on external factors.

semantic memory Memory for knowledge about the world.

sensation The sense organs' responses to external stimuli and the transmission of these responses to the brain.

sensitive periods Biologically determined time periods when specific skills develop most easily.

sensitization An increase in behavioral response following exposure to a threatening stimulus.

sensorimotor stage The first stage in Piaget's theory of cognitive development, during which infants acquire information about the world through their senses and respond reflexively.

sensory adaptation When an observer's sensitivity to stimuli decreases over time.

sensory memory Memory for sensory information that is stored briefly close to its original sensory form.

sensory neurons One of the three types of neurons, these afferent neurons detect information from the physical world and pass that information along to the brain.

seratonin A monoamine neurotransmitter important for a wide range of psychological activity, including emotional states, impulse control, and dreaming.

serial position effect The ability to recall items from a list depends on order of presentation, with items presented early or late in the list remembered better than those in the middle.

sexual response cycle A pattern of physiological responses during sexual activity.

sexual strategies theory Evolutionary theory that suggests men and women look for different qualities in their relationship partners because of gender-specific adaptive problems.

shaping A process of operant conditioning; it involves reinforcing behaviors that are increasingly similar to the desired behavior.

short-term memory (STM) A limited-capacity memory system that holds information in awareness for a brief period.

signal detection theory (SDT) A theory of perception based on the idea that the detection of a faint stimulus requires a judgment—it is not an all-or-none process.

situational attributions Explanations that refer to external events, such as the weather, luck, accidents, or the actions of other people.

situationism The theory that behavior is determined more by situations than by personality traits.

sleep apnea A disorder in which a person stops breathing while asleep.

social development The maturation of skills or abilities that enable people to live in a world with other people.

social facilitation When the mere presence of others enhances performance.

social integration The quality of a person's social relationships.

social loafing The tendency for people to work less hard in a group than when working alone.

social norms Expected standards of conduct, which influence behavior.

social psychology The study of group dynamics in relation to psychological processes.

sociocultural model A diagnostic model that views psychopathology as the result of the interaction between individuals and their cultures.

sociometer An internal monitor of social acceptance or rejection.

somatic markers Bodily reactions that arise from the emotional evaluation of an action's consequences.

somatic nervous system A major component of the peripheral nervous system; it transmits sensory signals to the CNS via nerves.

sound wave The pattern of the changes in air pressure through time that results in the percept of a sound.

source amnesia A type of amnesia that occurs when a person shows memory for an event but cannot remember where he or she encountered the information.

source misattribution Memory distortion that occurs when people misremember the time, place, person, or circumstances involved with a memory.

spatial memory Memory for the physical environment; it includes things such as location of objects, direction, and cognitive maps.

split brain A condition in which the corpus callosum is surgically cut and the two hemispheres of the brain do not receive information directly from each other.

spontaneous recovery A process in which a previously extinguished response reemerges following presentation of the conditioned stimulus.

standard deviation A statistical measure of how far away each value is, on average, from the mean.

stereotype threat Apprehension about confirming negative stereotypes related to one's own group.

stereotypes Cognitive schemas that allow for easy, fast processing of information about people based on their membership in certain groups.

stimulus discrimination A differentiation between two similar stimuli when only one of them is consistently associated with the unconditioned stimulus.

stimulus generalization Occurs when stimuli that are similar but not identical to the conditioned stimulus produce the conditioned response.

storage The retention of encoded representations over time that corresponds to some change in the nervous system that registers the event.

stream of consciousness A phrase coined by William James to describe one's continuous series of ever-changing thoughts.

stress A pattern of behavioral and physiological responses to events that match or exceed an organism's abilities to respond.

stressor An environmental event or stimulus that threatens an organism.

structuralism An approach to psychology based on the idea that conscious experience can be broken down into its basic underlying components or elements.

subliminal perception Information processed without conscious awareness.

substance P A neurotransmitter involved in pain perception.

subtractive color mixing A way to produce a given spectral pattern in which the mixture occurs within the stimulus itself and is actually a physical, not psychological, process.

suggestibility The development of biased memories when people are provided with misleading information.

superego In psychodynamic theory, the internalization of societal and parental standards of conduct.

symbolic representation An abstract mental representation that does not correspond to the physical features of an object or idea.

sympathetic division of ANS A division of the autonomic nervous system; it prepares the body for action.

synapse, or synaptic cleft The site for chemical communication between neurons, which contains extracellular fluid.

synaptic pruning A process whereby the synaptic connections in the brain that are frequently used are preserved, and those that are not are lost.

synesthesia Cross-sensory experience (in which, e.g., a visual image has a taste).

taste buds Sensory receptors that transduce taste information.

telegraphic speech The tendency for children to speak using rudimentary sentences that are missing words and grammatical markings but follow a logical syntax.

temperaments Biologically based tendencies to feel or act in certain ways.

temporal lobes The lower region of the cerebral cortex, important for processing auditory information and for memory.

tend-and-befriend response Females' tendency to protect and care for their offspring and form social alliances rather than flee or fight in response to threat.

teratogens Environmental agents that harm the embryo or fetus.

terminal buttons Small nodules, at the ends of axons, that release chemical signals from the neuron to the synapse.

thalamus The gateway to the brain; it receives almost all incoming sensory information before that information reaches the cortex.

theory A model of interconnected ideas and concepts that explains what is observed and makes predictions about future events.

theory of mind The term used to describe the ability to explain and predict other people's behavior as a result of recognizing their mental state.

third variable problem When the experimenter cannot directly manipulate the independent variable and therefore cannot be confident that another, unmeasured variable is not the actual cause of differences in the dependent variable.

top-down processing A hierarchical model of pattern recognition in which information at higher levels of processing can also influence lower, "earlier" levels in the processing hierarchy.

trait approach An approach to studying personality that focuses on the extent to which individuals differ in personality dispositions.

transcranial magnetic stimulation (TMS) The use of strong magnets to briefly interrupt normal brain activity as a way to study brain regions.

transduction A process by which sensory receptors produce neural impulses when they receive physical or chemical stimulation.

transience The pattern of forgetting over time.

Type A behavior pattern A pattern of behavior characterized by competitiveness, achievement orientation, aggressiveness, hostility, restlessness, inability to relax, and impatience with others.

Type B behavior pattern A pattern of behavior characterized by relaxed, noncompetitive, easygoing, and accommodating behavior.

unconditioned response (UR) A response that does not have to be learned, such as a reflex.

unconditioned stimulus (US) A stimulus that elicits a response, such as a reflex, without any prior learning.

unconscious The mental processes that operate below the level of conscious awareness.

validity The extent to which the data collected address the research hypothesis in the way intended.

variability In a set of numbers, how widely dispersed the values are from each other and from the mean.

variable Something in the world that can be measured and that can vary.

variable schedule A schedule in which reinforcement is applied at different rates or at different times.

vestibular sense Perception of balance.

vicarious learning Learning that occurs when people learn the consequences of an action by observing others being rewarded or punished for performing the action.

well-being A positive state that includes striving for optimal health.

working memory (WM) An active processing system that keeps different types of information available for current use.

Yerkes-Dodson law The psychological principle that behavioral efficiency increases with arousal up to an optimum point, after which it decreases with increasing arousal.

REFERENCES

Abramson, L. Y., Metalsky, G., & Alloy, L. (1989). Hopelessness depression: A theory-based subtype of depression. *Psychological Review, 96,* 358–372.

Ackerman, P. L., Beier, M. E., & Boyle, M. O. (2005). Working memory and intelligence: The same or different constructs? *Psychological Bulletin, 131,* 30–60.

Adair, J., & Kagitcibasi, C. (1995). Development of psychology in developing countries: Factors facilitating and impeding its progress. *International Journal of Psychology, 30,* 633–641.

Adams, R. B., Jr., Gordon, H. L., Baird, A. A., Ambady, N., & Kleck, R. E. (2003, June 6). Effects of gaze on amygdala sensitivity to anger and fear faces. *Science, 300,* 1536–1537.

Adolphs, R. (2003). Cognitive neuroscience of human social behavior. *Nature Reviews Neuroscience, 1,* 165–178.

Adolphs, R., Gosselin, F., Buchanan, T. W., Tranel, D., Schyns, P., & Damasio, A. R. (2005). A mechanism for impaired fear recognition after amygdala damage. *Nature, 433,* 68–72.

Adolphs, R., Sears, L., & Piven, J. (2001). Abnormal processing of social information from faces in autism. *Journal of Cognitive Neuroscience, 13,* 232–240.

Adolphs, R., Tranel, D., & Damasio, A. R. (1998). The human amygdala in social judgment. *Nature, 393,* 470–474.

Agawu, K. (1995). *African rhythm: A northern ewe perspective.* Cambridge, UK: Cambridge University Press.

Ali, S. R., Liu, W. M., & Humedian, M. (2004). Islam 101: Understanding the religion and therapy implications. *Professional Psychology Research and Review, 35,* 635–642.

Alicke, M. D., Klotz, M. L., Breitenbecher, D. L., Yurak, T. J., & Vredenburg, D. S. (1995). Personal contact, individuation, and the better-than-average effect. *Journal of Personality and Social Psychology, 68,* 804–825.

Alicke, M. D., LoSchiavo, F. M., Zerbst, J., & Zhang, S. (1997). The person who outperforms me is a genius: Maintaining perceived competence in upward social comparisons. *Journal of Personality and Social Psychology, 73,* 781–789.

Allport, G. W. (1954). *The nature of prejudice* (8th ed.). Oxford, UK: Addison-Wesley.

Allport, G. W. (1961). *Pattern and growth in personality.* New York: Holt, Rinehart & Winston.

Amanzio, M., & Benedetti, F. (1999). Neuropharmacological dissection of placebo analgesia: Expectation-activated opioid systems versus conditioning-activated specific subsystems. *Journal of Neuroscience, 19,* 484–494.

Amaral, D. G., Schumann, C. M., & Nordahl, C. W. (2008). Neuroanatomy of autism. *Trends in Neurosciences, 3,* 137–45.

Amato, P. R. (2001). Children of divorce in the 1990s: An update of the Amato and Keith (1991) meta-analysis. *Journal of Family Psychology, 15,* 355–370.

Amato, P. R., Johnson, D., Booth, A., & Rogers, S. J. (2003). Continuity and change in marital quality between 1980 and 2000. *Journal of Marriage and Family, 65,* 1–22.

Amato, P. R., & Keith, B. (1991). Parental divorce and the well-being of children: A meta-analysis. *Psychological Bulletin, 110,* 26–46.

Ambady, N., Hallahan, M., & Conner, B. (1999). Accuracy of judgments of sexual orientation from thin slices of behavior. *Journal of Personality and Social Psychology, 77,* 538–547.

Ambady, N., & Rosenthal, R. (1993). Half a minute: Predicting teacher evaluations from thin slices of nonverbal behavior and physical attractiveness. *Journal of Personality and Social Psychology, 64,* 431–441.

American Academy of Pediatrics. (2000, July 26). Joint statement on the impact of entertainment violence on children. Congressional Public Health Summit. Retrieved from http://www.aap.org/advocacy/releases/jstmtevc.htm

American Academy of Pediatrics, Committee on Bioethics. (1988). Fetal therapy: Ethical considerations. *Pediatrics, 81,* 898–899.

American Academy of Pediatrics, Committee on Drugs. (1998). Neonatal drug withdrawal. *Pediatrics, 10,* 1079–1088.

American College of Obstetricians and Gynecologists, Committee on Ethics. (2004). Patient choice in the maternal–fetal relationship. In *Ethics in obstetrics and gynecology* (2nd ed.). Washington, DC: Author. Retrieved from http://www.acog.org/from_home/publications/ethics/ethics034.pdf

American Psychiatric Association. (2000). Practice guidelines for the treatment of patients with eating disorders (revised). *American Journal of Psychiatry, 157*(Suppl.), 1–39.

American Psychological Association. (2007, August 5). *Exercise and mental stimulation both boost mouse memory late in life* [Press release]. Retrieved from http://www.apa.org/releases/mental_exercise.html

American Psychological Association, Health Psychology Division 38. (n.d.). *What is health psychology?* Retrieved August 4, 2008, from http://www.health-psych.org

Amminger, G. P., Pape, S., Rock, D., Roberts, S. A., Ott, S. L., Squires-Wheeler, E., et al. (1999). Relationship between childhood behavioral disturbance and later schizophrenia in the New York high-risk project. *American Journal of Psychiatry, 156,* 525–530.

Anderson, A. K., Christoff, K., Stappen, I., Panitz, D., Ghahremani, D. G., Glover, G., et al. (2003). Dissociated neural representations of intensity and valence in human olfaction. *Nature Neuroscience, 6,* 196–202.

Anderson, A. K., & Phelps, E. A. (2000). Expression without recognition: Contributions of the human amygdala to emotional communication. *Psychological Science, 11,* 106–111.

Anderson, C. A., Berkowitz, L., Donnerstein, E., Huesmann, L. R., Johnson, J., Linz, D., et al. (2003). The influence of media violence on youth. *Psychological Science in the Public Interest, 4*, 81–110.

Anderson, I. M. (2000). Selective serotonin reuptake inhibitors versus tricyclic antidepressants: A meta-analysis of efficacy and tolerability. *Journal of Affective Disorders, 58*, 19–36.

Anderson, N. B. (with Anderson, P. E.). (2003). *Emotional longevity: What really determines how long you live*. New York: Viking.

Anderson, S. W., Bechara, A., Damasio, H., Tranel, D., & Damasio, A. R. (1999). Impairment of social and moral behavior related to early damage in human prefrontal cortex. *Nature Neuroscience, 2*, 1032–1037.

Andreasen, N. C. (1984). *The broken brain: The biological revolution in psychiatry*. New York: Harper & Row.

Andrew, F. M. (1991). Stability and change in levels and structure of subjective well-being: USA 1972–1988. *Social Indicators Research, 25*, 1–30.

Angold, A., & Costello, E. J. (2001). The epidemiology of depression in children and adolescents. In I. M. Goodyer (Ed.), *The depressed child and adolescent* (2nd ed., pp. 143–178). New York: Cambridge University Press.

Antonuccio, D., & Burns, D. (2004). Adolescents with depression [Letter to the editor]. *Journal of the American Medical Association, 292*, 2577.

Aouizerate, B., Cuny, E., Martin-Guehl, C., Guehl, D., Amieva, H., Benazzouz, A., et al. (2004). Deep brain stimulation of the ventral caudate nucleus in the treatment of obsessive-compulsive disorder and major depression: Case report. *Journal of Neurosurgery, 101*, 574–575.

Arias, E., MacDorman, M. F., Strobino, D. M., & Guyer, B. (2003). Annual summary of vital statistics: 2002. *Pediatrics, 112*, 1215–1230.

Armony, J. L., Chochol, C., Fecteau, S., & Belin, P. (2007). Laugh (or cry) and you will be remembered: Influence of emotional expression on memory for vocalizations. *Psychological Science, 18*, 1027–1029.

Aronson, E., & Mills, J. (1959). The effects of severity of initiation on liking for a group. *Journal of Abnormal and Social Psychology, 59*, 177–181.

Asberg, M., Shalling, D., Traskman-Bendz, L., & Wagner, A. (1987). Psychobiology of suicide, impulsivity, and related phenomena. In H. Y. Melzer (Ed.), *Psychopharmacology: The third generation of progress* (pp. 655–668). New York: Raven Press.

Asch, S. E. (1955). Opinions and social pressure. *Scientific American, 193*, 31–35.

Ashby, F. G., Isen, A. M., & Turken, A. U. (1999). A neuropsychological theory of positive affect and its influence on cognition. *Psychological Review, 106*, 529–550.

Assad, L. K., Donnellan, M. B., & Conger, R. D. (2007). Optimism: An enduring resource for romantic relationships. *Journal of Personality and Social Psychology, 93*, 285–297.

Averill, J. R. (1980). A constructivist view of emotion. In R. Plutchik & H. Kellerman (Eds.), *Theories of emotion* (pp. 305–339). New York: Academic Press.

Aylward, E. H., Reiss, A. L., Reader, M. J., & Singer, H. S. (1996). Basal ganglia volumes in children with attention-deficit hyperactivity disorder. *Journal of Child Neurology, 11*, 112–115.

Baars, B. (1988). *A cognitive theory of consciousness*. Cambridge, UK: Cambridge University Press.

Badcock, C., & Crespi, B. (2008). Battle of the sexes may set the brain. *Nature, 454*, 1054–1055.

Baddeley, A. D. (2002). Is working memory still working? *European Psychologist, 7*, 85–77.

Bailey, A., Le Couteur, A., Gottesman, I., Bolton, P., Simonoff, E., Yuzda, E., et al. (1995). Autism as a strongly genetic disorder: Evidence from a British twin study. *Psychological Medicine, 25*, 63–78.

Baillargeon, R. (1995). Physical reasoning in infancy. In M. S. Gazzaniga (Ed.), *The cognitive neurosciences* (pp. 181–204). Cambridge, MA: MIT Press.

Baillargeon, R. (2008). Innate ideas revisited: For a principle of persistence in infants' physical reasoning. *Perspectives on Psychological Science, 3*, 2–13.

Baillargeon, R., Li, J., Ng, W., & Yuan, S. (2009). A new account of infants' physical reasoning. In A. Woodward & A. Needham (Eds.), *Learning and the infant mind* (pp. 66–116). New York: Oxford University Press.

Baker, T. B., Brandon, T. H., & Chassin, L. (2004). Motivational influences on cigarette smoking. *Annual Review of Psychology, 55*, 463–491.

Baldwin, D. A. (1991). Infants' contribution to the achievement of joint reference. *Child Development, 62*, 875–890.

Baldwin, D. A., & Baird, J. A. (2001). Discerning intentions in dynamic human action. *Trends in Cognitive Sciences, 5*, 171–178.

Baler, R. D., & Volkow, N. D. (2006). Drug addiction: The neurobiology of disrupted self-control. *Trends in Molecular Medicine, 12*(12), 559–566.

Ballantyne, J. C., & LaForge, K. S. (2007). Opioid dependence and addiction during opioid treatment of chronic pain. *Pain, 129*, 235–255.

Balthazard, C. G., & Woody, E. Z. (1992). The spectral analysis of hypnotic performance with respect to 'absorption.' *International Journal of Clinical and Experimental Hypnosis, 40*, 21–43.

Baltimore, D. (2001). Our genome unveiled. *Nature, 409*, 814–816.

Banaji, M. R., & Greenwald, A. G. (1995). Implicit gender stereotyping in judgments of fame. *Journal of Personality and Social Psychology, 68*, 181–198.

Bandura, A. (1977). *Social learning theory*. Englewood Cliffs, NJ: Prentice-Hall.

Bandura, A., Ross, D., & Ross, S. (1961). Transmission of aggression through imitation of aggressive models. *Journal of Abnormal and Social Psychology, 66*, 3–11.

Bandura, A., Ross, D., & Ross, S. (1963). Vicarious reinforcement and imitative learning. *Journal of Abnormal and Social Psychology, 67*, 601–607.

Barch, D. M., Sheline, Y. I., Csernansky, J. G., & Snyder, A. Z. (2003). Working memory and prefrontal cortex dysfunction: Specificity to schizophrenia compared with major depression. *Biological Psychiatry, 53*, 376–384.

Bargh, J. A. (2006). What have we been priming all these years? On the development, mechanisms, and ecology of nonconscious social behavior. *European Journal of Social Psychology, 36*(147), 168.

Bargh, J. A., & Chartrand, T. L. (1999). The unbearable automaticity of being. *American Psychologist, 54*, 462–479.

Bargh, J. A., Chen, M., & Burrows, L. (1996). Automaticity of social behavior: Direct effects of trait construct and stereotype activation on action. *Journal of Personality and Social Psychology, 71*, 230–244.

Bargh, J. A., & Ferguson, M. J. (2000). Beyond behaviorism: On the automaticity of higher mental processes. *Psychological Bulletin, 126*, 925–945.

Bargh, J. A., & Morsella, E. (2008). The unconscious mind. *Perspectives on Psychological Science, 3*, 73–79.

Bar-Haim, Y., Ziv, T., Lamy, D., & Hodes, R. (2006). Nature and nurture in own-race face processing. *Psychological Science, 17*, 159–163.

Barkley, R. A. (1997). *ADHD and the nature of self-control.* New York: Guilford Press.

Barlow, D. H. (2002). *Anxiety and its disorders: The nature and treatment of anxiety and panic* (2nd ed.). New York: Guilford Press.

Barlow, D. H. (2004). Psychological treatments. *American Psychologist, 59*, 869–878.

Barlow, D. H., Gorman, J. M., Shear, M. K., & Woods, S. W. (2000). Cognitive-behavioral therapy, imipramine, or their combination for panic disorder: A randomized controlled trial. *Journal of the American Medical Association, 283*, 2529–2536.

Barnett, R. C., & Hyde, J. S. (2001). Women, men, work, and family. An expansionist theory. *American Psychologist, 56*, 781–796.

Baron, A. S., & Banaji, M. R. (2006). The development of implicit attitudes. *Psychological Science, 17*, 53–58.

Baron-Cohen, S., Wheelwright, S., & Jolliffe, T. (1997). Is there a "language of the eyes"? Evidence from normal adults and adults with autism or Asperger Syndrome. *Visual Cognition, 4*, 311–332.

Barr, A. M., Panenka, W. J., MacEwan, G. W., Thornton, A. E., Lang, D. J., Honer, W. G., et al. (2006). The need for speed: An update on methamphetamine addiction. *Journal of Psychiatry & Neuroscience, 31*(5), 301–13.

Barrett, L. F., Mesquita, B., Ochsner, K. N., & Gross, J. J. (2007). The experience of emotion. *Annual Review of Psychology, 58*, 373–403.

Bartels, A., & Zeki, S. (2004). The neural correlates of maternal and romantic love. *Neuroimage, 21*, 1155–1166.

Bartels, J., Andreasen, D., Ehirim, P., Mao, H., Seibert, S., Wright, E. J., et al. (2008). Neurotrophic electrode: Method of assembly and implantation into human motor speech cortex. *Journal of Neuroscience Methods, 174*, 168–76.

Barton, D. A., Esler, M. D., Dawood, T., Lambert, E. A., Haikerwal, D., Brenchley, C., et al. (2008). Elevated brain serotonin turnover in patients with depression: effect of genotype and therapy. *Archives of General Psychiatry, 65*, 38–46.

Bartoshuk, L. M. (2000). Comparing sensory experiences across individuals: Recent psychophysical advances illuminate genetic variation in taste perception. *Chemical Senses, 25*, 447–460.

Batson, C. D., Dyck, J. L., Brandt, J. R., Batson, J. G., Powell, A. L., McMaster, M. R., et al. (1988). Five studies testing two new egoistic alternatives to the empathy-altruism hypothesis. *Journal of Personality and Social Psychology, 55*, 52–77.

Batson, C. D., Turk, C. L., Shaw, L. L., & Klein, T. (1995). Information function of empathic emotion: Learning that we value the other's welfare. *Journal of Personality and Social Psychology, 68*, 300–313.

Baumeister, R. F. (1991). *Escaping the self: Alcoholism, spirituality, masochism, and other flights from the burden of selfhood.* New York: Basic Books.

Baumeister, R. F. (2000). Gender differences in erotic plasticity: The female sex drive as socially flexible and responsive. *Psychological Bulletin, 126*, 347–374.

Baumeister, R. F., Campbell, J. D., Krueger, J. I., & Vohs, K. D. (2003). Does high self-esteem cause better performance, interpersonal success, happiness, or healthier lifestyles? *Psychological Science in the Public Interest, 4*, 1–44.

Baumeister, R. F., Campbell, J. D., Krueger, J. I., & Vohs, K. D. (2005, January). Exploding the self-esteem myth. *Scientific American, 292*, 84–91.

Baumeister, R. F., Catanese, K. R., & Vohs, K. D. (2001). Is there a gender difference in strength of sex drive? Theoretical views, conceptual distinctions, and a review of the relevant literature. *Social Psychology Review, 5*, 242–273.

Baumeister, R. F., Dale, K., & Sommers, K. L. (1998). Freudian defense mechanisms and empirical findings in modern social psychology: Reaction formation, projection, displacement, undoing, isolation, sublimation, and denial. *Journal of Personality, 66*, 1081–1124.

Baumeister, R. F., & Leary, M. R. (1995). The need to belong: Desire for interpersonal attachments as a fundamental human motivation. *Psychological Bulletin, 117*, 497–529.

Baumeister, R. F., Smart, L., & Boden, J. M. (1996). Relation of threatened egotism to violence and aggression: The dark side of high self-esteem. *Psychological Review, 103*, 5–33.

Baumeister, R. F., Stillwell, A. M., & Heatherton, T. F. (1994). Guilt: An interpersonal approach. *Psychological Bulletin, 115*, 243–267.

Baumrind, D., Larzelere, R. E., & Cowan, P. A. (2002). Ordinary physical punishment: Is it harmful? Comment on Gershoff (2002). *Psychological Bulletin, 128*, 580–589.

Baxter, L. R. (2000). Functional imaging of brain systems mediating obsessive-compulsive disorder. In D. S. Charney, E. J. Nestler, & B. S. Bunney (Eds.), *Neurobiology of mental illness* (pp. 534–547). New York: Oxford University Press.

Baxter, L. R., Schwartz, J. M., Bergman, K. S., Szuba, M. P., Guze, B., Mazziota, J. C., et al. (1992). Caudate glucose metabolic rate changes with both drug and behavior therapy for obsessive-compulsive disorder. *Archives of General Psychiatry, 49*, 681–689.

Beck, A. T. (1967). *Depression: Clinical, experimental and theoretical aspects.* New York: Harper & Row.

Beck, A. T. (1976). *Cognitive therapy and the emotional disorders.* New York: International Universities Press.

Beck, A. T., Brown, G., Seer, R. A., Eidelson, J. L., & Riskind, J. H. (1987). Differentiating anxiety and depression: A test of the cognitive content-specificity hypothesis. *Journal of Abnormal Psychology, 96*, 179–183.

Beck, A. T., Freeman, A., & Associates. (1990). *Cognitive therapy of personality disorders.* New York: Guilford Press.

Beck, A. T., & Rector, N. A. (2005). Cognitive approaches to schizophrenia: Theory and therapy. *Annual Review of Clinical Psychology, 1*, 577–606.

Beck, A. T., Rush, A. J., Shaw, B., & Emery, G. (1979). *Cognitive therapy of depression.* New York: Guilford Press.

Beck, A. T., Steer, R. A., & Brown, G. K. (1996). *Beck depression inventory manual.* San Antonio, TX: The Psychological Corporation.

Beck, A. T., Ward, C. H., Mendelson, M., Mock, J., & Erbaugh, J. (1961). An inventory for measuring depression. *Archives of General Psychiatry, 4*, 561–571.

Becker, D. V., Kenrick, D. T., Neuberg, S. L., Blackwell, K. C., & Smith, D. M. (2007). The confounded nature of angry men and happy women. *Journal of Personality and Social Psychology, 92*, 179–190.

Beggan, J. K. (1992). On the social nature of nonsocial perception: The mere ownership effect. *Journal of Personality and Social Psychology, 62*, 229–237.

Beggs, J. M., Brown, T. H., Byrne, J. H., Crow, T., LeDoux, J. E., LeBar, K., et al. (1999). Learning and memory: Basic mechanisms. In M. J. Zigmond, F. E. Bloom, S. C. Landis, J. L. Roberts, & L. R. Squire (Eds.), *Fundamentals of neuroscience* (pp. 1411–1454). San Diego, CA: Academic Press.

Behne, T., Carpenter, M., Call, J., & Tomasello, M. (2005). Unwilling versus unable: Infants' understanding of intentional action. *Developmental Psychology, 41*, 328–337.

Bellak, L., & Black, R. B. (1992). Attention-deficit hyperactivity disorder in adults. *Clinical Therapeutics, 14*, 138–147.

Belmaker, R. H., & Agam, G. (2008). Major depressive disorder. *New England Journal of Medicine, 358*, 55–68.

Belsky, J. (1990). Children and marriage. In F. D. Fincham & T. N. Bradbury (Eds.), *The psychology of marriage: Basic issues and applications* (pp. 172–200). New York: Guilford Press.

Bem, D. (1967). Self-perception: An alternative explanation of cognitive dissonance phenomena. *Psychological Review, 74*, 183–200.

Bem, D. J. (1996). Exotic becomes erotic: A developmental theory of sexual orientation. *Psychological Review, 103*, 320–335.

Bem, D. J., & Honorton, C. (1994). Does psi exist? Replicable evidence for an anomalous process of information transfer. *Psychological Bulletin, 115*, 4–18.

Bender, H. L., Allen, J. P., McElhaney, K. B., Antonishak, J., Moore, C. M., Kelly, H. O., et al. (2007). Use of harsh physical discipline and developmental outcomes in adolescence. *Development and Psychopathology, 19*, 227–242.

Benedetti, F., Mayberg, H. S., Wagner, T. D., Stohler, C. S., & Zubieta, J. K. (2005). Neurobiological mechanisms of the placebo effect. *Journal of Neuroscience, 25*, 10390–10402.

Benedetti, F., Serretti, A., Colombo, C., Campori, E., Barbini, B., di Bella, D., et al. (1999). Influence of a functional polymorphism within the promoter of the serotonin transporter gene on the effects of total sleep deprivation in bipolar depression. *American Journal of Psychiatry, 156*, 1450–1452.

Benjamin, L. T. (2005). A history of clinical psychology as a profession in America (and a glimpse at its future). *Annual Review of Clinical Psychology, 1*, 1–30.

Bentler, P. M., & Newcomb, M. D. (1978). Longitudinal study of marital success and failure. *Journal of Consulting and Clinical Psychology, 46*, 1053–1070.

Berger, K. S. (2004). *The developing person through the life span* (6th ed.). New York: Worth.

Berkman, L. F., & Syme, S. L. (1979). Social networks, host resistance, and mortality: A nine-year follow-up study of Alameda County residents. *American Journal of Epidemiology, 109*, 186–204.

Berkowitz, L. (1990). On the formation and regulation of anger and aggression: A cognitive-neoassociationistic analysis. *American Psychologist, 45*, 494–503.

Berns, G. S., Chappelow, J., Zink, C. F., Pagnoni, G., Martin-Skurski, M. E., & Richards, J. (2005). Neurobiological correlates of social conformity and interdependence during mental rotation. *Biological Psychiatry, 58*, 245–253.

Berscheid, E., & Regan, P. (2005). *The psychology of interpersonal relationships.* New York: Prentice-Hall.

Betancourt, H., & Lopez, S. R. (1993). The study of culture, ethnicity, and race in American psychology. *American Psychologist, 48*, 629–637.

Bickel, W. K., Odum, A. L., & Madden, G. J. (1999). Impulsivity and cigarette smoking: Delay discounting in current, never, and ex-smokers. *Psychopharmacology, 146*, 447–454.

Bickel, W. K., Miller, M. L., Yi, R., Kowal, B. P., Lindquist, D. M., & Pitcock, J. A. (2007). Behavioral and neuroeconomics of drug addiction: Competing neural systems and temporal discounting processes. *Drug and Alcohol Dependence, 90* (Suppl. 1), S85–S91.

Bickerton, D. (1998). The creation and re-creation of language. In C. B. Crawford & D. L. Krebs (Eds.), *Handbook of evolutionary psychology: Ideas, issues, and applications* (pp. 613–634). Mahwah, NJ: Erlbaum.

Bidell, T. R., & Fischer, K. W. (1995). Between nature and nurture: The role of agency in the epigenesis of intelligence. In R. Sternberg & E. Grigorenko (Eds.), *Intelligence: Heredity and environment.* New York: Cambridge University Press.

Biederman, J., Hirshfeld-Becker, D. R., Rosenbaum, J. F., Herot, C., Friedman, D., Snidman, N., et al. (2001). Further evidence of association between behavioral inhibition and social anxiety in children. *American Journal of Psychiatry, 158*, 1673–1679.

Biederman, J., Monuteaux, M. C., Spencer, T., Wilens, T. E., Macpherson, H. A., & Faraone, S. V. (2008). Stimulant therapy and risk for subsequent substance use disorders in male adults with ADHD: A naturalistic controlled 10-year follow-up study. *American Journal of Psychiatry, 165*, 597–603.

Biesanz, J., West, S. G., & Millevoi, A. (2007). What do you learn about someone over time? The relationship between length of acquaintance and consensus and self-other agreement in judgments of personality. *Journal of Personality and Social Psychology, 92*, 119–135.

Birbaumer, N., Grodd, W., Diedrich, O., Klose, U., Erb, M., Lotze, M., et al. (1998). fMRI reveals amygdala activation to human faces in social phobics. *Neuroreport, 9*, 1223–1226.

Blagys, M. D., & Hilsenroth, M. J. (2000). Distinctive feature of short-term psychodynamic-interpersonal psychotherapy: A review of the comparative psychotherapy process literature. *Clinical Psychology: Science and Practice, 7*, 167–188.

Blair, I. V. (2002). The malleability of automatic stereotypes and prejudice. *Personality and Social Psychology Review, 6*, 242–261.

Blair, R. J. (2001). Neurocognitive models of aggression, the antisocial personality disorders, and psychopathy. *Journal of Neurology, Neurosurgery, and Psychiatry, 71*, 727–731.

Blair, R. J. (2003). Neurobiological basis of psychopathy. *British Journal of Psychiatry, 182*, 5–7.

Blakemore, C. (1983). *Mechanics of the mind.* Cambridge, UK: Cambridge University Press.

Blakemore, S. J., Wolpert, D. M., & Frith, C. D. (1998). Central cancellation of self-produced tickle sensation. *Nature Neuroscience, 1*, 635–640.

Blakeslee, S. (2001, April 10). A reason we call our cheddar cheese "sharp" and shirts "loud." *The New York Times.* Retrieved from http://www.nytimes.com

Blanchard, R., & Ellis, L. (2001). Birth weight, sexual orientation, and the sex of preceding siblings. *Journal of Biosocial Science, 33*, 451–467.

Blass, T. (1991). Understanding behavior in the Milgram obedience experiment: The role of personality, situations, and their interactions. *Journal of Personality and Social Psychology, 60*, 398–413.

Bloom, B., & Cohen, R. A. (2007). Summary health statistics for U.S. children: National health interview survey, 2006 (Vital and Health Statistics, Series 10, No. 234). Hyattsville, MD: Centers for Disease Control and Prevention.

Blue, I., & Harpham, T. (1996). Urbanization and mental health in developing countries. *Current Issues in Public Health, 2*, 181–185.

Bogaert, A. F. (2006). Biological versus nonbiological older brothers and men's sexual orientation. *Proceedings of the National Academy of Sciences, USA, 103*, 10771–10774.

Bohus, M., Haaf, B., Simms, T., Limberger, M. F., Schmahl, C., Unckel, C., et al. (2004). Effectiveness of inpatient dialectical behavioral therapy for borderline personality disorder: A controlled trial. *Behavioral Research and Therapy, 42*, 487–499.

Bolles, R. C. (1970). Species-specific defense reactions and avoidance learning. *Psychological Review, 77*, 32–48.

Booth-Kewley, S., & Friedman, H. S. (1987). Psychological predictors of heart disease. *Psychological Bulletin, 101*, 343–362.

Bornstein, R. F. (1999). Criterion validity of objective and projective dependency tests: A meta-analytic assessment of behavioral prediction. *Psychological Assessment, 11*, 48–57.

Bosson, J. K., Lakey, C. E., Campbell, W. K., Zeigler-Hill, V., Jordan, C. H., & Kernis, M. H. (2008). Untangling the links between narcissism and self-esteem: A theoretical and empirical review. *Social and Personality Psychology Compass, 2*, 1415–1439.

Bouchard, T. J., Jr., Lykken, D. T., McGue, M., Segal, N. L., & Tellegen, A. (1990, October 12). Sources of human psychological differences: The Minnesota study of twins reared apart. *Science, 250*, 223–228.

Bouchard, C., Tremblay, A., Despres, J. P., Nadeau, A., Lupien, J. P., Theriault, G., et al. (1990). The response to long-term overfeeding in identical twins. *New England Journal of Medicine, 322*, 1477–1482.

Bouton, M. E. (1994). Context, ambiguity, and classical conditioning. *Current Directions in Psychological Science, 3*, 49–53.

Bouton, M. E., Westbrook, R. F., Corcoran, K. A., & Maren, S. (2006). Contextual and temporal modulation of extinction: Behavioral and biological mechanisms. *Biological Psychiatry, 60*, 352–360.

Bower, A. (2001). Attractive models in advertising and the women who loathe them: The implications of negative affect for spokesperson effectiveness. *Highly Journal of Advertising, 30*, 51–63.

Bradbury, T. N., & Fincham, F. D. (1990). Attributions in marriage: Review and critique. *Psychological Bulletin, 107*, 3–33.

Bramlett, M. D., & Mosher, W. D. (2002). *Cohabitation, marriage, divorce, and remarriage in the United States* (Vital and Health Statistics, Series 23, No. 22). Hyattsville, MD: Centers for Disease Control and Prevention.

Bransford, J. D., & Johnson, M. K. (1972). Contextual prerequisites for understanding: Some investigations of comprehension and recall. *Journal of Verbal Learning and Verbal Behavior, 11*, 717–726. (Reprinted and modified in *Human memory*, p. 305, by E. B. Zechmeister & S. E. Nyberg, 1982, Eds., Pacific Grove, CA: Brooks Cole)

Braunschweig, D., Ashwood, P., Krakowiak, P., Hertz-Picciotto, I., Hansen, R., Croen, L. A., et al. (2008). Autism: Maternally derived antibodies specific for fetal brain proteins. *Neurotoxicology, 29*, 226–231.

Brefczynski-Lewis, J. A., Lutz, A., Schaefer, H. S., Levinson, D. B., & Davidson, R. J. (2007). Neural correlates of attentional expertise in long-term meditation practitioners. *Proceedings of the National Academy of Sciences, USA, 104*, 1143–1148.

Breland, K., & Breland, M. (1961). The misbehavior of organisms. *American Psychologist, 16*, 681–684.

Brent, D. A. (2004). Antidepressants and pediatric depression: The risk of doing nothing. *New England Journal of Medicine, 351*, 1598–1601.

Brewer, J. B., Zhao, Z., Glover, G. H., & Gabrieli, J. D. E. (1998, August 21). Making memories: Brain activity that predicts how well visual experiences will be remembered. *Science, 281*, 1185–1187.

Brewer, M. B., & Caporael, L. R. (1990). Selfish genes vs. selfish people: Sociobiology as origin myth. *Motivation and Emotion, 14*, 237–243.

Brigham, J. C., & Malpass, R. S. (1985). The role of experience and contact in the recognition of faces of own- and other-races persons. *Journal of Social Issues, 41*, 139–155.

Broadbent, D. A. (1958). *Perception and communication.* New York: Pergamon.

Brody, A. L., Saxena, S., Stoessel, P., Gillies, L. A., Fairbanks, L. A., Alborzian, S., et al. (2001). Regional brain metabolic changes in patients with major depression treated with either paroxetine or interpersonal therapy: Preliminary findings. *Archives of General Psychiatry, 58*, 631–640.

Brody, J. E. (1997, December 30) Personal health: Despite the despair of depression, few men seek treatment. *The New York Times.* Retrieved from http://www.nytimes.com

Brody, J. E. (2000, December 12). Personal health: Exposing the perils of eating disorders. *The New York Times.* Retrieved from http://www.nytimes.com

Brody, N. (1992). *Intelligence.* San Diego, CA: Academic Press.

Bromley, S. M., & Doty, R. L. (1995). Odor recognition memory is better under bilateral than unilateral test conditions. *Cortex, 31*, 25–40.

Bronfenbrenner, U. (1995). The bioecological model from a life course perspective: Reflections of a participant observer. In P. Moen, G. H. Elder, Jr., & K. Luscher (Eds.), *Examining lives in context: Perspectives on the ecology of human development* (pp. 599–618). Washington, DC: American Psychological Association.

Brown, A. S. (1991). A review of the tip-of-the-tongue phenomenon. *Psychological Bulletin, 109*, 204–223.

Brown, B. B., Mounts, N., Lamborn, S. D., & Steinberg, L. (1993). Parenting practices and peer group affiliations in adolescence. *Child Development, 64*, 467–482.

Brown, G. W., & Harris, T. O. (1978). *Social origins of depression: A study of psychiatric disorders in women.* New York: Free Press.

Brown, J. D., & Kobayashi, C. (2002). Self-enhancement in Japan and America. *Asian Journal of Social Psychology, 5*, 145–168.

Brownell, C. A., & Brown, E. (1992). Peers and play in infants and toddlers. In V. Van Hasselt & M. Hersen (Eds.), *Handbook of social development: A lifespan perspective* (pp. 183–200). New York: Plenum Press.

Bruce, V., & Young, A. (1986). Understanding face recognition. *British Journal of Psychology, 77*, 305–327.

Bruck, M. L., & Ceci, S. (1993). Amicus brief for the case of State of New Jersey v. Michaels. Presented by Committee of Concerned Social Scientists. Supreme Court of New Jersey Docket No. 36,633. (Reprinted in *Psychology, Public Policy and Law, 1*, 1995, 272–322.)

Bruder, C. E., Piotrowski, A., Gijsbers, A. A., Andersson, R., Erickson, S., de Ståhl, T. D., et al. (2008). Phenotypically concordant and discordant monozygotic twins display different DNA copy-number-variation profiles. *American Journal of Human Genetics, 82*, 763–771.

Buckner, R. L., Kelley, W. M., & Petersen, S. E. (1999). Frontal cortex contributes to human memory formation. *Nature Neuroscience, 2*, 311–314.

Bug Labs. (n.d.). *Welcome BUG, status: Recompiling. . . .* Retrieved December 20, 2007, from http://www.buglabs.net/

Bureau of Labor Statistics, U. S. Department of Labor. (2007). *Occupational outlook handbook, 2008–2009 edition: psychologists.* Retrieved from http://www.bls.gov/oco/ocos056.htm

Burger, J. M. (2009). Replicating Milgram: Would people still obey today? *American Psychologist, 64,* 1–11.

Burke, B. L., Arkowitz, H., & Menchola, M. (2003). The efficacy of motivational interviewing: A meta-analysis of controlled clinical trials. *Journal of Consulting and Clinical Psychology, 71,* 843–861.

Bush, E. C., & Allman, J. M. (2004). The scaling of frontal cortex in primates and carnivores. *Proceedings of the National Academy of Sciences, USA, 101,* 3962–3966.

Bushman, B. J., & Anderson, C. A. (2001). Media violence and the American public: Scientific facts versus media misinformation. *American Psychologist, 56,* 477–489.

Bushman, B. J., & Baumeister, R. F. (1998). Threatened egotism, narcissism, self-esteem, and direct and displaced aggression: Does self-love or self-hate lead to violence? *Journal of Personality and Social Psychology, 75,* 219–229.

Bushman, B. J., & Huesmann, L. R. (2001). Effects of televised violence on aggression. In D. G. Singer & J. L. Singer (Eds.), *Handbook of children and the media* (pp. 223–254). Thousand Oaks, CA: Sage.

Buss, A. H., & Plomin, R. (1984). *Temperament: Early developing personality traits.* Hillsdale, NJ: Erlbaum.

Buss, D. M. (1989). Sex differences in human mate preferences: Evolutionary hypotheses tested in 37 cultures. *Behavioral and Brain Sciences, 12,* 1–49.

Buss, D. M. (1999). Human nature and individual differences: The evolution of human personality. In L. A. Pervin & O. P. John (Eds.), *Handbook of personality: Theory and research* (pp. 31–56). New York: Guilford Press.

Buss, D. M., & Greiling, H. (1999). Adaptive individual differences. *Journal of Personality, 67,* 209–243.

Buss, D. M., & Schmitt, D. P. (1993). Sexual strategies theory: An evolutionary perspective on human mating. *Psychological Review, 100,* 204–232.

Buss, D. M., & Shackelford, T. K. (2008). Attractive women want it all: Good genes, investment, parenting indicators, and commitment. *Evolutionary Psychology, 6,* 134–146.

Cacioppo, J. T., Hughes, M. E., Waite, L. J., Hawkley, L. C., & Thisted, R. A. (2006). Loneliness as a specific risk factor for depressive symptoms: Cross sectional and longitudinal analyses. *Psychology and Aging, 21,* 140–151.

Cahill, L. (2003). Sex-related influences on the neurobiology of emotionally influenced memory. *Annals of the New York Academy of Sciences, 985,* 163–167.

Cahill, L. (2006). Why sex matters in neuroscience. *Nature Reviews Neuroscience, 7,* 477–484.

Cahill, L., Haier, R. J., White, N. S., Fallon, J., Kilpatrick, L., Lawrence, C., et al. (2001). Sex-related difference in amygdala activity during emotionally influenced memory storage. *Neurobiology of Learning and Memory, 75,* 1–9.

Cahill, L., Haier, R. J., Fallon, J., Alkire, M. T., Tang, C., & Keator, D., et al. (1996). Amygdala activity at encoding correlated with long-term, free recall of emotional information. *Proceedings of the National Academy of Sciences, USA, 93,* 8016–8021.

Cahill, L., Prins, B., Weber, M., & McGaugh, J. L. (1994). Beta-adrenergic activation and memory for emotional events. *Nature, 371,* 702–704.

Cahn, B. R., & Polich, J. (2006). Meditation states and traits: EEG, ERP, and neuroimaging studies. *Psychological Bulletin, 132,* 180–211.

Cairns, R. B., & Cairns, B. D. (1994). *Lifelines and risks: Pathways of youth in our times.* Cambridge, UK: Cambridge University Press.

Caldwell, M., Skeem, J., Salekin, R., & Van Rybroek, G. (2006). Treatment response of adolescent offenders with psychopathy features: A 2-year follow-up. *Criminal Justice and Behavior, 33,* 571–596.

Callaghan, T., Rochat, P., Lillard, A., Claux, M. L., Odden, H., Itakura, S., et al. (2005). Synchrony in the onset of mental-state reasoning: Evidence from five cultures. *Psychological Science, 16,* 378–384.

Campbell, W. K., Bush, C. P., Brunell, A. B., & Shelton, J. (2005). Understanding the social costs of narcissism: The case of tragedy of the commons. *Personality and Social Psychology, 31,* 1358–1368.

Campbell, W. K., Foster, C. A., & Finkel, E. J. (2002). Does self-love lead to love for others? A story of narcissistic game playing. *Journal of Personality and Social Psychology, 83,* 340–354.

Campbell, W. K., & Sedikides, C. (1999). Self-threat magnifies the self-serving bias: A meta-analytic integration. *Review of General Psychology, 3,* 23–43.

Canli, T. (2006). *Biology of personality and individual differences.* New York: Guilford Press.

Canli, T., Desmond, J. E., Zhao, Z., & Gabrieli, J. D. (2002). Sex differences in the neural basis of emotional memories. *Proceedings of the National Academy of Sciences, USA, 99,* 10789–10794.

Cannon, T. D., Cadenhead, K., Cornblatt, B., Woods, S. W., Addington, J., Walker, E., et al. (2008). Prediction of psychosis in youth at high clinical risk: A multisite longitudinal study in North America. *Archives of General Psychiatry, 65,* 28–37.

Caporael, L. R. (2001). Evolutionary psychology: Toward a unifying theory and a hybrid science. *Annual Review of Psychology, 52,* 607–628.

Caramaschi, D., de Boer, S. F., & Koolhaus, J. M. (2007). Differential role of the 5-HT receptor in aggressive and non-aggressive mice: An across-strain comparison. *Physiology & Behavior, 90,* 590–601.

Carmena, J. M., Lebdev, M. A., Crist, R. E., O'Doherty, J. E., Santucci, D. M., Dimitrov, D. F., et al. (2003). Learning to control a brain-machine interface for reaching and grasping by primates. *PLoS Biology, 1,* 193–208.

Carmichael, M. (2007, March 26). Stronger, faster, smarter. *Newsweek, 149*(13). Retrieved from http://www.newsweek.com

Carmody, T. P. (1993). Nicotine dependence: Psychological approaches to the prevention of smoking relapse. *Psychology of Addictive Behaviors, 7,* 96–102.

Carnagey, N. L., Anderson, C. A., & Bartholow, B. D. (2007). Media violence and social neuroscience: New questions and new opportunities. *Current Directions in Psychological Science, 16,* 178–182.

Carnagey, N. L., Anderson, C. A., & Bushman, B. J. (2007). The effect of video game violence on physiological desensitization to real-life violence. *Journal of Experimental Social Psychology, 43,* 489–496.

Caro, T. M., & Hauser, M. D. (1992). Is there teaching in nonhuman animals? *Quarterly Journal of Biology, 67,* 151–174.

Carstensen, L. L. (1995). Evidence for a life-span theory of socioemotional selectivity. *Current Directions in Psychological Science, 4,* 151–156.

Carter, C. S. (2003). Developmental consequences of oxytocin. *Physiology & Behavior, 74*, 383–397.

Caruso, S., Intelisano, G., Farina, M., Di Mari, L., & Agnello, C. (2003). The function of sildenafil on female sexual pathways: A double-blind, cross-over, placebo-controlled study. *European Journal of Obstetrics & Gynecology and Reproductive Biology, 110*, 201–206.

Case, R. (1992). The role of the frontal lobes in development. *Brain and Cognition, 20*, 51–73.

Caspi, A. (2000). The child is father of the man: Personality continuities from childhood to adulthood. *Journal of Personality and Social Psychology, 78*, 158–172.

Caspi, A., & Herbener, E. S. (1990). Continuity and change: Assortative marriage and the consistency of personality in adulthood. *Journal of Personality and Social Psychology, 58*, 250–258.

Caspi, A., McClay, J., Moffit, T. E., Mill, J., Martin, J., Craig, I. W., et al. (2002). Role of genotype in the cycle of violence in maltreated children. *Science, 29*, 851–854.

Castellanos, F. X., Giedd, J. N., Eckberg, P., & Marsh, W. L. (1998). Quantitative morphology of the caudate nucleus in attention deficit hyperactivity disorder. *American Journal of Psychiatry, 151*, 1791–1796.

Catalyst. (2006). Different cultures, similar perceptions: Stereotypes of Western European business leaders. New York: Author.

Cattell, R. B. (1965). *The scientific analysis of personality*. London: Penguin.

Cattell, R. B. (1971). *Abilities: Their structure, growth, and action*. Boston: Houghton Mifflin.

Ceci, S. J. (1999). Schooling and intelligence. In S. J. Ceci & W. M. Williams (Eds.), *The nature-nurture debate: The essential readings* (pp. 168–175). Oxford, UK: Blackwell.

Ceci, S. J., & Bruck, M. (1995). Jeopardy in the courtroom: A scientific analysis of children's testimony. Washington, DC: American Psychological Association.

CensusScope. (2000). *Multiracial profile: United States*. Retrieved from http://www.censusscope.org/us/chart_multi.html

Centers for Disease Control and Prevention, National Center for Health Statistics. (2002, October 8). *HHS news: Obesity still on the rise, new data show* [Press release.]. Retrieved from http://www.cdc.gov/nchs/PRESSROOM/02news/obesityonrise.htm

Centers for Disease Control and Prevention. (2004). *Mean body weight, height, and body mass index, United States 1960–2002* [Advance data]. Retrieved January 22, 2008, from http://usgovinfo.about.com

Centers for Disease Control and Prevention, National Center on Birth Defects and Developmental Disabilities. (2004, July). *Fetal alcohol syndrome: Guidelines for referral and diagnosis*. Retrieved from http://www.cdc.gov/ncbddd/fas/publications/FAS_guidelines_accessible.pdf

Centers for Disease Control and Prevention. (2005). Tobacco use, access, and exposure to tobacco in media among middle and high school students—United States, 2004. *Morbidity and Mortality Weekly Report, 54*, 297–301.

Centers for Disease Control and Prevention, National Center for Health Statistics. (2006). *Data on injury* [Fact sheet]. Retrieved May 8, 2008, from http://www.cdc.gov/nchs/data/factsheets/injury.pdf

Centers for Disease Control and Prevention, National Center for Health Statistics. (2007). [Table 27, Life expectancy at birth, at 65 years of age, and at 75 years of age, by race and sex: United States, selected years 1900–2005]. *Health, United States, 2007*. Retrieved from http://www.cdc.gov/nchs/data/hus/hus07.pdf#027

Cepeda, N. J., Pashler, H., Vul, E., Wixted, J. T., & Rohrer, D. (2006). Distributed practice in verbal recall tasks: A review and quantitative synthesis. *Psychological Bulletin, 132*, 354–380.

Chabas, D., Taheri, S., Renier, C., & Mignot, E. (2003). The genetics of narcolepsy. *Annual Review of Genomics & Human Genetics, 4*, 459–483.

Chabris, C. (1999). Prelude or requiem for the "Mozart effect"? *Nature, 400*, 826–827.

Chamberlain, S. R., & Sahakian, B. J. (2007). The neuropsychiatry of impulsivity. *Current Opinions in Psychiatry, 20*, 255–261.

Chambers, D. W. (1983). Stereotypic images of the scientist: The draw-a-scientist test. *Science Education, 67*, 255–265.

Chase, V. D. (2006). *Shattered nerves: How science is solving modern medicine's most perplexing problem*. Baltimore: The Johns Hopkins University Press.

Chase, W. G., & Simon, H. A. (1973). Perception in chess. *Cognitive Psychology, 4*, 55–81.

Chassin, L., Presson, C. C., & Sherman, S. J. (1990). Social psychological contributions to the understanding and prevention of adolescent cigarette smoking. *Personality and Social Psychology Bulletin, 16*, 133–151.

Cherry, E. C. (1953). Some experiments on the recognition of speech, with one and two ears. *Journal of the Acoustic Society of America, 25*, 975–979.

Chess, S., & Thomas, A. (1984). *Origins and evolution of behavior disorders: From infancy to early adult life*. Cambridge, MA: Harvard University Press.

Cheung, F. M., Leung, K., Zhang, J. X, Sun, H. F., Gan, Y. G., Song, W. Z, et al. (2001). Indigenous Chinese personality constructs: Is the five-factor model complete? *Journal of Cross-Cultural Psychology, 32*, 407–433.

Chistyakov, A. V., Kaplan, B., Rubichek, O., Kreinin, I., Koren, D., Feinsod, M., et al. (2004). Antidepressant effects of different schedules of repetitive transcranial magnetic stimulation vs. clomipramine in patients with major depression: Relationship to changes in cortical excitability. *International Journal of Neuropsychopharmacology, 8*, 223–233.

Choi, I., Dalal, R., Kim-Prieto, C., & Park, H. (2003). Culture and judgment of causal relevance. *Journal of Personality and Social Psychology, 84*, 46–59.

Choleris, E., Gustafsson, J. A., Korach, K. S., Muglia, L. J., Pfaff, D. W., & Ogawa, S. (2003). An estrogen-dependent four-gene micronet regulating social recognition: A study with oxytocin and estrogen receptor-alpha and -beta knockout mice. *Proceedings of the National Academy of Sciences, USA, 100*, 6192–6197.

Christakis, N. A., & Fowler, J. H. (2007). The spread of obesity in a large social network over 32 years. *New England Journal of Medicine, 357*, 370–379.

Christensen-Szalanski, J., & Willham, C. F. (1991). The hindsight bias: A meta analysis. *Organizational Behavior and Human Decision Processes, 48*, 147–168.

Christianson, S. (1992). Emotional stress and eyewitness memory: A critical review. *Psychological Bulletin, 112*, 284–309.

Cheung, F. M., Cheung, S. F., & Leung, F. (2008). Clinical utility of the cross-cultural (Chinese) personality assessment inventory (CPAI-2) in the assessment of substance use disorders among Chinese men. *Psychological Assessment, 20*, 103–113.

Chua, H. F., Boland, J. E., & Nisbett, R. E. (2005). Cultural variation in eye movements during scene perception. *Proceedings of the National Academy of Sciences, USA, 102,* 12629–12633.

Cialdini, R. B. (2008). *Influence: Science and prejudice* (5th ed.). Boston: Allyn & Bacon.

Cialdini, R. B., Shaller, M., Houlihan, D., Arps, K., Fultz, J., & Beaman, A. L. (1987). Empathy-based helping: Is it selflessly or selfishly motivated? *Journal of Personality and Social Psychology, 52,* 749–758.

Clark, A. C., & Watson, D. (1999). Temperament: A new paradigm for trait psychology. In L. A. Pervin & O. P. John (Eds.), *Handbook of personality: Theory and research* (pp. 399–423). New York: Guilford Press.

Clark, L. A. (2007). Assessment and diagnosis of personality disorder: Perennial issues and an emerging reconceptualization. *Annual Review of Psychology, 58,* 227–257.

Clark, R. D., & Hatfield, E. (1989). Gender differences in receptivity to sexual offers. *Journal of Psychology and Human Sexuality, 2,* 39–55.

Clark, S. E., & Wells, G. L. (2008). On the diagnosticity of multiple-witness identifications. *Law and Human Behavior, 32,* 406–422.

Clarke-Stewart, K. A., Vandell, D. L., McCartney, K., Owen, M. T., & Booth, C. (2000). Effects of parental separation and divorce on very young children. *Journal of Family Psychology, 14,* 304–326.

Cloninger, C., Adolfsson, R., & Svrakic, N. (1996). Mapping genes for human personality. *Nature and Genetics, 12,* 3–4.

Cohen, G. L., Garcia, J., Apfel, N., & Master, A. (2006). "Reducing the racial achievement gap": A social-psychological intervention. *Science, 313,* 1307–1310.

Cohen, S., Alper, C. M., Doyle, W. J., Treanor, J. J., & Turner, R. B. (2006). Positive emotional style predicts resistance to illness after experimental exposure to rhinovirus or influenza A virus. *Psychomatic Medicine, 68,* 809–815.

Cohen, S., Doyle, W. J., Skoner, D. P., Rabin, B. S., & Gwaltney, J. M. J. (1997). Social ties and susceptibility to the common cold. *Journal of the American Medical Association, 277,* 1940–1944.

Cohen, S., Tyrrell, D. A. J., & Smith, A. P. (1991). Psychological stress and susceptibility to the common cold. *New England Journal of Medicine, 325,* 606–612.

Cohen, S., & Wills, T. A. (1985). Stress, social support, and the buffering hypothesis. *Psychological Bulletin, 98,* 310–357.

Colapinto, J. (2000). *As nature made him: The boy who was raised as a girl.* New York: HarperCollins.

Compton, W. M., Conway, K. P., Stinson, F. S., Colliver, J. D., & Grant, B. F. (2005). Prevalence, correlates, and comorbidity of DSM-IV antisocial personality syndromes and alcohol and specific drug use disorders in the United States: Results from the national epidemiologic survey on alcohol and related conditions. *Journal of Clinical Psychiatry, 66,* 677–685.

Conrad, A., Wilhelm, F. H., Roth, W. T., Spiegel, D., & Taylor, C. B. (2008). Circadian affective, cardiopulmonary, and cortisol variability in depressed and nondepressed individuals at risk for cardiovascular disease. *Journal of Psychiatric Research, 42,* 769–777.

Conway, A. R. A., Kane, M. J., Bunting, M. F. , Hambrick, D. Z., Wilhelm, O., & Engle, R. W. (2005). Working memory span tasks: A methodological review and user's guide. *Psychonomic Bulletin & Review, 12,* 769–786.

Conway, A. R. A., Kane, M. J., & Engle, R. W. (2003). Working memory capacity and its relation to general intelligence. *Trends in Cognitive Sciences, 7,* 547–552.

Conway, M. A., Anderson, S. J., Larsen, S. F, Donnelly, C. M., McDaniel, M. A., McClelland, A. G. R., et al. (1994). The formation of flashbulb memories. *Memory and Cognition, 22,* 326–343.

Conway, M., & Ross, M. (1984). Getting what you want by revising what you had. *Journal of Personality and Social Psychology, 47,* 738–748.

Cook, G. I., Marsh, R. L., Clark-Foos, A., & Meeks, J. T. (2007, February). Learning is impaired by activated intentions. *Psychonomic Bulletin and Review, 14,* 101–106.

Cook, M., & Mineka, S. (1989). Observational conditioning of fear to fear-relevant versus fear-irrelevant stimuli in rhesus monkeys. *Journal of Abnormal Psychology, 98,* 448–459.

Cooke, S. F., & Bliss, T. V. P. (2006). Plasticity in the human central nervous system. *Brain: A Journal of Neurology, 129,* 1659–1673.

Cooney, J., & Gazzaniga, M. S. (2003). Neurological disorders and the structure of human consciousness. *Trends in Cognitive Sciences, 7,* 161–165.

Cooper, L. A., & Shepard, R. N. (1973). Chronometric studies of the rotation of mental images. In W. G. Chase (Ed.), *Visual information processing* (pp. 75–176). New York: Academic Press.

Coopersmith, S. (1967). *The antecedents of self-esteem.* San Francisco: W. H. Freeman.

Corder, E. H., Saunders, A. M., Strittmatter, W. J., Schmechel, D. E., Gaskell, P. C., Small, G. W., et al. (1993). Gene dose of apolipoprotein E type 4 allele and the risk of Alzheimer's disease in late onset families. *Science, 261,* 921–923.

Coren, S., & Hakstian, A. R. (1987). Visual screening without the use of technical equipment: Preliminary development of a behaviorally validated questionnaire. *Applied Optics, 26,* 1468–1472.

Coren, S., & Hakstian, A. R. (1988). Color vision screening with the use of technical equipment: Scale development and cross-validation. *Perception & Psychophysics, 43*(2), 115–120.

Corkin, S., Amaral, D. G., Gonzalez, R. G., Johnson, K. A., & Hyman, B. T. (1997). H. M.'s medial temporal lobe lesion: Findings from magnetic resonance imaging. *Journal of Neuroscience, 17,* 3964–3979.

Cornish, J. W., Metzger, D., Woody, G. E., Wilson, D., McLellan, A. T., Vandergrift, B., et al. (1997). Naltrexone pharmacotherapy for opioid dependent federal probationers. *Journal of Substance Abuse Treatment, 14,* 529–534.

Correll, C. U., Leucht, S., & Kane, J. M. (2004). Lower risk for tardive dyskinesia associated with second-generation antipsychotics: A systematic review of 1-year studies. *American Journal of Psychiatry, 161,* 414–425.

Correll, J., Park, B., Judd, C. M., Wittenbrink, B., Sadler, M. S., & Keesee, T. (2007). Across the thin blue line: Police officers and racial bias in the decision to shoot. *Journal of Personality and Social Psychology, 92,* 1006–1023.

Cosmides, L., & Tooby, J. (1997). *Evolutionary psychology: A primer.* Retrieved May 24, 2002, from http://www.psych.ucsb.edu/research/cep/primer.html

Cosmides, L., & Tooby, J. (2000). The cognitive neuroscience of social reasoning. In M. S. Gazzaniga (Ed.), *The new cognitive neurosciences* (pp. 1259–1270). Cambridge, MA: MIT Press.

Cosmides, L., Tooby, J., & Kurzban, R. (2003). Perceptions of race. *Trends in Cognitive Sciences, 7,* 173–179.

Costa, P. T., & McCrae, R. R. (1992). *Revised NEO Personality Inventory (NEO-PI-R) and NEO Five-Factor Inventory (NEO-FFI) professional manual.* Odessa, FL: Psychological Assessment Resources.

Costa, P. T., Terracciano, A., & McCrae, R. R. (2001). Gender differences in personality traits across cultures: Robust and surprising findings. *Journal of Personality and Social Psychology, 81,* 322–331.

Courchesne, E., Pierce, K., Schumann, C. M., Redcay, E., Buckwalter, J. A., Kennedy, D. P., et al. (2007). Mapping early brain development in autism. *Neuron, 56,* 399–413.

Courchesne, E., Redcay, E., & Kennedy, D. P. (2004). The autistic brain: Birth through adulthood. *Current Opinion in Neurology, 17,* 489–496.

Craft, L. L., & Perna, F. M. (2004). The benefits of exercise for the clinically depressed. *Journal of Clinical Psychiatry, 6,* 104–111.

Crawford, H. J., Corby, J. C., & Kopell, B. (1996). Auditory event-related potentials while ignoring tone stimuli: Attentional differences reflected in stimulus intensity and latency responses in low and highly hypnotizable persons. *International Journal of Neuroscience, 85,* 57–69.

Crocker, J., & Major, B. (1989). Social stigma and self-esteem: The self-protective properties of stigma. *Psychological Review, 96,* 608–630.

Crosnoe, R., Cavanagh, S., & Elder, G. H., Jr. (2003). Adolescent friendships as academic resources: The intersection of friendship, race, and school disadvantage. *Sociological Perspectives, 46,* 331–352.

Crosnoe, R., & Elder, G. H. (2002). Successful adaptation in the later years: A life-course approach to aging. *Social Psychology Quarterly, 65,* 309–328.

Crowe, R. R. (2000). Molecular genetics of anxiety disorders. In D. S. Charney, E. J. Nestler, & B. S. Bunney (Eds.), *Neurobiology of mental illness* (pp. 451–462). New York: Oxford University Press.

Csikszentmihalyi, M. (1990). *Flow: The psychology of optimal experience.* New York: Harper and Row.

Csikszentmihalyi, M. (1999). If we are so rich, why aren't we happy? *American Psychologist, 54,* 821–827.

Cunningham, M. R., Barbee, A. P., & Druen, P. B. (1996). Social allergens and the reactions they produce: Escalation of annoyance and disgust in love and work. In R. M. Kowalski (Ed.), *Aversive interpersonal behaviors* (pp. 189–214). New York: Plenum Press.

Cunningham, M. R., Roberts, A. R., Barbee, A. P., Druen, P. B., & Wu, C. (1995). Their ideas of beauty are, on the whole, the same as ours: Consistency and variability in the cross-cultural perception of female physical attractiveness. *Journal of Personality and Social Psychology, 68,* 261–279.

Cunningham, W. A., Johnson, M. K., Raye, C. L., Gatenby, J. C., Gore, J. C., & Banaji, M. R. (2004). Separable neural components in the processing of black and white faces. *Psychological Science, 15,* 806–813.

Cupach, W. R., & Metts, S. (1990). Remedial processes in embarrassing predicaments. In J. Anderson (Ed.), *Communication yearbook* (pp. 323–352). Newbury Park, CA: Sage.

Curtis, C. E., & D'Esposito, M. (2003). Persistent activity in the prefrontal cortex during working memory. *Trends in Cognitive Sciences, 7,* 415–423.

Curtiss, S. (1977). *Genie: A psycholinguistic study of a modern day "wild child."* New York: Academic Press.

Dalton, M. A., Bernhardt, A. M., Gibson, J. J., Sargent, J. D., Beach, M. L., Adachi-Mejia, A. M., et al. (2005). "Honey, have some smokes." Preschoolers use cigarettes and alcohol while role playing as adults. *Archives of Pediatrics & Adolescent Medicine, 159,* 854–859.

Damasio, A. R. (1994). *Descartes' error.* New York: Avon Books.

Damasio, H., Grabowski, T., Frank, R., Galaburda, A. M., & Damasio, A. R. (1994, May 20). The return of Phineas Gage: Clues about the brain from the skull of a famous patient. *Science, 264,* 1102–1105.

Danaher, K., & Crandall, C. S. (2008). Stereotype threat in applied settings re-examined. *Journal of Applied Social Psychology, 38,* 1639–1655.

Darley, J. M., & Batson, C. D. (1973). "From Jerusalem to Jericho": A study of situational and dispositional variables in helping behavior. *Journal of Personality and Social Psychology, 27,* 100–108.

Dasgupta, A. G., & Greenwald, A. G. (2001). Exposure to admired group members reduces automatic intergroup bias. *Journal of Personality and Social Psychology, 81,* 800–814.

Davidson, J. R., Foa, E. B., Huppert, J. D., Keefe, F. J., Franklin, M. E., Compton, J. S., et al. (2004). Fluoxetine, comprehensive cognitive behavioral therapy, and placebo in generalized social phobia. *Archives of General Psychiatry, 61,* 1005–1013.

Davidson, R. J. (2000a). Affective style, psychopathology, and resilience: Brain mechanisms and plasticity. *American Psychologist, 55,* 1196–1214.

Davidson, R. J. (2000b). The functional neuroanatomy of affective style. In R. Lane & L. Nadel (Eds.), *Cognitive neuroscience of emotion* (pp. 371–388). New York: Oxford University Press.

Davidson, R. J., Pizzagalli, D., Nitschke, J. B., & Putnam, K. M. (2002). Depression: Perspectives from affective neuroscience. *Annual Review of Psychology, 53,* 545–574.

Davidson Ward, S. L., Bautisa, D., Chan, L., Derry, M., Lisbin, A., Durfee, M., et al. (1990). Sudden infant death syndrome in infants of drug abusing mothers. *Journal of Pediatrics, 117,* 876–887.

Davies, M. F. (1997). Belief persistence after evidential discrediting: The impact of generated versus provided explanations on the likelihood of discredited outcomes. *Journal of Experimental Social Psychology, 33,* 561–578.

Davis, K. L., Stewart, D. G., Friedman, J. I., Buchsbaum, M., Harvey, P. D., Hof, P. R., et al. (2003). White matter changes in schizophrenia: Evidence for myelin-related dysfunction. *Archives of General Psychiatry, 60,* 443–456.

Davis, M. (1997). Neurobiology of fear responses: The role of the amygdala. *Journal of Neuropsychological and Clinical Neuroscience, 9,* 382–402.

Davison, K., & Pennebaker, J. (1996). Social psychosomatics. In E. T. Higgins & A. W. Kruglanski (Eds.), *Social psychology: Handbook of basic principles* (pp. 102–130). New York: Guilford Press.

Deacon, B. J., & Abramowitz, J. S. (2004). Cognitive and behavioral treatments for anxiety disorders: A review of meta-analytic findings. *Journal of Clinical Psychology, 60,* 429–441.

Deary, I. J. (2000). *Looking down on human intelligence.* New York: Oxford University Press.

Deary, I. J. (2001). *Intelligence: A very short introduction.* New York: Oxford University Press.

Deary, I. J., & Der, G. (2005). Reaction time explains IQ's association with death. *Psychological Science, 16,* 64–69.

Debiec, J., LeDoux, J. E., & Nader, K. (2002). Cellular and systems consolidation in the hippocampus. *Neuron, 36,* 527–538.

de Bruin, W. B., Parker, A. M., & Fischoff, B. (2007). Individual differences in adult decision-making competence. *Journal of Personality and Social Psychology, 92,* 938–956.

DeCasper, A. J., & Fifer, W. P. (1980, June 6). Of human bonding: Newborns prefer their mothers' voices. *Science, 208,* 1174–1176.

DeCasper, A. J., & Spence, M. J. (1986). Prenatal maternal speech influences newborns' perception of speech sounds. *Infant Behavior and Development, 9*, 133–150.

deCharms, R. C., Maeda, F., Glover, G. H, Ludlow, D., Pauly, J. M., Soneji, D., et al. (2005). Control over brain activation and pain learned by using real-time functional MRI. *Proceedings of the National Academy of Sciences, USA, 102*, 18626–18631.

Deci, E. L., & Ryan, R. M. (1987). The support of autonomy and the control of behavior. *Journal of Personality and Social Psychology, 53*, 1024–1037.

Dehaene, S., Changeux, J. P., Naccache, L., Sackur, J., & Sergent, C. (2006). Conscious, preconscious, and subliminal processing: A testable taxonomy. *Trends in Cognitive Sciences, 10*, 204–211.

Dehaene-Lambertz, G., & Gliga, T. (2004). Common neural basis for phoneme processing in infants and adults. *Journal of Cognitive Neuroscience, 16*, 1375–1387.

Dejong, W., & Kleck, R. E. (1986). The social psychological effects of overweight. In C. P. Herman, M. P. Zanna, & E. T. Higgins (Eds.), *Physical appearance, stigma and social behavior: The Ontario Symposium* (pp. 65–87). Hillsdale, NJ: Erlbaum.

DeLong, M. R., & Wichmann, T. (2008). *The expanding potential of deep brain stimulation: The 2008 progress report on brain research.* New York: Dana Foundation.

Demerouti, E. (2006). Job characteristics, flow, and performance: The moderating role of conscientiousness. *Journal of Occupational Health Psychology, 11*(3), 266–280.

Demir, E., & Dickson, B. J. (2005). Fruitless: Splicing specifies male courtship behavior in drosophila. *Cell, 121*, 785–794.

Dennerstein, L., & Burrows, G. D. (1982). Hormone replacement therapy and sexuality in women. *Clinics in Endocrinology and Metabolism, 11*, 661–679.

Despues, D., & Friedman, H. S. (2007). Ethnic differences in health behaviors among college students. *Journal of Applied Social Psychology, 37*, 131–142.

Devine, P. G. (1989). Stereotypes and prejudice: Their automatic and controlled components. *Journal of Personality and Social Psychology, 56*, 5–18.

Diamond, A., & Doar, B. (1989). The performance of human infants on a measure of frontal cortex function, delayed response task. *Developmental Psychobiology, 22*, 271–294.

Diamond, D. M., Fleshner, M., Ingersoll, N., & Rose, G. (1996). Psychological stress impairs spatial working memory: Relevance to electrophysiological studies of hippocampal function. *Behavioural Brain Research, 62*, 301–307.

Diener, E. (2000). Subjective well-being: The science of happiness and a proposal for a national index. *American Psychologist, 55*, 34–43.

Diener, E., & Diener, C. (1996). Most people are happy. *Psychological Science, 7*, 181–185.

Diener, E., Gohm, C. L., Suh, E., & Oishi, S. (2000). Similarity of the relations between marital status and subjective well-being. *Journal of Cross-Cultural Psychology, 31*, 419–436.

Diener, E., & Wellborn, M. (1976). Effect of self-awareness on anti-normative behavior. *Journal of Research in Personality, 10*, 107–111.

Diener, E., Wolsic, B., & Fujita, F. (1995). Physical attractiveness and subjective well-being. *Journal of Personality and Social Psychology, 69*, 120–129.

Dijksterhuis, A. (2004). Think different: The merits of unconscious thought in preference development and decision making. *Journal of Personality and Social Psychology, 87*, 586–598.

Dijksterhuis, A., & Nordgren, L. F. (2006). A theory of unconscious thought. *Perspectives on Psychological Science, 1*, 95–109.

Dijksterhuis, A., & van Knippenberg, A. (1998). The relation between perception and behavior, or how to win a game of Trivial Pursuit. *Journal of Personality and Social Psychology, 74*, 865–877.

Diller, L. H., Tanner, J. L., & Weil, J. (1996). Etiology of ADHD: Nature or nurture. *American Journal of Psychiatry, 153*, 451–452.

Dion, K., Berscheid, E., & Walster, E. (1972). What is beautiful is good. *Journal of Personality and Social Psychology, 24*, 285–290.

Diotallevi, M. (2008). Testimonials versus evidence. *Canadian Medical Association Journal, 179*, 449.

Dobbs, D. (2006, August/September). Turning off depression. *Scientific American Mind*, 26–31.

Docherty, N. M. (2005). Cognitive impairments and disordered speech in schizophrenia: Thought disorder, disorganization, and communication failure perspectives. *Journal of Abnormal Psychology, 114*, 269–278.

Dohrenwend, B. P., Shrout, P. E., Link, B. G., Skodol, A. E., & Martin, J. L. (1986). Overview and initial results from a risk factor study of depression and schizophrenia. In J. E. Barrett (Ed.), *Mental disorders in the community: Progress and challenge* (pp. 184–215). New York: Guilford Press.

Dolan, R. J. (2000). Emotion processing in the human brain revealed through functional neuroimaging. In M. S. Gazzaniga (Ed.), *The new cognitive neurosciences* (pp. 115–131). Cambridge, MA: MIT Press.

Domhoff, G. W. (2003). *The scientific study of dreams: Neural networks, cognitive development, and content analysis.* Washington, DC: American Psychological Association.

Domino, M. E., Burns, B. J., Silva, S. G., Kratochvil, C. J., Vitiello, B., Reinecke, M. A., et al. (2008). Cost-effectiveness of treatments for adolescent depression: Results from TADS. *American Journal of Psychiatry, 165*, 588–596.

Donahue, A. B. (2000). Electroconvulsive therapy and memory loss: A personal journey. *Journal of ECT, 16*, 133–143.

Doraiswamy, P. M., & Xiong, G. L. (2007, September 28). Does meditation enhance cognition and brain longevity? *Annals of the New York Academy of Sciences.* Advance online publication. Abstract retrieved from http://www.annalsnyas.org

Doty, R. L., Shaman, P., Applebaum, S. L., Giberson, R., Siksorski, L., & Rosenberg, L. (1984). Smell identification ability: Changes with age. *Science, 226*, 1441–1443.

Dovidio, J. F., ten Vergert, M., Stewart, T. L., Gaertner, S. L., Johnson, J. D., Esses, V. M., et al. (2004). Perspective and prejudice: Antecedents and mediating mechanisms. *Personality and Social Psychology Bulletin, 30*, 1537–1549.

Doyal, L. (2001). Sex, gender, and health: The need for a new approach. *British Medical Journal, 323*, 1061–1063.

Drosopoulos, S., Schulze, C., Fischer, S., & Born, J. (2007). Sleep's function in the spontaneous recovery and consolidation of memories. *Journal of Experimental Psychology: General 136*(2), 169–183.

Drummond, S. P., Brown, G. G., Gillin, J. C., Stricker, J. L., Wong, E. C., & Buxton, R. B. (2000). Altered brain response to verbal learning following sleep deprivation. *Nature, 403*, 655–657.

Dubroski, E. (2000, April 19). Letter to the federal railroad administration from the Brotherhood of locomotive engineers [Electronic version]. Message archived at http://www.bleteam.org/naslbc/Reg_Leg_Issues/Horns/BLET_comments_04-19-2000.pdf

Dugatkin, L. A. (2004). *Principles of animal behavior.* New York: W. W. Norton.

Duncan, J., Burgess, P., & Emslie, H. (1995). Fluid intelligence after frontal lobe lesions. *Neuropsychologia, 33*, 261–268.

Duncker, K. (1945). On problem solving. *Psychological Monographs, 58* (5, Whole No. 70).

Dunn, J. (2004). Annotation: Children's relationships with their nonresident fathers. *Journal of Child Psychology and Psychiatry, 45*, 659–671.

Dutton, D. G., & Aron, A. P. (1974). Some evidence for heightened sexual attraction under conditions of high anxiety. *Journal of Personality and Social Psychology, 30*, 510–517.

Duval, S., & Wicklund, R. A. (1972). *A theory of objective self-awareness.* New York: Academic Press.

Dykman, B. M., Horowitz, L. M., Abramson, L. Y., & Usher, M. (1991). Schematic and situational determinants of depressed and nondepressed students' interpretation of feedback. *Journal of Abnormal Psychology, 100*, 45–55.

Eacott, M. J. (1999). Memory for the events of early childhood. *Current Directions in Psychological Science, 8*, 46–49.

Eagly, A. H., Karau, S. J., & Makhijani, M. G. (1995). Gender and the effectiveness of leaders: A meta-analysis. *Psychological Bulletin, 117*, 125–145.

Eaker, E. D., Sullivan, L. M., Kelly-Hayes, M., D'Agostino, R. B., Sr., & Benjamin, E. J. (2004). Anger and hostility predict the development of atrial fibrillation in men in the Framingham Offspring Study. *Circulation, 109*, 1267–1271.

Eberhardt, J. L., Goff, P. A., Purdie, V. J., & Davies, P. G. (2004). Seeing black: Race, crime, and visual processing. *Journal of Personality and Social Psychology, 87*, 876–893.

Egeland, J. A., Gerhard, D. S., Pauls, D. L., Sussex, J. N., Kidd, K. K., Allen, C. R., et al. (1987). Bipolar affective disorders linked to DNA markers on chromosome 11. *Nature, 325*, 783–787.

Eich, J. E., Weingartner, H., Stillman, R. C., & Gillin, J. C. (1975). State-dependent accessibility of retrieval cues in the retention of a categorized list. *Journal of Verbal Learning and Verbal Behavior, 14*, 408–417.

Eimas, P. D., Siqueland, E. R., Jusczyk, P., & Vigorito, J. (1971, January 22). Speech perception in infants. *Science, 171*, 303–306.

Einstein, G. O., & McDaniel, M. A. (2005). Prospective memory. Multiple retrieval processes. *Current Directions in Psychological Science, 14*, 286–290.

Eisenberg, N. (2000). Emotion, regulation, and moral development. *Annual Review of Psychology, 51*, 665–697.

Ekelund, J., Lichtermann, D., Jaervelin, M., & Peltonen, L. (1999). Association between novelty seeking and type 4 dopamine receptor gene in a large Finnish cohort sample. *American Journal of Psychiatry, 156*, 1453–1455.

Ekman, P., & Friesen, W. V. (1971). Constants across cultures in the face and emotion. *Journal of Personality and Social Psychology, 17*, 124–129.

Ekman, P., Levenson, R. W., & Friesen, W. V. (1983, September 16). Autonomic nervous system activity distinguishes among emotions. *Science, 221*, 1208–1210.

Ekman, P., Sorenson, E. R., & Friesen, W. V. (1969, April 4). Pan-cultural elements in facial displays of emotions. *Science, 164*, 86–88.

Elfenbein, H. A., & Ambady, N. (2002). On the universality of cultural specificity of emotion recognition: A meta-analysis. *Psychological Bulletin, 128*, 203–235.

Ellermeir, W., & Westphal, W. (1995). Gender differences in pain ratings and pupil reactions to painful stimuli. *Pain, 61*, 435–439.

Ellis, B. J., Bates, J. E., Dodge, K. A., Fergusson, D. M., Horwood, L. J., Pettit, G. S., et al. (2003). Does father absence place daughters at special risk for early sexual activity and teenage pregnancy? *Child Development, 74*, 801–821.

Else-Quest, N., Hyde, J. S., Goldsmith, H. H., & Van Hulle, C. A. (2006). Gender differences in temperament: A meta-analysis. *Psychological Bulletin, 132*, 33–72.

Emery, C. F., Kiecolt-Glaser, J. K., Glaser, R., Malarkey, W. B., & Frid, D. J. (2005). Exercise accelerates wound healing among healthy older adults: A preliminary investigation. *Journals of Gerontology, 60A*(11), 1432–1436.

Emslie, G. J., Rush, A. J., Weinberg, W. A., Kowatch, R. A., Hughes, C. W., Carmody, T., et al. (1997). A double-blind, randomized, placebo-controlled trial of fluoxetine in children and adolescents with depression. *Archives of General Psychiatry, 54*, 1031–1037.

Endo, Y., & Meijer, Z. (2004). Autobiographical memory of success and failure experiences. In Y. Kashima, Y. Endo, E. S. Kashima, C. Leung, & J. McClure (Eds.), *Progress in Asian social psychology* (Vol. 4, pp. 67–84). Seoul, Korea: Kyoyook-Kwahak-Sa Publishing.

Engle, R. W., & Kane, M. J. (2004). Executive attention, working memory capacity, and a two-factor theory of cognitive control. In B. Ross (Ed.), *The psychology of learning and motivation* (pp. 145–199). New York: Academic Press.

Engle, R. W., Tuholski, S. W., Laughlin, J. E., & Conway, A. R. A. (1999). Working memory, short-term memory, and general fluid intelligence: A latent variable approach. *Journal of Experimental Psychology: General, 128*, 309–331.

Enns, J. (2005). *The thinking eye, the seeing brain.* New York: W. W. Norton.

Era, P., Jokela, J., & Heikkinen, E. (1986). Reaction and movement times in men of different ages: A population study. *Perceptual and Motor Skills, 63*, 111–130.

Erikson, E. H. (1968). *Identity: Youth and crisis.* New York: W. W. Norton.

Eriksson, P. S., Perfilieva, E., Bjork-Eriksson, T., Alborn, A. M., Nordborg, C., Peterson, D. A., et al. (1998). Neurogenesis in the adult human hippocampus. *Nature Medicine, 4*, 1313–1317.

Eron, L. D. (1987). The development of aggressive behavior from the perspective of a developing behaviorism. *American Psychologist, 42*, 435–442.

Espie, C. A. (2002). Insomnia: Conceptual issues in the development, persistence, and treatment of sleep disorders in adults. *Annual Review of Psychology, 53*, 215–243.

Evers, S., & Suhr, B. (2000). Changes of the neurotransmitter serotonin but not of hormones during short time music perception. *European Archives of Psychiatry and Clinical Neuroscience, 250*, 144–147.

Eysenck, M. W., Mogg, K., May, J., Richards, A., & Matthews, A. (1991). Bias in interpretation of ambiguous sentences related to threat in anxiety. *Journal of Abnormal Psychology, 100*, 144–150.

Fagerström, K. O., & Schneider, N. G. (1989). Measuring nicotine dependence: A review of the Fagerström tolerance questionnaire. *Journal of Behavioral Medicine, 12*, 159–181.

Fallon, A. E., & Rozin, P. (1985). Sex differences in perceptions of desirable body shape. *Journal of Abnormal Psychology, 94*, 102–105.

Fantz, R. L. (1966). Pattern discrimination and selective attention as determinants of perceptual development from birth. In A. H. Kidd & L. J. Rivoire (Eds.), *Perceptual development in children* (pp. 143–173). New York: International Universities Press.

Farah, M. J. (1996). Is face recognition "special"? Evidence from neuropsychology. *Behavioural Brain Research, 76*, 181–189.

Farah, M. J., Betancourt, L., Shera, D. M., Savage, J. H., Giannetta, J. M., Malmud, E. K., et al. (2008). Environmental stimulation, parental nurturance and cognitive development in humans. *Developmental Science, 11*, 793–801.

Farah, M. J., Shera, D. M., Savage, J. H., Betancourt, L., Giannetta, J. M., Brodsky, N. L., et al. (2006). Childhood poverty: Specific associations with neurocognitive development. *Brain Research, 1110*, 166–174.

Farooqi, I. S., Bullmore, E., Keogh, J., Gillard, J., O'Rahilly, S., & Fletcher, P. C. (2007, September 7). Leptin regulates striatal regions and human eating behavior. *Science, 317*, 1355.

Farwell, L. A., & Donchin, E. (1991). The truth will out: Interrogative polygraphy ("lie detection") with event-related brain potentials. *Psychophysiology, 28*, 531–547.

Farwell, L. A., & Smith, S. S. (2001) Using brain MERMER testing to detect knowledge despite efforts to conceal. *Journal of Forensic Science, 46*(1), 135–143.

Fawcett, J. (1992). Suicide risk factors in depressive disorders and in panic disorders. *Journal of Clinical Psychiatry, 53*, 9–13.

Fazio, R. H. (1995). Attitudes as object-evaluation associations: Determinants, consequences, and correlates of attitude accessibility. In R. E. Petty & J. A. Krosnick (Eds.), *Attitude strength: Antecedents and consequences* (pp. 247–282). Hillsdale, NJ: Erlbaum.

Fazio, R. H., Eisner, J. R., & Shook, N. J. (2004). Attitude formation through exploration: Valence asymmetries. *Journal of Personality and Social Psychology, 87*, 293–311.

Feingold, A. (1994). Gender differences in personality: A meta-analysis. *Psychological Bulletin, 116*, 429–456.

Feldman Barrett, L., Lane, R. D., Sechrest, L., & Schwartz, G. E. (2000). Sex differences in emotional awareness. *Personality and Social Psychology Bulletin, 26*, 1027–1035.

Feldman, R., Weller, A., Zagoory-Sharon, O., & Levine, A. (2007). Evidence for a neuroendocrinological foundation of human affiliation: Plasma oxytocin levels across pregnancy and the postpartum period predict mother-infant bonding. *Psychological Science, 18*, 965–970.

Ferguson, J. N., Young, L. J., Hearn, E. F., Matzuk, M. M., Insel, T. R., & Winslow, J. T. (2000). Social amnesia in mice lacking the oxytocin gene. *Nature Neuroscience, 25*, 284–288.

Ferguson, T. J., & Stegge, H. (1995). Emotional states and traits in children: The case of guilt and shame. In J. P. Tangney & K. W. Fischer (Eds.), *Self-conscious emotions* (pp. 174–197). New York: Guilford Press.

Fernald, A. (1989). Intonation and communicative intent in mothers' speech to infants: Is the melody the message? *Child Development, 60*, 1497–1510.

Ferrari, P. F., Gallese, V., Rizzolatti, G., & Fogassi, L. (2003). Mirror neurons responding to the observation of ingestive and communicative mouth actions in the monkey ventral premotor cortex. *European Journal of Neuroscience, 17*, 1703–1714.

Ferry, G. (Writer/Broadcaster). (2002, 12 & 19 November). Hearing colours, eating sounds. *BBC Radio 4, Science*. Retrieved from BBC, http://www.bbc.co.uk/radio4/science/hearingcolours.shtml

Festinger, L. (1954). A theory of social comparison processes. *Human Relations, 7*, 117–140.

Festinger, L. (1987). A personal memory. In N. E. Grunberg, R. E. Nisbett, J. Rodin, & J. E. Singer (Eds.), *A distinctive approach to psychological research: The influence of Stanley Schachter* (pp. 1–9). New York: Erlbaum.

Festinger, L., & Carlsmith, J. M. (1959). Cognitive consequences of forced compliance. *Journal of Abnormal and Social Psychology, 58*, 203–210.

Festinger, L., Riecken, H. W., & Schachter, S. (1956). *When prophecy fails*. Minneapolis: University of Minnesota Press.

Festinger, L., Schachter, S., & Back, K. W. (1950). *Social pressures in informal groups*. New York: Harper.

Fillingim, R. B. (2003). Sex-related influences on pain: A review of mechanisms and clinical implications. *Rehabilitation Psychology, 48*, 165–174.

Fillipek, P. A., Semrud-Clikeman, M., Steingard, R. J., Renshaw, P. F., Kennedy, D. N., & Biederman, J. (1997). Volumetric MRI analysis comparing subjects having attention–deficit hyperactivity disorder with normal controls. *Neurology, 48*, 589–600.

Fine, I., Wade, A. R., Brewer, A. A., May, M. G., Goodman, D. F., Boynton, G. M., et al. (2003). Long-term deprivation affects visual perception and cortex. *Nature Neuroscience, 6*, 915–916.

Finger, S. (1994). *Origins of neuroscience*. Oxford, UK: Oxford University Press.

Fink, M. (2001). Convulsive therapy: A review of the first 55 years. *Journal of Affective Disorders, 63*, 1–15.

Finkelstein, E. A., Fiebelkorn, I. C., & Wang, G. (2003). National medical spending attributable to overweight and obesity: How much, and who's paying? *Health Affairs, 10*(Suppl. W3), 219–226.

Fischer, K. (1980). A theory of cognitive development: The control and construction of hierarchies of skills. *Psychological Review, 87*, 477–531.

Fischoff, B. (1975). Hindsight does not equal foresight: The effect of outcome knowledge on judgment under uncertainty. *Journal of Experimental Psychology: Human Perception and Performance, 1*, 288–299.

Fisher, H. E., Aron, A., & Brown, L. L. (2006). Romantic love: A mammalian brain system for mate choice. *Philosophical Transactions of the Royal Society of London, 361B*, 2173–2186.

Fitzgerald, P. B., Brown, T. L., Marston, N. A., Daskalakis, Z. J., De Castella, A., & Kulkarni, J. (2003). Transcranial magnetic stimulation in the treatment of depression: A double-blind, placebo-controlled trial. *Archives of General Psychiatry, 60*, 1002–1008.

Fixx, J. F. (1978). *Solve it*. New York: Doubleday.

Flynn, J. (2007, October/November). IQ gains and the real world. *Scientific American Mind*, 24–31.

Flynn, J. R. (1981). The mean IQ of Americans: Massive gains 1932 to 1978. *Psychological Bulletin, 95*, 29–51.

Flynn, J. R. (1987). Massive IQ gains in 14 nations: What IQ tests really measure. *Psychological Bulletin, 101*, 171–191.

Foa, E. B., Liebowitz, M. R., Kozak, M. J., Davies, S., Campeas, R., Franklin, M. E., et al. (2005). Randomized, placebo-controlled trial of exposure and ritual prevention, clomipramine, and their combination in the treatment of obsessive-compulsive disorder. *American Journal of Psychiatry, 162*, 151–161.

Foley, K. M. (1993). Opioids. *Neurologic Clinics, 11*, 503–522.

Folkman, S., & Lazarus, R. S. (1988). Coping as a mediator of emotion. *Journal of Personality and Social Psychology, 54*, 466–475.

Folkman, S., & Moskowitz, J. T. (2000). Positive affect and the other side of coping. *American Psychologist, 55*, 647–654.

Forgas, J. P. (1998). Asking nicely: Mood effects on responding to more or less polite requests. *Personality and Social Psychology Bulletin, 24*, 173–185.

Forth, A. E., Kosson, D., & Hare, R. D. (2003). *Psychopathy checklist: Youth version.* Toronto, Ontario, Canada: Multi-Health Systems.

Fost, N. (1989). Maternal-fetal conflicts: Ethical and legal considerations. *Annals of the New York Academy of Sciences, 56*, 248–254.

Foster, J., Brewer, C., & Steele, T. (2003). Naltrexone implants can completely prevent early (1-month) relapse after opiate detoxification: A pilot study of two cohorts totalling 101 patients with a note on naltrexone blood levels. *Addiction Biology, 8*(211), 217.

Fox, N. A., Henderson, H. A., Marshall, P. J., Nichols, K. E., & Ghera, M. M. (2005). Behavioral inhibition: Linking biology and behavior within a developmental framework. *Annual Review of Psychology, 56*, 235–262.

Fox, R., Aslin, R. N., Shea, S. L., & Dumais, S. T. (1980, January 18). Stereopsis in human infants. *Science, 207*, 323–324.

Fraley, R. C., & Shaver, P. R. (2000). Adult romantic attachment: Theoretical developments, emerging controversies, and unanswered questions. *Review of General Psychology, 4*, 132–154.

Frangou, S., Chitins, X., & Williams, S. C. (2004). Mapping IQ and gray matter density in healthy young people. *Neuroimage, 23*, 800–805.

Frank, E., Kupfer, D., Perel, I., Comes, C., Jarret, D., Mallinger, A., et al. (1990). Three-year outcomes for maintenance therapies in recurrent depression. *Archives of General Psychiatry, 47*, 1093–1099.

Frankl, V. E. (1959). *Man's search for meaning.* New York: Simon and Schuster.

Franken, R. E. (1998). *Human motivation.* Pacific Grove, CA: Brooks Cole.

Franklin, A. J. (2007). Gender, race and invisibility in psychotherapy with African American men. In J. C. Muran (Ed.), *Dialogues on difference: Studies of diversity in the therapeutic relationship* (pp. 117–131). Washington, DC: American Psychological Association.

Fratiglioni, L., Paillard-Borg, S., & Winblad, B. (2004). An active and socially integrated lifestyle in late life might protect against dementia. *Lancet Neurology, 3*, 343–353.

Fredrickson, B. L. (2001). The role of positive emotions in positive psychology: The broaden-and-build theory of positive emotions. *American Psychologist, 56*, 218–226.

Freedman, J. L. (1984). Effects of television violence on aggression. *Psychological Bulletin, 96*, 227–246.

Freedman, J. L., & Fraser, S. C. (1966). Compliance without pressure: The foot-in-the-door technique. *Journal of Personality and Social Psychology, 4*, 196–202.

Freud, A. (1936). *The ego and the mechanisms of defense.* New York: International Universities Press.

Frick, P. J. (1998). Conduct disorders and severe antisocial behavior. New York: Plenum Press.

Friedman, J. (2003, February 7). A war on obesity, not the obese. *Science, 299*, 856–858.

Frijda, N. H. (1994). Emotions are functional, most of the time. In P. Ekman & R. J. Davidson (Eds.), *The nature of emotion: Fundamental questions, Vol. 4. Series in affective science* (pp. 112–122). New York: Oxford University Press.

Frincke, J. L., & Pate, W. E. (2004, March). *Yesterday, today, and tomorrow. Careers in psychology: 2004. What students need to know.* Paper presented at the annual convention of the Southeastern Psychology Association, Atlanta, GA.

Funder, D. C. (1995). On the accuracy of personality judgment: A realistic approach. *Psychological Review, 102*, 652–670.

Funder, D. C. (2001). Personality. *Annual Review of Psychology, 52*, 197–221.

Fung, H. H., & Carstensen, L. L. (2004). Motivational changes in response to blocked goals and foreshortened time: Testing alternatives to socioemotional selectivity theory. *Psychology and Aging, 19*, 68–78.

Fung, M. T., Raine, A., Loeber, R., Lynam, D. R., Steinhauer, S. R., Venables, P. D., et al. (2005). Reduced electrodermal activity in psychopathy-prone adolescents. *Journal of Abnormal Psychology, 114*, 187–196.

Furnham, A., Wytykowska, A., & Petrides, K. V. (2005). Estimates of multiple intelligences: A study in Poland. *European Psychologist, 10*, 51–59.

Galea, L. A., & Kimura, D. (1993). Sex differences in route-learning. *Personality and Individual Differences, 14*(1), 53–65.

Gallistel, C. R. (2000). The replacement of general-purpose learning models with adaptively specialized learning modules. In M. S. Gazzaniga (Ed.), *The new cognitive neurosciences.* Cambridge, MA: MIT Press.

Gallup. (1995). *Disciplining children in America: A Gallup poll report.* Princeton, NH: Author.

Gangestad, S. W., Simpson, J. A., Cousins, A. J., Garver-Apgar, C. E., & Christensen, P. N. (2004). Women's preferences for male behavioral displays change across the menstrual cycle. *Psychological Science, 15*, 203–207.

Garcia, J., & Koelling, R. A. (1966). Relation of cue to consequence in avoidance learning. *Psychonomic Science, 4*, 123–124.

Gardner, D. (2008). Numbers are nice, but stories matter. *Canadian Medical Association Journal, 179*, 108.

Gardner, H. (1983). *Frames of mind: The theory of multiple intelligences.* New York: Basic Books.

Gardner, W. L., Pickett, C. L., Jefferis, V., & Knowles, M. (2005). On the outside looking in: Loneliness and social monitoring. *Personality and Social Psychology Bulletin, 31*, 1549–1560.

Garlick, D. (2002). Understanding the nature of the general factor of intelligence: The role of individual differences in neural plasticity as an explanatory mechanism. *Psychological Review, 109*, 116–136.

Garoff-Eaton, R. J., Slotnick, S. D., & Schacter, D. L. (2006). Not all false memories are created equal: The neural basis of false recognition. *Cerebral Cortex, 16*, 1645–1652.

Gazzaniga, M. S. (2000). Cerebral specialization and interhemispheric communication: Does the corpus callosum enable the human condition? *Brain, 123*, 1293–1326.

Geary, D., & Flinn, M. V. (2002). Sex differences in behavioral and hormonal response to social threat: Commentary on Taylor et al. (2000). *Psychological Review, 109*, 745–750.

Geddes, J. R., Burgess, S., Hawton, K., Jamison, K., & Goodwin, G. M. (2004). Long-term lithium therapy for bipolar disorder: Systematic review and meta-analysis of randomized controlled trials. *American Journal of Psychiatry, 161*, 217–222.

Geen, R. G. (1984). Preferred stimulation levels in introverts and extraverts: Effects on arousal and performance. *Journal of Personality and Social Psychology, 46*, 1303–1312.

Gentile, D. A., Saleem, M., & Anderson, C. A. (2007). Public policy and the effects of media violence on children. *Social Issues and Policy Review, 1*, 15–51.

George, M. S., Lisanby, S. H., & Sackheim, H. A. (1999). Transcranial magnetic stimulation: Applications in neuropsychiatry. *Archives of General Psychiatry, 56*, 300–311.

George, M. S., Wassermann, E. M., Williams, W. A., Callahan, A., Ketter, T. A., Basser, P., et al. (1995). Daily repetitive transcranial magnetic stimulation (rTMS) improves mood in depression. *Neuroreport, 6*, 1853–1856.

Gergely, G., & Csibra, G. (2003). Teleological reasoning in infancy: The naïve theory of rational action. *Trends in Cognitive Sciences, 7*, 287–292.

Gernsbacher, M. A., Dawson, M., & Goldsmith, H. H. (2005). Three reasons not to believe in an autism epidemic. *Current Directions in Psychological Science, 14*, 55–58.

Gershoff, E. T. (2002). Parental corporal punishment and associated child behaviors and experiences: A meta-analytic and theoretical review. *Psychological Bulletin, 128*, 539–579.

Gershon, E. S., Berrettini, W. H., & Goldin, L. R. (1989). Mood disorders: Genetic aspects. In H. I. Kaplan & B. J. Sadock (Eds.), *Comprehensive textbook of psychiatry* (5th ed.). Baltimore: Williams & Wilkins.

Geula, C., & Mesulam, M. (1994). Cholinergic systems and related neuropathological predilection patterns in Alzheimer disease. In R. D. Terry, R. Katzman, & K. Bick (Eds.), *Alzheimer disease* (pp. 263–291). New York: Raven Press.

Gibbons, M. B., Crits-Christoph, P., & Hearon, B. (2008). The empirical status of psychodynamic therapies. *Annual Review of Clinical Psychology, 4*, 93–108.

Gick, M. L., & Holyoak, K. J. (1983). Schema induction and analogical transfer. *Cognitive Psychology, 15*, 1–38.

Giedd, J. N., Castellanos, F. X., Rajapakse, J. C., Vaituzis, A. C., & Rapoport, J. L. (1997). Sexual dimorphism of the developing human brain. *Progress in Neuro-Psychopharmacology & Biological Psychiatry, 21*(8), 1185–1201.

Gigerenzer, G. (2004). Dread risk, September 11, and fatal traffic accidents. *Psychological Science, 15*, 286–287.

Gijsman, H. J., Geddes, J. R., Rendell, J. M., Nolen, W. A., & Goodwin, G. M. (2004). Antidepressants for bipolar depression: A systematic review of randomized, controlled trials. *American Journal of Psychiatry, 161*, 1537–1547.

Gilberg, C. (1980). Maternal age and infantile autism. *Journal of Autism and Developmental Disorders, 10*, 293–297.

Gilbert, D. T., Giesler, R. B., & Morris, K. A. (1995). When comparisons arise. *Journal of Personality and Social Psychology, 69*, 227–236.

Gilbert, D. T., Morewedge, C. K., Risen, J. L., & Wilson, T. D. (2004). Looking forward to looking backward: The misprediction of regret. *Psychological Science, 15*, 346–350.

Gilbert, D. T., Pinel, E. C., Wilson, T. D., Blumberg, S. J., & Wheatley, T. (1998). Immune neglect: A source of durability bias in affective forecasting. *Journal of Personality and Social Psychology, 75*, 617–638.

Gilbert, D. T., & Wilson, T. D. (2007, September). Prospection: Experiencing the future. *Science, 317*, 1351–1354.

Gillihan, S. J., & Farah, M. J. (2005). Is self special? A critical review of evidence from experimental psychology and cognitive neuroscience. *Psychological Bulletin, 131*, 76–97.

Gillogley, K. M., Evans, A. T., Hansen, R. L., Samuels, S. J., & Batra, K. K. (1990). The perinatal impact of cocaine, amphetamine, and opiate use detected by universal intrapartum screening. *American Journal of Obstetrics and Gynecology, 163*, 1535–1542.

Gilovich, T. (1991). *How we know what isn't so: The fallibility of human reason in everyday life.* New York: The Free Press.

Gilpin, E. A., Choi, W. S., Berry, C., & Pierce, J. P. (1999). How many adolescents start smoking each day in the United States? *Journal of Adolescent Health, 25*, 248–255.

Gintzler, A. R., & Liu, N. J. (2000). Ovarian sex steroids activate antinociceptive systems and reveal gender-specific mechanisms. In R. B. Fillingim (Ed.), *Sex, gender, and pain* (pp. 89–108). Seattle, WA: International Association for the Study of Pain (IASP) Press.

Gizewski, E. R., Krause, E., Karama, S., Baars, A., Senf, W., & Forsting, M. (2006). There are differences in cerebral activation between females in distinct menstrual phases during viewing of erotic stimuli: A fMRI study. *Experimental Brain Research, 174*, 101–108.

Gladwell, M. (2005). *Blink: The power of thinking without thinking.* New York: Little, Brown.

Godden, D. R., & Baddeley, A. D. (1975). Context-dependent memory in two natural environments: On land and underwater. *British Journal of Psychology, 66*, 325–331.

Goh, J. O., Chee, M. W., Tan, J. C., Venkatraman, V., Hebrank, A., Leshikar, E. D., et al. (2007). Age and culture modulate object processing and object-science binding in the ventral visual area. *Cognitive, Affective & Behavioral Neuroscience, 7*, 44–52.

Golby, A. J., Gabrieli, J. D. E., Chiao, J. Y., & Eberhardt, J. L. (2001). Differential responses in the fusiform region to same-race and other-race faces. *Nature Neuroscience, 4*, 845–850.

Gold, P. E., McIntyre, C., McNay, E., Stefani, M., & Korol, D. (2001). Neurochemical referees of dueling memory systems. In P. Gold & W. T. Greenough (Eds.), *Memory consolidation: Essays in honor of James L. McGaugh* (pp. 218–248). Washington, DC: American Psychological Association.

Goldapple, K., Segal, Z., Garson, C., Lau, M., Bieling, P., Kennedy, S., et al. (2004). Modulation of cortical-limbic pathways in major depression: Treatment-specific effects of cognitive behavior therapy. *Archives of General Psychiatry, 61*, 34–41.

Goldenberg, J. L., McCoy, S. K., Pyszczynski, T., Greenberg, J., & Solomon, S. (2000). The body as a source of self-esteem: The effects of mortality salience on identification with one's body, interest in sex, and appearance monitoring. *Journal of Personality and Social Psychology, 79*, 118–130.

Goldman-Rakic, P. S., Scalaidhe, S., & Chafee, M. (2000). Domain specificity in cognitive systems. In M. S. Gazzaniga (Ed.), *The new cognitive neurosciences* (pp. 733–742). Cambridge, MA: MIT Press.

Gong, Q., Sluming, V., Mayes, A., Keller, S., Barrick, T., Cezayirli, E., et al. (2005). Voxel-based morphometry and stereology provide convergent evidence of the importance of medial prefrontal cortex for fluid intelligence in healthy adults. *Neuroimage, 25*, 1175–1186.

Goodale, M. A., & Milner, A. D. (1992). Separate visual pathways for perception and action. *Trends in Neuroscience, 15*, 22–25.

Goodall, G. (1984). Learning due to the response-shock contingency in signaled punishment. *Quarterly Journal of Experimental Psychology, 36*, 259–279.

Goodman, R., & Stevenson, J. (1989). A twin study of hyperactivity-II. The aetiological role of genes, family relationships, and perinatal adversity. *Journal of Child Psychology and Psychiatry, 30*, 691–709.

Goodwin, D. W., Powell, B., Bremer, D., Hoine, H., & Stern, J. (1969, March 21). Alcohol and recall: State dependent effects in man. *Science, 163*, 1358.

Goodwin, F. K., & Jamison, K. R. (1990). *Manic-depressive illness.* New York: Oxford University Press.

Goodwin, R. D., Lieb, R., Hoefler, M., Pfister, H., Bittner, A., Beesdo, K., et al. (2004). Panic attack as a risk factor for severe psychopathology. *American Journal of Psychiatry, 161*, 2207–2214.

Gopnik, A., & Graf, O. (1988). Knowing how you know: Young children's ability to identify and remember the sources of their beliefs. *Child Development, 59*, 1366–1371.

Gosling, S. D. (1998). Personality dimensions in spotted hyenas (Crocuta crocuta). *Journal of Comparative Psychology, 112*, 107–118.

Gosling, S. D. (2001). From mice to men: What can we learn about personality from animal research? *Psychological Bulletin, 127*, 45–86.

Gosling, S. D., & John, O. P. (1999). Personality dimension in non-human animals: A cross-species review. *Current Directions in Psychological Science, 8*, 69–75.

Gosling, S. D., Kwan, V. S. Y., & John, O. P. (2003). A dog's got personality: A cross-species comparative approach to evaluating personality judgments. *Journal of Personality and Social Psychology, 85*, 1161–1169.

Gottesman, I. I. (1991). *Schizophrenia genesis: The origins of madness.* New York: Freeman.

Gottesman, I. I., & Hanson, D. R. (2005). Human development: Biological and genetic processes. *Annual Review of Psychology, 56*, 263–286

Gottfredson, L. S. (2004a). Intelligence: Is it the epidemiologists' elusive "fundamental cause" of social class inequalities in health? *Journal of Personality and Social Psychology, 86*, 174–199.

Gottfredson, L. S. (2004b, Summer). Schools and the g factor. *The Wilson Quarterly, 28*(3), 35–45.

Gottfredson, L., & Deary, I. J. (2004). Intelligence predicts health and longevity: But why? *Current Directions in Psychological Science, 13*, 1–4.

Gottman, J. (1994). *Why marriages succeed or fail.* New York: Simon & Schuster.

Gottman, J. M. (1998). Psychology and the study of marital processes. *Annual Review of Psychology, 49*, 169–197.

Gould, E., & Tanapat, P. (1999). Stress and hippocampal neurogenesis. *Biological Psychiatry, 46*, 1472–1479.

Grandin, T. (1995). *Thinking in pictures: And other reports from my life with autism.* New York: Doubleday.

Gray, J. R., & Thompson, P. M. (2004). Neurobiology of intelligence: Science and ethics. *Nature Reviews Neuroscience, 5*, 471–482.

Green, L., Myerson, J., Lichtman, D., Rosen, S., & Fry, A. (1996). Temporal discounting in choice between delayed rewards: The role of age and income. *Psychological Science, 11*, 79–94.

Greenberg, B. D., Gabriels, L. A., Malone, D. A., Jr., Rezai, A. R., Friehs, G. M., Okun, M. S., et al. (2008). Deep brain stimulation of the ventral internal capsule/ventral striatum for obsessive-compulsive disorder: Worldwide experience. *Molecular Psychiatry.* Advance online publication. Retrieved May 20, 2008. doi: 10.1038/mp.2008.55

Greenberg, J. (2008). Understanding the vital human quest for self-esteem. *Perspectives on Psychological Science, 3*, 48–55.

Greenberg, J., Solomon, S., & Pyszczynski, T. (1997). Terror management theory of self-esteem and cultural worldviews: Empirical assessments and conceptual refinements. In M. P. Zanna (Ed.), *Advances in Experimental Social Psychology* (Vol. 29, pp. 61–136). New York: Academic Press.

Greene, B. (2007). How difference makes a difference. In J. C. Muran (Ed.), *Dialogues on difference: Studies of diversity in the therapeutic relationship* (pp. 47–63). Washington, DC: American Psychological Association.

Greenwald, A. G. (1992). New look 3: Reclaiming unconscious cognition. *American Psychologist, 47*, 766–779.

Greenwald, A. G., & Banaji, M. R. (1995). Implicit social cognition: Attitudes, self-esteem, and stereotypes. *Psychological Review, 102*, 4–27.

Greenwald, A. G., McGhee, D., & Schwartz, J. (1998). Measuring individual differences in implicit cognition: The implicit association test. *Journal of Personality and Social Psychology, 74*, 1464–1480.

Greenwald, A. G., Oakes, M. A., & Hoffman, H. (2003). Targets of discrimination: Effects of race on responses to weapons holders. *Journal of Experimental Social Psychology, 39*, 399–405.

Greenwald, A. G., Poehlman, T. A., Uhlmann, E., & Banaji, M. R. (in press). Understanding and using the Implicit Association Test: III. Meta-analysis of predictive validity. *Journal of Personality and Social Psychology.*

Gregory, A. H., Worrall, L., & Sarge, A. (1996). The development of emotional responses to music in young children. *Motivation and Emotion, 20*, 341–348.

Gretton, H. M., Hare, R. D., & Catchpole, R. E. H. (2004). Psychopathy and offending from adolescence to adulthood: A 10-year follow-up. *Journal of Consulting and Clinical Psychology, 72*, 636–645.

Grill-Spector, K., Knouf, N., & Kanwisher, N. (2004). The fusiform face area subserves face perception, not generic within-category identification. *Nature Neuroscience, 7*, 555–562.

Groebel, J. (1998). *The UNESCO global study on media violence: A joint project of UNESCO, the world organization of the Scout movement and Utrecht University, the Netherlands. Report Presented to the Director General of UNESCO.* Paris: UNESCO.

Gross, J. J. (1999). Emotion and emotion regulation. In L. A. Pervin & O. P. John (Eds.), *Handbook of personality: Theory and research* (2nd ed., pp. 525–552). New York: Guilford Press.

Grossman, L. (2005, January 24). Grow up? Not so fast. *Time, 165*, 42–53.

Grossman, M., & Wood, W. (1993). Sex differences in intensity of emotional experience: A social role interpretation. *Journal of Personality and Social Psychology, 65*, 1010–1022.

Gruber, S. A., Silveri, M. M., & Yurgelun-Todd, D. A. (2007). Neuropsychological consequences of opiate use. *Neuropsychological Review, 17*, 299–315.

Gruzelier, J. H. (2000). Redefining hypnosis: Theory, methods, and integration. *Contemporary Hypnosis, 17*, 51–70.

Guerin, B. (1994). What do people think about the risks of driving? Implications for traffic safety interventions. *Journal of Applied Social Psychology, 24*, 994–1021.

Guerri, C. (2002). Mechanisms involved in central nervous system dysfunctions induced by prenatal ethanol exposure. *Neurotoxicity Research, 4*(4), 327–335.

Guimond, S. (2008). Psychological similarities and differences between women and men across cultures. *Social and Personality Psychology Compass, 2*, 494–510.

Guimond, S., Branscombe, N. R., Brunot, S., Buunk, A. P., Chatard, A., Desert, M., et al. (2007). Culture, gender, and the self: Variations and impact of social comparison processes. *Journal of Personality and Social Psychology, 92*, 1118–1134.

Gunderson, J. G. (1984). *Borderline personality disorder.* Washington, DC: American Psychiatric Press.

Gur, R. C., & Gur, R. E. (2004). Gender differences in the functional organization of the brain. In M. J. Legato (Ed.), *Principles of gender-specific medicine* (pp. 63–70). Amsterdam: Elsevier.

Gutchess, A. H., Welsh, R. C., Boduroglu, A., & Park, D. C. (2006). Cultural differences in neural function associated with object processing. *Cognitive, Affective, and Behavioral Neuroscience, 6*, 102–109.

Haier, R. J., Jung, R. E., Yeo, R. A., Head, K., & Alkire, M. T. (2005). The neuroanatomy of general intelligence: Sex matters. *Neuroimage, 25*, 320–327.

Halligan, P. W., & Marshall, J. C. (1998). Neglect of awareness. *Consciousness and Cognition, 7*, 356–380.

Halpern, C. T., Udry, J. R., & Suchindran, C. (1997). Testosterone predicts initiation of coitus in adolescent females. *Psychosomatic Medicine, 59*, 161–171.

Halpern, D. F. (2000). *Sex differences in cognitive abilities* (3rd ed.). Mahwah, NJ: Erlbaum.

Halpern, D. F. (2003). *Thought and knowledge: An introduction to critical thinking* (4th ed.). Mahwah, NJ: Erlbaum.

Halpern, D. F., Benbow, C., Geary, D., Gur, D., Hyde, J., & Gernsbacher, M. A. (2007). The science of sex-differences in science and mathematics. *Psychological Science in the Public Interest, 8*, 1–51.

Halpern, D. F., & Cheung, F. M. (2009). *Women at the top: Powerful leaders tell us how to combine work and family.* New York: Wiley-Blackwell.

Halpern, D. F., & Collaer, M. L. (2005). Sex differences in visuospatial abilities: More than meets the eye. In P. Shah & A. Miyake (Eds.), *The Cambridge handbook of visuospatial thinking* (pp. 170–212). Cambridge, UK: Cambridge University Press.

Hamann, S. B., Ely, T. D., Grafton, D. T., & Kilts, C. D. (1999). Amygdala activity related to enhanced memory for pleasant and aversive stimuli. *Nature Neuroscience, 2*, 289–293.

Hamann, S., Herman, R. A., Nolan, C. L., & Wallen, K. (2004). Men and women differ in amygdala response to visual sexual stimuli. *Nature Neuroscience, 7*, 411–416.

Hambrecht, M., Maurer, K., Hafner, H., & Sartorius, N. (1992). Transnational stability of gender differences in schizophrenia: Recent findings on social skills training and family psychoeducation. *Clinical Psychology Review, 11*, 23–44.

Hamilton, N. A., Gallagher, M. W., Preacher, K. J., Stevens, N., Nelson, C. A., Karlson, C., et al. (2007). Insomnia and well-being. *Journal of Consulting and Clinical Psychology, 75*, 939–946.

Hammen, C. (2005). Stress and depression. *Annual Review of Clinical Psychology, 1*, 293–319.

Hancock, P. J., Bruce, V. V., & Burton, A. M. (2000). Recognition of unfamiliar faces. *Trends in Cognitive Sciences, 4*, 330–337.

Handleman, J. S., Gill, M. J., & Alessandri, M. (1988). Generalization by severely developmentally disabled children: Issues, advances, and future directions. *Behavior Therapist, 11*, 221–223.

Haney, C., Banks, C., & Zimbardo, P. (1973). Interpersonal dynamics in a simulated prison. *International Journal of Criminology and Penology, 1*, 69–97.

Hansen, C. J., Stevens, L. C., & Coast, J. R. (2001). Exercise duration and mood state: How much is enough to feel better? *Health Psychology, 20*, 267–275.

Hansen, W. B., Graham, J. W., Sobel, J. L., Shelton, D. R., Flay, B. R., & Johnson, C. A. (1987). The consistency of peer and parental influences on tobacco, alcohol, and marijuana use among young adolescents. *Journal of Behavioral Medicine, 10*, 559–579.

Haque, A. (2004). Psychology from Islamic perspective: Contributions of early Muslim scholars and challenges to contemporary Muslim psychologists. *Journal of Religion & Health, 43*(4), 357–377.

Harburger, L. L., Nzerem, C. K., & Frick, K. M. (2007). Single enrichment variables differentially reduce age-related memory decline in female mice. *Behavioral Neuroscience, 121*(4), 679–688.

Harding, C. M., Zubin, J., & Strauss, J. S. (1987). Chronicity in schizophrenia: Fact, partial fact, or artifact? *Hospital and Community Psychiatry, 38*, 477–486.

Hare, R. D. (1993). *Without conscience: The disturbing world of the psychopaths among us.* New York: Pocket Books.

Hare, R. D. (2003). *Hare psychopathy checklist—revised (PCL-R)* (2nd technical manual ed.). North Tonawanda, NY: Multi-Health Systems.

Hare, R. D., McPherson, L. M., & Forth, A. E. (1988). Male psychopaths and their criminal careers. *Journal of Consulting and Clinical Psychology, 56*, 710–714.

Hariri, A. R., Mattay, V. S., Tessitore, A., Kolachana, B., Fera, F., Goldman, D., et al. (2002, July 19). Serotonin transporter genetic variation and the response of the human amygdala. *Science, 297*, 400–403.

Harlow, H. F., Harlow, M. K., & Meyer, D. R. (1950). Learning motivated by a manipulation drive. *Journal of Experimental Psychology, 40*, 228–234.

Harpur, T. J., & Hare, R. D. (1994). Assessment of psychopathy as a function of age. *Journal of Abnormal Psychology, 103*, 604–609.

Harris, G. T., Rice, M. E., & Cormier, C. A. (1991). Psychopathy and violent recidivism. *Law and Human Behavior, 15*, 625–637.

Harris, J. R. (1995). Where is the child's environment? A group socialization theory of development. *Psychological Review, 102*, 458–489.

Harrison, G. (1976). This song. On *Thirty Three & 1/3* [record]. Los Angeles: Dark Horse.

Hart, S. D., & Hare, R. D. (1997). Psychopathy: Assessment and association with criminal conduct. In D. M. Stoff, J. Breiling, & J. D. Maser (Eds.), *Handbook of antisocial behavior.* New York: Wiley.

Hartford, J., Kornstein, S., Liebowitz, M., Pigott, T., Russell, J., Detke, M., et al. (2007). Duloxetine as an SNRI treatment for generalized anxiety disorder: Results from a placebo and active-controlled trial. *International Clinical Psychopharmacology, 22,* 167–174.

Hartsough, C. S., & Lambert, N. M. (1985). Medical factors in hyperactive and normal children: Prenatal, developmental, and health history findings. *American Journal of Orthopsychiatry, 55,* 190–201.

Hauk, O., Johnsrude, I., & Pulvermüller, F. (2004). Somatotopic representation of action words in human motor and premotor cortex. *Neuron, 41,* 301–307.

Hazan, C., & Shaver, P. R. (1987). Romantic love conceptualized as an attachment process. *Journal of Personality and Social Psychology, 52,* 511–524.

Hazard, R. (1981). Girls just want to have fun [Recorded by Cyndi Lauper]. On *She's So Unusual* [record]. New York: Portrait.

Heatherton, T. F., & Baumeister, R. F. (1991). Binge eating as escape from self-awareness. *Psychological Bulletin, 110,* 86–108.

Heatherton, T. F., Herman, C. P., & Polivy, J. (1991). Effects of physical threat and ego threat on eating behavior. *Journal of Personality and Social Psychology, 60,* 138–143.

Heatherton, T. F., & Vohs, K. D. (2000). Interpersonal evaluations following threats to self: Role of self-esteem. *Journal of Personality and Social Psychology, 78,* 725–736.

Heatherton, T. F., & Weinberger, J. L. (1994). *Can personality change?* Washington, DC: American Psychological Association.

Hebl, M. R., & Heatherton, T. F. (1998). The stigma of obesity in women: The difference is black and white. *Personality and Social Psychology Bulletin, 24,* 417–426.

Hedden, T., Ketay, S., Aron, A., Markus, H. R., & Gabrieli, J. D. E. (2008). Cultural influences on neural substrates of attentional control. *Psychological Science, 19,* 12–17.

Heilbrun, K., Hart, S., Hare, R., Gustofson, D., Nunez, C., & White, A. (1998). Inpatient and post-discharge aggression in mentally disordered offenders: The role of psychopathy. *Journal of Interpersonal Violence, 13,* 514–527.

Heine, S. J. (2003). An exploration of cultural variation in self-enhancing and self-improving motivations. In V. Murphy-Berman & J. J. Berman (Eds.), *Nebraska symposium on motivation: Vol. 49. Cross-cultural differences in perspectives on the self* (pp. 101–128). Lincoln: University of Nebraska Press.

Heine, S. J. (2005). Where is the evidence for pancultural self-enhancement? A reply to Sedikides, Gaertner, & Toguchi. *Journal of Personality and Social Psychology, 89,* 531–538.

Heine, S. J., Buchtel, E., & Norenzayan, A. (2008). What do cross-national comparisons of self-reported personality traits tell us? The case of conscientiousness. *Psychological Science, 19,* 309–313.

Heine, S. J., & Hamamura, T. (2007). In search of East Asian self-enhancement. *Personality and Social Psychology Review, 11,* 4–27.

Heine, S. J., Buchtel, E. E., & Norenzayan, A. (2008). What do cross-national comparisons of personality traits tell us? The case of conscientiousness. *Psychological Science, 19,* 309–313.

Helmreich, R., Aronson, E., & LeFan, J. (1970). To err is humanizing sometimes: Effects of self-esteem, competence, and a pratfall on interpersonal attraction. *Journal of Personality and Social Psychology, 16,* 259–264.

Henderson, L., & Zimbardo, P. G. (1998). Shyness. In *Encyclopedia of mental health* (Vol. 3, pp. 497–509). San Diego, CA: Academic Press.

Herbert, T. B., & Cohen, S. (1993). Stress and immunity in humans: A meta-analytic review. *Psychosomatic Medicine, 55,* 364–379.

Hering, E. (1964). *Outlines of a theory of the light sense* (L. M. Hurvich & D. Jameson, Trans.). Cambridge, MA: Harvard University Press. (Original work published 1878).

Herlitz, A., & Kabir, Z. N. (2006). Sex differences in cognition among illiterate Bangladeshis: A comparison with literate Bangladeshis and Swedes. *Scandinavian Journal of Psychology, 47,* 441–447.

Hernstein, R. J., & Murray, C. (1994). *The bell curve: Intelligence and class structure in American life.* New York: Free Press.

Herz, R. S., & Cahill, E. D. (1997). Differential use of sensory information in sexual behavior as a function of gender. *Human Nature, 8,* 275–285.

Hetherington, E. M., Bridges, M., & Insabella, G. M. (1998). What matters? What does not? Five perspectives on the association between marital transitions and children's adjustment. *American Psychologist, 53,* 167–184.

Higgins, L. T., & Zheng, M. (2002). An introduction to Chinese psychology—its historical roots until the present day. *The Journal of Psychology, 136*(2), 225–239.

Higgins, S. C., Gueorguiev, M., & Korbonits, M. (2007). Ghrelin, the peripheral hunger hormone. *Annals of Medicine, 39,* 116–136.

Higley, J. D., Mehlman, P. T., Higley, S. B., Fernald, B., Vickers, J., Lindell, S. G., et al. (1996). Excessive mortality in young free-ranging male non-human primates with low cerebrospinal fluid 5-hydroxyindoleacetic acid concentrations. *Archives of General Psychiatry, 53,* 537–543.

Hilgard, E. R., & Hilgard, J. R. (1975). *Hypnosis in the relief of pain.* Los Altos, CA: Kaufmann.

Hines, T. (2003). *Pseudoscience and the paranormal.* Amherst, NY: Prometheus.

Ho, B. C., Andreasen, N. C., Nopoulos, P., Arndt, S., Magnotta, V., & Flaum, M. (2003). Progressive structural brain abnormalities and their relationship to clinical outcome: A longitudinal magnetic resonance imaging study early in schizophrenia. *Archives of General Psychiatry, 60,* 585–594.

Hobson, J. A. (1995). *Sleep.* New York: Scientific American Library.

Hobson, J. A. (1999). Sleep and dreaming. In M. J. Zigmond, F. E. Bloom, S. C. Landis, J. L. Roberts, & L. R. Squire (Eds.), *Fundamentals of neuroscience* (pp. 1207–1225). San Diego, CA: Academic Press.

Hobson, J. A., Pace-Schott, E. F., & Stickgold, R. (2000). Consciousness: Its vicissitudes in waking and sleep. In M. S. Gazzaniga (Ed.), *The new cognitive neurosciences* (pp. 1341–1354). Cambridge, MA: MIT Press.

Hofmann, S. G., & Smits, J. A. J. (2008). Cognitive-behavioral therapy for adult anxiety disorders: A meta-analysis of randomized placebo-controlled trials. *Journal of Clinical Psychiatry, 69,* 621–632.

Holden, C. (2005, June 10). Sex and the suffering brain. *Science, 308,* 1574.

Holland, P. C. (1977). Conditioned stimulus as a determinant of the form of the Pavlovian conditioned response. *Journal of Experimental Psychology: Animal Behavior Processes, 3,* 77–104.

Hollander, E., Bartz, J., Chaplin, W., Phillips, A., Sumner, J., Soorya, L., et al. (2007). Oxytocin increases retention of social cognition in autism. *Biological Psychiatry, 61,* 498–503.

Hollander, E., Novotny, S., Hanratty, M., Yaffe, R., DeCaria, C. M., Aronowitz, B. R., et al. (2003). Oxytocin infusion reduces repetitive behaviors in adults with autistic and Asperger's disorders. *Neuropsychopharmacology, 28,* 193–198.

Hollis, K. L. (1997). Contemporary research on Pavlovian conditioning: A "new" functional analysis. *American Psychologist, 52,* 956–965.

Hollon, S. D., Stewart, M. O., & Strunk, D. (2006). Enduring effects for cognitive behavior therapy in the treatment of depression and anxiety. *Annual Review of Psychology, 57,* 285–315.

Hollon, S. D., Thase, M. E., & Markowitz, J. C. (2002). Treatment and prevention of depression. *Psychological Science in the Public Interest, 3,* 39–77.

Hooley, J. (2007). Expressed emotion and relapse of psychopathology. *Annual Review of Clinical Psychology, 3,* 329–352.

Hooley, J. M., & Gotlib, I. H. (2000). A diathesis-stress conceptualization of expressed emotion and clinical outcome. *Applied and Preventive Psychology, 9,* 135–152.

Horn, J. L. (1968). Organization of abilities and the development of intelligence. *Psychological Review, 75,* 242–259.

Horn, J. L., & Hofer, S. M. (1992). Major abilities and development in the adult period. In R. J. Sternberg & C. A. Berg (Eds.), *Intellectual development* (pp. 44–99). New York: Cambridge University Press.

Horn, J. L., & McArdle, J. J. (2007). Understanding human intelligence since Spearman. In R. Cudeck & R. C. MacCallum (Eds.), *Factor analysis at 100: Historical developments and future directions* (pp. 205–247). Mahwah, NJ: Erlbaum.

Hoshino, Y., Kumashiro, H., Yashima, Y., Tachibana, R., Watanabe, M., & Furukawa, H. (1980). Early symptoms of autism in children and their diagnostic significance. *Japanese Journal of Child and Adolescent Psychiatry, 21,* 284–299.

Hothersall, D. (1995). *History of psychology.* New York: McGraw-Hill.

House, J. S., Landis, K. R., & Umberson, D. (1988, July 29). Social relationships and health. *Science, 241,* 540–545.

Hovland, C. I., Janis, I. L., & Kelley, H. H. (1953). *Communication and persuasion: Psychological studies of opinion change.* New Haven, CT: Yale University Press.

Howlin, P., Mawhood, L., & Rutter, M. (2000). Autism and developmental receptive language disorder—A follow-up comparison in early adult life. II: Social, behavioural, and psychiatric outcomes. *Journal of Child Psychology and Psychiatry and Allied Disciplines, 41,* 561–578.

Hubel, D. H., & Wiesel, T. N. (1962). Receptive fields, binocular interaction, and functional architecture in the cat's visual cortex. *Journal of Physiology* (London), *160,* 106–154.

Hudson, W. (1967). The study of the problem of pictorial perception among unacculturated groups. *International Journal of Psychology, 2,* 89–107.

Huesmann, L. R. (1998). The role of social information processing and cognitive schemas in the acquisition and maintenance of habitual aggressive behavior. In R. G. Geen & E. Donnerstein (Eds.), *Human aggression: Theories, research, and implications for policy* (pp. 73–109). New York: Academic Press.

Hull, J. G., & Bond, C. F. (1986). Social and behavioral consequences of alcohol consumption and expectancy: A meta-analysis. *Psychological Bulletin, 99,* 347–360.

Hulse, G. K., Milne, E., English, D. R., & Holman, C. D. J. (1998). Assessing the relationship between maternal opiate use and antepartum haemorrhage. *Addiction, 93,* 1553–1558.

Hunsley, J., & Mash, E. J. (2007). Evidence-based assessment. *Annual Review of Clinical Psychology, 3,* 29–51.

Hurley, S. (2004). Imitation, media violence, and freedom of speech. *Philosophical Studies, 117,* 165–218.

Ikier, S., Tekcan, A. I., Gülgöz, S., & Küntay, A. (2003). Whose life is it anyway? Adoption of each other's autobiographical memories by twins. *Applied Cognitive Psychology, 17,* 237–247.

Ilan, A. B., Smith, M. E., & Gevins, A. (2004). Effects of marijuana on neurophysiological signals of working and episodic memory. *Psychopharmacology, 176,* 214–222.

Insel, T. R., & Charney, D. S. (2003). Research on major depression. *Journal of the American Medical Association, 289,* 3167–3168.

Insel, T. R., & Young, L. J. (2001). The neurobiology of attachment. *Nature Reviews Neuroscience, 2,* 129–136.

Isen, A. M. (1993). Positive affect and decision making. In M. Lewis & J. M. Haviland (Eds.), *Handbook of emotions* (pp. 261–277). New York: Guilford Press.

Ivanovic, D. M., Leiva, B. P., Perez, H. T., Olivares, M. G., Diaz, N. S., Urrutia, M. S., et al. (2004). Head size and intelligence, learning, nutritional status and brain development: Head, IQ, learning, nutrition and brain. *Neuropsychologia, 42,* 1118–1131.

Iyengar, S. S., & Lepper, M. R. (2000). When choice is demotivating: Can one desire too much of a good thing? *Journal of Personality and Social Psychology, 79,* 995–1006.

Izard, C. E., & Malatesta, C. Z. (1987). Perspectives on emotional development. In J. Osofsky (Ed.), *Handbook of infant development* (pp. 494–554). New York: Wiley.

Jablensky, A. (1989). Epidemiology and cross-cultural aspects of schizophrenia. *Psychiatric Annals, 19,* 516–524.

Jackson, B., Kubzansky, L. D., Cohen, S., Jacobs, D. R., Jr., & Wright, R. J. (2007). Does harboring hostility hurt? Associations between hostility and pulmonary function in the coronary artery risk development in (young) adults (CARDIA) Study. *Health Psychology, 26*(3), 333–340.

Jackson, S. A., Thomas, P. R., Marsh, H. W., & Smethurst, C. J. (2001). Relationships between flow, self-concept, psychological skills, and performance. *Journal of Applied Sport Psychology, 13,* 129–153.

Jacoby, L. L., Kelley, C., Brown, J., & Jasechko, J. (1989). Becoming famous overnight: Limits on the ability to avoid unconscious influences of the past. *Journal of Personality and Social Psychology, 56,* 326–338.

James, W. (1890). *The principles of psychology.* New York: Henry Holt.

Jamieson, G. A. (2007). *Hypnosis and conscious states: The cognitive neuroscience perspective.* New York: Oxford University Press.

Jamison, K. R. (1993). *Touched with fire: Manic-depressive illness and the artistic temperament.* New York: Simon & Schuster.

Jamison, K. R. (1995). *An unquiet mind.* New York: Vintage Books.

Jang, K. L., Hu, S., Lively, W. J., Angleitner, A., Riemann, R., Ando, J., et al. (2001). Covariance structure of neuroticism and agreeableness: A twin and molecular genetic analysis of the role of the serotonin transporter gene. *Journal of Personality and Social Psychology, 81,* 295–304.

Janssen, E., Carpenter, D., & Graham, C. A. (2003). Selecting films for sex research: Gender differences in erotic film preference. *Archives of Sexual Behavior, 32,* 243–251.

Jencks, C. (1979). *Who gets ahead? The determinants of economic success in America.* New York: Basic Books.

Jensen, A. R. (1998). *The g factor: The science of mental ability.* Westport, CT: Praeger.

Jensen, P. S., Arnold, L. E., Swanson, J. M., Vitiello, B., Abikoff, H. B., Greenhill, L. L., et al. (2007). 3-year follow-up of the NIMH MTA study. *Journal of the American Academy of Child and Adolescent Psychiatry, 46*, 989–1002.

Jensen, P. S., Hinshaw, S. P., Swanson, J. M., Greenhill, L. L., Conners, C. K., Arnold, L. E., et al. (2001). Findings from the NIMH multimodal treatment study of ADHD (MTA): Implications and applications for primary care providers. *Journal of Developmental and Behavioral Pediatrics, 22*, 60–73.

Jiang, Y., Sheikh, K., & Bullock, C. (2006). Is there a sex or race difference in stroke mortality? *Journal of Stroke and Cerebrovascular Disease 15*(5), 179–186.

John, O. P. (1990). The "Big Five" factor taxonomy: Dimensions of personality in the natural language and in questionnaires. In L. A. Pervin & O. P. John (Eds.), *Handbook of personality: Theory and research* (pp. 66–100). New York: Guilford Press.

John, O. P., & Srivastava, S. (1999). The Big Five trait taxonomy: History, measurement, and theoretical perspectives. In L. A. Pervin & O. P. John (Eds.), *Handbook of personality: Theory and research* (2nd ed., pp. 102–138). New York: Guilford Press.

Johnson, D. L., Wiebe, J. S., Gold, S. M., Andreasen, N. C., Hichwa, R. D., Watkins, G. L., et al. (1999). Cerebral blood flow and personality: A positron emission tomography study. *American Journal of Psychiatry, 156*, 252–257.

Johnson, K. (2008, January 28). For many of USA's inmates, crime runs in the family. *USA Today*. Retrieved from http://www.usatoday.com

Johnson, K. L., Gill, S., Reichman, V., & Tassinary, L. G. (2007). Swagger, sway, and sexuality: Judging sexual orientation from body motion and morphology. *Journal of Personality and Social Psychology, 93*, 321–334.

Johnson, W., Jung, R. E., Colom, R., & Haier, R. J. (2008). Cognitive abilities independent of IQ correlate with regional brain structure. *Intelligence, 36*, 18–28.

Joiner, T. E., Coyne, J. C., & Blalock, J. (1999). On the interpersonal nature of depression: Overview and synthesis. In T. E. Joiner & J. C. Coyne (Eds.), *The interactional nature of depression: Advances in interpersonal approaches* (pp. 3–19). Washington, DC: American Psychological Association.

Joiner, T. E., Jr., Walker, R. L., Pettit, J. W., Perez, M., & Cukrowicz, K. C. (2005). Evidence-based assessment of depression in adults. *Psychological Assessment, 17*, 267–277.

Jones, S. S., Collins, K., & Hong, H. (1991). An audience effect on smile production in 10-month-old infants. *Psychological Science, 2*, 45–49.

Jope, R. S. (1999). Anti-bipolar therapy: Mechanism of action of lithium. *Molecular Psychiatry, 4*, 117–128.

Jorde, L. B., Mason-Brothers, A., Waldman, R., Ritvo, E. R., Freeman, B. J., Pingree, C., et al. (1990). The UCLA-University of Utah epidemiologic survey of autism: Genealogical analysis of familial aggregation. *American Journal of Medical Genetics, 36*, 85–88.

Judge, T. A., & Cable, D. M. (2004). The effect of physical height on workplace success and income: Preliminary test of a theoretical model. *Journal of Applied Psychology, 89*, 428–441.

Jureidini, J. N., Doecke, C. J., Mansfield, P. R., Haby, M., Menkes, D. B., & Tonkin, A. L. (2004). Efficacy and safety of antidepressants for children and adolescents. *British Medical Journal, 328*, 879–883.

Kagan, J., & Snidman, N. (1991). Infant predictors of inhibited and uninhibited profiles. *Psychological Science, 2*, 40–44.

Kahneman, D. (2007, July 20–22). *A short course in thinking about thinking. A master class by Danny Kahneman.* [Online video.] Retrieved from *Edge, The Third Culture,* at http://www.edge.org/3rd_culture/kahneman07/kahneman07_index.html/

Kahneman, D., & Tversky, A. (1972). Subjective probability: A study of representativeness. *Cognitive Psychology, 3*, 430–454.

Kahneman, D., & Tversky, A. (1984). Choices, values, and frames. *American Psychologist, 39*, 341–350.

Kajantie, E. (2008). Physiological stress response, estrogen, and the male-female mortality gap. *Current Directions in Psychological Science, 17*, 348–352.

Kallio, S., & Revonsuo, A. (2003). Hypnotic phenomena and altered states of consciousness: A multi-level framework of description and explanation. *Contemporary Hypnosis, 20*, 111–164.

Kanazawa, S. (2004). General intelligence as a domain-specific adaptation. *Psychological Review, 111*, 512–523.

Kandall, S. R., & Gaines, J. (1991). Maternal substance use and subsequent sudden infant death syndrome (SIDS) in offspring. *Neurotoxicology and Teratology, 13*, 235–240.

Kandel, E. R., Schwartz, J. H., & Jessell, T. M. (1995). *Essentials of neural science and behavior.* Norwalk, CT: Appleton & Lange.

Kane, M. J., Hambrick, D. Z., & Conway, A. R. (2005). Working memory capacity and fluid intelligence are strongly related constructs: Comment on Ackerman, Beier, and Boyle (2005). *Psychological Bulletin, 131*, 66–71.

Kanwisher, N., Tong, F., & Nakayama, K. (1998). The effect of face inversion on the human fusiform face area. *Cognition, 68*, 1–11.

Kaplan, A. L. (2006). Ethical issues surrounding forced, mandated, or coerced treatment. *Journal of Substance Abuse Treatment, 31*, 117–120.

Kaplan, R. M. (2007). Should Medicare reimburse providers for weight loss interventions? *American Psychologist, 62*, 217–219.

Kappenberg, E. S., & Halpern, D. F. (2006). Kinship center attachment questionnaire: Development of a caregiver-completed attachment measure for children under six years of age. *Educational and Psychological Measurement, 66*, 852–873.

Kapur, S. E., Craik, F. I. M., Tulving, E., Wilson, A. A., Houle, S., & Brown, G. R. (1994). Neuroanatomical correlates of encoding in episodic memory: Levels of processing effects. *Proceedings of the National Academy of Sciences, USA, 91*, 2008–2011.

Karasek, R. A., & Theorell, T. (1990). *Healthy work: Stress, productivity, and the reconstruction of working life.* New York: Basic Books.

Karney, B. R., & Bradbury, T. N. (1995). The longitudinal course of marital quality and stability: A review of theory, methods, and research. *Psychological Bulletin, 118*, 3–34.

Kasari, C., Paparella, T., Freeman, S., & Jahromi, L. B. (2008). Language outcomes in autism: Randomized comparison of joint attention and play interventions. *Journal of Counseling and Clinical Psychology, 76*, 125–137.

Kawachi, I., Kennedy, B., & Glass, R. (1999). Social capital and self-rated health: A contextual analysis. *American Journal of Public Health, 89*(8), 1187–1193.

Kawakami, K., Dovidio, J. F., Moll, J., Hermsen, S., & Russin, A. (2000). Just say no (to stereotyping): Effects of training in the negation of stereotypic associations on stereotype activation. *Journal of Personality and Social Psychology, 78*, 871–888.

Kay, K. N., Naselaris, T., Prenger, R. J., & Gallant, J. L. (2008). Identifying natural images from human brain activity. *Nature, 452,* 352–355.

Kazdin, A. E. (1994). Methodology, design, and evaluation in psychotherapy research. In A. E. Bergin & S. L. Garfield (Eds.), *International handbook of behavior modification and behavior change* (4th ed., pp. 19–71). New York: Wiley.

Kazdin, A. E. (2008). Evidence-based treatment and practice: New opportunities to bridge clinical research and practice, enhance the knowledge base, and improve patient care. *American Psychologist, 63,* 146–159.

Kazdin, A. E., & Benjet, C. (2003). Spanking children: Evidence and issues. *Current Directions in Psychological Science, 12,* 99–103.

Keane, M. (1987). On retrieving analogues when solving problems. *Quarterly Journal of Experimental Psychology, 39A,* 29–41.

Keel, P. K., Baxter, M. G., Heatherton, T. F., & Joiner, T. E. (2007). A 20-year longitudinal study of body weight, dieting, and eating disorder symptoms. *Journal of Abnormal Psychology, 116,* 422–432.

Keel, P. K., & Mitchell, J. E. (1997). Outcome in bulimia nervosa. *American Journal of Psychiatry, 154,* 313–321.

Keith, S. J., Regier, D. A., & Rae, D. S. (1991). Schizophrenic disorders. In L. N. Robins & D. A. Regier (Eds.), *Psychiatric disorders in America: The epidemiological catchment areas study.* New York: Free Press.

Keller, J., & Bless, H. (2008). Flow and regulatory compatibility: An experimental approach to the flow model of intrinsic motivation. *Personality and Social Psychology Bulletin, 34,* 196–209.

Keller, M. B., & Baker, L. A. (1991). Bipolar disorder: Epidemiology, course, diagnosis, and treatment. *Bulletin of the Menninger Clinic, 55,* 172–181.

Keller, M. B., McCullough, J. P., Klein, D. N., Arnow, B., Dunner, D. L., Gelenberg, A. J., et al. (2000). A comparison of nefazodone, a cognitive behavioral analysis system of psychotherapy, and their combination for the treatment of chronic depression. *New England Journal of Medicine, 342,* 1462–1470.

Kelley, W. T., Macrae, C. N., Wyland, C., Caglar, S., Inati, S., & Heatherton, T. F. (2002). Finding the self? An event-related fMRI study. *Journal of Cognitive Neuroscience, 14,* 785–794.

Kellman, P. J., Spelke, E. S., & Short, K. R. (1986). Infant perception of object unity from translatory motion in depth and vertical translation. *Child Development, 57,* 72–86.

Kelly, D. J., Quinn, P. C., Slater, A., Lee, K., Ge, L., & Pascalis, O. (2007). The other-race effect develops during infancy: Evidence of perceptual narrowing. *Psychological Science, 18,* 1084–1089.

Kelly, G. A. (1955). *The psychology of personal constructs.* New York: W. W. Norton.

Keltner, D., & Anderson, C. (2000). Saving face for Darwin: The functions and uses of embarrassment. *Current Directions in Psychological Science, 9,* 187–192.

Keltner, D., & Bonanno, G. A. (1997). A study of laughter and dissociation: Distinct correlates of laughter and smiling during bereavement. *Journal of Personality and Social Psychology, 73,* 687–702.

Keltner, D., Young, R. C., Heerey, E. A., Oemig, C., & Monarch, N. D. (1998). Teasing in hierarchical and intimate relations. *Journal of Personality and Social Psychology, 75,* 1231–1247.

Kennedy, Q., Mather, M., & Carstensen, L. L. (2004). The role of motivation in the age-related positivity effect in autobiographical memory. *Psychological Science, 15,* 208–214.

Kenrick, D. T., & Funder, D. C. (1991). The person-situation debate: Do personality traits really exist? In V. J. Derlega, B. A. Winstead, & W. H. Jones (Eds.), *Personality: Contemporary theory and research* (pp. 149–174). Chicago: Nelson Hall.

Kenrick, D. T., Montello, D. R., Gutierres, S. E., & Trost, M. R. (1993). Effects of physical attractiveness on affect and perceptual judgments: When social comparison overrides social reinforcement. *Personality and Social Psychology Bulletin, 19,* 195–199.

Kersh, R., & Morone, J. (2002). The politics of obesity: Seven steps to government action. *Health Affairs, 21*(6), 142–153.

Kessler, R. C., Adler, L., Barkley, R., Biederman, J., Conners, C. K., Demler, O., et al. (2006). The prevalence and correlates of adult ADHD in the United States: Results from the national comorbidity survey replication. *American Journal of Psychiatry, 163,* 716–723.

Kessler, R. C., Berglund, P., Demler, O., Jin, R., Koretz, D., Merikangas, K., et al. (2003). The epidemiology of major depressive disorder: Results from the national comorbidity survey replication (NCS-R). *Journal of the American Medical Association, 289,* 3095–3105.

Kessler, R. C., Chiu, W. T., Demler, O., & Walters, E. E. (2005a). Prevalence, severity, and comorbidity of twelve-month DSM-IV disorders in the national comorbidity survey replication (NCS-R). *Archives of General Psychiatry, 62,* 617–627.

Kessler, R. C., Demler, O., Frank, R. G., Olfson, M., Pincus, M. A., Walters, E. E., et al. (2005b). Prevalence and treatment of mental disorders, 1990 to 2003. *New England Journal of Medicine, 352,* 2515–2523.

Kessler, R. C., McGonagle, K. A., Zhao, S., Nelson, C. B., Hugh, M., Eshleman, S., et al. (1994). Lifetime and 12-month prevalence of DSM-III-R psychiatric disorders in the United States: Results from the national comorbidity study. *Archives of General Psychiatry, 51,* 8–19.

Kessler, R. C., Merikangas, K. R., & Wang, P. S. (2007). Prevalence, comorbidity, and service utilization for mood disorders in the United States at the beginning of the twenty-first century. In S. Nolen-Hoeksema, T. Cannon, & T. Widiger (Eds.), *Annual review of clinical psychology: Volume 3* (pp. 137–158). Palo Alto, CA: Annual Reviews.

Kessler, R. C., Sonnega, A., Bromet, E., Hughes, M., & Nelson, C. B. (1995). Posttraumatic stress disorder in the national comorbidity survey. *Archives of General Psychiatry, 52,* 1048–1060.

Kessler, R. C., & Wang, P. S. (2008). The descriptive epidemiology of commonly occurring mental disorders in the United States. *Annual Review of Public Health, 29,* 115–129.

Keyes, Daniel. (1981). *The minds of billy milligan.* New York: Random House.

Keys, A., Brozek, J., Henschel, A. L., Mickelsen, O., & Taylor, H. L. (1950). *The biology of human starvation.* Minneapolis: University of Minnesota Press.

Khan, M. M. (2005). Suicide prevention and developing countries. *Journal of the Royal Society of Medicine, 98,* 459–463.

Kiecolt-Glaser, J. K., & Glaser, R. (1988). Immunological competence. In E. A. Blechman & K. D. Brownell (Eds.), *Handbook of behavioral medicine for women* (pp. 195–205). Elmsford, NY: Pergamon Press.

Kiecolt-Glaser, J. K., Malarkey, W. B., Chee, M., & Newton, T. (1993). Negative behavior during marital conflict is associated with immunological down-regulation. *Psychosomatic Medicine, 55,* 395–409.

Kiecolt-Glaser, J. K., & Newton, T. L. (2001). Marriage and health: His and hers. *Psychological Bulletin, 127*(4), 472–503.

Kihlstrom, J. F. (1985). Hypnosis. *Annual Review of Psychology, 36,* 385–418.

Kihlstrom, J. F. (2005). Dissociative disorder. *Annual Review of Clinical Psychology, 1*, 227–253.

Kihlstrom, J. F., & Eich, E. (1994). Altering states of consciousness. In D. Druckman & R. A. Bjork (Eds.), *Learning, remembering, and believing: Enhancing performance* (pp. 207–248). Washington, DC: National Academy Press.

Kilbride, P. L., & Robbins, M. C. (1969). Pictorial depth perception and acculturation among the Baganda. *American Anthropologist, 71*, 293–301.

Kim, J. B., Zaehres, H., Wu, G., Gentile, L., Ko, K., Sebastiano, V., et al. (2008). Pluripotent stem cells induced from adult neural stem cells by reprogramming with two factors. *Nature, 454*, 646–650.

Kim, J. J., & Jung, M. W. (2006). Neural circuits and mechanisms involved in Pavlovian fear conditioning: A critical review. *Neuroscience & Biobehavioral Reviews, 30*(2), 188–202.

Kim, S. J., Lyoo, I. K., Hwang, J., Chung, A., Hoon Sung, Y., Kim, J., et al. (2006). Prefrontal grey-matter changes in short-term and long-term abstinent methamphetamine abusers. *The International Journal of Neuropsychopharmacology, 9*, 221–228.

Kirsch, I., & Lynn, S. J. (1995). The altered state of hypnosis: Changes in the theoretical landscape. *American Psychologist, 10*, 846–858.

Klauer, M. H., Musch, J., & Naumer, B. (2000). On belief bias in syllogistic reasoning. *Psychological Review, 107*, 852–884.

Kleinmuntz, B., & Szucko, J. J. (1984). Lie detection in ancient and modern times: A call for contemporary scientific study. *American Psychologist, 39*, 766–776.

Klin, A., Jones, W., Schultz, R., & Volkmar, F. (2003). The enactive mind, or from actions to cognition: Lessons from autism. *Philosophical Transactions of the Royal Society of London, 358B*, 345–360.

Klump, K. L., & Culbert, K. M. (2007). Molecular genetic studies of eating disorders: Current status and future directions. *Current Directions in Psychological Science, 16*, 37–41.

KMBC-TV 9, Kansas City News. (2008, January 7). Judge rules in Baby Max custody case [Online news report]. Retrieved from http://www.kmbc.com/news/14994541/detail.html

Knight, R. (1953). Borderline states. *Bulletin of the Menninger Clinic, 17*, 1–12.

Knox, S. S., Weidner, G., Adelman, A., Stoney, C. M., & Ellison, R. C. (2004). Hostility and physiological risk in the national heart, lung, and blood institute family heart study. *Archives of Internal Medicine, 164*, 2442–2447.

Knutson, B., Fong, G. W., Adams, C. M., Varner, J. L., & Hommer, D. (2001). Dissociation of reward anticipation and outcome with event-related fMRI. *NeuroReport, 12*, 3683–3687.

Knutson, B., Wolkowitz, O. M., Cole, S. W., Chan, T., Moore, E. A., Johnson, R. C., et al. (1998). Selective alteration of personality and social behavior by serotonergic intervention. *American Journal of Psychiatry, 155*, 373–379.

Kobasa, S. C. (1979). Personality and resistance to illness. *American Journal of Community Psychology, 7*, 413–423.

Koch, J. L. (1891). *Die psychopathischen Minderwertigkeiten*. Ravensburg, Germany: Maier.

Kocsis, J. H., Rush, A. J., Markowitz, J. C., Borian, F. E., Dunner, D. L., Koran, L. M., et al. (2003). Continuation treatment of chronic depression: A comparison of nefazodone, cognitive behavioral analysis system of psychotherapy, and their combination. *Psychopharmacology Bulletin, 37*, 73–87.

Koh, K., Joiner, W. J., Wu, M. N., Yue, Z., Smith, C. J., Sehgal, A. (2008). Identification of SLEEPLESS, a sleep-promoting factor. *Science, 321*, 372–376.

Kohlberg, L. (1984). *Essays on moral development: Vol. 2. The psychology of moral development*. San Francisco: Harper & Row.

Kohler, W. (1925). *The mentality of apes*. New York: Harcourt Brace.

Kohn, D. (2008, March 11). Cases without borders: Psychotherapy for all. *The New York Times*. Retrieved from http://www.nytimes.com

Kolar, D. W., Funder, D. C., & Colvin, C. R. (1996). Comparing the accuracy of personality judgments by the self and knowledgeable others. *Journal of Personality, 64*, 311–337.

Kontsevich, L. L., & Tyler, C. W. (2004). What makes Mona Lisa smile? *Vision Research, 44*, 1493–1498.

Koole, S. L., Dijksterhuis, A., & van Knippenberg, A. (2001). What's in a name: Implicit self-esteem and the automatic self. *Journal of Personality and Social Psychology, 80*, 669–685.

Korn, M. L., Kotler, M., Molcho, A., Botsis, A. J., Grosz, D., Chen, C., et al. (1992). Suicide and violence associated with panic attacks. *Biological Psychiatry, 31*, 607–612.

Kosslyn, S. M., Thompson, W. L., Constantine-Ferrando, M. F., Alpert, N. M., & Spiegel, D. (2000). Hypnotic visual illusion alters color processing in the brain. *American Journal of Psychiatry, 157*, 1279–1284.

Kosslyn, S., & Koenig, O. (1995). *Wet mind: The new cognitive neuroscience*. New York: Free Press.

Kosslyn, S. M., Thompson, W. L., Kim, I. J., & Alpert, N. M. (1995). Topographical representations of mental images in primary visual cortex. *Nature, 378*, 496–493.

Kowalski, P., & Taylor, A. K. (2004). Ability and critical thinking as predictors of change in students' psychological misconceptions. *Journal of Instructional Psychology, 31*, 297.

Kozorovitskiy, Y., & Gould, E. (2004). Dominance hierarchy influences adult neurogenesis in the dentate gyrus. *Journal of Neuroscience, 24*, 6755–6759.

Krantz, D. S., & McCeney, M. K. (2002). Effects of psychological and social factors on organic disease: A critical assessment of research on coronary heart disease. *Annual Review of Psychology, 53*, 341–369.

Krendl, A. C., Richeson, J. A., Kelley, W. M., & Heatherton, T. F. (2008). The negative consequences of threat: An fMRI investigation of the neural mechanisms underlying women's underperformance in math. *Psychological Science, 19*, 168–175.

Kringelbach, M. L., Lehtonen, A., Squire, S., Harvey, A. G., Craske, M. G., Holliday, I. E., et al. (2008). A specific and rapid neural signature for parental instinct. *PLoS ONE, 3*(2), e1664. Retrieved from www.plosone.org

Kristensen, P., & Bjerkedal, T. (2007, June 22). Explaining the relation between birth order and intelligence. *Science, 316*, 1717.

Krueger, R. F., & Markon, K. E. (2006). Understanding psychopathology: Melding behavior genetics, personality, and quantitative psychology to develop an empirically based model. *Current Directions in Psychological Science, 15*, 113–117.

Kruesi, M. J., Hibbs, E. D., Zahn, T. P., Keysor, C. S., Hamburger, S. D., Bartko, J. J., et al. (1992). A 2-year prospective follow-up study of children and adolescents with disruptive behavior disorders. Prediction by cerebrospinal fluid 5-hydroxyindoleacetic acid, homovanillic acid, and autonomic measures. *Archives of General Psychiatry, 49*, 429–435.

Krumhansl, C. (2002). Music: A link between cognition and emotion. *Current Directions in Psychological Science, 11*, 45–50.

Kuhl, P. (2006). Is speech learning "gated" by the social brain? *Developmental Science, 10*, 110–120.

Kuhl, P. K. (2004). Early language acquisition: Cracking the speech code. *Nature Reviews Neuroscience, 5*, 831–843.

Kuhl, P. K., Stevens, E., Hayashi, A., Deguchi, T., Kiritani, S., & Iverson, P. (2006). Infants show a facilitation effect for native language phonetic perception between 6 and 12 months. *Developmental Science, 9*, F13–F21.

Kuhl, P. K., Tsao, F. M., & Liu, H. M. (2003). Foreign-language experience in infancy: effects of short-term exposure and social interaction on phonetic learning. *Proceedings of the National Academy of Sciences, USA, 100*, 9096–9101.

Kuhn, C., Swartzwelder, S., & Wilson, W. (2003). *Buzzed: The straight facts about the most used and abused drugs from alcohol to ecstasy* (2nd ed.). New York: W. W. Norton.

Kulhara, P., & Chakrabarti, S. (2001). Culture and schizophrenia and other psychotic disorders. *Psychiatric Clinics of North America, 24*, 449–464.

Kuncel, N. R., Hezlett, S. A., & Ones, D. S. (2004). Academic performance, career potential, creativity, and job performance: Can one construct predict them all? *Journal of Personality and Social Psychology, 86*, 148–161.

Kunda, Z., & Spencer, S. J. (2003). When do stereotypes come to mind and when do they color judgment? A goal-based theoretical framework for stereotype activation and application. *Psychological Bulletin, 129*, 522–544.

Kunz Center, University of Cincinnati. (2005). *Work and family in America*. Retrieved February 28, 2008, from http://asweb.artsci.uc.edu/sociology/kunzctr/stats.htm

Kurdek, L. A., & Sinclair, R. J. (2000). Psychological, family, and peer predictors of academic outcomes in first- through fifth-grade children. *Journal of Educational Psychology, 92*, 449–457.

Kurzban, R., Tooby, J., & Cosmides, L. (2001). Can race be erased? Coalitional computation and social categorization. *Proceedings of the National Academy of Sciences, USA, 98*, 15387–15392.

Kyllonen, P. C., & Christal, R. E. (1990). Reasoning ability is (little more than) working-memory capacity?! *Intelligence, 14*, 389–433.

LaFrance, M. L., & Banaji, M. (1992). Toward a reconsideration of the gender-emotion relationship. In M. Clarke (Ed.) *Review of personality and social psychology* (pp. 178–201). Beverly Hills, CA: Sage.

Laird, J. D. (1974). Self-attribution of emotion: The effects of expressive behavior on the quality of emotional experience. *Journal of Perspectives in Social Psychology, 29*, 475–486.

Lambert, J., Fernandez, S., & Frick, K. (2005). Different types of environmental enrichment have discrepant effects on spatial memory and synaptophysin levels in female mice. *Neurobiology of Learning and Memory, 83*, 206–216.

Lamm, C., Batson, C. D., & Decety, J. (2007). The neural substrate of human empathy: Effects of perspective-taking and cognitive appraisal. *Journal of Cognitive Neuroscience, 19*, 42–58.

Landa, R., Holman, K., & Garrett-Mayer, E. (2007). Social and communication development in toddlers with early and later diagnosis of autism spectrum disorders. *Archives of General Psychiatry, 64*, 853–864.

Langleben, D. D., Schroeder, L., Maldjian, J. A., Gur, R. C., McDonald, S., Ragland, J. D., et al. (2002). Brain activity during simulated deception: An event-related functional magnetic resonance study. *Neuroimage, 15*, 727–732.

Langlois, J. H., Kalakanis, L., Rubenstein, A. J., Larson, A., Hallam, M., & Smoot, M. (2000). Maxims or myths of beauty? A meta-analytic and theoretical review. *Psychological Bulletin, 126*, 390–423.

Langlois, J. H., Ritter, J. M., Casey, R. J., & Sawin, D. B. (1995). Infant attractiveness predicts maternal behaviors and attitudes. *Developmental Psychology, 31*, 464–472.

Langlois, J. H., & Roggman, L. A. (1990). Attractive faces are only average. *Psychological Science, 1*, 115–121.

Larsen, J. T., McGraw, A. P., & Cacioppo, J. T. (2001). Can people feel happy and sad at the same time? *Journal of Personality and Social Psychology, 81*, 684–696.

Latané, B., & Darley, J. M. (1968). Group inhibition of bystander intervention in emergencies. *Journal of Personality and Social Psychology, 10*, 215–221.

Latané, B., Williams, K., & Harkins, S. G. (1979). Many hands make light the work: The causes and consequences of social loafing. *Journal of Personality and Social Psychology, 37*, 822–832.

Laureys, S. (2007, May). Eyes open, brain shut. *Scientific American, 296*, 84–89.

Lautenschlager, N. T., Cox, K. L., Flicker, L., Foster, J. K., van Bockxmeer, F. M., Xiao, J., et al. (2008). Effect of physical exercise on cognitive function in older adults at risk for Alzheimer disease. *Journal of the American Medical Association, 300*, 1027–1037.

Law and Neuroscience Project, University of California, Santa Barbara. (2007). *Network on addiction and antisocial behavior*. Retrieved from http://lawandneuroscienceproject.org

Lawton, C. A. (1994). Gender differences in way-finding strategies: Relationship to spatial ability and spatial anxiety. *Sex Roles, 30*(11–12), 765–779.

Layton, M. (1995, May/June). Emerging from the shadows. *Family Therapy Networker*, 35–41.

Lazarus, R. S. (1993). From psychological stress to the emotions: A history of changing outlooks. *Annual Review of Psychology, 44*, 1–21.

Leary, M. R. (2004). The function of self-esteem in terror management theory and sociometer theory: Comment on Pyszczynski et al., *Psychological Bulletin, 130*, 478–482.

Leary, M. R., Tambor, E. S., Terdal, S. K., & Downs, D. L. (1995) Self-esteem as an interpersonal monitor: The sociometer hypothesis. *Journal of Personality and Social Psychology, 68*, 518–530.

Leary, M. R., & MacDonald, G. (2003). Individual differences in self-esteem: A review and theoretical integration. In M. R. Leary & J. P. Tangney (Eds.), *Handbook of self and identity* (pp. 401–418). New York: Guilford Press.

Leckman, J. F., Elliott, G. R., Bromet, E. J., Campbell, M., Cicchetti, D., Cohen, D. J., et al. (1995). Report card on the national plan for research on child and adolescent mental disorders: The midway point. *Archives of General Psychiatry, 34*, 715–723.

LeDoux, J. E. (2007). The amygdala. *Current Biology, 17*, R868–R874.

LeDoux, J. E. (1996). *The emotional brain: The mysterious underpinnings of emotional life*. New York: Simon & Schuster.

LeDoux, J. E. (2002). *Synaptic self*. New York: Viking.

Leff, J., Sartorius, N., Jablensky, A., Korten, A., & Ernberg, G. (1992). The international pilot study of schizophrenia: Five-year follow-up findings. *Psychological Medicine, 22,* 131–145.

Lehrner, J. P. (1993). Gender differences in long-term odor recognition memory: Verbal versus sensory influences and the consistency of label use. *Chemical Senses, 18,* 17–26.

Leichsenring, F., Rabung, S., & Leibing, E. (2004). The efficacy of short-term psychodynamic psychotherapy in specific psychiatric disorders: A meta-analysis. *Archives of General Psychiatry, 61,* 1208–1216.

Leigh, B. C., & Schafer, J. C. (1993). Heavy drinking occasions and the occurrence of sexual activity. *Psychology of Addictive Behaviors, 7,* 197–200.

Leigh, B. C., & Stacy, A. W. Alcohol expectancies and drinking in different age groups. *Addiction, 99,* 215–217.

Lemeshow, A. R., Fisher, L., Goodman, E., Kawachi, I., Berkey, C., & Colditz, G. A. (2008). Subjective social status in the school and change in adiposity in female adolescents: Findings from a prospective cohort study. *Archives of Pediatrics & Adolescent Medicine, 162,* 23–28.

Lenneberg, E. (1967). *The biological foundations of language.* New York: Wiley.

Lenzenweger, M. F., Lane, M. C., Loranger, A. W., & Kessler, R. C. (2007). DSM-IV personality disorders in the national comorbidity survey replication. *Biological Psychiatry, 62,* 553–564.

Lepper, M. R., Greene, D., & Nisbett, R. E. (1973). Undermining children's intrinsic interest with extrinsic reward: A test of the "overjustification" hypothesis. *Journal of Personality and Social Psychology, 28,* 129–137.

Lesniak, K. T., & Dubbert, P. M. (2001). Exercise and hypertension. *Current Opinion in Cardiology, 16,* 356–359.

Leuchter, A. F., Cook, I. A., Witte, E. A., Morgan, M., & Abrams, M. (2002). Changes in brain function of depressed subjects during treatment with placebo. *American Journal of Psychiatry, 159,* 122–129.

Levant, R. F., Good, G. E., Cook, S. W., O'Neil, J. M., Smalley, K. B., Owen, K. A., & Richmond, K. (2006). Validation of the normative male alexithymia scale: Measurement of a gender-linked syndrome. *Psychology of Men & Masculinity, 7*(4), 212–224.

LeVay, S. (1991, August 30). A difference in hypothalamic structure between heterosexual and homosexual men. *Science, 253,* 1034–1037.

Leventhal, H., & Cleary, P. D. (1980). The smoking problem: A review of research and theory in behavioral risk modification. *Psychological Bulletin, 88,* 370–405.

Lewin, C., & Herlitz, A. (2002). Sex differences in face recognition: Women's faces make the difference. *Brain and Cognition, 50,* 121–128.

Lewinsohn, P. M., Allen, N. B., Seeley, J. R., & Gotlib, I. H. (1999). First onset versus recurrence of depression: Differential processes of psychosocial risk. *Journal of Abnormal Psychology, 108,* 483–489.

Lewinsohn, P. M., Rodhe, P. D., Seeley, J. R., & Hops, H. (1991). Comorbidity of unipolar depression: I. Major depression with dysthymia. *Journal of Abnormal Psychology, 98,* 107–116.

Lewontin, R. C. (1976). Race and intelligence. In N. J. Block & G. Dworkin (Eds.), *The IQ controversy.* New York: Pantheon Books.

Li, N. P., Kenrick, D. T., Bailey, J. M., Linsenmeier, J. A. W. (2002). The necessities and luxuries of mate preferences: Testing the tradeoffs. *Journal of Personality and Social Psychology, 82,* 947–955.

Lieb, K., Zanarini, M. C., Schmahl, C., Linehan, M. M., & Bohus, M. (2004). Borderline personality disorder. *Lancet, 364,* 453–461.

Lieberman, M. D. (2000). Intuition: A social cognitive neuroscience approach. *Psychological Bulletin, 126,* 109–137.

Lieberman, M. D., Ochsner, K. N., Gilbert, D. T., & Schacter, D. L. (2001). Do amnesiacs exhibit cognitive dissonance reduction? The role of explicit memory and attention in attitude change. *Psychological Science, 121,* 135–140.

Lilienfeld, S. O. (2007). Psychological treatments that cause harm. *Perspectives on Psychological Science, 2,* 53–67.

Lindemann, B. (2001). Receptors and transduction in taste. *Nature, 413,* 219–225.

Linehan, M. M. (1987). Dialectical behavior therapy for borderline personality disorder: Theory and method. *Bulletin of the Menninger Clinic, 51,* 261–276.

Linehan, M. M., Armstrong, H. E., Suarez, A., Allmon, D., & Heard, H. (1991). Cognitive behavioral treatment of chronically parasuicidal borderline patients. *Archives of General Psychiatry, 48,* 1060–1064.

Linehan, M. M., Heard, H., & Armstrong, H. E. (1993). Naturalistic follow-up of a behavioral treatment for chronically parasuicidal borderline patients. *Archives of General Psychiatry, 50,* 971–974.

Liu, J., Raine, A., Venables, P. H., & Mednick, S. A. (2004). Malnutrition at age 3 years and externalizing behavior problems at ages 8, 11, and 17 years. *American Journal of Psychiatry, 161,* 2005–2013.

Livingston, R. W., & Drwecki, B. B. (2007). Why are some individuals not racially biased? Susceptibility to affective conditioning predicts nonprejudice toward blacks. *Psychological Science, 18,* 816–823.

Ljungberg, T., Apicella, P., & Schultz, W. (1992). Responses of monkey dopamine neurons during learning of behavioral reactions. *Journal of Neurophysiology, 67,* 145–163.

Lledo, P. M., Gheusi, G., & Vincent, J. D. (2005). Information processing in the mammalian olfactory system. *Physiological Review, 85,* 281–317.

Locke, E. A., & Latham, G. P. (1990). *A theory of goal setting and task performance.* Englewood Cliffs, NJ: Prentice-Hall.

Loewenstein, G. F., Weber, E. U., Hsee, C. K., & Welch, N. (2001). Risk as feelings. *Psychological Bulletin, 127,* 267–286.

Loftus, E. F., Miller, D. G., & Burns, H. J. (1978). Semantic integration of verbal information into a visual memory. *Journal of Experimental Psychology: Human Learning and Memory, 4,* 19–31.

Loftus, E. F., & Palmer, J. C. (1974). Reconstruction of automobile destruction: An example of the interaction between language and memory. *Journal of Learning and Verbal Behavior, 13,* 585–589.

Logan, J. M., Sanders, A. L., Snyder, A. Z., Morris, J. C., & Buckner, R. L. (2002). Under-recruitment and nonselective recruitment: Dissociable neural mechanisms associated with aging. *Neuron, 33,* 1–20.

Loo, C. K., & Mitchell, P. B. (2005). A review of the efficacy of transcranial magnetic stimulation (TMS) treatment for depression, and current and future strategies to optimize efficacy. *Journal of Affective Disorders, 88,* 255–267.

Lovaas, O. I. (1987). Behavioral treatment and normal educational and intellectual functioning in young autistic children. *Journal of Consulting and Clinical Psychology, 55,* 3–9.

Lowe, P. (2001, October 12). No prison for Candace's adoptive mom. *Denver Rocky Mountain News,* p. 26A.

Lubinski, D. (2004). Introduction to the special section on cognitive abilities: 100 years after Spearman's (1904) "'General intelligence,' objectively determined and measured." *Journal of Personality and Social Psychology, 86,* 96–111.

Lubinski, D., & Benbow, C. P. (2000). States of excellence. *American Psychologist, 55,* 137–150.

Luchins, A. S., (1942). Mechanization in problem solving. *Psychological Monographs, 54* (Whole No. 248).

Lykken, D. T. (1957). A study of anxiety in the sociopathic personality. *Journal of Abnormal Social Psychology, 55,* 6–10.

Lykken, D. T. (1995). *The antisocial personalities.* Hillsdale, NJ: Erlbaum.

Lykken, D. T. (2000). The causes and costs of crime and a controversial cure. *Journal of Personality, 68*(3), 560–605.

Lykken, D. T., McGue, M., Tellegen, A., & Bouchard, T. J., Jr. (1992). Emergenesis: Genetic traits that may not run in families. *American Psychologist, 47,* 1565–1577.

Lykken, D. T., & Tellegen, A. (1996). Happiness is a stochastic phenomenon. *Psychological Science, 7,* 184–189.

Lynam, D. R., Loeber, R., & Stouthamer-Loeber, M. (2008). The stability of psychopathy from adolescence into adulthood: The search for moderators. *Criminal Justice and Behavior, 35,* 228–243.

Lynch, T. R., Trost, W. T., Salsman, N., & Linehan, M. M. (2007). Dialectical behavior therapy for borderline personality disorder. *Annual Review of Clinical Psychology, 3,* 181–205.

Lyubomirsky, S., King, L., & Diener, E. (2005). The benefits of frequent positive affect: Does happiness lead to success? *Psychological Bulletin, 131,* 803–855.

Lyubomirsky, S., & Nolen-Hoeksema, S. (1995). Effects of self-focused rumination on negative thinking and interpersonal problem solving. *Journal of Personality and Social Psychology, 69,* 176–190.

Lyubomirsky, S., Sheldon, K. M., & Schkade, D. (2005). Pursuing happiness: The architecture of sustainable change. *Review of General Psychology, 9,* 111–131.

Maccoby, E. E., & Jacklin, C. N. (1974). *The psychology of sex differences.* Stanford, CA: Stanford University Press.

MacDonald, G., & Leary, M. R. (2005). Why does social exclusion hurt? The relationship between social and physical pain. *Psychological Bulletin, 131,* 202–223.

Macklin, R. (1990). Maternal-fetal conflict: An ethical analysis. *Women's Health Issues, 1,* 28–30.

MacKay, D. G. (1973). Aspects of a theory of comprehension, memory and attention. *Quarterly Journal of Experimental Psychology, 25,* 22–40.

Macrae, C. N., Alnwick, K. A., Milne, A. B., & Schloerscheidt, A. M. (2002). Person perception across the menstrual cycle: Hormonal influences on social-cognitive functioning. *Psychological Science, 13,* 532–536.

Macrae, C. N., Bodenhausen, G. V., & Calvini, G. (1999). Contexts of cryptomnesia: May the source be with you. *Social Cognition, 17,* 273–297.

Macrae, C. N., Moran, J. M., Heatherton, T. F., Banfield, J. F., & Kelley, W. M. (2004). Medial prefrontal activity predicts memory for self. *Cerebral Cortex, 14,* 647–654.

Madden, G. J., Petry, N. M., Badger, G. J., & Bickel, W. K. (1997). Impulsivity and self-control choices in opioid-dependent patients and non-drug-using control participants: Drug and monetary rewards. *Experimental and Clinical Psychopharmacology, 5,* 256–262.

Magnier, M. (2008, May 26). China quake survivors show signs of post-traumatic stress. *Los Angeles Times,* p. 1.

Magnussen, S., Adersson, J., Cornoldi, C., De Beni, R., Endestad, T., Goodman, G., et al. (2006). What people believe about memory. *Memory, 14,* 595–613.

Maguire, E. A., Spiers, H. J., Good, C. D., Hartley, T., Frackowiak, R. S., & Burgess, N. (2003). Navigation expertise and the human hippocampus: A structural brain imaging analysis. *Hippocampus, 13,* 250–259.

Maguire, E. A., Frackowiak, R. S. J., & Frith, C. D. (1997). Recalling routes around London: Activation of the right hippocampus in taxi drivers. *Journal of Neuroscience, 17,* 7103–7110.

Maguire, E. A., Gadian, D. G., Johnsrude, I. S., Ashburner, C. D., Frackowiak, R. S. J., & Frith, C. D. (2000). Navigation-related structural change in the hippoccampi of taxi drivers. *Proceedings of the National Academy of Sciences, USA, 97,* 4398–4403.

Maier, N. R. F. (1931). Reasoning in humans, II: The solution of a problem and its appearance in consciousness. *Journal of Comparative Psychology, 12,* 181–194.

Main, M., & Solomon, J. (1986). Discovery of a new, insecure-disorganized/disoriented attachment pattern. In T. B. Brazelton & M. Yogman (Eds.), *Affective development in infancy* (pp. 95–124). Norwood, NJ: Ablex.

Malle, B. F., Knobe, J., & Nelson, S. (2007). Actor-observer asymmetries in behavior explanations: New answers to an old question. *Journal of Personality and Social Psychology, 93,* 491–514.

Manderscheid, R. W., Witkin, M. J., Rosenstein, M. J., Milazzo-Sayre, L. J., Bethel, H. E., & MacAskill, R. L. (1985). In C. A. Taube & S. A. Barrett (Eds.), *Mental health, United States, 1985.* Washington DC: National Institute of Mental Health.

Maner, J. K., Luce, C. L., Neuberg, S. L., Cialdini, R. B., Brown, S., & Sagarin, B. J. (2002). The effects of perspective taking on motivations for helping: Still no evidence for altruism. *Personality and Social Psychology Bulletin, 28,* 1601–1610.

Manhart, K. (2004, December). The limits of multi-tasking. *Scientific American Mind,* 62–67.

Manning, R., Levine, M., & Collins, A. (2007). The Kitty Genovese murder and the social psychology of helping: The parable of the 38 witnesses. *American Psychologist, 62,* 555–562.

Mannuzza, S., Klein, R. G., Bonagura, N., Malloy, P., Giampino, T. L., & Addalli, K. A. (1991). Hyperactive boys almost grown up. Replications of psychiatric status. *Archives of General Psychiatry, 48,* 77–83.

Mannuzza, S., Klein, R. G., Truong, N. L., Moulton, J. L., III, Roizen, E. R., Howell, K. H., et al. (2008). Age of methylphenidate treatment initiation in children with ADHD and later substance abuse: Prospective follow-up into adulthood. *American Journal of Psychiatry, 165,* 604–609.

March, J. S., Silva, S., Petrycki, S., Curry, J., Wells, K., Fairbank, J., et al. (2007). The Treatment for Adolescents With Depression Study (TADS): Long-term effectiveness and safety outcomes. *Archives of General Psychiatry, 64,* 1132–1143.

Marcus, G. F. (2004). *The birth of the mind.* New York: Basic Books.

Marcus, G. F. (1996). Why do children say "breaked"? *Current Directions in Psychological Science, 5,* 81–85.

Marcus, G. F., Pinker, S., Ullman, M., Hollander, M., Rosen, T. S., & Xu, F. (1992). Overregularization in language acquisition. *Monographs of the Society for Research in Child Development, 57* (4, serial No. 228), 181.

Markon, J. (2001, October 8). Elderly judges handle 20 percent of U.S. caseload. *The Wall Street Journal*, p. A15.

Markowitz, J. C., & Weissman, M. M. (1995). Interpersonal psychotherapy. In E. E. Beckham & W. R. Leber (Eds.), *Handbook of depression* (2nd ed., pp. 376–390). New York: Guilford Press.

Markus, H. R. (1977). Self-schemata and processing information about the self. *Journal of Personality and Social Psychology, 35*, 63–78.

Markus, H. R., & Kitayama, S. (1991). Culture and the self: Implications for cognition, emotion, and motivation. *Psychological Review, 98*, 224–253.

Marlatt, G. A. (1999). Alcohol, the magic elixir? In S. Peele & M. Grant (Eds.), *Alcohol and pleasure: A health perspective* (pp. 233–248). Philadelphia: Brunner/Mazel.

Marlowe, D. B. (2006). Depot naltrexone in lieu of incarceration: A behavioral analysis of coerced treatment for addicted offenders. *Journal of Substance Abuse Treatment, 31*, 131–139.

Marsella, A. J., & Yamada, A. M (2007). Culture and psychopathology: Foundations, issues, directions. In S. Kitayama & D. Cohen (Eds.), *Handbook of cultural psychology* (pp. 797–819). New York: Guilford Press.

Marsland, A. L., Pressman, S., & Cohen, S. (2007). Positive affect and immune function. *Psychoneuroimmunology, 2*, 761–779.

Martin, L. A., Ashwood, P., Braunschweig, D., Cabanlit, M., Van de Water, J., & Amaral, D. G. (in press). Stereotypes and hyperactivity in rhesus monkeys exposed to IgG from mothers of children with autism. *Brain, Behavior, and Immunity, 22*, 804–805.

Martin, S. S., Butzin, C. A., Saum, S. A., & Inciardi, J. A. (1999). Three-year outcomes of therapeutic community treatment for drug-involved offenders in Delaware. *Prison Journal, 79*, 294–320.

Martire, L. M., & Schulz, R. (2007). Involving family in psychosocial interventions for chronic illness. *Current Directions in Psychological Science, 16*, 90–94.

Maruta, T., Colligan, R. C., Malinchoc, M., & Offord, K. P. (2002). Optimism-pessimism assessed in the 1960s and self-reported health status 30 years later. *Mayo Clinic Proceedings, 77*, 748–753.

Maslow, A. (1968). *Toward a psychology of being.* New York: Van Nostrand.

Massachusetts Institute of Technology, Sloan School of Management. (Producer). (2007). Intellectual capital: Arnie Barnett finds safety in numbers [Video]. *MIT Tech TV.* Podcast retrieved from http://techtv.mit.edu/

Masuda, T., & Nisbett, R. E. (2006). Culture and change blindness. *Cognitive Science, 30*, 381–399.

Mather, M., & Carstensen, L. L. (2003). Aging and attentional biases for emotional faces. *Psychological Science, 14*, 409–415.

Matthews, V. P., Kronenberger, W. G., Want, Y., Lurito, J. T., Lowe, M. J., & Dunn, D. W. (2005). Media violence exposure and frontal lobe activation measure by functional magnetic resonance imaging in aggressive and nonaggressive adolescents. *Journal of Computer Assisted Tomography, 29*, 287–292.

Mayberg, H. S., Lozano, A. M., Voon, V., McNeely, H. E., Seminowicz, D., Hamani, C., et al (2005). Deep brain stimulation for treatment-resistant depression. *Neuron, 45*, 651–660.

McAdams, D. P. (1999). Personal narratives and the life story. In L. A. Pervin & O. P. John (Eds.), *Handbook of personality: Theory and research* (2nd ed., pp. 478–500). New York: Guilford Press.

McAdams, D. P. (2001). The psychology of life stories. *Review of General Psychology, 5*, 100–122.

McCarthy, G., Puce, A., Gore, J. C., & Allison, T. (1997). Face-specific processing in the human fusiform gyrus. *Journal of Cognitive Neuroscience, 9*, 605–610.

McClelland, D. C. (1987). *Human motivation.* New York: Cambridge University Press.

McClelland, D. C., Koestner, R., & Weinberger, J. (1989). How do self-attributed and implicit motives differ? *Psychological Review, 96*, 690–702.

McCrae, R. R., & Costa, P. T., Jr. (1990). *Personality in adulthood.* New York: Guilford Press.

McCrae, R. R., & Costa, P. T., Jr. (1999). A five-factor theory of personality. In L. A. Pervin & O. P. John (Eds.), *Handbook of personality: Theory and research* (2nd ed., pp. 139–153). New York: Guilford Press.

McCrae, R. R., Costa, P. T., Ostendorf, F., Angleitner, A., Hrebickova, M., Avia, M. D., et al. (2000). Nature over nurture: Temperament, personality, and life span development. *Journal of Personality and Social Psychology, 78*, 173–186.

McCrink, K., & Wynn, K. (2004). Large-number addition and subtraction in infants. *Psychological Science, 15*, 776–781.

McCullough, J. P. (2000). *Treatment for chronic depression: Cognitive Behavioral Analysis System of Psychotherapy (CBASP).* New York: Guilford Press.

McDaniel, M. A., & Einstein, G. O. (2000). Strategic and automatic processes in prospective memory retrieval: A multiprocess framework. *Applied Cognitive Psychology, 14*, S127–S144.

McDaniel, M. A. (2005). Big-brained people are smarter: A meta-analysis of the relationship between in vivo brain volume and intelligence. *Intelligence, 33*, 337–346.

McDougle, C. (1997). Psychopharmacology. In D. Cohen & R. Volkmar (Eds.), *Handbook of autism and pervasive developmental disorders* (2nd ed., pp. 707–729). New York: Wiley.

McEwen, B. S. (2000). The effects of stress on structural and functional plasticity in the hippocampus. In D. S. Charney, E. J. Nestler, & B. S. Bunney (Eds.), *Neurobiology of mental illness* (pp. 475–493). New York: Oxford University Press.

McEwen, B. S., & Lasley, E. N. (2002). *The end of stress as we know it* (12th ed.). Washington, DC: Joseph Henry Press.

McEwen, B. S., & Lasley, E. N. (2007). Allostatic load: When protection gives way to damage. In A. Monat, R. S. Lazarus, & G. Reevy (Eds.), *The Praeger handbook on stress and coping* (Vol. 1, pp. 99–109). Westport, CT: Praeger.

McGlashan, T. H. (1988). A selective review of recent North American long-term follow-up studies of schizophrenia. *Schizophrenia Bulletin, 14*, 515–542.

McGough, J. J., & Barkley, R. A. (2004). Diagnostic controversies in adult attention deficit hyperactivity disorder. *American Journal of Psychiatry, 161*, 1948–1956.

McGue, M., Bacon, S., & Lykken, D. T. (1993). Personality stability and change in early adulthood: A behavioral genetic analysis. *Developmental Psychology, 29*, 96–109.

McInnis, M. G., McMahon, F. J., Chase, G. A., Simpson, S. G., Ross, C. A., & DePaulo, J. R. (1993). Anticipation in bipolar affective disorder. *American Journal of Human Genetics, 53*, 385–390.

McNeely, H. E., Mayberg, H. S., Lozano, A. M., & Kennedy, S. H. (2008). Neuropsychological impact of Cg25 deep brain stimulation for treatment-resistant depression: Preliminary results over 12 months. *The Journal of Nervous and Mental Disease, 196,* 405–410.

McNeil, D. G., Jr. (2006, November 23). For rare few, taste is in the ear of the beholder. *The New York Times.* Retrieved from http://www.nytimes.com

Meddis, R. (1977). *The sleep instinct.* London: Routledge & Kegan Paul.

Mednick, S. A., Gabrielli, W. F., & Hutchings, B. (1987). Genetic factors in the etiology of criminal behavior. In S. A. Mednick, T. E. Moffitt, & S. A. Stacks (Eds.), *The causes of crime: New biological approaches* (pp. 267–291). Cambridge, MA: Cambridge University Press.

Mednick, S. A., Huttunen, M. O., & Machon, R. A. (1994). Prenatal influenza infections and adult schizophrenia. *Schizophrenia Bulletin, 20,* 263–267.

Medvec, V. H., Madey, S. F., & Gilovich, T. (1995). When less is more: Counterfactual thinking and satisfaction among Olympic medalists. *Journal of Personality and Social Psychology, 69,* 603–610.

Mehler, J., & Bever, T. G. (1967, October 6). Cognitive capacity of very young children. *Science, 158,* 141–142.

Mehler, J., Jusczyk, P. W., Lambertz, G., Halsted, N., Bertoncini, J., & Amiel-Tison, C. (1988). A precursor of language acquisition in young infants. *Cognition, 29,* 143–178.

Melcher, J. M., & Schooler, J. W. (1996). The misremembrance of wines past: Verbal and perceptual expertise differentially mediate verbal overshadowing of taste memory. *Journal of Memory and Language, 35,* 231–245.

Meltzoff, A. N. (1995). Understanding the intentions of others: Re-enactment of intended acts by 18-month-old children. *Developmental Psychology, 31,* 838–850.

Melzack, R., & Wall, P. D. (1982). *The challenge of pain.* New York: Basic Books.

Mennella, J. A., Jagnow, C. P., & Beauchamp, G. K. (2006). Prenatal and postnatal flavor learning by human infants. *Pediatrics.* Available from http://www.pubmedcentral.nih.gov

Messias, E., Kirkpatrick, B., Bromet, E., Ross, D., Buchanan, R. W., Carpenter, W. T., Jr., et al. (2004). Summer birth and deficit schizophrenia: A pooled analysis from 6 countries. *Archives of General Psychiatry, 61,* 985–989.

Meston, C. M., & Frohlich, P. F. (2000). The neurobiology of sexual function. *Archives of General Psychiatry, 57,* 1012–1030.

Metcalfe, J., & Mischel, W. (1999). A hot/cool-system analysis of delay of gratification: Dynamics of willpower. *Psychological Review, 106,* 3–19.

Mezulis, A. H., Abramson, L. Y., Hyde, J. S., & Hankin, B. L. (2004). Is there a universal positivity bias in attributions? A meta-analytic review of individual, developmental, and culture differences in the self-serving attributional bias. *Psychological Bulletin, 130,* 711–747.

Mickelson, K. D., Kessler, R. C., & Shaver, P. R. (1997). Adult attachment in a nationally representative sample. *Journal of Personality and Social Psychology, 73,* 1092–1106.

Miller, G. (2005, July 1). How are memories stored and retrieved? *Science, 309,* 92–93.

Miller, G. E., Freedland, K. E., Carney, R. M., Stetler, C. A., & Banks, W. A. (2003). Cynical hostility, depressive symptoms, and the expression of inflammatory risk markers for coronary heart disease. *Journal of Behavioral Medicine, 26,* 501–515.

Miller, I. W., Norman, W. H., & Keitner, G. I. (1989). Cognitive-behavioral treatment of depressed inpatients: Six- and twelve-month follow-up. *American Journal of Psychiatry, 146,* 1274–1279.

Miller, L. C., & Fishkin, S. A. (1997). On the dynamics of human bonding and reproductive success: Seeking windows on the adapted-for human-environmental interface. In J. Simpson & D. T. Kenrick (Eds.), *Evolutionary social psychology* (pp. 197–236). Mahwah, NJ: Erlbaum.

Miller, R. S. (1996). *Embarrassment: Poise and peril in everyday life.* New York: Guilford Press.

Miller, R. S. (1997). We always hurt the ones we love: Aversive interactions in close relationships. In R. M. Kowalski (Ed.), *Aversive interpersonal behaviors* (pp. 11–29). New York: Plenum Press.

Miller, W. T. (2000). Rediscovering fire: Small interventions, large effects. *Psychology of Addictive Behaviors, 14,* 6–18.

Milton, J., & Wiseman, R. (2001). Does psi exist? Reply to Storm and Ertel (2001). *Psychological Bulletin, 127,* 434–438.

Mineka, S., Davidson, M., Cook, M., & Keir, R. (1984). Observational conditioning of snake fear in rhesus monkeys. *Journal of Abnormal Psychology, 93,* 355–372.

Miniño, A. M., Heron, M. P., & Smith, B. L. (2006). [Table 1, Deaths: Final data for 2004]. *National Vital Statistics Reports.* Hyattsville, MD: Centers For Disease Control and Prevention, National Center for Health Statistics.

Mirsky, A. F., Bieliauskas, L. A., French, L. M., Van Kammen, D. P., Jonsson, E., & Sedvall, G. (2000). A 39-year followup of the Genain quadruplets. *Schizophrenia Bulletin, 26,* 699–708.

Mischel, W., & Shoda, Y. (1995). A cognitive-affective system theory of personality: Reconceptualizing situations, dispositions, dynamics, and invariance in personality structure. *Psychological Review, 102,* 246–268.

Mischel, W., Shoda, Y., & Rodriguez, M. L. (1989, May 26). Delay of gratification in children. *Science, 244,* 933–938.

Mitelman, S. A., Shihabuddin, L., Brickman, A. M., Hazlett, E. A., & Buchsbaum, M. S. (2005). Volume of the cingulate and outcome in schizophrenia. *Schizophrenia Research, 72,* 91–108.

Mittal, V. A., Neumann, C., Saczawa, M., & Walker, E. F. (2008). Longitudinal progression of movement abnormalities in relation to psychotic symptoms in adolescents at high risk of schizophrenia. *Archives of General Psychiatry, 65,* 165–171.

Miyamoto, Y., & Kitayama, S. (2002). Cultural variation in correspondence bias: The critical role of attitude diagnosticity of socially constrained behavior. *Journal of Personality and Social Psychology, 83,* 1239–1248.

Mizerski, R. (1995). The relationship between cartoon trade character recognition and attitude toward product category in young children. *Journal of Marketing, 59,* 58–70.

Mobbs, D., Greicius, M. D., Abdel-Azim, E., Menon, V., & Reiss, A. L. (2003). Humor modulates the mesolimbic reward centers. *Neuron, 40,* 1041–1048.

Moffat, S. D., Hampson, E., & Hatzipantelis, E. (1998). Navigation in a "virtual" maze: Sex differences and correlation with psychometric measures of spatial ability in humans. *Evolution and Human Behavior, 19,* 73–87.

Moffitt, T. E. (2003). Life-course persistent and adolescence-limited antisocial behaviour. In B. B. Lahey, T. E. Moffit, & A. Caspi (Eds.), *Causes of conduct disorder and juvenile delinquency* (pp. 49–77). New York: Guilford Press.

Moffitt, T. E., Brammer, G. L., Caspi, A., Fawcett, J. P., Raleigh, M., Yuwiler, A., et al. (1998). Whole blood serotonin relates to violence in an epidemiological study. *Biological Psychiatry, 43,* 446–457.

Moises, H. W., & Gottesman, I. I. (2004). Does glial asthenia predispose to schizophrenia? *Archives of General Psychiatry, 61,* 1170.

Monteith, M. J. (1993). Self-regulation of prejudiced responses: Implications for progress in prejudice reduction efforts. *Journal of Personality and Social Psychology, 65,* 469–485.

Monteith, M. J., Ashburn-Nardo, L., Voils, C. I., & Czopp, A. M. (2002). Putting the brakes on prejudice: On the development and operation of cues for control. *Journal of Personality and Social Psychology, 83,* 1029–1050.

Montepare, J. M., & Vega, C. (1988). Women's vocal reactions to intimate and casual male friends. *Personality and Social Psychology Bulletin, 14,* 103–113.

Montgomery, G. H., DuHamel, K. N., & Redd, W. H. (2000). A meta-analysis of hypnotically induced analgesia: How effective is hypnosis? *International Journal of Clinical and Experimental Hypnosis, 48,* 138–153.

Morgan, R. K. (n.d.) *Information for majors.* Retrieved April 23, 2008, from http://homepages.ius.edu/RMORGAN

Morris, N. M., Udry, J. R., Khan-Dawood, F., & Dawood, M.Y. (1987). Marital sex frequency and midcycle female testosterone. *Archives of Sexual Behavior, 16,* 27–37.

Morris, W. N. (1992). A functional analysis of the role of mood in affective systems. In M. S. Clark (Ed.), *Emotion: Review of personality and social psychology* (Vol. 13, pp. 256–293). Newbury Park, CA: Sage.

Morrison, M. (n.d.) *Sports superstitions.* Retrieved November 11, 2008, from http://www.infoplease.com/spot/superstitions1.html

Morton, J., & Johnson, M. H. (1991). CONSPEC and CONLERN: A two-process theory of infant face recognition. *Psychological Review, 98,* 164–181.

Moscovitch, M. (1995). Confabulation. In D. L. Schacter (Ed.), *Memory distortions: How minds, brains, and societies reconstruct the past* (pp. 226–251). Cambridge, MA: Harvard University Press.

Moskowitz, A. K. (2004). "Scared stiff": Catatonia as an evolutionary-based fear response. *Psychological Bulletin, 111,* 984–1002.

Mowery, P. D., Brick, P. D., & Farrelly, M. (2000). Pathways to established smoking: Results from the 1999 national youth tobacco survey (Legacy First Look Report No. 3). Washington, DC: American Legacy Foundation.

Mroczek, D. K., & Kolarz, C. M.(1998). The effect of age on positive and negative affect: A developmental perspective on happiness. *Journal of Personality and Social Psychology, 75,* 1333–1349.

Mufson, L., Dorta, K. P., Wickramaratne, P., Nomura, Y., Olfson, M., & Weissman, M. M. (2004). A randomized effectiveness trial of inter-personal psychotherapy for depressed adolescents. *Archives of General Psychiatry, 61,* 577–584.

Muhle, R., Trentacoste, S.V., & Rapin, I. (2004). The genetics of autism. *Pediatrics, 113,* 472–486.

Mumford, D. B., Saeed, K., Ahmad, I., Latif, S., & Mubbashar, M. H. (1997). Stress and psychiatric disorder in rural Punjab. A community survey. *British Journal of Psychiatry, 170,* 473–478.

Munson, M. L., & Sutton, P. D. (2004). *Births, marriages, divorces, and deaths: Provisional data for May 2004* (National Vital Statistics Reports, Vol. 53, No. 8). Hyattsville, MD: Centers for Disease Control and Prevention, National Center for Health Statistics.

Murata, M. (2000). Secular trends in growth and changes in eating patterns of Japanese children. *American Journal of Clinical Nutrition, 72,* 1379–1383.

Musgrave, D. S., Vogt, M. T., Nevitt, M. C., & Cauley, J. A. (2001). Back problems among postmenopausal women taking estrogen replacement therapy: The study of osteoporotic fractures. *Spine, 26,* 1606–1612.

Mustanski, B. S., Chivers, M. L., & Bailey, J. M. (2002). A critical review of recent biological research on human sexual orientation. *Annual Review of Sex Research, 13,* 89–140.

Myers, D. G. (2000). The funds, friends, and faith of happy people. *American Psychologist, 55,* 56–67.

Nakano, K., & Kitamura, T. (2001). The relation of the anger subcomponent of type A behavior to psychological symptoms in Japanese and foreign students. *Japanese Psychological Research, 43*(1), 50–54.

Naqvi, N. H., Rudrauf, D., Damasio, H., & Bechara, A. (2007, January 27). Damage to the insula disrupts addiction to cigarette smoking. *Science, 315,* 531–534.

Nash, M., & Barnier, A. (2008). *The Oxford handbook of hypnosis.* New York: Oxford University Press.

National Human Genome Research Institute. (n.d.). *Learning about sickle cell disease.* Retrieved October 12, 2007, from http://www.genome.gov/10001219

National Institute of Drug Abuse. (2007). *NIDA InfoFacts: High School and Youth Trends* [Fact sheet]. Retrieved from http://www.nida.nih.gov/Infofacts/HSYouthtrends.html

National Institute of Drug Abuse. (2006). *NIDA Research Report: Methamphetamine Abuse and Addiction.* (NIH Publication No. 06–4210). Retrieved from http://www.nida.nih.gov/ResearchReports/methamph/methamph.html

National Research Council, Committee on Educational Interventions for Children with Autism. (2001). *Educating young children with autism.* Washington, DC: National Academy Press.

National Television Violence Study. (1997). *Technical report, 2.* Thousand Oaks, CA: Sage.

National Television Violence Study. (1998). *Technical report, 3.* Thousand Oaks, CA: Sage.

Neidemeyer, E., & Naidu, S. B. (1997). Attention deficit hyperactivity disorder (ADHD) and frontal-motor cortex disconnection. *Clinical Electroencephalography, 28,* 130–135.

Neisser, U., Boodoo, G., Bouchard, T. J., Jr., Boykin, A. W., Brody, N., Ceci, S. J., et al. (1996). Intelligence: Knowns and unknowns. *American Psychologist, 51,* 77–101.

Neisser, U., & Harsch, N. (1993). Phantom flashbulbs: False recollections of hearing the news about Challenger. In E. Winograd & U. Neisser (Eds.), *Affect and accuracy in recall: Studies of "flashbulb" memories* (pp. 9–31). New York: Cambridge University Press.

Nelson, G. (1998, April 29). The observatory: You don't have to be a rocket scientist to think like one. *Minneapolis Star Tribune,* p. 14.

Nelson, K. B., Grether, J. K., Croen, L. A., Dambrosia, J. M., Dickens, B. F., Jelliffe, L. L., et al. (2001). Neuropeptides and neurotrophins in neonatal blood of children with autism or mental retardation. *Annals of Neurology, 49,* 597–606.

Nelson, R. M., & DeBacker, T. K. (2008). Achievement motivation in adolescents: The role of peer climate and best friends. *Journal of Experimental Education, 76*(2), 170–189.

Neylan, T. C., Canick, J. D., Hall, S. E., Reus, V. I., Spolosky, R. M., & Wolkowitz, O. M. (2001). Cortisol levels predict cognitive impairment induced by electroconvulsive therapy. *Biological Psychiatry, 50,* 331–336.

Ng, D. M., & Jeffrey, E. W. (2003). Relationships between perceived stress and health behaviors in a sample of working adults. *Health Psychology, 22,* 638–642.

Nicholas, J. G., & Geers, A. E. (2006). Effects of early auditory experience on the spoken language of deaf children at 3 years of age. *Ear & Hearing, 27*(3), 286–298.

Nicolini, H., Bakish, D., Duenas, H., Spann, M., Erickson, J., Hallberg, C., et al. (2008). Improvement of psychic and somatic symptoms in adult patients with generalized anxiety disorder: Examination from a duloxetine, venlafaxine extended-release and placebo-controlled trial. *Psychological Medicine, 19,* 1–10.

Nisbett, R. E. (2003). *The geography of thought.* New York: Free Press.

Nisbett, R. E., Peng, K., Choi, I., & Norenzayan, A. (2001). Culture and systems of thought: Holistic versus analytic cognition. *Psychological Review, 108,* 291–310.

Nisbett, R. E., & Ross, L. (1980). *Human inferences: Strategies and shortcomings of social judgment.* Englewood Cliffs, NJ: Prentice-Hall.

Nisbett, R. E., & Wilson, T. D. (1977). Telling more than we can know: Verbal reports on mental processes. *Psychological Review, 84,* 231–259.

Nishino, S. (2007). Narcolepsy: Pathophysiology and pharmacology. *Journal of Clinical Psychiatry, 68*(Suppl. 13), 9–15.

Noftle, E. E., & Robins, R. W. (2007). Personality predictors of academic outcomes: Big five correlates of GPA and SAT scores. *Journal of Personality and Social Psychology, 93,* 116–130.

Norem, J. K. (1989). Cognitive strategies as personality: Effectiveness, specificity, flexibility and change. In D. M. Buss & N. Cantor (Eds.), *Personality psychology: Recent trends and emerging issues* (pp. 45–60). New York: Springer-Verlag.

Norman, K. A., Polyn, S. M., Detre, G. J., & Haxby, J. V. (2006). Beyond mind-reading: Multi-voxel pattern analysis of fMRI data. *Trends in Cognitive Sciences, 10,* 424–423.

Norton, M. I., Frost, J. A., & Ariely, D. (2007). Less is more: The lure of ambiguity, or why familiarity breeds contempt. *Journal of Personality and Social Psychology, 92,* 97–106.

Novotny, S. L., Hollander, E., Allen, A., Aronowitz, B. R., DeCaria, C., Cartwright, C., et al. (2000). Behavioral response to oxytocin challenge in adult autistic disorders. *Biological Psychiatry, 47,* 52.

Noyes, R. (1991). Suicide and panic disorder: A review. *Journal of Affective Disorders, 22,* 1–11.

Nurco, D. N., Hanlon, T. E., & Kinlock, T. W. (1991). Recent research on the relationship between illicit drug use and crime. *Behavioral Sciences and the Law, 9,* 221–249.

Nurnberger, J. J., Goldin, L. R., & Gershon, E. S. (1994). Genetics of psychiatric disorders. In G. Winokur & P. M. Clayton (Eds.), *The medical basis of psychiatry* (pp. 459–492). Philadelphia: W. B. Saunders.

O'Brien, C., & Cornish, J. W. (2006). Naltrexone for probationers and parolees. *Journal of Substance Abuse Treatment, 31,* 107–111.

Oberauer, K., Schulze, R., Wilhelm, O., & Süß, H. M. (2005). Working memory and intelligence—their correlation and their relation: Comment on Ackerman, Beier, and Boyle (2005). *Psychological Bulletin, 131,* 61–65.

Obot, I. S., & Room, R. (2005). *Alcohol, gender and drinking problems: Perspectives from low and middle income countries.* Geneva, Switzerland: World Health Organization.

O'Brien, C. P., Woody, G. E., & McLellan, A. T. (1986). A new tool in the treatment of impaired physicians. *Philadelphia Medicine, 82,* 442–446.

Ochsner, K. N., Bunge, S. A., Gross, J. J., & Gabrieli, J. D. E. (2002). Rethinking feelings: An fMRI study of the cognitive regulation of emotion. *Journal of Cognitive Neuroscience, 14,* 1215–1299.

Oei, N. Y. L., Everaerd, W. T. A. M., Elzinga, B. M., Van Well, S. & Bermond, B. (2006). Psychosocial stress impairs working memory at high loads: An association with cortisol levels and memory retrieval. *Stress, 9,* pp. 133–141.

Ogbu, J. U. (1994). From cultural differences to differences in cultural frames of reference. In P. M. Greenfield & R. R. Cocking (Eds.), *Cross cultural roots of minority child development* (pp. 365–392). Hillsdale, NJ: Erlbaum.

O'Kane, G. O., Kensinger, E. A., & Corkin, S. (2004). Evidence for semantic learning in profound amnesia: An investigation with the patient H. M. *Hippocampus, 14,* 417–425.

Olanow, C. W., Goetz, C. G., Kordower, J. H., Stoessl, A. J., Sossi, V., Brin, M. F., et al. (2003). A double-blind controlled trial of bilateral fetal nigral transplantation in Parkinson's disease. *Annals of Neurology, 54,* 403–414.

Olds, J. (1962). Hypothalamic substrates of reward. *Psychological Review, 42,* 554–604.

Olds, J., & Milner, P. (1954). Positive reinforcement produced by electrical stimulation of the septal area and other regions of the rat brain. *Journal of Comparative and Physiological Psychology, 47,* 419–428.

O'Leary, S. G. (1995). Parental discipline mistakes. *Current Directions in Psychological Science, 4,* 11–13.

Olfson, M., Marcus, S. C., Druss, B., Elinson, L., Tanielian, T., & Pincus, H. A. (2002). National trends in the outpatient treatment of depression. *Journal of the American Medical Association, 287,* 203–209.

Olfson, M., Shaffer, D., Marcus, S. C., & Greenberg, T. (2003). Relationship between antidepressant medication treatment and suicide in adolescents. *Archives of General Psychiatry, 60,* 978–982.

Olson, R., Hogan, L., & Santos, L. (2006). Illuminating the history of psychology: Tips for teaching students about the Hawthorne studies. *Psychology Learning and Teaching, 5,* 110–118.

Olsson, A., Ebert, J. P., Banaji, M. R., & Phelps, E. A. (2005, July 29). The role of social groups in the persistence of learned fear. *Science, 309,* 785–787.

Olsson, A., Nearing, K. I., & Phelps, E. A. (2007). Learning fears by observing others: The neural systems of social fear transmission. *Social Cognitive and Affective Neuroscience Advance Access, 2,* 3–11.

Olsson, A., & Phelps, E. A. (2007). Social learning of fear. *Nature Neuroscience, 10,* 1095–1102.

Oltmans, T. F., Neale, J. M., & Davison, G. C. (Eds.). (1999). *Case studies in abnormal psychology.* New York: Wiley.

O'Neal, J. M. (1984). First person account: Finding myself and loving it. *Schizophrenia Bulletin, 10,* 109–110.

O'Neil, J. (2004, December 29). Slow-motion miracle: One boy's journey out of autism's grasp. *The New York Times,* p. B8.

O'Neil, S. (1999). Flow theory and the development of musical performance skills. *Bulletin of the Council for Research in Music Education, 141*, 129–134.

Onishi, K. H., & Baillargeon, R. (2005, April 8). Do 15-month-old infants understand false beliefs? *Science, 308*, 255–258.

Ortigue, S., Bianchi-Demicheli, F., Hamilton, C., & Grafton, S. T. (2007, July). The neural basis of love as a subliminal prime: An event-related functional magnetic resonance imaging study. *Journal of Cognitive Neuroscience, 19*(7), 1218–1230.

Osterling, J., & Dawson, G. (1994). Early recognition of children with autism: A study of first birthday home videotapes. *Journal of Autism and Developmental Disorders, 24*, 247–257.

O'Toole, A. J., Jiang, F., Abdi, H., & Haxby, J.V. (2005). Partially distributed representations of objects and faces in ventral temporal cortex. *Journal of Cognitive Neuroscience, 17*, 580–590.

Ottieger, A. E., Tressell, P. A., Inciardi, J. A., & Rosales, T. A. (1992). Cocaine use patterns and overdose. *Journal of Psychoactive Drugs, 24*, 399–410.

Owen, A. M., Coleman, M. R., Boly, M., Davis, M. H., Laureys, S., & Pickard, J. D. (2006). Detecting awareness in the vegetative state. *Science, 313*, 1402.

Pagnoni, G., & Cekic, M. (2007). Age effects on gray matter volume and attentional performance in Zen meditation. *Neurobiology of Aging, 28*, 1623–1627.

Paller, K. A., & Wagner, A. D. (2002). Observing the transformation of experience into memory. *Trends in Cognitive Science, 6*, 93–102.

Panksepp, J. (1992). Oxytocin effects on emotional processes: Separation distress, social bonding, and relationships to psychiatric disorders. *Annals of the New York Academy of Sciences, 652*, 243–252.

Papadimitrious, G. N., Zervas, I. M., & Papakostas, Y. G. (2001). Unilateral ECT for prophylaxis in affective illness. *Journal of ECT, 17*, 229–231.

Paquette, V., Levesque, J., Mensour, B., Leroux, J. M., Beaudoin, G., Bourgouin, P., et al. (2003). "Change the mind and you change the brain": Effects of cognitive-behavioral therapy on the neural correlates of spider phobia. *Neuroimage, 18*, 401–409.

Pascual-Leone, A. Catala, M. D., & Pascual-Leone, P. A. (1996). Lateralized effect of rapid-rate transcranial magnetic stimulation of the prefrontal cortex on mood. *Neurology, 46*, 499–502.

Pasupathi, M., & Carstensen, L. L. (2003). Age and emotional experience during mutual reminiscing. *Psychology and Aging, 18*, 430–442.

Patterson, B. W. (2004). The "tyranny of the eyewitness." *Law & Psychology Review, 28*, 195–203.

Patterson, C. M., & Newman, J. P. (1993). Reflectivity and learning from aversive events: Toward a psychological mechanism for the syndromes of disinhibition. *Psychological Review, 100*, 716–736.

Patterson, D., & Jensen, M. (2003). Hypnosis and clinical pain. *Psychological Bulletin, 129*(4), 495–521.

Paul-Labrador, M., Polk, D., Dwyer, J. H., Velasquez, I., Nidich, S., Rainforth, M., et al. (2006). Effects of a randomized controlled trial of transcendental meditation on components of the metabolic syndrome in subjects with coronary heart disease. *Archives of Internal Medicine, 166*, 1218–1224.

Pauls, D. L. (2008). The genetics of obsessive compulsive disorder: A review of the evidence. *American Journal of Medical Genetics, 148C*, 133–139.

Pavot, W., & Diener, E. (1993). Review of the satisfaction with life Scale. *Psychological Assessment, 5*, 164–172.

Paykel, E. S. (2003). Life events and affective disorders. *Acta Psychiatrica Scandinavica, 108*, 61–66.

Payne, B. K. (2001). Prejudice and perception: The role of automatic and controlled processes in misperceiving a weapon. *Journal of Personality and Social Psychology, 81*, 181–192.

Paz-Elizur, T., Krupsky, M., Blumenstein, S., Elinger, D., Schechtman, E., & Livneh, Z. (2003). DNA repair activity for oxidative damage and risk of lung cancer. *Journal of the National Cancer Institute, 95*, 1312–1331.

Pegna, A. J., Khateb, A., Lazeyras, F., & Seghier, M. L. (2005). Discriminating emotional faces without primary visual cortices involves the right amygdala. *Nature Neuroscience, 8*, 24–25.

Pelham, W. E., McBurnett, K., Harper, G. W., Milich, R., Murphy, D. A., Clinton, J., et al. (1990). Methylphenidate and baseball playing in ADHD children: Who's on first? *Journal of Consulting and Clinical Psychology, 58*, 130–133.

Pelham, W., & Bender, M. E. (1982). Peer relationships in hyperactive children: Description and treatment. In K. D. Gadow & I. Bailer (Eds.), *Advances in learning and behavioral disabilities: A research annual*. Greenwich, CT: JAI Press.

Penfield, W., & Jasper, H. (1954). *Epilepsy and the functional anatomy of the human brain*. Boston: Little, Brown.

Pennebaker, J. W. (1990). *Opening up: The healing power of confiding in others*. New York: Morrow.

Pennebaker, J. W. (1995). *Emotion, disclosure, & health*. Washington, DC: American Psychological Association.

Pennebaker, J. W., Barger, S. D., & Tiebout, J. (1989). Disclosure of traumas and health among Holocaust survivors. *Psychosomatic Medicine, 51*(5), 577–589.

Pennebaker, J. W., & Beall, S. K. (1986). Confronting a traumatic event: Toward an understanding of inhibition and disease. *Journal of Abnormal Psychology, 95*, 274–281.

Pennebaker, J. W., Mayne, T. J., & Francis, M. E. (1997). Linguistic predictors of adaptive bereavement. *Journal of Personality and Social Psychology, 72*, 863–871.

Pennisi, E. (2007, December 21). Breakthrough of the year. Human genetic variation. *Science, 318*, 1842–1843.

Penton-Voak, I. S., Perrett, D. I., Castles, D., Burt, M., Koyabashi, T., & Murray, L. K. (1999). Female preference for male faces changes cyclically. *Nature, 399*, 741–742.

Peretz, I. (1996). Can we lose memory for music? A case of music agnosia in a nonmusician. *Journal of Cognitive Neuroscience, 8*, 481–496.

Peretz, I., & Zatorre, R. J. (2005). Brain organization for music processing. *Annual Review of Psychology, 56*, 89–114.

Perkins, W. J. (2007, February/March). How does anesthesia work? *Scientific American Mind*, 84.

Perrett, D. I., May, K. A., & Yoshikawa, S. (1994). Facial shape and judgments of female attractiveness. *Nature, 368*, 239–242.

Pessiglione, M., Schmidt, L., Draganski, B., Kalisch, R., Lau, H., Dolan, R. J., et al. (2007, May 11). How the brain translates money into force: A neuroimaging study of subliminal motivation. *Science, 316*, 904–906.

Petitto, L. A. (2000). On the biological foundations of human language. In H. Lane & K. Emmorey (Eds.), *The signs of language revisited* (pp. 447–471). Mahwah, NJ: Erlbaum.

Petitto, L. A., & Seidenberg, M. S. (1979). On the evidence for linguistic abilities in signing apes. *Brain and Language, 8,* 162–183.

Petrie, K. J., Fontanilla, I., Thomas, M. G., Booth, R. J., & Pennebaker, J. W. (2004). Effect of written emotional expression on immune function in patients with human immunodeficiency virus infection: A randomized trial. *Psychosomatic Medicine, 66,* 272–275.

Petronis, A., & Kennedy, J. L. (1995). Unstable genes—unstable mind? *American Journal of Psychiatry, 152,* 164–172.

Pett, M. A., Wampold, B. E., Turner, C. W., & Vaughan-Cole, B. (1999). Paths of influence of divorce on preschool children's psychosocial adjustment. *Journal of Family Psychology, 13,* 145–164.

Petty, R. E., & Cacioppo, J. T. (1986). Communication and persuasion: Central and peripheral routes to attitude change. New York: Springer-Verlag.

Phelan, J. (2006). Foreword. In A. Ziv, *Breeding between the lines: Why interracial people are healthier and more attractive.* Lanham, MD: National Book Network.

Phelps, E. A. (2004). Human emotion and memory: Interactions of the amygdala and hippocampal complex. *Current Opinion in Neurobiology, 14,* 198–202.

Phelps, E. A. (2006). Emotion and cognition: Insights from studies of the human amygdala. *Annual Review of Psychology, 57,* 27–53.

Phelps, E. A., O'Connor, K. J., Cunningham, W. A., Funayama, E. S., Gatenby, J. C., Gore, J. C., et al. (2000). Performance on indirect measures of race evaluation predicts amygdala activation. *Journal of Cognitive Neuroscience, 12,* 729–738.

Phinney, J. S. (1990). Ethnic identity in adolescents and adults: Review of research. *Psychological Bulletin, 108,* 499–514.

Pinker, S. (1984). *Language learnability and language development.* Cambridge, MA: Harvard University Press.

Pinker, S. (1994). *The language instinct.* New York: Morrow.

Pitman, R., Sanders, K., Zusman, R., Healy, A., Cheema, F., Lasko, N., et al. (2002). Pilot study of secondary prevention of posttraumatic stress disorder with propranolol. *Biological Psychiatry, 51,* 189–192.

Piven, J., Arndt, S., Bailey, J., Havercamp, S., Andreasen, N. C., & Palmer, P. (1995). An MRI study of brain size in autism. *American Journal of Psychiatry, 152,* 1145–1149.

Plakun, E. M., Burkhardt, P. E., & Muller, A. P. (1985). Fourteen-year follow-up of borderline and schizotypal personality disorders. *Comprehensive Psychiatry, 26,* 448–455.

Plant, E. A., Hyde, J. S., Keltner, D., & Devine, P. G. (2000). The gender stereotyping of emotions. *Psychology of Women Quarterly, 24,* 81–92.

Plant, E. A., & Peruche, M. (2005). The consequences of race for police officers' responses to criminal suspects. *Psychological Science, 16,* 180–183.

Plomin, R., & Caspi, A. (1999). Behavioral genetics and personaliity. In L. A. Pervin & O. P. John (Eds.), *Handbook of personality: Theory and research* (2nd ed., pp. 251–276). New York: Guilford Press.

Plomin, R., & Spinath, F. M. (2002). Genetics and general cognitive ability (g). *Trends in Cognitive Sciences, 6,* 169–176.

Plomin, R., & Spinath, F. M. (2004). Intelligence: Genetics, genes, and genomics. *Journal of Personality and Social Psychology, 86,* 112–129.

Polivy, J., & Herman, C. P. (1985). Dieting and bingeing: A causal analysis. *American Psychologist, 40,* 193–201.

Pollock, K. M. (2004). Exercise in treating depression: Broadening the psychotherapist's role. *Journal of Clinical Psychology, 57,* 1289–1300.

Posner, M. I., & DiGirolamo, G. J. (2000). Cognitive neuroscience: Origins and promise. *Psychological Bulletin, 126,* 873–889.

Premack, D. (1970). Mechanisms of self-control. In W. A. Hunt (Ed.), *Learning mechanisms in smoking* (pp. 107–123). Chicago: Aldine.

Prentiss, D., Power, R., Balmas, G., Tzuang, G., & Israelski, D. (2004). Patterns of marijuana use among patients with HIV/AIDS followed in a public health care setting. *Journal of Acquired Immune Deficiency Syndromes, 35*(1), 38–45.

President's Council on Bioethics. (2003, March). *"Better" memories? The promise and perils of pharmacological interventions* (Staff Working Paper). Retrieved from http://www.bioethics.gov/background/better_memories.html

President's Council on Bioethics. (2003, January). *Ethical aspects of sex control* (Staff Working Paper). Retrieved from http://www.bioethics.gov/background/sex_control.html

Price, D. D., Harkins, S. W., & Baker, C. (1987). Sensory-affective relationships among different types of clinical and experimental pain. *Pain, 28,* 297–307.

Program on International Policy Attitudes (PIPA)/Knowledge Networks Poll. (2004, October 21). *Bush supporters still believe Iraq had WMD or major program, supported al Qaeda* [Press release]. Retrieved from http://www.pipa.org/OnlineReports/Iraq/IraqRealities_Oct04/IraqRealitiesOct04rpt.pdf

Pylyshyn, Z. (1984). *Computation and cognition.* Cambridge, MA: MIT Press.

Pyszczynski, T., Greenberg, J., Solomon, S., Arndt, J., & Schimel, J. (2004). Why do people need self-esteem? A theoretical and empirical review. *Psychological Bulletin, 130,* 435–468.

Raesaenen, S., Pakaslahti, A., Syvaelahti, E., Jones, P. B., & Isohanni, M. (2000). Sex differences in schizophrenia: A review. *Nordic Journal of Psychiatry, 54,* 37–45.

Raine, A. (1989). Evoked potentials and psychopathy. *International Journal of Psychopathology, 8,* 1–16.

Raine, A., Mellingen, K., Liu, J., Venables, P., & Mednick, S. A. (2003). Effects of environmental enrichment at ages 3–5 years on schizotypal personality and antisocial behavior at ages 17 and 23 years. *American Journal of Psychiatry, 160,* 1627–1635.

Rainville, P., Duncan, G. H., Price, D. D., Carrier, B., & Bushnell, M. C. (1997, August 15). Pain affect encoded in human anterior cingulate but not somatosensory cortex. *Science, 277,* 968–971.

Rainville, P., Hofbauer, R. K., Bushnell, M. C., Duncan, G. H., & Price, D. D. (2002). Hypnosis modulates activity in brain structures involved in the regulation of consciousness. *Journal of Cognitive Neuroscience, 14,* 887–901.

Rakic, P. (2000). Molecular and cellular mechanisms of neuronal migration: Relevance to cortical epilepsies. *Advances in Neurology, 84,* 1–14.

Raleigh, M. J., McGuire, M. T., Brammer, G. L., Pollack, D. B., & Yuwiler, A. (1991). Serotonergic mechanisms promote dominance in adult male vervet monkeys. *Brain Research, 559,* 181–190.

Ramachandran, V. S. (2003). Lecture 2: Synapses and the self. Retrieved from BBC Radio 4, *The Reith Lectures 2003: The emerging mind website* at http://www.bbc.co.uk/print/radio4/reith2003/lecture2.shtml

Ramachandran, V. S., & Hirstein, W. (1998). The perception of phantom limbs: The D. O. Hebb lecture. *Brain, 121*, 1603–1630.

Ramachandran, V. S., & Hubbard, E. M. (2001). Psychophysical investigations into the neural basis of synaesthesia. *Proceedings of the Royal Society of London, 268B*, 979–983.

Ramachandran, V. S., & Hubbard, E. M. (2003, May). Hearing colors, tasting shapes: Color-coded world. *Scientific American, 288*(5) 42–49.

Rampon, C., Jiang, C. H., Dong, H., Tang, Y., Lockhart, D. J., Schultz, P. G., et al. (2000). Effects of environmental enrichment on gene expression in the brain. *Proceedings of the National Academy of Sciences, USA, 97*, 12880–12884.

Rapoport, J. (1990). *The boy who couldn't stop washing: The experience and treatment of obsessive-compulsive disorder.* New York: Penguin.

Rapoport, J. L. (1989, March). The biology of obsessions and compulsions. *Scientific American, 260*, 83–89.

Rapoport, J. L. (1991). Recent advances in obsessive-compulsive disorder. *Neuropsychopharmacology, 5*, 1–10.

Rauch, S. L., van der Kolk, B. A., Fisler, R. E., & Alpert, N. M. (1996). A symptom provocation study of posttraumatic stress disorder using positron emission tomography and script-driven imagery. *Archives of General Psychiatry, 53*, 380–387.

Rauscher, F. H., Shaw, G. L., & Ky, K. N. (1993). Usic and spatial task performance. *Nature, 365*, 611.

Rayner, K., Foorman, B. R., Perfetti, C. A., Pesetsky, D., & Seidenberg, M. S. (2001). How psychological science informs the teaching of reading. *Psychological Science in the Public Interest, 2*, 31–74.

Raz, A., Fan, J., & Posner, M. I. (2005). Hypnotic suggestion reduces conflict in the human brain. *Proceedings of the National Academy of Sciences, USA, 102*, 9978–9983.

Raz, A., Shapiro, T., Fan, J., & Posner, M. I. (2002, December). Hypnotic suggestion and the modulation of Stroop interference. *Archives of General Psychiatry, 59*, 1155–1161.

Read, J. P., & Brown, R. A. (2003). The role of exercise in alcoholism treatment and recovery. *Professional Psychology: Research and Practice, 34*, 49–56.

Reeves, L. M., & Weisberg, R. W. (1994). The role of content and abstract information in analogical transfer. *Psychological Bulletin, 115*, 381–400.

Regard, M., & Landis, T. (1997). "Gourmand syndrome": Eating passion associated with right anterior lesions. *Neurology, 48*, 1185–1190.

Rehman, J., & Herlitz, A. (2006). Women remember more faces than men do. *Acta Psychologica, 124*, 344–355.

Reinders, A. A., Nijenhuis, E. R., Paans, A. M., Korf, J., Willemsen, A. T., & den Boer, J. A. (2003). One brain, two selves. *Neuroimage, 20*, 2119–2125.

Reis, D. L., Brackett, M. A., Shamosh, N. A., Kiehl, K. A., Salovey, P., & Gray, J. R. (2007). Emotional intelligence predicts individual differences in social exchange reasoning. *Neuroimage, 35*, 1385–1391.

Renfrow, P. J., & Gosling, S. D. (2003). The do re mi's of everyday life: The structure and personality correlates of music preferences. *Journal of Personality and Social Psychology, 84*, 1236–1256.

Rescorla, R. (1966). Predictability and number of pairings in Pavlovian fear conditioning. *Psychonomic Science, 4*, 383–384.

Rescorla, R. A., & Wagner, A. R. (1972). A theory of Pavlovian conditioning: Variations in the effectiveness of reinforcement and non-reinforcement. In A. H. Black & W. F. Prokosy (Eds.), *Classical conditioning II: Current research and theory* (pp. 64–99). New York: Appleton-Century-Crofts.

Revonsuo, A. (2000). *Prospects for a scientific research program on consciousness—neural correlates of consciousness.* Cambridge, MA: MIT Press.

Rhodes, G., Byatt, G., Michie, P. T., & Puce, A. (2004). Is the fusiform face area specialized for faces, individuation, or expert individuation? *Journal of Cognitive Neuroscience, 16*, 189–203.

Rhodewalt, F., & Morf, C. C. (1998). On self-aggrandizement and anger: A temporal analysis of narcissism and affective reactions to success and failure. *Journal of Personality and Social Psychology, 74*, 672–685.

Richeson, J. A., Baird, A. A., Gordon, H. L., Heatherton, T. F., Wyland, C. L., Trawalter, S., et al. (2003). An fMRI investigation of the impact of interracial contact on executive function. *Nature Neuroscience, 6*, 1323–1328.

Richeson, J. A., & Trawalter, S. (2008). The threat of appearing prejudiced and race-based attentional biases. *Psychological Science, 19*, 98–102.

Richman, L. S., Kubzansky, L., Maselko, J., Kawachi, I., Choo, P., & Bauer, M. (2005). Positive emotion and health: Going beyond the negative. *Health Psychology, 24*(4), 422–429.

Ridley, M. (2003). *Nature versus nurture: Genes, experience, and what makes us human.* New York: HarperCollins.

Rifkin, A., & Rifkin, W. (2004). Adolescents with depression. *Journal of the American Medical Association, 292*, 2577–2578.

Rinck, M., Reinecke, A., Ellwart, T., Heuer, K., & Becker, E. S. (2005). Speeded detection and increased distraction in fear of spiders: Evidence from eye movements. *Journal of Abnormal Psychology, 114*, 235–248.

Rizzolatti, G., & Arbib, M. A. (1998). Language within our grasp. *Trends in Neuroscience, 21*, 188–194.

Rizzolatti, G., & Craighero, L. (2004). The mirror-neuron system. *Annual Reviews in Neuroscience, 27*, 169–192.

Rizzolatti, G., Fadiga, L., Gallese, V., & Fogassi, L. (1996). Premotor cortex and the recognition of motor actions. *Cognitive Brain Research, 3*, 131–141.

Roberts, B. W., Walton, K. E., & Viechtbauer, W. (2006). Patterns of mean-level change in personality traits across the life course: A meta-analysis of longitudinal studies. *Psychological Bulletin, 132*, 3–21.

Roberts, D. F. (2000). Media and youth: Access, exposure, and privatization. *Journal of Adolescent Health 27*(Suppl.), 8–14.

Roberts, S. (2006, November 15). A neuroscientist life's work: Analyzing brains to study structure and cognition. *The New York Times.* Retrieved from http://www.nytimes.com

Robins, L. N., Helzer, J. E., & Davis, D. H. (1975). Narcotic use in Southeast Asia and afterward: An interview study of 898 Vietnam returnees. *Archives of General Psychiatry, 32*, 955–961.

Robins, L. N., & Regier, D. A. (1991). *Psychiatric disorders in America: The epidemiological catchment areas study.* New York: Free Press.

Rock, I. (1984). *Perception.* New York: Scientific American Books.

Roediger, H. L., III, & Karpicke, J. D. (2006). The power of testing memory: Basic research and implications for educational practice. *Psychological Science, 1*, 181–210.

Roediger, H. L., & McDermott, K. B. (1995). Creating false memories: Remembering words not presented in lists. *Journal of Experimental Psychology: Learning, Memory, and Cognition, 21*, 803–814.

Rogan, M. T., Stäubli, U. V., & LeDoux, J. E. (1997). Fear conditioning induces associative long-term potentiation in the amygdala. *Nature, 390*, 604–607.

Rogers, T. B., Kuiper, N. A., & Kirker, W. S. (1977). Self-reference and the encoding of personal information. *Journal of Personality and Social Psychology, 35*, 677–688.

Roisman, G. I., Clausell, E., Holland, A., Fortuna, K., & Elieff, C. (2008). Adult romantic relationships as contexts of human development: A multimethod comparison of same-sex couples with opposite-sex dating, engaged, and married dyads. *Developmental Psychology, 44*, 91–101.

Rolls, B. J., Roe, L. S., & Meengs, J. S. (2007). The effect of large portion sizes on energy intake is sustained for 11 days. *Obesity Research, 15*, 1535–1543.

Rolls, E. T. (2007). Sensory processing in the brain related to the control of food intake. *Proceedings of the Nutritional Society, 66*, 96–112.

Rolls, E. T., Burton, M. J., & Mora, F. (1980). Neurophysiological analysis of brain-stimulation reward in the monkey. *Brain Research, 194*, 339–357.

Rolls, E. T., Murzi, E., Yaxley, S., Thorpe, S. J., & Simpson, S. J. (1986). Sensory-specific satiety: Food-specific reduction in responsiveness of ventral forebrain neurons after feeding in the monkey. *Brain Research, 368*, 79–86.

Rosenbluth, M., & Silver, D. (1992). The inpatient treatment of borderline personality disorder. In D. Silver & M. Rosenbluth (Eds.), *Handbook of borderline disorders.* Madison, CT: International Universities Press.

Rosenman, R. H., Brand, R. J., Jenkins, C. D., Friedman, M., Straus, R., & Wurm, M. (1975). Coronary heart disease in the Western Collaborative Group Study: Final follow-up experience of $8\frac{1}{2}$ years. *Journal of the American Medical Association, 233*, 872–877.

Rosenstein, D., & Oster, H. (1988). Differential facial responses to four basic tastes in newborns. *Child Development, 59*, 1555–1568.

Rosenthal, D., (Ed). (1963). *The Genain quadruplets.* New York: Basic Books.

Rosenzweig, M. R., Bennett, E. L., & Diamond, M. C. (1972, February). Brain changes in response to experience. *Scientific American, 226*, 22–29.

Ross, D. M., & Ross, S. A. (1982). *Hyperactivity: Research, theory, and action.* New York: Wiley.

Roth, T. (2007). Narcolepsy: Treatment issues. *Journal of Clinical Psychiatry, 68*(Suppl. 13), 16–19.

Rothbaum, B. O., Hodges, L., Alarcon, R., Ready, D., Shahar, F., Graap, K., et al. (1999). Virtual reality exposure therapy for PTSD Vietnam veterans: A case study. *Journal of Traumatic Stress, 12*, 263–271.

Rothemund, Y., Preuschhof, C., Bohner, G., Bauknecht, H. C., Klingebiel, R., Flor, H., et al. (2007). Differential activation of the dorsal striatum by high-calorie visual food stimuli in obese individuals. *Neuroimage, 37*, 410–421.

Rotter, J. B. (1954). *Social learning and clinical psychology.* New York: Prentice-Hall.

Rovee-Collier, C. (1999). The development of infant memory. *Current Directions in Psychological Science, 8*, 80–85.

Rowe, D. C., Chassin, L., Presson, C., & Sherman, S. J. (1996). Parental smoking and the "epidemic" spread of cigarette smoking. *Journal of Applied Social Psychology, 26*, 437–445.

Rozin, P. (1996). Sociocultural influences on human food selection. In E. D. Capaldi (Ed.), *Why we eat what we eat: The psychology of eating* (pp. 233–263). Washington, DC: American Psychological Association.

Rozin, P., & Kalat, J. W. (1971). Specific hungers and poison avoidance as adaptive specializations of learning. *Psychological Review, 78*, 459–486.

Rubenstein, A. J., Kalakanis, L., & Langlois, J. H. (1999). Infant preferences for attractive faces: A cognitive explanation. *Developmental Psychology, 35*, 848–855.

Rudman, L. A., & Goodwin, S. A. (2004). Gender differences in automatic in-group bias: Why do women like women more than men like men? *Journal of Personality and Social Psychology, 87*, 494–509.

Rusbult, C. E., & Van Lange, P. A. M. (1996). Interdependence processes. In E. T. Higgins & A. Kruglanski (Eds.), *Social psychology: Handbook of basic principles* (pp. 564–596). New York: Guilford Press.

Ruscio, A. M., Brown, T. A., Chiu, W. T., Sareen, J., Stein, M. B., & Kessler, R. C. (2008). Social fears and social phobia in the USA: Results from the national comorbidity survey replication. *Psychological Medicine, 35*, 15–28.

Russell, C. A., Clapp, J. D., & Dejong, W. (2005). Done 4: Analysis of a failed social norms marketing campaign. *Health Communication, 17*(1), 57–65.

Russell, J. A. (1980). A circumplex model of affect. *Journal of Personality and Social Psychology, 39*, 1161–1178.

Russell, J. A. (1994). Is there universal recognition of emotion from facial expressions? A review of the cross-cultural studies. *Psychological Bulletin, 115*, 102–141.

Russell, J. A., & Barrett, L. F. (1999). Core affect, prototypical emotional episodes, and other things called emotion: Dissecting the elephant. *Journal of Personality and Social Psychology, 76*, 805–819.

Russell, M. A. H. (1990). The nicotine trap: A 40-year sentence for four cigarettes. *British Journal of Addiction, 85*, 293–300.

Rutter, M. (2005). Incidence of autism disorders: Changes over time and their meaning. *Acta Paediatrica, 94*, 2–15.

Ruys, K. I., & Stapel, D. A. (2008). Emotion elicitor or emotion messenger? Subliminal priming reveals two faces of facial expressions. *Psychological Science, 19*, 593–600.

Rymer, R. (1993). *Genie: A scientific tragedy.* New York: HarperCollins.

Sabol, S. Z., Nelson, M. L., Fisher, C., Gunzerath, L., Brody, C. L., Hu, S., et al. (1999). A genetic association for cigarette smoking behavior. *Health Psychology, 18*, 7–13.

Sacks, O. (1995). *An anthropologist on Mars: Seven paradoxical tales.* New York: Knopf.

Saha, S., Chant, D. C., Welham, J. L., & McGrath, J. J. (2006). The incidence and prevalence of schizophrenia varies with latitude. *Acta Psychiatrica Scandinavica, 114*, 36–39.

Salekin, R. T., Rogers, R., & Sewell, K. W. (1996). A review and meta-analysis of the psychopathy checklist and psychopathy checklist—revised: Predictive validity of dangerousness. *Clinical Psychology: Science and Practice, 3*, 203–213.

Salovey, P., & Grewal, D. (2005). The science of emotional intelligence. *Current Directions in Psychological Science, 14*, 281–286.

Salovey, P., & Mayer, J. D. (1990). Emotional intelligence. *Imagination, Cognition, and Personality, 9*, 185–211.

Salthouse, T. (1992). The information-processing perspective on cognitive aging. In R. Sternberg & C. Berg (Eds.), *Intellectual development* (pp. 261–277). Cambridge, UK: Cambridge University Press.

Sanderson, W. C., & Barlow, D. H. (1990). A description of patients diagnosed with DSM-III-R generalized anxiety disorder. *The Journal of Nervous and Mental Disease, 178*, 588–591.

Sapolsky, R. M. (1994). *Why zebras don't get ulcers*. New York: Freeman.

Sapolsky, R. M. (2004, December). Stressed-out memories. *Scientific American Mind*, 28.

Sargent, J. D., Beach, M. L., Adachi-Mejia, A. M., Gibson, J. J., Titus-Ernstoff, L. T., Carusi, C. P., et al. (2005). Exposure to movie smoking: Its relation to smoking initiation among US adolescents. *Pediatrics, 116*, 1183–1191.

Savic, I., Berglund, H., & Lindström, P. (2005). Brain responses to putative pheromones in homosexual men. *Proceedings of the National Academy of Sciences, USA, 102*, 7356–7361.

Savitz, J. B., & Ramesar, R. S. (2004). Genetic variants implicated in personality: A review of the more promising candidates. *American Journal of Medical Genetics, 131B*, 20–23.

Saxena, S., Maulik, P. K., Sharan, P., Levav, I., & Saraceno, B. (2004). Mental health research on low- and middle-income countries in indexed journals: A preliminary assessment. *Journal of Mental Health Policy and Economics, 7*, 127–131.

Sayette, M. A. (1993). An appraisal-disruption model of alcohol's effects on stress responses in social drinkers. *Psychological Bulletin, 114*, 459–476.

Scarr, S., & McCarthy, K. (1983). How people make their own environments: A theory of genotype 1 environment effects. *Child Development, 54*, 424–435.

Schab, F. R. (1991). Odor memory: Talking stock. *Psychological Bulletin, 109*, 242–251.

Schacter, D. L. (1996). *Searching for memory: The brain, the mind, and the past*. New York: Basic Books.

Schacter, D. L. (1999). The seven sins of memory: Insights from psychology and cognitive neuroscience. *American Psychologist, 54*, 182–203.

Schachter, S. (1951). Deviation, rejection, and communication. *Journal of Abnormal Psychology, 46*, 190–207.

Schachter, S. (1959). *The psychology of affiliation*. Stanford, CA: Stanford University Press.

Schachter, S., & Singer, J. (1962). Cognitive, social, and physiological determinants of emotional state. *Psychological Review, 69*, 379–399.

Schaie, K. W. (1990). Intellectual development in adulthood. In J. E. Birren & K. W. Schaie (Eds.), *Handbook of the psychology of aging* (3rd ed., pp. 291–319). New York: Van Nostrand Reinhold.

Schank, R. C., & Abelson, R. P. (1977). Scripts, plans, goals, and understanding. Hillsdale, NJ: Erlbaum.

Scheerer, M. (1963). Problem-solving. *Scientific American, 208*, 118–128.

Schiff, N. D., Giacino, J. T., Kalmar, K., Victor, J. D., Baker, K., Gerber, M., et al. (2007). Behavioural improvements with thalamic stimulation after severe traumatic brain injury. *Nature, 448*, 600–603.

Schiffman, J., Walker, E., Ekstrom, M., Schulsinger, F., Sorensen, H., & Mednick, S. (2004). Childhood videotaped social and neuromotor precursors of schizophrenia: A prospective investigation. *American Journal of Psychiatry, 161*, 2021–2027.

Schmader, T., & Johns, M. (2003). Converging evidence that stereotype threat reduces working memory capacity. *Journal of Personality and Social Psychology, 85*, 440–452.

Schmader, T., Johns, M., & Forbes, C. (2008). An integrated process model of stereotype threat effects on performance. *Psychological Review, 115*, 336–356.

Schmajuk, N. A., Lamoureux, J. A., & Holland, P. C. (1998). Occasion setting: A neural network approach. *Psychological Review, 105*, 3–32.

Schmidt, F. L., & Hunter, J. (2004). General mental ability in the world of work: Occupational attainment and job performance. *Journal of Personality and Social Psychology, 96*, 162–173.

Schmitt, D. P., Alcalay, L., Allik, J., Angleitner, A., Ault, L., Austers, I., et al. (2003). Universal sex differences in the desire for sexual variety: Tests from 52 nations, 6 continents, and 13 islands. *Journal of Personality and Social Psychology, 85*, 85–104.

Schmitt, D. P., Allik, J., McCrae, R. R., & Benet-Martinez, V. (2007). The geographic distribution of big five personality traits: Patterns and profiles of human self-description across 56 nations. *Journal of Cross-Cultural Psychology, 38*, 173–212.

Schmitt, D. P., Realo, A., Voracek, M., & Allik, J. (2008). Why can't a man be more like a woman? *Journal of Personality and Social Psychology, 94*, 168–182.

Schmitzer-Torbert, N. (2007). Place and response learning in human virtual navigation: Behavioral measures and gender differences. *Behavioral Neuroscience, 121*(2), 277–290.

Schneider, B., & Csikszentmihalyi, M. (2000). *Becoming adult: How teenagers prepare for the world of work*. New York: Basic Books.

Schoenemann, P. T., Sheehan, M. J., & Glotzer, L. D. (2005). Prefrontal white matter volume is disproportionately larger in humans than in other primates. *Nature Neuroscience, 8*, 242–252.

Schooler, J. W. (2002). Verbalizaton produces a transfer inappropriate processing shift. *Applied Cognitive Psychology, 16*, 989–997.

Schooler, J. W., & Engstler-Schooler, T. Y. (1990). Verbal overshadowing of visual memories: Some things are better left unsaid. *Cognitive Psychology, 22*, 36–71.

Schreiber, F. R. (1974). *Sybil: The true story of a woman possessed by sixteen personalities*. London: Penguin.

Schultz, P. W., Nolan, J. M., Cialdini, R. B., Goldstein, N. J., & Griskevicius, V. (2007). The constructive, destructive, and reconstructive power of social norms. *Psychological Science, 18*, 429–434.

Schulz, K. P., Fan, J., Tang, C. Y., Newcorn, J. H., Buchsbaum, M. S., Cheung, A. M., et al. (2004). Response inhibition in adolescents diagnosed with attention deficit hyperactivity disorder during childhood: An event-related fMRI study. *American Journal of Psychiatry, 161*, 1650–1657.

Schuur, Diane. (1999, July 14). Heroes and icons: Helen Keller. *Time*. Retrieved from http://www.time.com/time/time100/heroes/profile/keller01.html

Schwartz, B. (2004). *The paradox of choice: Why more is less*. New York: Ecco.

Schwartz, C. E., Wright, C. I., Shin, L. M., Kagan, J., & Rauch, S. L. (2003, June 20). Inhibited and uninhibited infants "grown up": Adult amygdalar response to novelty. *Science, 300*, 1952–1953.

Schwartz, J. M., Stoessel, P. W., Baxter, L. R., Martin, K. M., & Phelps, M. E. (1996). Systematic changes in cerebral glucose metabolic rate after successful behavior modification treatment of obsessive-compulsive disorder. *Archives of General Psychiatry, 53*, 109–113.

Schwarz, N., & Clore, G. L. (1983). Mood, misattribution, and judgments of well-being: Informative and directive functions of affective states. *Journal of Personality and Social Psychology, 45*, 513–523.

Science Daily. (2006, November 29). *Violent video games leave teenagers emotionally aroused* [Online news report]. Retrieved from http://www.sciencedaily.com/releases/2006/11/061128140804.htm

Scislowska, M. (2007, June 4). Man wakes from 19-year coma to "prettier" Poland. Railway worker is shocked at radical changes. *Associated Press*. Retrieved from http://www.associatedpress.com

Sclafani, A., & Springer, D. (1976). Dietary obesity in adult rats: Similarities to hypothalamic and human obesity syndromes. *Physiology and Behavior, 17*, 461–471.

Sedikides, C., Gaertner, L., & Toguchi, Y. (2003). Pancultural self-enhancement. *Journal of Personality and Social Psychology, 84*, 60–79.

Sedikides, C., & Gregg, A. (2008). Self-enhancement: Food for thought. *Perspectives on Psychological Science, 3*, 102–116.

Sedlmeier, P., & Gigerenzer, G. (1997). Intuitions about sample size: The empirical law of large numbers. *Journal of Behavioral Decision Making, 10*, 33–51.

Segall, M. H., Campbell, D. T., & Herskovits, M. J. (1966). *The influence of culture on visual perception.* New York: Bobbs-Merrill.

Segerstrom, S. C., & Miller, G. E. (2004). Psychological stress and the human immune system: A meta-analytic study of 30 years of inquiry. *Psychological Bulletin, 130*, 601–630.

Seguin, J. R. (2004). Neurocognitive elements of antisocial behavior: Relevance of an orbitofrontal cortex account. *Brain and Cognition, 55*, 185–197.

Seligman, M. (1970). On the generality of the laws of learning. *Psychological Review, 77*, 406–418.

Seligman, M. E. P. (1974). Depression and learned helplessness. In R. J. Friedman & M. M. Katz (Eds.), *The psychology of depression: Contemporary theory and research* (pp. 83–113). Washington, DC: V. H. Winston.

Seligman, M. E. P. (1975). *Helplessness: On depression, development, and death.* San Francisco: W. H. Freeman.

Seligman, M. E. P., & Csikszentmihalyi, M. (2000). Positive psychology: An introduction. *American Psychologist, 55*, 5–14.

Seligman, M. E. P., Steen, T. A., Park, N., & Peterson, C. (2005). Positive psychology progress: Empirical validation of interventions. *American Psychologist, 60*, 410–421.

Seligman, M. E. P., Walker, E. F., & Rosenhan, D. L. (2001). *Abnormal psychology.* New York: W. W. Norton.

Shallice, T., & Warrington, E. (1969). Independent functioning of verbal memory stores. *Quarterly Journal of Experimental Psychology, 22*, 261–273.

Shedler, J., & Block, J. (1990). Adolescent drug use and psychological health: A longitudinal inquiry. *American Psychologist, 45*, 612–630.

Sheese, B. E., Brown, E. L., & Graziano, W. G. (2004). Emotional expression in cyberspace: Searching for moderators of the Pennebaker disclosure effect via e-mail. *Health Psychology, 23*, 457–464.

Sher, L. (2000). Sociopolitical events and technical innovations may affect the content of delusions and the course of psychotic disorders. *Medical Hypotheses, 55*, 507–509.

Sherman, D. K., McGue, M. K., & Iacono, W. G. (1997). Twin concordance for attention deficit hyperactivity disorder: A comparison of teacher's and mother's reports. *American Journal of Psychiatry, 154*, 532–535.

Sherman, S. J., Presson, C., Chassin, L., Corty, E., & Olshavsky, R. (1983). The false consensus effect in estimates of smoking prevalence: Underlying mechanisms. *Personality and Social Psychology Bulletin, 9*, 197–207.

Sherwin, B. B. (1988). A comparative analysis of the role of androgen in human male and female sexual behavior: Behavioral specificity, critical thresholds, and sensitivity. *Psychobiology, 16*, 416–425.

Sherwin, B. B. (1994). Sex hormones and psychological functioning in postmenopausal women. *Experimental Gerontology, 29*, 423–430.

Sherwood, R. A., Keating, J., Kavvadia, V., Greenough, A., & Peters, T. J. (1999). Substance misuse in early pregnancy and relationship to fetal outcome. *European Journal of Pediatrics, 158*, 488–492.

Shettleworth, S. J. (2001). Animal cognition and animal behaviour. *Animal Behaviour, 61*, 277–286.

Shih, M., Pittinsky, T. L., & Ambady, N. (1999). Stereotype susceptibility: Identity salience and shifts in quantitative performance. *Psychological Science, 10*, 80–83.

Siegel, J. M. (2008). Do all animals sleep? *Trends in Neuroscience, 31*, 208–213.

Siegel, S. (1984). Pavlovian conditioning and heroin overdose: Reports by overdose victims. *Bulletin of the Psychonomic Society, 22*, 428–430.

Siegel, S., Hinson, R. E., Krank, M. D., & McCully, J. (1982). Heroin "overdose" death: Contribution of drug-associated environmental cues. *Science, 216*, 436–437.

Siegler, I. C., Costa, P. T., Brummett, B. H., Helms, M. J., Barefoot, J. C., Williams, R. et al. (2003). Patterns of change in hostility from college to midlife in the UNC alumni heart study predict high-risk status. *Psychosomatic Medicine, 65*, 738–745.

Sigurdsson, T., Doyère, V., Cain, C. K., & LeDoux, J. E. (2007). Long-term potentiation in the amygdala: A cellular mechanism of fear learning and memory. *Neuropharmacology, 52*, 215–227.

Silbersweig, D., Clarkin, J. F., Goldstein, M., Kernberg, O. F., Tuescher, O., Levy, K. N., et al. (2007). Failure of frontolimbic inhibitory function in the context of negative emotion in borderline personality disorder. *American Journal of Psychiatry, 64*, 1832–1841.

Silva, C. E., & Kirsch, I. (1992). Interpretive sets, expectancy, fantasy proneness, and dissociation as predictors of hypnotic response. *Journal of Personality and Social Psychology, 63*, 847–856.

Silva, P. A., & Stanton, W. (1996). *From child to adult: The Dunedin study.* Oxford, UK: Oxford University Press.

Simner, J., Mulvenna, C., Sagiv, N., Tsakanikos, E., Witherby, S. A., Fraser, C., et al. (2006). Synaesthesia: The prevalence of atypical cross-modal experiences. *Perception, 35*, 1024–1033.

Simner, J., & Ward, J. (2006). Synaesthesia: The taste of words on the tip of the tongue. *Nature, 44*, 438–439.

Simon, T. (2003). Photographer's foreword to *The Innocents.* [Electronic version]. Retrieved from http://www.pbs.org/wgbh/pages/frontline/shows/burden/innocents/

Simons, D. J., & Ambinder, M. S. (2005). Change blindness: Theory and consequences. *Current Directions in Psychological Science, 14*, 44–48.

Simons, D. J., & Levin, D. T. (1998). Failure to detect changes to people during a real-world interaction. *Psychonomic Bulletin and Review, 5*, 644–649.

Simpson, H. B., Foa, E. B., Liebowitz, M. R., Ledley, D. R., Huppert, J. D., Cahill, S., et al. (2008). A randomized, controlled trial of cognitive-behavioral therapy for augmenting pharmacotherapy in obsessive-compulsive disorder. *American Journal of Psychiatry, 165,* 621–630.

Simpson, J. A., Collins, A., Tran, S., & Haydon, K. C. (2007). Attachment and the experience and expression of emotions in romantic relationships: A developmental perspective. *Journal of Personality and Social Psychology, 92,* 355–367.

Sims, H. E. A., Goldman, R. F., Gluck, C. M., Horton, E., Kelleher, P., & Rowe, D. (1968). Experimental obesity in man. *Transactions of the Association of American Physicians, 81,* 153–170.

Singer, T., Seymour, B., O'Doherty, J., Kaube, H., Dolan, R. J., & Frith, C. D. (2004, February 20). Empathy for pain involves the affective but not sensory components of pain. *Science, 303,* 1157–1162.

Sirois, B. C., & Burg, M. M. (2003). Negative emotion and coronary heart disease: A review. *Behavior Modification, 27,* 83–102.

Skinner, B. F. (1971). *Beyond freedom and dignity.* New York: Wiley.

Skodol, A. E., Siever, L. J., Livesley, W. J., Gunderson, J. G., Pfohl, B., & Widiger, T. A. (2002). The borderline diagnosis II: Biology, genetics, and clinical course. *Biological Psychiatry, 51,* 951–963.

Slovic, P., Finucane, M., Peters, E., & MacGregor, D. (2002). The affect heuristic. In T. Gilovich, D. Griffin, & D. Kahneman (Eds.), *Heuristics and biases: The psychology of intuitive judgment* (pp. 397–420). New York: Cambridge University Press.

Smith, C., & Lapp, L. (1991). Increases in number of REMs and REM density in humans following an intensive learning period. *Sleep, 14,* 325–330.

Smith, D. M., Langa, K. M., Kabeto, M. U., & Ubel, P. A. (2005). Health, wealth, and happiness: Financial resources buffer subjective well-being after the onset of a disability. *Psychological Science, 16,* 663–664.

Smith, M. T., & Perlis, M. L. (2006). Who is a candidate for cognitive-behavioral treatment for insomnia? *Health Psychology, 25,* 15–19.

Smith, S. M., Glenberg, A. M., & Bjork, R. A. (1978). Environmental context and human memory. *Memory and Cognition, 6,* 342–353.

Smith, T. L. (2007, August 9). Testimony at U.S. House of Representatives hearing on federal, state, and local roles in rail safety [Electronic version]. Retrieved from the Brotherhood of Locomotive Engineers and Trainmen at http://www.bletdc.org/legislation/testimony/Smith%2020070809.pdf

Smith, T. W., Orleans, C. T., & Jenkins, C. D. (2004). Prevention and health promotion: Decades of progress, new challenges, and an emerging agenda. *Health Psychology, 23,* 126–131.

Snider, L. A., & Swedo, S. E. (2004). PANDAS: Current status and directions for research. *Molecular Psychiatry, 9,* 900–907.

Snyder, E. E., Walts, B. M., Chagnon, Y. C., Pérusse, L., Weisnagel, S. J., Chagnon, Y. C., et al. (2004). The human obesity gene map: The 2003 update. *Obesity Research, 12,* 369–438.

Snyder, M., & Cantor, N. (1998). Understanding personality and personal behavior: A functionalist strategy. In D. T. Gilbert, S. T. Fiske, & G. Lindzey (Eds.), *Handbook of social psychology* (pp. 635–679). New York: McGraw-Hill.

Snyder, M., Tanke, E. D., & Berscheid, E. (1977). Social perception and interpersonal behavior: On the self-fulfilling nature of social stereotypes. *Journal of Personality and Social Psychology, 35,* 656–666.

Solms, M. (2000). Dreaming and REM sleep are controlled by different brain mechanisms. *Behavioral and Brain Sciences, 23,* 793.

Somerville, L. H., Kim, H., Johnstone, T., Alexander, A. L., & Whalen, P. J. (2004). Human amygdala responses during presentation of happy and neutral faces: Correlations with state anxiety. *Biological Psychiatry, 55,* 897–903.

Sommerville, J. A., & Woodward, A. L. (2005). Pulling out the intentional structure of action: The relation between action processing and action production in infancy. *Cognition, 95,* 1–30.

Sorensen, T., Holst, C., Stunkard, A. J., & Skovgaard, L. T. (1992). Correlations of body mass index of adult adoptees and their biological and adoptive relatives. *International Journal of Obesity and Related Metabolic Disorders, 16,* 227–236.

Spanos, N. P., & Coe, W. C. (1992). A social-psychological approach to hypnosis. In E. Fromm & M. Nash (Eds.), *Contemporary hypnosis research* (pp. 102–130). New York: Guilford Press.

Spearman, C. (1904). "General intelligence," objectively determined and measured. *American Journal of Psychology, 15,* 201–293.

Spence, S. A., Kaylor-Hughes, C. J., Brook, M. L., Lankappa, S. T., & Wilkinson, I. D. (2007). 'Munchausen's syndrome by proxy' or a 'miscarriage of justice'? An initial application of functional neuroimaging to the question of guilt versus innocence. *European Psychiatry, 23*(4), 309–314.

Spencer, M. B., & Markstrom-Adams, C. (1990). Identity processes among racial and ethnic minority children in America. *Child Development, 56,* 564–572.

Sperling, G. (1960). The information available in brief visual presentations. *Psychological Monographs, 74,* 1–29.

Spitzer, R. L., Skodol, A. E., Gibbon, M., & Williams, J. B. W. (1983). *Psychopathology, a case book.* New York: McGraw-Hill.

Spitzer, R. L., Williams, J. B., Gibbon, M., & First, M. B. (1992). The structured clinical interview for DSM-III-R (SCID). I: History, rationale, and description. *Archives of General Psychiatry, 49,* 624–629.

Spurr, K. F., Graven, M. A., & Gilbert, R. W. (2008). Prevalence of unspecified sleep apnea and the use of continuous positive airway pressure in hospitalized patients, 2004 national hospital discharge survey. *Sleep and Breathing, 12,* 229–234.

Squire, L. R., & Moore, R. Y. (1979). Dorsal thalamic lesion in a noted case of human memory dysfunction. *Annals of Neurology, 6,* 503–506.

Squire, L. R., Stark, C. E. L., & Clark, R. E. (2004). The medial temporal lobe. *Annual Review of Neuroscience, 27*(27), 279–306.

Srivastava, S., John, O. P., Gosling, S. D., & Potter, J. (2003). Development of personality in early and middle adulthood: Set like plaster or persistent change? *Journal of Personality and Social Psychology, 84,* 1041–1053.

Srivastava, S., McGonigal, K. M., Richards, J. M., Butler, E. A., & Gross, J. J. (2006). Optimism in close relationships: How seeing things in a positive light makes them so. *Personality Processes and Individual Differences, 91*(1), 143–153.

Srull, T. K., & Wyer, R. S. (1979). The role of category accessibility in the interpretation of information about persons: Some determinants and implications. *Journal of Personality and Social Psychology, 37,* 1660–1672.

Starcevic, V., Linden, M., Uhlenhuth, E. H., Kolar, D., & Latas, M. (2004). Treatment of panic disorder with agoraphobia in an anxiety disorders clinic: Factors influencing psychiatrists' treatment choices. *Psychiatry Research, 125,* 41–52.

Stark, S. (2000, December 22). "Cast Away" lets Hanks fend for himself. *The Detroit News.* Retrieved from http://www.detnews.com

Steffenburg, S., Gillberg, C., Helgren, L., Anderson, L., Gillberg, L., Jakobsson, G., et al. (1989). A twin study of autism in Denmark, Finland, Iceland, Norway, and Sweden. *Journal of Child Psychological Psychiatry, 30,* 405–416.

Stein, J., & Richardson, A. (1999). Cognitive disorders: A question of misattribution. *Current Biology, 9,* R374–R376.

Stein, M. B., & Stein, D. J. (2008). Social anxiety disorder. *Lancet, 371,* 1115–1125.

Steiner, J. E. (1977). Facial expressions of the neonate infant indicating the hedonics of food-related chemical stimuli. In J. M. Weiffenbach (Ed.), *Taste and development* (pp. 173–189). Bethesda, MD: National Institutes of Health.

Stellar, J. R., Kelley, A. E., & Corbett, D. (1983). Effects of peripheral and central dopamine blockade on lateral hypothalamic self-stimulation: Evidence for both reward and motor deficits. *Pharmacology, Biochemistry, and Behavior, 18,* 433–442.

Steriade, M. (1992). Basic mechanisms of sleep generation. *Neurology, 42*(Suppl. 6), 9–18.

Sternberg, R. J. (1986). A triangular theory of love. *Psychological Review, 93,* 119–135.

Sternberg, R. J. (1999). The theory of successful intelligence. *Review of General Psychology, 3,* 292–316.

Stevensen, H. W., & Stigler, J. W. (1992). Learning gap: Why our schools are failing and what we can learn from Japanese and Chinese education. New York: Summit Books.

Stewart, J. Y. (2007, June 4). Bettye Travis, 55; activist for the overweight [Obituary.]. *Los Angeles Times,* p. B7.

Stickgold, R., Whidbee, D., Schirmer, B., Patel, V., & Hobson, J. A. (2000). Visual discrimination task improvement: A multi-step process occurring during sleep. *Journal of Cognitive Neuroscience, 12,* 246–254.

Stokstad, E. (2001, October 5). New hints into the biological basis of autism. *Science, 294,* 34–37.

Stoleru, S., Gregoire, M. C., Gerard, D., Decety, J., Lafarge, E., Cinotti, L., et al. (1999). Neuroanatomical correlates of visually evoked sexual arousal in human males. *Archives of Sexual Behavior, 28,* 1–21.

Stone, A. A., Neale, J. M., Cox, D. S., & Napoli, A. (1994). Daily events are associated with a secretory immune response to an oral antigen in men. *Health Psychology, 13,* 440–446.

Stone, M. H., Stone, D. K., & Hurt, S. W. (1987). The natural history of borderline patients treated by intensive hospitalization. *Psychiatric Clinics of North America, 10,* 185–206.

Stone, V. E., Baron-Cohen, S., & Knight, R. T. (1998). Frontal lobe contributions to theory of mind. *Journal of Cognitive Neuroscience, 10,* 640–656.

Strayer, D. L., & Drews, F. A. (2007). Cell-phone-induced driver distraction. *Current Directions in Psychological Science, 16,* 128–131.

Strentz, T., & Auerbach, S. M. (1988). Adjustment to the stress of simulated captivity: Effects of emotion-focused versus problem-focused preparation on hostages differing in locus of control. *Journal of Personality and Social Psychology, 55,* 652–660.

Stricker, L. J., & Ward, W. C. (2004). Stereotype threat, inquiring about test takers' ethnicity and gender, and standardized test performance. *Journal of Applied Social Psychology, 34,* 665–693.

Stricker, L. J., & Ward, W. C. (2008). Stereotype threat in applied settings re-examined: A reply. *Journal of Applied Social Psychology, 38,* 1656–1663.

Stunkard, A. J. (1996). Current views on obesity. *American Journal of Medicine, 100,* 230–236.

Sturm, R. (2002). The effects of obesity, smoking, and drinking on medical problems and costs. *Health Affairs, 21*(2), 245–253.

Sturm, R. (2003). Increases in clinically severe obesity in the United States, 1986–2000. *Archives of Internal Medicine, 163,* 2146–2148.

Stuss, D. T. (1991). Self, awareness, and the frontal lobes: A neuropsychological perspective. In J. Strauss & G. R. Goethals (Eds.), *The self: Interdisciplinary approaches* (pp. 255–278). New York: Springer-Verlag.

Stuss, D. T., Gow, C. A., & Hetherington, C. R. (1992). "No longer Gage": Frontal lobe dysfunction and emotional changes. *Journal of Consulting and Clinical Psychology, 60,* 349–359.

Sulin, R. A., & Dooling, D. J. (1974). Intrusion of a thematic idea in retention of prose. *Journal of Experimental Psychology, 103,* 255–262.

Süß, H. M., Oberauer, K., Wittman, W. W., Wilhelm, O., & Schulze, R. (2002). Working-memory capacity explains reasoning ability—and a little bit more. *Intelligence, 30,* 261–288.

Svenson, O. (1981). Are we all less risky and more skillful than our fellow drivers? *Acta Psychologica, 47,* 143–148.

Swaab, D. F., & Fliers, E. (2007). A sexually dimorphic nucleus in the human brain. In G. Einstein (Ed.), *Sex and the brain* (pp. 321–325). Cambridge, MA: MIT Press.

Swartz, M. S., Blazer, D., George, L., & Winfield, I. (1990). Estimating the prevalence of borderline personality disorder in the community. *Journal of Personality Disorders, 4,* 257–272.

Swenson, C. R., Sanderson, C., Dulie, R. A., & Linehan, M. M. (2001). The application of dialectical behavior therapy for patients with borderline personality disorder on inpatient units. *Psychiatric Quarterly, 72,* 307–324.

Szatzmari, P., Jones, M. B., Tuff, L., Bartolucci, G., Fisman, S., & Mahoney, W. (1993). Lack of cognitive impairment in first-degree relatives of children with pervasive developmental disorders. *Journal of the American Academy of Child and Adolescent Psychiatry, 32,* 1264–1273.

Tajfel, H., & Turner, J. C. (1979). An integrative theory of intergroup conflict. In W. G. Austin & S. Worchel (Eds.), *The social psychology of intergroup relations* (pp. 33–47). Monterey, CA: Brooks/Cole.

Talley, P. R., Strupp, H. H., & Morey, L. C. (1990). Matchmaking in psychotherapy: Patient-therapist dimensions and their impact on outcome. *Journal of Consulting and Clinical Psychology, 58,* 182–188.

Tandon, R., Keshavan, M. S., & Nasrallah, H. A. (2008). Schizophrenia, "Just the facts." What we know in 2008. 2. Epidemiology and etiology. *Schizophrenia Research, 102,* 1–18.

Tang, Y. P., Wang, H., Feng, R., Kyin, M., Tsien, J. Z. (2001). Differential effects of enrichment on learning and memory function in NR2B transgenic mice. *Neuropharmacology, 41,* 779–790.

Tang, Y. Y., Ma, Y. H., Wang, J. H., Fan, Y. X., Feng, S. G., Lu, Q. L., et al. (2007). Short-term meditation training improves attention and self-regulation. *Proceedings of the National Academy of Sciences, USA, 104,* 17152–17156.

Tateyama, M., Asai, M., Kamisada, M., Hashimoto, M., Bartels, M., & Heimann, H. (1993). Comparison of schizophrenic delusions between Japan and Germany. *Psychopathology, 26,* 151–158.

Taylor, S. E. (2006). Tend and befriend: Biobehavioral bases of affiliation under stress. *Current Directions in Psychological Science, 15,* 273–277.

Taylor, S. E., & Brown, J. D. (1988). Illusion and well-being: A social psychological perspective on mental health. *Psychological Bulletin, 103*, 193–210.

Taylor, S. E., Lewis, B. P., Gruenewald, T. L., Gurung, R. A. R., Updegraff, J. A., & Klein, L. C. (2002). Sex differences in biobehavioral responses to threat: Reply to Geary and Flinn. *Psychological Review, 109*, 751–753.

Teller, D. Y., Morse, R., Borton, R., & Regal, C. (1974). Visual acuity for vertical and diagonal gratings in human infants. *Vision Research, 14*, 1433–1439.

Terracciano, A., Abdel-Khalek, A. M., Ádám, N., Adamovová, L., Ahn, C. K., Ahn, H. N., et al. (2005, October 7). National character does not reflect mean personality trait levels in 49 cultures. *Science, 310*, 96–100.

Tesser, A. (1988). Toward a self-evaluation maintenance model of social behavior. *Advances in Experimental Social Psychology, 21*, 181–227.

Tesser, A. (1993). The importance of heritability: The case of attitudes. *Psychological Review, 100*, 129–142.

Tettamanti, M., Buccino, G., Saccuman, M. C., Gallese, V., Danna, M., Scifo, P., et al. (2005). Listening to action-related sentences activates fronto-parietal motor circuits. *Journal of Cognitive Neuroscience, 17*, 273–281.

Thigpen, C. H., & Cleckley, H. (1954). A case of multiple personality. *Journal of Abnormal Psychology, 49*, 135–151.

Thomas, M. S. C., & Johnson, M. H. (2008). New advances in understanding sensitive periods in brain development. *Current Directions in Psychological Science, 17*, 1–5.

Thompson, P. (1980). Margaret Thatcher: A new illusion. *Perception, 9*, 483–484.

Thompson, P. M., Hayashi, K. M., Simon, S. L., Geaga, J. A., Hong, M. S., Sui, Y., et al. (2004). Structural abnormalities in the brains of human subjects who use methamphetamine. *Journal of Neuroscience, 24*, 6028–6036.

Thompson, W. F., Schellenberg, E. G., & Husain, G. (2001). Arousal, mood, and the Mozart effect. *Psychological Science, 12*, 248–251.

Thorgeirsson, T. E., Geller, F., Sulem, P., Rafnar, T., Wiste, A., Magnusson, K. P., et al. (2008). A variant associated with nicotine dependence, lung cancer and peripheral arterial disease. *Nature, 452*, 638–642.

Tickle, J. J., Sargent, J. D., Dalton, M. A., Beach, M. L., & Heatherton, T. F. (2001). Favorite movie stars, their tobacco use in contemporary movies and its association with adolescent smoking. *Tobacco Control, 10*, 16–22.

Tienari, P., Lahti, I., Sorri, A., Naarala, M., Moring, J., Kaleva, M., et al. (1990). Adopted-away offspring of schizophrenics and controls: The Finnish adoptive family study of schizophrenia. In L. Robins & M. Rutter (Eds.), *Straight and devious pathways from childhood to adulthood* (pp. 365–379). New York: Cambridge University Press.

Tienari, P., Wynne, L. C., Moring, J., Lahti, I., Naarala, M., Sorri, A., et al. (1994). The Finnish adoptive family study of schizophrenia: Implications for family research. *British Journal of Psychiatry, 23*(Suppl.), 20–26.

Tiggermann, M., & McGill, B. (2004). The role of social comparison in the effect of magazine advertisements on women's mood and body dissatisfaction. *Journal of Social and Clinical Psychology, 23*, 23–44.

Tollesfson, G. D. (1995). Selective serotonin reuptake inhibitors. In A. F. Schatzberg & C. B. Nemeroff (Eds.), *The American Psychiatric Press textbook of psychopharmacology* (1st ed., pp. 161–182). Washington, DC: American Psychiatric Press.

Tomasello, M. (1999). *The cultural origins of human cognition*. Cambridge, MA: Harvard Press.

Tombs, S., & Silverman, I. (2004). Pupillometry: A sexual selection approach. *Evolution and Human Behavior, 25*, 221–228.

Tomkins, S. S. (1963). *Affect imagery consciousness: Volume 2. The negative affects*. New York: Tavistock/Routledge.

Tong, F., Nakayama, K., Vaughan, J. T., & Kanwisher, N. (1998). Binocular rivalry and visual awareness in human extrastriate cortex. *Neuron, 21*, 753–759.

Tooby, J., & Cosmides, L. (1990). On the universality of human nature and the uniqueness of the individual: The role of genetics and adaptation. *Journal of Personality, 58*, 17–68.

Torgersen, S., Kringlen, E., & Cramer, V. (2001). The prevalence of personality disorders in a community sample. *Archives of General Psychiatry, 58*, 590–596.

Torrey, E. F. (1999). Epidemiological comparison of schizophrenia and bipolar disorder. *Schizophrenia Research, 39*, 101–106.

Torrey, E. F., Torrey, B. B., & Peterson, M. R. (1977). Seasonality of schizophrenic births in the United States. *Archives of General Psychiatry, 34*, 1065–1070.

Trebay, G. (2008, February 7). The vanishing point. *The New York Times*. Retrieved from http://www.nytimes.com/2008/02/07/fashion/shows/07DIARY.html?_r=1&th=&oref=slogin&emc=th&pagewanted=all

Treatment for Adolescents with Depression Study (TADS) Team. (2004). Fluoxetine, cognitive-behavioral therapy, and their combination for adolescents with depression: Treatment for adolescents with depression study (TADS) randomized controlled trial. *Journal of the American Medical Association, 292*, 807–820.

Treffert, D. A., & Christensen, D. D. (2006, June/July). Inside the mind of a savant. *Scientific American Mind*, 50–55.

Treisman, A., & Gelade, G. (1980). A feature-integration theory of attention. *Cognitive Psychology, 12*, 97–136.

Tremblay, P. F., Graham, K., & Wells, S. (2008). Severity of physical aggression reported by university students: A test of the interaction between trait aggression and alcohol consumption. *Personality and Individual Differences, 45*(1), 3–9.

Triandis, H. C. (1989). The self and social behavior in differing cultural contexts. *Psychological Review, 96*, 506–520.

Trivers, R. L. (1971). The evolution of reciprocal altruism. *Quarterly Review of Biology, 46*, 35–57.

Trzaska, K. A., & Rameshwar, P. (2007). Current advances in the treatment of Parkinson's disease with stem cells. *Current Neurovascular Research, 4*(2), 99–109.

Trzesniewski, K. H., Donnellan, M. B., & Roberts, R. W. (2008). Is "generation me" really more narcissistic than previous generations? *Journal of Personality, 76*, 903–918.

Tsien, J. Z. (2000, April). Building a brainier mouse. *Scientific American, 282*, 62–68.

Tugade, M. M., & Fredrickson, B. L. (2004). Resilient individuals use positive emotions to bounce back from negative emotional experiences. *Journal of Personality and Social Psychology, 86*, 320–333.

Twenge, J. M., & Campbell, W. K. (2003). "Isn't it fun to get the respect that we're going to deserve?" Narcissism, social rejection, and aggression. *Personality and Social Psychology Bulletin, 29*, 261–272.

Twenge, J. M., Konrath, S., Foster, J. D., Campbell, K. W., & Bushman, B. J. (2008). Egos inflating over time: A cross-temporal meta-analysis of the narcissistic personality inventory. *Journal of Personality, 76*, 875–902.

Uchino, B. N., Cacioppo, J. T., & Kiecolt-Glaser, J. K. (1996). The relationship between social support and physiological processes: A review with emphasis on underlying mechanisms and implications for health. *Psychological Bulletin, 119*, 488–531.

Ungerleider, L. G., & Mishkin, M. (1982). Two cortical visual systems. In D. J. Ingle, Mansfield, R. J. W., & M. S. Goodale (Eds.), *The analysis of visual behavior* (pp 549–586). Cambridge, MA: MIT Press.

United States Department of Energy, Office of Science. (n.d.). *Human genome project information. Behavioral genetics.* Retrieved January 14, 2008, from http://genomics.energy.gov

United States Department of Health and Human Services. (1999). *Mental health: A report of the surgeon general.* Washington, DC: Department of Health and Human Services.

United States Department of Health and Human Services. (2001, 8 January). *Preventing disease and death from tobacco use* [Press release]. Retrieved from http://www.hhs.gov/news/press/2001pres/01stbco.html

United States Department of Health and Human Services, Office of the Surgeon General (2004, May 27). *The health consequences of smoking: A report of the Surgeon General.* Available from http://www.surgeongeneral.gov/library/smokingconsequences

Upton, N. (1994). Mechanisms of action of new antiepileptic drugs: Rational design and serendipitous findings. *Trends in Pharmacological Sciences, 15*, 456–463.

Üstün, T. B., Ayuso-Mateos, J. L., Chatterji, S., Mathers, C., & Murray, C. J. (2000). Global burden of depressive disorders in the year 2000. *British Journal of Psychiatry, 184*, 386–392.

Uvnas-Moberg, K. (1998). Oxytocin may mediate the benefits of positive social interaction and emotions. *Psychoneuroendocrinology, 23*, 819–835.

Vallabha, G. K., McClelland, J. L., Pons, F., Werker, J. F., & Amano, S. (2007). Unsupervised learning of vowel categories from infant-directed speech. *Proceedings of the National Academy of Sciences, USA, 104*, 13273–13278.

van IJzendoorn, M. H., & Juffer, F. (2005). Adoption is a successful natural intervention enhancing adopted children's IQ and school performance. *Current Directions in Psychological Science, 14*, 326–330.

Vanchieri, C. (1998). Lessons from the tobacco wars edify nutrition war tactics. *Journal of the National Cancer Institute, 90*, 420–424.

Vargha-Khadem, F., Gadian, D. G., Watkinds, K., Connelly, A., Can Paesschen, W., & Mishkin, M. (1997, July 18). Differential effects of early hippocampal pathology on episodic and semantic memory. *Science, 277*, 376–380.

Varley, C. K. (1984). Attention deficit disorder (the hyperactivity syndrome): A review of selected issues. *Developmental and Behavioral Pediatrics, 5*, 254–258.

Vazire, S., & Mehl, M. R. (2008). Knowing me, knowing you: The accuracy and unique predictive validity of self and other ratings of daily behavior. *Journal of Personality and Social Psychology, 95*, 1202–1216.

Ventura, P., Pattamadilok, C., & Fernandes, T. (2008). Schooling in Western culture promotes context-free processing. *Journal of Experimental Child Psychology, 100*(2), 79–88.

Vernon, P. A., Wickett, J. C., Bazana, P. G., Stelmack, R. M., & Sternberg, R. J. (2000). The neuropsychology and psychophysiology of human intelligence. In R. J. Sternberg (Ed.), *Handbook of intelligence* (pp. 245–264). Cambridge, UK: Cambridge University Press.

Vohs, K. D., & Heatherton, T. F. (2004). Ego threat elicits different social comparison processes among high and low self-esteem people: Implications for interpersonal perceptions. *Social Cognition, 22*, 168–190.

Volkmar, F., Chawarska, K., & Klin, A. (2005). Autism in infancy and early childhood. *Annual Review of Psychology, 56*, 1–21.

Volkow, N. D. (2007, September). This is your brain on food. Interview by Kristin Leutwyler-Ozelli. *Scientific American, 297*, 84–85.

Volkow, N. D., Wang, G. J., Telang, F., Fowler, J. S., Logan, J., Childress, A. R., et al. (2008). Dopamine increases in striatum do not elicit craving in cocaine abusers unless they are coupled with cocaine cues. *Neuroimage, 39*, 1266–1273.

Volpicelli, J. R., Alterman, A. I., Hayashida, M., & O'Brien, C. P. (1999). Naltrexone in the treatment of alcohol dependence. *Archives of General Psychiatry, 49*, 876–880.

von Neumann, J., & Morgenstern, O. (1947). *Theory of games and economic behavior.* Princeton, NJ: Princeton University Press.

von Restorff, H. (1933). Uber die wirkung von bereichsbildungen im spurenfeld [On the effect of spheres' formations in the trace field]. *Psychologische Forschung, 18*, 299–342.

Vouloumanos, A., Kiehl, K. A., Werker, J. F., & Liddle, P. F. (2001). Detection of sounds in the auditory stream: Event-related fMRI evidence for differential activation to speech and nonspeech. *Journal of Cognitive Neuroscience, 13*, 994–1005.

Wadhwa, P. D., Sandman, C. A., & Garite, T. J. (2001). The neurobiology of stress in human pregnancy: Implications for prematurity and development of the fetal central nervous system. *Progress in Brain Research, 133*, 131–142.

Wager, T. D. (2005). Placebo effects in the brain: Linking mental and physiological processes. *Brain, Behavior, and Immunity, 19*(4), 281–282.

Wager, T. D., & Smith, E. E. (2003). Neuroimaging studies of working memory: A meta-analysis. *Cognitive, Affective, and Behavioral Neuroscience, 3*, 255–274.

Wagner, A. D., Schacter, D. L., Rotte, M., Koutstaal, W., Maril, A., Dale, A. M., et al. (1998, August 21). Building memories: Remembering and forgetting of verbal experiences as predicted by brain activity. *Science, 281*, 1188–1191.

Wagner, U., Gals, S., Haider, H., Verleger, R., & Born, J. (2004). Sleep inspires insight. *Nature, 427*, 352–356.

Walker, E., Kestler, L., Bollini, A., & Hochman, K. M. (2004). Schizophrenia: Etiology and course. *Annual Review of Psychology, 55*, 401–430.

Walker, M. P., & Stickgold, R. (2006). Sleep, memory, and plasticity. *Annual Review of Psychology, 57*, 139–166.

Walsh, T., McClellan, J. M., McCarthy, S. E., Addington, A. M., Pierce, S. B., Cooper, G. M., et al. (2008, March 27). Rare structural variants disrupt multiple genes in neurodevelopmental pathways in schizophrenia. *Science, 320*, 539–543.

Waltrip, R. W., Buchanan, R. W., Carpenter, W. T., Kirkpatrick, B., Summerfelt, A., Breier, A., et al. (1997). Borna disease virus antibodies and the deficit syndrome of schizophrenia. *Schizophrenia Research, 23,* 253–257.

Wang, S.-H., & Baillargeon, R. (2008). Detecting impossible changes in infancy: a three-system account. *Trends in Cognitive Sciences, 12,* 17–23.

Watson, D., & Clark, L. A. (1997). Extraversion and its positive emotional core. In R. Hogan, J. Johnson, & S. Briggs (Eds.), *Handbook of personality psychology* (pp. 767–793). San Diego, CA: Academic Press.

Watson, D., Wiese, D., Vaidya, J., & Tellegen, A. (1999). The two general activation systems of affect: Structural findings, evolutionary considerations, and psychobiological evidence. *Journal of Personality and Social Psychology, 76,* 820–838.

Watson, J. B. (1924). *Behaviorism.* New York: W. W. Norton.

Weber, N., & Brewer, N. (2004). Confidence-accuracy calibration in absolute and relative face recognition judgments. *Journal of Experimental Psychology: Applied, 10,* 156–172.

Wegner, D., Shortt, J., Blake, A., & Page, M. (1990). The suppression of exciting thoughts. *Journal of Personality and Social Psychology, 58,* 409–418.

Weiner, B. (1974). *Achievement motivation and attribution theory.* Morristown, NJ: General Learning Press.

Weiss, A., Bates, T. C., & Luciano, M. (2008). Happiness is a personal(ity) thing: The genetics of personality and well-being in a representative sample. *Psychological Science, 19,* 205–210.

Weiss, A., King, J. E., & Perkins, L. (2006). Personality and subjective well-being in orangutans (pongo pygmaeus and pongo abelli). *Journal of Personality and Social Psychology, 90,* 501–511.

Weiss, G., & Hechtman, L. T. (1993). *Hyperactive children grown up.* New York: Guilford Press.

Weissman, M. M., Bland, R. C., Canino, G. J., Greenwald, S., Hwu, H. G., Lee, C. K., et al. (1994). The cross national epidemiology of obsessive compulsive disorder. The cross national collaborative group. *Journal of Clinical Psychiatry, 55,* 5–10.

Wells, G. L. (2008). Field experiments on eyewitness identification: Towards a better understanding of pittfalls and prospects. *Law and Human Behavior, 32,* 6–10.

Wells, G. L., Small, M., Penrod, S., Malpass, R. S., Fulero, S. M., & Brimacombe, C. A. E. (1998). Eyewitness identification procedures: Recommendations for lineups and photospreads. *Law and Human Behavior, 22,* 603–647.

Werker, J. F., Gilbert, J. H., Humphrey, K., & Tees, R. C. (1981). Developmental aspects of cross-language speech perception. *Child Development, 52,* 349–355.

Westen, D. (1998). The scientific legacy of Sigmund Freud: Toward a psychodynamically informed psychological science. *Psychological Bulletin, 124,* 333–371.

Westen, D., Novotny, C. M., & Thompson-Brenner, H. (2004). The empirical status of empirically supported psychotherapies: Assumptions, findings, and reporting in controlled clinical trials. *Psychological Bulletin, 130,* 631–663.

Whalen, C. K. (1989). Attention deficit and hyperactivity disorders. In T. H. Ollendick & M. Herson (Eds.), *Handbook of child psychopathology* (2nd ed., pp. 131–169). New York: Plenum Press.

Whalen, P. J., Kagan, J., Cook, R. G., Davis, F. C., Kim, H., Polis, S., et al. (2004, 17 December). Human amygdala responsivity to masked fearful eye-whites. *Science, 306,* 2061.

Whalen, P. J., Rauch, S. L., Etcoff, N. L., McInerney, N. L., Lee, M. B., & Jenike, M. A. (1998). Masked presentations of emotional facial expressions modulate amygdala activity without explicit knowledge. *Journal of Neuroscience, 18,* 411–418.

Whalen, P. J., Shin, L. M., McInerney, S. C. L., Fischer, H., Wright, C. I., & Rauch, S. L. (2001). A functional MRI study of human amygdala responses to facial expressions of fear versus anger. *Emotion, 1,* 70–83.

Wheatley, T., & Haidt, J. (2005). Hypnotic disgust makes moral judgments more severe. *Psychological Science, 16,* 780–784.

Wheeler, M. E., & Fiske, S. T. (2005). Controlling racial prejudice: Social-cognitive goals affect amygdala and stereotype activation. *Psychological Science, 16,* 56–63.

Whiteside, S. P., Port, J. D., & Abramowitz, J. S. (2004). A meta-analysis of functional neuroimaging in obsessive-compulsive disorder. *Psychiatry Research, 15,* 69–79.

Widiger, T. A., & Corbitt, E. M. (1995). Are personality disorders well-classified in DSM-IV? In W. J. Lively (Ed.), *The DSM-IV personality disorders* (pp. 103–126). New York: Guilford Press.

Widom, C. S. (1978). A methodology for studying noninstitutionalized psychopaths. In R. D. Hare & D. A. Schalling (Eds.), *Psychopathic behavior: Approaches to research* (pp. 72ff). Chichester, UK: Wiley.

Wiesel, T. N., & Hubel, D. H. (1963). Single-cell responses in striate cortex of kittens deprived of vision in one eye. *Journal of Neurophysiology, 26,* 1003–1017.

Wilens, T. E., Faraone, S. V., & Biederman, J. (2004). Attention-deficit/hyperactivity disorder in adults. *Journal of the American Medical Association, 292,* 619–623.

Wilke, M., Sohn, J. H., Byars, A. W., & Holland, S. K. (2003). Bright spots: Correlations of gray matter volume with IQ in a normal pediatric population. *Neuroimage, 20,* 202–215

Williams, L. E., & Bargh, J. A. (2008). Keeping one's distance: The influence of spatial distance cues on affect and evaluation. *Psychological Science, 19,* 302–308.

Williams, L. E., & Bargh, J. A. (2008, October 24). Experiences of physical warmth influence interpersonal warmth. *Science, 322,* 606–607.

Williams, R. B., Jr. (1987). Refining the type A hypothesis: Emergence of the hostility complex. *American Journal of Cardiology, 60,* 27J–32J.

Wills, T. A., DuHamel, K., & Vaccaro, D. (1995). Activity and mood temperament as predictors of adolescent substance use: Test of a self-regulation mediational model. *Journal of Personality and Social Psychology, 68,* 901–916.

Wilsnack, R. W., Wilsnack, S. C., & Obot, I. S. (2005). Why study gender, alcohol and culture? In I. S. Obot & R. Room (Eds.), *Alcohol, gender and drinking problems: Perspectives from low and middle income countries* (pp. 1–23). Geneva, Switzerland: World Health Organization.

Wilson, M. A., & McNaughton, B. L. (1994, July 29). Reactivation of hippocampal ensemble memories during sleep. *Science, 265,* 676–679.

Wilson, R. S., Schneider, J. A., Arnold, S. E., Tang, Y., Boyle, P. A., & Bennett, D. A. (2007). Olfactory identification and incidence of mild cognitive impairment in older age. *Archives of General Psychiatry, 64,* 802–808.

Wilson, T. D., & Gilbert, D. T. (2003). Affective forecasting. In M. Zanna (Ed.), *Advances in experimental social psychology* (Vol. 35, pp. 345–411). New York: Elsevier.

Wilson, T. D., & Gilbert, D. T. (2005). Affective forecasting: Knowing what to want. *Current Directions in Psychological Science, 14,* 131–134.

Winberg, J., & Porter, R. H. (1998). Olfaction and human neonatal behaviour: Clinical implications. *Acta Paediatrica, 87*, 6–10.

Winfried, R., & Hofmann, S. G. (2008). The missing data problem in meta-analyses. *Archives of General Psychiatry, 65*, 238.

Wise, R. A., & Rompre, P. P. (1989). Brain dopamine and reward. *Annual Review of Psychology, 40*, 191–225.

Wiseman, C. V., Harris, W. A., & Halmi, K. A. (1998). Eating disorders. *Medical Clinics of North America, 82*, 145–159.

Wishaw, I. Q., Drigenberg, H. C., & Comery, T. A. (1992). Rats (rattus norvegicus) modulate eating speed and vigilance to optimize food consumption: Effects of cover, circadian rhythm, food deprivation, and individual differences. *Journal of Comparative Psychology, 106*, 411–419.

Wolfe, J. M., & Horowitz, T. S. (2004). What attributes guide the deployment of visual attention and how do they do it? *Nature Reviews Neuroscience, 5*, 495–501.

Wolford, G. L., Miller, M. B., & Gazzaniga, M. (2000). The left hemisphere's role in hypothesis formation. *Journal of Neuroscience, 20*, 1–4.

Woller, K. M., Buboltz, W. C. J., & Loveland, J. M. (2007). Psychological reactance: Examination across age, ethnicity, and gender. *American Journal of Psychology, 120*(1), 15–24.

Wolpe, J. (1997). Thirty years of behavior therapy. *Behavior Therapy, 28*, 633–635.

Wolpe, P. R., Foster, K. R., & Langleben, D. D. (2005). Emerging neurotechnologies for lie-detection: Promises and perils. *American Journal of Bioethics, 5*(2), 39–49.

Wolraich, M. L., Wilson, D. B., & White, J. W. (1995). The effects of sugar on behavior or cognition in children: A meta-analysis. *Journal of the American Medical Association, 274*, 1617–1621.

Wood, J. M., Garb, H. N., Lilienfeld, S. O., & Nezworski, M. T. (2002). Clinical assessment. *Annual Review of Psychology, 53*, 519–543.

Woodward, S. A., McManis, M. H., Kagan, J., Deldin, P., Snidman, N., Lewis, M., et al. (2001). Infant temperament and the brainstem auditory evoked response in later childhood. *Developmental Psychology, 37*, 533–538.

Woodworth, M., & Porter, S. (2002). In cold blood: Characteristics of criminal homicides as a function of psychopathy. *Journal of Abnormal Psychology, 111*, 436–445.

World Health Organization. (2002). *The world health report.* Geneva, Switzerland: World Health Organization.

World Health Organization. (2008). *WHO Report on global tobacco epidemic.* Retrieved from http://www.who.int/tobacco/mpower/en/

Worley, H. (2006, June). *Depression: A leading contributor to global burden of disease: Myriad obstacles—particularly stigma—block better treatment in developing countries.* Retrieved November 10, 2008, from http://www.prb.org/Articles/2006/DepressionaLeadingContributortoGlobalBurdenofDisease.aspx

Yamagata, S., Suzuki, A., Ando, J., Ono, Y., Kijima, N., Yoshimura, K., et al. (2006). Is the genetic structure of human personality universal? A cross-cultural twin study from North America, Europe, and Asia. *Journal of Personality and Social Psychology, 90*, 987–998.

Yamaguchi, S., Greenwald, A. G., Banaji, M. R., Murakami, F., Chen, D., Shiomura, K., et al. (2007). Apparent universality of positive implicit self-esteem. *Psychological Science, 18*, 498–500.

Yerkes, R. M., & Dodson, J. D. (1908). The relation of strength of stimulus to rapidity of habit formation. *Journal of Comparative Neurology & Psychology, 18*, 459–482.

Yoo, S. S., Hu, P. T., Gujar, N., Jolesz, F. A., & Walker, M. P. (2007). A deficit in the ability to form new human memories without sleep. *Nature Neuroscience, 10*, 385–392.

Yucel, M., Harrison, B. J., Wood, S. J., Fornito, A., Wellard, R. M., Pujol, J., et al. (2007). Functional and biochemical alterations of the medial frontal cortex in obsessive-compulsive disorder. *Archives of General Psychiatry, 64*, 946–955.

Yuille, J. C., & Cutshall, J. L. (1986). A case study of eyewitness memory of a crime. *Journal of Applied Psychology, 71*, 291–301.

Zahn-Waxler, C., & Radke-Yarrow, M. (1990). The origins of empathic concern. *Motivation and Emotion, 14*, 107–130.

Zahn-Waxler, C., & Robinson, J. (1995). Empathy and guilt: Early origins of feelings of responsibility. In J. P. Tangney & K. W. Fischer (Eds.), *Self-conscious emotions: The psychology of shame, guilt, embarrassment, and pride* (pp. 143–173). New York: Guilford Press.

Zajonc, R. B. (1965, July 15). Social facilitation. *Science, 149*, 269–274.

Zajonc, R. B. (1968). Attitudinal effects of mere exposure. *Journal of Personality and Social Psychology Monographs, 9*, 1–27.

Zajonc, R. B. (1980). Feeling and thinking: Preferences need no inferences. *American Psychologist, 35*, 151–175.

Zajonc, R. B. (2001). Mere exposure: A gateway to the subliminal. *Current Directions in Psychological Science 10*, 224–228.

Zak, P. J., Kurzban, R., & Matzner, W. T. (2005). Oxytocin is associated with human trustworthiness. *Hormones and Behavior, 48*(5), 522–527.

Zametkin, A. J., Nordahl, T. E., Gross, M., King, A. C., Stemple, W. E., Rumsey, J., et al. (1990). Cerebral glucose metabolism in adults with hyperactivity of childhood onset. *New England Journal of Medicine, 323*, 1361–1366.

Zebian, S., Alamuddin, R., Mallouf, M., & Chatila, Y. (2007). Developing an appropriate psychology through culturally sensitive research practices in the Arab-speaking world: A content analysis of psychological research published between 1950 and 2004. *Journal of Cross-Cultural Psychology, 38*, 91–122.

Zentall, S. S., Sutton, J. E., & Sherburne, L. M. (1996). True imitative learning in pigeons. *Psychological Science, 7*, 343–346.

Zihl, J., von Cramon, D., & Mai, N. (1983). Selective disturbance of movement vision after bilateral brain damage. *Brain, 106*, 313–340.

Zorrilla, E. P., Iwasaki, S., Moss, J. A., Chang, J., Otsuji, J., Inoue, K., et al. (2006). Vaccination against weight gain. *Proceedings of the National Academy of Sciences, USA, 103*, 13226–13231.

Zuckerman, M. (1994). *Behavioral expressions and biosocial bases of sensation seeking.* New York: Cambridge University Press.

Zuckerman, M. (1995). Good and bad humors: Biochemical bases of personality and its disorders. *Psychological Science, 6*, 325–332.

ANSWER KEY FOR MEASURING UP EXERCISES AND FOR PRACTICE TESTS

CHAPTER 1: INTRODUCTION

Measuring Up, p. 16
For each example below, indicate which of the seven themes of psychological science apply. *Answers: a. 7; b. 2 (could also be 6); c. 1; d. 6 (could also be 4); e. 4; f. 3*

Measuring Up, p. 24
Identify the school of thought that each of the following statements characterizes. *Answers: a. behaviorism; b. functionalism; c. cognitive; d. social; e. Gestalt; f. structuralism; g. psychoanalysis*

Measuring Up, p. 29
1. Critical thinking is _____. *Answer: b. using specific thinking skills to reach reasonable conclusions*

2. Psychology is relevant _____. *Answer: b. in all aspects of life*

Practice Test, p. 31
1. When you mention to your family that you enrolled in a psychology course, your family members share their understanding of the field. Which comment best reflects the nature of psychological science? *Answer: c. "I think you'll be surprised by the range of questions psychologists ask about the mind, the brain, and behavior, not to mention the methods they use to answer these questions."*

2. Match each definition with one of the following ideas from evolutionary theory: adaptation, natural selection, survival of the fittest. *Answers: a. adaptations; b. survival of the fittest; c. natural selection*

3. Titles of recent research articles appear below. Indicate which of the four levels of analysis—cultural, social, individual, or biological—each article likely addresses. *Answers: a. social; b. biological; c. cultural; d. individual*

4. True or false? Psychology as a field of inquiry developed almost exclusively from Western thinking. *Answer: false*

5. Indicate which school or schools of thought each of the following scholars is associated with: John Dewey, William James, Wolfgang Kohler, Kurt Lewin, George Miller, B. F. Skinner, Edward Titchener, Edward Tolman, John B. Watson, Max Wertheimer, Wilhelm Wundt. *Answers: a. Titchener, Wundt; b. Dewey, James; c. Kohler, Wertheimer; d. Skinner, Watson; e. Kohler, Miller, Tolman; f. Lewin*

6. Match each description with one of the following theoretical ideas: field theory, information processing theory, introspection, phenomenological approach, stream of consciousness. *Answers: a. introspection; b. field theory; c. phenomenological approach; d. stream of consciousness; e. information processing theory*

7. Imagine you have decided to seek mental health counseling. You mention this to a few of your friends. Each friend shares an opinion with you. Based on your understanding of psychological science, which friend offers the strongest advice? *Answer: c. "That's great! Psychologists do research to figure out which interventions are most helpful for people with different concerns."*

8. Which of the following practices are hallmarks of critical thinking? *Answer: All are correct.*

9. Your brother reads that research shows eating ice cream makes people more intelligent. He starts downing a pint of ice cream every day to increase his intelligence. To help your brother better understand this claim (and avoid obesity), which of the following questions would you ask? *Answers: b. "Does the article say how the researchers measured intelligence?"; d. "I wonder how the researchers designed the study. Were they doing good science?"; e. "I'd want to know who sponsored the study. Would you believe these results if the study was paid for and conducted by researchers at the world's largest ice cream company?"*

CHAPTER 2: RESEARCH METHODOLOGY

Measuring Up, p. 37
1. How are theories, hypotheses, and research different? *Answer: b. Theories are broad conceptual frameworks, hypotheses are derived from theories and are used to design research that will support or fail to support a theory, and research is a test of the hypotheses.*

2. How does psychological research differ from relying on personal experience or intuition as a way of understanding thought, emotions, and behavior? *Answer: b. Carefully designed research is the most objective method for understanding thoughts, emotions, and behaviors.*

Measuring Up, p. 50
1. The main reason researchers randomly assign participants to different groups in an experiment is that _____. *Answer: d. random assignment is the only way to ensure that the participants are (on average) equal and that any difference in the dependent variables must have been caused by their being in different groups*

2. Match each of the main methods of conducting research with the advantages and disadvantages listed below. *Answers: a. experimental; b. descriptive; c. correlational; d. cross-sectional; e. descriptive; f. longitudinal; g. experimental; h. correlational*

Measuring Up, p. 65
For each example below, indicate which data collection method would work best. *Answers: 1. case study; 2. survey or interview; 3. description/observation [in the wild is best]; 4. experience sampling; 5. meta-analysis; 6. brain imaging; 7. transcranial magnetic stimulation*

Measuring Up, p. 72

1. When researchers want to summarize in a single number all the data they collect, they compute a measure of central tendency. Here are hypothetical data for a study in which 10 women in a sample indicated how many hours they worked that day and then used a rating scale to indicate how much they wanted to have fun. . . . For each set of data, compute the mean, median, and mode. *Answer: Mean for number of hours worked = 5.7; mean ratings of how much they want to have fun = 6.4; median number of hours worked = 5.5; median ratings of how much they want to have fun = 6; mode for number of hours worked = 5, 6, and 8 are all tied for mode—all occur twice; mode for ratings of how much they want to have fun = 5.*

   Now, using a grid like the ones in Figure 2.22, draw a scatterplot of the data in question 1. When you are finished, look at the plot and decide if it represents a positive, negative, or no (linear) relationship between these two variables. Explain what the scatterplot is showing in your own words. *Answer:* There appears to be a positive linear relationship between numbers of hours worked and ratings of fun. This means that as the number of hours the women worked increased, the women gave higher ratings for how much fun they wanted to have. Because this is a correlation, we cannot say that working more hours caused the women to want to have more fun, because there may be a third variable. (Perhaps the women who worked more hours had more money than those who worked fewer hours, or having more money to spend may make women want to have fun.)

2. Which is an accurate description of the rationale for inferential statistics? *Answer: d. When the means of two sample groups are significantly different, we can infer that the populations the groups were selected from are different.*

Practice Test, p. 75

1. Which of the following is a technique that increases scientists' confidence in the findings from a given research study? *Answer: c. replication*

2. Which hypothesis is stronger? Why? *Answer: b, because it offers a specific prediction*

3. Which sampling method is strongest? Why? *Answer: a, because it is random*

4. Which set of conditions should be included in the study? Why? *Answer: c, because it includes experimental and control groups*

5. How should participants be chosen for each condition? Why? *Answer: a, because it uses random assignment*

6. Which operational definition of the dependent variable, stress, is stronger? Why? *Answer: b, because it describes how the variable will be measured*

7. Should you conduct the study in a lab or in a natural setting (e.g., in the campus dining hall)? Why? *Answer: natural setting, because you want to know what people do in their daily lives*

8. Should you use written descriptions of what is heard or a running tally of prespecified categories of behavior? Why? *Answer: prespecified categories of behavior, because you want to know whether a specific behavior, discussing politics, occurs; a simple tally of "yes" or "no" would answer this question.*

9. Should participants know you are observing them? Why? *Answer: No, because doing so will create reactivity.*

10. Indicate which quality of good data is violated by each description. *Answers: a. validity; b. reliability; c. accuracy*

CHAPTER 3: BIOLOGICAL FOUNDATIONS

Measuring Up, p. 91

1. The difference between genotype and phenotype is that _____. *Answer: a. genotype refers to an organism's genetic makeup; phenotype refers to observable characteristics that result from genetic and environmental influences*

2. What is the principle behind knockout gene research? *Answer: b. By rendering a single gene inactive, we can study that gene's effects on behavior.*

Measuring Up, p. 103

1. Neurons communicate by firing. Put the following steps in the correct order so they describe this process. *Answer: e, c, d, b, f, g, h, a*

2. Match each major neurotransmitter with its major functions. *Answers: a. 4; b. 3; c. 5; d. 1; e. 6; f. 2; g. 7*

Measuring Up, p. 113

1. Match each lobe of the brain with its functions. *Answers: a. 2; b. 4; c. 3; d. 1*

2. Match each of the following brain structures with its role or function. *Answers: a. 7; b. 8; c. 6; d. 5; e. 2; f. 1; g. 3; h. 4*

Measuring Up, p. 119

1. Match each statement with one or more of the following terms: peripheral nervous system (PNS); somatic nervous system; autonomic nervous system (ANS); sympathetic division; parasympathetic division. *Answers: a. sympathetic; b. parasympathetic; c. somatic; d. PNS; e. autonomic*

2. Which of the following statements are true? *Answers: Choices b, d, e, f, and h are true.*

Measuring Up, p. 128

1. A person's brain changes in response to environment, including all of that person's experiences. Place an X next to the statements below that support this idea. *Answers: Choices b, c, e, and g are all examples of environment's effect on the brain. Choice f is an extreme effect caused by a brain injury.*

2. Indicate whether the following statements, about the ways in which females' and males' brains differ, are true or false. *Answers: a. true; b. false; c. false; d. false; e. false*

Practice Test, p. 131

1. Complete the following analogy: Genes are to chromosomes as _____ are to _____. *Answer: c. bricks, walls*

2. Which of the following statements are true regarding the relationship between genetic makeup and environment? *Answers: Choices a, b, and c are true.*

3. Which *two* labels accurately describe neurons that detect information from the physical world and pass that information along to the brain? *Answers: b. sensory neuron, e. afferent neuron*

4. You witness a major car accident on your way to school. You pull over and rush to help one of the victims, who has severe cuts across his forehead and legs. . . . Which neurochemical is likely keeping the man pain free despite of his obvious injuries? *Answer: d. endorphins*

5. Who do you predict would have a larger hippocampus? *Answer: a. someone who plays computer games requiring the exploration of complex virtual worlds*

6. Someone suffers a stroke that causes damage to the left motor cortex. Which of the following impairments will the person most likely exhibit? *Answer: d. paralysis of the right side of the body*

7. Because it determines other glands' activities, the _____ is sometimes called "the master gland." *Answer: a. pituitary*

8. The adage *You can't teach an old dog new tricks* is consistent with which phenomenon? *Answer: b. critical periods*

9. True or false: Differences in the brains of people from different cultures necessarily reveal underlying differences in biology. *Answer: False*

CHAPTER 4: THE MIND AND CONSCIOUSNESS

Measuring Up, p. 149

1. Which of the following statements are correct, according to our understanding of consciousness? *Answers: Choices b, e, f, g, and h are correct.*

2. In split-brain patients, the interpreter _____. *Answer: c. makes sense of actions directed by the right hemisphere*

Measuring Up, p. 158

1. When people sleep, _____. *Answer: b. brain activity goes through several cycles of different stages, and each stage has its own characteristic pattern of brain waves*

2. Select the hypothesized reasons why we dream. *Answers: b. Dreams are a way of making sense of neural firing patterns.; c. Dreams allow us to rehearse coping strategies for anxiety producing events.*

Measuring Up, p. 165

Mark each statement below with an "S" if it supports the conclusion that hypnosis is a real phenomenon. Put an "F" next to any false statement. *Answers a. S; b. F; c. S; d. Neither S nor F; e. F; f. F; g. F*

Measuring Up, p. 175

1. All drugs work by _____. *Answer: d. activating neurotransmitter systems*

2. Match each of the following drugs or drug categories with as many true statements as apply. *Answers: a. alcohol; b. marijuana; c. opiates; d. opiates; e. stimulants; f. MDMA; g. alcohol; h. stimulants; i. MDMA*

Practice Test, p. 176

1. What is a key distinction between a person in a persistent vegetative state and a person in a minimally conscious state? *Answer: c. The person in the minimally conscious state shows some degree of brain activity, whereas the person in the persistent vegetative state shows no brain activity.*

2. A researcher asks study participants to play a word game in which they unscramble letters to form words. . . . After participants complete the word game, they meet and interact with a stranger. What do you predict participants' behavior during that interaction will reveal? *Answer: b. Participants in Condition A will be more friendly toward the stranger than will participants in Condition B.*

3. A study participant who has a severed corpus callosum is asked to focus on a dot in the middle of a computer screen. After a few seconds, a car appears on the left half of the screen while an automobile tire appears on the right half of the screen. How will the participant most likely respond if asked to describe the objects in the pictures? *Answer: a. The participant will say he saw a tire and will draw a car.*

4. For each description below, name the sleep disorder: insomnia, apnea, narcolepsy, or somnambulism. *Answers: a. narcolepsy; b. somnambulism; c. insomnia; d. apnea*

5. Which of the following pieces of evidence suggest sleep is an adaptive behavior? *Answers: b. All animals sleep.; c. It is impossible to resist indefinitely the urge to sleep.; e. Animals die when deprived of sleep for extended periods.*

6. Four students discuss a hypnotist's performance on campus. Which student's claim about hypnotism is most consistent with current evidence? *Answer: d. "It's pretty cool that a hypnotist could help those people enter an altered state of consciousness."*

7. Which of the following instruction sets would a yoga teacher trained in concentrative meditation be most likely to give? *Answer: b. "Lying on your back, rest your hands gently on your abdomen. As you breathe in and out, focus attention on your breath. Notice the rhythmic rise and fall of your abdomen and the slow, deep movement of your chest."*

8. Match each of the following drugs with the appropriate description of a user's typical response: alcohol, marijuana, MDMA, opiates, stimulants. *Answers: a. stimulants; b. marijuana; c. alcohol; d. MDMA; e. opiates*

9. A group of people are talking about their weekend plans. Which of the following statements suggest the most understanding regarding alchohol's effects? *Answers: c. "I won't drink tonight because I really need a good night's sleep and I always wake up insanely early after I drink."; d. "I think a beer or two will give me the liquid courage I need to ask Jordan out on a date."*

10. Which of the following phenomena are best described as symptoms of physical dependence? *Answers: a. strong cravings for the substance; b. elevated tolerance for the substance*

CHAPTER 5: SENSATION AND PERCEPTION

Measuring Up, p. 186

1. Suppose you are designing an experiment to determine the absolute threshold for detecting a salty taste. You plan to give participants plain water that _____. *Answer: b. sometimes has a small amount of salt in it and sometimes has no salt*

   You plan to have them sip a small amount of water and tell you _____. *Answer: a. whether they taste salt or no salt*

   You will use the participants' responses to calculate an absolute threshold for tasting salt by _____. *Answer: a. comparing hits and false alarms*

2. What is Weber's law? *Answer: d. The amount of physical energy needed to detect a change in sensation depends on the proportional change from the original stimulus.*

Measuring Up, p. 212

1. The sensory systems _____. *Answer: b. use only a small portion of the available energy in their environment*

2. A general principle regarding sensation is that _____. *Answer: a. the combined firing of many different receptors and the neurons they connect with creates our sensations*

3. An intense stimulus, such as a loud sound or a heavy touch, is coded by _____. *Answer: b. an increase in the number of neurons that respond to the stimulation*

Measuring Up, p. 231

1. Match each of the following monocular depth cues with its description: familiar size, linear perspective, occlusion, position relative to the horizon, relative size, texture gradient. *Answers: a. linear perspective; b. occlusion; c. familiar size; d. relative size; e. texture gradient; f. position relative to the horizon*

2. What is binocular disparity? *Answer: b. a cue to depth caused by the formation of a slightly different image in each eye*

3. Perceptual constancy _____. *Answer: a. allows us to see objects as stable even when there are large fluctuations in the sensory information we receive*

Practice Test, p. 233

1. Which answer accurately lists the order in which these structures participate in sensation and perception (except for smell)? *Answer: a. specialized receptors, thalamus, cortex*

2. While listening to a string quartet, you find you can easily decipher the notes played by the violins, by the viola, and by the cello. When you focus on the viola, you find some of the notes especially loud and others barely discernable. Which of the following statements best describes your sensations of the quartet? *Answer: c. You can decipher qualitative differences among the instruments because of the involvement of specific sensory receptors, whereas you can make quantitative distinctions—recognizing variations in the notes' intensity—due to the rate of firing of your sensory neurons.*

3. When the violist plays a solo, you cannot hear it. Which of the following statements is the most likely explanation? *Answer: b. The intensity of the auditory stimulation does not exceed the minimum threshold needed for you to detect a sensation.*

4. Imagine you have a steady, radiating pain across your lower back. No matter how you position yourself, you cannot make the pain go away. Select the answer choices most relevant to this type of pain. *Answers: a. activated by chemical changes in tissue; e. nonmyelinated axons; f. slow fibers*

5. A one-year-old girl skins her knees on a rough sidewalk. The girl cries in pain. Which of the following interventions will most likely calm her? *Answer: d. Directing the girl's hand on a quick touching tour of the nearby environment and saying things such as "Feel this tree's rough bark. Touch the grass; it tickles. Feel how smooth this rock is!"*

6. After hours of waiting, a bird watcher hears the call of rare bird species. The bird watcher instinctively turns his head about 45 degrees to the left and sees the bird. Which of the following statements best describes how the bird watcher knew where to turn his head? *Answer: a. The call reached the bird watcher's left ear before it reached his right ear; the call was less intense in the bird watcher's right ear than in his left ear.*

7. In which lobe of the brain (frontal, occipital, parietal, temporal) does each of the following sensory cortices reside? *Answers: a. temporal; b. parietal; c. occipital*

8. Imagine you are preparing to conduct a brain imaging study of visual processing. Which pathway—dorsal or ventral—do you hypothesize will be activated by each of the following experimental tasks? *Answers: dorsal ("where") pathway activated by a and e; ventral ("what") pathway activated by b, c, d*

CHAPTER 6: LEARNING

Measuring Up, p. 249

1. Which of the following are true statements about conditioning? *Answers: Choices a, d, f, and j are true.*

2. John B. Watson had planned to extinguish Little Albert's conditioned response to, for example, the rat. Which of the following techniques would have achieved that goal? *Answer: a. Repeatedly showing Little Albert the rat without making a loud sound.*

Measuring Up, p. 260

1. Indicate whether each of the following phenomena is related to operant or classical conditioning. *Answers: a. classical; b. operant; c. operant; d. operant; e. classical; f. operant; g. operant; h. operant*

2. Suppose a mother is trying to get her eight-year-old to stop cursing. Each time the child curses, the mother waits until the child's father is present before spanking the child. Select the better answers: *Answers: a. The time interval between the cursing and the punishment is ___x___ too long for optimal learning.; b. One likely outcome to the continued use of this punishment is ___x___ the child will curse at times he or she is unlikely to be caught.; c. Generalization is likely to occur such that ___x___ the child comes to fear the father and mother.; d. What is the child likely to learn? ___x___ Do not get caught cursing.; e. A more effective approach would be to ___x___ provide rewards for not cursing.*

Measuring Up, p. 268

1. How do cultural beliefs about learning affect human performance? *Answer: b. Students from cultures that view learning as the result of persistence work harder and therefore achieve more than students from cultures with other beliefs.*

2. The critical finding from Bandura's Bobo doll research was that _____. *Answer: a. children exhibited more aggressive behaviors toward the doll after viewing an actor being rewarded for acting aggressively toward the doll than did children in the control condition*

3. Mirror neurons _____. *Answer: a. fire when we are watching motor activity in other people*

Measuring Up, p. 275

1. What can we learn from the superlearner Doogie mice? *Answer: a. NMDA receptors are important in producing learning.*

2. What is the evidence that dopamine is a critical neurotransmitter for reinforcers' effects on behavior? *Answer: b. Rats will work continuously to deliver electrical stimulation to a portion of the brain that uses dopamine in its neural processes.*

Practice Test, p. 277

1. Every night for a few weeks, you feed your pet rat while watching the evening news. Eventually, the rat learns to sit by its food dish when the news program's opening theme song plays. In this example of classical conditioning, what are the US, UR, CS, and CR? *Answers: US is food, UR is going to the food dish to eat the food, CS is the program's theme song, CR is going to the food dish to eat the food when the theme song plays.*

2. At a psychology lecture, each student receives 10 lemon wedges. The professor instructs the students to bite into a lemon wedge anytime a large blue dot appears within her slide presentation. Nearly every time the students bite into lemons, their mouths pucker. The 11th time a blue dot appears on the screen, many students' mouths pucker visibly. In this case, what are the US, UR, CS and CR? *Answers: US is lemon, UR is a pucker, CS is a blue dot, CR is a pucker at the sight of the blue dot.*

3. A few minutes later in that same psychology lecture, the professor projects the image of a turquoise dot. How will the students likely respond to this image? *Answer: c. The students will experience puckering responses, because of stimulus generalization.*

4. Which pairing of stimuli will most quickly create a learned association? *Answer: b. Eating a box of raisins and experiencing extreme nausea a few hours later.*

5. Identify each statement as an example of negative punishment, positive punishment, negative reinforcement, or positive reinforcement. *Answers: a. positive reinforcement; b. positive punishment; c. negative reinforcement; d. negative punishment (removal of affection)*

6. Match each scenario with one of the following reinforcement schedules: fixed ratio, variable ratio, fixed interval, variable interval. *Answers: a. fixed interval; b. variable interval; c. fixed ratio; d. variable ratio*

7. Recently, Albert Bandura has employed serial television dramas to address global social issues such as illiteracy and overpopulation. He believes principles of social learning should apply when viewers observe fictional characters engaging in behaviors relevant to a particular issue. Based on what you have read about social learning, which of the following factors do Bandura and his collaborators likely consider when creating these shows? *Answers: They likely consider factors a, c, d, f, and g. One example of the effectiveness of Bandura's approach is that a million people sought out literacy skills classes after one of these serial dramas addressed the issue of illiteracy in Mexico.*

8. Hebb's postulate states that _____. *Answer: b. cells that fire together wire together*

9. _____ is more closely associated with long-term potentiation than with reinforcement. *Answers: b. The hippocampus; c. NMDA*

CHAPTER 7: ATTENTION AND MEMORY

Measuring Up, p. 286

1. Which statement correctly describes the two stages of attention? *Answer: b. Attention has a rapid process that searches for one feature together and a slower, serial process that searches for multiple features one at a time.*

2. What happens to information when we are not paying attention? *Answer: a. Some of the unattended information is passed on for further processing, but it is weaker than attended information.*

Measuring Up, p. 294

1. Indicate how long each of the three stages of memory holds information, and indicate its capacity. *Answers: a. Duration: ii, Capacity: iii; b. Duration: iv, Capacity: ii; c. Duration: v, Capacity: iv*

2. Which memory system is responsible for your ability to remember the first word in this question? *Answer: b. working memory*

Measuring Up, p. 299

Indicate whether each of the following examples of memory is prospective, implicit, or explicit; if it is explicit, also indicate whether it is episodic or semantic. *Answers: a. implicit; b. semantic and explicit; c. semantic and explicit; d. explicit and either semantic or episodic, depending on whether you remember when and where you learned it; e. prospective; f. implicit*

Measuring Up, p. 304

1. Which is the best way to teach scuba divers how to surface safely? *Answer: b. Teach them underwater because the situation will provide retrieval cues for when they need to use the knowledge.*

2. One strategy for improving memory is to relate something you are learning to information you already know. Why would that strategy be effective? *Answer: a. Because the known information can act as a retrieval cue to help you remember the new information when you need it.*

Measuring Up, p. 311

1. What changes occur at the synapses when people learn and remember? *Answers: a. Neuronal connections are strengthened.; c. Neurons make more synaptic connections.*

2. One difference between females' and males' underlying brain mechanisms for memory is found in _____. *Answer: b. emotional memory*

Measuring Up, p. 316

1. Indicate whether each of the following is an example of retroactive interference or proactive interference or neither. *Answers: a. retroactive; b. proactive; c. proactive*

2. Which of the following examples reflects an accurate understanding of cultural differences in change blindness? *Answer: b. North Americans tend to be more individualistic and therefore tend to notice changes to a central figure faster than East Asians do, whereas East Asians notice changes in background information faster.*

Measuring Up, p. 325

1. Which principles must be balanced in a court of law when considering memories' accuracy? *Answer: d. What are the costs of letting a possible felon go free, and what are the costs of incarcerating someone who may be innocent?*

2. Flashbulb memories _____. *Answer: c. are often distorted in the same way as other memories, but "feel" true to the people whose memories they are*

3. Suppose a teacher accuses you of plagiarizing a term paper. . . . Of course, you did not commit plagiarism—you would never do that. Which of the following phenomena might be cited in your defense? *Answer: a. cryptomnesia*

Practice Test, p. 329

1. The card game Set requires players to attend to four features (shape, color, shading, and number) across 12 cards in an effort to identify a "Set." . . . Playing this game requires participants to engage in a _____, which is _____. *Answer: a. conjunction task; effortful*

2. Sarah and Anna are chatting at a coffee shop. . . . Which strategy could Anna use to effectively pull Sarah's attention back to the conversation? *Answer: d. Anna should use Sarah's name in a sentence.*

3. Imagine you are a manager seeking to hire a new employee. Before leaving work Monday afternoon, you look through a stack of 30 resumes organized alphabetically by last name. When you return to work Tuesday morning, which job applicant are you most likely to remember? *Answer: a. Alvarado*

4. You are asked to memorize a list of words. Which encoding strategy will likely result in the best recall performance? *Answer: d. As you read each word, think of a synonym for it.*

5. You ask a friend to memorize the following list: bed, rest, night, tired, blanket, pillow, relaxed. . . . In addition to remembering some of the words, your friend lists the word *sleep*, which did not appear on the original list. Which of the following phenomena is most related to your friend's error in recall? *Answer: c. networks of associations*

6. Damage to which area of the brain (amygdala, frontal lobe, hippocampus) would most likely lead to each of the following impairments? *Answers: a. hippocampus; b. frontal lobe; c. amygdala*

7. Which "sin of memory" is demonstrated in each of the following examples? *Answers: a. absentmindedness; b. blocking*

8. Fill in the blanks. People experiencing _____ amnesia are unable to recall memories from the past, whereas people experiencing _____ amnesia are unable to form new memories. *Answers: retrograde; anterograde*

CHAPTER 8: THINKING AND INTELLIGENCE

Measuring Up, p. 341

1. Indicate whether each of the following examples is an analogical or symbolic representation. *Answers: a. analogical; b. symbolic; c. analogical; d. symbolic; e. analogical; f. analogical; g. analogical*

2. Which of the following is an advantage of scripts? *Answer: a. They provide quick and almost effortless guides to behavior in different situations.*

3. Which of the following is a disadvantage of scripts? *Answer: a. They tend to reinforce stereotypical behaviors.*

Measuring Up, p. 356

1. For each of the following terms, identify the appropriate definition(s). *Answers: reasoning—c, f; decision making—a; problem solving—b, e*

2. In performing affective forecasting, _____. *Answer: a. most people are poor judges of how they will feel about something in the future*

Measuring Up, p. 375

1. While discussing with his grandmother what he has been studying at college, Dave was impressed by how much she knows. . . . His grandmother's general knowledge exemplifies her _____ intelligence, whereas her ability to figure out the cell phone exemplifies her _____ intelligence. *Answer: b. crystallized, fluid*

2. If you wanted to reduce the effects of stereotype threat, you could _____. *Answer: d. tell test takers that the upcoming test will not reflect group differences.*

Practice Test, p. 377

1. Which of the following statements reflect incorrect assumptions in the *defining attribute model* of concepts? *Answers: a. All attributes of a category are equally salient.; b. All members of a category fit equally well into that category.; e. Membership within a category is on an all-or-none basis.*

2. Which of the following fruits will most likely be considered prototypical? Which will least likely be considered prototypical? *Answers: a is most likely; c is least likely.*

3. On the first day of the semester, students enter a new class. . . . Based on our script for the first day of class, what will students most likely do? *Answer: a. Students will settle into their seats and perhaps glance over the handout. People who already know each other might converse, but they most likely will not discuss the questions.*

4. Label each of the following statements as an example of deductive reasoning or inductive reasoning. *Answers: a. inductive; b. deductive; c. deductive; d. inductive; e. inductive*

5. Label each of the following scenarios as an example of affective forecasting, the availability heuristic, a framing effect, or the representativeness heuristic. *Answers: a. framing effect; b. availability heuristic; c. representativeness heuristic*

6. _____ is an indicator of current levels of skill or knowledge, whereas _____ is an indicator of future potential. *Answer: a. achievement, aptitude*

7. Casey is very empathic. It is as if he can read the minds of the people around him, knowing instantly if someone is uncomfortable with a topic of conversation, interested in garnering someone's affections, stressed out, and so on. We would expect Casey to score well on which indicators of intelligence? *Answers: b. EQ; e. interpersonal intelligence*

8. Which one of the following comments most accurately reflects the facts about the roles of nature and of nuture in intelligence? *Answer: d. "Group differences in intelligence cannot be attributed to genetic differences if there are environmental differences between the groups."*

CHAPTER 9: MOTIVATION AND EMOTION

Measuring Up, p. 390

1. Arrange the levels of Maslow's need hierarchy in the correct order, with lowest needs at the bottom, and then match each example with the correct level. *Answers: c. 1; e. 2; a. 4; d. 3; b. 5*

2. Indicate whether the motivation in each of the following scenarios is intrinsic or extrinsic. *Answers: a. intrinsic; b. extrinsic; c. intrinsic; d. extrinsic*

Measuring Up, p. 395

Imagine you are asked to design a program for people who need to lose weight. Based on the information in this chapter about the processes that regulate eating, what suggestions would you make in each of the following areas? *Answers: 1. a; 2. a; 3. a; 4. a*

Measuring Up, p. 404

1. Identify whether each of the following statements about human sexual behavior best describes a biological, cultural, or evolutionary perspective. *Answers: a. biological and evolutionary; b. evolutionary; c. cultural; d. cultural and evolutionary; e. biological; f. biological; g. biological and evolutionary*

2. Arrange the stages of the human sexual response cycle in order, and match each stage with its description. *Answers: excitement—d; plateau—b; orgasm—c; resolution—e; refractory—a*

Measuring Up, p. 413

1. A display rule is _____. *Answer: b. a rule that specifies when and how certain people can express an emotion*

2. What is a likely explanation for blushing? *Answer: a. It is a nonverbal way of admitting a mistake.*

Measuring Up, p. 423

For each of the three main theories of emotions—James-Lange, Cannon-Bard, and two-factor—select as many all of the descriptive statements and examples that apply to each theory. *Answers: James-Lange—4, 5, c; Cannon-Bard—1, 5, d; two-factor—1, 3, 4, a, b*

Practice Test, p. 425

1. Students enrolled in a difficult class are preparing to give end-of-term presentations, which will count 50 percent toward final grades. Which student below is likely to perform the best? *Answer: b. Sonya is somewhat anxious about this presentation. She knows her stuff but recognizes how much is riding on the quality of this presentation. This anxious energy motivates her to polish her slides and practice her talk.*

2. A classmate tells you he is having a hard time remembering which eating outcomes are associated with damage to different parts of the hypothalamus. Which of the following verbal mnemonics would be most helpful to your classmate? *Answers: b. Organisms with damage to the lateral area of the hypothalamus (LH) eat little.; d. Organisms with damage to the ventromedial region of the hypothalamus (VMH) eat very much.*

3. Which statement below is backed by empirical findings? *Answer: c. Prenatal exposure to hormones is associated with sexual orientation.*

4. Which neurotransmitter is *not* implicated in the sexual response? *Answer: b. GABA*

5. Which of the following phrases statements likely describe somatic markers? *Answers: b. "I have butterflies in my stomach."; c. "My heart is pounding so hard it is going to jump out of my chest."*

6. People [can / cannot] experience positive and negative affect simultaneously. *Answer: can*

7. Positive affective states are associated with increased levels of [GABA / dopamine]. *Answer: dopamine*

8. Negative affective states are associated with increased levels of [dopamine / norepinephrine]. *Answer: norepinephrine*

9. Which of these statements are true regarding involvement of the amygdala in emotion? *Answers: All three choices are true.*

10. Would you expect activity in the left or right prefrontal cortex in response to pictures of dead and decomposing livestock? *Answer: b. right*

CHAPTER 10: HEALTH AND WELL-BEING

Measuring Up, p. 433

1. Of the following possibilities, select one way that our behaviors contribute to reduced health. *Answer: a. We can make unhealthy choices such as eating a poor diet and smoking.*

2. Which of the following statements exemplifies the biopsychosocial model? *Answer: b. By engaging in healthy behaviors, we can strengthen our immune systems.*

Measuring Up, p. 444

1. Match each stage in the general adaptation syndrome—alarm, resistance, and exhaustion—with one of the following examples. *Answers: alarm—b; resistance—c; exhaustion—a*

2. How does long-term stress affect health? *Answer: a. The extended physiological response damages organs such as the heart.*

Measuring Up, p. 456

1. How does exercise affect the brain? *Answer: d. Exercise causes the growth of new neurons and new neural connections, especially in brain areas associated with memory and cognition.*

2. Why do restrictive diets rarely work in reducing obesity? *Answer: b. The body learns to conserve calories, so restrictive dieting may lead ultimately to greater weight gain.*

Measuring Up, p. 462

1. Which of the following statements explains how researchers concluded that oxytocin causes people to be more trusting? *Answer: d. When researchers sprayed oxytocin in the noses of people playing the trust game, the players acted in a more trusting way than did the placebo control group.*

2. What aspects of social support are most important in creating a positive effect on health? *Answer: c. It is most important that people around you genuinely care about your well-being.*

Practice Test, p. 467

1. Which of the following comments most accurately represents health psychologists' current understanding of illness? *Answer: d. "Genetic predispositions to some illnesses exist. But living healthily can help reduce the chances we'll develop an illness."*

2. The correct answer to the previous question is consistent with the _____ of health and illness. *Answer: b. biopsychosocial model*

3. Latasha is normally an engaged and satisfied employee. For a few months, she becomes very dissatisfied, grumpy, and uninterested in her job. Shortly after participating in a weekend-long seminar about the secrets of success, Latasha begins enjoying her work life again. Which of the following attributions for her improved satisfaction at work best reflects the concept of regression to the mean? *Answer: a. "Well, I figured I couldn't stay in that funk forever. Things eventually had to start looking up again."*

4. Which of the following individuals is most at risk for developing heart disease, assuming equal levels of physiological risk factors such as blood pressure and cholesterol level? *Answer: b. People describe Patti as a complainer. She always finds something to gripe about, whether it is poor service at a restaurant, a driver's failure to use turn signals, or a loud talker on a cell phone.*

5. Individuals who are hardy _____. *Answers: a. are committed to daily activities; e. see challenges as opportunities for growth; f. see themselves as able to control their own lives*

6. Which of the following statements are true? *Answer: All the choices are true.*

7. Label each of the following statements as applying to anorexia nervosa (AN) and/or bulimia nervosa (BN). *Answers: a. AN and BN (though BN is seldom fatal); b. BN; c. AN; d. AN; e. BN; f. AN; g. AN; h. BN; i. BN; j. AN and BN*

8. Imagine your grandparent is preparing to move to a retirement community. Which of the following might you say if you wanted to help her or him promote physical and mental health? *Answers: b. "Know that I care about you and am here for you if there's anything I can do to help with the transition to your new home."; c. "Make a point of meeting a lot of other residents."; d. "Make sure to stay in touch with your close friends."*

9. Which of the following statements are true regarding oxytocin? *Answers: b. Oxytocin is released when people feel empathy.; d. Participants dosed with oxytocin behave more trustingly than control participants do.; e. Women release oxytocin when they breast-feed infants.*

CHAPTER 11: HUMAN DEVELOPMENT

Measuring Up, p. 482

1. Which of the following research findings would support the idea that humans have sensitive learning periods? *Answers: c. Children with minimal exposure to language before age 12 can learn to speak, but their learning will happen poorly and with great difficulty*

2. Identify the type of attachment that each of the following statements describes. *Answers: a. disorganized; b. avoidant; c. secure; d. anxious / ambivalent*

Measuring Up, p. 502

1. Match each of Piaget's stages of cognitive development with its description. *Answers: a. preoperational; b. formal operational; c. sensorimotor; d. concrete operational*

2. Indicate whether each of the following statements about language learning is true or false. *Answers: a. false; b. false; c. true; d. false; e. false*

Measuring Up, p. 511

1. Choose the statement that is true about divorce. *Answer: d. Reduced income and, often, poverty follow divorce and may be responsible for some of the negative effects of divorce on children.*

2. The case study of Bruce/Benda Reimer shows that _____. *Answer: a. gender identity has a strong biological component*

Measuring Up, p. 519

1. Erikson proposed that certain challenges typify the passage through adulthood to old age. Which of the following statements represents these challenges? *Answer: c. In adulthood, people face the challenge of creating and maintaining close relationships, giving back to society, and responding well to the lives they have lived.*

2. Indicate whether the following statements describe cognitive aging. Either mark the statement "CA" or leave it blank. *Answers: a. CA; c. CA; e. CA*

Practice Test, p. 521

1. A one-week-old infant normally can _____. *Answers: a. differentiate between sweet and nonsweet tastes; c. grasp a caregiver's finger; d. make eye contact; e. orient toward loud sounds; i. turn his or her head toward the smell of the mother's breast milk; j. turn toward a nipple near his or her mouth*

2. Which of the following statements best summarizes the key finding from Harry Harlow's study of infant rhesus monkeys? *Answer: d. Contact with comforting "mothers" promoted normal social development.*

3. A nine-month-old child watches as three cubes are covered by a panel, then as three more cubes appear to move behind the panel. Once the panel is lifted, only three cubes appear. Which of the following statements describes the infant's likely reaction? *Answer: d. The infant will stare at the three remaining cubes for a relatively long time.*

4. Imagine reading a young child a story. In the story, Schuyler calls Emma a mean name. Emma retaliates by biting Schuyler. You ask the child what she thinks about the fact that Emma bit Schuyler. Three possible responses appear below. Label each as typical of one of the levels of moral reasoning described by Kohlberg: preconventional, conventional, or postconventional. *Answers: a. preconventional; b. postconventional; c. conventional*

5. Indicate whether each of the following phenomena is associated with the scholarship of Chomsky or with that of Vygotsky. *Answers: c, d, g, h are associated with Chomsky; a, b, e, f are associated with Vygotsky.*

6. Which of the following conclusions about the relationship between parenting style and child well-being is supported by empirical research? Optimal social development occurs when _____. *Answer: d. the parenting style fits the child's temperament*

7. Which of the following comments violate the critical thinking skills addressed in this chapter: understanding that some does not mean all and avoiding either/or thinking? *Answers: b shows a lack of awareness that some does not mean all; c demonstrates either/or thinking*

8. Igor is 83 years old. Which of his behaviors and cognitions are consistent with the socioemotional selectively theory? *Answers: Choices b, d, e are consistent.*

9. Which of the following characteristics describe most older adults? *Answers: a. happy; b. mentally healthy; c. feeling more positive emotions than negative ones; e. physically well*

CHAPTER 12: SOCIAL PSYCHOLOGY

Measuring Up, p. 532

1. Identify the attitude formation(s) or change process(es) described in each of the following examples. *Answers: a. mere exposure; b. persuasion and socialization; c. conditioning; d. cognitive dissonance*

2. For each of the following scenarios, indicate whether the attitude is likely to predict the subsequent behavior. In a few words, explain why or why not. *Answers: a. No, attitude is not strong; b. Yes, attitude is strong and highly accessible; c. No, attitude lacks specificity.*

Measuring Up, p. 544

1. Label each of the following statements as an example of stereotyping, prejudice, or discrimination. *Answers: a. stereotyping; b. prejudice; c. discrimination*

2. Max was arrested for driving while under the influence of alcohol. Label each of the following statements as an example of personal attribution, situational attribution, or fundamental attribution error. *Answers: a. situational attribution; b. fundamental attribution error; c. personal attribution*

Measuring Up, p. 552

1. Label each of the following scenarios as an example of conformity, compliance, or obedience. *Answers: a. conformity; b. obedience; c. compliance*

2. Match each of the following social influence constructs with the correct definition: deindividuation, group polarization, social facilitation, and social loafing. *Answers: a. deindividuation; b. social loafing; c. group polarization; d. social facilitation*

Measuring Up, p. 559

1. Indicate whether each of the following statements supports a biological, individual-differences, or sociocultural explanation for aggression. *Answers: Choices a, f, g, h support a biological explanation; b, i support an individual-differences explanation; c, d, e support a sociocultural explanation.*

2. For each of the following scenarios, indicate whether the individuals are likely to evidence bystander apathy. Briefly explain why or why not. *Answers: a. no (no ambiguity, no opportunity to diffuse responsibility, no anonymity); b. yes (high cost-benefit ratio, driver can remain anonymous, opportunity for diffusion of responsibility); c. yes (situation is ambiguous, opportunity for diffusion of responsibility).*

Measuring Up, p. 566

1. Label each of the following characteristics as an attribute of passionate love or companionate love. *Answers: Choices a, b, e, g are attributes of passionate love; c, d, f, h are attributes of companionate love.*

2. For each of the following situations, select the comment that, according to empirical findings, indicates a lasting relationship. *Answers: Situation 1—b; Situation 2—a*

Practice Test, p. 568

1. Which of the following scenarios illustrates postdecisional dissonance? *Answer: b. Adrianna wants to go on a community service trip during her spring break. . . . When asked to explain why she made this decision, she says, "The Mexico trip will give me a chance to travel outside the United States, which I've always wanted to do. Plus, the Louisiana trip sounded pretty stale."*

2. Which of the following scenarios illustrates justification of effort? *Answer: a. David's boss regularly asks him to do a lot of extra tasks around*

the office. . . . When asked why he does all these extra tasks, David replies, "I'm happy to do whatever it takes to make our office as welcoming and efficient as possible."

3. Some of the following statements illustrate cognitive or behavioral outcomes of stereotyping. As appropriate, label those statements as examples of illusory correlation, ingroup favoritism, outgroup homogeneity, and self-fulfilling prophecy. *Answers: a. ingroup favoritism; b. illusory correlation; c. outgroup homogeneity*

4. Dorm A and Dorm B have a long-standing rivalry. . . . A couple students from each dorm encourage the students to get together to brainstorm possible strategies for easing the tension. According to the ideas presented in this chapter, which suggestion would be most effective? *Answer: d. "We can hold an all-campus competition, where teams of dorms would compete for prizes. Dorm A and Dorm B could be on one team; Dorm C and Dorm D could be on the other team."*

5. Which of the following examples of social norms marketing would most likely be most effective? *Answer: b. 80 percent of the residents in your neighborhood recycle. Keep up the great work!*

6. Some of the following scenarios illustrate compliance strategies discussed in this chapter. As appropriate, label each scenario as an example of door in the face, foot in the door, or low-balling. *Answers: a. low-balling, b. door in the face, c. no response choice is appropriate*

7. Which of the following examples most accurately describes the relationship between relationship length and frequency of sex? *Answer: a. After an initial period of frequent sex, there is a negative correlation between relationship length and frequency of sex.*

8. Match each definition below with the appropriate term: altruism, inclusive fitness, kin selection, reciprocal helping. *Answers: a. kin selection; b. altruism; c. reciprocal helping; d. inclusive fitness*

9. Which statement below about Shelly, who is very attractive, is most consistent with the "what is beautiful is good" stereotype? *Answer: b. "Shelly is easily the happiest person I know!"*

CHAPTER 13: PERSONALITY

Measuring Up, p. 581

1. Indicate which theorists are associated with each of the following four approaches to studying personality: psychodynamic, humanistic, type and trait, and learning and cognition. *Answers: psychodynamic approaches—c, d, f, j, m; humanistic approaches—a, e, k; type and trait approaches—h, i, l; learning and cognition—b, g, n*

2. Indicate which concepts are associated with each of the four approaches to studying personality (see question 1). *Answers: psychodynamic approaches—a, b, j, m; humanistic approaches—e, l; type and trait approaches—c, g, h, k; learning and cognition approaches—d, f, i*

Measuring Up, p. 588

1. Match the strengths and limitations listed below to the following assessment methods: California Q-Sort, NEO Personality Inventory, Rorschach inkblot test, Thematic Apperception Test. *Answers: California Q-Sort—a, d, e; NEO Personality Inventory—a, e; Rorschach inkblot test—b, f, g; Thematic Apperception Test—b, c*

2. For each scenario, indicate which person is most likely to engage in the behavior described and explain why. *Answers: Situation 1—a, because conscientiousness is centrally important to Hayley's personality; Situation 2—b, because a bar is a weak situation and thus less likely to dictate behavior*

Measuring Up, p. 601

1. Which of the following statements are true regarding the relationships among environment, genes, personality traits, and temperament? *Answers: Choices b, c, and d are true.*

2. Which of the following findings support biological bases of personality? *Answers: Choices a, f, and g support biological bases.*

Measuring Up, p. 612

1. Imagine that while browsing the shelves of a local bookstore, you discover a series of books about self-esteem. Which of the following three theoretical perspectives is most likely addressed in each book: self-evaluation maintenance theory, sociometer theory, or terror management theory? *Answers: a. self-evaluation maintenance theory; b. terror management theory; c. sociometer theory*

2. Sort the following list of attributes into two groups: those more often evidenced in collectivist cultures and those more often evidenced in individualist cultures. *Answers: collectivist cultures—a, e, f, h, j, k, l; individualist cultures—b, c, d, g, i*

Practice Test, p. 615

1. Your psychology instructor asks the students in your class to form groups of five and then take turns answering the question *What do we need to know about you to truly know you?* The people in your group give the following answers; label each as representative of psychodynamic, humanistic, type and trait perspectives, or learning and cognitive perspectives. *Answers: a. type and trait; b. learning and cognition; c. psychodynamic; d. humanistic*

2. June asks people to watch a five-minute recording of a play in which two characters find themselves in a dangerous situation. Then she asks her research participants to write an ending to the story, which she codes to reveal features of each participant's personality. This proposed measure of personality can best be described as _____ and _____. *Answer: a. idiographic; projective*

3. Which of the following statements might explain why our close acquaintances sometimes are better able to predict our behaviors than we are? *Answers: b. Predictions of our own behaviors may be biased in favor of our subjective perceptions (how we think we act) rather than our objective behaviors (how we do act).; c. We tend to pay more attention to others than to ourselves and thus fail to notice our own behavior; others notice how we behave and are better able to predict our future behaviors.*

4. Which of the following are associated with the behavioral approach system (BAS), and which are associated with the behavioral inhibition system (BIS)? *Answers: BAS—a, d; BIS—b, c, e*

5. Which of the following statements best describes the distinctions among traits, temperaments, and characteristic adaptations? *Answer: a. Temperaments, which are broader than traits, influence personality throughout development. Situational demands can lead to characteristic adaptations, which, although they do not reflect changes in the underlying dispositions, can reflect changes in how these dispositions are expressed.*

6. By extrapolating from research on self-schemas, indicate which of the following memorization techniques should be most effective in memorizing a list of nouns. *Answer: b. Imagine yourself doing something with each noun (e.g., "I wiggle my toes inside my shoe").*

7. A professional athlete makes the following statements during an interview with a sports reporter. Which statements are most likely to be positive illusions? *Answers: b. "I'm sure that wearing my lucky socks helped."; d. "I'm done with injuries. From here on out, I'll have a clean bill of health."*

8. Braunwin prides herself on her musical ability. Which of the following successes would most likely lead Braunwin to feel bad about herself? Which would most likely lead her to feel good? Why? *Answers: Braunwin is most likely to feel bad if c (best friend asked to play a solo) because this person is close to her and is succeeding in a domain that is important to Braunwin; she is most likely to feel good if d (sister receives a prestigious athletic scholarship) because this person is close to her and is succeeding in a domain that is not as important to Braunwin.*

CHAPTER 14: DISORDERS OF THE MIND AND BODY

Measuring Up, p. 630

1. Indicate whether each of the following scenarios is best described as a mental status exam, a structured interview, an unstructured interview, a behavioral test, a psychological test, or a neuropsychological test. *Answers: a. neuropsychological testing, given the emphasis on memory, a brain function; b. mental status exam; c. structured interview*

2. While at a conference on mental disorders, you attend a symposium titled *Understanding the Origins of Mental Health.* Excerpts from three of the presentations appear below. Match each excerpt to one of the etiological models discussed in this chapter: diathesis-stress model, biological model, family systems model, sociocultural model, and cognitive-behavioral approach. *Answers: a. biological; b. family systems model; c. diathesis-stress model*

Measuring Up, p. 636

1. Which of the following symptoms commonly are experienced by people with anxiety disorders? *Answers: a. exaggerated startle response; b. excessive fidgeting; d. feelings of apprehension; e. impaired ability to concentrate; f. muscular tension; h. sleep disruptions*

2. Indicate whether each of the following empirical findings supports a cognitive, situational, or biological underpinning of anxiety disorders. *Answers: a. biological; b. cognitive; c. biological; d. situational; e. cognitive*

Measuring Up, p. 641

1. Indicate whether each of the symptoms and causes listed below is associated with major depression, bipolar disorder, or both. *Answers: a. major depression; b. major depression; c. major depression; d. bipolar disorder; e. bipolar disorder; f. bipolar disorder; g. major depression and bipolar disorder; h. major depression; i. bipolar disorder; j. major depression and bipolar disorder; k. major depression and bipolar disorder; l. major depression and bipolar disorder*

2. Which of the following statements represent dysfunctional cognitive patterns believed to cause depression? If a statement is an example of dysfunctional cognition, briefly describe why. *Answers: a. shows evidence of overgeneralizing based on a single event; c. shows a perceived powerlessness to avoid negative events*

Measuring Up, p. 647

1. Indicate whether each of the following phenomena is a negative or a positive symptom of schizophrenia. *Answers: a. negative; b. negative; c. positive; d. positive; e. negative; f. positive*

2. Indicate whether each of the following phenomena is a biological or an environmental factor contributing to schizophrenia. *Answers: a. biological; b. biological; c. environmental; d. biological; e. environmental; f. environmental*

Measuring Up, p. 655

The *DSM-IV* groups together seemingly different disorders—such as borderline personality disorder, antisocial personality disorder, and mental retardation. What features of these disorders justify this grouping? *Answers: a. They last throughout the life span.; c. There is no expectation of significant change.*

Measuring Up, p. 661

1. Children with autism exhibit deficits in which of the following categories? *Answers: a. awareness of other people; b. communication; e. restricted activities and interests*

2. Compared with people without ADHD, people with ADHD show _____ activation in the _____ of the brain. *Answer: a. less; frontal lobes and limbic regions*

Practice Test, p. 663

1. Which of the following questions would a clinician ask to determine whether a behavior represents psychopathology? *Answers: a. Does the behavior deviate from cultural norms?; b. Is the behavior causing the individual personal distress?; c. Is the behavior maladaptive?*

2. Two students visit the campus health center. Student A describes feeling constantly fearful and anxious. Student B describes feeling persistently agitated and often exhibiting violent outbursts. Student A's symptoms are consistent with an _____ disorder, which are more common in _____; student B's symptom's are consistent with an _____ disorder, which are more common in _____. Choose from the following pairs of words to fill in the blanks. *Answer: c. internalizing, females; externalizing, males*

3. Indicate whether each of the following constellations of symptoms is best described as phobic disorder, generalized anxiety disorder, panic disorder, or obsessive-compulsive disorder. *Answers: a. generalized anxiety disorder; b. phobic disorder*

4. Indicate whether each of the following constellations of symptoms is best described as major depression, dysthymia, or bipolar disorder. *Answers: a. dysthymia; b. major depression*

5. Match each of the following statements with the correct label for that symptom of schizophrenia: delusion of grandeur, delusion of persecution, flat affect, hallucination, loosening of associations, social withdrawal. *Answers: a. loosening of associations; b. delusion of persecution; c. hallucination*

6. Which of the following statements describe key objections to categorizing personality disorders as true mental disorders? *Answers: b. Overlap in the characteristics of different disorders suggests that the categories may not be conceptually clear cut.; c. Some features of personality disorders are not as stable as researchers once thought.; d. The features of personality disorders are merely extreme versions of normal personality traits.*

7. Royce takes swimming lessons at the community pool. . . . Based on this description, which of the following disorders does Royce most likely have? *Answer: b. attention-deficit/hyperactivity disorder*

8. Are females or males more likely to be diagnosed with each of the following disorders? *Answers: Females are more likely to be diagnosed with d. borderline personality disorder, e. depression, f. generalized anxiety disorder, g. obsessive-compulsive disorder, h. panic disorder; males are more likely to be diagnosed with a. antisocial personality disorder, b. attention-deficit/hyperactivity disorder, c. autism.*

CHAPTER 15: TREATING DISORDERS OF THE MIND AND BODY

Measuring Up, p. 677

1. Identify the psychotherapeutic orientation each of the following scenarios typifies. *Answers: a. cognitive-behavioral therapy; b. psychodynamic therapy; c. client-centered therapy*

2. Identify the disorder most commonly treated with each medication. *Answers: a. schizophrenia; b. depression; c. anxiety*

Measuring Up, p. 695

Indicate whether cognitive-behavioral therapy, drug therapy, or a combination of the two is the recommended treatment for each disorder listed. *Answers: Drug therapy is most effective for choices a, g; CBT is most effective for c, d, e, f; a combination of drug therapy and CBT is most effective for b.*

Measuring Up, p. 699

Why are personality disorders so difficult to treat? *Answers: a. People with personality disorders are difficult to engage in therapy because they do not believe their actions cause their problems; b. People with personality disorders believe their problems are caused by their environments.*

Measuring Up, p. 708

1. Label each point below as an argument either for or against the practice of prescribing SSRI medications to adolescents with depression. *Answers: Choices b, d, e, and f support the use of SSRIs in treating adolescent depression; a and c argue against the use of SSRIs in this population.*

Practice Test, p. 711

1. Which of the following statements are true regarding how culture can affect the therapeutic process? *Answers: Choices a, b, and e are true.*

2. Which of the following statements are true regarding pseudotherapies? *Answers: Choices a, b, c, and d are true.*

3. Barlow advocates distinguishing between psychological treatments and general talk therapy. Which of the following attributes characterize psychological treatments? *Answers: a. Treatments should be based on evidence of their effectiveness.; b. Treatments should be appropriate for the particular disorders.; c. Specific techniques for treatment should be developed in the laboratory by psychological scientists.*

4. Dialectical behavior therapy takes place in three stages. Place the descriptions of the three stages below in the correct order. *Answer: The correct order is c, a, b.*

5. During his early adult years, Joshua was diagnosed with antisocial personality disorder. Joshua is now 40. Over the coming years, his friends and family will likely see a decrease in which of the following behaviors? *Answer: c. Joshua's tendency to get into fistfights.*

6. Label each point below as an argument either for or against the practice of prescribing Ritalin (methylphenidate) to children with ADHD. *Answers: Choices a and d support the use of Ritalin in treating ADHD; b, c, e, and f argue against the use of Ritalin in this population.*

7. Three-year old Marley recently received a diagnosis of autism. Which of the following are true about her likely treatment? *Answers: Choices a, b, and d are likely true.*

8. Imagine you are asked to evaluate the quality of the following two methodologies for an empirical evaluation of a new treatment for ADHD. Label each of the methodologies as strong or weak. If a methodology is strong, briefly explain why. If a methodology is weak, provide a brief recommendation for strengthening it. *Answers: a. weak, would be improved if random assignment to condition were used; b. strong because of the use of treatment and control groups*

PERMISSIONS ACKNOWLEDGMENTS

CHAPTER 1

Chapter Opener: Sue Bennett/Alamy.

Fig. 1.01a: AP/Wide World Photos.

Fig. 1.01b: Timothy A. Clary/AFP/Getty Images.

Fig. 1.02: From Phelps et al. (2000). *Journal of Cognitive Neuroscience, 12,* 729–738. Images courtesy Elizabeth A. Phelps, Phelps Lab.

Fig. 1.03a: *Time,* January 28, 2008, cover.

Fig. 1.03b: *Newsweek,* March 19, 2007, cover.

Fig. 1.03c: *Time,* January 29, 2007, cover.

Fig. 1.04: Chris Hondros/Getty Images.

Fig. 1.05: The Granger Collection, New York.

Fig. 1.06: Imagno/Getty Images.

Fig. 1.07: James Cavallini/Photo Researchers.

Fig. 1.08: Bettmann/Corbis.

Fig. 1.09: Courtesy Professor Joseph J. Campos, University of California, Berkeley.

Fig. 1.10: Luke Duggleby/OnAsia.

Fig. 1.11a: From Phelps et al. (2000). *Journal of Cognitive Neuroscience, 12,* 729–738. Images courtesy Elizabeth A. Phelps, Phelps Lab.

Fig. 1.11b: Stockbyte/Alamy.

Fig. 1.11c: Somos Images LLC/Alamy.

Fig. 1.11d: Bruno De Hogues/Getty.

Fig. 1.12: Rischgitz/Getty Images.

Fig. 1.13: Bettmann/Corbis.

Fig. 1.14: Archives of the History of American Psychology, University of Akron.

Fig. 1.15: *American Journal of Psychology.* © 1974 by the Board of Trustees of the University of Ilinois. Used with permission of the University of Illinois Press.

Fig. 1.16: From *Mind Sights* by Roger N. Shepard. © 1990 by Roger N. Shepard. Henry Holt and Company, LLC.

Fig. 1.17: Archives of the History of American Psychology, University of Akron.

Fig. 1.18: Bettmann/Corbis.

Fig. 1.19: Archives of the History of American Psychology, University of Akron.

Fig. 1.20: Courtesy George Miller, Princeton University © 2001, Pryde Brown Photographs, Princeton, NJ.

Fig. 1.21: Archives of the History of American Psychology, University of Akron.

Fig. 1.23b: AP Photo/Hermann J. Knippertz.

Cartoon 1.1: *The Far Side* ® by Gary Larson © 1982 FarWorks, Inc. All rights reserved. Used with permission.

Cartoon 1.2: © The *New Yorker* Collection 1998, Sam Gross from cartoonbank.com. All rights reserved.

CHAPTER 2

Chapter Opener: Photodisc/Getty Images.

P. 33: "Girls Just Want to Have Fun," lyrics by Robert Hazard, as performed by Cyndi Lauper. © 1984 Sony/ATV Tunes LLC. All rights on behalf of Sony/ATV Tunes LLC, administered by Sony/ATV Music Publishing, 8 Music Square West, Nashville, TN 37203. All rights reserved. Used by permission.

Fig. 2.02a: Women Singing Karaoke—Image © Howard Pyle/zefa/Corbis.

Fig. 2.02b: Howard Pyle/zefa/Corbis.

Fig. 2.02c: Dave & Les Jacobs/JupiterImages.

Fig. 2.02e: Christy Varonfakis Johnson/Alamy.

Fig. 2.03a: Karl Ammann/Corbis.

Fig. 2.03b: Lawrence S. Sugiyama/University of Oregon.

Fig. 2.04: A Granada Television Production, photo courtesy of First Run Features.

Fig. 2.05a: Digital Vision/Alamy.

Fig. 2.05b: Image Source Black/Alamy.

Fig. 2.07: Bob Daemmrich/The Image Works.

Fig. 2.10a, b: Corbis/SuperStock.

Fig. 2.11c, d: © Peter Menzel/www.menzelphoto.com.

Fig. 2.12a, b: © 2007 President and Fellows of Harvard College; all rights reserved.

CHAPTER 5

Chapter Opener: John-Francis Bourke/Photonica/Getty Images.

Fig. 5.1: New England Historic Genealogical Society.

Fig. 5.5a, b: AP/Peter Kramer.

Fig. 5.7: Jonathan Olley/Getty Images.

Fig. 5.8: Marcy Maloy/Getty Images.

Fig. 5.9a, b: John-Francis Bourke/Photonica/Getty Images.

Fig. 5.10a: Steven Errico/Getty.

Fig. 5.10b: Jose Luis Pelaez Inc./Getty.

Fig. 5.11: Jochen Sand/Agefotostock.

Fig. 5.12: AP/John Bazemore.

Fig. 5.14: Mario Tama/Getty Images.

Fig. 5.15: Stanley Coren and A. Ralph Hakstian, "Color Vision Screening Inventory" from "Color vision screening without the use of technical equipment: Scale development and cross-validation," *Perception and Psychophysics,* Vol. 43, 1988. Reprinted with permission of S. Coren and R. Hakstian (Inventory is copyright of SC Psychological Enterprises Ltd.).

Fig. 5.16b: Stephen Dalton/NHPA.

Fig. 5.17a: James King-Holmes/Photo Researchers.

Fig. 5.17b: AP Photo/*The Sun,* Larry Steagall.

Fig. 5.18: Cheyenne Rouse/Getty.

Fig. 5.23: Stanley Coren and A. Ralph Hakstian, "Hearing Screening Inventory" from "The development and cross-validation of a self-report inventory to assess pure tone threshold hearing sensitivity," *Journal of Speech and Hearing Research,* Vol. 35, August 1992. Reprinted with permission of S. Coren and R. Hakstian (Inventory is copyright of SC Psychological Enterprises Ltd.).

Fig. 5.25: P. Zimbardo, *Psychology and Life,* 15th ed. (Figure 3.11—page 118). © 1999. Reproduced by permission of Pearson Education, Inc.

Fig. 5.26: From Celeste McCollough, "Color adaptation of edge detectors in the human visual system," *Science* 149:1115 (9/3/1965). Reprinted with permission from AAAS.

Fig. 5.27: Figure "Color contrast and color appearance: Brightness constancy and color" from *Vision and Visual Perception,* ed. C. H. Graham (New York: Wiley, 1965).

Fig. 5.28a: Kitaoka, A. "Colored ray illusion," Illusion Designology (7), *Nikkei Science,* 31(8), 66–68. Reprinted by permission of Akiyoshi Kitaoka.

Fig. 5.28b: Kitaoka, A. "Colored ray illusion #2," Illusion Designology (7), *Nikkei Science,* 31(8), 66–68. Reprinted by permission of Akiyoshi Kitaoka.

Fig. 5.28c: Kitaoka, A. "Light of Sweden illusion." Reprinted by permission of Akiyoshi Kitaoka.

Fig. 5.31: Todd Heatherton/Dartmouth.

Fig. 5.32a: B. Bird/zefa/Corbis.

Fig. 5.32b: Robert van der Hilst/Corbis.

Fig. 5.33a–b: Figure 8.4(a) and (b) from p. 280 of *Psychology* by Peter Gray. © 1991, 1994, 1999 by Worth Publishers. Used with permission.

Fig. 5.33e (i): Kanizsa, G. "Subjective Contours" from *Scientific American* 234. Copyright © 1976. Reprinted by permission of Jerome Kuhl.

Fig. 5.33e (ii): Figure from Varin, D., "Fenomeni di contrasto e diffusione cromatica," *Rivista di Psicologia* 65 (1970).

Fig. 5.34: Selfridge, Oliver, "Context influences perception (pattern recognition)" from *Proceedings of the Western Computer Conference.* Copyright © 1955 by IEEE.

Fig. 5.38: From McCarthy, G., Price, A., & Allison, T. (1997). *Journal of Cognitive Neuroscience, 9I,* 605–610.

Fig. 5.39: Courtesy Peter Thompson, University of York.

Fig. 5.41a: www.news.bbc.co.uk.

Fig. 5.41b: AP/Wide World Photos.

Fig. 5.42: Zafer Kizilkaya/Images and Stories.

Fig. 5.44a, b: © 2002 Magic Eye Inc.

Fig. 5.45: Munch, Edvard (1863–1944) © ARS, NY. *Evening on Karl Johan Street,* c. 1892. Historical Museum, Bergen, Norway. Scala/Art Resource, NY.

Fig. 5.47: Drawings used by Hudson (1967) and Kilbride and Robbins (1969).

Fig. 5.48: Joel Sartore/Getty.

Fig. 5.49: Courtesy of Todd Heatherton.

Fig. 5.53a, b: Honoré Daumier, from *O Lune! … inspire-moi ce soir* (1844).

Fig. 5.55: Illustration "Turning Tables" illusion from *Mind Sights* by Roger N. Shepard. Copyright © 1990 by Roger N. Shepard. Reprinted by permission of Henry Holt and Company, LLC.

Fig. 5.56: Figure from *The Art Pack* by Christopher Frayling, Helen Frayling, and Ron Van der Meer. Copyright © 1992 Van der Meer Paper Design Ltd.

Fig. 5.57a, b: © 2004 by W. W. Norton & Co., Inc.

Cartoon 5.1: © The *New Yorker* Collection, Pat Byrnes from cartoonbank.com.

CHAPTER 6

Chapter Opener: Ryan McVay/Getty.

Fig. 6.1: Bettmann/Corbis.

Fig. 6.2: Bettmann/Corbis.

Fig. 6.6: Jun Sato/WireImage/Getty.

Fig. 6.7a: Benjamin Harris, U. New Hampshire.

Fig. 6.7b: Archives of the History of American Psychology/University of Akron.

Fig. 6.8: Childress, A. R., Mozey, P. D., McElgin, W., Fitzgerald, J., Revich, M., & O'Brien, C. P. (1999).

Fig. 6.9a, b: Lincoln P. Brower.

Fig. 6.10a: Paul Popper/Popperfoto/Getty Images.

Fig. 6.10b: AP Photo/Evan Vucci.

Fig. 6.11a: Yerkes, Robert M., Manuscripts & Archives, Yale University.

Fig. 6.13a: Nina Leen/Time/Pix Images.

Fig. 6.14: AP/Wide World Photos.

Fig. 6.17: Lynn M. Stone/Naturepl.com.

Fig. 6.19: © Frans de Waal.

Fig. 6.20: Albert Bandura, Dept. of Psychology, Stanford University.

Fig. 6.21: Susan Mineka, Northwestern University.

Fig. 6.22: Geri Engberg/The Image Works.

Fig. 6.23: D. Hurst/Alamy.

Fig. 6.24a: Pegaz/Alamy.

Fig. 6.24b: Jonathan Storey/Getty.

Fig. 6.25: Courtesy Daniel Miller, Dept. of Neurology, Carthage College.

Fig. 6.27: Biophoto/Associates/Photo Researchers, Inc.

Fig. 6.29: AP/Wide World Photos.

Cartoon 6.1: © The *New Yorker* Collection 1993, Tom Cheney from cartoonbank.com.

CHAPTER 7

Chapter Opener: Dean Freeman/Lensmodern.

Fig. 7.3b: Alamy.

Fig. 7.6a, b, c: Simons, D. J., & Levin, D. T. (1998). Failure to detect changes to people during a real-world interaction. *Psychonomic Bulletin and Review, 5,* 644–649. From Simon & Levin study (1998), © 1998 Psychonomic Society, Inc. Figure courtesy Daniel J. Simons.

Fig. 7.9: Newscom.

Fig. 7.13a: David Turnley/Getty Images.

Fig. 7.13b: Newscom.

Fig. 7.14: Maria Teijeiro/Getty Images.

Fig. 7.15: Jose Luis Pelaez/Getty.

Fig. 7.18a: Bjorn Svensson/Alamy.

Fig. 7.18b: Chris A. Crumley/Alamy.

Fig. 7.20: Wheeler, M. E., Petersen, S. E., & Buckner, R. L. (2000). Memory's echo: vivid remembering reactivates sensory specific cortex. *Proceedings of the National Academy of Sciences, 97,* 11125–11129.

Fig. 7.23: *Why Sex Matters for Neuroscience* by Larry Cahill, *Neuroscience,* AOP, published online 10 May 2006; doi: 10.1038/nrn 1909.

Fig. 7.24: Photofest.

Fig. 7.25: Photofest.

Fig. 7.27: AP Photo/Robert E. Klein.

Fig. 7.28: AP Photo/John Froschauer.

Fig. 7.29a: Kennedy Space Center/NASA.

Fig. 7.29b: Tom Stoddart/Getty Images.

Fig. 7.30: Joe Raedle/Getty Images.

Fig. 7.31: AP/Wide World Photos.

Fig. 7.32a, b: From Loftus, Miller, & Burns, 1978. Courtesy Elizabeth Loftus.

Fig. 7.33: AP Photo/Tony Gutierrez.

Fig. 7.34: Courtesy Radiological Society of North America.

Cartoon 7.2: © The *New Yorker* Collection 1998, Mick Stevens from cartoonbank.com.

CHAPTER 8

Chapter Opener: Mark Katzman/Halo Images.

Fig. 8.1a: AP Photo/Carmen Taylor.

Fig. 8.1b: AP Photo/Rick Bowmer.

Fig. 8.3: Eysenck, M. W., Figures 7.6 and 7.7, *Cognitive Psychology: A Student's Handbook,* 2nd ed., Lawrence Erlbaum Associates. Copyright © 1990. Reprinted by permission.

Fig. 8.6: Eysenck, M. W., Figure 8.3, *Cognitive Psychology: A Student's Handbook,* 2nd ed., Lawrence Erlbaum Associates. Copyright © 1990. Reprinted by permission.

Fig. 8.8a: Imagebroker/Alamy.

Fig. 8.8b: Steven Vidler/Eurasia Press/Corbis.

Fig. 8.8c: Warner Bros./Photofest.

Fig. 8.8d: Artisan Entertainment/Photofest.

Fig. 8.9: Yann Arthus-Bertrand/Corbis.

Fig. 8.10a: Jeff Greenberg/PhotoEdit.

Fig. 8.10b: Erik Dreyer/Getty.

Fig. 8.10c: Corbis.

Fig. 8.11a: Mario Tama/Getty Images.

Fig. 8.11b: Vesa Moilanen/AFP/Getty Images.

Fig. 8.12a: Imageshop/Alamy.

Fig. 8.12b: Blend Images/Getty.

Fig. 8.12c: Glowimages/Getty.

Fig. 8.12d: Alamy.

Fig. 8.12e: Agency Design Pics Inc./Alamy.

Fig. 8.12f: Photodisc/Getty.

Fig. 8.15: AP Photo/Adam Butler.

Fig. 8.20a: Courtesy of Bug Labs.

Fig. 8.20b: Serzhol/Dreamstime.com.

Fig. 8.21: Alamy.

Fig. 8.22: The Photo Works.

Fig. 8.23: The Granger Collection, New York.

Fig. 8.26a: Duomo/Corbis.

Fig. 8.26b: Reuters New Media Inc./Corbis.

Fig. 8.26c, d: AP/World Wide Photos.

Fig. 8.30: Jim Ross/*The New York Times.*

Fig. 8.31: Courtesy of The Stephen Wiltshire Gallery.

Fig. 8.33: From Kristensen and Bjer, "Explaining the relation between birth order and intelligence," *Science* 316:1717 (6/22/2007). Reprinted with permission from AAAS.

Fig. 8.35: AP/World Wide Photos.

Fig. 8.36a: RubberBall/Alamy.

Fig. 8.36b: Courtesy Brains and Emotions Research, University of Wisconsin–Madison.

Fig. 8.36c: Rebecca Saxe/Saxelab, MIT.

Cartoon 8.1: © Leo Cullum November 30, 1998. *New Yorker* cartoon, cartoonbank.com.

CHAPTER 9

Chapter Opener: Tim A. Hetherington/Panos.

Fig. 9.1: "Management of malignant tumors," Bulsara et al., *Neurosurg Focus 13(4),* Art. 5, 2002, Fig. 1.

Fig. 9.05: Archives of the History of American Psychology.

Fig. 9.7: Jacob E. Steiner, PhD, Laboratory of Oral Physiology, The Hebrew University.

Fig. 9.8: Alamy.

Fig. 9.10: Saxpix.com/Agefotostock.

Fig. 9.12: Bob Daemmrich/The Image Works.

Fig. 9.13: Reuters/Corbis.

Fig. 9.14: AP Photo/The Rockefeller University.

Fig. 9.15: Simone van den Berg/FeaturePics.

Fig. 9.17a: Alex Mares-Manton/Agefotostock.

Fig. 9.17b: Seishiro Akiyama/Getty.

Fig. 9.17c: Alex Mares-Manton/Agefotostock.

Fig. 9.19: Brent Sims, Joseph Taravella and Eva Olielska and Pail Zei.

Fig. 9.20: Courtesy of W. W. Norton & Co., Inc.

Fig. 9.21: Ekman (1972–2004).

Fig. 9.24: Tim Graham/Getty Images.

Fig. 9.26: Courtesy of W. W. Norton & Co., Inc.

Fig. 9.31: Chris Lisle/Corbis.

Cartoon 9.1: Bob Zahn from cartoonbank.com.

CHAPTER 10

Chapter Opener: Tony Anderson/Digital Vision/Getty Images.

Fig. 10.1: Jim Mahoney/*Dallas Morning News.*

Fig. 10.4: Adam Gault/Photo Researchers.

Fig. 10.5a: Alaska Stock LLC/Alamy.

Fig. 10.5b: Alamy.

Fig. 10.9: Alamy.

Fig. 10.10: Universal/The Kobal Collection.

Fig. 10.12a: Douglas Peebles.

Fig. 10.12b: Eric Johnson/*The New York Times.*

Fig. 10.13a: Teh Eng Koon/AFP/Getty Images.

Fig. 10.13b: Travel Ink/Getty Images.

Fig. 10.14: Granger Collection.

Fig. 10.15: Ana Nance/Redux.

Fig. 10.16: AFP/Getty Images.

Fig. 10.18: Jack Geuz/AFP/Getty Images.

Fig. 10.21: Alamy.

Cartoon 10.1: © The *New Yorker* Collection. 1987 Donald Reilly/cartoonbank.com. All rights reserved.

CHAPTER 11

Chapter Opener: Photodisc/Getty Images.

Fig. 11.3a: Dr. Yorgos Nikas/Phototake.

Fig. 11.3b: Petit Format/Photo Researchers.

Fig. 11.3c: Biophoto Associates/Photo Researchers.

Fig. 11.4: Courtesy of Sterling K. Clarren, MD, Clinical Professor of Pediatrics, University of British Columbia Faculty of Medicine.

Fig. 11.6: Michael S. C. Thomas and Mark H. Johnson, Figure 2 from "New advances in understanding sensitive periods in brain development," *Current Directions in Psychological Science* 17.1, Feb. 2008, pp. 1–5. Copyright © 2008 Association for Psychological Science. Reproduced with permission of Blackwell Publishing Ltd.

Fig. 11.7: Nina Leen/TimePix/Getty Images.

Fig. 11.8a, b: Harlow Primate Laboratory, University of Wisconsin.

Fig. 11.10: Stock Boston, LLC/Spencer Grant.

Fig. 11.11: Courtesy Velma Dobson, University of Arizona.

Fig. 11.13a, b: © Dr. Carolyn Rovee-Collier, Director, Rutgers Early Learning Project.

Fig. 11.14: Bettman/Corbis.

Fig. 11.15a: Sally and Richard Greenhill/Alamy.

Fig. 11.15b: Tom Mareschal/Alamy.

Fig. 11.15c: Alamy.

Fig. 11.15d: Jon Feingersh/Getty Images.

Fig. 11.16a–c: Michael Newman/PhotoEdit.

Fig. 11.22a: Caroline Penn/Panos Pictures.

Fig. 11.22b: Panos Pictures.

Fig. 11.23: Alamy.

Fig. 11.25: Figure 2 from Kuhl, P. K., Tsao, F.-M., & Liu, H.-M., "Foreign-language experience in infancy: effects of short-term exposure and social interaction on phonetic learning," *Proceedings of the National Academy of Sciences,* Vol. 100, No. 15: 9096–9101. © 2003 National Academy of Sciences, U.S.A. Reprinted by permission.

Fig. 11.26: Alamy.

Fig. 11.27: Tomas Munita/*The New York Times*/Redux.

Fig. 11.28: Ellen Senisi/The Image Works.

Fig. 11.29: Courtesy of Laura Ann Petitto.

Fig. 11.30: AP Photo/Billings Gazette, Larry Mayer.

Fig. 11.31: Monica Almeida/*The New York Times*/Redux.

Fig. 11.32: Courtesy of Frank Caston.

Fig. 11.34a: Alamy.

Fig. 11.34b: Jeff Greenberg/The Image Works.

Fig. 11.35: Photo courtesy David Reimer. From Colapinto, John, *As Nature Made Him: The Boy Who Was Raised as a Girl* (2000), HarperCollins Publishers Inc.

Fig. 11.36: Reuters Newsmedia Inc./Corbis.

Fig. 11.37: *Psychological Science,* 2006 Feb., 17(2): 159–63.

Fig. 11.38a: Alamy.

Fig. 11.38b: R. Matina/Agefotostock.

Fig. 11.38c: Alamy.

Fig. 11.39: Chris McGrath/Getty Images.

Fig. 11.40a: Stephanie Maze/Corbis.

Cartoon 11.1: © The *New Yorker* Collection 2003, Donald Reilly from cartoonbank.com. All rights reserved.

Cartoon 11.2: © The *New Yorker* Collection 2001, Edward Koren from cartoonbank.com. All rights reserved.

Cartoon 11.3: © The *New Yorker* Collection 1994, Sidney Harris from cartoonbank.com. All rights reserved.

CHAPTER 12

Chapter Opener: Holly Wilmeth/Aurora Photos.

Fig. 12.01a: AP Photo.

Fig. 12.1b: © Philip G. Zimbardo, PhD.

Fig. 12.2: Najlah Feanny/Corbis.

Fig. 12.02a: AP Photo/Morry Gash.

CHAPTER 15

NAME INDEX

SUBJECT INDEX

Page numbers in *italics* refer to figures.

autonomic nervous system (ANS), 114–16, *114*, 130, 631
autoreception, 97–98
autoreceptors, 103
autostereogram, 223, *223*
availability heuristic, 346, *347*
averaging, 47, 71
avoidance behavior, 666, 669
avoidant attachment, 480
avoidant personality disorder, 648
awareness:
    brain areas involved in, 130, 147
    and mental disorders, 624
    and perception, 213
    and scientific foundations of psychology, 30
    self-, 545–46, 602–3
    and stereotypes, 542
    and study of consciousness, *148*, 149, 176
    and treatment of mental disorders, 679
    see also autism; consciousness
axons:
    and basic structure and functions of brain, 111
    definition of, 93
    and development, 474
    and development of brain, 120
    and nervous system, 93, 94, 96, 103, 114
    and perception, 214
    and sensation, 192, 194, 201

babbling, 497, 707
"baby in the box" incident, 236, *236*
Baganda people, 225
balance, 209–10
barn owls, 198–99, *199*
Barnum, P.T., 105
basal ganglia, 109, 110, 130, 660, 662
basic tendencies, 600, *600*
Bauby, Jean-Dominique, 133–34
Bayer Aspirin Company, 168, *168*
Beck Depression Inventory, 622
behavior:
    affecting physical health, 428–30, 445–56, 466
    appropriate, 341
    assessments of, 622
    and attitudes, 525–31, 568
    crowd, 546
    and culture, 12–13
    and death, 429–31, 465
    definition of, 5
    deviant, 523–25
    disorganized and inappropriate, 644
    and genetics/genes, 9–10, 78–79, 83–87, 130, 428, 445–47, 448, 451, 453
    groups' influence on individual, 545–47
    influence of neurotransmission on, 98–104, 119, 130
    as learned, 669
    and levels of analysis, 12–13
    measurement of, 51
    and mental disorders, 23, 619, 622, 631, 635, 642, 644, 646, 657, 658, 661, 710
    and mind, 24
    and motivation, 380–90

and overview of psychological science, 5
and personality, 572–73
predicting, 23, 25–26
purpose of, 18, 30
and race/ethnicity, 455, 466
and research methodology, 37–50
and scientific foundations of psychology, 22–23, 30
and scripts, 340–41
situations as shaping, 23
and social factors, 24
and study of consciousness, 144–46, 176
and themes of psychological science, 5, 9–10, 11, 12–13, *12*, 29, 30
thin slices of, 533, 544
and thought/thinking, 22–23, 30
unconscious processing as influence on, 144–46
see also behavioral approach system; behavioral genetics; behavioral inhibition system; behavioral therapy; behaviorism; behavior modification; cognitive-behavioral therapy; dialectical behavior therapy; emotions; learning; motivation; rewards; social psychology; *specific mental disorder; type of behavior*
behavioral approach system (BAS), 596, *596*, 616
behavioral economics approach, 259–60
behavioral genetics, 83–87, 89–90, 91, 368–69, 402, 601
behavioral inhibition system (BIS), 596–97, *596*, 616
behavioral therapy:
    and choosing a practitioner, 692–94
    and treatment of mental disorders, 23, 669–71, 681–82, 695, 696, 697, 703–4, 708, 709, 710
    see also cognitive-behavioral therapy
behaviorism:
    definition of, 21
    and development, 477
    founding of, 236, 237, 249
    influence of, 237
    and learning, 237–49, 257–59, 275, 276
    and mental disorders, 627, 628, 667
    and personality, 576, 579–80
    and research methodology, 61
    and scientific foundations of psychology, 21–23, 30
behavior modification, 236, 255–57, 667, 669, 670, 703–4
    and scientific foundations of psychology, 21–22, 23, 30
belief persistence, 408–9
beliefs:
    and adaptation, 12–13
    and development, 481, 503, 505, 508, 509, 519
    and identity, 503, 508, 509
    and memory, 297, 323
    and mental disorders, 628
    and personality, 572–73, 576, 580, 614
    and scientific foundations of psychology, 23

and situations, 567
and social influence, 551
and themes of psychological science, 12–13
and treatment of mental disorders, 669, 692, 697
benzodiazepines, 101, 673
beta blockers, 312
beta waves, 150, *150*, 151
better-than-average effect, 608
Bhutto, Benazir, 247
bias:
    attention, 310
    attributional, 534–35
    correspondence, 534
    and critical thinking, 26, 30
    hindsight, 657–58, *658*
    ingroup-outgroup, 533, 538–39, *538*, 568
    and memory, 319–20, *319*, 323, 325
    "my side," 409
    observer, 40, 41, 56
    and research methodology, 34, 37, 40, 41, 46, 56
    response, 185, *185*
    self-report, 56
    self-serving, 535, 568, 608, 609, 610–12
    and sensation, 185, *185*, 186
    and stereotypes, 568
Big Five, 579, *579*, 583, 586, 592, 597, 599, 614
Binet-Simon Intelligence Scale, 358
binge eating, 449, 450
binocular depth cues, 222–23, *223*, 232
binocular disparity, 222–23, *223*
biocultural systems theory, 502–3
biological needs, 252, 383, 384, 391
biological preparedness, 246
biological revolution, 9–10, 30
biological rhythms, 640, 662
biological therapies:
    and brain stimulation, 676, *676*, 682, 686–87, *687*, 695, 710
    limitation of, 667
    and magnetic fields, 674
    and pseudotherapies, 676–77
    and psychosurgery, 674–75, 676, 682, 689
    and treatment of mental disorders, 666–67, 674–76, 691, 695, 706, 710
    see also alternative treatments
biology:
    of addiction, 174
    and application of psychological science, 25
    and brain, 5, 126
    constraints of, 257, *257*
    and development, 504, 520
    as foundation of psychology, 76–131
    and gender, 509–10, 520
    and harming and helping others, 553–54, 568
    and identity, 509–10
    and intelligence, 358
    and learning, 257–59, 260, 268–74, 276
    and mental disorders, 24, 101, 625–26, *626*, 629, 630, 631, 634–35, 639–41, 647, 654, 658–60, 661–62
    and motivation, 402–3, 423
    and operant conditioning, 257–59, 276

and memory, 302
  of mental disorders, 620
  of race/ethnicity, 511, 520
  and stereotypes, 536–38, 541, 544, 567
  and thought/thinking, 336–39, 343–44
catharsis, 671
CAT scan, 185
caudate, 635, *635*, 682
causality, and research methodology, 41, 42, 43,
    45–46, 50
Celexa, 589
cell bodies, 93, 103
cells:
  and genetic basis of psychological science, 79,
    82
  see also type of cells
Center for Science in the Public Interest, 451
Centers for Disease Control, 452
central executive component, 290–91, 328
central nervous system (CNS), 104, 114–15,
    114, 119, 192, 196, 202, 626, 702
central tendency, 68
cerebellum, 108, *108*, 113, 130
cerebral asymmetry, 419
cerebral cortex:
  and basic structure and functions of brain,
    108, *108*, 109, 110–13, 130
  and development of brain, 121
  and memory, 321
  and perception, 213, 214
  size of, 110
  and sleep, 155
  see also left hemisphere; right hemisphere
Challenger space shuttle, 317, *317*
chance results, 71–72
"change blindness" phenomenon, 284–85, *284*,
    286, 315
characteristic adaptations, 600–601, *600*, 614
cheating, 11, 411, 602
childhood amnesia, 321
children:
  and crime, 653
  effects of divorce on, 505–7
  having, 518
  and life transitions, 515
  marriage for sake of, 506–7
  and mental disorders, 634, *634*, 635, 646–47,
    653, 655–60, *655*, 662, 698, 699–708, 710
  and violence, 653
  what shapes, 470–76
  see also adolescence; parent-child relationship;
    parenting, style of
Children's Hospital (Los Angeles, California),
    470
chlorpromazine, 689, 690
Cho, Seung-Hui, 54, 55, *55*
choices, and problem solving, 146, 354–55, *354*
Christene (patient), 624
chromosomes, 79–80, *79*, 82
chronic pulmonary disease, 441
chronosystems, 503
chunking, 289–90, *289*, 293, 294, 301, 328
cigarettes, *see* smoking
circadian rhythms, 153, 154, 155, 176

circumplex model, 414–15
clang associations, 644
classical conditioning:
  and attitudes, 525
  definition of, 238
  and emotions, 417
  and learning, 237, 238–40, *238, 239,* 242–48,
    243, 249–60, 271, 274, 275, 276
  and memory, 297, 305–6
  and mental disorders, 628, 669
  and motivation, 174
  operant conditioning as different than,
    249–60, 276
  and rewards, 271
client-centered therapy, 668
client-practitioner relationship, 692, 694, 697
clinical interview, 621
clinical psychologists, 693
clinical psychology, 24
Clinton, Bill, 546
clomipramine, 681
closed-ended questions, 55
closure, 217, *217*
clozapine, 674, 689–90, *690,* 710
coarse coding, 182
Coca-Cola, and cocaine, 166–67, 168, *168*
cocaine, 98, 166, 169, 244, *244,* 271
  and Coca-Cola, 166–67, 168, *168*
cochlea, 196, *197*, 199–200
cochlear implants, 199–200, *199*
cocktail party effect, 283, 603
codeine, 168
coding, *see* encoding
cognition:
  and adulthood, 512
  and aging, 515–16, 517–18, 520
  and application of psychological science, 27
  and attitudes, 531
  definition of, 333–34
  and development, 470–76, 481, 482, 487–89,
    499, 502, 519, 520
  and drugs, 357
  and emotions, 408–11, 414, 419–21, 422, 466
  and exercise, 454–55
  and gender, 520
  and harming and helping others, 554
  and health, 428–29
  and influence of neurotransmission, 101
  information-processing theories of, 22
  innate, 489–92, 501
  and intelligence, 358, 365–67, 376
  and language, 499
  and learning, 248, 257–59, 260, 276
  and levels of analysis, 14–15
  and mental disorders, 23–24, 631, 634–35,
    639–41, *640,* 642, 662
  and moral values, 494
  and operant conditioning, 257–59, 276
  and personality, 573, 579–80, 581, 613, 614
  Piaget's stages of development for, 36,
    487–89, 501, 520
  and research methodology, 36, 57–58
  and scientific foundations of psychology,
    23–24

and self-knowledge, 602
  and sensation, 194, 195
  and sleep, 154, 157, 158
  and social psychology, 527–28, 532, 554, 568,
    602
  and themes of psychological science, 30
  and treatment of mental disorders, 691, 706,
    710
  see also cognitive-behavioral therapy (CBT);
    cognitive dissonance; cognitive
    restructuring; cognitive therapy; decision
    making; problem solving; representations,
    mental; schemas; thought/thinking
cognitions, hot/cold, 387
Cognitive-Affective Personality System (CAPS),
    580, *580,* 614
cognitive-behavioral therapy (CBT):
  and sleep, 152
  and treatment of mental disorders, 24,
    627–28, 630, 666, 669–71, 680–82, 684,
    685, 688, 691, 692, 695, 700, 710
cognitive dissonance, 527–28, *527, 528,* 531,
    568
cognitive maps, 258
cognitive-neoassociationistic model, 554
cognitive neuroscience, 5, 22, *22*
cognitive psychology, and scientific foundations
    of psychology, 22
cognitive restructuring, 669, *669,* 670, 710
cognitive-social theories, of personality, 580, 581
cognitive therapy:
  and scientific foundations of psychology, 17
  and treatment of mental disorders, 24, 666,
    669–71, 678–82, 695, 696, 697, 710
  see also cognitive-behavioral therapy
cognitive triad, 640
collective self, 610, *611,* 612
College Board Examination Survey, 608
color, 204–9, *205,* 212, 215, 230, 232, 282
color vision screening inventory (CVSI), 206,
    206
coma, 134, *134,* 138–39
  see also persistent vegetative state
common sense, 8, 145, 524
communication:
  and adaptation, 12
  of animals, 501
  and basic structure and functions of brain,
    110
  and development, 470
  and mental disorders, 656–57, 662, 705, 706
  and nervous system, 92–95, 96
  neuron integration into systems of, 103,
    114–19
  and specialization of neurons, 92–95
  and themes of psychological science, 12
  see also language; speech
comorbidity, 623, *623,* 632, *632*
companionate love, 562, *563,* 568
comparison groups, 43
compensation, and perception, 228–29
compliance, 549–50, 551, 568
compulsions, *see* obsessive-compulsive disorder

computers:
    brain analogous to, 22
    and memory, 286, *287*, 288, 291
    and PET scans, 59, 60
    and scientific foundations of psychology, 22
concepts:
    definition of, 337
    and research methodology, 37
    as symbolic representations, 336–39, 341, 376
concordance rates, 639, 654, 658, 659
concrete operational stage, 488–89, 520
conditional syllogisms, 343–44
conditioned food aversion, 245, *245*, 248
conditioned response (CR), 237–42, 680
conditioned stimulus (CS), 237–42, 245–48, 274
conditioning:
    and attitudes, 525, 568
    and choosing a practitioner, 692–94
    and emotions, 417
    and learning, 237, 238–42, 274, 275
    and mental disorders, 628, 635, *635*
    second-order, 241–42
    vicarious, 268
    see also classical conditioning; operant
        conditioning
conditioning trials, 238
conduct disorder, 653, 698, 710
cones, 201, 202, *202*, 204, *205*, 208, 212, 232,
    483
confabulation, 321–22, 328, 486
"confessional" therapies, 671, 710
confidentiality, 62–63
conflict, 506, 564, 565, 566, 568
    and scientific foundations of psychology, 21
conformity, 547–49, *548*, 551, 566, 568
confounds, 45–46
Confucius, 16, *16*
conjunction tasks, 282, *282*
conscience, 575
conscientiousness, 579, 586–87, 590–91
consciousness:
    and alcohol, 169–72
    altered, 138, 158–74
    and coma, 138–39
    and decision making, 356
    definitions of, 134, *134*, 135, 176
    and drugs, 138, 165–74, *166*
    and escapism, 164, *164*
    and flow, 163–64
    and hypnosis, 159–61, *160*
    and immersion in action/activities, 163–64,
        163
    levels of, 575, 600, *600*
    and meditation, 162–63, *162*
    and memory, 295–97, 298–99
    and mental disorders, 628, 635, 642
    and overview of psychological science, 5
    and personality, 574, *574*, 613
    and problem solving, 353–54, 356
    and scientific foundations of psychology, 17,
        18, 21, 30
    sleep as altered state of, 150–53, 158, 176
    and split brain, 139–44, *141*, *142*
    study of, 132–77, *134*, *136*

summary of principles of, 176
    and themes of psychological science, 9
    variations in, 138–39, *139*
consolidation process, and memory, 306–8, 309,
    310, 311, 328
contact comfort, 470, 478
context-dependent memory, 303, *303*
contiguity, and learning, 240, 245
continuous reinforcement, 255, 256
control, 193–95, 385, 633, 703
    and research methodology, 37, 43, 45
    see also locus of control; self-regulation
convenience sampling, 46, *47*, 50
conventional morals, 494
cooperation, 542–44, *543*, 567, 568
coping:
    and appraisals, 442–43, 444
    and behaviors affecting health, 464
    and exercise, 454
    and individual differences, 443
    and mental disorders, 626, 696, 703
    as process, 442–44
    with stress, 434–44, 454, 464, 466
    types of, 442–43
coping response, 434–35
cornea, 200–201
corpus callosum, 111, 127, 140, 367
correlational studies, and research methodology,
    37, 40–43, *43*, 49–50, 69–71, *70*, 72
correlation coefficient, 69, 72
correspondence bias, 534
cortex:
    and basic structure and functions of brain,
        110
    and development, 472
    and development of brain, 124, 128
    and perception, 219, 222, 232
    reorganization of, 124, *124*
    and seizures, 139
    specialization of, 106
    see also cerebral cortex; visual cortex; *specific
        cortex*
cortical maps, 124, *124*
cortisol, 435, 436, 438, 441, 686
counseling psychologists, 693
crack cocaine, 166
creative intelligence, 363, 376
creativity:
    and motivation, 384–85
    and scientific foundations of psychology, 18
creole, 499–500, *499*
criminals:
    children as, 653
    and mental disorders, 623–24, 651–52, 653,
        654, 697, 698
    self-esteem of, 606
critical periods, 121, 476, 520
critical thinking, *see* thought/thinking, critical
critical trials, 238
cross-cultural studies, 52
cross-sectional studies, and research
    methodology, 39–40, *40*
cross-sensory experience, *see* synesthesia
crowd behavior, 546

cryptomnesia, 318, *318*, 328
crystallized intelligence, 362, 366, 376, 518, 520
cultural neuroscience, 121
culture:
    and adaptation, 10–11, 12–13
    and aging, 515
    and alcohol abuse, 671
    and anxiety, 671
    and behavior, 12–13, *12*
    definition of, 52
    and depression, 671, 672
    and development, 121–22, 128, 129, 470, 495,
        499–500, 501, 508–10, 520
    East-West, 12–13, 218
    and eating, 392, *392*, 424
    and emotions, 406–8, *407*, 413, 672
    and euphemisms, 672
    evolution of, 12–13
    and gender, 508, 520
    and harming and helping others, 554–56,
        555, 558, 568
    and identity, 502, 508–10, 511, 520
    and impressions, 535
    and ingroup-outgroup bias, 538–39
    and intelligence, 360–61, *360*, 376
    and language, 499–500, 520
    and learning, 261, 275, 276
    and levels of analysis, 13
    and memory, 301, 315, 316
    and mental disorders, 619, 627, *627*, 628–29,
        639, 642, 643, 671–72, 692
    and motivation, 392, 398–402
    and nature/nurture debate, 7
    and obesity, 447, *447*, 466
    and perception, 218, 220, *220*, 224–26, *225*,
        232
    and personality, 572–73, 575, 579, 586–87,
        587, 588, 595, *600*
    and problem solving, 355
    and psychotherapy, 671–72, *672*, 710
    and research methodology, 40, 51, 52–53, *52*,
        56–57
    and schizophrenia, 671
    and scripts, 340
    and self-knowledge, 606, 610–12
    and self-serving bias, 610–12
    and sensation, 189, 195
    and sexual behavior, 398–401, 424
    and stress, 671
    and themes of psychological science, 10–11,
        12–14, *12*, 29, 30
culture-bound syndromes, 629, *629*, 630
culture of honor, 555–56, *556*
curiosity, 384
Cymbalta, 679

Dahmer, Jeffrey, 651
Darwinism, 18
    see also evolution
data:
    analysis and evaluation of, 65–73, 74
    collection of, 51–66, 74
    and research methodology, 35, 37, 65–73, 74
David (patient), 624

and treatment of mental disorders, 693, 698
virtual, 679, 680
see also experience
enzyme deactivation, 97–98, 103
epilepsy, 105, 128, 139, 140, 280, 417
epinephrine, 99–100, 309, 328
episodic memory, 290, 291, 296, *296*, 297, 299, 308, 328
equilibrium, 382
equipotentiality, 106, 305
equivalent groups, 46–47
erogenous zones, 574
erotica, 398
erotic plasticity, 399
errors, and research methodology, 67
escapism, 164, *164*
ESP (extrasensory perception), 210–11, 232
estrogen, 117, 119, 195, 397, 401
estrus, 117
ethics:
    and altering memory, 312
    and cochlear implants, 199–200
    code of, 28, 29, 30
    and Declaration of Helsinki, 64
    and dilemmas, 28, 29, 139, 170, *170*
    and drugs, 589
    and involuntary treatment, 691
    and learning, 274
    and Nuremberg Code, 64
    and obesity, 451
    and personality, 589
    and pregnancy, 473
    and research methodology, 62–64
ethnicity, *see* race/ethnicity
ethnomusicology, 14
ethyl alcohol, 101
etiology, 620, 667, 699, 708
eugenics, 84
euphemisms, for mental disorders, 672
eustress, 435
evidence-based assessment, 623, 630
evidence-based treatments, 678
evil, 23
evolution:
    of brain, 11–12
    of culture, 12–13
    and emotions, 408, 413, 417
    and harming and helping others, 554, 557
    and impressions, 532
    and ingroup-outgroup bias, 538, 539
    and learning, 245–46, 252, 257
    and memory, 294, 312, 327
    of mind, 29
    and motivation, 399, 400–401, 423
    and personality, 597, 601
    and scientific foundations of psychology, 18
    and self-knowledge, 605
    and sexual behavior, 399, 400–401
    of speech, 265
    and stereotypes, 538, 541
    and stress, 436
    and themes of psychological science, 10–13, *10*, 29

excitation:
    centers of, 392
    and eating, 392
    and motivation, 392
    and nervous system, 95, 96, 102, 103
excitation phase, 396
excitation transfer, 421
executive functions, 602
exemplars, 339, *339*, 341, 376
exercise:
    and acculturation, 455
    and consciousness, 163
    and health, 430, 439, 445, 454–55, 463, 465, 466
    and life expectancies, 455
    and stress, 439, 463
    as therapy, 686, 695
exosystems, 503
expectancy, and research methodology, 40
expectations:
    and mental disorders, 627
    and perception, 218, *218*
    and personality, 572, 580, *580*, 614
expected utility theory, 345, 355
experience:
    and attitudes, 525, 531, 568
    and development, 126, 470, 507, 520
    and development of brain, 120–21
    and Gestalt psychology, 19
    and how the brain is divided, 130, 142–44, 176
    and learning, 237, 238
    and memory, 280–81, 286, 294, 296, 297, 309–10, 328
    and mental disorders, 667, 668
    and nature/nurture debate, 7
    openness to new, 505, 579, 614
    and perception, 180–81, 222
    and personality, 573, 576–77, 579, 614
    and scientific foundations of psychology, 18, 19, 30
    and sensation, 186
    and study of consciousness, 136
    see also environment; *type of experience*
experience sampling, 56
experiment, definition of, 43
experimental groups, 43, 45, 47
experimental psychology, 17–18
experimental studies:
    and research methodology, 37, 43–46, *45*, 49
    and scientific foundations of psychology, 5, 17–18, 23
experimenter expectancy effects, 40
explanation, and research methodology, 37
explicit attitudes, 526, 568
explicit memory, 295–97, *296*, 299, 300, 306, 328
exposure, 669, *670*, 679, 680, 681–82, 695
expressed emotion, 670
externalizing disorders, 628, *628*, 630, 638
extinction, 240–41, *240*, 243, 276, 680
extraversion, 579, 586–87, 590–92, 614
extraverts, 577, 578, 585, 586, 595–97, 600, 614
extrinsic motivation, 384–86

eyes, 121–22, 200–202, 221–22, 232
eyewitnesses, 318–20, *318*, 325, 328

face, *see* facial attractiveness; facial expressions; facial recognition; fusiform face area
facial attractiveness, 562
facial expressions:
    and basic structure and functions of brain, 110
    and development, 122, 123, 476–77
    and emotions, 122, *123*, 405–7, *406*, 413, *413*, 418
    and fear, 122, *123*
    and impression formation, 533
    and personality, 597
facial feedback hypothesis, 415, *415*
facial recognition:
    and basic structure and functions of brain, 112
    and mental disorders, 634, *634*
    and perception, 219–21, *219*, *220*, *221*
    and study of consciousness, 147
factor analysis, 361
faking bad, 622
false belief test, 493, 494
false-consensus effect, 452
false fame effect, 297, 318, 536
false memories, 321–24, 328
family-focused intervention, 443–44
family systems model, 626, 662
family therapy, 670–71, *671*, 710
fear:
    and adaptation, 11, *11*
    as adaptive, 631, 633
    and brain, 5, 110, 417, 418
    and facial expressions, 122, *123*
    hierarchy of, 679, *679*
    and learning, 242–44, 245–46, 254, 263, *263*, 274, 276, 306, 628, 679, 693
    and memory, 306, 309, 310, 311
    and mental disorders, 23, 634, 654, 662
    neurochemistry of, 309, 310, 311
    and personality, 597
    and relationships, 560
    and scientific foundations of psychology, 23
    and social influence, 549
    and themes of psychological science, 11
    see also agoraphobia; neophobia; phobias
feature search tasks, *see* visual search tasks
feelings, *see* emotions
fetal alcohol syndrome, 472, 473, *473*
fetal cells, 101, 120, 128
    see also stem cells
field theory, 23
fight-or-flight response, 435, 436, 438, 444, 466
filter theory, 283–84
Fish, Mardy, 349, *349*
five-factor theory, 579, *579*
    see also Big Five
fixation, 574
fixed interval schedule, 255
fixed schedules, 255, *255*
flashbulb memories, 317, *317*, 325, 328
flow, 163–64

objectified self, 602
objective method:
    for personality assessment, 583–84, 588, 614
    and research methodology, 52
object perception, 216–22
object permanence, 488, 489, 490
object relations theory, 575
observation:
    and actor-observer discrepancy, 535–36, *535*
    and learning, 238, 261–68, *262*, 276, 580
    as method of psychological science, 5
    naturalistic, 38–39
    participant, 38–39
    and personality, 582, 583, 584, 588, 614
    and research methodology, 34, 38–40, 52–54
    and scientific foundations of psychology, 17, 22, 24, 26
    see also eyewitnesses
observational studies, *see* descriptive studies
observer bias, 40, 41
obsessions, definition of, 633
obsessive-compulsive disorder, 101, 633, *633*, 635, *635*, 648–49, 662, 670, 676, 681–82, *681*, 683, 695, 706, 710
occasion setter, 248
occipital lobe:
    and basic structure and functions of brain, 110–11, 112, 113, *148*
    and perception, 214, *214*, 232
    and sleep, 151
odorants, 190, *190*
Oedipus complex, 574
O'Keeffe, Georgia, 639
olfaction, *see* smell
olfactory bulb, 190, *190*, 232
olfactory epithelium, 190–91, *190*
olfactory hallucinations, 643
O'Neil, James, 707–8, *708*
open-ended questions, 55, *56*
openness to new experience, 505, 579, 590–92, 614
operant conditioning:
    and attitudes, 525
    and behavior modification, 255–57
    biology's influence on, 257–59, 276
    classical conditioning as different from, 249–60, 276
    cognition's influence on, 257–59, 276
    and learning, 237, 249–60, *250*, 271, 275, 276
    and mental disorders, 628, 635, *635*
    and rewards, 271
    and schedules of reinforcement, 255–57, 276
    and treatment of mental disorders, 669
operational definitions, 38
opiates, 168, 172, 174
optical illusions, 226–27, *226*
optic chiasm, 202, *203*
optic nerves, 201–2, *202*, *203*, 208
optimal foraging theory, 259
oral personalities, 574
oral stage, 574
orgasm, 396, 397
orgasm phase, 396
orienting reflex, 483

orienting response, 272
ossicles, 196, *197*
Oswald, Lee Harvey, 316
outer ears, 196, *197*
outgroup homogeneity effect, 539, 543, 568
outgroups, 12
overlearning, 293, 326
overprotectiveness, 505
oxytocin, 397, 437, 460–62, 466, 481, 520, 658, 662, 706

pain:
    and attitudes, 528
    and basic sensory processes, 192–96, *194*, 232
    and childbirth, 195
    gate-control theory of, 193–95, *194*
    and gender, 195
    and hormones, 195
    and humor, 422
    and hypnosis, 161
    and influence of neurotransmission, 102, *102*, 103, 130
    as motivation, 384, 415
    and personality, 596
    phantom, 193
    types of, 193–94, *194*
panic, 632–33, *632*, 662, 665–66, *666*, 680–81, 683, 695, 710
paradoxical sleep, *see* REM sleep
parallel processing, 282, *282*
paralysis, 128, 137, *137*
paranoid personality, 648
paraprofessionals, 693
parasympathetic division, 115–16, *115*, 130
parent-child relationship:
    and development, 470, 480–81, 494–95, 503–4
    and identity, 503–4
    and personality, 574, 576, 593, 614
    and social development, 470
    see also attachment
parenting:
    and life transitions, 515
    style of, 495, *495*, 504–5, 520, 593
parents:
    development role of, 470, 480–81, 494–95, 503–5, 520
    divorce of, 505–7
    and identity, 503–4
    and mental disorders, 658, 659, 661, 662, 702, 707–8
    and personality, 504
    single, 506
    see also parent-child relationship; parenting
parietal lobes, 110–12, 113, *148*, 214, *214*, 691
Parkinson's disease, 101, 128, 676, 687, 689–90
partial-reinforcement, 255, 256
partial reinforcement-extinction effect, 256
participant observation, 38–39
passionate love, 562, *563*, 568
Pavlovian conditioning, *see* classical conditioning
Paxil, 589, *589*
Peek, Kim, 367

peer pressure, 524
peers, *see* friendships
pegs, 327
"pendulum" experiment, 351
Penny Quiz, *293*
perception:
    and aging, 517
    and application of psychological science, 25
    basic processes of, 213–31
    and basic sensory processing systems, 186–87, 210
    and "best" forms, 217
    and bottom-up and top-down processing, 218–19, 232
    and brain, 180–81, *180*, 209, 213–16, 219, 221–23, 228–30
    and color, 204–9, *205*, 212, 215, 230, 232
    and compensatory factors, 228–29
    constancies in, 229–30, *230*, 232
    constructive nature of, 182, 216–22
    and culture, 218, 220, *220*, 224–26, *225*, 232
    definition of, 180
    depth, 222–24, *225*, *226*, 232, 483–84
    and development, 470, 474, 482–84, 490, *490*, 520
    distance, 226–27, 232
    and emotions, 418
    and environment, 180, *180*
    and expectations, 218, *218*
    and experience, 180–81, 222
    and figure and ground, 218
    Gestalt principles of, 24, 30, 216–17, *217*, 229, 232
    and hearing, 214, *214*, 230, 232
    and how we sense the world, 180–81, *180*
    and illusions, 230, *230*
    and learning, 501
    and levels of analysis, 14–15
    and location of objects, 222–24
    and memory, 218, 288, 306, 311
    and mental disorders, 642
    and motion, 226, 228–29, *229*, 232
    object, 216–22
    overview about, 179–80, 231
    and overview of psychological science, 5
    and proximity and similarity, 217, *217*
    and research methodology, 57–58
    and scientific foundations of psychology, 19–20, 24, 30
    and shape, 230, *230*
    and sixth sense, 210–11, *210*
    size, 226–27, 230, *230*, 232
    and smell, 213, 231
    and spatial relationships, 214, 216, 222–24
    and stereotypes, 539–40, *540*
    and study of consciousness, 136, *136*, 147
    and survival, 219, 231
    and taste, 214, *214*, 231
    and themes of psychological science, 10, 30
    and touch, 214, *214*, 231, 232
    and vision, 180, 208, 209, 210, 214–15, *214*, 221–22, 228–29, 230–31, 232
    and what versus where, 215–16, 219
performance, and motivation, 383

performance anxiety, 538

performatives, 497

peripheral nervous system (PNS), 104, 114–16, *114*, 119, 130

persistent vegetative state, 134, 138–39, *139*
   see also coma

personal attributions, 534, 535

personal constructs, 579

personality:
   and adaptation, 597–98, 600–601, *600*, 614
   and age, 599, *599*
   of animals, 590–92, *591*
   assessment of, 582–87, 614
   basic elements of, 576–77
   and behavior, 572–73
   and behavioral genetics, 601
   and behaviorism, 576, 579–80
   biological basis of, 573, 590–98, 599, 600, *600*, 601, 613, 614
   and brain, 105, *105*, 113, 589, 590, 596–97, 600–601, 613
   change in, 601
   and cognition, 573, 579–80, 581, 613, 614
   and consciousness, 574, 613
   and culture, 572–73, 575, 579, 586–87, *587*, 588, 595, *600*
   definition of, 572, 573, 584
   and development, 480, 574, 594–96
   and drugs, 589
   and emotions, 572–73, 576–77, 578, 580
   and environment, 580, 581, 588, 590, 595, 596, 597, 599, 601, 614
   and ethics, 589
   and evolution, 597, 601
   and experience, 573, 576–77, 579, 614
   and gender, 586–87, 588, 595
   and genetics, 87, 88, 590, 592–94, 597, 599, 613, 614
   and Gestalt psychology, 20
   and health, 440–41
   hierarchical model of, 578, *578*, 614
   how scientists have studied, 573–80
   humanistic approach to, 576–77, 581, 583, 614
   and identity, 504
   and inconsistency, 584–85
   interactionist approach to, 585–86, 613, 614
   and learning, 579–80, 596, 614
   and mental disorders, 623–25, 637, 648–54, 662, 695–98, 710
   and motivation, 576, 580, 581, 583, 596
   and neo-Freudians, 575, 614
   overview about, 613–14
   parents' role in development of, 504
   and prediction, 572, 580, 582–87, 594, 598, 614
   psychodynamic theories of, 573–75, 581, 614
   and relationships, 560, *560*, 566, 574, 576, 614
   schizo-affective, 598
   and scientific foundations of psychology, 20
   and self-construals, 610, *610*
   and self-regulation, 580

and single-cause explanations, 598

and situations, 572, 580, 584–85, 588, 596, 597, 599, 600, *600*

and snobbery, 605–6, *605*

socio-cognitive approach to, 580, 581

stability of, 584–85, 598–601, 614

and stereotypes, 586–87, 588, 592

structural model of, 575

and temperament, 594–96, *595*, 598, 601, 613, 614

and themes of psychological science, 29, 30

types of, 577–79, 614

and unconsciousness, 573–75, 581, 583, 613–14

personality psychologists, 25

personal myths, 582, 588

person-centered approach, and personality, 576

persuasion, 528–31, 568

phallic phase, 574, 575

phantom limbs, 124, 125

phantom pain, 193

pharmacology, and treatment of mental disorders, 683–84, 689–92, 702–3, 706, 710

phenomena, definition of, 34

phenomenology, 19, 414, 576, 668

phenotypes, 81–82, *81*, 83, 86, 130

phenylketonuria (PKU), 82

pheromones, 402

philosophy, 17

phi movement, 229

phobias, 242–45, *243*, 276, 631–32, *631*, 634, *634*, 662, 669–70, 679–80, 710

phonemes, 496, *497*, 520

phonics, 500–501, *501*

phonological loop, 290–91, *290*, 294, 328

phototherapy, 685, 710

phrenology, 106, *106*

physical activity, and sleep, 154

physical attractiveness, 560–62, *561*, 566

physical condition:
   and aging, 512, 515–16
   and mental disorders, 621

physical dependence, 172–74, *173*

physical development, 470–76, *471*, 481, 520

physics, understanding of, 490, 520

physiology, 17, 414, 415–19, 422, 495, 626

Picasso, Pablo, 363

pidgin, 499–500

pineal gland, 155, *155*

Pitt, Brad, 525, 526

pituitary gland, 118, 130, 435

placebo/placebo effect, 431–33, *433*, 461, 466, 681, 682, 683–84, 706

place cells, 307, 328

planning, 101, 130, 366

plaque, and heart disease, 440, 441

plasticity, *see* brain, plasticity of

plateau phase, 396

Plato, 16

play, 384–85, 403, 705

pleasure:
   and learning, 269–70, *270*, 271, 276
   as motivation, 384, *384*, 415, 423
   and personality, 573, 575

and rewards, 270–71, 276

pleasure principle, 384, 573, 575

polarization:
   group, 546
   and nervous system, 94–95

polygenic effects, 82

polygraphs, *see* lie-detector tests

pons, 107, 108, 157

Ponzo illusion, 226, 227, *227*, 232

population, research, 46–48, *47*, 50, 56

positive activation, 414–15

positive psychology, 456, *456*

positive psychology movement, 576, 614

positive punishment, 253, *253*, 254

positive reappraisal, 443

positive reinforcement, 253, *253*, 254, 255, 271, 605

positive symptoms, of schizophrenia, 642–45, 662, 690, 710

positron emission tomography (PET), 59, 60, *101*, 516, 622, 626, 635, *635*
   see also brain imaging

possessiveness, 564

postconventional morals, 494

postdecisional dissonance, 527

posthypnotic suggestion, 159

postsynaptic neurons, 96, 98, 100, 102, 103

posttraumatic stress disorder (PTSD), 7, *7*, 310, 311, 312, 628, *628*, 633, 676

potassium, and nervous system, 94–95, 103

potentiation, long-term, 273–74, *273*, 275, 276

practical intelligence, 363, 366, 376

practice, and memory, 293, 326

practitioners, *see* therapists

prayer, 163

preconscious, 574

preconventional morals, 494

prediction:
   and application of psychological science, 25–26
   and attitudes, 531
   of behavior, 23, 25–26
   and development, 492
   and impressions, 531
   and learning, 248, 259
   and personality, 572, 580, 582–87, 594, *595*, 598, 614
   and research methodology, 34, 35, 37, 71–72
   and scientific foundations of psychology, 23

predispositions, and mental disorders, 626, 661

preferential looking technique, 483, 520

prefontal lobotomy, *see* lobotomies

prefrontal cortex:
   and basic sensory processes, 190, *191*
   and basic structure and functions of brain, 112–13, *148*, *417*, 418–19
   and eating, 394
   and emotions, 414, 418–19, 495
   and learning, 244
   and mental disorders, 635, 640, 683, 687, 689
   and motivation, 394
   and personality, 596
   and sleep, 154

reaction times, 57–58, 365
reactivity effect, 53
reading, learning, 500–501
reality:
 and delusions, 643
 virtual, 679, 680
reality principle, 575
reasoning:
 abstract, 489
 and brain structure and function, 366
 counterfactual, 374
 and decision making, 355
 deductive, 342–44, *343*, 355, 376
 definition of, 342
 and emotions, 410
 inductive, 342–44, *343*, 355, 376, 495
 and intelligence, 374, 375
 moral, 494
 and Piaget's cognitive development stages,
  489
 and premises, 343
 and problem solving, 342–45, *343*, 355
 see also thought/thinking
rebound effect, 422
recency effect, 292, *292*
receptive fields, 203–4, *204*, *209*, 215
receptors:
 and addiction, 172
 definition of, 96–97
 and motivation, 394
 and nervous system, 93, 96–97, 103
 and sensation, 181–83, *181*, 186–87, *186–87*,
  190–94, *190–91*, *192–93*, *194*, 197–98,
  197, 208, 209, 212, 232
 see also sensation; *type of receptors*
reciprocal helping, 557, 568
recognition:
 and aging, 517
 false, 321–22
 see also facial recognition
reconsolidation process, and memory, 306–7
"recreational drugs," 165, 169
reflected appraisal, 604
reflective listening, 668
reflexes, 107–8, 113, 474, 488
refraction process, 200–201
Regan (case study), 624
regression to the mean, 431, *431*
reification, 361, 371
Reimer, Bruce and Brian, 509–10, *509*
reinforcement:
 absence of, 259
 and choosing among reinforcers, 259–60
 as conditioning, 252
 and definition of reinforcer, 251
 and development, 477
 and economic principles, 259–60, 276
 and learning, 251–57, 260, 271, 276
 natural, 271
 and personality, 576, 579–80, 596
 as positive or negative, 253–54, *253*, 276
 and potency of reinforcers, 253
 and rewards, 269–71
 schedules of, 255–57, *255*, 276

secondary, 477
and self-knowledge, 605
and treatment of mental disorders, 697, 705
value of, 579–80, *580*
vicarious, 264
see also rewards
relationships:
 and aging, 520
 client-practitioner, 692, 694, 697
 and development, 470, 503–4
 and emotions, 405, 411–13, 418, 466
 and Erikson's stage theory of identity, 512
 and learning, 254
 and life transitions, 513–15
 and mental disorders, 640, 649, 650–52, 659,
  662, 668, 669
 and personality, 574, 576, 614
 quality of, 560–66, 568
 romantic, 512, 562–63, *563*, 566, *566*, 568
 and self-knowledge, 605
 and treatment of mental disorders, 696
 see also attachment; friendships; parent-child
  relationship; social interaction
relaxation techniques, 666, 679
 see also meditation
releasing factor, 118
reliability, 66–67, *68*
religion, 462, 464, 466, 672
religious ecstasy, 163, *163*, 466
REM behavior disorder, 153
REM sleep, 151, 153, 155, 156–57, *156*, 158,
 176, 308, 640
repetition priming, 297–98, 299
replication, 35
representations:
 analogical, 334–36, *334*, *335*, *336*, 341
 and decision making, 341
 functions of, 341
 and memory, 300
 mental, 332–42
 overview about, 341
 and Piaget's cognitive development stages,
  487–89
 and problem solving, 352–53
 restructuring, 352, 353
 symbolic, 334, *334*, 335–39, *336*, 341
representativeness heuristic, 347
repressed memories, 322–23, 328
repression, 322–23, 575, 678
reproduction:
 and adaptation, 10–11
 and depression, 687
 and emotions, 410
 and genetic basis of psychological science,
  80–83, 130
 and heredity, 80–81
 and life transitions, 515
 and motivation, 384, 388, 397, 399, 423
 and personality, 597
 and self-knowledge, 605
 and sexual behavior, 397, 399, 424
 and stress, 436
 and themes of psychological science, 10–11
Rescorla-Wagner model, 248

research methodology, 32–75
 and alternative explanations, 45–46
 and animals, 61
 and asking approach, 55–57
 and averaging, 47
 and bias, 34, 37, 40, 41, 46, 56
 and case studies, 54–55, *55*
 and causality, 41, 42, 43, 45–46, 50
 and concepts, 37
 and control, 37, 43, 45
 and correlational studies, 37, 40–43, *43*,
  49–50, 69–71, *70*, 72
 and cross-cultural studies, 52, *52*
 and cross-sectional studies, 39–40, *40*
 and data, 35, 37, 51–73, 74
 and descriptive studies, 37–40, *39*, 49
 and empirical process, 37
 and ethics, 62–64
 and experimental studies, 37, 43–46, *45*, 49
 and explanation, 37
 and generalizing, 46
 and hypotheses, 34–36
 and law of large numbers, 49
 and levels of analysis, 47
 and longitudinal studies, 39, *39*
 and meta-analysis, 47, 71
 and objectivity, 52
 and observation, 34, 38–40, 52–54
 overview about, 33–34, 74
 population for, 46–48, 50, 56
 and prediction, 34, 35, 37, 71–72
 and questions, 55–57
 and scientific inquiry, 34–37, 74
 and scientific method, 34–36, *34*, *35*
 and statistical procedures, 66–72, *68*
 and theories, 34–35
 and types of studies, 37–50, 74
 and unexpected findings, 36, 37
 and variables, 40–43, 45–46
reserpine, 689
resolution phase, 396
response:
 accuracy of, 57–58
 bias, 185, *185*
 and scientific foundations of psychology,
  21–22
 and sensation, 182–86, *182*
response performance, 57–58, *58*
response-prevention therapy, 681–82, 695
responsibility:
 diffusion of, 558, 568
 and mental disorders, 662, 703
rest, and sleep, 153–54
resting membrane potential, 94–95, *94*
restrained eating, 448–49
restrictive dieting, 430, 448–49, 466
restructuring:
 cognitive, 669, 670, 710
 of representations, 352, 353, 376
reticular formation, 108, 113, 155
retina, 200–203, *202*, 208, 209, 214, 222–23,
 223, 226, 228–29, *229*, 232, 483
retrieval, of memory, 281, 287, *287*, 299–300,
 302–4, 308, 309, 311, 328

sensory coding, 181, *182*
   see also encoding, sensory
sensory memory, 287–88, *287, 288, 290,* 294
sensory neurons, 92, *92*
sensory-specific satiety, 391
sensory thresholds, 182–83, *183*
separation anxiety, 478
September 11, 2001, 317, 331–32, *332,* 430, 443, *443*
septum, 553
serial position effect, 292, *292*
serotonin:
   and addiction, 168
   and brain chemistry, 14
   definition of, 100
   functions of, 99, 100–101, 103
   and harming and helping others, 554, *554*
   and influence of neurotransmission, 100–101, 103
   and levels of analysis, 14
   and mental disorders, 640, 651, 662, 673, 674, 679, 681, 689, 706, 710
   and motivation, 397
   and personality, 589, 593, 597
   and sexual behavior, 397
   and sleep, 154
set-points, 382–83, 394, 424, 448
seven sins of memory, 313–14, 318
sex determination, 84
sexual behavior:
   and adaptive behavior, 401
   and addiction, 172
   and behaviors affecting health, 464
   and biology, 396–98, 402, 424
   and brain, 109–10, 402
   and depression, 638, 683
   and endocrine system, 117, 130
   and environment, 402
   and evolution, 399
   and frequency of sex, 562
   and gender, 117, 399–400, *400,* 403, 424
   and hormones, 117, 396–97, 404, 424
   and instincts, 574–75
   and love, 564
   and mating strategies, 400–401, 424
   and mental disorders, 651
   and motivation, 384, 395–404, 423, 424
   and nervous system, 117, 130
   overview about, 404
   and personality, 574–75
   and relationships, 562, 564, 566
   and safe sex, 464
   and scientific foundations of psychology, 21
   and sexual orientation, 401–3, *403*
sexual dimorphism, 126
sexual dysfunction, 638, 674, 677, 683
sexual identity, 511, 539
sexual reproduction, *see* reproduction
sexual response cycle, 396, *396*
sexual strategies theory, 400–401
shading, 232
shadowing, 283, *283*
shame, 495

sham surgery, 101, 678
   see also placebo/placebo effect
shape perception, 230, *230*
shaping, 252, *252*
shock experiments, 550–52, *550, 551, 552*
short-term memory:
   and aging, 517, 520
   long-term memory distinguished from, 291–93, 294
   as stage of memory, 280–81, *287, 288*–91, *290,* 294
shyness, 595, 597, 634
sibling studies, 369
sickle-cell disease, 83, *83*
Sight Savers International, 222
signal-detection theory, 184–85, *185,* 232
sign language, 200, 498, *498,* 501
Simon, Taryn, 320, *320*
simple cells, 215, *215*
simple models of learning, 271–72, *272*
simultaneous contrast, 204, 206, *208,* 209, *209*
single-cause explanations, 598, *598*
situation, and sensation, 186
situationism, 584
situations:
   and adaptation, 11
   and attitudes, 566
   and brain, 22
   and development, 509–10
   and evil, 23
   and gender, 509–10
   and harming and helping others, 554, 557–58
   and identity, 509–10
   and impressions, 534, 536, 544, 568
   influence on behavior of, 524, 567
   and learning, 23
   and mental disorders, 7, 619, 632, 634–35, 639–41, 662
   and personality, 572, 580, 584–86, 588, 596, 597, 599, 600, *600*
   and relationships, 560–62, 568
   and research methodology, 38
   and scientific foundations of psychology, 23, 30
   and social influence, 544, 551
   and social psychology, 524–25, 534, 536, 544, 551, 554, 557–62, 567, 568
   strong, 585, *585*
   and themes of psychological science, 9, 11
   and treatment of mental disorders, 684
   weak, 585, *585*
sixth senses, 210–11, *210*
size perception, 226–27, 230, *230,* 232
skepticism, 26, 37
Skinner, Deborah, 236, *236*
Skinner box, 251–52
sleep:
   as adaptive behavior, 153–55, 176
   as altered state of consciousness, 150–53, 158, 176
   amount of, 150
   and basic structure and functions of brain, 109
   and brain, 130, 149–58, *150*

   and cognitive behavioral therapy, 152
   definition of, 158
   deprivation of, 152–54, 326
   and development, 471
   disorders, 152–53, *153*
   and memory, 308, 326
   and mental disorders, 631, 632, 637, 638, 640, 651, 660
   and moods, 154
   and nervous system, 100, 120
   purpose of, 150, 153
   regulation of, 130, 155
   and restoration, 153–54
   and sleep-wake cycles, 118
   stages of, 150–51, *150, 151,* 158
   what is, 149–58, 176
   see also dreams; REM sleep
sleeper effect, 318
sleep spindles, 151
"slippery slope," 169
slow-wave sleep, 151, 155
smell, 109, 189–92, *190–91,* 213, 231
Smith, Timothy L., 312
smoking, 42, 173, *173,* 259, 264, 430, 438, 439, 445, 452–53, *452, 453,* 455, 464, 466
   and children, 173
snobbery, 605–6
sociability, 594
social anxiety disorder, 632, *632,* 634, *634*
   see also social phobia
social comparisons, 389, 608, *609*
social competence, 554
social development, 121–22, 470, 476–81, 501, 502–11, 518
social exclusion, 11, 549
social facilitation, 545, *545,* 551, 568
social factors:
   and behavior, 24
   and emotions, 411–13
   and genetic basis of psychological science, 88, 130
   and mental disorders, 632, 634, 644, 656, 661, 706, 707
   and scientific foundations of psychology, 24
   and themes of psychological science, 29, 30
   and treatment of mental disorders, 710
   see also relationships
social influence, 545–52, 568
social integration, 458–60
social interaction:
   and aging, 520
   and development, 486–89, 520
   and intelligence, 518, 520
   and language, 520
   and mental disorders, 644, 656, *656,* 661
   and treatment of mental disorders, 690, 695, 705, 706, 707
   see also relationships
socialization:
   and attitudes, 525–26, 531, 568
   and development, 470, 520
   and emotions, 407, 411
   and gender, 508, 509
   and group socialization theory, 504

Sullivan, Anne, 179–80, *180*
superego, 575, 614
superordinate goals, 544
superordinate traits, 578, 596
superstitions, 267, *267*
supertasters, 188, *188*
support, social:
    and health, 458–60, 465, 466
    and stress, 443–44, 458, 466
    and treatment of mental disorders, 669, 686,
        696
suppression, thought, 422
surgery, and mental disorders, 674–75, 676, 682,
    689
surrogate mothers, *see* mothers, surrogate
survival:
    and adaptation, 11, 12
    and basic structure and functions of brain,
        107–8, 113, 130
    and development, 470, 476–81, 520
    and emotions, 405, 410, 411
    and harming and helping others, 556, 568
    and ingroup-outgroup bias, 539
    and learning, 246, 276
    and memory, 294, 327
    and mental disorders, 661
    and motivation, 381, 384, 388, 423
    and perception, 219, 231
    and personality, 597, 614
    and self-knowledge, 605
    and sensation, 231
    and stress, 435
    and themes of psychological science, 11, 12
survival of the fittest, 11
syllogisms, 343, 376
symbolic knowledge, 376
symbolic representations, 334, *334*, 335–39,
    336, 341
symbolism, and Piaget's cognitive development
    stages, 488
sympathetic division, 115–16, *115*, 130
sympathetic nervous system, 441
sympathy, 494
synapse/synapses:
    definition of, 93
    and development, 474–76, *475*, 520
    and exercise, 455
    and intelligence, 369–70
    and learning, 271–73, 275, 276
    and memory, 309
    and mental disorders, 673
    and nervous system, 93, 96–97, 100, 102, 103,
        129, 130
    and sensation, 202
    and termination of synaptic transmission, 98
synaptic cleft, 93, 96, 98, 103
synaptic pruning, 474, 520
synaptic transmission, 122
synesthesia, 77–78, *78*, 124–25, 128, 130
syntax, 496, 501
systematic desensitization, 679
systematic errors, 67
systems approach, 670

taboos, 392, 395
tabula rasa, *see* blank slate, mind as
talking, and health, 458–59
"talk" psychotherapy, 459, 668, 671, 678–79
    see also psychoanalysis; psychodynamic
        theories
tardive dyskinesia, 674, 689–90, 710
taste, 186–89, *186–87*, *188*, *189*, 214, *214*, 231,
    232, 391, 394, 424, 474
taste buds, *186*, 187–88, *188*, 232
technology, 5
telegraphic speech, 498
temperament:
    definition of, 480, 504
    and development, 480, 504, 505
    and divorce, 505
    and gender, 594–95
    and mental disorders, 634, 660
    and personality, 594–96, *595*, 598, 601, 613,
        614
temporal lobes:
    and basic structure and functions of brain,
        111–12, *111*, 113, *148*
    and memory, 280, *280*, 292, 305–8, 309, 316
    and mental disorders, 646, 662
    and perception, 214, *214*
tend-and-befriend response, 460, 436–37, 466
teratogens, 472, 520
terminal buttons, 93, 98
terrorism, 317, 553
terror management theory, 606
testing:
    aptitude, 358, 372–73
    intelligence, 365, 366, 370–71, 372–73, 376,
        518
    as measurement of intelligence, 358–75
    and mental disorders, 622, *622*, 630, 652, 662
    neuropsychological, 622, *622*
    psychological, 541, *541*, 622, *622*, 630, 652,
        662
    validity of, 359–60, 376
    see also type of test
testosterone, 117, 119, 397, 398, 401–2, 461
texture gradient, 224, *224*
thalamus:
    and basic structure and functions of brain,
        109, 110, 113, 130
    and development, 472
    and emotions, 417
    and memory, 316
    and mental disorders, 635, *635*
    and perception, 139, 213, 214, *214*
    and sensation, 180, *187*, 190, *193*, 202
thalidomide, 472
Thatcher, Margaret, 220, *220*, 317, *317*
Thatcher illusion, 220, *220*
THC (tetrahydrocannabinol), 166
Thematic Apperception Test (TAT), 583, *583*
theories, and research methodology, 34–35
theory of mind, 492–94, *493*, 501, 520, 656
therapists:
    caring, 710
    choosing, 692–94, *693*
    client relationship with, 692, 694, 697

cost of, 694
    manipulation of, 696
theta waves, 150–51, *150*
thin slices of behavior, 533, 544
third-variable problem, 42, 50
thought/thinking:
    abstract, 489, 520
    and aging, 516
    amount of, 342
    and application of psychological science, 26,
        30
    and behavior, 22, 30
    and categorization, 336–39, 343–44
    complex, 520
    critical, 26–28, 29, 30, 44–45, 47–49, 90–91,
        126, 169, 183–84, *184*, 211–12, 247, 267,
        285, 320, 375, 386, 408–9, 432–33,
        480–81, 507, 598, 605–6, 694, 704
    distorted, 661
    egocentric, 492
    influence of neurotransmission on, 98–104
    and mental disorders, 23, 628, 661
    overview about, 331–32, 374–75
    rational, 575
    and representations, 332–42
    and scientific foundations of psychology, 18,
        22, 23, 30
    and structural model of personality, 575
    see also cognition; decision making; mind;
        problem solving; reasoning; representations
threat-rehearsal strategies, dreams as, 157–58
threats, 634
thresholds, 182–83, *183*, 186
tickling, 193
time sequences, 308
tip-of-the-tongue phenomenon, 314–15, 316,
    328
token economies, 256
tolerance, 172, 245, 276
top-down processing, 218–19, 232
touch, 192–94, *192–93*, *194*, 214, *214*, 231, 232,
    474
Tourette's syndrome, 271, 655, 680
"Tower of Hanoi" problem, 350, *350*
toxins, and influence of neurotransmission, 98,
    99–100
traits, personality:
    and adaptation, 597–98
    of animals, 590–92, *591*
    as approach for studying personality, 577–79,
        580, 581, 614
    assessment of, 583–84, 586–87, 588, 614
    as behavioral dispositions, 577–79
    central, 582
    consistency of, 573
    definition of, 573
    and hierarchical model, 578, *578*
    and person-situation debate, 585
    secondary, 582
    stability of, 598–601, 614
tranquilizers, 672, 679, 680, 689
transcendental meditation, 162
transcranial magnetic stimulation (TMS), 60, 61,
    675, *675*, 686, 695, 710